June 15–19, 2015
Portland, Oregon, USA

Association for
Computing Machinery

Advancing Computing as a Science & Profession

SIGMETRICS'15

Proceedings of the 2015 ACM SIGMETRICS International Conference on
Measurement and Modeling of Computer Systems

(part of FCRC)

Sponsored by:

ACM SIGMETRICS

Supported by:

Akamai, Facebook, Hewlett-Packard, IBM, Intel, and NSF

Association for
Computing Machinery

Advancing Computing as a Science & Profession

The Association for Computing Machinery
2 Penn Plaza, Suite 701
New York, New York 10121-0701

Notice to Past Authors of ACM-Published Articles

ACM intends to create a complete electronic archive of all articles and/or other material previously published by ACM. If you have written a work that has been previously published by ACM in any journal or conference proceedings prior to 1978, or any SIG Newsletter at any time, and you do NOT want this work to appear in the ACM Digital Library, please inform permissions@acm.org, stating the title of the work, the author(s), and where and when published.

ISBN: 978-1-4503-3486-0

Additional copies may be ordered prepaid from:

ACM Order Department
PO Box 30777
New York, NY 10087-0777, USA

Phone: 1-800-342-6626 (USA and Canada)
+1-212-626-0500 (Global)
Fax: +1-212-944-1318
E-mail: acmhelp@acm.org
Hours of Operation: 8:30 am – 4:30 pm ET

Printed in the USA

Message from the General Chairs

It is our great pleasure and distinct honor to welcome you to the 2015 SIGMETRICS Conference on Measurement and Modeling of Computer Systems, and to Portland, Oregon! Once again, SIGMETRICS is being held this year as part of the Federated Computer Research Conference (FCRC), which provides our attendees with the opportunity to mingle with the attendees from other FCRC conferences and workshops. On Monday, June 15, the conference starts with three affiliated workshops being held in parallel (NetEcon, DCC, and MAMA), each with a great program. The main conference is being held over three days from Tuesday, June 16 to Thursday, June 18, consisting of 32 regular papers, about 20 posters, a SIGMETRICS Achievement Award lecture (Prof. Bruce Hajek), and a SIGMETRICS Rising Star Award lecture (TBD). We also have three tutorials on Friday, June 19, one on Bandit Optimizations, another on Social Search and Social Recommendations, and the third on Learning with Strategic Agents.

Organizing a conference like SIGMETRICS is a very substantial undertaking and would not be possible without substantial contributions from a great team of co-organizers. We would like to thank all of them for their time and dedication. In particular, we would like to thank our Technical Program Committee Co-Chairs, Sudipta Sengupta and Devavrat Shah, for their immense efforts. They, together with a distinguished program committee, worked hard to put together a very high quality and exciting technical program this year. It has been a pleasure to work closely with them, and we are very thankful for their outstanding job. In addition, Florin Ciucu helped put together a great set of workshops and tutorials. Alex Liu secured funding for us from NSF to support student travel, and coordinated the student travel grants and student activities. Niklas Carlsson made sure that the conference was well publicized. David Goldberg worked with Sheridan Communications and authors to ensure that papers get to publication. Ashwin Lall handled participants' registration. Finally, Ping Yin helped with the website.

On behalf of SIGMETRICS 2015, we are also extremely grateful to the US National Science Foundation for providing travel grants to 21 student authors, and to our industry supporters Akamai, Facebook, HP, IBM and Intel for their generous support and continuing engagement with SIGMETRICS. In addition, we would like to thank everyone at ACM and on the FCRC organizing team for helping guide us through the planning process. Finally, we would like to thank all the authors for their contributions of outstanding papers and posters and all the attendees of SIGMETRICS 2015 for their participation in the conference. We hope you enjoy the program and your interactions with your fellow researchers!

Bill Lin
SIGMETRICS 2015 General Co-Chair
University of California, San Diego

Jun (Jim) Xu
SIGMETRICS 2015 General Co-Chair
Georgia Tech

Program Chairs' Welcome

Welcome to SIGMETRICS 2015. SIGMETRICS is the flagship conference of the ACM special interest group for the computer systems performance evaluation community. This year marks the forty-second anniversary since SIGMETRICS (under its prior name, SIGME) held the First National SIGME Symposium on Measurement and Evaluation in 1973. The past four decades have seen enormous changes in the field of computer science, but the importance of measurement, modeling, and performance evaluation remains as critical as ever.

This year's conference includes papers on topics that have been a mainstay since the founding of our SIG, including queuing, scheduling, resource allocation, and performance measurement. Application areas that have emerged in recent years, such as data center and cloud, big data, solid-state storage, machine learning, crowdsourcing, energy optimization, continue to be represented in our program. We received 239 submissions to this year's conference, of which 32 appear in the program as full papers, which is a highly competitive acceptance ratio below 14%. An additional 24 submissions appear in the abbreviated form of poster presentations and extended abstracts.

As in some prior years, we performed reviews in three rounds. In the first round, each paper was assigned to three reviewers. In the second round, papers were up for discussion among the reviewers, especially those with highly divergent review opinions. In some cases, additional reviews were necessary to ensure that every paper would receive at least three reviews. Based on this and immediately prior to the TPC meeting, papers were bucketed into "accept", "reject", and "discuss at TPC meeting" buckets. Finally, in the TPC meeting at MIT (Cambridge, MA), we entertained comments and objections on papers in the "accept" and "reject" buckets and discuss all papers in the "discuss at TPC meeting" bucket.

It was no mean feat to winnow a set of nearly two hundred and fifty submissions down to a set of appropriate size for a three-day conference. We offer tremendous thanks to the 57 members of the program committee who collectively performed this daunting task. We are grateful for the support of the SIGMETRICS board during the lengthy process of selecting this year's conference program.

There are many conference organizers whose efforts have been critical to pulling this event together, but as program chairs, we are most directly indebted to three of them: Our webmaster, Ping Yin, was outstandingly responsive to every online update we requested. Our publications chair, David Goldberg, was very helpful with the work items involved in getting to a final published program after the decisions were made on the papers. It has been a pleasure working with the general chairs, Bill Lin and Jun (Jim) Xu.

It has been our honor to serve as this year's program co-chairs. We look forward to an engaging, interactive, and productive conference.

Sudipta Sengupta
SIGMETRICS'15 Program Co-chair
Microsoft Research, USA

Devavrat Shah
SIGMETRICS'15 Program Co-chair
MIT, USA

Table of Contents

Session: Machine learning and Crowdsourcing

Session: Ads and Information Dissemination

Session: Benchmarking with Traces

Session: Queueing and More

Session: Networking

Poster Session

SIGMETRICS 2015 Conference Organization

Organizing Committee

General Chairs	Bill Lin	*University of California, San Diego*
	Jun (Jim) Xu	*Georgia Tech*
TPC Chairs	Sudipta Sengupta	*Microsoft Research*
	Devavrat Shah	*Massachusetts Institute of Technology*
Workshops & Tutorials Chair	Florin Ciucu	*University of Warwick*
Publicity Chair	Niklas Carlsson	*Linkoping University*
Publications Chair	David Goldberg	*Georgia Tech*
Student Activities Chair	Alex Liu	*Michigan State University*
Registration Chair	Ashwin Lall	*Denison University*
Webmaster	Ping Yin	*University of California, San Diego*

Technical Program Committee

Mohammad Alizadeh	*Insieme Networks*
Lakshmi Bairavasundaram	*Datrium*
Randall Berry	*Northwestern University*
Sem Borst	*Eindhoven U. of Technology and Alcatel-Lucent Bell Labs*
Ana Busic	*INRIA*
John C S Lui	*CUHK*
Y Charlie Hu	*Purdue University*
Mark Crovella	*Boston University*
Peter Desnoyers	*Northeastern University*
Ayalvadi Ganesh	*University of Bristol*
Javad Ghaderi	*Columbia University*
Philip Gibbons	*Intel Research Pittsburgh*
Leana Golubchik	*University of Southern California*
Varun Gupta	*University of Chicago*
Bruce Hajek	*UIUC*
Mor Harchol-Balter	*CMU*
John Hasenbein	*UT Austin*
Kyomin Jung	*Seoul National University*
Amin Karbasi	*Yale University*
Ramana Kompella	*Purdue University*
Alex Liu	*Michigan State University*
Peter Marbach	*University of Toronto*
Athina Markopoulou	*UC Irvine*

Technical Program Committee (Continued)

Vishal Misra	*Columbia University*
Eytan Modiano	*MIT*
Jason Nieh	*Columbia University*
Sewoong Oh	*UIUC*
Alexandre Proutiere	*France Telecom*
Konstantinos Psounis	*University of Southern California*
Kavita Ramanan	*Brown University*
Rhonda Righter	*UC Berkeley*
Dan Rubenstein	*Columbia University*
Saswati Sarkar	*University of Pennsylvania*
Srinivas Shakkottai	*Texas A&M University*
Mayank Sharma	*IBM T. J. Watson Research Center*
Jinwoo Shin	*KAIST*
Evgenia Smirni	*College of William and Mary*
Alex Snoeren	*UCSD*
Mark Squillante	*IBM T. J. Watson Research Center*
Alexander (Sasha) Stolyar	*Alcatel-Lucent Bell Labs*
Ryan Stutsman	*Microsoft Research*
Lakshmi Subramanian	*NYU*
Vijay Subramanian	*Northwestern University*
Wee Peng Tay	*Nanyang Technological University*
Don Towsley	*University of Massachusetts Amherst*
Milan Vojnovic	*Microsoft Research*
Neil Walton	*University of Amsterdam*
Jia Wang	*AT&T Research*
Adam Wierman	*California Institute of Technology*
Lau Wing-Cheong	*CUHK*
Cathy Xia	*Ohio State University*
Kuang Xu	*Stanford*
Tauhid Zaman	*MIT*
Li Zhang	*IBM T. J. Watson Research Center*
Zhi-Li Zhang	*University of Minnesota*
Yuan Zhong	*Columbia University*
Gil Zussman	*Columbia University*
Bert Zwart	*CWI*

SIGMETRICS 2015 Sponsor & Supporters

Sponsor:

Supporters:

Bounds Implied by Drift and Applications

Bruce Hajek
Department of Electrical and Computer Engineering
and the Coordinated Science Laboratory
University of Illinois at Urbana-Champaign
b-hajek@illinois.edu

ABSTRACT

A recurring theme in the design of control schemes for computer communication networks has been to identify the drift of critical quantities such as queue lengths, and then devise control strategies that close the loop. A useful tool for the performance analysis of such strategies are bounds on deviations from the expected trajectory. This talk identifies an incomplete list of such tools that have been used in a broad class of applications, for both stochastic and deterministically constrained models of load.

Categories and Subject Descriptors

C.2 [**Computer Commun. Networks**]: Miscellaneous; G.3 [**Probability and Statistics**]: Stochastic process

Keywords

drift analysis, Lyapunov function, stability

1. OVERVIEW OF PRESENTATION

Aside from general work on Lyapunov stability and martingales, Kingman's early work gave simple intuitive bounds implied by drift for queues[8, 9]. As a tool to address stability of controlled ALOHA, [3] introduced simple related bounds for time-dependent processes with exponential tails. The bounds came in handy for large-time analysis of the global optimization algorithm simulated annealing [5] and state-space collapse [1]. The Lyapunov stability method[11] continues to be a workhorse tool for network stability. The stability of fluid limits implies stability of both stochastic systems [10] and systems with regulated bursty traffic [6, 2]. Variations of bounds implied by drift appear as comparison theorems for diffusions [4] or maximal inequalities for supermartingales [7].

2. BIOGRAPHICAL INFORMATION

Dr. Hajek has been on the faculty at the University of Illinois since 1979. He received a BS in Mathematics and MS in Electrical Engineering from the University of Illinois at Urbana-Champaign and the Ph. D. in Electrical Engineering from the University of California at Berkeley. Prof. Hajek's research interests include communication networks, wireless communications, auctions and mechanism design, stochastic analysis, optimization, and control. He served as Editor-in-Chief for the IEEE Transactions on Information Theory, and as President of the IEEE Information Theory Society. He is coauthor of the book *Stochastic Processes in Engineering Systems* with E. Wong, and author of the book *Random Processes for Engineers*, 2015. Dr. Hajek is a Fellow of IEEE, he received the IEEE Kobayashi Award for Computer Communication and he is a member of the US National Academy of Engineering.

SIGMETRICS'15, June 15-19, 2015, Portland, OR, USA.
ACM 978-1-4503-3486-0/15/06
http://dx.doi.org/10.1145/2745844.2745902.

3. REFERENCES

[1] A. Eryilmaz and R. Srikant. Asymptotically tight steady-state queue length bounds implied by drift conditions. *Queueing Systems*, 72(3-4):311–359, 2012.

[2] D. Gamarnik. Using fluid models to prove stability of adversarial queueing networks. *IEEE Trans Automatic Control*, 45(4):741–746, 2000.

[3] B. Hajek. Hitting-time and occupation-time bounds implied by drift analysis with applications. *Advances in Applied probability*, 14:502–525, 1982.

[4] B. Hajek. Mean stochastic comparison of diffusions. *Zeitschrift für Wahrscheinlichkeitstheorie und verwandte Gebiete*, 68(3):315–329, 1985.

[5] B. Hajek. Cooling schedules for optimal annealing. *Math Operations Research*, 13(2):311–329, 1988.

[6] B. Hajek. Large bursts do not cause instability. *IEEE Trans Automatic Control*, 45(1):116–118, 2000.

[7] B. Hajek. A maximal inequality for supermartingales. *Elect. Commun. Probability*, 19:1–10, 2014.

[8] J. Kingman. Some inequalities for the queue GI/G/1. *Biometrika*, 49(3/4):315–324, December 1962.

[9] J. Kingman. A martingale inequality in the theory of queues. *Cambridge Phiolos. Soc.*, 59:359–361, 1964.

[10] A. L. Stolyar. On the stability of multiclass queueing networks: A relaxed sufficient condition via limiting fluid processes. *Markov Processes and Related Fields*, 1(4):491–512, 1995.

[11] L. Tassiulas and A. Ephremides. Stability properties of constrained queueing systems and scheduling policies for maximum throughput in multihop radio networks. *IEEE Trans Automatic Control*, 37(12):1936–1948, 1992.

Online Auctions in IaaS Clouds: Welfare and Profit Maximization with Server Costs

Xiaoxi Zhang
Dept. of Computer Science
The University of Hong Kong
xxzhang2@cs.hku.hk

Zhiyi Huang
Dept. of Computer Science
The University of Hong Kong
zhiyi@cs.hku.hk

Chuan Wu
Dept. of Computer Science
The University of Hong Kong
cwu@cs.hku.hk

Zongpeng Li
Dept. of Computer Science
University of Calgary
zongpeng@ucalgary.ca

Francis C.M. Lau
Dept. of Computer Science
The Univeristy of Hong Kong
fcmlau@cs.hku.hk

ABSTRACT

Auction design has recently been studied for dynamic resource bundling and VM provisioning in IaaS clouds, but is mostly restricted to the one-shot or offline setting. This work targets a more realistic case of online VM auction design, where: (i) cloud users bid for resources into the future to assemble customized VMs with desired occupation durations; (ii) the cloud provider dynamically packs multiple types of resources on heterogeneous physical machines (servers) into the requested VMs; (iii) the operational costs of servers are considered in resource allocation; (iv) both social welfare and the cloud provider's net profit are to be maximized over the system running span. We design truthful, polynomial time auctions to achieve social welfare maximization and/or the provider's profit maximization with good competitive ratios. Our mechanisms consist of two main modules: (1) an online primal-dual optimization framework for VM allocation to maximize the social welfare with server costs, and for revealing the payments through the dual variables to guarantee truthfulness; and (2) a randomized reduction algorithm to convert the social welfare maximizing auctions to ones that provide a maximal expected profit for the provider, with competitive ratios comparable to those for social welfare. We adopt a new application of Fenchel duality in our primal-dual framework, which provides richer structures for convex programs than the commonly used Lagrangian duality, and our optimization framework is general and expressive enough to handle various convex server cost functions. The efficacy of the online auctions is validated through careful theoretical analysis and trace-driven simulation studies.

Categories and Subject Descriptors

C.4 [**Performance of Systems**]: Design studies; Modeling techniques; I.1.2 [**Algorithms**]: Analysis of algorithms

General Terms

Algorithms; Design; Economics

DOI: http://dx.doi.org/10.1145/2745844.2745855.

Keywords

Cloud Computing; Auction; Resource Allocation; Pricing; Online Algorithms; Truthful Mechanisms

1. INTRODUCTION

As a major model in cloud computing services, Infrastructure-as-a-Service (IaaS) clouds are proliferating in today's Internet. An IaaS cloud meets users' realtime resource demands through virtualization technologies, which pack resources (*e.g.*, CPU, RAM, disk) into virtual machines (VMs). Major IaaS providers today typically offer pre-configured VM instances of fixed types, with the number of types increasing over the years. For example, Amazon EC2 currently provides 7 categories and 23 types of VMs [1], a substantial growth from a few years ago. A few recently emerged cloud platforms start to allow customized VMs that bundle various resources at user-specified amounts [2][3]. Although the granularity of resource provisioning keeps improving, fixed pricing policies are still dominant in practice, charging customers a fixed amount for each pre-configured VM [1] or each unit of resources [2][3]. Despite their apparent simplicity, fixed-price policies inherently lack market agility and efficiency, jeopardizing both the provider's profit and customers' utility. Amazon EC2's Spot Instance is a first-step attempt to apply a market-based auction mechanism on VM provisioning, but its prices have been discovered to be often not market-driven [4], which can lead to untruthful bidding.

Towards better market-based pricing, auctions have recently been designed for cloud resource allocation, for pre-configured VMs of limited types [5][6], or for customized VMs with user-specified resource bundles [7][8][9]. Most of the mechanisms have focused on the *one-shot* or *offline* setting, solving for resource allocation and payments assuming that the bids are given all at once. Online VM auctions, where bidders come and go at wish and allocations and charging decisions are to be made on the spot, have only been investigated in very limited setups. Wang *et al.* [10] and Zhang *et al.* [11] consider only one type of VMs available to all users in their online auctions. Shi *et al.* [7] study auctions over multiple rounds, which are coupled together by an overall budget at each user, while each acquired VM is still used for a single round. The social welfare and revenue optimization in [9] is achieved based on a strong assumption of allowing preemption of resources already occupied by a user, which is arguable at best in practice.

This work targets a more realistic and general setup in online VM auction design with the following features. (I) User-specified VM (future) start/end time and time-varying resource bundle: Each cloud user bids for a customized bundle of resources to constitute her VM, which can start execution at any future time for any specified duration. Besides, the resource composition of the VM can vary over its duration, according to the projected need of user workload. (II) Heterogeneous servers with various resource capacities and operational costs: The cloud provider dynamically packs multiple types of resources on heterogeneous physical machines (servers) into the requested VMs. Various server cost functions under different server operational models are considered in resource allocation, which have *not* been modeled in previous cloud auctions. (III) Social welfare maximization as well as profit maximization: We design auctions that maximize the social welfare on aggregate gain of the cloud provider and the users (system efficiency), and auctions that maximize the cloud provider's net profit (another realistic objective), while guaranteeing other desirable properties including truthful bidding, individual rationality and computationally efficiency over the entire system running span.

The design of online allocation algorithms in our setup is indeed challenging, when one aims to pursue social welfare or profit that closely approaches that in the optimal offline solution, computed using complete information in the system span. Even in the offline setting, packing multiple types of resources on heterogeneous servers into customized VMs of time-varying resource composition and different durations involves NP-hard combinatorial optimization problems. In the online algorithm, the decision on packing or reserving resources (if the VM is to start at a future time) for the requested VM should be made upon receipt of each bid, without the assistance of any future information. What's more, even when an online approximate allocation algorithm is in place, it can be difficult to design a payment rule that works with the allocation algorithm to guarantee desired properties such as truthfulness [12]. The classic VCG mechanism, essentially the only type of auction that guarantees both truthfulness and economic efficiency in the offline setting [13], does not directly work in the online case, since it requires the computation of exact optimal allocation to guarantee truthfulness, which cannot be calculated for the future requests.

The challenge further escalates when our auction model involves operational costs of servers in the computation of social welfare and profit. Most existing auction designs ignore such (production) costs of resources, but consider social welfare as only the overall value of accepted bids and profit as the overall payment. Significant difficulties are involved, preventing good results, when the costs of resources are deducted in calculating social welfare and profit, especially in the online setting: The allocation problem with server costs contains a mixture of packing and covering constraints (packing VM requests within resource capacities, and covering accepted requests by producing enough resources and paying server costs) —such problems are known to be more challenging than problems with only packing constraints such as the previous models without server costs [14]. Further, we seek to consider more generic server cost functions that are convex instead of linear, and there were no appropriate techniques for handling such non-linear costs until very recently (see Sec. 2 for details).

Our Contributions. This paper leverages a set of latest, novel primal-dual online optimization techniques and randomized reduction techniques, to design a set of truthful, polynomial-time online auctions for social welfare maximization or profit maximization with good competitive ratios. Our mechanisms consist of two main modules: (1) an online primal-dual optimization framework for VM allocation to maximize the social welfare with server costs, and for revealing the payments through the dual variables to guarantee truthfulness; and (2) a randomized reduction algorithm to convert the social welfare maximizing auctions to ones that glean a maximal expected profit for the provider, with competitive ratios comparable to those for social welfare.

First, we model the social welfare (profit) maximization problem using a primal-dual optimization framework, and adopt a new application of Fenchel duality for the dual, which provides richer structures for convex programs that guide the design and analysis of online auctions, than the commonly used Lagrangian duality. Our optimization framework is general and expressive enough to handle various convex server cost functions, *e.g.*, cubic, linear, or zero infinity, representing different server operation models in real-world IaaS clouds.

Second, we design efficient primal-dual online auctions for social welfare maximization, which extend the existing online primal-dual resource allocation framework to handle departures of resource requests, such that resources released by completed VM requests can be reused by later bids. Existing online primal-dual resource allocation algorithms (e.g., [15][16]) do not handle resource re-use and time-varying resource demands in each request. To the best of our knowledge, the only online primal-dual algorithms that address departure of resource requests are those for online scheduling (e.g., [17]), which is structurally different from our problem and the techniques cannot be easily translated to our setting. Other highlights of the design include meticulously designed pricing functions for updating the marginal prices per unit resource according to the current resource usage levels, which play a key role in achieving truthfulness and good competitive ratio.

Third, we extend our social welfare maximizing auctions to profit maximizing ones using randomized reduction, with minor losses in competitive ratios. To obtain good competitive ratios in terms of profit with super-linear server costs (Sec. 4), we introduce a new online primal-dual analysis for profit. Previous techniques usually compare the profit of online auctions with the optimal social welfare, and do not easily generalize to our model with server costs. In contrast, we compare the profit of our auctions with the dual objective of the social welfare maximization convex program. To our knowledge, our online primal dual analysis for profit is novel in the literature and may be of further interest for other profit maximization problems.

Organization. We discuss related work in Sec. 2, and define the problem model in Sec. 3. Sec. 4 presents our online auction design under super-linear server cost functions. Sec. 5 discusses the online auctions under linear server cost models. Simulations are presented in Sec. 6. Sec. 7 concludes the paper.

2. RELATED WORK

Allocating pre-configured types of VMs in an IaaS cloud to serve user jobs has been extensively studied with different focuses. Beloglazov *et al.* [18] study energy-efficient allocation algorithms for scheduling VMs to serve computing tasks. Joe-Wong *et al.* [19] seek to balance efficiency and fairness when allocating VMs to users. Maguluri *et al.* [20] investigate stochastic models and algorithms for load balancing and VM allocation to handle randomly arriving workloads. None of them investigates online optimized packing of customized VMs at user-specified resource amounts, which is the focus of this work.

Auction mechanisms have been at the focal point of recent literature on VM pricing. Lin *et al.* [6] propose a second price auction for computing capacity allocation and pricing. Zaman and Grosu [5] study on-demand VM allocation through a truthful auction, and show through experiments that a higher revenue can be achieved for the cloud provider. Their models do not include tailormade VM assembling. Wang *et al.* [21] model VM allocation and pricing as a multi-unit combinatorial auction, apply the critical value method, and derive a mechanism that is truthful and collusion-resistant. Zhang *et al.* [8] study customized VM provisioning within one data center, and design a truthful auction by applying an LP decomposition technique, achieving a 2.72-approximation in social welfare in typical scenarios. All these studies consider only one-round auctions with all bids given, neglecting the dynamical nature of users' demands.

Wang *et al.* [10] model a dynamic auction where bidders may request to occupy a VM for more than one decision interval, and propose an online auction mechanism. With simulations, they show their mechanism to be truthful and asymptotically optimal in provider revenue when demand is sufficiently high. However, the auction model is over-simplified and considers one type of VM only. In the VM auction of Zhang *et al.* [11], the bidding language and the user valuation models capture the heterogeneous demands in a cloud market. However, only a single type of VM is considered, significantly simplifying the underlying social welfare maximization. Shi *et al.* [7] investigate auctions over multiple rounds which are coupled together by the overall budget of each user, while each acquired VM is still used for only one round. We investigate a more practical online setup, where each VM can be running for various durations into the future, where it is significantly more challenging to guarantee truthfulness and efficiency. Online VM allocation is also studied in [9], but a strong assumption is made on allowing preemption of resources already occupied by a user. In addition, none of existing cloud auctions consider server costs in the social welfare or provider's profit, which will be included in our model.

The online primal dual framework (see [15] for a survey) has been used to design online algorithms and auctions for various problems, such as the ski rental problem, metrical task system problem and ad auctions. The original online primal dual framework focuses on linear programs, which does not naturally model the convex cost functions considered in this work.

Recently, there have been studies on extending the online primal dual framework to problems modeled by convex programs, such as online scheduling on speed-scalable machines [17][22], and online combinatorial auctions with production costs [16][23]. The former is structurally different from our problem. The latter does not handle departures of resource requests, while in practical scenarios of VM allocations, each VM only occupies the requested resources for a limited period of time, and the resources can be released and reused afterwards. This work extends the primal-dual framework to handle VM departures and resource recycling.

3. PROBLEM MODEL

3.1 Cloud System and the Auction

We consider an IaaS cloud system consisting of S servers, offering users R types of resources, as exemplified by CPU, RAM, disk storage and bandwidth. We use $[X]$ to denote the set $\{1, 2, ..., X\}$. Each server $s \in [S]$ can provide a maximum amount C_{rs} of resource $r \in [R]$. Cloud users arrive over time, and each requests one or multiple tailor-made VMs for workload execution, with the amount of resources needed for each VM specified. The IaaS cloud provider acts as the auctioneer and sells the VMs through auctions.

A user submits a bid for each VM she requests upon her arrival. A total number of I bids are submitted in a large time span $1, 2, \ldots, T$. Let B_i denote the ith bid submitted at t_i (we allow multiple bids to be submitted at the same time and order simultaneous bids randomly). t_i^- is the start time to run the VM if B_i is accepted and t_i^+ is the end time, where $t_i \le t_i^- < t_i^+$.

Let $d_{ir}(t)$ denote the amount of type-r resource required by bid i at time t. By allowing $d_{ir}(t)$ to resume different values over $t \in [t_i^-, t_i^+]$, we enable each VM to consume a different amount of each type of resource over time. For example, at different stages of a MapReduce job, different CPU and bandwidth capacities are needed [24]. $d_{ir}(t)$'s are specified in the bid based on the projected resource need of the bidder's workload at different times, *e.g.*, according to previous execution of similar workloads. Dynamic scaling of resources occupied by a running VM is practically feasible through "hotplug" technologies that adjust CPU cycles, memory and disks allocated to a running VM, as supported in various virtualization environments including Xen, VMWare and VirtualBox [25][26]. Let b_i be the overall willingness-to-pay submitted in bid i for the tailor-made VM to run between t_i^- and t_i^+, and v_i be the true valuation of the respective bidder. A bid can be expressed as (*bidding language*):

$$B_i = \{t_i^-, t_i^+, \{d_{ir}(t)\}_{r\in[R], t\in[t_i^-, t_i^+]}, b_i\}. \qquad (1)$$

Upon receiving each bid, the cloud provider decides whether to accept it, and on which server to provision the requested VM if accepted. A binary variable x_{is} is set to 1 if bid i is accepted with resources allocated on server s, and 0 otherwise. The provider also computes a payment $\hat{p}_i$ for each winning bid i.

In practice, most cloud data centers keep their servers on, which remain in the low-power idle mode if no jobs are running, to avoid time-consuming booting up if switched completely off [27]. The decisions of server provisioning happen at a much larger time scale than those for VM allocation, *e.g.*, Amazon EC2 adjusts its server provisioning roughly once per month, according to discussions with Amazon employees. Therefore, we realistically assume that all S servers are turned on in the span T under our investigation. Each server consumes a basic amount of power with no VM running, and the power usage increases with the increase of resource occupied on the server. The operational cost of a server is mainly due to the power cost, following a similar increasing trend with power consumption. We use $f_{rs}(\cdot)$ to denote the cost function of server s on the amount of type-r resource used on the server, as indicated by $y_{rs}(t)$. The cost function is defined as follows:

$$f_{rs}(y_{rs}(t)) = \begin{cases} h_{rs} y_{rs}(t)^{1+\beta_{rs}}, & y_{rs}(t) \in [0, C_{rs}] \\ +\infty, & y_{rs}(t) > C_{rs} \end{cases} \qquad (2)$$

Parameter $\beta_{rs} \ge 0$ decides the shape of the cost function, according to different operational models of the server. For example, Dynamic Voltage Frequency Scaling (DVFS) has been widely supported in virtualization platforms, which adjusts the frequency or voltage of a CPU on the fly (often in response to the workload) to conserve its power consumption [28]. When the CPU voltage is elevated with the utilization, the CPU power usage renders a cubic increase with the CPU voltage [29], and hence we can approximately use $\beta_{rs} = 2$ in (2) where r denotes the CPU. If DVFS is not enabled, measurements have shown that the server power consumption increases roughly linearly with the utilization of CPU, memory, disk I/O and network I/O [30], and hence we set $\beta_{rs} = 0$ in this case. h_{rs} indicates the relative weight of the cost due to each type of resource in the overall server cost. It has also been shown that power consumption of memory, disk I/O and network I/O are significantly lower than that of the CPU, further ranked in a decreasing order among themselves [31], and the power usage due to different resources is additive [30], confirming our additive model of the costs due to different resources.

3.2 Mechanism Design Goals

We target the following properties in our auction design.

(i) *Truthfulness*: For any bidder, declaring her true valuation of the VM and true information (*e.g.*, bid arrival time) in her bid always maximizes her utility, regardless of other users' bids. (ii) *Computational efficiency*: Polynomial-time algorithms for resource allocation and payment calculation are needed for the auction to run efficiently in an online fashion. (iii) *Individual rationality*: Each bidder obtains a non-negative utility by participating in the auction, and the cloud provider receives a non-negative net profit. (iv) *Social welfare maximization or provider's profit maximization*: The cloud provider's profit equals the aggregate user payment minus server costs, *i.e.*,

$$\sum_{i\in[I]} \hat{p}_i \sum_{s\in[S]} x_{is} - \sum_{t\in[T]} \sum_{s\in[S]} \sum_{r\in[R]} f_{rs}(y_{rs}(t)). \quad (3)$$

Bid i's utility is $v_i - \hat{p}_i$. The social welfare over system span T is the sum of the provider's profit and the bidders' aggregate utility, $\sum_{i\in[I]}(v_i - \hat{p}_i)\sum_{s\in[S]} x_{is}$ (valuation minus payment of all winning bids), which equals the aggregate valuation of the winning bids minus the server costs,

$$\sum_{i\in[I]} v_i \sum_{s\in[S]} x_{is} - \sum_{t\in[T]} \sum_{s\in[S]} \sum_{r\in[R]} f_{rs}(y_{rs}(t)),$$

and

$$\sum_{i\in[I]} b_i \sum_{s\in[S]} x_{is} - \sum_{t\in[T]} \sum_{s\in[S]} \sum_{r\in[R]} f_{rs}(y_{rs}(t))$$

under truthful bidding. A cloud system operates at the maximal efficiency if social welfare is maximized over the running span, benefiting both the cloud provider and users. An equally natural goal is to maximize the provider's profit, which we will also pursue with efficient online auction design.

The offline VM allocation and winner determination problem can be formulated as follows, supposing all I bids within system span T are known and truthful bidding is guaranteed. The objective in (4) indicates social welfare maximization, and can be easily changed to profit maximization by replacing the social welfare with the provider's profit in (3).

$$\text{maximize} \quad \sum_{i\in[I]} \sum_{s\in[S]} b_i x_{is} - \sum_{t\in[T]} \sum_{s\in[S]} \sum_{r\in[R]} f_{rs}(y_{rs}(t)) \quad (4)$$

subject to:

$$\sum_{s\in[S]} x_{is} \le 1, \ \forall i \in [I] \ (4a)$$

$$\sum_{\substack{i\in[I]:\\ t_i^- \le t \le t_i^+}} d_{ir}(t) x_{is} \le y_{rs}(t), \ \forall r \in [R], s \in [S], t \in [T] \ (4b)$$

$$x_{is} \in \{0,1\}, y_{rs}(t) \ge 0, \ \forall r \in [R], s \in [S], i \in [I], t \in [T] \ (4c)$$

Here, constraint (4a) indicates that each requested VM is provisioned on at most one server. (4b) sums up the amount of type-r resource needed by all accepted bids on server s at t (counting only bids whose VMs are running at t) into $y_{rs}(t)$. Recall the definition of the cost function in (2): by setting $f_{rs}(y_{rs}(t)) = +\infty$ when $y_{rs}(t)$ exceeds C_{rs} (the overall capacity of type-r resource on server s), it is (implicitly) guaranteed that the allocation of each type of resource on any server will not go beyond the capacity limit.

The offline problem in (4) is a convex mixed integer program with a concave objective function and linear constraints. We relax the integrality constraints $x_{is} \in \{0,1\}$ to $x_{is} \ge 0$ (constraint (4a) guarantees $x_{is} \le 1$), and apply Fenchel duality [32] to the relaxed convex program. As compared to the well-known Lagrangian duality defined generically for convex and non-convex programs, Fenchel duality is defined only for convex programs, and the derived Fenchel dual problems typically present richer structures that guide the design and analysis of primal-dual online algorithms.

Table 1: Notation

I	# of bids	T	# of time slots
R	# of resource types	S	# of servers
t_i	arrival time of bid i	t_i^- (t_i^+)	start (end) time of bid i
$d_{ir}(t)$	demand of resource r at t of bid i		
C_{rs}	capacity of resource r of server s		
x_{is}	serve bid i on server s (1) or not (0)		
$\alpha_1, 2\alpha_2$	competitive ratios of algorithms PD_1 and PD_2		
U_r	$\max_{i\in[I]} b_i / \sum_{t\in[t_i^-,t_i^+]} d_{ir}(t)$		
L_r	$\min_{i\in[I]} b_i / \sum_{t\in[t_i^-,t_i^+]} d_{ir}(t)$		
$y_{rs}(t)$	amount of allocated resource r on s at t		
u_i	utility of bid i		
$p_{rs}(t)$	marginal payment of type-r resource on s at t		
$f_{rs}(y_{rs}(t))$	cost function of type-r resource on s		
$f_{rs}^*(p_{rs}(t))$	conjugate of $f_{rs}(\cdot)$		
$\hat{p}_i$	payment of bid i in PD_1 and PD_2		

Let u_i and $p_{rs}(t)$ be the dual variables associated with (4a) and (4b), respectively. The Fenchel dual [32] of the relaxed convex program is as follows:

$$\text{minimize} \quad \sum_{i\in[I]} u_i + \sum_{t\in[T]} \sum_{r\in[R]} \sum_{s\in[S]} f_{rs}^*(p_{rs}(t)) \quad (5)$$

subject to:

$$u_i \ge b_i - \sum_{t\in[t_i^-,t_i^+]} \sum_{r\in[R]} d_{ir}(t) p_{rs}(t), \ \forall s \in [S], i \in [I] \ (5a)$$

$$p_{rs}(t) \ge 0, \ \forall r \in [R], s \in [S], t \in [T] \ (5b)$$

$$u_i \ge 0, \ \forall i \in [I] \ (5c)$$

where $f_{rs}^*(p_{rs}(t))$ is the conjugate of the cost function $f_{rs}(\cdot)$, defined as

$$f_{rs}^*(p_{rs}(t)) = \sup_{y_{rs}(t)\ge 0} \{p_{rs}(t) y_{rs}(t) - f_{rs}(y_{rs}(t))\} \quad (6)$$

PROPOSITION 1. *The conjugate of $f_{rs}(y_{rs}(t))$ defined in (2) is*

$$f_{rs}^*(p_{rs}(t)) = \begin{cases} \left(\frac{p_{rs}(t)}{1+\beta_{rs}}\right)^{\frac{1+\beta_{rs}}{\beta_{rs}}} \frac{\beta_{rs}}{(h_{rs})^{\frac{1}{\beta_{rs}}}}, & y_{rs}^0(t) \le C_{rs} \\ C_{rs} p_{rs}(t) - h_{rs}(C_{rs})^{1+\beta_{rs}}, & y_{rs}^0(t) > C_{rs} \end{cases} \quad (7)$$

where $y_{rs}^0(t) = \left(\frac{p_{rs}(t)}{h_{rs}(1+\beta_{rs})}\right)^{\frac{1}{\beta_{rs}}}$.

See Appendix A for the proof.

The offline allocation problem and its Fenchel dual are established assuming complete knowledge about the system over its entire lifespan. In practice, with the arrival of bids, the variables and constraints emerge gradually. For example, on the arrival of bid i, there is a set of new primal variables x_{is} for $s \in [S]$ subject to $\sum_{s\in[S]} x_{is} \le 1$. The cloud provider must decide immediately whether to serve bid i and on which server, as well as the bidder's payment if served. In the following, we design online primal-dual allocation algorithms and payment schemes based on (4) and (5).

4. ONLINE AUCTIONS FOR SOCIAL WELFARE AND PROFIT MAXIMIZATION

In this section, we focus on the case of superlinear server cost functions, *i.e.*, $h_{rs} > 0$ and $\beta_{rs} > 0$ in (2), and design online auctions for social welfare maximization (Sec. 4.1) and profit maximization (Sec. 4.2). We will discuss the case of linear server cost functions (with zero server cost as a special case) in Sec. 5.

4.1 Online Auction for Social Welfare Maximization

4.1.1 Auction Design

Deciding whether to serve a new bid i and on which server is equivalent to choosing a feasible assignment for the new primal variables x_{is}. If the cloud provider decides to serve bid i on some server s_i, then let $x_{is_i} = 1$, and increase the amount of allocated resources $y_{rs_i}(t)$ by $d_{ir}(t)$ on server s_i for all resources $r \in [R]$ and for all time slots $t \in [t_i^-, t_i^+]$. As a result, the total server cost of s_i, $\sum_{t\in[T]} \sum_{r\in[R]} f_{rs_i}(y_{rs_i}(t))$, increases accordingly. Otherwise, x_{is} will be zero for all servers $s \in [S]$.

VM Allocation. The question is how to decide whether to serve bid i and on which server. For this we will look into the dual program and resort to the KKT conditions [33]. With bid i, there is a new dual variable $u_i \geq 0$ subject to constraints (5a), that is, $u_i \geq b_i - \sum_{t\in[t_i^-,t_i^+]} \sum_{r\in[R]} d_{ir}(t)p_{rs}(t)$ for all $s \in [S]$. The KKT conditions indicate that in the offline primal and dual solutions to (4) and (5), x_{is} must be zero unless constraint (5a) is tight for server s. Thus, we let u_i be the maximal of 0 and the right hand side (RHS) of constraints (5a), that is,

$$u_i = \max\left\{0, \max_{s\in[S]}\left\{b_i - \sum_{t\in[t_i^-,t_i^+]} \sum_{r\in[R]} d_{ir}(t)p_{rs}(t)\right\}\right\}. \tag{8}$$

Accordingly, we adopt the following method to decide whether to accept a bid and on which server: the cloud provider does not serve bid i, *i.e.*, $x_{is} = 0$ for all $s \in [S]$, if no server s achieves a non-negative value on the RHS of (5a) (*i.e.*, $u_i = 0$), and otherwise serves bid i on the server s_i that maximizes the RHS (*i.e.*, $x_{is_i} = 1$, and $x_{is} = 0, \forall s \neq s_i$).

The rationale is as follows: If we interpret $p_{rs}(t)$ as the marginal price (a.k.a. payment) per unit of type-r resource on server s at time t, then the second term on the RHS of (5a) becomes the total payment that bid i should pay for the requested resources, *i.e.*,

$$\hat{p}_i = \sum_{t\in[t_i^-,t_i^+]} \sum_{r\in[R]} d_{ir}(t)p_{rs}(t). \tag{9}$$

So the RHS of (5a) for a given s is the utility of bid i if it would be served on server s (valuation minus payment, assuming truthful bidding). Therefore, the above method effectively assigns bid i to the server that maximizes its utility, and u_i is bid i's utility. In this way, we target utility maximization for each bid, which leads to truthfulness and social welfare maximization.

Payment Design. Furthermore, the cloud provider updates the marginal prices $p_{rs}(t)$ as the amounts of allocated resources $y_{rs}(t)$ change, after calculating payment $\hat{p}_i$ of accepted bid i using (9), to ensure that: (i) the gain in social welfare when a bid is served outweighs the loss in total server cost, and (ii) the cloud does not allocate all resources to low value bids that come early at the risk of having no capacity left for high value bids in the future. Indeed, designing the online pricing rules is the key to obtain a good competitive ratio in social welfare, as compared to the offline optimum.

Again, our method of pricing is driven by the structure of the offline primal and dual solutions. Let $\ddot{y}_{rs}(t)$ be total demand of resource r on server s at time t, and $\ddot{p}_{rs}(t)$ be the respective marginal prices in the offline primal and dual solutions. If $\ddot{y}_{rs}(t)$ is smaller than the capacity C_{rs}, the marginal price $\ddot{p}_{rs}(t)$ shall be equal to the marginal cost per unit of the resource, $f'_{rs}(\ddot{y}_{rs}(t))$; if the demand meets its capacity, the marginal price shall serve as a threshold to filter out the low value bids, such that the demand subject to the prices is equal to the capacity.

In this online setting, however, the cloud provider can see only the current demands of resources, not the final demands. Therefore, it will predict the final demands based on the current ones and set prices accordingly. Our approach is predicting the final demand of a resource r on server s to be δ_{rs} times its current demand if the predicted final demand does not exceed the capacity, for a fixed parameter $\delta_{rs} > 1$ to be determined later, and set the marginal price to be $p_{rs}(t) = f'_{rs}(\delta_{rs} y_{rs}(t))$. If the above predicted final demand exceeds the capacity, the cloud provider needs to predict the final threshold price (subject to which the demand equals the capacity) and use it as the marginal price. For this we use the state-of-the-art technique in online resource allocation (e.g., [34]), and let the marginal price increase exponentially in the current demand, *i.e.*, $p_{rs}(t) = f'_{rs}(C_{rs}) \exp(\theta_{rs}(y_{rs}(t) - C_{rs}/\delta_{rs}))$, where θ_{rs} is a parameter to be determined later, if the predicted final demand exceeds the capacity. In summary, the marginal price for each resource on each server at each time, $p_{rs}(t)$, is defined to be a function on $y_{rs}(t)$ (for all $r \in [R]$, $s \in [S]$, and $t \in [T]$):

$$p_{rs}(y_{rs}(t)) = \begin{cases} f'_{rs}(\delta_{rs} y_{rs}(t)), & y_{rs}(t) \leq \frac{C_{rs}}{\delta_{rs}} \\ f'_{rs}(C_{rs}) e^{\theta_{rs}(y_{rs}(t) - \frac{C_{rs}}{\delta_{rs}})}, & y_{rs}(t) > \frac{C_{rs}}{\delta_{rs}} \end{cases} \tag{10}$$

We will show in Sec. 4.1.2 that such a price function leads to nice properties, guaranteeing competitiveness of the online auction.

Auction Mechanism. Directed by the discussions above, we design the online auction algorithm PD_1, as given in Alg. 1, with the

---

Algorithm 1: Primal-Dual Online Auction PD_1

```
Input: S, R, C, h, β
Output: x, p
DEFINE f_rs(y_rs(t)) according to (2), ∀s ∈ [S], r ∈ [R];
DEFINE p_rs(y_rs(t)) according to (10), ∀s ∈ [S], r ∈ [R];
INITIALIZE x_is = 0, y_rs(t) = 0, u_i = 0, p_rs(t) = 0, ∀i ∈ [I], s ∈ [S], r ∈ [R], t ∈ [T];
Upon the arrival of the ith bid
Get bidding language B_i according to (1);
(x_i, p̂_i, p, y) = CORE(S, R, B_i, p, y, p(y));
if ∃s ∈ [S], x_is = 1 then
    Accept the ith bid and allocate resources on server s to
    provision the VM requested in bid i;
    Charge the ith bid at p̂_i;
else
    Reject the ith bid;
end
```

Algorithm 2: One-Round Auction Algorithm CORE

```
Input: S, R, B_i, p, y, p(y)
Output: x_i, p̂_i, p, y
Update the dual variable u_i (utility) according to (8);
if u_i > 0 then
    s_i = argmax_{s∈[S]} {b_i − Σ_{t∈[t_i^-, t_i^+]} Σ_{r∈[R]} d_ir(t) p_rs(t)};
    Calculate the payment of the ith bid:
    p̂_i = Σ_{t∈[t_i^-, t_i^+]} Σ_{r∈[R]} d_ir(t) p_{rs_i}(t).;
    Update the primal variables:
    x_{is_i} = 1, and x_is = 0 for all s ≠ s_i;
    y_{rs_i}(t) = y_{rs_i}(t) + d_ir(t)    ∀r ∈ [R], t ∈ [t_i^-, t_i^+];
    Update the dual marginal price variables:
    p_{rs_i}(t) = p_{rs_i}(y_{rs_i}(t))    ∀r ∈ [R], t ∈ [t_i^-, t_i^+];
else
    x_is = 0 for all s ∈ [S];
end
```

one-round algorithm CORE given in Alg. 2. Upon arrival of each bid, we calculate the payment for an accepted bid by summing up the product of resource demand and current marginal price on the selected server s_i to serve bid i for all resources over the occupation period (line 5, Alg. 2). We update primal variables by setting x_{is_i} to 1 (line 7), and increase the utilization $y_{rs_i}(t)$ for different resources for future time slots $t \in [t_i^-, t_i^+]$, according to the demand of bid i (line 8). We update the dual marginal price variables $p_{rs_i}(t)$'s according to (10) (line 10). Recycling of resources is implicitly handled by increasing $y_{rs}(t)$'s with bid i's resource demand, only for time slots within specified duration $[t_i^-, t_i^+]$.

4.1.2 *Analysis*

(i) Truthfulness, Individual Rationality, and Polynomial Time

THEOREM 1. *The online auction* PD$_1$ *in Alg. 1 is truthful and individually rational, and processes each bid in $O(RST)$ time.*

The detailed proof can be found in Appendix B.

(ii) Competitiveness in Social Welfare

We next analyze the competitive ratio of our online auction, *i.e.*, the worst-case upper-bound ratio of the social welfare achieved by the offline solution of (4) to the overall social welfare achieved by our online auction at the end of T. We start by introducing an online primal-dual analysis framework, which bounds the ratio according to a bound between the increase of primal objective value and the increase of dual objective value at each step of the online algorithm.

Let $P^0 = 0$ and D^0 be the initial values of the primal and dual objectives. Let P^i and D^i denote the primal and dual objective values after handling bid i. $y_{rs}^i(t)$ denotes the amount of allocated type-r resource on server s after handling bid i, and $p_{rs}^i(t)$ denotes the corresponding marginal price. Note that P^I and D^I are the primal and dual objective values at the end of T. Let OPT be the optimal primal objective value of (4), *i.e.*, the offline optimal social welfare.

LEMMA 1. *If (i) there is a constant $\alpha \geq 1$ such that the incremental increase of the primal and dual objective values differ by at most an α factor,* i.e., $P^i - P^{i-1} \geq \frac{1}{\alpha}(D^i - D^{i-1})$, *for every step i, and (ii) the initial dual objective value D^0 is at most $\frac{1}{2}OPT$, then the algorithm is 2α competitive.*

PROOF. Summing up the inequality of each step i, we have

$$P^I = \textstyle\sum_i (P^i - P^{i-1}) \geq \frac{1}{\alpha}\sum_i (D^i - D^{i-1}) = \frac{1}{\alpha}(D^I - D^0).$$

Here, we use the fact that $P^0 = 0$. By weak duality [33], $D^I \geq OPT$. Further by our assumption that $D^0 \leq \frac{1}{2}OPT$, we have $P^I \geq \frac{1}{2\alpha}OPT$. So the algorithm is 2α competitive. □

In fact, the initial dual value of our algorithm PD$_1$ is $D^0 = 0$. According to the above proof, we can show that our algorithm is α (instead of 2α) competitive, if we can find the smallest $\alpha \geq 1$ such that $P^i - P^{i-1} \geq \frac{1}{\alpha}(D^i - D^{i-1})$ for all steps i, since it achieves $P^I = \frac{1}{\alpha}(D^I - D^0) = \frac{1}{\alpha}D^I \geq \frac{1}{\alpha}OPT$.

The key to identify this α is to show that our constructed marginal pricing function $p_{rs}(t)$ in (10) satisfies an *Allocation-Payment Relationship* contingent on this α, which is sufficient to guarantee the inequality in Lemma 1, based on Theorem 2.

DEFINITION 1. *The* Allocation-Payment Relationship *for a given parameter $\alpha \geq 1$ is*

$$p_{rs}^{i-1}(t)\big(y_{rs}^i(t) - y_{rs}^{i-1}(t)\big) - \big(f_{rs}(y_{rs}^i(t)) - f_{rs}(y_{rs}^{i-1}(t))\big) \geq \tfrac{1}{\alpha}\big(f_{rs}^\star(p_{rs}^i(t)) - f_{rs}^\star(p_{rs}^{i-1}(t))\big), \quad (11)$$

for all $i \in [I]$, $r \in [R]$, $s \in [S]$, and $t \in [t_i^-, t_i^+]$.

The *Allocation-Payment Relationship* shows that the difference between payment for type-r resource on server s (according to the old price before handling i) and the incremental cost of server s due to bid i's additional use of resource r, is no smaller than $\frac{1}{\alpha}$ of the value increase of the conjugate $f_{rs}^\star$ due to the adjustment of the marginal price. Since the payment of bid i according to the adjusted price is no smaller than $p_{rs}^{i-1}(t)d_{ir}(t)$, it guarantees that the payment from a bid if served can cover the loss in the server cost to a guaranteed extent. Concretely, the following lemma shows that the net profit is lower bounded by a constant fraction of the increase in the dual objective due to the increase of dual prices $p_{rs}(t)$.

LEMMA 2. *If the Allocation-Payment Relationship holds for $\alpha \geq 1$, then for every accepted bid i and the corresponding server s_i*

$$\hat{p}_i - \textstyle\sum_{t\in[t_i^-,t_i^+]}\sum_{r\in[R]}\big(f_{rs_i}(y_{rs_i}^i(t)) - f_{rs_i}(y_{rs_i}^{i-1}(t))\big) \geq \frac{1}{\alpha}(D^i - D^{i-1} - u_i)$$

PROOF. Recall that $\hat{p}_i = \sum_{t\in[t_i^-,t_i^+]}\sum_{r\in[R]} d_{ir}(t)p_{rs_i}^{i-1}(t) = \sum_{t\in[t_i^-,t_i^+]}\sum_{r\in[R]}\big(y_{rs}^i(t) - y_{rs}^{i-1}(t)\big)p_{rs_i}^{i-1}(t)$ and that

$$D^i - D^{i-1} = u_i + \textstyle\sum_{t\in[t_i^-,t_i^+]}\sum_{r\in[R]}\big(f_{rs_i}^\star(p_{rs_i}^i(t)) - f_{rs_i}^\star(p_{rs_i}^{i-1}(t))\big)$$

The lemma follows by summing the Allocation-Payment Relationship (11) over all $r \in [R]$ and $t \in [t_i^-, t_i^+]$. □

THEOREM 2. *If the Allocation-Payment Relationship holds for $\alpha \geq 1$, then $P^i - P^{i-1} \geq \frac{1}{\alpha}(D^i - D^{i-1})$ for all $i \in [I]$.*

PROOF. If bid i is rejected, then $P^i - P^{i-1} = D^i - D^{i-1} = 0$. Next, assume bid i is accepted and let s_i be the server to which bid i is allocated ($x_{is_i} = 1$). The change of primal objective is

$$P^i - P^{i-1} = b_i - \textstyle\sum_{t\in[t_i^-,t_i^+]}\sum_{r\in[R]}\big(f_{rs_i}(y_{rs_i}^i(t)) - f_{rs_i}(y_{rs_i}^{i-1}(t))\big)$$

Note that $b_i = u_i + \hat{p}_i$. By Lemma 2, we get that

$$P^i - P^{i-1} \geq u_i + \tfrac{1}{\alpha}(D^i - D^{i-1} - u_i)$$

By $u_i \geq 0$ and $\alpha \geq 1$, we have $P^i - P^{i-1} \geq \frac{1}{\alpha}(D^i - D^{i-1})$. □

We next find the smallest $\alpha \geq 1$ for which our marginal price functions satisfy the respective *Allocation-Payment Relationship.* Note that each inequality (11) in Definition 1 involves only quantities about the same resource r and the same server s. Therefore, we will identify a separate ratio $\alpha_{rs} \geq 1$ for each pair of r and s, such that the marginal pricing functions on r and s satisfy the *Differential Allocation-Payment Relationship* decided by this α_{rs} (Definition 2). We can then take α as the maximum of all α_{rs}'s, *i.e.*, $\alpha = \max_{r\in[R],s\in[S]}\alpha_{rs}$, to satisfy (11) for all r and s.

Without loss of generality, we assume in the following discussions that the demands $d_{ir}(t)$ are much smaller compared to the server capacity C_{rs}. Then we can derive a differential version of the Allocation-Payment Relation (11) based on $d_{ir}(t) = \mathrm{d}y_{rs}(t)$ for all $s \in [S], t \in [t_i^-, t_i^+]$, as follows:

DEFINITION 2. *The* Differential Allocation-Payment Relationship *for a given parameter $\alpha_{rs} \geq 1$ is*

$$p_{rs}(t)\mathrm{d}y_{rs}(t) - f_{rs}'(y_{rs}(t))\mathrm{d}y_{rs}(t) \geq \tfrac{1}{\alpha_{rs}} f_{rs}^{\star\prime}(p_{rs}(t))\mathrm{d}p_{rs}(t),$$
$$\forall i \in [I], r \in [R], s \in [S], t \in [t_i^-, t_i^+]. \quad (12)$$

LEMMA 3. *The marginal payment function defined in* (10) *satisfies the Differential Allocation-Payment Relationship for*

$$\alpha_{rs} = \max\Big\{4(1+\beta_{rs}), \tfrac{2(1+\beta_{rs})}{\beta_{rs}}\ln\Big(\tfrac{U_r}{h_{rs}(1+\beta_{rs})C_{rs}^{\beta_{rs}}}\Big)\Big\},$$

with parameters

$$\delta_{rs} = \max\{2, (1+\beta_{rs})^{\frac{1}{\beta_{rs}}}\},$$
$$\theta_{rs} = \max\{\tfrac{\delta_{rs}}{C_{rs}}\beta_{rs}, \tfrac{\delta_{rs}}{C_{rs}(\delta_{rs}-1)}\ln(\tfrac{U_r}{h_{rs}(1+\beta_{rs})C_{rs}^{\beta_{rs}}})\},$$

where
$$U_r = \max_{i\in[I]} \frac{b_i}{\sum_{t\in[t_i^-,t_i^+]} d_{ir}(t)}$$

is the maximum value per unit of resource r per unit of time.

We will need the following lemma, which states that the marginal payment is greater than the marginal cost by at least a $1+\beta_{rs}$ factor.

LEMMA 4. *For $y_{rs}(t) \in [0, C_{rs}]$ and the corresponding $p_{rs}(t)$,*
$$p_{rs}(t) \geq (1+\beta_{rs})f'_{rs}(y_{rs}(t)) = h_{rs}(1+\beta_{rs})^2 y_{rs}(t)^{\beta_{rs}} \ ,$$
for the parameters in Lemma 3.

The proofs of Lemma 4 and Lemma 3 are given in Appendices C and D. We next obtain the competitive ratio of online auction PD_1.

THEOREM 3. *The online auction PD_1 in Alg. 1 is α_1-competitive in social welfare, for*
$$\alpha_1 = \max_{r\in[R],s\in[S]} \alpha_{rs}$$
with the parameters given in Lemma 3.

PROOF. By Lemma 3, the marginal prices used by online auction PD_1 satisfies the Differential Allocation-Payment Relationship defined in (12) for α_1. By the assumption that each $dy_{rs_i} = y^i_{rs_i}(t) - y^{i-1}_{rs_i}(t) = d_{ir}(t)$ is very small compared to the capacity (and that $dy_{rs}(t) = y^i_{rs}(t) - y^{i-1}_{rs}(t) = 0$ for $s \neq s_i$), we get that
$$f_{rs}(y^i_{rs}(t)) - f_{rs}(y^{i-1}_{rs}(t)) = f'_{rs}(y^{i-1}_{rs}(t))(y^i_{rs}(t) - y^{i-1}_{rs}(t))$$
$$f^\star_{rs}(p^i_{rs}(t)) - f^\star_{rs}(p^{i-1}_{rs}(t)) = f^{\star\prime}_{rs}(p^{i-1}_{rs}(t))(p^i_{rs}(t) - p^{i-1}_{rs}(t)) \ .$$
So (12) holds implies that (11) also holds for α_1. Then, by Lemma 1, Theorem 2, the theorem follows. □

4.2 Online Auction for Profit Maximization

Next, we present an online auction for profit maximization based on the social welfare maximizing online auction PD_1, inspired by a randomized reduction technique [35]. While the idea of increasing the payment by a randomly chosen power-of-2 factor is similar to [35], the analysis of [35] does not extend to our setting with server costs and our analysis is fundamentally different. In particular, we will use an online primal-dual analysis, comparing the expected profit of our online auction to the dual objective value of the social welfare optimization problem. To the best of our knowledge, using the online primal dual framework to analyze profit is new in the literature, and the only known technique for analyzing profit with resource costs is the work by Blum *et al.* [23]. However, the competitive ratio achieved by their technique grows logarithmically in the number of bids, which is undesirable as we are interested in systems involving a large number of bids. In contrast, our competitive ratio is independent on the number of bids. Further, the technique of [23] incurs an additive loss in profit (other than the multiplicative competitive ratio) while our technique does not.

4.2.1 Auction Design

We first introduce a few parameters: $\beta_{\min}$ is the minimum of β_{rs}; L_r and U_r are the lower and upper bounds of a user's value per unit of resource per unit of time, respectively.

Algorithm 3: Randomized Online Auction RPD_1

Input: $S, R, \mathbf{C}, \mathbf{h}, \beta, L_r, U_r$
Output: $\mathbf{x}, \mathbf{p}$
DEFINE $\chi = \max_{r\in[R]} \frac{RU_r}{L_r}$;
INITIALIZE $x_{is} = 0, y_{rs}(t) = 0, u_i = 0, p_{rs}(t) = 0, \forall i \in [I], s \in [S], r \in [R], t \in [T]$;
Upon the arrival of the i**th bid**
Get *bidding language* B_i according to (1);
$(\mathbf{x}_i, \hat{p}_i, \mathbf{p}, \mathbf{y}) = \text{CORE}(S, R, B_i, \mathbf{p}, \mathbf{y}, \mathbf{p}(\mathbf{y}))$;
if $\exists s \in [S], x_{is} = 1$ **then**
  Update
  $$\tilde{p}_i = \max\{\sum_{r\in[R]}\sum_{t\in[t_i^-,t_i^+]} d_{ir}(t)\tfrac{L_r}{R}, \hat{p}_i\}$$
  Generate a random number η such that:
  $$\eta = \begin{cases} 1 & \text{with prob. } \frac{1}{2} \\ 2^j & \text{with prob. } \frac{1}{2\log_2\chi} \text{ for } j = 1, \ldots, \log_2\chi \end{cases} \quad (13)$$
  if $b_i \geq \eta\tilde{p}_i$ **then**
    Accept the ith bid, allocate the VM on server s, and charge $\eta\tilde{p}_i$;
  else
    Reject the ith bid;
  end
else
  Reject the ith bid;
end

$$\beta_{\min} = \min_{s\in[S],r\in[R]} \beta_{rs}$$
$$L_r = \min_{i\in[I]} \frac{b_i}{\sum_{t\in[t_i^-,t_i^+]} d_{ir}(t)} \quad U_r = \max_{i\in[I]} \frac{b_i}{\sum_{t\in[t_i^-,t_i^+]} d_{ir}(t)} \quad (14)$$

(assuming truthful bidding such that $v_i = b_i$).

The online auction RPD_1 is presented in Alg. 3. The idea is to use PD_1 to first obtain a tentative allocation and payment for each bid, and then re-examine each tentatively accepted bid with a boosted payment to improve profit. If the bidding price of the bid is larger than the respective boosted payment, it will be accepted; otherwise it will be rejected. Here, PD_1 serves as a pre-screening step that filters out low-value bids, giving us a set of bids whose total value is comparable to the offline optimal social welfare (according to the competitive analysis of PD_1). The problem is that the payment chosen by PD_1 for, say, the ith bid, could be much smaller than its true value b_i, leaving us with little profit.

To resolve this problem, RPD_1 increases the tentative payment in two steps to guarantee that it is close to the true value v_i with non-trivial probability. First note that for any resource r, by the definition of L_r, the true value (bid price) of the ith bid is at least
$$b_i \geq \sum_{t\in[t_i^-,t_i^+]} d_{ir}(t)L_r \ .$$
Since the above holds for any resource, we further get that
$$b_i \geq \sum_{r\in[R]}\sum_{t\in[t_i^-,t_i^+]} d_{ir}(t)\tfrac{L_r}{R}$$
In light of this observation, RPD_1 raises the tentative payment to
$$\tilde{p}_i = \max\{\sum_{r\in[R]}\sum_{t\in[t_i^-,t_i^+]} d_{ir}(t)\tfrac{L_r}{R}, \hat{p}_i\}$$

The above payment can still be very far from the true value v_i. Hence, RPD$_1$ further multiply $\tilde{p}_i$ by a randomly chosen power of 2, denoted as η, which is drawn from a carefully chosen distribution (*i.e.*, (13)). By doing so, the final payment is within a factor of 2 (and lower than) the true value v_i with non-trivial probability.

We note that Alg. 3 requires U_r and L_r as input, whose exact values are not known before all bids have arrived. Instead, we adopt estimated values of the upper and lower bounds as input to our online algorithm, *e.g.*, based on past experience. We will show in the simulations good performance of the auction even if the estimation is quite different from the actual value.

4.2.2 *Analysis*

(i) Truthfulness, Individual Rationality, and Polynomial Time

THEOREM 4. *The randomized online auction* RPD$_1$ *in Alg. 3 is truthful and individually rational, and processes each bid in* $O(RST)$ *time.*

The proof is given in Appendix E.

(ii) Competitiveness in Profit

THEOREM 5. *The randomized online auction* RPD$_1$ *in Alg. 3 is* $O(\alpha_1+\log_2\chi)$*-competitive in expected profit, where* α_1 *is given in Theorem 3,* $\chi = \max_{r\in[R]} \frac{RU_r}{L_r}$ *with* U_r *and* L_r *defined in* (14).

PROOF. Let R^i denote the expected profit that RPD$_1$ generates from the first i bids ($R^0 = 0$). We will use an analysis similar to the online primal dual approach, and show that for any $i \in [I]$,

$$O\big(\alpha_1 + \log_2\chi\big)\cdot(R^i - R^{i-1}) \geq D^i - D^{i-1} \tag{15}$$

where D_i is dual objective of primal dual auction PD$_1$ after handling the first i bids. The theorem follows because the expected profit of RPD$_1$ at the end of the instance satisfies $O\big(\alpha_1+\log_2\chi\big)R^I \geq D^I - D^0 \geq OPT$, where the last inequality holds because $D^I \geq OPT$ (weak duality) and $D^0 = 0$ (definition of PD$_1$).

It remains to prove (15). If bid i is not accepted by PD$_1$, it is not accepted by RPD$_1$ either. Therefore, both sides of (15) are zero.

Next, suppose bid i is accepted by PD$_1$. Let

$$c_i = \textstyle\sum_{t\in[t_i^-,t_i^+]}\sum_{r\in[R]} f'_{rs_i}\big(y_{rs_i}(t)\big)\mathrm{d}y_{rs_i}(t) \tag{16}$$

denote the increase of server costs if bid i is accepted. Then,

$$\begin{aligned}
&R^i - R^{i-1}\\
&= \Pr[\eta=1](\tilde{p}_i - c_i) + \sum_{j=1}^{\log_2\chi}\Pr[\eta=2^j]\mathbf{1}_{b_i\geq 2^j\tilde{p}_i}\cdot 2^j(\tilde{p}_i - c_i)\\
&= \tfrac{1}{2}(\tilde{p}_i - c_i) + \tfrac{1}{2\log_2\chi}\textstyle\sum_{j=1}^{\log_2\chi}\mathbf{1}_{b_i\geq 2^j\tilde{p}_i}\cdot(2^j\tilde{p}_i - c_i)
\end{aligned} \tag{17}$$

where $\mathbf{1}_{b_i\geq 2^j\tilde{p}_i}$ equals 1 if $b_i \geq 2^j\tilde{p}_i$, and equals 0 otherwise.

By Lemma 2, 3 (recall the definition of c_i in (16)), we have

$$\tilde{p}_i - c_i \geq \hat{p}_i - c_i \geq \tfrac{1}{\alpha_1}(D^i - D^{i-1} - u_i) \tag{18}$$

So the first term of (17) alone is almost sufficient for showing (15) modulo the u_i term.

The rest of the proof is divided into two cases depending on whether $b_i < 2\tilde{p}_i$ (only the first term in (17) is non-zero, but b_i and, thus, u_i are small), or not (b_i and, thus, u_i are large, but we get positive contribution from the second term of (17)).

Case 1: $b_i < 2\tilde{p}_i$. Note that

$$\tilde{p}_i \geq \hat{p}_i = \textstyle\sum_{r\in[R]}\sum_{t\in[t_i^-,t_i^+]} p_{rs_i}(t)\mathrm{d}y_{rs_i}(t)\ .$$

By Lemma 4, $\tilde{p}_i$ is at least

$$\textstyle\sum_{r\in[R]}\sum_{t\in[t_i^-,t_i^+]}(1+\beta_{rs})f'_{rs_i}\big(y_{rs}(t)\big)\mathrm{d}y_{rs_i}(t) \geq (1+\beta_{\min})c_i$$

Note that $\mathbf{1}_{b_i\geq 2^j\tilde{p}_i} = 0$ for all $j \geq 1$. We get that

$$\begin{aligned}
&R^i - R^{i-1}\\
&= \tfrac{1}{2}(\tilde{p}_i - c_i)\\
&\geq \tfrac{1}{6}(\hat{p}_i - c_i) + \tfrac{1}{3}(\tilde{p}_i - c_i) && (\tilde{p}_i \geq \hat{p}_i)\\
&\geq \tfrac{1}{6}(\hat{p}_i - c_i) + \tfrac{\beta_{\min}}{3(1+\beta_{\min})}\tilde{p}_i && (\tilde{p}_i \geq (1+\beta_{\min})c_i)\\
&\geq \tfrac{1}{6}(\hat{p}_i - c_i) + \tfrac{\beta_{\min}}{6(1+\beta_{\min})}u_i && (u_i \leq b_i < 2\tilde{p}_i)\\
&\geq \tfrac{1}{6\alpha_1}(D^i - D^{i-1} - u_i) + \tfrac{\beta_{\min}}{6(1+\beta_{\min})}u_i && (\text{by } (18))
\end{aligned}$$

By definition, $\alpha_{rs} \geq 1 + \frac{1}{\beta_{rs}}$. Recall $\alpha_1 = \max_{r\in[R],s\in[S]}\alpha_{rs}$. So $\alpha_1 \geq 1 + \frac{1}{\beta_{\min}}$. Putting together, (15) follows because

$$R^i - R^{i-1} \geq \tfrac{1}{6\alpha_1}(D^i - D^{i-1} - u_i) + \tfrac{\beta_{\min}}{6}u_i \geq \tfrac{1}{6\alpha_1}(D^i - D^{i-1})$$

Case 2: $b_i \geq 2\tilde{p}_i$. On one hand, by our choice of $\tilde{p}_i$, it is at least

$$\tilde{p}_i \geq \textstyle\sum_{r\in[R]}\sum_{t\in[t_i^-,t_i^+]} d_{ir}(t)\frac{L_r}{R}\ .$$

On the other hand, by the definition of U_r, the true value is at most

$$b_i \leq \textstyle\sum_{r\in[R]}\sum_{t\in[t_i^-,t_i^+]} d_{ir}(t)U_r$$

So $\frac{b_i}{\tilde{p}_i} \leq \frac{RU_r}{L_r} \leq \chi$. Since η is a randomly chosen power of 2 between 1 and χ, with probability $\frac{1}{2\log_2\chi}$, η satisfies $\frac{1}{2}b_i \leq \eta\tilde{p}_i \leq b_i$ and, thus, RPD$_1$ accepts bid i and obtains profit at least $\frac{1}{2}b_i$. Therefore, $R^i - R^{i-1} \geq \frac{1}{2}(\tilde{p}_i - c_i) + \frac{1}{2\log_2\chi}\frac{1}{2}b_i$ (recall (17)). By (18), the first term is at least $\frac{1}{2\alpha_1}(D^i - D^{i-1} - u_i)$. The second term is at least $\frac{1}{4\log_2\chi}u_i$ because bid i's utility is at most its value. Putting together, the expected profit from bid i is at least

$$\begin{aligned}
R^i - R^{i-1} &\geq \tfrac{1}{2\alpha_1}(D^i - D^{i-1} - u_i) + \tfrac{1}{4\log_2\chi}u_i\\
&\geq \tfrac{1}{2\alpha_1+4\log_2\chi}(D^i - D^{i-1} - u_i) + \tfrac{1}{2\alpha_1+4\log_2\chi}u_i\\
&= \tfrac{1}{2\alpha_1+4\log_2\chi}(D^i - D^{i-1})
\end{aligned}$$

So the theorem holds in case 2 as well. □

(iii) Competitiveness in Social Welfare

THEOREM 6. *Randomized online auction* RPD$_1$ *in Alg. 3 is* $2\alpha_1$*-competitive in expected social welfare, where* α_1 *is given in Theorem 3.*

PROOF. Consider any bid i that is accepted by PD$_1$. By the definition if RPD$_1$, it will tentatively accept the bid and then reexamine it with randomly chosen boosted payment. With probability $\frac{1}{2}$, $\eta = 1$. Further note that when $\eta = 1$, $b_i \geq \eta\tilde{p}_i$ and, thus, RPD$_1$ will accept bid i. In sum, for every bid i that is accepted by PD$_1$, RPD$_1$ would accepted it with probability at least $\frac{1}{2}$. Therefore, the expected social welfare of RPD$_1$ is at least a half of the social welfare of PD$_1$. □

5. EXTENSION TO LINEAR SERVER COSTS

We extend the auction design in Sec. 4 to the setting of linear server cost functions, *i.e.*, $\beta_{rs} = 0$ in (2) such that

$$f_{rs}(y_{rs}(t)) = \begin{cases} h_{rs}y_{rs}(t), & y_{rs}(t) \in [0, C_{rs}]\\ +\infty, & y_{rs}(t) > C_{rs}\end{cases} \tag{19}$$

which says that the marginal cost per unit of resource usage is a constant (h_{rs}) within the capacity constraint.

Algorithm 4: Primal-Dual Online Auction PD_2

Input: S, R, $\mathbf{C}$, $\mathbf{h}$, σ
Output: $\mathbf{x}, \mathbf{p}$
DEFINE $f_{rs}(y_{rs}(t))$ according to (19);
DEFINE $p_{rs}(y_{rs}(t))$ according to (21);
INITIALIZE $x_{is}=0, y_{rs}(t)=0, u_i=0, p_{rs}(t)=\frac{L_r-h_{rs}}{2\sigma RS}+h_{rs}, \forall i\in[I], s\in[S], r\in[R], t\in[T]$;
Upon the arrival of the i**th bid**
Get *bidding lauguage* B_i according to (1);
$(\mathbf{x}_i,\hat{p}_i,\mathbf{p},\mathbf{y})=\text{CORE}(S,R,B_i,\mathbf{p},\mathbf{y},\mathbf{p}(\mathbf{y}))$;
if $\exists s\in[S], x_{is}=1$ **then**
  Accept the ith bid on server s, and charge it at $\hat{p}_i$;
else
  Reject the ith bid;
end

PROPOSITION 2. *The conjugate of $f_{rs}(y_{rs}(t))$ defined in* (19) *is*

$$f^{\star}_{rs}(p_{rs}(t))=\begin{cases}0, & p_{rs}(t)\le h_{rs}\\ (p_{rs}(t)-h_{rs})C_{rs}, & p_{rs}(t)>h_{rs}\end{cases} \quad (20)$$

The proof can be found in Appendix F.

5.1 Social Welfare Maximization

We adapt online auction PD_1 to online auction PD_2 for linear cost functions, as given in Alg. 4. Among the input, $\sigma>0$ is a parameter such that $\frac{T}{\sigma}$ is the minimum resource occupation time span among all bids (which can be an estimated lower bound). We define a new marginal payment function:

$$p_{rs}(y_{rs}(t))=\frac{L_r-h_{rs}}{2\sigma RS}\left(\frac{2\sigma RS(U_r-h_{rs})}{L_r-h_{rs}}\right)^{\frac{y_{rs}(t)}{C_{rs}}}+h_{rs}\ , \quad (21)$$

where L_r and U_r are defined in (14). For any bid i such that $b_i/\sum_{t\in[t_i^-,t_i^+]}d_{ir}(t)\le h_{rs}$, its value is smaller than the server cost needed to serve it and, thus, will be rejected. So we can assume without loss of generality that $L_r>h_{rs}$.

The marginal price $p_{rs}(t)$ is a function of the amount of currently allocated resource $y_{rs}(t)$. $p_{rs}(t)$ is higher than marginal operational cost h_{rs} to guarantee non-negative utility of the provider. The initial marginal price is low enough such that any bid (subject to L_r which lower bounds a bid's value per unit of resource per unit of time) will be accepted. Then, the marginal price $p_{rs}(t)$ increases as $y_{rs}(t)$ increases to ensure that a server will not allocate all capacity of a resource to low value bids. Finally, the marginal price is high enough (larger than U_r – upper bound of a bid's value per unit of resource per unit of time) when $y_{rs}(t)>C_{rs}$ to make sure a server will not allocate more resources than its capacity.

PD_2 also uses CORE as a sub-routine. The only difference between PD_1 and PD_2 are the marginal price functions and initial values of the marginal prices, due to different server cost functions.

THEOREM 7. *The online auction* PD_2 *in Alg. 4 is truthful and individually rational, and runs in polynomial time.*

The proof is similar to the proof of Theorem 1 and thus omitted.

THEOREM 8. *The online auction* PD_2 *in Alg. 4 is $2\alpha_2$-competitive in social welfare with*

$$\alpha_2=\max_{r\in[R],s\in[S]}\ln\left(\frac{2\sigma RS(U_r-h_{rs})}{L_r-h_{rs}}\right)\ , \quad (22)$$

assuming that the offline optimal social welfare is at least

$$OPT\ge\frac{1}{RS}\sum_{r\in[R]}\sum_{s\in[S]}\frac{T}{\sigma}(L_r-h_{rs})C_{rs}\ .$$

Before we get to the proof of the theorem, let us first explain how to interpret the assumed lower bound on the offline optimal social welfare. Recall that $\frac{T}{\sigma}$ is the minimum time span that a bid occupies the requested resources for. L_r-h_{rs} is the minimum social welfare generated by a bid that demands resource r and is allocated to server s, per unit of resource r and per unit of time. Thus, $\frac{T}{\sigma}(L_r-h_{rs})C_{rs}$ is the minimal social welfare generated by all bids that demand resource r and are allocated to server s if the entire capacity of resource r on server s is occupied for each time slot. So the assumption in the above theorem is essentially saying that in the offline solution, there are enough workloads to exhaust at least one resource on one server at a time slot, which is easily satisfied in real-world cloud systems.

PROOF. Let $\alpha_{rs}=\ln\frac{2\sigma RS(U_r-h_{rs})}{L_r-h_{rs}}$. We will show that the marginal payment function defined in (21) satisfies the Differential Allocation-Payment Relationship for all resource r, server s, and time t with parameter α_{rs}, i.e.,

$$p_{rs}(t)\mathrm{d}y_{rs}(t)-f'_{rs}(y_{rs}(t))\mathrm{d}y_{rs}(t)\ge\frac{1}{\alpha_{rs}}f^{\star\prime}_{rs}(p_{rs}(t))\mathrm{d}p_{rs}(t)$$

and that the initial value of the dual objective is at most $\frac{1}{2}OPT$. Then, given $\alpha_2=\max_{r\in[R],s\in[R]}\alpha_{rs}$, the theorem will follow from Lemma 1 and Theorem 2. According to (19) and (20),

$$f'_{rs}(y_{rs}(t))=\begin{cases}h_{rs}, & 0\le y_{rs}(t)\le C_{rs}\\ +\infty, & y_{rs}(t)>C_{rs}\end{cases}$$

$$f^{\star\prime}_{rs}(p_{rs}(t))=\begin{cases}0, & 0\le p_{rs}(t)<h_{rs}\\ C_{rs} & p_{rs}(t)\ge h_{rs}\end{cases}$$

By (21), we get $p_{rs}(t)>U_r$ when the demand exceeds the capacity, i.e., $y_{rs}(t)>C_{rs}$. So by our choice of $p_{rs}(t)$, the cloud provider will never allocate more resources than its capacity, *i.e.*, $y_{rs}(t)\le C_{rs}$. In addition, the initial marginal price $p_{rs}(0)=\frac{L_r-h_{rs}}{2\sigma RS}+h_{rs}>h_{rs}$, and the marginal prices are non-decreasing. Therefore in the rest of the discussion, we may assume that $f'_{rs}(y_{rs}(t))=h_{rs}$ and $f^{\star\prime}_{rs}(p_{rs}(t))=C_{rs}$. Putting them into the above differential inequality, it becomes $(p_{rs}(t)-h_{rs})\mathrm{d}y_{rs}(t)\ge\frac{C_{rs}}{\alpha_{rs}}\mathrm{d}p_{rs}(t)$, which holds with equality by our choice of $p_{rs}(t)$ and that $\alpha_{rs}=\ln\frac{2\sigma RS(U_r-h_{rs})}{L_r-h_{rs}}$.

Finally, according to (5) and (20),

$$\begin{aligned} D^0 &= \textstyle\sum_{t\in[T]}\sum_{s\in[S]}\sum_{r\in[R]}C_{rs}(p_{rs}(0)-h_{rs})\\ &= \textstyle\sum_{t\in[T]}\sum_{s\in[S]}\sum_{r\in[R]}C_{rs}\left(\frac{L_r-h_{rs}}{2\sigma RS}\right)\\ &= \textstyle\frac{1}{2}\frac{1}{RS}\sum_{r\in[R]}\sum_{s\in[S]}\frac{T}{\sigma}(L_r-h_{rs})C_{rs}\\ &\le \textstyle\frac{1}{2}OPT. \end{aligned}$$

The last inequality is based on the assumption in the theorem. □

5.2 Profit Maximization

Next, we present an extension of PD_2 *i.e.*, Alg. 5, that achieves a competitive ratio comparable to $2\alpha_2$ in provider's profit. Similar to how RPD_1 extends PD_1, RPD_2 first use PD_2 as a black box to obtain a tentative allocation x_i and payment $\hat{p}_i$ for each bid i. Then it raises the payment by a factor of $\eta\ge 1$ and accepts the bid only when its value is higher than the new payment. The difference lies in the different values of χ, which decides the distribution from which η is sampled.

THEOREM 9. *The online auction* RPD_2 *in Alg. 5 is truthful and individually rational, and runs in polynomial time.*

The proof is similar to the proof of Theorem 4 and thus omitted.

Algorithm 5: Randomized Online Auction RPD_2

Input: S, R, $\mathbf{C}$, $\mathbf{h}$, σ, L_r, U_r
Output: $\mathbf{x}, \mathbf{p}$
DEFINE $f_{rs}(y_{rs}(t))$ according to (19);
DEFINE $p_{rs}(y_{rs}(t))$ according to (21);
DEFINE $\chi = \max_{r\in[R],s\in[S]} \frac{2\sigma RS(U_r - h_{rs})}{L_r - h_{rs}}$;
INITIALIZE $x_{is} = 0, y_{rs}(t) = 0, u_i = 0, p_{rs}(t) = \frac{L_r - h_{rs}}{2\sigma RS} + h_{rs}, \forall i \in [I], s \in [S], r \in [R], t \in [T]$;
Upon the arrival of the ith bid
Get *bidding language* B_i according to (1);
$(\mathbf{x}_i, \hat{p}_i, \mathbf{p}, \mathbf{y}) = \text{CORE}(S, R, B_i, \mathbf{p}, \mathbf{y}, \mathbf{p}(\mathbf{y}))$;
if $\exists s \in [S], x_{is} = 1$ **then**
  Generate a random number η such that:

$$\eta = \begin{cases} 1 & \text{with prob. } \frac{1}{2} \\ 2^j & \text{with prob. } \frac{1}{2\log_2 \chi} \text{ for } j = 1, \ldots, \log_2 \chi \end{cases} \tag{23}$$

  if $b_i \geq \eta \hat{p}_i$ **then**
    Accept the ith bid on server s, and charge $\eta \hat{p}_i$;
  else
    Reject the ith bid;
  end
else
  Reject the ith bid;
end

The profit guarantee will be presented in Theorem 10. We first show a few technical lemmas that are needed for the proof of Theorem 10 (proofs of lemmas given in appendices G—I). Let $A^\star$ be the set of bids accepted by social welfare maximizing online auction PD_2, and $O^\star$ be the set of bids accepted by the offline omniscient optimal algorithm for social welfare maximization. c_i is the cost occurs by an accepted bid i in (16).

LEMMA 5. *The optimal profit of any truthful and individually rational auction (online or offline) in our system is upper bounded by*

$$\sum_{i\in A^\star}(b_i - c_i) + \sum_{i\in O^\star : b_i < \hat{p}_i}(b_i - c_i). \tag{24}$$

LEMMA 6. *The first term of* (24) *is upper bounded by* $4\log_2 \chi$ *times the expected profit of online auction* RPD_2.

LEMMA 7. *The second term of* (24) *can be upper bounded by* α_2 *times the profit of online auction* PD_2, *i.e.,*

$$\sum_{i\in O^\star : b_i < \hat{p}_i}(b_i - c_i) \leq \alpha_2 \sum_{i\in A^\star}(\hat{p}_i - c_i) \tag{25}$$

where α_2 *is defined in* (22).

LEMMA 8. *The expected profit of* RPD_2 *is at least a half of the profit of* PD_2.

PROOF. It follows from that for every bid i, RPD_2 uses the same allocation and payment as in PD_2 with probability $\frac{1}{2}$. □

THEOREM 10. *The randomized online auction* RPD_2 *in Alg. 5 is* $\left(\frac{4}{\ln 2} + 2\right)\alpha_2$*-competitive in terms of expected profit.*

PROOF. Combining Lemmas 5, 6, 7 and 8, the optimal profit is upper bounded by $4\log_2 \chi + 2\alpha_2$ times the expected profit of RPD_2. By the choice of $\chi = \max_{r\in[R],s\in[S]} \frac{2\sigma RS(U_r - h_{rs})}{L_r - h_{rs}}$ and the definition of α_2 in (22), we get that $\log_2 \chi = \frac{1}{\ln 2}\ln \chi = \frac{1}{\ln 2}\alpha_2$. So the theorem follows. □

We also give the competitiveness in social welfare achieved by RPD_2 in the following theorem, with proof given in Appendix J.

THEOREM 11. *The randomized online auction* RPD_2 *in Alg. 5 is* $4\alpha_2$*-competitive in terms of expected social welfare.*

Finally, we note that as a special case, the online auctions in this section also handle the case with no server costs within the capacity, which is equivalent to having $h_{rs} = 0$, and the server cost functions as the following zero infinity functions:

$$f_{rs}(y_{rs}(t)) = \begin{cases} 0, & y_{rs}(t) \in [0, C_{rs}] \\ +\infty, & y_{rs}(t) > C_{rs} \end{cases} \tag{26}$$

All the properties that we have shown for linear cost functions apply to zero infinity costs, with proofs omitted due to duplicity.

6. PERFORMANCE EVALUATION

We evaluate our auctions using trace-driven simulations, exploiting Google cluster-usage data [36], which contains information including resource demands (CPU, RAM, Disk) for each job submitted to the Google cluster, job arrival times and durations. We translate each job into a VM bid, requesting $R = 3$ types of resources at the demands extracted from the traces (note demand $d_{ir}(t)$ here is not much smaller than C_{rs}, though our theoretical analysis assumed so). Each time slot is 10 seconds [37], and a bid arrives every $[1, 10]$ time slot(s) (we set this arrival rate relatively low to test our algorithm in extreme scenarios, since the more bids arrive concurrently, the closer our online algorithm is to the offline one). The duration of each VM is between 10 and 3600 time slots. We set the bidding price of each bid by multiplying the overall resource demands in the bid by unit prices randomly picked within different ranges, according to the upper and lower bounds of users' value per unit of resource per unit of time, U_r and L_r, which will be varied in different experiments. We will vary the span between bid arrival time and the VM start time. We simulate servers with heterogenous resource capacities (C_{rs}) following the distribution of server configurations summarized from the Google data as follows (CPU and Memory units are normalized so that the maximum capacity is 1):

# of machines (percentage)	6732 (53%)	3863 (30%)	1001 (8%)	795 (6%)	126 (3%)
CPU	0.50	0.50	0.50	1.00	0.25
Memory	0.50	0.25	0.750	1.00	0.25

Since the Google data does not provide disk configurations, we set the disk storage capacity of servers randomly within $[320, 800](GB)$. The total capacity of each type of resource to provision, and hence the number of servers to simulate, is roughly according to the total amount of demand from all bids multiplying a random number in $[0.4, 0.8]$. The total number of time slots T is set to $5I + 3600$, since on average a bid arrives in 5 time slots and an extra 3600 time slots are reserved to serve long-running bids that come near the end of the batch. h_{rs} is set within $[0.4, 0.6]$ for CPU (different for different servers s), and within $[0.005, 0.02]$ for RAM and disk, roughly following the percentage measured in [31]. For superlinear cost functions, we set β_{rs} within $[1.7, 2.2]$ for CPU and within $[0.5, 1]$ for RAM and disk [29][31]. By default, $\sigma = 500$, $U_r = 50$, $L_r = 1$.

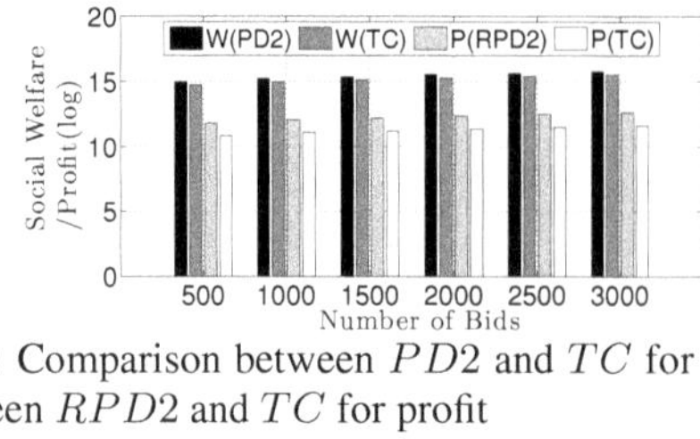

Figure 7: Comparison between $PD2$ and TC for social welfare, and between $RPD2$ and TC for profit

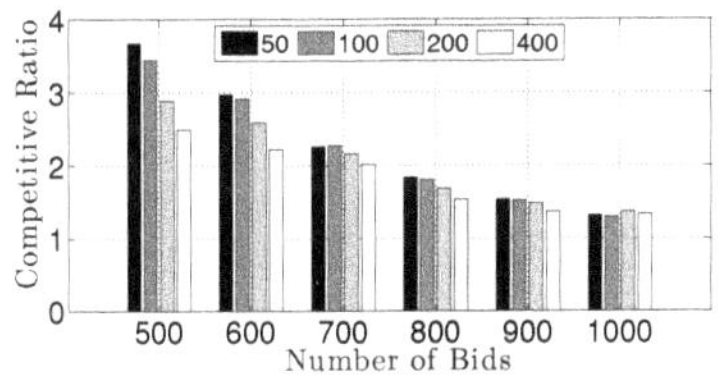

Figure 1: Competitive ratio of PD_1 in social welfare among different Γ

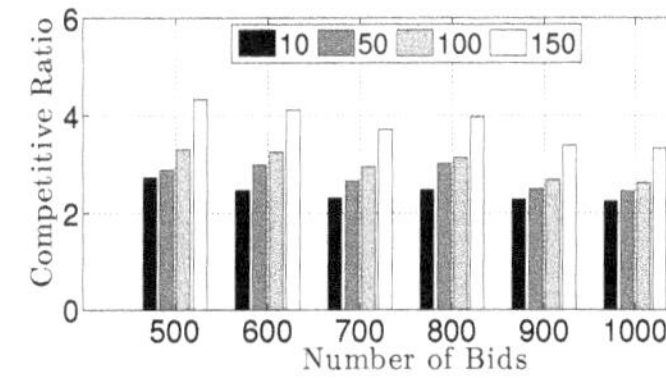

Figure 2: Competitive ratio of RPD_1 in profit among different U_r

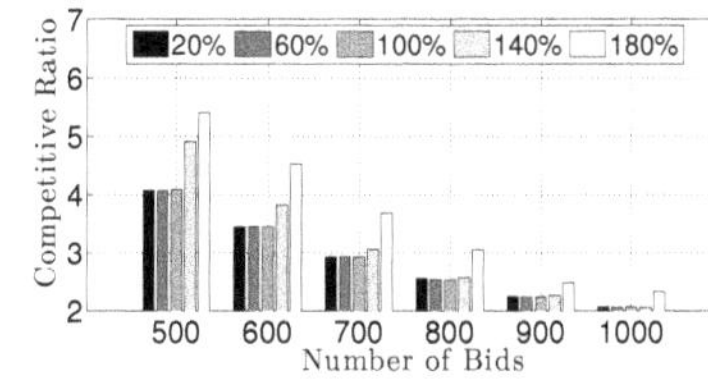

Figure 3: Competitive ratio of RPD_1 in profit over different percentages of estimation over real U_r

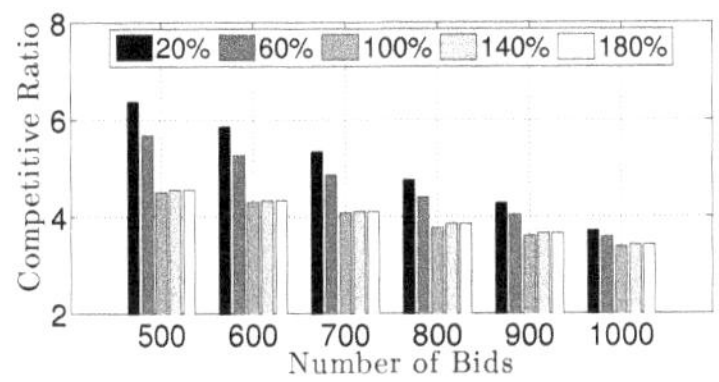

Figure 4: Competitive ratio of RPD_1 in profit over different percentages of estimation over real L_r

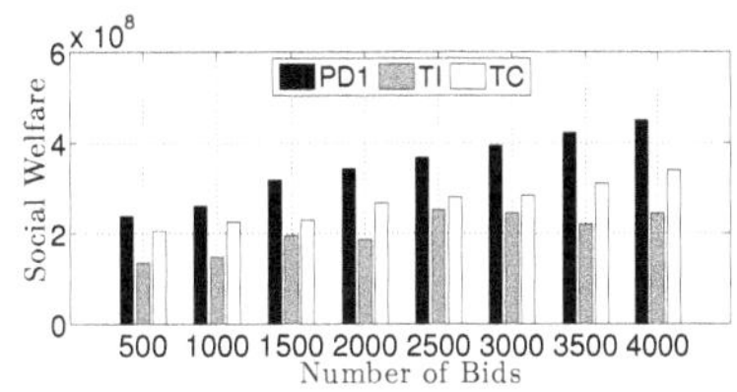

Figure 5: Comparison among $PD1$, TC and TI

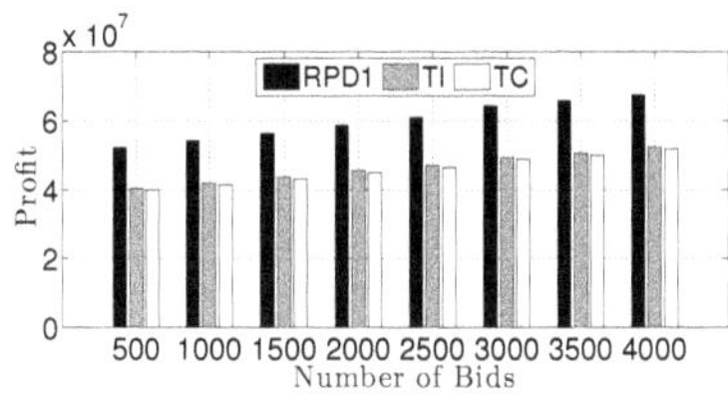

Figure 6: Comparison among $RPD1$, TC, TI

We compare our algorithms with the offline optimum, as well as two existing schemes *Twice-the-Cost* (TC) and *Twice-the-Index* (TI) [23] (we identified a lack of comparable approaches from the VM auction literature). TC and TI share similar basic ideas with our online auctions, but adopt different marginal pricing functions: For TC, $p_{rs}(y_{rs}(t)) = 2f'_{rs}(y_{rs}(t))$, *i.e.*, the current marginal payment is twice of the current marginal cost; for TI, $p_{rs}(y_{rs}(t)) = f'_{rs}(2y_{rs}(t))$, *i.e.*, the current marginal payment is the marginal cost on twice of the current resource usage.

6.1 Comparison with Offline Optimum

We first study the competitive ratios achieved by our online auctions, computed by dividing the offline optimal social welfare obtained by solving (4) exactly using Gurobi Optimizer, by the social welfare or profit achieved by the respective online algorithm. Due to the high time complexity of solving the offline convex program with a large number of variables, we set the largest number of bids to be 1000 in this set of experiments.

Fig. 1 illustrates that a smaller competitive ratio comes with a larger Γ, which is the average number of time slots between the bid arrival time to its specified VM start time over all the bids. Considering the online setting, this result is interesting but quite reasonable: a group of bids apply for a future occupation duration; the earlier they arrive before their actual resource occupation starts, the more future information the system can learn, and better allocation and payment decisions can be made. Fig. 2 shows that the competitive ratio of expected profit with RPD_1 becomes larger with the increase of U_r. According to Theorem 5, a larger U_r not only negatively influences the competitive ratio of RPD_1, but also determines the distribution of η that further increases the ratio. In Fig. 3 and 4, we use estimated values of U_r or L_r as input to RPD_1, which are at different percentages as divided by the real U_r or L_r. We see that both overestimation and underestimation have minor influence in the performance, as compared to that achieved by the real U_r or L_r (the case of 100% in the figures), and underestimation of U_r and overestimation of L_r are more desirable.

In addition, all figures show that the competitive ratio becomes smaller with the increase of the number of bids. According to our setup, when the number of bids increases, the total demands of resources increase, and more servers are provisioned. In our online auctions, we always choose a cheapest server for each coming bid in (8), and hence the solution space becomes larger when the number of servers increases, leading to better competitive ratios. The results for PD_2 and RPD_2 are similar to the cases of PD_1 and RPD_1, and we omit them here due to space constraints.

6.2 Comparison with Existing Schemes

We next compare the social welfare and profit achieved by our auctions with TC and TI at larger scales of the system. Fig. 5 shows that the social welfare achieved by our PD_1 outperforms those by TC and TI. Especially, we observe through our experiments that the marginal payment function in TC can not filter out low value bids when the used resource of a server approaches its full capacity, and with TI, maximally only half of the capacity on a server can be allocated due to the $+\infty$ part of the cost function, both leading to lower social welfare. Fig. 6 further reveals the higher profit achieved by our RPD_1, as compared to TC and TI.

Due to space limit, we compare PD_2 and RPD_2 with TC in terms of social welfare ($W(\cdot)$) and profit ($P(\cdot)$), respectively, in the same Fig. 7 (note the values are in log scale). Our algorithms outperform TC in both cases.

7. CONCLUDING REMARKS

This work designs truthful and efficient online VM auctions where cloud users bid for resources into the future for tailor-made VMs with different running durations, targeting social welfare maximization and cloud provider's profit maximization. We consider server costs in our auction model, and handle the resulting significantly more challenging mechanism design by leveraging a set of latest novel primal-dual online optimization and randomized reduction techniques. Our primal-dual framework adopts a new application of Fenchel duality and handles various convex server cost functions. It further allows request departures and resource recycling while guaranteeing good competitive ratios, which existing online primal-dual resource allocation frameworks do not handle. For profit maximization, we introduce a new online primal-dual analysis to obtain good competitive ratios with super-linear server costs, which is new in the literature and can be of further interest for other profit maximization problems in general. Trace driven simulations validate our theoretical analysis and show good performance of our mechanisms as compared to the offline solution and existing mechanisms on similar frameworks.

8. ACKNOWLEDGMENTS

This work was supported in part by grants from Hong Kong RGC under the contracts HKU 718513 and HKU 27200214E, the Natural Sciences and Engineering Research Council of Canada (NSERC), and Wedge Networks.

9. REFERENCES

[1] "Amazon EC2 Instances," http://aws.amazon.com/ec2/instance-types/.

[2] "ProfitBricks," https://www.profitbricks.com.

[3] "CloudSigma," https://www.cloudsigma.com.

[4] O. Agmon Ben-Yehuda, M. Ben-Yehuda, A. Schuster, and D. Tsafrir, "Deconstructing Amazon EC2 Spot Instance Pricing," in *Proc. of IEEE CloudCom*, 2011.

[5] S. Zaman and D. Grosu, "Combinatorial Auction-based Allocation of Virtual Machine Instances in Clouds," *Journal of Parallel and Distributed Computing*, vol. 73, no. 4, pp. 495–508, 2013.

[6] W.-Y. Lin, G.-Y. Lin, and H.-Y. Wei, "Dynamic Auction Mechanism for Cloud Resource Allocation," in *IEEE/ACM CCGrid*, 2010.

[7] W. Shi, L. Zhang, C. Wu, Z. Li, and F. C. Lau, "An Online Auction Framework for Dynamic Resource Provisioning in Cloud Computing," in *Proc. of ACM SIGMETRICS*, 2014.

[8] L. Zhang, Z. Li, and C. Wu, "Dynamic Resource Provisioning in Cloud Computing: A Randomized Auction Approach," in *Proc. of IEEE INFOCOM*, 2014.

[9] W. Shi, C. Wu, and Z. Li, "RSMOA: A Revenue and Social Welfare Maximizing Online Auction for Dynamic Cloud Resource Provisioning," in *Proc. of IWQoS*, 2014.

[10] W. Wang, B. Liang, and B. Li, "Revenue Maximization with Dynamic Auctions in IaaS Cloud Markets," in *Proc. of IEEE ICDCS*, 2013.

[11] H. Zhang, B. Li, H. Jiang, F. Liu, A. V. Vasilakos, and J. Liu, "A Framework for Truthful Online Auctions in Cloud Computing with Heterogeneous User Demands," in *Proc. of IEEE INFOCOM*, 2013.

[12] N. Buchbinder, K. Jain, and J. S. Naor, "Online Primal-Dual Algorithms for Maximizing Ad-Auctions Revenue," in *Proc. of the 15th Annual European Symposium on Algorithms*, 2007.

[13] A. Mu'Alem and N. Nisan, "Truthful Approximation Mechanisms for Restricted Combinatorial Auctions," *Games and Economic Behavior*, vol. 64, no. 2, pp. 612–631, 2008.

[14] Y. Azar, U. Bhaskar, L. Fleischer, and D. Panigrahi, "Online Mixed Packing and Covering," in *Proc. of ACM-SIAM SODA*, 2013.

[15] N. Buchbinder and J. Naor, "The Design of Competitive Online Algorithms via a Primal-dual Approach," *Foundations and Trends in Theoretical Computer Science*, vol. 3, no. 2–3, pp. 93–263, 2009.

[16] Z. Huang and A. Kim, "Welfare Maximization with Production Costs: a Primal Dual Approach," in *Proc. of the ACM-SIAM SODA*, 2015.

[17] N. R. Devanur and Z. Huang, "Primal Dual Gives Almost Optimal Energy Efficient Online Algorithms," in *Proc. of ACM-SIAM SODA*, 2014.

[18] A. Beloglazov, J. Abawajy, and R. Buyya, "Energy-Aware Resource Allocation Heuristics for Efficient Management of Data Centers for Cloud Computing," *Future Generation Computer Systems*, vol. 28, no. 5, pp. 755–768, 2012.

[19] C. Joe-Wong, S. Sen, T. Lan, and M. Chiang, "Multi Resource Allocation: Fairness-Efficiency Tradeoffs in a Unifying Framework," in *Proc. of IEEE INFOCOM*, 2012.

[20] S. T. Maguluri, R. Srikant, and L. Ying, "Stochastic Models of Load Balancing and Scheduling in Cloud Computing Clusters," in *Proc. of IEEE INFOCOM*, 2012.

[21] Q. Wang, K. Ren, and X. Meng, "When Cloud meets eBay: Towards Effective Pricing for Cloud Computing," in *Proc. of IEEE INFOCOM*, 2012.

[22] S. Anand, N. Garg, and A. Kumar, "Resource Augmentation for Weighted Flow-time Explained by Dual Fitting," in *Proc. of ACM-SIAM SODA*, 2012.

[23] A. Blum, A. Gupta, Y. Mansour, and A. Sharma, "Welfare and Profit Maximization with Production Costs," in *Proc. of IEEE FOCS*, 2011.

[24] R. Grandl, G. Ananthanarayanan, S. Kandula, S. Rao, and A. Akella, "Multi-Resource Packing for Cluster Schedulers," in *Proc. of ACM SIGCOMM*, 2014.

[25] P. Barham, B. Dragovic, K. Fraser, S. Hand, T. Harris, A. Ho, R. Neugebauer, I. Pratt, and A. Warfield, "Xen and the Art of Virtualization," in *Proc. of ACM SOSP*, 2003.

[26] "KVM CPU Hotplug," http://www.linux-kvm.org/page/CPUHotPlug.

[27] H. Chen, M. C. Caramanis, and A. K. Coskun, "Reducing the Data Center Electricity Costs Through Participation in Smart Grid Programs," in *Proc. of IGCC*, 2014.

[28] "Xen DVFS," http://lists.xen.org/archives/html/xen-devel/2009-09/msg00585.html.

[29] K. H. Kim, A. Beloglazov, and R. Buyya, "Power-aware Provisioning of Virtual Machines for Real-time Cloud Services," *Concurrency and Computation: Practice and Experience archive*, vol. 23, no. 13, pp. 1491–1505, 2011.

[30] B. Krishnan, H. Amur, A. Gavrilovska, and K. Schwan, "VM Power Metering: Feasibility and Challenges," *ACM SIGMETRICS Performance Evaluation Review*, vol. 38, no. 3, pp. 56–60, 2010.

[31] J. Kansal, F. Zhao, J. Liu, N. Kothari, and A. A. Bhattacharya, "Virtual Machine Power Metering and Provisioning," in *Proc. of ACM SoCC*, 2010.

[32] N. R. Devanur and Z. Huang, "Primal dual gives optimal energy efficient online algorithms," in *Proc. of ACM-SIAM SODA*, 2014.

[33] S. Boyd and L. Vandenberghe, *Convex Optimization*. Cambridge University Press, 2004.

[34] N. Buchbinder and J. Naor, "Online Primal-Dual Algorithms for Covering and Packing Problems," in *Algorithms–ESA 2005*. Springer, 2005, pp. 689–701.

[35] B. Awerbuch, Y. Azar, and A. Meyerson, "Reducing Truth-telling Online Mechanisms to Online Optimization," in *Proc. of ACM STOC*, 2003.

[36] C. Reiss, J. Wilkes, and J. L. Hellerstein, "Google cluster-usage traces: format + schema," Google Inc., Mountain View, CA, USA, Technical Report, Nov. 2011, revised 2012.03.20. Posted at URL http://code.google.com/p/googleclusterdata/wiki/TraceVersion2.

[37] C. Reiss, A. Tumanov, G. R. Ganger, R. H. Katz, and M. A. Kozuch, "Heterogeneity and Dynamicity of Clouds at Scale: Google Trace Analysis," in *Proc. of ACM SoCC*, 2012.

[38] S. Chawla, J. D. Hartline, D. L. Malec, and B. Sivan, "Multi-Parameter Mechanism Design and Sequential Posted Pricing," in *Proc. of ACM STOC*, 2010.

APPENDIX

A. PROOF OF PROPOSITION 1

PROOF. $f^{\star}_{rs}(p_{rs}(t)) =$

$$\sup_{y\geq 0}\left\{\begin{array}{ll} p_{rs}(t)y_{rs}(t) - h_{rs}y_{rs}(t)^{1+\beta_{rs}}\mathbf{1}, & y_{rs}(t)\in[0,C_{rs}] \\ p_{rs}(t)y_{rs}(t) - \infty\mathbf{2}, & y_{rs}(t) > C_{rs} \end{array}\right.$$

Observe that $\mathbf{2}$=$-\infty$. Then we only need to obtain the conjugate of $f_{rs}(\cdot)$ from $\mathbf{1}$.

Let $g_{rs}(y_{rs}(t)) = p_{rs}(t)y_{rs}(t) - h_{rs}y_{rs}(t)^{1+\beta_{rs}}$. Differentiate $g_{rs}(t)$ with respect to $y_{rs}(t)$ and set

$$(p_{rs}(t)\times y_{rs}(t) - h_{rs}y_{rs}(t)^{1+\beta_{rs}})' = 0. \tag{27}$$

We obtain the solution of the equation as $y^0_{rs}(t) = (\frac{p_{rs}(t)}{h_{rs}(1+\beta_{rs})})^{\frac{1}{\beta_{rs}}}$.

Note that the domain of $g_{rs}(t)$ is $y_{rs}(t)\in[0,C_{rs}]$. Hence the supremum happens at $y^0_{rs}(t)$ only if $y^0_{rs}(t)$ lies in $[0,C_{rs}]$. Otherwise when $y^0_{rs}(t) > C_{rs}$, $(p_{rs}(t)\times y_{rs}(t) - h_{rs}y_{rs}(t)^{1+\beta_{rs}})' > 0$, such that $g_{rs}(y_{rs}(t))$ monotonically increases with y_{rs} in $[0,C_{rs}]$ and the supremum happens at C_{rs}.

Merging the two cases, we derive the conjugate of the cost function:

$$f^{\star}_{rs}(p_{rs}(t)) = \left\{\begin{array}{ll} (\frac{p_{rs}(t)}{1+\beta_{rs}})^{\frac{1+\beta_{rs}}{\beta_{rs}}}\frac{\beta_{rs}}{h_{rs}^{\frac{1}{\beta_{rs}}}}, & y^0_{rs}(t)\leq C_{rs} \\ C_{rs}p_{rs}(t) - h_{rs}C_{rs}^{1+\beta_{rs}}, & y^0_{rs}(t) > C_{rs} \end{array}\right. \tag{28}$$

□

B. PROOF OF THEOREM 1

PROOF. *(Truthfulness in bidding price)* The marginal prices that the cloud provider presents to bid i depend only on the demands of resources before the arrival of bid i and the demand of bid i, thus, are independent on bid i's bidding price. Further, the cloud provider always assigns bids to servers to maximize each bid's utility given the current marginal prices. So it falls into the family of sequential posted price mechanisms (e.g., [38]) and, thus, a bidder cannot improve its utility by lying about its bidding price. *(Truthfulness in arrival time)* Since the marginal prices are non-decreasing in the amount of allocated resources, which is non-decreasing over the resource allocation time, *i.e.*, let $y_{rs}(t_i,t)$ denote the amount of resource r on s in t which has been allocated by t_i ($t_i\leq t$) and $y_{rs}(t_i,t)$ is non-decreasing over t_i. Hence a bidder cannot decrease the total price of the resource that it requests by delaying its arrival. Note that the arrival time of a bid is the first time the bidder is aware of her demands so the arrival time can not be earlier. *(Truthfulness in resource occupation times)* Dropping part of the true resource occupation duration in the request would risk failing to complete the job. So no bidder would do that. On the other hand, the marginal prices are non-negative according to (10). So requesting a superset of the true resource occupation duration increases a bidder's payment and decreases her utility.

(Individually rational) According to (8), the utility of a bidder is always non-negative. The profit of the provider is also non-negative based on (10) which implies $p_{rs}(y_{rs}(t)) > f'_{rs}(y_{rs}(t))$.

(Polynomial running time) We assume that the algorithm can compute the differentials of marginal server cost functions, *i.e.*, f'_{rs} in constant time. (Otherwise, the running time will be $O(RST)$ times the time complexity of computing f'_{rs}.) To process a bid i, the algorithm first sums up the marginal prices for all requested resources over the occupation duration for each server $s\in[S]$ to compute the payment that bid i should pay if it would be served on server s. This step runs in $O(RST)$ time. Then, the algorithm computes u_i and decides the allocation and payment of bid i by checking the utility of the bid if it would be served on each server s, which can be done in $O(S)$ time. Finally, the algorithm updates the amount of allocated resources $y_{rs}(t)$ and the respective marginal prices $p_{rs}(t)$, which can be done in $O(RST)$ time. □

C. PROOF OF LEMMA 4

PROOF. It is easy to verify that the inequality in the lemma holds with equality when $y_{rs}(t)\leq\frac{C_{rs}}{\delta_{rs}}$ according to (10) and the choice of δ_{rs} in Lemma 3. Next, assume that $y_{rs}(t)\geq\frac{C_{rs}}{\delta_{rs}}$. In this case, $p_{rs}(t) = h_{rs}(1+\beta_{rs})C_{rs}^{\beta_{rs}}e^{\theta_{rs}(y_{rs}(t)-\frac{C_{rs}}{\delta_{rs}})}$. So the inequality is equivalent to $\frac{e^{\theta_{rs}y_{rs}(t)}}{y_{rs}(t)^{\beta_{rs}}}\geq\frac{(1+\beta_{rs})e^{\frac{\theta_{rs}C_{rs}}{\delta_{rs}}}}{C_{rs}^{\beta_{rs}}}$. Recall that $\delta_{rs}\geq(1+\beta_{rs})^{1/\beta_{rs}}$. It is easy to verify that the above inequality holds with equality for $y_{rs}(t) = \frac{C_{rs}}{\delta_{rs}}$. Next, it suffices to show that $\frac{e^{\theta_{rs}y_{rs}(t)}}{y_{rs}(t)^{\beta_{rs}}}$ is non-decreasing as $y_{rs}(t)$ increases. Its derivative is $\frac{e^{\theta_{rs}y_{rs}(t)}(\theta_{rs}y_{rs}(t)-\beta_{rs})}{y_{rs}(t)^{1+\beta_{rs}}}$. By our choice of $\theta_{rs}\geq\frac{\delta_{rs}\beta_{rs}}{C_{rs}}$ and the assumption that $y_{rs}(t)\geq\frac{C_{rs}}{\delta_{rs}}$, $\theta_{rs}y_{rs}(t)-\beta_{rs}\geq 0$ and the above derivative is non-negative. So the lemma follows. □

D. PROOF OF LEMMA 3

PROOF. First, we explicitly write down the differentials of the server cost functions (in (2)) and their convex conjugates (in (6)):

$$f'_{rs}(y_{rs}(t)) = \left\{\begin{array}{ll} h_{rs}(1+\beta_{rs})y_{rs}(t)^{\beta_{rs}}, & y_{rs}(t)\in[0,C_{rs}] \\ +\infty, & y_{rs}(t) > C_{rs} \end{array}\right.$$

$$f^{\star\prime}_{rs}(p_{rs}(t)) = \left\{\begin{array}{ll} (\frac{p_{rs}(t)}{(1+\beta_{rs})h_{rs}})^{\frac{1}{\beta_{rs}}}, & p_{rs}(t)\leq h_{rs}(1+\beta_{rs})C_{rs}^{\beta_{rs}} \\ C_{rs}, & p_{rs}(t) > h_{rs}(1+\beta_{rs})C_{rs}^{\beta_{rs}} \end{array}\right.$$

By $\theta_{rs}\geq\frac{\delta_{rs}}{C_{rs}(\delta_{rs}-1)}\ln(\frac{U_r}{h_{rs}(1+\beta_{rs})C_{rs}^{\beta_{rs}}})$ and the definition of marginal payment in (10), we get that when $y_{rs}(t) = C_{rs}$,

$$p_{rs}(t) = h_{rs}(1+\beta_{rs})C_{rs}^{\beta_{rs}}e^{\theta_{rs}(C_{rs}-\frac{C_{rs}}{\delta_{rs}})}\geq U_r\ .$$

By our choice of $p_{rs}(t)$, the cloud provider will never allocate more resources than its capacity, *i.e.*, $y_{rs}(t)\leq C_{rs}$. Therefore, we may assume in the rest of the proof that $y_{rs}(t)\leq C_{rs}$ and, thus, $f'_{rs}(y_{rs}(t)) = h_{rs}(1+\beta_{rs})y_{rs}(t)^{\beta_{rs}}$. Next, according to the piece-wise definition of $f^{\star\prime}_{rs}$, the proof is divided into two cases.

Case 1: $y_{rs}(t)\leq\frac{C_{rs}}{\delta_{rs}}$.

In this case, the Differential Allocation-Payment Relationship is

$$\begin{aligned}(p_{rs}(t) - h_{rs}(1+\beta_{rs})y_{rs}(t)^{\beta_{rs}})\mathrm{d}y_{rs}(t) \\ \geq\frac{1}{\alpha_{rs}}\big(\frac{1}{h_{rs}(1+\beta_{rs})}p_{rs}(r)\big)^{\frac{1}{\beta_{rs}}}\mathrm{d}p_{rs}(t)\end{aligned} \tag{29}$$

By the marginal payment definition in (10),

$$p_{rs}(t) = f'_{rs}(\delta_{rs}y_{rs}(t)) = h_{rs}(1+\beta_{rs})\delta_{rs}^{\beta_{rs}}y_{rs}(t)^{\beta_{rs}}. \tag{30}$$

Putting them together, (29) is equivalent to (cancelling common terms of both sides) $(\delta_{rs}^{\beta_{rs}}-1)\geq\frac{1}{\alpha_{rs}}\beta_{rs}\delta_{rs}^{\beta_{rs}+1}$. If $\beta_{rs}\geq 1$, then $\delta_{rs} = \max\{2,(1+\beta_{rs})^{\frac{1}{\beta_{rs}}}\} = 2$ and $\delta_{rs}^{\beta_{rs}+1} = 2\delta_{rs}^{\beta_{rs}} = 4\delta_{rs}^{\beta_{rs}} - 2\delta_{rs}^{\beta_{rs}}\leq 4\delta_{rs}^{\beta_{rs}} - 4$. So we get that $\frac{\beta_{rs}\delta_{rs}^{\beta_{rs}+1}}{\delta_{rs}^{\beta_{rs}}-1}\leq 4\beta_{rs} <$

α_{rs}. If $\beta_{rs} < 1$, then $\delta_{rs} = (1+\beta_{rs})^{\frac{1}{\beta_{rs}}}$, and

$$\frac{\beta_{rs}\delta_{rs}^{\beta_{rs}+1}}{\delta_{rs}^{\beta_{rs}}-1} = \delta_{rs}(1+\beta_{rs}) \le e(1+\beta_{rs}) < \alpha_{rs} \ .$$

Case 2: $\frac{C_{rs}}{\delta_{rs}} \le y_{rs}(t) \le C_{rs}$.

In this case, the Differential Allocation-Payment Relationship is

$$\left(p_{rs}(t) - h_{rs}(1+\beta_{rs})y_{rs}(t)^{\beta}\right)\mathrm{d}y_{rs}(t) \ge \frac{1}{\alpha_{rs}}C_{rs}\mathrm{d}p_{rs}(t) \quad (31)$$

Recall that when $y_{rs}(t) \ge \frac{C_{rs}}{\delta_{rs}}$, the marginal payment is

$$p_{rs}(t) = h_{rs}(1+\beta_{rs})C_{rs}^{\beta_{rs}} e^{\theta_{rs}(y_{rs}(t) - \frac{C_{rs}}{\delta_{rs}})} \quad (32)$$

By Lemma 4, to show (31), it suffices to show $\frac{\beta_{rs}}{1+\beta_{rs}} p_{rs}(t)\mathrm{d}y_{rs}(t) \ge \frac{1}{\alpha_{rs}}C_{rs}\mathrm{d}p_{rs}(t)$. On the other hand, by the definition of the marginal payment in (32), we have $\mathrm{d}p_{rs}(t) = \theta_{rs}p_{rs}(t)dy_{rs}(t)$. So it remains to show that $\theta_{rs} \le \frac{\beta_{rs}}{C_{rs}(1+\beta_{rs})}\alpha_{rs}$. By our choice of parameters, either

$$\begin{aligned}
\theta_{rs} &= \frac{\delta_{rs}}{C_{rs}}\beta_{rs} \le \frac{e}{C_{rs}}\beta_{rs} && (\delta_{rs} \le e)\\
&= \frac{\beta_{rs}}{C_{rs}(1+\beta_{rs})}e(1+\beta_{rs}) \le \frac{\beta_{rs}}{C_{rs}(1+\beta_{rs})}\alpha_{rs} \ ,\\
\text{or } \ \theta_{rs} &= \frac{\delta_{rs}}{C_{rs}(\delta_{rs}-1)}\ln\left(\frac{U_r}{h_{rs}(1+\beta_{rs})C_{rs}^{\beta_{rs}}}\right)\\
&\le \frac{2}{C_{rs}}\ln\left(\frac{U_r}{h_{rs}(1+\beta_{rs})C_{rs}^{\beta_{rs}}}\right) && (\delta_{rs} \ge 2)\\
&= \frac{\beta_{rs}}{C_{rs}(1+\beta_{rs})}\frac{2(1+\beta_{rs})}{\beta_{rs}}\ln\left(\frac{U_r}{h_{rs}(1+\beta_{rs})C_{rs}^{\beta_{rs}}}\right)\\
&\le \frac{\beta_{rs}}{C_{rs}(1+\beta_{rs})}\alpha_{rs} \ .
\end{aligned}$$

So the lemma holds in case 2. □

E. PROOF OF THEOREM 4

PROOF. RPD_1 also posts a take-it-or-leave-it price for each bid i and serves the bid if and only if its bidding price is larger than the posted price, while changing the payment from $\hat{p}_i$ in PD_1 to $\eta_1\tilde{p}_i$, where η_1 and $\tilde{p}_i$ are independent of b_i's bidding price. So it is still a sequentially posted pricing mechanism and, thus, truthful in terms of bidding price. The proof of truthfulness in bid arrival time and duration times, individual rationality, and time complexity of bid processing follows similarly to the proof of Theorem 1, and is hence omitted. □

F. PROOF OF PROPOSITION 2

PROOF. The conjugate of $f_{rs}(y_{rs}(t))$ is defined in (6). By the definition of f_{rs}, $p_{rs}(t)y_{rs}(t) - f_{rs}(y_{rs}(t))$ is equal to $(p_{rs}(t) - h_{rs})y_{rs}(t)$ if $y_{rs}(t) \le C_{rs}$, and is $-\infty$ if $y_{rs}(t) > C_{rs}$. If $p_{rs}(t) - h_{rs} < 0$, then the right hand side of (6) is maximized when $y_{rs}(t) = 0$ with maximum value 0; if $p_{rs}(t) - h_{rs} \ge 0$, then it is maximized when $y_{rs}(t) = C_{rs}$ with maximum value $(p_{rs}(t) - h_{rs})C_{rs}$. □

G. PROOF OF LEMMA 5

PROOF. The profit of any truthful and individually rational auction is upper bounded by its social welfare and, thus, by the optimal social welfare, *i.e.*,

$$\begin{aligned}
\textstyle\sum_{i\in O^\star}(b_i - c_i) &= \textstyle\sum_{i\in O^\star: b_i \ge \hat{p}_i}(b_i - c_i) + \sum_{i\in O^\star: b_i < \hat{p}_i}(b_i - c_i)\\
&\le \textstyle\sum_{i: b_i \ge \hat{p}_i}(b_i - c_i) + \sum_{i\in O^\star: b_i < \hat{p}_i}(b_i - c_i)\\
&= \textstyle\sum_{i\in A^\star}(b_i - c_i) + \sum_{i\in O^\star: b_i < \hat{p}_i}(b_i - c_i)
\end{aligned}$$

□

H. PROOF OF LEMMA 6

PROOF. Due to the linear cost function in this case, the incurred cost by an accepted bid i is $c_i = \sum_{t\in[t_i^-,t_i^+]}\sum_{r\in[R]} d_{ir}(t)h_{rs_i}$, where s_i is the server that serves the ith bid. By the definition of PD_2, for any tentatively accepted bid $i \in A^\star$, the tentative profit from bid i is at least

$$\begin{aligned}
\hat{p}_i - c_i &= \textstyle\sum_{r\in[R]}\sum_{t\in[t_i^-,t_i^+]}\left(d_{ir}(t)p_{rs}(t) - d_{ir}(t)h_{rs}\right)\\
&\ge \textstyle\sum_{r\in[R]}\sum_{t\in[t_i^-,t_i^+]} d_{ir}(t)\left(p_{rs}(0) - h_{rs}(t)\right)
\end{aligned}$$

Since $p_{rs}(0) = \frac{L_r - h_{rs}}{2\sigma RS} + h_{rs}$, we further have

$$\hat{p}_i - c_i \ge \textstyle\sum_{r\in[R]}\sum_{t\in[t_i^-,t_i^+]} d_{ir}(t)\frac{L_r - h_{rs}}{2\sigma RS}$$

On the other hand, the maximum profit from bid i is at most $b_i - c_i \le \sum_{r\in[R]}\sum_{t\in[t_i^-,t_i^+]} d_{ir}(t)(U_r - h_{rs})$. We have that $\frac{b_i - c_i}{\hat{p}_i - c_i} \le \frac{2\sigma RS(U_r - h_{rs})}{L_r - h_{rs}} = \chi$. By the definition of η in (23), η is a randomly chosen power of 2 between 1 and χ and, thus, satisfies that $\frac{1}{2}(b_i - c_i) \le \eta(\hat{p}_i - c_i) \le (b_i - c_i)$ with probability at least $\frac{1}{2\log_2\chi}$. In this case, RPD_2 will accept the ith bid and generate profit $\eta(\hat{p}_i - c_i) \ge \frac{1}{2}(b_i - c_i)$ from the ith bid. Therefore, the expected profit generated by RPD_2 from every bid $i \in A^\star$ (that is, tentatively accepted by PD_2) is at least $\frac{1}{2\log_2\chi}\cdot\frac{1}{2}(b_i - c_i)$. The expected profit of RPD_2 is at least $\frac{1}{4\log_2\chi}\sum_{i\in A^\star}(b_i - c_i)$. □

I. PROOF OF LEMMA 7

PROOF. Consider a virtual instance of our online problem where the ith bid in the virtual instance has the same demands $d_{ir}(t)$ over $[t_i^-, t_i^+]$ as in the original instance, but has bidding prices $\min\{b_i, \hat{p}_i\}$ instead of b_i. Then, the online auction PD_2 would accept the same set of bids in the virtual instance as in the original instance. The social welfare of PD_2 in the virtual instance is therefore $\sum_{i\in A^\star}(\hat{p}_i - c_i)$. Further note that choosing all $i \in O^\star$ such that $b_i < \hat{p}_i$ is a feasible solution in the virtual instance and gets social welfare $\sum_{i\in O^\star: b_i < \hat{p}_i}(b_i - c_i)$. The lemma now follows from the competitive ratio of online algorithm PD_2. □

J. PROOF OF THEOREM 11

PROOF. The set of accepted bids of the online auction RPD_2 is a subset of that of PD_2. Let $B^\star$ denote the set of accepted bids of RPD_2. Recall $A^\star$ denotes the set of accepted bids of PD_2.

Define a random variable b_i' as follows:

$$b_i' = \begin{cases} b_i & \text{if } b_i \ge \eta\hat{p}_i \\ 0 & \text{if } b_i < \eta\hat{p}_i \end{cases} \quad (33)$$

The expected social welfare of RPD_2 is:

$$E\left[\textstyle\sum_{i\in B^\star}(b_i - c_i)\right] = E\left[\textstyle\sum_{i\in A^\star}(b_i' - c_i)\right] \ . \quad (34)$$

Note that $A^\star = \{i : b_i \ge \hat{p}_i\}$. By linearity of expectation,

$$\begin{aligned}
(34) \ &= \ E\left[\textstyle\sum_{i:b_i\ge\hat{p}_i}(b_i' - c_i)\right] = \textstyle\sum_{i:b_i\ge\hat{p}_i} E\left[b_i' - c_i\right]\\
&= \ \textstyle\sum_{i:b_i\ge\hat{p}_i}(b_i - c_i)\cdot\Pr[b_i \ge \eta\hat{p}_i]\\
&\ge \ \textstyle\sum_{i:b_i\ge\hat{p}_i}(b_i - c_i)\cdot\Pr[b_i \ge \hat{p}_i]\cdot\Pr[\eta = 1]\\
&\ge \ \textstyle\frac{1}{2}\sum_{i\in A^\star}(b_i - c_i)
\end{aligned}$$

Therefore, the expected social welfare of RPD_2 is at least half of that of PD_2. The theorem then follows from Theorem 8. □

Distributed Proportional Fair Load Balancing in Heterogenous Systems

Se-Young Yun
MSR-INRIA
Paris, France
seyoung.yun@inria.fr

Alexandre Proutiere*
KTH
Stockholm, Sweden
alepro@kth.se

ABSTRACT

We consider the problem of distributed load balancing in heterogenous parallel server systems, where the service rate achieved by a user at a server depends on both the user and the server. Such heterogeneity typically arises in wireless networks (e.g., servers may represent frequency bands, and the service rate of a user varies across bands). We assume that each server equally shares in time its capacity among users allocated to it. Users initially attach to an arbitrary server, but at random instants of time, they probe the load at a new server and migrate there if this improves their service rate. The dynamics under this distributed load balancing scheme, referred to as Random Local Search (RLS), may be interpreted as those generated by strategic players updating their strategy in a load balancing game. In closed systems, where the user population is fixed, we show that this game has pure Nash Equilibriums (NEs), and that these equilibriums get close to a Proportionally Fair (PF) allocation of users to servers when the user population grows large. We provide an anytime upper bound of the gap between the allocation under RLS and the PF allocation. In open systems, where users randomly enter the system and leave upon service completion, we establish that the RLS algorithm stabilizes the system whenever this it at all possible under centralized load balancing schemes, i.e., it is throughput-optimal. The proof of this result relies on a novel Lyapounov analysis that captures the dynamics due to both users' migration and their arrivals and departures. To our knowledge, the RLS algorithm constitutes the first fully distributed and throughput-optimal load balancing scheme in heterogenous parallel server systems. We extend our analysis to various scenarios, e.g. to cases where users can be simultaneously served by several servers. Finally we illustrate through numerical experiments the efficiency of the RLS algorithm.

1. INTRODUCTION

Load balancing is an essential component in computer systems; it ensures high resource utilization and guarantees satisfactory quality of service. Traditionally, load balancing is performed when tasks arrive in the system: a task is assigned to a carefully selected server, and stays there until service completion. In this paper, we investigate systems where tasks are initially assigned to arbitrary servers, but may be re-assigned to other servers during their services. An additional important property of the systems considered here lies in their *heterogeneity*: the service speed of a task at a given server depends on both the task and the server.

Our work is motivated by two important problems in radio communication networks. (1) Dynamic Spectrum Access. Transmitters are today able to exploit a large part of the radio spectrum, and can switch frequency bands rapidly. The service rate achieved on a link operating on a given frequency band depends on the load of this band (i.e., the number of competing links exploiting on the same band), and on the channel conditions which in turn depend on the band and the link (this phenomenon is known as *frequency selective fading*). When joining the system, transmitters are not aware of the load of each frequency band, and they select an arbitrary band (or may be that with the best channel conditions). However they may explore new bands, and migrate there if this improves their throughput. The overall system performance then strongly relies on the distributed resampling and switching strategy. (2) Access Point Selection. When users in a wireless network may attach to various access points, we get a similar situation. The throughput experienced by a user depends on the load of the selected access point, and on the geographical proximity of this access point. In both examples, the network can be modelled as an heterogenous parallel server system: servers correspond to either frequency bands or access points, and the heterogeneity stems from frequency selective fading or from the heterogenous channel conditions to the various access points.

In this paper, we consider a generic heterogenous system of parallel servers fairly sharing their resources in time among users (they implement a Processor Sharing discipline). Users initially pick a server randomly, and may later switch servers during their services. For such systems, we aim at identifying efficient and fair distributed resampling algorithms. We analyze the performance of the Random Local Search (RLS) algorithm introduced and studied in [1] in the specific case of homogenous systems (all users are served at the same speed at any server). Under RLS, a user resamples a server randomly selected at the instants of a Poisson process, and moves there if this improves her service rate. RLS is evaluated in both *closed* and *open* systems. In closed systems, the user population is fixed, and we compare the performance of RLS to that obtained under an ideal Proportionally Fair (PF) allocation of users to servers. We also study the rate at which RLS converges. In open systems, users arrive according to Poisson processes and leave upon service completion. In such scenarios, we are primarily interested in the throughput region of the RLS algorithm, i.e.,

*This work has been supported by the ERC grant 308267, VR, and SSF.

SIGMETRICS'15, June 15–19, 2015, Portland, OR, USA.

DOI: http://dx.doi.org/10.1145/2745844.2745861.

on the set of user arrival rates such that the system is stable under RLS. We compare this region to the maximal throughput region, defined as the set of arrival rates such that there exists a centralized load balancing scheme stabilizing the system. Using an usual terminology, a load resampling algorithm with maximal throughput region is called *throughput optimal*.

In [1], the performance of the RLS algorithm is investigated in the case of homogenous systems. The analysis of the latter systems is much simpler. Indeed in such systems, allocations where each server roughly handles the same number of users are efficient, and they are easy to identify and reach. In heterogenous systems, characterizing and finding efficient allocations turns out to be much more challenging, as users have individual preferences for servers (this problem ressembles a max-weight matching problem). Also note that in open homogenous systems, the design of throughput optimal algorithms is simplified by the fact that to stabilize the system, it is essentially sufficient to keep all servers active. In [1], this simple observation is used to prove that RLS is throughput optimal. A similar result in heterogenous systems would be more surprising, and much more difficult to establish.

Our contributions are as follows:

- Closed systems. Under RLS, the system dynamics correspond to those in an ordinal potential game where players (here users) sequentially and selfishly update their strategy (the selected server). Hence under RLS, the system converges to pure Nash Equilibriums (NEs). We study the efficiency of these NEs. We prove that when the user population grows large, pure NEs get closer to a Proportionally Fair (PF) allocation of users to servers. We provide an upper bound of the gap between the welfares of NEs and of this ideal allocation depending on user population. This gap scales at most as $\frac{S}{n}\log(n+S)$ where n and S denote the number of users and servers, respectively. We further study the time it takes, under RLS, for the system to reach the PF allocation within a certain margin. More precisely, when the user population is large enough, after a time $\frac{S\log(S)}{\epsilon}$, the expected system welfare under RLS is at a distance at most ϵ of the welfare of the PF allocation.

- Open systems. We establish that RLS is throughput optimal. To do so, we use the analysis of the system dynamics under RLS in closed systems to build an appropriate Lyapunov function. In this construction, we need to explicitly account for the interactions between user migrations across servers, and user population dynamics. This contrasts with the analysis of homogenous systems, where the throughput optimality of RLS was simply due to the fact that the algorithm keeps all servers active when the user population grows large.

- Our results in closed and open systems suggest that RLS is optimal when the system is heavily loaded. However, it might yield poor performance when the user population is small. To improve the performance in such scenarios, we propose mRLS, an extension of RLS where each user maintains a connection with $m > 1$ servers. All result are extended to this scenario. We finally consider a limiting regime where m grows large. In this regime, users behave as if they were bidding with a fixed budget to acquire services from the various servers. We devise an algorithm, referred to as Water-Filling (WF), under which users update their bids to the various servers in such a way that the resulting limiting allocation corresponds to the PF allocation. The WF algorithm is hence efficient even for small user populations, and we also establish its throughput optimality.

2. RELATED WORK

Distributed load resampling strategies can be analyzed using game theoretical techniques, and there have been many studies in the analysis of load balancing games, see [2] for a survey. Most of the analysis aim at characterizing the inefficiency of NEs in these games, through the notion of price of anarchy [3]. Researchers have also looked at the time it takes to balance the system under various strategies, including best-response or Nash dynamics (such strategies require that users are aware of the load at all servers) [4], and more distributed strategies, see [5] and references therein. Please also refer to [1] for a more detailed discussion. As far as we know, all existing results concern homogenous systems. In heterogenous systems, the underlying games are more involved, as they do not belong to the class of potential games [6–9]. This significantly complicates the analysis of the efficiency of NEs in the case of finite user population, and very little is known about the time it takes to reach these NEs. Our approach to study such games departs from existing techniques. The use of the ideal and pivotal PF allocation to analyze NEs is novel, and turns out to be powerful to derive results in both closed and open systems.

Accounting for the user population dynamics is rare in game theory. In [10], the authors analyze the performance of a logit algorithm in congestion games where the set of players may vary over time. However, these variations are exogenous, and the authors do not investigate the interaction between users' strategic behaviors and user population dynamics. Note however that handling this interaction is crucial to analyze the system stability. As already mentioned in the introduction, we extend the results of [1] to heterogenous systems. These extensions required the development of new methods. Of course, there is an abundant literature on the performance of classical load balancing schemes in open systems, where users are not allowed to switch servers. For example, in [11], the throughput optimality of the so called min drift routing policy is established. To our knowledge, except [1], natural load resampling strategies have not been studied in open systems. There is also an abundant literature on dynamic spectrum access and on the access point selection problem, see e.g. [12] and references therein. To our knowledge, none of this literature looks at the transient system behavior (convergence time), and at user population dynamics precisely.

3. MODELS

We consider a set $\mathcal{S}$ of S servers shared by n users. The latter are categorized into a set $\mathcal{K}$ of K classes. Users of class k may access to a subset $\mathcal{S}_k \subset \mathcal{S}$ of servers. We denote by $\mathcal{K}_s$ the set of classes whose users may be served by server s. At a given time t, the state of the system is represented by a vector $\boldsymbol{n}(t)$ describing the numbers of users of the different classes attached to the various servers. When the system state is $\boldsymbol{n} = (n_{ks})_{k\in\mathcal{K},s\in\mathcal{S}} \in \mathbb{N}^{K\times S}$, n_{ks} denotes the number of class-k users attached to server s. Note that $n_{ks} = 0$ if $s \notin \mathcal{S}_k$. For $s \in \mathcal{S}$, we further denote by $n^s = \sum_{k\in\mathcal{K}} n_{ks}$ the number of users attached to server s, and for $k \in \mathcal{K}$, $n_k = \sum_{s\in\mathcal{S}_k} n_{ks}$ is the number of class-k users.

An alternative way of representing the system state is to use the user population n and the proportions of users of different classes and attached to the various servers, $\boldsymbol{\alpha} = (\alpha_{ks})_{k\in\mathcal{K},s\in\mathcal{S}} \in \Delta^{K\times S}$, where Δ^p is the simplex of dimension p, i.e., $\boldsymbol{x} \in \Delta^p$ if $\sum_i x_i = 1$ and for all i, $x_i \geq 0$. We write $\boldsymbol{n} \sim (n, \boldsymbol{\alpha})$ if $n = \sum_k n_k$, and for all k, s, $n_{ks} = \alpha_{ks} n$.

Each server fairly shares its capacity in time among users attached to it. We consider heterogenous systems: users are served at different speeds at different servers. Specifically, let μ_{ks} be the service speed of a class-k user at server s. Hence, when the system is in state $\boldsymbol{n}$, each class-k user attached to server s is served at rate μ_{ks}/n^s. We denote by $\mu_{\min} = \min_{k\in\mathcal{K}} \min_{s\in\mathcal{S}_k} \mu_{ks} > 0$ and by $\mu_{\max} = \max_{k\in\mathcal{K}} \max_{s\in\mathcal{S}_k} \mu_{ks}$ the minimum and maximum speed at which users can be served, and define $\xi = \mu_{\max}/\mu_{\min}$.

3.1 Distributed Load Balancing Algorithms

Users have a myopic view of the system in the sense that they are aware of their current service rate, but they do not know the rate at which they would be served at other servers. We consider natural distributed load balancing strategies, where users independently resample and switch servers to selfishly improve their rates. The two first proposed strategies, referred to as Random Local Search (RLS) and Random Load Oblivious (RLO) algorithms, respectively, have been introduced in [1], and analyzed in homogenous scenarios where users are served at the same speed when attached to the same server, namely for all s and all $k \in \mathcal{K}_s$, μ_{ks} does not depend on k. We shall compare these two first algorithms to the Best Response (BR) algorithm, under which when a user decides to switch server, she picks the one offering the best service rate.

- *The RLS and RLO algorithms.* At the instants of a Poisson process of intensity β, a user randomly selects a new server (if the user is of class k, this choice is uniform over $\mathcal{S}_k$). Under RLS, she migrates to it if this would increase her service rate, whereas under RLO, she migrates to it blindly. Assume that the system is in state $\boldsymbol{n}$, and that a class-k user attached to server s considers switching servers. Let s' be the randomly selected server. Under RLS, the user migrates to s' if $\mu_{ks'}/(n^{s'}+1) > \mu_{ks}/n^s$, and under RLO, she migrates even if this would decrease her service rate.

- *The BR algorithm.* Each user switches servers at the instants of a Poisson process of intensity β. If the system is in state $\boldsymbol{n}$, when the opportunity arises, a class-k user attached to server s migrates to $s' \in \arg\max_{c\in\mathcal{S}_k} \mu_{kc}/(n^c + 1_{s'\neq s})$. Observe that to implement the BR algorithm, users need to know the service rates they would achieve at the various servers, which can be costly.

3.2 Closed Systems

In a *closed* system, the numbers of users of the various classes are fixed, and we are interested in the system dynamics under the RLS and BR algorithms (under the RLO algorithm, the loads at the various servers evolve somewhat arbitrarily, and this algorithm is not relevant here). Let $n_{[1-K]} = (n_1, \dots, n_K)$ represent the fixed population of users of the various classes, and let $\mathcal{N}(n_{[1-K]})$ denote the set of feasible system states having n_k class-k users for all $k \in \mathcal{K}$: $\mathcal{N}(n_{[1-K]}) = \{\boldsymbol{m} \in \mathbb{N}^{K\times S} : \forall k \in \mathcal{K}, \forall s \in \mathcal{S}, \sum_{s\in\mathcal{S}_k} m_{ks} = n_k, (m_{ks} > 0 \Rightarrow s \in \mathcal{S}_k)\}$.

To investigate the system state dynamics under the RLS and BR algorithms, we interpret $\boldsymbol{n}(t)$ as the set of strategies used at time t by the various players in a dynamic load balancing game. In this game, the set of pure strategies available to a class-k user or player is just the set of servers $\mathcal{S}_k$, and her payoff corresponds to her service rate. In what follows, we study the existence and efficiency of pure Nash Equilibriums in this load balancing game, and characterize the speed at which $\boldsymbol{n}(t)$ converges to these equilibriums under the RLS and BR algorithms.

3.3 Open Systems

In *open* systems, the user population evolves over time. Users of class k arrive in the system according to a Poisson process of intensity ρ_k, and each user has an exponentially distributed service requirement with unit mean. Upon arrival, a class-k user randomly selects a server uniformly at random in $\mathcal{S}_k$. User arrivals are hence characterized by a *load* vector $\boldsymbol{\rho} = (\rho_1, \dots, \rho_K)$. Users leave the system upon service completion, and in view of our assumptions, when the system is in state $\boldsymbol{n}$, a class-k user attached to server s leaves the system at rate μ_{ks}/n^s. Under the RLS, RLO, and BR algorithms, the system state $(\boldsymbol{n}(t))_{t\geq 0}$ is a continuous-time Markov chain, and we are interested in providing conditions under which this process is positive recurrent. More precisely, we analyzed the throughput region of each of the three algorithms, defined as the set of load vectors $\boldsymbol{\rho}$ such that $(\boldsymbol{n}(t))_{t\geq 0}$ is positive recurrent.

Define the maximal throughput region as the set of $\boldsymbol{\rho}$ such that there exists a centralized load balancing algorithm (possibly depending on $\boldsymbol{\rho}$) under which $(\boldsymbol{n}(t))_{t\geq 0}$ is positive recurrent. The following lemma is classical (see e.g. [13]):

LEMMA 3.1. *$\boldsymbol{\rho}$ lies in the maximal throughput region if and only if there exists $\boldsymbol{\lambda} \in \mathcal{R}$ such that $\boldsymbol{\rho} < \boldsymbol{\lambda}$ component-wise, where*

$$\mathcal{R} = \{\boldsymbol{r} \in \mathbb{R}_+^K : \exists \boldsymbol{\omega} \in \Omega : \forall k \in \mathcal{K}, r_k = \sum_{s\in\mathcal{S}_k} \omega_{ks}\mu_{ks}\},$$

and where Ω is the set of $\boldsymbol{\omega} = (\omega_{ks})_{k\in\mathcal{K}, s\in\mathcal{S}}$ such that (i) for all k, s, $\omega_{ks} \geq 0$, (ii) for all s, $\omega_{ks} = 0$ if $k \notin \mathcal{K}_s$, and (iii) $\sum_{k\in\mathcal{K}_s} \omega_{ks} \leq 1$.

In the above lemma, ω_{ks} may be interpreted as the proportion of time s serves class-k users. It is worth remarking that $\mathcal{R}$ is also the maximal throughput region when jointly considering user association (or load balancing) strategy and service discipline policies at each server. We say that a load resampling algorithm is throughput optimal if its throughput region coincides with $\mathcal{R}$.

4. CLOSED SYSTEMS

This section is devoted to the analysis of the system state dynamics under the RLS and BR algorithms in closed systems. The numbers of users of various classes are fixed and represented by a vector $n_{[1-K]} = (n_1, \dots, n_K)$ where n_k is the number of class-k users. For all $t \geq 0$, $\boldsymbol{n}(t) \in \mathcal{N}(n_{[1-K]})$. The initial allocation of users to servers $\boldsymbol{n}(0)$ is arbitrary. As mentioned previously, we may interpret the evolution of $\boldsymbol{n}(t)$ under RLS and BR as the evolving strategies of players or users in a dynamic load balancing game. In this game, $\boldsymbol{n} \in \mathcal{N}(n_{[1-K]})$ constitutes a pure NE if and only if:

$$\forall k \in \mathcal{K}, \forall s \in \mathcal{S}_k : n_{ks} > 0, \forall s' \in \mathcal{S}_k, \frac{\mu_{ks}}{n^s} \geq \frac{\mu_{ks'}}{n^{s'}+1}.$$

The above inequality states that in state $\boldsymbol{n}$, a class-k user attached to server s has no incentive to move to server s'. We show that pure NEs exist, and that under both RLS and BR, $\boldsymbol{n}(t)$ converges to a pure NE as t grows large. The existence of pure NEs is simply due to the fact that the game admits an *ordinal potential* function. We also study the efficiency of the pure NEs, and the rate at which $\boldsymbol{n}(t)$ converges to an equilibrium under the RLS and BR algorithms. We establish that for large user populations, the equilibriums are close to the proportionally fair allocation, and provide an upper bound of the distance to this ideal allocation depending on the numbers of users and servers.

The analysis of the rate of convergence to equilibrium under RLS and BR turns out to be challenging. This is mainly due to the system heterogeneity. Recall that in [1], this rate of convergence was studied for homogenous systems with servers of equal capacities, i.e., $\mu_{ks} = 1$ for all k and s, which significantly simplifies the analysis. To analyze RLS and BR in heterogenous systems, our idea is to track the evolution over time of the distance between $\boldsymbol{n}(t)$ and the ideal proportionally fair allocation. To this aim, we establish a relationship between the expected drifts in social welfare (defined with logarithmic utilities) and in the ordinal potential. In turn, this allows us to quantify the rate of convergence of the system state under the RLS and BR algorithms when the user population is typically large.

4.1 Ordinal Potential and Social Welfare

4.1.1 *An ordinal potential game*

In our load balancing game, the system state $\boldsymbol{n}$ determines the strategies played by all users (n_{ks} is the number of class-k users playing or selecting server s). As shown in [14], due to the system heterogeneity, the game does not belong to the class of potential games [15]. Indeed in general, one cannot find a set of increasing functions $u_k : \mathbb{R}_+ \to \mathbb{R}$, and a potential function $\psi : \mathcal{N}(n_{[1-K]}) \to \mathbb{R}$ such that: for any $k \in \mathcal{K}$ and any $s, s' \in \mathcal{S}_k$, $\psi(\boldsymbol{n} + e_{ks'} - e_{ks}) - \psi(\boldsymbol{n}) = u_k(\frac{\mu_{ks'}}{n^{s'}+1}) - u_k(\frac{\mu_{ks}}{n^s})$ for all $\boldsymbol{n} \in \mathcal{N}(n_{[1-K]})$. Here $\boldsymbol{n} + e_{ks'} - e_{ks}$ denotes the system state obtained from $\boldsymbol{n}$ by moving one class-k user from server s to server s'. In fact, our load balancing game is a *congestion game with player-specific utilities* as introduced in [6]. It can be readily checked that there exists a function $\psi : \mathcal{N}(n_{[1-K]}) \to \mathbb{R}$ such that for all $\boldsymbol{n} \in \mathcal{N}(n_{[1-K]})$, for all k, s, s' such that $n_{ks} > 0$, $\frac{\mu_{ks}}{n^s} < \frac{\mu_{ks'}}{n^{s'}+1} \Rightarrow \psi(\boldsymbol{n}) < \psi(\boldsymbol{n} + e_{ks'} - e_{ks})$. Such a function ψ is referred to an ordinal potential function. A possible ordinal potential function ψ is defined by: for all $\boldsymbol{n} \in \mathcal{N}(n_{[1-K]})$,

$$\psi(\boldsymbol{n}) = -\sum_{s\in\mathcal{S}} \log(n^s!) + \sum_{s\in\mathcal{S}}\sum_{k\in\mathcal{K}} n_{ks}\log(\mu_{ks}).$$

The existence of an ordinal potential function ensures that pure NEs exists, and that the system dynamics under the RLS and BR algorithms converge to a pure NE [16].

4.1.2 *Proportionally Fair allocation*

When the user population is large, $\boldsymbol{n}$ is a pure NE if and only if: for all k, let $s \in \mathcal{S}_k$ such that $n_{ks} > 0$, then for any $s' \in \mathcal{S}_k$, $n_{ks'} > 0$ iff $\frac{\mu_{ks'}}{n^{s'}} = \frac{\mu_{ks}}{n^s}$, and $n_{ks'} = 0$ iff $\frac{\mu_{ks'}}{n^{s'}} < \frac{\mu_{ks}}{n^s}$. These conditions actually coincide with the KKT conditions of the following convex program:

$$\begin{aligned} \text{maximize} \quad & W(\boldsymbol{x}) = \sum_{k\in\mathcal{K}}\sum_{s\in\mathcal{S}_k} x_{ks}\log\left(\frac{\mu_{ks}}{\sum_{k\in\mathcal{K}} x_{ks}}\right) \quad (1)\\ \text{over} \quad & \boldsymbol{x} \in \mathcal{N}^R(n_{[1-K]}), \end{aligned}$$

where $\mathcal{N}^R(n_{[1-K]}) = \{\boldsymbol{y} \in \mathbb{R}_+^{K\times S} : \forall k, s, \sum_{s\in\mathcal{S}_k} y_{ks} = n_k,$ $(y_{ks} > 0 \Rightarrow s \in \mathcal{S}_k)\}$. In what follows, we denote by $x^\star$ the solution of (1), and $W^\star = W(x^\star)$. The above observation suggests that when the number of users grows large, the pure NEs become efficient in the sense that the allocation of users to servers is proportionally fair [17]. In the following subsection, we formalize this observation more precisely.

Define the social welfare in state $\boldsymbol{n} \in \mathcal{N}(n_{[1-K]})$ as:

$$W(\boldsymbol{n}) = \sum_{k\in\mathcal{K}}\sum_{s\in\mathcal{S}_k} n_{ks}\log\left(\frac{\mu_{ks}}{n^s}\right).$$

The proportionally fair allocation $\boldsymbol{n}^\star$ maximizes $W(\boldsymbol{n})$ over all $\boldsymbol{n} \in \mathcal{N}(n_{[1-K]})$. Note that typically, the social welfare scales as $-n\log(n)$ when n is large (the service of a user scales as $1/n$). Hence it may be more informative to work on a scaled version of the welfare. For $\boldsymbol{\alpha} \in \Delta^{K\times S}$, define $w(\boldsymbol{\alpha})$ as:

$$w(\boldsymbol{\alpha}) = \sum_{k\in\mathcal{K}}\sum_{s\in\mathcal{S}_k} \alpha_{ks}\log\left(\frac{\mu_{ks}}{\sum_\ell \alpha_{\ell s}}\right).$$

Note that when $\boldsymbol{n} \sim (n, \boldsymbol{\alpha})$, we have: $W(\boldsymbol{n}) = nw(\boldsymbol{\alpha}) - n\log(n)$. Now observe that $x^\star = (n, \boldsymbol{\alpha}^\star)$ if and only if $\boldsymbol{\alpha}^\star$ solves the following convex program:

$$\begin{aligned} \text{maximize} \quad & w(\boldsymbol{\alpha}) = \sum_{k\in\mathcal{K}}\sum_{s\in\mathcal{S}_k} \alpha_{ks}\log\left(\frac{\mu_{ks}}{\sum_\ell \alpha_{\ell s}}\right) \quad (2)\\ \text{subject to} \quad & \forall k, \sum_{s\in\mathcal{S}_k} \alpha_{ks} = \frac{n_k}{n}, \quad \forall s, \alpha_{ks} \geq 0. \end{aligned}$$

$\alpha^\star$ represents the proportionally fair allocation of users to servers when the system size n is large.

It will also turn useful to introduce a slightly different notion of social welfare: $V(\boldsymbol{n}) = \sum_{k\in\mathcal{K}} n_k \log\left(\sum_{s\in\mathcal{S}_k} \frac{n_{ks}}{n_k} \times \frac{\mu_{ks}}{n^s}\right)$. $V(\boldsymbol{n})$ may be interpreted as the social welfare of a system where users of a given class fairly share the sum of the services rates of users of the same class. The following lemma relates the welfares $W(\boldsymbol{n})$ and $V(\boldsymbol{n})$ and states that these welfares coincide when they are maximized.

LEMMA 4.1. *(i) For all $\boldsymbol{n}$, $V(\boldsymbol{n}) \geq W(\boldsymbol{n})$.*
(ii) Let $\boldsymbol{x}' \in \arg\max_{x\in\mathcal{N}^R(n_{[1-K]})} V(\boldsymbol{x})$, and $V^\star = V(\boldsymbol{x}')$, then $W^\star = W(x') = V^\star$, i.e., $x^\star = x'$.

4.2 Efficiency of Nash Equilibriums

Pure NEs can be quite inefficient when the user population is small. For example, consider a system with two users and two servers, where users have a different preferred server (say user i has a greater service speed at server i, for $i = 1, 2$). It might well be that the allocation where both users are attached to their un-preferred server is a pure NE, which is indeed inefficient.

When the user population grows large, the allocations corresponding to pure NEs become more efficient, and get close to the ideal proportionally fair allocation. Our objective here is to quantify this observation precisely: we provide upper bounds on the difference between the social welfare achieved under the proportionally fair allocation and under pure NEs.

4.2.1 *Average potential drift*

We first establish a crucial result relating the average drift in the ordinal potential function ψ to the system welfare under the RLS algorithm. Let $(t_i)_{i\geq1}$ be the increasing sequence of epochs at which one user has the opportunity to switch servers under the RLS algorithm. This sequence is the superposition of n Poisson processes of intensity β, and hence corresponds to the instants of a Poisson process of intensity $n\beta$.

THEOREM 4.1. *For all $i \geq 1$, the expected drift in the potential under RLS after the update taking place at time t_{i+1} satisfies:*

$$\begin{aligned} &\mathbb{E}\left[\psi(\boldsymbol{n}(t_{i+1})) - \psi(\boldsymbol{n}(t_i))|\boldsymbol{n}(t_i)\right] \\ &\geq \frac{1}{nS}\Big(W^\star - W(\boldsymbol{n}(t_i)) - S\log\big(e\xi(n+S)\big)\Big). \quad (3) \end{aligned}$$

4.2.2 *Social Welfare in pure NEs*

Assume that at time t_i, the system has reached a pure NE. Then the subsequent average potential drifts vanish, i.e.,

$$\mathbb{E}\left[\psi(\boldsymbol{n}(t_{i+1})) - \psi(\boldsymbol{n}(t_i))|\boldsymbol{n}(t_i)\right] = 0.$$

As a consequence, from the previous theorem, we deduce that:

COROLLARY 4.1. *If $\boldsymbol{n}$ is a pure NE, then*

$$W^\star - W(\boldsymbol{n}) \leq S \log\big(e\xi(n+S)\big), \quad (4)$$

$$V^\star - V(\boldsymbol{n}) \leq S \log\big(e\xi(n+S)\big). \quad (5)$$

(5) is obtained by combining (4) and the claim (i) of Lemma 4.1. To interpret Corollary 4.1, it is convenient to look at the scaled version of the social welfare. Let $\boldsymbol{n} \sim (n, \boldsymbol{\alpha})$ be a pure NE, then according to (4), we have: $w(\boldsymbol{\alpha}^\star) - w(\boldsymbol{\alpha}) \leq \frac{S}{n}\log\big(e\xi(n+S)\big)$. The above inequality implies that when the user population grows large, the allocation $\boldsymbol{\alpha}$ of users to servers in a pure NE converges to the proportionally fair allocation $\boldsymbol{\alpha}^\star$. The inequality also quantifies how fast this convergence occurs.

4.3 Convergence Rate

We are now interested in the system dynamics under the RLS and BR algorithms, and in particular, we wish to analyze the rate at which the system approaches pure NEs under these algorithms. To do so, we take a detour, and provide an upper bound of the difference between $W^\star$ and the welfare of the system at time t under one of these algorithms. In turn, in view of Corollary 4.1, this allows us to estimate the rate of convergence of RLS and BR when the user population is large.

THEOREM 4.2. *For any initial condition $\boldsymbol{n}(0)$, under the RLS algorithm, we have for all t:*

$$\mathbb{E}\left[W^\star - W(\boldsymbol{n}(t))\right] \leq \frac{nS}{\beta t}\log(S\xi) + S\log\big(e\xi n(n+S)\big).$$

Let $\boldsymbol{\alpha}(t)$ denote the fractions of users of various classes attached to the different servers at time t under the RLS algorithm, i.e., $\boldsymbol{n}(t) \sim (n, \boldsymbol{\alpha}(t))$. Theorem 4.2 states that:

$$\mathbb{E}\left[w(\boldsymbol{\alpha}^\star) - w(\boldsymbol{\alpha}(t))\right] \leq \frac{S}{\beta t}\log(S\xi) + \frac{S}{n}\log\big(e\xi n(n+S)\big).$$

Applying Markov inequality, we deduce that for large systems ($n \to \infty$), after time t, the system state has a scaled welfare within ϵ of $w(\boldsymbol{\alpha}^\star)$ with probability at least $1-\delta$ as soon as $t \geq \frac{S\log(\xi S)}{\epsilon\delta}$. In particular, the convergence time towards the proportionally fair allocation does not depend on the user population.

Under the BR algorithm, the system converges typically more rapidly than under RLS, as stated in the following theorem (whose proof is omitted – it is similar to that of Theorem 4.2).

THEOREM 4.3. *For any initial condition $\boldsymbol{n}(0)$, under the BR algorithm, we have for all t:*

$$\mathbb{E}\left[W^\star - W(\boldsymbol{n}(t))\right] \leq \frac{n}{\beta t}\log(S\xi) + S\log\big(e\xi n(n+S)\big).$$

4.4 Proofs

4.4.1 *Proof of Theorem 4.1*

Under the RLS algorithm, at time t_i, the probability that a class-k user attached to server s has the opportunity to switch servers is $n_{ks}(t_i)/n$. The probability that the probed server is $c \in \mathcal{S}_k$ is $1/S_k \geq 1/S$ where S_k is the cardinality of $\mathcal{S}_k$. This user migrates to the new server only if $\frac{\mu_{kc}}{n^c(t_i)+1} > \frac{\mu_{ks}}{n^s(t_i)}$. Hence the expected drift in the ordinal potential satisfies: for any $\boldsymbol{n} \in \mathcal{N}(n_{[1-K]})$,

$$\begin{aligned}
&\mathbb{E}\big[\psi(\boldsymbol{n}(t_{i+1})) - \psi(\boldsymbol{n}(t_i)) | \boldsymbol{n}(t_i) = \boldsymbol{n}\big] \\
&\geq \sum_{k\in\mathcal{K}}\sum_{s\in\mathcal{S}_k}\sum_{c\in\mathcal{S}_k}\frac{n_{ks}}{nS}\max\{0, \log\frac{\mu_{kc}}{n^c+1} - \log\frac{\mu_{ks}}{n^s}\} \\
&\geq \sum_{k\in\mathcal{K}}\sum_{s\in\mathcal{S}_k}\frac{n_{ks}}{nS}\max\{0, \max_{c\in\mathcal{S}_k}\log\frac{\mu_{kc}}{n^c+1} - \log\frac{\mu_{ks}}{n^s}\} \\
&\geq \sum_{k\in\mathcal{K}}\left(\frac{n_k}{nS}\max_{s\in\mathcal{S}_k}\log\frac{\mu_{ks}}{n^s+1} - \sum_{s\in\mathcal{S}_k}\frac{n_{ks}}{nS}\log\frac{\mu_{ks}}{n^s}\right).
\end{aligned}$$

It remains to show that:

$$\begin{aligned}
&\sum_{k\in\mathcal{K}}\left(n_k\max_{s\in\mathcal{S}_k}\log\frac{\mu_{ks}}{n^s+1} - \sum_{s\in\mathcal{S}_k}n_{ks}\log\frac{\mu_{ks}}{n^s}\right) \\
&\qquad \geq W^\star - W(\boldsymbol{n}(t_i)) - S\log\big(e\xi(n+S)\big). \quad (6)
\end{aligned}$$

Let $\boldsymbol{n} \in \mathcal{N}(n_{[1-K]})$, and let $\boldsymbol{n}'$ be a system state such that each server has one more users than in state $\boldsymbol{n}$. Hence $n' = n+S$, and for all s, $n'^s = n^s+1$. For all k and s, $n_{ks} \leq n'_{ks} \leq n_{ks}+1$. Define $\boldsymbol{\delta} = (\delta_{ks} = n'_{ks} - n_{ks})_{k\in\mathcal{K},s\in\mathcal{S}}$. Let $\mathcal{N}(n'_{[1-K]})$ the set of all possible states of a closed system starting from $\boldsymbol{n}'$. Define $\boldsymbol{x}'^\star = \arg\max_{\boldsymbol{x}\in\mathcal{N}^R(n'_{[1-K]})} W(\boldsymbol{x})$. We have:

$$W^\star - W(\boldsymbol{n}) = A + B + W(\boldsymbol{n}') - W(\boldsymbol{n}), \quad (7)$$

where $A = W^\star - W(\boldsymbol{x}'^\star)$ and $B = W(\boldsymbol{x}'^\star) - W(\boldsymbol{n}')$. From the definitions of $W^\star$ and $W(\boldsymbol{x}'^\star)$,

$$\begin{aligned}
A &= W^\star - \max_{\boldsymbol{x}'\in\mathcal{N}^R(n'[1-K])} W(\boldsymbol{x}') \\
&\leq W^\star - W(\boldsymbol{x}^\star + \boldsymbol{\delta}) \leq \nabla W(\boldsymbol{x}^\star+\boldsymbol{\delta})^T \cdot (-\boldsymbol{\delta}) \\
&\leq -S\left(\log\frac{\mu_{\min}}{n+S} - 1\right), \quad (8)
\end{aligned}$$

where we used the concavity of W in the second inequality. Again, using the concavity of W, B satisfies:

$$\begin{aligned}
B &\leq \nabla W(\boldsymbol{n}')^T \cdot (\boldsymbol{x}'^\star - \boldsymbol{n}') \\
&\leq \max_{\boldsymbol{x}'\in\mathcal{N}^R(n'[1-K])} \nabla W(\boldsymbol{n}')^T \cdot \boldsymbol{x}' - \nabla W(\boldsymbol{n}')^T \cdot \boldsymbol{n}' \\
&\leq \sum_{k\in\mathcal{K}} n'_k \max_{s\in\mathcal{S}_k}\log\frac{\mu_{ks}}{n^s+1} - \sum_{k\in\mathcal{K}}\sum_{s\in\mathcal{S}_k} n'_{ks}\log\frac{\mu_{ks}}{n^s+1} \\
&\leq \sum_{k\in\mathcal{K}} n_k \max_{s\in\mathcal{S}_k}\log\frac{\mu_{ks}}{n^s+1} + S\log\mu_{\max} - W(\boldsymbol{n}') \quad (9)
\end{aligned}$$

Combining (7), (8), and (9), we get (6). □

4.4.2 *Proof of Theorem 4.2*

To prove the theorem, we first state and prove three preliminary lemmas. The first lemma provides an upper bound of the difference between the maximum and the minimal values of the ordinal potential function ψ over $\mathcal{N}(n_{[1-K]})$.

LEMMA 4.2. *Let $\psi_{\max} = \max_{\boldsymbol{n}\in\mathcal{N}(n_{[1-K]})}\psi(\boldsymbol{n})$ and $\psi_{\min} = \min_{\boldsymbol{n}\in\mathcal{N}(n_{[1-K]})}\psi(\boldsymbol{n})$. Then:*

$$\psi_{\max} - \psi_{\min} \leq n\log(S\xi).$$

Proof. We first provide a lower and an upper bound of $\sum_s \log(n^s!)$. To this aim, we note that $n! = \Gamma(n+1)$ and use the convexity of $\log\Gamma(\cdot)$. We have:

$$\begin{aligned}\sum_{s\in\mathcal{S}}\log(n^s!) &= \sum_{s\in\mathcal{S}}\log(n^s!) + n\log S - n\log S\\ &= \sum_{s\in\mathcal{S}}\sum_{m=1}^{n^s}\log(Sm) - n\log S\\ &\overset{(a)}{\geq} \frac{1}{S}\sum_{s\in\mathcal{S}}\log((Sn^s)!) - n\log S\\ &\overset{(b)}{\geq} \frac{1}{S}\sum_{s\in\mathcal{S}}\log((Sn^s)!) - n\log S\\ &\quad - \frac{1}{S}\sum_{s\in\mathcal{S}}\log\Gamma(Sn^s+1) + \log(n!)\\ &= -n\log S + \log(n!),\end{aligned}$$

where (a) comes the combinatorial inequality $\frac{(Sn)!}{(n!)^S} \leq S^{Sn}$, and (b) is due to the convexity of $\log\Gamma(\cdot)$.

The upper bound of $\sum_{s\in\mathcal{S}}\log(n^s!)$ follows from the fact that: $\sum_{s\in\mathcal{S}}\log(n^s!) \leq \log(n!)$. For $\boldsymbol{n}\in\mathcal{N}(n_{[1-K]})$, $\psi(\boldsymbol{n})$ satisfies

$$\begin{aligned}\psi(\boldsymbol{n}) &= -\sum_{s\in\mathcal{S}}\log(n^s!) + \sum_{k\in\mathcal{K}}\sum_{s\in\mathcal{S}_k} n_{ks}\log(\mu_{ks})\\ &\leq n\log S - \log(n!) + \sum_{k\in\mathcal{K}} n_k \max_{s\in\mathcal{S}_k}\log(\mu_{ks}),\end{aligned}$$

and

$$\psi(\boldsymbol{n}) \geq -\log(n!) + \sum_{k\in\mathcal{K}} n_k \min_{s\in\mathcal{S}_k}\log(\mu_{ks}).$$

We deduce that:

$$\psi_{\max} - \psi_{\min} \leq n\log S + \sum_{k\in\mathcal{K}} n_k \log\frac{\max_{s\in\mathcal{S}_k}\mu_{ks}}{\min_{s\in\mathcal{S}_k}\mu_{ks}},$$

which concludes the proof. □

In the next lemma, we provide an upper bound of the minimum average gap between the maximum welfare $W^\star$ and the welfare after $i \leq I$ updates under the RLS algorithm.

LEMMA 4.3. *Let $I\in\mathbb{N}$. We have:*

$$\begin{aligned}&\min_{i\leq I}\mathbb{E}\left[W^\star - W(\boldsymbol{n}(t_i))\right]\\ &\quad\leq \frac{nS}{I+1}\cdot n\log(S\xi) + S\log\big(e\xi(n+S)\big).\end{aligned}$$

Proof. From Theorem 4.1, we have:

$$\begin{aligned}&\mathbb{E}\left[\psi(\boldsymbol{n}(t_{I+1})) - \psi(\boldsymbol{n}(0))\right]\\ &= \sum_{i=0}^{I}\mathbb{E}\left[\psi(\boldsymbol{n}(t_{i+1})) - \psi(\boldsymbol{n}(t_i))\right]\\ &\geq \sum_{i=0}^{I}\mathbb{E}\left[\frac{1}{nS}\Big(W^\star - W(\boldsymbol{n}(t_i)) - S\log\big(e\xi(n+S)\big)\Big)\right].\end{aligned}$$

By Lemma 4.2, $\psi(\boldsymbol{n}(t_{I+1})) - \psi(\boldsymbol{n}(0)) \leq n\log(S\xi)$. Thus,

$$\begin{aligned}&\min_{i\leq I}\mathbb{E}[W^\star - W(\boldsymbol{n}(t_i))]\\ &\leq \frac{nS}{I+1}\mathbb{E}[\psi(\boldsymbol{n}(t_{I+1})) - \psi(\boldsymbol{n}(0))] + S\log(e\xi(n+S))\\ &\leq \frac{nS}{I+1}n\log(S\xi) + S\log(e\xi(n+S)).\end{aligned}$$

□

Our third lemma provides an upper bound of the evolution over time of the difference between the social welfare and the potential.

LEMMA 4.4. *For all i and j,*

$$\big|\big(W(\boldsymbol{n}(t_i)) - \psi(\boldsymbol{n}(t_i))\big) - \big(W(\boldsymbol{n}(t_j)) - \psi(\boldsymbol{n}(t_j))\big)\big| \leq S\log n.$$

Proof. By definition,

$$W(\boldsymbol{n}) - \psi(\boldsymbol{n}) = \sum_{s\in\mathcal{S}}\Big(\log(n^s!) - n^s\log(n^s)\Big).$$

Using $\int_1^{n^s}\log(x)dx \leq \log(n^s!) \leq \int_1^{n^s+1}\log(x)dx$, we get:

$$\begin{aligned}&W(\boldsymbol{n}) - \psi(\boldsymbol{n})\\ &\leq \sum_{s\in\mathcal{S}}\Big((n^s+1)\log(n^s+1) - (n^s+1) - n^s\log(n^s)\Big)\\ &= \sum_{s\in\mathcal{S}} n^s\log(1+\frac{1}{n^s}) + \sum_{s\in\mathcal{S}}\log(1+n^s) - n - S\\ &\leq S + S\log n - n,\end{aligned}$$

and

$$\begin{aligned}W(\boldsymbol{n}) - \psi(\boldsymbol{n}) &\geq \sum_{s\in\mathcal{S}}(n^s\log n^s - n^s + 1 - n^s\log n^s)\\ &\geq S - n.\end{aligned}$$

We conclude that for all i and j,

$$\big|\big(W(\boldsymbol{n}(t_i)) - \psi(\boldsymbol{n}(t_i))\big) - \big(W(\boldsymbol{n}(t_j)) - \psi(\boldsymbol{n}(t_j))\big)\big| \leq S\log n.$$

□

We are now ready to prove Theorem 4.2. Let τ be the number of times users get an opportunity to switch servers up to time t under the RLS algorithm. From Lemma 4.3, given $\tau = I$, there exists $i^\star \leq I$ such that:

$$\begin{aligned}&\mathbb{E}\left[W^\star - W(\boldsymbol{n}(t_{i^\star}))|\tau = I\right]\\ &\leq \frac{nS}{I+1}\cdot n\log(S\xi) + S\log(e\xi(n+S)),\end{aligned}$$

and, by Lemma 4.4, for all $i^\star \leq i \leq I$,

$$W(\boldsymbol{n}(t_i)) \geq W(\boldsymbol{n}(t_{i^\star})) - \psi(\boldsymbol{n}(t_{i^\star})) + \psi(\boldsymbol{n}(t_i)) - S\log n.$$

Thus,

$$\begin{aligned}&\mathbb{E}\left[W^\star - W(\boldsymbol{n}(t))|\tau = I\right]\\ &\leq \mathbb{E}\left[W^\star - W(\boldsymbol{n}(t_{i^*}))\right]\\ &\qquad + \mathbb{E}\left[\psi(\boldsymbol{n}(t_{i^*})) - \psi(\boldsymbol{n}(t_i))\right] + S\log(n)\\ &\overset{(a)}{\leq} \mathbb{E}\left[W^\star - W(\boldsymbol{n}(t_{i^*}))\right] + S\log(n)\\ &\leq \frac{n^2S}{I+1}\log(S\xi) + S\log(e\xi(n+S)) + S\log(n),\end{aligned}$$

where (a) comes from the fact that the potential increases over time. Now, since τ has a Poisson distribution with mean $\lambda = \beta nt$, we have $\mathbb{E}[\frac{1}{I+1}] = \sum_{I=0}^{\infty}\frac{\lambda^I e^{-\lambda}}{I!(I+1)} \leq \frac{1}{\lambda}$. Finally, we obtain:

$$\mathbb{E}\left[W^\star - W(\boldsymbol{n}(t))\right] \leq \frac{Sn}{\beta t}\log(S\xi) + S\log(e\xi n(n+S)).$$

□

5. OPEN SYSTEMS

This section is devoted to open systems: users arrive in the system randomly and leave upon service completion. Refer to §3.3 for a full description of the model.

5.1 Throughput Regions

In the following two theorems, we characterize the throughput region (i.e., the set of arrivals rates stabilizing the system) of the RLO, RLS, and BR algorithms. Define:

$$\mathcal{R}^{\text{RLO}} = \{\boldsymbol{r} \in \mathbb{R}_+^K : \exists \boldsymbol{\theta} \in \Delta^K : \forall k \in \mathcal{K}, \\ r_k \leq \sum_{s \in \mathcal{S}_k} \mu_{ks} \frac{\theta_k / S_k}{\sum_{\ell \in \mathcal{K}_s} \theta_\ell / S_\ell}\},$$

THEOREM 5.1. *(Throughput region of RLO) Assume that there exists $\boldsymbol{r} \in \mathcal{R}^{\text{RLO}}$ such that $\boldsymbol{\rho} < \boldsymbol{r}$, then under the RLO algorithm, the Markov process $(\boldsymbol{n}(t))_{t \geq 0}$ is positive Harris recurrent. Conversely, if $\boldsymbol{\rho} > \boldsymbol{r}$ for all $\boldsymbol{r} \in \mathcal{R}^{\text{RLO}}$, the process is transient.*

THEOREM 5.2. *(Throughput Optimality of RLS and BR) Assume that there exists $\boldsymbol{r} \in \mathcal{R}$ such that $\boldsymbol{\rho} < \boldsymbol{r}$, then under the RLS (or BR) algorithm, the Markov process $(\boldsymbol{n}(t))_{t \geq 0}$ is positive Harris recurrent.*

In view of Lemma 3.1 and Theorem 5.2, RLS is throughput optimal. Hence a simple fully distributed and selfish load balancing scheme is able to stabilize the system whenever this is at all possible. This seems surprising. In closed systems, RLS converges to pure NEs, and the latter become efficient only when the user population is large. In addition, even if these pure NEs are efficient in heavily loaded systems, it takes time to reach efficient allocations when the user population changes (there is a priori no time-scale separation). The proof of Theorem 5.2 exploits the results derived in the previous section about the efficiency of pure NEs and the convergence rate to these NEs under the RLS algorithm in closed systems. These results allow us to build a Lyapunov function whose drift becomes negative when the user population is large.

In homogenous systems, i.e., when each server offers the same service speed to all users (μ_{ks} does not depend on k), RLO and RLS are throughput optimal [1]. The throughput optimality of RLS directly follows from the observation that to stabilize the system, it is enough to keep all servers active. In particular, the stability analysis of RLS in homogenous systems does not require a detailed analysis of closed systems. This contrasts with the case of heterogenous systems, where characterizing the throughput region of RLS calls for a more precise understanding of the way user migrations and user arrivals and departures interact.

In heterogenous systems, the RLO algorithm is no longer throughput optimal as stated in Theorem 5.1. This intuitive result was first mentioned in [13]. To prove it, we can combine the coupling argument used in [1] (to analyze the stability of RLO in homogenous systems) and the Lyapunov function used in [13]. The proof is omitted here. Note that to analyze the stability of systems with user migrations (whose rate is proportional to the number of users), it is wise not to consider fluid limits, as the corresponding limit theorems are extremely challenging to justify [18], see [1] for a detailed discussion. The inefficiency of the RLO algorithm can be illustrated through the example of a simple symmetric system with two user classes and two servers: $\mu_{11} = \mu_{22}$, $\mu_{12} = \mu_{21} < \mu_{11}$, and $\rho_1 = \rho_2 = \rho$. In this case, it can be readily shown that $(\rho,\rho) \in \mathcal{R}^{\text{RLO}}$ if and only if $\rho \leq \frac{1}{2}(\mu_{11}+\mu_{12})$, whereas $(\rho,\rho) \in \mathcal{R}$ as long as $\rho \leq \mu_{11}$. Hence when $\mu_{12} \ll \mu_{11}$, the system can support almost twice more traffic under RLS than under RLO.

5.2 Proofs

5.2.1 *Stability of Markov processes*

To investigate stability, we use a Foster-Lyapunov criterion for positive Harris recurrence of Markov processes with values in a locally compact and separable metric space $(\mathcal{X}, \mathcal{B}(\mathcal{X}))$ – refer to [19] for more details. Here our process has a countable state space, so we do not really need to apply this general criterion; however, we use it in the proofs of results in Section 7. Let $\Phi = (\Phi(t))_{t \geq 0}$ be a time-homogeneous Markov process with state space $(\mathcal{X}, \mathcal{B}(\mathcal{X}))$ and transition functions P^t. Assume that Φ is non-explosive (which is always the case in our systems because the total arrival rate is bounded). Let $\mathcal{A}$ be the generator of Φ, i.e., for all real-valued measurable function F on $\mathcal{X}$,

$$\mathcal{A}F(x) := \lim_{h \downarrow 0} \frac{\mathbb{E}\left[F(\Phi(h)) - F(\Phi(0)) | \Phi(0) = x\right]}{h}.$$

Further define, for a given distribution ν on $\mathbb{R}_+$, the Markov transition function K_ν as: $K_\nu(x, \cdot) := \int P^t(x, \cdot)\nu(dt)$. A set $C \in \mathcal{B}(\mathcal{X})$ is called ϕ_ν*-petite* if ϕ_ν is a non-trivial measure on $\mathcal{B}(\mathcal{X})$ and ν is a distribution on $(0, \infty)$ which satisfy $K_\nu(x, \cdot) \geq \phi_\nu(\cdot)$ for all $x \in C$.

For all $A \in \mathcal{B}(\mathcal{X})$, define the stopping time $\tau_A = \inf\{t \geq 0 : \Phi(t) \in A\}$. Φ is *Harris recurrent* if there exists some σ-finite measure ν such that $P\{\tau_A < \infty | \Phi(0) = x\} = 1$ for any $x \in \mathcal{X}$, whenever $\nu(A) > 0$. If $\boldsymbol{\Phi}$ is Harris recurrent, it has a unique invariant measure π. If, in addition, π is finite, $\boldsymbol{\Phi}$ is called *positive Harris recurrent.*

THEOREM 5.3 (THEOREM 4.2 [19]). *Let Φ be a non-explosive Markov process. Assume that there exist a closed petite set $M \in \mathcal{B}(\mathcal{X})$, a non-negative measurable function F bounded on M, a function $f \geq 1$, and constants $d, c > 0$ such that:*

$$\mathcal{A}F(x) \leq -cf(x) + d1_M(x), \quad \forall x \in \mathcal{X}.$$

Then Φ is positive Harris recurrent.

5.2.2 *Proof of Theorem 5.2*

The state space of the Markov process $(\boldsymbol{n}(t))_{t \geq 0}$ is

$$\mathcal{X} = \bigcup_{n_{[1-K]} \in \mathbb{N}^K} \mathcal{N}(n_{[1-K]}).$$

Since $\mathcal{X}$ is countable, for all finite n_0, it is easy to see that $B_{n_0} = \{\boldsymbol{n} \in \mathcal{X} : n \leq n_0\}$ is petite. In what follows, we will show that there exist F and a finite integer n_0 such that the drift $\mathcal{A}F(\boldsymbol{n})$ satisfies the condition of Theorem 5.3 with $M = B_{n_0}$.

The maximum social welfares for the user population of $\boldsymbol{n} \in \mathcal{N}(n_{[1-K]})$ are defined by: $V^\star(\boldsymbol{n}) = \max_{\boldsymbol{x} \in \mathcal{N}^R(n_{[1-K]})} V(\boldsymbol{x})$ and $W^\star(\boldsymbol{n}) = \max_{\boldsymbol{x} \in \mathcal{N}^R(n_{[1-K]})} W(\boldsymbol{x})$. We denote by $d_k(\boldsymbol{n})$ the departure rate of class-k users: $d_k(\boldsymbol{n}) = \sum_{s \in \mathcal{S}} \frac{n_{ks}}{n_k} \frac{\mu_{ks}}{n^s}$, and $\boldsymbol{d}(\boldsymbol{n}) = (d_1(\boldsymbol{n}), \ldots, d_K(\boldsymbol{n}))$. We also define utility function J as: for all $\boldsymbol{x} \in \mathbb{R}_+^K$, $J(\boldsymbol{x}, \boldsymbol{n}) = \sum_{k \in \mathcal{K}} n_k \log(x_k/n_k)$. Note that $J(\boldsymbol{d}(\boldsymbol{n}), \boldsymbol{n}) = V(\boldsymbol{n})$ and $J^\star(\boldsymbol{n}) := \max_{\boldsymbol{x} \in \mathcal{R}} J(\boldsymbol{x}, \boldsymbol{n}) = V^\star(\boldsymbol{n})$ (cf. Proposition 2 of [13]). We use the following Lyapunov function: $F(\boldsymbol{n}) = Y(\boldsymbol{n}) + Z(\boldsymbol{n})$ where

$$Y(\boldsymbol{n}) = \sum_{k \in \mathcal{K}} \frac{n_k^2}{\rho_k} \quad \text{and} \quad Z(\boldsymbol{n}) = \frac{2S}{\beta} \cdot \left(\psi_{\max}(\boldsymbol{n}) - \psi(\boldsymbol{n})\right).$$

We show that the drift $\mathcal{A}F(\boldsymbol{n})$ is negative when the number of users is sufficiently large.

Step 1. We first study the drift $\mathcal{A}Y(\boldsymbol{n})$.

$$\begin{aligned}\mathcal{A}Y(\boldsymbol{n}) &= \sum_{k\in\mathcal{K}} 2\frac{n_k}{\rho_k}(\rho_k - d_k(\boldsymbol{n})) + \sum_{k\in\mathcal{K}} \frac{\rho_k + d_k(\boldsymbol{n})}{\rho_k} \\ &\leq \sum_{k\in\mathcal{K}} 2\frac{n_k}{\rho_k}(\rho_k - d_k(\boldsymbol{n})) + 2KS\xi \\ &= 2\nabla J(\boldsymbol{\rho},\boldsymbol{n})^T \cdot (\boldsymbol{\rho} - \boldsymbol{d}(\boldsymbol{n})) + 2KS\xi \\ &\overset{(a)}{\leq} 2\Big(J(\boldsymbol{\rho},\boldsymbol{n}) - J(\boldsymbol{d}(\boldsymbol{n}),\boldsymbol{n})\Big) + 2KS\xi \\ &= 2\Big(V^\star(\boldsymbol{n}) - V(\boldsymbol{n})\Big) - 2\Big(J^*(\boldsymbol{n}) - J(\boldsymbol{\rho},\boldsymbol{n})\Big) + 2KS\xi \quad (10)\end{aligned}$$

where (a) comes from concavity of J.

Step 2. We now investigate the drift $\mathcal{A}Z(\boldsymbol{n})$. This drift has two components, one due to the movements of users between servers and another one due to an arrival or a departure of a user.

$$\begin{aligned}\mathcal{A}Z(\boldsymbol{n}) \leq &-2\Big(W^\star(\boldsymbol{n}) - W(\boldsymbol{n}) - S\log\big(e\xi(n+S)\big)\Big) \\ &+ \frac{4\mu_{\max}S^2}{\beta}\log(n\xi). \quad (11)\end{aligned}$$

The first part in the r.h.s. in the above inequality comes from the movements of users, and is derived from Theorem 4.1. The second part is due to arrivals and departures: the maximum drift due to one arrival or one departure is $\log(n\xi)$ and the arrival and departure rate cannot exceed $S\mu_{\max}$. Hence the drift due to arrivals and departures is upper bounded by $\frac{4\mu_{\max}S^2}{\beta}\log(n\xi)$.

Step 3. We are now ready to estimate $\mathcal{A}F(\boldsymbol{n})$. For notational simplicity, we define

$$R(\boldsymbol{n}) = 2KS\xi + 2S\log\big(e\xi(n+S)\big) + \frac{4\mu_{\max}S^2}{\beta}\log(n\xi).$$

Then, from (10) and (11), we get:

$$\begin{aligned}\mathcal{A}F(\boldsymbol{n}) =& \mathcal{A}Y(\boldsymbol{n}) + \mathcal{A}Z(\boldsymbol{n}) \\ \leq& 2\Big(V^\star(\boldsymbol{n}) - V(\boldsymbol{n})\Big) - 2\Big(W^\star(\boldsymbol{n}) - W(\boldsymbol{n})\Big) \\ &- 2\Big(J^*(\boldsymbol{n}) - J(\boldsymbol{\rho},\boldsymbol{n})\Big) + R(\boldsymbol{n}) \\ \leq& -2\Big(J^*(\boldsymbol{n}) - J(\boldsymbol{\rho},\boldsymbol{n})\Big) + R(\boldsymbol{n}). \quad (12)\end{aligned}$$

Observe that, since there exists $\boldsymbol{r} \in \mathcal{R}$ and $\delta > 0$ such that $(1+\delta)\boldsymbol{\rho} < \boldsymbol{r}$,

$$J^\star(\boldsymbol{n}) \geq J((1+\delta)\boldsymbol{\rho},\boldsymbol{n}) = J(\boldsymbol{\rho},\boldsymbol{n}) + n\log(1+\delta). \quad (13)$$

From (13) into (12), we obtain:

$$\mathcal{A}F(\boldsymbol{n}) \leq -2n\log(1+\delta) + R(\boldsymbol{n}).$$

Finally, since $R(\boldsymbol{n}) = \Theta(\log n)$, there exists a finite n_0 and $d > 0$ such that for all $\boldsymbol{n} \in \mathcal{X}$,

$$\mathcal{A}F(\boldsymbol{n}) \leq -2n\log(1+\delta) + R(\boldsymbol{n}) \leq -1 + d1_{B_{n_0}}(\boldsymbol{n}).$$

□

6. MULTI-SERVER ALLOCATIONS

In this section, we consider scenarios where each user can open several connections to the various servers – her service rate is the sum of the rates achieved on her connections. In wireless networks, this arises when devices have several radio interfaces. As before, servers share their time fairly among their connections. Each user is assumed to open $m > 1$ connections.

We introduce the following notation. In closed systems, the set of users is $\mathcal{U} = \{1,\ldots,n\}$ and we denote by $\mathcal{U}_k$ the set of class-k users. The system state is represented by a vector $\boldsymbol{m} = (m_{us})_{u\in\mathcal{U},s\in\mathcal{S}} \in \mathbb{N}^{n\times S}$, where m_{us} is the number of connections of user u to server s. When the numbers of users of the different classes are $n_{[1-K]}$, $\mathcal{M}(n_{[1-K]})$ denotes the set of possible system states, i.e., $\boldsymbol{m} \in \mathcal{M}(n_{[1-K]})$ if (i) $m_{us} > 0$ only if $s \in \mathcal{S}_{k(u)}$ where $k(u)$ is the class of user u, (ii) $\sum_s m_{us} = m$, and (iii) $\sum_{u\in\mathcal{U}} 1_{k(u)=k} = n_k$. Finally, m^s denotes the number of connections to server s in state $\boldsymbol{m}$. In state $\boldsymbol{m}$, the service rate of user u is $\sum_s \frac{m_{us}\mu_{k(u)s}}{m^s}$.

To devise an efficient and distributed load resampling strategy, we use game theoretical techniques as earlier, but with a key difference. If we consider a game where players correspond to users, then this game is similar to a multi-path routing game as considered in [20,21]. Unfortunately, this game does not always admit a pure NE [21]. A simple way to circumvent this difficulty consists in considering a game played by the connections (each connection aims at selfishly maximizing its service rate). This game is the same as that studied in Section 4, except that n is now replaced by nm. The analysis made in Sections 4 and 5 can be directly adapted. Following this approach, the RLS algorithm is simply replaced by the so-called mRLS algorithm described below.

The mRLS algorithm. Each user has a Poisson clock ticking at rate β. When the clock of a class-k user ticks, this user selects one of her active connections uniformly at random, say from server s, and a server s' uniformly at random in $\mathcal{S}_k$. She migrates the selected connection to the new server if this would increase the service rate of the connection, i.e., if $\mu_{ks}/m^s < \mu_{ks'}/(m^{s'}+1)$.

6.1 Ordinal Potential and Social Welfare

If $n_{[1-K]}$ is fixed, the system dynamics $\boldsymbol{m}(t)$ under the mRLS algorithm may be interpret as those observed in a load balancing game where nm strategic connections try to switch servers to improve their service rates. $\boldsymbol{m} \in \mathcal{M}(n_{[1-K]})$ is a pure NE of the game if and only if: $\forall u \in \mathcal{U}, \forall s \in \mathcal{S}_{k(u)} : m_{us} > 0$, $\forall s' \in \mathcal{S}_{k(u)}$, $\frac{\mu_{k(u)s}}{m^s} \geq \frac{\mu_{k(u)s'}}{m^{s'}+1}$. As shown in Section 4, this game is an ordinal potential game. A possible ordinal potential function is defined by: for all $\boldsymbol{m} \in \mathcal{M}(n_{[1-K]})$,

$$\psi(\boldsymbol{m}) = -\sum_{s\in\mathcal{S}} \log(m^s!) + \sum_{s\in\mathcal{S}}\sum_{k\in\mathcal{K}_s}\sum_{u\in\mathcal{U}_k} m_{us}\log(\mu_{ks}).$$

Under the mRLS algorithm, the ordinal potential $\psi(\boldsymbol{m}(t))$ increases over time, and $\boldsymbol{m}(t)$ converges to a pure NE.

Once again, the proportionally fair allocation of connections to servers plays an important role in the analysis of the system dynamics. We define the social welfare of state $\boldsymbol{m}$ as:

$$W(\boldsymbol{m}) = \sum_{u\in\mathcal{U}} \log\left(\sum_s \frac{\mu_{k(u)s}m_{us}}{m^s}\right).$$

Note that this welfare is defined from the users' perspective, not from the connections' point of view. The proportionally fair allocation maximizes $W(\boldsymbol{m})$ over all $\boldsymbol{m} \in \mathcal{M}(n_{[1-K]})$. To analyze the efficiency of multi-server allocations, we take as a reference the proportionally fair allocation in the ideal scenario where each user controls a large number of connections, in which case the system state is represented by a vector $\boldsymbol{x} \in \mathcal{M}^R(n_{[1-K]})$ where

$$\mathcal{M}^R(n_{[1-K]}) = \Big\{ \boldsymbol{x} \in \mathbb{R}_+^{n \times S} : \forall u, x_{us} = 0 \text{ if } s \notin \mathcal{S}_{k(u)}, \sum_{s \in \mathcal{S}_{k(u)}} x_{us} = m, \sum_u 1_{k(u)=k} = n_k \Big\}$$

Let $\boldsymbol{x}^\star$ be the maximizer of $W(\boldsymbol{x})$ over $\boldsymbol{x} \in \mathcal{M}^R(n_{[1-K]})$, and $W^\star = W(\boldsymbol{x}^\star)$. We further introduce two different notions of social welfare that help our analysis: for $\boldsymbol{m} \in \mathcal{M}(n_{[1-K]})$,

$$V(\boldsymbol{m}) = \sum_k n_k \log(\sum_{u \in \mathcal{U}_k} \sum_{s \in \mathcal{S}_k} \frac{m_{us}\mu_{ks}}{n_k m^s}),$$

$$U(\boldsymbol{m}) = \sum_{u \in \mathcal{U}} \sum_{s \in \mathcal{S}_{k(u)}} m_{us} \log(\frac{\mu_{us}}{m^s}).$$

Note that U is the welfare defined from the connections' perspective and it corresponds to the welfare W defined in Section 4 but with nm users. As in Lemma 4.1, we can show that $\frac{1}{m}U(\boldsymbol{m}) \le W(\boldsymbol{m}) \le V(\boldsymbol{m})$, and that if $\boldsymbol{x}' \in \arg\max_{x \in \mathcal{M}^R(n_{[1-K]})} V(\boldsymbol{x})$, then $W^\star = W(\boldsymbol{x}') = V(\boldsymbol{x}') = \frac{1}{m}U(\boldsymbol{x}')$.

6.2 Efficiency of NEs, Convergence Rate, and Stability

The results presented below are direct applications of those derived in Section 4.

6.2.1 *Closed Systems*

Under the mRLS algorithm, the system converges to a pure NE. Let $(t_i)_{i \ge 1}$ be the increasing sequence of epochs at which one user has the opportunity to update her allocation under mRLS. Then:

THEOREM 6.1. *For all $i \ge 1$, under mRLS, the expected drift in the potential after the update taking place at time t_{i+1} satisfies:*

$$\begin{aligned}\mathbb{E}\big[\psi(\boldsymbol{m}(t_{i+1})) - \psi(\boldsymbol{m}(t_i)) | \boldsymbol{m}(t_i)\big] \\ \ge \frac{1}{mnS}\Big(mW^\star - U(\boldsymbol{m}(t_i)) - S\log\big(e\xi(mn+S)\big)\Big) \\ \ge \frac{1}{nS}\Big(W^\star - W(\boldsymbol{m}(t_i)) - \frac{S}{m}\log\big(e\xi(mn+S)\big)\Big). \quad (14)\end{aligned}$$

From the above theorem, we may quantify the efficiency of pure NEs:

COROLLARY 6.1. *If $\boldsymbol{m}$ is a pure NE, then:*

$$W^\star - W(\boldsymbol{m}) \le \frac{S}{m}\log\big(e\xi(mn+S)\big).$$

Thus when users control more than one connection, the pure NEs become more efficient. Note that when m grows large, any pure NE $\boldsymbol{m}$ is efficient as $W^\star - W(\boldsymbol{m})$ tends to 0. However, as stated in the theorem below, it also takes more time to converge to these equilibriums.

THEOREM 6.2. *For any initial condition $\boldsymbol{n}(0)$, under the mRLS algorithm, we have for all t:*

$$\mathbb{E}\left[W^\star - W(\boldsymbol{n}(t))\right] \le \frac{mnS}{\beta t}\log(S\xi) + \frac{S}{m}\log\big(e\xi mn(mn+S)\big).$$

6.2.2 *Open Systems*

When the user population evolves over time, we may use the results derived for closed systems to analyze the stability of the system under mRLS. The analysis is the same as that presented in Section 5. Again, mRLS turns out to be throughput optimal. With arrivals and departures, under the mRLS algorithm, the system state $\boldsymbol{m}(t)$ is a continuous-time Markov chain with countable state space $\cup_{n_{[1-K]} \in \mathbb{N}^K} \mathcal{M}(n_{[1-K]})$.

THEOREM 6.3. *(Throughput Optimality of mRLS) Assume that there exists $\boldsymbol{r} \in \mathcal{R}$ such that $\boldsymbol{\rho} < \boldsymbol{r}$, then under the mRLS algorithm, the Markov process $(\boldsymbol{m}(t))_{t \ge 0}$ is positive Harris recurrent.*

Note that the maximal stability region in the case where users control several connections remains $\mathcal{R}$. However, when the load of the system is relatively low, controlling m connections improves the average sojourn time (in very lightly loaded systems, this sojourn time is divided by a factor m provided that $m \le S_k, \forall k$).

7. CONTINUOUS ALLOCATIONS

We have seen that when each user controls m connections, a natural extension of RLS is shown to be throughput optimal. Opening m connections improves the system performance in light or moderate load scenarios. Observe however that when the user population is finite, there is still a gap between the socially optimal allocation and that realized under mRLS (see Theorem 6.1).

To close this gap, we investigate a scenario where users control an infinite number of connections ($m = \infty$). We may interpret such a scenario as follows: Users have a constant budget, say equal to 1, and bid on the various servers to obtain resources of these servers. We use the notation of the previous section. The system state is represented by a vector $\boldsymbol{w} = (w_{us})_{u \in \mathcal{U}, s \in \mathcal{S}} \in \mathbb{R}_+^{n \times S}$, where w_{us} is the weight or bid of user u on server s. When the numbers of users of the different classes are $n_{[1-K]}$, $\mathcal{W}(n_{[1-K]})$ denotes the set of possible states, i.e., $\boldsymbol{w} \in \mathcal{W}(n_{[1-K]})$ if (i) $w_{us} > 0$ only if $s \in \mathcal{S}_{k(u)}$, (ii) $\sum_s w_{us} = 1$ for all u, s, and (iii) $\sum_{u \in \mathcal{U}} 1_{k(u)=k} = n_k$. Finally $w^s = \sum_{u \in \mathcal{U}} w_{us}$ is the total weight at server s. Servers fairly share their service capacity among users, and in state $\boldsymbol{w}$, the rate of users is $\sum_s \frac{w_{us}\mu_{k(u)s}}{w^s}$. This allocation can be seen as the limiting allocation considered in Section 6 when $m \to \infty$, and is referred to as the weighted proportional allocation [22].

7.1 Social Welfares

As in the previous section, we define the following social welfares:

$$\begin{aligned} W(\boldsymbol{w}) &= \sum_{u \in \mathcal{U}} \log(\sum_{s \in \mathcal{S}_{k(u)}} \frac{\mu_{k(u)s} w_{us}}{w^s}) \\ V(\boldsymbol{w}) &= \sum_{k \in \mathcal{K}} n_k \log\left(\sum_{u \in \mathcal{U}_k} \sum_{s \in \mathcal{S}_k} \frac{\mu_{ks} w_{us}}{w^s n_k}\right) \\ U(\boldsymbol{w}) &= \sum_{u \in \mathcal{U}} \sum_{s \in \mathcal{S}_{k(u)}} w_{us} \log(\frac{\mu_{k(u)s}}{w^s}). \end{aligned}$$

W captures users' utility, V corresponds to a per-class utility, and U is the social utility of a "non-atomic" system (each infinitesimal quantity composing the weight w_{us} is considered as a player). Denote by $\boldsymbol{w}^\star \in \mathcal{W}(n_{[1-K]})$ the weights maximizing W, and $W^\star = W(\boldsymbol{w}^\star)$. The following lemma states that W, V, and U achieve their maximum at the same point, so that to maximize W, we just need to either identify a maximizer for V or U.

LEMMA 7.1. *(i) For all $\boldsymbol{w}$, $V(\boldsymbol{w}) \geq W(\boldsymbol{w}) \geq U(\boldsymbol{w})$.*
(ii) Let $\boldsymbol{w}' \in \arg\max_{\boldsymbol{w}\in\mathcal{W}(n_{[1-K]})} U(\boldsymbol{w})$, then $\boldsymbol{x}'$ also maximizes V and W.

7.2 The Water-Filling Algorithm

Assume that the user population is fixed and described by $n_{[1-K]}$. Further assume that the system state is $\boldsymbol{w} = (w_u, \boldsymbol{w}_{-u})$, where w_u and $\boldsymbol{w}_{-u}$ represent the weights of user u and of all other users, respectively. As earlier, we propose a distributed load resampling scheme that corresponds to users' selfish moves. Again, if users update their weights so as to maximize their service rates, then the system dynamics become difficult to analyze. Instead when a user, say of class k, has the opportunity to update her weights, she does it so as to solve the convex program:

$$\max_{w_u} \sum_{s\in\mathcal{S}_{k(u)}} (w_{us} + w^s_{-u}) \log\left(\frac{\mu_{k(u)s}}{w_{us} + w^s_{-u}}\right)$$
$$\text{s.t.} \sum_{s\in\mathcal{S}_{k(u)}} w_{us} = 1,$$

where w^s_{-u} denotes the sum of the weights that all users except u put on server s. We can readily see that the above optimization problem is solved using a *water-filling* procedure:

$$\forall s, \quad w_{us} = \max\left\{0, \mu_{k(u)s}\lambda - w^s_{-u}\right\}, \tag{15}$$

where the water level λ is uniquely defined by $\sum_{s\in\mathcal{S}_k} w_{us} = 1$ (the Lagrange multiplier corresponding to the constraint $\sum_s w_{us} = 1$ is given by $\log\lambda + 1$).

The Water-Filling (WF) algorithm. Each user has a Poisson clock ticking at rate β. When the clock of a class-k user ticks, this user updates her weights according to (15).

7.3 Efficiency, Convergence Rate, and Stability

7.3.1 Closed Systems

Under the WF algorithm, the system state converges to an allocation maximizing the social welfare U. Indeed when user u updates her weights, the welfare U increases, for the components in U that depend on w_{us}, $s \in \mathcal{S}_{k(u)}$ reduce to:

$$\sum_{s\in\mathcal{S}_{k(u)}} w_{us}\log(\frac{\mu_{k(u)s}}{w^s}) + \sum_{u'\neq u}\sum_{s\in\mathcal{S}_{k(u)}} w_{u's}\log(\frac{1}{w^s})$$
$$= \sum_{s\in\mathcal{S}_{k(u)}} \left(w^s\log(\frac{1}{w^s}) + w_{us}\log(\mu_{k(u)s})\right)$$
$$= \sum_{s\in\mathcal{S}_{k(u)}} \left(w^s\log(\frac{\mu_{k(u)s}}{w^s}) - w^s_{-u}\log(\mu_{k(u)s})\right).$$

Hence in view of Lemma 7.1, WF converges to an allocation maximizing W, i.e., to the proportionally fair allocation. This result was expected (see Theorem 6.1 with $m \to \infty$).

LEMMA 7.2. *Under the WF algorithm, $\boldsymbol{w}(t)$ converges to $\boldsymbol{w}$ such that $W(\boldsymbol{w}) = W^\star$.*

We also establish that the rate at which the system converges is similar to that at which the system converges under RLS (users control a single connection). This is due to the fact that each user simultaneously updates her weights to all servers, which contrasts with mRLS where only one connection can be updated at a time. Let $(t_i)_{i\geq 1}$ be the increasing sequence of epochs at which one user has the opportunity to update her allocation under the WF algorithm. Then:

		Server				
		1	2	3	4	5
Class	1	5	3	1	0.1	0.1
	2	0.1	5	3	1	0.1
	3	0.1	0.1	5	3	1
	4	1	0.1	0.1	5	3
	5	3	1	0.1	0.1	5

Table 1: Service speeds

THEOREM 7.1. *For all $i \geq 1$, under WF, the expected drift in the utility U after the update taking place at time t_{i+1} satisfies:*

$$\mathbb{E}\left[U(\boldsymbol{w}(t_{i+1})) - U(\boldsymbol{w}(t_i))|\boldsymbol{w}(t_i)\right]$$
$$\geq \frac{1}{n}\Big(U^\star - U(\boldsymbol{w}(t_i)) - 2S\log\left(e\xi(n+S)\right)\Big). \tag{16}$$

THEOREM 7.2. *For any initial condition $\boldsymbol{w}(0)$, under the WF algorithm, we have for all t:*

$$\mathbb{E}\left[W^* - W(\boldsymbol{w}(t))\right] \leq \frac{n}{\beta t}\log(S\xi) + 2S\log\left(e\xi n(n+S)\right).$$

The proofs of the above theorems are similar to those of Theorems 4.1 and 4.2, and are presented in appendix for completeness.

7.3.2 Open System

The water-filling algorithm is throughput-optimal: under WF, $\boldsymbol{w}(t)$ is a continuous time Markov process with state space:

$$\mathcal{X} = \bigcup_{n_{[1-K]}\in\mathbb{N}^K} \mathcal{W}(n_{[1-K]}).$$

We show that if $\boldsymbol{\rho}$ is in $\mathcal{R}$ (note again that the maximal stability region remains equal to $\mathcal{R}$), $(\boldsymbol{w}(t))_{t\geq 0}$ is positive Harris recurrent. The state space $\mathcal{X}$ is not countable, which complicates the analysis. We introduce a metric on $\mathcal{X}$ so that the latter is a locally compact and separable metric space and use Theorem 5.3 to show stability.

THEOREM 7.3. *(Throughput Optimality of WF) Assume that there exists $\boldsymbol{r} \in \mathcal{R}$ such that $\boldsymbol{\rho} < \boldsymbol{r}$, then under the WF algorithm, the Markov process $(\boldsymbol{w}(t))_{t\geq 0}$ is positive Harris recurrent.*

The proof of Theorem 7.3 is similar to the proof of Theorem 5.2. Please refer to Appendix B.3.

8. NUMERICAL EXPERIMENTS

In this section, we present numerical experiments to illustrate our theoretical results using two examples of simple systems.

8.1 Case 1: A Toy Example

We first consider a toy example with 5 servers and 5 user classes. The service speeds μ_{ks} are given in Table 1. We set the number of connections $m = 2$ in the mRLS algorithm.

8.1.1 Closed System

We fix $\beta = 1$. In Fig. 1(a), we plot the evolution over time of the scaled social welfare w under BR and RLS algorithms for an initial system state where $n_{ks} = 5$ for $k \in \mathcal{K}$ and $s \in \mathcal{S}$. Both algorithms converge to an allocation that is approximately optimal, and RLS takes roughly twice as much time as BR to converge.

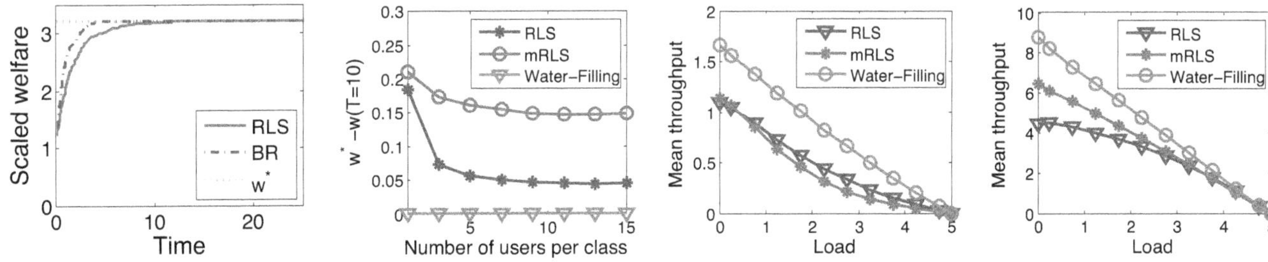

(a) Scaled social welfare vs. time (b) Social welfare gap at $t = 10$ (c) Mean throughput ($\beta = 1$) (d) Mean throughput ($\beta = 100$)

Figure 1: [Results for Case 1] Closed systems (a) and (b); Open systems (c) and (d).

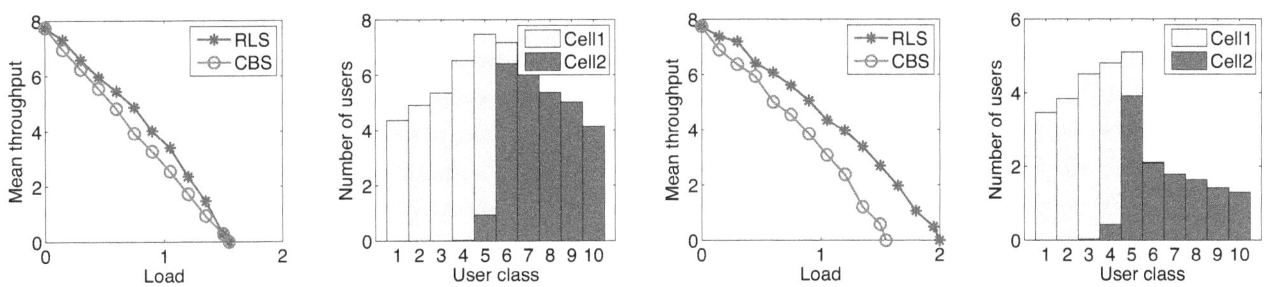

(a) Mean throughput ($\beta = 10$) (b) Average number of users ($\rho = 1.5$) under RLS (c) Mean throughput ($\beta = 10$) (d) Average number of users ($\rho = 1.95$) under RLS

Figure 2: [Results for Case 2] Homogeneous loads (a) and (b); Heterogeneous loads (c) and (d).

In Fig. 1(b), we compare the RLS, mRLS, and WF algorithms. We present the gap in terms of scaled welfare under the three algorithms at time 10 as a function of the number of users per class (each class has the same number of users). This gap is equal to $w^\star - w(t = 10)$, where $w^\star = \frac{1}{n}(W^\star + n\log(n))$ with $W^\star = \max_{\boldsymbol{n}\in\mathcal{N}^R(n_{[1-K]})} W(\boldsymbol{n})$ and $w(t = 10)$ is $\frac{1}{n}(W(t = 10) + n\log(n))$. Note that the definition of W depends on the systems considered (one connection, multiple connections, or continuous connections), but $W^\star$ is common to all systems, e.g.
$W^\star = \max_{\boldsymbol{m}\in\mathcal{M}^R(n_{[1-K]})} W(\boldsymbol{m})$. In the initial state, users are spread randomly over all servers. Under the WF algorithm, users find the best allocation rapidly; it converges to the optimal allocation before $t = 10$ with high probability, whereas this is not the case for RLS and mRLS. On the other hand, since only one connection may move at each update under mRLS, its convergence rate is proportional to $1/m$ and thus the convergence of mRLS is slower than that of RLS (see Theorem 6.2). Also observe that the gap under RLS and mRLS decreases as the number of users per class increases. This illustrates Theorems 4.2 and 6.2, i.e., the pure NEs may be inefficient when the number of users is small.

8.1.2 Open System

For open systems, we assume that the service requirements are i.i.d. exponentially distributed with unit mean. Users of the various classes arrive according to Poisson processes. The performance of the algorithms are illustrated using the *mean throughput*, equal to the inverse of the average sojourn time of users. We consider a symmetric scenario, where $\rho_k = \rho$ for all k.

Fig. 1(c) and 1(d) present the mean throughput as a function of the load ρ under RLS, mRLS, and WF when $\beta = 1$ and $\beta = 100$, respectively. First observe that as expected, all algorithms are throughput optimal. They are stable when the load is smaller than 5 – as if all users were always served at maximum speed 5.

Also note that β has a strong impact on performance. In lightly loaded systems, the mean throughput increases with the rate at which users may switch servers. When β is very large, each user moves frequently and rapidly finds the best server. For example, when ρ_k is close to 0, if $\beta = 100$, under RLS, users are served at rate almost equal to 5 in average. In contrast, when β is small, users may well not move before they leave the system, which explains their low mean throughput, see Fig. 1(c). The impact of β is here exacerbated by the large difference between the service speeds at the worst and best servers (from 0.1 to 5).

In general opening multiple connections increases the performance, especially in lightly loaded systems. In this case, a single user can simultaneously exploit the resources of multiple servers. The performance gain typically decreases with the load, and tends to vanish in heavy traffic. It should be observed that mRLS may well yield lower performance than RLS. Again, this is due to the fact that mRLS only moves at most one connection at each update – the benefit of having multiple connections is mitigated by the low convergence rate. Note that under WF, the convergence is quick, and users always exploit multiple resources of multiple servers. WF always provides the best quality of service.

8.2 Case 2: A Cellular System

In wireless cellular networks, the channel capacities between the users and the base stations (the servers) depend on their respective locations. Users close the base station experience a better channel quality, and are served at a high rate. Thus, in general, it makes sense to attach users to the closest base station (BS), an algorithm referred to as "Closest BS Selection (CBS)". In this section, we compare RLS with CBS in a simple scenario. Consider a network with two base stations and 10 user classes. We denote by $\mathcal{S} = \{1, 2\}$ and $\mathcal{K} = \{1, \ldots, 10\}$ the sets of base stations and user classes, respectively. We define the service speed of class-k users as follows: $\mu_{k1} = 11 - k$ at cell 1 and $\mu_{k2} = k$ at cell 2. Then, under CBS, class-k users select BS 1 if $1 \leq k \leq 5$ and the other users select BS 2.

We investigate open systems only. When users of the various classes have the same arrival rate (homogeneous loads), CBS and RLS exhibit very similar performance. Fig. 2(a) shows the mean throughput of the system, where $\rho_k = \rho$ for all k. Both CBS and RLS stabilize the system as long as $\rho < 1.55$ (this is the maximal load compatible with stability $1/(1/10+1/9+1/8+1/7+1/6) \simeq 1.55$). RLS performs slightly better than CBS. This little gain comes from the fact that when one of the base stations becomes idle, RLS can utilize its resource by balancing the load. Since the arrival rates are symmetric, almost all users of class $k \in \{1, \ldots, 5\}$ stay in cell 1 and users of class $k' \in \{6, \ldots, 10\}$ in cell 2 even under RLS, which is captured in Fig. 2(b).

When user arrival pattern is asymmetric, CBS performance becomes poor. Consider the heterogeneous scenario where $\rho_k = \rho$ for $1 \leq k \leq 5$ and $\rho_k = \rho/2$ for $6 \leq k \leq 10$. Then, under CBS, the overall load in cell 1 is 2 times higher than that in cell 2. Fig. 2(c) presents the mean throughput in this scenario. RLS can stabilize the system as long as $\rho < 2$ while the mean throughput of CBS is 0 for $\rho > 1.55$, i.e., it is unstable. Under RLS, the loads on two cells get balanced by the migration of class-5 users, which is shown in Fig. 2(d) where about 80% of class-5 users are in cell 2 although $\mu_{51} > \mu_{52}$.

9. CONCLUSION

In this paper, we have analyzed the performance of the RLS algorithm, a very simple distributed load resampling strategy for heterogenous parallel server systems. In scenarios where the user population is fixed, we were able to quantify at any time the efficiency of the allocation of users to servers under this algorithm. Using this result, we proved that when users arrive and leave the system upon service completion, RLS is throughput optimal, i.e., it stabilizes the system whenever this is at all possible. In other words, RLS is able to fully exploit the system heterogeneity when the user population is large, which is quite surprising.

There are many interesting directions for future work. It would be for example useful to derive estimates of the mean user sojourn times under the RLS algorithm and its extensions. This could be done by studying the system in various limiting regimes. We can use mean field asymptotics to analyze systems with a large number of servers. We may also look at systems in heavy traffic.

10. REFERENCES

[1] A. Ganesh, S. Lilienthal, D. Manjunath, A. Proutiere, and F. Simatos, "Load balancing via random local search in closed and open systems," in *Proc. ACM SIGMETRICS*, 2010, pp. 287–298.

[2] N. Nisan, T. Roughgarden, E. Tardos, and V. V. Vazirani, *Algorithmic Game Theory*. New York, NY, USA: Cambridge University Press, 2007.

[3] E. Koutsoupias and C. Papadimitriou, "Worst-case equilibria," in *Proc. STACS*, 1999, pp. 404–413.

[4] A. Orda, R. Rom, and N. Shimkin, "Competitive routing in multiuser communication networks," *IEEE/ACM Trans. Netw.*, vol. 1, no. 5, pp. 510–521, Oct. 1993.

[5] P. Berenbrink, T. Friedetzky, I. Hajirasouliha, and Z. Hu, "Convergence to equilibria in distributed, selfish reallocation processes with weighted tasks," *Algorithmica*, vol. 62, no. 3-4, pp. 767–786, 2012.

[6] I. Milchtaich, "Congestion games with player-specific payoff functions," *Games and Economic Behavior*, vol. 13, no. 1, pp. 111 – 124, 1996.

[7] V. Anantharam, "On the nash dynamics of congestion games with player-specific utility," in *Proc. IEEE CDC*, vol. 5, 2004, pp. 4673–4678 Vol.5.

[8] J. Ackermann, "Pure nash equilibria in player-specific and weighted congestion games," *Theoretical Computer Science*, vol. 410, no. 17, pp. 1552 – 1563, 2009.

[9] M. Gairing and M. Klimm, "Congestion games with player-specific costs revisited," in *Proc. SAGT*, 2013, pp. 98–109.

[10] D. Shah and J. Shin, "Dynamics in congestion games," in *Proc. ACM SIGMETRICS*, 2010, pp. 107–118.

[11] A. L. Stolyar, "Optimal routing in output-queued flexible server systems," *Probab. Eng. Inf. Sci.*, vol. 19, no. 2, pp. 141–189, Apr. 2005.

[12] R. Etkin, A. Parekh, and D. Tse, "Spectrum sharing for unlicensed bands," *IEEE JSAC*, vol. 25, no. 3, pp. 517–528, 2007.

[13] S. Borst, A. Proutiere, and N. Hegde, "Capacity of wireless data networks with intra- and inter-cell mobility," in *Proc. IEEE INFOCOM*, 2006, pp. 1–12.

[14] G. Kasbekar and A. Proutiere, "Opportunistic medium access in multi-channel wireless systems: A learning approach," in *Proc. Allerton*, 2010.

[15] D. Monderer and L. S. Shapley, "Potential games," *Games and Economic Behavior*, vol. 14, no. 1, pp. 124 – 143, 1996.

[16] M. Voorneveld and H. Norde, "A characterization of ordinal potential games," *Games and Economic Behavior*, vol. 19, no. 2, pp. 235–242, May 1997.

[17] F. Kelly, A. Maulloo, and D. Tan, "Rate control for communication networks: shadow prices, proportional fairness and stability," *Journal of the Operational Research Society*, no. 3, pp. 237–252, 1998.

[18] F. Simatos and D. Tibi, "Spatial homogenization in a stochastic network with mobility," *Ann. Appl. Probab.*, vol. 20, no. 1, pp. 312–355, 2010.

[19] S. P. Meyn and R. L. Tweedie, "Stability of Markovian processes III: Foster-Lyapunov criteria for continuous-time processes," *Advances in Applied Probability*, vol. 25, no. 3, pp. 518–548, Sep. 1993.

[20] P. Key, L. Massoulié, and D. Towsley, "Path selection and multipath congestion control," *Commun. ACM*, vol. 54, no. 1, pp. 109–116, Jan. 2011.

[21] P. Key and A. Proutiere, "Routing games with elastic traffic," *SIGMETRICS Perform. Eval. Rev.*, vol. 37, no. 2, pp. 63–64, Oct. 2009.

[22] T. Nguyen and M. Vojnovic, "Weighted proportional allocation," in *Proc. ACM SIGMETRICS*, 2011, pp. 173–184.

APPENDIX

A. PROOFS OF LEMMAS

A.1 Proof of Lemma 4.1

(i) By concavity of the log function:

$$\log\left(\sum_{s\in\mathcal{S}}\frac{n_{ks}\mu_{ks}}{n_k n^s}\right)\geq\sum_{s\in\mathcal{S}}\frac{n_{ks}}{n_k}\log(\frac{\mu_{ks}}{n^s}),$$

which implies $V(\boldsymbol{n})\geq W(\boldsymbol{n})$.

(ii) It was shown in [13] that V is maximized at $\boldsymbol{x}$ when the following conditions hold: a. when $x_{ks}>0$, $\frac{\mu_{ks}}{n^s}=\frac{\mu_{ks'}}{n^{s'}}$ if $x_{ks'}>0$; b. when $x_{ks}=0$. $\frac{\mu_{ks}}{n^s}\leq\frac{\mu_{ks'}}{n^{s'}}$ if $x_{ks'}>0$. For $\boldsymbol{x}$ satisfying these two conditions, it is clear that $W(\boldsymbol{x})=V(\boldsymbol{x})$, and hence in view of (i), $\boldsymbol{x}$ also maximizes W. □

A.2 Proof of Lemma 7.1

(i) Since log is a concave function,

$$\log\left(\sum_{s\in\mathcal{S}_{k(u)}}w_{us}\frac{\mu_{k(u)s}}{w^s}\right)\geq\sum_{s\in\mathcal{S}_{k(u)}}w_{us}\log(\frac{\mu_{k(u)s}}{w^s}).$$

Therefore, $W(\boldsymbol{w})\geq U(\boldsymbol{w})$.

(ii) In (i), the equality holds when every class k satisfies that

$$\frac{\mu_{ks}}{w^s}=\frac{\mu_{ks'}}{w^{s'}}$$

for all s and s' having positive weight $w_{ks},\ w_{ks'}>0$. This is the KKT condition of V and W. □

B. PROOFS OF THEOREMS

B.1 Proof of Theorem 7.1

The proof is similar to that of Theorem 4.1.

$$\begin{aligned}
&n\mathbb{E}\big[U(\boldsymbol{w}(t_{i+1}))-U(\boldsymbol{w}(t_i))|\boldsymbol{w}(t_i)=\boldsymbol{w}\big]\\
&\geq\sum_{u\in\mathcal{U}}\sum_{s\in\mathcal{S}_{k(u)}}w_{us}\max\{0,\max_{c\in\mathcal{S}_{k(u)}}\log\frac{\mu_{k(u)c}}{w^c+1}-\log\frac{\mu_{k(u)s}}{w^s-1}\}\\
&\geq\sum_{u\in\mathcal{U}}\sum_{s\in\mathcal{S}_{k(u)}}w_{us}\left(\max_{c\in\mathcal{S}_{k(u)}}\log\frac{\mu_{k(u)c}}{w^c+1}-\log\frac{\mu_{k(u)s}}{w^s-\delta^*_{k(u)s}}\right)\\
&=\sum_{u\in\mathcal{U}}\sum_{s\in\mathcal{S}_{k(u)}}w_{us}\left(\max_{c\in\mathcal{S}_{k(u)}}\log\frac{\mu_{k(u)c}}{w^c+1}-\log\frac{\mu_{k(u)s}}{w^s}\right)\\
&\quad-\sum_{u\in\mathcal{U}}\sum_{s\in\mathcal{S}_{k(u)}}w_{us}\log\frac{w^s}{w^s-\delta^*_{k(u)s}}\\
&\overset{(a)}{\geq}U^\star-U(\boldsymbol{w})-S\log(e\xi(n+S))-S-S\log(\xi n),
\end{aligned}$$

where

$$\delta^*_{ks}=\arg\min_{\delta\in[0,1]}\left|\max_{c\in\mathcal{S}_k}\log\frac{\mu_{kc}}{w^c+1}-\log\frac{\mu_{ks}}{w^s-\delta^*_{ks}}\right|.$$

It remains to prove inequality (a). As in the proof of Theorem 4.1, we can easily show that:

$$\begin{aligned}
&\sum_{u\in\mathcal{U}}\sum_{s\in\mathcal{S}_{k(u)}}w_{us}\left(\max_{c\in\mathcal{S}_{k(u)}}\log\frac{\mu_{k(u)c}}{w^c+1}-\log\frac{\mu_{k(u)s}}{w^s}\right)\\
&\qquad\geq U^\star-U(\boldsymbol{w})-S\log(e\xi(n+S)).
\end{aligned}$$

Moreover, since $\frac{1}{\xi}\leq w^s-\delta^*_{ks}\leq w^s$,

$$\max_{k\in\mathcal{K},s\in\mathcal{S}_k}\log\frac{w^s}{w^s-\delta^*_{ks}}\leq\log(\xi n).\qquad(17)$$

Thus,

$$\begin{aligned}
\sum_{k\in\mathcal{K}}\sum_{s\in\mathcal{S}_k}w_{ks}\log\frac{w^s}{w^s-\delta^*_{ks}}&\leq S\log(\xi n)+\sum_{s\in\mathcal{S}}w'^s\log\frac{w^s}{w'^s}\\
&\leq S\log(\xi n)+S\log(e),
\end{aligned}$$

where $w'^s=\max\{0,w^s-1\}$. This completes the proof of inequality (a). □

B.2 Proof of Theorem 7.2

To prove the theorem, we first provide a lower and an upper bound of $U(\boldsymbol{w})$. For all $\boldsymbol{w}\in\mathcal{W}(n_{[1-K]})$, we have:

$$\begin{aligned}
U(\boldsymbol{w})&=\sum_{u\in\mathcal{U}}\sum_{s\in\mathcal{S}_{k(u)}}w_{us}\log\mu_{k(u)s}-\sum_{s\in\mathcal{S}}w^s\log(w^s)\\
&\leq n\mu_{\max}-\sum_{s\in\mathcal{S}}\frac{w^sS}{S}\log(w^sS)+n\log S\\
&\leq n\mu_{\max}-n\log(n)+n\log S \qquad(18)
\end{aligned}$$

and

$$U(\boldsymbol{w})\geq n\mu_{\min}-\sum_{s\in\mathcal{S}}w^s\log(w^s)\geq n\mu_{\min}-n\log(n).\quad(19)$$

From (18) and (19),

$$U_{\max}-U_{\min}\leq n\log(\xi)+n\log S,\qquad(20)$$

where we let $U_{\max}=\max_{\boldsymbol{w}\in\mathcal{W}(n_{[1-K]})}U(\boldsymbol{w})$ and $U_{\min}=\min_{\boldsymbol{w}\in\mathcal{W}(n_{[1-K]})}U(\boldsymbol{w})$.

Next, as in Lemma 4.3, we provide an upper bound of the minimum average gap between the maximum welfare $U^\star$ and the welfare after $i\leq I$ updates under the WF algorithm. From Theorem 7.1, we have:

$$\begin{aligned}
&\mathbb{E}\left[U(\boldsymbol{w}(t_{I+1}))-U(\boldsymbol{w}(0))\right]\\
&=\sum_{i=0}^{I}\mathbb{E}\left[U(\boldsymbol{w}(t_{i+1}))-U(\boldsymbol{w}(t_i))\right]\\
&\geq\sum_{i=0}^{I}\mathbb{E}\left[\frac{1}{n}\Big(U^\star-U(\boldsymbol{w}(t_i))-2S\log\big(e\xi(n+S)\big)\Big)\right].(21)
\end{aligned}$$

From (20) and (21),

$$\begin{aligned}
&\min_{i\leq I}\mathbb{E}[U^\star-U(\boldsymbol{w}(t_i))]\\
&\leq\frac{n}{I+1}\mathbb{E}[U(\boldsymbol{w}(t_{I+1}))-U(\boldsymbol{w}(0))]+2S\log(e\xi(n+S))\\
&\leq\frac{n}{I+1}n\log(S\xi)+2S\log(e\xi(n+S)).\qquad(22)
\end{aligned}$$

We are now ready to prove Theorem 7.2. Let τ be the number of times up to time t users get an opportunity to update their weights under the WF algorithm. From (22), given $\tau=I$, there exists $i^\star\leq I$ such that:

$$\begin{aligned}
&\mathbb{E}\left[U^\star-U(\boldsymbol{w}(t_{i^\star}))|\tau=I\right]\\
&\leq\frac{n^2}{I+1}\cdot\log(S\xi)+2S\log(e\xi(n+S)),
\end{aligned}$$

and, since, for all i, $U(\boldsymbol{w}(t_{i+1})) - U(\boldsymbol{w}(t_{i+1})) \geq 0$,

$$\begin{aligned}\mathbb{E}\left[U^\star - U(\boldsymbol{w}(t)) | \tau = I\right] &\leq \mathbb{E}\left[U^\star - U(\boldsymbol{w}(t_{i^*}))\right] \\ &\leq \frac{n^2}{I+1}\log(S\xi) + 2S\log(e\xi(n+S)).\end{aligned}$$

Now, since τ has a Poisson distribution with mean $\lambda = \beta n t$, we have $\mathbb{E}[\frac{1}{I+1}] = \sum_{I=0}^{\infty} \frac{\lambda^I e^{-\lambda}}{I!(I+1)} \leq \frac{1}{\lambda}$.
Finally, we obtain:

$$\begin{aligned}\mathbb{E}\left[W^\star - W(\boldsymbol{w}(t))\right] &\leq \mathbb{E}\left[U^\star - U(\boldsymbol{w}(t))\right] \\ &\leq \frac{n}{\beta t}\log(S\xi) + 2S\log(e\xi(n+S)).\end{aligned}$$

□

B.3 Proof of Theorem 7.3

Let $\boldsymbol{x} \in \mathcal{X}$. We denote by $n(\boldsymbol{x})$ the corresponding number of users, by $n_k(\boldsymbol{x})$ the number of class-k users, and by $n_{[1-K]}(\boldsymbol{x}) = (n_1(\boldsymbol{x}), \cdots, n_K(\boldsymbol{x}))$. Users are indexed by $u = 1, \ldots, n(\boldsymbol{x})$, and $k_{\boldsymbol{x}}(u)$ the class of user u. We introduce the following metric on $\mathcal{X}$:

$$\begin{aligned}d(\boldsymbol{x},\boldsymbol{y}) = &\sum_{u=1}^{\min\{n(\boldsymbol{x}),n(\boldsymbol{y})\}} \sum_{s\in\mathcal{S}} |x_{us} - y_{us}| \cdot 1_{k_{\boldsymbol{x}}(u)=k_{\boldsymbol{y}}(u)} \\ + &\sum_{u=1}^{\min\{n(\boldsymbol{x}),n(\boldsymbol{y})\}} \sum_{s\in\mathcal{S}} 2 \cdot 1_{k_{\boldsymbol{x}}(u)\neq k_{\boldsymbol{y}}(u)} + 2|n(\boldsymbol{x}) - n(\boldsymbol{y})|.\end{aligned}$$

Note that, in this metric, the order in which users appear in $\boldsymbol{x}$ matters may not seem natural. We could have defined a metric that does not depend on this order, but this is not needed here. Let $\mathbf{0}$ denote the empty state and define $\|\boldsymbol{x}\| = d(\boldsymbol{x}, \mathbf{0})$. Then $\mathcal{X}$ is a locally compact and separable metric space. The Markov process $(\boldsymbol{w}(t))_{t\geq 0}$ takes its values in $\mathcal{X}$, and has transition rates such that when there is an arrival or a departure, users are relabeled randomly. When a user updates her weights, we do not change the labels of users. The precise order in which users are labeled in the construction of the Markov process $(\boldsymbol{w}(t))_{t\geq 0}$ does not really matter: in fact to study its positive Harris recurrence, we use a Lyapunov function whose drift does not depend on the order in which users are considered in the state.

Let us first identify a closed petite set:

LEMMA B.1. *Let $n_0 > 0$. The set $C_{n_0} : \{\boldsymbol{x} \in \mathcal{X} : \|\boldsymbol{x}\| \leq n_0\}$ is a closed petite set.*

Proof. Let $\boldsymbol{x} \in C_{n_0}$. Then, there is a strictly positive probability that the system starting in $\boldsymbol{x}$ is in state $\mathbf{0}$ at time $t = 1$ (we can construct paths with only departures – no moves, and no arrivals). Hence choosing for example $\nu(\cdot) = \delta_1(\cdot)$, we can prove that there exists $\varepsilon > 0$ such that $K_\nu(\boldsymbol{x}, \mathbf{0}) = P^1(\boldsymbol{x}, \mathbf{0}) > \varepsilon$ for all $\boldsymbol{x} \in C_{n_0}$. Therefore, C_{n_0} is ϕ_ν-petite where $\phi_\nu(A) = \varepsilon$ if $\mathbf{0} \in A$ and $\phi_\nu(A) = 0$ otherwise. □

LEMMA B.2. *Let $\mathcal{A}$ denote the generator of the Markov process $(\boldsymbol{w}(t))_{t\geq 0}$. Let $F(\boldsymbol{w}) = \sum_{k=1}^{K} \frac{n_k(\boldsymbol{w})^2}{\rho_k} + \frac{2}{\beta} \cdot \big(U^\star(\boldsymbol{w}) - U(\boldsymbol{w})\big)$. Then, there exists n_0 such that for some $a, b > 0$*

$$\mathcal{A}F(\boldsymbol{w}) \leq -a + b 1_{C_{n_0}}.$$

Proof. The proof is similar to that of Theorem 5.2. $\boldsymbol{d}$, Y and Z are defined as

$$d_k = d_k(\boldsymbol{w}) = \sum_{u\in\mathcal{U}_k} \sum_{s\in\mathcal{S}_k} \frac{w_{us}}{n_k(\boldsymbol{w})} \frac{\mu_{ks}}{w^s},$$

$$Y(\boldsymbol{w}) = \sum_{k\in\mathcal{K}} \frac{n_k(\boldsymbol{w})^2}{\rho_k} \quad \text{and} \quad Z(\boldsymbol{w}) = \frac{2}{\beta} \cdot \big(U^\star(\boldsymbol{w}) - U(\boldsymbol{w})\big),$$

where $U^\star(\boldsymbol{w}) = \max_{\boldsymbol{x}\in\mathcal{W}^R(n_{[1-K]}(\boldsymbol{w}))} U(\boldsymbol{x})$.

The analysis of the drift $\mathcal{A}Y(\boldsymbol{w})$ is the same as in the proof of Theorem 5.2:

$$\begin{aligned}\mathcal{A}Y(\boldsymbol{w}) - 2KS\xi &\leq 2\Big(J(\boldsymbol{\rho},\boldsymbol{w}) - J(\boldsymbol{d},\boldsymbol{w})\Big) \\ &= 2\Big(U^\star(\boldsymbol{w}) - V(\boldsymbol{w})\Big) - 2\Big(U^\star(\boldsymbol{w}) - J(\boldsymbol{\rho},\boldsymbol{w})\Big), \quad (23)\end{aligned}$$

where J is defined as in the proof of Theorem 5.2: for all $\boldsymbol{x} \in \mathbb{R}_+^K$,

$$J(\boldsymbol{x},\boldsymbol{w}) = \sum_{k\in\mathcal{K}} n_k(\boldsymbol{w}) \log(x_k / n_k(\boldsymbol{w})).$$

By Theorem 7.1, we deduce that the drift $\mathcal{A}Z(\boldsymbol{w})$ satisfies:

$$\begin{aligned}\mathcal{A}Z(\boldsymbol{w}) \leq &-2\Big(U^\star(\boldsymbol{w}) - U(\boldsymbol{w})\Big) \\ &+ 4S\log\big(e\xi(n+S)\big) + \frac{4\mu_{\max}S}{\beta}\log(n\xi), \quad (24)\end{aligned}$$

where $n = n(\boldsymbol{w})$ (to simplify the notation). Therefore, if we define

$$R(\boldsymbol{w}) := 2KS\xi + 4S\log\big(e\xi(n+S)\big) + \frac{4\mu_{\max}S}{\beta}\log(n\xi),$$

we get:

$$\begin{aligned}\mathcal{A}F(\boldsymbol{w}) &\leq -2\Big(U^\star(\boldsymbol{w}) - J(\boldsymbol{\rho};\boldsymbol{n})\Big) + R(\boldsymbol{w}) \\ &\leq -2n\log(1+\delta) + R(\boldsymbol{w}). \quad (25)\end{aligned}$$

We conclude exactly as in the proof of Theorem 5.2. □

Multi-Resource Fairness: Objectives, Algorithms and Performance

Thomas Bonald*
Télécom ParisTech, Paris, France
thomas.bonald@telecom-paristech.fr

James Roberts
IRT-SystemX, Paris-Saclay, France
james.roberts@irt-systemx.fr

ABSTRACT

Designing efficient and fair algorithms for sharing multiple resources between heterogeneous demands is becoming increasingly important. Applications include compute clusters shared by multi-task jobs and routers equipped with middleboxes shared by flows of different types. We show that the currently preferred objective of Dominant Resource Fairness (DRF) has a significantly less favorable efficiency-fairness tradeoff than alternatives like Proportional Fairness and our proposal, Bottleneck Max Fairness. We propose practical algorithms to realize these sharing objectives and evaluate their performance under a stochastic demand model. It is shown, in particular, that the strategyproofness property that motivated the choice of DRF for an assumed fixed set of jobs or flows, is largely irrelevant when demand is dynamic.

Categories and Subject Descriptors

C.2.1 [**Computer communication networks**]: Network Architecture and Design—*packet-switching networks*; C.4 [**Performance of systems**]: [modeling techniques, performance attributes]

General Terms

Algorithms, Performance

Keywords

Dominant resource fairness, proportional fairness, bottleneck max fairness, multi-resource sharing, cluster computing

1. INTRODUCTION

Multi-resource fairness has recently received a lot of attention thanks mainly to two papers by A. Ghodsi and coauthors [6, 5]. In the present paper we argue that the objective of dominant resource fairness (DRF), advocated by Ghodsi *et al.* for resource sharing in compute clusters and routers equipped with middleboxes, respectively, is not preferable to more classical sharing objectives like proportional fairness (PF) which achieve a better efficiency-fairness tradeoff. Such objectives were discarded by Ghodsi *et al.* as being vulnerable to manipulation by users seeking to gain more than their fair share by falsely stating their requirements. The advocated *strategyproofness* property, possessed by DRF but not PF in a context of *static* demand, is not in fact discriminating when considering the more realistic context of *dynamic* demand.

Multi-resource sharing in a compute cluster consists in launching appropriate numbers of tasks of multi-task jobs. Each task of a given job has its particular requirements for CPU, RAM and other resources. In practice, various constraints on the placement of tasks on physical machines need to be taken into account but, for present purposes, we follow Ghodsi *et al.* [6] and assume resources of the same type are assembled in homogeneous pools. The question is, how should a central scheduler determine the numbers of simultaneous tasks to run for all the currently active jobs, ensuring efficiency and some measure of fairness.

Routers increasingly employ middleboxes to process packets and these constitute potential bottlenecks for flows, in addition to link bandwidth. Different flows have different per-packet resource requirements (e.g., some require complex packet processing, others none) and the issue here is what packet rates should be imposed for concurrent flows in order to efficiently and fairly share all types of resource of these software routers.

Bandwidth sharing in a network is a particular form of multi-resource sharing. The problem is generally simpler since all flows sharing a given link are assumed to have identical requirements. This assumption is not true, however, for some wireless links where the resource to be allocated is spectrum time and the amount required to realize a given bit rate varies considerably between terminals, depending on their particular radio conditions. It is important to share wireless and wired links in a manner that adequately balances efficiency and fairness.

We have already made the case in a recent paper for proportional fair sharing of compute cluster resources [2]. Here we extend those arguments to the case of router resources and networks and introduce a new allocation objective called bottleneck max fairness (BMF). BMF is a pragmatic alternative to PF to which it has similar performance in all three application areas.

*Both authors are members of the LINCS, Paris, France. See www.lincs.fr.

SIGMETRICS'15, June 15–19, 2015, Portland, OR, USA.

http://dx.doi.org/10.1145/2745844.2745869.

In addition to the introduction of BMF, the main contributions of the paper are

- a characterization of the properties of BMF including, in Theorem 1, a first result on the stability conditions of this sharing objective,
- practical algorithms allowing the implementation of PF and BMF allocations, the algorithms for BMF being rather simpler than those for PF,
- results on the impact of falsely declared resource requirements, illustrating the practical strategyproofness of PF and BMF allocations under dynamic demand.

We first describe DRF, PF and BMF sharing objectives in abstract terms common to the above three application contexts. We define the corresponding allocations and discuss their significant characteristics. Algorithms are then discussed for realizing the respective allocations and we propose practical, low-complexity algorithms to realize PF and BMF sharing in compute clusters, software routers and networks, respectively. The following section on performance includes an important theorem on BMF stability and presents numerical results that justify our claim that DRF is not in fact the preferred objective. Under dynamic demand, where jobs or flows arrive over time and have finite size, completion times are consistently and significantly smaller with either PF or BMF allocations. We further highlight the implausibility of players being able to game the system when these allocations are applied to a dynamic population of jobs or flows.

2. OBJECTIVES

We define DRF, PF and BMF multi-resource sharing objectives with respect to a fluid model where resources are assumed infinitely divisible. The model is abstract and, rather than jobs or flows, we refer to *transactions*. These are assumed divisible into a large number of infinitesimal components (representing tasks or packets, for instance) having homogeneous resource usage characteristics.

2.1 The fluid model

Consider R infinitely divisible resources of normalized capacity 1 to be shared by n transactions indexed by i. Each transaction i requires amounts of each resource in fixed proportions and the amount allocated determines the rate at which the transaction progresses. We denote the requirements of transaction i by a vector $a_i = (a_{i1}, \ldots, a_{iR})$. We say that transaction i requires resouce j if $a_{ij} > 0$. A resource j for which $a_{ij} = \max_k\{a_{ik}\}$ is called a *dominant resource* for transaction i.

An allocation is defined by a vector of real numbers $\varphi = (\varphi_1, \ldots, \varphi_n)$ such that $\varphi_i a_{ij}$ is the fraction of resource j allocated to transaction i. The allocation must satisfy capacity constraints:

$$\sum_{i=1}^{n} \varphi_i a_{ij} \leq 1, \quad \text{for } j = 1, \ldots, R. \tag{1}$$

We say that resource j is *saturated* if $\sum_{i=1}^{n} \varphi_i a_{ij} = 1$. We refer to such a resource as a bottleneck.

2.2 Sharing properties

The allocation φ should arguably possess the following properties [6, 2]:

Pareto-efficiency. Each transaction requires some resource which is saturated.

Envy-freeness. No transaction should prefer the allocation of some other transaction.

Sharing-incentive. Each transaction gets no less than a $1/n$ share of its dominant resource.

Single-resource fairness. Resource shares $\varphi_i a_{i1}$ are all equal to $1/n$ when $R = 1$.

Single-bottleneck fairness. The shares $\varphi_i a_{ij}$ of resource j are all equal to $1/n$ whenever j is the only bottleneck.

Strategyproofness. The resource shares of any transaction do not increase if this transaction modifies its vector of resource requirements.

Scale-invariance. The resource shares remain the same when the vector of resource requirements of any transaction is multiplied by a scaling factor.

It is straightforward to check that single-resource fairness is a rather crucial requirement in that it is realized by any Pareto-efficient allocation that fulfills any one of the other properties.

2.3 Dominant resource fairness

Dominant resource fairness (DRF) is the unique Pareto efficient allocation where transactions obtain fractions of their dominant resource that are as equal as possible. Equality may not be possible if some transactions require only a subset of the resources [15]. DRF in fact corresponds to *weighted max-min fairness* where the weight of transaction i is inversely proportional to its dominant resource requirement $\max_j\{a_{ij}\}$.

DRF satisfies all properties listed in §2.2 except single-bottleneck fairness [6, 2]: even in the presence of a single bottleneck, the shares of this resource are not equal and depend on requirements for non-saturated resources. The main advantage of DRF over other allocations is that it is *strategyproof*. This means a transaction cannot gain a greater share of resources by boosting some component of its requirement vector.

2.4 Proportional fairness

An allocation φ is proportional fair (PF) if, for any other allocation φ' satisfying (1), the sum of proportional changes is non-positive, $\sum_i (\varphi'_i - \varphi_i)/\varphi_i \leq 0$ [12]. Equivalently, φ maximizes $\sum_i \log \varphi_i$ subject to (1) and can thus be said to maximize social welfare assuming a logarithmic utility function.

While PF was introduced in [12] as an objective for sharing bandwidth in a wired network, it was advocated independently by Tse and co-authors as the preferred allocation for a time-shared wireless downlink channel [19].

By the Karush-Kuhn-Tucker theorem, PF is uniquely characterized in terms of Lagrange multipliers ν_j. We have,

$$\frac{1}{\varphi_i} = \sum_{j=1}^{R} a_{ij} \nu_j, \tag{2}$$

for $i = 1, \ldots, n$, where $\nu_j \geq 0$ and $\nu_j > 0$ if and only if resource j is a bottleneck.

PF is clearly Pareto-efficient. In fact, it satisfies all properties of §2.2 except strategyproofness. The proof of envy-freeness is given below; other properties are proved in [2].

PROPOSITION 1. *The PF allocation is envy-free.*

PROOF. For any two transactions i_1, i_2, it follows from (2) that

$$\sum_{j=1}^{R} \nu_j(\varphi_{i_1} a_{i_1 j} - \varphi_{i_2} a_{i_2 j}) = 0.$$

Since not all Lagrange multipliers are zero, this implies that $\varphi_{i_1} a_{i_1 j} \geq \varphi_{i_2} a_{i_2 j}$ for some resource j: transaction i_1 does not prefer the allocation of transaction i_2. □

PF is the only utility maximizing allocation that is single-resource fair [2]. In particular, none of the properties except Pareto-efficiency is satisfied by a utility maximizing allocation other than PF.

To see why PF is not strategyproof, consider the following example: we have $R = 2$ resources and $n = 2$ transactions with requirements $a_1 = (1/2, 1)$ and $a_2 = (1, 1/2)$. The PF allocation is then $\varphi = (2/3, 2/3)$. If transaction 1 claims requirement $a'_1 = (2/3, 1)$, we find $\varphi' = (3/4, 1/2)$ yielding a bigger share for transaction 1 at the expense of transaction 2. Note, however, that if a user does not know the other requirements, an ill-chosen modification can instead lead to it receiving a smaller share. Continuing the above example, if transaction 1 claims $a'_1 = (1, 1)$, the PF allocation would be $\varphi' = (1/2, 1/2)$. Both transactions lose out compared to the result of the truthful declaration, $a_1 = (1/2, 1)$.

It is interesting to note that, for $n = 2$, one can characterize the maximum gain a transaction can obtain by a false declaration. We have the following proposition.

PROPOSITION 2. *For $n = 2$ transactions, the relative gain obtained by a transaction declaring false requirements cannot exceed 50% under PF.*

PROOF. Without loss of generality, we can assume that $R = 2$ (whenever $R > 2$, one of the resources is never saturated since its requirements are dominated by those of another resource). By scale invariance, we can take $a_{12} = a_{21} = 1$ and $a_{11}, a_{22} \leq 1$. Assume transaction 1 declares false requirement a'_{11} on resource 1. If $\frac{1}{2}(1/a_{11} + a_{22}) < 1$ then resource 1 is the single bottleneck and no winning strategy exists. Otherwise, resource 2 is a bottleneck for the true requirement and transaction 1 gets the maximum share of this resource, given by:

$$\varphi_1 = \min\left(\frac{1}{2}, \frac{1 - a_{22}}{1 - a_{11}a_{22}}\right).$$

The best strategy for transaction 1 is to increase a_{11} until it gets the maximum share of both resource 1 and resource 2, that is to set

$$a'_{11} = \frac{1}{2 - a_{22}},$$

in which case the allocation is given by

$$\varphi'_1 = 1 - \frac{a_{22}}{2}.$$

It can be verified that the relative gain satisfies

$$\frac{\varphi'_1 - \varphi_1}{\varphi_1} \leq \frac{1}{2},$$

with equality for $a_{11} = 0$, $a_{22} = 1/2$, that is $a'_{11} = 2/3$. □

2.5 Bottleneck max fairness

Dolev *et al.* proposed the "no justified complaints" objective as an alternative to DRF [4]. To be concise, we adopt a simplified version of this objective: a transaction has no justified complaint if it receives at least a fraction $1/n$ of at least one bottleneck. Pareto efficient allocations fulfilling this objective for all users are said to realize "bottleneck-based fairness" [24, 9].

There are in fact many allocations that are bottleneck-based fair. We restrict the class of such allocations somewhat by requiring in addition that every transaction i receives an allocation $\varphi_i a_{ij}$ of some bottleneck resource j that is *maximal* for that resource. We call such allocations "bottleneck max fair" (BMF).

Discussions on bottleneck-based fairness in [4] and [9] suggest the existence of a BMF allocation is far from obvious. The following proposition, proved in the appendix, establishes the existence of a BMF allocation.

PROPOSITION 3. *A BMF allocation always exists.*

Like PF, BMF meets all properties of §2.2 except strategyproofness. It is Pareto-efficient by definition and envy-free since, for any transaction i, there is some resource j such that $\varphi_i a_{ij}$ is maximal over all transactions. The no justified complaints objective clearly implies BMF has the sharing-incentive property. It is both single-resource fair and single-bottleneck fair since all transactions attain the maximum allocation of the resource in question and this is necessarily equal to $1/n$. It is scale-invariant since the definition involves the resource shares $\varphi_i a_{ij}$ only.

It turns out that BMF is not necessarily unique. The following proposition, also proved in the appendix, shows however that BMF is unique for $R = 2$ resources.

PROPOSITION 4. *The BMF allocation is unique for two resources.*

That uniqueness does not extend to more than 2 resources is established by the following counter-example. Consider a 3 resource system with 3 transactions having requirement vectors (1, 1, 1), (1, 1/2, 3/4) and (1/2, 1, 3/4). Allocations $\varphi^{(0)} = (2/5, 2/5, 2/5)$ and $\varphi^{(1)} = (1/3, 4/9, 4/9)$ both satisfy the definition. In fact, allocations $\varphi^{(x)} = (2/5 - x/15, 2/5 + 2x/45, 2/5 + 2x/45)$ for $0 \leq x \leq 1$ are all BMF. Note that the absence of uniqueness is not necessarily problematic since all the allocations may be considered satisfactory with respect to the considered properties.

The fact that BMF is not strategyproof follows on observing that BMF coincides with PF for $n = 2$ transactions, so that the counterexample of §2.4 applies to BMF as well. BMF and PF in fact coincide for any two homogeneous populations of transactions.

PROPOSITION 5. *BMF coincides with PF for two types of transactions.*

PROOF. We assume without loss of generality that $R = 2$ (see the proof of Proposition 2). Take n_1 transactions with resource requirements a_1 and n_2 transactions with resource requirements a_2. By scale invariance, we can assume that $a_{11}a_{22} \neq a_{12}a_{21}$ (otherwise, there is actually a single type of transaction and each transaction gets a fraction $1/n$ of the most constraining resource).

Assume resource 1 is the single bottleneck. By single-bottleneck fairness, the allocation φ is the same under PF and BMF and given by $\varphi_1 a_{11} = \varphi_2 a_{21} = 1/n$. Since resource 2 is not saturated, we obtain

$$\frac{1}{n}\left(n_1\frac{a_{12}}{a_{11}} + n_2\frac{a_{22}}{a_{21}}\right) < 1. \tag{3}$$

Similarly, resource 2 is the single bottleneck if and only if

$$\frac{1}{n}\left(n_1\frac{a_{11}}{a_{12}} + n_2\frac{a_{21}}{a_{22}}\right) < 1, \tag{4}$$

in which case PF and BMF coincide. Now assume that neither (3) nor (4) hold. Then both resources are bottlenecks under both BMF and PF. We deduce that

$$\begin{cases} n_1\varphi_1 a_{11} + n_2\varphi_2 a_{21} = 1, \\ n_1\varphi_1 a_{12} + n_2\varphi_2 a_{22} = 1, \end{cases}$$

which has a unique solution whenever $a_{11}a_{22} \neq a_{12}a_{21}$. □

It is worth noting that the proof of the above proposition is based on the following three properties of BMF and PF only: scale-invariance, Pareto efficiency and single-bottleneck fairness. This means in particular that, for two types of transaction, there is no other allocation that satisfies these three properties. By the counterexample of §2.4, this allocation is not strategyproof, which shows that there is no allocation meeting all properties listed in §2.2. Any Pareto-efficient, scale-invariant allocation is either strategyproof (like DRF) or single-bottleneck fair (like PF and BMF).

3. ALGORITHMS

We discuss algorithms to realize DRF, PF and BMF, successively for the fluid model, for a compute cluster shared by multi-task jobs and for router or network resources shared by flows of packets.

3.1 Dominant resource fairness

Since DRF corresponds to max-min fair sharing with weights equal to the dominant resource requirements, the allocation can be computed through a water-filling algorithm [6, 15]: the φ_i are increased at rates inversely proportional to the dominant resource requirements $\max_j\{a_{ij}\}$ until some resource is fully used; transactions using that resource are frozen while rates of the others with non-zero requirements on non-saturated resources are further increased at their respective rates until a second resource is full; the process continues until all the φ_i are frozen. The complexity of this algorithm is of order $O(Rn)$.

Ghodsi *et al.* [6] show how the DRF allocation can be realized in practice for compute cluster resources. As resources are freed on task completion they are re-allocated preferentially to the most deprived job. This is the job with the smallest share on its dominant resource. Tasks are assigned when jobs arrive, if resources are available, or when other tasks end. If available resources are insufficient to accommodate a task of the most deprived job, allocations are frozen until a sufficient number of other tasks end or some other job takes over the most-deprived status. Note that we continue to assume resources are pooled though the assignment algorithm could be adapted to account for additional practical constraints such as assigning CPU and RAM on the same physical server, say [16], or meeting other compatibility constraints [7].

To share router resources between flows, we can apply the DRFQ algorithm defined by Ghodsi *et al.* [5]. To highlight parallels with similar algorithms defined below for PF and BMF, we adopt a slightly different specification of DRFQ.

DRFQ approximately realizes weighted max-min fairness by applying the start-time fair queuing (SFQ) algorithm at each resource [8]. This algorithm serves waiting packets in increasing order of their virtual start time. The virtual start time S_{ij}^k of packet k of flow i at resource j is determined recursively,

$$S_{ij}^k = \max\left(V_j(u_{ij}^k), S_{ij}^{k-1} + \max_j\{a_{ij}\}\right), \tag{5}$$

where u_{ij}^k is the packet arrival time at resource j and the virtual time functions $V_j(t)$ of real time t are set equal to the largest start time at t of any packet to have begun service at that resource. Each resource needs to maintain a sorted list of virtual start times, yielding a complexity of $O(\log n)$ per packet arrival.

As long as each resource is aware of the weight to apply (i.e., the dominant resource requirement $\max_j\{a_{ij}\}$), the scheduling can be applied independently at each resource, even when the resources are separated geographically as in the network application. There is no constraint on the order in which resources are used and processing can proceed in parallel, if possible, without compromising the DRF properties.

Note that the virtual time functions determine how the first packet of a burst is inserted into the schedule while the second term in the max operator of (5) ensures fairness between flows that are backlogged. DRFQ basically inherits the latency and fairness properties of SFQ and is satisfactory as long as packet processing times are small, as is usual.

3.2 Proportional fairness

The optimization problem defining PF is computationally expensive in general. An approximate solution can be obtained by the gradient descent algorithm applied iteratively to the Lagrange multipliers,

$$\nu_j \leftarrow \max\left(\nu_j + \theta\left(\sum_{i=1}^{n}\psi_i a_{ij} - 1\right), 0\right), \tag{6}$$

where $\theta > 0$ is a sufficiently small step size and

$$\psi_i = \frac{1}{\sum_{j=1}^{R} a_{ij}\nu_j},$$

for $i = 1, \ldots, n$. The allocation is then given by (2).

This approximate solution can be used in a practical task-based algorithm for sharing a compute cluster. This consists in applying the same "most deprived job" approach from §3.1. Specifically, the most deprived job is that whose ratio of actual to ideal allocation is smallest.

An algorithm for packet-based PF can be derived on extending the analysis of Massoulié and Roberts for network bandwidth sharing [14]. This relies on an assumption that resources are used consecutively and not in parallel. Each flow maintains a fixed window of W packets. This window might be realized within a router by creating an ingress queue and only admitting packet k to any internal buffer when packet $k - W$ has finished processing at all resources. Denote the number of flow i packets waiting or in service at resource j by Q_{ij} and let $Q_j = \sum_i Q_{ij}$. We have the conservation equation,

$$W = \sum_{j=1}^{R} Q_{ij}. \tag{7}$$

Assume the system attains a stable regime where the Q_{ij} are positive constants when resource j is a bottleneck, or zero otherwise. This corresponds to the fluid limit regime where W tends to infinity, as considered for instance by Schweitzer [17] and Walton [20]. In practice, assuming constant packet sizes, it is sufficient that $W \geq R$ so that each flow is backlogged on some resource. It turns out that serving packets at rates proportional to Q_{ij}/a_{ij} yields the PF allocation. We have,

$$\sum_{i=1}^{n} \varphi_i a_{ij} = 1 \implies \frac{Q_{kj}}{Q_{ij}} = \frac{\varphi_k a_{kj}}{\varphi_i a_{ij}}$$

and summing over k yields $Q_{ij} = \varphi_i a_{ij} Q_j$. On substituting for Q_{ij} in (7) we derive,

$$\frac{1}{\varphi_i} = \sum_j a_{ij} \frac{Q_j}{W}$$

where $Q_j \geq 0$ and $Q_j > 0$ if and only if $\sum_i \varphi_i a_{ij} = 1$. Comparison with (2) shows that the variables Q_j/W coincide with the Lagrange multipliers ν_j and, therefore, that φ is indeed the unique PF allocation.

To realize the required packet rates we can again adapt the SFQ algorithm. Start times S_{ij}^k are defined recursively and independently for each resource j,

$$S_{ij}^k = \max\left(V_j(u_{ij}^k), S_{ij}^{k-1} + a_{ij}/Q_{ij}\right), \tag{8}$$

where notation is as defined above in §3.1. Complexity is still $O(\log n)$.

This algorithm is not entirely satisfactory. The assumption that resources are visited sequentially by each packet is restrictive for the software router application. Moreover, for the network application, it would be necessary to take account of non-zero propagation times between visits to successive resources. This case is considered in [14] where it is shown that, even with homogeneous resource requirements, the algorithm only realizes PF approximately if the window W is large compared to the bandwidth delay product, i.e., the product of φ_i and the round trip propagation time of flow i.

3.3 Bottleneck max fairness

For small systems, it is possible to determine a BMF allocation by testing the feasibility of all possible one-to-one mappings of transactions to potential bottlenecks. For a mapping to be feasible, it must be possible to find values φ_i satisfying (1) such that every resource j with at least one mapped transaction is a bottleneck and all transactions mapped to j have the maximum share of j. Fortunately, it is not necessary to apply this algorithm in any practical implementation, as discussed below.

The most deprived job approach can be adapted to realize BMF in a compute cluster. For every job i we note its rank at each resource j: jobs with the biggest allocation have rank 1, jobs of rank k for $k > 1$ have a smaller share than $k-1$ other jobs. The deprivation status of job i is its highest rank on a bottleneck resource. A resource is considered a bottleneck here if its residual capacity is less than the maximal requirement for that resource over all transactions. Tasks are launched preferentially for the job whose current status is furthest from 1. Each resource maintains a sorted list of n jobs, yielding a complexity of $O(\log n)$ per task arrival or departure.

For the router application, BMF can be realized by imposing local weighted max-min fairness at each resource with respective weights $1/a_{ij}$. To demonstrate this, we again assume the existence of a steady state and extend arguments from [14]. We assume each flow i maintains a window of W_i packets and, to include the possibility of remotely located resources (as in the network application), we introduce the round trip propagation times T_i. The following conservation relations generalize (7),

$$W_i = \varphi_i T_i + \sum_{j=1}^{R} Q_{ij}. \tag{9}$$

Relation (9) shows that for every flow i, as long as W_i is sufficiently large, there is at least one bottleneck resource j such that $Q_{ij} > 0$ (assuming constant packet sizes, it is in fact sufficient that $W_i > \varphi_i T_i + R$ to ensure that flow i is backlogged at some resource). Moreover, the weighted fair queuing scheduler at j ensures $\varphi_i a_{ij} = \max_k(\varphi_k a_{kj})$, completing the BMF defining conditions.

To realize BMF using SFQ, start times must be calculated as follows,

$$S_{ij}^k = \max\left(V_j(u_{ij}^k), S_{ij}^{k-1} + a_{ij}\right), \tag{10}$$

where notation is again as defined above in §3.1. Complexity is $O(\log n)$.

Note that this algorithm is much simpler than that of PF in not requiring knowledge of queue lengths or imposing the same window for all flows. Like DRFQ, it can be applied independently of whether the resources are visited in parallel or sequentially and it does not depend on propagation times beyond the requirement that W_i be big enough to maintain a positive queue at bottlenecks.

4. PERFORMANCE

While the sharing algorithms are defined above with respect to a fixed set of n transactions, their behavior can only be realistically appraised under dynamic demand where transactions occur over time, each bringing a finite amount of work to be accomplished. We propose a simple Markovian demand model and use it to compare the performance of DRF, PF and BMF.

4.1 Markovian demand model

We suppose transactions belong to one of K classes and transactions of class k arrive as a Poisson process of rate λ_k. Class k transactions have requirement $a_k = (a_{k1}, \ldots, a_{kR})$ and bring a random amount of work with an exponential distribution with parameter μ_k. This work corresponds to the job duration for the computer cluster application and to the flow size in bits for the network application, for instance.

The state vector $\vec{n} = (n_1, \ldots, n_K)$, giving the current number of transactions of each class in progress, is then a Markov process with component-k birth rate λ_k and death rate $\phi_k \mu_k$, where $\phi = (n_1 \varphi_1, \ldots, n_K \varphi_K)$ denotes the per-class allocation vector. The Markovian model is adopted for the sake of simplicity. We expect, however, in view of the approximate insensitivity of fair resource sharing systems, that the comparative performance of DRF, PF and BMF will be similar under more accurate demand models (see [1], for example, for a discussion on the insensitivity property in the context of bandwidth sharing).

Capacity constraints (1) can be written

$$\sum_{k=1}^{K} \phi_k a_{kj} \leq 1, \qquad (11)$$

for $j = 1, \ldots, R$. When the allocation ϕ is DRF or PF, known results for bandwidth sharing in networks (e.g., [23]) allow us to conclude that the above process is stable as long as loads $\rho_k = \lambda_k / \mu_k$ satisfy the following inequalities,

$$\sum_{k=1}^{K} \rho_k a_{kj} < 1, \qquad (12)$$

for $j = 1, \ldots, R$. This follows for DRF since the objective is just a particular weighted max-min allocation. The BMF allocation is not included in the class of allocations considered by Ye [23] and it proves difficult to establish the stability condition for a general system. The following theorem, proved in the appendix, shows that condition (12) is sufficient for a system limited to two resources with homogeneous mean service requirements, $\mu_1 = \ldots = \mu_K$. We believe that, like DRF and PF, this result in fact extends to any number of resources and is insensitive to the distributions of service requirement beyond the means.

THEOREM 1. *Conditions* (12) *are sufficient to ensure the stability of BMF in the case of two resources with homogeneous mean service requirements.*

In the following we assume the system is stable and has a stationary distribution $\pi(\vec{n})$ from which we can compute performance measures like expected completion times. We compare algorithm performance via the mean service rate γ_k, defined as the ratio of the mean work $1/\mu_k$ to the mean completion time. Using Little's law, we find $\gamma_k = \rho_k / \mathbb{E}(n_k)$ where $\mathbb{E}(n_k)$ is the mean number of class k transactions in progress. Observe that, if there are only class-k transactions with normalized dominant resource requirement, that is $\max_j a_{kj} = 1$, the model reduces to a processor-sharing queue with arrival rate λ_k and service rate μ_k. In particular, $\mathbb{E}(n_k) = \rho_k/(1 - \rho_k)$ and $\gamma_k = 1 - \rho_k$: the relative service rate decreases linearly with the system load.

4.2 Performance of the fluid model

We illustrate the relative performance of DRF, PF and BMF using a numerical example. Two resources are shared by 3 classes of transaction with requirement vectors $a_1 = (.1, 1)$, $a_2 = (1, .1)$, $a_3 = (1, 1)$. The figures plot realized service rates γ_k against the load of the heaviest loaded resource, $\text{argmax}_{j=1,2} \sum_{k=1}^{K} \rho_k a_{kj}$.

Figure 1 corresponds to balanced load $\rho_1 = \rho_2 = \rho_3$ and shows performance is similar for all three allocations. BMF is very close to PF while both are somewhat better than DRF, especially at high load.

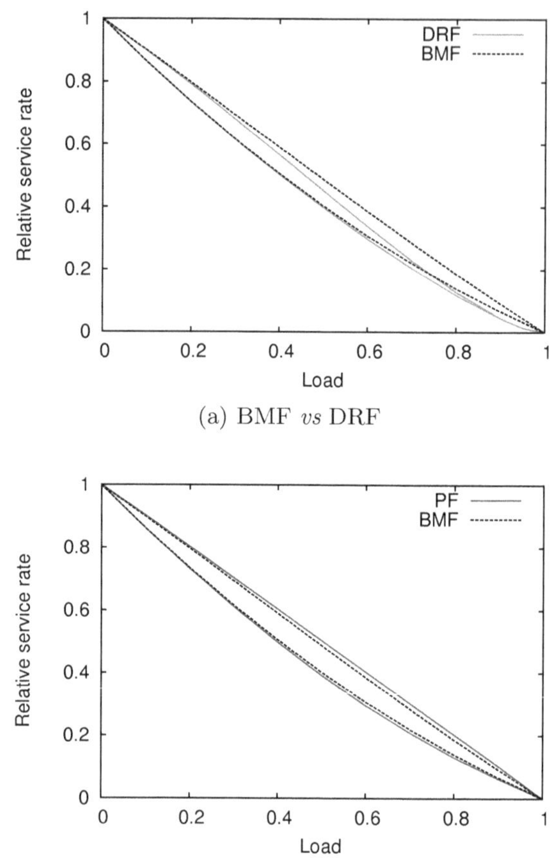

(a) BMF *vs* DRF

(b) BMF *vs* PF

Figure 1: Service rates γ_k against resource load for BMF and DRF with balanced load: $a_1 = (.1, 1)$, $a_2 = (1, .1)$, $a_3 = (1, 1)$; $\rho_1 = \rho_2 = \rho_3$; $\gamma_1 = \gamma_2 > \gamma_3$.

The difference in performance is accentuated under unbalanced load, as illustrated in Figure 2 for the case $\rho_1 = 4\rho_2 = 4\rho_3$. In this scenario resource 1 has less than half the load of resource 2. The plots show that strict fairness imposed by DRF prevents class 2 transactions from fully exploiting this. The service rates of PF and BMF are roughly equivalent, both yielding a better efficiency-fairness tradeoff with a significant gain in γ_2 for negligible reductions in γ_1, γ_3.

The generality of these results for DRF and PF was discussed in [2] where light and heavy load behavior was determined for two resources and two transaction classes. It is noteworthy that the performance advantage of PF for unbalanced load arises due to the fact that DRF sacrifices single-bottleneck fairness in the interest of strategyproofness.

4.3 Strategyproofness

The strategyproof property in §2.2 relates to a static population of transactions. We demonstrate in this subsection that the absence of this property for PF and BMF is hardly a disadvantage in dynamic traffic. Even if some transaction knows some statistics about the resource requirements of competing transactions, it does not know how many transactions are active or how this number will evolve and thus can hardly define a consistent strategy to improve its service rate by lying about its resource requirements.

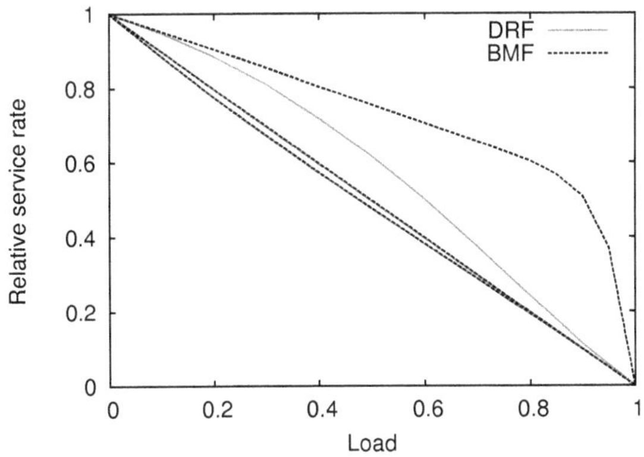

(a) BMF *vs* DRF

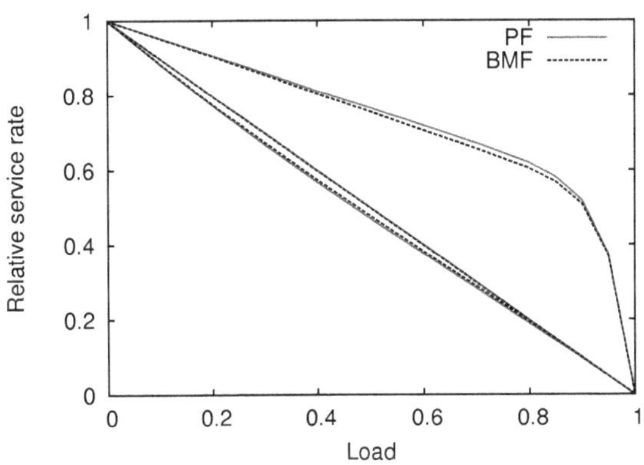

(b) BMF *vs* PF

Figure 2: Service rates γ_k against resource 2 load for BMF and DRF with unbalanced load: $a_1 = (.1, 1)$, $a_2 = (1, .1)$, $a_3 = (1, 1)$; $\rho_1 = 4\rho_2 = 4\rho_3$; $\gamma_2 > \gamma_1 > \gamma_3$.

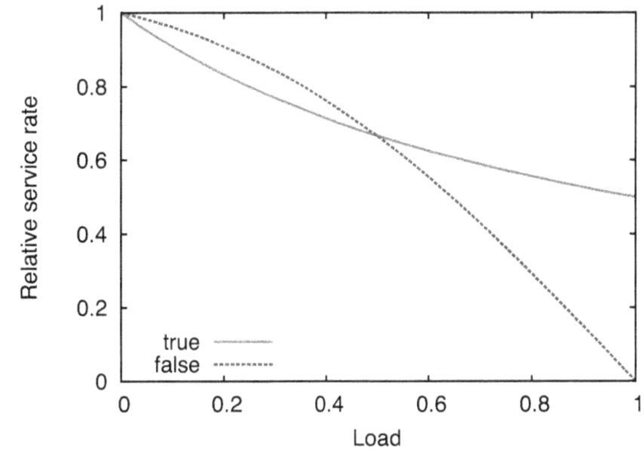

(a) Very short transaction

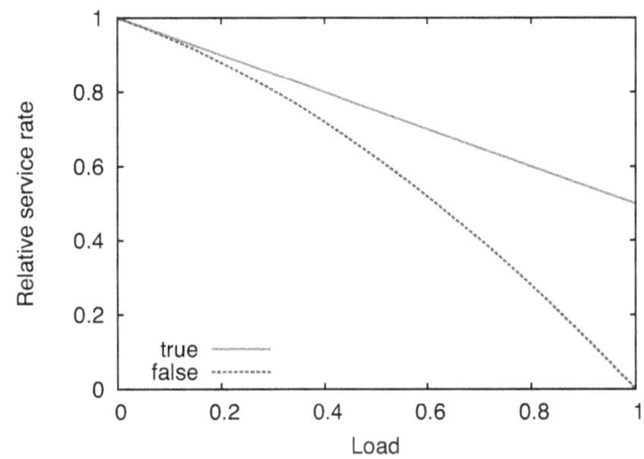

(b) Very long transaction

Figure 3: Service rate of a test transaction against class 2 load: the test transaction requires (0,1) but falsely declares (2/3,1) and competes with a dynamic population of transactions of profile (1,1/2).

Consider the potential for gaming when some test transaction competes with a homogeneous population of other transactions evolving according to the model of §4.1. Recall from Proposition 5 that PF and BMF allocations are identical for this case (since only two resources can be limiting).

From Proposition 2, the greatest gain for two resources and two transactions is obtained for $a_1 = (0, 1)$ and $a_2 = (1, 1/2)$ with transaction 1 falsely declaring $a_1' = (2/3, 1)$. Suppose first that transaction 1 truly declares $a_1 = (0, 1)$. The service rate of transaction 1 is then $\phi_1 = 1$ for $n_2 = 0$ and $\phi_1 = 1/2$ otherwise, while $\phi_2 = 1$ for any n_2. In particular, n_2 has a geometric distribution with parameter ρ_2. If transaction 1 is infinitesimally small, n_2 remains constant during its service. We deduce that the mean duration of transaction 1 is proportional to $1 - \rho_2 + 2\rho_2$ for an infinitesimally small size, yielding

$$\gamma_1 = \frac{1}{1 + \rho_2}.$$

If transaction 1 is infinitely large, the service rates average and we get

$$\gamma_1 = 1 - \rho_2 + \frac{\rho_2}{2} = 1 - \frac{\rho_2}{2}.$$

Now assume transaction 1 claims requirement $a_1' = (2/3, 1)$. The service rate of transaction 1 is then $\phi_1 = 1$ for $n_1 = 0$ and $\phi_1 = 3/(2(n_2 + 1))$ otherwise, while $\phi_2 = n_2/(n_2 + 1)$ for any n_2. If transaction 1 is infinitesimally small then n_2 still has a geometric distribution with parameter ρ_2 and the mean duration of transaction 1 is proportional to

$$1 - \rho_2 + \frac{2}{3} \sum_{n_2 \geq 1} (n_2 + 1)(1 - \rho_2)\rho_2^{n_2},$$

yielding

$$\gamma_1 = \frac{1 - \rho_2}{1 - \frac{2}{3}\rho_2 + \frac{\rho_2^2}{3}}.$$

If transaction 1 is infinitely large, the probability of state $(1, n_2)$ is proportional to $(n_2 + 1)\rho_2^{n_2}$ so that

$$\gamma_1 = (1 - \rho_2)^2 (1 + \frac{3}{2} \sum_{n_2 \geq 1} \rho_2^{n_2}) = (1 - \rho_2)(1 + \frac{\rho_2}{2}),$$

which is less that the original service rate for any load ρ_2.

Figure 3(a) shows how the service rate of transaction 1 behaves with the false declaration $a_1' = (2/3, 1)$ as a function of ρ_2 when this transaction occurs at an arbitrary instant and is infinitesimally small. The maximum gain in this configuration is only 10% compared to the 50% gain realized under static load. Moreover, this gain is realized only under a very particular configuration and rapidly disappears as the worst case conditions are relaxed. For example, Figure 3(b) confirms that if transaction 1 is not small but very large, there is no gain from the false declaration at any load.

The fact that transaction 1's competitors all have the profile (1,1/2) further exaggerates the scope for illicit gain. Transaction 1 can take no additional rate from any concurrent transactions with the same dominant resource (i.e., having a profile $(a_{11}, 1)$ for $a_{11} \leq 1$). In any mixed demand scenario, it is clear that the maximum gain is considerably less than 10%. Moreover, we note from the results of Figure 3 that the false requirements only ever yield a marginal improvement in the smallest completion times. Longer completion times, because load is heavy, as on the right of Fig. 3(a), or because the transaction is intrinsically long, as in Fig. 3(b), will be increased and not decreased.

The above clearly does not show that PF and BMF are strategyproof. Indeed they are not in case of static demand. However, the results do suggest it is rather implausible that any transaction can define a winning strategy when demand is dynamic.

4.4 Task-based allocations

While the fluid models analyzed above are useful in appraising the relative merits of alternative fairness objectives, it is necessary in practice to account for the fact that jobs are not infinitely divisible. In this section we relax this assumption. We compare the performance of task-based versions of DRF, PF and BMF through the results of simulation experiments. We follow the proposal in [6] in seeking to realize the fairness objective by preferentially launching tasks of the most deprived job with respect to the objective fairness criterion. The respective criteria for defining deprivation status were presented in §3.

Figure 4 plots the results of simulations showing how the algorithms perform in a particular configuration. Two resources (e.g., CPU and RAM) are shared by jobs of three classes with profiles (.1,1), (1,.1) and (1,1) and demand is unbalanced with $\rho_1 = 4\rho_2 = 4\rho_3$. This is the same data used for the fluid model in Figure 2. The present results show the service rate is much smaller for the task-based allocation. This is due to the finite task size which invalidates the infinite divisibility assumption of the fluid model.

We have assumed here that each job has 500 tasks to run, each having an independent exponential duration, and that the capacities of CPU and RAM are 100. For very low load, each job is alone with high probability and 100 of its tasks are processed in parallel while there remain at least 100 to run. From then on, the task completion rate decreases with the number of remaining tasks in progress from 99 to 1. It is possible in this case to compute the maximum service rate of 0.54 [2]. The discrepancy with respect to the fluid model is smaller when the task duration is less variable or when the number of tasks to run is much greater than the resource capacity.

The figure shows that PF and BMF still significantly outperform DRF for the class of jobs whose dominant resource is the least loaded (class 2 and resource 1 in this case). The algorithm for BMF is rather more effective than that of PF and yields greater service rates whereas the fluid results were virtually the same.

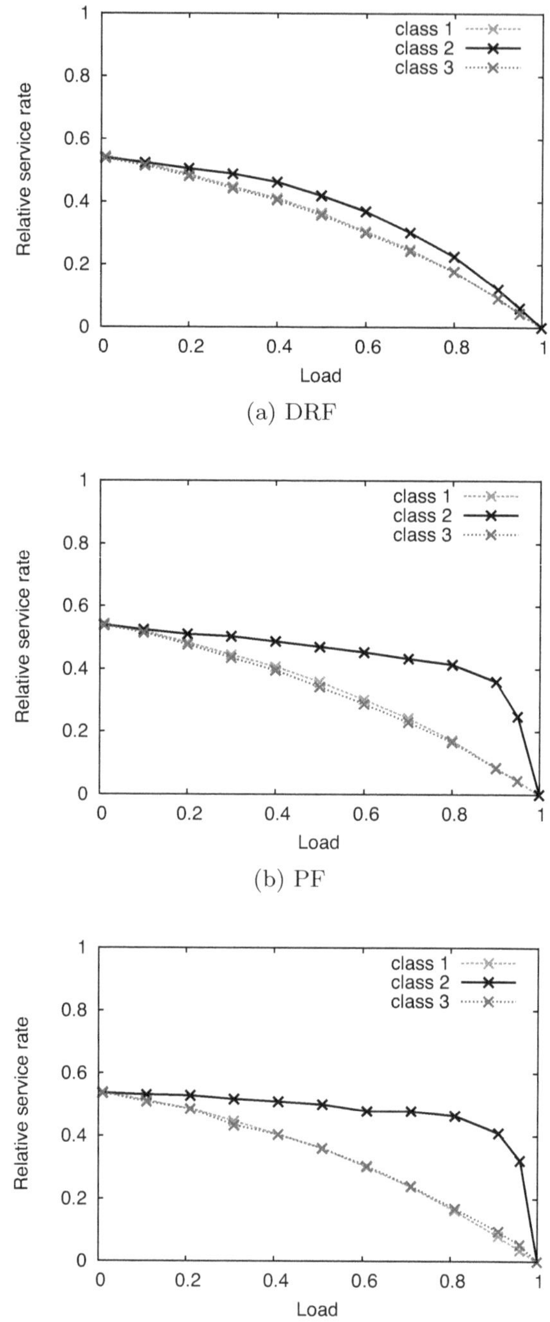

(a) DRF

(b) PF

(c) BMF

Figure 4: Cluster sharing: service rates γ_k against resource 2 load for unbalanced load: $a_1 = (.1, 1)$, $a_2 = (1, .1)$, $a_3 = (1, 1)$; $\rho_1 = 4\rho_2 = 4\rho_3$.

4.5 Packet-based allocations

In this section we evaluate by simulation the effectiveness of the SFQ-based algorithms defined in §3 for router resource sharing. The simulations assume two resources (e.g., CPU and bandwidth) are used *successively* by flow packets. The number of packets in each flow has a geometric distribution of mean 20000. For all algorithms we set the window W to 30 for all flows. We have verified that these parameter choices do not critically impact the presented results.

Service rates are shown in Figure 5 for the same unbalanced load scenario used in the previous section. Crosses are results of packet-based simulations for 10^5 flow arrivals and lines are the fluid model results from Figure 2. The results show that all three packet-based algorithms closely approximate the service rates of the ideal allocations, confirming the performance advantage of PF and BMF over DRF.

From a practical point of view, BMF is preferable to PF in that the algorithm is simpler to implement and more robust. Like DRF, BMF sharing is also realized by the same algorithm when some resources can be used simultaneously and not sequentially. Crucially for the network application, BMF is also applicable when propagation times are non-zero.

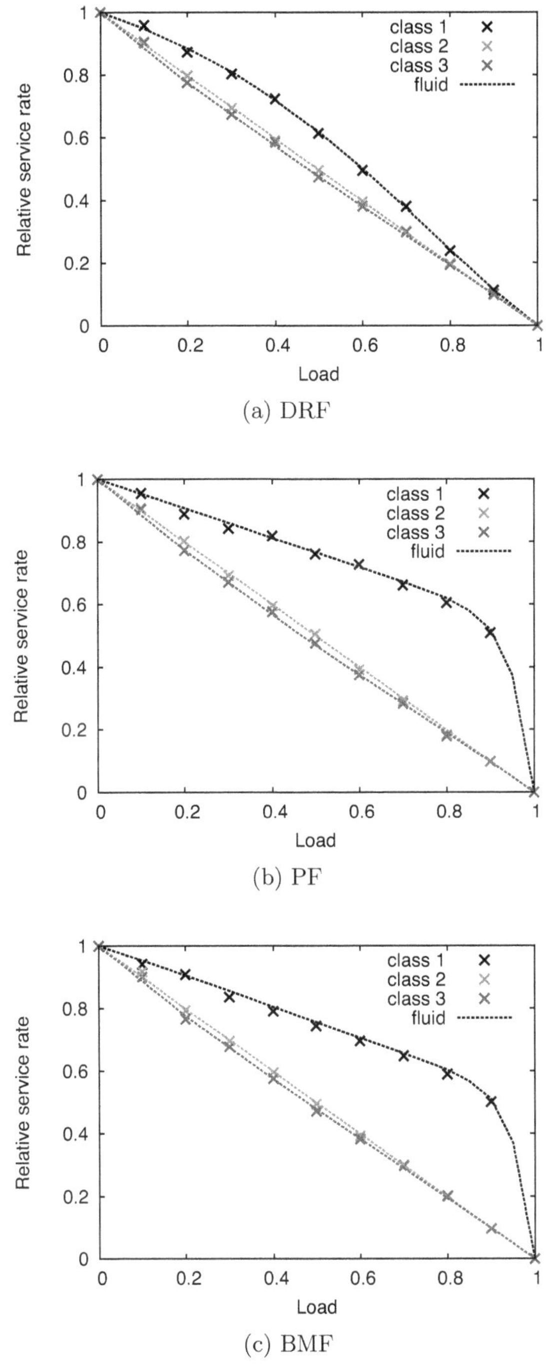

Figure 5: Router sharing: service rates γ_k against resource 2 load for unbalanced load: $a_1 = (.1, 1)$**,** $a_2 = (1, .1)$**,** $a_3 = (1, 1)$**;** $\rho_1 = 4\rho_2 = 4\rho_3$**.**

5. RELATED WORK

DRF [6] and "no justified complaints" [4] were placed in a more general economics framework in the work of Gutman and Nisan [9]. Joe-Wang *et al.* also generalized DRF by introducing two families of allocations that allow a controlled tradeoff between efficiency and fairness [11]. However, all these objectives are evaluated assuming static demand. It would be necessary to reappraise the impact of such generalizations under the more realistic assumption of dynamic, stochastic demand.

The "serve the most deprived job" approach introduced in [6] proves very versatile. It is used by Zeldes and Feitelson [24] to implement bottleneck-based fairness and by Ghodsi and co-authors [7] to account for compatibility constraints in task placement. Our proposed implementations of PF and BMF for sharing cluster resources are further illustrations of this versatility. It would be not difficult to account for possible placement constraints in these implementations.

The packet-based algorithms designed by Ghodsi *et al.* [5] to realize DRFQ for shared router resources are based on start-time fair queuing. Wang and co-authors have proposed alternative realizations that adapt Deficit Round Robin [18] to the multi-resource context [22]. Our implementations of PF and BMF rely on SFQ though it would be straightforward to substitute alternative fair queuing mechanisms.

The need to evaluate the performance of resource sharing objectives under dynamic demand is still not widely recognized. The paper by Massoulié and Roberts [13] was perhaps the first to note the importance of this while some of the most significant subsequent findings are summarized by Bonald *et al.* [1]. Our earlier paper [2] and the present work extend this analysis to the domain of multi-resource sharing.

The stability of network bandwidth sharing under various allocation objectives, with and without Markovian demand assumptions, is discussed by Walton and Mandjes [21]. Their paper surveys the literature on the stability question and illustrates its inherent difficulty. While existing results can be applied to prove the stability of DRF and PF, this is not the case for BMF.

6. CONCLUSIONS

Multi-resource sharing for efficiency and fairness is an old issue in networking with challenging new variants occurring in the domains of cluster computing and software routers. Recent prominent publications have led to the emergence of DRF and its apparent acceptance as the preferred sharing objective. DRF is implemented in the Hadoop Next Generation Fair Scheduler, for instance.

We have argued in this paper that this popularity is misplaced since alternative objectives like PF display a better efficiency-fairness tradeoff. This result is revealed on considering the completion time performance of alternative objectives under the realistic and crucial assumption that demand is dynamic: jobs and flows occur over time and their completion times depend critically on the implemented resource sharing objective.

We have proposed BMF as a pragmatic alternative to PF. It has similar performance and can be realized more simply, especially when sharing router and network resources between flows. It is clearly the most practical objective for a network integrating radio access and wired backhaul. Independent schedulers simply share their own resource equitably. BMF thus generalizes network-wide max-min fairness that is known to be realized by fair schedulers acting independently on each link [10].

Concerns about the vulnerability of objectives like PF and BMF to malicious gaming have been shown to be largely unfounded. While users can manipulate allocations by falsely boosting their declared requirement of non-dominant resources, their gain depends critically on knowing the requirements of competitors. Such knowledge is hardly conceivable in the context of highly dynamic populations of active transactions occurring in a realistic model of demand. Moreover, we have shown that the falsification is counter-productive in most cases, especially for large transactions.

While BMF is relatively straightforward to implement, it remains difficult to completely characterize its essential properties. We have proved that the usual per-resource stability conditions are sufficient in a system limited to two resource types. However, the extension of this result to more than two resources is a challenging open problem.

7. REFERENCES

[1] T. Bonald, L. Massoulié, A. Proutière, and J. Virtamo. A queueing analysis of max-min fairness, proportional fairness and balanced fairness. *Queueing Syst. Theory Appl.*, 53(1-2):65–84, June 2006.

[2] T. Bonald and J. Roberts. Enhanced cluster computing performance through proportional fairness. *Performance Evaluation*, 79(0):134 – 145, 2014. Special Issue: Performance 2014.

[3] G. De Veciana, T.-J. Lee, and T. Konstantopoulos. Stability and performance analysis of networks supporting elastic services. *Networking, IEEE/ACM Transactions on*, 9(1):2–14, 2001.

[4] D. Dolev, D. G. Feitelson, J. Y. Halpern, R. Kupferman, and N. Linial. No justified complaints: On fair sharing of multiple resources. In *Proceedings of the 3rd Innovations in Theoretical Computer Science Conference*, ITCS '12, pages 68–75, New York, NY, USA, 2012. ACM.

[5] A. Ghodsi, V. Sekar, M. Zaharia, and I. Stoica. Multi-resource fair queueing for packet processing. In *Proceedings of ACM SIGCOMM 2012*, pages 1–12, New York, NY, USA, 2012. ACM.

[6] A. Ghodsi, M. Zaharia, B. Hindman, A. Konwinski, S. Shenker, and I. Stoica. Dominant resource fairness: Fair allocation of multiple resource types. In *Proceedings of the 8th USENIX Conference on Networked Systems Design and Implementation*, NSDI'11, pages 24–24, Berkeley, CA, USA, 2011. USENIX Association.

[7] A. Ghodsi, M. Zaharia, S. Shenker, and I. Stoica. Choosy: Max-min fair sharing for datacenter jobs with constraints. In *Proceedings of the 8th ACM European Conference on Computer Systems*, EuroSys '13, pages 365–378, New York, NY, USA, 2013. ACM.

[8] P. Goyal, H. Vin, and H. Cheng. Start-time fair queueing: a scheduling algorithm for integrated services packet switching networks. *Networking, IEEE/ACM Transactions on*, 5(5):690–704, Oct 1997.

[9] A. Gutman and N. Nisan. Fair allocation without trade. In *Proceedings of the 11th International Conference on Autonomous Agents and Multiagent Systems - Volume 2*, AAMAS '12, pages 719–728, Richland, SC, 2012. International Foundation for Autonomous Agents and Multiagent Systems.

[10] E. Hahne. Round-robin scheduling for max-min fairness in data networks. *Selected Areas in Communications, IEEE Journal on*, 9(7):1024–1039, Sep 1991.

[11] C. Joe-Wong, S. Sen, T. Lan, and M. Chiang. Multi-resource allocation: Fairness-efficiency tradeoffs in a unifying framework. In *INFOCOM, 2012 Proceedings IEEE*, pages 1206–1214, 2012.

[12] F. P. Kelly, A. K. Maulloo, and D. K. H. Tan. Rate control for communication networks: Shadow prices, proportional fairness and stability. *The Journal of the Operational Research Society*, 49(3):pp. 237–252, 1998.

[13] L. Massoulié and J. Roberts. Bandwidth sharing and admission control for elastic traffic. *Telecommunication Systems*, 15(1-2):185–201, 2000.

[14] L. Massoulié and J. Roberts. Bandwidth sharing: Objectives and algorithms. *IEEE/ACM Trans. Netw.*, 10(3):320–328, June 2002.

[15] D. C. Parkes, A. D. Procaccia, and N. Shah. Beyond dominant resource fairness: extensions, limitations, and indivisibilities. In *ACM Conference on Electronic Commerce*, pages 808–825. ACM, 2012.

[16] C.-A. Psomas and J. Schwartz. Beyond beyond dominant resource fairness : Indivisible resource allocation in clusters. Tech Report Berkeley, 2013.

[17] P. J. Schweitzer. Bottleneck determination in networks of queues. In R. Disney and T. Ott, editors, *Applied Probability-Computer Science: The Interface Volume 1*, volume 2 of *Progress in Computer Science*, pages 471–485. Springer, 1982.

[18] M. Shreedhar and G. Varghese. Efficient fair queueing using deficit round robin. *SIGCOMM Comput. Commun. Rev.*, 25(4):231–242, Oct. 1995.

[19] P. Viswanath, D. Tse, and R. Laroia. Opportunistic beamforming using dumb antennas. *Information Theory, IEEE Transactions on*, 48(6):1277–1294, Jun 2002.

[20] N. S. Walton. Proportional fairness and its relationship with multi-class queueing networks. *The Annals of Applied Probability*, 19(6):2301–2333, 2009.

[21] N. S. Walton and M. R. Mandjes. A stability conjecture on bandwidth sharing networks. *Queueing Syst. Theory Appl.*, 68(3-4):237–250, Aug. 2011.

[22] W. Wang, B. Li, and B. Liang. Multi-resource round robin: A low complexity packet scheduler with dominant resource fairness. In *ICNP 2013*, 2013.

[23] H.-Q. Ye. Stability of data networks under an optimization-based bandwidth allocation. *Automatic Control, IEEE Transactions on*, 48(7):1238–1242, July 2003.

[24] Y. Zeldes and D. G. Feitelson. On-line fair allocations based on bottlenecks and global priorities. In *Proceedings of the 4th ACM/SPEC International Conference on Performance Engineering*, ICPE '13, pages 229–240, New York, NY, USA, 2013. ACM.

APPENDIX

Proposition 3 – Existence of BMF

It is convenient here to abandon the normalization of resource capacities and define the vector $C = (C_1, ..., C_R)$ associated with capacity constraints

$$\sum_{i=1}^{n} \varphi_i a_{ij} \leq C_j, \quad \text{for } j = 1, \ldots, R.$$

We prove by induction on n that there exists a BMF allocation φ which is a continuous function of the vector C. For $n = 1$ transaction, we take $\varphi_1 = \min_{j:a_{1j}>0} C_j/a_{1j}$, which is a continuous function of C. Now assume that the property holds for $n-1$ transactions, for some $n \geq 2$. For any non-negative $\theta < \min_{j:a_{1j}>0} C_j/a_{1j}$, there exists a bottleneck-max fair allocation $\varphi^{(\theta)}$, which is a continuous function of θ, for the system restricted to transactions $2, \ldots, n-1$ and the capacity vector $C^{(\theta)} = C - \theta a_1$. For any sufficiently small θ, we have, for all $j = 1, \ldots, R$,

$$\sum_{i=2}^{n} \varphi_i^{(\theta)} a_{ij} = C_j^{(\theta)} \quad \Longrightarrow \quad \theta a_{1j} < \max_{i=2,\ldots,n} \{\varphi_i^{(\theta)} a_{ij}\}. \quad (13)$$

Let θ_1 be the largest number such that this property is satisfied for all $\theta < \theta_1$. Observe that, by the continuity of $\varphi^{(\theta)}$ in θ, this property is violated for $\theta = \theta_1$. In particular, there exists some resource j_1 such that

$$\sum_{i=2}^{n} \varphi_i^{(\theta_1)} a_{ij_1} = C_{j_1}^{(\theta_1)}$$

and

$$\theta_1 a_{1j_1} \geq \max_{i=2,\ldots,n} \{\varphi_i^{(\theta_1)} a_{ij_1}\}. \quad (14)$$

Now define $\varphi_1 = \theta_1$ and $\varphi_i = \varphi_i^{(\theta_1)}$ for $i = 2, \ldots, n$. In view of (14), transaction 1 gets the maximum share of bottleneck resource j_1 under allocation φ. Now take any increasing sequence $\theta(1), \theta(2), \ldots$ tending to θ_1 such that for each transaction $i = 2, \ldots, n$, there is some bottleneck resource j_i in the system restricted to transactions $2, \ldots, n$ whose transaction-i share $\varphi_i^{(\theta)} a_{ij_i}$ is maximum over all transactions $2, \ldots, n$, for all $\theta = \theta(1), \theta(2), \ldots$ Such a sequence exists because $\varphi^{(\theta)}$ is bottleneck-max fair and there is a finite number of resources. It follows from (13) that $\theta a_{1j_i} < \varphi_i^{(\theta)} a_{ij_i}$ for all transactions $i = 2, \ldots, n$ and all $\theta = \theta(1), \theta(2), \ldots$. Taking the limit, it follows from the continuity of $\varphi^{(\theta)}$ that each transaction i gets the maximum share of resource j_i under allocation φ: the allocation is BMF. It remains to prove the continuity of the function φ in C, which follows from that of $\varphi^{(\theta)}$ in θ and that of θ_1 in C. □

Proposition 4 – Uniqueness of BMF

We first assume that $a_{ij} > 0$ for all i, j and number the transactions in increasing order of a_{i2}/a_{i1}. Observe that $\varphi_1 a_{11} \geq \varphi_2 a_{21} \geq \ldots \geq \varphi_n a_{n1}$ (if $\varphi_1 a_{11} < \varphi_2 a_{21}$ for instance then $\varphi_1 a_{12} \leq \varphi_1 a_{11} \times a_{22}/a_{21} < \varphi_2 a_{22}$ so that the bottleneck-max property is violated for transaction 1). Similarly, $\varphi_1 a_{12} \leq \varphi_2 a_{22} \leq \ldots \leq \varphi_n a_{n2}$. Without loss of generality, we can assume that $n \geq 2$ and

$$\frac{a_{12}}{a_{11}} < 1 < \frac{a_{n2}}{a_{n1}}. \quad (15)$$

Otherwise, one of the two resources is not limiting and the allocation is unique by single-bottleneck fairness.

We consider three cases:

- Case $\frac{1}{n}\sum_{i=1}^{n} a_{i2}/a_{i1} \leq 1$. The allocation φ such that $(\varphi_1 a_{11}, \ldots, \varphi_n a_{n1}) = (1/n, \ldots, 1/n)$ is BMF. Assume there is another BMF allocation, say $\varphi' \neq \varphi$. We have

$$\sum_{i=1}^{n} \varphi'_i a_{i2} = \frac{1}{n}\sum_{i=1}^{n} \frac{a_{i2}}{a_{i1}} + \sum_{i=1}^{n} \frac{a_{i2}}{a_{i1}}(\varphi'_i a_{i1} - \frac{1}{n}). \quad (16)$$

Since $\varphi' \neq \varphi$, $\varphi'_1 a_{11} > 1/n > \varphi'_n a_{n1}$. Let k be the maximum index i such that $\varphi'_i a_{i1} > 1/n$ and define

$$\theta = \sum_{i=1}^{k} (\varphi'_i a_{i1} - \frac{1}{n}) > 0.$$

Observe that

$$\sum_{i=k+1}^{n} (\frac{1}{n} - \varphi'_i a_{i1}) \geq \sum_{i=1}^{k} (\varphi'_i a_{i1} - \frac{1}{n}) = \theta.$$

Then

$$\begin{aligned}\sum_{i=1}^{n} \frac{a_{i2}}{a_{i1}}(\varphi'_i a_{i1} - \frac{1}{n}) &= \sum_{i=1}^{k} \frac{a_{i2}}{a_{i1}}(\varphi'_i a_{i1} - \frac{1}{n}) \\ &\quad - \sum_{i=k+1}^{n} \frac{a_{i2}}{a_{i1}}(\frac{1}{n} - \varphi'_i a_{i1}), \\ &\leq (\frac{a_{k,2}}{a_{k,1}} - \frac{a_{k+1,2}}{a_{k+1,1}})\theta \leq 0,\end{aligned}$$

where one of the last two inequalities is strict in view of (15). Using (16), we get

$$\sum_{i=1}^{n} \varphi'_i a_{i2} < \frac{1}{n}\sum_{i=1}^{n} \frac{a_{i2}}{a_{i1}} \leq 1.$$

By single-bottleneck fairness, this implies $\varphi' = \varphi$, a contradiction.

- Case $\frac{1}{n}\sum_{i=1}^{n} a_{i1}/a_{i2} \leq 1$. We prove similarly that the BMF allocation is unique.

- Case $\frac{1}{n}\sum_{i=1}^{n} a_{i2}/a_{i1} > 1$ and $\frac{1}{n}\sum_{i=1}^{n} a_{i1}/a_{i2} > 1$. By the bottleneck-max property, there exists some index $k < n$ such that $\alpha_1 = \varphi_1 a_{11} = \ldots = \varphi_k a_{k1} \geq \varphi_{k+1} a_{k+1,1}$

and $\alpha_2 = \varphi_{k+1}a_{k+1,2} = \ldots = \varphi_n a_{n2} \geq \varphi_k a_{k2}$. Without loss of generality, we can assume that $\alpha_1 > \varphi_{k+1}a_{k+1,1}$ (we take index $k+1$ instead of k otherwise). We have

$$\begin{cases} k\alpha_1 + S_2(n-k)\alpha_2 = 1, \\ S_1(k)\alpha_1 + (n-k)\alpha_2 = 1, \end{cases}$$

where

$$S_1(k) = \sum_{i=1}^{k} \frac{a_{i2}}{a_{i1}} \quad \text{and} \quad S_2(k) = \sum_{i=n-k+1}^{n} \frac{a_{i1}}{a_{i2}}.$$

Now

$$\frac{S_1(k)}{k}\frac{S_2(n-k)}{n-k} \leq \frac{a_{k,2}}{a_{k,1}} \times \frac{a_{k+1,1}}{a_{k+1,2}} \leq 1,$$

where one of the last two inequalities is strict in view of (15). Then $S_1(k)S_2(n-k) < k(n-k)$ and

$$\alpha_1 = \frac{n-k-S_2(n-k)}{k(n-k) - S_1(k)S_2(n-k)},$$

$$\alpha_2 = \frac{k - S_1(k)}{k(n-k) - S_1(k)S_2(n-k)}.$$

In particular, $S_1(k) < k$ and $S_2(n-k) < n-k$.

It remains to prove the uniqueness of the index k. Define $\delta_k = \alpha_2/\alpha_1$. Note that

$$\frac{a_{k,2}}{a_{k,1}} \leq \delta_k < \frac{a_{k+1,2}}{a_{k+1,1}}. \tag{17}$$

Let P_k be the property that $S_1(k) < k$ and $S_2(n-k) < n-k$. In view of (15), there exists some index i_1 such that

$$\frac{a_{i_1,2}}{a_{i_1,1}} \leq 1 < \frac{a_{i_1+1,2}}{a_{i_1+1,1}}.$$

If P_k holds and $k < i_1$ then P_{k+1} holds; similarly if P_k holds and $k > i_1 + 1$ then P_{k-1} holds. Thus the set of indices k such that P_k holds is of the form $\{k_1, \ldots, k_2\}$ with $k_1 \leq k_2$. For all $k = k_1 + 1, \ldots, k_2$,

$$\begin{aligned}
&\delta_k \geq \frac{a_{k2}}{a_{k1}}, \\
\iff \quad & k - S_1(k) \geq \frac{a_{k2}}{a_{k1}}(n-k-S_2(n-k)), \\
\iff \quad & k - S_1(k-1) \geq \frac{a_{k2}}{a_{k1}}(n-k+1-S_2(n-k)), \\
\iff \quad & k - 1 - S_1(k-1) \geq \\
&\frac{a_{k2}}{a_{k1}}(n-k+1-S_2(n-k+1)), \\
\iff \quad & \delta_{k-1} \geq \frac{a_{k2}}{a_{k1}},
\end{aligned}$$

where we have used the fact that $S_1(k) = S_1(k-1) + a_{k2}/a_{k1}$ and $S_2(n-k) = S_2(n-k+1) - a_{k1}/a_{k2}$. Now assume that k satisfies (17). If $k > k_1$ then $\delta_k \geq a_{k2}/a_{k1}$ implies $\delta_{k-1} \geq a_{k2}/a_{k1} \geq a_{k-1,2}/a_{k-1,1}$ and, by induction, $\delta_l \geq a_{l+1,2}/a_{l+1,1}$ for all $l = k_1, \ldots, k-1$. Similarly, if $k < k_2$ then $\delta_k < a_{k+1,2}/a_{k+1,1}$ implies $\delta_{k+1} < a_{k+1,2}/a_{k+1,1} \leq a_{k+2,2}/a_{k+2,1}$ and, by induction, $\delta_l < a_{l,2}/a_{l,1}$ for all $l = k+1, \ldots, k_2$. We conclude that there is at most one index k such that P_k holds and (17) is satisfied.

We now relax the assumption that $a_{ij} > 0$ for all i, j. We still number the transactions in increasing order of a_{i2}/a_{i1}, with $a_{i2}/a_{i1} = +\infty$ if $a_{i1} = 0$. Again, we consider three cases:

- Case $\frac{1}{n}\sum_{i=1}^n a_{i2}/a_{i1} \leq 1$. This implies that $a_{i1} > 0$ for all $i = 1, \ldots, n$ and we prove in the same way that the allocation φ such that $(\varphi_1 a_{11}, \ldots, \varphi_n a_{n1}) = (1/n, \ldots, 1/n)$ is the unique BMF allocation.
- Case $\frac{1}{n}\sum_{i=1}^n a_{i1}/a_{i2} \leq 1$. This implies that $a_{i2} > 0$ for all $i = 1, \ldots, n$ and the allocation φ such that $(\varphi_1 a_{12}, \ldots, \varphi_n a_{n2}) = (1/n, \ldots, 1/n)$ is the unique BMF allocation.
- Case $\frac{1}{n}\sum_{i=1}^n a_{i2}/a_{i1} > 1$ and $\frac{1}{n}\sum_{i=1}^n a_{i1}/a_{i2} > 1$. By the bottleneck-max property, there exists some index $k < n$ such that $\alpha_1 = \varphi_1 a_{11} = \ldots = \varphi_k a_{k1} \geq \varphi_{k+1}a_{k+1,1}$ and $\alpha_2 = \varphi_{k+1}a_{k+1,2} = \ldots = \varphi_n a_{n2} \geq \varphi_k a_{k2}$. Observe in particular that, by the sharing-incentive property, $a_{i1} > 0$ for all $i \leq k$ and $a_{i2} > 0$ for all $i > k$. The rest of the proof is identical.

Theorem 1 – Stability of BMF

Assume that $\max(a_{k1}, a_{k2}) = 1$ for all k; this assumption is not restrictive by scale invariance. We know by the proof of Proposition 4 that resource 1 is the single bottleneck if and only if $a_{k1} > 0$ for all k and $\sum_{k=1}^K n_k \frac{a_{k2}}{a_{k1}} < n$, which implies $\vec{n}.a_2 < \vec{n}.a_1$ since

$$\begin{aligned}
\vec{n}.(a_2 - a_1) &= \sum_{k=1}^K n_k \frac{a_{k2} - a_{k1}}{a_{k1}} + \sum_{k=1}^K n_k \frac{a_{k2} - a_{k1}}{a_{k1}}(a_{k1} - 1), \\
&\leq \left(\sum_{k=1}^K n_k \frac{a_{k2}}{a_{k1}}\right) - n < 0.
\end{aligned}$$

In particular, $\vec{n}.a_2 \geq \vec{n}a_1$ implies that resource 2 is a bottleneck; similarly, $\vec{n}.a_1 \geq \vec{n}a_2$ implies that resource 1 is a bottleneck.

Let V be the function defined by $V(x) = \max(x.a_1, x.a_2)$ for all $x \in \mathbb{R}_+^K$. Observe that the sets $\{\vec{n} : V(\vec{n}) \leq m\}$ are finite for any $m > 0$ so that V is a Lyapunov function for the Markov process $\vec{n}(t)$. The drift is given by

$$\begin{aligned}
\Delta V(\vec{n}) = &\sum_{k=1}^K \lambda_k (V(\vec{n} + e_k) - V(\vec{n})) \\
&+ \sum_{k:n_k>0} \mu\phi_k(\vec{n})(V(\vec{n} - e_k) - V(\vec{n})),
\end{aligned}$$

where e_k denotes the unit vector on component k and $\mu = \mu_1 = \ldots = \mu_k$. For any state $\vec{n}$ such that $\vec{n}.(a_1 - a_2) \geq 0$ and $(\vec{n} \pm e_k).(a_1 - a_2) \geq 0$ for all k, resource 1 is a bottleneck both in state $\vec{n}$ and after any jump from state $\vec{n}$. In particular, $V(\vec{n}) = \vec{n}.a_1$ and

$$\Delta V(\vec{n}) = \mu \left(\sum_{k=1}^K \rho_k a_{k1} - 1\right) \leq -\mu\delta,$$

where $\delta = 1 - \max_{j=1,2} \sum_{k=1}^K \rho_k a_{kj}$ is a positive constant.

Similarly, in any state $\vec{n}$ such that $\vec{n}.(a_2 - a_1) \geq 0$ and $(\vec{n} \pm e_k).(a_2 - a_1) \geq 0$ for all k, resource 2 is a bottleneck both in state $\vec{n}$ and after any jump from state $\vec{n}$ and $\Delta V(\vec{n}) \leq -\mu\delta$. Since V is a continuous, piecewise linear function and the transition rates of the Markov process $\vec{n}(t)$ are bounded, there exists some smoothened version W of V, which is a Lyapunov function for $\vec{n}(t)$ and such that $\Delta W(\vec{n}) \leq -\mu\delta/2$ outside a compact set [3]. By Foster's criterion, the Markov process $\vec{n}(t)$ is ergodic.

Exchange of Services in Networks: Competition, Cooperation, and Fairness

Leonidas Georgiadis
Dept. of ECE, AUTH, Greece,
leonid@auth.gr

George Iosifidis
Dept. of ECE, UTH, and CERTH, Greece,
giosifid@uth.gr

Leandros Tassiulas
Dept. of Elec. Eng., and YINS, Yale University,
leandros.tassiulas@yale.edu

ABSTRACT

Exchange of services and resources in, or over, networks is attracting nowadays renewed interest. However, despite the broad applicability and the extensive study of such models, e.g., in the context of P2P networks, many fundamental questions regarding their properties and efficiency remain unanswered. We consider such a service exchange model and analyze the users' interactions under three different approaches. First, we study a centrally designed service allocation policy that yields the fair total service each user should receive based on the service it offers to the others. Accordingly, we consider a competitive market where each user determines selfishly its allocation policy so as to maximize the service it receives in return, and a coalitional game model where users are allowed to coordinate their policies. We prove that there is a unique equilibrium exchange allocation for both game theoretic formulations, which also coincides with the central fair service allocation. Furthermore, we characterize its properties in terms of the coalitions that emerge and the equilibrium allocations, and analyze its dependency on the underlying network graph. That servicing policy is the natural reference point to the various mechanisms that are currently proposed to incentivize user participation and improve the efficiency of such networked service (or, resource) exchange markets.

Categories and Subject Descriptors

C.2 [**Computer-Communication Networks**]: Misc.

Keywords

Network Economics; Competitive Equilibriums

1. INTRODUCTION

Motivation. Today we are witnessing a renewed interest about models for exchanging services and resources in (or, over) networks, that go beyond the well-known peer-to-peer (P2P) file sharing idea. Some examples in communication

SIGMETRICS'15, June 15–19, 2015, Portland, OR, USA.

http://dx.doi.org/10.1145/2745844.2745860

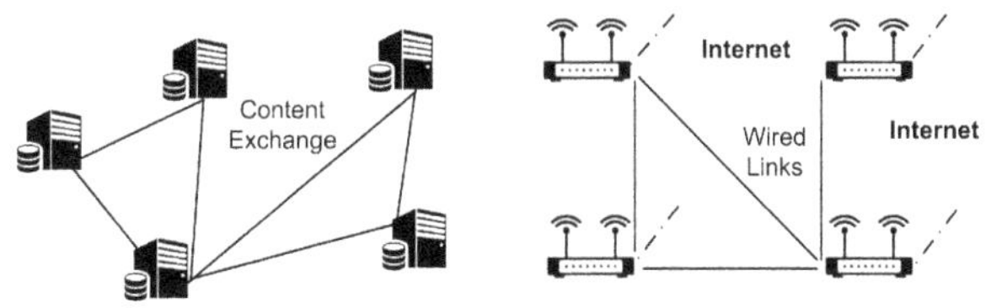

Figure 1: Instances of Service Exchange in Networks: a content sharing network, and an Internet sharing community mesh network.

networks are the WiFi sharing communities [9], [29], the mobile data sharing applications [24], the commercial or community mesh networks [6], [31], and various peer-assisted services [19], Fig. 1. Similar schemes have been studied and implemented for other technological systems as well, e.g., for renewable energy sharing over smart grid [26] where users share their energy surpluses with each other. Finally, there is nowadays a plethora of online platforms, motivated by the sharing economy concept [8], which facilitate the exchange of commodities and services among users who are co-located or have common interests [12], [14], [22], [28].

In essence, all the above scenarios apply the idea of collaborative consumption [8] of underutilized resources (such as the Internet access) to networks with autonomous and self-interested nodes (or, users). Whenever a user has some idle resource, he offers it to other users who at that time have excess needs, and benefits in exchange from the resources they offer to him in the future [11]. The goal is to exploit the nodes' complementarity in resource availability and demand, and increase the benefits for all the participants. Such models capture also more static settings where users have different preferences for the various resources, and exchange them in order to acquire those that are more valuable to them [30]. There is a broad consensus that these models are of major importance for the economy, society and technological evolution [23]. However, despite their significance and wide applicability, and although they have been subject to extensive research (e.g., in the context of P2P networks [4], [34]), some very important related questions remain unanswered.

Definition and Properties of a Fair Exchange Policy. This is one of the most critical issues in these cooperation schemes. Ideally, from a system design point of view, each user should receive service (or, resource) commensurate to its contribution. However, this is not always possible because there is an underlying graph that prescribes, for each user, the subset of the users it can serve and receive services from[1]. Additionally, there may be multiple feasible service exchange solutions that differ on the amount of service each user receives. We would prefer to select among them a *fair* outcome that balances the exchanges as much as possible. The existence and the characterization of the properties of such fair policies (e.g., their dependency on the underlying graph) is an important and currently open question.

Existence and Fairness of Competitive Equilibriums. Additionally, most often these systems are not controlled by a central entity that can exogenously impose such a fair solution. Instead, each user tries to greedily maximize its own benefit by allocating its idle resource to those users from which it expects to receive more service in return. A first question here is if such a competitive interaction among the nodes admits an equilibrium allocation, where each node cannot unilaterally improve the resource it accumulates. Also, we need to analyze how these equilibriums are affected by the graph structure and the nodes' resources. Finally, it is important to understand if such equilibriums are related to the centrally designed fair policy discussed above.

Robustness of the Fair Exchange Policy. The latter question is related to the robustness of the fair policy: when a central designer proposes such a fair policy, is it possible for a user to deviate from it and improve his performance? More interestingly, in many cases it is possible to have a subset of users that deviate from the fair policy by forming a coalition and excluding non-members from bartering. For example, in a WiFi community a subset of users may decide to serve only each other, expecting that this will increase their benefits. Such strategies are very likely to deteriorate the overall system performance. A key challenge is to explore whether the fair policy is robust to such group deviations.

Methodology and Contributions. In order to shed light on these questions, we employ a general model that abstracts all the above scenarios. We consider a set of nodes, where each one has a certain idle resource that it allocates to its neighbors, and unsaturated demand for the resources of others. The model captures situations where the nodes have complementary resource availability over time, or generic static bartering markets where nodes simply have different preferences for the resources. Neighborhood relationships are described by a bidirectional connected graph. The *exchange ratio* (or, simply *ratio*) of total received over allocated resource[2] characterizes the performance of each node, as it quantifies the resource that it receives for each resource unit it offers.

From a system point of view, a central designer would prefer to have a vector of exchange ratios where each coordinate, that corresponds to a node, has value equal to one. Often this will not be possible due to the graph exchange constraints and asymmetries in nodes' resource availability. For that cases, the lexicographically maximum (lex-optimal), or max-min, exchange vector is a meaningful performance criterion as it is Pareto optimal and balances the exchanged resources as much as possible [21].

In the absence of a network controller however, we assume that each node makes greedy myopic allocation decisions so as to maximize the aggregate resource it receives in return. The interactions of the nodes give rise to a competitive market, which however differ from previous similar models [25], [3], [34] due to the existence of the graph and the absence of side-payments (money) among the nodes (bartering). We introduce the concept of exchange equilibrium that is appropriate for this setting, characterize the equilibrium allocations, and study its relation to the max-min fair policy.

Accordingly, we assume that subset of nodes can coordinate and form coalitions exchanging resources only with each other. A coalitional graph-constrained game with non-transferable utility (NTU) is identified in the above set-up. We focus on the existence and properties of stable equilibrium allocations. Given a certain global allocation, if there is a subset of nodes that when they reallocate their own resources among themselves manage to improve the exchange ratio of *at least one* node in the subset, then they have an incentive to deviate from the global allocation (and hence destabilize it). Therefore, when an allocation is in equilibrium, it should be *strongly stable* and no such subset should exist.

We study the above frameworks, that differ on the assumptions about the system control and the users behavior, and find a surprising connection among them. In particular:

(i) We prove that there is a unique equilibrium exchange ratio vector that is a solution for the competitive market, and lies in the core of the NTU graph-constrained coalitional game, being also strongly stable. This is the max-min fair (lex-optimal) ratio vector. It reveals that a centrally designed meaningful fair solution can be reached by nodes who act independently and selfishly, and it is also robust to group deviations. This finding has many implications for the applicability of such fair policies to decentralized and autonomous graph-constrained systems.

(ii) We show that the equilibrium exhibits rich structure and a number of interesting properties. For example, in the equilibrium allocation there is exchange of resources only among the nodes with the lowest exchange ratios and the nodes with the highest ratios, the nodes with the second lowest ratios with the set of the second highest ratios, and so on. We also study how the exchange ratios are affected by the graph properties, such as the node degree. This latter aspect is particularly important from a network design point of view as it reveals, among others, the impact a link removal or addition has on the equilibrium. Our findings hold for any graph, and therefore they can help a controller to predict or even dictate the exchange equilibrium.

(iii) We provide a polynomial-time algorithm that finds the lex-optimal exchange ratio vector and the resource exchange strategies that lead to it. Hence, it can also be used to find the equilibriums of the respective competitive and coalitional games. This is a highly non-trivial task in such exchange markets, that is further compounded here due to the graph constraints.

The rest of this paper is organized as follows. In Sec. 2 we introduce the model, and in Sec. 3 we analyze the properties of the lex-optimal exchange policy. In Sec. 4 we define and solve the coalitional and the competitive games. In Sec. 5 we provide a polynomial algorithm for computing the lex-optimal ratios. We present several numerical examples in Sec. 6. In Sec. 7 we discuss related works, and conclude in Sec. 8. In the Appendix we provide the additional proofs. Finally, the reader is kindly requested to access the online report [36] with an additional proof which could not be included here due to lack of space.

[1]For example, in mesh networks the graph captures which nodes are within communication range.

[2]The idle resource can be the Internet bandwidth a user shares within a WiFi community during a month, and the demand the average request for additional bandwidth. Hereafter, we will use the term resource and service interchangeably.

2. MODEL AND PROBLEM STATEMENT

We consider a service exchange market that is modeled as an undirected connected graph $G = (\mathcal{N}, \mathcal{E})$ with node and edge set $\mathcal{N}$ and $\mathcal{E}$, respectively. Let $\mathcal{N}_i = \{j : (i,j) \in \mathcal{E}\}$ be the set of neighbors of node $i \in \mathcal{N}$, and $D_i > 0$ its idle resource (endowment). Let $d_{ij} \geq 0$ be the resource that node i allocates to node $j \in \mathcal{N}_i$. We assume that each non-isolated node allocates all its (idle) resource[3], i.e.,

$$\sum_{j \in \mathcal{N}_i} d_{ij} = D_i, \ \forall\, i \in \mathcal{N},\ \mathcal{N}_i \neq \emptyset. \quad (1)$$

A vector $\boldsymbol{d} = (d_{ij})_{(i,j)\in\mathcal{E}}$ satisfying (1) is called "allocation". The set of allocations is denoted by $\mathbb{D}$. Note that as long as not all nodes are isolated, i.e., $\mathcal{E} \neq \emptyset$, it holds $\mathbb{D} \neq \emptyset$.

This model captures either (i) a static setting where each user has a certain amount of a perfectly divisible resource which wishes to trade with other resources that are more valuable to him, or (ii) a dynamic setting where users have at random time instances a single unit of unsplittable excess resource which they allocate to one of their neighbors expecting similar benefits in the future. This latter dynamic setting will become more clear in the sequel.

A vector $\boldsymbol{r}$ of received resources induced by an allocation $d \in \mathbb{D}$ is called feasible. The set of feasible received resource vectors when $\mathcal{E} \neq \emptyset$ is defined as:

$$\mathbb{R} = \{\boldsymbol{r} = (r_i)_{i\in\mathcal{N}} : r_i = \sum_{j\in\mathcal{N}_i} d_{ji},\ i \in \mathcal{N},\ \boldsymbol{d} \in \mathbb{D}\}, \quad (2)$$

where we adopt the convention that for any isolated node i it is $r_i = 0$. In case $\mathcal{E} = \emptyset$, we define $\mathbb{R} = \{\boldsymbol{r} : r_i = 0, i \in \mathcal{N}\}$.

Throughout this work, we will be interested in the *exchange ratio* (or, simply *ratio*) vector $\boldsymbol{\rho} = (\rho_i = r_i/D_i : i \in \mathcal{N})$, where the ith coordinate quantifies the aggregate amount of resource that node i receives per unit of resource that offers to its neighbors. Notice that, under assumption (1), maximizing ρ_i ensures the maximization of r_i. We denote by $\mathbb{P}$ the set of all feasible ratio vectors. In the sequel, we consider three different problem formulations based on the above model.

2.1 Fairness Framework

In this setting, the total allocated resource is always equal to $\sum_{i\in\mathcal{N}} D_i$, and therefore the various allocations differ on how they split this amount across the nodes. A centrally designed policy for this cooperative setting would ideally allocate to every node $i \in \mathcal{N}$ resource equal to its contribution, i.e., $r_i = D_i$. However, due to the graph that constraints resource exchanges, and the different resource endowments of the nodes, such policies will not be realizable in general. Given this, the designer would prefer to ensure the most balanced allocation.

A suitable method to achieve this goal is to employ the lexicographic optimal (or, lex-optimal) criterion, which has been extensively used for resource allocation and load balancing in communication networks [10], [21], [32]. This multi-objective optimization method first increases as much as possible the allocated resource to the node with the smaller exchange ratio. Next, if there are many choices, it attempts to increase the resource allocated to the node with the second smaller exchange ratio, and so on. The resulting allocation is max-min fair, thus as balanced as possible. Next we provide the necessary definitions.

[3]For example, in P2P overlays, each node allocates all its uplink bandwidth, and in other settings it exchanges resources for which it has zero valuation (e.g., excess food).

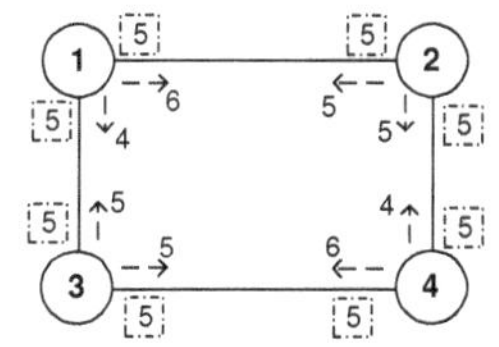

Figure 2: A 4-node graph with node resource $D_i = 10$, $\forall i$. Dashed arrows indicate resource exchange under two different allocations (values shown internal and external of the graph). Both allocations yield ratios $\rho_i = 1$, $\forall i$.

Definition 1. Lexicographical order. Let $\boldsymbol{x}$ and $\boldsymbol{y}$ be N-dimensional vectors, and $\phi(\boldsymbol{x})$ and $\phi(\boldsymbol{y})$ the respective N-dimensional vectors that are created by sorting the components of $\boldsymbol{x}$ and $\boldsymbol{y}$ respectively, in non-decreasing order. We say that $\boldsymbol{x}$ is lexicographically larger than $\boldsymbol{y}$, denoted by $\boldsymbol{x} \succ \boldsymbol{y}$, if the first non-zero component of the vector $\phi(\boldsymbol{x}) - \phi(\boldsymbol{y})$ is positive. The notation $\boldsymbol{x} \succeq \boldsymbol{y}$ means that either $\boldsymbol{x} \succ \boldsymbol{y}$ or, $\boldsymbol{x} = \boldsymbol{y}$.

It is easy to see that the set of received resource vectors $\mathbb{R}$ defined in (2) is compact and convex. Hence, as is shown in [32], there is a unique lex-optimal $\boldsymbol{r}^* \in \mathbb{R}$ such that, with $\boldsymbol{\rho}^* = (r_i^*/D_i)_{i\in\mathcal{N}}$ and for any $\boldsymbol{\rho} = (r_i/D_i)_{i\in\mathcal{N}} \in \mathbb{P}$, it holds $\boldsymbol{\rho}^* \succeq \boldsymbol{\rho}$, $\forall \boldsymbol{r} \in \mathbb{R}$. We are also interested in the respective *lex-optimal* allocations $\boldsymbol{d}$, which are those that result in the unique lex-optimal ratio vector. Note that there may be *many* allocations $\bar{\boldsymbol{d}}$ for which $\bar{\boldsymbol{\rho}} = \boldsymbol{\rho}^*$, as shown in Fig. 2. *Within this framework, we are interested in studying the properties of the lex-optimal exchange ratio vector, and the respective lex-optimal allocations, for any graph $G = (\mathcal{N}, \mathcal{E})$ and any endowments $\{D_i\}_{i\in\mathcal{N}}$.*

2.2 Coalitional Framework

Before providing the details of this framework, let us introduce some additional notation. We denote by $G_{\mathcal{S}} = (\mathcal{S}, \mathcal{E}_{\mathcal{S}})$ the subgraph of G induced by a nonempty set of nodes $\mathcal{S} \subseteq \mathcal{N}$, i.e., the graph with node set $\mathcal{S}$, and edge set the edges $(i,j) \in \mathcal{E}$, with $i, j \in \mathcal{S}$. By "allocation on $\mathcal{S}$", we mean a vector $\boldsymbol{d}_{\mathcal{S}} = \{d_{ij}\}_{(i,j)\in\mathcal{E}_{\mathcal{S}}}$ defined on graph $G_{\mathcal{S}} = (\mathcal{S}, \mathcal{E}_{\mathcal{S}})$ satisfying (1) (with $\mathcal{N} \leftarrow \mathcal{S}$ and $\mathcal{E} \leftarrow \mathcal{E}_{\mathcal{S}}$). We denote by $\mathbb{D}_{\mathcal{S}}$ the set of all allocations on $\mathcal{S}$, and by $\mathbb{R}_{\mathcal{S}}$ the set of all received resource vectors on $\mathcal{S}$ which can be obtained by any allocation on $\mathcal{S}$. By definition it is $\mathbb{R}_{\{i\}} = \{0\}$, $\forall\, i \in \mathcal{N}$.

We assume here that the nodes are able to coordinate with each other, form coalitions and deviate from the proposed fair solution if this will ensure higher resources for one or more of them. In game theoretic terms, this behavior leads to a coalitional (or, cooperative) game [20] played by the nodes. Specifically, we call any subset of nodes $\mathcal{S} \subseteq \mathcal{N}$ a coalition when they allocate their resources only among each other. That is, there is no resource exchange among nodes in $\mathcal{S}$ and nodes in its complement set $\mathcal{S}^c = \mathcal{N} - \mathcal{S}$. Hence, the feasible resource vectors that nodes in $\mathcal{S}$ get, are the vectors of the set $\mathbb{R}_{\mathcal{S}}$. We also refer to the set $\mathcal{N}$ as the grand coalition. This coalitional game is one with non-transferable utilities, as the received resource vector $\boldsymbol{r}$ cannot be split arbitrary among the nodes, due to the exchange constraints imposed by the graph and the lack of side payments. More formally, we define [20]:

Definition 2. Coalitional Service Exchange Game. A non-transferable utility (NTU) game in graph form consists of the triplet $< \mathcal{N}, G, \{\mathbb{R}_{\mathcal{S}}, \mathcal{S} \in \mathcal{N}\} >$, where $\mathcal{N}$ is the set of players (nodes) with initial resource endowments $\{D_i\}_{i\in\mathcal{N}}$, and $G = (\mathcal{N}, \mathcal{E})$ is the graph describing the service exchange possibilities among the nodes. Moreover, $\mathbb{R}_{\mathcal{S}}$, $\mathcal{S} \subseteq \mathcal{N}$, is the set of feasible $|\mathcal{S}|$-dimensional vectors of players' received resources $\{\boldsymbol{r}_i\}_{i\in\mathcal{S}}$, satisfying properties (i) $\mathbb{R}_{\{i\}} = \{0\}$, $\forall i \in \mathcal{N}$, (ii) $\mathbb{R}_{\mathcal{S}}$ is closed and bounded.

Our goal is to study the existence and the properties of self-enforcing allocations. This property is formally captured by the notion of stability for the grand coalition.

Definition 3. Stability. An allocation $\boldsymbol{d}$, and the respective resource vector $\boldsymbol{r}$ is called *strongly* stable if for any node set $\mathcal{S} \subseteq \mathcal{N}$, there is no allocation $\widehat{\boldsymbol{d}}_{\mathcal{S}}$ on the induced subgraph $G_{\mathcal{S}} = (\mathcal{S}, \mathcal{E}_{\mathcal{S}})$, such that $\hat{r}_i \geq r_i$ for all $i \in \mathcal{S}$, and $\hat{r}_j > r_j$ for at least one node $j \in \mathcal{S}$. The allocation is called *weakly* stable if for any node set $\mathcal{S} \subseteq \mathcal{N}$, there is no allocation $\widehat{\boldsymbol{d}}_{\mathcal{S}}$ such that $\hat{r}_i > r_i$ for all $i \in \mathcal{S}$.

Note that strong stability implies weak stability but not the other way around. In particular, the concept of weak stability for the grand coalition is directly related to the concept of the *core* which is formally defined[4] [20]:

Definition 4. Core. Given an NTU coalitional game $< \mathcal{N}, G, \{\mathbb{R}_{\mathcal{S}}, \mathcal{S} \in \mathcal{N}\} >$, the *core* of $\mathbb{R}$ is defined as the subset of $\mathbb{R}$ which consists of all received resource vectors $\boldsymbol{r} \in \mathbb{R}$, such that for any possible coalition $\mathcal{S}$ and any allocation $\hat{\boldsymbol{d}} \in \mathbb{D}^{|\mathcal{S}|}$, if $\hat{r}_i > r_i$, for all $i \in \mathcal{S}$, then $\hat{\boldsymbol{r}} \notin \mathbb{R}_{\mathcal{S}}$.

In this coalitional framework, we ask the question: *Is there a (weakly or strongly) stable allocation for this service exchange coalitional game, and if yes, what are its properties in terms of allocations and exchange ratios?*

2.3 Competitive Framework

Assume now that each node $i \in \mathcal{N}$ is an independent decision maker, devising its allocation vector $\boldsymbol{d}_i = \left(d_{ij}\right)_{j\in\mathcal{N}_i}$ so as to maximize the resource r_i it receives. In such a competitive market setting, the nodes are allowed to select any policy that satisfies eq. (1), i.e., allocating their entire resource (market clearing condition). Namely, the solution concept for this market is related to the competitive (or, Walrasian) equilibrium [3], [18], which has been also applied in communication networks [4], and extended to graphical economies (which exhibit *localities*) [16], [17]. However, for the problem under consideration, there do not exist explicit price variables (or, price signals), and hence we employ a different equilibrium concept:

Definition 5. *Exchange Equilibrium.* An allocation $\boldsymbol{d}$ is an exchange equilibrium, if and only if (iff) for any node $i \in \mathcal{N}$ it holds (i) $d_{ji} = \rho_i d_{ij}$ for all $j \in \mathcal{N}_i$, and (ii) if $d_{ji} > 0$ for some $j \in \mathcal{N}_i$ then $\rho_j = \min_{k\in\mathcal{N}_i} \rho_k$.

In other words, at the equilibrium each node i exchanges services only with its neighbors that trade in the lowest exchange ratio, so as to receive the maximum possible total service. Additionally, all the nodes that interact with i, have the same exchange ratio, while there may exist neighbors that do not allocate any resource to it. These latter nodes will certainly have higher exchange ratios, i.e., reciprocate with less resource for each unit of resource they receive. In this context, the question we want to tackle is the following: *Does this game have exchange equilibrium(s), and if so, what are its properties and how does it depend on the graph G.*

[4]With a slight abuse of terminology we refer both to the received resource vectors and the respective allocations as stable.

3. LEX-OPTIMAL ALLOCATIONS

In this section we study the properties of the lex-optimal vector $\boldsymbol{\rho}^*$ and the respective allocations. These results hold for any graph $G = (\mathcal{N}, \mathcal{E})$, and resource endowments $\{D_i\}_{i\in\mathcal{N}}$. To avoid trivial cases, we assume that there are no isolated nodes in the network[5]. We give first some notations. We denote the set of neighbors of nodes in a set $\mathcal{S}$, that do not belong to $\mathcal{S}$, by $\mathcal{N}(\mathcal{S}) = \cup_{i\in\mathcal{S}}\mathcal{N}_i - \mathcal{S}$. Given an allocation $\boldsymbol{d}$, for each node $i \in \mathcal{N}$ we define the subset $\mathcal{D}_i = \{j \in \mathcal{N}_i : d_{ij} > 0\}$ of nodes that receive resource from i, and the subset of nodes that don't receive resource $\mathcal{H}_i = \mathcal{N}_i - \mathcal{D}_i = \{j \in \mathcal{N}_i : d_{ij} = 0\}$. Also, we define the subset $\mathcal{R}_i = \{j \in \mathcal{N}_i : d_{ji} > 0\}$ of nodes that give resource to i.

For a given $\boldsymbol{r}$, the set of *different values (levels)* the coordinates of vector $\boldsymbol{\rho}$ take, will be denoted by l_k, $i = 1, ..., K \leq N$, where $l_1 < l_2 < ... < l_K$. The index of the level to which ρ_i is equal, is denoted by $k(i)$, i.e., $l_{k(i)} = \rho_i$. We call $k(i)$ the "level of node i". The set of nodes with level m is denoted by $\mathcal{L}_m = \{i \in \mathcal{N} : k(i) = m\}$. If a subset of nodes $\mathcal{S} \subseteq \mathcal{N}$ has the same level under an allocation $\boldsymbol{d}$, then we denote the index of this level by $k(\mathcal{S})$. Note that the above quantities depend on the allocation $\boldsymbol{d}$, and hence, in order to facilitate notation, we will use the same overline symbol for them whenever applicable.

Properties. An important well-known property of the lex-optimal policy is that it is *Pareto efficient* [18], [21], i.e., we cannot increase the exchange ratio for one node without decreasing the ratio of another node. The first property of the lex-optimal allocations that we prove is that the neighbors of each node $i \in \mathcal{N}$, that receive non-zero resource from i, belong to the same exchange ratio level set[6]. Moreover, all the neighbors that do not receive resource from i, have a higher level index. Specifically:

Lemma 1. Let $\boldsymbol{d}^*$ be a lex-optimal allocation, and let $i \in \mathcal{N}$. Then all nodes $j \in \mathcal{D}_i^*$ have the same level $l^*_{k(\mathcal{D}_i^*)}$ and hence belong to the same set $\mathcal{L}^*_{k(\mathcal{D}_i^*)}$. Moreover, for any node $j \in \mathcal{H}_i^*$, it is $l^*_{k(j)} \geq l^*_{k(\mathcal{D}_i^*)}$.

Proof. Consider a lex-optimal allocation $\bar{\boldsymbol{d}}$ and let j_1, j_2 be such that $\bar{d}_{ij_1} > 0$, $\bar{d}_{ij_2} > 0$, but $j_1 \in \mathcal{L}^*_m$ and $j_2 \in \mathcal{L}^*_n$ with $m < n$. Recall that the lex-optimal price vectors - and hence the respective level sets - are unique so we use the star $(*)$ notation for them. We can then move some resource from j_2 and give it to j_1 while ensuring that with the resulting allocation $\widehat{\boldsymbol{d}}$, it is $l^*_{k(j_1)} < \widehat{l}_{k(j_1)} \leq \widehat{l}_{k(j_2)} < l^*_{k(j_2)}$. Since the received resources of all other nodes remain the same, it follows that $\widehat{\boldsymbol{r}} \succ \bar{\boldsymbol{r}} = \boldsymbol{r}^*$, which is a contradiction as we assumed that it is lex-optimal. Assume next that $d^*_{ij} = 0$ for a node $j \in \mathcal{N}_i$ for which it holds that $l^*_{k(j)} < l^*_{k(\bar{\mathcal{D}}_i)}$. Using a similar argument we arrive at a contradiction again. □

Note that this lemma shows already that lex-optimal allocations have some of the required properties of exchange equilibriums. As will be shown later there are lex-optimal allocations that are in fact exchange equilibriums.

[5]If a graph G has a set of isolated nodes $\mathcal{I}$ then we set $\rho_i = 0$ for all $i \in \mathcal{I}$ and we proceed by considering the graph $G_{\mathcal{N}-\mathcal{I}}$.

[6]Recall that this ratio is determined by the total resource each of these nodes receives, i.e., not only from that allocated by node i.

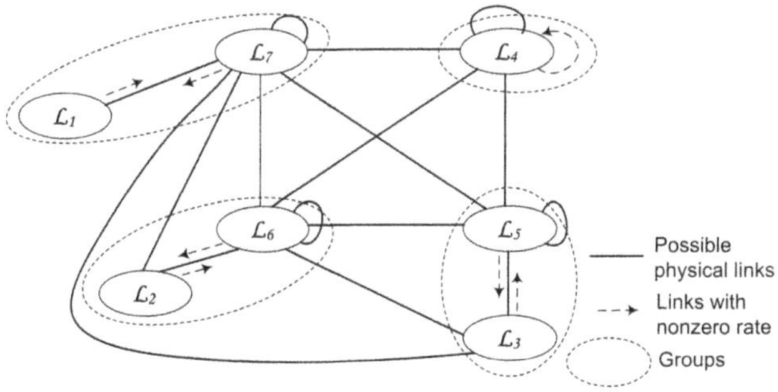

Figure 3: Structure of a graph with $K^* = 7$ levels.

We need some additional notation at this point. Let $\boldsymbol{d} \in \mathbb{D}$ and assume $K \geq 2$, i.e., the allocation has at least two levels. Define $\mathcal{Q}_1 = \mathcal{N}$, and for $K \geq 3$:

$$\mathcal{Q}_k = \mathcal{N} - \cup_{m=1}^{k-1} (\mathcal{L}_m \cup \mathcal{L}_{K-m+1}), \ 2 \leq k \leq \lceil K/2 \rceil.$$

For example, $\mathcal{Q}_2$ consists of the nodes in $\mathcal{N}$ that remain after removing those that belong to the level sets $\mathcal{L}_1$ and $\mathcal{L}_K$. In the sequel, a quantity X referring to induced subgraph $G_{\mathcal{Q}_k} = (\mathcal{Q}_k, \mathcal{E}_{\mathcal{Q}_k})$ is denoted $X_{\mathcal{Q}_k}$. The next Theorem describes the structure of a lex-optimal allocation.

Theorem 1. If an allocation $\boldsymbol{d}^*$ is lex-optimal and $K \geq 2$, then the following Properties hold:

1. $\mathcal{L}_k^*$ is an independent set in graph $G_{\mathcal{Q}_k}$, for $k = 1, ..., \lfloor \frac{K}{2} \rfloor$.
2. $\mathcal{L}_{K-k+1}^* = \mathcal{N}_{\mathcal{Q}_k}(\mathcal{L}_k^*)$, for $k = 1, ..., \lfloor \frac{K}{2} \rfloor$.
3. $l_k^* l_{K-k+1}^* = 1$, for $k = 1, ..., \lfloor K/2 \rfloor$.
4. $\sum_{i \in \mathcal{L}_k^*} r_i^* = \sum_{i \in \mathcal{L}_{K-k+1}^*} D_i$, for $k = 1, ..., \lfloor \frac{K}{2} \rfloor$.

Interestingly, sufficiency of this result holds as well:

Theorem 2. If an allocation $\boldsymbol{d}$ with $K \geq 2$ has properties 1-4 of Theorem 1, then it is lex-optimal.

Finally, when there is only one level set, it holds:

Theorem 3. If an allocation $\boldsymbol{d}^*$ is lex-optimal, and $K^* = 1$, then $l_1^* = 1$. Also, if an allocation $\boldsymbol{d}$ has $K = 1$, then $l_1 = 1$ and it is lex-optimal.

3.1 Analysis and Discussion

Let us now discuss the implications of the above theorems. Under a lex-optimal allocation, the nodes are classified in disjoint sets of different levels, in a fashion that depends both on their resource endowments and on the graph G. For the discussion below, please refer to Fig. 3, that presents an example of the structure for $K^* = 7$ levels. In this graph, we depict with solid lines the physical connections that may exist among the different sets of nodes. Notice that the actual nodes and their detailed connections are not shown.

Exchange ratios Structure. According to Property 3 of Theorem 1, the exchange ratios have a certain structure. Specifically, the highest level of ratios is inversely proportional to the lowest level of ratios ($l_7^* = 1/l_1^*$), the second highest exchange ratio level is inversely proportional to the second lowest ratio level ($l_6^* = 1/l_2^*$), and so on. Additionally, resource exchanges satisfy Property 4. For example, in Fig. 3 all the nodes of the highest ratio set $\mathcal{L}_7^*$, allocate their entire resources to the nodes belonging to the lowest level set $\mathcal{L}_1^*$. Moreover, the latter receive resource only from the nodes in $\mathcal{L}_7^*$. Similarly, the nodes in level set $\mathcal{L}_6^*$ allocate all their received resources to nodes in set $\mathcal{L}_2^*$ which are served only by these former nodes, and so on. Interestingly, when K^* is odd, there is one set of nodes, here the set $\mathcal{L}_4^*$, which exchange resource only with each other.

Topological Properties. On the other hand, Properties 1 and 2 reveal the *impact of the network topology on the max-min solution.* First, from Property 2, we can find the possible neighbors for each node, based on the level set it belongs to. For example, when $K^* = 7$, it holds $\mathcal{L}_7^* = \mathcal{N}(\mathcal{L}_1^*)$, i.e., the neighbors of nodes in $\mathcal{L}_1^*$, that do not have ratios l_1^*, belong only to set $\mathcal{L}_7^*$. Moreover, since Property 1 states that the set $\mathcal{L}_1^*$ in independent in the graph $G_{\mathcal{Q}_1} \triangleq G$, we understand that $\mathcal{L}_1$ nodes have neighbors only in $\mathcal{L}_7$.

Similarly, it holds that $\mathcal{L}_6^* = \mathcal{N}_{\mathcal{Q}_2}(\mathcal{L}_2^*)$. Hence, the nodes in set $\mathcal{L}_2^*$ can have links only with nodes in set $\mathcal{L}_6^*$ and possibly with nodes in $\mathcal{L}_7^*$ (since the latter do not belong in $G_{\mathcal{Q}_2}$). However, from Lemma 1 it follows that nodes in $\mathcal{L}_2^*$ exchange resource only with nodes in $\mathcal{L}_6^*$. With the same reasoning, it is easy to see that nodes in set $\mathcal{L}_3^*$ can be physically connected with nodes in $\mathcal{L}_7^*$, $\mathcal{L}_6^*$ and $\mathcal{L}_5^*$, but they exchange resource only with nodes in the latter set. Finally, nodes in set $\mathcal{L}_4^*$ exchange resources only with each other.

These properties reveal how the graph affects the lex-optimal fair solution. For example, by adding a link between two nodes initially belonging to $\mathcal{L}_1^*$ (which is independent), the lex-optimal solution changes and places these (now connected) nodes to another set. This dependency among the graph structure and the lex-optimal exchange ratio vector will become more evident in the sequel.

3.2 Proofs of Theorems

In this subsection we provide the proofs of Theorems 3 and 1, while Theorem 2 is proved in the Appendix.

3.2.1 PROOF of Theorem 3. Before proceeding with the proof, we provide some additional notation, lemmas and propositions. We denote the sum of received resources that are incoming to, and outgoing from set $\mathcal{S} \subseteq \mathcal{N}$, under allocation $\boldsymbol{d}$, as follows:

$$\text{In}(\mathcal{S}) = \sum_{i \in \mathcal{S}} \sum_{j \in \mathcal{N}_i \cap \mathcal{S}^c} d_{ji}, \ \text{Out}(\mathcal{S}) = \sum_{i \in \mathcal{S}} \sum_{j \in \mathcal{N}_i \cap \mathcal{S}^c} d_{ij}, \quad (3)$$

where $\mathcal{S}^c = \mathcal{N} - \mathcal{S}$ is the complement set of $\mathcal{S}$. By definition it is $\text{In}(\mathcal{N}) = \text{Out}(\mathcal{N}) = 0$, and also:

$$\text{In}(\mathcal{S}) = \text{Out}(\mathcal{S}^c), \ \text{Out}(\mathcal{S}) = \text{In}(\mathcal{S}^c). \quad (4)$$

Lemma 2. For any set $\mathcal{S} \subseteq \mathcal{N}$, under any feasible allocation $\boldsymbol{d} \in \mathbb{D}$, it holds

$$\sum_{i \in \mathcal{S}} r_i + \text{Out}(\mathcal{S}) = \sum_{i \in \mathcal{S}} D_i + \text{In}(\mathcal{S}). \quad (5)$$

$$\text{Out}(\mathcal{S}) \leq \sum_{i \in \mathcal{S}} D_i \quad (6)$$

with equality holding iff all nodes in $\mathcal{S}$ give their resource only to nodes outside $\mathcal{S}$. Also, it is:

$$\text{In}(\mathcal{S}) \leq \sum_{i \in \mathcal{S}} r_i \quad (7)$$

with equality holding iff all nodes in $\mathcal{S}$ get resource only from nodes outside $\mathcal{S}$.

Proof. Note that for any node set $\mathcal{S}$, the following holds:

$$\sum_{i \in \mathcal{S}} \sum_{j \in \mathcal{N}_i \cap \mathcal{S}} d_{ji} = \sum_{i \in \mathcal{S}} \sum_{j \in \mathcal{N}_i \cap \mathcal{S}} d_{ij}. \quad (8)$$

Also, by definition

$$r_i = \sum_{j\in\mathcal{N}_i\cap\mathcal{S}} d_{ji} + \sum_{j\in\mathcal{N}_i\cap\mathcal{S}^c} d_{ji}, \tag{9}$$

by feasibility of $\boldsymbol{d} \in \mathbb{D}$,

$$D_i = \sum_{j\in\mathcal{N}_i\cap\mathcal{S}} d_{ij} + \sum_{j\in\mathcal{N}_i\cap\mathcal{S}^c} d_{ij}. \tag{10}$$

Hence we calculate

$$\begin{aligned}\sum_{i\in\mathcal{S}} r_i &= \sum_{i\in\mathcal{S}}\sum_{j\in\mathcal{N}_i\cap\mathcal{S}} d_{ji} + \sum_{i\in\mathcal{S}}\sum_{j\in\mathcal{N}_i\cap\mathcal{S}^c} d_{ji} \text{ by (9)}\\ &= \sum_{i\in\mathcal{S}}\sum_{j\in\mathcal{N}_i\cap\mathcal{S}} d_{ij} + \mathrm{In}(\mathcal{S}) \quad \text{by (8), (3)}\\ &= \sum_{i\in\mathcal{S}}\sum_{j\in\mathcal{N}_i\cap\mathcal{S}} d_{ij} + \sum_{i\in\mathcal{S}}\sum_{j\in\mathcal{N}_i\cap\mathcal{S}^c} d_{ij} + \mathrm{In}(\mathcal{S}) - \mathrm{Out}(\mathcal{S})\\ &= \sum_{i\in\mathcal{S}} D_i + \mathrm{In}(\mathcal{S}) - \mathrm{Out}(\mathcal{S}) \quad \text{by (10)}\end{aligned}$$

Inequalities (6), (7) follow directly from the definitions. □

Lemma 3. Let $\boldsymbol{d} \in \mathbb{D}$. If $K = 1$ then $l_1 = 1$. If $K > 1$, then $l_1 < 1$ and $l_K > 1$.

Proof. If $K = 1$, we have $r_i = l_1 D_i$ for all $i \in \mathcal{N}$. From Lemma 2 (applied with $\mathcal{S} \leftarrow \mathcal{N}$) we then have $l_1 \sum_{i\in\mathcal{N}} D_i = \sum_{i\in\mathcal{N}} D_i$, hence $l_1 = 1$. Let now $K > 1$. If $l_1 \geq 1$, then since $l_K > l_1$, we have

$$\sum_{i\in\mathcal{N}} r_i = \sum_{k=1}^{K} l_k \sum_{i\in\mathcal{L}_k} D_i > \sum_{i\in\mathcal{N}} D_i \tag{11}$$

which contradicts Lemma 2. Similarly is shown $l_K > 1$. □

Proposition 4. Let $\bar{\boldsymbol{d}} \in \mathbb{D}$. If $\bar{K} = 1$ then $\bar{\boldsymbol{d}}$ is lex-optimal.

Proof. From Lemma 3, $\bar{l}_1 = 1$ and hence $\bar{r}_i = D_i$, $i \in \mathcal{N}$. If there is another allocation $\hat{\boldsymbol{d}}$ such $\hat{\boldsymbol{r}} \succ \bar{\boldsymbol{r}}$, then it should hold $\hat{r}_i \geq r_i = D_i$ $\forall i \in \mathcal{N}$ and $\hat{r}_j > \bar{r}_j = D_j$ for at least one $j \in \mathcal{N}$. But then, it would be $\sum_{i\in\mathcal{S}} \hat{r}_i > \sum_{i\in\mathcal{S}} D_i$, which contradicts (5) (applied with $\mathcal{S} \leftarrow \mathcal{N}$). □

Now we are ready to provide the proof of Theorem 3: From Lemma 3 we have that for a feasible allocation $\boldsymbol{d} \in \mathbb{D}$, with $K = 1$, it is $l_1 = 1$. From Proposition 4 we also get that this is a lex-optimal allocation. Moreover, since a lex-optimal allocation $\boldsymbol{d}^*$ is also feasible, when $K^* = 1$, it is also $l_1^* = 1$ from Lemma 3.

3.2.2 PROOF of Theorem 1. First, we need the following corollary.

Corollary 1. If under a lex-optimal allocation $\bar{\boldsymbol{d}}$ it holds $k(\bar{\mathcal{D}}_i) = K^*$ for some $i \in \mathcal{N}$, then $\mathcal{N}_i \subseteq \mathcal{L}_K^*$.

Proof. Since under a lex-optimal allocation there can be no node with level higher that l_{K^*}, Lemma 1 is applied with the equality, i.e., $\forall j \in \bar{\mathcal{H}}_i$, it holds $l^*_{k(j)} = l^*_{k(\bar{\mathcal{D}}_i)} = K^*$. Since the same also holds by definition for all nodes in $\bar{\mathcal{D}}_i$, the results follows. □

We introduce some additional definitions and results. Consider a lex-optimal allocation $\bar{\boldsymbol{d}}$ and let $\bar{\mathcal{Z}}$ be the subset of nodes in $\mathcal{L}_K^*$, with the property: $i \in \bar{\mathcal{Z}}$ iff $\mathcal{L}^*_{k(\bar{\mathcal{D}}_i)} = K^*$. Hence any node i in $\bar{\mathcal{Z}} \subset \mathcal{L}_K^*$ gives resource only to nodes in $\mathcal{L}_K^*$. The next lemma shows that the set $\bar{\mathcal{Z}}$ is empty if $K^* \geq 2$.

Lemma 5. Let $\bar{\boldsymbol{d}}$ be a lex-optimal allocation. If $K^* \geq 2$, then $\bar{\mathcal{Z}} = \emptyset$, i.e., the nodes in $\mathcal{L}_K^*$ give all their resource to nodes outside $\mathcal{L}_K^*$. Hence[7],

$$\overline{\mathrm{Out}}\,(\mathcal{L}_K^*) = \sum_{i\in\mathcal{L}_K^*} D_i. \tag{12}$$

Proof. According to Corollary 1 all neighbors of any node $i \in \bar{\mathcal{Z}}$ are in $\mathcal{L}_K^*$. It follows that a node i in $\bar{\mathcal{Z}}$ gets resource only from nodes in $\bar{\mathcal{Z}}$: if node i was getting resource from a neighbor node $j \notin \bar{\mathcal{Z}}$, then since as the previous sentence says $j \in \mathcal{L}_K^*$, node j should belong to $\bar{\mathcal{Z}}$ by definition; which is a contradiction. This implies that $\overline{\mathrm{In}}\,(\bar{\mathcal{Z}}) = 0$ and hence according to Lemma 2:

$$\sum_{i\in\bar{\mathcal{Z}}} r_i^* \leq \sum_{i\in\bar{\mathcal{Z}}} D_i.$$

If $\bar{\mathcal{Z}} \neq \emptyset$, then since $r_i^* = l_K^* D_i$, $\forall i \in \bar{\mathcal{Z}}$, we conclude from (3.2) that $l_K^* \leq 1$, which contradicts Lemma 3. Equality (12) follows immediately: since $\bar{\mathcal{Z}} = \emptyset$, the nodes in $\mathcal{L}_K^*$ give all their resource to nodes outside $\mathcal{L}_K^*$ and hence (6) applies with equality. □

Let $\bar{\mathcal{G}}$ be the set of nodes from which nodes in $\mathcal{L}_K^*$ get resource, i.e., $\bar{\mathcal{G}} = (i \in \mathcal{N} : k(\bar{\mathcal{D}}_i) = K^*)$. It holds:

Lemma 6. Let $\bar{\boldsymbol{d}}$ be a lex-optimal allocation and $K^* \geq 2$. It holds $\mathcal{L}_K^* \cap \bar{\mathcal{G}} = \emptyset$. Moreover, the set $\bar{\mathcal{G}}$ is nonempty, independent, it holds $\mathcal{N}\left(\bar{\mathcal{G}}\right) = \mathcal{L}_K^*$, and

$$\overline{\mathrm{In}}\left(\bar{\mathcal{G}} \cup \mathcal{L}_K^*\right) = 0. \tag{13}$$

Proof. According to Lemma 5, $\mathcal{L}_K^* \cap \bar{\mathcal{G}} = \bar{\mathcal{Z}} = \emptyset$. Also, according to (5), (12), and the definition of $\bar{\mathcal{G}}$, it is

$$\sum_{i\in\mathcal{L}_K^*} r_i^* = \overline{\mathrm{In}}\,(\mathcal{L}_K^*) \leq \sum_{i\in\bar{\mathcal{G}}} D_i.$$

Since $\sum_{i\in\mathcal{L}_K^*} r_i^* = l_K^* \sum_{i\in\mathcal{L}_K^*} D_i > 0$, we get $\bar{\mathcal{G}} \neq \emptyset$. According to Corollary 1 and the definition of $\bar{\mathcal{G}}$, it holds $\mathcal{N}_i \subseteq \mathcal{L}_K^*$, $\forall i \in \bar{\mathcal{G}}$. Since $\mathcal{L}_K^* \cap \bar{\mathcal{G}} = \emptyset$, $\bar{\mathcal{G}}$ is independent.

To show that $\mathcal{N}\left(\bar{\mathcal{G}}\right) = \mathcal{L}_K^*$ we argue as follows. According to Corollary 1, it is $\mathcal{N}\left(\bar{\mathcal{G}}\right) \subseteq \mathcal{L}_K^*$. Also, if $\mathcal{L}_K^* - \mathcal{N}\left(\bar{\mathcal{G}}\right) \neq \emptyset$, there would be a node $i \in \mathcal{L}_K^*$ not connected to any of the nodes in $\bar{\mathcal{G}}$; but since by definition of $\bar{\mathcal{G}}$ node i gets resource only from nodes in $\bar{\mathcal{G}}$, we would then have $r_i^* = l_K^* D_i = 0$, a contradiction since $l_K^* > 1$ and $D_i > 0$.

Notice next that $\mathcal{N}\left(\bar{\mathcal{G}}\right) = \mathcal{L}_K^*$ and the set $\bar{\mathcal{G}}$ is independent, all neighbors of nodes in $\bar{\mathcal{G}}$ are in $\mathcal{L}_K^*$, and hence nodes in $\bar{\mathcal{G}}$ can get resource only from nodes in $\mathcal{L}_K^*$. Since by definition nodes $\mathcal{L}_K^*$ get resource only from $\bar{\mathcal{G}}$, (13) holds. □

Lemma 7. Let $\bar{\boldsymbol{d}}$ be a lex-optimal allocation and $K^* \geq 2$. Let k_0 be the index of the smallest level in $\bar{\mathcal{G}}$. Then $l_K^* l_{k_0}^* \leq 1$. Strict inequality holds if

1. either $\overline{\mathrm{Out}}\left(\bar{\mathcal{G}} \cup \mathcal{L}_K^*\right) > 0$,

2. or $\overline{\mathrm{Out}}\left(\bar{\mathcal{G}} \cup \mathcal{L}_K^*\right) = 0$ and $\bar{\mathcal{G}} - \mathcal{L}_{k_0}^* \neq \emptyset$.

[7]To facilitate the reader, we repeat the notation: $\overline{\mathrm{Out}}$ and $\bar{\mathcal{Z}}$ are annotated with the bar symbol since they depend on $\bar{\boldsymbol{d}}$, while the optimal level sets and the received resources are unique and hence annotated with the star symbol.

If $\overline{\text{Out}}\left(\bar{\mathcal{G}} \cup \mathcal{L}_K^*\right) = 0$ and $\bar{\mathcal{G}}_K - \mathcal{L}_{k_0}^* = \emptyset$, then $l_K^* l_{k_0}^* = 1$.

Proof. Since by Lemma 6 $\bar{\mathcal{G}}$ is independent, and $\mathcal{N}\left(\bar{\mathcal{G}}\right) \subseteq \mathcal{L}_K^*$, the nodes in $\bar{\mathcal{G}}$ can give resource only to nodes in $\mathcal{L}_K^*$. Hence only nodes in $\mathcal{L}_K^*$ give resource to nodes in $\left(\bar{\mathcal{G}} \cup \mathcal{L}_K^*\right)^c$, hence:

$$\overline{\text{Out}}\left(\mathcal{L}_K^*\right) = \overline{\text{In}}\left(\bar{\mathcal{G}}\right) + \overline{\text{Out}}\left(\bar{\mathcal{G}} \cup \mathcal{L}_K^*\right).$$

Taking into account (12) we conclude:

$$\overline{\text{In}}\left(\bar{\mathcal{G}}\right) = \sum_{i \in \mathcal{L}_K^*} D_i - \overline{\text{Out}}\left(\bar{\mathcal{G}} \cup \mathcal{L}_K^*\right). \tag{14}$$

Since nodes in $\bar{\mathcal{G}}$ constitute an independent set it follows:

$$\overline{\text{Out}}\left(\bar{\mathcal{G}}\right) = \sum_{i \in \bar{\mathcal{G}}} D_i. \tag{15}$$

From Lemma 2 applied to set $\bar{\mathcal{G}}$, and using (14-15) we get

$$\sum_{i \in \bar{\mathcal{G}}} r_i = \overline{\text{In}}\left(\bar{\mathcal{G}}\right) = \sum_{i \in \mathcal{L}_K^*} D_i - \overline{\text{Out}}\left(\bar{\mathcal{G}} \cup \mathcal{L}_K^*\right), \text{ or}$$

$$\sum_{k=k_0}^{K^*-1} l_k^* \sum_{i \in \mathcal{L}_k^* \cap \bar{\mathcal{G}}} D_i = \sum_{i \in \mathcal{L}_K^*} D_i - \overline{\text{Out}}\left(\bar{\mathcal{G}} \cup \mathcal{L}_K^*\right). \tag{16}$$

Next, since nodes in $\mathcal{L}_K^*$ get resource only from nodes in $\bar{\mathcal{G}}$ (and all of it) we have

$$l_K^* \sum_{i \in \mathcal{L}_K^*} D_i = \sum_{i \in \bar{\mathcal{G}}} D_i. \tag{17}$$

Multiplying (16) and (17), and rearranging terms:

$$\sum_{k=k_0}^{K^*-1} l_K^* l_k^* \sum_{i \in \mathcal{L}_k^* \cap \bar{\mathcal{G}}} D_i = \sum_{i \in \bar{\mathcal{G}}} D_i - \frac{\sum_{i \in \bar{\mathcal{G}}} D_i}{\sum_{i \in \mathcal{L}_K^*} D_i} \overline{\text{Out}}\left(\bar{\mathcal{G}} \cup \mathcal{L}_K^*\right). \tag{18}$$

Eq. (18) implies that $l_K^* l_{k_0}^* \leq 1$: if $l_K^* l_{k_0}^* > 1$ then, because it will also hold $l_K^* l_k^* > 1$, $\forall k \geq k_0$, (18) would not hold.

Now, if $\overline{\text{Out}}\left(\bar{\mathcal{G}} \cup \mathcal{L}_K^*\right) > 0$ then from (18) we have:

$$\sum_{k=k_0}^{K^*-1} l_K^* l_k^* \sum_{i \in \mathcal{L}_k^* \cap \bar{\mathcal{G}}} D_i < \sum_{i \in \bar{\mathcal{G}}} D_i$$

and arguing as above we see that necessarily $l_K^* l_{k_0}^* < 1$. If $\overline{\text{Out}}\left(\bar{\mathcal{G}} \cup \mathcal{L}_K^*\right) = 0$ and $\bar{\mathcal{G}} - \mathcal{L}_{k_0}^* \neq \emptyset$ then again $l_K^* l_{k_0}^* < 1$. To see this, notice that if $l_K^* l_{k_0}^* \geq 1$ and $\bar{\mathcal{G}} - \mathcal{L}_{k_0}^* \neq \emptyset$ then it would hold:

$$l_K^* l_k^* \sum_{i \in \mathcal{L}_k^* \cap \bar{\mathcal{G}}} D_i \geq \sum_{i \in \mathcal{L}_k^* \cap \bar{\mathcal{G}}} D_i \;\forall\, k \geq k_0. \tag{19}$$

Also, since $\bar{\mathcal{G}} - \mathcal{L}_{k_0}^* \neq \emptyset$, for some $k > k_0$ there must be a nonempty set $\mathcal{L}_k^* \cap \bar{\mathcal{G}}$ which implies that the inequality is strict for some $k > k_0$. Adding inequalities (19) we would then get,

$$\sum_{k=k_0}^{K^*-1} l_K^* l_k^* \sum_{i \in \mathcal{L}_k^* \cap \bar{\mathcal{G}}} D_i > \sum_{i \in \bar{\mathcal{G}}} D_i,$$

which contradicts (18).

Assume finally that $\overline{\text{Out}}\left(\bar{\mathcal{G}} \cup \mathcal{L}_K^*\right) = 0$ and $\bar{\mathcal{G}} - \mathcal{L}_{k_0}^* = \emptyset$. From (18) we have $l_K^* l_{k_0}^* \sum_{i \in \bar{\mathcal{G}}} D_i = \sum_{i \in \bar{\mathcal{G}}} D_i$, and since $\bar{\mathcal{G}} \neq \emptyset$ implies $\sum_{i \in \bar{\mathcal{G}}} D_i > 0$, we get $l_K^* l_{k_0}^* = 1$. □

Lemma 8. If $K^* \geq 2$, then the set $\mathcal{L}_1^*$ is independent.

Proof. Assume that for some pair $i, j \in \mathcal{L}_1^*$, it is $(i,j) \in \mathcal{E}$. Consider the largest set $\mathcal{C} \subseteq \mathcal{L}_1^*$ such that a) $\mathcal{C}$ contains both i and j, b) the induced subgraph of $\mathcal{C}$ is connected. Therefore, each node in $\mathcal{C}$ has a node in $\mathcal{C}$, and hence a node in $\mathcal{L}_1^*$ as neighbor. By Lemma 1 we have that under any lex-optimal allocation $\boldsymbol{d}$, it holds $\mathcal{L}_{k(\mathcal{D}_i)}^* = 1$ for all $i \in \mathcal{C}$. That is, all nodes in $\mathcal{C}$ give resource only to other nodes in $\mathcal{C}$, hence, $\text{Out}(\mathcal{C}) = 0$. It follows from (5) that $\sum_{i \in \mathcal{C}} r_i^* \geq \sum_{i \in \mathcal{C}} D_i$. But we also have

$$\sum_{i \in \mathcal{C}} r_i^* \;=\; l_1^* \sum_{i \in \mathcal{C}} D_i < \sum_{i \in \mathcal{C}} D_i,$$

since $l_1^* < 1$ by Lemma 3, which is a contradiction. □

Lemma 9. Let $\bar{\boldsymbol{d}}$ be a lex-optimal allocation and $K^* \geq 2$. It holds $\mathcal{L}_1^* \subseteq \bar{\mathcal{G}}$.

Proof. Let $\bar{\mathcal{F}}_k \triangleq \left(\bar{\mathcal{G}} \cup \mathcal{L}_K^*\right)^c \cap \mathcal{L}_k^*$, $k = 1, ..., K^*-1$. It suffices to show that $\bar{\mathcal{F}}_1 = \emptyset$. Assume that $\bar{\mathcal{F}}_1 \neq \emptyset$. Let $\bar{\mathcal{B}}$ be the set of nodes in $\left(\bar{\mathcal{G}} \cup \mathcal{L}_K^*\right)^c$ that are neighbors of nodes in $\bar{\mathcal{F}}_1$. The set $\bar{\mathcal{B}}$ is nonempty because otherwise, since $\mathcal{L}_1^*$ (and hence $\bar{\mathcal{F}}_1$) is an independent set and by Lemma 6 it is $\mathcal{N}\left(\bar{\mathcal{G}}\right) \subseteq \mathcal{L}_K^*$, all neighbors of any node in $\bar{\mathcal{F}}_1$ would be in $\mathcal{L}_K^*$ which implies that $\bar{\mathcal{F}}_1 \subseteq \bar{\mathcal{G}}$, a contradiction.

Notice next that (13) and Lemma 1 imply that all nodes in $\bar{\mathcal{B}}$ give resource only to nodes in $\bar{\mathcal{F}}_1$. Hence

$$l_1^* \sum_{i \in \bar{\mathcal{F}}_1} D_i \geq \sum_{i \in \bar{\mathcal{B}}} D_i.$$

Also, since by Lemma 8 the set $\bar{\mathcal{F}}_1$ is independent, and by (13) nodes in $\bar{\mathcal{F}}_1$ do not give resource to nodes in $\mathcal{L}_K^*$, all nodes in this set give resource only to nodes in $\bar{\mathcal{B}}$ and (notice that since $\bar{\mathcal{B}} \neq \emptyset$, is should hold $K^* - 1 \geq 2$),

$$\sum_{k=2}^{K^*-1} l_k^* \sum_{i \in \bar{\mathcal{F}}_k \cap \bar{\mathcal{B}}} D_i \geq \sum_{i \in \bar{\mathcal{F}}_1} D_i.$$

Multiplying the last two inequalities and canceling terms:

$$\sum_{k=2}^{K^*-1} l_1^* l_k^* \sum_{i \in \bar{\mathcal{F}}_k \cap \bar{\mathcal{B}}} D_i \geq \sum_{i \in \bar{\mathcal{B}}} D_i,$$

which implies that $l_1^* l_{K-1}^* \geq 1$. But $l_{k_0}^* l_K^* > l_1^* l_{K-1}^*$, $k_0 \geq 1$ and hence $l_{k_0}^* l_K^* > 1$, which contradicts Lemma 7. □

Now we are ready to prove the following proposition.

Proposition 10. Let $\boldsymbol{d}^*$ be a lex-optimal allocation and $K^* \geq 2$. The set $\mathcal{L}_1^*$ is independent, $\mathcal{N}\left(\mathcal{L}_1^*\right) = \mathcal{L}_K^*$, and

$$l_1^* l_K^* = 1, \tag{20}$$

$$\sum_{i \in \mathcal{L}_1^*} r_i^* = \sum_{i \in \mathcal{L}_K^*} D_i, \tag{21}$$

$$\overline{\text{In}}\left(\mathcal{L}_1^* \cup \mathcal{L}_K^*\right) = \overline{\text{Out}}\left(\mathcal{L}_1^* \cup \mathcal{L}_K^*\right) = 0, \tag{22}$$

Proof. By Lemma 1 the nodes in the set $\mathcal{N}\left(\mathcal{L}_1^*\right) = \cup_{i \in \mathcal{L}_1} \mathcal{N}_i - \mathcal{L}_1^* = \cup_{i \in \mathcal{L}_1} \mathcal{N}_i$ (the last equality hold because $\forall i \in \mathcal{L}_i^*$, it is $\mathcal{N}_i \cap \mathcal{L}_1^* = \emptyset$) give resource only to nodes in $\mathcal{L}_1^*$, hence

$$\overline{\text{In}}\left(\mathcal{L}_1^*\right) = \sum_{i \in \mathcal{N}\left(\mathcal{L}_1^*\right)} D_i.$$

Also, since $\mathcal{L}_1^*$ is an independent set, its nodes give all their resource to nodes in $\mathcal{N}(\mathcal{L}_1^*)$, hence it is:

$$\overline{\text{Out}}(\mathcal{L}_1^*) = \sum_{i \in \mathcal{L}_1^*} D_i .$$

Applying (5) to the set $\mathcal{L}_1^*$, we then have

$$\sum_{i \in \mathcal{L}_1^*} r_i^* = l_1^* \sum_{i \in \mathcal{L}_1^*} D_i = \sum_{i \in \mathcal{N}(\mathcal{L}_1^*)} D_i \tag{23}$$

On the other hand, since according to Lemma 5 the nodes in $\mathcal{N}(\mathcal{L}_1^*) \subseteq \mathcal{L}_K^*$ give all their resource to nodes outside $\mathcal{L}_K^*$, according to (6) applied with equality, we get

$$\overline{\text{Out}}(\mathcal{N}(\mathcal{L}_1^*)) = \sum_{i \in \mathcal{N}(\mathcal{L}_1^*)} D_i . \tag{24}$$

Moreover, $\mathcal{L}_1^*$ is an independent set and thus the nodes in $\mathcal{N}(\mathcal{L}_1^*)$ get all the resource from nodes in $\mathcal{L}_1^*$. Hence:

$$\overline{\text{In}}(\mathcal{L}_K^*) \geq \sum_{i \in \mathcal{N}(\mathcal{L}_1^*)} D_i .$$

Applying now (5) to the set $\mathcal{N}(\mathcal{L}_1^*)$ we have:

$$\sum_{i \in \mathcal{N}(\mathcal{L}_1^*)} r_i^* = l_K^* \sum_{i \in \mathcal{N}(\mathcal{L}_1^*)} D_i \geq \sum_{i \in \mathcal{L}_1^*} D_i . \tag{25}$$

Multiplying (23), (25) we get $l_K^* l_1^* \geq 1$. If $\overline{\text{Out}}(\bar{\mathcal{G}} \cup \mathcal{L}_K^*) > 0$, from Lemma 7 we have $l_K^* l_1^* < 1$, i.e., a contradiction. If $\overline{\text{Out}}(\bar{\mathcal{G}} \cup \mathcal{L}_K^*) = 0$ and $\bar{\mathcal{G}} - \mathcal{L}_1^* \neq \emptyset$ then from the same lemma we have $l_K^* l_1^* < 1$, again a contradiction.

The only case that remains is $\overline{\text{Out}}(\bar{\mathcal{G}} \cup \mathcal{L}_K^*) = 0$ and $\bar{\mathcal{G}} - \mathcal{L}_1^* = \emptyset$ (i.e., $\bar{\mathcal{G}} \subseteq \mathcal{L}_1^*$) which again by the lemma implies $l_K^* l_1^* = 1$. Also, Lemma 9 implies $\bar{\mathcal{G}} = \mathcal{L}_1^*$. $\mathcal{N}(\mathcal{L}_1^*) = \mathcal{L}_K^*$ follows from Lemma 6, and (21) follows from (23). □

We can now proceed with the proof for Theorem 1: For $k = 1$, Items 1- 4 follow from Proposition 10. Hence the theorem is true when $K \in \{2, 3\}$. Assume now that $K \geq 4$. Since according to Proposition 10 it is $\text{Out}(\mathcal{L}_1 \cup \mathcal{L}_K) = \text{In}(\mathcal{L}_1 \cup \mathcal{L}_K) = 0$, the restriction $\boldsymbol{d}_{\mathcal{Q}_2} = \{d_{ij}\}_{(i,j) \in \mathcal{E}_{\mathcal{Q}_2}}$ of $\boldsymbol{d}$ in $\mathcal{Q}_2$, is an allocation on the graph with $K - 2$ levels. But then $\boldsymbol{d}_{\mathcal{Q}_2}$ must be a lex-optimal allocation in $G_{\mathcal{Q}_2} = (\mathcal{Q}_2, \mathcal{E}_{\mathcal{Q}_2})$ since otherwise we could combine an allocation $\hat{\boldsymbol{d}}_{\mathcal{Q}_2} \succ \boldsymbol{d}_{\mathcal{Q}_2}$ with the components of $\boldsymbol{d}$ in $\mathcal{E} - \mathcal{E}_{\mathcal{Q}_2}$ and get a lexicographically better allocation on the original graph. Moreover, by construction we have for the lowest level set in $G_{\mathcal{Q}_2}$: $\mathcal{L}_{\mathcal{Q}_2,1} = \mathcal{L}_2$ and $\mathcal{L}_{\mathcal{Q}_2,K-2} = \mathcal{L}_{K-1} = \mathcal{L}_{K-2+1}$. Hence properties 1- 4 hold for $k = 2$ and we can repeat the same arguments for the graph $G_{\mathcal{Q}_2}$ to deduce inductively the stated properties for all $k = 1, ..., \lfloor K/2 \rfloor$.

4. GAME-THEORETIC ANALYSIS

4.1 Coalitional Game

We consider two notions for coalition stability [20], namely weak and strong stability[8]. The latter is a more restrictive condition, and preferable as it ensures there is no other allocation that will yield a strictly better payoff *even* for one user. The main result in this context is:

[8]Please note that this service exchange game does not posses the *comprehensive property*, due to the fact that nodes allocate their entire idle resource, and hence we cannot define the inner core and the Shapley values and compare them with our solution [20].

Theorem 4. Any lex-optimal allocation $\boldsymbol{d}^*$ yields a received resource vector $\boldsymbol{r}^*$, that lies in the core of the NTU service exchange game, and it is strongly stable.

Therefore, no subset of nodes can deviate and improve the total received resource, *for at least one* of its members, without reducing the total received resource of at least another one of its members. Combining Theorems 1 and 4 we have the following corollary:

Corollary 2. Let $K^* \geq 2$. Under any lex-optimal allocation $\boldsymbol{d}^*$, the respective received resource vector $\boldsymbol{r}^*$, belongs to the core of the NTU coalitional servicing game, and has the following structure:

1. The set of nodes $\mathcal{N}$ is partitioned into disjoint groups $\mathcal{M}_1^*, ..., \mathcal{M}_L^*$, where $\lceil K^*/2 \rceil$, and each group contains nodes with exchange ratios belonging to at most two different levels.

2. There are exactly $\lfloor K^*/2 \rfloor$ groups with 2 levels. For group $\mathcal{M}_k^*$, $1 \leq k \leq \lfloor K^*/2 \rfloor$ it holds $\mathcal{M}_k^* = \mathcal{L}_k^* \cup \mathcal{L}_{K-k+1}^*$.

3. If K^* is odd, there is also a group with one ratio level, i.e., $\mathcal{M}_{\lceil K^*/2 \rceil}^* = \mathcal{L}_{\lceil K^*/2 \rceil}^*$.

4. It holds, $l_k^* l_{K-k+1}^* = 1$, $1 \leq k \leq \lfloor K^*/2 \rfloor$ and if K^* is odd, the single level group has ratio $l_{\lceil K^*/2 \rceil}^* = 1$.

5. The set $\cup_{k=1}^{\lfloor K^*/2 \rfloor} \mathcal{L}_k^*$ is independent.

Finally, if $K^* = 1$, there is one group of nodes with $l^* = 1$. For the proofs of the above corollary and theorem the reader is kindly requested to access the online technical report [36].

Analysis and Discussion. Existence of Core. The above results reveal that this coalitional service exchange NTU game has always a non-empty core, for any graph G, and any resource endowments $\{D_i\}_{i \in \mathcal{N}}$. Moreover, the core contains all lex-optimal allocations, which are also strongly stable. This is a more demanding condition than the non-emptiness of the core.

Groups of Nodes. Within the grand coalition, not all the nodes interact with each other. For example, in Figure 3 where $K^* = 7$, all the lex-optimal allocations result in 4 groups (denoted with the dotted circles): $\mathcal{M}_1^* = \mathcal{L}_1^* \cup \mathcal{L}_7^*$, $\mathcal{M}_2^* = \mathcal{L}_2^* \cup \mathcal{L}_6^*$, $\mathcal{M}_3^* = \mathcal{L}_3^* \cup \mathcal{L}_5^*$, and $\mathcal{M}_4^* = \mathcal{L}_4^*$. Each group consists of nodes belonging to one or two exchange ratio level sets, and none of them exchange resources with nodes in different groups[9]. These properties are very useful for network design. For example, for a given network we can predict which nodes will interact in the fair and stable allocation policy, and remove the redundant physical links, which in certain cases induce additional cost [15].

4.2 Competitive Market

In the competitive market framework, each node acts greedily, without any information about the graph or the other nodes' resources, and allocates its resource so as to maximize the total resource it receives in return. Interestingly, equilibriums always exist in this autonomous and decentralized setting, and lead to lex-optimal exchange ratio vectors:

[9]Notice that these groups do not constitute separate coalitions according to the given definitions.

Theorem 5. The following hold: **(i)** There is a lex-optimal allocation $\boldsymbol{d}^*$ under which each node $i \in \mathcal{N}$ gives resource to its neighbors in proportion to what it gets from them, i.e., $d^*_{ij} = d^*_{ji} D_i / r^*_i$, or $d^*_{ji}/d^*_{ij} = r^*_i / D_i = l^*_{k(i)}$, $j \in \mathcal{N}_i$, and the neighbors not receiving resource from i have higher exchange ratio, i.e., $l^*_{k(j)} \geq 1/l^*_{k(i)} = l^*_{k(\mathcal{D}_i)}$, $j \in \mathcal{H}_i$. **(ii)** if the allocation satisfies the above conditions, then the allocation is lexicographically optimal.

The proof of the theorem is provided in the Appendix.

Analysis and Discussion. This theorem states that there is a fair lex-optimal allocation, where every node $i \in \mathcal{N}$ serves its neighbors $j \in \mathcal{D}_i$ with a resource d_{ij}, so as to have a constant and equal exchange ratio d_{ij}/d_{ji} with all of them. Therefore, the lex-optimal allocation is an exchange equilibrium, and, additionally, any possible exchange equilibrium is also a lex-optimal allocation. In other words, the competitive interactions of rational users embedded in a graph, lead to the same allocation point that a central designer would have selected for such a system.

Dynamic Model. An important aspect to notice it that this framework can capture both models where infinitely divisible resources are exchanged among users with different preferences, and also dynamic settings where users exchange indivisible resources over time, exploiting their diverse resource availability. To make the latter case more clear, consider a dynamic resource exchange system which operates in the continuous time domain. Every node $i \in \mathcal{N}$ creates service opportunities for its neighbors (or, *tokens*[10]) according to a Poisson process with possibly different rate $\lambda_i > 0$. A meaningful strategy from the perspective of the nodes is the following: each node i allocates a token generated at time t to its neighbor that has, until then, given to i the largest number of service tokens (per received token from i).

A rational user, with no information about the graph and the nodes' endowments, is reasonable to expect that this strategy can increase its benefit. Besides, this type of best response policies have been considered before, e.g., for P2P networks [34] where it was shown that they converge to a steady state. In our case however, the scheme is decentralized and totally asynchronous. Interestingly, numerical results in Sec. 6 indicate that such myopic policies do converge to a steady state which moreover satisfies Theorem 5. This means that this dynamic model has a steady state that asymptotically coincides with the respective static model, and the equilibrium can be found if we set $D_i = \lambda_i, \forall i \in \mathcal{N}$. This is very important as it reveals that the results of this work do not apply only for the above static models, but also characterize the steady state allocations and equilibriums of more dynamic systems, where idle resources or service opportunities are created and allocated by each node asynchronously, greedily, and with no global network information (i.e., beyond the one hop neighbors).

5. LEX-OPTIMAL ALGORITHMS

In this section, we provide a polynomial (in $|\mathcal{N}|$) time algorithm that finds the lex-optimal allocation, and the respective exchange ratio vectors. The proposed algorithm uses the idea of max-min programming algorithm proposed in [32] and takes advantage of the structure of lex-optimal exchange ratio vector described in Theorem 1 to improve performance. The algorithm is based on the following result.

Lemma 11. Let $\bar{\boldsymbol{d}} \in \mathbb{D}$ and $K \geq 2$. If the set $\bar{\mathcal{L}}_1$ is independent and

$$\sum_{i \in \bar{\mathcal{L}}_1} \bar{r}_i = \sum_{i \in \mathcal{N}(\bar{\mathcal{L}}_1)} D_i, \tag{26}$$

then:

1. For any allocation $\hat{\boldsymbol{d}}$ that solves the problem
$$\underset{\boldsymbol{d} \in \mathbb{D}}{\text{maximize}} \min_{j \in \mathcal{N}} \frac{r_j}{d_j} \tag{27}$$
it holds $\bar{\mathcal{L}}_1 \subseteq \widehat{\mathcal{L}}_1$ and $\bar{l}_1 = \hat{l}_1$.
2. The set $\bar{\mathcal{L}}_1$ coincides with the respective set of the lex-optimal ratio vector, i.e., $\bar{\mathcal{L}}_1 = \mathcal{L}^*_1$ and $\bar{l}_1 = l^*_1$.

Proof. 1) Since $\hat{\boldsymbol{d}}$ solves (27) it holds $\hat{l}_1 \geq \bar{l}_1$ and hence $\frac{\hat{r}_i}{D_i} \geq \hat{l}_1 \geq \bar{l}_1 = \frac{\bar{r}_i}{D_i}$, $i \in \bar{\mathcal{L}}_1$ i.e.,

$$\hat{r}_i \geq \bar{r}_i, \quad i \in \bar{\mathcal{L}}_1. \tag{28}$$

We will show next that equality holds in (28) which implies that $\bar{\mathcal{L}}_1 \subseteq \widehat{\mathcal{L}}_1$. To see this notice that if strict inequality holds for at least one $i \in \bar{\mathcal{L}}_1$ then

$$\sum_{i \in \bar{\mathcal{L}}_1} \hat{r}_i > \sum_{i \in \bar{\mathcal{L}}_1} \bar{r}_i. \tag{29}$$

But since $\bar{\mathcal{L}}_1$ is an independent set, we have

$$\sum_{i \in \bar{\mathcal{L}}_1} \hat{r}_i = \widehat{\text{In}}\left(\bar{\mathcal{L}}_1\right) \leq \sum_{i \in \mathcal{N}(\bar{\mathcal{L}}_1)} D_i = \sum_{i \in \bar{\mathcal{L}}_1} \bar{r}_i \tag{30}$$

where the inequality holds by definition of inflow, and the last equality by assumption. This result contradicts (29).

2) Since any lex-optimal allocation $\hat{\boldsymbol{d}}$ solves (27), we have $\bar{\mathcal{L}}_1 \subseteq \hat{\mathcal{L}}_1 = \mathcal{L}^*_1$. If $\bar{\mathcal{L}}_1$ were a strict subset of $\hat{\mathcal{L}}_1$, then $\bar{\boldsymbol{d}}$ would be lexicographically better that $\hat{\boldsymbol{d}}$, a contradiction. □

Algorithm 1 provides the details. Recall the definition of graphs $G_{\mathcal{Q}_k} = (\mathcal{Q}_k, \mathcal{E}_{\mathcal{Q}_k})$ used in Theorem 1. The number of iterations of the algorithm is equal to the number of sets $\mathcal{Q}_k$, i.e., $\lceil K^*/2 \rceil$. Since each of the level sets contains at least 2 nodes, it holds $K^* \leq N/2$, and hence the number of iterations is at most $\lceil N/4 \rceil$.

In Step 3, l^*_k is computed as the optimal value of optimization problem (1.1.), as ensured by Lemma 11. The latter optimization problem can be transformed to a linear programming problem and hence can be solved in polynomial time. Note that the dimensionality of the problem is reduced at each iteration. If the conditions in Steps 5 and 10 are satisfied, then the lex-optimal allocation has been determined on all links and the algorithm terminates.

The implementation and polynomial complexity of Step 6 will be discussed shortly. This step determines the set $\mathcal{L}^*_k$, and hence $\mathcal{L}^*_{K^*-k+1} = \mathcal{N}(\mathcal{L}^*_k)$ and $l^*_{K^*-k+1} = 1/l^*_k$. Also, at the exit from this step, the allocated resources of all outgoing links from nodes in $\mathcal{L}^*_{K^*}$ to nodes in $\mathcal{N} - (\mathcal{L}^*_{K^*} \cup \mathcal{L}^*_1)$, will be zero and the allocated resources of all outgoing links from nodes in $\mathcal{L}^*_{K^*}$ to nodes in $\mathcal{L}^*_1$ will be determined.

Step 8 sets to zero all allocations of incoming links from nodes in $\mathcal{Q}_k - \left(\mathcal{L}^*_{\mathcal{Q}_k,1} \cup \mathcal{L}^*_{\mathcal{Q}_k,2}\right)$ to nodes in $\mathcal{L}^*_{\mathcal{Q}_k,2}$, as is required by Theorem 1. Step 9 determines allocations d^*_{ij}, $i \in$

[10]These are 0-1 token allocation decisions: whenever a user has an idle resource, e.g., an amount of unused bandwidth or energy, it can allocate it to one of its neighbors.

Algorithm 1: Finding the Lex-optimal allocation

1 $k \leftarrow 1$;
2 **while** *1* **do**
3 Find $\hat{\boldsymbol{r}}$ and $\hat{\boldsymbol{d}}$ solving: $\underset{\boldsymbol{d} \in \mathbb{D}_{\mathcal{Q}_k}}{\text{maximize}} \min_{j \in \mathcal{N}_{\mathcal{Q}_k}} \frac{r_j}{D_j}$; (1.1)
4 Set $l^*_{\mathcal{Q}_k,1}$ to the value of the solution to (1.1.)
5 **If** $(\hat{r}_i / D_i = 1 \ i \in \mathcal{Q}_k)$ **then** $K^* = k$; Exit;
6 Find the set $\mathcal{L}^*_{\mathcal{Q}_k,1}$;
7 Determine set $\mathcal{L}^*_{\mathcal{Q}_k,2} = \mathcal{N}\left(\mathcal{L}^*_{\mathcal{Q}_k,1}\right)$ and level value $l^*_{\mathcal{Q}_k,2} = 1/l^*_{\mathcal{Q}_k,1}$
8 $d_{ji} \leftarrow 0, \ \forall \ (j,i) \ i \in \mathcal{L}^*_{\mathcal{Q}_k,2}, \ j \in \mathcal{Q}_{\mathcal{Q}_k}$ - $(\mathcal{L}^*_{\mathcal{Q}_k,1} \cup \mathcal{L}^*_{\mathcal{Q}_k,2})$;
9 Find lex-optimal allocations on links (i,j), $i \in \mathcal{L}^*_{\mathcal{Q}_k,1}$, $j \in \mathcal{L}^*_{\mathcal{Q}_k,2}$;
10 **If** $\left(\mathcal{L}^*_{\mathcal{Q}_k,1} \cup \mathcal{L}^*_{\mathcal{Q}_k,2} = \mathcal{Q}_k\right)$ **then** $K^* = k$; Exit;
11 $k \leftarrow k+1$;
end

$\mathcal{L}^*_k$, $j \in \mathcal{L}^*_{K^*-k+1}$. Since it is known by Theorem 1 that

$$\sum_{j \in \mathcal{N}_i} d^*_{ji} = 1/l^*_k, \ i \in \mathcal{L}^*_{K^*-k+1},$$

this steps is equivalent to finding a feasible solution to a linear programming problem and hence it takes polynomial time to execute.

Algorithm 2: Finding the set $\mathcal{L}^*_1$

1 $\mathcal{L} = \widehat{\mathcal{L}}_1$; $r_{ij} = \widehat{r}_{ij}$; /* *on exit* $\mathcal{L} = \mathcal{L}^*_1$ */
2 **while** $\exists (i,j)$ *where* $i, j \in \mathcal{L}$ ***and*** $d_{ij_1} > 0$ *for some* $j_1 \in \mathcal{N}(\mathcal{L})$ **do**
3 Reallocate resource from link (i, j_1) to link (i,j) ensuring that with the new allocation $\min\{r_j/D_i, \ r_{j_1}/D_i\} > l^*_1$;
4 Set $\mathcal{L} \leftarrow \mathcal{L} - \{j\}$;
end
/**on exit the set* $\mathcal{L}$ *is independent**/
5 **while** $\exists (i, j_1)$, $i \in \mathcal{N}(\mathcal{L})$, $j_1 \in \mathcal{N} - \mathcal{L}$ *with* $r_{ij_1} > 0$, **do**
6 Reallocate resource from node j_1 to a node j in $\mathcal{N}(i)$ ensuring that with the new allocation $\min\{r_j/D_i, \ r_{j_1}/D_i\} > l^*_1$;
7 Set $\mathcal{L} \leftarrow \mathcal{L} - \{j\}$; /* *on exit, set* $\mathcal{L}$ *satisfies (26)* */
end

It remains to show that Step 6 has polynomial complexity. According to Lemma 11, the solution to (27) determines $l^*_1 < 1$ and in general provides a solution $\widehat{\mathcal{L}}_1$ which is a superset of $\mathcal{L}^*_1$. Furthermore, if by reallocating some of the link resources $\widehat{d}_{ij}$ we are able to create an allocation $\boldsymbol{d}$ such that (i) the set $\bar{\mathcal{L}}_1$ is independent, and (ii) the relation $\sum_{i \in \bar{\mathcal{L}}_1} \bar{r}_i = \sum_{i \in \mathcal{N}(\bar{\mathcal{L}}_1)} D_i$ holds, then it will be $\mathcal{L}^*_1 = \bar{\mathcal{L}}_1$.

The resource reallocation is described in Algorithm 2. There are two iteration loops. First, starting from the set $\mathcal{L} = \widehat{\mathcal{L}}_1$, if there is a link (i,j) such that $i, j \in \mathcal{L}$ then we select a node $j_1 \in \mathcal{N}(\mathcal{L})$, with $d_{ij_1} > 0$, and transfer resource from link (i, j_1) to the link (i,j). This selection is always possible since otherwise the condition "for all links (i,j) such that $i, j \in \mathcal{L}$ there is no node $j_1 \in \mathcal{N}(\mathcal{L})$, with $d_{ij_1} > 0$" would hold; however, this implies that $l^*_1 = 1$ which is excluded because at this point we have $K^* \geq 2$. The transfer of resource from(i, j_1) to link (i,j) in Step 3 of the algorithm ensures that the received resource ratios of nodes j and j_1 are larger than l^*_1 and hence j necessarily does not belong to $\mathcal{L}^*_1$. Hence on exit from the while loop in Step 2 the set $\mathcal{L}$ is independent. However, in order to ensure equality to $\mathcal{L}^*_1$ we may need to further modify $\mathcal{L}$ to ensure that the condition (26) holds. This is done in the second while loop that starts at Step 5. Also, at the exit from the algorithm, as a result of this reallocation process, the allocated resources of all outgoing links from nodes in $\mathcal{L}^*_{K^*}$ to nodes in $\mathcal{N} - (\mathcal{L}^*_{K^*} \cup \mathcal{L}^*_1)$ will be zero and, the allocated resources of all outgoing links from nodes in $\mathcal{L}^*_{K^*}$ to nodes in $\mathcal{L}^*_1$ will be determined. As is clear from the above description, Algorithm 1 and 2 take polynomial time to execute.

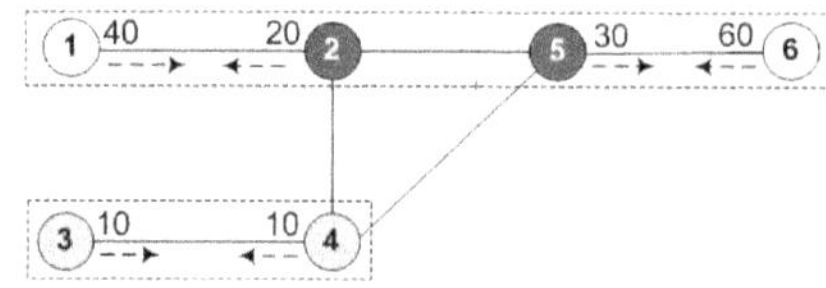

Figure 4: A network with 6 nodes that create 2 groups, each one marked with the dotted-line rectangle. There are 3 different levels of exchange ratios. The color of each node is analogous to its exchange ratio value (increasing from white to black colour). The received resources are $r^*_1 = 20$, $r^*_2 = 40$, $r^*_3 = 10$, $r^*_4 = 10$, $r^*_5 = 60$, and $r^*_6 = 30$. The exchange ratios for the nodes belonging to each set are $l^*_1 = 0.5$, $l^*_2 = 1$, and $l^*_3 = 2$ respectively.

6. NUMERICAL EXAMPLES

In this section, we analyze representative numerical examples to shed light on the above results. Consider first the network of Fig. 4 which has 6 nodes. Solid lines represent the physical connections of each node and dotted arrows indicate resource allocation. Next to each node i we depict its resource endowment. At the lex-optimal point, we have $K^* = 3$ levels with 3 node sets $\mathcal{L}^*_1 = \{1,6\}$, $\mathcal{L}^*_2 = \{3,4\}$, $\mathcal{L}^*_3 = \{2,5\}$ which are marked with different colors.

Let us now verify the properties that the lex-optimal allocation should have according to Theorem 1. First, notice that set $\mathcal{L}^*_1$ is independent in graph G. Moreover, all the neighbors of nodes in set $\mathcal{L}^*_3$, i.e., nodes 2 and 5, belong in $\mathcal{L}^*_1$. Although nodes in $\mathcal{L}^*_3$ are physically connected, they only allocate resource to nodes in $\mathcal{L}^*_1$ and it holds $\sum_{i \in \mathcal{L}^*_3} D_i = \sum_{i \in l_1} r_i = 20 + 30$. Moreover, the highest and the lowest levels satisfy the condition $l^*_1 l^*_3 = 1$.

Similarly, we can verify that the structure of the lex-optimal allocation satisfies Corollary 2. The nodes are partitioned into 2 disjoint groups $\mathcal{M}^*_1 = \mathcal{L}^*_1 \cup \mathcal{L}^*_3$ and $\mathcal{M}^*_2 = \mathcal{L}^*_2$, each one containing nodes with at most two levels. Also, the nodes in $\mathcal{L}^*_1$ are connected only to nodes in the set $\mathcal{L}^*_3$, and it is $l^*_2 = 1$. Finally, the conditions of Theorem 5 are satisfied. For example, node 2 allocates resource only to node 1, with $l_{k(1)} = 1/l_{k(2)}$, and not to node 4 since it is $l_{k(4)} = 1 > 0.5 = l_{k(\mathcal{D}_2)}$, where $l_{k(\mathcal{D}_2)} = l_{k(1)}$.

For the example of Fig. 5 we used a network with 13 nodes that yields $K^* = 6$ levels, with $l^*_1 = 0.25$, $l^*_2 = 0.43$, $l^*_3 = 0.77$, $l^*_4 = 2.34$, $l^*_5 = 1.3$, and $l^*_6 = 4$. The sets are $\mathcal{L}^*_1 = \{12, 13\}$, $\mathcal{L}^*_2 = \{4, 6, 8, 10\}$, $\mathcal{L}^*_3 = \{2\}$, $\mathcal{L}^*_4 = \{1\}$, $\mathcal{L}^*_5 = \{3, 5, 7, 9\}$, and $\mathcal{L}^*_6 = \{11\}$. Sets $\mathcal{L}^*_1$, $\mathcal{L}^*_2$, and $\mathcal{L}^*_3$ are independent in graphs $G_{\mathcal{Q}_1}$, $G_{\mathcal{Q}_2}$, $G_{\mathcal{Q}_3}$, and the set $\mathcal{L}^*_1 \cup \mathcal{L}^*_2 \cup$

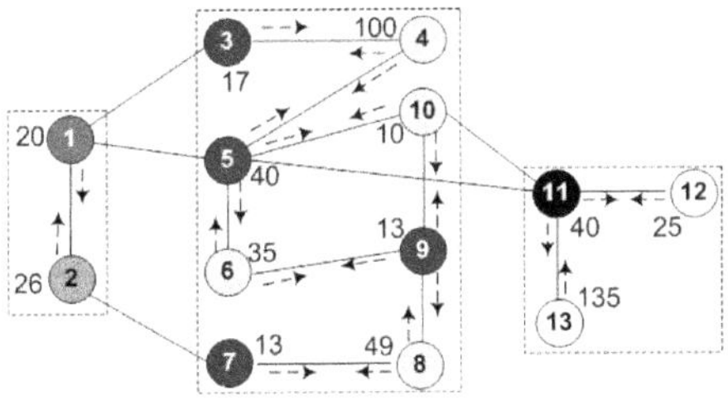

Figure 5: A network with 13 **nodes which create** 3 **groups. Received resources are** $r_1^* = 26$, $r_2^* = 20$, $r_3^* = 39.74$, $r_4^* = 42.78$, $r_5^* = 93.49$, $r_6^* = 14.97$, $r_7^* = 30.38$, $r_8^* = 20.96$, $r_9^* = 30.38$, $r_{10}^* = 4.28$, $r_{11}^* = 160$, $r_{12}^* = 6.25$, **and** $r_{13}^* = 33.75$.

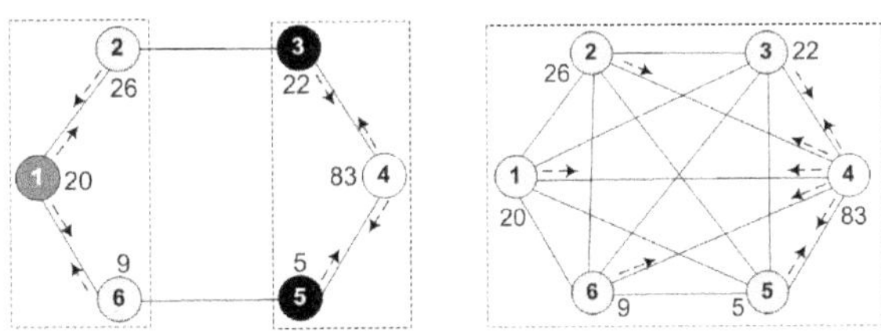

Figure 6: A complete graph of 6 **nodes with** 1 **coalition and** 2 **levels.**

$\mathcal{L}_3^*$ is independent in G. Moreover, it is $\mathcal{L}_6^* = \mathcal{N}_{\mathcal{Q}_1}(\mathcal{L}_1^*)$, $\mathcal{L}_5^* = \mathcal{N}_{\mathcal{Q}_2}(\mathcal{L}_2^*)$ and $\mathcal{L}_4^* = \mathcal{N}_{\mathcal{Q}_3}(\mathcal{L}_3^*)$, and holds $l_6^* l_1^* = l_5^* l_2^* = l_4^* l_3^* = 1$. In this example we have 3 disjoint groups $\mathcal{M}_1^* = \mathcal{L}_1^* \cup \mathcal{L}_6^*$, $\mathcal{M}_2^* = \mathcal{L}_2^* \cup \mathcal{L}_5^*$, and $\mathcal{M}_3^* = \mathcal{L}_3^* \cup \mathcal{L}_4^*$. We see that links $(10, 11)$, $(5, 11)$, $(1, 3)$, $(1, 5)$ and $(2, 7)$ are redundant and can be removed without affecting the lex-optimal allocation.

Figure 6 (right) depicts a complete graph with 6 nodes, where node $i = 4$ has level $l_1^* = 0.988$ while the other nodes have level $l_2^* = 1.012$. In general for complete graphs, from Property 6 of Corollary 2 and the fact that independent sets in such graphs contain only one node, it follows that lex-optimal allocations may have at most two levels. Moreover a complete graph has two levels iff the resource of node i_0 with the maximum endowment is larger than the sum of the resources of the rest of the nodes, and it is $\mathcal{L}_1 = \{i_0\}$. On the other hand, for the respective 6-node ring graph, the lex-optimal solution yields 2 groups and 4 levels.

Finally, we show that the naive best response strategy of the nodes in any graph-constrained dynamic resource exchange market, converges to a steady state point. Moreover, the latter coincides with the lex-optimal point of a static market in which every node has an average resource that is equal to the respective token generation rate of the dynamic market, i.e., $\lambda_i = D_i, \forall i \in \mathcal{N}$. In Figure 7 we present the quite fast convergence (each slot corresponds to the creation of a service opportunity) of this scheme for the above four networks, where we see that the system converges to the expected ratio values.

7. RELATED WORKS

The model we consider is generic and representative for many communication or economic networks. For example, such models arise in graphical economies [16], [17], which extend the classical Walrasian equilibrium [18] and Arrow - Debreu analysis [3] by imposing graph constraints on the subsets of buyers and sellers that can trade. However, our model

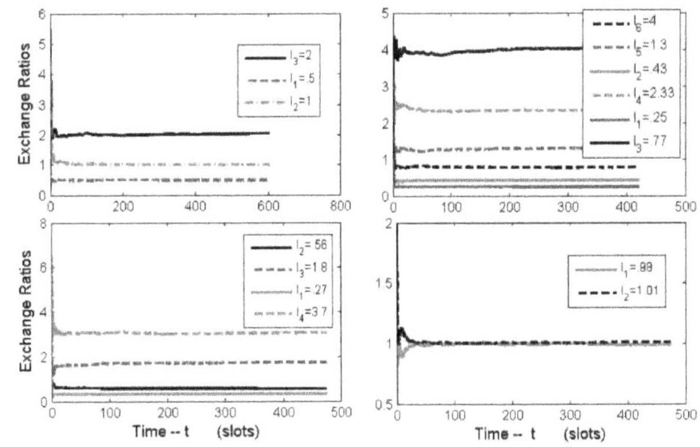

Figure 7: Convergence results for the dynamic interaction of nodes, for networks in Fig. 4 (upper left), Fig. 5 (upper right), Fig. 6-ring graph (lower left), and Fig. 6-complete graph (lower right).

does not presume any type of money transfers, i.e., there is no budget constraints (as in typical exchange economies) and the nodes do not value money (as in market games) [25]. Similar bartering models have been studied for housing markets [27] or timeshare exchanges [33], where the focus has been to prove existence of equilibriums.

Here, we fully characterize the equilibriums, relate them to the max-min fair solution, and study how they are affected by the graph. We also prove that these exchange equilibriums lie within the core of the respective NTU game. Although this relation is known for market games and the respective coalitional games [25], to the best of our knowledge this is the first result for NTU coalitional graph-constrained games without money. This property is also related to *strong* Nash equilibriums (see [1] and references therein), for which however there are no general existence results, nor they are appropriate for this competitive framework. Finally, [13], and [15] studied also core solutions of coalitional graph games where the nodes are allowed to create new or severe existing connections. In our model the graph is exogenously given, e.g., based on the location of the nodes.

The problem of cooperation in networks is of paramount importance and has been considered in different contexts, such as for ad hoc networks [5], WiFi sharing models [7], mesh networks [35], and P2P overlays [4]. This is a problem that gains increasing interest in communication networks [29], [31], [9], [6], and in social and economic networks as well [16], [15]. Unlike previous works, our model does not presume any kind of infrastructure, e.g., for transaction or reputation systems. Instead, we show numerically that asynchronous best response algorithms, with no information about the graph and resource endowments, converge to a fair and robust exchange equilibrium.

Previous works e.g., [34] have studied similar mechanisms for P2P overlays, without characterizing its properties and relation to competitive and coalitional equilibriums. The max-min fair criterion is natural for this setting, as it is defined with respect to each user's contribution. Also, while our model is similar to previous works, e.g., see [4] and references therein, our analysis provides novel insights for the structure and properties of the resulting equilibriums, and we also propose polynomial-time algorithms for their calculations. These algorithms can be also used for deriving the competitive equilibriums in graphical economies [17], [16].

8. DISCUSSION AND CONCLUSIONS

We considered a service (or, resource) exchange model among self-interested nodes embedded in a graph that prescribes their possible interactions. This is a key network model that represents Internet sharing communities [9], [29], [31], [6], P2P file sharing [4], [19], energy sharing networks [26], graphical economies [16], [17] and many online resource sharing platforms [22], [28], [14]. Such systems can be dynamic where the users share their resource surpluses that they have in different (and diverse) time instances, or static where users having different resource preferences barter with each other so as to acquire the resources they value higher. Despite the large interest of the research community and the previous contributions for specific related models (e.g., for P2P overlays), the fundamental properties of these systems remain unexplored.

We showed that the max-min fair policy exhibits a very rich structure, and characterized its properties for any given graph and node resource endowments. More importantly, we proved that this policy coincides with the exchange equilibrium of the respective competitive game, and lies in the core of the respective NTU coalitional game. This important result reveals that there is a unifying approach that solves the resource allocation problem for graph-constrained systems (or, economies), for different node behaviors. In other words, we can apply the max-min fair criterion, that has been extensively used for load balancing in centralized communication networks (e.g., see [21] and references therein), to service exchange models with autonomous and selfish nodes.

Finally, our findings contribute to the game theoretic literature since the connection between the competitive equilibrium for this graph-constrained model and the core of the respective NTU coalitional game is a new finding. We also proved the more strict *strong stability* property. A special aspect of our model is that we do not consider side payments (money), not even in the form of budget constraints. This renders the analysis significantly different than most of the previous models [25], [34], yet very appropriate for the considered problem. We believe that these results open many fascinating directions for future work. Among them, it is important to relax the common assumption of large demand that exceeds resource availability for the users (considered also in [4], [34], [26], [16], [17], [20], [7]), and provide a formal proof for the convergence of the dynamic asynchronous user interaction model.

Acknowledgements

This research has been co-financed by the European Union (European Social Fund - ESF) and Greek national funds through the Operational Program "Education and Lifelong Learning" of the National Strategic Reference Framework (NSRF) - Research Funding Program: Thales, Investing in knowledge society through the European Social Fund, for the project SOCONET.

9. REFERENCES

[1] N. Andelman, M. Feldman, Y. Mansour, "Strong Price of Anarchy", *in Proc. of ACM SODA*, 2007.

[2] R. Anderson, I. Ashlagi, D. Gamarnik, and Y. Kanoria, "A Dynamic Model of Barter Exachange", *in Proc. of ACM SODA*, 2015.

[3] K. Arrow, and G. Debreu, "Existence of an Equilibrium for a Competitive Economy", *Econom.*, 22(3), 1954.

[4] C. Aperjis, R. Johari, and M. Freedman, "Bilateral and Multilateral Exchanges for Peer-Assisted Content Distribution", *IEEE/ACM Tran. on Netw.*, 19(5), 2011.

[5] L. Buttyan, J. Hubaux, "Stimulating Cooperation in Self-organizing Mobile Ad Hoc Networks", *ACM J. Mobile Networks*, vol. 8, 2003.

[6] EU FP7 Project Confine, "A Case for Research with and on Community Networks", *ACM CCR*, July 2013.

[7] E. C. Efstathiou, P. A. Frangoudis, G. C. Polyzos, "Controlled Wi-Fi Sharing in Cities: A Decentralized Approach Relying on Indirect Reciprocity", *IEEE Trans. on Mob. Comp.*, 9(8), 2010.

[8] M. Felson, and J. L. Spaeth, "Community Structure and Collaborative Consumption", *Amer. Behav. Sc.*, 1978.

[9] FON, 2007, www.fon.com.

[10] L. Georgiadis, P. Georgatsos, K. Floros, and S. Sartzetakis, "Lexicographically Optimal Balanced Networks", *IEEE/ACM Transactions on Networking*, vol. 10, no. 5, 2002.

[11] L. Georgiadis, G. Iosifidis, and L. Tassiulas, "Dynamic Algorithms for Cooperation in User-provided Network Services", *in Proc. of NetGCoop*, 2014.

[12] GetRidApp, http://getridapp.com/.

[13] P. Herings, G. V. Laan, and D. Talman, "Cooperative Games in Graph Structure", *Res. Memoranda, Maastricht*, vol. 3, no. 11, 2002.

[14] HomeExchange, www.homeexchange.com

[15] M. Jackson, and A. Wolinsky, "A Strategic Model of Social and Economic Networks", *Journal of Econ. Th.*, 71(1), 1996.

[16] S. Kakade, M. Kearns, and L. Ortiz, "Graphical Economics", *in Springer Conf. on Learning*, 2004.

[17] S. Kakade, M. Kearns, L. Ortiz, R. Pemantle, S. Suri, "Economic Properties of Social Networks", *Advances in NIPS*, 2004.

[18] A. Mas-Colell, M. D. Whinston, J. R. Green, "Microeconomic Theory", *Oxford Un. Press*, 1995.

[19] V. Misra, S. Ioannidis, A. Chaintreau, and L. Massoulie, "Incentivizing Peer-assisted Services: A Shapley Value Approach", *ACM Sigmetrics*, 2010.

[20] R. Myerson, "Game Theory: Analysis of Conflict", *Harvard Press*, 1997.

[21] D. Nace, and M. Pioro, "Max-Min Fairness and Its Applications to Routing and Load-Balancing in Communication Networks: A Tutorial", *IEEE Comm. Surveys and Tutorials*, vol. 10, no. 4, 2008.

[22] Neighborgoods, http://neighborgoods.net/.

[23] NY Times, "It's Not Just Nice to Share, It's the Future", Jun. 2013.

[24] Open Garden, 2013, http://opengarden.com/.

[25] M. J. Osborne, A. Rubinstein, "A Cource in Game Theory", *MIT Press*, 1994.

[26] W. Saad, Z. Han, and V. H. Poor, "Coalitional Game Theory for Cooperative Micro-Grid Distribution Networks", *in Proc. of IEEE ICC*, 2011.

[27] L. Shapley, and H. Scarf, "On Cores and Indivisibility", *Journal of Math. Econ.*, vol. 1, 1974.

[28] Swap, www.swap.com

[29] R. Sofia, and P. Mendes, "User-Provided Networks: Consumer as Provider", *IEEE Comm. Mag.*, 46(12), 2008.

[30] T. Sonmez, and M. U. Unver, "Matching, Allocation, and Exchange of Discrete Resources", *in Handbook of Social Economics*, vol. 1A, 2011, pp. 781-852.
[31] Telefonica BeWiFi, 2014, http://www.bewifi.es/
[32] B. Radunovic, and J. Y. Le Boudec, "A Uunified Framework for Max-min and Min-max Fairness with Applications", *IEEE/ACM Trans. on Net.*, 15(5), 2007.
[33] Y. Wang, and A. Krishna, "Timeshare Exchange Mechanisms", *Management Science*, vol. 52, no. 8, 2006, pp. 1223-1237.
[34] F. Wu, and L. Zhang, "Proportional Response Dynamics Leads to Market Equilibrium", *in Proc. of IEEE FOCS*, 2010.
[35] F. Wu, T. Chen, S. Zhong, L. E. Li, and Y. R. Yang, "Incentive-Compatible Opportunistic Routing for Wireless Networks", *in Proc. of ACM Mobicom*, 2008.
[36] L. Georgiadis, G. Iosifidis, and L. Tassiulas, "Exchange of Services in Networks: Competition, Cooperation, and Fairness", *Online at arXiv*, http://arxiv.org/abs/1504.02052, 2015.

Appendix

We provide the additional proofs for the theorems and the lemmas. Due to lack of space, we very kindly request the reader to access the online technical report [36] for some more proofs related to Section 4.1.

Proof of Theorem 5

We begin with **(i)**. Let $\bar{\boldsymbol{d}}$ be a lex-optimal allocation. Starting from $\bar{\boldsymbol{d}}$ we will construct $\boldsymbol{d}$ by a sequence of link resource reallocations. Notice that for any allocation $\hat{\boldsymbol{d}}$, it holds:

$$\hat{r}_i = \hat{l}_{\hat{k}(i)} D_i = \sum_{j\in\mathcal{N}_i} \left(\hat{l}_{\hat{k}(i)} \hat{d}_{ij}\right) = \sum_{j\in\mathcal{N}_i} \hat{d}_{ji} \quad (31)$$

where the first equality is by definition of $\hat{l}_{\hat{k}(i)}$, the second by (1), and the last by definition of r_i. Hence under any allocation $\hat{\boldsymbol{d}}$ we have the following fact.

$$\begin{aligned} &\hat{l}_{\hat{k}(i)}\hat{d}_{ij_1} > \hat{d}_{j_1 i} \text{ for some } j_1 \in \mathcal{N}_i, \\ &\text{iff } \hat{l}_{k(i)}\hat{d}_{ij_2} < \hat{d}_{j_2 i} \text{ for another } j_2 \in \mathcal{N}_i. \end{aligned} \quad (32)$$

Let $\mathcal{Y}_0$ be the set of links (i,j) for which it holds $\bar{l}_{\bar{k}(i)}\bar{d}_{ij} > \bar{d}_{ji}$. If $\mathcal{Y}_0$ is nonempty, we will show that we can reallocate resource so that under the new allocaton $\boldsymbol{d}_1$, the resources the nodes receive remain the same, while for at least one of the links (i,j) in $\mathcal{Y}_0$ it holds, $\bar{l}_{\bar{k}(i)}\bar{d}_{ij} = \bar{d}_{ji}$ while the rest of the inequalities still hold in their original direction. Hence the new allocation $\boldsymbol{d}_1$ is also lex-optimal, while $\mathcal{Y}_1 = \mathcal{Y}_0 - \{(i,j)\}$. Proceeding in this manner we will arrive at an allocation $\boldsymbol{d}$ which is still lex-optimal but for which $\mathcal{Y} = \emptyset$. Based on (32) we will then conclude that the last allocation satisfies

$$d^*_{ji}/d^*_{ij} = r^*_i/D_i = l^*_{k(i)},\ j \in \mathcal{N}_i, \quad (33)$$

as stated in **(i)**. Also, let (i_1, i_0) be a link such $\bar{l}_{\bar{k}(i_1)}\bar{d}_{i_1 i_0} > \bar{d}_{i_0 i_1} \geq 0$ (hence $\bar{l}_{\bar{k}(i_1)} > 0$). Then according to (32) there must be a link (i_1, i_2) such that $\bar{l}_{\bar{k}(i_1)}\bar{d}_{i_1 i_2} < \bar{d}_{i_2 i_1}$ or

$$\frac{1}{\bar{l}_{\bar{k}(i_1)}}\bar{d}_{i_2 i_1} > \bar{d}_{i_1 i_2} \geq 0.$$

But due to lex optimality of $\bar{\boldsymbol{d}}$, we conclude from Corollary 2 Property 4 that $\bar{l}_{\bar{k}(i_2)} = \left(1/\bar{l}_{\bar{k}(i_1)}\right)$ and hence the above becomes $\bar{l}_{\bar{k}(i_2)}\bar{d}_{i_2 i_1} > \bar{d}_{i_1 i_2}$. Repeating this procedure we find a sequence of links (i_m, i_{m-1}), $m = 1, 2, ..$ for which it holds:

$$\bar{l}_{\bar{k}(i_m)}\bar{d}_{i_m i_{m-1}} > \bar{d}_{i_{m-1} i_m}. \quad (34)$$

Since the number of nodes is finite, we will eventually find a simple (no repeated nodes) cycle that satisfies (34). For all nodes $m = 1, 2, ..M$ on this cycle, subtract resource δ from $\bar{d}_{i_m i_{m-1}}$ and increase by δ the resource $\bar{d}_{i_m i_{m+1}}$. In addition, we require that the following relation must be satisfied for all nodes m on the cycle,

$$\bar{l}_{i_m}(\bar{d}_{i_m i_{m-1}} - \delta) \geq \bar{d}_{i_{m-1} i_m} + \delta,\ m = 1, 2, ..., M, \text{ or} \quad (35)$$

$$0 < \delta \leq \frac{\bar{l}_{i_m}\bar{d}_{i_m i_{m-1}} - \bar{d}_{i_{m-1} i_m}}{\bar{l}_{i_m} + 1},\ m = 1, 2, ..., M$$

This choice of δ ensures that the increase-decrease of resource allocation gives a new allocation and that with the new allocation inequalities (34) either still hold in their original direction or become equalities Since we have a cycle, this increase-decrease does not alter the resource the nodes of the cycle get. Since the resources of the rest of the nodes in the network are not changed, the resulting allocation is still lex-optimal. We now pick

$$\delta_1 = \max_m \left\{\frac{\bar{l}_{i_m}\bar{d}_{i_m i_{m-1}} - \bar{d}_{i_{m-1} i_m}}{\bar{l}_{i_m} + 1}\right\} > 0.$$

This choice ensures that at least one of the inequalities (34) become equality for some node in the cycle as desired.

Next we prove **(ii)**. First, we need a useful result: if an allocation $\boldsymbol{d}$ satisfies $d^*_{ji} = d^*_{ij} l^*_{k(i)}$, $j \in \mathcal{N}_i$, then for any node $j \in \mathcal{D}_i$ it holds:

$$l_{k(j)} > 0, \text{ and } l_{k(j)} = 1/l_{k(i)} \quad (36)$$

To see this, note that since $j \in \mathcal{D}_i$, by definition $d_{ij} > 0$, hence $l_{k(j)} = (r_j/D_j) \geq (d_{ij}/D_j) > 0$ and since by assumption

$$d_{ij} = l_{k(j)} d_{ji}, \quad (37)$$

it also holds $d_{ji} > 0$. Next, since by assumption

$$d_{ji} = l_{k(i)} d_{ij}, \quad (38)$$

multiplying (37) (38) and canceling (the nonzero) terms we have $l_{k_i} l_{k_j} = 1$. Therefore (37) holds.

Now, notice first that any node i gives resource to at least one node j, hence $d_{ij} > 0$. Therefore, it follows from eq. (36) that $l_1 > 0$. If under allocation $\boldsymbol{d}$ there is only one level, i.e., $K = 1$, then by Proposition 4, it is lex-optimal. Hence we concentrate on the case $K \geq 2$. We will show that allocation $\boldsymbol{d}$ satisfies the properties of Theorem 1 and hence, by Theorem 2, it is lex-optimal.

Consider first $k = 1$. The nodes in $\mathcal{L}_1$ constitute an independent set. To see this note that $d_{ij} = 0$ for all links (i,j) with $i, j \in \mathcal{L}_1$ since otherwise (i.e., $d_{ij} > 0$) by eq. (36), and the fact that $l_{k(1)} = l_{k(2)} = l_1$ it will follow that $l_1 = 1$, which contradicts Lemma 3. Hence all nodes in $\mathcal{L}_1$ give their resource to nodes in higher layers. Using again eq. (36), we conclude that all nodes in $\mathcal{L}_1$ give resource to nodes at level with value $1/l_1$. Now, if there is a link $(i,j) \in \mathcal{E}$ with $i, j \in \mathcal{L}_1$ then since $d_{ij} = 0$, the condition in **(i)**, i.e., "the neighbors not receiving resource from i have higher exchange ratio" (which holds according to Lemma 1), implies that $l_{k(j)} \geq 1/l_1$ and since $l_{k(j)} = l_1$, we conclude

$l_1 \geq 1$, a contradiction. Hence Item 1 of Theorem 1 holds for $k = 1$.

Consider now the nodes in $\mathcal{N}(\mathcal{L}_1)$. Nodes in $\mathcal{N}(\mathcal{L}_1)$ give resource only to nodes in $\mathcal{L}_1$. To see this, note that if node $j \in \mathcal{N}(\mathcal{L}_1)$ were giving resource to a node $i \notin \mathcal{L}_1$, then, since there are neighbors of j in $\mathcal{L}_1$ by a similar reasoning ("the neighbors not receiving resource from i have higher exchange ratio", Lemma 1), it would hold $l_1 \geq l_{k(i)}$, i.e., $l_1 = l_{k(i)}$, which contradicts the fact that $i \notin \mathcal{L}_1$. Since all nodes in $\mathcal{N}(\mathcal{L}_1)$ give resource to nodes in $\mathcal{L}_1$ it follows from (36) that all nodes in $\mathcal{N}(\mathcal{L}_1)$ are at the same level and $l_{k(\mathcal{N}(\mathcal{L}_1))} = 1/l_1$.

We claim now that for any node $i \in \mathcal{N} - \mathcal{N}(\mathcal{L}_1)$ it holds, $l_{k(i)} < l_{k(\mathcal{N}(\mathcal{L}_1))}$ which implies that $\mathcal{L}_K = \mathcal{N}(\mathcal{L}_1)$ and hence Item 2 of Theorem 1 holds for $k = 1$. Indeed, assume that $l_{k(i)} \geq l_{k(\mathcal{N}(\mathcal{L}_1))} = 1/l_1$. Then since node i gives resource to at least another neighbor node j, by (36) we would have $l_{k(j)} = \left(1/l_{k(i)}\right) \leq l_1$ hence $l_{k(j)} = l_1$, i.e., $j \in \mathcal{L}_1$ which contradicts the fact that $i \in \mathcal{N} - \mathcal{N}(\mathcal{L}_1)$.

The fact that Item 3 of Theorem 1 holds for $k = 1$, follows again from (36). Also, Item 4 of Theorem 1 holds since as shown above, all nodes in $\mathcal{L}_1 = \mathcal{N}(\mathcal{L}_1)$ give their resource to nodes in $\mathcal{L}_1$. If $K = 2$, the lex- optimality of $\boldsymbol{d}$ follows from Theorem 2. Consider next $K \geq 3$. According to Lemma 12, it holds

$$\mathrm{In}\left(\mathcal{L}_k \cup \mathcal{L}_{K-k+1}\right) = \mathrm{Out}\left(\mathcal{L}_k \cup \mathcal{L}_{K-k+1}\right) = 0,$$

hence the restriction of $\boldsymbol{d}$ on $\mathcal{Q}_2$, $\boldsymbol{d}_{\mathcal{Q}_2}$ constitutes an allocation on $G_{\mathcal{Q}_2}$with $K_{\mathcal{Q}_2} = K - 2$ levels. Moreover, since no nodes at levels $\mathcal{L}_1$ and $\mathcal{L}_K$ are in $\mathcal{Q}_2$, we have $\mathcal{L}_{\mathcal{Q}_2,1} = \mathcal{L}_2$, and $\mathcal{L}_{\mathcal{Q}_2,K_{\mathcal{Q}_2}} = \mathcal{L}_{K-1}$. Also, (36) and **(ii)** continue to hold for $\boldsymbol{d}_{\mathcal{Q}_2}$ on $G_{\mathcal{Q}_2}$. If $K = 3$, then we have $K_{\mathcal{Q}_2} = 1$, hence Item of Theorem 1 holds. If $K \geq 4$, we can apply now the arguments we used for $k = 1$ to show that Items 1-4 hold for $k = 2$. Proceeding iteratively we show that all properties in Theorem 1 hold for $\boldsymbol{d}$ and hence it is lex-optimal.

PROOF of Theorem 2

Before proving Theorem 2, we need the following lemma.

Lemma 12. If an allocation $\boldsymbol{d}$ with $K \geq 2$ satisfies Properties 1- 4 of Theorem 1, it holds for $k = 1, ..., \lfloor K/2 \rfloor$:

$$\mathrm{In}\left(\mathcal{L}_k \cup \mathcal{L}_{K-k+1}\right) = \mathrm{Out}\left(\mathcal{L}_k \cup \mathcal{L}_{K-k+1}\right) = 0. \quad (39)$$

Proof. Let $k = 1$. Since by Property 1 of Theorem 1 the set $\mathcal{L}_1$ is independent, we have $\sum_{i\in\mathcal{L}_1} r_i = \mathrm{In}(\mathcal{L}_1)$. Also, since only nodes in $\mathcal{N}_{Q_1}(\mathcal{L}_1) = \mathcal{N}(\mathcal{L}_1) = \mathcal{L}_K$ may have links with nodes in $(\mathcal{L}_1 \cup \mathcal{L}_K)^c$, we have $\mathrm{Out}(\mathcal{L}_K) = \mathrm{Out}(\mathcal{L}_1 \cup \mathcal{L}_K) + \mathrm{In}(\mathcal{L}_1)$, and hence:

$$\sum_{i\in\mathcal{L}_K} D_i \geq \mathrm{Out}(\mathcal{L}_K) = \mathrm{Out}(\mathcal{L}_1 \cup \mathcal{L}_K) + \mathrm{In}(\mathcal{L}_1)$$
$$= \mathrm{Out}(\mathcal{L}_1 \cup \mathcal{L}_K) + \sum_{i\in\mathcal{L}_1} r_i = \mathrm{Out}(\mathcal{L}_1 \cup \mathcal{L}_K) + \sum_{i\in\mathcal{L}_K} D_i,$$

where the last equality is due to Property 4 of Th. 1. The last equality implies that $\mathrm{Out}(\mathcal{L}_1 \cup \mathcal{L}_K) = 0$ and:

$$\mathrm{Out}(\mathcal{L}_K) = \sum_{i\in\mathcal{L}_K} D_i. \quad (40)$$

Next, we have for the nodes in $\mathcal{L}_K$:

$$\sum_{i\in\mathcal{L}_K} r_i + \mathrm{Out}(\mathcal{L}_K) = \sum_{\mathcal{L}_K} D_i + \mathrm{In}(\mathcal{L}_K)$$

Since by independence of $\mathcal{L}_1$ it holds:

$$\mathrm{In}(\mathcal{L}_K) = \sum_{i\in\mathcal{L}_1} D_i + \mathrm{In}(\mathcal{L}_1 \cup \mathcal{L}_K),$$

and taking into account (40), we conclude from (5):

$$\sum_{i\in\mathcal{L}_K} r_i = \sum_{i\in\mathcal{L}_1} D_i + \mathrm{In}(\mathcal{L}_k \cup \mathcal{L}_K), \quad (41)$$

or since $r_i = l_K D_i$, $i \in \mathcal{L}_K$, it is:

$$l_K \sum_{i\in\mathcal{L}_K} D_i = \sum_{i\in\mathcal{L}_1} D_i + \mathrm{In}\left(\mathcal{L}_k \cup \mathcal{N}_{Q_k}(\mathcal{L}_k)\right).$$

Similarly, from the equality in Property 4 we have

$$l_1 \sum_{i\in\mathcal{L}_1} D_i = \sum_{i\in\mathcal{L}_K} D_i. \quad (42)$$

Multiplying the last two equalities and rearranging terms we get:

$$l_1 l_K = 1 + \frac{\mathrm{In}(\mathcal{L}_1 \cup \mathcal{L}_K)}{\left(\sum_{i\in\mathcal{L}_1} D_i\right)\left(\sum_{i\in\mathcal{L}_K} r_i\right)}. \quad (43)$$

But since by Item 3 of Theorem 1 it hold $l_1 l_K = 1$, we conclude that $\mathrm{In}(\mathcal{L}_1 \cup \mathcal{L}_K) = 0$.

Hence, if $K \in \{2, 3\}$ the lemma holds. Next, assume $K \geq 4$ and observe that since (39) holds for $k = 1$, the restriction $\boldsymbol{d}_{\mathcal{Q}_2}$ of $\boldsymbol{d}$ to $\mathcal{Q}_2$ is an allocation on $\mathcal{Q}_2$ with $K - 2$ levels and by construction $\mathcal{L}_{\mathcal{Q}_2,1} = \mathcal{L}_2$, $\mathcal{L}_{\mathcal{Q}_2,K-2} = \mathcal{L}_{K-1} = \mathcal{L}_{K-2+1}$. Therefore, we can repeat the arguments above for $k = 2$ and inductively show that the lemma holds for $k = 1, ..., \lfloor K^*/2 \rfloor$. □

Proof of Theorem 2: For $k = 1$, since by Properties 1 and 4 of Theorem 1 $\mathcal{L}_1$ is an independent set and $\sum_{i\in\mathcal{L}_1} r_1^* = \sum_{i\in\mathcal{N}(\mathcal{L}_1)} D_i$, it follows from Lemma 11 that $\mathcal{L}_1^* = \mathcal{L}_1$ and $l_1^* = l_1$. Also, by Properties 2, 3 of Theorem 1 we have $l_K = l_{K^*}^*$ and $\mathcal{L}_K = \mathcal{N}(\mathcal{L}_1) = \mathcal{N}(\mathcal{L}_1^*) = \mathcal{L}_{K^*}^*$, where the last equality follows from Proposition 10. If $K = 2$, then since $\mathcal{N} = \mathcal{L}_1 \cup \mathcal{L}_2 = \mathcal{L}_1^* \cup \mathcal{L}_{K^*}^*$ we have necessarily $K^* = 2$ and we conclude that $\boldsymbol{d}$ is lex-optimal. Assume now that $K = 3$. From Proposition 10 we then have $\mathrm{In}(\mathcal{L}_1 \cup \mathcal{L}_3) = \mathrm{Out}(\mathcal{L}_2 \cup \mathcal{L}_3) = 0$. Hence the restriction $\boldsymbol{d}_{\mathcal{Q}_2}$ is an allocation on $G_{\mathcal{Q}_2}$ with $K_{\mathcal{Q}_2} = 1$. It follows by Proposition 4 that $\boldsymbol{d}_{\mathcal{Q}_2}$ is lex-optimal in $G_{\mathcal{Q}_2}$ and $l_2 = 1$. This implies that any lex-optimal allocation allocation on $G_{\mathcal{Q}_2}$ has $K_{\mathcal{Q}_2}^* = 1$ and $l_2^* = 1$. We then conclude that $K^* = 3$ and arguing as in the case $K = 2$, that $\boldsymbol{d}$ is lex-optimal.

We will use induction to show the Theorem for allocations $\boldsymbol{d}$ with arbitray K. Assume that the theorem holds for allocation with up to $K - 1$, $K \geq 4$ levels and let next $K \geq 4$. By (22), the vector $\boldsymbol{d}_{\mathcal{Q}_2}$ constitutes an allocation on graph $G_{\mathcal{Q}_2}$. Since this allocation has $K - 2$ levels we can apply the inductive hypothesis to conclude that the allocation $\boldsymbol{d}_{\mathcal{Q}_2}$ is lex-optimal in $G_{\mathcal{Q}_2}$. But the same holds for the restriction $\hat{\boldsymbol{d}}_{\mathcal{Q}_2}$ to $G_{\mathcal{Q}_2}$, of any lex-optimal allocation $\hat{\boldsymbol{d}}$. By uniqueness of lex optimality we conclude that all levels l_k, level sets $\mathcal{L}_k$ and received resource r_i of $\boldsymbol{d}_{\mathcal{Q}_2}$ for $k = 2, ..., K - 1$ are identical to those of any lex-optimal allocation. It follows that $K = K^*$ and we already showed that $\mathcal{L}_1^* = \mathcal{L}_1$, $l_1 = l_1^*$ $\mathcal{L}_K = \mathcal{L}_{K^*}^*$, and $l_K = l_{K^*}^*$. The lex-optimality of $\boldsymbol{d}$ follows.

Whittle Index Approach to Size-aware Scheduling with Time-varying Channels

Samuli Aalto
Aalto University, Finland
samuli.aalto@aalto.fi

Pasi Lassila
Aalto University, Finland
pasi.lassila@aalto.fi

Prajwal Osti
Aalto University, Finland
prajwal.osti@aalto.fi

ABSTRACT

We consider the optimal opportunistic scheduling problem for downlink data traffic in a wireless cell with time-varying channels. The scheduler itself operates in a very fast timescale of milliseconds, but the objective function is related to minimizing the holding costs in a much longer timescale, at the so-called flow level. The Whittle index approach is a powerful tool in this context, since it renders the flow-level optimization problem with heterogeneous users tractable. Until now, this approach has been applied to the opportunistic scheduling problem to generate non-anticipating index policies that may depend on the amount of attained service but do not utilize the exact size information. In this paper, we produce a size-aware (i.e., anticipating) index policy by applying the Whittle index approach in a novel way. By a numerical study based on simulations, we demonstrate that the resulting size-aware index policy systematically improves performance. As a side result, we show that the opportunistic scheduling problem is indexable when the file sizes follow the Pascal distribution, and we derive the corresponding Whittle index, which generalizes earlier results.

Categories and Subject Descriptors

C.4 [**Performance of Systems**]: Performance attributes; F.2.2 [**Nonnumerical Algorithms and Problems**]: Sequencing and scheduling; C.2.1 [**Network Architecture and Design**]: Wireless communication

Keywords

opportunistic scheduling, size-based scheduling, Whittle index, stochastic optimization

1. INTRODUCTION

Channel-aware (a.k.a. opportunistic) schedulers for wireless systems may improve the system capacity substantially by utilizing the channel variations in the users' radio access. The pioneering work was already done in [15], and probably the best known opportunistic scheduler implemented in real systems is the *Proportionally Fair* (PF) scheduler [6, 13].

SIGMETRICS'15, June 15–19, 2015, Portland, OR, USA.

http://dx.doi.org/10.1145/2745844.2745851.

In this paper, we consider the optimal opportunistic scheduling problem for downlink data traffic in a wireless cell with time-varying channels. The scheduler itself operates in a very fast timescale of milliseconds, but the objective function is related to minimizing the holding costs at the flow level, e.g., the mean downloading time of a digital document (file).

The problem itself is tricky: there is no exact optimal solution for the dynamic version of the problem when the number of users varies randomly. Even the corresponding static problem, where there is a finite number of users (each with its own file to be downloaded) but no new arrivals, is challenging. A promising approach is to utilize the *Whittle index* originally developed in the context of restless multi-armed bandits [23]. The key idea is to first relax the strict requirement that the scheduler should serve (at most) one user in each timeslot and replace it by a looser one that this should be the case only in the long run, i.e., the scheduler should serve, on average, at most one user per timeslot. In this way, the scheduling problem becomes *separable*, which allows one to calculate an index value for each user separately. By computing the index values in each timeslot and always scheduling the user with the highest index gives a good heuristic policy for the original, more constrained scheduling problem, even in a dynamic and heterogeneous setting with new arrivals and heterogeneous users.

The Whittle index approach for the opportunistic scheduling problem has recently been utilized in a series of papers. The problem is shown to be indexable for geometric file sizes and i.i.d. (independent and identically distributed) channel variations, and the corresponding Whittle index is derived in [4]. The resulting scheduling rule for the original problem is called *Potential Improvement* (PI). The result is generalized for Markovian channel models that allow two different channel states in [12]. Markovian channel models with multiple channels states are considered in [10]. However, in this case, the authors are no longer able to prove that the problem is indexable, but they are still able to generate good approximative index policies. While in all three papers mentioned above the file sizes are assumed to be geometric, two very recent papers ([19, 20]) apply the Whittle index approach to the opportunistic scheduling problem with general file size distributions but restricting themselves to i.i.d. channel variations. In [19], it is assumed that there are only two different channel states, and the more general case with multiple channel states is considered in [20]. Again, the authors are not able to prove that the problem is indexable, but they are able to generate good approximative index policies. For general file size distributions, the index values are dependent on the amount of attained service (i.e., the number of bits that have already been downloaded). In [20], the authors define such an approximative index policy called *Attained Service dependent Potential Improvement* (ASPI).

Another approach for the opportunistic scheduling problem utilizes so-called *timescale separation*, which is based on the idea that the downloading times are typically much longer than the timeslots of the scheduler, see, e.g., [8, 9, 7]. In this approach, the scheduling decisions are made in a much longer timescale (at the flow level) by choosing the current service rate vector from the set of achievable rate vectors, called the capacity region. For *homogeneous users* (with the same model for channel variations), it is sometimes possible to solve the static version of the flow-level scheduling problem (with a finite number of users in the beginning but no new arrivals) as demonstrated in [17, 2, 3]. However, the general case with *heterogeneous users* has remained intractable in this approach.

The stability of opportunistic schedulers at the flow level in the dynamic system with randomly varying number of users have been studied in [1, 5, 14]. Assuming time-scale separation, it has been heuristically justified first in [1] that all schedulers that give the highest priority for the users whose channel state is the best possible among the states that are available for that user are maximally stable. This result has been formally proven without the time-scale separation for i.i.d. arrivals, geometric file sizes, and i.i.d. channel variations in [5]. In [14], the result is generalized to Markovian channel models. Interestingly, e.g., the well-known *MaxWeight* scheduler [21], which has many nice properties if the flow-level variations are not taken into account, is not necessarily stable at the flow level [22]. On the other hand, it is shown in [9] that PF and many other so-called utility-based scheduling policies are maximally stable in this context.

Power of the Whittle index approach is that it renders the flow-level optimization problem with heterogeneous users tractable. Until now, this approach has been applied to the opportunistic scheduling problem to generate *non-anticipating* index policies that may depend on the amount of attained service but do not utilize the exact size information. In this paper, to further improve the performance, our aim is to produce a *size-aware* (i.e., anticipating) index policy by applying the Whittle index approach in a novel way. The trick needed is to approximate the exact size by a (shifted) Pascal distribution. Since a Pascal random variable can be constructed from a finite series of i.i.d. geometric phases, we call this a *phase-type* approximation.

Our main contributions in this paper are as follows: *(i)* We show that the opportunistic scheduling problem is indexable under the assumptions that the file sizes follow the (shifted) Pascal distribution and the channel variations are i.i.d. with two possible rate values for each user, and we derive the corresponding Whittle index, which generalizes the results of [4]. *(ii)* By approximating a deterministic value with the (shifted) Pascal distribution, we are able to determine a size-aware Whittle index, which is a novel result. *(iii)* The resulting size-aware index policy is proved to be maximally stable for geometric file sizes. *(iv)* If the channel variations are so negligible that they can be ignored and the holding cost rates are equal for all users, the resulting size-aware index policy is shown to be even optimal (and not only a good heuristic). *(v)* By a numerical study based on simulations, we demonstrate that the resulting size-aware index policy gives systematically better performance than PF, PI, and ASPI.

The paper is organized as follows. In Section 2, we formulate the size-aware opportunistic scheduling problem. Our approach to solve this problem by a phase-type approximation is then described in Section 3. In Section 4, we present the relaxed version of the problem. The relaxed problem is shown to be indexable in this context, and the corresponding Whittle index is derived in Section 5. A secondary index for tie-breaking purposes is derived in Section 6. In Section 7, we return to the original problem and define a size-aware Whittle index policy, the performance of which is evaluated by simulations in Section 8. Section 9 concludes the paper.

2. THE SIZE-AWARE OPPORTUNISTIC SCHEDULING PROBLEM

Consider the following discrete time scheduling problem. We measure time in *timeslots*[1] indexed with $t = 0, 1, \ldots$. At time 0 (i.e., in the beginning of the first timeslot), there are K *jobs*[2] indexed with $i \in \{1, \ldots, K\}$. For any timeslot t, the scheduler chooses one of the (uncompleted) jobs for service according to some scheduling policy π. Let $A_i^\pi(t) = 1$ if job i is chosen in timeslot t under policy π; otherwise $A_i^\pi(t) = 0$. Thus, for any policy π and timeslot t, we have the constraint[3]

$$\sum_{i=1}^{K} A_i^\pi(t) \le 1. \tag{1}$$

Let x_i denote the original size (i.e, the number of bits to be transmitted totally) of job i. In addition, let $Y_i^\pi(t)$ denote the remaining size of job i in the beginning of timeslot t when policy π is applied. For any π and i,

$$Y_i^\pi(0) = x_i.$$

We assume that the scheduling policies may utilize this size information, i.e., policy π is aware of the remaining sizes $\{Y_1^\pi(t), \ldots, Y_K^\pi(t)\}$.

The actual service time of job i is not only depending on its size x_i but also on the channel state process $R_i(t)$ and the scheduling policy π applied. Channel state $r \ge 1$ refers to the amount of service given (i.e., the number of bits transmitted) during one timeslot. Thus, if job i with remaining size of y_i is scheduled at time t and $R_i(t) = r$, its service is completed if and only if $y_i \le r$. We assume that, for each job i, there are two different channel states $r_{i,1}$ ("bad") and $r_{i,2}$ ("good") with

$$r_{i,1} < r_{i,2}, \tag{2}$$

[1]The length of the timeslot in current wireless cellular systems is of the order of 1 ms.

[2]The generic term job refers to the file to be downloaded by some user.

[3]In fact, we could, as well, have used a constraint, where 1 on the right hand side of (1) is replaced by any $M \in \{1, 2, \ldots\}$ as, e.g., in [12], and still we would have resulted in the exactly same size-aware Whittle index.

which are chosen independently in each timeslot t with probabilities

$$P\{R_i(t) = r_{i,1}\} = 1 - q_i, \quad P\{R_i(t) = r_{i,2}\} = q_i. \quad (3)$$

In addition, let $\bar{r}_i$ denote the mean value of the channel state,

$$\bar{r}_i = E[R_i(t)] = (1 - q_i)r_{i,1} + q_i r_{i,2}. \quad (4)$$

We assume that the scheduling policies may utilize this channel state information, i.e., policy π is aware of the channel states $\{R_1(t), \dots, R_K(t)\}$.

Note that, if policy $\pi_i(r)$ schedules job i only when the channel state is r, the service time of job i (i.e., the number of scheduled timeslots) under this policy is equal to

$$s^{\pi_i(r)} = \lceil x_i/r \rceil \approx x_i/r. \quad (5)$$

For any job i, holding costs are accrued with rate $c_i > 0$ until its service is completed. Thus, the expected total holding costs are as follows:

$$E\left[\sum_{t=0}^{\infty}\sum_{i=1}^{K} c_i 1_{\{Y_i^\pi(t)>0\}}\right], \quad (6)$$

where $Y_i^\pi(0) = x_i$, $P\{R_i(0) = r_{i,1}\} = 1-q_i$, and $P\{R_i(0) = r_{i,2}\} = q_i$ for all jobs i. The *original scheduling problem* is to find the optimal policy π that minimizes the expected total holding costs (6) subject to the capacity constraint (1) for all t.

3. PHASE-TYPE APPROXIMATION

Our approach to solve the original problem is based on an approximation where the deterministic size x_i is approximated by a discrete *phase type* distribution, which seems to be novel in this context.

For the approximation, we assume that the x_i's are so large that there is $J \in \{1, 2, \dots\}$ such that, for each i,

$$x_i > J r_{i,2}. \quad (7)$$

Denote by X_i a random variable comprised of J consecutive phases

$$X_i = X_{i,1} + \dots + X_{i,J}, \quad (8)$$

where each phase $X_{i,j}$ is independently and geometrically distributed with state space $\{1, 2 \dots\}$ and completion probability $p_i = J/x_i$,

$$P\{X_{i,j} = n\} = (1 - p_i)^{n-1}p_i, \quad E[X_{i,j}] = x_i/J.$$

Thus, $X_i - J$ obeys the Pascal distribution with parameters J and p_i so that, for any $n \in \{J, J+1, \dots\}$,

$$P\{X_i = n\} = \frac{(n-1)!}{(n-J)!(J-1)!}(1 - p_i)^{n-J}p_i^J, \quad (9)$$

which is referred to as the *shifted Pascal distribution* in this paper. Now

$$E[X_i] = x_i, \quad \frac{\mathrm{Var}[X_i]}{E[X_i]^2} = \frac{1}{J} - \frac{1}{x_i}.$$

Thus, if x_i and J are large, the relative variance (i.e., the squared coefficient of variation) of X_i is small, and the deterministic value x_i is reasonably approximated by the random variable X_i.

From this on until the end of Section 6, we consider jobs i with an initial random size X_i following the shifted Pascal distribution as defined in (9). The task is still to schedule one of the jobs in each timeslot (as long as there are uncompleted jobs). Instead of knowing the exact remaining size, we assume here that the scheduler is aware of the current phase of each job.

We take the random channel variations into account by modifying the phase completion probability according to the channel state. Thus, if job i is scheduled at time t and $R_i(t) = r$, its current phase is completed with probability $p_i r = Jr/x_i$. Naturally, if job i is not scheduled at time t, it completes its current phase with probability 0.

Thus, for policy $\pi_i(r)$, which schedules job i only when the channel state is r, the mean service time of job i is equal to

$$E[S_i^{\pi_i(r)}] = E[\lceil X_i/r \rceil] \approx x_i/r,$$

which is in line with (5). In addition, its relative variance is approximately the same as for X_i,

$$\frac{\mathrm{Var}[S_i^{\pi(r)}]}{E[S_i^{\pi(r)}]^2} \approx \frac{1}{J} - \frac{1}{x_i},$$

which is small if x_i and J are large.

Let $Z_i^\pi(t)$ refer to the number of *remaining* service phases of job i at time t. Thus, the service of job i is completed as soon as $Z_i^\pi(t) = 0$. At time $t = 0$, all the jobs are "fresh" so that $Z_i^\pi(0) = J$ for any policy π and job i. Note that the state of job i at time t under policy π is completely described by the pair $(Z_i^\pi(t), R_i(t))$. We assume that when making the scheduling decision at time t, the scheduler is aware of states $(Z_i^\pi(t), R_i(t))$ of all jobs $i = 1, \dots, K$.

For any job i, we still assume that the holding costs are accrued with rate c_i until the service is completed (i.e., all J phases have been completed). Thus, the expected total holding costs f^π under scheduling policy π are as follows:

$$f^\pi = E\left[\sum_{t=0}^{\infty}\sum_{i=1}^{K} c_i 1_{\{Z_i^\pi(t)>0\}}\right], \quad (10)$$

where $Z_i^\pi(0) = J$, $P\{R_i(0) = r_{i,1}\} = 1 - q_i$, and $P\{R_i(0) = r_{i,2}\} = q_i$ for all jobs i. The target is now to find the optimal policy π that minimizes the expected total holding costs (10) subject to the capacity constraint (1) for all t.

4. RELAXED OPPORTUNISTIC SCHEDULING PROBLEM

Our scheduling problem with objective function (10) belongs to the class of *restless multi-armed bandit* (RMAB) problems. To derive a heuristic solution for this kind of an RMAB problem, Whittle proposes to consider its relaxed version in his seminal work [23]. In the relaxed version, the strict capacity constraint of the scheduler (such as (1) in our problem) is replaced by an averaged one.

As also originally described in [23], the relaxed scheduling problem can be approached by the Lagrangian methods. In our case, the *Lagrangian version of the relaxed scheduling problem* is to find the optimal policy π that minimizes the following objective function:

$$f^\pi + \nu g^\pi, \quad (11)$$

where $\nu > 0$ can be interpreted as the unit price of work, the expected total costs f^π is given by (10), and the expected total amount of work g^π is as follows:

$$g^\pi = E\left[\sum_{t=0}^{\infty}\sum_{i=1}^{K} A_i^\pi(t)\right]. \tag{12}$$

Since

$$f^\pi + \nu g^\pi = \sum_{i=1}^{K}\left(E\left[\sum_{t=0}^{\infty} c_i 1_{\{Z_i^\pi(t)>0\}}\right] + \nu E\left[\sum_{t=0}^{\infty} A_i^\pi(t)\right]\right),$$

this problem is *separable*. Thus, for any i, we try to find the optimal policy π_i that minimizes the objective function

$$f_i^{\pi_i} + \nu g_i^{\pi_i}, \tag{13}$$

where

$$f_i^{\pi_i} = E\left[\sum_{t=0}^{\infty} c_i 1_{\{Z_i^{\pi_i}(t)>0\}}\right], \quad g_i^{\pi_i} = E\left[\sum_{t=0}^{\infty} A_i^{\pi_i}(t)\right].$$

The separable subproblems of the Lagrangian version of the relaxed scheduling problem can be considered in the context of *Markov decision processes*. Since the state space $\mathcal{S}_i$ and the action space $\mathcal{A}$,

$$\mathcal{S}_i = \{0,1,\ldots,J\} \times \{r_{i,1}, r_{i,2}\}, \quad \mathcal{A} = \{0,1\},$$

are finite, there is a stationary policy π_i^* (described by a function from the state space $\mathcal{S}_i$ to the action space $\mathcal{A}$) that minimizes (13), see, e.g., [16]. In addition, the optimal policy π_i^* is characterized by the following *optimality equations*:

$$\begin{aligned}
&v_i(0,r;\nu) = 0,\\
&v_i(j,r;\nu) = \min\{\\
&\quad c_i + (1-q_i)v_i(j,r_{i,1};\nu) + q_i v_i(j,r_{i,2};\nu),\\
&\quad c_i + \nu +\\
&\quad p_i r((1-q_i)v_i(j-1,r_{i,1};\nu) + q_i v_i(j-1,r_{i,2};\nu)) +\\
&\quad (1-p_i r)((1-q_i)v_i(j,r_{i,1};\nu) + q_i v_i(j,r_{i,2};\nu))\},\\
&\quad j = 1,\ldots,J,
\end{aligned} \tag{14}$$

where $v_i(j,r;\nu)$ denotes the optimal expected total costs (13) for the initial state (j,r),

$$v_i(j,r;\nu) = \min_{\pi_i} E_{j,r}\left[\sum_{t=0}^{\infty}(c_i 1_{\{Z_i^{\pi_i}(t)>0\}} + \nu A_i^{\pi_i}(t))\right], \tag{15}$$

where $j \in \{0,1,\ldots,J\}$, $r \in \{r_{i,1}, r_{i,2}\}$.

5. WHITTLE INDEX

In this section we show that the optimal solution for the relaxed opportunistic scheduling problem with objective function (13) can be characterized by the Whittle index, for which we have an explicit expression (Theorem 1). We start by giving an auxiliary result (Proposition 1), then define the indexability property, and finally prove the main result.

From the optimality equations (14), we see that, for any $j \in \{1,\ldots,J\}$ and $r \in \{r_{i,1}, r_{i,2}\}$, decision 0 (not to schedule job i) is optimal in state (j,r) if and only if

$$\nu \geq p_i r(\bar{v}_i(j;\nu) - \bar{v}_i(j-1;\nu)), \tag{16}$$

where we have defined

$$\bar{v}_i(j;\nu) = (1-q_i)v_i(j,r_{i,1};\nu) + q_i v_i(j,r_{i,2};\nu). \tag{17}$$

As it is easy to see from (16), the following result, saying essentially that the difference $\bar{v}_i(j;\nu) - \bar{v}_i(j-1;\nu)$ is the same for all j, will be crucial in the sequel.

PROPOSITION 1. *For any $j \in \{1,\ldots,J\}$,*

$$\bar{v}_i(j;\nu) - \bar{v}_i(j-1;\nu) = \begin{cases} \dfrac{c_i + q_i\nu}{p_i q_i r_{i,2}}, & \nu \geq \dfrac{c_i}{q_i(\frac{r_{i,2}}{r_{i,1}} - 1)};\\[2ex] \dfrac{c_i + \nu}{p_i \bar{r}_i}, & \nu < \dfrac{c_i}{q_i(\frac{r_{i,2}}{r_{i,1}} - 1)}. \end{cases} \tag{18}$$

PROOF. Let $j \in \{1,\ldots,J\}$. It follows from the optimality equations (14) that

$$\begin{aligned}
&\bar{v}_i(j;\nu) = c_i + \bar{v}_i(j;\nu) +\\
&\quad (1-q_i)\min\{0, \nu - p_i r_{i,1}(\bar{v}_i(j;\nu) - \bar{v}_i(j-1;\nu))\} +\\
&\quad q_i \min\{0, \nu - p_i r_{i,2}(\bar{v}_i(j;\nu) - \bar{v}_i(j-1;\nu))\},
\end{aligned}$$

which implies that the difference

$$\Delta_i(\nu) = \bar{v}_i(j;\nu) - \bar{v}_i(j-1;\nu).$$

does *not* depend on the phase index j and it satisfies the equation

$$\begin{aligned}
&c_i + (1-q_i)\min\{0, \nu - p_i r_{i,1}\Delta_i(\nu)\} +\\
&\quad q_i \min\{0, \nu - p_i r_{i,2}\Delta_i(\nu)\} = 0.
\end{aligned} \tag{19}$$

Below we show that this equation uniquely determines the function $\Delta_i(\nu)$ as given in (18).

1° Consider first the case $\nu - p_i r_{i,2}\Delta_i(\nu) \geq 0$. Since $r_{i,2} > r_{i,1}$, we also have $\nu - p_i r_{i,1}\Delta_i(\nu) \geq 0$, implying, by (19), that $c_i = 0$, which is a contradiction, since we have assumed that $c_i > 0$. Thus, we deduce that, for all ν,

$$\nu - p_i r_{i,2}\Delta_i(\nu) < 0.$$

2° Assume now that $\nu - p_i r_{i,1}\Delta_i(\nu) \geq 0$. From 1° and (19), it follows that

$$c_i + q_i(\nu - p_i r_{i,2}\Delta_i(\nu)) = 0.$$

Thus, in this case,

$$\Delta_i(\nu) = \frac{c_i + q_i\nu}{q_i p_i r_{i,2}}.$$

By requiring that $\nu - p_i r_{i,1}\Delta_i(\nu) \geq 0$ and applying the previous expression for $\Delta_i(\nu)$, we get the condition for its validity:

$$\nu \geq \frac{c_i}{q_i(\frac{r_{i,2}}{r_{i,1}} - 1)}.$$

3° Assume finally that $\nu - p_i r_{i,1}\Delta_i(\nu) < 0$. From 1° and (19), we easily get

$$\begin{aligned}
&c_i + (1-q_i)(\nu - p_i r_{i,2}\Delta_i(\nu)) + q_i(\nu - p_i r_{i,2}\Delta_i(\nu)) =\\
&\quad c_i + \nu - p_i \bar{r}_i \Delta_i(\nu) = 0,
\end{aligned}$$

which implies that

$$\Delta_i(\nu) = \frac{c_i + \nu}{p_i \bar{r}_i}.$$

By requiring that $\nu - p_i r_{i,1}\Delta_i(\nu) < 0$ and applying the previous expression for $\Delta_i(\nu)$, we get the condition for its validity:

$$\nu < \frac{c_i}{\frac{\bar{r}_i}{r_{i,1}} - 1} = \frac{c_i}{q_i(\frac{r_{i,2}}{r_{i,1}} - 1)},$$

which concludes the proof. □

DEFINITION 1. *We say that the optimization problem with objective function (13) is indexable if, for any $j \in \{1,\ldots,J\}$ and $r \in \{r_{i,1}, r_{i,2}\}$, there exists $\nu_i^*(j,r) \in [0,\infty]$ such that*

(i) it is optimal to schedule job i in state (j,r) if $\nu_i^*(j,r) \geq \nu$;

(ii) it is optimal not to schedule job i in state (j,r) if $\nu_i^*(j,r) \leq \nu$.

It is well-known that not all RMAB problems are indexable. However, our problem has this property as explicitly shown below.

THEOREM 1. *The optimization problem with objective function (13) is indexable, and the corresponding Whittle index is given by*

$$\nu_i^*(j,r_{i,1}) = \frac{c_i}{q_i(\frac{r_{i,2}}{r_{i,1}} - 1)}, \quad \nu_i^*(j,r_{i,2}) = \infty, \qquad (20)$$

for any $j \in \{1,\ldots,J\}$.

PROOF. 1° Let $j \in \{1,\ldots,J\}$ and consider first state $(j,r_{i,2})$. By (16), decision 0 (not to schedule job i) is optimal in state $(j,r_{i,2})$ if and only if

$$\nu \geq p_i r_{i,2}(\bar{v}_i(j;\nu) - \bar{v}_i(j-1;\nu)).$$

However, in part 1° of the proof of Proposition 1, we already concluded that this is never the case for any finite ν.

2° Consider now state $(j,r_{i,1})$. Again, by (16), decision 0 (not to schedule job i) is optimal in state $(j,r_{i,1})$ if and only if

$$\nu \geq p_i r_{i,1}(\bar{v}_i(j;\nu) - \bar{v}_i(j-1;\nu)).$$

From parts 2° and 3° of the proof of Proposition 1, we see that this condition is equivalent with

$$\nu \geq \frac{c_i}{q_i(\frac{r_{i,2}}{r_{i,1}} - 1)},$$

which concludes the proof. □

Remarks: Since $\nu_i^*(j,r_{i,2}) = \infty$, it is always optimal (for the relaxed optimization problem) to schedule job i when the channel state is the best possible. A natural secondary (tie-breaking) index to be applied in the original optimization problem among the jobs that have their best channel state is considered below in Section 6.

It is also interesting to observe that, for the bad channel state $r_{i,1}$, the Whittle index does not depend at all on the "size-related" parameters p_i and j nor directly on the absolute values of $r_{i,1}$ and $r_{i,2}$ of the channel model but just on their ratio $r_{i,2}/r_{i,1}$.

Finally we note that, for the geometric job size distribution (i.e., $J = 1$), the result of Theorem 1 originally appeared in [4].

6. SECONDARY INDEX

In order to derive a secondary index, we consider the discounted version of the separable relaxed problem. We prove that the problem is indexable, and we also derive an explicit expression for the corresponding Whittle index (Theorems 2 and 3). The discounted version proves to be technically more challenging. To justify the two main results, we need to derive a number of auxiliary results (Propositions 2-7) in this section. The secondary index itself is finally given in (46).

In the *discounted version* of the separable relaxed problem, the aim is to minimize, separately for any i, the objective function

$$f_{i,\beta}^{\pi_i} + \nu g_{i,\beta}^{\pi_i}, \qquad (21)$$

where $\beta \in (0,1)$ is the discount factor and

$$f_{i,\beta}^{\pi_i} = E\left[\sum_{t=0}^{\infty} \beta^t c_i 1_{\{Z_i^{\pi_i}(t)>0\}}\right], \quad g_{i,\beta}^{\pi_i} = E\left[\sum_{t=0}^{\infty} \beta^t A_i^{\pi_i}(t)\right].$$

Note that, according to our earlier notation,

$$\lim_{\beta\to 1} f_{i,\beta}^{\pi_i} = f_i^{\pi_i}, \quad \lim_{\beta\to 1} g_{i,\beta}^{\pi_i} = g_i^{\pi_i}.$$

This problem can also be considered in the context of Markov decision processes. Since the state space $\mathcal{S}_i$ and the action space $\mathcal{A}$,

$$\mathcal{S}_i = \{0,1,\ldots,J\} \times \{r_{i,1}, r_{i,2}\}, \quad \mathcal{A} = \{0,1\},$$

are finite, there is a stationary policy π_i^* that minimizes (21), see, e.g., [16]. In addition, the optimal policy π_i^* is characterized by the following *optimality equations*:

$$\begin{aligned}
&v_{i,\beta}(0,r;\nu) = 0,\\
&v_{i,\beta}(j,r;\nu) = \min\{\\
&\quad c_i + \beta((1-q_i)v_{i,\beta}(j,r_{i,1};\nu) + q_i v_{i,\beta}(j,r_{i,2};\nu)),\\
&\quad c_i + \nu +\\
&\quad \beta p_i r((1-q_i)v_{i,\beta}(j-1,r_{i,1};\nu) + q_i v_{i,\beta}(j-1,r_{i,2};\nu)) +\\
&\quad \beta(1-p_i r)((1-q_i)v_{i,\beta}(j,r_{i,1};\nu) + q_i v_{i,\beta}(j,r_{i,2};\nu))\},\\
&\quad j = 1,\ldots,J, \qquad (22)
\end{aligned}$$

where $v_{i,\beta}(j,r;\nu)$ denotes the optimal expected discounted costs for the initial state (j,r),

$$v_{i,\beta}(j,r;\nu) = \min_{\pi_i} E_{j,r}\left[\sum_{t=0}^{\infty} \beta^t (c_i 1_{\{Z_i^{\pi_i}(t)>0\}} + \nu A_i^{\pi_i}(t))\right], \qquad (23)$$

where $j \in \{0,1,\ldots,J\}$, $r \in \{r_{i,1}, r_{i,2}\}$. Note that, according to our earlier notation, for any $j \in \{1,\ldots,J\}$ and $r \in \{r_{i,1}, r_{i,2}\}$,

$$v_{i,\beta}(j,r;\nu) \leq \lim_{\beta\to 1} v_{i,\beta}(j,r;\nu) = v_i(j,r;\nu). \qquad (24)$$

PROPOSITION 2. *For any $j \in \{1,\ldots,J\}$ and $r \in \{r_{i,1}, r_{i,2}\}$,*

$$v_{i,\beta}(j,r;\nu) \leq \frac{c_i}{1-\beta}. \qquad (25)$$

PROOF. For the policy π_i° that *never* schedules job i, we clearly have

$$f_{i,\beta}^{\pi_i^\circ} = \sum_{t=0}^{\infty} \beta^t c_i = \frac{c_i}{1-\beta}, \quad g_{i,\beta}^{\pi_i^\circ} = 0$$

implying that

$$v_{i,\beta}(j,r;\nu) \leq v_{i,\beta}^{\pi_i^\circ}(j,r;\nu) = f_{i,\beta}^{\pi_i^\circ} + \nu g_{i,\beta}^{\pi_i^\circ} = \frac{c_i}{1-\beta},$$

which completes the proof. □

In addition, we note that the optimality equation (22) can be written as follows:

$$\begin{aligned}
v_{i,\beta}(j,r;\nu) = {} & c_i + \beta\bar{v}_{i,\beta}(j;\nu) +\\
& \min\{0, \nu - \beta p_i r(\bar{v}_{i,\beta}(j;\nu) - \bar{v}_{i,\beta}(j-1;\nu))\}, \quad (26)
\end{aligned}$$

where we have defined

$$\bar{v}_{i,\beta}(j;\nu) = (1-q_i)v_{i,\beta}(j,r_{i,1};\nu) + q_i v_{i,\beta}(j,r_{i,2};\nu). \qquad (27)$$

PROPOSITION 3. *For any $j \in \{1,\ldots,J\}$ and $r \in \{r_{i,1}, r_{i,2}\}$,*

(i) decision 0 is optimal in state (j,r) if and only if

$$\nu \geq \beta p_i r(\bar{v}_{i,\beta}(j;\nu) - \bar{v}_{i,\beta}(j-1;\nu)); \quad (28)$$

(ii) decisions 0 and 1 are equally good in state (j,r) if and only if

$$\nu = \beta p_i r(\bar{v}_{i,\beta}(j;\nu) - \bar{v}_{i,\beta}(j-1;\nu)); \quad (29)$$

(iii) decision 1 is optimal in state (j,r) if and only if

$$\nu \leq \beta p_i r(\bar{v}_{i,\beta}(j;\nu) - \bar{v}_{i,\beta}(j-1;\nu)). \quad (30)$$

PROOF. These results follow immediately from (26). □

PROPOSITION 4. *For any $j \in \{1,\dots,J\}$, function $\bar{v}_{i,\beta}(j;\nu)$ satisfies the following recursion:*

$$\bar{v}_{i,\beta}(j;\nu) - \bar{v}_{i,\beta}(j-1;\nu) = \quad (31)$$

$$\begin{cases} \dfrac{c_i - (1-\beta)\bar{v}_{i,\beta}(j-1;\nu)}{1-\beta}, & \nu \geq B; \\ \dfrac{c_i + q_i\nu - (1-\beta)\bar{v}_{i,\beta}(j-1;\nu)}{1-\beta+\beta p_i q_i r_{i,2}}, & A \leq \nu < B; \\ \dfrac{c_i + \nu - (1-\beta)\bar{v}_{i,\beta}(j-1;\nu)}{1-\beta+\beta p_i \bar{r}_i}, & \nu < A, \end{cases}$$

where

$$A = \frac{\beta p_i r_{i,1}(c_i - (1-\beta)\bar{v}_{i,\beta}(j-1;\nu))}{1-\beta+\beta p_i q_i(r_{i,2}-r_{i,1})},$$

$$B = \frac{\beta p_i r_{i,2}(c_i - (1-\beta)\bar{v}_{i,\beta}(j-1;\nu))}{1-\beta}.$$

PROOF. Let $j \in \{1,\dots,J\}$ and denote

$$\Delta_{i,\beta}(j;\nu) = \bar{v}_{i,\beta}(j;\nu) - \bar{v}_{i,\beta}(j-1;\nu).$$

It follows readily from the optimality equations (22) that

$$\begin{aligned} \bar{v}_{i,\beta}(j;\nu)(1-\beta) = c_i + \\ (1-q_i)\min\{0, \nu - \beta p_i r_{i,1}\Delta_{i,\beta}(j;\nu)\} + \\ q_i \min\{0, \nu - \beta p_i r_{i,2}\Delta_{i,\beta}(j;\nu)\}, \end{aligned} \quad (32)$$

Below we show that recursion (31) follows from (32).

1° Consider first the case $\nu - \beta p_i r_{i,2}\Delta_{i,\beta}(j;\nu) \geq 0$. Since $r_{i,2} > r_{i,1}$, we also have $\nu - \beta p_i r_{i,1}\Delta_{i,\beta}(j;\nu) \geq 0$, implying, by (32), that

$$\bar{v}_{i,\beta}(j;\nu) = \frac{c_i}{1-\beta}.$$

Thus,

$$\Delta_{i,\beta}(j;\nu) = \frac{c_i - (1-\beta)\bar{v}_{i,\beta}(j-1;\nu)}{1-\beta}.$$

By requiring that $\nu - p_i r_{i,2}\Delta_{i,\beta}(j;\nu) \geq 0$ and applying the previous expression for $\Delta_{i,\beta}(j;\nu)$, we get the required condition for its validity: $\nu \geq B$.

2° Assume now that $\nu - \beta p_i r_{i,2}\Delta_{i,\beta}(j;\nu) < 0$ and $\nu - \beta p_i r_{i,1}\Delta_{i,\beta}(j;\nu) \geq 0$. From 1° and (32), it follows that

$$\bar{v}_{i,\beta}(j;\nu) = \frac{c_i + q_i(\nu - \beta p_i r_{i,2}\Delta_{i,\beta}(j;\nu))}{1-\beta}.$$

After some manipulation, we get

$$\bar{v}_{i,\beta}(j;\nu) = \frac{c_i + q_i\nu + \beta p_i q_i r_{i,2}\bar{v}_{i,\beta}(j-1;\nu)}{1-\beta+\beta p_i q_i r_{i,2}},$$

which implies that

$$\Delta_{i,\beta}(j;\nu) = \frac{c_i + q_i\nu - (1-\beta)\bar{v}_{i,\beta}(j-1;\nu)}{1-\beta+\beta p_i q_i r_{i,2}}.$$

By first requiring that $\nu - \beta p_i r_{i,2}\Delta_{i,\beta}(j;\nu) < 0$ and $\nu - \beta p_i r_{i,1}\Delta_{i,\beta}(j;\nu) \geq 0$ and then applying the previous expression for $\Delta_{i,\beta}(j;\nu)$, we get the required condition for its validity: $A \leq \nu < B$.

3° Assume finally that $\nu - \beta p_i r_{i,1}\Delta_{i,\beta}(j;\nu) < 0$. From 1° and (32), we easily get

$$\bar{v}_{i,\beta}(j;\nu) = \frac{c_i + \nu - \beta p_i \bar{r}_i \Delta_{i,\beta}(j;\nu)}{1-\beta},$$

which, after some manipulation, gives

$$\Delta_{i,\beta}(j;\nu) = \frac{c_i + \nu - (1-\beta)\bar{v}_{i,\beta}(j-1;\nu)}{1-\beta+\beta p_i \bar{r}_i}.$$

By requiring that $\nu - \beta p_i r_{i,1}\Delta_{i,\beta}(j;\nu) < 0$ and applying the previous expression for $\Delta_{i,\beta}(j;\nu)$, we get the required condition for its validity: $\nu < A$. □

PROPOSITION 5. *For any $j \in \{1,\dots,J\}$,*

(i) if decision 0 is optimal in state $(j, r_{i,2})$, then

$$\bar{v}_{i,\beta}(j;\nu) - \bar{v}_{i,\beta}(j-1;\nu) = \frac{c_i - (1-\beta)\bar{v}_{i,\beta}(j-1;\nu)}{1-\beta}; \quad (33)$$

(ii) if decision 1 is optimal in state $(j, r_{i,2})$ and decision 0 is optimal in state $(j, r_{i,1})$, then

$$\bar{v}_{i,\beta}(j;\nu) - \bar{v}_{i,\beta}(j-1;\nu) = \frac{c_i + q_i\nu - (1-\beta)\bar{v}_{i,\beta}(j-1;\nu)}{1-\beta+\beta p_i q_i r_{i,2}}; \quad (34)$$

(iii) if decision 1 is optimal in state $(j, r_{i,1})$, then

$$\bar{v}_{i,\beta}(j;\nu) - \bar{v}_{i,\beta}(j-1;\nu) = \frac{c_i + \nu - (1-\beta)\bar{v}_{i,\beta}(j-1;\nu)}{1-\beta+\beta p_i \bar{r}_i}. \quad (35)$$

PROOF. These results follow immediately from Propositions 3 and 4. □

PROPOSITION 6. *For any $j \in \{1,\dots,J\}$,*

$$\bar{v}_{i,\beta}(j;\nu) \geq \bar{v}_{i,\beta}(j-1;\nu). \quad (36)$$

PROOF. By (25), we have

$$\bar{v}_{i,\beta}(j-1;\nu) \leq \frac{c_i}{1-\beta},$$

which clearly implies that

$$c_i + \nu \geq c_i + q_i\nu \geq c_i \geq (1-\beta)\bar{v}_{i,\beta}(j-1;\nu),$$

from which the claim follows by Proposition 4. □

Next we define the indexability property for the discounted cost problem, and show that such indices exist.

DEFINITION 2. *We say that the optimization problem with objective function (21) is indexable if, for any $j \in \{1,\dots,J\}$ and $r \in \{r_{i,1}, r_{i,2}\}$, there exists $\nu^*_{i,\beta}(j,r) \in [0,\infty]$ such that*

(i) it is optimal to schedule job i in state (j,r) if $\nu^*_{i,\beta}(j,r) \geq \nu$;

(ii) it is optimal not to schedule job i in state (j,r) if $\nu^*_{i,\beta}(j,r) \leq \nu$.

THEOREM 2. *The optimization problem with objective function (21) is indexable. In addition, for all $j \in \{1, \dots, J\}$,*

$$\nu^*_{i,\beta}(j, r_{i,2}) \geq \nu^*_{i,\beta}(j, r_{i,1}), \tag{37}$$

and, for all $j \in \{2, \dots, J\}$ and $r \in \{r_{i,1}, r_{i,2}\}$,

$$\nu^*_{i,\beta}(j-1, r) \geq \nu^*_{i,\beta}(j, r), \tag{38}$$

PROOF. 1° Let $j \in \{1, \dots, J\}$, and consider first state $(j, r_{i,2})$. By (28), decision 0 (not to schedule job i) is optimal in state $(j, r_{i,2})$ if and only if

$$\nu \geq \beta p_i r_{i,2}(\bar{v}_{i,\beta}(j;\nu) - \bar{v}_{i,\beta}(j-1;\nu)).$$

From parts 1° and 2° of the proof of Proposition 4, we see that this condition is equivalent with

$$\nu + \beta p_i r_{i,2} \bar{v}_{i,\beta}(j-1;\nu) \geq \frac{\beta p_i r_{i,2} c_i}{1-\beta}.$$

Since the left hand side is clearly an increasing and continuous function of ν and the right hand side is constant with respect to ν, there is $\nu^*_{i,\beta}(j, r_{i,2}) \in [0, \infty]$ satisfying the indexability property as given in Definition 2. In addition, if $j \geq 2$, then the previous inequality implies also that (38) holds for $r = r_{i,2}$, since $\bar{v}_{i,\beta}(j-1;\nu) \geq \bar{v}_{i,\beta}(j-2;\nu)$ by (36).

2° Consider now state $(j, r_{i,1})$. Again, by (28), decision 0 is optimal in state $(j, r_{i,1})$ if and only if

$$\nu \geq \beta p_i r_{i,1}(\bar{v}_{i,\beta}(j;\nu) - \bar{v}_{i,\beta}(j-1;\nu)).$$

From parts 2° and 3° of the proof of Proposition 4, we see that this condition is equivalent with

$$\nu + \frac{\beta(1-\beta) p_i r_{i,1} \bar{v}_{i,\beta}(j-1;\nu)}{1-\beta+\beta p_i q_i (r_{i,2} - r_{i,1})} \geq \frac{\beta p_i r_{i,1} c_i}{1-\beta+\beta p_i q_i (r_{i,2} - r_{i,1})}.$$

Since the left hand side is clearly an increasing and continuous function of ν and the right hand side is constant with respect to ν, there is $\nu^*_{i,\beta}(j, r_{i,1}) \in [0, \infty]$ satisfying the indexability property as given in Definition 2. In addition, if $j \geq 2$, then the previous inequality implies also that (38) holds for $r = r_{i,1}$, since $\bar{v}_{i,\beta}(j-1;\nu) \geq \bar{v}_{i,\beta}(j-2;\nu)$ by (36).

3° Finally, since $r_{i,2} > r_{i,1}$, we see from (28) that if decision 0 is optimal for state $(j, r_{i,2})$, then it is also optimal for state $(j, r_{i,1})$. Thus, (37) holds. □

The remaining task is to determine the Whittle index as β approaches 1. For that we need the following auxiliary result.

PROPOSITION 7. *Let $j \in \{1, \dots, J\}$. If*

$$\nu^*_{i,\beta}(j, r_{i,2}) \geq \nu^*_{i,\beta}(1, r_{i,1}),$$

then

(i) for any $\nu^*_{i,\beta}(1, r_{i,1}) \leq \nu \leq \nu^*_{i,\beta}(j, r_{i,2})$,

$$\bar{v}_{i,\beta}(j;\nu) = \frac{c_i + q_i \nu}{1-\beta}\left(1 - \left(\frac{\beta p_i q_i r_{i,2}}{1-\beta+\beta p_i q_i r_{i,2}}\right)^j\right); \tag{39}$$

(ii) for any $\nu \leq \nu^*_{i,\beta}(j, r_{i,1})$,

$$\bar{v}_{i,\beta}(j;\nu) = \frac{c_i + \nu}{1-\beta}\left(1 - \left(\frac{\beta p_i \bar{r}_i}{1-\beta+\beta p_i \bar{r}_i}\right)^j\right). \tag{40}$$

PROOF. 1° Consider first the case $j = 1$. Since $\nu^*_{i,\beta}(1, r_{i,2}) \geq \nu^*_{i,\beta}(1, r_{i,1})$, it is optimal to make decision 0 in state $(1, r_{i,1})$ and decision 1 in state $(1, r_{i,2})$ for any $\nu^*_{i,\beta}(1, r_{i,1}) \leq \nu \leq \nu^*_{i,\beta}(1, r_{i,2})$. Thus, it follows from (34) that, for any $\nu^*_{i,\beta}(1, r_{i,1}) \leq \nu \leq \nu^*_{i,\beta}(1, r_{i,2})$, we have

$$\begin{aligned}\bar{v}_{i,\beta}(1;\nu) &\overset{(34)}{=} \frac{c_i + q_i \nu}{1-\beta+\beta p_i q_i r_{i,2}} \\ &= \frac{c_i + q_i \nu}{1-\beta}\left(1 - \frac{\beta p_i q_i r_{i,2}}{1-\beta+\beta p_i q_i r_{i,2}}\right),\end{aligned}$$

implying that claim (i) is true for $j = 1$. In addition, since $\nu^*_{i,\beta}(1, r_{i,2}) \geq \nu^*_{i,\beta}(1, r_{i,1})$, it is optimal to make decision 1 in both states $(1, r_{i,1})$ and $(1, r_{i,2})$ for any $\nu \leq \nu^*_{i,\beta}(1, r_{i,1})$. Thus, it follows from (35) that, for any $\nu \leq \nu^*_{i,\beta}(1, r_{i,1})$, we have

$$\begin{aligned}\bar{v}_{i,\beta}(1;\nu) &\overset{(35)}{=} \frac{c_i + \nu}{1-\beta+\beta p_i \bar{r}_i} \\ &= \frac{c_i + \nu}{1-\beta}\left(1 - \frac{\beta p_i \bar{r}_i}{1-\beta+\beta p_i \bar{r}_i}\right),\end{aligned}$$

implying that also claim (ii) is true for $j = 1$.

2° Now let $j \in \{2, \dots, J\}$ and assume that

$$\nu^*_{i,\beta}(j, r_{i,2}) \geq \nu^*_{i,\beta}(1, r_{i,1}). \tag{41}$$

In addition, we make an induction assumption that Proposition 7 is true for $j-1$.

Assumption (41) and Theorem 2 together imply that

$$\nu^*_{i,\beta}(j-1, r_{i,2}) \geq \nu^*_{i,\beta}(j, r_{i,2}) \geq \nu^*_{i,\beta}(1, r_{i,1}) \geq \nu^*_{i,\beta}(j, r_{i,1})$$

so that we may apply claims (i) and (ii) for $j-1$. In this case, it is optimal to make decision 0 in state $(j, r_{i,1})$ and decision 1 in state $(j, r_{i,2})$ for any $\nu^*_{i,\beta}(1, r_{i,1}) \leq \nu \leq \nu^*_{i,\beta}(j, r_{i,2})$. Thus, it follows from (34) and the induction assumption (i.a.) that, for any $\nu^*_{i,\beta}(1, r_{i,1}) \leq \nu \leq \nu^*_{i,\beta}(j, r_{i,2})$, we have

$$\begin{aligned}\bar{v}_{i,\beta}(j;\nu) &\overset{(34)}{=} \frac{c_i + q_i \nu + \beta p_i q_i r_{i,2} \bar{v}_{i,\beta}(j-1;\nu)}{1-\beta+\beta p_i q_i r_{i,2}} \\ &\overset{\text{i.a.}}{=} \frac{(c_i + q_i \nu)}{1-\beta+\beta p_i q_i r_{i,2}} \times \\ &\quad \left(1 + \frac{\beta p_i q_i r_{i,2}}{1-\beta}\left(1 - \left(\frac{\beta p_i q_i r_{i,2}}{1-\beta+\beta p_i q_i r_{i,2}}\right)^{j-1}\right)\right) \\ &= \frac{c_i + q_i \nu}{1-\beta}\left(1 - \left(\frac{\beta p_i q_i r_{i,2}}{1-\beta+\beta p_i q_i r_{i,2}}\right)^j\right),\end{aligned}$$

implying that claim (i) is true for j. Furthermore, in this case, it is optimal to make decision 1 in both states $(j, r_{i,1})$ and $(j, r_{i,2})$ for any $\nu \leq \nu^*_{i,\beta}(j, r_{i,1})$. Thus, it follows from (35) and the induction assumption (i.a.) that, for any $\nu \leq \nu^*_{i,\beta}(j, r_{i,1})$, we have

$$\begin{aligned}\bar{v}_{i,\beta}(j;\nu) &\overset{(35)}{=} \frac{c_i + \nu + \beta p_i \bar{r}_i \bar{v}_{i,\beta}(j-1;\nu)}{1-\beta+\beta p_i \bar{r}_i} \\ &\overset{\text{i.a.}}{=} \frac{(c_i + \nu)}{1-\beta+\beta p_i \bar{r}_i} \times \\ &\quad \left(1 + \frac{\beta p_i \bar{r}_i}{1-\beta}\left(1 - \left(\frac{\beta p_i \bar{r}_i}{1-\beta+\beta p_i \bar{r}_i}\right)^{j-1}\right)\right) \\ &= \frac{c_i + \nu}{1-\beta}\left(1 - \left(\frac{\beta p_i \bar{r}_i}{1-\beta+\beta p_i \bar{r}_i}\right)^j\right),\end{aligned}$$

implying that also claim (ii) is true for j. □

THEOREM 3. *There is $\tilde\beta < 1$ such that, for any $\beta \in (\tilde\beta, 1)$, the Whittle index for the optimization problem with objective function (21) is given by*

$$\nu^*_{i,\beta}(j, r_{i,1}) = \frac{\frac{r_{i,1}}{\bar r_i}(\beta p_i \bar r_i)^j c_i}{(1-\beta+\beta p_i \bar r_i)^j - \frac{r_{i,1}}{\bar r_i}(\beta p_i \bar r_i)^j}, \quad (42)$$

$$\nu^*_{i,\beta}(j, r_{i,2}) = \frac{\frac{1}{q_i}(\beta p_i q_i r_{i,2})^j c_i}{(1-\beta+\beta p_i q_i r_{i,2})^j - (\beta p_i q_i r_{i,2})^j} \quad (43)$$

for any $j \in \{1, \ldots, J\}$.[4]

PROOF. 1° Consider first state $(1, r_{i,2})$. From (37) we see that, for $\nu = \nu^*_{i,\beta}(1, r_{i,2})$, it is optimal to make decision 0 in state $(1, r_{i,1})$ and both decisions (0 and 1) are equally good in state $(1, r_{i,2})$. Thus, it follows from (29) and (34) that we have, for $\nu = \nu^*_{i,\beta}(1, r_{i,2})$,

$$\nu \overset{(29)}{=} \beta p_i r_{i,2} \bar v_{i,\beta}(1;\nu) \overset{(34)}{=} \beta p_i r_{i,2} \frac{c_i + q_i \nu}{1-\beta+\beta p_i q_i r_{i,2}},$$

implying that

$$\nu = \frac{\beta p_i r_{i,2} c_i}{1-\beta},$$

which is in line with (43) for $j = 1$.

2° Consider now state $(1, r_{i,1})$. From (37) we see that, for $\nu = \nu^*_{i,\beta}(1, r_{i,1})$, both decisions (0 and 1) are equally good in state $(1, r_{i,1})$ and it is optimal to make decision 1 in state $(1, r_{i,2})$. Thus, it follows from (29) and (35) that we have, for $\nu = \nu^*_{i,\beta}(1, r_{i,1})$,

$$\nu \overset{(29)}{=} \beta p_i r_{i,1} \bar v_{i,\beta}(1;\nu) \overset{(35)}{=} \beta p_i r_{i,1} \frac{c_i + \nu}{1-\beta+\beta p_i \bar r_i},$$

implying that

$$\nu = \frac{\beta p_i r_{i,1} c_i}{1-\beta+\beta p_i q_i (r_{i,2} - r_{i,1})},$$

which is in line with (42) for $j = 1$. In addition, we note that

$$\lim_{\beta\to 1} \nu^*_{i,\beta}(1, r_{i,1}) = \frac{c_i}{q_i(\frac{r_{i,2}}{r_{i,1}} - 1)} < \infty. \quad (44)$$

3° Now let $j \in \{2, \ldots, J\}$, and consider state $(j, r_{i,2})$. Theorem 2 implies that

$$\nu^*_{i,\beta}(j-1, r_{i,2}) \ge \nu^*_{i,\beta}(j, r_{i,2}).$$

Consider now what happens if we assume that

$$\nu^*_{i,\beta}(j, r_{i,2}) \ge \nu^*_{i,\beta}(1, r_{i,1}) \quad (45)$$

so that

$$\nu^*_{i,\beta}(j-1, r_{i,2}) \ge \nu^*_{i,\beta}(j, r_{i,2}) \ge \nu^*_{i,\beta}(1, r_{i,1}).$$

In this case, for $\nu = \nu^*_{i,\beta}(j, r_{i,2})$, it is optimal to make decision 0 in state $(j, r_{i,1})$ and both decisions (0 and 1) are equally good in state $(j, r_{i,2})$. Thus, it follows from (29), (34), and (39) that, for $\nu = \nu^*_{i,\beta}(j, r_{i,2})$, we have

$$\begin{aligned}\nu &\overset{(29)}{=} \beta p_i r_{i,2}(\bar v_{i,\beta}(j;\nu) - \bar v_{i,\beta}(j-1;\nu)) \\ &\overset{(34)}{=} \beta p_i r_{i,2} \frac{c_i + q_i\nu - (1-\beta)\bar v_{i,\beta}(j-1;\nu)}{1-\beta+\beta p_i q_i r_{i,2}} \\ &\overset{(39)}{=} \frac{\beta p_i r_{i,2}}{1-\beta+\beta p_i q_i r_{i,2}} \times \\ &\quad \left(c_i + q_i\nu - (c_i + q_i\nu)\left(1 - \left(\frac{\beta p_i q_i r_{i,2}}{1-\beta+\beta p_i q_i r_{i,2}}\right)^{j-1}\right)\right) \\ &= \frac{1}{q_i}(c_i + q_i\nu)\left(\frac{\beta p_i q_i r_{i,2}}{1-\beta+\beta p_i q_i r_{i,2}}\right)^j,\end{aligned}$$

from which (43) clearly follows.

By letting $\beta \to 1$, we see from (43) that $\nu^*_{i,\beta}(j, r_{i,2}) \to \infty$. Since $\nu^*_{i,\beta}(1, r_{i,1})$ is bounded by (44), there is $\tilde\beta_j < 1$ such that (45) holds for any $\beta \in (\tilde\beta_j, 1)$.

4° Finally, let $j \in \{2, \ldots, J\}$, and consider state $(j, r_{i,1})$. Theorem 2 implies that

$$\nu^*_{i,\beta}(1, r_{i,1}) \ge \nu^*_{i,\beta}(j-1, r_{i,1}) \ge \nu^*_{i,\beta}(j, r_{i,1}).$$

Let $\beta \in (\tilde\beta_j, 1)$ so that (45) holds, and we have

$$\nu^*_{i,\beta}(j, r_{i,2}) \ge \nu^*_{i,\beta}(1, r_{i,1}) \ge \nu^*_{i,\beta}(j-1, r_{i,1}) \ge \nu^*_{i,\beta}(j, r_{i,1}).$$

In this case, for $\nu = \nu^*_{i,\beta}(j, r_{i,1})$, both decisions (0 and 1) are equally good in state $(j, r_{i,1})$ while decision 1 is optimal in state $(j, r_{i,2})$. Thus, it follows from (29), (35), and (40) that, for $\nu = \nu^*_{i,\beta}(j, r_{i,1})$, we have

$$\begin{aligned}\nu &\overset{(29)}{=} \beta p_i r_{i,1}(\bar v_{i,\beta}(j;\nu) - \bar v_{i,\beta}(j-1;\nu)) \\ &\overset{(35)}{=} \beta p_i r_{i,1} \frac{c_i + \nu - (1-\beta)\bar v_{i,\beta}(j-1;\nu)}{1-\beta+\beta p_i \bar r_i} \\ &\overset{(40)}{=} \beta p_i r_{i,1} \frac{c_i + \nu - (c_i+\nu)\left(1 - \left(\frac{\beta p_i \bar r_i}{1-\beta+\beta p_i \bar r_i}\right)^{j-1}\right)}{1-\beta+\beta p_i \bar r_i} \\ &= \frac{r_{i,1}}{\bar r_i}(c_i + \nu)\left(\frac{\beta p_i \bar r_i}{1-\beta+\beta p_i \bar r_i}\right)^j,\end{aligned}$$

from which (42) clearly follows.

The proof is completed by choosing $\tilde\beta = \max_j \tilde\beta_j$. □

Remarks: Note that, according to our earlier notation,

$$\lim_{\beta\to 1} \nu^*_{i,\beta}(j, r_{i,1}) = \frac{c_i}{q_i(\frac{r_{i,2}}{r_{i,1}} - 1)} = \nu^*_i(j, r_{i,1}),$$

$$\lim_{\beta\to 1} \nu^*_{i,\beta}(j, r_{i,2}) = \infty = \nu^*_i(j, r_{i,2}).$$

In addition, we have

$$\lim_{\beta\to 1}(1-\beta)\nu^*_{i,\beta}(j, r_{i,1}) = 0,$$

$$\lim_{\beta\to 1}(1-\beta)\nu^*_{i,\beta}(j, r_{i,2}) = \frac{c_i p_i r_{i,2}}{j}. \quad (46)$$

The latter one can be used as the *secondary (tie-breaking) index* among the jobs that have their best channel state when $\beta \to 1$. Interestingly, the secondary index coincides with the *Gittins index* [11] for a job with j remaining geometric phases in a discrete-time single server queueing system specified by the fixed phase completion probability of $p_i r_{i,2}$. In addition, at time 0 when the number of remaining phases is equal to J for *all* jobs i, we have

$$\lim_{\beta\to 1}(1-\beta)\nu^*_{i,\beta}(J, r_{i,2}) = \frac{c_i p_i r_{i,2}}{J} = \frac{c_i r_{i,2}}{x_i},$$

[4]For the geometric job size distribution (i.e., $J = 1$), the index values $\nu^*_{i,\beta}(j, r_{i,1})$ and $\nu^*_{i,\beta}(j, r_{i,2})$ differ by a factor of β from those given in [4], which is due to a slight difference in the cost models: While we "pay" the holding cost c_i for job i even in the timeslot where its service is completed, this is not the case in the cost model of [4].

since $p_i = J/x_i$. This limit is also used as our secondary index for the original jobs i with sizes x_i.

Finally, we note that, for the geometric job size distribution (i.e., $J = 1$), the limiting index values are the same as those in [4].

7. SIZE-AWARE WHITTLE INDEX POLICY

In this section, we return to our original setup (described in Section 2) where we have K jobs with known original sizes x_i, $i \in \{1, \dots, K\}$, and define a size-aware index policy that satisfies the constraint (1) and is based on our phase-type approximations utilizing the results related to the Whittle index for shifted Pascal job sizes derived in Sections 5 and 6.

DEFINITION 3. *Assume that there are K jobs with remaining sizes of y_i. For any $r \in \{r_{i,1}, r_{i,2}\}$, the primary index of job i is defined by*

$$\nu_i^{\mathrm{SW}}(y_i, r_{i,1}) = \frac{c_i}{q_i(\frac{r_{i,2}}{r_{i,1}} - 1)}, \quad \nu_i^{\mathrm{SW}}(y_i, r_{i,2}) = \infty, \tag{47}$$

and the secondary index by

$$\tilde{\nu}_i^{\mathrm{SW}}(y_i, r_{i,1}) = 0, \quad \tilde{\nu}_i^{\mathrm{SW}}(y_i, r_{i,2}) = \frac{c_i r_{i,2}}{y_i}. \tag{48}$$

The scheduling rule that

(i) gives an absolute priority to the jobs whose channel state is "good", breaking ties among these jobs by choosing the job i with the highest secondary index $\tilde{\nu}_i^{\mathrm{SW}}(y_i, r_{i,2})$, and

(ii) if there are no jobs whose channel state is "good", chooses the job i with the highest primary index $\nu_i^{\mathrm{SW}}(y_i, r_{i,1})$, breaking ties among these jobs randomly,

is called Size-aware Whittle index policy *(SW).*

While the development of the SW policy is based on a static setting (with a fixed number of jobs), it has some nice properties in the corresponding dynamic setting (taking into account random variations in the number of jobs). Below we assume that, in the dynamic setting, the arrivals take place always at the end of timeslot. Jobs are still indexed with i. Now we let $i \in \{1, 2, \dots\}$.

PROPOSITION 8. *The SW policy is maximally stable in the dynamic setting under the assumptions of i.i.d. arrivals (with a finite second moment) and geometric job sizes.*

PROOF. Since SW gives an absolute priority to the jobs i whose channel state is their own best possible (i.e., $r_{i,2}$), it belongs to so-called Best Rate (BR) policies, which are shown to be maximally stable under the given conditions for i.i.d. channel variations in [5, Theorem 5.2]. □

PROPOSITION 9. *The SW policy is optimal (minimizing the average holding costs under constraint (1)) in the dynamic setting with arbitrary arrivals if $q_i = 1$ and $c_i = 1$ for all i.*

PROOF. Assume that $q_i = 1$ and $c_i = 1$ for all i. Define $\tilde{x}_i = r_{i,2}\lceil(x_i/r_{i,2})\rceil$. Let $N^{\mathrm{SW}}(t)$ denote the number of jobs at time $t \in \{0, 1, \dots\}$ in the discrete-time system with job sizes x_i under the SW policy. Consider then the corresponding continuous time system with the same job arrival times but with job sizes $\tilde{x}_i$, and let $\tilde{N}^{\mathrm{SRPT}}(u)$ denote the number of jobs at time $u \geq 0$ under the Shortest Remaining Procesing Time policy (SRPT). It is easy to see that, for any $u \geq 0$,

$$\tilde{N}^{\mathrm{SRPT}}(u) = N^{\mathrm{SW}}(\lfloor u \rfloor).$$

Since SRPT is known to minimize the number of jobs at any time u in each sample path (with arbitrary arrivals) [18], the equation above guarantees that SW minimizes the number of jobs in the discrete time system for any t. Thus, SW also minimizes the average holding costs, as well. □

8. NUMERICAL RESULTS

In this section, we evaluate, by simulations, the performance of the proposed size-aware scheduler SW in a dynamic setting with randomly varying number of jobs and i.i.d. channel variations. We demonstrate that SW gives systematically better performance than PF, PI, and ASPI (mentioned in Section 1). Each of these policies is a similar index rule as SW, however, with their own indices.

Consider a job i with a *random* size of X_i with mean $E[X_i] = 1/\mu_i$. Let a_i denote the attained service of job i (in bits) and d_i the time that it has already spent in the system (at the decision time). Thus, the throughput of job i at that time is equal to a_i/d_i. The PF rule uses only a single (primary) index, which depends on the current channel state and the throughput as follows:

$$\nu_i^{\mathrm{PF}}(a_i, d_i, r_{i,1}) = \frac{r_{i,1}}{a_i/d_i}, \quad \nu_i^{\mathrm{PF}}(a_i, d_i, r_{i,2}) = \frac{r_{i,2}}{a_i/d_i}.$$

The PI and ASPI policies use instead both the primary and the secondary indices. However, PI does not utilize the attained service information at all (unlike ASPI). The primary index of this job under the PI policy [4] is given by

$$\nu_i^{\mathrm{PI}}(r_{i,1}) = \frac{c_i}{q_i(\frac{r_{i,2}}{r_{i,1}} - 1)}, \quad \nu_i^{\mathrm{PI}}(r_{i,2}) = \infty,$$

and the secondary index by

$$\tilde{\nu}_i^{\mathrm{PI}}(r_{i,1}) = 0, \quad \tilde{\nu}_i^{\mathrm{PI}}(r_{i,2}) = c_i \mu_i r_{i,2}.$$

Under the ASPI policy [20], the primary index of this job is given by

$$\nu_i^{\mathrm{ASPI}}(a_i, r_{i,1}) = \frac{c_i}{q_i(\frac{\mu_i(a_i, r_{i,2})}{\mu_i(a_i, r_{i,1})} - 1)}, \quad \nu_i^{\mathrm{ASPI}}(a_i, r_{i,2}) = \infty,$$

and the secondary index by

$$\tilde{\nu}_i^{\mathrm{ASPI}}(a_i, r_{i,1}) = 0, \quad \tilde{\nu}_i^{\mathrm{ASPI}}(a_i, r_{i,2}) = c_i \mu_i(a_i, r_{i,2}),$$

where $\mu_i(a_i, r) = P\{X_i \leq a_i + r \mid X_i > a_i\}$.

Note that, for geometric job sizes with state space $\{1, 2, \dots\}$ and mean $E[X_i] = 1/\mu_1$, we have

$$\mu_i(a_i, r) = 1 - (1 - \mu_i)^r \approx r\mu_i,$$

where the approximation is justified if $E[X_i]/r$ is large. In this case, ASPI is essentially the same policy as PI. By a similar argument, this is the case also for exponential job sizes with mean $E[X_i] = 1/\mu_i$.

In what follows, we construct various scenarios for the study of the Size-aware Whittle index (SW) policy and compare its performance against other scheduling rules discussed above. To validate our implementations of the other policies, we include two experiments, which coincide with earlier work ([4, Scenario 1] and [20, Scenario 2]). For each load value, the simulations are conducted for a duration that corresponds to approximately 1 000 000 job arrivals. Unless otherwise stated, the holding costs are assumed to accrue with rate $c = 1$ and the timeslot duration is 1 ms.

8.1 Homogeneous users

Our first scenario (S1) is the same as Scenario 2 in [20] with *homogeneous users*. Since there is only a single class of jobs, we leave out the subscript i in this subsection.

We assume that jobs are i.i.d. and the job size distribution for all jobs is Pareto with the tail function given by

$$P\{X > x\} = \left(\frac{1}{1+\gamma x}\right)^{\alpha}, \quad x > 0,$$

where $\alpha = 1.5$ and $\gamma = 4 \cdot 10^{-7}$ 1/b so that $E[X] = 5.0$ Mb. In addition, the channel model is the same for all jobs with

$$r_1 = 8.4\,\text{kb}, \quad r_2 = 33.6\,\text{kb}, \quad q = 0.5.$$

New jobs arrive according to a Poisson process with rate λ (arrivals per timeslot) and the system load is denoted by $\rho = \lambda E[X]/r_2$.

The results are given in Figure 1, which shows the mean holding costs as a function of the system load ρ for the four schedulers. We observe the ASPI is clearly better than PI or PF. Thus, the performance of PI is suffering from the erroneous assumption about the job size distribution in this case. However, the most prominent result is that SW is systematically performing better than all other policies. We also observe that the results for PF and ASPI coincide with those in [20, Figure 7]. Furthermore, in this case with homogeneous users, the PI policy corresponds to the so-called *Max Rate* (MR) scheduler, and our results for PI are in line with those of MR in [20, Figure 7]. Finally, although not shown in Figure 1, we have also simulated the TR-OPT policy from our earlier paper [3] that applies the optimal static (no new arrivals) size-aware policy in the dynamic setting, and the results are practically identical to those of our new SW policy.

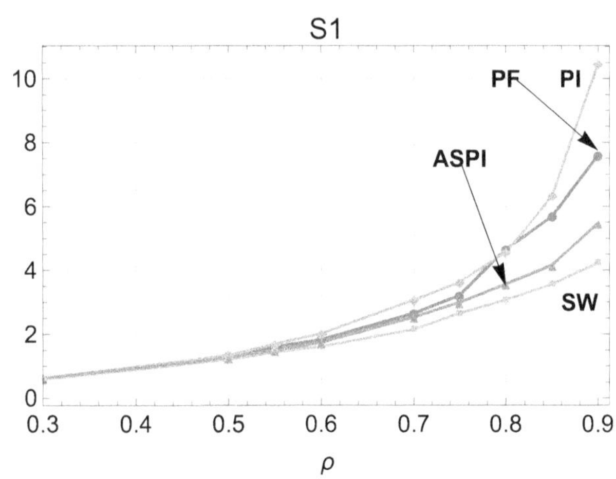

Figure 1: The mean holding cost (which is the same as the mean number of jobs in this case) as a function of the system load, ρ, for scenario S1 with homogeneous users.

8.2 Heterogeneous users

Our following three scenarios are related to *heterogeneous users* with two different job classes $k = 1, 2$. In this case, subscript k refers to the job class. Here we assume that the job sizes are exponential, implying that the PI and ASPI policies are essentially the same.

For each class k, jobs are i.i.d. and the job size distribution is exponential with mean $E[X_k]$. The channel model for class $k = 1$ is specified by parameters

$$r_{k,1} = 8.4\,\text{kb}, \quad r_{k,2} = 33.6\,\text{kb}, \quad q_k = 0.5. \qquad (49)$$

These rates have been taken from [20, Table 1]. Moreover, new class-k jobs arrive according to a Poisson process with rate λ_k (arrivals per timeslot), and the system load is denoted by $\rho = \rho_1 + \rho_2$, where

$$\rho_k = \lambda_k E[X_k]/r_{k,2}.$$

When the load is varying, we choose the arrival rates in the two classes so that the classwise loads remain equal ($\rho_1 = \rho_2$).

In our *first heterogeneous scenario* (S2a), we study the effect of the mean job size by having $E[X_1] = 0.5$ Mb and $E[X_2] = 5.0$ Mb. The channel model for class $k = 2$ is the same (49) as for class 1, as well as the holding cost rate ($c_1 = c_2 = 1$).

In our *second heterogeneous scenario* (S2b), we study the effect of different holding cost rates by having $c_1 = 5$ and $c_2 = 1$. The channel model for class $k = 2$ is again the same (49) as for class 1, as well as the mean job size ($E[X_1] = E[X_2] = 5.0$ Mb).

In our *third heterogeneous scenario* (S2c), we study the effect of different channel models by letting

$$r_{2,1} = 8.4\,\text{kb}, \quad r_{2,2} = 16.8\,\text{kb}, \quad q_2 = 0.5, \qquad (50)$$

while the mean job sizes ($E[X_1] = E[X_2] = 5.0$ Mb) and the holding cost rates ($c_1 = c_2 = 1$) are the same in both classes. Again, the rates have been taken from [20, Table 1].

The results are given in Figure 2, which shows the mean holding costs as a function of the system load ρ for the three schedulers. Again, we observe that the SW policy is consistently better than the other two policies. When we observe the class-wise results (included in the Appendix) the performance of SW is better in both the classes in S2a and S2b. However in scenario S2c, PI performs better in the class with larger maximum possible service rate (class 1). However, as shown in Figure 2(c), the overall performance of SW is still the best among the three when both the classes are considered together.

8.3 Multiple channel states

Our last scenario (S3) is the same as Scenario 1 in [4]. We consider *heterogeneous users* with two different job classes $k = 1, 2$, but now the channel state in each class has more than two possible states. The job sizes are geometric, implying that the PI and ASPI policies are essentially the same.

Let $q_{k,n} = P\{R_k(t) = r_{k,n}\}$, where $n \in \{1, \ldots, N_k\}$ and

$$r_{k,1} < \ldots < r_{k,N_k}.$$

We assume that $N_1 = 5$, $N_2 = 3$, and $r_{k,n}, q_{k,n}$ are taking values as given in [4, Table 1]. For each class k, jobs are i.i.d. and the job size distribution is geometric with mean $E[X_k] = 1/\mu_k = 102.57$ kb. New class-k jobs arrive according to a

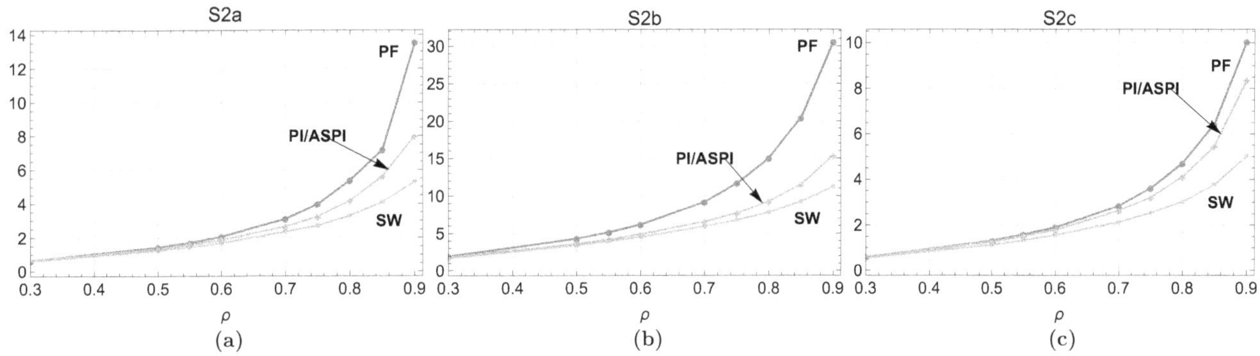

Figure 2: Mean holding cost incurred by both classes at different system load values, ρ, for scenarios S2a, S2b and S2c with heterogeneous users.

Poisson process with rate λ_k (arrivals per timeslot), and the system load is denoted by $\rho = \rho_1 + \rho_2$, where

$$\rho_k = \lambda_k E[X_k]/r_{k,N_k}.$$

The load of class 2 is kept constant $\rho_2 = 0.5$, while the load of class 1 is changed. In this experiment, the length of the timeslot is 1.67 ms.

Since there are now multiple possible channel states, we need to enlarge the definitions of the scheduling policies. The PF rule uses still a single (primary) index defined, for any $k \in \{1, 2\}$ and $n \in \{1, \ldots, N_k\}$, as follows:

$$\nu_k^{\mathrm{PF}}(a_i, d_i, r_{k,n}) = \frac{r_{k,n}}{a_i/d_i},$$

where a_i and d_i are defined as earlier for a job i belonging to class k. The primary index of the PI policy [4] is given, for each class k, by

$$\nu_k^{\mathrm{PI}}(r_{k,n}) = \frac{c_k}{\sum_{m>n} q_{k,m}(\frac{r_{k,m}}{r_{k,n}} - 1)}, \quad \nu_k^{\mathrm{PI}}(r_{k,N_k}) = \infty,$$

and the secondary index by

$$\tilde{\nu}_k^{\mathrm{PI}}(r_{k,n}) = 0, \quad \tilde{\nu}_k^{\mathrm{PI}}(r_{k,N_k}) = c_k \mu_k r_{k,N_k},$$

where $n \in \{1, \ldots, N_k - 1\}$. A natural extension of SW is defined by letting the primary index take values

$$\nu_k^{\mathrm{SW}}(y_i, r_{k,n}) = \frac{c_k}{\sum_{m>n} q_{k,m}(\frac{r_{k,m}}{r_{k,n}} - 1)}, \quad \nu_k^{\mathrm{SW}}(y_i, r_{k,N_k}) = \infty,$$

and the secondary index values

$$\tilde{\nu}_k^{\mathrm{SW}}(y_i, r_{k,n}) = 0, \quad \tilde{\nu}_k^{\mathrm{SW}}(y_i, r_{k,N_k}) = \frac{c_k r_{k,N_k}}{y_i},$$

where $n \in \{1, \ldots, N_k - 1\}$ and y_i is the remaining size of job i belonging to class k (as earlier).

The results are given in Figure 3. Figure 3(a) shows the mean holding costs (i.e., the mean number of jobs in this case) as a function of the system load ρ for the three schedulers. Again, we observe that SW is performing better than both PF and PI for any load ρ. The gain comes mainly from the class that has fewer possible service rates (class 2 in this scenario). However, in the class with the larger number of possible service rates (class 1 in this scenario), the performances of these three schedulers are very close to each other except at very high loads, as seen from Figure 3(b).

In Figures 3(b) and 3(c) we show the indifference maps of the mean number of jobs and the mean delay of jobs, respectively, in the two classes of this scenario. The points in the dotted gray line are the values of mean number of jobs or delays corresponding to the same values of the load ρ. From Figure 3(b), we see that both PF and PI keep the number of jobs in both the classes fairly balanced, while the differences in the mean delays in the two classes are clearly the smallest for SW, as seen in Figure 3(c).

Finally note that results for PI in Figures 3 coincide with those in [4, Figures 1&3]. PF has not been evaluated in [4].

9. CONCLUSIONS

The Whittle index approach provides a tractable technique to optimizing the flow-level performance of opportunistic scheduling with heterogeneous users, e.g., with respect to their channel characteristics. In this approach, by an appropriate relaxation of the original extremely difficult opportunistic scheduling problem, the task can be decomposed into one where the optimization just depends on each user alone.

Our main contribution was the derivation of a novel size-aware Whittle index policy, the SW policy. This was done for a two-state i.i.d. wireless channel by approximating the original size with a discrete phase-type distribution, i.e., a (shifted) Pascal distribution, for which the indexability property was proved both for minimizing the mean cost and the discounted cost, and the explicit Whittle index expressions were derived. The SW policy was also shown to be maximally stable. Our extensive simulation experiments with dynamic traffic, including scenarios with more channel states than two, demonstrated that our SW policy outperformed all other reference policies (the non-anticipating policies PI and ASPI, based on the Whittle index approach, and the well-known PF policy).

Thus, it appears that a size-aware policy in the time-varying capacity case is indeed a promising approach for improving the performance. A size-aware policy can also be considered more robust than a non-anticipating one since one does not need to rely on distributional assumptions or estimates, which may be inaccurate or even erroneous. As further work, we will consider the size-aware Whittle index for more general wireless channel models.

10. ACKNOWLEDGEMENTS

This research was partially supported by the TOP-Energy project funded by Academy of Finland (grant no. 268992).

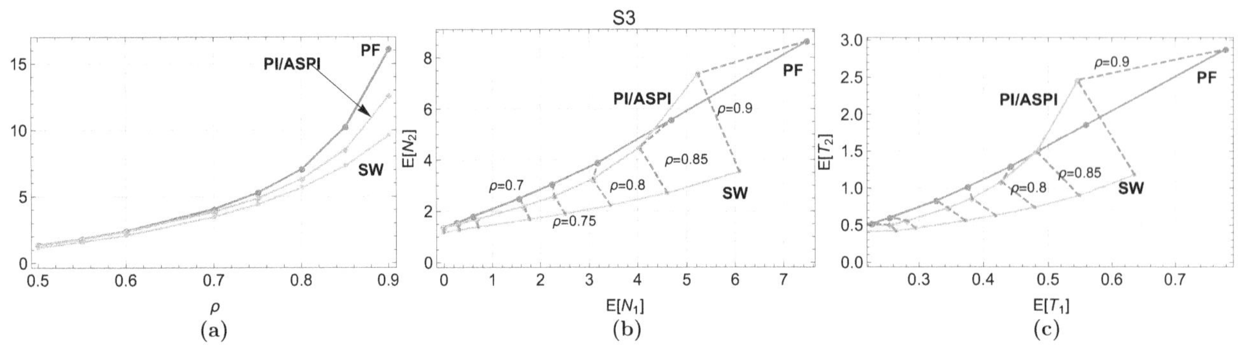

Figure 3: Performance of scenario S3 with multiple channel states. Panel (a) shows the mean holding cost or equivalently, in this case, the mean number of jobs at various values of system load, ρ. Panel (b) shows the plot of mean number of jobs in class 2 as a function of the mean number of jobs in class 1. Panel (c) shows the mean delay of class-2 jobs as a function of the mean delay of class-1 jobs. In panels (b) and (c), the isolines in gray color are drawn to indicate the same value of system load ρ.

11. REFERENCES

[1] S. Aalto and P. Lassila. Flow-level stability and performance of channel-aware priority-based schedulers. In *Proc. of NGI*, 2010.

[2] S. Aalto, A. Penttinen, P. Lassila, and P. Osti. On the optimal trade-off between SRPT and opportunistic scheduling. In *Proc. of ACM Sigmetrics*, pages 185–195, June 2011.

[3] S. Aalto, A. Penttinen, P. Lassila, and P. Osti. Optimal size-based opportunistic scheduler for wireless systems. *Queueing Systems*, 72:5–30, 2012.

[4] U. Ayesta, M. Erasquin, and P. Jacko. A modeling framework for optimizing the flow-level scheduling with time-varying channels. *Performance Evaluation*, 67:1014–1029, 2010.

[5] U. Ayesta, M. Erausquin, M. Jonckheere, and I. Verloop. Scheduling in a random environment: stability and asymptotic optimality. *IEEE/ACM Transactions on Networking*, 21:258–271, 2013.

[6] P. Bender, P. Black, M. Grob, R. Padovani, N. Sindhushyana, and S. Viterbi. CDMA/HDR: a bandwidth efficient high speed wireless data service for nomadic users. *IEEE Communications Magazine*, 38(7):70–77, 2000.

[7] T. Bonald, S. Borst, N. Hegde, M. Jonckheere, and A. Proutiére. Flow-level performance and capacity of wireless networks with user mobility. *Queueing Systems*, 63:131–164, 2009.

[8] S. Borst. User-level performance of channel-aware scheduling algorithms in wireless data networks. *IEEE/ACM Transactions on Networking*, 13:636–647, 2005.

[9] S. Borst and M. Jonckheere. Flow-level stability of channel-aware scheduling algorithms. In *Proc. of WiOpt*, April 2006.

[10] F. Cecchi and P. Jacko. Scheduling of users with Markovian time-varying transmission rates. In *Proc. of ACM Sigmetrics*, pages 129–140, June 2013.

[11] J. Gittins, K. Glazebrook, and R. Weber. *Multi-armed Bandit Allocation Indices.* Wiley, second edition, 2011.

[12] P. Jacko. Value of information in optimal flow-level scheduling of users with Markovian time-varying channels. *Performance Evaluation*, 68:1022–1036, 2011.

[13] A. Jalali, R. Padovani, and R. Pankaj. Data throughput of CDMA-HDR a high efficiency-high data rate personal communication wireless system. In *Proc. of IEEE VTC 2000 Spring*, pages 1854–1858, May 2000.

[14] J. Kim, B. Kim, J. Kim, and Y. Bae. Stability of flow-level scheduling with Markovian time-varying channels. *Performance Evaluation*, 70:148–159, 2013.

[15] R. Knopp and P. Humblet. Information capacity and power control in single-cell multiuser communications. In *Proc. of IEEE ICC*, pages 331–335, June 1995.

[16] S. Ross. *Applied Probability Models with Optimization Applications.* Holden-Day, 1970.

[17] B. Sadiq and G. de Veciana. Balancing SRPT prioritization vs opportunistic gain in wireless systems with flow dynamics. In *Proc. of ITC-22*, September 2010.

[18] L. Schrage. A proof of the optimality of the shortest remaining processing time discipline. *Operations Research*, 16:687–690, 1968.

[19] I. Taboada, P. Jacko, U. Ayesta, and F. Liberal. Opportunistic scheduling of flows with general size distribution in wireless time-varying channels. In *Proc. of ITC-26*, September 2014.

[20] I. Taboada, F. Liberal, and P. Jacko. An opportunistic and non-anticipating size-aware scheduling proposal for mean holding cost minimization in time-varying channels. *Performance Evaluation*, 79:90–103, 2014.

[21] L. Tassiulas and A. Ephremides. Dynamic server allocation to parallel queues with randomly varying connectivity. *IEEE Transactions on Information Theory*, 39:466–478, 1993.

[22] P. van de Ven, S. Borst, and S. Shneer. Instability of MaxWeight scheduling algorithms. In *Proc. of IEEE Infocom*, pages 1701–1709, April 2009.

[23] P. Whittle. Restless bandits: activity allocation in a changing world. *Journal of Applied Probability*, 25A:287–298, 1988.

APPENDIX

Classwise results for scenarios S2a, S2b and S2c

Here we present the classwise results for scenarios S2a, S2b and S2c, all of which have two classes of users as described in Section 8.2. The holding costs incurred in the two classes of the scenarios S2a, S2b, and S2c are shown in Figures 4, 5 and 6, respectively. The respective results for the total holding cost incurred in both the classes are shown in Figure 2.

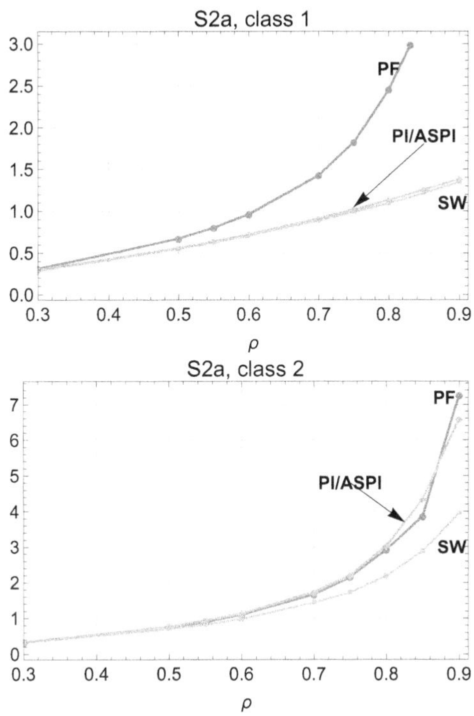

Figure 4: Mean holding cost incurred by class 1 (panel(a)) and class 2 (panel (b)) at different system load values, ρ, for scenario S2a. The total holding cost for both classes is shown in Figure 2 (a).

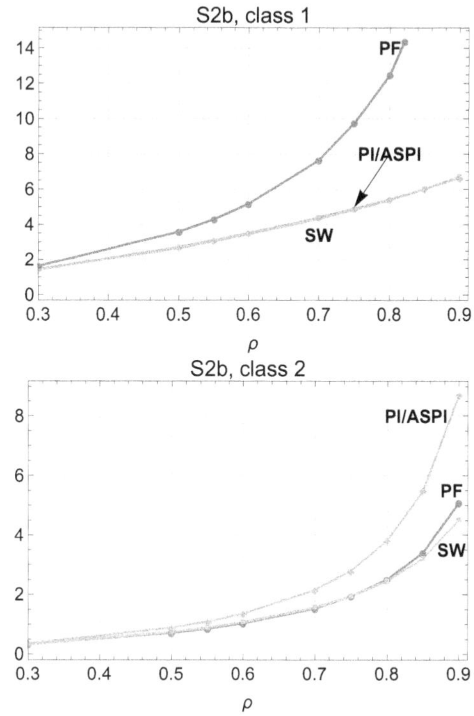

Figure 5: Mean holding cost incurred by class 1 (panel(a)) and class 2 (panel (b)) at different system load values, ρ, for scenario S2b. The total holding cost for both classes is shown in Figure 2 (b).

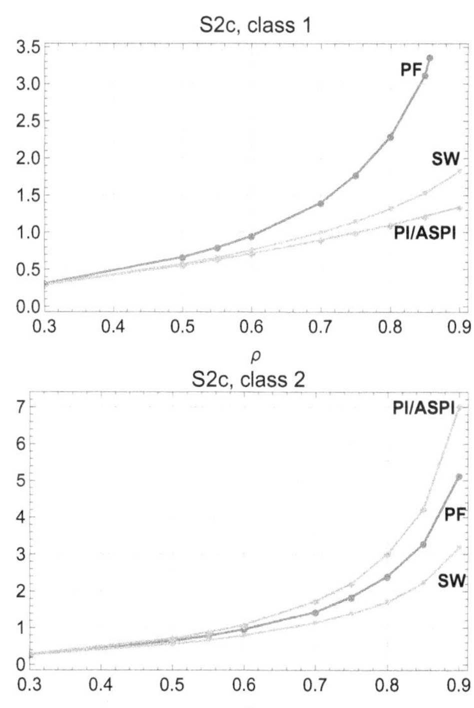

Figure 6: Mean holding cost incurred by class 1 (panel(a)) and class 2 (panel (b)) at different system load values, ρ, for scenario S2c. The total holding cost for both classes is shown in Figure 2 (c).

60 GHz Indoor Networking through Flexible Beams: A Link-Level Profiling

Sanjib Sur, Vignesh Venkateswaran, Xinyu Zhang, Parmesh Ramanathan
{sur2, vvenkateswar}@wisc.edu, {xyzhang, parmesh}@ece.wisc.edu
University of Wisconsin-Madison, USA

ABSTRACT

60 GHz technology holds tremendous potential to upgrade wireless link throughput to Gbps level. To overcome inherent vulnerability to attenuation, 60 GHz radios communicate by forming highly-directional electronically-steerable beams. Standards like IEEE 802.11ad have tailored MAC/PHY protocols to such flexible-beam 60 GHz networks. However, lack of a reconfigurable platform has thwarted a realistic proof-of-concept evaluation. In this paper, we conduct an in-depth measurement of indoor 60 GHz networks using a first-of-its-kind software-radio platform. Our measurement focuses on the link-level behavior with three major perspectives: *(i)* coverage and bit-rate of a single link, and implications for 60 GHz MIMO; *(ii)* impact of beam-steering on network performance, particularly under human blockage and device mobility; *(iii)* spatial reuse between flexible beams. Our study dispels some common myths, and reveals key challenges in maintaining robust flexible-beam connection. We propose new principles that can tackle such challenges based on unique properties of 60 GHz channel and cognitive capability of 60 GHz links.

Categories and Subject Descriptors

C.2.1 [**Computer-Communication Networks**]: Network Architecture and Design - Wireless communication;
C.4 [**Performance of Systems**]: Measurement techniques

Keywords

60 GHz, millimeter-wave, IEEE 802.11ad, software-radio

1. INTRODUCTION

Driven by the growing population of mobile devices and bandwidth-hungry applications, mobile network traffic is set to explode in our near future. Industry research predicts that aggregate wireless traffic will increase by 1000× within the next decade [1]. Legacy WiFi and cellular networks fall short of such demand because of the scarce spectrum resources in the underlying microwave band, despite tremendous research efforts in improving spectrum efficiency. Moving to higher frequencies, however, copious spectrum exists. Most remarkably, the 57 GHz – 64 GHz spectrum, colloquially known as the 60 GHz millimeter-wave (mmWave) band, allows for unlicensed access across majority of the world. Two IEEE 60 GHz MAC/PHY standards, 802.11ad [2] and 802.15.3c [3], have recently been ratified for local and personal area networking. With up to 7 Gbps of data rate, they are ready to support next-generation wireless applications, *e.g.*, uncompressed video streaming, cordless computing, and even wireless data centers [4]. A similar paradigm has been advocated by industry to realize 5G cellular networks [5].

Nonetheless, the eventual success of such conceptual development depends on system designs that account for the unique characteristics of 60 GHz networks. In particular, 60 GHz links are highly vulnerable to attenuation. The free-space path loss scales as $1/\lambda^2$, where λ is the carrier wavelength [6]. So, 60 GHz is 21.6 dB worse than 5 GHz and 28 dB worse than 2.4 GHz that is being used for current WiFi. On the other hand, 60 GHz links can be made highly directional by compacting many miniature antenna elements into a *phased-array*. Given the same form-factor, directivity gain scales as $1/\lambda^2$, which can compensate the path loss drawback. In IEEE 802.11ad, for example, a link quality gain of 20 dB can be easily achieved using a 16-element phased-array [7]. However, highly directional links induce a new sets of challenges, particularly due to human blockage and device mobility. Although phased-arrays are envisioned to overcome the hindrance by electronically steering beams, little experimental research has been conducted to validate the efficacy.

To date, evaluation of 60 GHz protocols mostly relies on simulations complemented by analytical/empirical propagation models [6]. However, given the diverse beam patterns and sophisticated multipath reflections, it is virtually infeasible to faithfully reproduce mmWave channel profiles with a unified model. This problem becomes especially pronounced in dynamic environment with human blockage, device mobility, and interference between directional beams. Recent commercial-off-the-shelf (COTS) 60 GHz devices [8, 9] enabled transport and application layer throughput profiling. However, lack of access to their propriety MAC/PHY implementation has left many open conjectures *w.r.t.* how 60 GHz networks behave especially under environment dynamics.

SIGMETRICS'15, June 15–19, 2015, Portland, OR, USA.

http://dx.doi.org/10.1145/2745844.2745858.

In this paper, we conduct a microscopic measurement of 802.11ad-based 60 GHz indoor WLAN, with an emphasis on how the flexible beams impact link-layer performance, and how they react under blockage/mobility. To this end, we build a first-of-its-kind 60 GHz software-radio testbed, called *WiMi*. A WiMi transmitter can reconfigure its carrier frequency, output power and waveform, which can be detected and processed by a receiver in real-time. Link-level statistics, such as Received Signal Strength (RSS), can be monitored in fine-resolution ($\leq$ 2 ms) even without higher-layer association between transmitter and receiver (unlike COTS devices). WiMi uses mechanically steerable horn antennas to emulate 802.11ad phased-array, and allows plug-and-play installation of antennas with different beamwidths.

Profiling Link-level Characteristics. We leverage WiMi's reconfigurability to examine 60 GHz flexible-beam links in indoor environment from three perspectives:

(i) Single static link. We identify key factors that determine the attenuation models a 60 GHz link should follow in indoor environment. Such factors explain the inconsistencies in prior channel measurement studies that use channel sounder hardware [10, 11] or COTS devices [4]. We then investigate the feasibility of establishing a mmWave MIMO link, by transforming WiMi into a virtual MIMO platform. We further analyze how the link rate/range scales with narrower beamwidth under regulatory power constraints.

(ii) Link behavior under environment dynamics. 802.11ad transmitters and receivers rely heavily on a beam searching protocol that aligns their beam directions to maximize link SNR, or detours obstacles via reflection paths. We examine the efficacy and cost of beam searching, along with other pathologies that may eventually nullify the benefits of flexible beams. In addition, we identify design principles that can minimize the impact of link outage caused by human blockage or device motion.

(iii) Multi-link spatial reuse. Indoor 60 GHz beams differ from the ideal fan-shaped patterns in theoretical models. We measure the impacts of such imperfectness on spatial reuse. Further, we investigate the impact of environment dynamics on 802.11ad-like MAC, which realize spatial reuse by establishing a conflict graph between directional beams.

Summary of insights from measurement study. Our measurement study leads to several interesting sets of insights, which we summarize as follows:

(i) Existing propagation models typically abstract narrow-beam advantage into an antenna gain factor. We found that beamwidth, along with factors like antenna height, also determine how closely the signal attenuation follows theoretical models. Unlike conventional perception that 60 GHz beams behave in a pseudo-optical manner, we found highly directional beams suffer less penetration loss across typical obstacles (except human body) in an office environment, and coverage can be achieved beyond a single room. A side discovery is that 60 GHz MIMO gain becomes correlated with link distance, instead of antenna distance as assumed in communications-theoretic models [6].

(ii) In device motion scenarios, we found the 802.11ad's beam searching algorithm costs more channel time than the Gbps data transmission, and thus degrades throughput even for a 22.5° beam with a relatively small search space. 802.11ad proposes a quasi-omni mode aiming to accelerate the AP-client discovery procedure by widening beams, yet we found this rarely helps because the 60 GHz channel itself exhibits a densely concentrated Angle-Of-Arrival (AOA) pattern. We also discover, for the first time, that 802.11ad links themselves tend to be asymmetric due to sophisticated interaction between beam patterns and environment dynamics.

In human blockage scenario, we found the effectiveness of beam searching is sensitive to blockage position and reflectivity of environment. From both scenarios, we derive and validate two principles that can combat link dynamics: (a) sparsity of AOA can be leveraged to reduce beam searching space and thus overhead; (b) sensitivity of 60 GHz links themselves can be exploited to detect blockage/motion and tackle link outage in a proactive way.

(iii) Due to reflection and strong antenna side lobes, even super-narrow beams (*e.g.* 3.4°) can leak signals causing interference and degrade spatial reuse. Conflict-graph based approach, albeit effective in static scenarios [12], can significantly disturb network performance due to a tradeoff between responsiveness and overhead. It is more sensible to detect device motion, and isolate mobile nodes by allocating separate TDMA slots.

Our Contributions. General properties of 60 GHz channel, such as directionality and vulnerability to blockage, are already well known in communications models [10, 11, 13]. The new contributions of this study lie in its microscopic perspectives on *network* performance, and particularly in: *(i)* novel link-layer measurement methodologies based on a 60 GHz software-radio platform; *(ii)* new measurement observations on the link-level behavior of flexible, directional 60 GHz beams under environment dynamics; *(iii)* new design principles to realize efficient beam searching and adaptation to blockage/mobility, harnessing the inherent sparsity and sensitivity of 60 GHz channels. The data set from this measurement study will be released to the research community through our project repository [14]. The empirical traces can drive the simulation of design choices such as network architecture, scheduling mechanisms and adaptation algorithms to combat blockage/mobility.

2. BACKGROUND AND METHODOLOGY

2.1 IEEE 802.11ad Standard for 60 GHz WLANs

An 802.11ad WLAN comprises multiple stations (STAs) that can establish peer-to-peer (P2P) mode connection between each other, or infrastructure mode connection with an access point (AP). Each node executes a beamforming and beam-steering mechanism to form directional transmit/receive beams using a phased-array antenna. The AP maintains a hybrid MAC scheduler to centrally coordinate all the directional links in the network.

Beamforming and Beam-steering: A phased-array antenna comprises multiple omni-directional antenna elements that together form a radio-frequency "lens". Beamforming is equivalent to reshaping the lens to form different beam patterns (widths and directions). More specifically, each beam pattern is generated by assigning a vector of phase-shifts to the antenna elements. Given M elements, a discrete set of $2M$ beam patterns can be generated by an 802.11ad phased-array [2]. The actual beamwidth and direction depends on the phase-shift values, and the narrowest beamwidth depends on how large M is.

802.11ad runs an iterative beam searching protocol to align the transmitter and receiver's beams (details in Section 4.1). Besides, a *quasi-omni* beam pattern (Figure 1), which

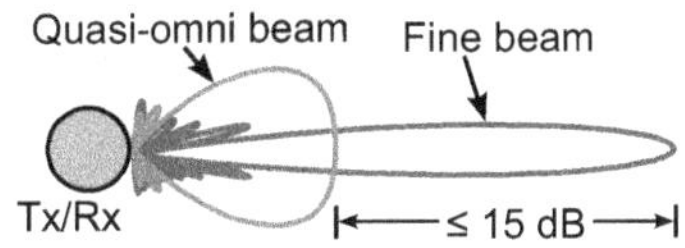

Figure 1: **Fine beam and its quasi-omni beam.**

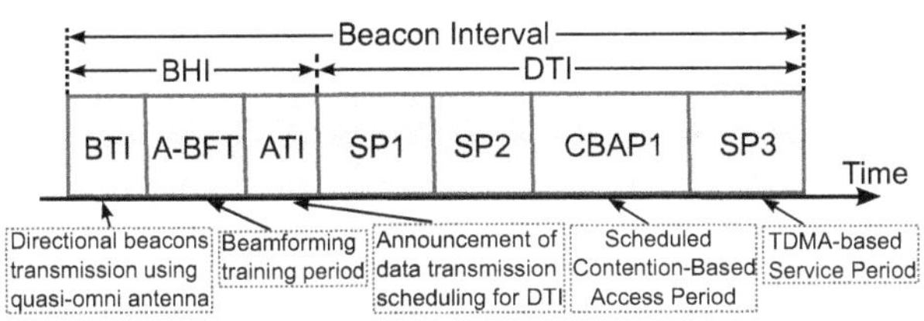

Figure 2: **IEEE 802.11ad beacon interval structure.**

is relatively wider, is used opportunistically to improve the rendezvous probability between AP and STAs' beams. The antenna gain of a quasi-omni beam can be at most 15 dB lower than that of the narrowest beam [2].

Hybrid MAC Layer: 802.11ad uses a hybrid MAC to coordinate the directional communication between multiple devices. Simply put, in infrastructure mode, the AP can enforce a *deterministic TDMA schedule* (*a.k.a.* Service Period) to communicate with multiple STAs, whose beam directions are trained periodically at the beginning of a beacon interval. In P2P mode, a *semi-contention scheduler* is used, where a STA can contend to reserve channel by sending a RTS request to the AP. The AP confirms the reservation with a CTS. The AP learns the interference relation between P2P links by collecting periodic interference reports from them (Section 5.2). It uses CTS to permit non-interfering links to transmit concurrently with the one who initiated RTS.

Timing in 802.11ad is based on beacon intervals (Figure 2), separated by directional beacons from the AP at the beginning of the interval (BTI). The AP uses quasi-omni beams to broadcast beacons through all spatial directions. Then, the AP and STAs execute a beam training (searching) procedure in an A-BFT slot, followed by an ATI, where AP announces the schedules for the immediate data transmission interval. The different scheduling modes are allocated in orthogonal time frames but the duration and allocation strategy can be customized and left as implementation dependent.

2.2 Measurement Methodology

We now introduce our 60 GHz software-radio that is built for measurement purpose. The software-radio provides signal-level visibility, and is engineered to profile link-level characteristics of 802.11ad devices using a combination of over-the-air transmission and emulation.

2.2.1 Building the WiMi Software-Radio

Existing COTS 60 GHz platforms (*e.g.*, Wilocity radio [9, 15] and HXI Gigalink radio [4]) can only report higher-layer throughput statistics or long-term average RSS, after a link is established. However, our link-level measurement requires a 60 GHz "sniffer" that can measure fine-grained link statistics even without connecting to the transmitter. This is crucial in studying dynamic scenarios with blockage/mobility, where link outages become the norm. In addition, the measurement platform needs to be programmable *w.r.t.* output power, beam patterns, and signal waveforms. Despite plenty of 2.4/5 GHz reconfigurable radios [16–18], we are unaware of a 60 GHz counterpart. Therefore, we have assembled our own testbed, *WiMi*, to satisfy the measurement requirements. WiMi is a 60 GHz software-radio that leverages the WARP FPGA [16] as baseband signal processing unit, along with a high-speed ADC/DAC module connected to a 60 GHz RF development board [19]. Figure 3 illustrates a pair of WiMi transmitter and receiver and their major building blocks.

Figure 3: **WiMi software-radio platform.**

2.2.2 Creating and Measuring 60 GHz Links on WiMi

RSS, bit-rate and throughput measurement. Each WiMi node is hosted by a PC that controls the radio hardware and executes MAC/PHY operations through a mix of MATLAB/C drivers. We have developed customized drivers that allow WiMi to send/receive 60 GHz packets at a fine-granularity of 2 ms per packet, each lasting up to 800 μs. The receiver computes RSS on a per-packet basis, by calculating the average signal power across the 800 μs. This suffices for evaluating link dynamics caused by environment change.

Due to hardware limitation, WiMi's bandwidth (245.76 MHz) is incommensurate with 802.11ad radios (2.16 GHz), so it cannot achieve Gbps data-rate. However, the measured RSS and noise floor can be translated into achievable bit-rate following an 802.11ad specific rate table (Table 2 in Appendix C). Such extrapolation approach has been adopted and verified in existing measurement studies [4, 9].

Unless noted otherwise, the transmit power of a WiMi node is always calibrated such that the RSS matches the minimum sensitivity required for the highest data rate, before starting any experiment. The protocol stack on the PC host emulates the 802.11ad MAC components that are pertinent to this study. The emulator uses a virtual clock when enforcing protocol actions including packetization with preambles, beam searching, inter-frame spacing, RTS/CTS, ACK, *etc.* that respect 802.11ad's default timing parameters. Link throughput is calculated taking into account the achievable bit-rate along with such overhead.

Adapting antenna beam width and directions. Due to the lack of any COTS electronically steerable phased-array antenna at 60 GHz, we emulate 802.11ad's beam-steering by using a mechanically steerable horn antenna with beamwidth 3.4° and antenna gain of 34 dBi (equivalent to a phased-array with 50×50 antenna elements). Besides, an omni-directional antenna can be plugged in and moved to create a virtual MIMO antenna (Appendix B). We further create a variety of different beam patterns by "reshaping" WiMi's built-in waveguide module. According to our measurement (Figure 24 in Appendix A), the waveguide pro-

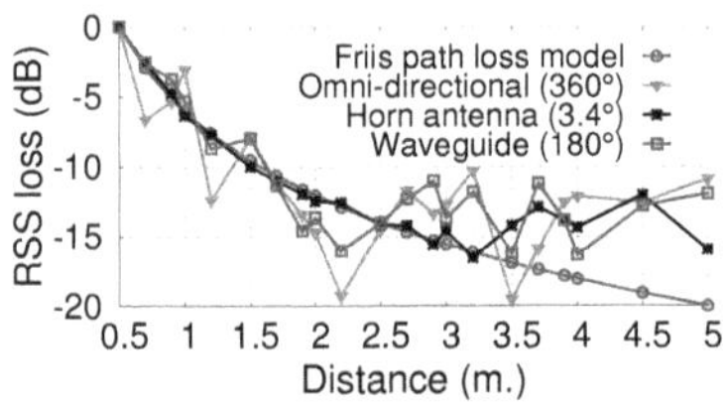

Figure 4: **Impact of beamwidth on LOS path loss. Antenna height is** 30 cm.

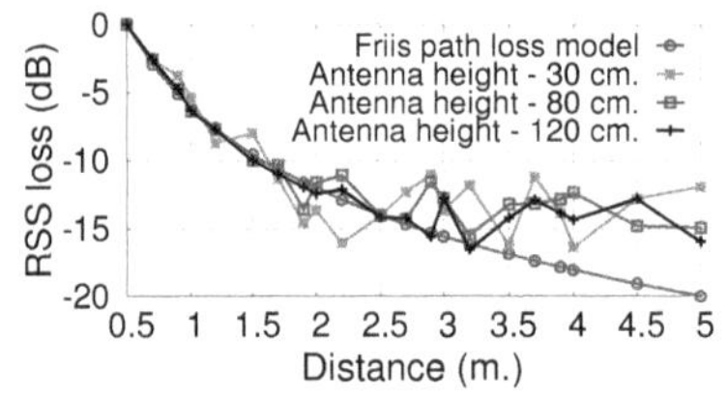

Figure 5: **Impact of antenna height on LOS path loss. Beamwidth is** 180°.

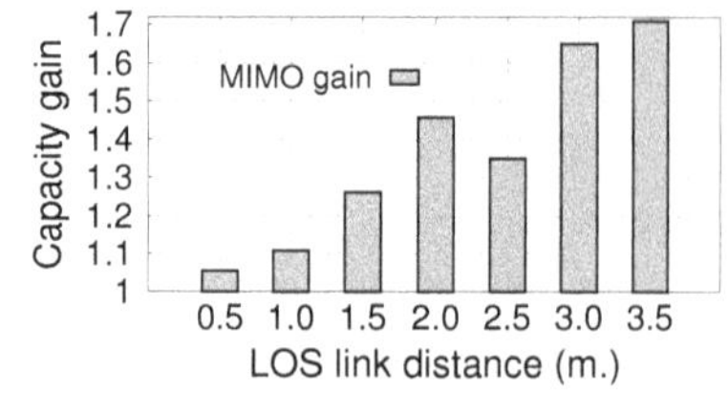

Figure 6: 2×2 **MIMO capacity gain for different link distances.**

vides approximately 180° beamwidth in horizontal and vertical plane. We leverage mmWave absorbers [20] and create conical shapes opening in front of the waveguide according to the beamwidth requirement. Examples beam patterns generated using this approach are verified in Appendix A. Similar to the horn antenna, beam directions of the emulated beam patterns can be steered mechanically.

3. PROFILING A SINGLE STATIC LINK

We first inspect the coverage and capacity of a standalone 60 GHz link, with a particular emphasis on 802.11ad directional beams.

3.1 Line-of-Sight (LOS) Links

In ideal free-space setting, RF signals' attenuation loss follows the Friis model (in dB scale):

$$PL(d) = 20\log_{10}(\frac{4\pi d}{\lambda}) = 20\log_{10}(4\pi d \cdot \frac{f}{c}) \\ = 20\log_{10}(d) + 20\log_{10}(f) - 147.56 \quad (1)$$

where d is the link distance, and λ, f, c are the carrier wavelength, signal frequency and light speed, respectively.

Whereas measurement of COTS 60 GHz links showed almost perfect fit to the Friis model [4,21], PHY-layer channel sounding tests revealed drastic deviations [10,11]. Owing to the flexibility of WiMi, we have identified two factors that can account for such discrepancies.

Attenuation of different beamwidth. We vary the distance of a LOS link, and measure the propagation loss relative to a reference distance $d_0 = 0.5$ m. The results (Figure 4) highlight two immediate observations: *(i)* A narrower beam follows the Friis model more closely. *(ii)* The shorter the distance, the closer the path loss is to the Friis model. In effect, both phenomena may be explained by the multipath reflections that disturb the model at further distances where the wavefront hits obstacles. To corroborate this point, we further vary the antenna position that affects how severe multipath is at certain distance.

Impacts of antenna positioning. We mount a pair of nodes with 180° beamwidth on a variety of heights above the floor. Figure 5 shows that, higher the antennas are, closer the loss is to Friis model, because it takes longer distance before the beams hit the floor to cause multipath reflections. It should be cautioned that the Friis model, being ideal, is not necessarily optimistic. At further distances, measured path loss can be even lower than that in free-space. This is due to a *waveguide effect*, where multipath are chambered to strengthen each other in indoor environment [13].

Implications for 60 GHz MIMO links. Next-generation 60 GHz MIMO network standard is already charted by the IEEE NG60 group [22], aiming to achieve 30+ Gbps rate by delivering parallel streams of data through multiple omnidirectional antennas simultaneously. Such *multiplexing gain* is achievable only if the antennas experience *uncorrelated* multipath channels [23]. However, the foregoing experiments hint that co-located antennas may experience *similar* Friis loss pattern, thus impairing the MIMO potential. We verify this hypothesis by building a 2×2 virtual MIMO on WiMi (see Appendix B), with half-wavelength separation between co-located antennas to minimize coupling effects. We then measure the capacity gain of MIMO over corresponding SISO link, with nodes mounted 30 cm above a table. Theoretically, this setup should achieve close to $2\times$ gain. Yet the results (Figure 6) show the MIMO gain is marginal ($< 1.26\times$) when link distance falls below 1.5 m, and gradually approaches 2 over longer distances. This is again because the parallel MIMO links experience random, uncorrelated multipath only beyond a certain distance.

3.2 Non-Line-of-Sight (NLOS) Links

It is a common perception that 60 GHz signals propagate in a pseudo-light manner and cannot penetrate walls or other obstacles indoor. We now examine this perception in an office environment, with floor plan shown in Figure 7(b).

Blockage loss by common objects indoor. We measure the penetration loss by placing the transmitter and receiver 1 m apart with obstacles in between, and compare with a LOS link of the same distance.

Table 1 shows that, for a 3.4° beam, penetration loss across drywall, wooden door, and cubicle partitions are below 1 dB, leading to only 7.5% of throughput degradation. Both whiteboard and metal sheet (0.1 cm) cause more than 4 dB of RSS loss and 33% of throughput degradation. Given equal beamwidth (30°), 60 GHz suffers more penetration loss than WiFi. However, the loss is significantly lower when using a 3.4° highly directional beam, likely because of less diffusion effects along a concentrated beam. To our knowledge, this phenomenon has not been reported in prior measurement studies that use inflexible channel sounder [10,11] or COTS devices [8,9]. As it is easier to build small form-factor directional antennas at 60 GHz [6], this advantage can partly compensate for the vulnerability to penetration loss.

Remarkably, 60 GHz signals experience dramatic attenuation when going through human body or water bottle. When a transmitter sends 3.4° and 30° beams and is fully blocked by a close-by human body, the receiver senses no signal. In contrast, the 30° WiFi link can still maintain connectivity, though at around 43% of throughput loss.

Coverage under penetration loss. Given the surprisingly low penetration loss across typical obstacles, we expect 60 GHz links can cover beyond a single room. For a quantitative validation, we first place a transmitter on a corner, and survey the receiver's spatial throughput distribution by

Material (thickness)	60 GHz (3.4°)		60 GHz (30°)		WiFi (30°)	
	RSS	Tput	RSS	Tput	RSS	Tput
Drywall (15 cm.)	0.53 dB	7.5%	3.2 dB	23%	1.5 dB	12.5%
Wooden door (4.5 cm.)	0.73 dB	7.5%	4 dB	33.3%	1.2 dB	12.5%
Office cubicle separator (5 cm.)	0.4 dB	7.5%	2.9 dB	23%	0.2 dB	12.5%
Office white board (2.5 cm.)	4.2 dB	33%	7.6 dB	48.7%	2.6 dB	14.3%
Metal sheet (0.1 cm.)	6.5 dB	38.5%	10.1 dB	58.9%	8 dB	25%
Human body	31.2 dB	100%	30.9 dB	100%	12.5 dB	42.9%
Water bottle	29.19 dB	100%	-	-	-	-

Table 1: **RSS and throughput loss due to obstacles.**

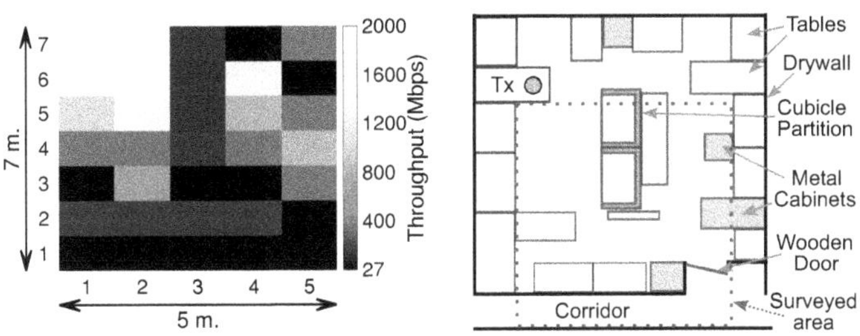

(*a*) (*b*)

Figure 7: (*a*) **Spatial throughput distribution of a 180° link inside an office and in corridor. Black spots denote grids with lowest throughput.** (*b*) **Floor plan of the office.**

dividing the measurement region into 1m × 1m grids. Within each grid, we sample the RSS at 4 random points, each lasting 20 s, and calculate the average. Both nodes are configured to a wide beam of 180°, corresponding to the lowest antenna gain and most conservative rate/coverage estimation.

From the result (Figure 7(a)), we see that even the 180° beam can sustain Gbps throughput within 1 to 2 m, and can maintain link connectivity with lowest data rate almost across the entire room and even outside, despite all the obstructions.

To further explore the coverage limit of directional 60 GHz links beyond room level, we configure the nodes to use two different antennas, and measure the rate degradation over distance and across a whiteboard, drywall and wooden door. The transmit power is calibrated, such that a receiver 50 cm away can have minimum RSS required to achieve highest rate. For comparison, we also calibrate a 2.4 GHz WiFi link such that the RSS at 50 cm is 28 dB higher than 60 GHz (to account for the Friis loss, see Section 3.1). Figure 8 shows that an omni-directional link quickly reaches a coverage limit of 5 m, especially after wall obstruction. Antenna gain from directional beams can significantly extend the range (*e.g.*, by 3× when 3.4° beam is used). Moreover, directional beams experience less rate loss across the obstacles, which is consistent with our penetration test. Interestingly, at lowest modulation rate, the range of a 3.4° 60 GHz link (27.5 Mbps) is *comparable to* WiFi (6 Mbps). This is partly due to the directionality gain, and partly because 802.11ad trades the ultra-wide bandwidth (2.16 GHz) for more robust connectivity at low rate.

Although the preceding experimental setup cannot represent all indoor scenarios, it clearly demonstrates that 60 GHz links can provide reasonable room-level coverage despite NLOS obstructions. Admittedly, compared with 2.4 GHz WiFi, 60 GHz links are more vulnerable to human

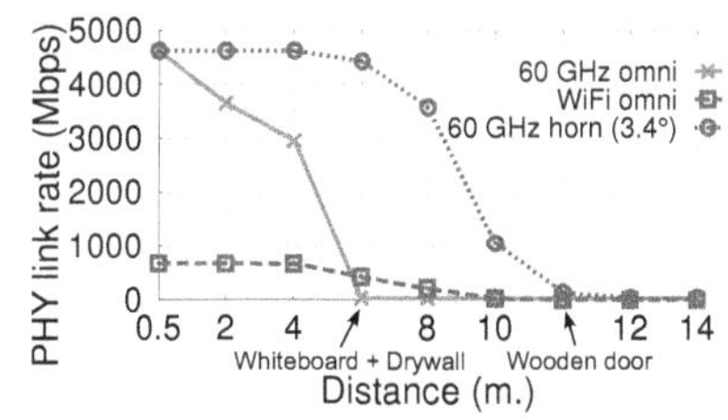

Figure 8: **Throughput and coverage in indoor environment. Transmit power of 60 GHz links are calibrated to match minimum RSS required for highest data rate at 50 cm. WiFi is calibrated to have 28 dB higher gain than 60 GHz.**

blockage, which necessitates new adaptation strategies (Section 4).

3.3 Rate/Range Scaling with Beamwidth

Given the directionality gain, it might be tempting to narrow the beamwidth indefinitely to improve link rate/range, as theoretically range improves quadratically with reduction in beamwidth (contribution via transmitter's and receiver's beam). However, ultimately the achievable performance is limited by the FCC's rule on 60 GHz spectrum, intended to confine the signal radiation for safety and interference management.

Specific to indoor environment, the maximum output power P_t (fed into antenna) is limited to 500 mW (27 dBm). A narrow-beam antenna amplifies the signal and increases its power by G_t dBi, *i.e.*, the antenna gain value. But the ultimate $P_t + G_t$, so called *Effective Isotropic Radiated Power (EIRP)*, must be limited to 40 dBm [24]. The joint effect of these two limits is depicted in Figure 9(a). When beamwidth is larger than 11.25°, EIRP increases proportionally as beamwidth decreases, even though P_t is capped to the 500 mW limit. As beamwidth narrows down to below 11.25°, EIRP saturates and is bounded by the 40 dBm limit. Thus, although a further decrease of transmitter beamwidth improves G_t, the P_t has to be decreased to enforce the EIRP limit[1].

However, it should be noted that the EIRP limit only bounds the effective power from the *transmitter*. Link quality can still be boosted as the receiver narrows its beamwidth, thus increasing the receiving antenna gain G_r. To evaluate the ultimate rate/range scaling as a function of beamwidth and under regulation constraints, we follow long-range indoor channel model in [13] to calculate the link budget, considering Friis loss within 1 m distance and log-distance path loss model with exponent 1.6 and a shadowing factor with standard deviation 1.8 dB. Figure 9(b) shows the LOS range scaling under different data rates and beamwidth. In the P_t-bounded region (beamwidth above 11.25°), maximum range increases quadratically as beamwidth decreases. Whereas in the EIRP-bounded region (beamwidth below 11.25°), only the receiver's narrower beamwidth contributes to RSS increase, and thus the range extension saturates compared with ideal case without EIRP regulation. Note the absolute range values here does not necessarily match all indoor environment. Yet the relative scaling should still hold.

[1]Note that the regulation differs in outdoor environment, which allows EIRP to increase by 2 dB for every 1 dB of additional antenna gain, until it reaches a maximum EIRP of 82 dBm [24].

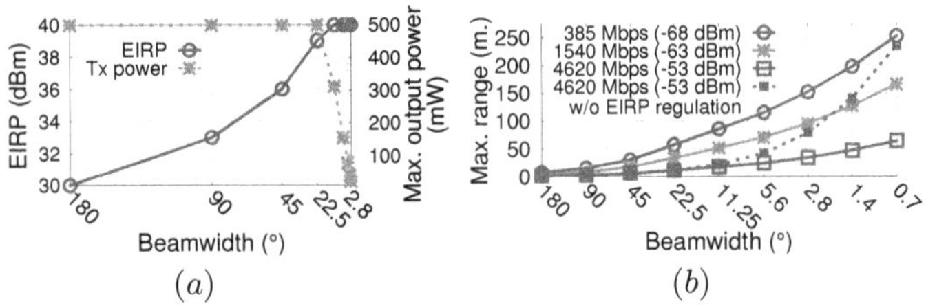

Figure 9: ***(a)*** **EIRP and maximum output power variation considering FCC's regulation.** ***(b)*** **Range/rate tradeoffs for different modulation rates and beamwidth.**

4. FLEXIBLE BEAMS UNDER LINK DYNAMICS

In this section, we investigate the effectiveness of 802.11ad's beam searching protocol in establishing high-capacity directional 60 GHz links in various environments, and maintaining the connection under human blockage or device motion. We unveil new challenges in this networking paradigm, and identify potential solution mechanisms that build on unique properties of 60 GHz links.

4.1 Impact of Beam Searching

4.1.1 A primer on 802.11ad beam searching: complexity and overhead

The 802.11ad standard employs a three-phase beam-training mechanism (Figure 10) to search for the optimal transmit and receive beam direction that maximizes link SNR. The *first phase* involves an initiator and a responder performing sector-level sweeping (SLS), *i.e.*, both the transmitter and receiver configure themselves to a *quasi-omni* mode and sweep through discrete directions. The receiver measures the SNR of each direction combination and reports it to the transmitter. This process yields initial coarse-grained sector-shaped beams with low directionality. In the *second phase*, called MID (Multiple sector ID Detection), a group of Tx quasi-omni directions are tested against a number of finer-grained Rx beams within the best Rx sector. This process is used to refine the Tx sector found in the SLS phase, which might have been suboptimal due to the use of quasi-omni Rx directions. A best Tx sector is estimated in this phase which is subsequently used for further refinement in the *third phase* called BC (Beamforming Combining). Here, a set of up to γ fine-grained directions ($\gamma \leq 7$) in the Tx and Rx sector, identified as top candidates in the previous phases, perform pairwise SNR testing.

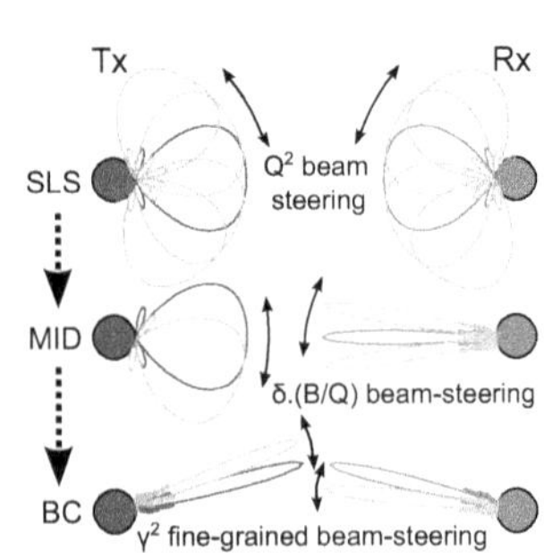

Figure 10: **Beamforming training procedure in 802.11ad.**

Denote B as the number of fine-grained transmit/receive beam directions, Q as the number of quasi-omni beam directions ($Q = c \cdot B$, where $c < 1$ is a constant defined in the standard [2]), and δ (≥ 2) as the number of candidate Tx sectors in the MID phase. Then the *timing complexity of the beam training* equals $BF_\tau = Q^2 + \delta \cdot \frac{B}{Q} + \gamma^2$. The SNR testing of each possible beam combination requires sending a separate training frame or sequence, which costs extra channel time. Figure 11 plots the resulting latency for different beamwidths[2], assuming the same number of antenna elements on the transmitter and receiver.

Due to the exhaustive search in the first phase, the BF_τ grows quadratically ($O(B^2)$) with the number of beam directions. The latency is several orders of magnitude higher than a typical 1KB packet sent at Gbps bit-rate. In Section 4.2, we will evaluate how such latency translates into throughput degradation, depending on how frequently the training process is invoked. By default, 802.11ad triggers beam searching whenever *link outage* occurs (*i.e.*, SNR cannot support the lowest Data PHY rate of 385 Mbps), which could be caused by either human blockage or device motion (beam misalignment).

4.1.2 Link asymmetry: a pathology from flexible beams

Due to the use of discrete phase-shifts on antenna elements, a practical 802.11ad phased-array cannot generate homogeneous beams across all directions [6]. Figure 12 shows an example. Both the AP and STA have 16 antenna elements, with narrowest beamwidth of 11.25° and widest 45°. Due to relative orientation, link SNR is maximized if a 11.25° beam from the STA aligns with a 45° beam from the AP.

Theoretically, even with asymmetric beam patterns, both uplink and downlink should have the same total antenna gains, so that the channel should still be reciprocal. However, we found this no longer holds in the presence of human blockage and environment dynamics.

Specifically, we set up a LOS link with AP orientation of 90° and beamwidth of 90°, and STA orientation of 30° and beamwidth of 22.5°. A human walks and cuts the link across at approximately 2 s intervals while the downlink and uplink packet transmission is ongoing alternately. Beam searching is disabled to isolate the impact of training overhead. The experiment lasts for about 5 minutes and throughput CDF across 50 ms. windows is plotted in Figure 13.

We found that the downlink provides 210 Mbps higher median throughput than uplink. Our further examination reveals that, a narrow receiver beam has higher channel coherence time[3] than a wide one *irrespective of the transmitter beamwidth*, resulting in less SNR variation and throughput turbulence in the presence of human movement/blockage. This explains the higher downlink throughput with a narrower beam STA. Such link asymmetry breaks the assumption in many conventional MAC operations (*e.g.*, reciprocity based link quality estimation).

4.1.3 AP discovery using quasi-omni beams

[2]The relationship between minimum beamwidth Θ and number of steering directions B is given by, $B = (\frac{360}{\Theta})^2$.

[3]Channel coherence time is the duration over which the channel states remain highly correlated (correlation coefficient ≥ 0.9) [25].

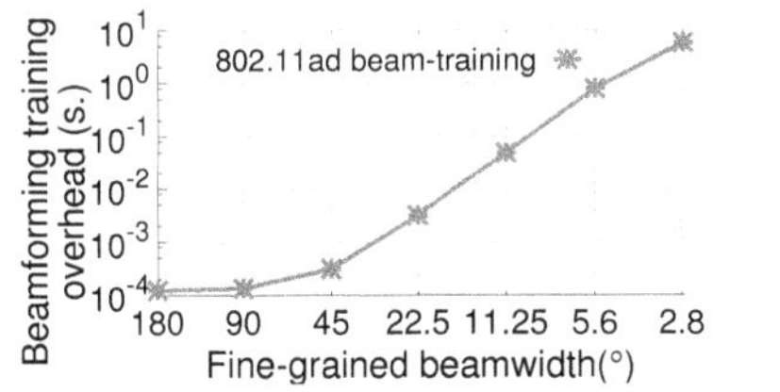

***Figure 11*: Beamforming training overhead in 802.11ad.**

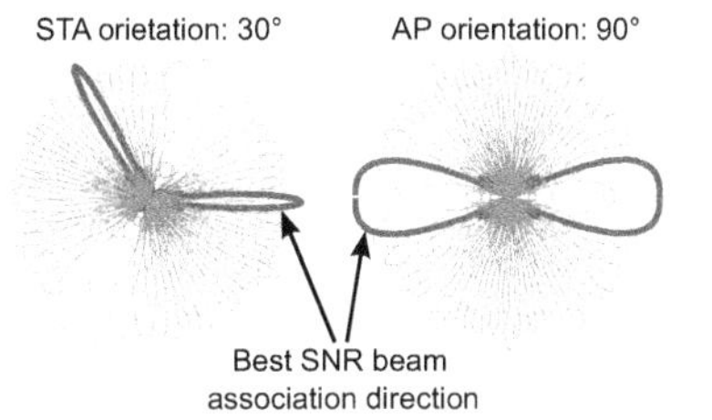

***Figure 12*: Simulated asymmetric association between AP and STA. Both are using 16-element linear phased-array.**

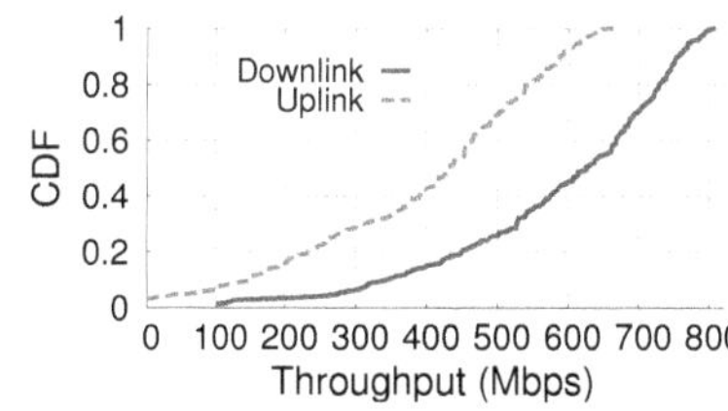

***Figure 13*: Throughput distribution in presence of human movement/blockage across the link.**

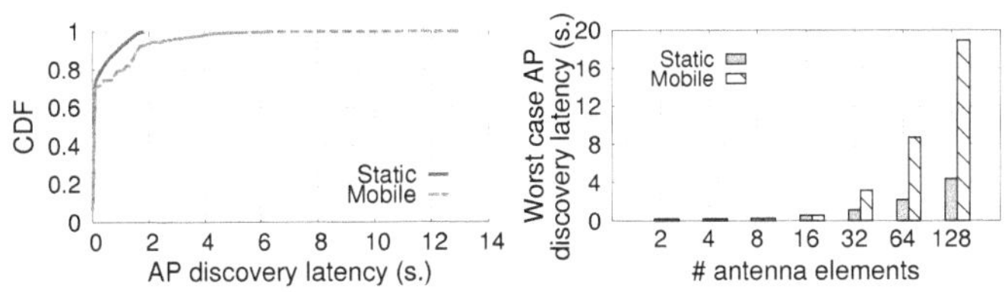

(*a*) (*b*)

***Figure 14*: AP discovery challenges: (*a*) Distribution of AP discovery latency using quasi-omni directional antenna. (*b*) Worst-case discovery latency.**

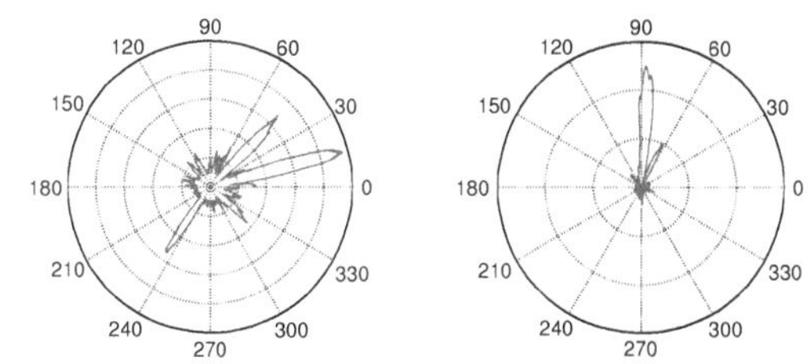

(*a*) (*b*)

***Figure 15*: Examples of omni-directional transmission's AOA pattern captured at two different receiver's location.**

An 802.11ad AP broadcasts beacons periodically, which can be leveraged by newly joining clients for AP discovery and association. To improve the reliability of beaconing, the AP needs to repeat beacons through all its quasi-omni directions. Conceptually, this allows the clients to quickly hear the beacons irrespective of their own beam orientation.

We verify the efficacy of such an AP discovery scheme for both static and mobile clients. Due to the limitation of our experimental platform that requires mechanical steering of horn antenna, we emulate the mobile client using channel traces. Specifically, we move the WiMi receiver and sample spatial channel at discrete points along a pre-defined trajectory, separated 15 cm apart. Each sample requires the client to measure the angular-distribution of RSS by rotating at a granularity of 0.04°. Meanwhile, the AP is fixed at omni-mode, with appropriate power control to match the quasi-omni gain. The resulting traces can thus determine the RSS when the client and AP are configured to any beamwidth and direction. A beacon can be received if the RSS exceeds the receiver sensitivity (−78 dBm) corresponding to the lowest modulation level. Following the 802.11ad specification [2], we configure the AP's quasi-omni beamwidth to ensure its antenna gain is around 15 dB lower than the client's beam.

Figure 14(a) plots the resulting CDF of AP discovery latency among 6 static locations (10^5 trials each), and along the trajectory of a mobile node. The beacon period equals the default 100 ms. We observe that, unlike legacy WiFi, discovery latency in 802.11ad depends heavily on *location and mobility*. For a static client, the latency ranges from 5 ms to 1.8 s, whereas for a mobile client, it can rise to 12.9 s!

Such long latency might seem counter-intuitive, given that the AP is emulating omni-directional transmission by sending beacons through all quasi-omni directions. To identify the root cause, we use WiMi's mechanical rotator to test the receiver's angular RSS distribution while the transmitter is using an omni-directional antenna. It is commonly assumed that, no matter which direction it points to, the receiver can hear an omni-directional transmitter. Besides AP discovery, such assumption is often leveraged in directional MAC protocols as a means of broadcast signaling [26]. However, example tests in two locations (Figure 15) disproves the perception. The receiver's angular RSS is sparsely distributed and largely pronounced on several narrow directions spanning a few degrees. This is likely attributed to the presence of a few strong reflecting objects indoor, and thus independent of the beamwidth of transmitter. Hence, unless both the transmitter's and receiver's quasi-omni beams are tuned to cover the reflecting directions, the beacon will be missed, resulting in prolonged discovery time.

We proceed to evaluate the scenarios with different number of antenna elements (*i.e.*, beamwidths). For each location, the measured angular RSS distribution is sectorized and calibrated in accordance to the quasi-omni beamwidth generated by a given number of antenna elements. In each experiment, the STA picks a random sector to listen to, and moves to the next sector if the AP beacon is not heard within the 100 ms beacon interval. The experiment is repeated over 10^5 random STA orientations. From the results (Figure 14(b)), we see that the worst-case latency grows proportionally with the number of antenna elements. Mobile nodes experience significantly higher latency than static ones (*e.g.* 5 s and 18 s, for 64 and 128 antenna elements respectively), which will clearly hinder the adoption of 60 GHz mobile devices.

The deficiency of quasi-omni transmission/reception can affect a wide range of signaling mechanisms in 802.11ad. For example, to resolve inter-cell interference in TDMA mode, an AP needs to send a *Quieting Adjacent BSS (QAB)* message to adjacent APs to suppress their transmission, in a similar way to periodic beaconing. Latency of such QAB signaling would be similar to the beaconing, thus resulting in substantial interference before the APs can respect each other. Although enforcing omni-directional signaling at both ends may alleviate the situation, it will substan-

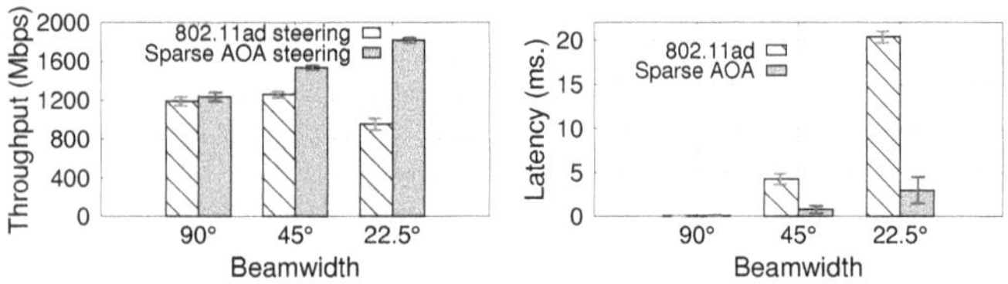

(a) (b)

***Figure 16*: Performance of beam-steering algorithms in presence of user motion. (*a*) Packet throughput. (*b*) Steering latency. Measurements are averaged over 1 s window.**

tially reduce range (Section 3.2). Alternative PHY-layer technologies, *e.g.* spread-spectrum, that trades bit-rate for range, may be a complementary solution, but is beyond the scope of this work.

4.2 Efficient Beam Searching based on AOA Sparsity

Although the sparse clustering of angular RSS plagues AP discovery, we found it can be exploited to curtail the overhead in beam searching. Below we propose a heuristic algorithm that can find near optimal beam direction without exhausting the full beam space.

Suppose two stations STA_a and STA_b search for the beam configuration that maximizes link SNR. Our basic idea is to allow STA_a to transmit beam training frames in *omni-directional* mode, while STA_b sweeps its receive beam directions using fine-beams (instead of quasi-omni) and evaluates the SNR. In this way, a consistent sparse AOA pattern is maintained throughout the training procedure, and the receiver is guaranteed to rendezvous with the angle with strongest signals. The role gets reversed when STA_a wants to identify its own beam direction. Overall, this simple algorithm can reduce search complexity to $O(B)$, substantially lower than 802.11ad (Section 4.1).

To validate the mechanism, we set up 10 different links each using 3 different beamwidths and collect RSS traces for 15 min. Multiple people move around the room and unintentionally block the links. From the trace data of RSS changes we evaluate the frequency of invoking an 802.11ad beam-searching. We then run the MAC emulator in WiMi that accounts for both the link rate and overhead. The results in Figure 16(a) show that, for 802.11ad, narrower beamwidth actually provides worse performance as antenna gain (SNR improvement) is nullified by the beam-steering overhead, even with an intermediate beamwidth of 22.5°. Figure 16(b) further contrasts the latency of beam-steering. Latency of the sparse-AOA based algorithm shows a linear growth while the 802.11ad has a quadratic growth as beamwidth narrows down (thus increasing beam search space), which explains its relatively higher throughput for narrower beams. It should be noted that the maximum link distance during beam searching may differ from that in data transmission. Depending on the sum of transmit/receive antenna gains during the quasi-omni mode SLS, 802.11ad's beam searching range can be either higher or lower than sparse-AOA.

4.3 Beam Switching to Overcome Blockage

Besides aligning the transmitter and receiver's beam directions to maximize link SNR, a crucial functionality of beam searching is to overcome human blockage and track mobile users, which we evaluate in this section.

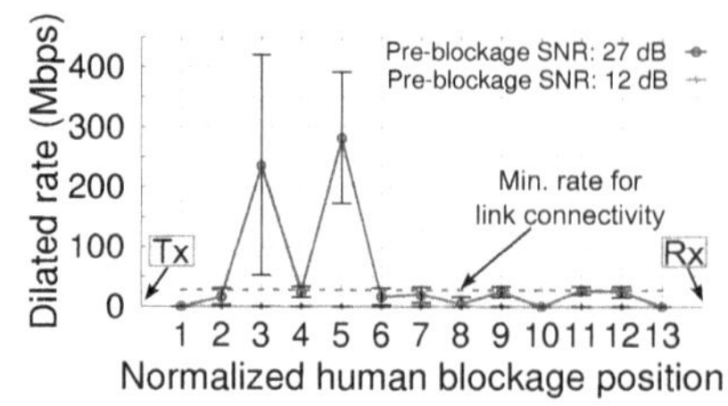

***Figure 17*: Link improvement due to beam dilation *w.r.t.* normalized human blockage position.**

4.3.1 Adapting Beamwidths to Overcome Blockage

One intuitive solution to human blockage is dilating the transmitter/receiver's beamwidth, such that part of the beam circumvents the human body. We now test the reliability of this approach in a controlled setting, with one LOS link (7 m distance). The original beamwidth is 3.4° and when the link is blocked, the transmitter switches to 19.2° (corresponding to its widest quasi-omni beam) without changing its direction. Figure 17 plots the link rate when the human blocks different position of the link (normalized *w.r.t.* link distance). Evidently, when the original link was operating at high rate of 4.6 Gbps (with a minimum SNR of 27 dB), the link can still sustain connectivity, but mostly using the lowest 27.5 Mbps Control PHY rate, and occasionally upgraded to a higher rate when blockage occurs in mid-link. In contrast, when the original SNR was low (12 dB with minimum Data PHY rate of 385 Mbps), no link connectivity is possible irrespective of the blockage position.

Therefore, under human blockage, beam dilation can help maintain link connectivity, but only if the original link SNR is high, and when blockage is sufficiently far away from the transmitter/receiver, such that only part of the beam is blocked. Regardless, the link rate will degrade substantially.

4.3.2 Steering Beam Direction

Alternatively, the transmitter can steer its beam direction to find a detour path that bounces off reflective objects. IEEE 802.11ad invokes this scheme (Section 4.1) automatically whenever the link quality suffers. To evaluate its efficacy, we define a *beam-steering effectiveness* metric η as follows,

$$\eta = (R_1 - R_0)/R_0 \tag{2}$$

where R_0 denotes the LOS link rate before blockage and R_1 means the best achievable rate after beam-steering. η should thus satisfy, $-1 \le \eta < \infty$. $\eta = -1$ if none of the secondary paths can establish connectivity. A positive η implies that secondary path after beam-steering provides a higher rate than the original LOS path. This can happen when the LOS path itself is weaker. Note that, RSS increase of as small as 1 dB can improve η by 0.3 on average [4]. Here we only focus on the rate change before/after beam steering to isolate the impact of searching overhead.

Figure 18(a) and 18(b) plot the η in an office and corridor environment, respectively. For each beamwidth setting, we test 10 links with transmitter and receiver randomly placed inside the test region, link distance ranging from 3 m to 7 m.

[4]Calculated using the rate table 2 in Appendix C and considering an operating RSS in the range −78 to −53 dBm.

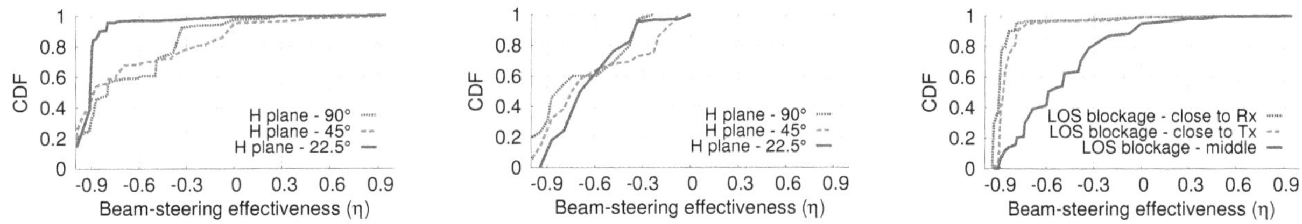

(a) Regular office environment

(b) Corridor environment with reflective structures

(c) Under human blockage at different positions (Beamwidth: 22.5°)

***Figure 18*: Beam-steering effectiveness (η) in indoor environment.**

We see that the η of a narrow beam (22.5°) is remarkably lower than that of wider beams (45° & 90°). Recall the partitions and drywalls in the office environment mostly pass instead of reflecting 60 GHz signals (Section 3.2), whereas candidate reflecting surfaces (mostly from 4 tall metal cabinets and book shelves) are sparsely distributed. Thus, the narrow beam can rarely find an opportunistic path to detour towards the receiver. Amid its lower rate, a wider beam is more resilient, as long as it can be steered to the best secondary path.

Reflective paths in the corridor environment show up differently — all beamwidths exhibit a reasonable level of η, owing to a more open space and existence of brick walls and concrete poles. For 45° and 90°, around 6% and 20% of links experience zero rate even after beam-steering, primarily because of the reflection loss and low antenna gain. Note that in both environments, we are only steering the beams around the azimuthal plane. Depending on reflectivity of ground/ceiling, the effects on the elevation dimension would show up following the same principles.

Figure 18(c) further plots the impact of human blocking position on η, for a 22.5° beam in corridor. We see that η can be much higher if blockage occurs in mid-link, in which case the beam is more likely to find a detour path. When blockage is close to either transmitter or receiver, η is degraded to around -0.9, *i.e.*, 90% of rate is lost.

In summary, *despite higher rate, a narrow beam is more susceptible to blockage as it owns fewer escape paths. Beam-steering can be effective in reflective environment, but barely helps when blockage occurs in close proximity of transmitter/receiver, e.g., human holding a device.*

4.4 Assisting Link Recovery via mmWave Sensing

The above micro-benchmark measurement directly compares possible beam dilation/steering options to overcome blockage. A practical protocol has to choose beam pattern based on its observation of link status. The 802.11ad adopts an *SNR maximization* strategy that tracks the beam pattern to maximize link SNR, which we evaluate below.

For the device motion experiment, we program WiMi's motion controller and create random orientation/position trajectory to emulate typical scenarios when user is holding a mmWave mobile device within the AP's LOS. Real-time RSS traces are collected for a 3.4° link and corresponding 19.2° quasi-omni mode used for beam dilation. The throughput distribution across 1800 time windows (each 50 ms) is plotted in Figure 19(a). Due to dramatic link quality variation, the 802.11ad beam searching is frequently invoked, resulting in substantial overhead. Consequently, dilating the beam to quasi-omni leads to 3× higher throughput, despite its lower bit-rate (when steering overhead is not considered).

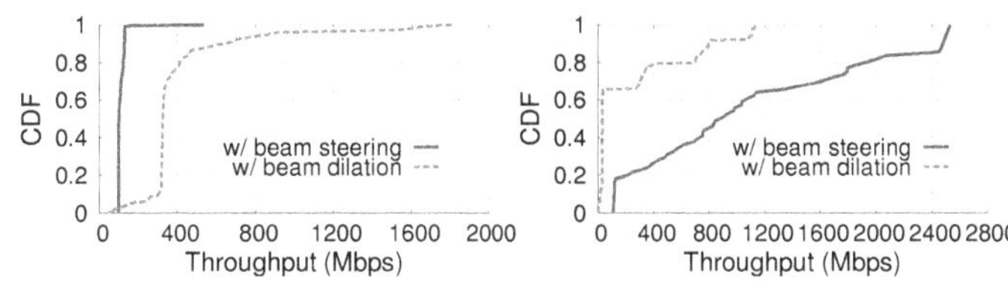

(*a*) (*b*)

***Figure 19*: Throughput of beam-steering and beam-dilation approach: (*a*) Device motion. (*b*) Human blockage.**

For the human blockage experiment, the transmitter and receiver are static and within LOS. A human walks and cuts the link across repeatedly for 90 seconds. Due to intermittent blocking effects, a dilated beam degrades throughput to the lowest value for more than 50% of the times (note this differs from the experiment in Section 4.3.1 where blockage is permanent). In contrast, median throughput of the narrower 3.4° beam is an order of magnitude higher. Beam steering is invoked infrequently – only when the beam is being cut, followed by periodic update in the beginning of beacon interval (Section 2.1). Thus, beam steering overhead is much smaller compared with the device motion case, and SNR-maximizing beam-steering can still be effective.

To summarize, *naïve SNR maximization leads to substantial overhead and low throughput for mobile devices, but can still be effective for a static devices even under human blockage. Thus, it is necessary to execute this metric according to the root cause of link dynamics.*

The natural question thus follows is: how can we diagnose the link outage and invoke proper protocol reaction? We observe that the inherent sensitivity of mmWave links can be harnessed to realize the diagnosis.

Figure 20(a) shows an example of RSS variation over short period of time due to human blockage (cutting the link) and device motion of a 3.4° link. Clearly, human blockage causes a more regular pattern of RSS change, which can serve as a signature to distinguish it from device motion. Let $RSS(t)$ denote the receiver's RSS at time t. We capitalize on the second order statistics of RSS values at the receiver side gathered over a time window of T, calculated as follows,

$$\partial^2 RSS(t,T) = \frac{\partial^2}{\partial^2 t}\Big[RSS(t), \ldots, RSS(t+T)\Big], \qquad (3)$$
$$N_{\partial^2 RSS} = Var\{\partial^2 RSS(t,T)\}$$

where $Var\{\cdot\}$ denotes the variance of sequence of observations. A window is classified as blockage if $N_{\partial^2 RSS}$ falls below

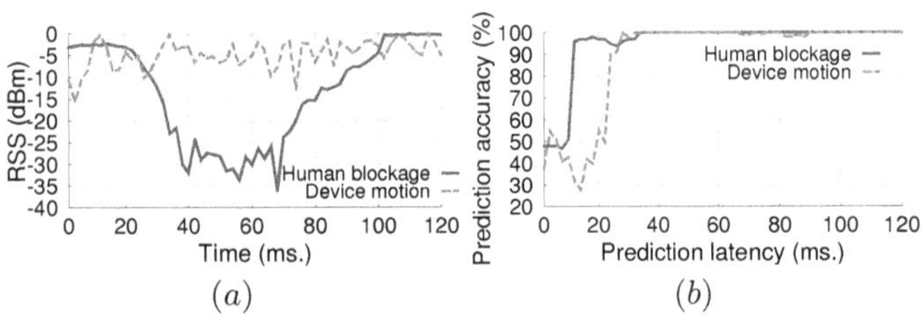

Figure 20: **(*a*) Example of RSS variation due to human blockage and device motion. (*b*) Accuracy of classification for human blockage and device motion. Beamwidth: 3.4°.**

a threshold Θ_{block}, and motion if $N_{\partial^2 RSS}$ exceeds an upper threshold Θ_{motion}. We then accumulate the confidence of classification over time until it rises above 0.95, or exceeds a detection latency bound t_{pred} (see Algorithm 1). The two thresholds are empirically set to 0.002 and 0.2. Since they are far away from each other, we found the detection performance is insensitive to minor parameter adjustment.

To verify this approach in realistic environment, we repeat the human blockage and device motion each for 50 times. We evaluate the classification accuracy for a given t_{pred}, computed over all 50 trials. From the Figure 20(b), we see that the accuracy increases sharply beyond a certain period of confidence accumulation. Given 30 ms or above, both motion and blockage can be classified with close to 100% accuracy. Although the 30 ms latency may leave the link in a temporarily outage/low-throughput state, it helps making a throughput maximizing choice immediately afterwards, instead of relentlessly seeking for SNR maximization, which may result in multiple folds of throughput reduction (Figure 19).

Algorithm 1 Detecting device motion and human blockage

Initialize $t = 0$, $T = T_{win}$, $C = 1$, $\alpha_{\{block,motion\}} = 0$.
while $\alpha \leq 0.95$ /* 95% confidence */
  Calculate the variance of second order statistics of RSS samples $N_{\partial^2 RSS}$, from Equation 3.
  if $N_{\partial^2 RSS} \leq \Theta_{block}$ **then** $\alpha_{block} = \alpha_{block} + 1$;
  else if $N_{\partial^2 RSS} \geq \Theta_{motion}$ **then** $\alpha_{motion} = \alpha_{motion} + 1$;
  end if
  if $\alpha_{block} > \alpha_{motion}$ **then** $\alpha = \alpha_{block}/C$;
  else $\alpha = \alpha_{motion}/C$;
  end if
  $T = T + T_{win}$; $C = C + 1$;
  if $T \geq t_{pred}$ /* Is it too late for prediction? */
    Update t, $T = T_{win}$, $C = 1$, $\alpha_{\{block,motion\}} = 0$;
  end if
end while

Note that, the above device motion experiments were conducted in LOS. In practical usage scenario of mobile mmWave devices, human blockage and device motion can occur together (*e.g.* human holding a device and blocking the AP), where neither beam-steering nor dilation is guaranteed to work. 802.11ad has proposed a fast session transfer mechanism to relocate the link to 2.4/5 GHz, thus salvaging the connection. Measurement and evaluation of such mechanisms is left as our future exercise.

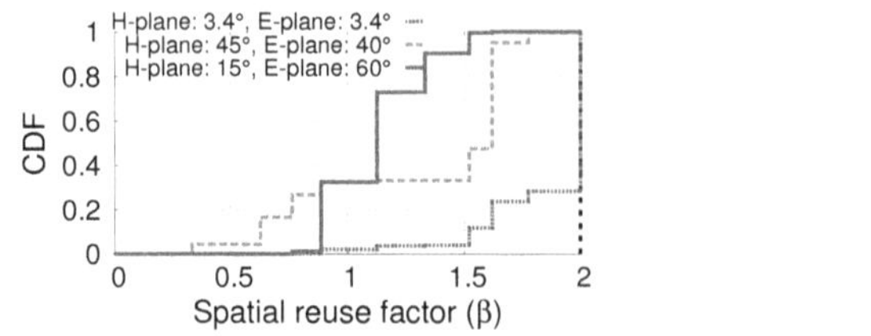

Figure 21: **Distribution of spatial reuse factor (β) with 3 different beamwidths.**

5. SPATIAL REUSE BETWEEN FLEXIBLE-BEAM LINKS

We now study the spatial reuse between narrow-beam 60 GHz links in both static and dynamic scenarios.

5.1 Imperfect Spatial Reuse Between Static Links

Existing modeling/measurement of spatial reuse in flexible-beam directional antenna networks presented bifurcated views: measurement of switched-beam WiFi radios in indoor environment [27] showed that directional beams provide little advantage of spatial reuse due to strong multipath reflections; on the other hand, ray-tracing modeling of outdoor 60 GHz networks [28] claims that the narrow directional links can be abstracted as pseudo-wire with no leakage interference. We now measure the realistic spatial reuse in indoor environment, characterized by a spatial reuse factor, defined as [27]:

$$\beta = \frac{\textit{Sum rate of concurrent links}}{\textit{Average rate of isolated links}} \quad (4)$$

Ideally, two coexisting links can achieve $\beta = 2$, should there be no mutual interference. The smaller β is, the stronger mutual interference becomes, and the worse spatial reuse.

Distribution of spatial reuse factor. We evaluate β in the office environment. For each beamwidth configuration, we randomly create 10 pairs of links, measure the SINR of each link, and then translate it into link rate (using Table 2) and β. Node locations are created under an amenable configuration such that interfering transmitter does not point directly to unintended receiver. Figure 21 plots the CDF of β across all pairs. In general, wider beams experience smaller spatial reuse. For a 3.4° narrow beam, perfect spatial reuse is achieved in 75% of cases. Yet there still exist a sizable fraction of cases with $\beta < 2$. Therefore, unlike 2.4 GHz networks [27], perfect spatial reuse is practical in the common cases for highly directional 60 GHz beams indoor, but leakage or reflected interference is still non-negligible, and thus the pseudo-wire abstraction does not hold.

Impact of side lobes. Existing modeling and simulation typically use a fan-shape to represent the spatial footprint of a 60 GHz link [28]. However, practical 60 GHz phased-array antennas inevitably have spurious side lobes that leak signals [6]. To evaluate the impact on spatial reuse, we place a static receiver on 7 different positions (out of the 10 locations in the previous experiment) and a interferer on 3 locations.

We measure interference on the unintended receiver locations, with and without side lobe effect. The transmitter is a COTS device [15] that uses a main beamwidth of 30° and has side lobes as shown in Figure 22(b). For contrast purpose, we also emulate the scenario without side lobes by enclosing the transmitter's antenna with two 50 dB mmWave

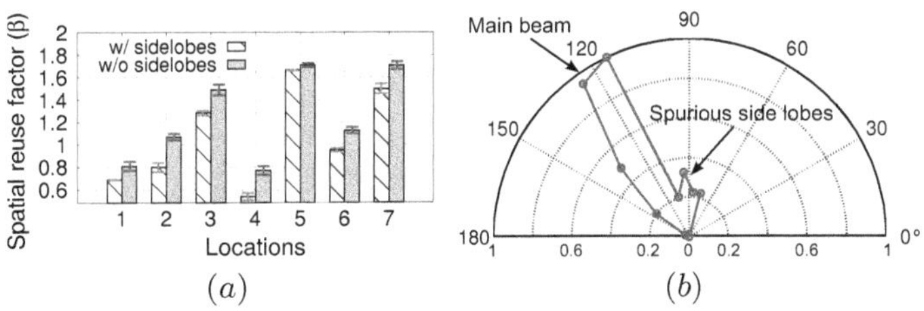

Figure 22: **(*a*) Measured spatial reuse factor (β) using 30° beamwidth across 7 different locations. (*b*) Example of measured beam pattern from the Wilocity 60 GHz radio.**

absorber boards, which form a 30° conical-shape opening and attenuate the side lobes to a negligible level.

Figure 22(a) plots the resulting β factor across 7 receiver locations. We see that side lobes can degrade β by 6% to 25%, translating into 250 Mbps to 700 Mbps of aggregate link throughput reduction. Thus, *to be precise, an interference model must take into account such imperfectness of practical phased-array antennas, instead of abstracting links as fan shapes or pseudo-wires.*

5.2 Spatial Reuse Under Link Dynamics

To maximize spatial reuse, an 802.11ad AP runs an interference aware scheduler that builds a conflict graph between directional links. While one link is transmitting, others can sense and periodically report the overheard RSS (interference) level to the AP. The AP then groups those links with close-to-zero mutual interference into the same TDMA slot to maximize spatial reuse, and regroups if interference recurs. One natural question is: will such interference-aware scheduling be able to cope with link dynamics?

We answer the question through a micro-benchmark experiment illustrated in Figure 23(a). The setup contains two links Tx1→Rx1 and Tx2→Rx2, each with 22.5° beamwidth. Initially both are static and orthogonal to each other, and thus grouped for concurrent transmission. Then, we move Rx1 at walking speed, passing by Rx2. While Tx1 is tracking Rx1, its beam covers and interferes with Rx2.

An 802.11ad AP handles such situations by recomputing a schedule in every beacon period (100 ms by default). We compare this scheme with two alternatives: *(i)* a fine-grained scheduler that requires STAs to report to the AP immediately whenever it wants to execute a beam-steering procedure (with another STA) so that the AP can take appropriate action if the conflict graph is changed due to new beam direction; *(ii)* a TDMA scheduler that intentionally allocates a separate slot to the mobile link. We plot the resulting CDF of throughput across every 50 ms window in Figure 23(b). 802.11ad's beacon-level granularity is too low to respond to node mobility, and thus its throughput is much lower than the isolated TDMA in majority of cases. On the other hand, the fine-grained scheduler incurs too much feedback overhead, and thus even lower throughput. The isolated TDMA performs best on average, yet its throughput in a small fraction of high-end cases is lower, mainly because it conservatively separates the two links even before they become conflicting.

To summarize, *an interference-aware scheduler must balance responsiveness and overhead. To make the best tradeoff, a mobile link should be opportunistically isolated from others and regrouped when appropriate.* The motion detection

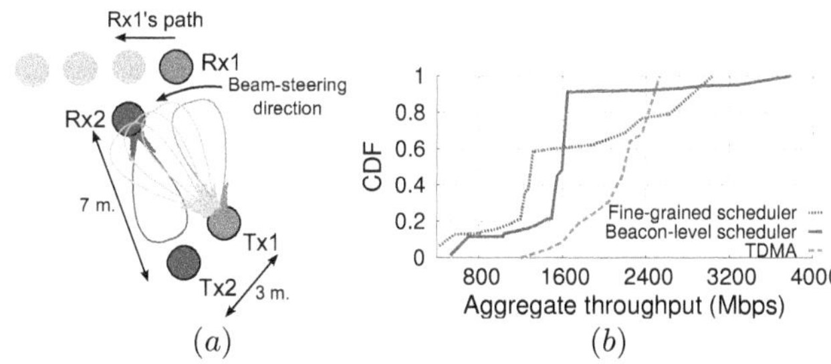

Figure 23: **(*a*) Example of interference map change in presence of mobile client. (*b*) Distribution of aggregate throughput under the influence of mobile client.**

algorithm (Section 4.4), combined with interference prediction (leveraging movement direction and relative position of links), hold potential to make such cognitive decisions.

6. RELATED WORK

60 GHz measurement and modeling. Prior literature on 60 GHz measurement has been extensively focused on characterizing and modeling the channel propagation profile, both indoor [10, 11, 13] & outdoor [29, 30]. Dedicated channel sounder hardware is used to extract statistical properties, such as path loss exponent, delay spread and AOA distribution that can be fit into a general analytical model. Few works measured [31] or simulated [32] the impacts of human blockage, again emphasizing RSS attenuation of a fixed beam, instead of behaviors of flexible-beam protocols.

Recently, Zhu *et al.* [9] used COTS 60 GHz radios for a reality-check of pico-cellular networks, focusing on outdoor coverage and transport-layer throughput. Appealing prospects were revealed: human can rarely block links owing to base-station height (above 6 m); beams can bounce off concrete buildings to reach users; interference can be avoided through base-station coordination. Our measurement found that many of the conclusions no longer hold in indoor 802.11ad WLANs. In particular, human blockage and device mobility pose grand challenges, and the efficacy of beam steering becomes highly sensitive to environment. More importantly, we identify protocol-level issues in operating flexible beams, such as link asymmetry, association latency, beam searching overhead, *etc.* Tie *et al.* [8] also conducted indoor 60 GHz measurement. But similar to [9], only coarse-grained TCP level statistics can be collected due to lack of access to COTS devices' MAC/PHY layers.

Directional-antenna networking over lower frequencies. Research issues in mmWave networking share certain similarities with the vast literature of directional antenna networking, which focused on MAC/routing protocols for ad-hoc networks with directional antennas (see [26] and the references therein). Steerable phased-array antennas have also been employed to improve spatial reuse between indoor WiFi links [12], enable high-capacity communication and robust outdoor vehicular networking [33]. The 60 GHz 802.11ad and 802.15.3c standards partly assimilated these research ideas, particularly in its hybrid MAC design. However, mmWave networking faces many unique challenges imposed by ultra-narrow beams (an order of magnitude narrower than those assumed in microwave-band), sensitivity to path loss/blockage, *etc.*, which have been testified in our contrasting experiments with WiFi (Section 3.2). In addition, unique capabilities of 60 GHz devices, *e.g.*, fine-grained beam switching, blockage/motion sensing, smaller spatial footprint, deserve new system design and measurement investigation.

7. CONCLUSION

In this paper, we have presented a link-level measurement of indoor 60 GHz networks using a software-radio platform. The measurement reveals new challenges pertinent to MAC protocols involving ultra-directional, flexible 60 GHz beams. In particular, 60 GHz links become highly sensitive to human blockage and device motion, posing non-trivial trade-offs between link quality and responsiveness, especially *w.r.t.* the beam searching and interference-aware scheduling. On the other hand, abundant opportunities exist. For example, a 60 GHz ultra-directional link can cover beyond a single room (unlike the common perception of pseudo-optical propagation). Its sensitivity can be harnessed to diagnose link outage, thereby facilitating judicious protocol reactions. We believe a new class of protocols need to be designed to incorporate such challenges/opportunities.

Acknowledgement

We sincerely thank the anonymous reviewers for their valuable comments and feedback. The work reported in this paper was supported in part by the NSF under Grant CNS-1318292, CNS-1343363, CNS-1350039 and CNS-1404613.

8. REFERENCES

[1] Qualcomm Inc., "The 1000x data challenge," https://www.qualcomm.com/1000x, 2014.
[2] IEEE Standards Association, "IEEE Standards 802.11ad-2012: Enhancements for Very High Throughput in the 60 GHz Band," 2012.
[3] ——, "IEEE Standards 802.15.3c-2009: Millimeter-wave-based Alternate Physical Layer Extension," 2009.
[4] X. Zhou, Z. Zhang, Y. Zhu, Y. Li, S. Kumar, A. Vahdat, B. Y. Zhao, and H. Zheng, "Mirror Mirror on the Ceiling: Flexible Wireless Links for Data Centers," in *Proc. of ACM SIGCOMM*, 2012.
[5] T. Rappaport, S. Sun, R. Mayzus, H. Zhao, Y. Azar, K. Wang, G. Wong, J. Schulz, M. Samimi, and F. Gutierrez, "Millimeter Wave Mobile Communications for 5G Cellular: It Will Work!" *IEEE Access*, vol. 1, 2013.
[6] T. S. Rappaport, R. W. H. Jr., R. C. Daniels, and J. N. Murdock, *Millimeter Wave Wireless Communications*. Prentice Hall, 2014.
[7] H. Pan, M. Park, and H. Alavi, "Array Analysis Using High Efficiency mm-wave Antenna for Gigabit Plus Throughput Wireless Communication," in *IEEE Antennas and Propagation Society International Symposium*, 2009.
[8] X. Tie, K. Ramachandran, and R. Mahindra, "On 60 GHz Wireless Link Performance in Indoor Environments," in *PAM*, 2011.
[9] Y. Zhu, Z. Zhang, Z. Marzi, C. Nelson, U. Madhow, B. Y. Zhao, and H. Zheng, "Demystifying 60GHz Outdoor Picocells," in *Proc. of ACM MobiCom*, 2014.
[10] H. Xu, V. Kukshya, and T. Rappaport, "Spatial and Temporal Characteristics of 60-GHz Indoor Channels," *IEEE Journal on Selected Areas in Communications*, vol. 20, no. 3, 2002.
[11] C. Anderson and T. Rappaport, "In-Building Wideband Partition Loss Measurements at 2.5 and 60 GHz," *IEEE Transactions on Wireless Communications*, vol. 3, no. 3, 2004.
[12] X. Liu, A. Sheth, M. Kaminsky, K. Papagiannaki, S. Seshan, and P. Steenkiste, "DIRC: Increasing Indoor Wireless Capacity Using Directional Antennas," in *Proc. of ACM SIGCOMM*, 2009.
[13] P. F. M. Smulders, "Statistical Characterization of 60-GHz Indoor Radio Channels," *IEEE Transactions on Antennas and Propagation*, vol. 57, no. 10, 2009.
[14] X. Zhang and P. Ramanathan, "WiMi Project Website," 2014. [Online]. Available: http://xyzhang.ece.wisc.edu/wimi
[15] "Wilocity 802.11ad Multi-Gigabit Wireless Chipset," http://wilocity.com, 2013.
[16] Rice University, "Wireless Open-Access Research Platform," http://warp.rice.edu/trac/wiki, 2013.
[17] Ettus Inc., "USRP," http://www.ettus.com.
[18] K. Tan, J. Zhang, J. Fang, H. Liu, Y. Ye, S. Wang, Y. Zhang, H. Wu, W. Wang, and G. M. Voelker, "Sora: High performance software radio using general purpose multi-core processors," in *Proc. of USENIX NSDI*, 2009.
[19] "60 GHz Transmit/Receive Development Systems," http://www.pasternack.com, 2014.
[20] TDK RF Solutions Inc., "Absorber for Microwave and Millimeter Wave Test Chambers," 2014.
[21] Y. Zhu, X. Zhou, Z. Zhang, L. Zhou, A. Vahdat, B. Y. Zhao, and H. Zheng, "Cutting the Cord: a Robust Wireless Facilities Network for Data Centers," in *Proc. of ACM MobiCom*, 2014.
[22] IEEE 802.11 NG60 Study Group, "Next Generation 60 GHz (NG60)," 2012.
[23] D. Tse and P. Viswanath, *Fundamentals of Wireless Communication*. Cambridge University Press, 2005.
[24] "FCC 13-112," https://apps.fcc.gov/edoc-public/attachmatch/FCC-13-112A1.pdf, 2013.
[25] X. Xie and X. Zhang, "Adaptive Feedback Compression for MIMO Networks," in *Proc. of ACM MobiCom*, 2013.
[26] O. Bazan and M. Jaseemuddin, "A Survey On MAC Protocols for Wireless Adhoc Networks with Beamforming Antennas," *IEEE Communications Surveys and Tutorials*, vol. 14, no. 2, 2012.
[27] S. Lakshmanan, K. Sundaresan, S. Rangarajan, and R. Sivakumar, "The Myth of Spatial Reuse with Directional Antennas in Indoor Wireless Networks," in *PAM*, 2010.
[28] S. Singh, R. Mudumbai, and U. Madhow, "Interference Analysis for Highly Directional 60 GHz Mesh Networks: the Case for Rethinking Medium Access Control," *IEEE/ACM Transactions on Networking*, vol. 19, no. 5, 2011.
[29] E. J. Violette, R. H. Espeland, and G. R. Hand, "Millimeter-wave Urban and Suburban Propagation Measurements Using Narrow and Wide Bandwidth Channel Probes," *NASA Tech Report*, 1985.
[30] T. Rappaport, F. Gutierrez, E. Ben-Dor, J. Murdock, Y. Qiao, and J. Tamir, "Broadband Millimeter-Wave Propagation Measurements and Models Using Adaptive-Beam Antennas for Outdoor Urban Cellular Communications," *IEEE Transactions on Antennas and Propagation*, vol. 61, no. 4, 2013.
[31] S. Collonge, G. Zaharia, and G. Zein, "Influence of the Human Activity on Wide-Band Characteristics of the 60 GHz Indoor Radio Channel," *IEEE Trans. on Wireless Comm.*, vol. 3, no. 6, 2004.
[32] M. Park and H. K. Pan, "Effect of Device Mobility and Phased Array Antennas on 60 GHz Wireless Networks," in *ACM mmCom*, 2010.
[33] V. Navda, A. P. Subramanian, K. Dhanasekaran, A. Timm-Giel, and S. Das, "MobiSteer: Using Steerable Beam Directional Antenna for Vehicular Network Access," in *Proc. of ACM MobiSys*, 2007.

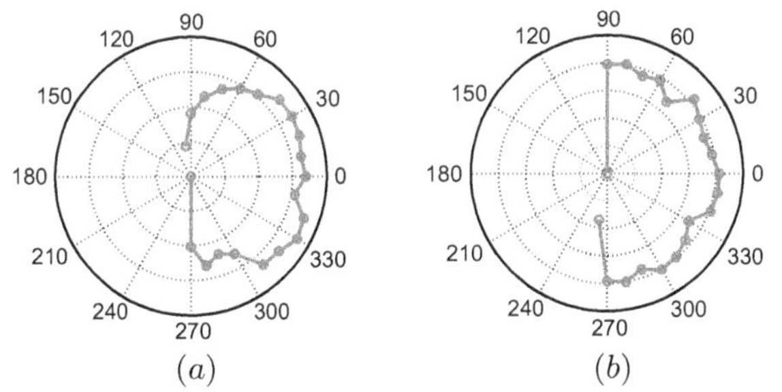

Figure 24: **WiMi waveguide antenna beam pattern: (*a*) Horizontal plane. (*b*) Vertical plane.**

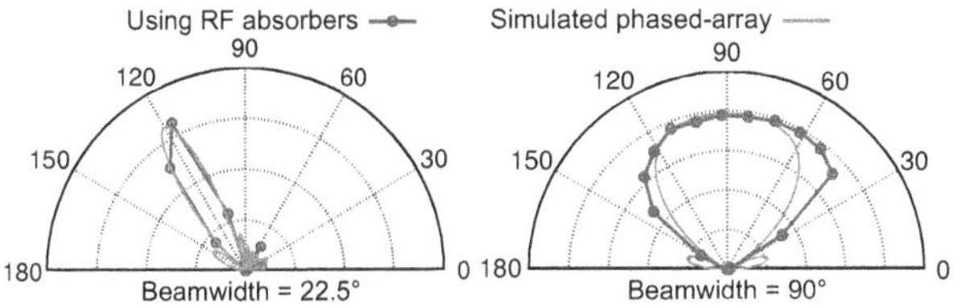

Figure 25: **Examples of simulated beam pattern vs. beam pattern generated using mmWave absorbers.**

APPENDIX

A. EMULATING FLEXIBLE BEAM PATTERNS ON WIMI

We exploit WiMi's quasi-omni directional antenna waveguide, together with multiple mmWave absorbers [20], to create a variety of beam patterns. The RF front-end is pre-built with a waveguide that provides $\sim 180^\circ$ beamwidth, which we have verified by placing a WiMi receiver around and sniffing its angular RSS distribution (Figure 24). The absorbers are placed in front of the waveguide in conical shape to create the desired beam patterns. Examples of beam pattern generated using this emulation approach is shown in Figure 25, which closely matches the ideal beam pattern. Thus, the emulated beams suffice for evaluating the impact of different beamwidths. We have attached the absorbers to the RF front-end, and mount them together on WiMi's motion control system, which allows for programmable pan/tilt/linear movement, thus ready for emulating beam steering and device motion.

B. EMULATING 60 GHZ MIMO ON WIMI

Due to lack of a commercial 60 GHz MIMO array, we create a virtual array of antennas to emulate a 2×2 MIMO node on WiMi.

A WiMi radio has only one Tx/Rx RF chain, supporting one Tx/Rx antenna. We overcome this constraint by creating a virtual MIMO Tx/Rx through antenna displacements. Specifically, we use the motion controller to slide an omni-directional Tx antenna to 2 different positions, separated by half-wavelength (2.5 mm). Meanwhile, the Rx antenna measures the channel gain (phase and magnitude). The measurement is then repeated for 2 Rx antenna positions, to obtain a 2×2 matrix representing the MIMO channel.

To ensure the matrix represents a "snapshot" of the MIMO channel, all the 4 element-wise channels must remain stable across the entire measurement. To validate this condition is satisfied, we first measure the channel stability, characterized by the *coherence time*. Correlation between two instances of channel samples, separated by T, is defined as [23]:

$$\mathcal{K}(T) = \frac{L}{L-T} \cdot \frac{|\sum_{t=0}^{L-T-1} h(t)h^*(t+T)|}{\sum_{t=0}^{L-1} |h(t)||h^*(t)|} \tag{5}$$

where L is the total length of the sequence of sampled channel gains. Coherence time is represented by an instance $T_{0.9}$ when correlation drops below 0.9, *i.e.*, $T_{0.9} = \mathcal{K}^{-1}(0.9)$. Figure 26 shows that the channel remains highly stable within 50 seconds window, whereas our MIMO channel matrix measurement only takes around 35 to 40 seconds (due to mechanical adjustment), which verifies the effectiveness of our MIMO emulation.

So, how can we measure MIMO capacity based on the emulator? Lets assume H_f forms the channel matrix between the N_T transmit and N_R receive antennas for frequency subcarrier f. Further if $\lambda_1 \geq \lambda_2 \geq \ldots \lambda_{rank(H_f)}$ are the ordered eigen values of the channel matrix H_f. Then, the capacity of the MIMO channel is given by [23],

$$\mathbf{C} = \mathbb{E}_H \Big[\sum_{i=1}^{rank(H_f)} log_2(1 + \frac{P}{N_0 N_T} \cdot \lambda_i^2) \Big] \tag{6}$$

where P denotes the combined output transmit power from N_T transmit antennas and is distributed equally among them. N_0 specifies a constant noise floor across all the received antennas.

In our trace driven emulation, we placed the transmitting and receiving antenna in LOS condition and collected channel matrix traces between the N_T and N_R antenna elements by using virtual sets of omni-directional antennas as described earlier. The channel matrix is collected across 256 different frequency subcarriers in order to capture frequency diversity within the environment. We derived the channel capacity of 60 GHz in the above scenario under a fixed power from the transmitting device according to the Equation 6.

C. MODULATION AND CODING SCHEMES IN IEEE 802.11AD

IEEE 802.11ad introduces three heterogeneous PHY layers dedicated to different application scenarios. The *Control* PHY is designed for very low SNR operation prior to beamforming. The *Single Carrier (SC)* PHY enables power efficient and low complexity transceiver implementation by using less robust coding protocol and using up to 16-QAM complex modulation scheme. The *OFDM* PHY provides high performance in frequency selective channels achieving highest data rates. The data rates, corresponding receiver sensitivity and coding schemes for *Control* and *SC* PHY are shown in Table 2. This table is used to map measured RSS into packet bit-rate throughout our experiments, in a similar way to existing studies [4,9].

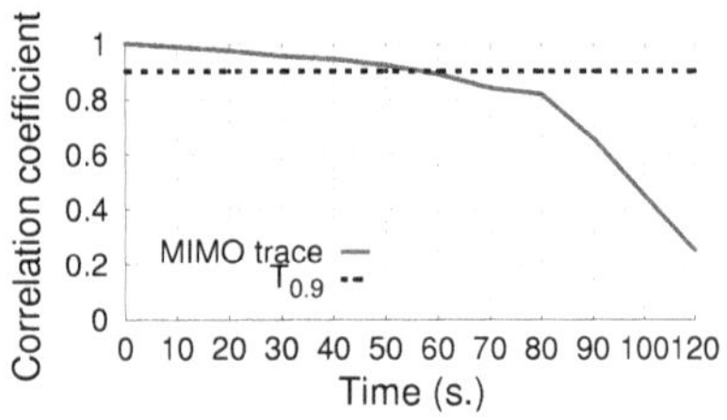

***Figure 26*: Channel stability during MIMO trace collection.**

Modulation	Coding Rate	Receive sensitivity (dBm)	Data Rate (Mbps)
DBPSK	1/64	−78	27.5
π/2-BPSK	1/4	−68	385
π/2-BPSK	1/2	−66	770
π/2-BPSK	5/8	−65	962.5
π/2-BPSK	3/4	−64	1155
π/2-BPSK	13/16	−62	1251.25
π/2-QPSK	1/2	−63	1540
π/2-QPSK	5/8	−62	1925
π/2-QPSK	3/4	−61	2310
π/2-QPSK	13/16	−59	2502.5
π/2-16QAM	1/2	−55	3080
π/2-16QAM	5/8	−54	3850
π/2-16QAM	3/4	−53	4620

***Table 2*: 802.11ad Control and Single Carrier rates.**

Sponsored Data Plan: A Two-Class Service Model in Wireless Data Networks

Liang Zhang†, Weijie Wu#, Dan Wang†‡
†Department of Computing, The Hong Kong Polytechnic University
‡The Hong Kong Polytechnic University Shenzhen Research Institute
#School of Electronic, Information and Electrical Engineering, Shanghai Jiao Tong University
{cslizhang, csdwang}@comp.polyu.edu.hk, weijiewu@sjtu.edu.cn

ABSTRACT

Data traffic demand over the Internet is increasing rapidly, and it is changing the pricing model between Internet service providers (ISPs), content providers (CPs) and end users. One recent pricing proposal is *sponsored data plan*, i.e., when accessing contents from a particular CP, end users do not need to pay for that volume of traffic consumed, but the CP will sponsor for this data consumption. In this paper, our goal is to understand the rationale behind this new pricing model, as well as its impacts to the wireless data market, in particular, who will benefit and who will be hurt from this scheme. We build a two-class service model to analyze the consumers' traffic demand under the sponsored data plan with consideration of QoS. We use a two-stage Stackelberg game to characterize the interaction between CPs and the ISP and reveal a number of important findings. Our conclusions include: 1) When the ISP's capacity is sufficient, the sponsored data plan benefits consumers and CPs in the short run, but the ISP does not have incentives to further improve its service in the long run. 2) When ISP's capacity is insufficient, the ISP and end users may achieve a win-win trade, while the ISP and CPs always compete for the revenue. 3) The sponsored data plan may enlarge the unbalance in revenue distribution between different CPs; CPs with higher unit income and poorer technology support are more likely to prefer the sponsored data plan.

Categories and Subject Descriptors

C.4 [**Performance of Systems**]: Modeling techniques, Performance attributes; J.4 [**Social and Behavioral Sciences**]: Economics

General Terms

Theory; Algorithm

Keywords

Sponsored Data; Stackelberg Game

SIGMETRICS'15, June 15–19, 2015, Portland, OR, USA.

http://dx.doi.org/10.1145/2745844.2745863.

1. INTRODUCTION

With the popularity of bandwidth-intensive mobile devices like smart phones and tablet computers, data traffic is increasing fast recently. The trend of intensive interactions of mobile devices and public clouds suggests that the amount of future wireless data traffic can be even daunting. This poses huge burden to the Internet service providers (ISPs) since supporting such demand-supply gap requires large investments. To share such costs with users, flat-rate pricing plans used in broadband networks are phasing out. ISPs now propose pricing plans with a cap. By paying a flat fee, users can consume any traffic volume below this cap, but they are either not allowed or highly charged for consuming traffic volume beyond this cap. This cap is usually conservative. For example, Google revealed that almost 85% of the plans offer less than 10 GB data per month, and 36% offer less than 1 GB per month [1]. Such caps would be easily reached in less than seven hours under the current 3G bandwidth [2]. There is thus a great demand on better pricing models. One research direction is time dependent pricing [3, 4]. The key observation is that the user traffic demands are not uniform at different times. Therefore, higher (lower) prices can be applied to peak (off-peak) hours so as to change the users' consumption patterns over times.

Another recent proposal is *sponsored data plan*, originated from 1-800 services of phone calls [5]. In particular, ISPs provide platforms for the content providers (CPs) to sponsor their end users, but with some payments or indirectly sharing advertising revenue, such that when end users access the content from one CP joining the sponsored data plan, their traffic from this CP is partially or fully exempted from their data caps. For example, Google has joined with India's Bharti Airtel to offer free access to certain Google-based services such as Gmail, Google+ and first pages of websites via Google search without ringing up data charges [6]. This pricing strategy is expected to create a positive cycle: End users will access more contents which will be exempted from their caps; content providers can attract more users and earn more from advertisement incomes; ISPs can obtain higher revenue to support better quality of service (QoS) and carry out technology upgrades. Early works [7, 8] have confirmed its benefits to CPs and end users.

Nevertheless, a key problem is whether such a plan may lead to unfair competition advantage to certain parties. Similar debates, e.g., network neutrality, appeared in the past. Opponents, including network neutrality advocates and representatives from public interest groups, concern that such a plan will favor rich and big CPs over small ones [9]. This may impede Internet innovation and ultimately hurt consumers. Proponents, mostly ISPs and some CPs, argue that this plan can promote competition and improve efficiency [10]; ultimately, consumers will benefit from better services and cheaper traffic. The pioneer ISP, AT&T, expressed confidence that the sponsored data plan complies with Federal Communications Commission (FCC) network neutrality rules. The core of network neutrality is that packet flows at the ISP level should not bear priorities[1]. Otherwise, when congestion occurs, low priority flows can be dropped before high priority ones, causing unfair competition in QoS among different CPs. Sponsored content, in fact, does not trigger differentiated services at the ISP flow level. When congestion occurs, packet flows of sponsored contents have the same probability to get dropped as non-sponsored ones. The FCC is inclined to side with proponents though its chairman claimed that the commission will carefully watch the sponsored data program and intervene if it finds the sponsored content practice violates the Open Internet Order [11]. After a long time of planning, AT&T finally announced its sponsored data program in January 2014. Its sponsored data partner, Syntonic Wireless, launched "toll-free" content store six months later [12].

In this paper, we show that an unfair competition advantage may still exist. In particular, there might be a competition disadvantage for certain CPs, such that tiered services will be created and ultimately users might be hurt. Under this plan, there will be a sponsored class services and an ordinary class services, where the sponsored class brings higher revenue to CPs. Yet to join the sponsored class, CPs need to pay a non-trivial premium for each unit of content it delivers. Only CPs with high unit profit can afford such a premium. This discriminates CPs in the sense that they need to compete for capital, i.e., the capability they pay a premium for their content, rather than their services, i.e., the quality of the contents or the quality of services. In addition, we find that in the long run, the ISP has no incentives to enlarge its traffic cap when its traffic capacity is sufficient; this greatly hurts consumers and CPs. Although these results seem discouraging for the sponsored data plan, we also show that if the traffic cap is regulated properly so as to guarantee the majority part of capacity being allocated to the ordinary class, then the ISP's optimal strategy is aligned with the consumers' surplus.

In this paper, we study a set of CPs, a monopolistic ISP and a set of users[2]. We model the users' traffic demand dynamics under the sponsoring plan with QoS consideration (Sec. III-A and III-B). Based on this, we develop a Stackelberg game framework (Sec. III-C and III-D) and analyze the interactions between the ISP, end users, and CPs (Sec. IV and V). In particular, we find that the equilibrium may not always exist and discuss the outcome of the interactions. We also develop efficient polynomial time algorithms to search the outcome in the exponential solution space. Finally, we determine and characterize the actions of the ISP and CPs in the steady state, i.e., the solution to the Stackelberg game. Our major findings are:

- If the ISP's capacity is sufficient, then the sponsored data plan benefits consumers and CPs in the short run; but in the long run, the ISP has no incentives to enlarge its traffic cap, which hurts consumers and CPs.
- If the ISP's capacity is insufficient, then the ISP has strong incentives to enlarge its capacity, which benefits both CPs and consumers. However, the ISP's optimal strategy to enlarge its profit is always contrary to CPs' surplus. If the traffic cap is regulated properly, then this strategy is aligned with the consumers' surplus.
- The sponsored data plan may enlarge the unbalance in the revenue distributions between different CPs; those with higher unit income and poorer technology support are more likely to prefer the sponsored data plan.

2. RELATED WORK

Sponsored data plan has become an attractive topic since it was proposed by AT&T. Under this plan, content providers can transfer part of their revenues to consumers so as to pursue higher traffic usage and remedy their consumers' low willingness to pay. Similar revenue transfer and sharing also happen between other interest groups with complementary requirements in the Internet [13, 14, 15, 16]. Based on the seminal work of two-sided markets by Armstrong [17], prior works [15, 16] studied the two-sided markets in the Internet, i.e., CPs and end users are the two sides that interact in a market enabled by the platform of ISPs. Njoroge et al. [15] found that through CP-side pricing, ISPs could extract higher surplus and maintain higher investment levels. Hande et al. [16] set up a two-sided model in a rate allocation market and concluded that subsidizing end users' cost of connectivity by pricing content providers may benefit both end users and CPs. Xu et al. [18] proposed a cooperative profit-distribution model for eyeball ISPs and peer-assisted content providers based on Nash Bargaining Solution. Authors in [13, 14] studied the profit-sharing mechanism of multi-lateral ISP settlements. Ma et al. [13] proposed a Shapley profit-sharing mechanism. At the Nash equilibrium, the routing and connecting/peering strategies maximize aggregate network profits. Wu et al. [14] proposed a Nash bargaining process and found that all ISPs are simultaneously better than the noncooperative equilibrium.

The sponsored data plan faces new challenges due to the complexity of users' behaviors and attracts lots of research interests. From the economic point of view, Andrews et al. [7] studied the contractual relationship between CPs and ISPs with random demand. They concluded that a coordinating contract can maximize the total system profit, and that the additional profit caused by sponsored data plan can be split between CPs and ISPs in an arbitrary manner. Zhang and Wang [8] formulated a competition problem between one large CP and one small CP to show whether sponsored content indeed favors large and rich CPs. Ma [19] captured the regulated subsidization competition among CPs under a neutral network and concluded that certain CPs might be harmed with a main reason being the high access prices instead of the existence of subsidization. Joe-Wong et al. [20] formulated the interaction among ISPs, CPs and heterogeneous users and derived their optimal behaviors. They found that sponsorship favors less cost-constrained CPs and more cost-constrained users, exacerbating CP inequalities

[1]Priorities for traffic engineering might be acceptable; yet priorities targeting on certain application types (e.g., P2P) or some particular CPs (e.g., Google), should be prohibited.
[2]In this paper, we use the terms "users" and "consumers" interchangeably.

but making user demand even more. From technical point of view, Raj et al. [2] developed a new computing abstraction, called SIMlet, based on the idea of split billing. Andrews et al. [21] developed a detailed methodology for extracting the parameters required by models in their previous work [7] and discussed how to select the proper sites to join the sponsored data plan.

The above works provide initial analysis on the sponsored data plan; however, further understandings are still limited. In particular, much is unknown on whether this strategy brings unfair competition and hurts consumers, as well as how end users behave and QoS changes upon the adoption of this plan. In this paper, we model the sponsored data plan as a two-class service model, which has been widely adopted by [22, 23, 24, 25, 26]. Li et al. [26] provided the technical support for two-class services with different QoS using a multicast protocol. Shetty et al. [23] investigated the effects of transition from a single-service class to two-service classes in the Internet by considering the interaction between end users and multiple ISPs. Yuksel et al. [24] focused on transit ISPs and quantified the extra capacity requirement for an over-provisioned classless network compared with the class network. Hermalin and Katz [25] examined the welfare effects of product-line restrictions and analyzed the case of two technologically restricted quality levels. However, all the above works focused on the ISP's side but not the CPs' choices. We have only found that Ma and Misra [22] considered the problem from similar directions with us. We adopt a similar methodology with Ma and Misra [22, 27] to obtain the equilibrium of the Stackelberg game. However, we do not consider QoS differentiation, but we focus on the sponsored data plan.

3. GENERAL MODEL

In this section, we model the wireless data market with three parties: a set of CPs $\mathcal{N}$ ($N = |\mathcal{N}|$), a monopolistic ISP and a set of end users with a total number M. The CPs provide services to end users. We assume that one CP supplies only one service. If a CP provides multiple services, then we treat it as multiple virtual CPs, each serving one particular service. The ISP provides Internet access services to CPs and end users. Usually, there is a transmission bottleneck for the connection services between CPs and end users. We define the traffic capacity (or capacity for short) of the ISP, denoted by μ, as the maximal possible amount of traffic volume that can be transmitted through the bottleneck during a fixed period[3]. Based on the above model, we can use a triple $(\mathcal{N}, \mu, M)$ to represent the whole system.

3.1 Users' Traffic Demand

Users have different preferences towards various contents and services of CPs. We use *valuation* to present this preference. Facing different choices in the service set, a user prefers accessing a service with a high per unit valuation when he has a usage limitation (or traffic cap). We assume a user's per-unit traffic valuation has a decreasing trend. For example, a user may have a high valuation on a VoIP service since he needs to have an important discussion with his friend, but when he finishes this discussion, the extra traffic he consumes, e.g., for telling jokes, is with a low valuation. In other words, the marginal valuation decreases with the traffic volume consumed. We define a strictly decreasing *valuation density function* $g_i(\cdot)$ to capture this feature, and the total valuation of consuming x_i amount of traffic is given by $\int_0^{x_i} g_i(s)ds$. Further, we assume $\int_0^{\infty} g_i(s)ds < \infty$.

Each service requires a certain bandwidth to achieve good QoS. For instance, a bandwidth of 500 Kbps is required for YouTube videos. We denote this maximal requirement for the service of CP i (or service i for short) as $\hat{b}_i$. However, in reality it may not be totally satisfied due to ISP's insufficient capacity. We denote the achievable bandwidth as b_i. Obviously, we have $b_i \le \hat{b}_i$. When the maximal bandwidth requirement cannot be satisfied, QoS decreases, resulting phenomenons like frequent screen freeze in video display. We define $q_i = b_i/\hat{b}_i$ as the ratio of the achievable bandwidth over the maximal bandwidth requirement. It reflects the extent of QoS degradation; when $q_i < 1$, it may lead to a reduction of users' valuations. In later parts of this paper, we call q_i the "*QoS index*". We capture this effect by a *QoS satisfaction function*: $h_i(\cdot) : [0,1] \to [0,1]$, where $h_i(0) = 0$ and $h_i(1) = 1$. We assume that it is a non-decreasing and continuous function in q_i. When $q_i < 1$, the marginal valuation decreases to $g_i(\cdot)h_i(q_i)$, and thus the total valuation for consuming x_i amount of traffic becomes $\int_0^{x_i} g_i(s)h_i(q_i)ds$.

We assume that an end user accesses a service if and only if his per unit traffic valuation of this service is higher than a pre-set threshold denoted by t_i. This threshold may come from the cost of bearing irritating pop-ups. Since the marginal valuation of a service reduces, there is a *usage threshold* for a user where his marginal valuation is equal to t_i. We define the *usage threshold* for service i as

$$\theta_i = \max\{s : g_i(s)h_i(q_i) \ge t_i\},$$

which reflects the maximal possible traffic usage for service i. When the inverse function of $g_i(\cdot)$ exists, we denote it as $g_i^{-1}(\cdot)$, and we have $\theta_i = g_i^{-1}\left(\frac{t_i}{h_i(q_i)}\right)$. For any traffic usage $x_i \in [0, \theta_i]$, let us define the users' *utility* as[4]

$$\psi_i(x_i) = \int_0^{x_i} [g_i(s)h_i(q_i) - t_i]\, ds. \quad (1)$$

We assume that the utility of consuming different services are additive. Therefore, the utility of accessing all services with traffic usage $\mathbf{x} = (x_1, \cdots, x_N)$ is

$$\psi(\mathbf{x}) = \sum_{i \in \mathcal{N}} \int_0^{x_i} [g_i(s)h_i(q_i) - t_i]\, ds. \quad (2)$$

In later analysis, we also call it the *surplus* of a consumer.

Now let us observe the ISP's role in users' consumption decisions. An ISP usually applies a "flat-rate-like" pricing scheme but with a cap, i.e., by paying a flat rate, end users can use the traffic below the cap, but they are not allowed to consume traffic volume beyond this cap, or are charged by a much higher price for usage beyond[5]. Let us use C to denote this cap. In this paper, we assume that each user's data

[3]Please be noted that the definition of "*capacity*" is different from the ISP's *cap* announced to the users; the later concept refers to the maximal traffic that a user is allowed consume during a fixed period.

[4]We do not include the Internet access fee charged by the ISP into the formula, since the access fee is a constant and does not impact any result.

[5]For instance, in the "AT&T individual plan" for 4G smart phones, AT&T charges $10 for a traffic cap 1 GB per month, but another $5 for any additional 50 MB.

consumption is below this cap. This assumption is for mathematical tractability; in reality, users do usually limit their usage below this cap due to the high fee charged for beyond. Under the sponsored data plan, traffic consumption of a particular service can be partially or totally exempted from this cap. We denote $\mathcal{O}$ (or $\mathcal{S}$) as the set of ordinary (or sponsoring) content providers (or services). Content providers in $\mathcal{S}$ sponsor the total traffic volume consumed on their content, while those in $\mathcal{O}$ do not participate in the sponsored plan. Each CP in $\mathcal{N}$ is in either $\mathcal{S}$ or $\mathcal{O}$. Thus, given the QoS index vector $\mathbf{q} = (q_1, \cdots, q_N)$, an end user can decide his optimal traffic usage by maximizing his utility:

$$\begin{aligned} \max_{\mathbf{x}} \quad & \psi(\mathbf{x}) = \sum_{i \in \mathcal{N}} \int_0^{x_i} [g_i(s) h_i(q_i) - t_i] \, ds, \\ \text{s.t.} \quad & \sum_{i \in \mathcal{O}} x_i \leq C, \; 0 \leq x_i \leq \theta_i. \end{aligned} \tag{3}$$

Note that for end users, the total traffic usage for non-sponsored services should not exceed the cap. Given the choices of CPs, i.e., $(\mathcal{O}, \mathcal{S})$, the above optimization can be solved by KKT conditions [28]. We have the following lemma.

LEMMA 1. *A user's optimal data consumption of the content provided by CP i, denoted as x_i, is:*

$$x_i = \begin{cases} \max\left\{0, g_i^{-1}\left(\frac{t_i + \nu}{h_i(q_i)}\right)\right\} & i \in \mathcal{O}, \\ \theta_i & i \in \mathcal{S}, \end{cases} \tag{4}$$

where ν is the Lagrange multiplier associated with the cap constraint. In addition, ν is non-decreasing with respect to q_i, and non-increasing with respect to C.

PROOF. Please refer to the technical report [29]. □

Lemma 1 derives the optimal traffic consumption of end users. The traffic consumption for services in $\mathcal{S}$ always approaches the usage threshold, but that in $\mathcal{O}$ is constrained by the traffic cap and the usage threshold.

We define ν as the *level of competition* for the traffic cap, because a high ν indicates a low traffic cap, so CPs in $\mathcal{O}$ face intense competition to attract users' consumption within this limited cap. When C is large, the traffic consumption of services in $\mathcal{O}$ also approaches the usage threshold. Services in $\mathcal{S}$ has no impact on the demand of traffic in $\mathcal{O}$. Lemma 1 also states that the level of competition is also affected by the QoS index. A higher QoS index means a higher level of competition since it increases the traffic demand.

3.1.1 Discussion on QoS Satisfaction Functions

Users may have different requirements on QoS for different services. For example, for real-time applications like Netflix, the value of the QoS satisfaction function decreases dramatically with respect to q_i. This is because inadequate bandwidth for the realtime applications greatly hurts users' experience. In contrast, for delay-tolerant services like email, reduction in QoS does not hurt users' experience too much. Therefore, in this paper, we define the QoS satisfaction function in the following form:

$$h_i(q_i) = {q_i}^{\gamma_i}, \tag{5}$$

where γ_i is called the *quality sensitivity* for service i. A large γ_i represents a service with a high sensitivity on the quality, while a small γ_i represents one with a low sensitivity.

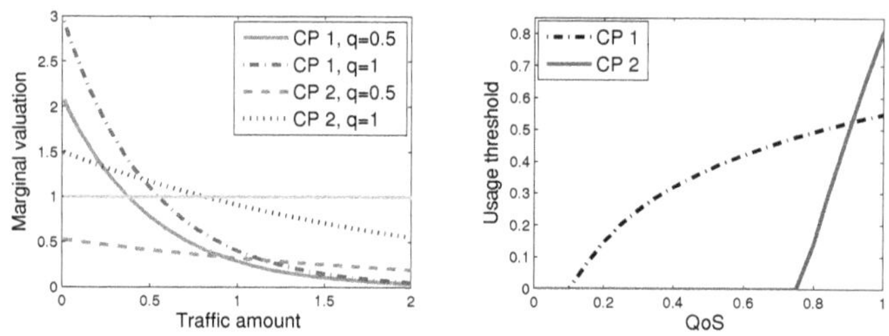

Figure 1: An example of consumers' valuation model

3.1.2 Discussion on Valuation Density Functions

Define $\alpha_i = \lim_{x_i \to 0} g_i(x_i)$. The value of the valuation density function approaches the maximum α_i when the user's consumption on service i approaches zero. As the traffic amount increases to infinity, the marginal valuation decreases to zero, i.e., $\lim_{x_i \to \infty} g_i(x_i) = 0$. The above requirement is needed to guarantee $\int_0^\infty g_i(s) ds < \infty$. In particular, we consider the following canonical form:

$$g_i(x_i) = \alpha_i e^{-\beta_i x_i}, \tag{6}$$

where β_i captures the *traffic sensitivity* on the valuation of service i. A higher traffic sensitivity indicates that the valuation of per unit traffic decreases more rapidly when more traffic is consumed by end users.

3.1.3 Illustration

We consider an example where two CPs are with parameters $(\alpha_1, \beta_1, \gamma_1) = (3, 2, 0.5)$ and $(\alpha_2, \beta_2, \gamma_2) = (1.5, 0.5, 1.5)$; CP 1 provides an Email type service with a high per unit valuation, a high traffic sensitivity and a low quality sensitivity, while CP 2 provides a video type service with a low per unit valuation, a low traffic sensitivity and a high quality sensitivity. Let the pre-set threshold be $t_i = 1$.

Figure 1 shows the marginal valuation with respect to the traffic consumed by both CPs (the left subfigure) and the usage threshold of the two CPs with respect to the QoS index (the right subfigure). The marginal valuation decreases with respect to the traffic amount consumed, and the decreasing trend becomes more rapid when congestion happens. For example, the marginal valuation of CP 1 decreases 63% when the traffic amount increases from 0.5 to 1. When the QoS index decreases, e.g., from 1 to 0.5, the marginal valuation of CP 1 decreases 28% further. A user consumes the traffic only when the marginal valuation is higher than the pre-set threshold. The critical point, i.e., the usage threshold, shifts to the left when congestion happens. When the marginal valuation line is all below the pre-set threshold line, the end user consumes no traffic and does not receive such service. The relationship between the usage threshold and the QoS index are shown in the right sub-figure. Each CP needs some QoS guarantee to attract its end users, while different CPs have different requirements. For example, CP 1 requires that the QoS index is larger than 0.1, while CP 2 requires it larger than 0.75. Comparing to CP 1, quality degradation has a more serious effect on CP 2. Decrease of the QoS index from 1 to 0.9 results in 39% reduction of the usage threshold for CP 2 but only 4% for CP 1.

Up till now we have captured end users' traffic demand under certain QoS. Next we will analyze the correlation between the end users' demand and QoS of the system.

3.2 Capacity Sufficiency and Rate Allocation Mechanism

In this subsection we analyze the aggregated traffic demand of all services, based on which we define the sufficiency and insufficiency of the ISP's capacity. Later, we capture the interactions between the traffic demand, sufficiency of capacity, and the quality of service.

Let us first consider the aggregated traffic demand of M end users receiving services in the sponsored class $\mathcal{S}$, i.e., $\sum_{i\in\mathcal{S}} Mx_i(\boldsymbol{q})$. According to lemma 1, the optimal usage for each service approaches the usage threshold, i.e., $x_i = \theta_i(q_i)$ for any $i \in \mathcal{S}$. The aggregated traffic demand for services in $\mathcal{S}$ is $\sum_{i\in\mathcal{S}} M\theta_i(q_i)$. Then let us consider the aggregated traffic demand in $\mathcal{O}$, i.e., $\sum_{i\in\mathcal{O}} Mx_i(\boldsymbol{q})$. When the traffic cap is sufficiently large, each end user's optimal traffic usage is the usage threshold, so the aggregated traffic demand in $\mathcal{O}$ is $\sum_{i\in\mathcal{O}} M\theta_i(q_i)$. Otherwise, if the cap for the users is smaller than $\sum_{i\in\mathcal{O}} M\theta_i(q_i)$, then the aggregated traffic demand is MC where C is the cap set by the ISP. Therefore, the aggregated demand for services in $\mathcal{O}$ is $M \min\left\{\sum_{i\in\mathcal{O}} \theta_i(q_i), C\right\}$. The aggregated traffic demand from all users is

$$D(\mathbf{q}) = \sum_{i\in\mathcal{S}} M\theta_i(q_i) + M \min\left\{\sum_{i\in\mathcal{O}} \theta_i(q_i), C\right\}. \quad (7)$$

Now let us formally define the sufficiency (insufficiency) of the ISP's capacity.

DEFINITION 1. *We say that the ISP's capacity C is sufficient if $C \geq D(\mathbf{1})$, or insufficient otherwise.*

When C is insufficient, we can by no means guarantee that each user receives each service under the best QoS; in other words, congestion happens. Lots of bandwidth allocating mechanisms have been used to address the rate allocation problem under congestion [22, 30]. One well adopted method is the proportional share mechanism [22], where each flow reduces the same percentage of rates under congestion. In other words, the ratios of the achievable bandwidth over the maximal bandwidth requirement for any two services i and j are the same, i.e., $b_i : \hat{b}_i = b_j : \hat{b}_j$, so the QoS indices for each service are the same, i.e., $q_i = q$ for any $i \in \mathcal{N}$.[6] Thus, the traffic demand function $D(\mathbf{q})$ can be simplified by $D(q)$. When $q < 1$, users' demand for each service reduces. When reaching a steady state, the traffic demand is equal to the capacity of the ISP:

$$D(q) = \mu. \quad (8)$$

We call the QoS index q that satisfies the above equation an *equilibrium QoS*. Let us define $\lambda = \mu/M$ as the average capacity (or per user capacity). Given the sets $(\mathcal{O}, \mathcal{S})$, the equilibrium QoS is captured by the following lemma.

LEMMA 2. *Given the sets $(\mathcal{O}, \mathcal{S})$, there is a unique equilibrium QoS $q \in [0, 1]$. Further, it is a non-decreasing function with respect to λ, and a non-increasing function with respect to C.*

PROOF. Please refer to the technical report [29]. □

[6]In practice, the QoS index q may be dynamic over time due to volatile traffic demand (e.g., high QoS index during valley period and low QoS index during peak period). However, the QoS index during peak period is relatively stable [31]. In this paper, we focus on the traffic capacity during peak period and treat q as the average QoS index over the period.

Lemma 2 shows that the ISP can improve QoS by enlarging its capacity, in particular, when $q < 1$. It is also interesting to note that if we merely increase the ISP's traffic cap, i.e., users are allowed to consume more traffic, then QoS becomes worse since the traffic demand from users increases but the ISP's capacity remains the same.

3.3 Utility of Content Providers and the ISP

Now let us formally define the utility functions of content providers and the Internet service provider. This serves as the foundation for our further game analysis.

3.3.1 *Utility of Content Providers*

We use v_i to denote the per unit revenue of CP i. Content providers may have quite different per unit revenue [32]. For example, Google search has a much higher per unit revenue than YouTube. The revenue can be generated by advertisements (e.g., YouTube), or value-added services (e.g., Tencent), or other e-commerce (e.g., Amazon). The cost of CP i consists of two parts: 1) the cost c_i for the connection service of per unit traffic, and 2) the additional cost p for per unit sponsored traffic. Thus, the utility of CP i, denoted by ϕ_i, is:

$$\phi_i(c_i, p) = \begin{cases} (v_i - c_i)x_i(q) & i \in \mathcal{O}, \\ (v_i - c_i - p)\theta_i(q) & i \in \mathcal{S}. \end{cases} \quad (9)$$

Content providers' surplus, defined as the summation of utilities of all CPs, can be expressed as

$$\phi = \sum_{i\in\mathcal{N}} \phi_i. \quad (10)$$

3.3.2 *Utility of the ISP*

We use the ISP's revenue to represent its utility[7], mainly from two sources: 1) the unit price charged to CPs for the connection service, i.e., c_i, and 2) the unit price charged to CPs for the sponsored traffic, i.e., p. We omit the price charged to end users because it is only a constant under the cap scheme. Thus, the utility (or surplus) of the ISP, denoted by π, is:

$$\pi(c_i, p) = \sum_{i\in\mathcal{S}} (c_i + p)\theta_i(q) + \sum_{i\in\mathcal{O}} c_i x_i(q). \quad (11)$$

Note that we treat the unit sponsoring price for different CPs as equal so as to cope with the network neutrality rules.

3.4 A Two-stage Stackelberg Game

We model the interactions of the ISP and CPs as a two-stage Stackelberg game in the system $(M, \mu, \mathcal{N})$. In particular, we have the following settings:

- *Players*: The ISP and the set of CPs.
- *Strategies*: The ISP decides the unit price charged to CPs for the sponsored traffic, and the traffic cap for end users, i.e., the ISP's strategy profile is $s_I \in \{(p, C) : p \geq 0, C \geq 0\}$. Each CP decides to join either the ordinary class or the sponsored class. We use $s_\mathcal{N} = (\mathcal{O}, \mathcal{S})$ to denote CPs' strategy profile, with $\mathcal{O} \cap \mathcal{S} = \emptyset$ and $\mathcal{O} \cup \mathcal{S} = \mathcal{N}$.

[7]We ignore the cost for delivering per unit traffic since the fixed cost is majority while the marginal cost is negligible.

- *Rules*: The ISP is the first mover who decides its price and traffic cap and announces them to CPs and end users. CPs are second movers and decide which class to join. Each CP makes its own decision independently.
- *Outcome*: The outcome is determined by backward induction. In particular, given any ISP's decision, each CP chooses which class to join to maximize its utility. Based on this knowledge, the ISP decides its optimal price and traffic cap that maximize its utility.

Note that we do not include the decision of c_i, i.e., the unit price for connection services, into the ISP's strategy profile. This is because we want to focus on the sponsored data scheme, which influences end users' decisions, but has limited impacts on c_i. Therefore we assume c_i is predetermined and known. We apply the Stackelberg game where the ISP is the first mover and CPs are second movers. This reflects the reality where ISPs usually have the monopolistic power and are active to promote the sponsored data plan. Once the ISP fixes its charging scheme, it cannot frequently change it as its contract with CPs and end users are normally of long term. After the ISP's decision, CPs decide whether they sponsor the content. Since CPs make their decisions simultaneously, we call their decision process a *simultaneous game* denoted by $(M, \mu, \mathcal{N}, s_I)$. Following the backward induction, we analyze the CPs' decisions, i.e., the simultaneous game, in Section 4, and later, the ISP's decision, in Section 5.

4. CONTENT PROVIDERS' DECISIONS

In this section, we analyze content providers' decisions, i.e., the outcome of the simultaneous game $(M, \mu, \mathcal{N}, s_I)$. In the decision phase, a CP joins a particular class ($\mathcal{O}$ or $\mathcal{S}$) where he can obtain a higher utility. Note that upon joining a particular class, this CP may impact the QoS index and the traffic consumption of other services. However, we consider when the number of CPs is large, this effect is ignorable, and thus define *competitive equilibrium* as follows:

DEFINITION 2. *A strategy profile $s_{\mathcal{N}} = (\mathcal{O}, \mathcal{S})$ is a competitive equilibrium of the game $(M, \mu, \mathcal{N}, s_I)$ if for any CP i, its utility satisfies:*

$$\frac{v_i - c_i - p}{v_i - c_i} \begin{cases} \leq \frac{x_i(\mathcal{O},\mathcal{S})}{\widetilde{\theta}_i(\mathcal{O},\mathcal{S})} & \text{if } i \in \mathcal{O}, \\ > \frac{\widetilde{x}_i(\mathcal{O},\mathcal{S})}{\theta_i(\mathcal{O},\mathcal{S})} & \text{if } i \in \mathcal{S}, \end{cases} \quad (12)$$

where $\widetilde{x}_i$ and $\widetilde{\theta}_i$ are the estimation of the ex-post traffic usage $x_i(\mathcal{O} \cup \{i\}, \mathcal{S}/\{i\})$ and $\theta_i(\mathcal{O}/\{i\}, \mathcal{S} \cup \{i\})$ accordingly.

Definition 2 states that under the competitive equilibrium, CPs in each class cannot obtain a higher profit by joining the other class. The competitive equilibrium depends on the estimation of the ex-post traffic usage for $\widetilde{x}_i$ and $\widetilde{\theta}_i$ which are obtained by $\widetilde{x}_i = g_i^{-1}\left(\frac{t_i+\widetilde{\nu}}{h_i(\widetilde{q})}\right)$ and $\widetilde{\theta}_i = g_i^{-1}\left(\frac{t_i}{h_i(\widetilde{q})}\right)$, i.e., we can calculate the ex-post traffic usage by estimating the ex-post QoS $\widetilde{q}$ and ex-post level of competition $\widetilde{\nu}$. This estimation for the two parameters $(\widetilde{\nu}, \widetilde{q})$, called *congestion metric*, alleviates each CP from estimating all other CPs' characteristics and greatly simplifies our analysis.

4.1 Outcome of the Simultaneous Game

Intuitively, we can use the competitive equilibrium to capture the steady state of the system, or the outcome of the simultaneous game. However, we will show later that there does not always exist a competitive equilibrium for the game. In this section, we derive the conditions for the existence of the competitive equilibrium, and explore how to determine the outcome of the game when there is no equilibrium. We also design an algorithm to quickly find out the unique outcome of the game over the feasible space of exponential size.

4.1.1 Sufficient Capacity

According to Definition 1, when the ISP has a sufficient capacity, it can support the traffic demand from all users when all services are with the best QoS, i.e., $q = 1$. This is the reality of the broadband (or wired) network, in particular, with fiber access. As for the wireless network, with the development of 4G LTE, the total demand may be fully satisfied in the future so as to fulfill a sufficient capacity condition. In this case, an end user's traffic consumption of service i is:

$$x_i = \begin{cases} \max\left\{0, g_i^{-1}(t_i + \widetilde{\nu})\right\} & i \in \mathcal{O}, \\ g_i^{-1}(t_i) & i \in \mathcal{S}. \end{cases} \quad (13)$$

To see each CP's decision, we first define the *relative priority* of CP i as:

$$\rho_i = g_i\left((v_i - c_i - p)g_i^{-1}(t_i)/(v_i - c_i)\right) - t_i. \quad (14)$$

This relative priority is the highest critical level of competition that CP i can tolerate in the ordinary class. A smaller relative priority of a CP means a higher incentive or priority to join the sponsored class $\mathcal{S}$. Then, CP i's choice is:

$$i \in \begin{cases} \mathcal{O} & \text{if } \rho_i \geq \widetilde{\nu}, \\ \mathcal{S} & \text{if } \rho_i < \widetilde{\nu}. \end{cases} \quad (15)$$

The key point to find an equilibrium is to decide the corresponding level of competition $\widetilde{\nu}$. We first relabel the CPs according to a non-increasing order of ρ_i such that $\rho_i \geq \rho_j$ if $i < j$. Then, we define set $\mathcal{H}_l$ as the set of first l CPs. Given the choices of CPs as $(\mathcal{H}_l, \mathcal{N}/\mathcal{H}_l)$, we can obtain the level of competition $\nu(\mathcal{H}_l)$ according to the optimization problem (3), and this value increases with respect to l. When the sequences $\{\nu(\mathcal{H}_l)\}$ and $\{\rho_l\}$ are smooth enough, i.e., the differences between any two neighboring elements are small enough, we can approximately view them as continuous sequences. The intersection points of these two sequences, if exist, are the levels of competition $\widetilde{\nu}$. Otherwise, the level of competition is zero or $\nu(\mathcal{H}_N)$. We use this rough description to illustrate the idea on finding the level of competition; in what follows we describe the detailed conditions for the existence of competitive equilibria based on this idea.

Theorem 1. *If there does not exist a positive number l such that $\nu(\mathcal{H}_{l-1}) < \rho_l < \nu(\mathcal{H}_l)$, then there exists at least one competitive equilibrium.*

PROOF. Please refer to the technical report [29]. □

When there exists a positive number l such that $\nu(\mathcal{H}_{l-1}) < \rho_l < \nu(\mathcal{H}_l)$, neither $\mathcal{S}$ nor $\mathcal{O}$ will be chosen by CP l. When CP l chooses $\mathcal{O}$, then $\mathcal{S}$ becomes a better choice since $\rho_l < \nu(\mathcal{H}_l)$; when CP l chooses $\mathcal{S}$, then $\mathcal{O}$ becomes a better choice since $\nu(\mathcal{H}_{l-1}) < \rho_l$. The intuition is that CP l's decision to join either class results in a jump on the level of competition, i.e., $\nu(\mathcal{H}_l) - \nu(\mathcal{H}_{l-1})$. This jump can in turn change the original decision of CP l.

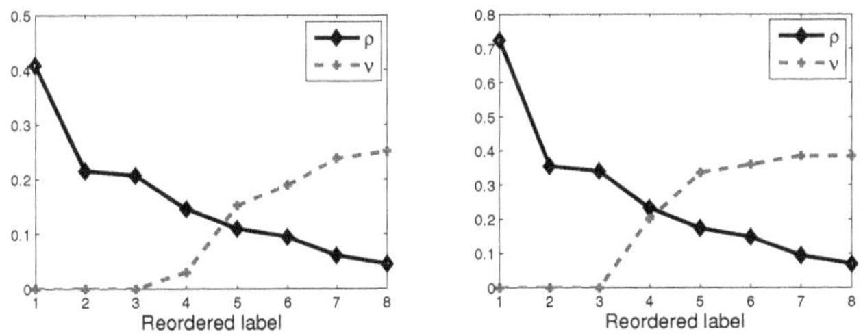

(a) $s_1 = (1,5)$ (b) $s_2 = (1.5,4)$

Figure 2: Examples of equilibria under sufficient capacity

When there is no competitive equilibrium, we still need to analyze the outcome of this game. Due to the fact that the sponsored data plan contracts between the ISP and CPs are usually of long term, it is impossible for CPs to always change their decisions, but in fact, their decisions will last for a relatively long time. To determine such decisions as the outcome of the game, we assume that any particular CP, say, CP l, makes its decision according to the following nearest point rule:

$$l \in \begin{cases} \mathcal{O} & \text{if } \nu(\mathcal{H}_l) - \rho_l \leq \rho_l - \nu(\mathcal{H}_{l-1}), \\ \mathcal{S} & \text{if } \nu(\mathcal{H}_l) - \rho_l > \rho_l - \nu(\mathcal{H}_{l-1}). \end{cases} \tag{16}$$

The key point for this rule is that the unstable CP joins the set with the level of competition nearer to its relative priority. A binary-search algorithm can be designed to find the outcome of the game when the ISP's capacity is sufficient. We denote the binary-search algorithm as $FindEqInt()$ with input $\{\rho_l\}$, $\{\mathcal{H}_l\}$ and $\{\nu(\mathcal{H}_l)\}$. It adopts half-interval search to find the intersection point between sorted sequences $\{\rho_l\}$ and $\{\nu(\mathcal{H}_l)\}$ according to the nearest point rule.

Numerical Example: To intuitively understand the outcome of the game, we give a numerical example of eight CPs with parameters $\alpha_i \in \{1,3\}$, $\beta_i \in \{1,2\}$ and $\gamma_i \in \{0.5, 1.5\}$.[8] We set $c_i = 1$ and $t_i = 0.5$. The per unit revenues for the eight CPs are $\{3, \cdots, 10\}$ accordingly.

Figure 2 shows the level of competition sequences $\{\nu(\mathcal{H}_l)\}$ and relative priority sequences $\{\rho_l\}$ under two cases of the ISP's strategies, i.e., $s_1 = (1,5)$ and $s_2 = (1.5,4)$. The set $\mathcal{H}_N = \{2,4,1,6,8,3,5,7\}$ and the first four CPs join $\mathcal{O}$ under both strategies s_1 and s_2 since $\rho_l > \nu(\mathcal{H}_l)$ for $l \in \{1,2,3,4\}$. Then let us consider CP 8 under s_1. When it joins $\mathcal{O}$, it finds $\rho_5 < \nu(\mathcal{H}_5)$ and thus joining $\mathcal{S}$ is a better choice. However, when it joins $\mathcal{S}$, it finds $\rho_5 > \nu(\mathcal{H}_4)$ and thus joining $\mathcal{O}$ is better. Therefore, there is no equilibrium for CP 8 under s_1. This oscillation does not happen under s_2 since $\rho_5 < \nu(\mathcal{H}_4)$. Thus CP 8 joins $\mathcal{S}$, and the equilibrium of the simultaneous game is $\mathcal{O} = \{2,4,1,6\}$ and $\mathcal{S} = \{8,3,5,7\}$. When we adopt the nearest point rule in Eq. 16, CP 8 joins the $\mathcal{O}$ under s_1, so the outcome of the game is $\mathcal{O} = \{2,4,1,6,8\}$ and $\mathcal{S} = \{3,5,7\}$.

4.1.2 Insufficient Capacity

[8]In this example, the sequence of parameters of CP i is given by $(\gamma\beta\alpha)_2 = (i-1)_{10}$, where $\alpha = 0$ indicates CP i chooses the first value of α_i, i.e., $\alpha_i = 1$; otherwise $\alpha_i = 3$ is chosen. Similarly, β_i and γ_i are determined by sequences β and γ.

Currently wireless data networks often lack capacity. ISPs often cannot support all traffic demand under the best possible QoS. Traffic cap is usually set to limit end users' traffic usage so as to alleviate the congestion problem. Finding an equilibrium of the game $(M, \mu, \mathcal{N}, s_I)$ under the insufficient capacity is complex since we need to consider a pair of parameters $(\widetilde{\nu}, \widetilde{q})$ rather than one single parameter $\widetilde{\nu}$. The interactions between $\widetilde{\nu}$ and $\widetilde{q}$ make the problem more complicated. To find an equilibrium, we first fix the QoS index q. Then we can obtain the relative priority sequence $\{\rho_l(q)\}$ under this QoS index. Similar to the sufficient capacity case, the competitive equilibrium $(\mathcal{O}(q), \mathcal{S}(q))$ can be calculated according to the binary-search algorithm. This equilibrium results in a new QoS index, i.e., $q'(\mathcal{O}(q), \mathcal{S}(q))$. When this new QoS index is equal to the original QoS index, i.e., $q'(\mathcal{O}(q), \mathcal{S}(q)) = q$, then we obtain a competitive equilibrium $(\mathcal{O}(q), \mathcal{S}(q))$. The following theorem quantifies the condition for the existence of competitive equilibria under the insufficient capacity case.

Theorem 2. *If there does not exist a QoS index q^* such that $q(\mathcal{O}(q^+), \mathcal{S}(q^+)) < q^* < q(\mathcal{O}(q^-), \mathcal{S}(q^-))$ where $q^- = q^* - \epsilon$, $q^+ = q^* + \epsilon$ (ϵ is any sufficiently small positive number), then there exists at least one competitive equilibrium.*

PROOF. Please refer to the technical report [29]. □

If there exists a QoS index q^* such that $q(\mathcal{O}(q^+), \mathcal{S}(q^+)) < q^* < q(\mathcal{O}(q^-), \mathcal{S}(q^-))$, then the choices of CPs oscillate. Under different choices of CPs, the QoS index changes around q^* but never converges to a stable point. Similarly, in order to capture the outcome of the simultaneous game, we also adopt the nearest point rule, i.e.,

$$(\mathcal{O}, \mathcal{S}) \leftarrow \begin{cases} (\mathcal{O}(q^-), \mathcal{S}(q^-)) & \text{if } q^* \geq \overline{q}, \\ (\mathcal{O}(q^+), \mathcal{S}(q^+)) & \text{if } q^* < \overline{q}, \end{cases} \tag{17}$$

where $\overline{q} = \frac{1}{2}\left(q\left(\mathcal{O}(q^-), \mathcal{S}(q^-)\right) + q\left(\mathcal{O}(q^+), \mathcal{S}(q^+)\right)\right)$.

Algorithm 1 FindEq()

Input: $(N, \mu, \mathcal{M}, s_I)$
Output: $(\mathcal{O}, \mathcal{S})$
1: Initialize $(\nu[0], q[0])$;
2: Calculate $(\mathcal{O}_{[0]}, \mathcal{S}_{[0]})$ induced by $(\nu[0], q[0])$;
3: $t \leftarrow 0$;
4: **do**
5: Calculate $\{\rho_l(q[t])\}$ and sort them according to a non-increasing order;
6: Calculate $\{\mathcal{H}_l[t]\}$ and $\{\nu(\mathcal{H}_l[t])\}$;
7: $(\mathcal{O}_{[t+1]}, \mathcal{S}_{[t+1]}) \leftarrow FindEqInt(\{\rho_l(q[t])\}, \{\mathcal{H}_l[t]\}, \{\nu(\mathcal{H}_l[t])\})$;
8: Calculate $(\nu'[t], q'[t])$ induced by $(\mathcal{O}_{[t+1]}, \mathcal{S}_{[t+1]})$;
9: $q[t+1] \leftarrow q[t] + g[t](q'[t] - q[t])$;
10: $t \leftarrow t+1$;
11: **until** $t < T$ or $(\mathcal{O}_{[t]}, \mathcal{S}_{[t]}) == (\mathcal{O}_{[t-1]}, \mathcal{S}_{[t-1]})$
12: **return** $(\mathcal{O}_{[t]}, \mathcal{S}_{[t]})$.

We design Algorithm 1, called *FindEq*(), to search the outcome of the game under the insufficient capacity. It starts with initializing congestion metric $(\nu[0], q[0])$ and calculating CPs' choices $(\mathcal{O}_{[0]}, \mathcal{S}_{[0]})$ (line 1 to 3). In each step t, after obtaining the relative priority of CPs under the QoS index $q[t]$, the algorithm calculates the outcome according to the binary-search algorithm $FindEqInt()$ (line 5 to 7).

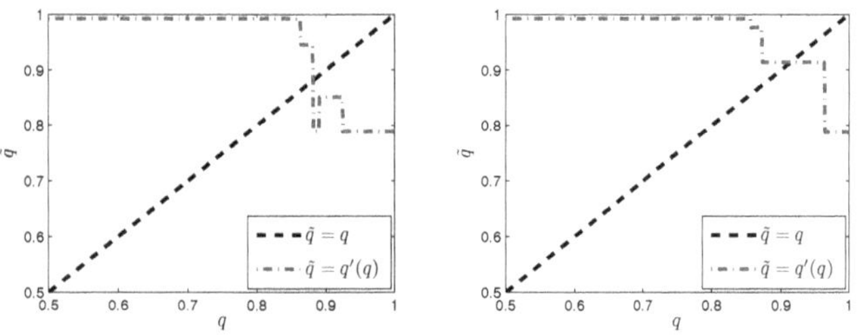

(a) $s_1 = (0.5, 5)$ (b) $s_2 = (1, 4)$

Figure 3: Examples of equilibria under insufficient capacity

Then it updates the QoS index $q[t+1]$ based on $q[t]$ and the induced QoS index $q'[t]$ (line 8 to 10). The step size parameter $g[t]$ can be time-static or decreasing in t. The algorithm terminates when the round time approaches the maximal number, i.e., T, or the outcome is stable (line 11).

Numerical Example: We provide a numerical example with the same CPs under the sufficient capacity case (in Section 4.1.1). We set the capacity as $\mu = 6$. Figure 3 shows the QoS index under the outcome for two ISP's strategies, i.e., $s_1 = (0.5, 5)$ and $s_2 = (1, 4)$. This QoS index is determined by the cross point of $\tilde{q} = q'(\mathcal{O}(q), \mathcal{S}(q))$ and $\tilde{q} = q$ as discussed previously. Figure 3(a) shows non-existence of equilibra. We have $q^* = 0.8815$ such that $q(\mathcal{O}(q^+), \mathcal{S}(q^+)) < q^* < q(\mathcal{O}(q^-), \mathcal{S}(q^-))$. The CPs' choices oscillate between $(\mathcal{O}, \mathcal{S}) = (\{2,6,8,4,5,7\}, \{1,3\})$ with QoS index $\tilde{q} = 0.9453$ and $(\mathcal{O}, \mathcal{S}) = (\{2,6,8,4,5\}, \{1,3,7\})$ with QoS index $\tilde{q} = 0.7891$. When we adopt the nearest point rule in Eq. 17, $\bar{q} = 0.8672 < q^*$, the outcome is $(\mathcal{O}, \mathcal{S}) = (\{2,6,8,4,5,7\}, \{1,3\})$. Figure 3(b) shows the case with no oscillation and thus there is a unique equilibrium $(\mathcal{O}, \mathcal{S}) = (\{2,4,1\}, \{3,5,6,7,8\})$.

4.2 Characteristics of the Outcome

Given the ISP's decision $s_I = (p, C)$, content providers play the simultaneous game $(M, \mu, \mathcal{N}, s_I)$. We denote the outcome of the game $(M, \mu, \mathcal{N}, s_I)$ as $(\mathcal{O}, \mathcal{S})$ and the corresponding congestion metric as (ν, q). Given different decisions of the ISP, CPs play different simultaneous games and may lead to different outcomes. We have the following theorem to quantify the condition that leads to the same outcome.

Theorem 3. *Consider a new decision of the ISP $s'_I \succeq s_I$ and denote the outcome of the new simultaneous game $(M, \mu, \mathcal{N}, s'_I)$ as $(\mathcal{O}', \mathcal{S}')$. If $(\mathcal{O}', \mathcal{S}') = (\mathcal{O}, \mathcal{S})$, then for any $\tilde{s}_I$ satisfying $s_I \preceq \tilde{s}_I \preceq s'_I$, $(\mathcal{O}, \mathcal{S})$ is also the outcome of the new game $(M, \mu, \mathcal{N}, \tilde{s}_I)$.*

PROOF. Please refer to the technical report [29]. □

Theorem 3 states that when two decisions of the ISP lead to the same outcome of the simultaneous game, then any decision in between has the same outcome. This stability of CPs' outcome provides some flexibility for the ISP's strategy. For example, the ISP may increase the price charged to the sponsored data and reduce the traffic cap slightly so as to increase its revenue and improve QoS, where the simultaneous game has the same outcome. As $N \to \infty$, this stability shrinks and finally disappears. Extended from the above theorem, we can easily obtain the following corollary.

COROLLARY 1. *Denote the relative priority of CP i under the outcome of the game $(M, \mu, \mathcal{N}, s_I)$ and the new game $(M, \mu, \mathcal{N}, s'_I)$ as ρ_i and ρ'_i, respectively. If $s'_I \succeq s_I$ and $(\mathcal{O}, \mathcal{S})$ is the outcome of both games, then $\rho'_i - \nu' \geq \rho_i - \nu$.*

Corollary 1 states that the gap between the relative priority and the level of competition for each CP increases when the ISP increases its price charged to the sponsored data or the traffic cap. According to CPs' choices in Eq. 15, this gives each CP higher incentives to join the ordinary class.

Theorem 4. *The congestion metric (ν', q') under the outcome of the new game $(M, \epsilon\mu, \mathcal{N}, s_I)(\epsilon \geq 1)$ satisfies at least one of the following properties: 1) $\nu' \leq \nu$; 2) $q' \geq q$.*

PROOF. Please refer to the technical report [29]. □

Theorem 4 states that if the ISP's capacity increases, then QoS improves, or the level of competition reduces. High QoS increases the traffic demand in $\mathcal{S}$, while low level of competition increases the traffic demand in $\mathcal{O}$. Therefore, when the ISP's capacity increases, it may benefit CPs in $\mathcal{S}$, or those in $\mathcal{O}$, or both.

Each CP's decision depends on their own features (v_i, c_i), the quality sensitivity γ_i, the pre-set threshold t_i of end users, and the traffic sensitivity β_i. To investigate the incentives of various CPs on joining the sponsored plan, we study a set $\mathcal{T}$ of CPs with the same pre-set threshold t_i and traffic sensitivity β_i but different features (v_i, c_i) and quality sensitivity γ_i. This setting represents those with similar services but differing in size or technology. We say that CPs in $\mathcal{T}$ are of the *same type*. We have the following theorem.

Theorem 5. *If CP $j \in \mathcal{T}$ joins $\mathcal{S}$ under the outcome of the game $(M, \mu, \mathcal{N}, s_I)$, then any other CP $i \in \mathcal{T}$ that satisfies $v_i - c_i \geq v_j - c_j$ and $\gamma_i \geq \gamma_j$ also joins $\mathcal{S}$.*

PROOF. Please refer to the technical report [29]. □

Theorem 5 indicates that for the same type of CPs, those with high per unit revenue or quality sensitivity usually have high incentives to join the sponsored class, and in turn they have potential to achieve higher revenue. This may result in unfair competition and encourage CPs to pursue capital instead of improving their quality of service.

5. MONOPOLISTIC ISP'S STRATEGY

In the previous section, we have analyzed the outcome of the simultaneous game, i.e., the second stage of the Stackelberg game. In this section, we discuss the first stage of the Stackelberg game, i.e., the monopolistic ISP's best choice, so that we can understand the outcome of the Stackelberg game and its impacts to CPs and end users.

5.1 Sufficient Capacity

When the ISP has a sufficient capacity, it can support all demands with the best QoS. However, this does not imply that the ISP has an incentive to release the cap to users.

Theorem 6. *Given any strategy $s_I = (p, C)$ of the ISP and a sufficiently small $\epsilon > 0$, the strategy s_I is dominated by $s_I^+ = (p, C + \epsilon)$ if and only if CPs' decisions remain unchanged under the new game $(M, \mu, \mathcal{N}, s_I^+)$.*

PROOF. Please refer to the technical report [29]. □

Theorem 6 states that the ISP has an incentive to enlarge its traffic cap until the CPs' decisions change. The intuition is that when CP's decisions remain unchanged, a large cap increases the revenue from $\mathcal{O}$. Yet, this may lead CPs in $\mathcal{S}$ switching to $\mathcal{O}$. When this happens, the profit from $\mathcal{S}$ has a jump of reduction. The total profit of the ISP increases if the profit increase from $\mathcal{O}$ dominates the loss from $\mathcal{S}$, or decreases otherwise. If the sponsored data plan is prohibited, i.e., $p \to \infty$, then the ISP will set the cap to infinity. This is because when the capacity is not a constraint, the ISP wants to attract users' demand as much as possible, so that it delivers as much traffic as possible for CPs, and this generates a large income to the ISP charged from CPs.

We conduct simulations with 100 CPs and one ISP to explore the key features of the ISP's strategy. The pre-set threshold t_i is randomly selected from $[0.1, 1]$[9]. The per unit traffic cost of connection services for each CP is normalized as $c_i = 1$. We set the CPs' per unit revenue v_i randomly distributed over $[1, 10]$ that excludes the CPs unable to afford connection services. The quality sensitivity γ_i is uniformly distributed over $[0, 2]$. The parameter pair (α_i, β_i) is chosen randomly from $[1, 10] \times [1, 2]$[10]. We set the ISP's per user capacity as 500, larger than the maximal capacity needed for one user, representing a sufficient capacity. Note that our simulations do not depend on particular settings, and our purpose is to show qualitative trends in general.

We first consider the ISP's optimal traffic cap under different prices, as shown in Figure 4(a). When the traffic cap is small, e.g., $C = 20$, the ISP's profit π decreases with the traffic cap. This means the profit loss from $\mathcal{S}$ dominates the increase from $\mathcal{O}$. Charging higher prices to CPs leads to a larger reduction of the ISP's profit when the traffic cap increases. When the traffic cap is large, e.g., $C = 100$, the ISP's profit π increases with respect to the traffic cap. This means the profit increase from $\mathcal{O}$ dominates the loss from $\mathcal{S}$. This happens when most CPs join $\mathcal{O}$. Enlarging the traffic cap increases the ISP's profit until the traffic usage in $\mathcal{O}$ approaches the maximal demand. Figure 4(b)(c) show that CPs' and consumers' utilities both increase with respect to the traffic cap.

We then show the ISP's optimal price under various traffic caps in Figure 5(a). When the price is low, e.g., $p = 0.1$, the ISP's profit increases with the price due to high revenue obtained from $\mathcal{S}$. When the price is high, e.g., $p = 7$, the ISP's profit reduces with the price since more CPs choose to join $\mathcal{O}$, resulting in the reduction of the sponsored traffic. The ISP decides the optimal price that balances the per unit income from the sponsored traffic, and the amount of this traffic. Figure 5(b)(c) show that CPs' and consumers' utilities decrease with respect to the traffic cap.

Remark: When the ISP's capacity is sufficient, the ISP, CPs and consumers all benefit from the sponsored data plan in the short run. However, the ISP may not have incentives to enlarge its traffic cap. Keeping a small traffic cap (e.g., $C = 10$) and charging a high price (e.g., $p = 4$) to the sponsored traffic can bring in more revenue for the ISP. This selfish strategy greatly hurts the benefits of both CPs and consumers in the long run. To remedy this problem, the authority may need to put some regulations to the ISP so as to protect the consumers' surplus in the long run. In general, there are two regulation methods. The first method is to allow the sponsored data plan but regulate the traffic cap, i.e., encouraging the ISP to enlarge the cap. The price for the sponsored data will also decrease accordingly. The other method is to forbid the sponsored data plan. In this case, the ISP has incentives to extend its traffic cap or even provide limitless usage service.

5.2 Insufficient Capacity

When the ISP's capacity is insufficient, the traffic cap set by the ISP is a good choice to limit the traffic of consumers. We analyze the ISP's strategy with insufficient capacity under the sponsored data plan. We also assume that $c_i = c$ in this subsection. We have the following theorem:

Theorem 7. *Given the ISP's strategy $s_I = (p, C)$ and a traffic cap $C' \le C$, s_I is always dominated by (p, C') if the outcome of the simultaneous game $(M, \mu, \mathcal{N}, s_I)$ satisfies $\mathcal{S} \neq \emptyset$ and $q < 1$.*

PROOF. Please refer to the technical report [29]. □

Theorem 7 says that the ISP is willing to set a small traffic cap so as to increase its profit. The reasons are: 1) the capacity is fully utilized, so it is good to limit users' consumption; and 2) the sponsored traffic brings in more profit to the ISP than the ordinary traffic. When a smaller traffic cap is given, more CPs will join $\mathcal{S}$, indicating a larger profit.

We also evaluate the effects of the sponsored strategy under an insufficient capacity via simulations. The basic settings are the same as the previous subsection. The price charged for the sponsored traffic is $p = 4$, and the average capacity is $\lambda = 100$ unless otherwise specified. We define the traffic cap ratio as $\kappa = C/\lambda$.

We first consider the effect of the ISP's capacity under various traffic caps, as shown in Figure 6. Figure 6(a) shows the ISP's profit π under different capacities. When the capacity is small, the ISP's profit increases linearly with respect to the capacity, i.e., $(c + (1 - \kappa)p)\lambda$. This happens when the capacity allocated to $\mathcal{S}$ (or sponsored capacity for short) is fully utilized. When this capacity is under-utilized, the ISP's profit reduces when the capacity increases since more CPs join $\mathcal{O}$. In addition, the ISP can obtain a higher profit by reducing the traffic cap. Figure 6(b) shows that the CPs' surplus increases with respect to the traffic capacity until all CPs join $\mathcal{O}$. Figure 6(c) shows that consumers' surplus increases with respect to the ISP's capacity. When the sponsored capacity is under-utilized, consumers' surplus increases at a much lower rate. In addition, CPs and consumers benefit more from the increasing cap. Figure 6(d) states that QoS improves with respect to the capacity as long as the sponsored capacity is fully utilized. Given a fixed capacity, a larger traffic cap may not indicate a higher QoS.

We then focus on the effect of the price charged to the sponsored traffic under various traffic caps, as shown in Figure 7. Figure 7(a) shows the ISP's profit π under different prices. When the price p is small, the ISP's profit increases linearly with respect to the price, i.e., $c\lambda + (1 - \kappa)\lambda p$. This happens when most CPs can afford the cost of the sponsored traffic so that the sponsored capacity is fully utilized. When

[9]We exclude the interval $[0, 0.1]$ since consumers always have non-ignorable t_i; otherwise they will consume infinite traffic.

[10]We exclude $[0, 1]$ for α_i to ensure non-zero traffic usage and narrow the range of β_i to avoid some CPs' traffic dominating the capacity.

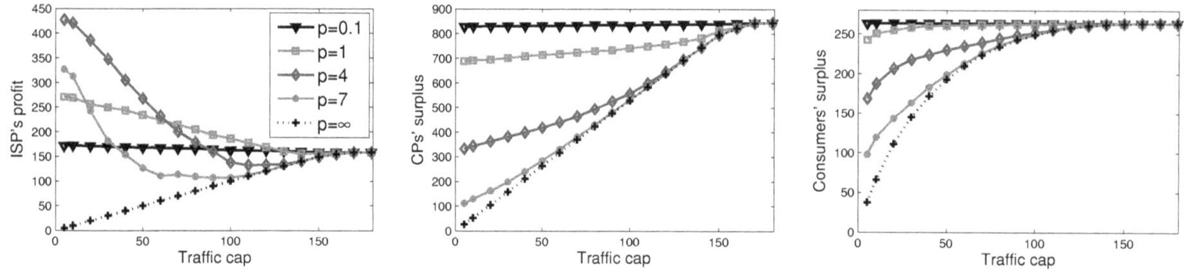

(a) π vs. traffic cap (b) ϕ vs. traffic cap (c) ψ vs. traffic cap

Figure 4: π, ϕ, ψ versus traffic cap with varying prices

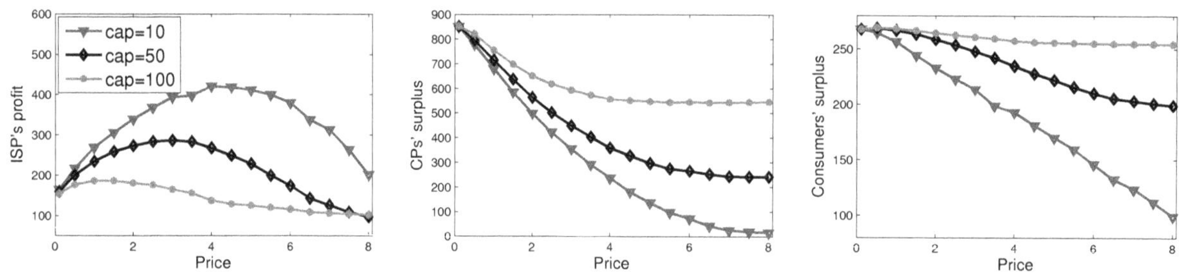

(a) π vs. price (b) ϕ vs. price (c) ψ vs. price

Figure 5: π, ϕ, ψ versus price with varying traffic caps

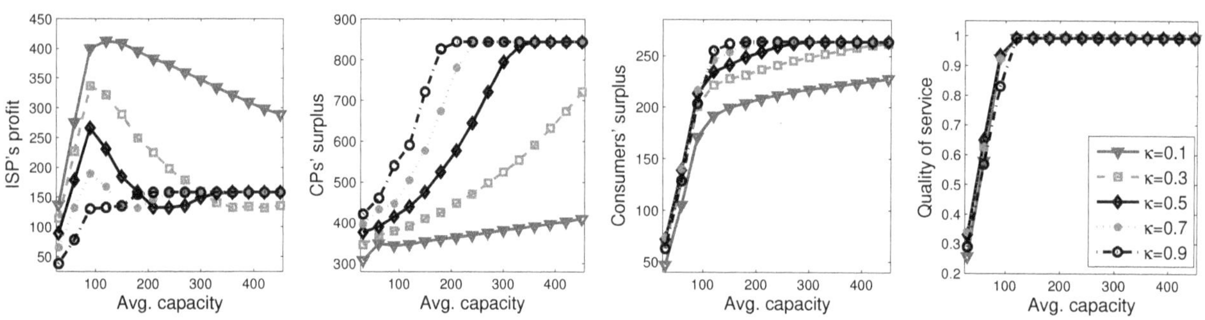

(a) π vs. capacity (b) ϕ vs. capacity (c) ψ vs. capacity (d) q vs. capacity

Figure 6: π, ϕ, ψ, q versus capacity

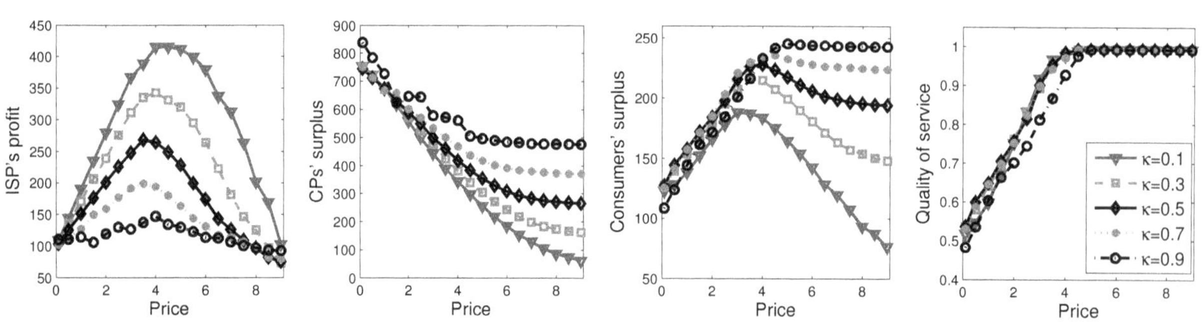

(a) π vs. price (b) ϕ vs. price (c) ψ vs. price (d) q vs. price

Figure 7: π, ϕ, ψ, q versus price

p is large, the ISP's profit reduces as the price increases. This happens when the sponsored capacity is under-utilized. The optimal price of the ISP is around $p = 4$. Figure 7(b) shows that CPs always prefer higher traffic cap and lower price charged to the sponsored traffic. Figure 7(c) shows that consumers' surplus is almost aligned with the ISP's profit. This happens when the traffic cap is not too small. The optimal price for end users is also around $p = 4$. The intuition is that a low price results in serious QoS degradation and reduces the valuation of per unit traffic, while a large price results in the sponsored capacity under-utilized and reduces the traffic amount. Figure 7(d) shows that the QoS index increases with respect to the price until it reaches its maximal value, i.e., $q = 1$, since more CPs join $\mathcal{O}$ and less traffic is consumed.

Remark: When the capacity is insufficient, the ISP still has no incentives to enlarge the traffic cap under the sponsored strategy. The traffic cap has a negligible effect on the QoS. Other factors, i.e., the price and the capacity, can be utilized to impact QoS. This may relieve the concerns of QoS degradation by the sponsored data plan. The ISP has a strong incentive to enlarge its traffic capacity until the best QoS achieves. This benefits both CPs and users. The ISP also prefers to set a high price due to a linear increase of its profit, i.e., $(c + (1-\kappa)p)\lambda$. Yet, when the price is too high, more CPs will join the ordinary class and the sponsored capacity may be under-utilized. A suitable traffic cap and price charged for the sponsored traffic can increase the ISP's profit so as to support it on enlarging the traffic capacity in the future. The CPs prefer the sponsored strategy with a large traffic cap and a low sponsored price, which is always on the contrary to the ISP's optimal strategy. The ISP's and consumers' surplus can increase simultaneously if the majority of capacity is allocated to the ordinary class.

6. DISCUSSION AND LIMITATION

Sponsored data plan was originated from the 1-800 services, but the market for wireless data networks is quite different. Currently, the main 3G and 4G LTE data plans set traffic caps to limit consumers' usage due to insufficient capacities. The sponsored data plan proposed by AT&T provides a method for specific CPs to traverse the traffic caps. A potentially higher revenue may support the investment for larger capacities and thus improve QoS. For the time being, AT&T only provides the toll-free services for its sponsored data plan, probably because consumers have a strong preference to a simple data plan. Our two-class service model (i.e., ordinary class and sponsored class) is built based on the data plans at status quo.

In fact, the sponsored data plan does not differentiate services from CPs in the ordinary and the sponsored classes. In other words, the quality of services is the same for both classes. This is different from PMP [33] or Public Option ISP [22]. However, CPs in the ordinary class face serious levels of competition. This is, in some sense, like the bad QoS challenge faced by CPs in the lower charged channel of PMP [33] or the public option ISP [22]. The ordinary class is mainly preferred by CPs with lower per unit revenue, e.g., startup companies. Content providers with higher per unit revenue, e.g., Google, prefer joining the sponsored class. This may also happen to CPs that are sensitive to QoS since they may fail to compete for the traffic from end users' scare traffic cap. Although the sponsored data plan opens a door for CPs to increases their traffic demand, it also brings the risk that when competition happens, it benefits more to CPs with higher per unit revenue, instead of those with better technology support.

The sponsored data plan brings higher revenue to ISPs. However, ISPs may prefer high prices for the sponsored data and small traffic caps (Theorem 7) under current wireless data networks. This selfish strategy hurts both consumers and CPs. Fortunately, the damage for consumers is negnigible when the majority capacity is allocated to the ordinary class (Figures 6(c) and 7(c)). ISPs can also relieve from the concerns of poor QoS caused by the sponsored data plan (Figures 6(d) and 7(d)). Suitable revenue encourages ISPs to provide more investment to extend the capacity, which benefit both consumers and CPs. Despite the potential risks, we believe that a fair and transparent sponsored data plan would provide a unified platform for competition among CPs and create a healthy ecosystem in wireless data networks.

Although we build our two-class service model based on the currently dominated data plans and capture the interactions among various components, our work has several limitations. First, our model may not capture the short-term off-equilibrium that usually happens in practice due to some players' non-rational or non-optimal decisions. Second, our two-class model only focuses on a single ISP and its fixed end users. We set up this model not only for mathematical simplicity, but also capture one ISP's monopoly access power for a majority of CPs even in the market with multiple ISPs. Current long-term contracts also limit end users' transition from one ISP to another. However, it is still interesting to explore the competitive market with multiple ISPs. Finally, our numerical evaluations are limited to capture qualitative trends. Carrying out real experiment or detailed validation could be very challenging, since it is quite difficult to obtain an accurate estimation on a number of parameters in our model. Despite these limitations, we still believe our analysis has captured some important insights and might help the scheme and regulation designs for future wireless data pricing markets.

7. CONCLUSION

In this paper, we propose a two-class service model, analyze the interaction among end users, content providers and the ISP, and study the impact of the sponsored data plan on the Internet service market. In particular, we focus its impact on the quality of service, the profit of CPs and the ISP, and on shaping the users' traffic consumption behaviors. Our interesting findings include: 1) when the ISP's capacity is sufficient, the sponsored data plan benefits consumers and CPs in the short run, but the ISP does not have incentives to further improve its service in the long run; 2) when the ISP's capacity is insufficient, the ISP and end users may both benefit from the scheme, while the ISP and CPs always compete for the revenue; and 3) the sponsored data plan may enlarge the unbalance in revenue distribution between different CPs and result in unfair competition. Our findings provide important insights to designing sponsored data plans and potentially necessary regulations. We believe that given proper regulations, a fair and transparent sponsored data plan would be a promising trend of pricing models for future wireless data networks.

8. ACKNOWLEDGMENT

The authors would like to thank the anonymous reviewers for their constructive comments. Dan Wang is supported in part by National Natural Science Foundation of China No. 61272464 and RGC/GRF PolyU 5264/13E. Weijie Wu is supported in part by National Natural Science Foundation of China No. 61402287 and Shanghai Yangfan Project No. 14YF1401900.

9. REFERENCES

[1] Google, "International broadband pricing study: Dataset for public use." http://policybythenumbers.blogspot.gr/2012/08 /international-broadband-pricing-study.html.

[2] H. Raj, S. Saroiu, A. Wolman, and J. Padhye, "Splitting the bill for mobile data with simlets," in *Proc. of ACM HotMobile*, 2013.

[3] S. Ha, S. Sen, C. J. Wang, Y. Im, and M. Chiang, "Tube: Time-dependent pricing for mobile data," in *Proc. of ACM SIGCOMM*, 2012.

[4] L. Zhang, W. Wu, and D. Wang, "Time-dependent pricing in wireless data networks: Flat-rate vs. usage-based schemes," in *Proc. of IEEE INFOCOM*, 2014.

[5] AT&T, "Sponsored data from at&t." http://developer.att.com/apis/sponsored-data.

[6] P. Goldstein, "Google joins with india's bharti airtel for toll-free wireless internet service." http://www.fiercemobileit.com/story/att-ceo-content-providers-asking-toll-free-data-plans/2012-07-18.

[7] M. Andrews, U. Ozen, M. I. Reiman, and Q. Wang, "Economic models of sponsored content in wireless networks with uncertain demand," in *Proc. of IEEE Smart Data Pricing Workshop*, 2013.

[8] L. Zhang and D. Wang, "Sponsoring content: Motivation and pitfalls for content service providers," in *Proc. of IEEE Smart Data Pricing Workshop*, 2014.

[9] S. Marek, "Verizon's shammo: Content providers see value in toll-free data model." http://www.fiercewireless.com/story/verizons-shammo-content-providers-see-value-toll-free-data-model/2013-05-22.

[10] J. Ankeny, "At&t ceo: Content providers asking for 'toll-free' data plans." http://www.fiercemobileit.com/story/att-ceo-content-providers-asking-toll-free-data-plans/2012-07-18.

[11] I. Fried, "Fcc chairman says at&t sponsored data plans warrant watching." http://recode.net/2014/01/09/fcc-chairman-says-att-sponsored-data-plans-worth-monitoring/.

[12] P. Goldstein, "At&t sponsored data partner syntonic wireless to launch 'toll-free' content store." http://www.fiercewireless.com/story/att-sponsored-data-partner-syntonic-wireless-launch-toll-free-content-store/2014-07-10.

[13] R. T. B. Ma, D. M. Chiu, J. C. S. Lui, V. Misra, and D. Rubenstein, "Internet economics: The use of shapley value for isp settlement," in *Proc. of ACM CoNEXT*, 2007.

[14] Y. Wu, H. Kim, P. H. Hande, M. Chiang, and D. H. Tsang, "Revenue sharing among isps in two-sided markets," in *Proc. of IEEE INFOCOM*, 2011.

[15] P. Njoroge, A. E. Ozdaglar, N. E. Stier-Moses, and G. Y. Weintraub, "Investment in two-sided markets and the net neutrality debate," *Review of Network Economics*, vol. 12, no. 4, pp. 355–402, 2013.

[16] P. Hande, M. Chiang, R. Calderbank, and S. Rangan, "Network pricing and rate allocation with content provider participation," in *Proc. of IEEE INFOCOM*, 2009.

[17] M. Armstrong, "Competition in two-sided markets," *RAND Journal of Economics*, vol. 47, no. 3, pp. 668–691, 2006.

[18] K. Xu, Y. Zhong, and H. He, "Can p2p technology benefit eyeball isps a cooperative profit," *IEEE Transactions on Parallel and Distributed Systems*, vol. 25, no. 11, pp. 1101–1111, 2014.

[19] R. T. B. Ma, "Subsidization competition: Vitalizing the neutral internet," in *Proc. of ACM CoNEXT*, 2014.

[20] C. Joe-Wong, S. Ha, and M. Chiang, "Sponsoring mobile data: An economic analysis of the impact on users and content providers," in *Proc. of IEEE INFOCOM*, 2015.

[21] M. Andrews, G. Bruns, and H. Lee, "Calculating the benefits of sponsored data for an individual content provider," in *Proc. of IEEE CISS*, 2014.

[22] R. T. B. Ma and V. Misra, "The public option: a non-regulatory alternative to network neutrality," in *Proc. of ACM CoNEXT*, 2011.

[23] N. Shetty, G. Schwartz, and J. Walrand, "Internet qos and regulations," *IEEE/ACM Transactions on Networkin*, vol. 18, no. 6, pp. 1725–1737, 2010.

[24] M. Yuksel, K. K. Ramakrishnan, S. Kalyanaraman, J. Houle, and R. Sadhvani, "Quantifying overprovisioning vs. class-of-service: Informing the net neutrality debate," in *Proc. of IEEE ICCCN*, 2010.

[25] B. E. Hermalin and M. L. Katz, "The economics of product-line restrictions with an application to the network neutrality debate," *Information Economics and Policy*, vol. 19, 2007.

[26] S. Li, K. Xu, Y. Liu, and J. Wu, "Edge overlay multicast to support comparable multi-class services," *Journal of High Speed Networks*, vol. 17, no. 1, pp. 13–36, 2008.

[27] R. T. B. Ma and V. Misra, "Congestion equilibrium for differentiated service classes," in *Proc. of 49th Annual Allerton Conference*, 2011.

[28] S. Boyd and L. Vandenberghe, "Convex optimization," *Cambridge, U.K.: Cambridge Univ. Press*, 2004.

[29] L. Zhang, W. Wu, and D. Wang, "Sponsored data plan: A two-class service model in wireless data networks," tech. rep. Available at http://www4.comp.polyu.edu.hk/~cslizhang/sigmetric15-TR.pdf.

[30] J. Mo and J. Walrand, "Fair end-to-end window-based congestion control," *IEEE/ACM Transactions on Networking*, vol. 8, no. 5, pp. 556–567, 2000.

[31] Citrix, "Mobile analytics report, otcober 2012." http://www.citrix.com/.

[32] A. Odlyzko, "The volume and value of information," *International Journal of Communication*, vol. 6, 2012.

[33] A. Odlyzko, "Paris metro pricing for the internet," in *Proc. of ACM EC*, 1999.

Queue-Proportional Rate Allocation with Per-Link Information in Multihop Networks

Bin Li
Coordinated Science Lab
University of Illinois at Urbana-Champaign
Urbana, IL 61801, USA
Email: lib@illinois.edu

R. Srikant
Coordinated Science Lab, Department of ECE
University of Illinois at Urbana-Champaign
Urbana, IL 61801, USA
Email: rsrikant@illinois.edu

ABSTRACT

The backpressure scheduling algorithm for multihop wireless networks is known to be throughput optimal, but it requires each node to maintain per-destination queues. Recently, a clever generalization of processor sharing has been proposed which is also throughput optimal, but which only uses per-link queues. Here we propose another algorithm called Queue Proportional Rate Allocation (QPRA) which also only uses per-link queues, and allocates service rates to links in proportion to their queue-lengths and employs the Serve-In-Random-Order (SIRO) discipline within each link. Through fluid limit techniques and using a novel Lyapunov function, we show that the QPRA achieves the maximum throughput. We demonstrate an advantage of QPRA by showing that, for the so-called primary interference model, it is able to develop a low-complexity scheduling scheme which approximates QPRA and achieves a constant fraction of the maximum throughput region, independent of network size.

Categories and Subject Descriptors

C.2.1 [**Computer-Communication Networks**]: Network communications, Store and forward networks, Wireless communication; G.3 [**Probability and Statistics**]: Markov processes, Queueing theory.

General Terms

Algorithms, Performance, Theory.

Keywords

Resource Allocation; Low-complexity Scheduler Design; Multihop Wireless Networks; Maximum Throughput; Lyapunov Functions; Fluid Limit Analysis.

1. INTRODUCTION

We consider the resource allocation problem in multihop wireless networks with fixed routing, where each packet may traverse multiple links before departure. The work of Tassiulas and Ephremides (see [28]) developed a throughput-optimal backpressure algorithm, which prioritizes activation of routes with the largest differential backlog awaiting service subject to network interference constraints. Here, the throughput-optimal strategy means that it can achieve any throughput subject to network stability that is achievable by any other scheduling strategy. A large body of work has extended throughput to other long-term metrics, such as fairness (e.g., [9, 21, 16, 27, 14]), average energy consumption (e.g., [22, 23, 4]), etc.; see [26] for an overview.

However, all the policies mentioned above make transmission decisions by maintaining per-destination queueing information at each node and frequently exchanging this information among neighboring nodes, which is usually a difficult task in large networks handling thousands of flows. Such a restriction has motivated recent research efforts to develop more practical throughput-optimal schedulers (e.g., [17, 12]) with reduced queueing information. For example, the authors in [12] developed a scheduling algorithm with per-link queueing information in limited network setups, where routes do not form loops. But, it is likely to happen in practice that different routes do form a loop, in which case the results in [12] do not apply. Additionally, the arrival rates are assumed to be either known or measured in this line of work.

More recently, motivated by the research activities in bandwidth sharing networks (e.g., [19, 1, 20, 25]), the author in [29] cleverly generalized the idea of processing-sharing in queueing networks, and proposed the throughput-optimal Proportional Scheduler that only utilizes per-link queueing information. Therefore, the Proportional Scheduler significantly simplifies the queueing structure compared to the well-known backpressure algorithm, since the number of traffic flows is generally orders of magnitude greater than the number of links in communication networks. However, the Proportional Scheduler requires the network to solve a concave optimization problem with the full knowledge of the capacity region and its low-complexity implementation still remains an open question.

In this work, we propose alternative throughput-optimal scheduling algorithm, called Queue-Proportional Rate Allocation (QPRA), which also makes scheduling decisions only based on per-link queueing information. The proposed QPRA algorithm is a natural generalization of the algorithm developed in [10] that has been shown to be throughput-optimal in single-hop networks, where packets immediately leave the network once they are served. In particular, the

SIGMETRICS'15, June 15–19, 2015, Portland, OR, USA.

http://dx.doi.org/10.1145/2745844.2745864.

QPRA algorithm allocates the service rates to links in proportion to their queue-lengths as in [10] and additionally employs the Service-In-Random-Order (SIRO) queueing discipline within each link. However, stability in a single-hop network does not necessarily imply stability in a multihop network (e.g., [18, 24, 3]).

By using fluid limit techniques and a novel Lyapunov function that intelligently groups the number of packets at neighboring links along a given route, we are able to prove that the proposed QPRA algorithm achieves maximum throughput. Further, for the commonly-used primary interference model (see, for example, [11]), we develop a low-complexity scheduling scheme approximating the QPRA algorithm that not only uses per-link queueing information but also achieves a constant fraction of the maximum throughput region, independent of network size. To the best of our knowledge, this is the first work that addresses the low-complexity scheduling design with only per-link queueing information in multihop networks. The following items list our main contributions along with references on where they appear in the text:

- In Section 3, we develop a scheduling algorithm that allocates service rates to links in proportion to their queue-lengths and employs the SIRO queueing discipline within each link. Then, we provide a simple proof of rate stability of our proposed algorithm for any arrival rate vector within the maximum throughput region. The proof of rate stability captures the intuition behind the QPRA algorithm, namely, the algorithm attempts to reduce the maximum queue length in the network.
- In Section 4, we introduce a novel concept, namely *section*, which intelligently groups the number of each route packets at each link. Based on this concept, we propose a Lyapunov function and show the throughput-optimality of our proposed algorithm through fluid limit arguments.
- To illustrate the advantage of our proposed algorithm, we develop an efficient low-complexity scheduling algorithm that mimics our proposed QPRA algorithm in Section 5, and show that it at least achieves a constant fraction of the maximum throughput region, independent of network size, in networks with primary interference.

A note on Notation: We use bold and script font to denote a vector and a set, respectively. Also, let $|\mathcal{A}|$ denote the cardinality of the set $\mathcal{A}$. We use $\text{Int}(\mathcal{A})$ to denote the set of interior points of the set $\mathcal{A}$. We use the convention that $0/0 = 0$.

2. SYSTEM MODEL

We consider a wireless network represented by a graph $\mathcal{G} = (\mathcal{N}, \mathcal{L})$, where $\mathcal{N}$ is the set of nodes and $\mathcal{L}$ is the set of links. A node represents a wireless transmitter or receiver, while a link represents a pair of transmitter and receiver that are within the transmission range of each other. We assume that the system operates in slotted time. For ease of exposition, we assume that each link can at most transfer one packet in one time slot. We consider the *link-based conflict model*, where links conflicting with each other cannot be active at the same time. We call a set of links that can be active simultaneously as a *feasible schedule* and denote it as $\mathbf{R}(t) \triangleq (R_l(t))_{l\in\mathcal{L}}$, where $R_l(t) = 1$ if the link l is scheduled in time slot t and $R_l(t) = 0$, otherwise. We define the *capacity region* Λ as the convex hull of all feasible schedules.

We consider a *multihop traffic model*, where packets traverse multiple links within the network before they depart. We assume that each route r consists of $K^{(r)}$ consecutive links that do not form a cycle. That is, a route r packet served at link $l_k^{(r)}$ must next go to link $l_{k+1}^{(r)}$ until it is served at the last link $l_{K^{(r)}}^{(r)}$, where $k = 1, 2, \cdots, K^{(r)} - 1$. Let $\mathcal{R}$ be a set of routes through the network. We use the notation $l \in r$ to denote that link l is part of route r. We also say pair (l, r) if $l \in r$. Further, we denote $l_-^{(r)}$ as the previous (upstream) link of link l on route r.

We use $A_{l,r}(t)$ to denote the number of *exogenous* route r packets arriving at the ingress link $l = l_1^{(r)}$ in time slot t. Note that $A_{l,r}(t) \equiv 0$ if $l \neq l_1^{(r)}$. Let $A_{l,r}^{\Sigma}(t) \triangleq \sum_{\tau=0}^{t-1} A_{l,r}(\tau)$ denote the cumulative number of route r packets arriving at the ingress link l up to time slot $t-1$. The arrival processes are assumed to satisfy the Strong Law of Large Numbers (SLLN), i.e.,

$$\lambda_{l,r} = \lim_{t\to\infty} \frac{A_{l,r}^{\Sigma}(t)}{t}, \text{ with probability 1,} \tag{1}$$

where $\lambda_{l,r} \triangleq \lambda_r \mathbb{1}_{\{l=l_1^{(r)}\}}$, and $\lambda_r > 0$ is the mean arrival rate of route r packets. For simplicity, here we will assume that the arrival process for each route are i.i.d., and independent across routes[1].

A queue is maintained for each link l with $Q_l(t)$ denoting its queue-length at the beginning of time slot t. Let $X_{l,r}(t)$ be the number of route r packets at link l in time t. Thus,

$$Q_l(t) = \sum_{r:l\in r} X_{l,r}(t), \quad \forall t \geq 0. \tag{2}$$

We use $H_l(t)$ to denote the number of packets departing from link l in time slot t. Let $D_{l,r}(t)$ be the number of route r packets departing from link l in time slot t. Therefore, we have

$$H_l(t) = \sum_{r:l\in r} D_{l,r}(t), \quad D_{l,r}(t) \leq X_{l,r}(t), \quad \forall t \geq 0. \tag{3}$$

Based on the above setup, the queueing dynamics of a multihop network can be described as follows:

$$X_{l,r}(t+1) = X_{l,r}(t) + A_{l,r}(t) + D_{l_-^{(r)},r}(t) - D_{l,r}(t), \tag{4}$$

holds for any pair (l, r) and $t \geq 0$. Here, we note that $D_{l_-^{(r)},r}(t) = 0$ if $l = l_1^{(r)}$.

In this paper, we consider the policies under which the system evolves as a Markov Chain. We call system *stable* if the underlying Markov Chain is positive recurrent. We define the *maximum throughput region* $\overline{\Lambda}$ as the set of arrival rate vectors $\boldsymbol{\lambda} \triangleq (\lambda_r)_{r\in\mathcal{R}}$ for which the network is stable under some policy. It has been shown in [28] that the maximum throughput region $\overline{\Lambda}$ can be represented as $\overline{\Lambda} \triangleq \{(\lambda_r)_{r\in\mathcal{R}} : (\sum_{r:l\in r} \lambda_r)_{l\in\mathcal{L}} \in \Lambda\}$, where we recall that Λ denotes the capacity region. We call an algorithm *throughput-optimal* if it makes the system stable for any arrival rate vector $\boldsymbol{\lambda}$ that lies strictly within the maximum throughput region $\overline{\Lambda}$, i.e., $\boldsymbol{\lambda} \in \text{Int}(\overline{\Lambda})$. An algorithm is said to achieve an *efficiency ratio* $\kappa \in (0, 1]$ if it can stabilize the system for any $\boldsymbol{\lambda}$ strictly within a fraction κ of the maximum throughput region $\overline{\Lambda}$, i.e., $\boldsymbol{\lambda} \in \text{Int}(\kappa\overline{\Lambda})$.

[1]Since we use fluid limit techniques, this assumption can be relaxed in many different ways at the cost of additional notation. In particular, we only need a Markovian description of the queueing system for our results to hold.

The aim of this work is to address the scheduler design with only per-link queueing information in multihop networks. We first present a centralized throughput-optimal algorithm that makes transmission decisions only based on the link queue-lengths. Then, we show that this algorithm can be easily modified for low-complexity implementations, which achieve a strictly positive efficiency ratio for certain interference models, independent of the network size.

3. QUEUE-PROPORTIONAL RATE ALLOCATION SCHEDULER

In this section, we present a throughput-optimal scheduling algorithm that makes transmission decisions only based on per-link queueing information.

3.1 Algorithm Description

Here we develop a scheduling algorithm that only utilizes per-link queueing information and achieves the maximum throughput region. Given the link queue-length vector $\mathbf{Q}(t) = (Q_l(t))_{l\in\mathcal{L}}$, the algorithm operates as follows:

Queue-Proportional Rate Allocation (QPRA):

(1) In each time slot t, first allocate the service rate $\sigma_l(t)$ for each link l, such that

$$\sigma_l(t) = 0, \text{whenever } Q_l(t) = 0,$$

$$\frac{\sigma_l(t)}{Q_l(t)} = \frac{\sigma_{l'}(t)}{Q_{l'}(t)}, \text{ whenever } Q_l(t) > 0 \text{ and } Q_{l'}(t) > 0,$$

and $\boldsymbol{\sigma}(t) = (\sigma_l(t))_{l\in\mathcal{L}}$ lies on the boundary of the capacity region Λ. That is, the allocated service rate vector $\boldsymbol{\sigma}(t)$ is the longest vector within the capacity region Λ that is along the same direction of the link queue-length vector $\mathbf{Q}(t)$. Let $\mathbf{R}(t)$ be a random vector with the support on the set of all feasible schedules and mean $\boldsymbol{\sigma}(t)$.

(2) Then, serve each link l according to Serve-In-Random-Order (SIRO) queueing discipline, i.e., serve packets at each link l uniformly at random. This implies that the average departure rate of each route at link l is proportional to the number of packets of its route, i.e.,

$$\mu_{l,r}(t) = 0, \text{ whenever } X_{l,r}(t) = 0,$$

$$\frac{\mu_{l,r}(t)}{X_{l,r}(t)} = \frac{\mu_{l,r'}(t)}{X_{l,r}(t)}, \text{ whenever } X_{l,r}(t) > 0 \text{ and } X_{l,r'}(t) > 0,$$

where $\mu_{l,r}(t)$ denotes the average departure rate of route r packets at link l in time slot t.

Unlike the well-known backpressure algorithm, the QPRA algorithm only requires the per-link queueing information to make transmission decisions and thus significantly simplifies the queueing structure of multihop networks. Here, we want to point out that the QPRA algorithm generalizes the algorithm proposed in [10] under the single-hop traffic model, i.e., packets immediately leave the network once they are served. In particular, the link rate allocation procedure of the QPRA algorithm was proposed in [10], where the authors showed that this link rate allocation scheme can achieve maximum throughput under the single-hop traffic model. However, as we mentioned in the Introduction, the stability in a single-hop system does not necessarily imply stability in a multihop system (e.g., [18, 24, 3]). Nevertheless, we are able to show that the QPRA algorithm achieves the maximum throughput under the multihop traffic model through fluid limit techniques. Next, we introduce the fluid limit and fluid model equations under the QPRA algorithm.

3.2 Fluid Model

In this subsection, we present the fluid limit and fluid model equations associated with the QPRA algorithm.

PROPOSITION 1. *Under the QPRA algorithm, with probability 1, for any positive sequence $w_n \to \infty$, there exists a subsequence w_{n_j} with $w_{n_j} \to \infty$ such that*

$$\frac{1}{w_{n_j}} X_{l,r}(w_{n_j}t) \to x_{l,r}(t), \quad \forall (l,r), \tag{5}$$

$$\frac{1}{w_{n_j}} Q_l(w_{n_j}t) \to q_l(t), \quad \forall l \in \mathcal{L}, \tag{6}$$

hold uniformly over compact intervals[2], *where the limiting functions $x_{l,r}(t)$ and $q_l(t)$ are Lipschitz-continuous in $[0,\infty)$, which implies that these limiting functions are differentiable for almost all t. Let $\mathcal{T}$ be the set of time instants where these functions are differentiable. Then, the following equations hold for all $t \in \mathcal{T}$:*

$$q_l(t) = \sum_{r:l\in r} x_{l,r}(t), \quad \forall l \in \mathcal{L}, \tag{7}$$

$$\frac{d}{dt} x_{l,r}(t) = \lambda_{l,r} + \mu_{l_-^{(r)},r}(t) - \mu_{l,r}(t), \quad \forall (l,r), \tag{8}$$

where $\boldsymbol{\mu}(t) \triangleq (\mu_{l,r}(t))_{r\in\mathcal{R},l\in\mathcal{L}}$ satisfies

$$\mu_{l_-^{(r)},r}(t) = 0, \text{ whenever } l = l_1^{(r)}, \tag{9}$$

$$\mu_{l,r}(t) = \frac{x_{l,r}(t)}{q_l(t)} \sigma_l(t), \tag{10}$$

and $\boldsymbol{\sigma}(t) \triangleq (\sigma_l(t))_{l\in\mathcal{L}}$ lies on the boundary of the capacity region Λ satisfying

$$\sigma_l(t) = 0, \text{ whenever } q_l(t) = 0, \tag{11}$$

$$\frac{\sigma_l(t)}{q_l(t)} = \frac{\sigma_{l'}(t)}{q_{l'}(t)}, \text{ whenever } q_l(t) > 0 \text{ and } q_{l'}(t) > 0. \tag{12}$$

The proof of Proposition 1 is somewhat standard and technical using the techniques developed in [8, 7, 15], and is available in Appendix A for completeness. Proposition 1 indicates that the stochastic queueing networks and its fluid model are strongly coupled. In particular, the queue-length dynamics (7) and (8) are equivalent to (2) and (4), respectively. Moreover, equations (9), (10), (11) and (12) follows from the QPRA algorithm. By [8, Theorem 4.2], the stability of the fluid model implies that the original stochastic system is positive recurrent, where the fluid model is *stable* if there exists a finite time $T \geq 0$ such that for every fluid limit model $\mathbf{x} \triangleq (x_{l,r}(t))_{r\in\mathcal{R},l\in\mathcal{L}}$ with $\|\mathbf{x}(0)\| = 1$, $\mathbf{x}(t) = 0$ for all $t \geq T$. Therefore, it is sufficient to show that the fluid model is stable in the rest of the paper.

However, there are lots of detailed and subtle techniques involving in proving the stability of the fluid model associated with the QPRA algorithm. To get an insight of the proof, we first show that the fluid model is *weakly stable*,

[2] A sequence of functions $\{f_n(\cdot)\}_{n\geq 1}$ is said to converge to a function $f(\cdot)$ *uniformly over compact (u.o.c.)* intervals if for all $t \geq 0$, $\lim_{n\to\infty} \sup_{0\leq t'\leq t} |f_n(t') - f(t')| = 0$.

i.e., for every fluid limit model $\mathbf{x} \triangleq (x_{l,r}(t))_{r\in\mathcal{R},l\in\mathcal{L}}$ with $\mathbf{x}(0) = 0$, $\mathbf{x}(t) = 0$ for all $t \geq 0$, for any arrival rate vector $\boldsymbol{\lambda}$ within the maximum throughput region. This in turn implies that the original system is rate stable (see [7, Theorem 3]), i.e., the average departure rate is equal to the average arrival rate at each link, for any arrival rate vector $\boldsymbol{\lambda}$ inside the maximum throughput region.

3.3 Weak Stability of the Fluid Model

In this subsection, we will show that the fluid model is weakly stable under the QPRA algorithm for any arrival rate vector within the maximum throughput region $\overline{\Lambda}$. We first state the following two simple lemmas that will be used for the stability proof.

LEMMA 1. *If $f(x) = \max_{i=1,2,...,K} f_i(x)$ and $f_i(x), \forall i$, are locally Lipschitz continuous*[3], *then, we have*

$$\frac{D^+}{dx^+} f(x) \leq \max_{i\in\mathcal{K}} \left\{ \frac{D^+}{dx^+} f_i(x) \right\}, \tag{13}$$

where $\mathcal{K} \triangleq \{i | f_i(x) = f(x)\}$, and $\frac{D^+}{dx^+} f(x)$ is defined as

$$\frac{D^+}{dx^+} f(x) \triangleq \limsup_{u\downarrow 0} \frac{f(x+u) - f(x)}{u}.$$

This lemma relaxes the assumption of differentiability of $f_i(x), \forall i = 1, 2, ..., K$ in [2, Proposition 2.3.2] to the case when these functions are locally Lipschitiz continuous. The proof is quite similar to that in [2, Proposition 2.3.2] and is available in Appendix B for completeness.

LEMMA 2. *Let $g : [0,\infty) \to [0,\infty)$ be a locally Lipschitz continuous function.*

(i) Assume that $g(0) = 0$ and $\frac{D^+}{dt^+} g(t) \leq 0$ whenever $g(t) > 0$. Then, $g(t) = 0$ for all $t \geq 0$;

(ii) Assume that $g(0) > 0$ and $\frac{D^+}{dt^+} g(t) \leq -\gamma$ for some $\gamma > 0$ whenever $g(t) > 0$. Then, there exists a $T \geq 0$ such that $g(t) = 0$ for all $t \geq T$.

The proof of Lemma 2 is available in Appendix C.

Next, we give the following lemma that is quite important in establishing the system stability. It shows that if $\theta(\sum_{r:l\in r} \lambda_r)_{l\in\mathcal{L}} \in \Lambda$ for some $\theta > 0$, and the pair (l^*, r^*) achieves the maximum of $x_{l,r}/\lambda_r$ over all pairs (l, r), then the departure rate of route r^* at link l^* is at least $\theta\lambda_{r^*}$ under the QPRA algorithm. Intuitively, the QPRA algorithm tries to reduce the maximum of $x_{l,r}/\lambda_r$ over all pairs (l, r), which keeps the system stable.

LEMMA 3. *Assume $\theta(\sum_{r:l\in r} \lambda_r)_{l\in\mathcal{L}} \in \Lambda$ for some $\theta > 0$. If $\mathbf{x} \neq 0$ and $(l^*, r^*) \in \arg\max_{(l,r)} \frac{x_{l,r}}{\lambda_r}$, then $\mu_{l^*,r^*} \geq \theta\lambda_{r^*}$.*

PROOF. The proof generalizes [15, Lemma 5] to the multihop setup. Since $\mathbf{x} \neq 0$, we have $x_{l^*,r^*} > 0$. Assume $\mu_{l^*,r^*} < \theta\lambda_{r^*}$. Then, for any route r within the link l ($r \neq r^*$ or $l \neq l^*$), there are two cases:

(i) If $x_{l,r} = 0$, then $\mu_{l,r} = 0$.

(ii) If $x_{l,r} > 0$, then we have

$$\mu_{l,r} \overset{(a)}{=} \frac{x_{l,r}}{x_{l^*,r^*}} \mu_{l^*,r^*} = \frac{x_{l,r}/\lambda_r}{x_{l^*,r^*}/\lambda_{r^*}} \frac{\lambda_r}{\lambda_{r^*}} \mu_{l^*,r^*}$$
$$\overset{(b)}{\leq} \lambda_r \frac{\mu_{l^*,r^*}}{\lambda_{r^*}} \overset{(c)}{<} \theta\lambda_r, \tag{14}$$

where the step (a) follows from equations (10) and (12); (b) is true since $\frac{x_{l^*,r^*}}{\lambda_{r^*}} = \max_{l,r} \frac{x_{l,r}}{\lambda_r}$; (c) follows from the assumption.

Combining (i) and (ii), we have $\mu_{l,r} < \theta\lambda_r$ for any pair (l, r). Therefore, for each link l, if $q_l > 0$, then, by equations (7) and (10), we have $\sigma_l = \sum_{r:l\in r} \mu_{l,r} < \theta \sum_{r:l\in r} \lambda_r$; if $q_l = 0$, then $\sigma_l = 0 < \theta \sum_{r:l\in r} \lambda_r$. Hence, we have $\sigma_l < \theta \sum_{r:l\in r} \lambda_r$ for each link $l \in \mathcal{L}$. This contradicts the fact that the allocated service rate vector $(\sigma_l)_{l\in\mathcal{L}}$ lies on the boundary of the capacity region Λ, since $\theta(\sum_{r:l\in r} \lambda_r)_{l\in\mathcal{L}} \in \Lambda$. Therefore, we have the desired result. □

Having shown Lemma 3, we are ready to prove that the fluid model is weakly stable for any arrival rate vector within the maximum throughput region $\overline{\Lambda}$.

PROPOSITION 2. *The fluid model for the multihop network under the QPRA algorithm is weakly stable for any arrival rate vector that is inside the maximum throughput region $\overline{\Lambda}$.*

PROOF. Given any arrival rate vector $\boldsymbol{\lambda} \in \overline{\Lambda}$, there always exists a real number $\epsilon \geq 0$ such that $(1+\epsilon)(\sum_{r:l\in r} \lambda_r)_{l\in\mathcal{L}} \in \Lambda$. Choose Lyapunov function

$$L(\mathbf{x}) \triangleq \max_{(l,r)} \frac{x_{l,r}}{\lambda_r}. \tag{15}$$

We would like to show $\frac{D^+}{dt^+} L(\mathbf{x}(t)) \leq 0$ whenever $L(\mathbf{x}(t)) > 0$, which implies the desired result according to Lemma 2. According to Lemma 1, we have

$$\frac{D^+}{dt^+} L(\mathbf{x}(t)) \leq \max_{(l^*,r^*)\in\mathcal{K}^*} \frac{1}{\lambda_{r^*}} \frac{d}{dt} x_{l^*,r^*}(t), \tag{16}$$

where $\mathcal{K}^* \triangleq \left\{(l^*, r^*) : L(\mathbf{x}(t)) = \frac{x_{l^*,r^*}(t)}{\lambda_{r^*}}\right\}$. In the rest of proof, we omit the time index t for concision.

We consider the case when $L(\mathbf{x}) > 0$, i.e., $x_{l^*,r^*} > 0$. According to equation (8), we have the following two cases:

(i) If l^* is not the ingress link for route r^*, then

$$\frac{1}{\lambda_{r^*}} \frac{d}{dt} x_{l^*,r^*} = \frac{1}{\lambda_{r^*}} \left(\mu_{l^*_-,r^*} - \mu_{l^*,r^*} \right). \tag{17}$$

If $x_{l^*_-,r^*} = 0$, then $\mu_{l^*_-,r^*} = 0$. By Lemma 3, we have $\frac{1}{\lambda_{r^*}} \frac{d}{dt} x_{l^*,r^*} = -\frac{\mu_{l^*,r^*}}{\lambda_{r^*}} \leq -(1+\epsilon)$. If $x_{l^*_-,r^*} > 0$, then, we have

$$\frac{1}{\lambda_{r^*}} \frac{d}{dt} x_{l^*,r^*} \overset{(a)}{=} \frac{1}{\lambda_{r^*}} \left(\frac{x_{l^*_-,r^*}}{q_{l^*_-}} \sigma_{l^*_-} - \frac{x_{l^*,r^*}}{q_{l^*}} \sigma_{l^*} \right)$$
$$\overset{(b)}{=} \left(\frac{x_{l^*_-,r^*}}{\lambda_{r^*}} - \frac{x_{l^*,r^*}}{\lambda_{r^*}} \right) \frac{\sigma_{l^*}}{q_{l^*}} \overset{(c)}{\leq} 0, \tag{18}$$

where the steps (a) and (b) use equations (10) and (12), respectively; (c) is true since $\frac{x_{l^*,r^*}}{\lambda_{r^*}} = \max_{l,r} \frac{x_{l,r}}{\lambda_r}$.

(ii) If l^* is the ingress link for route r^*, then

$$\frac{1}{\lambda_{r^*}} \frac{d}{dt} x_{l^*,r^*} = \frac{1}{\lambda_{r^*}} (\lambda_{r^*} - \mu_{l^*,r^*}) \leq -\epsilon \leq 0, \tag{19}$$

where we use Lemma 3.

Therefore, by combining (i) and (ii), we have $\frac{1}{\lambda_{r^*}} \frac{d}{dt} x_{l^*,r^*} \leq 0$ for any pair $(l^*, r^*) \in \mathcal{K}^*$, which implies $\frac{D^+}{dt^+} L(\mathbf{x}) \leq 0$. □

Proposition 2 indicates that $L(\mathbf{x})$ is a promising Lyapunov function for establishing the throughput-optimality of the

[3]Locally Lipschitz continuity guarantees the existences (see [6]) of $\frac{D^+}{dx^+} f(x)$ and $\frac{D^+}{dx^+} f_i(x)$, $i = 1, 2, ..., K$.

QPRA algorithm. However, from the proof of Proposition 2, we can observe in (18) that even if the arrival rate vector is strictly within the maximum throughput region, i.e., $\epsilon > 0$, the derivative of the number of route r^* packets at link l^* is not strictly negative, because the arrival rate from the previous link may be arbitrarily close to the departure rate from l^*, due to the fact that the queue lengths at both links may be nearly equal. To resolve this issue, in the next section, we develop an intelligent grouping scheme for links with the same route, and then, based on this scheme, we propose a novel Lyapunov function to obtain the throughput optimality result.

4. THROUGHPUT OPTIMALITY

In this section, we show that the QPRA algorithm achieves throughput-optimality in multihop networks. To that end, we introduce a concept, called *section*, to carefully group links which have nearly the same queue lengths and belong to the same route.

Let $x_{\max}^{(r)} \triangleq \max_{l':l'\in r} x_{l',r}$ be the maximum number of route r packets at each link. Given any $\delta \in (0,1)$ and the queue-length vector $\mathbf{x}$, we define a *section* $\mathbf{S}^{(r)}$ for route r as a set of *consecutive* links satisfying: (i) the last link in the section has the maximum number of route r packets on the route while the number of route r packets at the next link on the route, if any, is strictly less than $x_{\max}^{(r)}$; (ii) the number of route r packets at all other links in the section is strictly greater than $(1-\delta)x_{\max}^{(r)}$. Without loss of generality, the section $\mathbf{S}^{(r)}$ can be represented as

$$\left(l_1^{(r,I)}, l_2^{(r,I)}, \ldots, l_{K_I^{(r)}}^{(r,I)}, l_1^{(r,II)}, l_2^{(r,II)}, \ldots, l_{K_{II}^{(r)}}^{(r,II)}\right), \quad (20)$$

where $(1-\delta)x_{\max}^{(r)} < x_{l_j^{(r,I)},r} < x_{\max}^{(r)}, \forall j = 1, \cdots, K_I^{(r)}$ for some $K_I^{(r)} \geq 0$, and $x_{l_j^{(r,II)},r} = x_{\max}^{(r)}, \forall j = 1, 2, \ldots, K_{II}^{(r)}$ for some $K_{II}^{(r)} \geq 1$.

Fig. 1 provides an example of a particular route in the network in time slot t. From Fig. 1, we know that links 4, 6, 7 and 9 contain the maximum number of this route's packets in time slot t. Given $\delta = 1/10$. There are three sections along this route: (2, 3, 4), (6, 7) and (9).

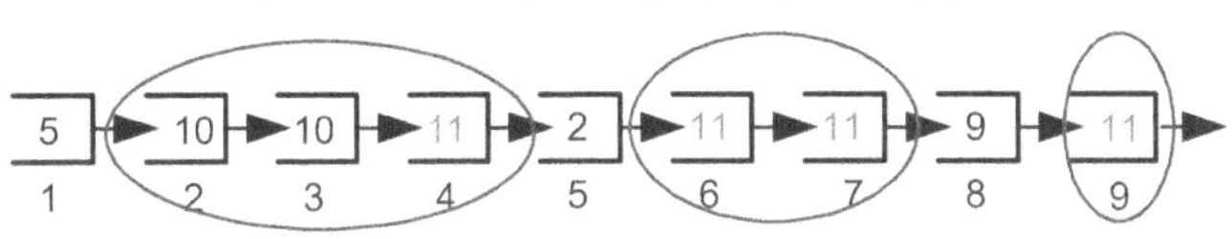

Figure 1: An example showing one route in slot t: the number inside the link represents the number of this route's packets in slot t while the number under the link is its index.

For each section $\mathbf{S}^{(r)}$, we define its weight $W_{\mathbf{S}^{(r)}}(\mathbf{x})$ as the average number of route r packets maintained at each link within this section, i.e.,

$$W_{\mathbf{S}^{(r)}}(\mathbf{x}) \triangleq \frac{1}{|\mathbf{S}^{(r)}|} \sum_{l\in\mathbf{S}^{(r)}} x_{l,r}, \quad (21)$$

where $|\mathbf{S}^{(r)}|$ denotes the number of links within the section $\mathbf{S}^{(r)}$. Let $\mathcal{S}^{(r)}$ be the collection of sections in route r.

Having introduced the concept of a section and its weight, we are in the position to establish the throughput optimality of the QPRA algorithm.

PROPOSITION 3. *The QPRA algorithm achieves throughput optimality, i.e., it stabilizes the system for any arrival rate vector that is strictly inside the maximum throughput region* $\overline{\Lambda}$.

Remark: While the proof of the Proposition 3 is long and quite technical, the intuition is the following. Instead of looking at the drift of the maximum queue lengths, we look at the drift of the maximum section in the network, where the maximum section is the section with the maximum weight (where the weight of a section is defined in (21)). The key steps in the proof are as follows: (i) if the maximum section does not contain the ingress link of its route, then its drift is upper bounded by the difference between the departure rate from the previous link and the departure rate from the last link of the maximum section, which is strictly negative by the definition of the section; (ii) if the maximum section includes the ingress link of its route, then its drift is upper bounded by the difference between the arrival rate and the departure rate from the last link of the maximum section, which is also strictly negative due to the fact that the maximum section has the weight very close to maximum queue-length and Lemma 3.

PROOF. Given any arrival rate vector $\boldsymbol{\lambda} \in \mathrm{Int}(\overline{\Lambda})$, there always exists a real number $\epsilon \in (0, 1/2)$ such that

$$(1+\epsilon)\left(\sum_{r:l\in r} \lambda_r\right)_{l\in\mathcal{L}} \in \Lambda. \quad (22)$$

We select $\delta = \epsilon/2 \in (0, 1/4)$. Consider the Lyapunov function

$$V(\mathbf{x}(t)) \triangleq \max_{r\in\mathcal{R}} \frac{1}{\lambda_r} \max_{\mathbf{S}^{(r)}(t)\in\mathcal{S}^{(r)}(t)} W_{\mathbf{S}^{(r)}(t)}(\mathbf{x}(t)). \quad (23)$$

We would like to show that $\frac{D^+}{dt^+}V(\mathbf{x}(t))$ is strictly negative whenever $V(\mathbf{x}(t)) > 0$, which implies the desired result according to Lemma 2 and [8, Theorem 4.2].

According to Lemma 1, we have

$$\frac{D^+}{dt^+}V(\mathbf{x}(t)) \leq \max_{\overline{r}\in\overline{\mathcal{K}}} \frac{1}{\lambda_{\overline{r}}} \frac{D^+}{dt^+} \max_{\mathbf{S}^{(\overline{r})}(t)\in\mathcal{S}^{(\overline{r})}(t)} W_{\mathbf{S}^{(\overline{r})}(t)}(\mathbf{x}(t)),$$

where

$$\overline{\mathcal{K}} \triangleq \left\{\overline{r} \in \mathcal{R} : V(\mathbf{x}(t)) = \frac{1}{\lambda_{\overline{r}}} \max_{\mathbf{S}^{(\overline{r})}(t)\in\mathcal{S}^{(\overline{r})}(t)} W_{\mathbf{S}^{(\overline{r})}(t)}(\mathbf{x}(t))\right\}.$$

Next, we consider the case when $V(\mathbf{x}(t)) > 0$, i.e.,

$$\max_{\mathbf{S}^{(\overline{r})}(t)\in\mathcal{S}^{(\overline{r})}(t)} W_{\mathbf{S}^{(\overline{r})}(t)}(\mathbf{x}(t)) > 0.$$

Recall that $(l^*, r^*) \in \arg\max_{(l,r)} \frac{x_{l,r}(t)}{\lambda_r}$. Then, we have

$$\frac{x_{l^*,r^*}(t)}{\lambda_{r^*}} \geq \frac{x_{\max}^{(\overline{r})}(t)}{\lambda_{\overline{r}}} \overset{(a)}{\geq} \frac{1}{\lambda_{\overline{r}}} \max_{\mathbf{S}^{(\overline{r})}(t)\in\mathcal{S}^{(\overline{r})}(t)} W_{\mathbf{S}^{(\overline{r})}(t)}(\mathbf{x}(t)) > 0,$$

where the step (a) follows from the fact that the weight of any section in route r should not be greater than $x_{\max}^{(r)}(t)$. Therefore, we have both $x_{l^*,r^*}(t) > 0$ and $x_{\max}^{(\overline{r})}(t) > 0$.

Next, we consider $\frac{D^+}{dt^+} \max_{\mathbf{S}^{(\overline{r})}(t)\in\mathcal{S}^{(\overline{r})}(t)} W_{\mathbf{S}^{(\overline{r})}(t)}(\mathbf{x}(t))$. Note that $x_{l,r}(t)$ is continuous for any pair (l, r). Since $x_{\max}^{(\overline{r})}(t) > 0$, according to the sign-preserving property of continuous functions, for a sufficiently small $u > 0$, we have the following two facts:

(i) The link with the maximum number of route $\overline{r}$ packets at time $t+u$ should also have the maximum number of route $\overline{r}$ packets at time t;

(ii) The link with the number of route $\overline{r}$ packets strictly less (or greater) than $(1-\delta)x_{\max}^{(\overline{r})}(t)$ at time t should also have the number of route $\overline{r}$ packets strictly less (or greater) than $(1-\delta)x_{\max}^{(\overline{r})}(t+u)$ at time $t+u$.

Indeed, If $\frac{x_{l,\overline{r}}(t)}{x_{\max}^{(\overline{r})}(t)} < 1$, then $\frac{x_{l,\overline{r}}(t+u)}{x_{\max}^{(\overline{r})}(t+u)} < 1$ since $\frac{x_{l,\overline{r}}(t)}{x_{\max}^{(\overline{r})}(t)} - 1$ is a continuous function of t. Hence, if a link does not contain the maximum number of route $\overline{r}$ packets at time t, then it cannot have the maximum number of route $\overline{r}$ packets at time $t+u$. This implies Fact (i). Similarly, if $\frac{x_{l,\overline{r}}(t)}{x_{\max}^{(\overline{r})}(t)} \leqslant 1-\delta$, then $\frac{x_{l,\overline{r}}(t+u)}{x_{\max}^{(\overline{r})}(t+u)} \leqslant 1-\delta$, which implies Fact (ii).

Hence, if there is a section at time $t+u$, then some of its links must also constitute a section at time t by Fact (i). Let $\left(l_1^{(\overline{r},I)}, l_2^{(\overline{r},I)}, ..., l_{K_I^{(\overline{r})}}^{(\overline{r},I)}, l_1^{(\overline{r},II)}, l_2^{(\overline{r},II)}, ..., l_{K_{II}^{(r)}}^{(\overline{r},II)}\right)$ be a section at time t, where most of its links constitute a *section with the maximum weight* at time $t+u$, $(1-\delta)x_{\max}^{(\overline{r})}(t) < x_{l_i^{(\overline{r},I)}}(t) < x_{\max}^{(\overline{r})}(t)$, $\forall i = 1, ..., K_I^{(\overline{r})}$ for some $K_I^{(\overline{r})} \geq 0$, and $x_{l_j^{(r,II)}}(t) = x_{\max}^{(\overline{r})}(t)$, $\forall j = 1, ..., K_{II}^{(\overline{r})}$ for some $K_{II}^{(\overline{r})} \geq 1$.

Therefore, by Fact (ii), we have $(1-\delta)x_{\max}^{(\overline{r})}(t+u) < x_{l_i^{(\overline{r},I)}}(t+u), \forall i = 1, 2, ..., K_I^{(\overline{r})}$ and $(1-\delta)x_{\max}^{(\overline{r})}(t+u) < x_{l_i^{(\overline{r},II)}}(t+u), \forall i = 1, 2, ..., K_{II}^{(\overline{r})}$. Without loss of generality, we assume that $l_{K_s^{(\overline{r})}}^{(\overline{r},II)} (K_s^{(\overline{r})} = 1, 2, ..., K_{II}^{(\overline{r})})$ is the largest index of link with the maximum number of route $\overline{r}$ packets within the section at time $t+u$. Consequently, we know that

$$\left(l_1^{(\overline{r},I)}, l_2^{(\overline{r},I)}, \cdots, l_{K_I^{(\overline{r})}}^{(\overline{r},I)}, l_1^{(\overline{r},II)}, l_2^{(\overline{r},II)}, \cdots, l_{K_s^{(\overline{r})}}^{(\overline{r},II)}\right)$$

is part of section with the maximum weight at time $t+u$. Also, we assume that $\left(l_1^{(\overline{r},0)}, l_2^{(\overline{r},0)}, ..., l_{K_0^{(\overline{r})}}^{(\overline{r},0)}\right)$ is a set of links with the number of route $\overline{r}$ packets equal to $(1-\delta)x_{\max}^{(\overline{r})}(t)$ that are included in a section at time $t+u$, i.e., $x_{l_j^{(\overline{r},0)}}(t+u) > (1-\delta)x_{\max}^{(\overline{r})}(t+u)$, where $j = 1, 2, \cdots, K_0^{(\overline{r})}$ for some $K_0^{(\overline{r})} \geq 0$. Hence, we have that

$$\left(l_1^{(\overline{r},0)}, \cdots, l_{K_0^{(\overline{r})}}^{(\overline{r},0)}, l_1^{(\overline{r},I)}, \cdots, l_{K_I^{(\overline{r})}}^{(\overline{r},I)}, l_1^{(\overline{r},II)}, \cdots, l_{K_s^{(\overline{r})}}^{(\overline{r},II)}\right)$$

is a section with the maximum weight at time $t+u$.

The relation between the sections in time t and $t+u$ is shown in Fig. 2. Since $x_{l_i^{(\overline{r},0)},\overline{r}}(t) < x_{l_j^{(\overline{r},I)},\overline{r}}(t) < x_{l_k^{(\overline{r},II)},\overline{r}}(t)$, $\forall i, j, k$, by Fact (ii), we have

$$x_{l_i^{(\overline{r},0)},\overline{r}}(t+u) < \min\left\{x_{l_j^{(\overline{r},I)},\overline{r}}(t+u), x_{l_k^{(\overline{r},II)},\overline{r}}(t+u)\right\}.$$

Therefore, we have

$$\max_{\mathbf{S}^{(\overline{r})}(t+u)\in\mathcal{S}^{(\overline{r})}(t+u)} W_{\mathbf{S}^{(\overline{r})}(t+u)}(\mathbf{x}(t+u))$$
$$\leq \frac{1}{K_I^{(\overline{r})} + K_s^{(\overline{r})}} \left(\sum_{j=1}^{K_I^{(\overline{r})}} x_{l_j^{(\overline{r},I)},\overline{r}}(t+u) + \sum_{j=1}^{K_s^{(\overline{r})}} x_{l_j^{(\overline{r},II)},\overline{r}}(t+u) \right). \quad (24)$$

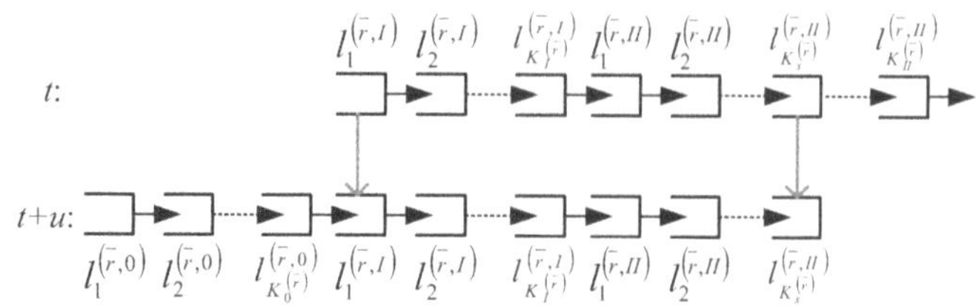

Figure 2: Relation between the sections in time t and $t+u$.

In addition, since $x_{l_i^{(\overline{r},I)},\overline{r}}(t) < x_{l_j^{(\overline{r},II)},\overline{r}}(t), \forall i, j$, we have

$$\max_{\mathbf{S}^{(\overline{r})}(t)\in\mathcal{S}^{(\overline{r})}(t)} W_{\mathbf{S}^{(\overline{r})}(t)}(\mathbf{x}(t))$$
$$\geq \frac{1}{K_I^{(\overline{r})} + K_s^{(\overline{r})}} \left(\sum_{j=1}^{K_I^{(\overline{r})}} x_{l_j^{(\overline{r},I)},\overline{r}}(t) + \sum_{j=1}^{K_s^{(\overline{r})}} x_{l_j^{(\overline{r},II)},\overline{r}}(t) \right). \quad (25)$$

By utilizing (24) and (25), we have

$$\frac{D^+}{dt^+} \max_{\mathbf{S}^{(\overline{r})}(t)\in\mathcal{S}^{(\overline{r})}(t)} W_{\mathbf{S}^{(\overline{r})}(t)}(\mathbf{x}(t))$$
$$= \limsup_{u\downarrow 0} \frac{1}{u}\Bigg(\max_{\mathbf{S}^{(\overline{r})}(t+u)\in\mathcal{S}^{(\overline{r})}(t+u)} W_{\mathbf{S}^{(\overline{r})}(t+u)}(\mathbf{x}(t+u)) - \max_{\mathbf{S}^{(\overline{r})}(t)\in\mathcal{S}^{(\overline{r})}(t)} W_{\overline{\mathbf{S}}^{(\overline{r})}(t)}(\mathbf{x}(t))\Bigg)$$
$$\leq \limsup_{u\downarrow 0} \frac{1}{K_I^{(\overline{r})} + K_s^{(\overline{r})}} \Bigg(\sum_{j=1}^{K_I^{(\overline{r})}} \frac{1}{u}\left(x_{l_j^{(\overline{r},I)},\overline{r}}(t+u) - x_{l_j^{(\overline{r},I)},\overline{r}}(t)\right) + \sum_{j=1}^{K_s^{(\overline{r})}} \frac{1}{u}\left(x_{l_j^{(\overline{r},II)},\overline{r}}(t+u) - x_{l_j^{(\overline{r},II)},\overline{r}}(t)\right)\Bigg)$$
$$= \frac{1}{K_I^{(\overline{r})} + K_s^{(\overline{r})}} \left(\sum_{j=1}^{K_I^{(\overline{r})}} \frac{d}{dt} x_{l_j^{(\overline{r},I)},\overline{r}}(t) + \sum_{j=1}^{K_s^{(\overline{r})}} \frac{d}{dt} x_{l_j^{(\overline{r},II)},\overline{r}}(t) \right).$$

In the rest of proof, we will omit the time index t for concision. According to (8), we have the following two cases: (i) If $l_1^{(\overline{r},I)}$ is not the ingress link for route $\overline{r}$, then

$$\frac{1}{\lambda_{\overline{r}}} \frac{D^+}{dt^+} \max_{\mathbf{S}^{(\overline{r})}\in\mathcal{S}^{(\overline{r})}} W_{\mathbf{S}^{(\overline{r})}}(\mathbf{x})$$
$$\leq \frac{1}{\lambda_{\overline{r}}\left(K_I^{(\overline{r})} + K_s^{(\overline{r})}\right)} \Bigg(\sum_{j=1}^{K_I^{(\overline{r})}} \left(\mu_{l_{j-}^{(\overline{r},I)},\overline{r}} - \mu_{l_j^{(\overline{r},I)},\overline{r}} \right) + \sum_{j=1}^{K_s^{(\overline{r})}} \left(\mu_{l_{j-}^{(\overline{r},II)},\overline{r}} - \mu_{l_j^{(\overline{r},II)},\overline{r}} \right)\Bigg)$$
$$= \frac{1}{\lambda_{\overline{r}}\left(K_I^{(\overline{r})} + K_s^{(\overline{r})}\right)} \left(\mu_{l_{1-}^{(\overline{r},I)},\overline{r}} - \mu_{l_{K_s^{(\overline{r})}}^{(\overline{r},II)},\overline{r}} \right). \quad (26)$$

If $x_{l_{1-}^{(\overline{r},I)},\overline{r}} = 0$, then $\mu_{l_{1-}^{(\overline{r},I)},\overline{r}} = 0$ and thus we have

$$\frac{1}{\lambda_{\overline{r}}} \frac{D^+}{dt^+} \max_{\mathbf{S}^{(\overline{r})}\in\mathcal{S}^{(\overline{r})}} W_{\mathbf{S}^{(\overline{r})}}(\mathbf{x}) \leq - \frac{\mu_{l_{K_s^{(\overline{r})}}^{(\overline{r},II)},\overline{r}}}{\lambda_{\overline{r}}\left(K_I^{(\overline{r})} + K_s^{(\overline{r})}\right)}, \quad (27)$$

Recall that $(l^*, r^*) \in \arg\max_{(l,r)} \frac{x_{l,r}}{\lambda_r}$. Hence, we have

$$\frac{x_{\max}^{(\overline{r})}}{\lambda_{\overline{r}}} \overset{(a)}{\geq} \frac{1}{\lambda_{\overline{r}}} \max_{\mathbf{S}^{(\overline{r})} \in \mathcal{S}^{(\overline{r})}} W_{\mathbf{S}^{(\overline{r})}}(\mathbf{x}) \overset{(b)}{\geq} \frac{1}{\lambda_{r^*}} \max_{\mathbf{S}^{(r^*)} \in \mathcal{S}^{(r^*)}} W_{\mathbf{S}^{(r^*)}}(\mathbf{x}) \overset{(c)}{\geq} \frac{(1-\delta)x_{l^*,r^*}}{\lambda_{r^*}}, \tag{28}$$

where the step (a) follows from the fact that the weight of any section in route r should not be greater than $x_{\max}^{(r)}$; (b) follows from the definition of the route $\overline{r}$; (c) is true since the weight of any section in route r should be greater than $(1-\delta)x_{\max}^{(r)}$. Thus, we have

$$\begin{aligned} \mu_{\overline{l}^{(\overline{r},II)}_{K_{II}^{(\overline{r})}},\overline{r}} &\overset{(a)}{=} \frac{x_{\overline{l}^{(\overline{r},II)}_{K_{II}^{(\overline{r})}},\overline{r}}}{x_{l^*,r^*}} \mu_{l^*,r^*} \\ &= \frac{x_{\max}^{(\overline{r})}/\lambda_{\overline{r}}}{x_{l^*,r^*}/\lambda_{r^*}} \frac{\lambda_{\overline{r}}}{\lambda_{r^*}} \mu_{l^*,r^*} \\ &\overset{(b)}{\geq} (1-\delta)(1+\epsilon)\lambda_{\overline{r}} \\ &\overset{(c)}{\geq} \left(1+\frac{\epsilon}{4}\right)\lambda_{\overline{r}}, \end{aligned} \tag{29}$$

where the step (a) follows from equations (10) and (12), and the fact that $x_{\overline{l}^{(\overline{r},II)}_{K_{II}^{(\overline{r})}},\overline{r}} = x_{\max}^{(\overline{r})} > 0$ and $x_{l^*,r^*} > 0$; (b) utilizes inequality (28) and Lemma 3; (c) is true since $\delta = \epsilon/2$ and $0 < \epsilon < 1/2$.

Hence, by substituting (29) into (27), we have

$$\frac{1}{\lambda_{\overline{r}}} \frac{D^+}{dt^+} \max_{\mathbf{S}^{(\overline{r})} \in \mathcal{S}^{(\overline{r})}} W_{\mathbf{S}^{(\overline{r})}}(\mathbf{x}) \leq -\frac{1+\epsilon/4}{K_I^{(\overline{r})} + K_s^{(\overline{r})}} \leq -\frac{1+\epsilon/4}{|\mathcal{L}|},$$

where the last step follows from the fact that each route is acyclic and thus the maximum number of links belonging to route $\overline{r}$ should not be greater than $|\mathcal{L}|$, i.e., $K_I^{(\overline{r})} + K_s^{(\overline{r})} \leq |\mathcal{L}|$.

If $x_{l_{1-}^{(\overline{r},I)},\overline{r}} > 0$, then, (26) becomes

$$\begin{aligned} &\frac{1}{\lambda_{\overline{r}}} \frac{D^+}{dt^+} \max_{\mathbf{S}^{(\overline{r})} \in \mathcal{S}^{(\overline{r})}} W_{\mathbf{S}^{(\overline{r})}}(\mathbf{x}) \\ &\overset{(a)}{\leq} \frac{1}{\lambda_{\overline{r}}\left(K_I^{(\overline{r})} + K_s^{(\overline{r})}\right)} \left(\frac{x_{l_{1-}^{(\overline{r},I)},\overline{r}}}{q_{l_{1-}^{(\overline{r},I)}}} \sigma_{l_{1-}^{(\overline{r},I)}} - \frac{x_{l^{(\overline{r},II)}_{K_s^{(\overline{r})}},\overline{r}}}{q_{l^{(\overline{r},II)}_{K_s^{(\overline{r})}}}} \sigma_{l^{(\overline{r},II)}_{K_s^{(\overline{r})}}} \right) \\ &\overset{(b)}{=} \frac{1}{\lambda_{\overline{r}}\left(K_I^{(\overline{r})} + K_s^{(\overline{r})}\right)} \left(x_{l_{1-}^{(\overline{r},I)},\overline{r}} - x_{l^{(\overline{r},II)}_{K_s^{(\overline{r})}},\overline{r}} \right) \frac{\sigma_{l^{(\overline{r},II)}_{K_s^{(\overline{r})}}}}{q_{l^{(\overline{r},II)}_{K_s^{(\overline{r})}}}} \\ &\overset{(c)}{\leq} \frac{-\delta x_{\max}^{(\overline{r})}}{\lambda_{\overline{r}}\left(K_I^{(\overline{r})} + K_s^{(\overline{r})}\right)} \frac{\sum_{l\in\mathcal{L}} \sigma_l}{\sum_{l\in\mathcal{L}} q_l}, \end{aligned} \tag{30}$$

where the steps (a) and (b) use equations (10) and (12), respectively; (c) follows from the fact that the previous link of $l_1^{(\overline{r},I)}$ does not belong to the section $\mathbf{S}^{(\overline{r})}$, the fact that $x_{l_{1-}^{(\overline{r},I)}} \leq (1-\delta)x_{\max}^{(\overline{r})}$ and $x_{l^{(\overline{r},II)}_{K_s^{(\overline{r})}},\overline{r}} = x_{\max}^{(\overline{r})}$, and the fact that

$$\frac{x_1}{y_1} = \frac{\sum_{i=1}^n x_i}{\sum_{i=1}^n y_i} \text{ if } \frac{x_1}{y_1} = \frac{x_2}{y_2} = \cdots = \frac{x_n}{y_n}.$$

Since $\frac{x_{l^*,r^*}}{\lambda_{r^*}} \geq \frac{x_{l,r}}{\lambda_r}, \forall (l,r)$, we have $x_{l,r} \leq \lambda_r \frac{x_{l^*,r^*}}{\lambda_{r^*}}$. Therefore, we have

$$q_l = \sum_{r:l\in r} x_{l,r} \leq \frac{x_{l^*,r^*}}{\lambda_{r^*}} \sum_{r:l\in r} \lambda_r \leq \frac{x_{l^*,r^*}}{\lambda_{r^*}}, \quad \forall l \in \mathcal{L},$$

where the last step follows from the fact that $\sum_{r:l\in r} \lambda_r \leq 1, \forall l \in \mathcal{L}$, which is due to the assumption that each link can at most transfer one packet in one slot and equation (22).

Hence, we have

$$\sum_{l\in\mathcal{L}} q_l \leq |\mathcal{L}| \frac{x_{l^*,r^*}}{\lambda_{r^*}}. \tag{31}$$

Since $\boldsymbol{\sigma}$ lies on the boundary of the capacity region Λ, we have

$$\sum_{l=1}^{L} \sigma_l \geq M, \tag{32}$$

where $M > 0$ is the minimum l_1-norm of rate vector lying on the boundary of the capacity region.

Hence, by using inequalities (28), (31) and (32), we have

$$\frac{x_{\max}^{(\overline{r})}}{\lambda_{\overline{r}}\left(K_I^{(\overline{r})} + K_s^{(\overline{r})}\right)} \frac{\sum_{l\in\mathcal{L}} \sigma_l}{\sum_{l\in\mathcal{L}} q_l} \geq \frac{(1-\delta)M}{\left(K_I^{(\overline{r})} + K_s^{(\overline{r})}\right)|\mathcal{L}|} \geq \frac{M(1-\delta)}{|\mathcal{L}|^2}, \tag{33}$$

where the last step follows from the fact that the route is acyclic and thus the maximum number of links belonging to route $\overline{r}$ should not be greater than $|\mathcal{L}|$, i.e., $K_I^{(\overline{r})} + K_s^{(\overline{r})} \leq |\mathcal{L}|$.

By substituting inequality (33) into (30), we have

$$\frac{1}{\lambda_{\overline{r}}} \frac{D^+}{dt^+} \max_{\mathbf{S}^{(\overline{r})} \in \mathcal{S}^{(\overline{r})}} W_{\mathbf{S}^{(\overline{r})}}(\mathbf{x}) \leq -\delta \frac{M(1-\delta)}{|\mathcal{L}|^2} \leq -\frac{3M\epsilon}{8|\mathcal{L}|^2},$$

where the last step follows from the fact that $\delta = \epsilon/2 \in (0, 1/4)$.

(ii) If $l_1^{(\overline{r})}$ is the ingress link for route $\overline{r}$, then, by following the same steps in deriving inequality (26), we have

$$\begin{aligned} &\frac{1}{\lambda_{\overline{r}}} \frac{D^+}{dt^+} \max_{\mathbf{S}^{(\overline{r})} \in \mathcal{S}^{(\overline{r})}} W_{\mathbf{S}^{(\overline{r})}}(\mathbf{x}) \\ &\leq \frac{1}{\lambda_{\overline{r}}\left(K_I^{(\overline{r})} + K_s^{(\overline{r})}\right)} \left(\lambda_{\overline{r}} - \mu_{\overline{l}^{(\overline{r},II)}_{K_{II}^{(\overline{r})}},\overline{r}} \right) \\ &\overset{(a)}{\leq} -\frac{\epsilon}{4\left(K_I^{(\overline{r})} + K_s^{(\overline{r})}\right)} \\ &\overset{(b)}{\leq} -\frac{\epsilon}{4|\mathcal{L}|}, \end{aligned} \tag{34}$$

where the step (a) uses inequality (29); (b) follows from the fact that $K_I^{(\overline{r})} + K_s^{(\overline{r})} \leq |\mathcal{L}|$.

Therefore, by combining (i) and (ii), we have that

$$\frac{1}{\lambda_{\overline{r}}} \frac{D^+}{dt^+} \max_{\mathbf{S}^{(\overline{r})} \in \mathcal{S}^{(\overline{r})}} W_{\mathbf{S}^{(\overline{r})}}(\mathbf{x}) \leq -\epsilon \min\left\{ \frac{3M}{8|\mathcal{L}|^2}, \frac{1}{4|\mathcal{L}|} \right\}, \tag{35}$$

holds for any route $\overline{r} \in \overline{\mathcal{K}}$, which implies that $\frac{D^+}{dt^+} V(\mathbf{x}) \leq -\epsilon \min\left\{ \frac{3M}{8|\mathcal{L}|^2}, \frac{1}{4|\mathcal{L}|} \right\}$. □

Even though the QPRA algorithm is throughput-optimal, it requires the knowledge of the full capacity region, which is generally unavailable in practice. Motivated by [15] and the QPRA Algorithm, we next propose an efficient low-complexity scheduling scheme that makes transmission decisions only based on per-link queueing information in multihop networks.

5. LOW-COMPLEXITY IMPLEMENTATION

In this section, we propose a low-complexity scheduling algorithm with only per-link queueing information.

We consider the primary interference model, where each link l interferes with all of its one-hop neighboring links. The capacity region Λ (see [11]) under the primary interference model is bounded by

$$\frac{2}{3}\Gamma \subseteq \Lambda \subseteq \Gamma, \tag{36}$$

where

$$\Gamma \triangleq \left\{ \boldsymbol{\eta} = (\eta_l)_{l\in\mathcal{L}} \middle| \sum_{l\in\mathcal{E}(i)} \eta_l \leq 1, \forall i \in \mathcal{N} \right\}, \tag{37}$$

and $\mathcal{E}(i)$ denotes the set of links that connect to the neighbors of node i.

Motivated by the QPRA Algorithm and [15], for any queue-length vector $\mathbf{Q} \neq 0$, let $\boldsymbol{\sigma} = (\sigma_l)_{l\in\mathcal{L}}$ be the longest vector in Γ such that $\sigma_l = \gamma Q_l, \forall l \in \mathcal{L}$, for some $\gamma \geq 0$. Therefore, it can be easily calculated that

$$\sigma_l = \frac{Q_l}{\max_{i\in\mathcal{N}} \sum_{l'\in\mathcal{E}(i)} Q_{l'}}, \quad \forall l \in \mathcal{L}. \tag{38}$$

Based on (38), we develop a low-complexity scheduling algorithm with only per-link queueing information.

Low-Complexity QPRA (LC-QPRA):

(1) In each time slot t, each link l attempts transmission with probability $\sigma_l(t)$ as follows:

$$\sigma_l(t) = \begin{cases} 0, & \text{if } Q_l(t) = 0; \\ \dfrac{Q_l(t)}{\max_{i\in\mathcal{N}} \sum_{k\in\mathcal{E}(i)} Q_k(t)}, & \text{if } Q_l(t) > 0. \end{cases} \tag{39}$$

(2) Then, each link l attempting transmission generates a uniformly distributed random variable over $(0, \Delta)$ with $0 < \Delta \ll 1$, and starts transmission after this random duration unless it senses another transmission before.

(3) Finally, serve each link l according to the SIRO queueing discipline as in the QPRA algorithm.

Remark: Here we need to know $\max_{i\in\mathcal{N}} \sum_{k\in\mathcal{E}(i)} Q_k(t)$ in each time slot. However, since the throughput performance is insensitive to the accuracy of the queue-lengths (e.g., [30, 13]), we may just need to update the attempt probability over a relative long period so that all links have enough time to learn this global information.

Due to the random-backoff procedure in the second part of the LC-QPRA algorithm, only a subset of links that attempt transmission will be active. Next, we show that if a link attempts to transmit, the conditional probability that it successfully transmits is at least 1/3.

LEMMA 4. *Under the LC-QPRA algorithm, the conditional probability that link l successfully transmits, conditioned on it attempts transmission, is at least $1/3$.*

The proof is similar to that in [15, Lemma 2] and is omitted here for brevity.

PROPOSITION 4. *The LC-QPRA Algorithm can achieve a constant efficient ratio of at least $\rho^2(1-\Delta)$ under the primary interference model, i.e., it stabilizes the system for any arrival rate vector that is strictly within the region $\rho^2(1-\Delta)\overline{\Lambda}$, where $\rho \triangleq 1/3$.*

PROOF. First we note that the capacity region Λ shrinks to $(1-\Delta)\Lambda$ due to the overhead of the LC-QPRA algorithm. Given any arrival rate vector $\boldsymbol{\lambda} \in \text{Int}(\rho^2(1-\Delta)\overline{\Lambda})$, there always exists a real number $\epsilon \in (0, 1/2)$ such that

$$\frac{1+\epsilon}{\rho^2}\left(\sum_{r:l\in r} \lambda_r\right)_{l\in\mathcal{L}} \in (1-\Delta)\Lambda.$$

The fluid model under the LC-QPRA algorithm is the same as that in Proposition 1 except the departure rate vector $\boldsymbol{\mu}(t) = (\mu_{l,r}(t))_{r\in\mathcal{R},l\in\mathcal{L}}$, which satisfies

$$\mu_{l,r}(t) = \frac{x_{l,r}(t)}{q_l(t)}\nu_l(t), \tag{40}$$

$$\sigma_l(t) \geq \nu_l(t) \geq \rho\sigma_l(t), \tag{41}$$

where $\nu_l(t)$ is the service rate for link l at time t and $\boldsymbol{\sigma}(t) = (\sigma_l(t))_{l\in\mathcal{L}}$ lies on the boundary of the region Γ satisfying

$$\sigma_l(t) = 0, \text{ whenever } q_l(t) = 0; \tag{42}$$

$$\sigma_l(t) = \frac{q_l(t)}{\max_{i\in\mathcal{N}} \sum_{l'\in\mathcal{E}(i)} q_{l'}(t)}, \text{ whenever } q_l(t) > 0, \tag{43}$$

Here we note that equation (41) follows from Lemma 4, and (40), (42) and (43) are from the LC-QPRA algorithm.

Given the queue-length vector $\mathbf{x}$, we introduce the section $\mathbf{S}^{(r)}$ (c.f. Section 4) by choosing $\delta = 1 - \rho + \rho\epsilon/2$. We use the same Lyapunov function $V(\mathbf{x}(t))$ as in the proof of Proposition 3 and consider the case when $V(\mathbf{x}(t)) > 0$. By employing the same techniques as in Proposition 3, we have

$$\begin{aligned} &\frac{D^+}{dt^+} \max_{\mathbf{S}^{(\overline{r})}(t)\in\mathcal{S}^{(\overline{r})}(t)} W_{\mathbf{S}^{(\overline{r})}(t)}(\mathbf{x}(t)) \\ &\leq \frac{1}{K_I^{(\overline{r})} + K_s^{(\overline{r})}} \left(\sum_{j=1}^{K_I^{(\overline{r})}} \frac{d}{dt} x_{l_j^{(\overline{r},I)},\overline{r}}(t) + \sum_{j=1}^{K_s^{(\overline{r})}} \frac{d}{dt} x_{l_j^{(\overline{r},II)},\overline{r}}(t) \right), \end{aligned}$$

where $\overline{r}$, $K_I^{(\overline{r})} \geq 0$ and $K_{II}^{(\overline{r})} \geq 1$ are defined in the proof of Proposition 3. Similar to the proof of Proposition 3, we have the following two cases:

(i) If $l_1^{(\overline{r},I)}$ is not the ingress link for route $\overline{r}$, then

$$\begin{aligned} &\frac{1}{\lambda_{\overline{r}}} \frac{D^+}{dt^+} \max_{\mathbf{S}^{(\overline{r})}\in\mathcal{S}^{(\overline{r})}} W_{\mathbf{S}^{(\overline{r})}}(\mathbf{x}) \\ &\leq \frac{1}{\lambda_{\overline{r}}\left(K_I^{(\overline{r})} + K_s^{(\overline{r})}\right)} \left(\mu_{l_{1-}^{(\overline{r},I)},\overline{r}} - \mu_{l_{K_s^{(\overline{r})}}^{(\overline{r},II)},\overline{r}} \right). \end{aligned} \tag{44}$$

If $x_{l_{1-}^{(\overline{r},I)},\overline{r}} = 0$, then $\mu_{l_{1-}^{(\overline{r},I)},\overline{r}} = 0$ and thus we have

$$\frac{1}{\lambda_{\overline{r}}} \frac{D^+}{dt^+} \max_{\mathbf{S}^{(\overline{r})}\in\mathcal{S}^{(\overline{r})}} W_{\mathbf{S}^{(\overline{r})}}(\mathbf{x}) \leq -\frac{\mu_{l_{K_s^{(\overline{r})}}^{(\overline{r},II)},\overline{r}}}{\lambda_{\overline{r}}\left(K_I^{(\overline{r})} + K_s^{(\overline{r})}\right)}, \tag{45}$$

Next, we consider the departure rate $\mu_{\bar{l}^{(\bar{r},II)}_{K_{II}^{(\bar{r})}},\bar{r}}$.

$$\begin{aligned}
\mu_{\bar{l}^{(\bar{r},II)}_{K_{II}^{(\bar{r})}},\bar{r}} &\overset{(a)}{=} \frac{x_{\bar{l}^{(\bar{r},II)}_{K_{II}^{(\bar{r})}},\bar{r}}}{q_{\bar{l}^{(\bar{r},II)}_{K_{II}^{(\bar{r})}}}} \nu_{\bar{l}^{(\bar{r},II)}_{K_{II}^{(\bar{r})}}} \\
&\overset{(b)}{\geq} \rho x^{(\bar{r})}_{max} \frac{\sigma_{\bar{l}^{(\bar{r},II)}_{K_{II}^{(\bar{r})}}}}{q_{\bar{l}^{(\bar{r},II)}_{K_{II}^{(\bar{r})}}}} \\
&\overset{(c)}{=} \rho x^{(\bar{r})}_{max} \frac{\sigma_{l^*}}{q_{l^*}} \\
&\overset{(d)}{\geq} \rho x^{(\bar{r})}_{max} \frac{\nu_{l^*}}{q_{l^*}} \\
&\overset{(e)}{=} \rho x^{(\bar{r})}_{max} \frac{\mu_{l^*,r^*}}{x_{l^*,r^*}} \\
&= \rho \frac{x^{(\bar{r})}_{\max}/\lambda_{\bar{r}}}{x_{l^*,r^*}/\lambda_{r^*}} \frac{\lambda_{\bar{r}}}{\lambda_{r^*}} \mu_{l^*,r^*} \\
&\overset{(f)}{\geq} \rho(1-\delta)(1+\epsilon)\frac{1}{\rho^2}\lambda_{\bar{r}} \\
&\overset{(g)}{\geq} (1+\epsilon/4)\,\lambda_{\bar{r}}, \qquad (46)
\end{aligned}$$

where the steps (a) and (e) use equation (40); (b) and (d) follow from inequality (41); (c) utilizes equation (43); (f) utilizes inequality (28) and Lemma 3; (g) is true since $\delta = 1-\rho+\rho\epsilon/2$ and $\epsilon \in (0, 1/2)$.

Hence, by substituting (46) into (45), we have

$$\frac{1}{\lambda_{\bar{r}}}\frac{D^+}{dt^+} \max_{\mathbf{S}^{(\bar{r})}\in\mathcal{S}^{(\bar{r})}} W_{\mathbf{S}^{(\bar{r})}}(\mathbf{x}) \leq -\frac{1+\epsilon/4}{|\mathcal{L}|}, \qquad (47)$$

where we use the fact that $K_I^{(\bar{r})} + K_s^{(\bar{r})} \leq |\mathcal{L}|$.

If $x_{l_{1-}^{(\bar{r},I)},\bar{r}} > 0$, then, (44) becomes

$$\begin{aligned}
&\frac{1}{\lambda_{\bar{r}}}\frac{D^+}{dt^+} \max_{\mathbf{S}^{(\bar{r})}\in\mathcal{S}^{(\bar{r})}} W_{\mathbf{S}^{(\bar{r})}}(\mathbf{x}) \\
&\overset{(a)}{\leq} \frac{1}{\lambda_{\bar{r}}\left(K_I^{(\bar{r})}+K_s^{(\bar{r})}\right)} \left(\frac{x_{l_{1-}^{(\bar{r},I)},\bar{r}}}{q_{l_{1-}^{(\bar{r},I)}}} \nu_{l_{1-}^{(\bar{r},I)}} - \frac{x_{l^{(\bar{r},II)}_{K_s^{(\bar{r})}},\bar{r}}}{q_{l^{(\bar{r},II)}_{K_s^{(\bar{r})}}}} \nu_{l^{(\bar{r},II)}_{K_s^{(\bar{r})}}} \right) \\
&\overset{(b)}{\leq} \frac{1}{\lambda_{\bar{r}}\left(K_I^{(\bar{r})}+K_s^{(\bar{r})}\right)} \left(\frac{x_{l_{1-}^{(\bar{r},I)},\bar{r}}}{q_{l_{1-}^{(\bar{r},I)}}} \sigma_{l_{1-}^{(\bar{r},I)}} - \frac{x_{l^{(\bar{r},II)}_{K_s^{(\bar{r})}},\bar{r}}}{q_{l^{(\bar{r},II)}_{K_s^{(\bar{r})}}}} \rho\sigma_{l^{(\bar{r},II)}_{K_s^{(\bar{r})}}} \right) \\
&\overset{(c)}{\leq} \frac{x_{l_{1-}^{(\bar{r},I)},\bar{r}} - \rho x_{l^{(\bar{r},II)}_{K_s^{(\bar{r})}},\bar{r}}}{\lambda_{\bar{r}}\left(K_I^{(\bar{r})}+K_s^{(\bar{r})}\right)} \frac{1}{\max_{i\in\mathcal{N}}\sum_{k\in\mathcal{E}(i)} q_k} \\
&\overset{(d)}{\leq} \frac{-\epsilon\rho x^{(\bar{r})}_{\max}}{2\lambda_{\bar{r}}\left(K_I^{(\bar{r})}+K_s^{(\bar{r})}\right)} \frac{1}{\max_{i\in\mathcal{N}}\sum_{k\in\mathcal{E}(i)} q_k}, \qquad (48)
\end{aligned}$$

where the steps (a), (b) and (c) use equations (40), (41), (43) respectively; (d) follows from the fact that the previous link of $l_1^{(\bar{r},I)}$ does not belong to the section $\mathbf{S}^{(\bar{r})}$ and the fact that $x_{l_{1-}^{(\bar{r},I)}} \leq (1-\delta)x^{(\bar{r})}_{\max}$, $\delta = 1-\rho+\rho\epsilon/2$, and $x_{l^{(\bar{r},II)}_{K_s^{(\bar{r})}},\bar{r}} = x^{(\bar{r})}_{\max}$.

By utilizing (31), we have

$$\max_{i\in\mathcal{N}} \sum_{k\in\mathcal{E}(i)} q_k \leq \sum_{l\in\mathcal{L}} q_l \leq |\mathcal{L}|\frac{x_{l^*,r^*}}{\lambda_{r^*}}. \qquad (49)$$

Hence, by using inequalities (28), (49) and $\delta = 1-\rho+\rho\epsilon/2$, we have

$$\begin{aligned}
&\frac{\rho x^{(\bar{r})}_{\max}}{2\lambda_{\bar{r}}\left(K_I^{(\bar{r})}+K_s^{(\bar{r})}\right)} \frac{1}{\max_{i\in\mathcal{N}}\sum_{k\in\mathcal{E}(i)} q_k} \\
&\geq \frac{\rho^2(1-\epsilon/2)}{2\left(K_I^{(\bar{r})}+K_s^{(\bar{r})}\right)|\mathcal{L}|} \geq \frac{3\rho^2}{8|\mathcal{L}|^2}, \qquad (50)
\end{aligned}$$

where the last step follows from the fact that the route is acyclic and thus the maximum number of links belonging to route $\bar{r}$ should not be greater than $|\mathcal{L}|$, i.e., $K_I^{(\bar{r})}+K_s^{(\bar{r})} \leq |\mathcal{L}|$.

By substituting inequality (50) into (48), we have

$$\frac{1}{\lambda_{\bar{r}}}\frac{D^+}{dt^+} \max_{\mathbf{S}^{(\bar{r})}\in\mathcal{S}^{(\bar{r})}} W_{\mathbf{S}^{(\bar{r})}}(\mathbf{x}) \leq -\epsilon\frac{3\rho^2}{8|\mathcal{L}|^2}. \qquad (51)$$

(2) If $\bar{l}_1^{(\bar{r})}$ is the ingress link for route $\bar{r}$, then, by following the same steps in deriving inequality (44), we have

$$\begin{aligned}
&\frac{1}{\lambda_{\bar{r}}}\frac{D^+}{dt^+} \max_{\mathbf{S}^{(\bar{r})}\in\mathcal{S}^{(\bar{r})}} W_{\mathbf{S}^{(\bar{r})}}(\mathbf{x}) \\
&\leq \frac{1}{\lambda_{\bar{r}}\left(K_I^{(\bar{r})}+K_s^{(\bar{r})}\right)} \left(\lambda_{\bar{r}} - \mu_{\bar{l}^{(\bar{r},II)}_{K_{II}^{(\bar{r})}},\bar{r}}\right) \\
&\leq -\frac{\epsilon}{4\left(K_I^{(\bar{r})}+K_s^{(\bar{r})}\right)} \leq -\frac{\epsilon}{4|\mathcal{L}|}, \qquad (52)
\end{aligned}$$

where we use (46) and the fact that $K_I^{(\bar{r})}+K_s^{(\bar{r})} \leq |\mathcal{L}|$.

Therefore, by combining (i) and (ii), we have that

$$\frac{1}{\lambda_{\bar{r}}}\frac{D^+}{dt^+} \max_{\mathbf{S}^{(\bar{r})}\in\mathcal{S}^{(\bar{r})}} W_{\mathbf{S}^{(\bar{r})}}(\mathbf{x}) \leq -\epsilon\min\left\{\frac{3\rho^2}{8|\mathcal{L}|^2}, \frac{1}{4|\mathcal{L}|}\right\},$$

holds for any route $\bar{r} \in \overline{\mathcal{K}}$, which implies that $\frac{D^+}{dt^+}V(\mathbf{x}) \leq -\epsilon\min\left\{\frac{3\rho^2}{8|\mathcal{L}|^2}, \frac{1}{4|\mathcal{L}|}\right\}$. Therefore, we have the desired result by [8, Theorem 4.2]. □

6. CONCLUSION

In this work, we first developed a scheduling algorithm that makes transmission decisions only based on the per-link queueing information, which significantly reduces the queueing complexity compared to the well-known backpressure algorithm. By introducing a novel concept of section that intelligently groups links belonging to the same route, we are able to establish the throughput optimality of our proposed algorithm through fluid limit arguments. We further proposed a low-complexity scheduling algorithm that approximates our proposed algorithm and showed that it achieves a constant fraction of the maximum throughput region, independent of network size.

7. ACKNOWLEDGEMENTS

This work is supported in part by NSF grant CNS-1161404, ONR Grant N00014-13-1-003, and DTRAgrant HDTRA1-13-1-0030.

8. REFERENCES

[1] T. Bonald and A. Proutiere. Insensitive bandwidth sharing in data networks. *Queueing Systems*, 44:69–100, 2003.

[2] J. M. Borwein and A. S. Lewis. *Convex Analysis and Nonlinear Optimization: Theory and Examples.* Springer, 2000.

[3] M. Bramson. Stability of queueing networks. *Probability Surveys*, 5:169–345, 2008.

[4] M. Chiang. Balancing transport and physical layers in wireless multihop networks: Jointly optimal congestion control and power control. *IEEE Journal on Selected Areas in Communications, special issue on Nonlinear Optimization of Communication Systems*, 23(1):104 – 116, January 2005.

[5] Y. S. Chow. On a strong law of large numbers for martingales. *The Annals of Mathematical Statistics*, 38:610, 1967.

[6] F. Clarke. *Optimization and Nonsmooth Analysis (Classics in Applied Mathematics)*. Society for Industrial Mathematics, 1987.

[7] J. Dai and B. Prabhakar. The throughput of data switches with and without speedup. In *Proc. IEEE International Conference on Computer Communications (INFOCOM)*, Tel Aviv, Israel, March 2000.

[8] J. G. Dai. On positive harris recurrence of multiclass queueing networks: A unified approach via fluid limit models. *Annals of Applied Probability*, 5:49–77, 1995.

[9] A. Eryilmaz and R. Srikant. Joint congestion control, routing and MAC for stability and fairness in wireless networks. *IEEE Journal on Selected Areas in Communications, special issue on Nonlinear Optimization of Communication Systems*, 14:1514–1524, August 2006.

[10] A. Eryilmaz, R. Srikant, and J. R. Perkins. Throughput-optimal scheduling for broadcast channels. In *Proceedings of ITCom (Modeling and Design of Wireless Networks)*, Denver, CO, August 2001.

[11] B. Hajek and G. Sasaki. Link scheduling in polynomial time. *IEEE/ACM Transactions on Information Theory*, 34(5):910–917, September 1988.

[12] B. Ji, C. Joo, and N. B. Shroff. Throughput-optimal scheduling in multihop wireless networks without per-flow information. *IEEE/ACM Transactions on Networking*, 21(2):634–647, April 2013.

[13] K. Kar, X. Luo, and S. Sarkar. Throughput-optimal scheduling in multichannel access point networks under infrequent channel measurements. *IEEE Transactions on Wireless Communications*, 7:2619 – 2629, 2008.

[14] B. Li, R. Li, and A. Eryilmaz. On the optimal convergence speed of wireless scheduling for fair resource allocation. *To appear in IEEE/ACM Transactions on Networking.*

[15] X. Lin and S. B. Rasool. Constant-time distributed scheduling policies for ad hoc wireless networks. *IEEE Transactions on Automatic Control*, 54(2):231–242, 2009.

[16] X. Lin and N. Shroff. The impact of imperfect scheduling on cross-layer rate control in multihop wireless networks. In *Proc. IEEE International Conference on Computer Communications (INFOCOM)*, Miami, FL, March 2005.

[17] S. Liu, E. Ekici, and L. Ying. Scheduling in multihop wireless networks without back-pressure. In *Proceedings of the Allerton Conference on Communications, Control and Computing*, Monticello, IL, October 2010.

[18] S. H. Lu and P. R. Kumar. Distributed scheduling based on due dates and buffer priorities. *IEEE Transactions on Automatic Control*, 36(12):1406–1416, December 1991.

[19] L. Massoulie and J. Roberts. Bandwidth sharing: Objectives and algorithms. *IEEE/ACM Transactions on Networking*, 10:320–328, 2002.

[20] J. Mo and J. Walrand. Fair end-to-end window-based congestion control. *IEEE/ACM Transactions on Networking*, 8(5):556–567, 2000.

[21] M. Neely, E. Modiano, and C. Li. Fairness and optimal stochastic control for heterogeneous networks. In *Proc. IEEE International Conference on Computer Communications (INFOCOM)*, Miami, FL, March 2005.

[22] M. Neely, E. Modiano, and C. Rohrs. Dynamic power allocation and routing for time varying wireless networks. In *Proc. IEEE International Conference on Computer Communications (INFOCOM)*, San Francisco, CA, April 2003.

[23] M. J. Neely. Energy optimal control for time varying wireless networks. In *Proc. IEEE International Conference on Computer Communications (INFOCOM)*, Miami, FL, March 2005.

[24] A. Rybko and A. Stolyar. Ergodicity of stochastic processes describing the operation of open queueing networks. *Problemy Peredachi Informatsii*, 28(3):3–26, 1992.

[25] D. Shah, N. Walton, and Y. Zhong. Optimal queue-size scaling in switched networks. In *Proc. ACM International Conference on Measurement and Modeling of Computer Systems (SIGMETRICS)*, London, United Kingdom, June 2012.

[26] R. Srikant and L. Ying. *Communication Networks: An Optimization, Control, and Stochastic Networks Perspective.* Cambridge University Press, 2014.

[27] A. L. Stolyar. Maximizing queueing network utility subject to stability: Greedy primal-dual algorithm. *Queueing Systems*, 50(4):401–457, August 2005.

[28] L. Tassiulas and A. Ephremides. Stability properties of constrained queueing systems and scheduling policies for maximum throughput in multihop radio networks. *IEEE Transactions on Automatic Control*, 36:1936–1948, December 1992.

[29] N. Walton. Concave switching in single and multihop networks. In *Proc. ACM International Conference on Measurement and Modeling of Computer Systems (SIGMETRICS)*, Austin, Texas, June 2014.

[30] L. Ying, R. Srikant, A. Eryilmaz, and G. E. Dullerud. Distributed fair resource allocation in cellular networks in the presence of heterogeneous delays. *IEEE Transactions on Automatic Control*, 52:129–134, 2007.

APPENDIX

A. PROOF OF PROPOSITION 1

For any integer $t \geq 1$, let $R_l^{\Sigma}(t) \triangleq \sum_{\tau=0}^{t-1} R_l(\tau)$ be the total amount of service available to link l from time slot 0 to $t-1$. Let $H_l^{\Sigma}(t) \triangleq \sum_{\tau=0}^{t-1} H_l(\tau)$ be the cumulative number of packets departing from link l up to time slot $t-1$. Let $D_{l,r}^{\Sigma}(t) \triangleq \sum_{\tau=0}^{t-1} D_{l,r}(\tau)$ denote the cumulative number of route r packets departing from link l up to time slot $t-1$. Further, let $R_l^{\Sigma}(0) = H_l^{\Sigma}(0) = D_{l,r}^{\Sigma}(0) = 0$. Then, the evolution of the queue-length can be rewritten as

$$X_{l,r}(t) = X_{l,r}(0) + A_{l,r}^{\Sigma}(t) - D_{l_-^{(r)},r}^{\Sigma}(t) + D_{l,r}^{\Sigma}(t), \tag{53}$$

for all pairs (l,r). Here we note that $D_{l_-^{(r)},r}^{\Sigma}(t) = 0$ if $l = l_1^{(r)}$.

For the purposes of our analysis, we interpolate the values of $A_{l,r}^{\Sigma}(t)$, $R_l^{\Sigma}(t)$, $H_l^{\Sigma}(t)$ and $D_{l,r}^{\Sigma}(t)$ to all real number $t \geq 0$ by linear interpolation between $\lfloor t \rfloor$ and $\lfloor t \rfloor + 1$, where $\lfloor t \rfloor$ denotes the largest integer no greater than t. Then, we have the following lemma.

LEMMA 5. *Under the QPRA algorithm, with probability 1, for any positive sequence $w_n \to \infty$, there exists a subsequence w_{n_j} with $w_{n_j} \to \infty$ such that the following convergence holds uniformly over compact intervals of time t:*

$$\frac{1}{w_{n_j}} A_{l,r}^{\Sigma}(w_{n_j} t) \to \lambda_{l,r} t, \quad \forall (l,r), \tag{54}$$

$$\frac{1}{w_{n_j}} R_l^{\Sigma}(w_{n_j} t) \to \sigma_l^{\Sigma}(t), \quad \forall l \in \mathcal{L}, \tag{55}$$

$$\frac{1}{w_{n_j}} H_l^{\Sigma}(w_{n_j} t) \to \phi_l^{\Sigma}(t), \quad \forall l \in \mathcal{L}, \tag{56}$$

$$\frac{1}{w_{n_j}} D_{l,r}^{\Sigma}(w_{n_j} t) \to \mu_{l,r}^{\Sigma}(t), \quad \forall (l,r), \tag{57}$$

$$\frac{1}{w_{n_j}} X_{l,r}(w_{n_j} t) \to x_{l,r}(t), \quad \forall (l,r), \tag{58}$$

$$\frac{1}{w_{n_j}} Q_l(w_{n_j} t) \to q_l(t), \quad \forall l \in \mathcal{L}, \tag{59}$$

where the limiting functions $\sigma_l^{\Sigma}(t), \phi_l^{\Sigma}(t), \mu_{l,r}^{\Sigma}(t), x_{l,r}(t), q_l(t)$ are Lipschitz-continuous in $[0,\infty)$, which implies that these limiting functions are differentiable for almost all t. Let $\mathcal{T}$ be the set of time instants where these functions are differentiable. Then, the following equations hold for all $t \in \mathcal{T}$:

$$\frac{d}{dt}\sigma_l^{\Sigma}(t) = \sigma_l(t), \quad \forall l \in \mathcal{L}, \tag{60}$$

$$\frac{d}{dt}\mu_{l,r}^{\Sigma}(t) = \mu_{l,r}(t), \quad \forall (l,r), \tag{61}$$

$$\frac{d}{dt}\phi_l^{\Sigma}(t) = \sigma_l(t), \forall l \in \mathcal{L}, \quad \text{whenever } q_l(t) > 0, \tag{62}$$

$$\phi_l^{\Sigma}(t) = \sum_{r:l\in r} \mu_{l,r}^{\Sigma}(t), \quad \forall (l,r), \tag{63}$$

$$q_l(t) = \sum_{r:l\in r} x_{l,r}(t), \quad \forall (l,r), \tag{64}$$

$$\frac{d}{dt}x_{l,r}(t) = \lambda_{l,r} + \mu_{l_-^{(r)},r}(t) - \mu_{l,r}(t), \quad \forall (l,r), \tag{65}$$

where $\mu_{l_-^{(r)},r}(t) = 0$ if $l = l_1^{(r)}$. Here $\boldsymbol{\sigma}(t) = (\sigma_l(t))_{l\in\mathcal{L}}$ is the longest vector within the capacity region Λ that is along the same direction of $\mathbf{q}(t)$ and $\boldsymbol{\mu}(t) = (\mu_{l,r})_{l\in\mathcal{L},r\in\mathcal{R}}$ satisfies

$$\mu_{l_-^{(r)},r}(t) = 0, \ \textit{whenever } l = l_1^{(r)} \tag{66}$$

$$\mu_{l,r}(t) = 0, \ \textit{whenever } x_{l,r}(t) = 0 \tag{67}$$

$$\frac{\mu_{l,r}(t)}{x_{l,r}(t)} = \frac{\mu_{l',r}(t)}{x_{l',r}(t)}, \tag{68}$$

for any route $r \in l, r' \in l'$ with $x_{l,r}(t) > 0$ and $x_{l',r'}(t) > 0$.

Thus, equations (9), (11) and (12) immediately follows from Lemma 5. By combining (61), (62), and (63), we have

$$\sigma_l(t) = \sum_{r:l\in r} \mu_{l,r}(t), \text{ if } q_l(t) > 0, \tag{69}$$

Since $\frac{\mu_{l,r}(t)}{x_{l,r}(t)} = \frac{\mu_{l,r'}(t)}{x_{l,r'}(t)}$ for all $r, r' \in l$ with $x_{l,r}(t) > 0$ and $x_{l,r'}(t) > 0$, the following equation

$$\frac{\mu_{l,r}(t)}{x_{l,r}(t)} = \frac{\sigma_l(t)}{q_l(t)}, \tag{70}$$

holds for any route $r \in l$ with $x_{l,r}(t) > 0$. Therefore, if $q_l(t) > 0$ we have

$$\mu_{l,r}(t) = \frac{x_{l,r}(t)}{q_l(t)}\sigma_l(t), \text{ whenever } x_{l,r}(t) > 0. \tag{71}$$

Noting the equation (67) and the convention $0/0 = 0$, we have equation (10).

Proof of Lemma 5: Equation (54) follows from the Functional Strong Law of Large Numbers if $l = l_1^{(r)}$. If $l \neq l_1^{(r)}$, then $A_{l,r}^{\Sigma}(w_{n_j} t) = \lambda_{l,r} = 0$ and thus equation (54) always holds.

Note that for any $0 \leq t_1 \leq t_2$, we have

$$0 \leq \frac{1}{w_n} R_l^{\Sigma}(w_n t_2) - \frac{1}{w_n} R_l^{\Sigma}(w_n t_1) \leq t_2 - t_1, \tag{72}$$

where we use the fact that each link l can at most transfer one packet in one time slot. Thus, the sequence of functions $\{\frac{1}{w_n} R_l^{\Sigma}(w_n t)\}$ is uniformly equicontinuous, and since $R_l^{\Sigma}(0) = 0$, the sequence is also uniformly bounded. Similarly, the sequence $\{\frac{1}{w_n} D_{l,r}^{\Sigma}(w_n t)\}$ is uniformly bounded and uniformly equicontinuous. Consequently, according to the Arzela-Ascoli Theorem, there must exist a subsequence of $\{w_n\}_{n\geq 1}$ for which both (55) and (57) hold. Since

$$\frac{1}{w_n} H_l^{\Sigma}(w_n t) = \sum_{r:l\in r} \frac{1}{w_n} D_{l,r}^{\Sigma}(w_n t),$$

$$\frac{1}{w_n} X_{l,r}(w_n t) = \frac{1}{w_n} A_{l,r}^{\Sigma}(w_n t) - \frac{1}{w_n} D_{l_-^{(r)},r}^{\Sigma}(w_n t) + \frac{1}{w_n} D_{l,r}^{\Sigma}(w_n t),$$

$$\frac{1}{w_n} Q_l^{\Sigma}(w_n t) = \sum_{r:l\in r} \frac{1}{w_n} X_{l,r}^{\Sigma}(w_n t),$$

we have (56), (58) and (59) by taking limits as $w_{n_j} \to \infty$.

Since the functions $R_l^{\Sigma}(t)$, $H_l^{\Sigma}(t)$, $D_{l,r}^{\Sigma}(t)$, $X_{l,r}(t)$, $Q_l(t)$ are Lipschitz continuous, the Lipschitz continuity of $\sigma_l^{\Sigma}(t)$, $\phi_l^{\Sigma}(t)$, $\mu_{l,r}^{\Sigma}(t)$, $x_{l,r}(t)$,$q_l(t)$ also follows. Hence, these limiting functions are differentiable for almost all t. In the rest of proof, we consider all $t \in \mathcal{T}$, where $\mathcal{T}$ is the set of time instants where the limiting functions are differentiable.

Next, we prove equation (60). Since $\sigma_l(\mathbf{q}(t))$ is continuous with respect to $\mathbf{q}$ when $q_l > 0$. Therefore, for any $\epsilon > 0$, there exists a $u > 0$ such that for all $t' \in [t, t+u]$, we have

$$\left|\sigma_l(\mathbf{q}(t')) - \sigma_l(\mathbf{q}(t))\right| \leq \epsilon. \quad (73)$$

Since $\frac{1}{w_{n_j}}\mathbf{Q}(\lfloor w_{n_j} t' \rfloor) \to \mathbf{q}(t')$ uniformly over compact intervals of time, and $\sigma_l(a\mathbf{Q}) = \sigma_l(\mathbf{Q})$ for any $a > 0$, we have $\sigma_l(\mathbf{Q}(\lfloor w_{n_j} t' \rfloor)) \to \sigma_l(\mathbf{q}(t'))$ with probability 1. Thus, there exists an integer $J > 0$ such that for all $j > J$ and $t' \in [t, t+u]$,

$$\sigma_l(\mathbf{q}(t')) - \epsilon \leq \sigma_l(\mathbf{Q}(\lfloor w_{n_j} t' \rfloor)) \leq \sigma_l(\mathbf{q}(t')) + \epsilon. \quad (74)$$

Combining with (73), we have

$$\sigma_l(\mathbf{q}(t)) - 2\epsilon \leq \sigma_l(\mathbf{Q}(\lfloor w_{n_j} t' \rfloor)) \leq \sigma_l(\mathbf{q}(t)) + 2\epsilon. \quad (75)$$

By the definition of the limit in (55), for any $t' \in [t, t+u]$, we have

$$\sigma_l^{\Sigma}(t') - \sigma_l^{\Sigma}(t) = \lim_{j\to\infty} \frac{1}{w_{n_j}} \sum_{k=\lfloor w_{n_j} t \rfloor}^{\lfloor w_{n_j} t' \rfloor - 1} R_l(k). \quad (76)$$

Define the filtration $\mathcal{F}_k, k = 1, 2, \cdots$, where $\mathcal{F}_k$ is the $\sigma-$algebra generated by the random variables $A_{l,r}^{\Sigma}(\lfloor w_{n_j} t \rfloor + k')$, $R_l^{\Sigma}(\lfloor w_{n_j} t \rfloor + k')$, $D_{l,r}^{\Sigma}(\lfloor w_{n_j} t \rfloor + k')$, $X_{l,r}(\lfloor w_{n_j} t \rfloor + k')$ for all pairs (l, r) and for $k' = 0, 1, 2, \cdots, k-1$. Let

$$Y_k = R_l(\lfloor w_{n_j} t \rfloor + k) - \mathbb{E}\left[R_l(\lfloor w_{n_j} t \rfloor + k) | \mathbf{Q}(\lfloor w_{n_j} t \rfloor + k)\right].$$

Therefore, $\sum_{m=0}^{k-1} Y_m, k = 1, 2, \cdots$, is a martingale with respect to the filtration $\mathcal{F}_k, k = 1, 2, \cdots$. Further, $\mathbb{E}\left[Y_k^2\right]$ is always bounded for all k. Hence, using a strong law of large numbers for martingales [5], we have

$$\lim_{k\to\infty} \frac{1}{k} \sum_{m=0}^{k-1} Y_m = 0, \text{ with probability 1}, \quad (77)$$

which implies that

$$\begin{aligned} \sigma_l^{\Sigma}(t') - \sigma_l^{\Sigma}(t) &= \lim_{j\to\infty} \frac{1}{w_{n_j}} \sum_{k=\lfloor w_{n_j} t \rfloor}^{\lfloor w_{n_j} t' \rfloor - 1} R_l(k) \\ &= \lim_{j\to\infty} \frac{1}{w_{n_j}} \sum_{k=\lfloor w_{n_j} t \rfloor}^{\lfloor w_{n_j} t' \rfloor - 1} \mathbb{E}\left[R_l(k) | \mathbf{Q}(k)\right] \\ &= \lim_{j\to\infty} \frac{1}{w_{n_j}} \sum_{k=\lfloor w_{n_j} t \rfloor}^{\lfloor w_{n_j} t' \rfloor - 1} \sigma_l\left(\mathbf{Q}(k)\right). \end{aligned} \quad (78)$$

By using (75), we have

$$(t'-t)(\sigma_l(\mathbf{q}(t)) - 2\epsilon) \leq \sigma_l^{\Sigma}(t') - \sigma_l^{\Sigma}(t) \leq (t'-t)(\sigma_l(\mathbf{q}(t)) + 2\epsilon),$$

for $t' \in [t, t+u]$. Since we assume that $\sigma_l^{\Sigma}(t)$ is differentiable at t (i.e., $t \in \mathcal{T}$), we have

$$\sigma_l(\mathbf{q}(t)) - 2\epsilon \leq \frac{d}{dt}\sigma_l^{\Sigma}(t) \leq \sigma_l(\mathbf{q}(t)) + 2\epsilon. \quad (79)$$

Finally, since this is true for any $\epsilon > 0$, equation (60) follows. The proof of equation (61) follows the similar technique and is omitted here for brevity.

Next, we consider equation (62). If $q_l(t) > 0$, then there exists a positive u such that for all $t' \in [t, t+u]$, $q_l(t') > 0$. This implies that for all sufficiently large j, the backlog $Q_l(\lfloor w_{n_j} t' \rfloor)$ at link l is larger than 1 for all $t' \in [t, t+u]$. Therefore, the available service to link l will be fully utilized between $\lfloor w_{n_j} t \rfloor$ and $\lfloor w_{n_j}(t+u) \rfloor$. We thus have

$$R_l^{\Sigma}(\lfloor w_{n_j} t' \rfloor) - R_l^{\Sigma}(\lfloor w_{n_j} t \rfloor) = H_l^{\Sigma}(\lfloor w_{n_j} t' \rfloor) - H_l^{\Sigma}(\lfloor w_{n_j} t \rfloor),$$

for all $t \leq t' \leq t+u$. Dividing both sides by w_{n_j} and taking limits as $w_{n_j} \to \infty$, we have

$$\sigma_l^{\Sigma}(t') - \sigma_l^{\Sigma}(t) = \phi_l^{\Sigma}(t') - \phi_l^{\Sigma}(t), \quad (80)$$

for all $t \leq t' \leq t+u$, which implies $\frac{d}{dt}\phi_l^{\Sigma}(t) = \frac{d}{dt}\sigma_l^{\Sigma}(t)$. By combining with (60), we have equation (62).

Equations (63) and (64) follow from the equation $H_l^{\Sigma}(t) = \sum_{r:l\in r} D_{l,r}^{\Sigma}(t)$ and $Q_l(t) = \sum_{r:l\in r} X_{l,r}(t)$ by taking limits as $w_{n_j} \to \infty$, respectively.

Finally, by using the queue-evolution equation (53) and taking limits as $w_{n_j} \to \infty$, we have

$$\frac{d}{dt}x_{l,r}(t) = \lambda_{l,r} + \frac{d}{dt}\mu_{l_-^{(r)},r}^{\Sigma}(t) - \frac{d}{dt}\mu_{l,r}^{\Sigma}(t). \quad (81)$$

By utilizing equation (61), we have equation (65).

B. PROOF OF LEMMA 1

We prove it by contradiction. Assume

$$\frac{D^+}{dx^+}f(x) > \max_{i\in\mathcal{K}}\left\{\frac{D^+}{dx^+}f_i(x)\right\}. \quad (82)$$

Then, for a sufficient small $\epsilon > 0$, there exist a decreasing sequence $\{u_k, k = 1, 2, ...\}$ with $\lim_{k\to\infty} u_k = 0$ such that

$$\frac{f(x+u_k) - f(x)}{u_k} \geq \max_{i\in\mathcal{K}}\left\{\frac{D^+}{dx^+}f_i(x)\right\} + \epsilon, \forall k = 1, 2, \cdots.$$

Note that $f(x) = f_i(x), \forall i \in \mathcal{K}$. Since there are a finite number of locally Lipschitz continuous functions $f_i(x), i = 1, 2, \cdots, K$, there must exist a $j \in \mathcal{K}$ and a decreasing subsequence $\{u_{t_k}, k = 1, 2, \cdots\}$ of $\{u_k, k = 1, 2, \cdots\}$ such that $f_j(x + u_{t_k}) = f(x + u_{t_k}) = \max_{i=1,2,\cdots,K} f_i(x + u_{t_k}), \forall k = 1, 2, \cdots$, which implies that

$$\frac{f_j(x+u_{t_k}) - f_j(x)}{u_{t_k}} \geq \max_{i\in\mathcal{K}}\left\{\frac{D^+}{dx^+}f_i(x)\right\} + \epsilon, \forall k = 1, 2, \cdots.$$

Therefore, we obtain the contradiction

$$\frac{D^+}{dx^+}f_j(x) \geq \max_{i\in\mathcal{K}}\left\{\frac{D^+}{dx^+}f_i(x)\right\} + \epsilon. \quad (83)$$

Hence, we have the desired result.

C. PROOF OF LEMMA 2

(i) Assume that there exist a $t_1 > 0$ and a $\zeta > 0$ such that $g(t_1) = \zeta$. Since $g(0) = 0$, according to the continuity property of the function $g(\cdot)$, there exists a $t_2 \in (0, t_1)$ such that $g(t_2) = \zeta/2$ and $g(t) \geq \zeta/2 > 0$ for any $t \in (t_2, t_1]$. Since $g(t) > 0$ for any $t \in [t_2, t_1]$ and $\frac{D^+}{dt^+}g(t) \leq 0$ whenever $g(t) > 0$, we have $g(t_1) \leq g(t_2)$, which contradicts that $g(t_1) = \zeta > g(t_2) = \zeta/2$. Therefore, $g(t) = 0$ for all $t \geq 0$.

(ii) Since $\frac{D^+}{dt^+}g(t) \leq -\gamma$ whenever $g(t) > 0$, the function $g(\cdot)$ will first hit zero at time $T = g(0)/\gamma$. Then, by using the technique in (i), we can show that $g(t) = 0$ for all $t \geq T$.

Resource Allocation and Rate Gains in Practical Full-Duplex Systems

Jelena Marašević[1], Jin Zhou[1], Harish Krishnaswamy[1], Yuan Zhong[2], Gil Zussman[1]
[1]Electrical Engineering Dept., [2]Industrial Engineering and Operations Research Dept.
Columbia University
New York, NY, 10027, USA
{jelena@ee., jz2495@, harish@ee., yz2561@, gil@ee.}columbia.edu

ABSTRACT

Full-duplex communication has the potential to substantially increase the throughput in wireless networks. However, the benefits of full-duplex are still not well understood. In this paper, we characterize the full-duplex rate gains in both single-channel and multi-channel use cases. For the single-channel case, we *quantify the rate gain as a function of the remaining self-interference and SNR values.* We also provide a sufficient condition under which the sum of uplink and downlink rates on a full-duplex channel is concave in the transmission power levels. Building on these results, we consider the multi-channel case. For that case, we *introduce a new realistic model of a small form-factor (e.g., smartphone) full-duplex receiver* and demonstrate its accuracy via measurements. We study the problem of jointly allocating power levels to different channels and selecting the frequency of maximum self-interference suppression, where the objective is maximizing the sum of the rates over uplink and downlink OFDM channels. We develop a *polynomial time algorithm which is nearly optimal under very mild restrictions.* To reduce the running time, we develop an efficient nearly-optimal algorithm under the high SINR approximation. Finally, we demonstrate via numerical evaluations the capacity gains in the different use cases and obtain insights into the impact of the remaining self-interference and wireless channel states on the performance.

Categories and Subject Descriptors

C.2.1 [**Computer-Communication Networks**]: Network Architecture and Design—*Wireless Communication*

Keywords

Full-Duplex; Modeling; Resource Allocation

1. INTRODUCTION

Full-duplex (FD) communication – simultaneous transmission and reception on the same frequency channel – is an emerging technology that holds great promise to substantially improve the throughput in wireless networks. The main challenge hindering the implementation of practical FD devices is high self-interference (SI) caused by signal leakage from the transmitter into the receiver circuit. The SI signal is usually many orders of magnitude higher than the desired signal at the receiver's input, requiring over 100dB of self-interference cancellation (SIC).[1]

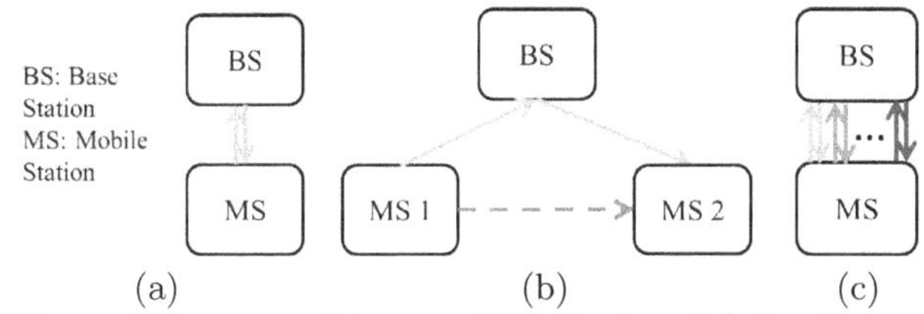

Figure 1: Some possible uses of full-duplex: (a) simultaneous uplink and downlink for one MS; (b) uplink and downlink used by two different MSs and caused inter-node interference (red dashed line), (c) simultaneous uplink and downlink over OFDM channels.

Cancelling SI is a very challenging problem. Even though ideas for different techniques of SIC were proposed over a decade ago, only recently practical circuit designs that provide sufficient SIC to be employed in Wi-Fi and cellular networks emerged (see [26] and references therein for an overview). Exciting progress has been made in the last few years by various research groups, demonstrating that a combination of SIC techniques employed both in the analog and digital domains can provide SIC levels that can support practical applications [3,5,8,9,11–14,17–21,24,28,29].

While there has been significant interest in FD from both industry and academia [2–5,7–9,11–15,17–22,24,27–31], *the exact rate gains resulting from the use of FD are not well understood.* The first implementations of FD receivers optimistically envisioned 100% rate improvement (e.g., [5,17]). To achieve such an increase in data rates, the FD receiver would need perfect SIC, namely to cancel SI to at least one order of magnitude below the noise floor to render it negligible. The highest reported SIC [5], however, suppresses the SI to the level of noise in the best case.

Despite this mismatch, much of the work on FD rate improvement assumes perfect SIC [4,15,27,31]. While non-negligible SI has also been considered [2,7,22], *there are still no explicit bounds on the rate gains for given FD circuit parameters and parameters of the wireless signal.* Moreover,

[1]Namely, it is required to reduce the SI signal power by 10^{10} times.

SIGMETRICS'15, June 15–19, 2015, Portland, OR, USA.

ACM 978-1-4503-3486-0/15/06 ...$15.00.
http://dx.doi.org/10.1145/2745844.2745872.

from a modeling perspective, the frequency selectivity of SIC has not been considered in any analytical work. This is *an important feature that is inherent in conventional compact implementations of an FD receiver, such as that found in small-form factor mobile devices (e.g., smartphones and tablets)*, where frequency selectivity is mainly a consequence of the cancellation in the RF domain.[2]

Hence, *the main contribution of this paper is a thorough analytical study of rate gains from FD under non-negligible SI.* We consider both *single-channel and multi-channel orthogonal frequency division multiplexing (OFDM) scenarios.* For the multi-channel case, *we develop a new model for frequency-selective SIC in small-form factor receivers.* Our results provide explicit guarantees on the rate gains of FD, as a function of receivers' signal-to-noise ratios (SNRs) and SIC profile. Our analysis provides several insights into the structure of the sum of rates under FD, which we believe will be useful for future work on FD scheduling and MAC layer algorithm design.

Specifically, we consider three different use cases of FD, as illustrated in Fig. 1: (i) a single channel bidirectional link, where one mobile station (MS) communicates with the base station (BS) both on the uplink and on the downlink (Fig. 1(a)); (ii) two single channel unidirectional links, where one MS communicates with the BS on the uplink, while another MS communicates with the BS on the downlink (Fig. 1(b)); and (iii) a multi-channel bidirectional link, where one MS communicates with the BS over multiple OFDM channels, both on the uplink and on the downlink (Fig. 1(c)).

For SI, we consider two different models. For the BS in all use cases and the MS in use case (i), we model the remaining SI after cancellation as a constant fraction of the transmitted signal. Such design is possible for devices that do not require a very small form factor (e.g., base stations), and was demonstrated in [5].

In the multi-channel case, we rely on the characteristics of radio-frequency integrated circuit (RFIC) receivers that we recently designed [32, 34] and *develop a frequency selective model for the remaining SI in a small form-factor device.* We demonstrate the accuracy of the developed model via measurements with our receivers [32, 34].

We note that a frequency-selective profile of SIC that we model is inherent to RF cancellers with flat amplitude and phase response (see Section 3). While a mixed-signal SIC architecture [28] does not necessarily have flat amplitude and phase response, we do not consider this architecture because it requires a separate up-conversion path which introduces its own noise and distortion, limiting the resultant RF SIC.

We primarily focus on the problem of maximizing the sum of uplink and downlink rates under FD (for brevity, in the rest of the paper we refer to the sum of uplink and downlink rates as the sum rate). This problem, in general, is neither concave nor convex in the transmission power levels, since the remaining SI after cancellation often depends on the transmission power level. Due to the lack of good problem structure, existing analytical results (see e.g., [2, 7, 22]) are often restricted to specialized settings. Yet, we obtain several analytical results on the FD rate gains, often under mild restrictions, by examining closely the structural properties of the sum rate function.

[2]See our recent work [32, 34] and Section 3 for more details.

In the single-channel cases, we prove that if any rate gain can be achieved from FD, then the gain is maximized by setting the transmission power levels to their respective maximum values. This result is somewhat surprising because of the lack of good structural properties of the sum rate function. We then derive a sufficient condition under which the sum rate is concave in both transmission power levels, and show that when this condition is not satisfied, one cannot gain more than 1b/s/Hz (additively) from FD as compared to time-division duplex (TDD). We note that although the model for the remaining SI in the single channel case is relatively simple, it nonetheless captures the main characteristics of the FD sum rate, with some results extending to the multi-channel setting.

In the multi-channel case, we use the frequency-selective SI model for the MS receiver, and study the problem of transmission power allocation over OFDM channels and frequency selection, where the objective is to maximize the sum of the rates over uplink and downlink OFDM channels (in this case, frequency refers to the frequency of maximum SIC of the SI canceller). Although in general it is hard to find an optimal solution to this problem, we develop a nearly optimal algorithm under two mild technical conditions. One condition ensures that the sum rate is concave in transmission power levels. This restriction is mild, since we prove that when it does not hold, the possible gains from FD are small. Another condition imposes bounds on the magnitude of the first derivative of the sum rate in terms of maximum SIC frequency, and can be easily satisfied in an OFDM system with a large number of channels.

Although the algorithm is nearly optimal and has polynomial time complexity, its running time is relatively high. Therefore, we consider a high SINR approximation of the sum rate, and derive fixed optimal power allocation and maximum SIC frequency setting that maximizes the sum rate up to an additive ϵ in time $O(K \log(1/\epsilon))$, for any given ϵ, where K is the number of channels.

Finally, we note that throughout the paper, we provide numerical results that quantify the rate gains in various use cases and illustrate the impact of different parameters on these gains. For example, for the multi-channel case, we evaluate the rate gains using measured SI of our RFIC receiver [32, 34]. We use algorithms for the general SINR regime and for the high SINR regime, and demonstrate that for rate gains of over 50%, the outputs of the two algorithms match closely.

The rest of the paper is organized as follows. Section 2 reviews related work and Section 3 outlines the challenges in implementing FD receivers. Section 4 introduces the new model for a small form factor FD receiver, and the model for the various use cases. Section 5 provides analysis and numerical evaluation for the sum rate maximization on a single channel for use case (i). Section 6 analyzes use case (ii) and Section 7 provides analysis, algorithms, and numerical evaluation for use case (iii). We conclude in Section 8. Due to space constraints, some of the proofs are omitted and are instead provided in a technical report [23].

2. RELATED WORK

Possible rate gains from FD have been studied in [2, 4, 7, 15, 22, 27, 31], with much of the work [4, 15, 27, 31] focusing on perfect SIC. Unlike this body of work, we focus on rate gains from FD communication under imperfect SIC.

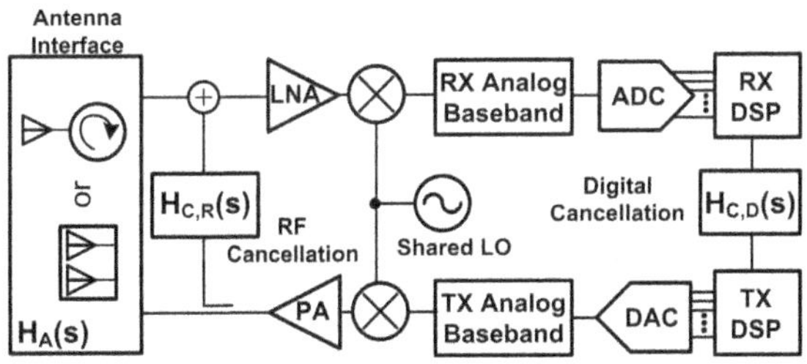

Figure 2: Block diagram of a full-duplex transceiver employing RF and digital cancellation.

Non-negligible SI has been considered in [2,7,22]. A sufficient condition for achieving positive rate gains from FD on a bidirectional link has been provided in [2], for the special case of equal SINRs on the uplink and downlink. This model takes into account the transmitter's phase noise, which is not considered in this paper. In [2], the FD capacity region is compared to the corresponding TDD capacity region, by normalizing power levels so that each station irradiates the same amount of power in both the FD and TDD regimes. In this paper, we provide explicit bounds on FD rate gains as a function of the remaining SI and uplink and downlink SNRs. Unlike [2], we bound the irradiated power of each station individually, which complies with all current Wi-Fi and cellular standards.

Power allocation over orthogonal bidirectional links was considered in [7] and [22] for MIMO and OFDM systems, respectively. The model used in [7] assumes the same amount of SIC and equal power allocation on all channels, which is a less general model than the one that we consider.

A more detailed model with different SIC over OFDM channels was considered in [22]. The model used in [22] does not consider dependence of SIC in terms of canceller frequency (although, unlike our work, it takes into account the transmitter's phase noise). Similar to [2], [22] compares the FD and TDD capacity regions of a bidirectional link by assuming equal irradiated power levels for the two duplexing methods. Optimal power allocation that maximizes one of the rates when the other is fixed is derived for equal power levels across channels, while for the general case of unequal power levels, [22] only provides a suboptimal solution.

Our work relies on structural properties of the sum rate to derive optimal power allocation and maximum SIC frequency setting that maximizes the sum rate. While the model we consider is different from [2,22], we provide a more specific characterization of achievable rate gains, and derive results that provide insights into the rate dependence on the power allocation. These results allow us to solve a very general problem of rate maximization.

3. FD IMPLEMENTATION CHALLENGES

Fig. 2 shows the block diagram of a full-duplex transceiver. There are two antenna interfaces that are typically considered for full-duplex operation: (i) an antenna pair and (ii) a circulator. The advantage of using a circulator is that it allows a single antenna to be shared between the TX and the RX. SIC must be performed in both the RF and digital domains to achieve in excess of 100dB SI suppression. The RF canceller taps a reference signal at the output of the power amplifier (PA) and performs SIC at the input of the low-noise amplifier (LNA) at the RX side [10].

(a) (b) (c)

Figure 3: (a) RFIC receiver with RF SI cancellation [32,34] and the two antenna interfaces used in our measurements: (b) an antenna pair and (c) a circulator.

Typically, 20-30dB of SIC is required from the RF, given that the antenna interface typically has a TX/RX isolation of 20-30dB [1]. Thus, an overall 50-60dB RF TX/RX isolation is achieved before digital SIC is engaged. This amount of RF TX/RX isolation is critical to alleviate the RX linearity and the analog-to-digital conversion (ADC) dynamic range requirements [10,26]. Digital cancellation further cancels the linear SI as well as the non-linear distortion products generated by the RX or the RF canceller.

A mixed-signal SIC architecture has been proposed in [28], where the digital TX signal is processed and upconverted to RF for cancellation. However, this requires a separate up-conversion path which introduces its own noise and distortion. Moreover, the noise and distortion of the TX analog and RF circuits (such as the power amplifier) are not readily captured in the cancellation signal, limiting the resultant RF SIC. In addition, the dedicated up-conversion path results in area and power overhead. Because of these reasons, we are not considering this SIC architecture in this paper.

For wideband SIC, the transfer function of the canceller must closely track that of the antenna interface across frequency. However, the frequency dependence of the inherent antenna interface isolation together with selective multi-path-ridden SI channels render this challenging for the RF canceller in particular. The net antenna interface isolation amplitude and phase response can vary significantly with frequency. A rapidly-varying phase response is representative of a large group delay, requiring bulky delay lines to replicate the selectivity in the RF canceller [5,10].

The fundamental challenge associated with wideband SIC at RF in a compact form-factor and/or using integrated circuits is the generation of large time delays. The amount of true time delay is linearly proportional to the dimension of the delay structure and inversely proportional to the wave velocity in the medium. To generate 1ns delay in a silicon integrated circuit, a transmission line of 15cm length is required as the relative dielectric constant of silicon oxide is 4. Therefore, a conventional integrated RF SI canceller with dimensions less than 1mm^2 will exhibit negligible delay, and *the amplitude and phase response of the canceller can be assumed to be flat with respect to frequency* when compared with antenna interface's isolation, limiting the cancellation bandwidth [26,32].

While achieving wideband RF SI cancellation using innovative RFIC techniques is an active research topic (e.g., frequency domain equalization based RF SI cancellation in [33]), in this paper we focus on compact flat amplitude- and phase-based RF cancellers, such as the one we implemented in the RFIC depicted in Fig. 3(a) [32,34].

We measured isolation amplitude and group delay response of (i) a PCB antenna pair (see Fig. 3(b)) and (ii) a commercial 2110-2170MHz miniature circulator from Skyworks [1] (see Fig. 3(c)). The results are shown in Fig. 4(a) and

$$RSI_{m,k} = (|H_A|^2 P_{m,k} + |H_{C,R}|^2 P_{m,k} - 2\sqrt{|H_A|^2 P_{m,k} |H_{C,R}|^2 P_{m,k}} \cdot \cos(\angle H_A(f_k) + \angle H_{C,R})) SIC_D^{-1}. \quad (1)$$

Fig. 4(b), respectively. The resultant TX/RX isolations using an RF canceller with flat amplitude and phase response after the antenna interfaces (i) and (ii) are shown in Fig. 4(c) and Fig. 4(d), respectively. As Fig. 4(c) and Fig. 4(d) suggest, for -60dB TX/RX isolation after RF cancellation, the bandwidths are about 4MHz and 2.5MHz, respectively.

4. MODEL

We consider three use cases of FD: (i) a bidirectional link, where one mobile station (MS) communicates with the base station (BS) both on the uplink and on the downlink (Fig. 1(a)), (ii) two unidirectional links, where one MS is communicating with the BS on the uplink, while another MS is communicating with the BS on the downlink (Fig. 1(b)), and (iii) multiple orthogonal bidirectional links (Fig. 1(c)). Note that in (ii) only the BS is operating in FD.

For the multi-channel FD (use case (iii)), we assume that the network bandwidth of size B is subdivided into K orthogonal frequency channels of width B/K each, and index the frequency channels with $k \in \{1, ..., K\}$. An example of such sub-channelization is OFDM with each frequency channel consisting of an integral number of subcarriers.

For all notation that relates to the BS, we will use b in the subscript. For the notation that relates to the MS in use cases (i) and (iii), we will use m in the subscript, while in the use case (ii) we will use m_1 and m_2 to refer to MS 1 and MS 2, respectively. Summary of the main notation is provided in Table 1.

The transmission power of a station $u \in \{b, m, m_1, m_2\}$ on channel k is denoted by $P_{u,k}$, where $k \in \{1, ..., K\}$. In use cases (i) and (ii), k is omitted from the subscript, since we consider a single channel.

4.1 Remaining SI

Single-channel FD. For single-channel FD, we assume that the remaining SI both at the BS and at an MS can be expressed as a constant fraction of the transmitted power. In particular, if the BS transmits at the power level P_b, the remaining SI is $RSI_b = g_b P_b$, where g_b is a constant determined by the hardware. Similarly, if an MS transmits at the power level P_m, its remaining SI is $RSI_m = g_m P_m$.

Multi-channel FD. We assume that the FD receiver at the BS has frequency-flat SIC profile, meaning that the remaining SI at the BS on channel k is $RSI_{b,k} = g_b P_{b,k}$, where g_b is a constant. We note that such FD receiver design is possible to implement in devices that do not require small form factor of the circuit (e.g., a BS or an access point (AP)), and has been reported in [5].

In the rest of this section, we describe the mathematical model of the remaining SI for a small form factor device (MS). We consider a compact/RFIC FD receiver with a *circulator* at the antenna interface, described in Section 3, and assume a frequency-flat amplitude and phase response of the canceller, denoted by $|H_{C,R}|$ and $\angle H_{C,R}$, respectively. The amplitude and phase response of the canceller are assumed to be programmable but constant with frequency.

For the antenna interface's TX/RX isolation, we assume a flat amplitude response $|H_A(f)| = const = |H_A|$ and a constant group delay equal to τ, so that $H_A(f) = |H_A| e^{-j2\pi f \tau}$ (recall that the measured amplitude and phase response are shown in Fig. 4(b)). For the digital SIC, denoted by SIC_D, we assume that the amount of cancellation is constant across frequency, as delay can be easily generated in the digital domain.

Let f_k denote the central frequency of the kth channel, so that $f_k = f_1 + (k-1)B/K$. Then, the remaining SI after cancellation can be written as (1).

We assume a common oscillator for the TX and RX, with the phase noise of the oscillator being good enough so that it does not affect the remaining SI.

The RF canceller's settings can be programmed in the field to adjust the frequency at which peak SIC is achieved [32, 34]. With the amplitude ($|H_{C,R}|$) and the phase ($\angle H_{C,R}$) of the RF canceller set to $|H_A|$ and $-\angle H_A(f_{c_i})$, respectively, peak SIC is achieved at frequency f_c. Therefore, the total remaining SI at the MS on channel k can be written as:

$$RSI_{m,k} = 2|H_A|^2 P_{m,k}(1 - \cos(2\pi\tau(f_k - f_c))) SIC_D^{-1},$$

where τ is the group delay from the antenna interface with a typical value at the order of 1ns (which agrees with the measured group delay in Fig. 4(b)). Frequency bands used by commercial wireless systems are at most 10s of MHz wide. It follows that $2\pi\tau(f_k - f_c) << 1$, and using the standard approximation $\cos(x) \approx 1 - x^2/2$ for $x << 1$, we further get:

$$RSI_{m,k} \approx |H_A|^2 P_{m,k} (2\pi\tau)^2 (f_k - f_c)^2 SIC_D^{-1}.$$

Recalling that $f_k = f_1 + (k-1)B/K = f_0 + kB/K$ for $f_0 = f_1 - B/K$, and writing f_c as $f_c = f_0 + cB/K$, for $c \in \mathbb{R}$, we can combine all the constant terms and represent the remaining SI as:

$$RSI_{m,k} = g_m P_{m,k}(k - c)^2, \quad (2)$$

where $g_m = |H_A|^2 (2\pi\tau)^2 (B/K)^2 SIC_D^{-1}$. Note that even though in this notation we allow c to take negative values, we will later show that in any solution that maximizes the sum rate it must be $c \in (1, K)$ (Lemma 7.3).

Fig. 4(d) shows the TX/RX isolation based on Eq. (2) and based on measurement results. The parameter g_m in Eq. (2) was determined via a least square estimation. The modeled TX/RX isolation based on Eq. (2) is also compared to the measured TX/RX isolation of the canceller with the antenna pair interface in Fig. 4(c). *As Fig. 4 shows, our model of the remaining SI closely matches the remaining SI that we measured with the RFIC FD receiver presented in* [32, 34].

4.2 Sum Rate

The total transmitted power of each station is assumed to be bounded as follows. In use cases (i) and (ii): $P_b \leq \overline{P_b}$, and each $P_m, P_{m_1}, P_{m_2} \leq \overline{P_m}$. In use case (iii): $\sum_{k=1}^{K} P_{u,k} \leq \overline{P_u}$, where $u \in \{b, m\}$, $\overline{P_u} > 0$. The channel gain from station u to station v on channel k is denoted by $h_{uv,k}$ in use case (iii) and by h_{uv} in use cases (i) and (ii). The noise level at station u is assumed to be equal on each channel and is denoted by N_u.

For the signal transmitted from u to v, where $u, v \in \{b, m, m_1, m_2\}$, $u \neq v$, and either $u = b$ or $v = b$, we let $\gamma_{uv,k} = \frac{h_{uv,k}}{N_v}$ denote signal to noise ratio (SNR) at v on channel k. Similarly as before, in use cases (i) and (ii), index k is omitted from the notation. In the use case (ii),

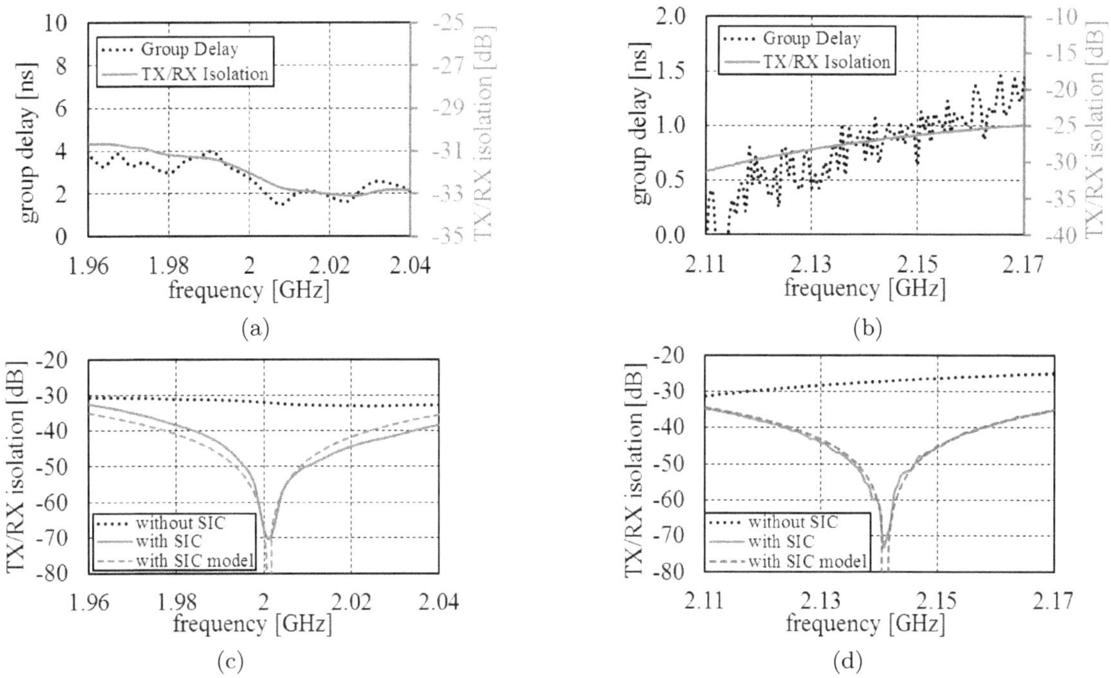

Figure 4: Measured isolation amplitude and group delay of (a) a PCB antenna pair and (b) a commercial 2110-2170 MHz miniature circulator from Skyworks [1], and the resultant TX/RX isolation using the integrated RF canceller with flat amplitude and phase response from [32,34] with (c) the antenna pair and (d) the circulator compared to the modeled SIC.

Table 1: Nomenclature.

m	Subscript notation for an MS
b	Subscript notation for the BS
K	Total number of OFDM channels
k	Channel index, $k \in \{1, ..., K\}$
u, v	Station indexes, $u, v \in \{b, m, m_1, m_2\}$
$P_{u,k}$	Transmission power of station u on channel k
$\overline{P_u}$	Maximum total power: $\sum_{k=1}^{K} P_{u,k} \leq \overline{P_u}$
g_b	Remaining SI at the BS per unit transmitted power
c	Position of the maximum SIC frequency, $c \in \mathbb{R}$
g_m	Remaining SI at an MS per unit transmitted power for $K = 1$; Remaining SI at an MS per unit transmitted power at unit distance from the maximum SIC frequency for $K > 1$
$h_{uv,k}$	Wireless channel gain for signal from u to v on channel k, for $u \neq v$
N_u	Thermal noise at station u
$\gamma_{uv,k}$	SNR of signal from u to v on channel k, where $u \neq v$
$\gamma_{uu,k}$	XINR at station u, channel k
$\gamma_{uv,k}^{\max}$	$\gamma_{uv,k}$ for $P_u = \overline{P_u}$
r_k	Total rate on channel k
r	Sum rate: $r = \sum_{k=1}^{K} r_k$
$r_{\text{TDD}}^{\max}$	Maximum TDD rate.

$\gamma_{m_1 m_2}$ denotes the (inter-node-)interference to noise ratio (INR). Self-interference to noise ratio (XINR) at the BS is denoted by $\gamma_{bb} = \frac{g_b P_b}{N_b}$ in use cases (i) and (ii), and by $\gamma_{bb,k} = \frac{g_b P_{b,k}}{N_b}$ in use case (iii). XINR at the MS is denoted by $\gamma_{mm} = \frac{g_m P_m}{N_m}$ and $\gamma_{mm,k} = \frac{g_m (k-c)^2 P_{m,k}}{N_m}$ in use cases (i) and (iii), respectively.

We use Shannon's capacity formula for spectral efficiency, and let log(.) denote the base 2 logarithm, ln(.) denote the natural logarithm. We use the terms "spectral efficiency" and "rate" interchangeably, as the spectral efficiency on a channel is the rate on that channel normalized by B/K.[3]

In use case (i), the sum rate on the channel is given as:

$$r = \log\left(1 + \frac{\gamma_{mb}}{1 + \gamma_{bb}}\right) + \log\left(1 + \frac{\gamma_{bm}}{1 + \gamma_{mm}}\right). \quad (3)$$

Observe that $\frac{\gamma_{mb}}{1+\gamma_{bb}}$ and $\frac{\gamma_{bm}}{1+\gamma_{mm}}$ are signal to interference-plus-noise ratios (SINRs) on the uplink and downlink, respectively. We will refer to $r_m = \log\left(1 + \frac{\gamma_{mb}}{1+\gamma_{bb}}\right)$ as the uplink rate and $r_b = \log\left(1 + \frac{\gamma_{bm}}{1+\gamma_{mm}}\right)$ as the downlink rate.

Similarly as for (i), the sum rate for use case (ii) is:

$$r = \log\left(1 + \frac{\gamma_{m_1 b}}{1 + \gamma_{bb}}\right) + \log\left(1 + \frac{\gamma_{bm_2}}{1 + \gamma_{m_1 m_2}}\right). \quad (4)$$

Finally, in use case (iii), the rate on channel k is given as:

$$r_k = \log\left(1 + \frac{\gamma_{mb,k}}{1 + \gamma_{bb,k}}\right) + \log\left(1 + \frac{\gamma_{bm,k}}{1 + \gamma_{mm,k}}\right), \quad (5)$$

while the sum rate (on all channels) is $r = \sum_{k=1}^{K} r_k$.

The objective in all problems considered in this paper is to maximize r subject to the upper bound on total transmitted power and non-negativity constraints. In use cases (i) and (ii), the variables are P_b and P_m, while in the use case (iii), the variables are c, $P_{b,k}$, and $P_{m,k}$, for $k \in \{1, ..., K\}$.

For the purpose of comparison to TDD systems, we will sometimes also consider TDD rates. A pair of uplink and downlink TDD rates $r_{\text{TDD},m}$ and $r_{\text{TDD},b}$ is feasible if there exist $a_m, a_b \geq 0$ such that $a_m + a_b \leq 1$ and $r_{\text{TDD},m} =$

[3]Note that this is true both in single-channel and multi-channel cases, since in the single-channel case $K = 1$.

$a_m \log(1+\gamma_{mb})$, $r_{\text{TDD},b} = a_b \log(1+\gamma_{bm})$. We let $r_{\text{TDD}}^{\max}$ denote the maximum of the sum $r_{\text{TDD},m} + r_{\text{TDD},b}$.

5. A BIDIRECTIONAL FD LINK

In this section, we derive general properties of the sum rate function for use case (i) (Fig. 1(a)).

First, we show that if it is possible for the FD sum rate to exceed the maximum TDD rate, it is always optimal for the MS and the BS to transmit at their maximum respective power levels (Lemma 5.1). This result is somewhat surprising, because in general, the FD sum rate function does not have good structural properties, i.e., it need not be convex or concave in the transmission power variables.

Building upon this insight, we quantify the FD rate gains by comparing the FD sum rate to corresponding TDD rates (Section 5.2). More specifically, we define a metric that characterizes by how much the FD capacity region extends the corresponding TDD capacity region, and provide a sufficient condition on the system parameters for rate gains to hold.

Finally, we establish a sufficient condition for the FD sum rate function to be concave in transmission power levels (Section 5.3). This condition imposes very mild restrictions on the XINRs at the BS and the MS. Moreover, the established condition extends to the multi-channel scenario (use case (iii)), where it plays a crucial role in deriving a nearly-optimal algorithm for the sum rate maximization (Section 7.2.1).

5.1 Power Allocation

LEMMA 5.1. *If there exists an FD sum rate r that is higher than the maximum TDD rate, then r is maximized for $P_m = \overline{P_m}$, $P_b = \overline{P_b}$.*

PROOF. From (3), the sum rate can be written as:

$$r = \log\left(1 + \frac{h_{mb}P_m}{N_b + g_b P_b}\right) + \log\left(1 + \frac{h_{bm}P_b}{N_m + g_m P_m}\right)$$

Taking partial derivatives of r directly does not provide conclusive information about the optimal power levels. Instead, we write r as an increasing function of another function that is easier to analyze. Specifically:

$$\begin{aligned} r &= \log\left(\left(1 + \frac{h_{mb}P_m}{N_b + g_b P_b}\right)\cdot\left(1 + \frac{h_{bm}P_b}{N_m + g_m P_m}\right)\right) \\ &= \log(1+\gamma), \quad \text{where} \\ \gamma &= \frac{h_{mb}P_m}{N_b + g_b P_b} + \frac{h_{bm}P_b}{N_m + g_m P_m} + \frac{h_{mb}P_m}{N_b + g_b P_b}\cdot\frac{h_{bm}P_b}{N_m + g_m P_m}. \end{aligned}$$

Since r is strictly increasing in γ, to maximize r it suffices to determine P_m, P_b that maximize γ.

The first and the second partial derivative of γ with respect to P_m are:

$$\frac{\partial \gamma}{\partial P_m} = \frac{h_{mb}}{N_b + g_b P_b} + \frac{h_{bm}P_b}{(N_m + g_m P_m)^2}\left(\frac{h_{mb}N_m}{N_b + g_b P_b} - g_m\right), \tag{6}$$

$$\frac{\partial^2 \gamma}{\partial {P_m}^2} = -2\frac{h_{bm}P_b g_m}{(N_m + g_m P_m)^3}\left(\frac{h_{mb}N_m}{N_b + g_b P_b} - g_m\right). \tag{7}$$

From (6) and (7):

1. If $\frac{h_{mb}N_m}{N_b + g_b P_b} - g_m \geq 0$, then $\frac{\partial^2\gamma}{\partial {P_m}^2} \leq 0$ and $\frac{\partial\gamma}{\partial P_m} > 0$, which implies that γ is concave and strictly increasing in P_m, and therefore maximized for $P_m = \overline{P_m}$.

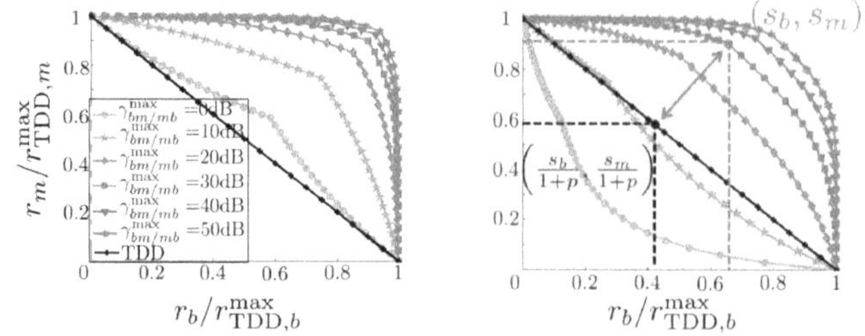

(a) (b)

Figure 5: TDD and FD capacity regions, and FD extension. The capacity region is plotted for equal maximum SNRs: $\gamma_{mb}^{\max} = \gamma_{bm}^{\max} \equiv \gamma_{bm/mb}^{\max}$ and two cases of maximum XINRs: (a) $\gamma_{bb}^{\max} = 1$, $\gamma_{mm}^{\max} = 1$ and (b) $\gamma_{bb}^{\max} = 1$, $\gamma_{mm}^{\max} = 10$.

2. If $\frac{h_{mb}N_m}{N_b + g_b P_b} - g_m < 0$, then $\frac{\partial^2\gamma}{\partial {P_m}^2} > 0$, which means that γ is strictly convex in P_m. Therefore, γ is maximized at either $P_m = 0$ or $P_m = \overline{P_m}$. Note that if $P_m = 0$, there is no signal on uplink, in which case FD rate equals the maximum TDD uplink rate.

A similar results follows for P_b by taking the first and the second partial derivative of γ with respect to P_b. □

5.2 Mapping Gain over SINR Regions

In this section we quantify the FD rate gains by comparing the FD capacity region to the corresponding TDD capacity region. Let $r_b = \log(1+\frac{\gamma_{bm}}{1+\gamma_{mm}})$, $r_m = \log(1+\frac{\gamma_{mb}}{1+\gamma_{bb}})$ denote downlink and uplink rates, respectively and let $r_{\text{TDD},b}^{\max} = \log(1+\gamma_{bm}^{\max})$, $r_{\text{TDD},m}^{\max} = \log(1+\gamma_{mb}^{\max})$ denote the maximum TDD rates. The FD capacity region is the set of all points (r_b, r_m) such that $P_m \in [0, \overline{P_m}]$, $P_b \in [0, \overline{P_b}]$, while the TDD capacity region is the convex hull of the points $(0,0)$, $(r_{\text{TDD},b}^{\max}, 0)$, and $(0, r_{\text{TDD},m}^{\max})$.

We also let $s_b = \log(1+\frac{\gamma_{bm}^{\max}}{1+\gamma_{mm}^{\max}})$ and $s_m = \log(1+\frac{\gamma_{mb}^{\max}}{1+\gamma_{bb}^{\max}})$ be the FD downlink and uplink rates when both stations transmit at their maximum power levels $\overline{P_b}, \overline{P_m}$.

Fig. 5 shows FD and TDD capacity regions for symmetric maximum SNRs $\gamma_{mb}^{\max} = \gamma_{bm}^{\max}$ and two cases of maximum XINRs: $\gamma_{bb}^{\max} = \gamma_{mm}^{\max} = 1$ and $\gamma_{bb}^{\max} = 1$, $\gamma_{mm}^{\max} = 10$. Here, the axes are normalized by $r_{\text{TDD},b}^{\max}$ and $r_{\text{TDD},m}^{\max}$, respectively. Note that FD capacity regions are not necessarily convex (e.g., Fig. 5(b) for $\gamma_{bm/mb}^{\max} = 0\text{dB}$ and $\gamma_{bm/mb}^{\max} = 10\text{dB}$).

Lemma 5.1 states that the maximizer of the FD sum rate is either $(r_{\text{TDD},b}^{\max}, 0)$, $(0, r_{\text{TDD},m}^{\max})$ or (s_b, s_m). In particular, to see whether FD operation increases the sum rate, it suffices to check whether $s_b + s_m > \max\{r_{\text{TDD},b}^{\max}, r_{\text{TDD},m}^{\max}\}$. This motivates us to focus on the pair (s_b, s_m) when considering by how much the FD capacity region extends the corresponding TDD capacity region. We introduce the following definition (see Fig. 5(b) for a geometric interpretation).

Definition 1. FD extends the corresponding TDD capacity region by $p \cdot 100\%$ if $p \geq 0$ is the smallest number for which $\frac{s_b}{1+p}, \frac{s_m}{1+p}$ is inside the TDD capacity region.

The following lemma provides a necessary and sufficient condition for the capacity region extension of $p \cdot 100\%$.

LEMMA 5.2. *FD extends the TDD capacity region by $p \cdot 100\%$, where $p \geq 0$, if and only if:*

$$\frac{\log\left(1 + \frac{\gamma_{bm}^{\max}}{1+\gamma_{mm}^{\max}}\right)}{\log(1+\gamma_{bm}^{\max})} + \frac{\log\left(1 + \frac{\gamma_{mb}^{\max}}{1+\gamma_{bb}^{\max}}\right)}{\log(1+\gamma_{mb}^{\max})} = 1 + p. \tag{8}$$

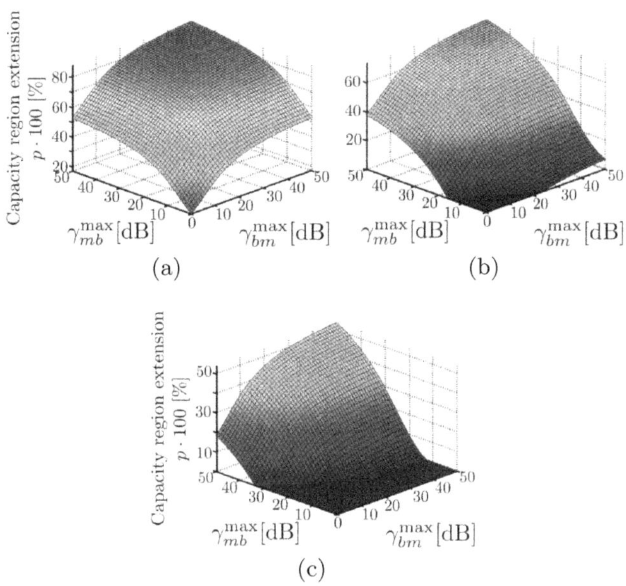

Figure 6: TDD capacity region extension due to FD as a function of SNRs for (a) $\gamma_{bb}^{\max} = 1$, $\gamma_{mm}^{\max} = 1$, (b) $\gamma_{bb}^{\max} = 1$, $\gamma_{mm}^{\max} = 10$, and (c) $\gamma_{bb}^{\max} = 1$, $\gamma_{mm}^{\max} = 100$.

PROOF SKETCH. The proof is based on the fact that since p is the smallest number for which the point $(\frac{s_b}{1+p}, \frac{s_m}{1+p})$ is in the TDD capacity region, $(\frac{s_b}{1+p}, \frac{s_m}{1+p})$ must lie on the line connecting $r_{\mathrm{TDD},b}^{\max}$ and $r_{\mathrm{TDD},m}^{\max}$ (Fig. 5(b)), and therefore: $\frac{s_m}{1+p} = r_{\mathrm{TDD},m}^{\max} - \frac{r_{\mathrm{TDD},m}^{\max}}{r_{\mathrm{TDD},b}^{\max}} \frac{s_b}{1+p}$, which is equivalent to $\frac{\log\left(1+\frac{\gamma_{bm}^{\max}}{1+\gamma_{mm}^{\max}}\right)}{\log(1+\gamma_{bm}^{\max})} + \frac{\log\left(1+\frac{\gamma_{mb}^{\max}}{1+\gamma_{bb}^{\max}}\right)}{\log(1+\gamma_{mb}^{\max})} = 1+p$. □

Fig. 6 shows the TDD capacity region extension due to FD operation, as a function of received signals' SNR, for BS FD receiver that cancels SI to the noise level and MS FD receiver that cancels SI to (i) the noise level (Fig. 6(a)), (ii) one order of magnitude above noise (Fig. 6(b)), and (iii) two orders of magnitude above noise (Fig. 6(c)). Somewhat surprisingly, even in the case when the MS cancels SI to two orders of magnitude above noise, capacity region extension can be as high as 50% for sufficiently high SNRs (Fig. 6(c)).

5.3 Sum Rate Concavity

In this section, we establish a sufficient condition for the sum rate to be (strictly) concave, and increasing in P_m and in P_b (Condition 5.3). We also show that when the condition fails, using FD does not provide appreciable rate gains, as compared to the maximum rate achievable by TDD operation.

CONDITION 5.3. $\gamma_{mm} \leq \frac{\gamma_{mb}}{1+\gamma_{bb}}$ *and* $\gamma_{bb} \leq \frac{\gamma_{bm}}{1+\gamma_{mm}}$.

PROPOSITION 5.4. *If* $\gamma_{mm} \leq \frac{\gamma_{mb}}{1+\gamma_{bb}}$, *the sum rate* r *is strictly concave and strictly increasing in* P_m. *Similarly, if* $\gamma_{bb} \leq \frac{\gamma_{bm}}{1+\gamma_{mm}}$, r *is strictly concave and strictly increasing in* P_b. *Thus, when Condition 5.3 holds,* r *is strictly concave and strictly increasing both in* P_m *and in* P_b. *Furthermore, when Condition 5.3 does not hold,* $r - r_{TDD}^{\max} < 1$*b/s/Hz.*

PROOF. From the proof of Lemma 5.1, we can express r as $r = \log(1+\gamma)$, where γ is strictly increasing and concave

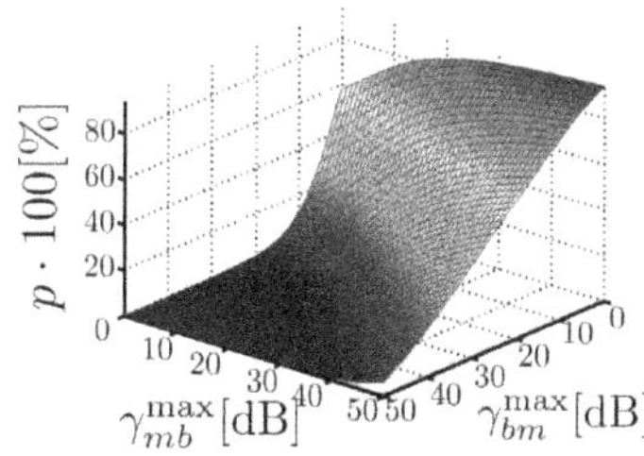

Figure 7: Capacity region extension when Condition 5.3 is not satisfied. Non-negligible gains are possible only when uplink SNR is at least an order of magnitude higher than the downlink SNR, a case that is irrelevant in practice.

in P_m whenever

$$\frac{h_{mb}N_m}{N_b + g_b P_b} - g_m \geq 0. \tag{9}$$

Multiplying both sides of (9) by $\frac{P_m}{N_m}$ and reordering terms:

$$\frac{h_{mb}P_m}{N_b + g_b P_b} \geq \frac{g_m P_m}{N_m} \quad \Leftrightarrow \quad \gamma_{mm} \leq \frac{\gamma_{mb}}{1+\gamma_{bb}}.$$

Whenever (9), or equivalently, the inequality $\gamma_{mm} \leq \frac{\gamma_{mb}}{1+\gamma_{bb}}$, holds, since $\gamma > 0$, $\frac{\partial \gamma}{\partial P_m} > 0$, $\frac{\partial^2 \gamma}{\partial {P_m}^2} \leq 0$:

$$\frac{\partial r}{\partial P_m} = \frac{1}{1+\gamma} \cdot \frac{\partial \gamma}{\partial P_m} > 0, \text{ and,}$$
$$\frac{\partial^2 r}{\partial {P_m}^2} = -\frac{1}{(1+\gamma)^2} \cdot \left(\frac{\partial \gamma}{\partial P_m}\right)^2 + \frac{1}{1+\gamma} \cdot \frac{\partial^2 \gamma}{\partial {P_m}^2} < 0,$$

and therefore r is strictly increasing and strictly concave in P_m. Similarly, whenever $\gamma_{bb} \leq \frac{\gamma_{bm}}{1+\gamma_{mm}}$, r is strictly increasing and strictly concave in P_b.

Now suppose that Condition 5.3 does not hold. Then, either $\gamma_{mm} > \frac{\gamma_{mb}}{1+\gamma_{bb}}$ or $\gamma_{bb} > \frac{\gamma_{bm}}{1+\gamma_{mm}}$. Suppose that $\gamma_{mm} > \frac{\gamma_{mb}}{1+\gamma_{bb}}$. Then:

$$\begin{aligned} r &= \log\left(1 + \frac{\gamma_{mb}}{1+\gamma_{bb}}\right) + \log\left(1 + \frac{\gamma_{bm}}{1+\gamma_{mm}}\right) \\ &< \log\left(1 + \frac{\gamma_{mb}}{1+\gamma_{bb}}\right) + \log\left(1 + \frac{\gamma_{bm}}{1+\frac{\gamma_{mb}}{1+\gamma_{bb}}}\right) \\ &= \log\left(1 + \gamma_{bm} + \frac{\gamma_{mb}}{1+\gamma_{bb}}\right) \\ &= \log\left(2 \cdot \left(1 + \frac{1}{2}\left(\gamma_{bm} + \frac{\gamma_{mb}}{1+\gamma_{bb}} - 1\right)\right)\right) \\ &= 1\text{b/s/Hz} + \log\left(1 + \frac{1}{2}\left(\gamma_{bm} + \frac{\gamma_{mb}}{1+\gamma_{bb}} - 1\right)\right). \end{aligned}$$

Since $\frac{1}{2}\left(\gamma_{bm} + \frac{\gamma_{mb}}{1+\gamma_{bb}} - 1\right) < \max\{\gamma_{mb}, \gamma_{bm}\}$, it follows that $r < 1\text{b/s/Hz} + r_{\mathrm{TDD}}^{\max}$, which completes the proof for $\gamma_{mm} > \frac{\gamma_{mb}}{1+\gamma_{bb}}$. The proof for the case $\gamma_{bb} > \frac{\gamma_{bm}}{1+\gamma_{mm}}$ follows the same line of argument and is omitted for brevity. □

When Condition 5.3 does not hold, the bound $r - r_{\mathrm{TDD}}^{\max} < 1$b/s/Hz limits the additive increase in FD rate. However, it does not bound the FD capacity region extension. Therefore, we plot an upper bound on the FD capacity region extension in Fig. 7 for a perfect SIC at the BS ($\gamma_{bb} = 0$) and $\gamma_{mm} = \frac{\gamma_{mb}}{1+\gamma_{bb}} = \gamma_{mb}$. As Fig. 7 shows, to have non-negligible capacity region extension, the uplink SNR γ_{mb} should be higher than the downlink SNR γ_{bm}. This is rarely the case in practice, since in cellular and Wi-Fi networks typically the opposite holds, i.e., $\gamma_{bm} > \gamma_{mb}$, due to better antenna gain and higher transmission power at the BS/AP.

Note that the condition for concavity in P_b, $\gamma_{bb} \leq \frac{\gamma_{bm}}{1+\gamma_{mm}}$, is relatively simple to satisfy, since in practice it is possible to achieve $\gamma_{bb} = 1$ [5], and the condition is satisfied for downlink SINR (SINR at the MS) $\geq$ 0dB.

6. TWO UNIDIRECTIONAL LINKS

Much of the analysis for use case (i) (Section 5) extends to use case (ii) (Fig. 1(b)), due to the similarity between the sum rate as a function of transmission power levels for these two use cases (see Eqs. (3) and (4)). However, there are also important differences. First, the interfering signal at MS 2 in use case (ii), unlike the self-interfering signal at the MS in the bidirectional link case, is not known at the receiver, and therefore, cannot be cancelled (unless an additional channel is used, which we do not consider). Second, in use case (ii), the channel gains between MSs cannot take arbitrary values. This is because the channel gains typically conform to a path loss model of propagation, where the SNR depends on distances between MSs, which in turn need to satisfy the triangle inequality. The following two lemmas are similar to Lemmas 5.1 and 5.2. We state them without proofs.

LEMMA 6.1. *If there exists an FD sum rate that is higher than the maximum TDD rate, then the FD sum rate is maximized at $P_{m_1} = \overline{P_m}$ for MS 1, and $P_b = \overline{P_b}$ for the BS.*

LEMMA 6.2. *FD extends the TDD capacity region by $p \cdot 100\%$ if and only if:*

$$\frac{\log\left(1+\frac{\gamma_{bm_2}^{\max}}{1+\gamma_{m_1 m_2}^{\max}}\right)}{\log(1+\gamma_{bm_2}^{\max})} + \frac{\log\left(1+\frac{\gamma_{m_1 b}^{\max}}{1+\gamma_{bb}^{\max}}\right)}{\log(1+\gamma_{m_1 b}^{\max})} = 1+p. \quad (10)$$

In a path loss model of propagation, the wireless channel gain between two stations is a function of the distance between the stations: $h_{uv} = \left(\frac{L}{d_{uv}}\right)^{\eta}$, where $u, v \in \{b, m_1, m_2\}$, $u \neq v$, η is the path loss exponent, and L is a constant. Therefore, since distances $d_{m_1 b}$, d_{bm_2}, and $d_{m_1 m_2}$ need to satisfy the triangle inequality, SNRs $\gamma_{m_1 b}$, γ_{bm_2} and INR $\gamma_{m_1 m_2}$ cannot take arbitrary values.

To evaluate rate gains in use case (ii), we consider path loss exponents from the set $\{2, 3, 4\}$, since typical range for the path loss exponent is between 2 and 4 [25]. We assume fixed maximum power levels at the BS and the MS 1, equal noise levels N at the BS and the MS 2, and we vary SNRs and the INR as the function of distance, as follows:

$$\gamma_{m_1 b} = \frac{h_{m_1 b}\overline{P_{m_1}}}{N} = \frac{h_{m_1 b}}{h_{m_1 b}^{\max}} \cdot \gamma_{m_1 b}^{\max} = \left(\frac{d_{m_1 b}}{d_{m_1 b}^{\min}}\right)^{\eta} \gamma_{m_1 b}^{\max},$$

$$\gamma_{m_1 m_2} = \frac{h_{m_1 m_2}\overline{P_{m_1}}}{N} = \frac{h_{m_2 m_2}}{h_{m_1 m_2}^{\max}} \cdot \gamma_{m_1 m_2}^{\max} = \left(\frac{d_{m_1 m_2}}{d_{m_1 m_2}^{\min}}\right)^{\eta} \gamma_{m_1 m_2}^{\max},$$

$$\gamma_{bm_2} = \frac{h_{bm_2}\overline{P_b}}{N} = \frac{h_{bm_2}}{h_{bm_2}^{\max}} \cdot \gamma_{bm_2}^{\max} = \left(\frac{d_{bm_2}}{d_{bm_2}^{\min}}\right)^{\eta} \gamma_{bm_2}^{\max},$$

where $d_{uv,min}$ is a reference distance at which $\gamma_{uv} = \gamma_{uv}^{\max}$ for $u, v \in \{b, m_1, m_2\}$, $x \neq y$.

For the purpose of comparison, we will assume that $d_{bm_2}^{\min} = d_{m_1 b}^{\min} = d_{m_1 m_2}^{\min} \equiv d^{\min}$, which would correspond to $\overline{P_b} = \overline{P_m}$, and normalize all distances to $d^{\min}$ (or, equivalently, take $d^{\min} = 1$). Note that by assuming $\overline{P_b} = \overline{P_m}$ we estimate an upper bound on the capacity region extension, since in practice $\overline{P_m} \leq \overline{P_b}$, and from Lemma 6.1 if FD rate can be greater than the maximum TDD rate, it is maximized when the transmission power levels are maximized.

Capacity region extension as a function of SNRs is shown in Fig. 8, for different values of the path loss exponent and $d_{m_1 m_2} = \rho(d_{m_1 b} + d_{bm_2})$, for $\rho \in \{0.25, 0.5, 0.75, 1\}$. For all combinations of SNRs at which the triangle inequality is not satisfied, we set the capacity region extension p to 0.

Fig. 8 suggests that to achieve over 50% capacity region extension, the environment needs to be sufficiently lossy, i.e., with the path loss exponent $\eta > 2$. Moreover, to achieve high capacity region extension, the SNRs at the BS and at the MS 2 need to be low enough, meaning that the corresponding distances $d_{m_1 b}$ and d_{bm_2} need to be large, since the differences in the SNR shown in all the graphs are due to different distances (and consequently different path loss).

7. OFDM BIDIRECTIONAL LINKS

In this section, we focus on the rate maximization for use case (iii) (Fig. 1(c)). Recall that in this use case the FD receiver at the MS has a frequency-selective SIC profile (Fig. 4(d)). Requiring two technical conditions (Conditions 7.2 and 7.4), we derive a nearly optimal algorithm for the sum rate maximization. While the derived algorithm is nearly optimal and has polynomial time complexity, its running time is high because it requires invoking a large number of gradient ascent methods. We therefore also consider a high SINR approximation of the sum rate, and develop an efficient power allocation algorithm for the sum rate maximization. We also prove that in the high SINR regime it is always optimal to set the maximum SIC frequency in the middle of the used frequency band. Interestingly, our numerical results (Section 7.3) suggest that for FD capacity region extension of over 50%, the high SINR approximation provides a solution that is very close to the optimal one.

7.1 Analysis of Sum Rate

7.1.1 *Dependence on Channel Power Levels*

The analysis of the sum rate in terms of transmission power levels extends from the single-channel case provided in Section 5. In particular:

OBSERVATION 7.1. *If*

$$\frac{g_m(k-c)^2}{N_m} \leq \frac{h_{mb,k}}{N_b + g_b P_{b,k}} \text{ and } \frac{g_b}{N_b} \leq \frac{h_{bm,k}}{N_m + g_m P_{m,k}(k-c)^2} \quad (11)$$

hold, then the sum rate is concave in both $P_{m,k}$ and $P_{b,k}$.

This result is simple to show, since $(k-c)^2$ term is independent of the transmission power levels, and $P_{b,k}$ and $P_{m,k}$ only appear in one summation term (r_k). Therefore, we get the same form of partial derivatives in $P_{b,k}$ and $P_{m,k}$ as in the case of a single channel (proof of Lemma 5.1). Similar to the case of a single channel, if condition (11) is not satisfied, then the achievable rate improvement is low (cf. Prop. 5.4).

The first inequality in (11) guarantees concavity in $P_{m,k}$, while the second one guarantees concavity in $P_{b,k}$. The condition (11) cannot be satisfied for any $P_{b,k} \geq 0$, $P_{m,k} \geq 0$ (e.g., the first inequality cannot be satisfied if $\frac{g_m(k-c)^2}{N_m} > \frac{h_{mb,k}}{N_m}$). However, since the role of condition (11) is to guar-

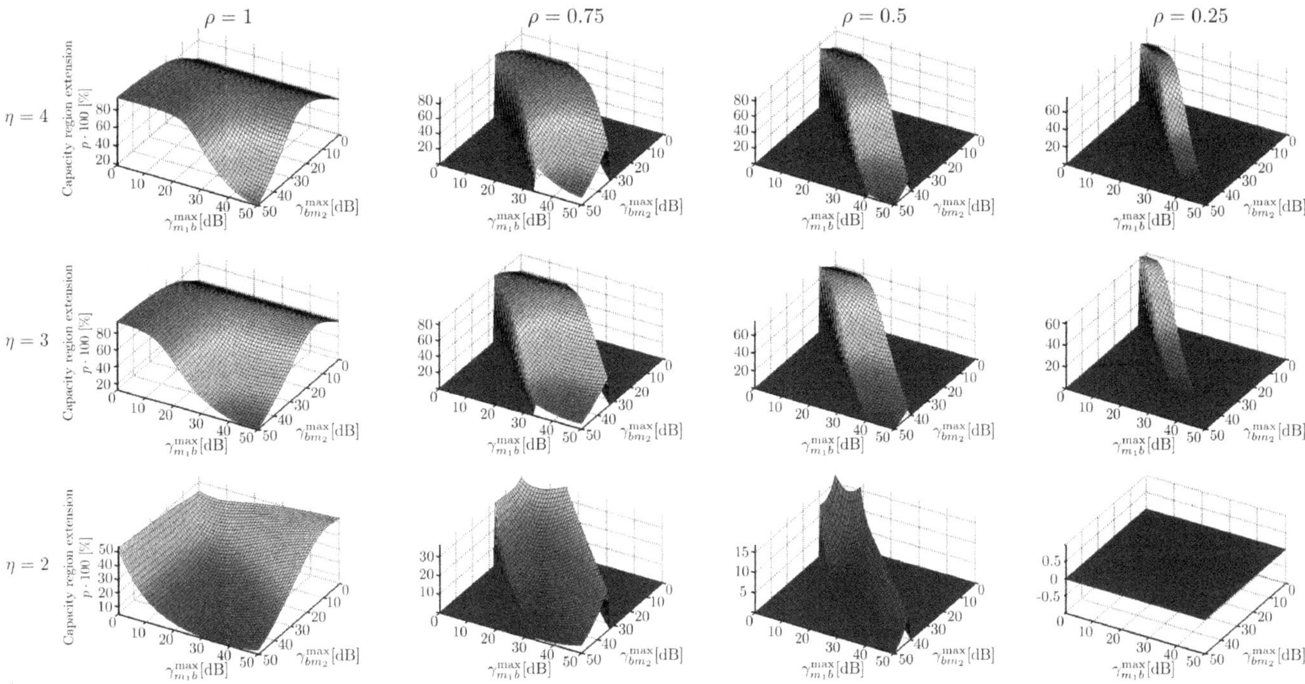

Figure 8: TDD capacity region extension due to FD as a function of SNRs, where SNRs change due to path loss with exponent η, and distance between MS 1 and MS 2 is $d_{m_1 m_2} = \rho(d_{m_1 b} + d_{b m_2})$. Transmission power levels are set to maximum. In SNR regions where the triangle inequality of the distances is not satisfied, p is set to 0.

antee concavity in the power levels, we can replace this condition by either $P_{m,k} = 0$ or $P_{b,k} = 0$, which implies rate concavity in $P_{m,k}, P_{b,k}$. Specifically, to guarantee that the sum rate is concave in all $P_{m,k}, P_{b,k}$, we require the following condition to hold:

Condition 7.2. *(a)* $\frac{g_m(k-c)^2}{N_m} \leq \frac{h_{mb,k}}{N_b + g_b P_{b,k}}$ *if* $\frac{g_m(k-c)^2}{N_m} < \frac{h_{mb,k}}{N_b}$*, otherwise* $P_{m,k} = 0$*, and*
(b) $\frac{g_b}{N_b} \leq \frac{h_{bm,k}}{N_m + g_m P_{m,k}(k-c)^2}$ *if* $\frac{g_b}{N_b} < \frac{h_{bm,k}}{N_m}$*; otherwise* $P_{b,k} = 0$ *if* $P_{m,k}$ *was not set to 0 by (a).*

Note that Condition 7.2 forces a channel k to be used in half-duplex (only one of $P_{m,k}, P_{b,k}$ is non-zero) whenever it is not possible to satisfy the sufficient condition (11) for the sum rate concavity in $P_{m,k}, P_{b,k}$ for any $P_{m,k} \geq 0$ and $P_{b,k} \geq 0$.

7.1.2 Dependence on Maximum SIC Frequency

The following lemma shows that choosing optimal c for a given power allocation $\{P_{b,k}, P_{m,k}\}$ is hard in general, since the sum rate r as a function of c is neither convex nor concave, and can have $\Omega(K)$ local maxima. Proofs of the following two lemmas are provided in [23].

Lemma 7.3. *The sum rate r is neither convex nor concave in c. All (local) maxima of $r(c)$ lie in the interval $(1, K)$. In general, the number of local maxima is $\Omega(K)$.*

Even though $r(c)$ can have multiple maxima in c, if we restrict the analysis to practically relevant values of $\gamma_{mb,k}$ and $\gamma_{mm,k}$, the selection of c, together with the power allocation, can be made tractable under the following condition:

Condition 7.4. $\frac{g_m P_{m,k}}{N_m} \leq \gamma_{mb,k}\ \forall k \in \{1, ..., K\}$.

Note that this condition is implied by Condition 7.2 for $|k-c| \geq 1$, and that there can be at most 2 channels with $|k-c| < 1$. For $|k-c| < 1$, this condition limits SI on channel k. The following lemma bounds the first partial derivative of r with respect to c. This bound will prove useful in maximizing r as a function of c and $\{P_{b,k}, P_{m,k}\}$ (Section 7.2.1).

Lemma 7.5. *If Condition 7.4 holds, then:*

$$\left|\frac{\partial r}{\partial c}\right| \leq \frac{2}{\ln 2}(\ln(K) + 1 + 2\sqrt{3}) \quad \forall c \in (1, K).$$

7.2 Parameter Selection Algorithms

7.2.1 General SINR Regime

The pseudocode of the algorithm for maximizing the sum rate in the general SINR regime is provided in Algorithm 1 – MaximumRate. We claim the following:

Lemma 7.6. *Under conditions 7.2 and 7.4,* MaximumRate *determines c and the power allocation $\{P_{b,k}, P_{m,k}\}$ that maximize sum rate up to an absolute error ϵ, for any $\epsilon > 0$. The running time of* MaximumRate *is polynomial in $\frac{1}{\epsilon}$ and K.*

Note that if Algorithm 1 only applied gradient ascent to maximize the sum rate without requiring Condition 7.2, it would not necessarily obtain an optimal or a near-optimal power allocation. This is because without Condition 7.2 the sum rate is not necessarily concave in the power variables, and gradient ascent methods could converge to a local (instead of global) optimum. Moreover, since the sum rate is highly nonlinear in the parameter c (Lemma 7.3), c cannot be used as a variable in the gradient ascent. Nevertheless,

Algorithm 1 MaximumRate(ϵ)

Input: $K, \overline{P_b}, \overline{P_m}, g_b, g_m, N_m, N_b$

1: $c_{\min} = 1$, $c_{\max} = K$, $\Delta c = \frac{\epsilon}{\frac{2}{\ln 2}(\ln(K)+1+2\sqrt{3})}$

2: $c^{\max} = r^{\max} = 0$, $\{P_{b,k}^{\max}\} = \{P_{m,k}^{\max}\} = \{0\}$

3: **for** $c = c_{\min}$, $c < c_{\max}$, $c = c + \Delta c$ **do**

4: Solve via gradient ascent:

$$\max \quad r = \sum_{k=1}^{K} r_k, \text{ where } r_k \text{ is given by (5)}$$

s.t. Conditions 7.2 and 7.4 hold

$$\sum_{k=1}^{K} P_{m,k} \le \overline{P_m}, \quad \sum_{k=1}^{K} P_{b,k} \le \overline{P_b}$$

$$P_{b,k} \ge 0, \quad P_{m,k} \ge 0 \quad \forall k \in \{1, ..., K\}.$$

5: **if** $r > r^{\max}$ **then**

6: $r^{\max} = r, \quad c^{\max} = c,$

7: $\{P_{b,k}^{\max}\} = \{P_{b,k}\}, \quad \{P_{m,k}^{\max}\} = \{P_{m,k}\}$

8: **return** $c^{\max}, \{P_{b,k}^{\max}\}, \{P_{m,k}^{\max}\}, r^{\max}$.

as a result of Lemma 7.5 that bounds the first derivative of r with respect to c when Condition 7.4 is applied, by examining a sufficient number of choices for c from the interval $(1, K)$ and determining an optimal power allocation for each such c, the algorithm determines a nearly-optimal solution.

Proof of Lemma 7.6. Consider the optimization problem in Step 4 of the algorithm. Since Condition 7.2 is required by the constraints, the objective r is concave in $P_{b,k}, P_{m,k}$. The feasible region of the problem from Step 4 is determined by linear inequalities and Conditions 7.2 and 7.4.

Condition 7.2 is either an inequality or an equality for each $P_{m,k}, P_{b,k}$ that (possibly rearranging the terms) is linear in $P_{m,k}, P_{b,k}$. Condition 7.4 is a linear inequality in $P_{m,k}$. Therefore, the feasible region in the problem of Step 4 is a polyhedron and therefore convex. It follows immediately that this problem can be solved optimally via a gradient ascent method in time polynomial in K.

The algorithm finds an optimal power allocation for each c from the set of $\frac{(K-1)(\frac{2}{\ln 2}(\ln(K)+1+2\sqrt{3}))}{\epsilon} - 2$ equally spaced points from the interval $(1, K)$, and chooses c and power allocation that provide maximum sum rate r.

What remains to prove is that by choosing any alternative $c \ne c^{\max}$ and accompanying optimal power allocation the sum rate cannot be improved by more than an additive ϵ.

Recall from Lemma 7.3 that optimal c must lie in $(1, K)$. Suppose that there exist $c^*, \{P_{b,k}^*, P_{m,k}^*\}$ such that $c^* \in (1, K)$, $c^* \ne c^{\max}$ and $r(c^*, \{P_{b,k}^*, P_{m,k}^*\}) > r^{\max} + \epsilon$.

From the choice of points c in the algorithm, there must exist at least one point c^a that the algorithm considers such that $|c^a - c^*| < \Delta c = \frac{\epsilon}{\frac{2}{\ln 2}(\ln(K)+1+2\sqrt{3})}$. From Lemma 7.5,

$$r(c^*, \{P_{b,k}^*, P_{m,k}^*\}) - r(c^a, \{P_{b,k}^*, P_{m,k}^*\}) <$$
$$\frac{\epsilon}{\frac{2}{\ln 2}(\ln(K)+1+2\sqrt{3})} \cdot \Big(\frac{2}{\ln 2}(\ln(K)+1+2\sqrt{3})\Big) = \epsilon,$$

since in any finite interval I any continuous and differentiable function $f(x)$ cannot change by more than the length of the interval I times the maximum value of its first derivative $f'(x)$ (a simple corollary of the Mean-Value Theorem).

Since the algorithm finds an optimal power allocation for each c, we have that $r(c^a, \{P_{b,k}^*, P_{m,k}^*\}) \le r(c^a, \{P_{b,k}^a, P_{m,k}^a\}) \le r^{\max}$. Therefore: $r(c^*, \{P_{b,k}^*, P_{m,k}^*\}) - r^{\max} < \epsilon$, which is a contradiction. □

7.2.2 High SINR Regime

A high SINR approximation of the sum rate is:

$$r \approx \sum_{k=1}^{K} \Big(\log\Big(\frac{\gamma_{mb,k}}{1+\gamma_{bb,k}}\Big) + \log\Big(\frac{\gamma_{bm,k}}{1+\gamma_{mm,k}}\Big)\Big). \tag{12}$$

While in the high SINR regime the dependence of sum rate on each power level $P_{b,k}, P_{m,k}$ for $k \in \{1, ..., K\}$ becomes concave (regardless of whether Condition 7.2 holds or not), the dependence on the parameter c remains neither convex nor concave as long as we consider a general power allocation. Therefore, we cannot derive a closed form expression for c in terms of an arbitrary power allocation. However, as we show in Lemma 7.9, when power allocation and the choice of parameter c are considered jointly, it is always optimal to place c in the middle of the interval $(1, K)$: $c = \frac{K+1}{2}$. The following proposition and lemma characterize the optimal power allocation for a given c.

Proposition 7.7. *Under high-SINR approximation and any power allocation $\{P_{m,k}\}$ at the MS and any choice of c, it is always optimal to allocate BS power levels as $P_{b,k} = \frac{\overline{P_b}}{K}$.*

Proof. Let P_b denote the total irradiated power by the BS. Write power levels on individual subchannels as $P_{b,k} = \beta_k P_b$, where $\beta_k \ge 0$, $\forall k \in \{1, ..., K\}$, and $\sum_{k=1}^{K} \beta_k = 1$. Then the sum rate can be written as:

$$r = \sum_{k=1}^{K} \Big(\log\Big(\frac{h_{mb,k} P_{m,k}}{N_b + g_b \beta_k P_b}\Big) + \log\Big(\frac{h_{bm,k}\beta_k P_b}{N_m + g_m (k-c)^2 P_{m,k}}\Big)\Big).$$

First, observe that

$$\frac{\partial r}{\partial P_b} = \sum_{k=1}^{K} \mathbb{1}_{\{\beta_k > 0\}} \Big(\frac{1}{P_b} - \frac{g_b \beta_k}{N_b + g_b \beta_k P_b}\Big)$$
$$= \sum_{k=1}^{K} \mathbb{1}_{\{\beta_k > 0\}} \Big({P_b}^{-1} - (N_b/(g_b\beta_k) + P_b)^{-1}\Big),$$

where $\mathbb{1}_{\{.\}}$ is an indicator function. Since $\beta_k \ge 0$ $\forall k \in \{1, ..., K\}$ and $\sum_{k=1}^{K} \beta_k = 1$, it follows that there exists at least one strictly positive β_k. For each such β_k, $\mathbb{1}_{\beta_k > 0}\Big(\frac{1}{P_b} - \frac{1}{\frac{N_b}{g_b\beta_k} + P_b}\Big) > 0$, since $P_b < \frac{N_b}{g_b \beta_k} + P_b$. Therefore, $\frac{\partial r}{\partial P_b} > 0$, which implies that it is optimal to choose $P_b = \overline{P_b}$.

Taking the first and the second partial derivative of r with respect to each β_k, it is simple to show that r has the same dependence on each β_k, and, moreover, is strictly concave in each β_k, as $\frac{\partial^2 r}{\partial {\beta_k}^2} = -\frac{1}{{\beta_k}^2} + \frac{1}{\big(\frac{N_b}{g_b P_b} + \beta_k\big)^2} < 0$, where the inequality follows from $\beta_k < \frac{N_b}{g_b P_b} + \beta_k$. Therefore, r is maximized for $\beta_k = \frac{1}{K}$. □

Lemma 7.8. *Under high-SINR approximation and for a fixed c, the optimal power allocation at the MS satisfies $P_{m,k} = \alpha_k \cdot \overline{P_m}$, where $\alpha_k \ge 0$, $\sum \alpha_k = 1$, and for $k \ne K$:*

(i) $\alpha_k = \Big(\frac{1}{\alpha_K} - \frac{1}{N_m/R_K + \alpha_K}\Big)^{-1}$ if $k = c$,

(ii) $\alpha_k = \frac{-N_m + \sqrt{{N_m}^2 + 4\alpha_K(N_m + R_K\alpha_K)R_k}}{2R_k}$ if $k \ne c$,

where $R_k = g_m(k-c)^2 \overline{P_m}$ for $k \in \{1, ..., K\}$.

PROOF. Let $P_{m,k} = \alpha_k \cdot P_m$, where $\alpha_k > 0$, $\forall k$, and $\sum_{k=1}^{K} \alpha_k = 1$. The sum rate can then be written as:

$$r = \sum_{k=1}^{K} \Big(\log \Big(\frac{h_{mb,k} \alpha_k P_m}{N_b + g_b P_{b,k}} \Big) + \log \Big(\frac{h_{bm,k} P_{b,k}}{N_m + g_m (k-c)^2 \alpha_k P_m} \Big) \Big).$$

Proving that at the optimal solution that maximizes r we necessarily have $P_m = \overline{P_m}$ is analogous to the proof given in Proposition 7.7 for $P_b = \overline{P_b}$, and it is therefore omitted.

As $\sum_{k=1}^{K} \alpha_k = 1$, only $K-1$ α_k's can be chosen independently, while the value of the remaining one is implied by their sum being equal to 1. Choose $\alpha_K = 1 - \sum_{k=1}^{K-1} \alpha_k$, and observe that that $K - c \neq 0$ (and therefore $R_K \neq 0$) is always true since, similar as in the proof of Lemma 7.3, at the optimum it must be $c \in (1, K)$.

If $R_k = g_m (k-c)^2 P_m = 0$, then the first and the second derivative of r with respect to α_k are given as:

$$\frac{\partial r}{\partial \alpha_k} = \frac{1}{\alpha_k} + \frac{1}{\alpha_K} \frac{\partial \alpha_K}{\partial \alpha_k} - \frac{R_K}{N_m + R_K \alpha_K} \frac{\partial \alpha_K}{\partial \alpha_k} = \frac{1}{\alpha_k} - \frac{1}{\alpha_K} + \frac{R_K}{N_m + R_K \alpha_K},$$

$$\frac{\partial^2 r}{\partial {\alpha_k}^2} = -\frac{1}{\alpha_k^2} - \Big(\frac{1}{\alpha_K^2} - \frac{{R_K}^2}{(N_m + R_K \alpha_K)^2} \Big) = -\frac{1}{\alpha_k^2} - \Big(\frac{1}{\alpha_K^2} - \frac{1}{(N_m / R_K + \alpha_K)^2} \Big) < 0.$$

It follows that r is concave in α_k and maximized for

$$\alpha_k = \big({\alpha_K}^{-1} - (N_m / R_K + \alpha_K)^{-1} \big)^{-1}, \tag{13}$$

where $R_K = g_m (K-c)^2 P_m$.

If $R_k \neq 0$, then the first and the second derivative are:

$$\frac{\partial r}{\partial \alpha_k} = \frac{1}{\alpha_k} - \frac{R_k}{N_i + R_k \alpha_k} - \frac{1}{\alpha_K} + \frac{R_K}{N_m + R_K \alpha_K},$$

$$\frac{\partial^2 r}{\partial {\alpha_k}^2} = -\frac{1}{\alpha_k^2} + \frac{{R_k}^2}{(N_m + R_k \alpha_k)^2} - \frac{1}{\alpha_K^2} + \frac{{R_K}^2}{(N_m + R_K \alpha_K)^2} = -\big(\alpha_k^{-2} - (N_m / R_k + \alpha_k)^{-2} \big) - \big(\alpha_K^{-2} - (N_m / R_k + \alpha_K)^{-2} \big) < 0.$$

It follows that r is concave in α_k and maximized for:

$$\frac{\partial r}{\partial \alpha_k} = \frac{1}{\alpha_k} - \frac{R_k}{N_i + R_k \alpha_k} - \frac{1}{\alpha_K} + \frac{R_K}{N_m + R_K \alpha_K} = 0. \tag{14}$$

After simplifying (14), we get:

$$\alpha_k (N_m + R_k \alpha_k) = \alpha_K (N_m + R_K \alpha_K). \tag{15}$$

Solving the quadratic equation (15) for α_k and using that $\alpha_k > 0$, it follows that r is maximized when α_k satisfies

$$\alpha_k = \frac{-N_m + \sqrt{{N_m}^2 + 4\alpha_K (N_m + R_K \alpha_K) R_k}}{2 R_k}, \tag{16}$$

where $R_k = g_m (k-c)^2 P_m$. □

It is relatively simple to show (using similar approach as in the proof of Lemma 7.3) that under general power allocation r can have up to K local maxima with respect to c. However, if c is considered jointly with the optimal power allocation corresponding to c (Proposition 7.7 and Lemma 7.8), it is always optimal to place c in the middle of the interval $(1, K)$, as the following lemma states.

LEMMA 7.9. *If $(c, \{P_{b,k}, P_{m,k}\})$ maximizes the sum rate under high SINR approximation, then $c = \frac{K+1}{2}$.*

Even though this result may seem intuitive because the optimal power allocation is always symmetric around c (Proposition 7.7 and Lemma 7.8), the proof does not follow directly from this property and requires many technical details. For this reason, the proof is provided in [23].

A simple corollary of Lemma 7.9 is that:

COROLLARY 7.10. *If $(c^*, \{P_{m,k}^{\max}, P_{b,k}^{\max}\})$ maximizes r under high SINR approximation, then the power allocation $\{P_{m,k}^{\max}\}$ is symmetric around $\frac{K+1}{2}$ and decreasing in $|k-c|$.*

PROOF. The first part follows directly from $c^{\max} = \frac{K+1}{2}$. The proof of the second part can be found in [23] (proof of Lemma 7.9, Claim (K2)). □

LEMMA 7.11. *A solution $(c^{\max}, \{P_{m,k}^{\max}, P_{b,k}^{\max}\})$ that maximizes r under high SINR approximation up to an absolute error ϵ can be computed in $O\big(K \log\big(\frac{1}{\epsilon}\big)\big)$ time.*

PROOF. From Proposition 7.7, at the optimum $P_{b,k}^{\max} = \frac{P_{b,\max}}{K}$, $\forall k \in \{1, ..., K\}$. This can be computed in constant time, and requires $\Theta(K)$ time to assign the values to all the $P_{b,k}$'s. From Lemma 7.9, $c^{\max} = \frac{K+1}{2}$.

From Lemma 7.8, $P_{m,k}^{\max} = \alpha_k \cdot \overline{P_m}$, where $\{\alpha_k\}$ are positive coefficients given by (13), (16) and $\sum_{k=1}^{K} \alpha_k = 1$. Recall that all the α_k's are given in terms of α_K, so we can determine the allocation $\{\alpha_k\}$ by performing a binary search for α_K until $\sum_{k=1}^{K} \alpha_k \in [1-\epsilon', 1]$. Corollary 7.10 implies that $\alpha_K \leq \frac{1}{K}$, so it is sufficient to perform the binary search for α_K only within the interval $\big[0, \frac{1}{K}\big]$. Such binary search requires $O\big(\log\big(\frac{1}{K\epsilon'}\big)\big)$ iterations, with each iteration requiring $O(K)$ time to compute $\{\alpha_k\}$ and evaluate $\sum_{k=1}^{K} \alpha_k$, for the total time $O\big(K \log\big(\frac{1}{K\epsilon'}\big)\big)$.

The last part of the proof is determining an appropriate ϵ' so that $r(c^{\max}, \{P_{m,k}^{\max}, P_{b,k}^{\max}\}) \geq \max r - \epsilon$, where the maximum is taken over all feasible points $(c, \{P_{m,k}, P_{b,k}\})$. Notice that we are only deviating from the optimal solution in that $\sum_{k=1}^{K} P_{m,k}^{\max} = \overline{P_m} \cdot \sum_{k=1}^{K} \alpha_k \in [\overline{P_m}(1-\epsilon'), \overline{P_m}]$ instead of $\sum_{k=1}^{K} P_{m,k}^{\max} = \overline{P_m}$. Therefore, $(c^{\max}, \{P_{m,k}^{\max}, P_{b,k}^{\max}\})$ is the optimal solution to the problem that is equivalent to the original problem, with maximum total power at the MS equal to $\overline{P_m} \cdot \sum_{k=1}^{K} \alpha_k$. Observe that:

$$\frac{\partial r}{\partial P_m} = \sum_{k=1}^{K} \Big(\frac{1}{P_m} - \frac{1}{\frac{N_m}{g_m (k-c)^2} + P_i} \cdot \mathbb{1}_{\{k \neq c\}} \Big) \leq \frac{K}{P_m}.$$

As $\frac{\partial r}{\partial P_m}(P_m) \leq \frac{K}{\overline{P_m}(1-\epsilon')}$ for $P_m \in [\overline{P_m}(1-\epsilon'), \overline{P_m}]$, it follows that: $\max r - r(c^{\max}, \{P_{m,k}^{\max}, P_{b,k}^{\max}\}) \leq \frac{K}{\overline{P_m}(1-\epsilon')} \cdot \overline{P_m} \epsilon'$. Setting: $\frac{K}{\overline{P_m}(1-\epsilon')} \cdot \overline{P_m} \epsilon' = \epsilon \;\Leftrightarrow\; \epsilon' = \frac{\epsilon}{K+\epsilon}$, we yield the total running time of: $O\big(K \log\big(\frac{K+\epsilon}{K\epsilon}\big)\big) = O\big(K \log\big(\frac{1}{\epsilon}\big)\big)$. □

We summarize the results from this section in Algorithm 2 – HSINR-MAXIMUMRATE.

7.3 Measurement-based Numerical Evaluation

This section presents numerical evaluations for use case (iii). Numerical evaluations for use cases (i) and (ii) were already provided in Sections 5 and 6, respectively.

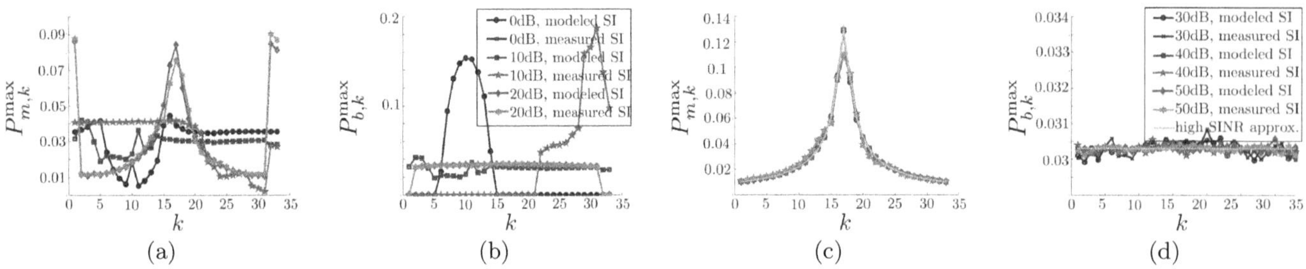

Figure 9: Power allocation over channels for SNR (a), (b) 0dB–20dB and (c), (d) 30dB–50dB. The graphs show the results obtained by running MAXIMUMRATE with measured SI and modeled SI at the input. Graphs (c) and (d) also show the power allocation computed by HSINR-MAXIMUMRATE. For SNR $\geq$ 30dB all three power allocations match closely.

Algorithm 2 HSINR-MAXIMUMRATE(ϵ)

```
Input: K, \bar{P_b}, \bar{P_m}, g_b, g_m, N_m, N_b
c^max = (K+1)/2
{P^max_{b,k}} = \bar{P_b}/K, ∀k ∈ {1, ..., K}
for α_K ∈ [0, 1/K], via a binary search do
    Compute α_k for 1 ≤ k ≤ K − 1 using (13) and (16)
    End binary search when Σ_{k=1}^{K} α_k ∈ [1 − ε/(K+ε), 1]
return c^max, {P^max_{b,k}}, {P^max_{m,k}}.
```

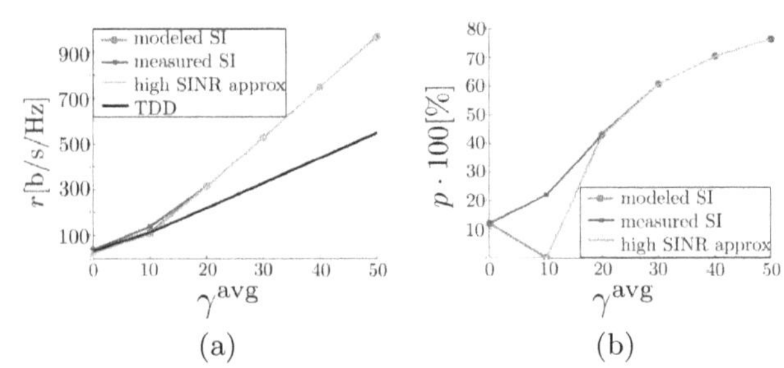

Figure 10: Evaluated (a) sum rate and (b) capacity region extension as a function of $\gamma^{\text{avg}} = \frac{h_{bm,k}\frac{1}{K}}{N_m} = \frac{h_{mb,k}\frac{1}{K}}{N_b}$. For $\gamma^{\text{avg}} \geq$ 20dB, sum rate and capacity region extension obtained from MAXIMUMRATE (both with measured and modeled SI profile) and HSINR-MAXIMUMRATE match closely.

We focus on the impact of a frequency-selective SIC profile in a small form factor hardware at the MS (Fig. 4(d)), and evaluate rate gains based on measurements and the model presented in Sections 3 and 4.1, respectively.

To determine the position $c^{\max}$ of maximum SIC and the power allocation $\{P_{m,k}^{\max}, P_{b,k}^{\max}\}$ that maximize the sum rate, we run an implementation of the MAXIMUMRATE algorithm separately for measured ([32,34] and Fig. 4(d)) and modeled (Eq. (1)) SIC profiles of the MS FD receiver. Additionally, we determine $c^{\max}, \{P_{m,k}^{\max}, P_{b,k}^{\max}\}$ for the high SINR approximation of the sum rate using HSINR-MAXIMUMRATE.

Since the measurements were performed only for the analog part of the FD receiver, we assume additional 50dB of cancellation from the digital domain.[4] Similar to [5], we assume that when either station transmits at maximum total power that is equally allocated across channels (so that $P_{m,k} = \frac{\overline{P_m}}{K}, P_{b,k} = \frac{\overline{P_b}}{K}$), the noise on each channel is 110dB below the transmitted power level.

[4]Note that Fig. 4(d) only shows isolation that results from the SIC in the analog domain.

We consider a total bandwidth of 20MHz in the range 2.13–2.15GHz, and take the distance between the measurement points as the OFDM channel width ($\approx$ 600kHz), so that there are $K = 33$ channels in the considered band. For the SIC at the BS, we take $g_b = 1$ [5].

We scale all the power variables so that $\overline{P_m} = \overline{P_b} = 1$, and normalize the SNR to the scaled values of power levels on channels. We consider flat frequency fading, and perform numerical evaluations for $\frac{h_{mb,k}}{N_b} = \frac{h_{bm,k}}{N_m} \equiv \gamma^{\text{avg}} \cdot K, \forall k$, where $\gamma^{\text{avg}} \in \{0, 10, 20, 30, 40, 50\}$ [dB].

We run MAXIMUMRATE for $\Delta c = 0.01$, which translates into an absolute error $\epsilon \approx 0.2$ for r. We evaluate the sum rate and the capacity region extension using the measurement data for the remaining SI and $c^{\max}, \{P_{m,k}^{\max}, P_{b,k}^{\max}\}$ returned by the algorithm. We assume that the SIC profile does not change as f_c (and correspondingly c) is varied. To run the algorithm for c positioned at any point between two neighboring channels, we interpolate the measurement data.

Since for the transmitted power of $1/K$ and c placed in the middle of the frequency band XINR at the first and the last channel is about 35 ($\approx$ 15dB), our numerical results suggest, as expected (see e.g., Fig. 5(b) and Fig. 6(b)), that to achieve high rate gain, γ^{avg} needs to be sufficiently high.

Fig. 9(a) and 9(b) show the power allocation at the MS and at the BS computed by MAXIMUMRATE for $\gamma^{\text{avg}} \in \{0, 10, 20\}$[dB] for measured and modeled SI. For γ^{avg} up to 10dB the algorithm selects most of the channels as half-duplex, where either $P_{m,k}^{\max} = 0$ or $P_{b,k}^{\max} = 0$. At $\gamma^{\text{avg}} =$ 20dB, all except for three channels at the edges of the frequency band are operating in FD.

Fig. 9(c) and 9(d) show the power allocation at the MS and at the BS computed by the MAXIMUMRATE algorithm for $\gamma^{\text{avg}} \in \{30, 40, 50\}$[dB] for the measured and modeled SI, and computed by the HSINR-MAXIMUMRATE algorithm for the high SINR approximation of the sum rate. In all the cases $\gamma^{\text{avg}} \in \{30, 40, 50\}$[dB] the power allocations returned by the algorithms for the measured and modeled SI and for the high SINR approximation of the sum rate match closely.

Fig. 10(a) shows the rate as a function of average SNR for $c_{\max}, \{P_{m,k}^{\max}, P_{b,k}^{\max}\}$ returned by the MAXIMUMRATE algorithm for the measured and modeled SI and returned by the HSINR-MAXIMUMRATE algorithm. Fig. 10(a) also shows the maximum TDD rate as a function of the average SNR. Fig. 10(b) shows the capacity region extension for $c_{\max}, \{P_{m,k}^{\max}, P_{b,k}^{\max}\}$ determined by the MAXIMUMRATE algorithm for the measured and modeled SI, and computed using the HSINR-MAXIMUMRATE algorithm. As suggested by Fig. 10(a) and 10(b), for low average SNR, mainly for

$\gamma^{\text{avg}} \leq 10$dB, the achievable rate improvements are low; in particular, capacity region extension is up to about 20%. (Recall from Fig. 9(a) and 9(b) that in that case most channels are selected as half-duplex by the MaximumRate.) For $\gamma^{\text{avg}} \geq 20$dB, when the power allocation is close to the high SINR approximation (see Fig. 9), more significant rate improvements are observed. In particular, for $\gamma^{\text{avg}} \geq 20$dB the capacity region extension is between 40% and 80%.

8. CONCLUSION AND FUTURE WORK

In this paper we considered three basic use cases of FD, including single- and multi-channel scenarios. In order to analyze the multi-channel scenario, we developed a new model that is grounded in realistic FD receiver implementations for small form factor devices. We characterized the rate gains in different scenarios and solved power allocation and frequency selection problems either analytically or algorithmically. Our numerical results demonstrate the gains from FD in scenarios and for receiver models that have not been studied before.

This is one of the first steps towards understanding the benefits and the complexities associated with FD. Hence, there are still many open problems to consider. In particular, SIC that has different impacts on different channels calls for the design of algorithms for OFDM networks with multiple access and MSs modeled as small form-factor devices. Moreover, we plan to develop scheduling algorithms that support the co-existence of half- and full-duplex users. While significant attention has been given to scheduling and resource allocation in half duplex OFDM networks [6,16], as demonstrated in this paper, the special characteristics of FD pose new challenges that have not been addressed.

9. ACKNOWLEDGEMENTS

This research was supported in part by the NSF grant CNS-10-54856, DARPA RF-FPGA program HR0011-12-1-0006, and the People Programme (Marie Curie Actions) of the European Union's Seventh Framework Programme (FP7/2007-2013) under REA grant agreement n°[PIIF-GA-2013-629740].11.

10. REFERENCES

[1] Skyfr-000709 miniature 2110-2170MHz single junction robust lead circulator data sheet.

[2] E. Ahmed, A. M. Eltawil, and A. Sabharwal. Rate gain region and design tradeoffs for full-duplex wireless communications. *IEEE Trans. Wireless Commun.*, 12(7):3556–3565, July 2013.

[3] E. Aryafar, M. A. Khojastepour, K. Sundaresan, S. Rangarajan, and M. Chiang. MIDU: enabling MIMO full duplex. In *Proc. ACM MobiCom'12*, 2012.

[4] J. Bai and A. Sabharwal. Distributed full-duplex via wireless side-channels: Bounds and protocols. *IEEE Trans. Wireless Commun.*, 12(8):4162–4173, Aug. 2013.

[5] D. Bharadia, E. McMilin, and S. Katti. Full duplex radios. In *Proc. ACM SIGCOMM'13*, 2013.

[6] S. C. Borst, M. G. Markakis, and I. Saniee. Distributed power allocation and user assignment in OFDMA cellular networks. In *IEEE Allerton'11*, 2011.

[7] W. Cheng, X. Zhang, and H. Zhang. Optimal dynamic power control for full-duplex bidirectional-channel based wireless networks. In *Proc. IEEE INFOCOM'13*, 2013.

[8] J. Choi, S. Hong, M. Jain, S. Katti, P. Levis, and J. Mehlman. Beyond full duplex wireless. In *Proc. IEEE Asilomar'12*, 2012.

[9] J. Choi, M. Jain, K. Srinivasan, P. Levis, and S. Katti. Achieving single channel, full duplex wireless communication. In *Proc. ACM MobiCom'10*, 2010.

[10] B. Debaillie, D.-J. van den Broek, C. Lavin, B. van Liempd, E. Klumperink, C. Palacios, J. Craninckx, B. Nauta, and A. Parssinen. Analog/RF solutions enabling compact full-duplex radios. *IEEE J. Sel. Areas Commun.*, 32(9):1662–1673, Sept 2014.

[11] M. Duarte, C. Dick, and A. Sabharwal. Experiment-driven characterization of full-duplex wireless systems. *IEEE Trans. Wireless Commun.*, 11(12):4296–4307, Dec. 2012.

[12] M. Duarte and A. Sabharwal. Full-duplex wireless communications using off-the-shelf radios: Feasibility and first results. In *Proc. IEEE Asilomar'10*, 2010.

[13] M. Duarte, A. Sabharwal, V. Aggarwal, R. Jana, K. Ramakrishnan, C. Rice, and N. Shankaranarayanan. Design and characterization of a full-duplex multiantenna system for WiFi networks. *IEEE Trans. Veh. Technol.*, 63(3):1160–1177, Mar. 2014.

[14] E. Everett, A. Sahai, and A. Sabharwal. Passive self interference suppression for full-duplex infrastructure nodes. *IEEE Trans. Wireless Commun.*, 13(2):680–694, Feb. 2014.

[15] S. Goyal, P. Liu, S. Panwar, R. DiFazio, R. Yang, J. Li, and E. Bala. Improving small cell capacity with common-carrier full duplex radios. In *Proc. IEEE ICC'14*, 2014.

[16] J. Huang, V. G. Subramanian, R. Agrawal, and R. A. B. . Downlink scheduling and resource allocation for OFDM systems. *IEEE Trans. Wireless Commun.*, 8(1):288–296, Jan. 2009.

[17] M. Jain, J. Choi, T. Kim, D. Bharadia, S. Seth, K. Srinivasan, P. Levis, S. Katti, and P. Sinha. Practical, real-time, full duplex wireless. In *Proc. ACM MobiCom'11*, 2011.

[18] A. Khandani. Two-way (true full-duplex) wireless. In *Proc. CWIT'13*, 2013.

[19] M. Khojastepour and S. Rangarajan. Wideband digital cancellation for full-duplex communications. In *Proc. IEEE Asilomar'12*, 2012.

[20] M. Khojastepour, K. Sundaresan, S. Rangarajan, X. Zhang, and S. Barghi. The case for antenna cancellation for scalable full-duplex wireless communications. In *Proc. ACM HotNets'11*, 2011.

[21] M. E. Knox. Single antenna full duplex communications using a common carrier. In *Proc. IEEE WAMICON'12*, 2012.

[22] W. Li, J. Lilleberg, and K. Rikkinen. On rate region analysis of half-and full-duplex OFDM communication links. *IEEE J. Sel. Areas Commun.*, 32(9):1688–1698, Sept. 2014.

[23] J. Marašević, J. Zhou, H. Krishnaswamy, Y. Zhong, and G. Zussman. Resource allocation and rate gains in practical full-duplex systems, Mar. 2015. arXiv preprint, `http://arxiv.org/abs/1503.08237`.

[24] J. McMichael and K. Kolodziej. Optimal tuning of analog self-interference cancellers for full-duplex wireless communication. In *IEEE Allerton'12*, 2012.

[25] T. S. Rappaport. *Wireless communications: principles and practice*, chapter 4. Prentice-Hall, 2 edition, 2002.

[26] A. Sabharwal, P. Schniter, D. Guo, D. Bliss, S. Rangarajan, and R. Wichman. In-band full-duplex wireless: Challenges and opportunities. *IEEE J. Sel. Areas Commun.*, 32(9):1637–1652, Sept. 2014.

[27] A. Sahai, S. Diggavi, and A. Sabharwal. On uplink/downlink full-duplex networks. In *Proc. IEEE Asilomar'13*, 2013.

[28] A. Sahai, G. Patel, C. Dick, and A. Sabharwal. Understanding the impact of phase noise on active cancellation in wireless full-duplex. In *IEEE Asilomar'12*, 2012.

[29] A. Sahai, G. Patel, and A. Sabharwal. Pushing the limits of full-duplex: Design and real-time implementation. *arXiv preprint arXiv:1107.0607*, 2011.

[30] N. Singh, D. Gunawardena, A. Proutiere, B. Radunovic, H. V. Balan, and P. Key. Efficient and fair MAC for wireless networks with self-interference cancellation. In *Proc. WiOpt'11*, 2011.

[31] X. Xie and X. Zhang. Does full-duplex double the capacity of wireless networks? In *Proc. IEEE INFOCOM'14*, 2014.

[32] J. Zhou, A. Chakrabarti, P. Kinget, and H. Krishnaswamy. Low-noise active cancellation of transmitter leakage and transmitter noise in broadband wireless receivers for FDD/co-existence. *IEEE J. Solid-State Circuits*, 49(12):1–17, Dec. 2014.

[33] J. Zhou, T.-H. Chuang, T. Dinc, and H. Krishnaswamy. A receiver with reconfigurable self-interference cancellation based on RF frequency-domain equalization supporting >20MHz cancellation bandwidth for FDD, co-existence and same-channel full duplex applications. In *Proc. IEEE ISSCC'15*, 2015.

[34] J. Zhou, P. R. Kinget, and H. Krishnaswamy. A blocker-resilient wideband receiver with low-noise active two-point cancellation of >0dBm TX leakage and TX noise in RX band for FDD/co-existence. In *Proc. IEEE ISSCC'14*, 2014.

Transient and Steady-state Regime of a Family of List-based Cache Replacement Algorithms

Nicolas Gast
Inria
Univ. Grenoble Alpes
CNRS, LIG, F-38000 Grenoble, France
nicolas.gast@inria.fr

Benny Van Houdt
Department of Mathematics
and Computer Science
University of Antwerp
benny.vanhoudt@uantwerpen.be

ABSTRACT

In this paper we study the performance of a family of cache replacement algorithms. The cache is decomposed into lists. Items enter the cache via the first list. An item enters the cache via the first list and jumps to the next list whenever a hit on it occurs. The classical policies FIFO, RANDOM, CLIMB and its hybrids are obtained as special cases. We present explicit expressions for the cache content distribution and miss probability under the IRM model. We develop an algorithm with a time complexity that is polynomial in the cache size and linear in the number of items to compute the exact miss probability. We introduce lower and upper bounds on the latter that can be computed in a time that is linear in the cache size times the number of items.

We further introduce a mean field model to approximate the transient behavior of the miss probability and prove that this model becomes exact as the cache size and number of items tends to infinity. We show that the set of ODEs associated to the mean field model has a unique fixed point that can be used to approximate the miss probability in case the exact computation becomes too time consuming.

Using this approximation, we provide guidelines on how to select a replacement algorithm within the family considered such that a good trade-off is achieved between the cache reactivity and its steady-state hit probability. We simulate these cache replacement algorithms on traces of real data and show that they can outperform LRU. Finally, we also disprove the well-known conjecture that the CLIMB algorithm is the optimal finite-memory replacement algorithm under the IRM model.

Categories and Subject Descriptors

D.4 [**Operating Systems**]: Storage Management ; C.4 [**Performance of Systems**]: Design studies, Modeling techniques.

SIGMETRICS'15, June 15–19, 2015, Portland, OR, USA.
Copyright is held by the owner/author(s). Publication rights licensed to ACM.
ACM 978-1-4503-3486-0/15/06 ...$15.00.
http://dx.doi.org/10.1145/2745844.2745850 .

Keywords

Cache Replacement Policies; Independent Reference Model; Storage Management; Self-organizing lists; Miss-ratio

1. INTRODUCTION

Caches are omnipresent in modern day computer systems to improve system performance. A plethora of cache replacement algorithms has been studied by various authors over the past few decades. Nevertheless, explicit expressions for the cache content distribution and miss probability under the well-known Independent Reference Model (IRM) are only available for a limited number of replacement algorithms such as FIFO, RANDOM, LRU, CLIMB and some simple hybrids thereof. Further, these results are of little practical use due to the curse of dimensionality (except for FIFO and RANDOM). As such many approximation methods have been proposed for single caches [9, 8, 13, 25, 5] as well as for networks of caches [23, 11, 26, 14, 25, 5]. While these approximations have often been shown to result in highly accurate predictions for the miss probability (under the IRM model), their theoretical support is most often rather limited. Further, these prior studies typically focus on the long term (steady state) behavior only, while the transient behavior of the miss probability is also of interest under more dynamic request patterns.

In this paper we study two broad classes of cache replacement algorithms that both organize the cache content in a number of lists (with a fixed size). Items enter the cache via the first list and are promoted to the next list whenever a hit occurs at the expense of demoting another item. The difference between the two classes of replacement algorithms exists in the manner in which the demoted item is selected. These two classes of cache replacement algorithms contain the well-known RANDOM, FIFO and CLIMB algorithm as well as some more advanced algorithms introduced in [2] as special cases.

The main contributions of the paper are as follows:

1. We show that both classes of algorithms perform alike under the IRM model by deriving an explicit expression for the cache content distribution and miss probability that is valid in both classes. We subsequently exploit this expression to devise fast algorithms to compute the exact overall and per-item miss probability, thereby avoiding the traditional curse of dimensionality. The time complexity to compute the overall miss probability is linear in the number of items and polynomial in the cache size (where the degree is equal to the number of lists used). We also derive upper and lower

bounds on the miss probability that can be computed in a time that is linear in the cache size.

2. We introduce a mean field model (for one of the two classes of replacement algorithms) that can be used to approximate the transient behavior of the miss probability under the IRM model and show that this model becomes exact as the number of items and cache size becomes infinitely large (under some mild conditions). We prove that the set of ODEs that characterizes the mean field model has a unique fixed point and demonstrate that this point can be used to get a highly accurate approximation of the miss probability whenever the exact computation becomes too time consuming.
3. We provide a number of guidelines on how to select the number of lists and list sizes by relying on various experiments using both the IRM model and trace-based simulations. These experiments demonstrate that the algorithms considered in this paper can outperform LRU. We also show that the well-known conjecture [2, page 135] that the CLIMB algorithm is the optimal finite-memory demand replacement algorithm under the IRM model is false.

The paper is structured as follows. We describe related work in Section 2. In Section 3, we describe the two classes of replacement algorithms. We derive the exact steady-state probabilities and miss probabilities as well as upper and lower bounds in Section 4. We develop our mean-field approximation and show its validity in Section 5. Finally, we provide empirical evidence on how the list sizes should be chosen in Section 6. We conclude in Section 7.

2. RELATED WORK

Cache replacement algorithms have been analyzed by various authors mostly under the well-known IRM model. While this model is not very suitable in the context of secondary memory management, it is argued by many authors to be a reasonable model in a web caching context. For instance, as stated in [7], for some purposes, one might model web accesses by a simple model that assumes independent references following a Zipf-like distribution and no correlation between request frequency and item size.

Explicit results under the IRM model for the cache content distribution and miss probability have been derived for FIFO and LRU [22, 2], RANDOM [15] and some simple hybrids thereof [1, 3]. LRU is shown to outperform FIFO in [29], while FIFO and RANDOM perform identical [15]. These expressions however can only be used directly to compute the miss probability of very small caches (e.g., 20 items). For FIFO, an algorithm to compute the exact miss probability in $O(mn)$ time is given in [10], where n is the number of items and m the cache size.

A number of approximations have been proposed to analyze caches of reasonable size. In [9] a fast iterative scheme is proposed for FIFO that coincides with the iterative algorithm proposed in [25] for RANDOM. For LRU the author of [9] introduce an $O(mn)$ time approximation, which is of limited use since the introduction of the well-known Che-approximation [8], for which theoretical support is provided in [13].

Recently, the idea of the Che-approximation was generalized to capture a broader class of replacement algorithms, both under the IRM model and in case of a renewal model [25]. While [25] also considers replacement policies that make use of multiple lists, all but these lists are assumed to be virtual lists that only store the item ids and not the actual items. Further, the algorithms are iterative in nature, but in general no proof of a unique fixed point or convergence towards a fixed point is provided. Renewal models were also considered in [21, 11, 5] for time-to-live caches which, in light of the Che-approximation, can be used to approximate capacity-driven replacement polices.

More practically oriented simulation based studies have also been performed and we do not attempt to provide an overview here. We would like to indicate that the idea of using multiple lists has been explored before, e.g., the $2Q$ and LIRS policies both combat the poor performance of LRU on *scan sequences* and typical database access patterns [20, 19].

Considerable efforts have also been made to develop approximation methods to analyze networks of caches [23, 11, 26, 14, 25, 5]. Some of these methods are iterative in nature and require the repeated solution of isolated caches, e.g., [26]. As such, studying isolated caches is useful in the study of networks of caches.

Fluid limits for the miss probability have been derived for LRU [18], 2Q [17] and RANDOM [28]. Our mean field result is more general compared to [17, 28] as these papers consider a system with Nn items, say $e_{i,j}$ with $1 \leq i \leq n$ and $1 \leq j \leq N$, such that the request probability of item $e_{i,j}$ does not depend on j, while N tends to infinity.

3. REPLACEMENTS ALGORITHMS

In this section we introduce two families of replacement algorithms that are obtained by slightly modifying a family of replacement algorithms introduced in [2]. We denote the members of this families as FIFO($\mathbf{m}$) and RAND($\mathbf{m}$), respectively, where $\mathbf{m} = (m_1, m_2, \dots, m_h)$, with $m_i \geq 1$ integer for $i = 1, \dots, h$.

The FIFO($\mathbf{m}$) replacement algorithm.

The FIFO($\mathbf{m}$) algorithm makes use of h lists, labeled 1 to h. The length of list i is equal to m_i, for $i = 1, \dots, h$, and the total cache size is equal to $m = \sum_{i=1}^{h} m_i$. Items enter the cache via list 1 and whenever hit while being part of list i they move up one list. More specifically, one of the following three events occurs when an item, say item k, is requested at some point in time:

1. Item k was not in the cache (miss) – in this case item k is inserted in position 1 of list 1. The remaining items in list 1 move back one position, while the item that was in the last position of list 1, that is, in position m_1, is removed from the cache.
2. Item k was in position j of list $i < h$ (hit) – in this case item k moves to position 1 of list $i+1$, all the items in list $i+1$ move back one position, the item that was in position m_{i+1} of list $i+1$ takes the former position of item k, that is, position j in list i.
3. Item k was part of list h (hit) – in this case no changes are made.

The RAND($\mathbf{m}$) replacement algorithm.

The RAND($\mathbf{m}$) algorithm operates in a manner similar to the FIFO($\mathbf{m}$) algorithm, except for two changes. First, when a miss occurs the item is inserted in a *random* position in list 1 (as opposed to position 1) and the item that was in this randomly selected position is removed from the cache. Second, when a hit occurs on an item part of list $i < h$, say in position j, the item is inserted in a *random* position in list $i+1$, while the item that was in this randomly selected position moves to position j of list i. In other words, only two items change position in case a hit in list $i < h$ occurs.

We will shown that the FIFO($\mathbf{m}$) and RAND($\mathbf{m}$) algorithm have the same steady state distribution for the cache content under the IRM model, which is a generalization of the well-known fact that FIFO and RANDOM perform alike under the IRM model [15]. In fact, one can even show that the steady state probabilities of FIFO($\mathbf{m}$) remain the same if we do not update the cache when a hit occurs unless the item hit is in the first position of some list i, for $i = 1, \ldots, h-1$.

A natural extension of these policies is to consider the two following variants: strict FIFO($\mathbf{m}$) and LRU($\mathbf{m}$):

- *strict FIFO($\mathbf{m}$)* – The difference between strict FIFO($\mathbf{m}$) and FIFO($\mathbf{m}$) is when a hit occurs on an item that is in position j of a list $i < h$. As before, item k moves to position 1 of list $i+1$ and all the items in list $i+1$ move back one position. The difference is that the item that was in position m_{i+1} of list $i+1$ moves to position 1 of list i and the items that were in position 1 to $j-1$ of list i move back one position.
- *LRU($\mathbf{m}$)* – The only difference between LRU($\mathbf{m}$) and strict FIFO($\mathbf{m}$) is when a hit occurs in position j of list h. In this case, this item is moved to the first position of list h and all the items in the positions 1 to $j-1$ of list h move back one position.

The strict FIFO($\mathbf{m}$) algorithm corresponds to the policy $\mathcal{A}^h_{m_h}(m_h, \ldots, m_1)$ of [2], while the LRU($\mathbf{m}$) algorithm is denoted as $\mathcal{A}^h_1(m_h, \ldots, m_1)$ in [2]. Note that the lists in [2] are labeled in the opposite order. The FIFO($\mathbf{m}$) and the strict FIFO($\mathbf{m}$) algorithms operate identical when $m_1 = \ldots = m_{h-1} = 1$. For this special case, closed-form results for the steady-state probabilities for the strict FIFO($\mathbf{m}$) algorithm under the IRM model were also derived in [2].

Although these algorithms are close to our definition of FIFO($\mathbf{m}$), simple closed-form expressions for the cache content distribution and miss probabilities do not appear to exist. In Section 6, we compare all these policies using trace-based simulation. We demonstrate that the hit probabilities of strict FIFO($\mathbf{m}$) and FIFO($\mathbf{m}$) are close to each other (unless m_1 is close to m), while LRU($\mathbf{m}$) outperforms these policies only marginally (at the expense of slightly more work).

4. STEADY STATE PROBABILITIES

Let $Y_{i,j}(t)$, with $(i,j) \in \mathcal{I}(\mathbf{m}) \triangleq \{(i,j)|i = 1, \ldots, h, j = 1, \ldots, m_i\}$, be the id of the item in position j of list i at time t, where we observe the cache whenever a request arrives. Let $\mathcal{C}_n(m)$ consists of all the sequences $(c_1, \ldots, c_m)$ of m distinct integers taken from the set $\{1, \ldots, n\}$. Under the IRM model the process $\mathbf{Y} = \{(Y_{i,j}(t), (i,j) \in \mathcal{I}(\mathbf{m})), t \geq 0\}$ is clearly a Markov chain on the state space $\mathcal{C}_n(m)$ for the FIFO($\mathbf{m}$) and RAND($\mathbf{m}$) algorithms. Denote $\pi_{\mathrm{A}}(\mathbf{c})$, with $\mathbf{c} = (c_1, \ldots, c_m)$, as the steady state probability of state $\mathbf{c}$, where A = FIFO($\mathbf{m}$) or RAND($\mathbf{m}$) denotes the replacement algorithm used.

To ease the notation denote $c_{\sum_{s=1}^{i-1} m_s + j}$ as $c(i,j)$ for $(i,j) \in \mathcal{I}(\mathbf{m})$, where we can think of $c(i,j)$ as the id of the item in position j at list i. The next theorem shows that the steady state probabilities of this Markov chain have a simple closed form for the FIFO($\mathbf{m}$) or RAND($\mathbf{m}$) algorithm:

THEOREM 1. *The steady state probabilities $\pi_{RAND(\mathbf{m})}(\mathbf{c})$ and $\pi_{FIFO(\mathbf{m})}(\mathbf{c})$, with $\mathbf{c} \in \mathcal{C}_n(m)$, can be written as*

$$\pi_{FIFO(\mathbf{m})}(\mathbf{c}) = \pi_{RAND(\mathbf{m})}(\mathbf{c}) =$$

$$\pi(\mathbf{c}) \triangleq \frac{1}{Z(\mathbf{m})} \prod_{i=1}^{h} \left(\prod_{j=1}^{m_i} p_{c(i,j)} \right)^i, \qquad (1)$$

where $Z(\mathbf{m}) = \sum_{\mathbf{c} \in \mathcal{C}_n(m)} \prod_{i=1}^{h} \left(\prod_{j=1}^{m_i} p_{c(i,j)} \right)^i$.

The proof consists in verifying the balance equations. It is detailed in Appendix A.

When $h = 1$ and $\mathbf{c} = (c_1, \ldots, c_m)$ we get

$$\pi(\mathbf{c}) = \frac{1}{Z(\mathbf{m})} \prod_{j=1}^{m} p_{c_j}.$$

These are the well-known steady state probabilities for the FIFO and RANDOM algorithm [22, 15]. When $h = m$, meaning m_i=1 for all i, the RAND($\mathbf{m}$) algorithm coincides with the so-called TRANSPOSITION rule or CLIMB algorithm [27, 16]. In this case the above theorem reduces to

$$\pi(\mathbf{c}) = \frac{1}{Z(\mathbf{m})} \prod_{j=1}^{m} p_{c_j}^j,$$

which are the steady state probabilities of the CLIMB algorithm as reported in [2, Section 4.2]. Theorem 1 also generalizes the results for the second family of replacement algorithms studied in [1] which corresponds to $m_1 = \ldots = m_{h-1} = 1$

$$\pi(\mathbf{c}) = \frac{1}{Z(\mathbf{m})} \prod_{j=1}^{m} p_{c_j}^{\min(j,h)}.$$

Due to Theorem 1 it is easy to check that the following corollary holds:

COROLLARY 1. *For the RAND($\mathbf{m}$) replacement algorithm the Markov chain $\mathbf{Y}$ is reversible,* i.e.,

$$\pi(\mathbf{c})\mathbf{P}[Y(t+1) = \mathbf{c}'|Y(t)=\mathbf{c}] = \pi(\mathbf{c}')\mathbf{P}[Y(t+1) = \mathbf{c}|Y(t)=\mathbf{c}'],$$

for any $\mathbf{c}, \mathbf{c}' \in \mathcal{C}_n(m)$.

Denote the hit probability of the RAND($\mathbf{m}$) and FIFO($\mathbf{m}$) algorithms as $H(\mathbf{m})$ and let $M(\mathbf{m}) = 1 - H(\mathbf{m})$ be the miss probability under the IRM model. Clearly, one can express the miss probability via the steady state probabilities

$$M(\mathbf{m}) = \sum_{\mathbf{c} \in \mathcal{C}_n(m)} \left(1 - \sum_{i=1}^{h} \sum_{j=1}^{m_i} p_{c(i,j)} \right) \pi(\mathbf{c}). \qquad (2)$$

This formula is however not very useful to compute $M(\mathbf{m})$, unless m is very small, as the number of terms is exponential in m. In the next two sections we indicate how to compute the overall and per item miss probability in a more efficient manner.

4.1 Exact overall miss probability

In this section we introduce Algorithm 1 that computes the steady-state miss probability in a time that is polynomial in the cache size m, where the degree of the polynomial is equal to h. This algorithm is a generalization of the methodology introduced in [10] for the FIFO algorithm (which corresponds to the case with $h = 1$). It uses a dynamic programming approach: to compute $M(\mathbf{m})$, we compute $M(\mathbf{m}')$ for any $\mathbf{m}' \leq \mathbf{m}$ (component-wise). In other words, the quantities $M(\mathbf{m}')$ are obtained as by-products of the computation of $M(\mathbf{m})$. Obtaining these quantities is useful when studying optimal list sizes. More precisely, define a first set of miss probabilities $\mathcal{M}_h^{\leq m} = \{M(m_1 \dots m_k) | k \leq h, m_i \leq m, \sum_{i=1}^{h'} m_i \leq m\}$ and a second set of miss probabilities $\mathcal{M}_h^{m_1 \dots m_h} = \{M(m'_1 \dots m'_k) | k \leq h, m'_i \leq m_i\}$. Our algorithm computes the set $\mathcal{M}_h^{\leq m}$ in $O(nh^2 m^h / h!)$ time and the set $\mathcal{M}_h^{m_1 \dots m_h}$ in $O(nh^2 \prod_{i=1}^h (m_i + 1))$ time. In the next section, we show how to compute the corresponding per item hit probabilities in $O(n^{3/2} h^2 m^h / h!)$ and $O(n^{3/2} h^2 \prod_{i=1}^h (m_i + 1))$ time, respectively.

Let $p_1, \dots, p_n$ be a *fixed* but arbitrary ordering of the request probabilities and $\mathbf{r} = (r_1, \dots, r_h)$ with r_i integer for all i and $r = \sum_i r_i$. Let $\mathbf{e}_j$ be the j-th row of the size h identity matrix. Define $E(\mathbf{0}, k) = 1$, $E(\mathbf{r}, k) = 0$ if $\sum_i r_i > k$ or $r_j < 0$ for some j and

$$E(\mathbf{r}, k) = \sum_{\mathbf{c} \in \mathcal{C}_k(r)} \prod_{i=1}^{h} \left(\prod_{j=1}^{r_i} p_{c(i,j)} \right)^i. \tag{3}$$

By using (2) we can express $M(\mathbf{m})$ via $E(\mathbf{r}, k)$:

$$M(\mathbf{m}) = \sum_{\mathbf{c} \in \mathcal{C}_n(m)} \left(\sum_{k \notin \mathbf{c}} p_k \right) \pi(\mathbf{c}) = \frac{E(\mathbf{m} + \mathbf{e}_1, n)}{E(\mathbf{m}, n)}.$$

Further, we have the following recursion for $E(\mathbf{r}, k)$ by noting that item k appears at most once in $\mathbf{c}$:

$$E(\mathbf{r}, k) = E(\mathbf{r}, k-1) + \sum_{j=1}^{h} r_j p_k^j E(\mathbf{r} - \mathbf{e}_j, k-1). \tag{4}$$

In principle we can use this recursion with $E(\mathbf{e}_j, 1) = p_1^j$ to compute the miss probabilities. However, $E(\mathbf{r}, k)$ decreases quickly in $\sum_i r_i$ and can easily cause underflows even for m values below 100 (as in [10] for the FIFO replacement policy). To avoid this problem, we define for $i = 1, \dots, h$:

$$F_i(\mathbf{r}, k) = \frac{E(\mathbf{r}, k)}{E(\mathbf{r} - \mathbf{e}_i, k)}, \tag{5}$$

for $\mathbf{r} = (r_1, \dots, r_h)$ with $r_j \geq 0$ for $j \neq i$ and $r_i \geq 1$. Let $F_i(\mathbf{r}, k) = 0$ if $\sum_i r_i > k$ or $r_j < 0$ for some j or $r_i \leq 0$. Note that the miss probability $M(\mathbf{m})$ equals

$$M(\mathbf{m}) = F_1(\mathbf{m} + \mathbf{e}_1, n).$$

The next theorem establishes a recursive relationship for the $F_i(\mathbf{r}, k)$ values that allows us to compute the miss probabilities without causing underflows.

THEOREM 2. *The miss probability $M(\mathbf{m}) = F_1(\mathbf{m} + \mathbf{e}_1, n)$ and the quantities $F_i(\mathbf{r}, k)$, for $i = 1, \dots, h$, $\mathbf{r} = (r_1, \dots, r_h)$ with $r_j \geq 0$ for $j \neq i$ and $r_i \geq 1$, obey the following recursion*

$$F_i(\mathbf{r}, k) = \frac{F_i(\mathbf{r}, k-1) + \sum_{j=1, j\neq i}^{h} p_k^j r_j \frac{F_i(\mathbf{r} - \mathbf{e}_j, k-1)}{F_j(\mathbf{r} - \mathbf{e}_i, k-1)} + p_k^i r_i}{1 + \sum_{j=1, j \neq i}^{h} \frac{p_k^j r_j}{F_j(\mathbf{r} - \mathbf{e}_i, k-1)} + \frac{p_k^i (r_i - 1) \mathbf{1}_{\{r_i > 1\}}}{F_i(\mathbf{r} - \mathbf{e}_i, k-1)}}, \tag{6}$$

and $F_i(\mathbf{e}_i, 1) = p_1^i$.

Input: The vectors $\mathbf{p}$ and $\mathbf{m}$
Output: The set $\mathcal{M}_h^{\leq m}$

for $i, j = 1$ *to* h **do**
  $F_j(\mathbf{e}_i, 1) = \mathbf{1}_{\{i=j\}} p_1^i$;
end
for $k = 1$ *to* n **do**
  for $\mathbf{r} \in \mathcal{R}_{\min(k, m+1), h}$ **do**
    for $i = 1$ *to* h **do**
      compute $F_i(\mathbf{r}, k)$ via (6);
    end
  end
end
for $M(\mathbf{m}) \in \mathcal{M}_h^{\leq m}$ **do**
  set $M(\mathbf{m}) = F_1(\mathbf{m} + \mathbf{e}_1, n)$
end

Algorithm 1: Algorithm to compute the overall miss probabilities in the set $\mathcal{M}_h^{\leq m}$.

PROOF. By applying (4) on the numerator and denominator of (5) we get that $F_i(\mathbf{r}, k)$ can be written[1] as

$$\frac{E(\mathbf{r}, k-1) + \sum_{j=1}^{h} p_k^j r_j E(\mathbf{r} - \mathbf{e}_j, k-1)}{E(\mathbf{r} - \mathbf{e}_i, k-1) + \sum_{j=1}^{h} p_k^j (r_j - \mathbf{1}_{\{i=j\}}) E(\mathbf{r} - \mathbf{e}_i - \mathbf{e}_j, k-1)}.$$

By dividing the numerator and denominator by $E(\mathbf{r} - \mathbf{e}_i, k-1)$ (which is well defined as $r_i > 0$ and differs from zero as $\sum_s r_s - 1 \leq k - 1$), we find

$$F_i(\mathbf{r}, k) = \frac{F_i(\mathbf{r}, k-1) + \sum_{j=1, j\neq i}^{h} p_k^j r_j \frac{E(\mathbf{r} - \mathbf{e}_j, k-1)}{E(\mathbf{r} - \mathbf{e}_i, k-1)} + p_k^i r_i}{1 + \sum_{j=1, j \neq i}^{h} \frac{p_k^j r_j}{F_j(\mathbf{r} - \mathbf{e}_i, k-1)} + \frac{p_k^i (r_i - 1) \mathbf{1}_{\{r_i > 1\}}}{F_i(\mathbf{r} - \mathbf{e}_i, k-1)}}.$$

The result follows by noting that $E(\mathbf{r} - \mathbf{e}_j, k-1) / E(\mathbf{r} - \mathbf{e}_i, k-1)$ can be written as $F_i(\mathbf{r} - \mathbf{e}_j, k-1) / F_j(\mathbf{r} - \mathbf{e}_i, k-1)$ when $r_j > 0$. □

Denote $\mathcal{R}_{k,h}$ as the set $\{(r_1, \dots, r_h) | r_i \in \{0, \dots, k\}, 1 \leq \sum_{i=1}^h r_i \leq k\}$. Algorithm 1 indicates how to use the above theorem to compute the values of $F_i(\mathbf{r}, k)$ for $i = 1, \dots, h$, $k \leq n$ and $\mathbf{r} \in \mathcal{R}_k$ in $O(nh^2 |\mathcal{R}_{m+1,h}|)$ time with $|\mathcal{R}_{m+1,h}| = O(m^h / h!)$. In other words we can determine the set of miss probabilities $\mathcal{M}_h^{\leq m}$ in $O(nh^2 m^h / h!)$ time, where n is the number of items. Similarly, one can compute the miss probabilities in the set $\mathcal{M}_h^{m_1, \dots, m_h}$ in $O(nh^2 \prod_{i=1}^h (m_i + 1))$ time.

For the CLIMB algorithm we have $m_1 = \dots = m_h = 1$ and $h = m$, meaning the miss probability can be computed in $O(nm^2 2^m)$ time, which is still exponential in m, but clearly a significant gain over directly relying on (2).

4.2 Per item miss probabilities

In this section we focus on the hit probability of item k, denoted as $H^{(k)}(\mathbf{m})$, for $k = 1, \dots, n$. We first show how to express $M^{(k)}(\mathbf{m}) = 1 - H^{(k)}(\mathbf{m})$ in terms of $F_i(\mathbf{m}, n-1)$. Recall that the items $p_1, \dots, p_n$ in the previous subsection were ordered in an arbitrary, but *fixed* order. To express $M^{(k)}(\mathbf{m})$ in terms of $F_i(\mathbf{m}, n-1)$, we order the items such that item k, with request probability p_k, is the *last* item. Thus, we need to recompute the $F_i(\mathbf{m}, n-1)$ values for each item k and we denote these values as $F_i^{(k)}(\mathbf{m}, n-1)$. A direct application of this result would therefore leads to

[1]We use the notation $\mathbf{1}_{\{i=j\}}$ equals 1 if $i = j$ and 0 otherwise.

an algorithm with a time complexity $O(n^2)$. We further indicate how to reduce this to an algorithm in $O(n^{3/2})$.

THEOREM 3. *The item k miss probability $M^{(k)}(\mathbf{m})$ is*

$$M^{(k)}(\mathbf{m}) = \frac{1}{1+\sum_{i=1}^{h}\frac{p_k^i m_i}{F_i^{(k)}(\mathbf{m},n-1)}},$$

if $\sum_{i=1}^h m_i < n$ *and* $M^{(k)}(\mathbf{m}) = 0$ *otherwise.*

PROOF. The hit probability of item k is identical to the steady state probability that item k is in the cache

$$M^{(k)}(\mathbf{m}) = 1 - \sum_{i=1}^{h}\sum_{j=1}^{m_i}\sum_{\mathbf{c}\in\mathcal{C}_n(m),c(i,j)=k}\pi(\mathbf{c}).$$

Let $E^{(k)}(\mathbf{r},k)$ be defined as $E(\mathbf{r},k)$ with the requirement that the items are ordered such that item k is in the last position. By means of (1), (3) and (4) we find

$$M^{(k)}(\mathbf{m}) = 1 - \frac{\sum_{i=1}^h p_k^i m_i E^{(k)}(\mathbf{m}-e_i,n-1)}{E(\mathbf{m},n)} \tag{7}$$

$$= \frac{1}{E^{(k)}(\mathbf{m},n-1)+\sum_{i=1}^h p_k^i m_i E^{(k)}(\mathbf{m}-e_i,n-1)}.$$

If $\sum_{i=1}^h m_i \geq n$, $E^{(k)}(\mathbf{m},n-1)$ and $M^{(k)}(\mathbf{m}) = 0$ (as all items fit in the cache), otherwise $E^{(k)}(\mathbf{m},n-1)$ differs from zero and the result follows from dividing the numerator and denominator by $E^{(k)}(\mathbf{m},n-1)$. □

Note that p_k has to be the last item in the order when computing the $F_i^{(k)}(\mathbf{r},n-1)$ values based on Theorem 2, thus for each k we must use a different order. However, it is also clear that if we only change the order of the last s items, the values of $F_i(\mathbf{r},n-s)$ do not change.

To take advantage of this observation, we partition the set of items $\{1,\ldots,n\}$ into $\sqrt{n}$ sets $S_1,\ldots,S_{\sqrt{n}}$ each holding $\sqrt{n}$ items (for ease of presentation we assume that n is a square). To compute the hitting probabilities of the item k belonging to set S_j, we fix the order such that all the items *not* belonging to S_j appear first (in an arbitrary fixed order), followed by an arbitrary order of items of S_j with k as the last item. Thus, the computation of the $F_i(\mathbf{r},n-\sqrt{n})$ values, with $r_i\in\{0,1,\ldots,m\}$ and $\sum_i r_i \leq m$, is identical for all the items belonging to S_j and takes $O(nh^2m^h/h!)$ time, while computing the $F_i(\mathbf{m},n-1)$ values from the $F_i(\mathbf{r},n-\sqrt{n})$ values takes $O(\sqrt{n}h^2m^h/h!)$ time for each item in S_j. This results in an overall time complexity of

$$\sqrt{n}\cdot\left[O(\frac{nh^2m^h}{h!})+\sqrt{n}\cdot O(\frac{\sqrt{n}h^2m^h}{h!})\right] = O(\frac{n^{3/2}h^2m^h}{h!}),$$

which is a significant gain over $O(n^2h^2m^h/h!)$ if the number of items n is large.

For $h=1$ we have $H^{(k)}(m) = p_k m/(p_k m + F_1^{(k)}(m,n-1))$ and the above algorithm to compute the per item hit probabilities has a time complexity of $O(mn^{3/2})$. An efficient algorithm to compute the per item hit probabilities of the RANDOM and FIFO scheme appears to be novel as [10] only considered the overall hit probabilities.

THEOREM 4. *For any* $\mathbf{m}$*, under the algorithms FIFO(*$\mathbf{m}$*) and RAND(*$\mathbf{m}$*),* $p_k > p_\ell$ *implies that* $M^{(k)}(\mathbf{m}) < M^{(\ell)}(\mathbf{m})$*, that is, more popular items have lower miss probabilities.*

policy	m	$M(\mathbf{m})$	lower bound
Optimal	RAND(1,1,4)	0.005284	0.004925
	RAND(1,1,3,1)	0.005299	0.004884
	RAND(1,1,2,2)	0.005317	0.004884
	RAND(1,1,2,1,1)	0.005321	0.004879
	RAND(1,1,1,3)	0.005338	0.004884
	RAND(1,1,1,2,1)	0.005343	0.004879
	RAND(1,1,1,1,2)	0.005347	0.004879
CLIMB	RAND(1,1,1,1,1,1)	0.005348	0.004878
	RAND(1,2,3)	0.005428	0.004925
	RAND(1,2,2,1)	0.005439	0.004884
LRU	LRU(6)	0.005880	–
RANDOM	RAND(6)	0.015350	0.015350

Table 1: CLIMB is not optimal for IRM model: $p = (49,49,49,49,7,1,1)/205$ **and** $m=6$**.**

The proof is given in Appendix B. It is a generalization of [32, Lemma 5] which established the same result for the CLIMB algorithm, that is, when $m_1=\ldots=m_h=1$.

4.3 Upper and lower bounds on the overall miss probability

In the previous subsections we developed fast algorithms to compute the overall and per item miss probabilities of the FIFO(**m**) and RAND(**m**) algorithm. In this section we present a lower and upper bound on the overall miss probability. Compared to Algorithm 1, that leads to an algorithm that is exponential in h, these bounds can be computed in a $O(mn)$ time (linear in the number of items times the cache size). The upper bound coincides with the miss probability of the original FIFO and RANDOM schemes.

THEOREM 5. *The miss ratio* $M(\mathbf{m})$ *of the FIFO(*$\mathbf{m}$*) and RAND(*$\mathbf{m}$*) algorithm is upper bounded by*

$$M(\mathbf{m}) \leq F_1((m+1)\mathbf{e}_1,n) = M_{\text{FIFO}}(\mathbf{m}),$$

and lower bounded by

$$F_1(\mathbf{e}_1+m\mathbf{e}_h,n) = \frac{\sum_{\mathbf{x}\in C_n(m)}\left(\prod_{j=1}^m p_{x_j}^h\right)(1-\sum_{j=1}^m p_{x_j})}{\sum_{\mathbf{x}\in C_n(m)}\left(\prod_{j=1}^m p_{x_j}^h\right)}$$

with $m=\sum_{i=1}^h m_i$*.*

These bounds can be computed in $O(mn)$ *time.*

The proof is given in Appendix C.

4.4 CLIMB is not optimal

Theorem 5 shows that the RANDOM algorithm achieves the worst performance (*i.e.*, the highest miss rate) for the class of RAND(**m**) algorithms with $\sum_i m_i = m$ under the IRM model. Hence, it is tempting to conjecture that separating a list into two smaller lists improves the performance and that the CLIMB algorithm, that is, having m lists of size 1, achieves the lowest miss rate within this class. In [2, p135] an even stronger conjecture is presented that states that CLIMB is optimal under the IRM model for all finite-memory demand replacement algorithms.

Figure 1 shows that both conjectures are false. The popularity distribution is $\mathbf{p} = (49,49,49,49,7,1,1)/205$ and the cache has a size $\sum_i m_i = 6$. Figure 1 lists the ten vectors $\mathbf{m}$ with $\sum_i m_i = 6$ that achieve the lowest miss probability $M(\mathbf{m})$, together with their corresponding $M(\mathbf{m})$ value.

For comparison, we also show the performance of RANDOM and LRU. This shows that CLIMB is not optimal. It further indicates that when fixing the number of lists h, the optimal choice for the length of each list is not necessarily setting $m_1 = \ldots = m_{h-1} = 1$: for instance, $\mathbf{m} = (1, 1, 3, 1)$ is better than $\mathbf{m} = (1, 1, 1, 3)$. This demonstrates that another of the *natural* conjectures formulated in [2, p135] is also false.

4.5 Miss probability is not Schur concave

A related question is whether the miss probability is a Schur-concave[2] function of the popularity distribution $\mathbf{p} = (p_1, \ldots, p_n)$ for the class of algorithms RAND($\mathbf{m}$). If the miss probability were Schur-concave, it would imply that putting more weight on the most popular items decreases the miss probability. The authors of [30] proved that the miss probability of the RANDOM algorithm, *i.e.*, when $h = 1$, is Schur-concave, which is almost immediate from [24, p80].

It is shown in the more recent paper [31] that the miss probability of the CLIMB algorithm is not a Schur-concave function of $\mathbf{p}$ by providing a simple counter-example with $m = 3$. We make use of the same example to demonstrate that a counter-example also exist for RAND($\mathbf{m}$) with $h = 2$. We consider the popularity distributions $\mathbf{p}_1 = (0.45, 0.45, 0.05, 0.05)$ and $\mathbf{p}_2 = (.75, .15, 0.05, 0.05)$ ($\mathbf{p}(x_1)$ is majorized by $\mathbf{p}(x_2)$). For p_1, the miss probability is $M(1, 2) = 0.05835$ while it is $M(1, 2) = 0.05994$ for p_2. This implies that $M(1, 2)$ is not a Schur-concave function of $\mathbf{p}$.

4.6 Number of lists

In this section we investigate the potential reduction in the miss probability by making use of multiple lists. To this end Figure 1 depicts the lower bounds established in Theorem 5 for various h values as a function of the cache size m when $n = 3000$ and $\mathbf{p}$ follows a Zipf-like distribution with $\alpha = 0.8$, that is, $p_i = A/i^\alpha$, where A is the normalizing constant. Furthermore, we also plotted the miss probability M($\mathbf{m}$) of the RAND($\mathbf{m}$) algorithm when $m_1 = \ldots = m_{h-1} = 1$.

The main conclusions are that these lower bounds appear to be very sharp under a Zipf-like workload (with $\alpha = 0.8$ and $n = 3000$ items). Second, the figure demonstrates that there is little room for further reducing the miss probability by using more than $h = 10$ lists. Most of the gain can be obtained by implementing a limited number of lists. This will be confirmed in Section 6 using trace-based simulations.

5. MEAN FIELD APPROXIMATION

In this section we develop an ODE approximation for the RAND($\mathbf{m}$) policy. We show that this approximation becomes exact as the number of items and the cache size tends to infinity. This approximation allows us to study fast and accurately the transient behavior of the RAND($\mathbf{m}$) algorithm. We use it to compute the time to fill an empty cache in Section 6. It can also be used to obtain a fast approximation of the steady-state miss probability, when the cache size or the number of lists make Algorithm 1 too time consuming.

5.1 Derivation of the equations and intuition

At a given time step t, item k is either part of some list $i \in \{1, \ldots, h\}$ or is not in the cache. If an item is not in the cache, we say that it is part of list 0. For an item $k \in \{1 \ldots n\}$ and a list $i \in \{0 \ldots h\}$, we define the random variables $X_{k,i}(t)$, where $X_{k,i}(t)$ equals 1 if the item k is part of list i at time t and 0 otherwise. The probability that item k is in list i at time t is $\mathbf{E}[X_{k,i}(t)]$.

Our mean-field approximation of the RAND($\mathbf{m}$) algorithm boils down to assuming that the evolution of two items is independent of each other. We approximate $\mathbf{E}[X_{k,i}(t)]$ by a deterministic quantity $x_{k,i}(t)$. The initial conditions of the ODE are $x_{k,i}(0) = 1$ if the item k is in the ith list of the cache at time $t = 0$ and 0 otherwise. Let $(x_{k,i}(t))_{k,i}$ be the unique[3] solution of the following set of ODEs, for $k \in \{1 \ldots n\}, i \in \{1 \ldots h\}$:

$$\dot{x}_{k,i}(t) = p_k x_{k,i-1}(t) - \sum_j p_j x_{j,i-1}(t) \frac{x_{k,i}(t)}{m_i} + \mathbf{1}_{\{i<h\}} \left(\sum_j p_j x_{j,i}(t) \frac{x_{k,i+1}(t)}{m_{i+1}} - p_k x_{k,i}(t) \right), \quad (8)$$

where $\mathbf{1}_{\{i<h\}}$ is equal to 1 if $i < h$ and 0 otherwise.

This equation can be understood as follows. Assume that item k is in list $i \in \{0 \ldots h-1\}$ at time t. With probability p_k, item k is requested and moves to list $i + 1$. With probability $H_{i-1}(t) = \sum_j p_j X_{j,i-1}(t)$, an item from list $i - 1$ is requested and is exchanged with an item from list i chosen at random. This item is item k with probability $1/m_i$. Hence, with probability $H_{i-1}(t)/m_i$, item k moves to list $i - 1$. If the list in which item k is and the variables $H_i(t)$ were independent, the behavior of item k would be described by a Markov chain whose transition matrix is represented in Figure 2.

If the probability p_k is small and the list sizes m_i, for $i = 1, \ldots, h$, are large, this Markov chain is well approximated by a continuous time Markov chain. If all items

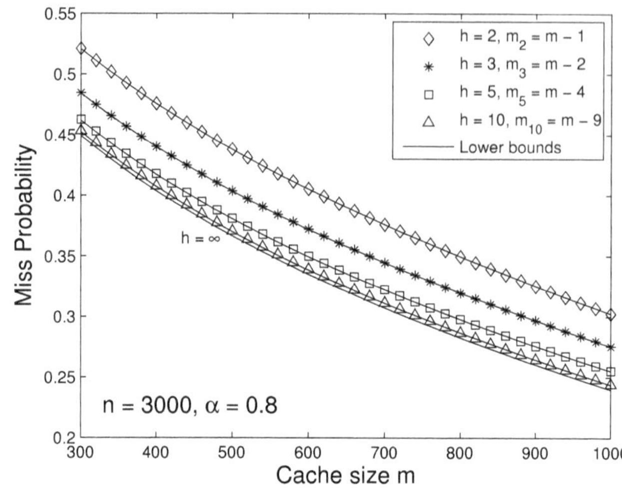

Figure 1: Lower bounds for $h = 2, 3, 5, 10$ and ∞ and the miss rate M(m) with $m_1 = \ldots = m_{h-1} = 1$ for $h = 2, 3, 5$ and 10 as a function of the cache size m, with $n = 3000$ and $\alpha = 0.8$.

[2] A function is Schur-concave if $\mathbf{p}$ majorizes $\mathbf{p}'$, implies that the miss probability is lower for $\mathbf{p}$ than for $\mathbf{p}'$.

[3] It should be clear that this ODE is Lipschitz-continuous and hence has a unique solution. Moreover, with the initial conditions indicated, the solution of the ODE satisfy that, for all time t: $\sum_{k=1}^n x_{k,i}(t) = m_i$ and $\sum_{i=0}^h x_{k,i}(t) = 1$.

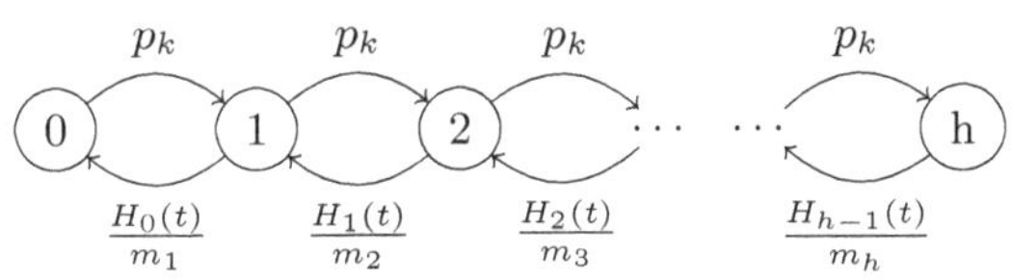

Figure 2: Evolution of the list in which item k is. When p_k is small and the m_is are large, the state of one item becomes independent of the hit rate in each box and its behavior can be approximated by a time-inhomogeneous continuous-time Markov chain. This is the mean-field approximation.

evolve independently, this leads to the mean-field approximation given by Equation (8). In the next section, we establish a theoretical result, Theorem 6, that guarantees that, as the cache size grows, the transient hit probability can indeed be described by the ODE (8). The accuracy of this mean field approximation is validated in Sections 5.4 and 6.1, where we compare simulation results and a numerical integration of the ODE.

5.2 Proof of the validity of the approximation

Let $H_i(t) = \sum_{k=1}^{n} p_k X_{k,i}(t)$ be the sum of the popularities of the items that are part of the ith list of the cache at time t and $H_0(t) = 1-\sum_{i=1}^{h} H_i(t)$ be the miss probability at time t. Let $\delta_i(t) = \sum_k p_k x_{k,i}(t)$, where $x_{k,i}(t)$ is the unique solution of ODE (8), with initial conditions $x_{k,i}(0) = X_{k,i}(0)$.

THEOREM 6. *For any $T > 0$, there exists a constant $C > 0$ that depends on T such that, for any probability distribution over n items and list sizes $m_1 \dots m_h$, we have:*

$$\mathbf{E}\left[\sup_{t\in\{0\dots\tau\},i\in\{0\dots h\}} |H_i(t)-\delta_i(t)|\right] \le C\sqrt{\max_{k=1}^{n} p_k + \max_{i=0}^{h}\frac{1}{m_i}},$$

where $\tau := \lceil T/(\max_{k=1}^{n} p_k + \max_{i=0}^{h}\frac{1}{m_i})\rceil$.

In particular, Theorem 6 implies that the ODE approximation becomes exact as the cache size goes to infinity and the probability of each item goes to 0. This results can be seen as a generalization of [28] for two reasons. First, [28] only considers the RANDOM policy, that is, RAND($\mathbf{m}$) with $h = 1$. More importantly, [28] assumed that there were a finite number of classes of items with an infinite number of items per class. Our results is more general as we assume any distribution for $\mathbf{p}$.

In fact, we believe that this result can also be extended to show that the ODE approximation becomes exact as the caches size goes to infinity, even if the probability of some items do not go to 0 (as it is the case for a Zipf distribution with $\alpha > 1$). Assume that item k has a probability $p_k \gg 1/m_h$. In such a case, as shown of Figure 2, the item k will quickly enter list h by having been hit multiple times, but will only exit list h with probability $O(1/m_h) \ll p_k$. We believe a result similar to Theorem 6 can therefore be obtained by separating the behavior of the popular and non-popular items.

PROOF. Let $a = \max_k p_k$ and $b = \max_i 1/m_i$. Recall that $X_{k,i}(t)$ is equal to 1 if item k is in the ith list of the cache at time t and 0 otherwise. For any $\alpha \in \mathbf{Z}^+$, and $i \in \{0\dots h\}$, we define $H_{i,\alpha}(t) = a^{1-\alpha}\sum_k (p_k)^\alpha X_{k,i}(t)$.

Let $\mathcal{H}$ be the set of infinite vectors $(\delta_{i,\alpha})_{i\in\{0\dots h\},\alpha\in\{1,2\dots\}}$ where $\delta_{i,\alpha} = a^{1-\alpha}\sum_k (p_k)^\alpha x_{k,i}$ for some $(x_{k,i})_{k,i}$ such that $\sup_{i,k}|x_{k,i}| < \infty$. We equip $\mathcal{H}$ with the ℓ_∞ norm: $\|h\|_\infty = \sup_{i,\alpha}|h|$ and define $\mathcal{H}_{\le 1}$ the set of $h\in\mathcal{H}$ such that $\|h\|_\infty \le 1$.

We define the function $f : \mathcal{H} \to \mathcal{H}$ by, for all $\delta \in \mathcal{H}$:

$$\begin{aligned} f_{i,\alpha}(\delta) &= a\delta_{i-1,\alpha+1}(t) - \frac{\delta_{i-1,1}(t)\delta_{i,\alpha}(t)}{m_i} \\ &\quad + \mathbf{1}_{\{i<h\}}\left(\frac{\delta_{i,1}(t)\delta_{i+1,\alpha}(t)}{m_{i+1}} - a\delta_{i,\alpha+1}(t)\right), \end{aligned} \tag{9}$$

where $\mathbf{1}_{\{i<h\}}$ equals 1 if $i < h$ and 0 otherwise.

To prove the result we rely on the following lemma, the proof of which is postponed to Appendix D.

LEMMA 1. *Let $(\mathcal{F}_t)$ be the filtration associated with process of the $(X_{k,i}(t))_{k,i}$, then:*

(i) $f(H(t))$ is the average variation of $H(t)$:

$$\mathbf{E}\left[H(t+1) - H(t)|\mathcal{F}_t\right] = f(H(t)) \tag{10}$$

(ii) the second moment is bounded:

$$\mathbf{E}\left[\|H(t+1) - H(t)\|_\infty^2 |\mathcal{F}_t\right] \le 2a^2 \tag{11}$$

(iii) there exists a constant L independent of the p_ks and the m_is such that the function f is Lipschitz-continuous of constant $L(a+b)$ on $\mathcal{H}_{\le 1}$, where $a = \max_k p_k$ and $b = \max_i 1/m_i$.

(iv) If $x_{k,i}(t)$ is the unique solution of ODE (8), with initial conditions $x_{k,i}(0) = X_{k,i}(0)$, then the infinite vector δ, defined by $\delta_{i,\alpha}(t) = a^{1-\alpha}\sum_k (p_k)^\alpha x_{k,i}(t)$ is the unique solution of $\dot\delta = f(\delta)$, that is:

$$\delta(t) = H(0) + \int_0^t f(\delta(s))ds.$$

Let $\bar H$ denote the continuous function equal to $H(t)$ when $t \in \mathbf{Z}^+$ and linear between t and $t+1$. A straightforward computation shows that for all $t \in \mathbf{Z}^+$: $H(t) \in \mathcal{H}_{\le 1}$ and that $\mathcal{H}_{\le 1}$ is convex. Hence, for all $t > 0$: $\bar H(t) \in \mathcal{H}_{\le 1}$.

Let $M(t) := \sum_{s=0}^{t-1} H(s+1) - H(s) - f(H(s))$. We have

$$\begin{aligned} \bar H(t) &= H(0) + \sum_{s=0}^{t-1} f(H(s)) + M(t) \\ &= H(0) + \int_{s=0}^t f(H(\lfloor s\rfloor))ds + M(t) \\ &= H(0) + \int_{s=0}^t f(\bar H(s))ds + M(t) \\ &\quad + \int_0^t \left(f(H(\lfloor s\rfloor)) - f(\bar H(s))\right)ds. \end{aligned} \tag{12}$$

Equation (9) implies that for $h \in \mathcal{H}_{\le 1}$, $\|f(h)\|_\infty \le 2(a+b)$. Hence, $\left\|H(\lfloor s\rfloor) - \bar H(s)\right\|_\infty \le 2(a+b)(\lfloor s\rfloor - s)$, which by Lemma 1*(iii)* implies that

$$\begin{aligned} \int_{s=0}^t \left\|f(H(\lfloor s\rfloor)) - f(\bar H(s))\right\|_\infty ds &\le tL(a+b)\int_0^1 2(a+b)sds \\ &= L(a+b)^2 t. \end{aligned}$$

Combined with (12) and Lemma 1*(iv)*, for $t < \tau$, this shows that $\left\|\bar H(t) - \delta(t)\right\|_\infty$ is less than

$$\int_0^t \left\|f(\bar H(s)) - f(\delta(s))\right\|_\infty ds + L(a+b)^2 t + \sup_{t\le\tau}\|M(t)\|_\infty,$$

which, by Lemma 1*(iii)* and Grönwall's lemma implies that $\sup_{t\leq\tau}\left\|\bar{H}(t)-\delta(t)\right\|_\infty$ is less than

$$\left(L(a+b)^2\tau+\sup_{t\leq\tau}\|M(t)\|_\infty\right)\exp(L(a+b)\tau) \qquad (13)$$

Moreover, by Lemma 1*(ii)*, we have $\mathbf{E}\left[\|M(\tau)\|_\infty^2\right]\leq 2a^2\tau$. By Lemma 1*(i)*, $M(t)$ is a martingale. Therefore, this implies that $\mathbf{E}\left[\sup_{t\leq\tau}\|M(t)\|_\infty\right]\leq a\sqrt{2\tau}\leq(a+b)\sqrt{2\tau}$. Replacing τ by $T/(a+b)$, Equation (13) is smaller than: $(LT(a+b)+\sqrt{a+b}\sqrt{2T})\exp(LT)$. By construction, $a+b\leq 2$, which implies that $a+b\leq\sqrt{2}\sqrt{a+b}$. Thus, setting $C=\sqrt{2}(LT+\sqrt{T})\exp(LT)$ gives the result. □

5.3 Steady-state behavior

Theorem 6 justifies the fact that the ODE is an approximation of the transient behavior of the hit probability of the original system. We now use this approximation to obtain a fixed-point equation for the steady-state hit probabilities. When $h=1$ this equation is identical to the one introduced in [9] for FIFO and used in [25] for the RANDOM algorithm.

The next theorem shows that the mean field approximation of our system, given by the ODE (8) has a unique fixed point. As indicated by [4], having a unique fixed-point is not, in general, a sufficient condition to show that the steady-state of the stochastic system concentrates on this point. In our case due to Corollary 1 the stochastic process of RAND($\mathbf{m}$) is reversible and for reversible processes that converge to an ODE [6] showed that the stationary measure of a reversible process concentrates on the fixed point of the ODE. Although we cannot directly apply the result of [6] to our setting, we expect that a similar argument can be used. As RAND($\mathbf{m}$) and FIFO($\mathbf{m}$) have the same steady-state hit probability, this fixed-point provides a very efficient numerical method to compute the steady-state performance of both policies.

THEOREM 7. *The mean-field model (8) has a unique fixed point. For this fixed point, the probability that item k is part of list i, for $k=1,\dots,n$ and $i=0,\dots,h$, is given by*

$$x_{k,i}=\frac{p_k^i z_i}{1+\sum_{j=1}^h p_k^j z_j},$$

where $\mathbf{z}=(z_1,\dots,z_h)$ is the unique solution of the equation

$$\sum_{k=1}^n\frac{p_k^i z_i}{1+\sum_{j=1}^h p_k^j z_j}=m_i. \qquad (14)$$

PROOF. Let $(x_{k,i})_{k,i}$ be a fixed point of the ODE (8) and let $H_{i-1}=\sum_{j=1}^n p_j x_{j,i-1}$ be the corresponding hit probability in box $i-1$. The fixed-point equations are:

$$p_k x_{k,i-1}-\frac{H_{i-1}}{m_i}x_{k,i}+\mathbf{1}_{\{i<h\}}\left(\frac{H_i}{m_{i+1}}x_{k,i+1}-p_k x_{k,i}\right)=0$$

As these equations correspond to the fixed-point equation of the birth-and-death process described in Figure 2, we have

$$x_{k,i}=\frac{p_k^i m_1\dots m_i}{H_0\dots H_{i-1}}x_{k,0}$$

Let $z_i=\prod_{j=0}^{i-1}m_{j+1}/H_j$ for $i\in\{1\dots h\}$. By using that $\sum_{i=0}^h x_{k,i}=1$, this implies that $x_{k,i}=p_k^i z_i/(1+\sum_{j=1}^h p_k^j z_j)$.

By using that $\sum_{k=1}^n x_{k,i}=m_i$, this yields

$$m_i=\sum_{k=1}^n x_{k,i}=\sum_{k=1}^n\frac{p_k^i z_i}{1+\sum_{j=1}^h p_k^j z_j} \qquad (15)$$

We now show that Equation (15) has a unique solution. For a vector $\mathbf{z}=(z_1\dots z_h)\in(\mathbf{R}^+)^h$, we define $D_i(\mathbf{z})$, for $i=1,\dots,h$, by

$$D_i(\mathbf{z})=\sum_{k=1}^n\frac{p_k^i z_i}{1+\sum_{j=1}^h p_k^j z_j}=\sum_{k=1}^n\frac{p_k^i}{1/z_i+\sum_{j=1}^h p_k^j z_j/z_i}$$

The function $D_i(\mathbf{z})$ is increasing in z_i and decreasing in z_j for $j\neq i$.

For a vector $\mathbf{z}=(z_1,\dots,z_h)$, $i\in\{1,\dots,h\}$ and $y>0$, we denote $\mathbf{z}_{-i}(y)$ the vector whose coordinates are all equal to the ones of $\mathbf{z}$ except for the ith one which is equal to y. $D_i(\mathbf{z}_{-i}(y))$ is increasing in y. Hence, the equation $D_i(\mathbf{z}_{-i}(y))=m_i$ has a unique solution that we denote $G_i(\mathbf{z})$ (it should be clear that, by definition, $G_i(\mathbf{z})$ does not depend on z_i). Moreover, as $D_j(\mathbf{z})$ is decreasing in z_j for $j\neq i$, $G_i(\mathbf{z})$ is increasing in z_j, for all $j\neq i$. This shows that G is increasing (componentwise) in $\mathbf{z}$: if for all i, $z_i\leq z'_i$, then for all i: $G_i(\mathbf{z})\leq G_i(\mathbf{z}')$.

We define the sequence $\mathbf{z}^t$ by $\mathbf{z}^0=(0,\dots,0)$ and $\mathbf{z}^{t+1}=G(\mathbf{z}^t)$ for $t\geq 0$. As $G(\mathbf{z})$ is componentwise increasing in $\mathbf{z}$, the sequence $\mathbf{z}^t$ is increasing. Moreover, by using that $\mathbf{z}=\mathbf{z}_{-i}^t(z_i^t)$ and $m_i=D_i(\mathbf{z}_{-i}^t(z_i^{t+1}))$, we have:

$$D_i(\mathbf{z}^t)=D_i(\mathbf{z}_{-i}^t(z_i^t))\leq D_i(\mathbf{z}_{-i}^t(z_i^{t+1}))=m_i$$

where the inequality from the fact that z_i^t is increasing in t and $D_i(\mathbf{z})$ is increasing in z_i. This shows for all t:

$$n-\sum_{i=1}^h m_i\leq n-\sum_{i=1}^h D_i(\mathbf{z}^t)=\sum_{k=1}^n\frac{1}{1+\sum_{j=1}^h p_k^j z_j^t},$$

which implies that the sequence $\mathbf{z}^t$ is bounded. As this sequence is increasing, it converges to a fixed point of G.

We now prove the uniqueness. Let $\lambda>1$. If we multiply all coordinates of $\mathbf{z}$ by λ, the $D(\lambda\mathbf{z})$ becomes:

$$\begin{aligned}D_i(\lambda\mathbf{z})&=\sum_{k=1}^n\frac{p_k^i z_i\lambda}{(1+\sum_{j=1}^h p_k^j z_j\lambda)}\\&=\sum_{k=1}^n\frac{p_k^i z_i}{(1/\lambda+\sum_{j=1}^h p_k^j z_j)}\\&>D_i(\mathbf{z}).\end{aligned}$$

This implies that $G_i(\lambda z)<\lambda G_i(\mathbf{z})$.

The function G satisfies the assumptions of a standard interference function I of [33], which, by [33, Theorem 2], implies that the fixed point of G is unique and that the iterations $\mathbf{z}^{t+1}=G(\mathbf{z}^t)$ converge, regardless of $\mathbf{z}^0$. □

5.4 Numerical algorithm and validation

The proof of Theorem 7 is based on the construction of an iterative scheme $\mathbf{z}^{t+1}=G(\mathbf{z}^t)$ that converges to the unique fixed point given by Equation (14). This iteration provides an efficient method to compute the fixed-point, as it converges exponentially fast to the fixed point and each iteration takes $O(nh)$ time, that is, is linear in the number of items times the number of lists. This is clearly a significant

α	n	m_1	m_2	exact	mean field
0.8	300	2	98	0.3466	0.3470
		30	70	0.3608	0.3612
		98	2	0.4239	0.4245
0.8	3000	20	980	0.3034	0.3035
		300	700	0.3159	0.3160
		980	20	0.3723	0.3724
1.1	300	2	98	0.1719	0.1722
		30	70	0.1832	0.1835
		98	2	0.2362	0.2367
1.1	3000	20	980	0.1110	0.1110
		300	700	0.1183	0.1183
		980	20	0.1531	0.1531

Table 2: Mean field model validation for $h = 2$ with Zipf-like popularity distributions.

m_1	m_2	m_3	m_4	exact	mean field
2	2	96	-	0.3166	0.3169
10	30	60	-	0.3296	0.3299
20	2	78	-	0.3273	0.3276
90	8	2	-	0.4094	0.4100
1	4	10	85	0.3039	0.3041
5	15	25	55	0.3136	0.3139
25	25	25	25	0.3345	0.3348
60	2	2	36	0.3514	0.3517

Table 3: Mean field model validation for $h = 3$ and $h = 4$ with $n = 300$ and a Zipf-like popularity distribution with $\alpha = 0.8$.

improvement over the $O(nhm^h/h!)$ time complexity of Algorithm 1, used to compute exact hit probabilities, especially for large cache size and/or a large number of lists.

In Tables 2 and 3, we compare the steady-state miss probabilities given by the mean-field approximation with the exact values given by Algorithm 1. The popularity distribution follows a Zipf-like distribution of parameter 0.8 or 1.1. These tables contain the results for various values of $\mathbf{m}$. We observe that, in all cases, the approximation is within 1% of the exact value. This holds even when the lists are small or with highly non-uniform distributions (Zipf with $\alpha > 1$).

When the number of lists exceeds five, the execution time of Algorithm 1 becomes prohibitive (it grows as m^h). We therefore compare the mean-field model with values obtained by simulation for $h = 10$ in Table 4. We show the results for various popularity models (Zipf 0.5 to Zipf 1.4) and diverse lists sizes: all lists have the same size ($m_i = 30$), increasing sizes ($m_i = 10i$ or $\mathbf{m} = (10, \dots, 10, 50, \dots, 50)$), varying ($m_i = 30 - (i-5)^2$), decreasing sizes ($m_i 8(11-i)$) or alternating ($\mathbf{m} = (80, 8, 80, 8 \dots)$). In all cases, the mean-field approximation was computed almost instantaneously on a regular laptop while the time to obtain our simulation results was several hours. The accuracy of the transient behavior of the ODE approximation is discussed in Section 6.1.

α	m_i	simul	mean field
0.5	30	.50113 ± .00011	.50116
0.75	$10 + 40 \cdot \mathbf{1}_{\{i>5\}}$	.32307 ± .00002	.32310
0.8	$10i$	.15836 ± .00003	.15838
0.9	$30 - (i-5)^2$	.29437 ± .00003	.29439
1.1	$8(11-i)$	.09412 ± .00007	.09417
1.4	$8 + 72 \cdot \mathbf{1}_{\{i \text{ is odd}\}}$	.02504 ± .00001	.02504

Table 4: Mean field model validation for $h = 10$ lists with $n = 1000$ and a Zipf-like popularity distribution based on 5 simulation runs.

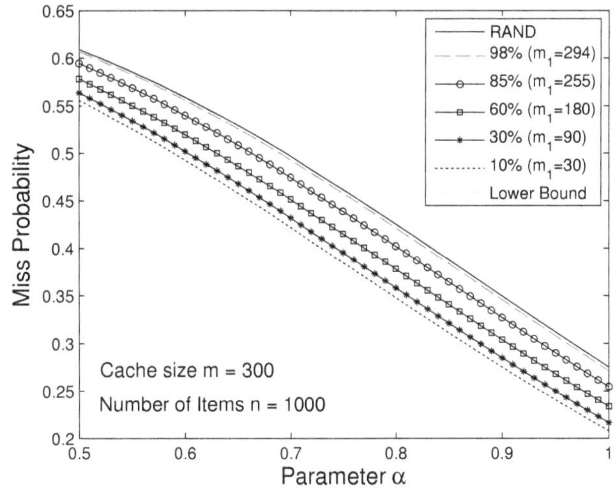

Figure 3: Impact of parameter α of the Zipf-like distribution on the miss probability $M(m_1, m_2)$, with $n = 1000$ and $m = 300$.

6. NUMERICAL RESULTS AND GUIDELINES

In this section, we wish to formulate some guidelines on how to select the number of lists and the list sizes m_1 to m_h. We first focus on the IRM model and study the trade-off between time to fill the cache and miss probability. We then explore traces of real data.

6.1 IRM model and time to fill the cache

In Figure 3 we study the impact of the size m_1 of the first list on the miss probability when $h = 2$, $m = 300$, $n = 1000$ and the popularity distribution $\mathbf{p}$ follows a Zipf-like distribution with α ranging from 0.5 to 1. The figure indicates that there is no need to make the size m_1 of the first list extremely small in order to have a miss probability that is close to the lower bound. This is important as we will show next that small m_1 values make it harder for items that suddenly become popular to enter the cache.

To this end, we study the transient behavior of the hit probability under the IRM model starting from an empty cache by making use of the mean field model (with $H_0(t) = 1$). We also validate the accuracy of the mean field model to capture the transient regime by plotting the corresponding simulation results (averaged over 5 or 25 runs to reduce the noise). Figure 4 shows the transient behavior of the hit probability as a function of the number of requests received under the IRM model with a Zipf-like popularity distribution with $\alpha = 0.5$ for $h = 2$ lists, $m = 200$, $n = 1000$ and various values for the size of the first list m_1. The figure indicates that the mean field model and the simulation based results are in perfect agreement. Further, as expected, it demonstrates that while decreasing m_1 improves the steady state hit probability (which is in agreement with Figure 3),

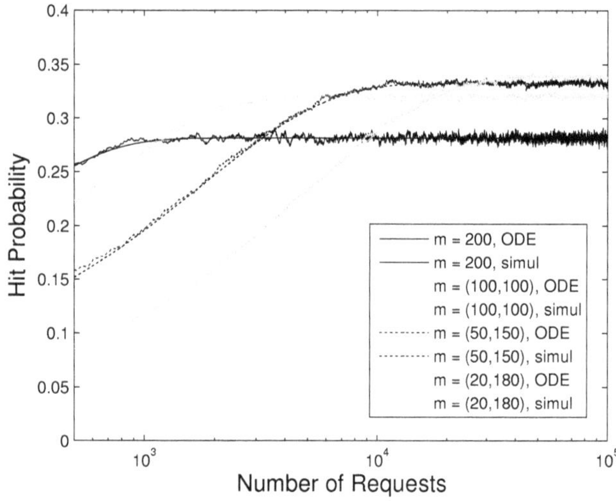

Figure 4: Evolution of the hit probability starting from an empty cache with $n = 1000$ and $\alpha = 0.5$. Simulation is based on 25 runs.

the time to reach the steady state increases as a function of m_1. Assigning a sufficient portion of the overall cache size, to the first list gives a significant increase in the hit probability while having a limited impact on the cache reactivity.

To obtain more insights on the time to fill the cache, let us focus on the case when $\mathbf{p}$ is a uniform distribution. In this case, the mean-field approximation (8) simplifies to

$$\dot{x}_i(t) =$$
$$\frac{x_{i-1}(t)}{n} - \frac{x_{i-1}(t)x_i(t)}{m_i} + \mathbf{1}_{\{i<h\}}\left(\frac{x_i(t)x_{i+1}(t)}{m_{i+1}} - \frac{x_i(t)}{n}\right).$$

When $m_1 \ll n$, items enter the first list at rate $1/n$ and leave it at rate $1/m_1$. This leads to $x_1(t) \approx (m_1/n)(1 - \exp(-t/m_1))$: the time to fill the first list is proportional to m_1. When list i contains x items, these items jump to

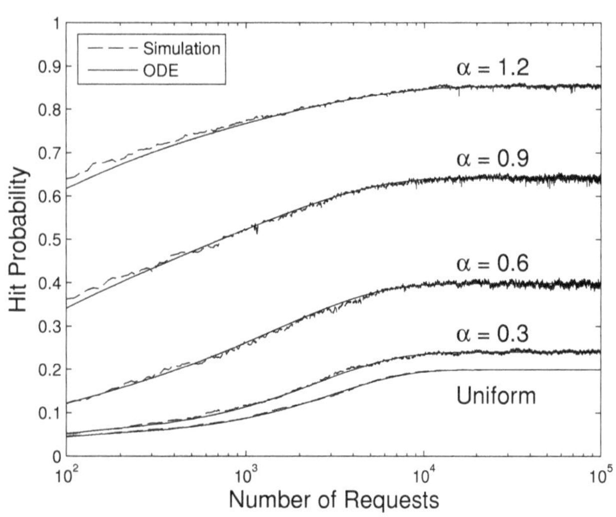

Figure 5: Evolution of the hit probability starting from empty cache with $n = 1000$ and $\mathbf{m} = (50, 150)$. Simulation is based on 5 runs.

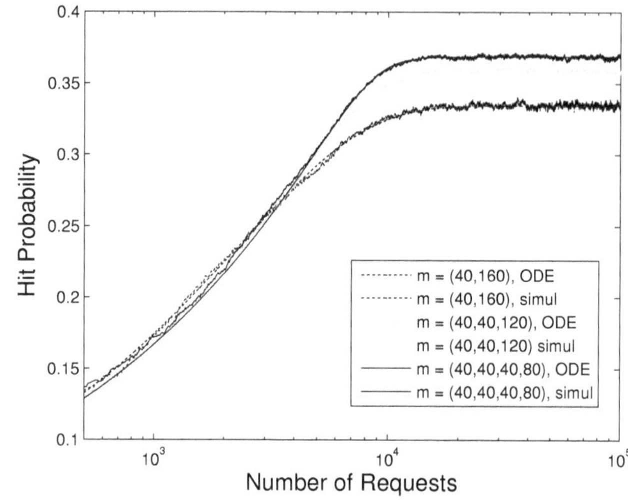

Figure 6: Evolution of the hit probability starting from empty cache with $n = 1000$ and $\alpha = 0.5$. Simulation is based on 25 runs.

the next list at rate x/n. This suggests that the time to fill the lists 2 to h is roughly proportional to $n(m_2/m_1 + m_3/m_2 + \cdots + m_h/m_{h-1})$. Hence, a natural choice is to set $m_1 = m_2 = \cdots = m_h$, which results in a total time to fill the cache of $1/m_1 + n(m - m_1)/m_1$.

Although this analysis only works for a uniform distribution, we show in Figure 5 that the impact of the parameter α of the Zipf-like popularity distribution $\mathbf{p}$ on time to reach the steady state hit probability is limited. This figure shows the hit probability as a function of the number of requests for $n = 1000$ items and $\mathbf{m} = (50, 150)$. Similarly, we depict the transient hit probability when $m_1 = 40$ for $h = 2, 3$ and 4 lists Figure 6. The main message of this figure is that the time to reach the steady state hit probability does not depend much on the list sizes m_2 to m_h. Hence, instead of working with just two lists, one can improve the steady state hit probability by relying on multiple lists without affecting the reactivity of the cache when the size of each of the lists is at least as large as the first one.

6.2 Trace-based simulations

To validate the insights obtained by studying the IRM model, we perform trace-based simulations using a publicly available YouTube trace that was collected at a campus network during a 14 day period in 2008 [34, Trace T5]. This trace contains a total of 611,968 requests for 303,331 different videos, meaning that, if we start with an initially empty cache, the miss probability is at least $303,331/611,968 \approx 0.496$ even if the cache has infinite capacity. Further, about 65.9% of these videos were requested only once during the trace, meaning the request pattern is quite different from the IRM model. We selected this particular trace among the ones discussed in [34] as it is by far the longest one.

We developed a simulation program for the FIFO($\mathbf{m}$), RAND($\mathbf{m}$), strict FIFO($\mathbf{m}$) and LRU($\mathbf{m}$) algorithms discussed in Section 3, for the scenario where the campus network relies on a single proxy cache. As only HTML-based control messages are available for trace T5, we have no information on the size of the requested videos. We therefore

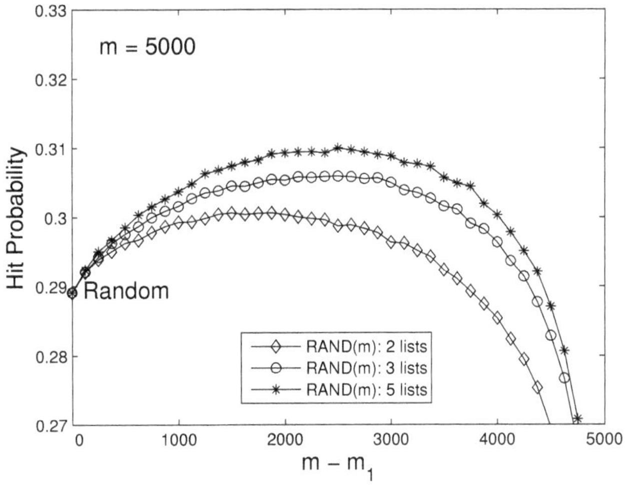

Figure 7: Trace-based hit probability of RAND(m) with $m_i = (m - m_1)/(h-1)$ for $i = 2, \ldots, h$ and $\sum_i m_i = 5000$.

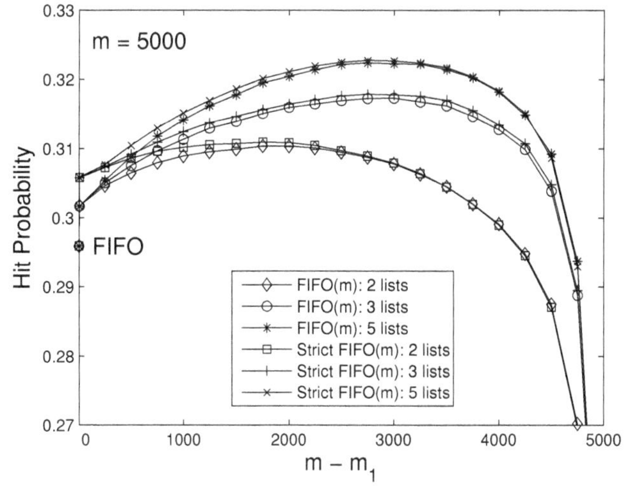

Figure 8: Trace-based hit probability of FIFO(m) and strict FIFO(m) with $m_i = (m - m_1)/(h - 1)$ for $i = 2, \ldots, h$ and $\sum_i m_i = 5000$.

assumed (for all the policies) that the cache size is expressed in the number of videos m that can be stored in the proxy cache (the average size of a video should be a few Mbyte). This should not impact the results much if the correlation between video popularity and video size is small.

When comparing the different replacement policies, we varied the size of the first list m_1 and divided the remaining cache capacity equally among the remaining $h-1$ lists. Figures 7 to 9 depict the hit probability as a function of the cache capacity assigned to list 2 to h when the total cache capacity is $m = 5000$ videos and we make use of $h = 2, 3$ or 5 lists. The following insights are provided by these figures. While the FIFO($\mathbf{m}$) and RAND($\mathbf{m}$) algorithm perform alike under the IRM model, RAND($\mathbf{m}$) results in a lower hit probability when using real data, as expected. The strict FIFO($\mathbf{m}$) and FIFO($\mathbf{m}$) algorithm do however perform very similar, especially if enough capacity is assigned to list 2 to h. The LRU($\mathbf{m}$) algorithm does outperform FIFO($\mathbf{m}$) when using two or three lists, but the gain becomes very limited when using $h = 5$ lists. We also note that FIFO($\mathbf{m}$) clearly outperforms a pure LRU cache.

In all cases, the hit probability is maximal when about 30 to 60% of the cache capacity is assigned to the first list. It quickly deteriorates as the size of the first list becomes small. This observation is in line with the earlier observation that the time to fill the cache is larger for small values of m_1, that make it harder to insert new items into the cache.

The increase in the hit probability as a function of the number of lists is the most pronounced when h is small, which is in agreement with earlier observations under IRM. In fact, further increasing the number of lists beyond 10 causes a decrease in the hit probability, mostly because the sizes of the lists 2 to h become small, making it harder to insert new items in the cache.

Both strict FIFO($\mathbf{m}$) and FIFO($\mathbf{m}$) exhibit a jump in the hit probability as soon as we add a second list, even if this list can only store a single item. For strict FIFO($\mathbf{m}$) this can be easily understood as the second list allows an item that is hit repeatedly to move to the front of the cache. In particular, strict FIFO$(m-1, 1)$ behaves very similar to a pure LRU, that is known to outperform pure FIFO [29]. The same happens to a lesser extent for FIFO($\mathbf{m}$), but items now move to a random position in the first list when being demoted. Still, on average it allows popular items that are in the back of the cache to move away from the back of the cache. RAND($\mathbf{m}$) does not exhibit such a behavior as being at the front or back in the first list makes no difference.

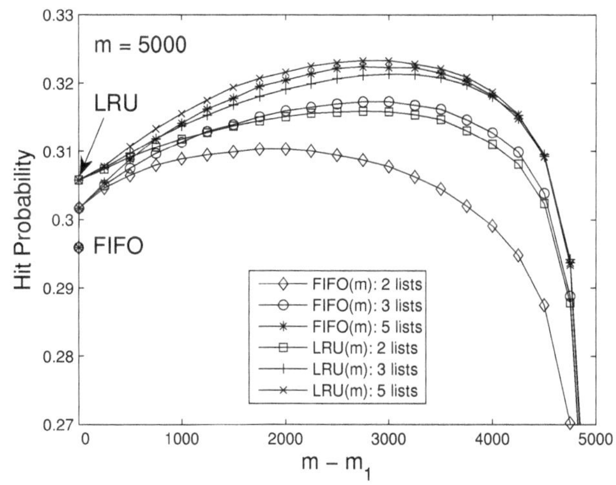

Figure 9: Trace-based hit probability of FIFO(m) and LRU(m) with $m_i = (m - m_1)/(h-1)$ for $i = 2, \ldots, h$ and $\sum_i m_i = 5000$.

7. CONCLUSION

In this paper, we studied a family of cache replacement algorithms FIFO($\mathbf{m}$) and RAND($\mathbf{m}$). We provided close-form results for the steady-state probabilities under the IRM model, as well as a polynomial algorithm to compute the steady-state miss probabilities. We further developed a mean-field approximation that provides a fast and accurate method for approximating the miss probabilities. We used this approximation to study the transient behavior of the cache and to provide guidelines of how to tune the number of lists and the list sizes. This suggests that the first few lists should be large enough and have equal sizes. By using these insights, we verify on real traces of cache requests that these policies perform well and can outperform other classical heuristics such as FIFO or LRU.

A direct extension of this work would be to consider a network of caches, by using the model of [11]. We also aim at obtaining close-form expression for the steady-state probabilities or the time to fill the cache when the distribution is Zipf(α) or develop an approximation for studying the transient behavior of FIFO($\mathbf{m}$) or the steady-state of LRU($\mathbf{m}$).

8. ACKNOWLEDGMENT

This work is partially supported by the EU project QUANTICOL, 600708.

APPENDIX

A. PROOF OF THEOREM 1

We start with the RAND($\mathbf{m}$) algorithm.

Denote $\mathbf{c}_{(i,j)\leftrightarrow(i',j')}$ as the vector $\mathbf{c}$ with $c(i,j)$ and $c(i',j')$ exchanged and $\mathbf{c}_{k\to(i,j)}$ as the vector $\mathbf{c}$ with entry $c(i,j)$ replaced by k. Using these notations we can express the global balance equation of state $\mathbf{c}$ as

$$\pi_{\text{RAND}(\mathbf{m})}(\mathbf{c})\left(1-\sum_{j=1}^{m_h} p_{c(h,j)}\right) = \sum_{k\neq c_1,\ldots,c_m}\sum_{u=1}^{m_1}\pi_{\text{RAND}(\mathbf{m})}(\mathbf{c}_{k\to(1,u)})\frac{p_{c(1,u)}}{m_1} + \sum_{i=1}^{h-1}\sum_{u=1}^{m_i}\sum_{v=1}^{m_{i+1}}\pi_{\text{RAND}(\mathbf{m})}(\mathbf{c}_{(i,u)\leftrightarrow(i+1,v)})\frac{p_{c(i+1,v)}}{m_{i+1}},$$

as we exit state $\mathbf{c}$ unless there is a hit on one of the entries in list h, while we can enter state $\mathbf{c}$ because there is a miss (and some item is inserted in a random position in list 1) or there is a hit on an item in list i that moves up to a random position at list $i+1$. Implicitly plugging in (1) and noting that $\pi(\mathbf{c}_{(i,u)\leftrightarrow(i+1,v)})/\pi(\mathbf{c}) = p_{c(i,u)}/p_{c(i+1,v)}$ and $\pi(\mathbf{c}_{k\to(1,u)})/\pi(\mathbf{c}) = p_k/p_{c(1,u)}$ holds for (1), yields

$$1-\sum_{j=1}^{m_h} p_{c(h,j)} = \sum_{k\neq c_1,\ldots,c_m} p_k + \sum_{i=1}^{h-1}\sum_{u=1}^{m_i} p_{c(i,u)},$$

which clearly holds as $\sum_{i=1}^n p_i = 1$.

For FIFO($\mathbf{m}$), let the vector $\mathbf{c}_{\text{miss}(k)}$ be identical to $\mathbf{c}$ except that $(c_{\text{miss}(k)}(1,1),\ldots,c_{\text{miss}(k)}(1,m_1))$ is equal to $(c(1,2),\ldots,c(1,m_1),k)$ and denote $\mathbf{c}_{\text{hit}(i,j)}$ as the vector $\mathbf{c}$ except that $(c_{\text{hit}(i,j)}(i+1,1),\ldots,c_{\text{hit}(i,j)}(i+1,m_{i+1})) = (c(i+1,2),\ldots,c(i+1,m_1),c(i,j))$ and $c_{\text{hit}(i,j)}(i,j) = c(i+1,1)$, then

$$\pi_{\text{FIFO}(\mathbf{m})}(\mathbf{c})\left(1-\sum_{j=1}^{m_h} p_{c(h,j)}\right) = \sum_{k\neq c_1,\ldots,c_m}\pi_{\text{FIFO}(\mathbf{m})}(\mathbf{c}_{\text{miss}(k)})p_{c(1,1)} + \sum_{i=1}^{h-1}\sum_{j=1}^{m_i}\pi_{\text{FIFO}(\mathbf{m})}(\mathbf{c}_{\text{hit}(i,j)})p_{c(i+1,1)}.$$

The result follows by noting that $\pi(\mathbf{c}_{\text{miss}(k)})/\pi(\mathbf{c}) = p_k/p_{c(1,1)}$ and $\pi(\mathbf{c}_{\text{hit}(i,j)})/\pi(\mathbf{c}) = p_{c(i,j)}/p_{c(i+1,1)}$ holds for (1).

B. PROOF OF THEOREM 4

PROOF. Due to (7), $M^{(k)}(\mathbf{m}) < M^{(\ell)}(\mathbf{m})$ is equivalent to

$$\sum_{i=1}^h p_\ell^i m_i E^{(\ell)}(\mathbf{m}-e_i,n-1) - \sum_{i=1}^h p_k^i m_i E^{(k)}(\mathbf{m}-e_i,n-1) < 0,$$

If we order the first $n-1$ entries in both cases such that items k and ℓ are in the last two positions and we use Equation (4), the above rewrites as

$$\begin{aligned}&\sum_{i=1}^h p_\ell^i m_i\Bigg(E(\mathbf{m}-e_i,n-2) + \sum_{j=1}^h p_k^j(m_j-\mathbf{1}_{\{i=j\}})E(\mathbf{m}-e_i-e_j,n-2)\Bigg)\\ &-\sum_{i=1}^h p_k^i m_i\Bigg(E(\mathbf{m}-e_i,n-2) + \sum_{j=1}^h p_\ell^j(m_j-\mathbf{1}_{\{i=j\}})E(\mathbf{m}-e_i-e_j,n-2)\Bigg)\\ &=\sum_{i=1}^h(p_\ell^i-p_k^i)m_iE(\mathbf{m}-e_i,n-2),\end{aligned}$$

which is negative as $p_k > p_\ell$. □

C. PROOF OF THEOREM 5

To establish the lower and upper bounds in Theorem 5 we rely on a Lemma of [29] based on the FKG inequality [12].

We order the items such that $p_1 \le p_2 \le \ldots \le p_n$. For $\mathbf{x},\mathbf{y} \in C_n(m)$ let $\mu(\mathbf{x}) = p_{x_1}p_{x_2}\ldots p_{x_m} > 0$ and define $\mathbf{x} \preceq \mathbf{y}$ if $x_i \le y_i$ for $i = 1,\ldots,m$. A function f from $C_n(m)$ to $\mathbb{R}$ is increasing if $\mathbf{x} \preceq \mathbf{y}$ implies that $f(\mathbf{x}) \le f(\mathbf{y})$, f is decreasing if $(-f)$ is increasing. Further, we state that f is permutation invariant if its value is independent of the order of its arguments $x_1,\ldots,x_m$.

LEMMA 2 (LEMMA OF [29]). *Let g be decreasing and permutation invariant on on $C_n(m)$. If f is increasing on $C_n(m)$, then*

$$\sum_{\mathbf{x}\in C_n(m)}\mu(\mathbf{x})f(\mathbf{x})g(\mathbf{x})\sum_{\mathbf{y}\in C_n(m)}\mu(\mathbf{y}) \le \sum_{\mathbf{x}\in C_n(m)}\mu(\mathbf{x})f(\mathbf{x})\sum_{\mathbf{y}\in C_n(m)}\mu(\mathbf{y})g(\mathbf{y}).$$

If f is decreasing on $C_n(m)$, then

$$\sum_{\mathbf{x}\in C_n(m)}\mu(\mathbf{x})f(\mathbf{x})g(\mathbf{x})\sum_{\mathbf{y}\in C_n(m)}\mu(\mathbf{y}) \ge \sum_{\mathbf{x}\in C_n(m)}\mu(\mathbf{x})f(\mathbf{x})\sum_{\mathbf{y}\in C_n(m)}\mu(\mathbf{y})g(\mathbf{y}).$$

PROOF OF THEOREM 5. We start with the upper bound. Define the function g on $C_n(\mathbf{m})$ as

$$g(\mathbf{x}) = 1 - p_{x_1} - p_{x_2} - \ldots - p_{x_h}.$$

The function g is clearly decreasing and permutation invariant on $C_n(\mathbf{m})$. Let $f(\mathbf{x})$ be defined as

$$f(\mathbf{x}) = \prod_{i=1}^{h}\left(\prod_{j=1}^{m_i} p_{x(i,j)}\right)^{i-1}.$$

where $x(i,j) = x_{\sum_{s=1}^{i-1} m_s + j}$. Due to (1) and (2) we have

$$\sum_{\mathbf{x}\in C_n(\mathbf{m})} \mu(\mathbf{x})f(\mathbf{x})g(\mathbf{x}) = Z(\mathbf{m})M(\mathbf{m}),$$

$$\sum_{\mathbf{x}\in C_n(\mathbf{m})} \mu(\mathbf{x})f(\mathbf{x}) = Z(\mathbf{m}),$$

while

$$\sum_{\mathbf{y}\in C_n(\mathbf{m})} \mu(\mathbf{y})g(\mathbf{y}) = Z(\mathbf{m})M_{FIFO}(\mathbf{m}) = Z(\mathbf{m})F_1((\mathbf{m}+1)\mathbf{e}_1, n)$$

and

$$\sum_{\mathbf{y}\in C_n(\mathbf{m})} \mu(\mathbf{y}) = Z(\mathbf{m}).$$

As f is increasing, the upper bound therefore follows from the first inequality of Lemma 2.

For the lower bound define $\tilde{\mu}(\mathbf{x}) = \mu(\mathbf{x})^h \geq 0$ and let $\mathbf{x}\wedge\mathbf{y} = (\min(x_1,y_1),\ldots,\min(x_m,y_m))$ and $\mathbf{x}\vee\mathbf{y} = (\max(x_1,y_1),\ldots,\max(x_m,y_m))$, then $\tilde{\mu}(\mathbf{x})\tilde{\mu}(\mathbf{y}) = \tilde{\mu}(\mathbf{x}\wedge\mathbf{y})\tilde{\mu}(\mathbf{x}\vee\mathbf{y})$ and $\tilde{\mu}$ is permutation invariant on $C_n(m)$. As a result, the proof of the Lemma in [29] can be repeated to show that Lemma 2 remains valid if μ is replaced by $\tilde{\mu}$. The result now follows from the second inequality of Lemma 2 (with μ replaced by $\tilde{\mu}$) by setting

$$f(\mathbf{x}) = \prod_{i=1}^{h}\left(\prod_{j=1}^{m_i} p_{x(i,j)}\right)^{i-h},$$

which is a decreasing function on $C_n(m)$ and noting that

$$\frac{\sum_{\mathbf{y}\in C_n(\mathbf{m})}\tilde{\mu}(\mathbf{y})g(\mathbf{y})}{\sum_{\mathbf{y}\in C_n(\mathbf{m})}\tilde{\mu}(\mathbf{y})} = F_1(\mathbf{e}_1 + \mathbf{m}\mathbf{e}_h, n).$$

Theorem 2 implies that

$$F_h(r_h\mathbf{e}_h, k) = \frac{F_h(r_h\mathbf{e}_h, k-1) + p_k^h r_h}{1 + \frac{p_k^h (r_h-1)\mathbf{1}_{\{r_h>1\}}}{F_h((r_h-1)\mathbf{e}_h, k-1)}},$$

and

$$F_1(\mathbf{e}_1 + r_h\mathbf{e}_h, k) = \frac{F_1(\mathbf{e}_1 + r_h\mathbf{e}_h, k-1) + p_k^h r_h \frac{F_1(\mathbf{e}_1+(r_h-1)\mathbf{e}_h, k-1)}{F_h(r_h\mathbf{e}_h, k-1)} + p_k}{1 + \frac{p_k^h r_h}{F_h(r_h\mathbf{e}_h, k-1)}}.$$

This shows that the quantities F_h and F_1 can be computed by induction on k and m. □

D. PROOF OF LEMMA 1

Let $\alpha \in \mathbf{Z}^+$ and $i \in \{1\ldots h\}$. Two types of events can modify the value of $H_{i,\alpha}(t)$:

- If at time t, the item k is requested and is in list $i-1$, then, it is exchanged with another item j that is chosen uniformly at random from list i. This occurs with probability $X_{k,i-1}(t)X_{j,i}(t)p_k/m_i$ and modifies $H_{i,\alpha}(t)$ in $H_{i,\alpha}(t) + a^{1-\alpha}(p_k^\alpha - p_j^\alpha)$.

  The average variation of $H_{i,\alpha}$ due to these events is:

$$\begin{aligned}&\sum_{k,j} X_{k,i-1}(t)X_{j,i}(t)a^{1-\alpha}(p_k^\alpha - p_j^\alpha)\frac{p_k}{m_i}\\ &= \sum_k X_{k,i-1}(t)a^{1-\alpha}p_k^{\alpha+1}\sum_j X_{j,i}(t)\frac{1}{m_i}\\ &\quad + \sum_k X_{k,i-1}(t)p_k \sum_j a^{1-\alpha}p_j^\alpha X_{j,i}(t)\frac{1}{m_i}\\ &= aH_{i-1,\alpha+1}(t) + \frac{H_{i-1,1}(t)H_{i,\alpha}(t)}{m_i},\end{aligned}$$

  where the last line comes from the fact that $\sum_j X_{j,i}(t) = m_i$ and $\sum_k p_k X_{k,i-1}(t) = H_{i-1,1}(t)$.

- If $i < h$ and if at time t, the item k is in cache i and is hit, then, it is exchanged with another item j that is chosen uniformly at random from cache $i+1$. This occurs with probability $X_{k,i}(t)X_{j,i+1}(t)p_k/m_{i+1}$ and modify $H_{i,\alpha}(t)$ in $H_{i,\alpha}(t) + a^{1-\alpha}(-p_k^\alpha + p_j^\alpha)$.

  This second type of events leads to an average variation of $aH_{i,\alpha+1}(t) + (H_{i,1}(t)H_{i+1,\alpha}(t))/m_{i+1}$ if $i < h$.

Summing the two terms implies *(i)*: for all i, α, we have

$$\mathbf{E}\left[H_{i,\alpha}(t+1) - H_{i,\alpha}(t)|\mathcal{F}_t\right] = f_{i,\alpha}(H(t)).$$

We now show that the second moment of the variation of H is bounded. For all k, j $0 \leq p_k, p_j \leq a$, which implies $a^{2-2\alpha}(p_k^\alpha - p_j^\alpha)^2 \leq a^2$. Therefore, by using the same two types of events as for the proof of *(i)*, we have

$$\begin{aligned}&\mathbf{E}\left[\sup_\alpha(H_{i,\alpha}(t+1) - H_{i,\alpha}(t))^2|\mathcal{F}_t\right]\\ &= \sum_{k,j} X_{k,i-1}(t)X_{j,i}(t)\sup_\alpha a^{2-2\alpha}(p_k^\alpha - p_j^\alpha)^2\frac{p_k}{m_i}\\ &\quad + \sum_{k,j} X_{k,i}(t)X_{j,i+1}(t)\sup_\alpha a^{2-2\alpha}(p_j^\alpha - p_k^\alpha)^2\frac{p_k}{m_{i+1}}\\ &\leq \sum_{k,j} X_{k,i-1}(t)X_{j,i}(t)a^2\frac{p_k}{m_i} + \sum_{k,j} X_{k,i}(t)X_{j,i+1}(t)a^2\frac{p_k}{m_{i+1}}\\ &= (H_{i-1,1}(t) + H_{i,1}(t))a^2\end{aligned}$$

This shows that

$$\begin{aligned}&\mathbf{E}\left[\|H(t+1) - H(t)\|_\infty^2|\mathcal{F}_t\right]\\ &= \mathbf{E}\left[\sup_{i,\alpha}(H_{i,\alpha}(t+1) - H_{i,\alpha}(t))^2|\mathcal{F}_t\right]\\ &\leq \mathbf{E}\left[\sum_i \sup_\alpha(H_{i,\alpha}(t+1) - H_{i,\alpha}(t))^2|\mathcal{F}_t\right]\\ &\leq \sum_i (H_{i-1,1}(t) + H_{i,1}(t))a^2 \leq 2a^2.\end{aligned}$$

The points *(iii)* and *(iv)* are easier as f is a sum of two terms: the first one is Lipschitz-continuous of constant a and the second is a second order polynomial function of h divided by m_i, which is therefore Lipschitz-continuous of constant C/m_i on all bounded sub-space of $\mathcal{H}$. Moreover, by plugging (8) into (11), we find that δ is the solution of $\dot{\delta} = f(\delta)$. □

E. REFERENCES

[1] O. I. Aven, L. B. Boguslavsky, and Y. A. Kogan. Some results on distribution-free analysis of paging algorithms. *IEEE Transactions on Computers*, 25(7):737–745, July 1976.

[2] O. I. Aven, E. G. Coffman, Jr., and Y. A. Kogan. *Stochastic Analysis of Computer Storage*. Kluwer Academic Publishers, Norwell, MA, USA, 1987.

[3] O. Babaoglu and D. Ferrari. Two-level replacement decisions in paging stores. *IEEE Trans. Comput.*, 32(12):1151–1159, Dec. 1983.

[4] M. Benaïm and J. Le Boudec. A class of mean field interaction models for computer and communication systems. *Performance Evaluation*, 65(11-12):823–838, 2008.

[5] D. S. Berger, P. Gland, S. Singla, and F. Ciucu. Exact analysis of TTL cache networks. *Performance Evaluation*, 79:2–23, 2014.

[6] J.-Y. L. Boudec. The stationary behaviour of fluid limits of reversible processes is concentrated on stationary points. *arXiv:1009.5021*, 2010.

[7] L. Breslau, P. Cao, L. Fan, G. Phillips, and S. Shenker. Web caching and Zipf-like distributions: Evidence and implications. In *INFOCOM'99*, volume 1, pages 126–134. IEEE, 1999.

[8] H. Che, Y. Tung, and Z. Wang. Hierarchical web caching systems: modeling, design and experimental results. *IEEE J.Sel. A. Commun.*, 20(7):1305–1314, 2002.

[9] A. Dan and D. Towsley. An approximate analysis of the LRU and FIFO buffer replacement schemes. *SIGMETRICS Perform. Eval. Rev.*, 18(1):143–152, Apr. 1990.

[10] R. Fagin and T. G. Price. Efficient calculation of expected miss ratios in the independent reference model. *SIAM J. Comput.*, 7:288–296, 1978.

[11] N. C. Fofack, P. Nain, G. Neglia, and D. Towsley. Analysis of TTL-based cache networks. In *Valuetools 2012*, pages 1–10. IEEE, 2012.

[12] C. M. Fortuin, P. W. Kasteleyn, and J. Ginibre. Correlation inequalities on some partially ordered sets. *Communications in Mathematical Physics*, 22(2):89–103, 1971.

[13] C. Fricker, P. Robert, and J. Roberts. A versatile and accurate approximation for lru cache performance. In *Proceedings of the 24th International Teletraffic Congress*, ITC '12, pages 8:1–8, 2012.

[14] M. Gallo, B. Kauffmann, L. Muscariello, A. Simonian, and C. Tanguy. Performance evaluation of the random replacement policy for networks of caches. *Performance Evaluation*, 72(0):16–36, 2014.

[15] E. Gelenbe. A unified approach to the evaluation of a class of replacement algorithms. *IEEE Trans. Comput.*, 22(6):611–618, June 1973.

[16] J. H. Hester and D. S. Hirschberg. Self-organizing linear search. *ACM Comput. Surv.*, 17(3):295–311, Sept. 1985.

[17] R. Hirade and T. Osogami. Analysis of page replacement policies in the fluid limit. *Oper. Res.*, 58:971–984, July 2010.

[18] P. Jelenkovic. Asymptotic approximation of the move-to-front search cost distribution and least-recently used caching fault probabilities. *Ann. Appl. Probab.*, 9(2):430–464, May 1999.

[19] S. Jiang and X. Zhang. LIRS: An efficient low inter-reference recency set replacement policy to improve buffer cache performance. *SIGMETRICS Perform. Eval. Rev.*, 30(1):31–42, June 2002.

[20] T. Johnson and D. Shasha. 2Q: A low overhead high performance buffer management replacement algorithm. In *VLDB '94*, pages 439–450, San Francisco, CA, USA, 1994.

[21] J. Jung, A. W. Berger, and H. Balakrishnan. Modeling TTL-based internet caches. In *INFOCOM 2003*, volume 1, pages 417–426. IEEE, 2003.

[22] W. F. King III. Analysis of demand paging algorithms. In *IFIP Congress (1)*, pages 485–490, 1971.

[23] N. Laoutaris, H. Che, and I. Stavrakakis. The LCD interconnection of LRU caches and its analysis. *Perform. Eval.*, 63(7):609–634, July 2006.

[24] A. W. Marshall and I. Olkin. *Inequalities: theory of majorization and its applications*. Academic Press, New York, 1979.

[25] V. Martina, M. Garetto, and E. Leonardi. A unified approach to the performance analysis of caching systems. In *INFOCOM 2014*, pages 2040–2048, 2014.

[26] E. J. Rosensweig, J. Kurose, and D. Towsley. Approximate models for general cache networks. In *INFOCOM'10*, pages 1100–1108, Piscataway, NJ, USA, 2010. IEEE Press.

[27] D. Starobinski and D. Tse. Probabilistic methods for web caching. *Perform. Eval.*, 46(2-3):125–137, Oct. 2001.

[28] N. Tsukada, R. Hirade, and N. Miyoshi. Fluid limit analysis of FIFO and RR caching for independent reference models. *Perform. Eval.*, 69(9):403–412, Sept. 2012.

[29] J. van den Berg and A. Gandolfi. LRU is better than FIFO under the independent reference model. *Journal of Applied Probability*, 29(1):pp. 239–243, 1992.

[30] J. van den Berg and D. F. Towsley. Properties of the miss ratio for a 2-level storage model with LRU or FIFO replacement strategy and independent references. *IEEE Trans. Computers*, 42(4):508–512, 1993.

[31] S. Vanichpun and A. M. Makowski. Comparing strength of locality of reference – popularity, majorization, and some folk theorems. In *INFOCOM*, 2004.

[32] S. Vanichpun and A. M. Makowski. The output of a cache under the independent reference model: Where did the locality of reference go? *SIGMETRICS Perform. Eval. Rev.*, 32(1):295–306, June 2004.

[33] R. D. Yates. A framework for uplink power control in cellular radio systems. *Selected Areas in Communications, IEEE Journal on*, 13(7):1341–1347, 1995.

[34] M. Zink, K. Suh, Y. Gu, and J. Kurose. Characteristics of YouTube network traffic at a campus network - measurements, models, and implications. *Comput. Netw.*, 53(4):501–514, Mar. 2009.

Memory Row Reuse Distance and its Role in Optimizing Application Performance

Mahmut Kandemir
Department of Computer Science and Engineering
The Pennsylvania State University
University Park, PA 16802
kandemir@cse.psu.edu

Hui Zhao
Department of Computer Science and Engineering
The Pennsylvania State University
University Park, PA 16802
hzz105@cse.psu.edu

Xulong Tang
Department of Computer Science and Engineering
The Pennsylvania State University
University Park, PA 16802
xzt102@cse.psu.edu

Mustafa Karakoy
Department of Computer Engineering
TOBB ETU
Ankara, Turkey
m.karakoy@yahoo.co.uk

ABSTRACT

Continuously increasing dataset sizes of large-scale applications overwhelm on-chip cache capacities and make the performance of last-level caches (LLC) increasingly important. That is, in addition to maximizing LLC hit rates, it is becoming equally important to reduce LLC miss latencies. One of the critical factors that influence LLC miss latencies is row-buffer locality (i.e., the fraction of LLC misses that hit in the large buffer attached to a memory bank). While there has been a plethora of recent works on optimizing row-buffer performance, to our knowledge, there is no study that quantifies the full potential of row-buffer locality and impact of maximizing it on application performance.

Focusing on multithreaded applications, the first contribution of this paper is the definition of a new metric called (memory) row reuse distance (RRD). We show that, while intra-core RRDs are relatively small (increasing the chances for row-buffer hits), inter-core RRDs are quite large (increasing the chances for row-buffer misses). Motivated by this, we propose two schemes that measure the maximum potential benefits that could be obtained from minimizing RRDs, to the extent allowed by program dependencies. Specifically, one of our schemes (Scheme-I) targets only intra-core RRDs, whereas the other one (Scheme-II) aims at reducing both intra-core RRDs and inter-core RRDs. Our experimental evaluations demonstrate that (i) Scheme-I reduces intra-core RRDs but increases inter-core RRDs; (ii) Scheme-II reduces inter-core RRDs significantly while achieving a similar behavior to Scheme-I as far as intra-core RRDs are concerned; (iii) Scheme-I and Scheme-II improve execution times of our applications by 17% and 21%, respectively, on average; and (iv) both our schemes deliver consistently good results under different memory request scheduling policies.

SIGMETRICS'15, June 15–19, 2015, Portland, OR, USA.

DOI: http://dx.doi.org/10.1145/2745844.2745867

Categories and Subject Descriptors

B.3.2 [**Memory Structures**]: Design Styles; C.1.2 [**Processor Architectures**]: Multiple Data Stream Architectures (Multiprocessors)

General Terms

Performance, Design

Keywords

Multicores, memory scheduling, row-buffer locality, row reuse distance

1. INTRODUCTION

With recent trends towards multicore systems and enormous dataset sizes, the memory system is increasingly becoming a bottleneck [1–5]. Unfortunately, traditional optimization techniques based on on-chip caches will have limited scope in coping with this memory bottleneck, simply because the growth in dataset sizes far exceeds the growth in on-chip cache capacities. Employing smart cache management strategies [6–10] can provide a temporary relief (delta improvement) but certainly not a long-term solution. Instead, to address this growing problem, solutions that consider the *entire path of data accesses* (not just cache performance) should be investigated. One of the components of this path is the last-level cache (LLC) misses (off-chip memory requests).

One of the critical factors that determine the performance of LLC misses in modern main memory systems is *row-buffer locality,* which refers to reusing data from a row-buffer, a buffer that acts as a cache for the most recently accessed memory row, as much as possible. There have been several recent papers [11–15] that proposed hardware-based techniques to maximize row-buffer locality (row-buffer hits). One popular memory-scheduling (reordering) scheme found in current commercial systems is FR-FCFS [11, 12], which gives priority to requests that target the current memory row in the row-buffer over other requests, including the older ones. More recent scheduling techniques [16–20, 36] try to coordinate memory controllers to achieve better row-buffer performance.

The row-buffer optimization techniques proposed in the literature are mostly ad-hoc architectural schemes that use different heuristics. One of the critical questions in this context is to understand the potential and limits of maximizing row-buffer performance. In other words, *what are the maximum benefits one could expect from an ideal scheme that maximizes row-buffer locality?* Motivated by this observation, this paper makes the following main contributions:

- We define a novel metric called intra-core and inter-core memory *row reuse distance* (RRD) and quantify it using a set of 12 multithreaded benchmarks. This characterization indicates that while intra-core RRDs are generally low, leading to good row-buffer performance (locality), inter-core RRDs are very high.
- We propose an ideal off-chip memory request (LLC miss) scheduling policy oriented towards minimizing only intra-core RRDs. The results collected through our experiments clearly show that while minimizing intra-core RRDs does bring performance improvements (17% execution time reduction on average), there is still scope for further improvement.
- We next study the potential of a strategy that considers *both* intra-core and inter-core RRDs. The results show that such an integrated approach generates a 26% better row-buffer performance (in terms of row-buffer hits), resulting in about 21% improvement (on average) in execution cycles. We also compared our schemes with two previous schemes proposed to improve row-buffer locality. Our evaluation shows that our schemes greatly outperform these previous schemes in reducing the programs' execution time.

Overall, our results motivate considering both intra-core and inter-core RRDs in optimizing for memory system performance. Furthermore, our results clearly show that if off-chip memory requests could be reorganized on the core side, we may not need sophisticated memory request schedulers on the memory controller side. To our knowledge, this is the first paper that formalizes the (memory) row reuse distance concept, and demonstrates the impact of optimizing (minimizing) it on the row-buffer locality and overall application performance.

The remainder of this paper is organized as follows. The next section gives an overview of modern memory systems employed by current multicore/manycore architectures, and explains the concept of row-buffer locality. Section 3 describes our experimental platform as well as application programs. Section 4 defines intra-core and inter-core RRDs and quantifies them in the original application codes. Section 5 gives our two schemes oriented towards minimizing RRDs by performing core-side memory request (LLC miss) scheduling. Section 6 gives detailed evaluations of our schemes. Section 7 discusses related work and Section 8 concludes the paper.

2. DRAM BASICS AND ROW-BUFFER LOCALITY

In this section, we introduce the background on contemporary DRAM memory architectures. We base our introduction on DDR3 SDRAM systems [21, 22]. The discussion below is also applicable to other DRAM memories that employ page-based memory architectures. We also provide an introduction to the state-of-the-art memory request scheduling schemes implemented in hardware.

2.1 SDRAM organization

Figure 1 shows the high-level view of a modern DRAM hierarchy. A DRAM consists of one or more building blocks called dual in-line memory modules (DIMMs). In each DIMM, there are several SDRAM ICs that consist of multiple memory banks. Accesses to different memory banks can be serviced in parallel. The actual elements that store memory data are the DRAM cells, and they are organized as a two-dimensional array in each bank. Read or write operations need to provide a DRAM address that contains bank, row, and column information in order to access the data in the DRAM.

Accesses to the two-dimensional memory cell array take place at the granularity of *rows*. To reduce the delay of accessing the memory array, there is a structure called *row-buffer* that can hold the data of an entire row of the memory array. After the row address is asserted, the contents of the accessed memory row are latched in the row-buffer so that subsequent memory accesses to the same row can be served promptly. Figure 2 illustrates how a memory access is executed. In this example, the memory access needs to read data from bank 1. First, the row address select signal is asserted and the data in the same row across all banks are selected (because a row is the basic accessing unit in the memory array). Following that, the selected row data is latched into the row-buffer. Next, the data can be read from the row-buffer using the bank address and column address. Consecutive memory accesses to data in the row-buffer are called *row-buffer hits*. However, if the successive memory requests access different rows, this will lead to a *row-buffer miss*. In such cases, a new row of memory data needs to be read into the row-buffer. Since memory accesses resulting in row-buffer misses need to access the memory array itself, this leads to longer access latencies. *Row buffer locality* refers to repeated accesses to the contents of a given row when its data is loaded into the row-buffer. Taking advantage of row-buffer locality can improve the performance by eliminating the cycles spent in accessing the memory arrays. A series of memory requests that generate a high row-buffer hit rate is said to have good row-buffer locality.

2.2 Impact of the row-buffer on memory access latencies

Since the row-buffer serves as a cache to the memory bank arrays, latencies of memory accesses are *not* uniform, depending on whether the data is found in the row-buffer or not. The memory access delay can be classified into three categories:

- *Row open with bank hit*: The row-buffer is loaded with data and the accessed data happens to be in the row-buffer. In this case, the memory latency incurred is the minimum

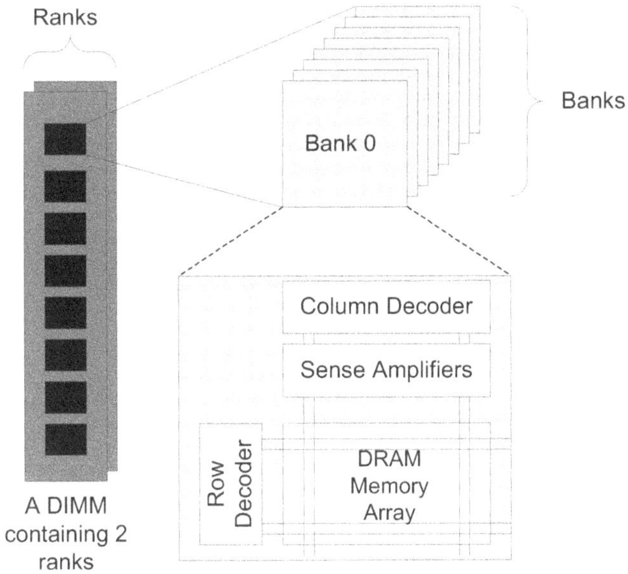

Figure 1: High-level view of a DDR3 SDRAM memory architecture.

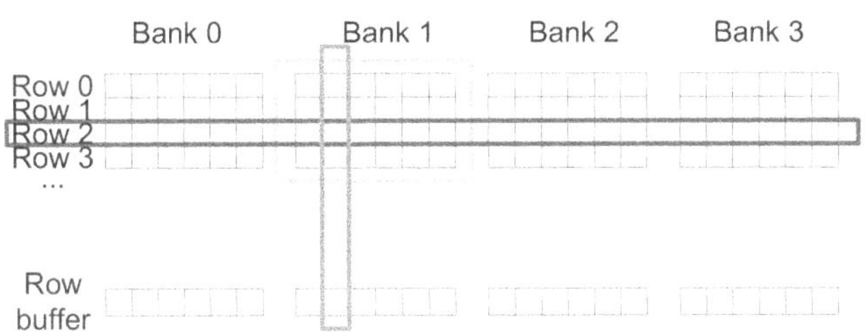

Figure 2: Accessing the memory data through a row-buffer.

and includes only the time to access the right column in the selected bank.

• *Row open with bank conflict*: The row-buffer is loaded with data but the desired data is not in the current row-buffer. The current row needs to be closed first, and the right bank needs to be precharged to load data into the row-buffer. The resulting memory access latency is the highest among all cases.

• *Row empty*: Row buffer is closed in this case and there is no data in the row-buffer. In such a situation, a new row of data need to be loaded into the row-buffer and then desired data can be accessed using column address.

2.3 Row buffer management policies

Existing row-buffer management policies[1] can be categorized into two classes: *open-page policy* and *close-page policy*.

• *Open-page* policy. In this policy, the row-buffer is kept open after every access. This policy is based on the speculation that once a row of data is brought to the row-buffer, the same row may be accessed again in the near future (as a side effect of locality of data). If the next memory access is made to the same row, its memory access latency can be reduced to the minimum since the row is already active and there is no need to access the memory array. However, in the case that the next access is to a different row of the same bank, the memory access latency is much larger, which includes the latency to precharge the DRAM array, access another row and perform the column access. In the open-page policy, the memory access latency is not predictable because a row-buffer hit can have much smaller delay than a row-buffer miss.

• *Close-page policy.* In contrast to the open-page policy, a DRAM page is closed immediately after every read or write operation. This policy does not take advantage of data locality to improve memory bandwidth, but it makes the latency of each memory access predictable and has lower design complexity. The close-page policy can have an edge over the open-page policy in situations where random DRAM pages are accessed frequently.

To summarize, a row-buffer management policy has an influence on the design of the memory system. It directly impacts several other design parameters, such as the memory address mapping and memory access scheduling in the memory controllers. Since our goal in this work is to maximize row-buffer locality, we employ the open-page policy.

2.4 Memory access scheduling in the memory controllers

Between processors and DRAM, there is an interface component called *memory controller*. The main functionality of memory controller is to orchestrate the DRAM banks, buses and buffering queues to effectively serve the memory requests from processors. Requests sent from the processors are first stored in the buffering queues. Based on their memory address, the requests are dispatched to the DRAM when there is bus bandwidth available. There is an important logic called *scheduler* (implemented in hardware) in the memory controller that decides the issue order of incoming requests to memory based on performance and priority requirements.

There have been various scheduling schemes proposed in prior work to improve the efficiency and/or fairness of the memory request scheduling. One of the well-known scheduling algorithms is the *First Come First Serve* algorithm (FCFS). In this policy, memory requests are serviced in their arriving order. Note that this policy may not perform well in some cases because it does not take advantage of the data locality in the row-buffer. Instead, the *First Ready-First Come and First Serve* algorithm (FR-FCFS) [11,12] was proposed to optimize the memory throughput. This scheduling policy gives the highest priority to ready memory requests. A memory request is considered ready when its data is available in an open row. If there is no request that leads to a row-buffer hit, the FR-FCFS then selects requests to serve in their arriving order as in the case of FCFS. Serving ready requests first can improve memory throughput by taking advantage of the row-buffer locality and can maximize row-buffer hit rate. The original FR-FCFS scheme was proposed to improve the memory performance (by improving row-buffer locality) in a single-core platform. Recently, there have been several memory scheduling schemes proposed for multi-core platforms to improve performance as well as fairness [20,23–25]. For example, Nesbit et al. [23] propose a scheduling scheme similar to the network fair-queuing strategies to fairly allocate memory bandwidth among applications. Similarly, in [24], a memory scheduling scheme is proposed to

[1]Note that these policies just decide whether an accessed row should be kept in the row-buffer for future accesses or not, and are different from memory scheduling policies that reorder requests to improve memory performance.

Table 1: Major platform parameters.

Parameter	Default Value
Cores	32 (each is two issue)
Cache Line	64 bytes (for all caches)
L1 Cache	32KB per core (private), 8-way, 4 cycle-latency
L2 Cache	256KB per core (private), 8-way, 12 cycle-latency
L3 Cache	16MB shared, 32-way, 32 cycle-latency (managed as SNUCA [43])
Data TLB	Two-level; L1: 64 entries, 4-way, L2: 512 entries, 4-way
On-Chip Network	4 × 8 mesh, 2-stage wormhole switched, VC flow control,6 VCs per port, 5 flit buffer depth
Main Memory	4 DDR3 Memory Controllers (MC), 8 ranks/MC, 2 banks/rank, FR-FCFS, 2KB row-buffer size, 1107 MHz memory clock, 64GB capacity, 32-entry memory queue size

reorder memory requests based on the average memory stall time of each processor.

3. TARGET SYSTEM, SIMULATION PLATFORM, AND MULTITHREADED APPLICATIONS

Table 1 gives the important features of the default 32-core system we modeled in the Sniper simulator infrastructure [26]. Sniper allows one to carry out timing simulations for both multi-program workloads and multi-threaded, shared-memory applications with tens of cores. Later in the paper, we modify the default values of some of the parameters shown in this table to perform sensitivity experiments.

In this work, we evaluated our approach over a set of 12 multithreaded programs listed in Table 2. The second column gives a brief description of each program, and the third column shows its total input size.[2] The last column on the other hand gives the LLC miss rates of these codes under our default simulation platform described in Table 1. In selecting these applications, we tried to strike a balance between *regular* and *irregular* data access patterns. For example, while benchmarks such as *mgrid* and *fma3d* represent application programs with regular access patterns, *hpcg* and *moldyn* have quite irregular data access patterns made through index arrays. We also tried to have input sizes ranging from relatively small values (210.8 MB) to much larger ones (1.58 GB) to put different amount of pressure on the memory system.

4. ROW REUSE DISTANCE (RRD)

4.1 Definition

The Row Reuse Distance (RRD) between two off-chip accesses (references), r_a and r_b, to the same memory row R_i that reside in memory bank B_j is defined as the number of accesses to different rows $R_k (\neq R_i)$ in the same bank that appear between these two off-chip accesses. For example, in Figure 3(a), the RRD between the two successive accesses to row R_3 (in bank B_1) is 4. Note that we exclude from the reuse distance the references that are targeted to different banks. We observe that RRD can be divided into two classes: *intra-core RRD* and *inter-core RRD*. As shown in Figure 3(b), if two references belong to the same core, the RRD in question is termed as intra-core RRD. On the other hand, if the references belong to different cores, the corresponding RRD is referred to as inter-core RRD. It is important to emphasize that RRD can be used as a *measure* of the row-buffer locality. More specifically, a small RRD (be it intra-core or inter-core) increases the chances for the second reference (r_b) to generate a row-buffer hit, compared to a large RRD. This is because a small RRD makes

[2]Note that the input sizes we use are larger than the default sizes of these benchmarks to stress the last-level cache (LLC).

Table 2: Applications used in our evaluations.

Application	Brief Description	Input Size	LLC Miss Rate
gs-solver [38]	Gauss-Seidel based iterative sparse solver	390.2MB	22.6%
equake [39]	Earthquake simulation	487.7MB	29.8%
miniFE [40]	Finite element mini application	654.1MB	16.1%
hpcg [42]	High performance preconditioned CG solver benchmark	210.8MB	27.7%
facerec [39]	Face recognition	436.1MB	18.1%
ammp [39]	Chemistry/biology	1.09GB	36.5%
mgrid [39]	Multigrid solver	771.6MB	26.2%
moldyn [41]	Generalized program for the evaluation of molecular dynamics models	336.2MB	21.4%
fma3d [39]	Crash simulation	1.58GB	47.2%
gafort [39]	Genetic algorithm	364MB	20.8%
swim [39]	Shallow water modeling	444.9MB	22.2%
wupwise [39]	Quantum chromodynamics	1.18GB	19.4%

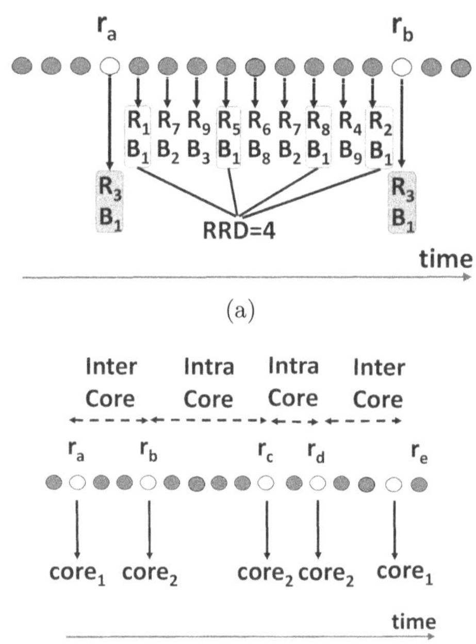

(b)

Figure 3: (a) Illustration of RRD for row R_3 in bank B_1. r_a and r_b are two requests to R_3. Note that intervening accesses to different rows in the same bank (B_1) contribute to RRD, whereas intervening accesses to different banks do not. (b) Difference between intra-core RRD and inter-core RRD.

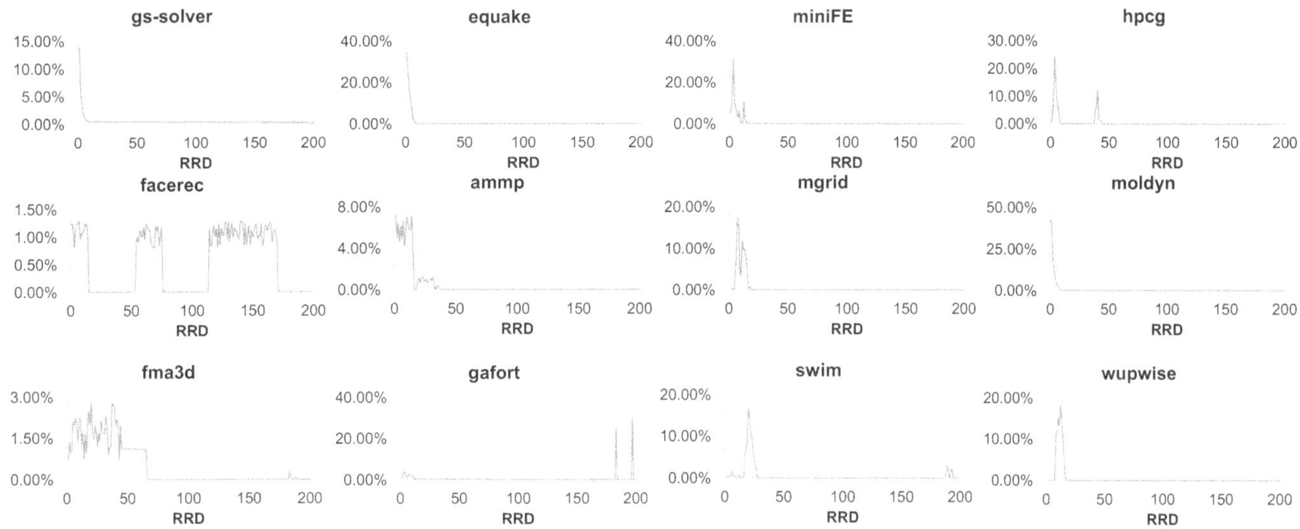

Figure 4: Intra-core RRDs for the original applications. The y-axis in each figure captures the frequency of occurance for different row reuse distances (given on the x-axis). The number of row reuse distances larger than 200 is negligible.

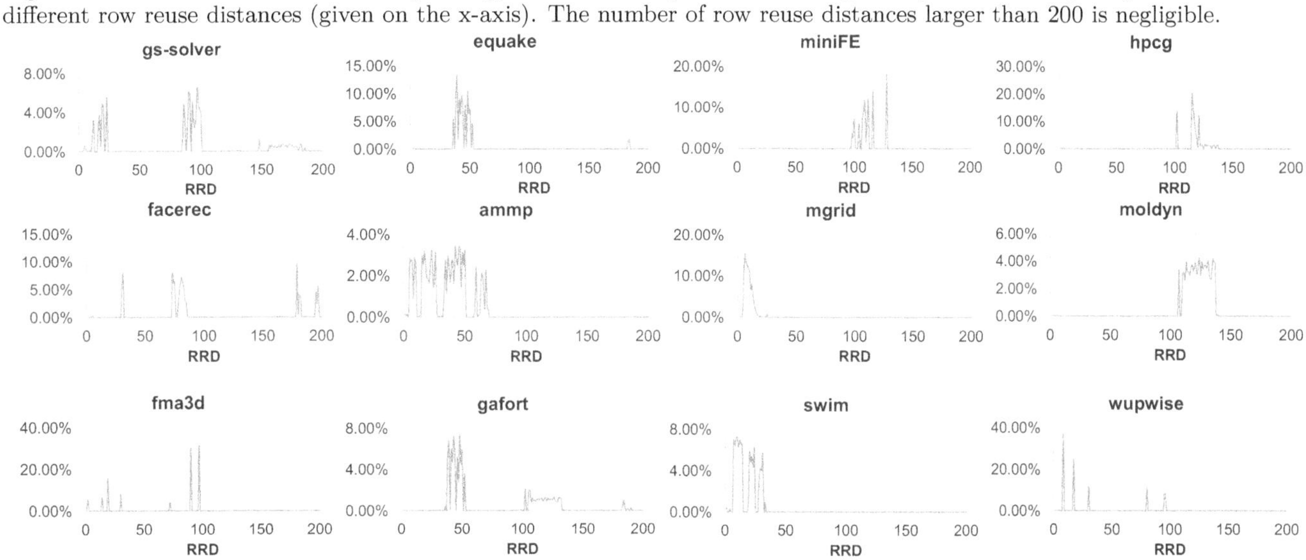

Figure 5: Inter-core RRDs for the original applications. The y-axis in each figure captures the frequency of occurrence for different row reuse distances (given on the x-axis). The number of row reuse distances larger than 200 is negligible.

it more likely for the second reference r_b to be located in the row-buffer, while the first reference (r_a) is in the row-buffer. This scenario results in a row-buffer hit (as opposed to row-buffer miss). Therefore, *one of the optimization strategies that could be built on top of RRDs is to reduce RRDs*, either through architectural techniques, software optimizations, or a combination of both. In the rest of this section, we present intra-core and inter-core RRDs of our multithreaded applications and show how these results translate to row-buffer locality and execution times.

4.2 RRDs of the original applications

Figure 4 and Figure 5 plot, respectively, the distribution of intra-core and inter-core RRDs in our original applications, when considering all rows and all banks. In obtaining the inter-core results, we considered all cores and banks, and similarly, in obtaining the intra-core results (for each core in isolation), all banks are taken into account (note that, in each figure, each point on the x-axis represents a specific RRD value, and the y-axis gives its frequency of occurrence). One can make two observations from these plots. First, intra-core RRDs are generally not very high except for a few applications (e.g., *facerec*, *gafort*, and *fma3d*). It needs to be noted however that only a subset of these row reuses can be converted into row-buffer locality at runtime, depending on the memory buffer size and the memory request scheduling algorithm employed. Specifically, as explained earlier, while FR-FCFS exploits row reuse for the requests waiting in the memory buffer, it cannot exploit any reuse that is not in the buffer. Second, most of the inter-core RRDs plotted in Figure 5 are very high compared to intra-core RRDs. For example, in applications such as *miniFE*, *hpcg* and *moldyn*, almost all RRDs are larger than 100.

While the distribution of RRDs is certainly important, one also needs to consider the contributions (frequency of occurrence) of the intra-core and inter-core row reuses. The plot given in Figure 6(a) shows this breakdown of row reuses between intra-core and inter-core cases. One can observe from this plot that, while in some applications such as *facerec* and *wupwise*, intra-core row reuse clearly dominates, in others such as *equake* and *gafort*, inter-core reuse takes a sizable portion. Figure 6(b) gives, under the FR-FCFS scheduling policy and the default values of our system parameters, the row-buffer hit rates of our applications within and across cores. We observe from this plot that the hit rates due to intra-core reuses range between 4% and 42%, averaging on 19%. In contrast, the inter-core hit rates range between 1% and 22%, leading to an average hit rate of 7%. That is, row reuses originated from the same core take much better advantage of row-buffers, compared to reuses across different cores. These hit rates along with the row reuse frequencies plotted in Figure 6(a) contribute to the execution times shown in Figure 6(c).

There have been studies in the past on cache reuse distance. Cache reuse distance [27–29] is a concept proposed to predict the data locality and is employed in techniques to improve cache performance. The cache reuse distance is defined as the number of distinct cache line addresses accessed between two consecutive accesses to the same address. Cache performance can be largely predicted by the reuse distance because it reflects the temporal locality of its data access. For example, in a fully-associative cache employing the LRU (Least Recently Used) replacement policy, we can forecast if a data access will result in a hit or a miss. If the reuse distance of one cache access is greater than the cache size, the next access to the same address will be a miss; otherwise, it will be a cache hit. In reality, cache performance is also affected by other factors such as cache configuration and replacement policies. However, the cache reuse distance can still help to predict the cache performance with certain level of accuracy. In fact, there have been several techniques proposed previously to improve the cache performance based on the reuse distance characteristics [19, 27–30].

Our proposed RRD and cache reuse distance have significant differences. First, our proposed RRD reflects characteristics of a program's off-chip memory requests, whereas cache reuse distance focuses on on-chip data accesses. Second, our proposed RRD takes into account the specific design of memory banks which is an important factor affecting the performance of memory accesses. For example, intervening accesses to different banks do not contribute to RRD, whereas intervening accesses to different rows of the same bank do. Third, the ways in which cache reuse distances and our RRDs are used for optimization are quite different. Specifically, cache reuse distances are used to improve cache hits, whereas our RRDs target the row-buffer locality of cache misses.

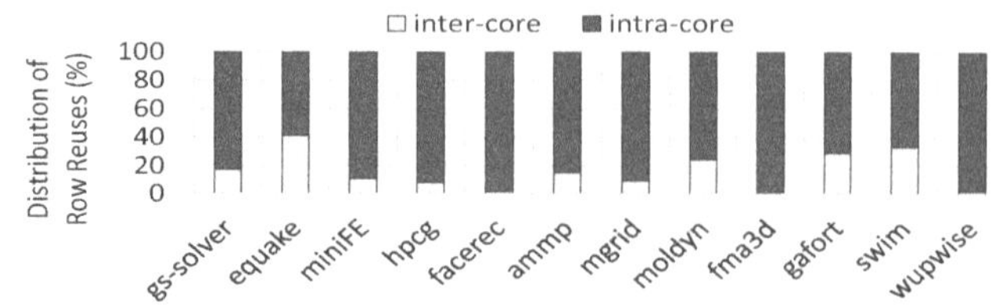

(a) Breakdown of row reuses between intra-core and inter-core cases.

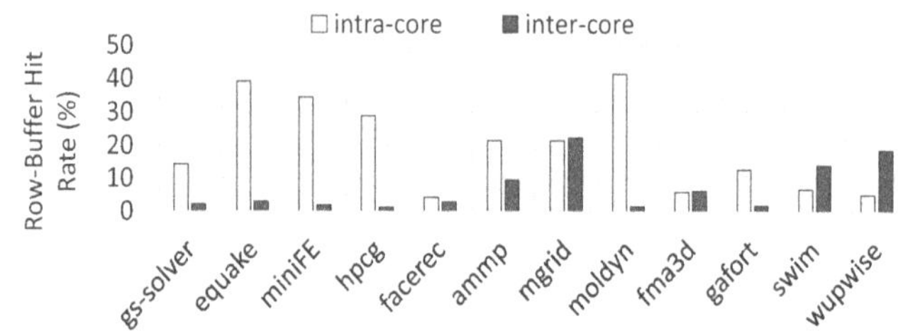

(b) Row-buffer hit rates of intra-core and inter-core row reuses.

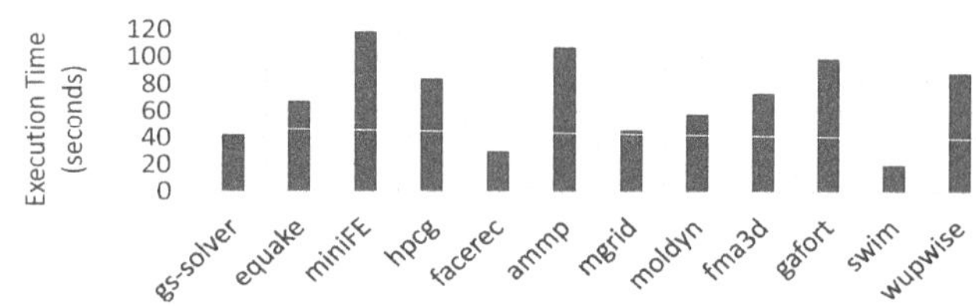

(c) Execution times of our original applications.

Figure 6: Characterization of row-buffer reuse.

5. MINIMIZING RRDS

The goal of this section is to present two schemes that aim to reduce RRDs. Both these schemes employ LLC miss reordering (restructuring) to reduce RRDs as much as possible, constrained only by program dependencies. The first of them focuses only on intra-core RRDs, whereas the second one considers both intra-core RRDs and inter-core RRDs. Below, we present the details of these two schemes. It needs to be emphasized that these schemes are in a sense *ideal* approaches, as far as optimizing for intra-core RRDs and intra-core + inter-core RRDs are concerned. Specifically, they do *not* represent any specific implementation; in fact, they cannot directly be implemented in practice. Rather, they indicate what would be the results if an ideal cache miss reordering strategy could be employed, constrained by only data and control dependencies in a given program code. In the remainder of this paper, we refer to these two (ideal) schemes as **Scheme-I** and **Scheme-II**.

5.1 Scheme-I: intra-core RRD optimization

Originally, off-chip accesses are sent over to their target memory controllers via the on chip network, and are then forwarded to their target memory banks. Scheme-I reorders those accesses from a single core's view before they reach the memory controllers. Since off-chip accesses are generated strictly following the time-line, to perform our reordering, we construct a very large queue (*buffer*) to temporarily buffer those accesses[3]. Note that initially this queue contains the memory access sequence in its original order. Because different memory banks accommodate disjoint rows, we focus on the row accesses within the same bank by splitting this queue into sub-queues based on the accessed bank's $bank_{id}$. Row buffer locality is then optimized within each of those sub-queues in an isolated fashion. The only factor that prevents Scheme-I from minimizing intra-core RRDs (by reordering the LLC misses in the 128K-entry buffer) is potential data and control dependencies in the program code. Although accesses to different row-buffers will not have memory location dependencies, data hazards from the

[3] In our experiments, we used a 128K-entry buffer. Increasing the size of this buffer further did not bring any additional benefits when all the requests in this buffer have been processed, we reload it with the next 128K LLC misses.

program will restrict the opportunities for maximizing row-buffer locality. Consider the following scenario as an example. In a three-instruction case, an arithmetic instruction first generates an access to row_2 due to an LLC miss. A load instruction then loads a value from row_1 to register t_1. Finally, a store instruction stores t_1 to row_2. In this scenario, one cannot swap the load and store instruction to achieve row_2 locality due to the load-store hazard. In general, any dependences between the instructions that access the same row can prevent Scheme-I from minimizing RRDs. Note that, in a practical implementation, memory dependencies can be handled in different layers, and we do not defend one possible implementation over the other. Rather, our goal is to take into account the impact of dependencies in an otherwise ideal (unimplementable) scheme that can perform core-side memory scheduling considering a very large buffer of references.

Our miss-reordering based approach to intra-core RRD optimization is given as a pseudo-code in Algorithm 1. In this pseudo-code, the body of the outermost loop is assumed to be executed for all cores in the system. X and Y are the number of channels and the number of banks per channel, respectively. Each bank has a link list as its queue, which is initialized in *line 27*. Our approach then distributes the accesses over the access sub-queues according to each access's $bank_{id}$, which is implemented by a loop between *line 28* and *line 30*. We then call the reorder function to optimize row-buffer locality. The first loop (*line 2*) in this function traverses all memory bank sub-queues, while the second loop (*line 4*) traverses all accesses within each queue. The while loop (*line 10*) is used to find accesses to the same row. Note that, in *line 12*, if a dependency is detected or the *RRD* is already very small (which can be captured by FR-FCFS anyway), we skip this access and go to the next one.

We now go over a simple example, shown in Figure 7, to illustrate how our scheme works in practice. Figure 7(a) depicts the original access sequence to two memory banks. All accesses are originally ordered following the time-line without considering row-buffer locality (representing the original LLC miss sequence). Figure 7(b) shows the sub-queues according to $bank_{id}$. Dependencies are marked by an arrow, and Figure 7(c) illustrates the reordered bank queues after applying our strategy. Originally, we have 6 row-buffer misses to $bank_1$ and 6 row-buffer misses to $bank_2$ in Figure 7(b). We reduce the row-buffer misses to 3 in $bank_1$ and 4 in $bank_2$, respectively. Note that, although the best order will give us 2 row misses to $bank_1$ because of the three row accesses in total, we cannot achieve that due to dependencies.

So far, we ordered the LLC misses from each core's perspective independently. It needs to be noted that, evaluating Scheme-I is important as it is relatively easier to incarnate a practical implementation from it, compared to Scheme-II (presented shortly). This is because the former does not require any inter-core coordination which would be very challenging to implement in practice without significant hardware complexity and runtime overheads. Also note that, although memory references from different cores interleave at memory controllers and banks, maintaining core-level locality of memory accesses is still expected to achieve some locality improvement (especially in cases where a given bank is shared – in a given period – by only few cores). However, Scheme-I may not be able to provide the optimal row lo-

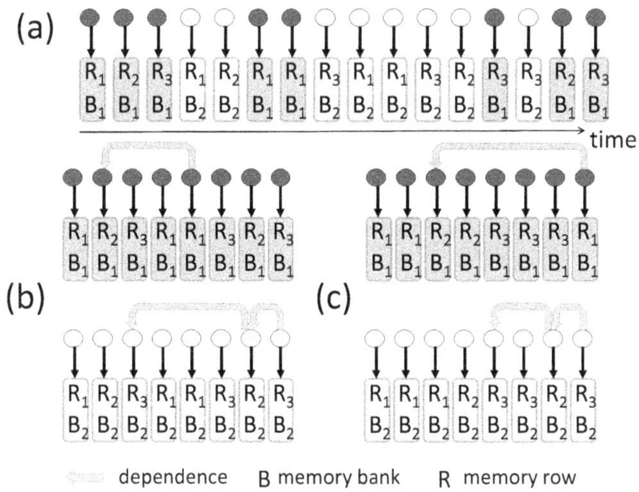

Figure 7: Example for intra-core RRD optimization.

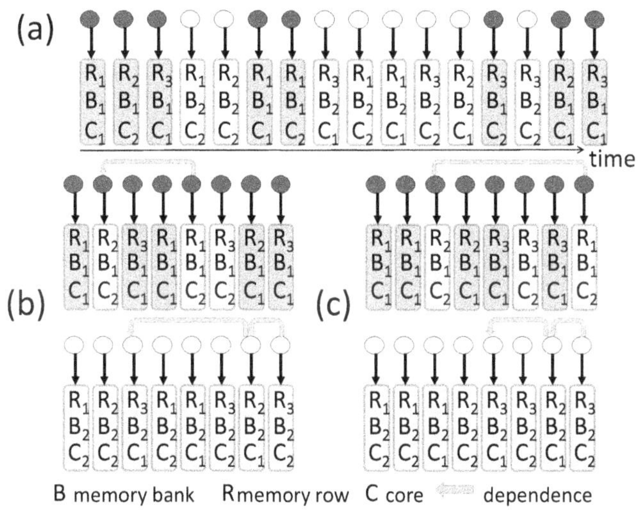

Figure 8: Example for inter-core RRD optimization.

cality, when accesses from all cores are considered together. Suppose, for example that, $core_1$ accesses row_1 and row_2, and $core_2$ accesses the row_3 and row_1 from the same memory bank after $core_1$ accesses row_1. In this case, the single core view adopted by Scheme-I will not be sufficient to optimize the locality of row_1, which leads us to our intra-core + inter-core RRD optimization.

5.2 Scheme-II: intra-core + inter-core RRD optimization

We now discuss an alternate scheme, which considers *both* intra-core row reuse and inter-core row reuse. Instead of focusing on each core in isolation, Scheme-II expands the scope to all the cores in the system, that is, it looks at the LLC misses coming from all cores at a given period of time (within a queue length of 128K entries). Recall that, in the scenario we discussed at the end of the previous section, $core_1$ accesses row_1 and then $core_2$ accesses row_3 and row_1. In this scenario, the two accesses from $core_2$ can be swapped to enable the row reuse with $core_1$. A pseudo-code version of this approach is provided in Algorithm 2.

Algorithm 1 Scheme-I

```
INPUT: # of Channels: X, # of Banks/channel: Y, Mem channel
   queue length: N, # of cores: K
 1: function ACCESSES-REORDER(X,Y)
 2:     for bank_j, j from 0 to X*Y do
 3:         num ← access misses in bank_j
 4:         for miss_k, k from 0 to num do
 5:             miss_var ← miss_k
 6:             if miss_var is marked as scanned then
 7:                 continue
 8:             end if
 9:             scan bank_j
10:              while next miss_l accesses the same row-buffer do
11:                 RRD ← distance between these two misses
12:                 if dependence_detected || RRD ≤ N then
13:                     miss_var ← miss_l
14:                 else
15:                     move miss_l next to miss_k
16:                     update bank_j
17:                     miss_var ← miss_l
18:                 end if
19:                 mark miss_l scanned
20:             end while
21:         end for
22:     end for
23: end function
24: // outermost loop
25: for core C_i, i from 0 to K do
26:     //initial all bank queue sets
27:     bank_j ← ∅   j from 0 to X * Y
28:     for each access miss do
29:         bank_{bank_id} ← access_{bank_id}
30:     end for
31:     //reorder access misses
32:     ACCESSES-REORDER(X,Y)
33: end for
```

Algorithm 2 Scheme-II

```
INPUT: # of Channels: X, # of Banks/channel: Y, Mem channel
   queue length: N, # of cores: K
1: //initial all bank queue sets
2: bank_j ← ∅   j from 0 to X * Y
3: for core C_i, i from 0 to K do
4:     for each access miss do
5:         bank_{bank_id} ← access_{bank_id}
6:     end for
7: end for
8: //reorder access misses
9: ACCESSE-REORDER(X,Y)
```

Instead of generating a separate bank queue for each core, we gather the accesses from all the cores and store them in a set of very large queues based on access arrival time and relative $bank_{id}$, (captured between *line 3* and *line 7*). We then apply our miss reordering strategy on the bank queues which now contain mixed accesses from all the cores.

Figure 8 shows an example illustrating how Scheme-II works in practice. In this example, the original queue contains accesses from two cores, as illustrated in Figure 8(a). Similar to the intra-core classification method, we build the queues according to access $bank_{id}$ in Figure 8(b). Figure 8(c) depicts the optimized access order. Note that without considering inter-core reuse, we would have an access order of $R_2R_1R_3$ for memory $bank_1$ of $core_2$. However, taking into account inter-core reuse, Scheme-II achieves an access order $R_2R_3R_1$, which benefits the row-buffer locality between $core_1$ and $core_2$ on accessing R_3.

It is to be noted that, as far as intra-core reuse is concerned, Scheme-II is expected to be almost as good as Scheme-I. This is because the main difference between these two schemes is that, in Scheme-II we mix all the core accesses together. Note also that the bank queue generation depends only on $bank_{id}$. Our reorder function only takes $bank_{id}$ and row_{id} as input parameters, which are orthogonal to $core_{id}$. As a result, all intra- and inter-core row reuses are captured.

5.3 Discussion

We want to emphasize that neither Scheme-I nor Scheme-II can be implemented in hardware as they are. They are meant to be used as bars against which results of practical implementations can be compared. In this subsection, we would like to discuss the hurdles that need to be addressed if one wants to come close to the performance of our ideal schemes. Let us start with Scheme-I first. A practical implementation that approximates Scheme-I should be able to (i) reorder off-chip references (LLC misses) in a very large buffer before sending them over to their respective target banks, and (ii) ensure that these requests are not reordered in the on-chip network. One difficulty in achieving (i) is the fact that one may not be able to afford to accommodate a very large buffer (e.g., 128K entries) on the core side. Another difficulty is that the potential dependences between off-chip requests need to be checked at the runtime, and costs of such checks usually increase with increasing buffer size. The issues here would be very similar to those encountered in designing re-order buffers (ROB [44]) in superscalar processor design. Point (ii) is even more problematic, because different requests can be delayed in on-chip network (between cores and memory controllers) by different amounts, thereby arriving controllers in a different order than they exit cores. Ensuring that the off-chip requests are not reordered in the network may not be trivial in practice. However, an alternate view of this problem could be to let the network routers themselves implement the desired ordering of off-chip memory requests. That is, each router can be attached with a reasonable-sized buffer using which the off-chip requests are ordered. If all routers implement this policy, one can potentially expect very good row-buffer performance on the DRAM side. Instead of modifying all network routers, one may also consider modifying only the ones that are close to the memory controllers. Coming to Scheme-II, it is certainly much more difficult to implement it in practice, because it requires a global coordination across all cores to decide on the best order of off-chip requests. Note however that the network router-based implementation alternative mentioned above can achieve, to some extent, the effect of Scheme-II, as each on-chip network router normally handles requests coming from different cores and destined to different channels/banks. In case one prefers to have a core-side implementation however (inside of a router-based one), software (e.g., OS) based implementation can read buffers attached to cores and reorder them from a global perspective. Clearly, minimizing the runtime overheads in this case will be a primary concern.

6. EXPERIMENTAL EVALUATION

6.1 Results with the default system parameters

We now quantify the impact and benefits brought by the two schemes discussed in the previous section when simulating a system whose major parameters are listed in Table 1. First, we present in Figure 9 and 10 the distribution of intra-core and inter-core RRDs, respectively, when Scheme-I is applied. One can observe from these results that, while, as

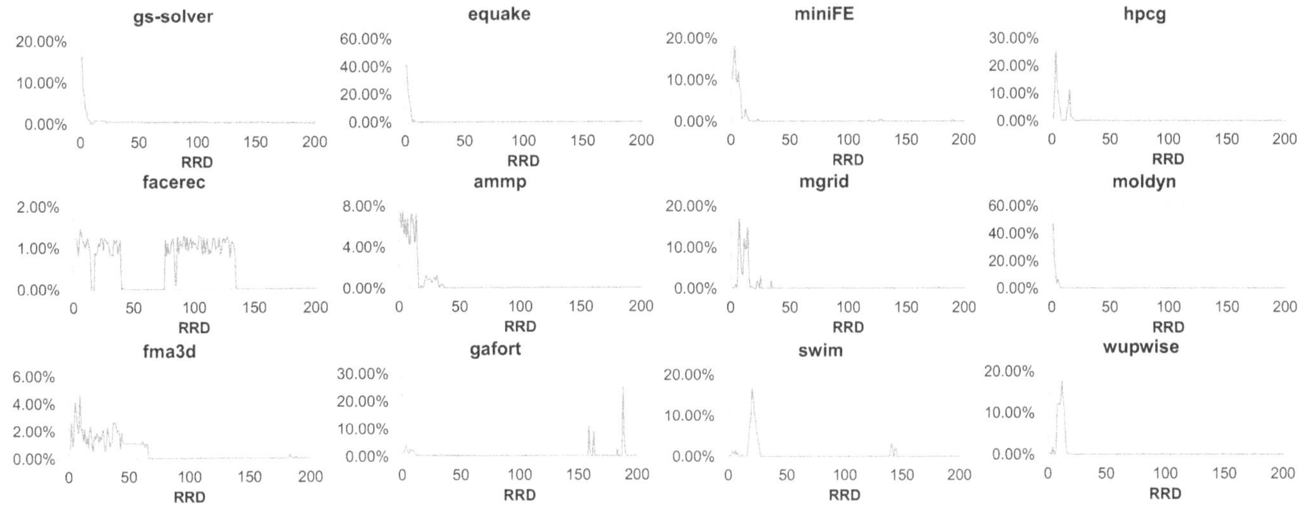

Figure 9: Intra-core RRDs with Scheme-I. The y-axis in each figure captures the frequency of occurrence for different row reuse distances (given the on x-axis). The number of row reuse distances larger than 200 is negligible.

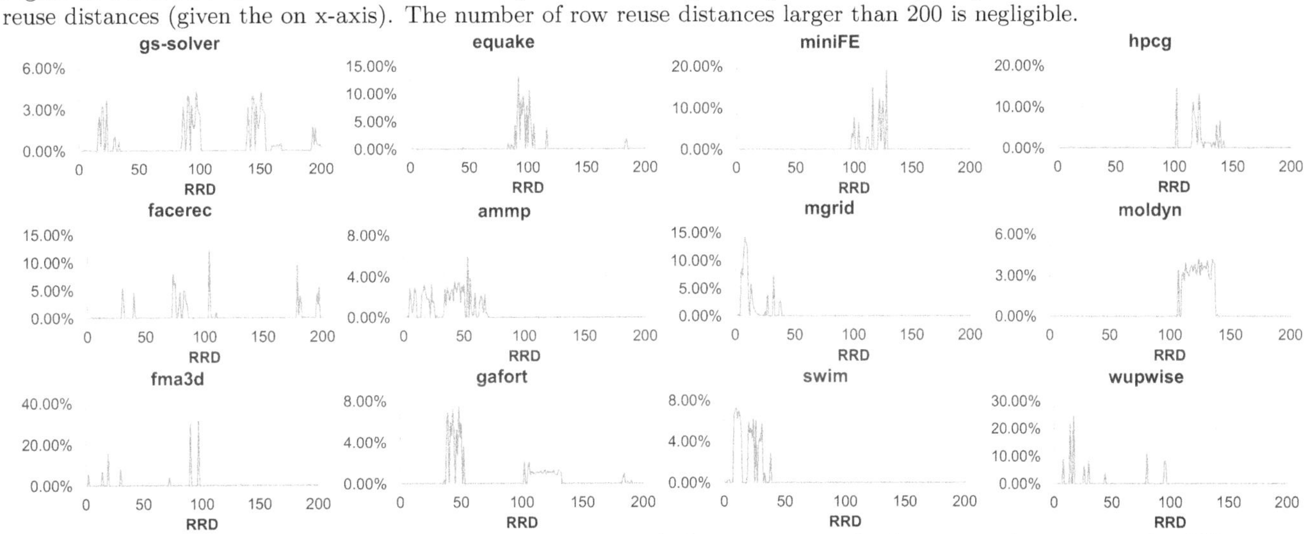

Figure 10: Inter-core RRDs with Scheme-I. The y-axis in each figure captures the frequency of occurrence for different row reuse distances (given on the x-axis). The number of row reuse distances larger than 200 is negligible.

expected, Scheme-I significantly reduces intra-core RRDs, it (unexpectedly) increases inter-core RRDs. This result means that optimizing row reuse from the perspective of each core in isolation does not necessarily generate good row-buffer locality from a global perspective. The first two groups of bars in Figure 13 give the row-buffer hit rates (higher is better) with this scheme. Comparing these results to those presented earlier in Figure 6 show that Scheme-I improves the intra-core row-buffer locality by 16% on an average. In turn, the impact of these row-buffer hit rate improvements on execution times are plotted in Figure 14 (the first bar for each benchmark), as *percentage improvements over the original case*. Overall, optimizing for only intra-core RRD results in an execution time reduction of 17%, when averaged over all 12 application programs we used.

Figures 11 and 12, on the other hand, give the distribution of intra-core and inter-core RRD distributions with Scheme-II. One can make two important observations from these results. First, the distribution of intra-core misses in Figure 11 is very similar to that in Figure 9. That is, considering inter-core row reuse does not significantly impact intra-core reuse distances. The second observation is that Scheme-II substantially reduces the inter-core RRDs. These results in turn translate to the row-buffer hit rates plotted in Figure 13 (the last two groups of bars), indicating an average row-buffer hit rate improvement of 12% for intra-core hits and 13% for inter-core hits. Finally, this scheme brings execution time improvements ranging between 7% (*facerec*) and 34% (*ammp*), as captured by the second bar for each benchmark in Figure 14.

6.2 Evaluation of the previously-proposed schemes

In this subsection, we report results from our implementation of two previously-proposed schemes that improve row-buffer locality and show how close they come to our savings reported above. This first of these schemes, by Awasthi et al. [18], employs adaptive first-touch page-placement and dynamic page-migration, and the execution time improvements it generates over the original execution case are given as the third bar for each application in Figure 14. It can be seen that this approach reduces execution time by 10%

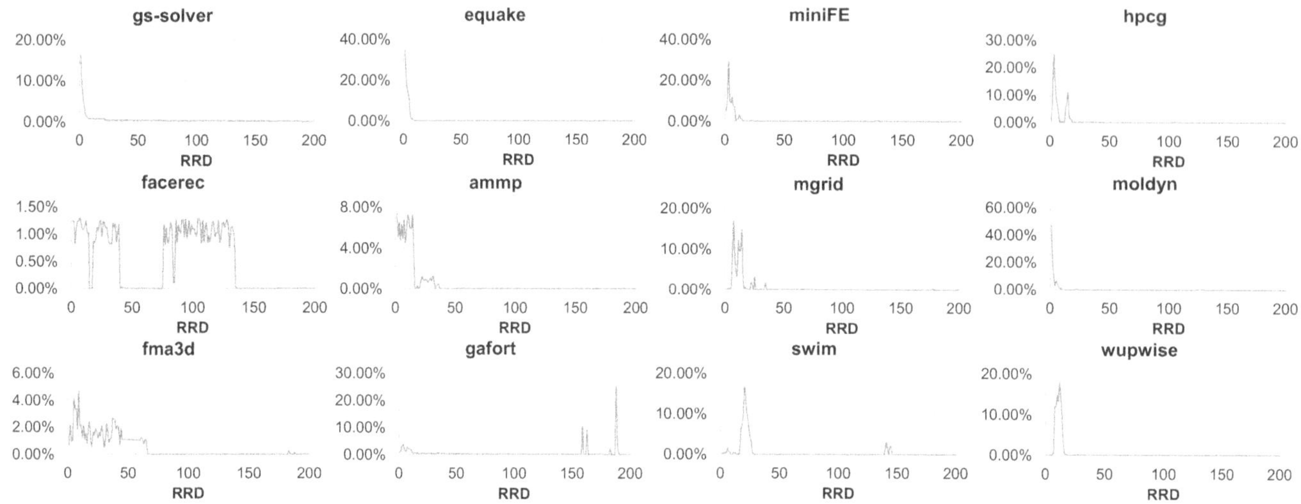

Figure 11: Intra-core RRDs with Scheme-II. The y-axis in each figure captures the frequency of occurrence for different row reuse distances (given on the x-axis). The number of row reuse distances larger than 200 is negligible.

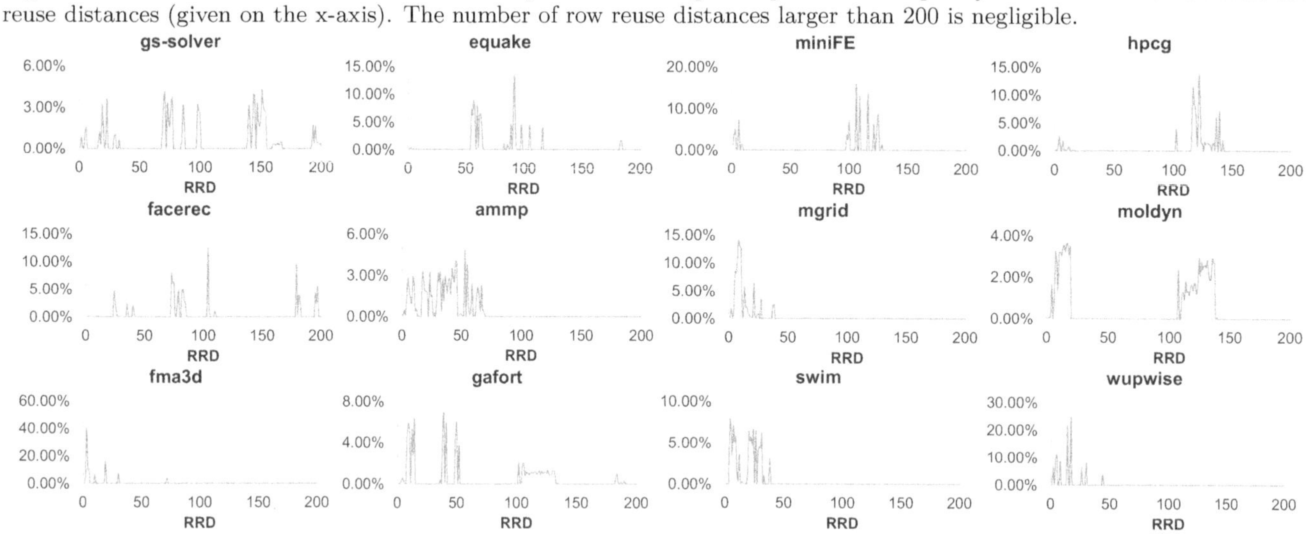

Figure 12: Inter-core RRDs with Scheme-II. The y-axis in each figure captures the frequency of occurance for different row reuse distances (given on the x-axis). The number of row reuse distances larger than 200 is negligible.

on an average. The second scheme we tested [37] is not specific to multithreaded applications but can be used for them. It orchestrates page frame allocation so that the pages that threads access are dispersed randomly across multiple banks so that each thread's access pattern is randomized. The execution time improvements it brings over the original case are plotted as the fourth bar in the same figure (9% average improvement). These results clearly show that, while both these practical schemes are effective in improving performance, there is a significant gap between them and our ideal schemes, motivating for further research on improving row-buffer locality.

6.3 Results from the sensitivity experiments

Our goal in this section is to evaluate our schemes under different values of our major system parameters. In each experiment, the value of only one parameter is modified; the remaining parameters retain their original values listed in Table 1. The results from these sensitivity experiments with Scheme-II are given in Figure 16. Our main observations from these experiments can be summarized as follows. First, when we increase the number of cores, the effectiveness of our scheme increases. This is mainly because a higher core count makes considering the row reuse across cores even more critical, increasing opportunities for Scheme-II. A similar observation, with a smaller variance though, can be made with the increased LLC (L3) capacity. This is due to the fact that a larger L3 causes the off-chip requests to spread apart more and become sparser over the memory space, this again benefits more from our scheme, which is oriented towards reducing large reuse distances. However, an opposite trend is observed when the row-buffer (memory row) size increased. This is because a larger memory row makes some of the memory accesses that would normally generate row-buffer misses result in row-buffer hits. Next, increasing the number of banks (by keeping the total memory space same) causes the off-chip accesses to spread more over the address space, again increasing the importance of row-buffer optimization. Finally, as expected, reducing the memory queue size helps our schemes generate better results, as a large memory queue captures some of the reuse that would otherwise be lost in the smaller queue. Overall, these sensitivity experiments clearly show that there is a great potential for

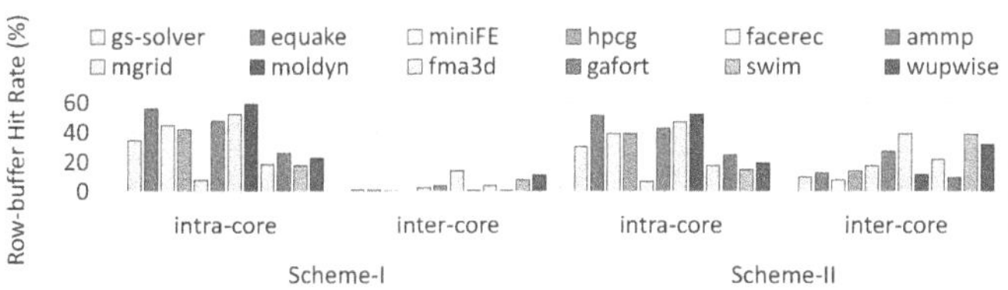

Figure 13: Row-buffer hit rates with our schemes.

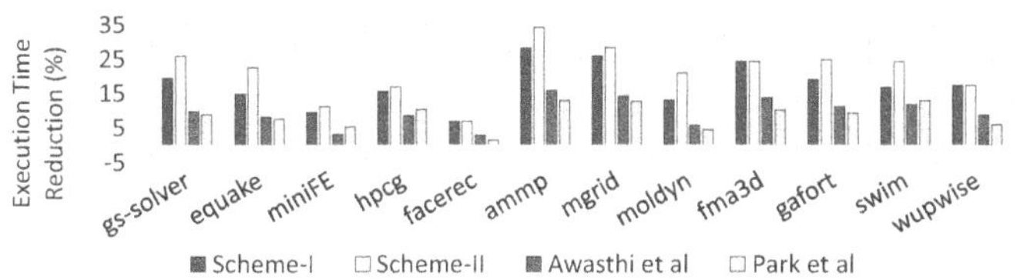

Figure 14: Execution time improvements with different schemes.

Scheme-II under various values of our major system parameters.

6.4 Results with different memory scheduling policies

Our final set of experiments measure the behavior of our two schemes under different memory request scheduling policies. Recall that the default memory scheduling policy used in our experiments so far was FR-FCFS, which re-orders the pending requests in the memory buffer to maximize row-buffer hits. Since our schemes also reorder the requests (on the core side) by looking at a much larger window (128K entries instead of 32K entries), it is interesting to test its impact under different memory scheduling policies. In the results presented in Figure 15, we use our approach with FCFS (simple first-come, first-served; which is basically FR-FCFS with no locality engagement), ATLAS [20], and TCM [35]. ATLAS [20] periodically orders threads based on the service they received from the memory controllers so far, and prioritizes the threads that have attained least service over others. In comparison, TCM [35] groups threads with similar memory access behavior into either the memory-non-intensive or the memory-intensive bin, and performs prioritization across these bins to maximize memory performance. In Figure 15, all bars for a given benchmark are *normalized* with respect to our approach (Scheme-II) running with FR-FCFS. Maybe the most striking observation from this plot is that these different memory scheduling policies generate very similar performance results (between -3% and 3% range), as long as they are used with our scheme. In other words, *the existence of our scheme makes the specifics of the underlying memory scheduling policy much less important.* This is a very important (and somewhat unexpected) result because, everything else being equal, it is always more cost efficient to employ the least complex policy at hardware. These results clearly show that, if we could reorder the off-chip requests on the core side, there is *no* need for any second-level request reordering (in hardware) at the memory bank queues.

7. RELATED WORK

Reuse distance has been studied in a lot of prior works to help design techniques that can improve the program's

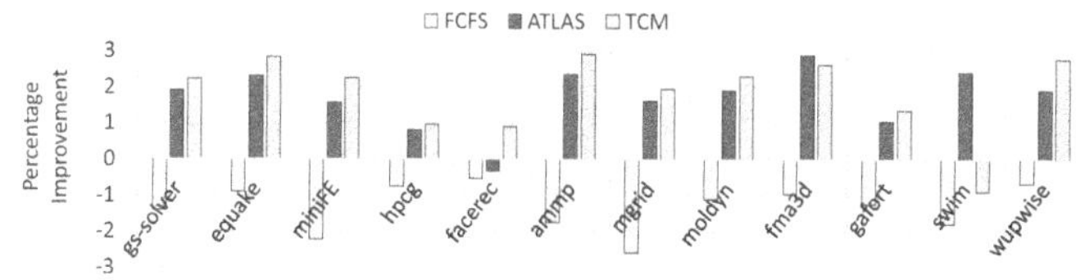

Figure 15: Results with different memory scheduling policies. For each benchmark, all bars are normalized to Scheme-II running with FR-FCFS.

performance [27–29, 31–34]. Chen and Zhong proposed a scheme to predict program locality by analyzing the data reuse distance with the help of profiling techniques [27]. They first employed distance-based sampling to a program's execution. Then they use a pattern recognition technique to analyze the data reuse distance to predict the program's data locality. Keramidas et al used reuse distance to improve the traditional LRU cache replacement policy [28]. Based on their observation that LRU is not effective for applications that have a large reuse distance, they proposed static and dynamic cache replacement policies in order to improve performance.

Zhang et al [19] investigated on multi-core data reuse. Their investigation shows that current on-chip cache hierarchies of multicore architectures and the state-of-the-art code/data optimizations are not able to fully exploit inter-core data reuse in parallel applications. They presented a compiler-based data locality optimization strategy that can balance both inter-core and intra-core reuse optimizations. Our work is different from [19] because we focus on row-buffer data locality.

There have also been many previously-proposed schemes to optimize the design of memory schedulers [13, 14, 18, 20, 23–25]. Zhang et al proposed a permutation-based scheme that dramatically increases the row-buffer hit rate to reduce memory stall time [13]. Their scheme employed the fast exclusive-OR operation to generate the bank index, so that data addresses are interleaved in a way to increase both the bank-level parallelism as well as data locality in the row-buffer. However, their scheme targets only on single processor platforms. In this work, we are more interested in measuring the impact of row-buffer locality on performance for multithreaded applications.

The past years have also seen many research works leveraging memory controller scheduling to improve the fairness for parallel applications [20, 23–25, 35, 36]. A scheme is proposed in [20] that periodically reorders threads based on the amount of service they have obtained from the memory controllers. Their scheme is based on Pareto Distribution which claims that a job running for a short time so far is expected to end soon. The proposed memory scheduling policy prioritizes threads receiving the least amount of service over others in each epoch in order to provide fairness to all threads. PAR-BS [25] is a memory scheduling scheme proposed to provide quality of service and also improve the system throughput. In the PAR-BS scheme, DRAM requests are processed in batches in order to provide fairness. PAR-BS also employs parallelism-aware DRAM scheduling by processing requests from a given thread in parallel across all the DRAM banks. As a result, the system performance

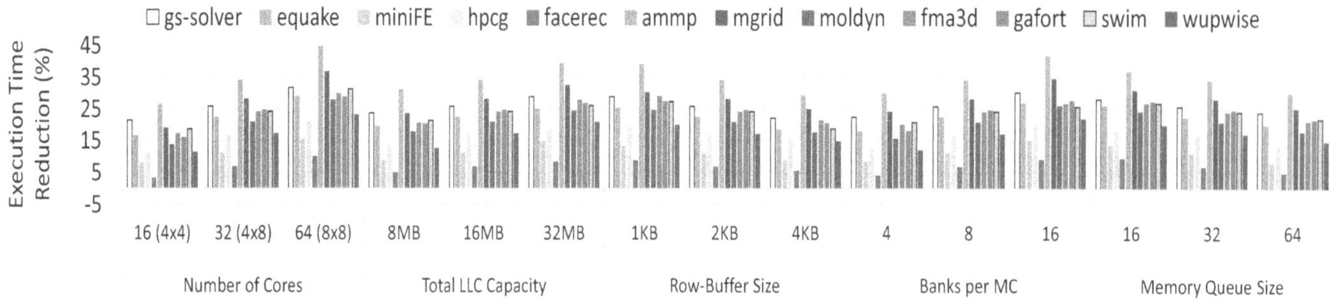

Figure 16: Results from the sensitivity experiments. In each sensitivity experiment, the middle group of bars represent the default value.

can be improved by reducing the memory stall time of the threads.

8. CONCLUDING REMARKS AND FUTURE WORK

In this paper, we make two main contributions. First, we define row reuse distance (RRD) both for a core and across different cores, and quantify it using a set of 12 multithreaded benchmarks and a detailed simulation infrastructure. Second, we evaluate two ideal schemes targeting (i) only intra-core row reuses and (ii) both intra- and inter-core memory row reuses. The results from this evaluation show that (i) the scheme that targets only intra-core row reuses results in an increase in inter-core reuse distances (despite the significant reduction in intra-core reuse distances), and (ii) the second scheme significantly improves inter-core row reuse distances while maintaining almost the same performance level of the first scheme regarding the intra-core row reuses. To our knowledge, ours is the first work that formalizes the concept of memory row reuse distance concept, and gives two schemes to optimize it. Overall, our experimental result indicate that the proposed two schemes can improve row-buffer buffer hit rates by 13% and 26% on average, which translate to average execution time improvements of 17% and 21%. The schemes evaluated in this work are not directly implementable. Our next step includes developing practical schemes that can approximate the behavior/performance of these ideal schemes. In particular, motivated by the observation that considering both intra-core and inter-core row reuse distances can bring significant execution time savings, we plan to explore low-overhead techniques that enable coordinated LLC miss scheduling across multiple cores.

9. ACKNOWLEDGMENTS

This work is supported in part by NSF grants 1213052, 1205618, 1439021, 0963839, and 1017882, as well as a grant from Intel.

10. REFERENCES

[1] M. Xie, D. Tong, K. Huang and X. Cheng, *Improving system throughput and fairness simultaneously in shared memory CMP systems via Dynamic Bank Partitioning*, HPCA, 2014.

[2] L. Subramanian, D. Lee, V. Seshadri, H. Rastogi, and O. Mutlu, *The Blacklisting Memory Scheduler: Achieving High Performance and Fairness at Low Cost*, ICCD, 2014.

[3] B. T. Davis, *Modern DRAM Architectures. PhD thesis*, University of Michigan, 2000.

[4] W. Ding, D. Guttman and M. Kandemir, *Compiler Support for Optimizing Memory Bank-Level Parallelism*, MICRO, 2014.

[5] S. O,Y. H. Son, N. S. Kim and J. H. Ahn, *Row-buffer decoupling: a case for low-latency DRAM microarchitecture*, ISCA, 2014.

[6] D. Chandra, F. Guo, S. Kim, and Y. Solihin. *Predicting inter-thread cache contention on a chip multi-processor architecture*, HPCA, 2005.

[7] J. Chang and G. S. Sohi, *Cooperative cache partitioning for chip multiprocessors*, ICS, 2007.

[8] A. Jaleel, W. Hasenplaugh, M. Qureshi, J. Sebot, S. Steely Jr. and J. Emer, *Adaptive insertion policies for managing shared caches*, PACT, 2008.

[9] M. Kandemir, S. P. Muralidhara, S. H. K. Narayanan, Y. Zhang, O. Ozturk, *Optimizing shared cache behavior of chip multiprocessors*, MICRO, 2009.

[10] S. Kim, D. Chandra and Y. Solihin *Fair cache sharing and partitioning in a chip multiprocessor architecture*, PACT, 2004.

[11] S. Rixner, *Memory controller optimizations for web servers*, MICRO, 2004.

[12] S. Rixner, W. J. Dally, U. J. Kapasi, P. Mattson, and J. D. Owens, *Memory access scheduling*, ISCA, 2000.

[13] Z. Zhang, Z. Zhu, and X. Zhang, *A permutation-based page interleaving scheme to reduce row-buffer conflicts and exploit data locality*, MICRO, 2000.

[14] S. M. Zahedi, and B. C. Lee, *REF: resource elasticity fairness with sharing incentives for multiprocessors*, ASPLOS, 2014.

[15] H. Wang, R. Singh, M. J. Schulte, and N. S. Kim, *Memory scheduling towards high-throughput cooperative heterogeneous computing*, PACT, 2014.

[16] J. Hasan, S. Chandra, and T. N. Vijaykumar, *Efficient Use of Memory Bandwidth to Improve Network Processor Throughput*, ISCA, 2003.

[17] H. Yoon, J. Meza, R. Ausavarungnirun, R. A. Harding and O. Mutlu, *Row Buffer Locality Aware Caching Policies for Hybrid Memories*, ICCD, 2012.

[18] K. Sudan, N. Chatterjee, D. Nellans, M. Awasthi, R. Balasubramonian and A. Davis, *Micro-Pages: Increasing DRAM Efficiency with Locality-Aware Data Placement*, ASPLOS, 2010.

[19] Y. Zhang, M. T. Kandemir and T. Yemliha, *Studying inter-core data reuse in multicores*, SIGMETRICS, 2011.

[20] Y. Kim, D. Han, O. Mutlu and M. Harchol-Balter, *ATLAS: A Scalable and High-Performance Scheduling Algorithm for Multiple Memory Controllers*, HPCA, 2010.

[21] JEDEC Solid State Technology Association, *DDR3 SDRAM Specification*, JESD79-3D edition, Sept, 2009

[22] *Calculating Memory System Power for DDR3*, Technical report, Micron Technology Inc., 2–7, TN-4-01, 2007.

[23] K. J. Nesbit, N. Aggarwal, J. Laudon, and J. E. Smith. *Fair queuing memory systems*, MICRO, 2006.

[24] O. Mutlu and T. Moscibroda. *Stall-time fair memory access scheduling for chip multiprocessor*, MICRO, 2007.

[25] O. Mutlu and T. Moscibroda, *Parallelism-aware batch scheduling: Enhancing both performance and fairness of shared DRAM systems*, ISCA, 2008.

[26] T. E. Carlson, W. Heirman, and L. Eeckhout, *Sniper: Exploring the level of abstraction for scalable and accurate parallel multi-core simulations*, SC, 2011.

[27] D. Chen and Y. Zhong, *Predicting whole-program locality through reuse distance analysis*, PLDI, 2003.

[28] G. Keramidas, P. Petoumenos and S. Kaxiras, *Cache Replacement Based on Reuse-Distance Prediction*, ICCD, 2007.

[29] A. Jaleel, K. B. Theobald, S. C. Steely Jr. and J. Emer, *High Performance Cache Replacement Using Re-Reference Interval Prediction*, ISCA, 2007.

[30] K. Beyls and E. H. D'Hollander, *Reuse distance as a metric for cache behavior*, IPDCS, 2001.

[31] G. Almasi, C. Cascaval and D. A. Padua, *Calculating stack distances efficiently*, SIGPLAN Not., 2003

[32] Y. Jiang, E. Z. Zhang, K. Tian, X. Shen, *Is reuse distance applicable to data locality analysis on chip multiprocessors?*, Compiler Construction, 2010.

[33] M. Kandemir, *A compiler technique for improving whole-program locality*, POPL, 2001.

[34] D. L. Schuff, M. Kulkarni, and V. S. Pai, *Accelerating multicore reuse distance analysis with sampling and parallelization*, PACT, 2010.

[35] Y. Kim, M. Papamichael, O. Mutlu and M. Harchol-Balter, *Thread Cluster Memory Scheduling: Exploiting Differences in Memory Access Behavior*, MICRO, 2010.

[36] M. Awasthi, D. Nellans, K. Sudan, R. Balasubramonian and A. Davis, *Handling the Problems and Opportunities Posed by Multiple On-Chip Memory Controllers*, PACT, 2010.

[37] H. Park, S. Baek, J. Choi, D. Lee and S. Noh, *Regularities considered harmful: forcing randomness to memory accesses to reduce row-buffer conflicts for multi-core, multi-bank systems*, ASPLOS, 2013.

[38] R. Barrett, R. Barrett, M. Berry3, T. F. Chan, J. Demmel, J. M. Donato, J. Dongarra, V. Eijkhout, R. Pozo, C. Romine, and H. Van der Vorst, *Templates for the Solution of Linear Systems: Building Blocks for Iterative Methods*, 2nd Edition, SIAM, 1994.

[39] V. Aslot, M. Domeika, R. Eigenmann, G. Gaertner, W. B. Jones, and B. Parady, *SPEComp: A new benchmark suite for measuring parallel computer performance*, WOMPEI, 2001.

[40] https://www.nersc.gov/users/computational-systems/cori/nersc-8-procurement/trinity-nersc-8-rfp/nersc-8-trinity-benchmarks.

[41] D J. Craik, A .Kumar, G. C. Levy, *MOLDYN: a generalized program for the evaluation of molecular dynamics models using nuclear magnetic resonance spin-relaxation data*, J. Chem. Inf. Comput. Sci., 1983.

[42] https://software.sandia.gov/hpcg/html/index.html.

[43] C. Kim, D. Burger, and S. Keckler, *An adaptive, non-uniform cache structure for wire-delay dominated on-chip caches*, ASPLOS, 2002.

[44] J. Hennessy and D. Patterson, *Computer Architecture: A Quantitative Approach, 4th Edition*, Morgan Kaufmann, 2012.

Smartphone Energy Drain in the Wild: Analysis and Implications

Xiaomeng Chen[†^] Ning Ding[†^] Abhilash Jindal[†^] Y. Charlie Hu[†^] Maruti Gupta[*] Rath Vannithamby[*]
[†]Purdue University [^]Mobile Enerlytics [*]Intel Corporation

ABSTRACT

The limited battery life of modern smartphones remains a leading factor adversely affecting the mobile experience of millions of smartphone users. In order to extend battery life, it is critical to understand where and how is energy drain happening on users' phones under normal usage, for example, in a one-day cycle.

In this paper, we conduct the first extensive measurement and modeling of energy drain of 1520 smartphone in the wild. We make two primary contributions. First, we develop a hybrid power model that integrates utilization-based models and FSM-based models for different phone components with a novel technique that estimates the triggers for the FSM-based network power model based on network utilization. Second, through analyzing traces collected on 1520 Galaxy S3 and S4 devices in the wild, we present detailed analysis of where the CPU time and energy are spent across the 1520 devices, inside the 800 apps, as well as along several evolution dimensions, including hardware, Android, cellular, and app updates. Our findings of smartphone energy drain in the wild have significant implications to the various key players of the Android phone eco-system, including phone vendors (*e.g.,* Samsung), Android developers, app developers, and ultimately millions of smartphone users, towards the common goal of extending smartphone battery life and improving the user mobile experience.

Categories and Subject Descriptors

C.4 [**Computer System Organization**]: Performance of Systems—*Modeling techniques*; D.2.8 [**Metrics**]: Performance measures

General Terms

Experimentation, Measurement, Performance

Keywords

Smartphones, battery drain, power model, screen-off energy

1. INTRODUCTION

The smartphone market has been growing at a phenomenal rate. eMarketer [2] estimates the smartphone users worldwide surpassed the 1 billion mark in 2012 and will be 1.75 billion in 2014, and expects smartphone adoption to continue on a fast-paced trajectory through 2017.

Despite the phenomenal market penetration of smartphones, the user experience has been severely limited by the phone battery life. For example, a survey in May 2014 by research company GMI [7] of 1000 Britons shows 89% rated long battery life as an "important" factor when buying a new smartphone – long battery life rated higher than all other features.

To improve the mobile experience of billions of smartphone users, it is critical to study ways of extending smartphone battery life. As the rechargeable battery technology has remained stagnant and seems unlikely to deliver the energy requirements, optimizing the energy drain is the more promising approach. Tackling this problem requires a thorough understanding of where energy drain is occurring inside the phone over the course of a typical battery recharge cycle, for example over the period of a day.

Understanding the energy drain of smartphones in normal users' daily life however cannot be easily done via controlled experiments in the lab, since the energy drain for a given device is affected by external conditions and user behavior in significant ways. First, the energy drain of wireless interfaces such as WiFi or cellular data, which accounts for a significant fraction of the total device energy drain, can be affected by the different signal strength the device experiences throughout the day [9]. Second, different users set very different device configurations (*e.g.,* notification and WiFi settings). Third, different users spend differing amounts of time each day on the phone. Fourth, different users install and play with different apps on their devices, which can have very different energy drain behavior. Fifth, even for the same app, different users can have very different usage patterns, resulting in different energy drain rates.

In this paper, we undertake to our knowledge the first effort towards performing such an energy analysis of smartphones in the wild. Conducting such a study faces two major challenges. First, to enable the measurement of hardware components and apps and services running on the phones in the wild, we need an accurate power model for smartphones that (1) does not rely on triggers that can only be collected by modifying the Android framework or the kernel of the phones, (2) does not rely on packet-level trace (*e.g.,* from tcpdump) which would require users to root their phones, violating the service plans for carriers such as AT&T and Verizon; and (3) can capture details of activities such as WiFi beaconing, cellular paging, and SOC suspension. We overcome this challenge by developing a hybrid model that combines utilization-based and FSM-based models for different phone components and estimates the triggers for the FSM-based network power model based on network utilization. The key insight is to strike a careful balance be-

SIGMETRICS'15, June 15–19, 2015, Portland, OR, USA.

ACM 978-1-4503-3486-0/15/06 ...$15.00.
DOI: http://dx.doi.org/10.1145/2745844.2745875.

tween the estimation error and granularity of the utilization logging which directly affects the estimation error and logging overhead.

A second challenge is to collect triggers for driving such a power model of real users' phones under the normal usage in their daily lives, while incurring low logging overhead. To this end, we developed a free app that performs logging and released it to Google Play so volunteers can download and contribute to the data collection.

We summarize our contributions and highlights of our findings as follows.

- We developed a hybrid power model for estimating energy drain of the hardware components and apps and services running on the smartphones in the wild. The model relies on light-weight logging that can be performed without modifying the Android framework or rooting the phones and hence is readily deployable.
- Through a carefully designed free app that performs low overhead logging, we collected all the triggers needed to drive our power model from 1520 Galaxy S3 and S4 devices, geographically distributed over 56 countries, covering a total of 49326 days and 199 mobile operators.
- Our in-depth analysis of the CPU usage time on the 1520 devices shows that: (1) During screen-on periods, the CPU on average, is idle for 73.5% of time, signifying that user activities do not use a lot of computational power. (2) On average, the total CPU busy time during screen-on and screen-off periods are 8.6% and 17.0% respectively, suggesting a significant portion of the total CPU busy time is spent during screen-off periods running apps and services in the background. (3) Out of the total CPU busy time (25.6%), background services which run on behalf of the apps account for about 11.9% (in absolute), which testifies to the uniqueness of the Android programming environment where much of the common tasks are abstracted and provided by the system as services which can be directly called by apps and hence simplify app programming. (4) On average, the devices spent 45.4% of the time connected to WiFi, 32.2% of the time connected to Cellular, and 22.5% of the time disconnected from both, showing a significant period of time the user has no network connectivity.
- Our analysis of the energy drain across the 1520 devices shows that: (1) On average the SOC suspend state, cellular paging, WiFi beacon, and WiFi scanning account for a total of 23.4% of the daily energy drain, of which cellular paging is a significant energy hog using up 12.5%. (2) Additionally, background apps and services during screen-off contribute to 16.1% of the total energy. (3) Overall, on average a whopping 45.0% of the total energy drain in a day occurs during screen-off periods. (4) Out of the 55.0% energy incurred during screen-on periods, a little less than half, 24.0%, is spent on the screen. (5) The energy drain from active networking over cellular (LTE and 3G) and over WiFi are 11.7% and 1.3%, respectively, showing cellular drains significantly more energy than WiFi. Further, a significant portion of the energy drain, 10.5% out of 11.7% for 3G/LTE and 1.2% out of the 1.3% for WiFi, are tail energy.
- We further study the 800 apps running on the 1520 devices which show that (1) Background energy can be significant for apps: accounting for more than 50% of the total energy for 22.5% of the apps, with an average of 27.1% across all 800 apps. (2) Within the foreground app energy, screen energy is the largest portion, at 46.2% on average across the apps. (3) Within either foreground or background periods, CPU and GPU dominate networking energy – the average ratios are 2.7x and 2.8x, respectively, across the 800 apps. (4) We further studied the app energy drain by different Google Play app categories and gained much insight into energy bottlenecks of the apps in different categories.
- Finally, we analyzed the energy drain of the 1520 devices along several evolution dimensions, including hardware evolution, Android evolution, cellular evolution, and app evolution. Our analysis shows that (1) the average CPU time of S4/Jellybean devices is 8.1% longer than S3/Jellybean devices, which translates into 11.3% energy drain increase; (2) the average CPU time of S3 and S4 KitKat devices are 33.2% and 22.5% higher than the corresponding Jellybean S3 and S4 devices, which translate into only 9.7% and 8.0% energy increase. (3) Popular apps such as Facebook and Chrome have many different versions running in the wild, and their average power draw during foreground runs fluctuates by up to 150.8%.

The detailed analysis and findings of the smartphone energy drain in the wild from our study have significant implications to the various key players of the Android phone eco-system, including phone vendors (*e.g.,* Samsung), Android developers, app developers, and ultimately millions of smartphone users, towards the common goal of extending smartphone battery life and improving user mobile experience.

The remaining paper is organized as follows. §2 presents the power model we developed for estimating the detailed energy drain of smartphones in the wild. §3 then presents the CPU time and energy analysis of the 1520 Galaxy S3 and S4 devices in the wild using the traces collected from these phones. §4 zooms into the apps and services running on the devices and analyzes their energy drain behavior, and §5 analyzes the energy drain of the 1520 devices along several evolution dimensions, including hardware, Android, cellular, and app evolutions. We discuss related work in §6 and conclude in §7.

2. POWER MODELING FOR PHONES IN THE WILD

The simplest way to measure the battery drain of a smartphone is to use a power meter [5]. However, such an approach suffers two drawbacks: (1) it cannot be used to measure phones in the wild; (2) it cannot measure the energy drain of individual apps and services concurrently running on the phone since the power meter outputs the total power draw of the phone. To measure the battery drain of apps and services of smartphones in the wild, we developed a hybrid power model that requires no modifications to the Android framework or the kernel or rooting the phone.

2.1 Background

Power models for mobile devices in general and wireless components such as WiFi, 3G and LTE radios have been actively studied in recent years, and the proposed power models fall into two major categories.

The first category of power models known as utilization-based models for smartphones (*e.g.,* [21, 24, 25]) are based on the intuitive assumption that the utilization of a hardware component (*e.g.,* NIC) corresponds to a certain power state and the change of utilization is what triggers the power state change of that component. Consequently, these models all use the utilization of a hardware component as the "trigger" in modeling power states and state transitions. Such models thus do not capture power behavior of modern wireless components that do not lead to active utilization such as the promotion and tail power behavior of 3G and LTE [19, 12], and thus can incur high modeling error.

The second category of power models capture the non-utilization-based power behavior of wireless components using finite state machines (FSMs), *e.g.,* [8, 15, 18, 16, 17, 9] for WiFi and 3G and [12] for LTE. In a nut shell, the built-in state machine of the wireless radio, *e.g.,* the RRC states and transitions in LTE, is reverse-engineered and represented in a finite state machine that annotates each power state or transition with measured power draw and dura-

Table 1: Summary of power model.

Hardware component power draw	Model trigger
CPU	frequency + utilization
GPU	frequency + utilization
Screen	brightness level
WiFi	FSM + signal strength
3G/LTE	FSM + signal strength
WiFi beacon	WiFi status
Cellular Paging	cellular status
SOC Suspension	constant

tion values. The triggers for the state transitions are either packet-level traces [19, 12] or networking system calls [17].

2.2 Challenges

The smartphone power model we need to enable measurement of energy drain of hardware components and apps and services running on the smartphones in the wild needs to satisfy the following requirements:

- The model cannot rely on triggers (*e.g.,* system calls) that can only be collected by modifying the Android framework or the kernel of the phones.
- Similarly, the model should not rely on packet-level trace (*e.g.,* from tcpdump) which would require users to root their phones. Rooting the phones would void the phone's warranty and violate the service plans for carriers such as AT&T and Verizon.
- Since we also want to measure the energy drain during screen-off periods, the model needs to incorporate behavior such as WiFi beaconing, cellular paging, and SOC suspension as they add up to significant energy drain over time.

2.3 Modeling Overview

Hardware components modeled. We focus on Galaxy S3 and S4 phones in our measurement study due to their popularity, accounting for 11% of the total Android phone market share [1]. We determined the set of phone components to be modeled by measuring the maximal power draw of all the major components using microbenchmarks one at a time, while keeping the load on other components steady. For example, to gauge the GPU power, we kept the CPU at a fixed frequency, and ran the GPU benchmark app [4] that performs 2D rendering. Based on these initial power measurements, we selected the set of components showing significant power draw, as shown in Table 1. We further confirmed the components are largely independent – our model described below which assumes different components are independent and add up to the total power drain of the phone has an error less than 10%.

When actively used, GPS can drain a non-trivial amount of power. We do not model GPS in our study as logging GPS requires explicit user permission and we found many users feel reluctant to give out this permission for privacy concerns.

A hybrid model. To accurately capture the power behavior of all the identified components, we developed a hybrid utilization-based and FSM-based power model that satisfies the above model requirements yet achieves good modeling accuracy. In particular, we resort to utilization-based modeling to capture power behavior of CPU and GPU whose power draw depend on utilization, we use FSM-based modeling for wireless interfaces such as WiFi/3G/LTE, we model WiFi beacon and cellular paging as constant power draws by averaging their power spikes over time, and finally we model SOC suspension power as a constant power draw.

In summary, the triggers for modeling all the components are shown in Table 1, and can be collected on unmodified user phones.

2.4 Modeling Details

Before we start, we distinguish two classes of programs consuming CPU time and energy on the smartphones: apps and system services. System services include kernel processes (with UID < 1000) and framework processes (with UID between 1000 and 9999) such as `LocationManagerService` which are exported from the Android framework for use by apps. Apps can be user-level programs or system apps such as `Calendar` and `Clock` and have UIDs > 10000, and an app can potentially invoke services exported by the Android framework or the kernel. In this paper, we simply refer to system services as *services.*

CPU. As specified in the previous section, we used CPU microbenchmarks to obtain the relationship between the CPU power draw and CPU operating frequency and also devised a methodology for accounting for multiple cores running at different frequencies. Further details can be found in Appendix A.

Screen. To model the power draw of Galaxy S3/S4 which are both AMOLED screens, we derived a power model based on screen brightness and ignored screen content to reduce our overhead. Details can be found in Appendix A.

GPU. We developed a power model for GPU based on the different power states as well as accounting for the operating frequency during each state. Details can be found in Appendix A.

To use the GPU power model, we log the duration of each GPU frequency and state combination every 1 second, and predict the GPU power draw of each interval based on the GPU model.

SOC during suspension. When the CPU and other hardware components are offline, the entire SOC is suspended and draws a constant current. We turn the screen and WiFi off, set the phone in airplane mode; soon after the SOC is put in suspension by the Linux power manager, and we measure the SOC base power draw in this state. The measured constant power draw of the SOC suspended state are 3.8 mA and 5.1 mA for Galaxy S3 and S4, respectively.

WiFi Beacon. When the WiFi radio is associated with an AP and in power saving mode, the WiFi radio wakes up at fixed intervals to receive beacons from the AP. Each beacon thus results in a power spike of the WiF radio, and we noticed that the width and shape of the spikes are independent of the WiFi version, channel frequency, or the AP. We average the energy of 50 spikes over the duration of the spikes and then model the WiFi beacon power as constant current over time over the base SOC power – 1.1 mA on both Galaxy S3 and S4.

WiFi scanning. When WiFi is enabled on the phone, whether in connected or disconnected state, it performs scanning, *i.e.,* to try to connect to a suitable network by searching all possible channels until it finds one to connect to. For example, the 2.4 GHz band (802.11/bg) has 11 channels and the 5GHz (802.11ac) band has 22 channels and all may have to be searched. Galaxy S3 and S4 devices are capable of both bands, though we found most of WiFi hotspots seem to operate at 2.4GHz. Our measurements showed that WiFi scanning on these two phones has a duration of 3.4 seconds and average power draw of 64 mA. When scanning completes, Android generates an event, `android.net.wifi.SCAN_RESULTS` We find out how many scanning events happened by logging such events.

Cellular paging. On a cellular network, the base station periodically broadcasts a message during the 3G/LTE Idle state to signal incoming downlink data or voice call or SMS. This is called paging. The power meter shows paging results in a power spike on the phone modem every 1.28s, and this happens regardless whether the phone has a SIM card or not, and with or without mobile data enabled. As with WiFi beacon, we average the spike energy over time and model the cellular paging as a constant current over time over the base SOC power – 8.3 mA on S3 and 2.3 mA on S4.

WiFi, 3G, LTE State Machine Models. WiFi, 3G, and LTE interfaces have multiple power states (see Appendix A) and the power draw and duration at the Active state is affected by the wireless signal strength [9]. Further, as in [11], we noticed significant CPU power draw during pure data transfer workload, due to interrupt handling and TCP/IP stack processing, and therefore we need to carefully decouple CPU power draw from the wireless interface power draw in training the model. To develop signal-strength-aware power models for the wireless interfaces for our phone, we connected the phone to the power meter and ran data transfer microbenchmarks. While the power meter collects the power profile, we also recorded the packets via tcpdump alongside signal strength values via Android APIs as well as CPU frequencies and the CPU utilization. We varied the signal strength received by the phone by adjusting the distance between the phone and the AP for WiFi experiments and changing the location of the phone for 3G/LTE experiments. In post-processing, we synchronized the power profile from the power meter, tcpdump and signal strength traces. We derived the power draw by the radio interface(s) by subtracting the CPU power from the total power. We inferred the different power states of WiFi, 3G, LTE following the procedure in [12, 9] and derived the various parameters of the signal-strength-aware power state machine for each interface. Tables 10 in Appendix A shows the WiFi and LTE power draw for Galaxy S3 and S4 under different signal strength.

Estimating network events from network usage. The above power-state-machine models for wireless interfaces are driven by network events collected in a packet trace or a network system call trace. However, on an unmodified user phone, we can only collect network usage information periodically. Thus we need a way to convert network usage to network events. Specifically, our objective is to convert the number of bytes sent N_{snd} and received N_{rcv} logged at each logging interval T into a sequence of network send and receive system calls, each with a time t_i and the number of bytes sent n^i_{snd} or received n^i_{rcv}.

To decide the rules of conversion, we first found out the distribution, timing and message sizes in popular apps. We played top 20 apps in Google Play on a Galaxy S3 phone many times and logged the network system calls using systemtap which requires modifying the Android framework. We found the average message size is 600 bytes with a variance of 200 bytes for a send call and 6200 bytes with a variance of 2000 bytes for a receive call. The timings of receive system calls in each interval across different apps follow a randomly uniform distribution. Thus in our heuristic, we assume system call timings to follow a random uniformly distribution within each interval, and rely on controlling the logging interval T to be small enough so that the estimation error is acceptable. We further found in the apps we played that a receive call will always be preceded by a send call which agrees with the natural client-server communication model.

Based on the above observation, we convert the network usage (N^i_{snd}, N^i_{rcv}) within a interval T_i to a sequence of $K = \lceil N_{rcv}/6200 \rceil$ network system calls $\{(n^i_{snd}, n^i_{rcv}, t^i)\}$, where i = 1, ..., K, $n^i_{rcv} = 6200$ if $i < K$, $n^i_{rcv} = N_{rcv}$ mod 6200 if $i = K$, and $n^i_{snd} = N_{snd}/K; t^i = random(0, T)$.

The logging interval T determines the tradeoff between the estimation accuracy and the logging overhead. To determine the network logging interval T, we performed what-if analysis and calculated the network energy estimation error under different values of T against the network energy derived from the actual system call sequence we logged. We found T = 1 second gives an acceptable error of 5.1% during screen-on intervals and T = 5 second gives an acceptable error of 7.4% during screen-off periods. We therefore used these two parameters in the field experiment. In future work, we plan to improve the estimation accuracy, by customizing the parameters according to app categories and individual user behavior.

2.5 Logging App Design

We have designed a free Android app called eStar that when downloaded to a user's phone, performs logging of all the required information needed for driving our power model. All the information collected (summarized below) are anonymized before uploaded to our server [1].

In principle, the more fine-grained utilization information we collect, the more accurate the power model will be in estimating the energy drain of each app by the CPU, GPU, and wireless interfaces, but also the higher the logging overhead. In designing the app, we carefully chose logging intervals to strike a balance between these two objectives.

Coarse-grained logging (every 5 minutes). Coarse-grained logging happens every 5 minutes, where the app logs app-wise CPU usage (from `/proc/[pid]/stat`), and the per-core CPU usage (from `/proc/stat`) and the duration staying on different frequencies (from `/sys/devices/system/cpu/cpu[id]/`).

Fine-grained logging (every 1 or 5 seconds). Fine-grained logging happens every 5 seconds during screen-off when the CPU is on and every 1 sccond during scree-on, where the app logs the network usage (in bytes) of all apps that had data transfer during the interval, by reading `/proc/uid_stat/[uid]/`.

Dynamic event logging. Finally, dynamic events are logged on demand. These include WiFi, mobile data, and screen being switched on and off, WiFi being associated and scanning, WiFi and cellular signal strength change, battery level change (1% granularity), and every app's start and stop.

Logging overhead. We measured three types of overhead of our logging app, CPU time, network bytes and total energy. On average across the 1520 devices where we collected traces (details in §3), the average logging overhead per day are: (1) CPU time 214.7s, 2.4% of total. (2) Network bytes 190 KB, 0.3% of total. (3) Energy 7.3 mAh, 0.6% of total.

2.6 Model Validation

We experimentally validated our power model by measuring the model accuracy in both screen-on periods and screen-off periods on a small set of user devices that have our app installed and running. The devices are connected to a Monsoon power meter, whose reading serves as ground truth. We note for our energy study energy estimation accuracy is much more relevant than instantaneous power estimation accuracy.

Component model validation. We first validate the component models for Galaxy S3 and S4 by generating synthetic workload on each component and comparing the predicted energy against the power meter reading. We run each experiment for 10 minutes and repeat 3 times, and show the cumulative energy over time by model prediction and by the power meter, as well as the cumulative energy error rate. Due to space limit, we only shows the results for Galaxy S3; the results for Galaxy S4 are similar and hence are omitted.

Note that for WiFi, LTE and GPU, we are comparing the component energy plus CPU energy since running benchmark requires the CPU to be on.

CPU: For CPU validation we turn off the screen, run worker processes on each core and set each core to random frequencies

[1] Our experiment using the app received exemption from the full requirement of 45 CFR 46 or 21 CFR 56 by the IRB of our organization.

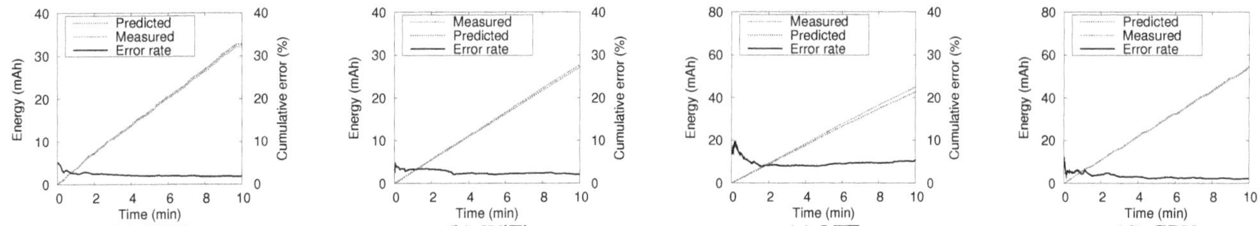

(a) CPU (b) WiFi (c) LTE (d) GPU

Figure 1: Model validation for CPU, WiFi, LTE and GPU – energy drain over time by estimation and by the power meter, and the relative estimation error as a function of duration (right y-axis).

every 10s. We log the frequency and utilization of each core and apply the CPU model to predict the CPU energy consumption. Figure 1(a) shows that the cumulative energy error rate starts at 5.0% and becomes smooth to 1.9% for 10 minutes duration.

CPU+Network: For network we place the phone at a medium signal strength location, turn off the screen, and run a simple C socket program to continuously download from a local server for 10 minutes. To minimize the CPU power in downloading, we only enable one core and set it to the lowest frequency, 384MHz. We log the network traffic and CPU frequency and utilization, and apply the network and CPU models to predict the total energy consumption for downloading. The total energy error rate is 1.9% for WiFi and 5.7% for LTE, as shown in Figure 1(b)(c).

CPU+Screen+GPU: For GPU we leave the display on and run 2 GPU benchmark apps [3] for 10 minutes. We log the GPU frequency and state, CPU frequency and utilization, and screen brightness, and apply the GPU, CPU and screen models to predict the total energy consumption. The overall energy error rate is 1.2% for benchmark 1, and 11.0% for benchmark 2. Figure 1(d) shows the result for benchmark 1.

Whole phone energy estimation. *Screen-on:* In screen-on tests, we installed 25 top apps on Google Play including 11 games, 7 online chat apps, 4 music apps and 3 news apps. The games are CPU-intensive and the rest are network-intensive. A normal user performed similar operations for the same type of apps, 2-3 minutes each, under WiFi and under LTE. Figures 2(a)(b) show the cumulative estimated energy drain over time closely matches that of the power meter output, with relative error converges to below 10% under WiFi and 10.3% under LTE beyond 20 minutes.

Screen-off: In screen-off tests, we installed the same 25 apps phone and logged in to the apps if necessary (*e.g.,* Facebook) using a normal user account. We then left the phone screen-off for 1 hour with either WiFi or LTE connectivity. At the end of each test, we compared the estimated energy from the power model and the power meter output to calculate the model accuracy. Figures 2(c)(d) show the cumulative estimated energy drain over time closely match that of the power meter output, with the relative error converges to below 4.1% under WiFi and 5.0% under LTE beyond 20 minutes.

3. CHARACTERIZING ENERGY DRAIN IN THE WILD

In this section, we first describe the trace collection and then present the energy analysis of the 1520 user phones in the wild using the power model developed in §2.

3.1 Trace Collection

Our trace was collected from 670 Galaxy S3 and 850 Galaxy S4 devices worldwide in October and November, 2014. Each user trace ranges from 10 days to 2 months in length, with an average of 32.5 days (median 34.0 days). The detailed characteristics of the trace are shown in Table 2.

Table 2: Trace statistics.

Devices > 10 days trace	1520
Aggregate trace duration	49326 days
Median trace duration	34.0 days
Countries of origin	56
Mobile operators	191
Unique phone types	2
Rate of mobile RSSI reading	when signal changes, effective: 1/min
Rate of network usage reading	screen-on: every 1 second, screen-off: every 5 seconds

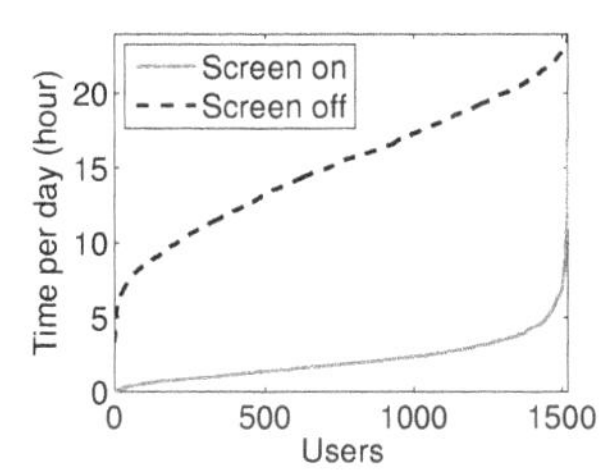

Figure 3: Distribution of avg. daily screen-off/on time across users.

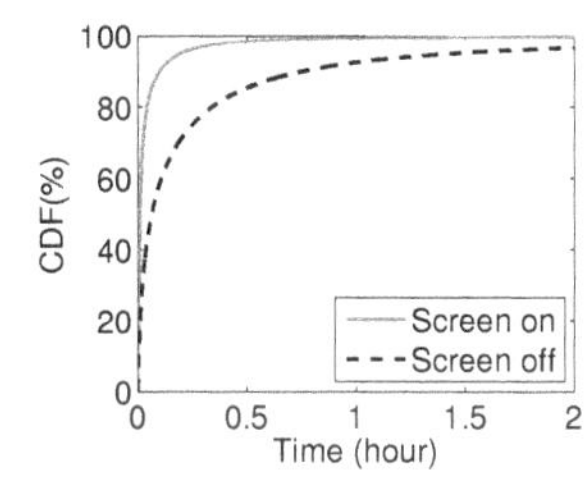

Figure 4: CDF of all screen-off/screen-on intervals for all users and all days.

3.2 Trace Overview

We start with an overview of the general usage behavior of smartphone users. Figure 3 shows the distribution of the average daily screen-off and screen-on time (seperately) across the 1520 users in the sorted order. The average, 10th percentile, and 90th percentile screen-on time are 129.5, 41.5, and 232.5 minutes, respectively. This is consistent with a recent study by Flurry [6], an app analytics firm, which found that users are spending 162 minutes per day on mobile devices, out of which mobile app usage accounts for 139 minutes.

Figure 4 shows the CDF of the duration of individual screen-off and screen-on intervals for all users across all days, truncated at 2 hours. We observe that as expected, the screen-off intervals tend to last much longer than screen-on intervals: the average, 10th percentile, and 90th percentile durations are 23.0 minutes, 15.0 seconds, and 45.6 minutes for screen-off intervals, and 5.2 minutes, 5.5 seconds, and 5.9 minutes for screen-on intervals, respectively.

Next we calculate the time spent by each device connected to different cellular technologies. We find that although it has been 5 years since LTE first started entering the commercial market, a majority of the devices, 8 and 960, respectively, could only connect to 2G and 3G from time to time, but the majority of the network traffic, about 90%, are transmitted over 3G and LTE.

Finally, Table 3 shows the breakdown of Android versions on the 1520 phones. We see 47.8% of the phones ran Android 4.2 Jellybean and 52.2% of the phones ran Android 4.4 KitKat, and no phone in our trace ran the latest Android 5.0 Lollypop.

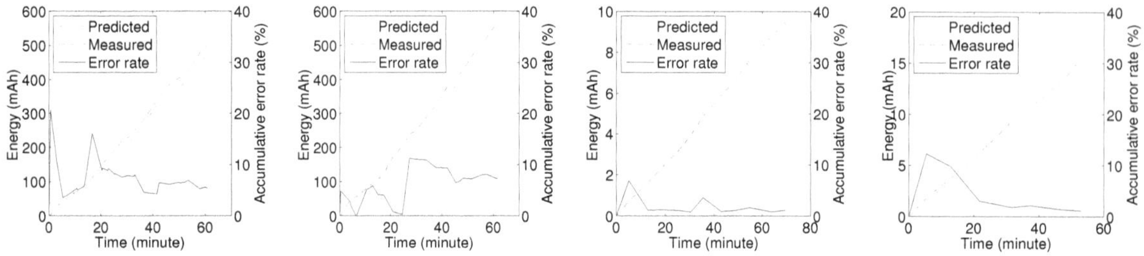

(a) Screen-on, using WiFi (b) Screen-on, using cellular (c) Screen-off, under WiFi (d) Screen-off, using cellular

Figure 2: Battery drain estimation error during screen-on and screen-off. Shown are energy drain over time by estimation and by the power meter, and the relative estimation error as a function of duration (right y-axis).

Table 3: Android version breakdown.

Android version	Percentage on S3	Percentage on S4
4.2 Jellybean	77.8%	24.0%
4.4 KitKat	22.2%	76.0%

3.3 CPU Time Analysis

Since a primary source of energy drain is the CPU, before we break down the energy drain, we first study the CPU time break down.

CPU time breakdown. To see the complete picture of how the CPU time is spent, we break down the total CPU time, *e.g.*, in a day, into the following seven main components:

- CPU busy time by background services during screen-off;
- CPU busy time by background apps during screen-off;
- CPU busy time by background services during screen-on;
- CPU busy time by background apps during screen-on;
- CPU busy time for foreground apps during screen on;
- CPU idle time during screen-on;
- CPU idle time during screen-off.

Note the rest of the time in a day, where the CPU is neither busy nor idle, is when it is in suspended state or the phone is powered off.

Figure 5(b) shows the average percentage breakdown of daily CPU time across all the users (the legends for different colors are in Figure 5(a)). We make the following observations about Figure 5(b). (1) **CPU idle:** Out of the total CPU time in a day, CPU is idle for 23.9% during screen-on and 50.4% during screen-off, which correspond to 73.5% and 74.8% of the total CPU time during screen-on and screen-off, respectively. In foreground, except for games that can be keeping CPU busy while the user is idle, most apps are not using the CPU when the user is not directly interacting with the app (*e.g.,* touch screen activities.) Thus the large idle CPU time suggests during screen-on periods, the users are idle for a significant portion of the time, *e.g.,* reading web pages, emails, or thinking. In screen-off periods, CPU idle time should ideally be close to zero as apps should keep the CPU on (*e.g.,* by holding wakelocks) only when they are actively computing something. However, we find that a huge portion (74.8%) of screen-off CPU time (67.4%) is spent idle (50.4%). (2) **Screen-on vs. screen-off:** On average, the total CPU busy time during screen-on and screen-off periods are 8.6% to 17.0%, suggesting a significant portion of the total CPU busy time is spent during screen-off periods running apps and services in the background. (3) **Services vs. apps:** Out of the total CPU busy time (25.6%), background services which run on behalf of the apps account for about 46.5% (11.9% in absolute). This testifies to the uniqueness of the Android programming environment where much of the common tasks are abstracted and

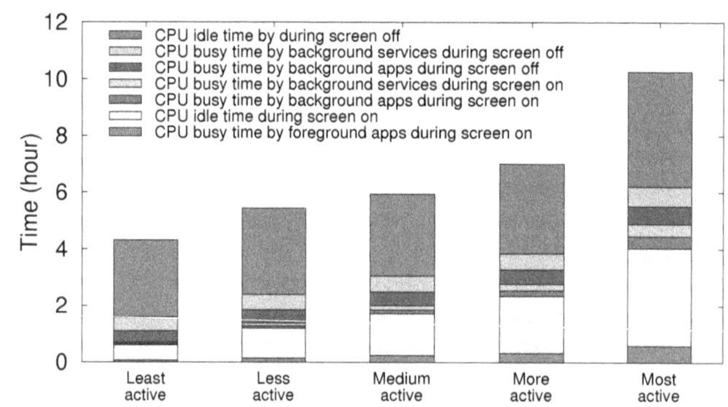

(a) Average daily CPU time breakdown of 5 groups of the 1520 users.

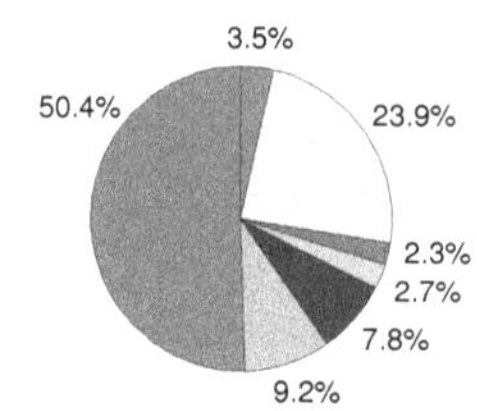

(b) Daily CPU time percentage breakdown, average over all users.

Figure 5: Daily CPU time breakdown.

provided by the system as services which can be directly called by apps and hence simplify app programming. We note that during screen-on periods, we cannot easily infer how much of the background service CPU time is due to foreground apps and how much is due to background apps; inferring such causality would require inserting logging hooks to the Android.

3.4 Energy Analysis

Energy breakdown by activities. We first break down the total energy per day per device among different activities as follows:

- Energy by WiFi beacon, WiFi scanning, cellular paging, and SOC base power during screen-off;
- Energy by background services and apps, respectively, during screen-off;
- Energy by background services and apps, respectively, during screen-on;
- CPU, GPU and network energy by foreground apps during screen-on;
- CPU idle energy during screen-on and screen-off respectively;
- Screen energy by foreground apps during screen-on.

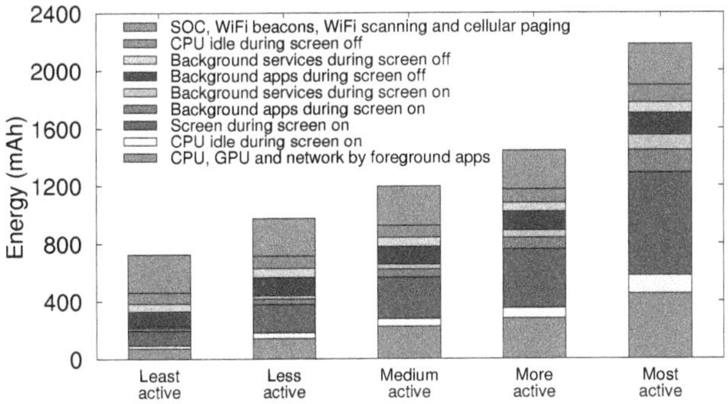

(a) Average daily energy drain breakdown of 5 groups of the 1520 users.

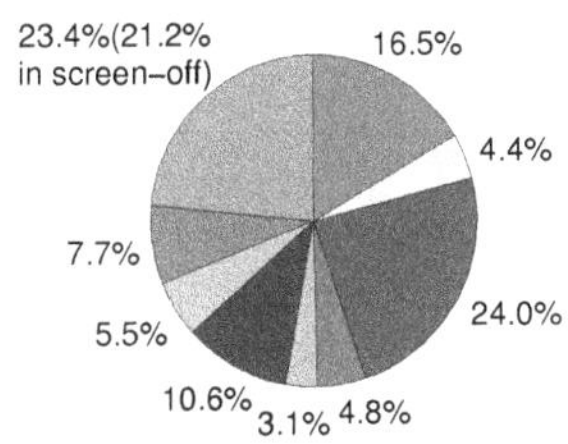

(b) Daily energy percentage breakdown, averaged over all users.

Figure 6: Daily energy breakdown by activities.

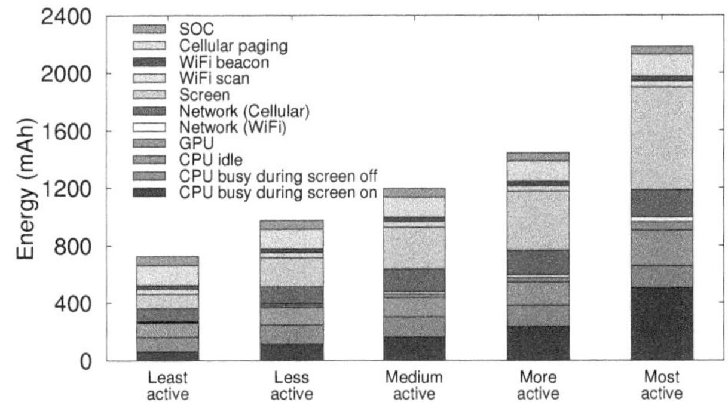

(a) Average daily energy drain breakdown of 5 groups of the 1520 users.

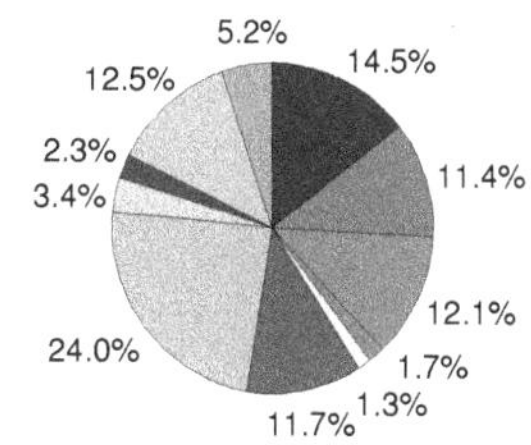

(b) Daily energy percentage breakdown, averaged over all users.

Figure 7: Daily energy breakdown by components.

Note each app and service energy component includes both CPU and networking energy. The reason we separate screen energy from other components is that they only happen for foreground apps during screen-on, and depend on non-app factors such as the brightness level.

For each device, we calculate the average daily energy of the 5 groups of users as before, as well as the average energy percentage breakdown across all users. We make the following observations about Figure 6(b). (1) **Overall screen-on vs. screen-off:** Overall, on average a whopping 45.0% of the total energy drain in a day occurs during screen-off periods. This is rather significant, and countering the expectation that when a phone is turned off and not used, it should consume little energy. (2) **Suspended state energy:** During screen-off periods, on average, the energy drain while the phone is suspended, *i.e.,* due to SOC base power, WiFi beacon, WiFi scanning and cellular paging activities, account for 21.2% of the total energy drain throughout a day. This is rather significant considering the energy drain does not contribute to any useful work. (3) **Screen energy:** Out of the 55.0% energy incurred during screen-on periods, a little less than half, 24.0% in absolute, is spent in screen energy. (4) **Useful energy in Screen-on vs. screen-off:** The background apps and services during screen-off together contribute to 16.1% of the total energy drain, in contrast to the 24.4% by background apps and services and foreground apps during screen-on. (5) **CPU idle energy:** Although on average the CPU spends 74.3% of the total CPU time in idle (Figure 5), it only drains on average 12.1% of the total energy. Two factors contributed to this contrast: (1) in entering the idle state, the CPU frequency quickly drops to the lowest possible, *e.g.,* 384MHz on Galaxy S3, and thus draws minimum power. (2) There are no networking activities during CPU idle while there can be networking activities during CPU busy which add to the energy drain during CPU busy.

Energy breakdown by components. To dissect energy drain by different phone components, we re-plot in Figure 7(b) the average percentage breakdown of daily energy drain among all users, this time among phone components. We make the following observations. (1) **SOC:** On average the SOC accounts for 5.2% of the daily total energy drain. (2) **Cellular paging vs. WiFi beacon:** The energy drain from cellular paging and WiFi beacon are 12.5% and 2.3%, respectively, showing cellular paging is a significant energy hog (3) **Screen:** The screen energy accounts for 24.0% of the total phone energy. (4) **Cellular vs. WiFi:** The energy drain from active networking over cellular (LTE and 3G) and over WiFi are 11.7% and 1.3%, respectively, showing cellular drains significantly more energy than WiFi. (Their correlation with traffic volume is discussed in §3.5.) Furthermore, a significant portion of wireless interface energy drain are tail energy, 89.3% out of total cellular energy is 3G/LTE tail energy, and 90.4% out of the total WiFi energy is WiFi tail energy. (5) **CPU:** The busy CPU energy during screen-on executing services and apps is comparable to that during screen-off, at 14.5% and 11.4%, respectively. (6) **GPU:** Finally, the GPU accounts for 1.7% of the total energy drain, used by foreground apps during screen-on periods.

3.5 Component Analysis

In this section, we take a close look at the power behavior of some individual phone components to gain insight into their overall energy drain in the previous section.

Screen. To understand the 24.0% of the total energy drain by the screen of the devices on average, we plot in Figure 8 the distribution of the devices' screen brightness level during screen-on intervals. Since a single device can experience multiple brightness levels, for each device we calculate and plot the average brightness level, weighted by the duration spent in each level. We observe an almost uniform distribution, with the average and median levels being 59.0% and 58.3%, respectively. Interestingly, about 16.0% of the devices appear to stay at the 100% brightness level all the time.

CPU. To understand the discrepancy between the CPU busy time ratio of 8.6% to 17.0% and CPU busy energy ratio of 24.4% to 16.1%, between screen-on and screen-off periods, we plot in Figure 9 the distribution of core-0 and core-1 CPU time spent in differ-

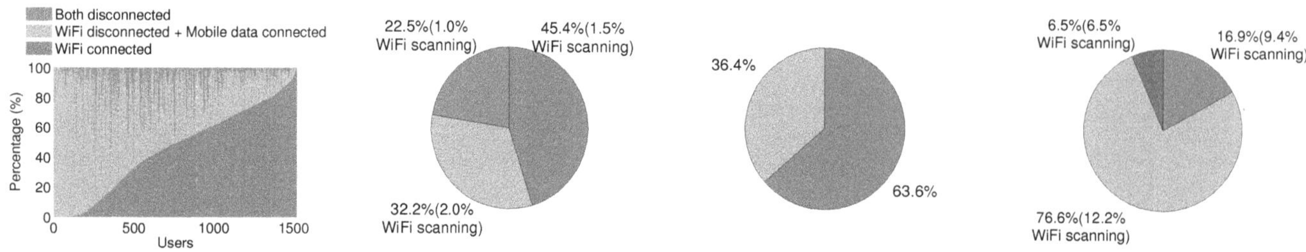

(a) Distribution of breakdown of time spent in WiFi and cellular states.

(b) Average percentage breakdown of time spent in WiFi and cellular.

(c) Average percentage breakdown of bytes transmitted in WiFi and cellular.

(d) Average percentage breakdown of wirless energy drain in different connection states.

Figure 10: Time and traffic comparison between WiFi and cellular.

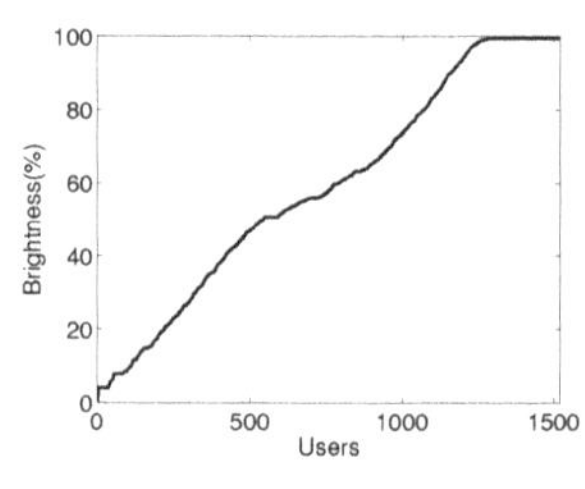

Figure 8: Distribution of average screen brightness level.

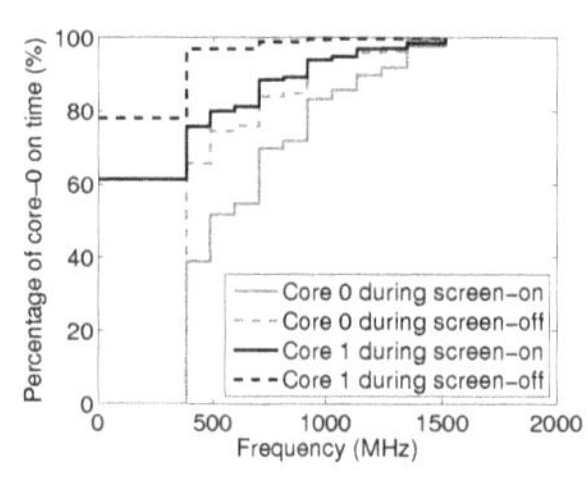

Figure 9: CDF of core-0 and core-1 time spent in different frequencies on S3.

ent frequencies during screen-on or screen-off periods on the 670 S3 devices. Note the fraction of core-1 time in different states and frequencies is normalized to the total core-0 on time, in screen-on and in screen-off, respectively. We make several observations. (1) Core-0 is idle at the lowest 384 MHz for 38.8% of the time during screen-on but 65.7% of the time during screen-off. This high idle time in screen-off happens because often in screen-off background apps/services wake up and acquire some wakelocks and then wait for responses from remote servers during which time the CPU cannot sleep but to stay idle. (2) Core-1 is turned off during 61.3% of the core-0 on time during screen-on, but 78.0% of the core-0 on time during screen-off, *i.e.,* during screen-on the chance of core-1 running when core-0 is running is higher than during screen-off. (3) Both core-0 and core-1 tend to be busy at higher frequencies during screen-on than during screen-off periods. For example, core-0 stays on less than 486 MHz and 1242 MHz for 51.7% and 91.9% of the time during screen-on, and 74.5% and 96.2% during screen-off periods, respectively. Similarly, core-1 stays on less than 486 MHz and 1242 MHz for 18.6% and 35.8% of the time during screen-on, and 18.9% and 21.8% during screen-off periods, respectively.

GPU. The GPU active power and average screen power (at brightness level 50%) are comparable, yet the energy breakdown shows that the GPU drains only 1.7% while the screen drains 24.0%. This is mainly due to the fact that most non-game apps use little GPU.

Networking. To understand the high energy drain ratio of cellular data over WiFi across the devices, we compare the time spent and bytes transmitted over the two types of wireless technologies. Figure 10(a) shows the distribution of time each device is spent in each of the three states: connected to WiFi, connected to mobile data, and connected to neither, across the 1520 devices. We observed an almost uniform distribution in terms of the percentage time spent in WiFi between 0% and 100%. Figure 10(b) then shows the average percentage breakdown of time in the three states across the devices: on average, the devices spent 45.5% of the time connected to WiFi, 32.2% of the time connected to mobile data, and 22.5% of the time disconnected from both. In all three states, WiFi rarely performed scanning, accounting for 1.5%, 2.0%, and 1.0% of the total time, respectively. In other words, WiFi did not perform much more scanning when disconnected compared to when connected. Figure 10(c) shows on average 63.6% of total traffic is transmitted over WiFi compared to 36.4% in cellular. Finally, Figure 10(d) shows although on average each device spent 1.4x more time in WiFi and transmitting 1.8x more bytes in WiFi, it drains 8.6x less energy in WiFi, excluding WiFi scanning energy. WiFi scanning, however, drains 28.1% of the total wireless energy exluding WiFi beacon and cellular paging. Finally, including WiFi beacon, WiFi scanning and cellular paging energy, the split between the total energy due to WiFi and due to cellular are 7.0% and 24.2% (Figure 7).

3.6 Light Users vs. Heavy Users

We have seen the screen-on time and hence usage level across the 1520 users in Figure 3 almost follows a uniform distribution except an exponential upward slope towards the end. To gain insight into the energy drain of users with different phone usage intensities, we divide up the users into 5 groups corresponding to the 5 20-percentiles in total screen-on time, and denote them as least active, less active, medium active, more active, and most active groups, respectively. We next compare the CPU time breakdown and energy breakdown of these 5 groups.

Figure 5(a) shows the average CPU time breakdown of users in each of the 5 groups. We observe that in moving from the least active group to the most active group, the time spent in screen-on periods, in particular, the total as well as time in the 4 different categories, grow more or less proportional to the total screen-on time, but the time spent in screen-off periods barely increased. For example, the total average screen-on time for the most active group is 7.0x that of the least active group, the corresponding increase in the average CPU busy time by foreground apps and the average CPU idle time during screen-on are 9.2x and 6.5x, but the increase in the total CPU time in screen-off is only 1.6x. As a result, the ratio of total CPU time during screen-off over screen-on goes down significantly, from 5.2x for the least active users to 1.1x for the most active users.

Figure 6(a) and Figure 7(a) shows the average energy breakdown of users in each of the 5 groups, by activities and by components, respectively. Here we see while the different portions of energy during screen-on grow more or less proportional to the screen-on CPU time as we move from the least to the most active groups, all the portions of screen-off energy by SOC, WiFi beacon, cellular paging, WiFi scan, and by the background apps and services during screen-off, remained largely constant, around 540 mAh. As a result, the relative energy drain during screen-off is quite different for different user groups – for the least active users, on average 68.9% of total device energy drain happens during screen-off, while for

Table 4: Highlights of average percentage energy breakdown across the 1520 devices.

Component	Energy Drain
Cellular paging	12.5%
WiFi scanning	3.4%
SOC suspended	5.2%
Screen	24.0%
CPU idle energy (screen-on)	4.4%
CPU idle energy (screen-off)	7.7%
3G/4G energy	11.7%
3G/4G tail energy	10.53%
Apps/services in screen-off	16.1%

the most active users, on average only 28.9% of total device energy drain happens during screen-off. Similarly, the constant energy drain accounts for a higher percentage for less active users than for more active users. For example, the absolute SOC energy drain is a constant, and hence its percentage is high for light phone users, and low for heavy phone users – the percentage is 9.0% for the 20% least active devices, but only 2.2% for the 20% most active devices.

3.7 Implications to Phone Vendors

Table 4 summarizes the highlights from the above energy drain analysis of the 1520 devices in the wild, which have a number of implications to the phone vendors, SOC vendors, and cellular carriers. As can be seen from the data, the energy spent in performing no direct useful work such as SOC suspension, cellular paging, WiFi scanning receiving beacons *etc.* is significant at 23.4%. For the cellular network components, cellular designers need to develop better air-interface protocols that consume less energy during activities designed to maintain connectivity such as paging by coming up with more efficient ideas on managing an always-on connectivity. In addition, since WiFi is much more energy-efficient at transporting data, than cellular interfaces, a lot more work needs to go into better energy optimized cellular data transfer, for example, by using WiFi more aggressively, and developing a more rigorous implementation of power management techniques such as DRX in the cellular domain. Given that the most energy consuming component in the smartphone is the screen at 24.0%, a context-aware algorithm to apply the right brightness level that can be applied for each user would save a lot of energy. Our data shows a great deal of variability in how power is consumed for each user, thus simple heuristics may not be enough, and algorithms that take into account user context are essential. Another major area of optimization is the amount of energy spent in running background apps and services by gathering and utilizing user-context information.

4. APP ENERGY ANALYSIS

The whole-device energy analysis in the previous section shows across the 1520 devices, on average 68.9% of the daily energy drain of a device is by apps and services running in screen-on (including screen energy) and screen-off periods. Since the rest of the energy drain such as SOC, WiFi beacon and scanning, cellular paging, are largely fixed for a given hardware, in this section, we zoom into these apps and services running on the devices to study their energy drain behavior. Understanding app energy drain is important as it can keep users informed of power-hungry apps and give app developers hints on where to tighten app energy drain.

Our trace from the 1520 devices consists of a total of 800 apps with no less than 10 users and no less than 10 minutes total foreground time each, which cover 67% of top 100 apps in Google Play. On average the top 5% most popular apps ran on 1009 devices each while the bottom 80% least popular apps ran on 20 devices each.

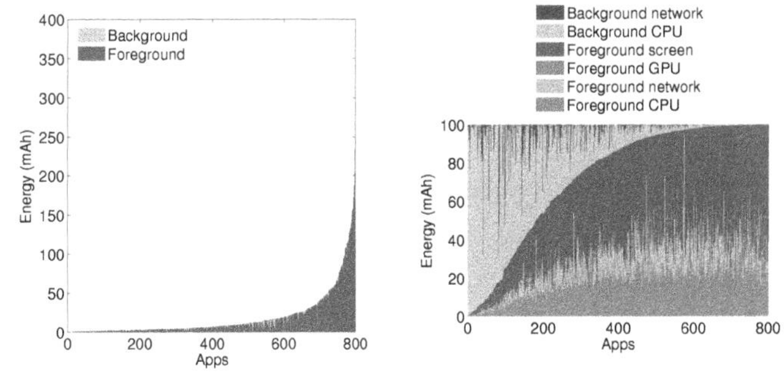

(a) Absolute breakdown (b) Relative breakdown

Figure 11: Distribution of daily energy breakdown across apps.

4.1 Energy Drain, Screen-on vs. Screen-off

Figure 11(a) shows the total daily energy drain of the 800 apps in the sorted order. We see that the energy drain follows an exponential distribution: the top 5% of apps drain an average of 133.6 mAh per day, while the bottom 80% drain an average of 6.8 mAh per day.

A common misconception is that apps only drain energy when running in the foreground during screen-on periods. Figure 11(a) further breaks down the total daily energy drain of each app into foreground and background energy drain. We see that the background energy drain fluctuates and there is no strong correlation between background energy and total energy drain of the apps. For a better view, Figure 11(b) shows the relative energy drain of different components by the apps when running in foreground and in background, sorted according to the increasing percentage of foreground energy percentages. We see that (1) background energy can be significant for many apps – the fraction of background energy is more than 50% for 22.5% of the apps, and the average fraction of background energy across the 1520 devices is 27.1%. (2) Within the foreground app energy, screen energy is the largest portion, at 46.2% on average across the 800 apps; (3) Within either foreground or background energy, CPU and GPU energy dominates networking energy – the average ratios are 2.7x and 2.8x for foreground and background energy, respectively, across the 800 apps.

4.2 App Energy Drain Rate

Since an app's total energy drain is the accumulation of its power draw over its runtime, the longer an app is played, the higher its energy. Thus the highest energy drain app may not be the most power-hungry app. To compare the power draw of the apps, we plot in Figure 12 the foreground energy drain rate (EDR), defined as the total foreground energy drain of an app divided by the total foreground time. We observe that over 92.6% of the apps have an average power draw between 200-400 mA. However, the last 4 apps, Speedtest.net, Deezer Music, BBC iPlayer, Kill Shot (0.5%) have average power draw between 600 mA and 832 mA. The first three apps (one WiFi test app and two music apps) consume 66.8%, 46.5% and 49.7% of the total app energy on network, respectively. On the other hand, the last app (a game) consumes 39.8% of the total app energy on CPU.

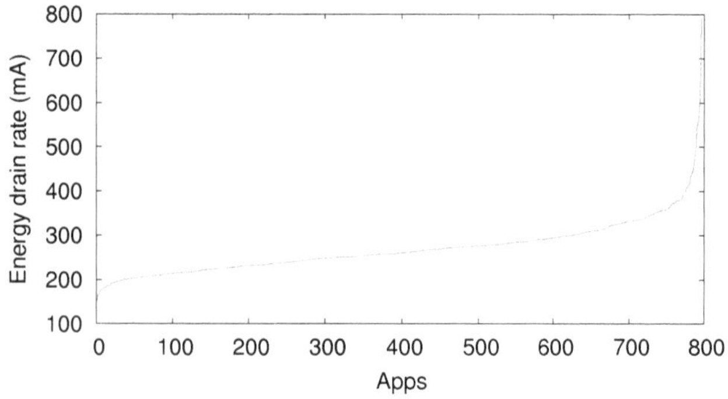

Figure 12: App energy drain rate.

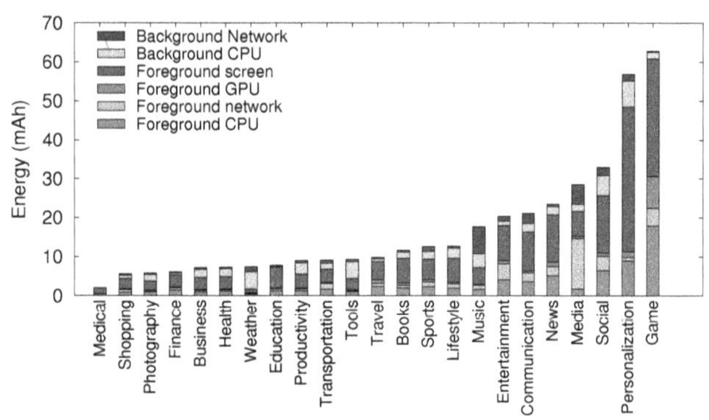

Figure 13: Average daily app energy drain by Google Play category.

4.3 App Categories

Next, we study the app energy drain by different app categories, where the categories follow from Google Play's classification.

Figure 13 shows the average foreground and background energy drain and the 6-way splits as before of the apps in each of the 23 app categories. We make the following observations. (1) **Total energy:** On average, apps in two app categories, Games and Personalization (*e.g.,* Candy Crush and Cover Lock Screen), drain far more energy each day than apps in the rest categories, *e.g.,* about 2.1x high than those in Social, Media and News categories, and about 9.7–8.2x high than those in Finance, Business, and Health categories. (2) **Background energy:** The fraction of background energy varies significantly across app categories and have little correlation with the total energy drain. For example, the Health, Weather, Education, Productivity categories have comparable EDR, but their average fractions of background energy, 32.5%, 76.9%, 5.3%, and 39.0%, are quite different. (3) **Screen energy:** The screen energy remains the dominating chunk of the total energy across all categories, ranging from 73.6% for Medical and 68.3% for Education to 13.0% for Weather and 22.3% for Media. (4) **GPU energy:** Game apps draw on average 12.9% of total energy on GPU, much higher than all other app categories, (5) **CPU energy:** The highest CPU energy draining categories are Game, Travel, and Finance, at 28.6%, 24.8%, and 24.1%, respectively. (6) **Network energy:** The top network energy draining app categories are Media and Music, where on average the network accounts for 62.8% and 45.1% of the total app energy drain.

5. EVOLUTION STUDY

In this section, we analyze the energy drain of the 1520 devices along several evolution dimensions, including hardware evolution, Android evolution, cellular evolution, and app evolution,

Table 5: Average daily CPU, GPU and network energy of foreground apps of the four groups of devices.

Devices	CPU (mAh)	GPU (mAh)	Network (mAh)
S3/JB	109.8	14.4	122.2
S4/JB	127.3	21.1	71.2
S3/KK	121.5	71.2	61.0
S4/KK	133.4	27.7	57.1

and draw implications to the various key players of the Android phone eco-system, including phone vendors (*e.g.,* Samsung), Android developers, mobile network carriers, app developers, and ultimately phone users.

5.1 Device Evolution: S3 vs. S4

Since both S3 and S4 devices could be running Android JellyBean and KitKat, to decouple of the impact of Android versions from device versions, we separately plot the daily CPU time breakdown and energy breakdown for four groups of devices: S3 devices running Jellybean (S3/JB), S3 devices running KitKat (S3/KK), S4 devices running Jellybean (S4/JB), and S4 devices running KitKat (S4/KK). The results are shown in Figure 14.

We first compare S3 devices with S4 devices. Figure 14(a) shows the average CPU time of S4/JB devices is 8.1% longer than S3/JB devices. The increase mainly comes from increased screen-on time (14.7%), within which CPU idle time increases by 72.3% and CPU busy time by foreground apps, background apps and background services shrink by 62.7%, 48.8% and 71.3% respectively.

The increase of screen-on time suggests users with S4 are more active. The decrease of CPU busy time during screen-on is mainly due to the faster CPU of S4 with more cores and higher maximum frequency and the CPU tends to turn on all the cores when there are tasks during screen-on period which we observe in the traces. On the other hand, during screen-off periods the CPU usually keeps one core on to process background tasks to save battery life, which explains the little change of background CPU busy time. We observed similar trend of changes between S3/KK and S4/KK devices.

Figure 14(b) shows that the 8.1% increase in total CPU time of S4/JB over S3/JB devices translates into 11.3% energy increase. In particular, during screen-on, the 72.3% CPU idle time increase translates to 15.1% energy increase, because the CPU power draw is minimal during CPU idle, but the 62.4% CPU busy time decrease translates to only 1.6% energy reduction, due to the faster CPU of S4 than S3; S3 has a dualcore 1.5GHz Krait CPU, and S4 has a quadcore 1.9GHz Krait 300 CPU. For the same amount of computation, more cores and higher frequency translate into less CPU time but also higher instantaneous CPU power, and the total CPU energy given by their product can be either higher or lower which determines the CPU energy efficiency.

To better understand the CPU efficiency of S3 and S4, we further break down foreground app energy into CPU, GPU and network in Table 5. If we assume users using different devices have similar behavior, the amount of computation for foreground apps can be measured by screen-on time. Figure 14(a) shows S4/JB devices have 14.7% more screen-on time than S3/JB, while Table 5 shows the foreground app CPU energy of S4/JB devices is 16.3% higher than S3/JB. This indicates the CPU of S3 is slightly more energy efficient than S4. The much higher network energy of S3/JB in Table 5 can be partly explained by the over 2x higher 3G power of S3 compared to S4 devices (see Table 10 in Appendix A).

Finally, the SOC, WiFi scanning, WiFi beacon and cellular paging energy of S4 increases by 39.1% since S4 has a higher SOC suspended power.

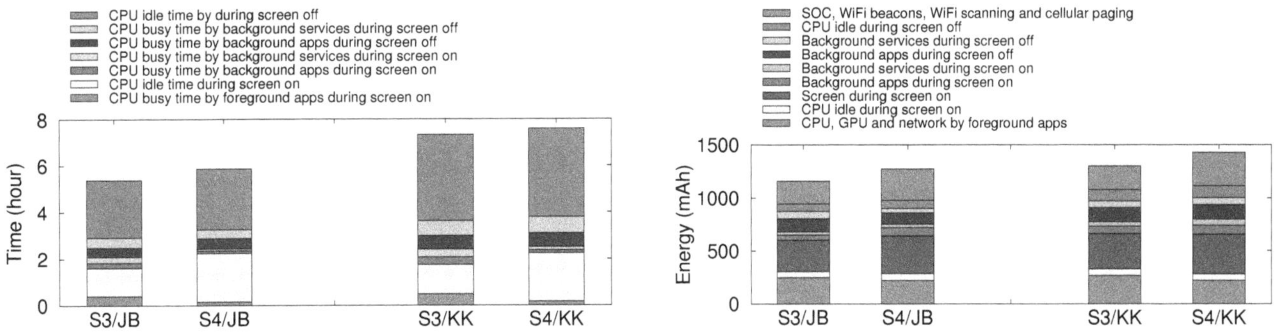

(a) Total CPU time breakdown

(b) Total energy breakdown

Figure 14: Comparison of CPU time and energy breakdown among Galaxy S3, Galaxy S4, JellyBean and KitKat.

5.2 Android Evolution: Jellybean vs. KitKat

We next measure the impact of Android versions on the usage pattern and energy drain of the devices. Figure 14(a) shows the average CPU time of S3/KK and S4/KK devices are 36.0% and 29.6% higher than the corresponding S3/JB and S4/JB. The increase appears to be mainly coming from increased background CPU time, 43.6% and 52.3%. To understand the reason for the increase, we calculated the average numbers of apps/services on the S3/JB, S4/JB, S3/KK and S4/KK devices which come out to be 67.2, 79.3, 79.0 and 86.4, respectively. Such higher numbers of apps/services on KitKat devices explain their higher background CPU busy time since more apps/services are likely to introduce more background tasks and traffic. It also indicates users with newer devices (*e.g.,* S4 compared to S3) tend to install more apps likely because of the perception of their faster CPU and larger storage.

The 36.0% and 29.6% increase in total CPU time of S3/KK and S4/KK over S3/JB and S4/JB devices translate into only 12.4% and 11.9% total energy increase. This is because although CPU idle during screen-off is increased by 22.7% and 20.5%, relative to the total CPU time of S3/JB and S4/JB, it only results in 3.0% and 2.7% energy increase, relative to the total energy of S3/JB and S4/JB. This is because the CPU power draw is low during CPU idle.

On the other hand, the high relative CPU time increase of background apps and services (43.6% from S3/JB to S3/KK and 52.3% from S4/JB to S4/KK), only results in a smaller relative energy increase of 35.9% and 25.3% during screen-on and 2.0% and 36.6% during screen-off, respectively. This small energy increase of background apps and services can be explained as follows.

KitKat offers a new API that allows apps to specify networking (or background activities) to happen within a window so the scheduler may co-locate them and thus aggregate CPU wakeups as well as networking activities which in turn translates into few network tails, saving network energy. Since in screen-off periods, our CPU logging is infrequent and network logging is every 1 second, we use networking activity per interval to estimate whether the CPU woke up in the interval. We calculated the number of wakeups during screen-off periods per day and found on average KitKat devices have 68.2% fewer wakeups than Jellybean devices. We further observed the number of 3G/LTE tails during screen-off per day to be 64.7% lower on KitKat devices. Finally, the aggregated network activities leads to the lower average normalized network energy of KitKat devices of 0.71 mAh/MB compared to 2.07 mAh/MB of JellyBean devices.

Finally, KitKat brings significant performance improvements on GPU acceleration and make it easily accessible: any apps that use RenderScript on a supported device will benefit from GPU acceleration, without any code updates or recompiling, and RenderScript functionality can be accessed directly from native code. Table 5 shows the average GPU energy drain of S3/KK and S4/KK are 5x and 1.3x higher than those of S3/JB and S4/JB, respectively.

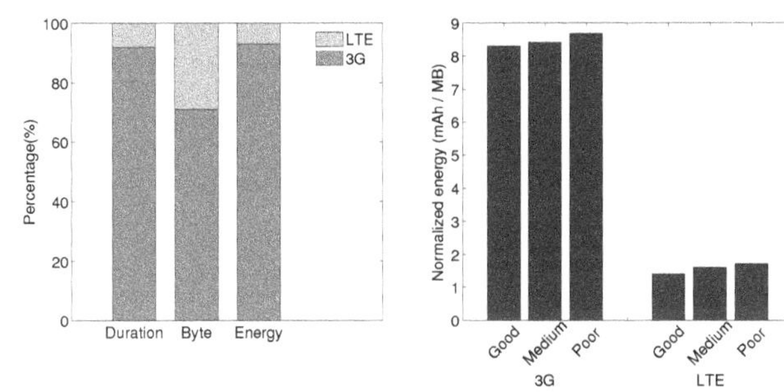

(a) Percentage energy, bytes, and duration

(b) Normalized energy by bytes

Figure 15: Traffic volume, duration and energy drain in 3G and LTE.

5.3 Cellular Evolution: 3G vs. LTE

We next study the impact of mobile data technology evolution on the energy drain of devices. The power model comparison of 3G and LTE in Appendix A suggests that the tail time of 3G and LTE are similar while the tail power of LTE is much lower than that of 3G. Since a same device can be using 3G and LTE during different time of the day, we first compare the average daily energy drain (excluding paging), bytes transmitted, and duration during connectivity with 3G and LTE across the 1520 devices. Figure 15(a) shows that although LTE accounts for 29.0% of total bytes are transmitted, it only accounts for 8.7% of the time connected to 3G/LTE and only consumes 6.9% of the total 3G/LTE network energy.

Since the two technologies offer different data rates, we also compare the energy drain normalized by the traffic volume under the two technologies. Figure 15(b) shows on average 3G drains 5.9x, 5.3x, and 5.1x more energy per MB transmitted under good, medium and poor signal strength, respectively, which are defined as -85dBm, -95dBm and -105dBm for 3G and -90dBm, -100dBm, and -110dBm for LTE.

5.4 App Evolution: App Updates

Finally, we study how the energy drain rate of apps change with app versions, *e.g.,* from different app updates. We pick 4 popular apps, Facebook, Dropbox, Chrome, and Gmail, and calculate the average app energy drain rate across their foreground runs on all the devices, as shown in Figure 16. We omit the background

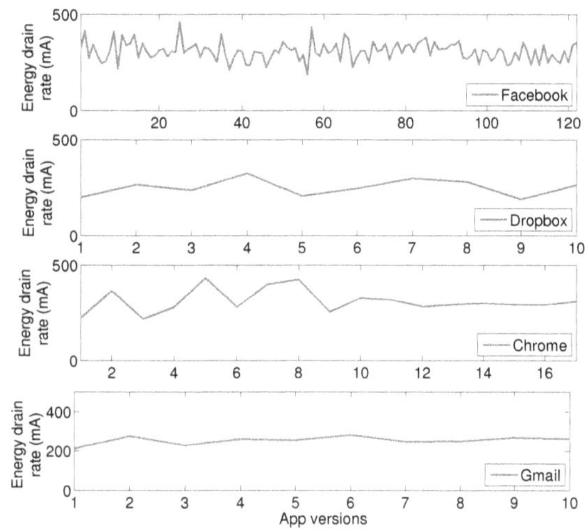

Figure 16: Comparison of average foreground energy drain rate of 4 popular apps over different versions.

energy drain analysis due to page limit. We make the following observations. (1) Across the different versions of the 4 popular apps, the average power draw fluctuates by up to 150.8%, 70.9%, 99.6%, 33.1%, respectively. (2) Facebook has more than 120 versions used by 1520 users within the two-mouth trace period, with each version used by 34 users on average. The foreground power fluctuates between 184.4 mA and 462.6 mA with an average of 307.3 mA. The fluctuating and high foreground power can be attributed to its frequently updated new features. (3) Dropbox and Gmail have less foreground power variation across their few versions (10 and 10, respectively) and a low average foreground power, 250.6 mA and 254.9 mA, respectively. This is mainly because these two apps usually synchronize with servers in background, minimizing foreground network energy. On the other hand, they both have simple UI which helps to lower the foreground CPU and GPU energy. (4) The Chrome foreground power has some repeating fluctuation among its earlier 9 versions but appears to stabilize in the more recent 8 versions. Since it is difficult for browsers to prefetch network traffic, the foreground power of Chrome, 311.0 mA on average, is higher than that of Dropbox and Gmail.

6. RELATED WORK

Power modeling of smartphones. We already discussed various previous work on power modeling of smartphones in §2.1.

Measurement study. There have been a number of work on measurement studies of smartphone apps and traffics. In [10], Falaki *et al.* characterize the smartphone traffic based on traffic trace collected from 43 users. In [14], Huang *et al.* study the 3G network performance using 3GTest data. In [23], Xu *et al.* study the smartphone usage pattern via network measurement from cellular network provider. AppInsight [20] monitors the performance of mobile apps in the wild by instrumenting app binary. In [22], Sommers and Barford study the WiFi and cellular performance using the Speedtest.net data. None of the work above however study the energy drain of mobile apps in the wild.

A few work study the energy consumption of mobile apps. In [13], Huang *et al.* collect traffic from 20 users and study screen-off radio energy consumption. In [21], Shye *et al.* derive a regression-based power model for HTC G1 phone which only has 2G EDGE and study component energy breakdown from a 20-user trace which does not include any app energy analysis. Different from these work, we collected trace from a much broader user base, developed a power model that captures both utilization-based and FSM-based components (for WiFI, 3G and LTE), and performed detailed activity and energy analysis across devices, components, apps, and technology and app evolutions.

7. CONCLUSIONS

In this paper, we undertook to our knowledge the first extensive effort towards understanding where and how energy drain happens in smartphones running in the wild. We developed a hybrid utilization-based and FSM-based model that accurately estimates energy breakdown among activities and phone components without changing the Android framework or rooting the phone. Our analysis of traces collected on 1520 Galaxy S3 and S4 devices in the wild covering 800 apps gained much insight on energy drain across devices (users), device components, apps, and multiple technology and app evolutions. These insights in turn allow us to draw implications to the phone vendors, SOC vendors, cellular carriers, and app developers on better system, network, and app design to extend battery life.

Acknowledgment

This work was supported in part by NSF grant CCF-1320764 and by Intel.

8. REFERENCES

[1] AppBrain, top android phones. `www.appbrain.com/stats/top-android-phones`.
[2] eMarketer, smartphone users worldwide will total 1.75 billion in 2014. `www.emarketer.com/Article/Smartphone-Users-Worldwide-Will-Total-175-`.
[3] Gpu benchmark 3d. `play.google.com/store/apps/details?id=com.kortenoeverdev.GPUbench`.
[4] GPU benchmark app. `play.google.com/store/apps/details?id=name.duzenko.farfaraway`.
[5] Monsoon power monitor. `www.msoon.com/LabEquipment/PowerMonitor/`.
[6] TechCrunch, mobile app usage increases in 2014, as mobile web surfing declines.
[7] theGuardian, your smartphone's best app? battery life, say 89% of britons. `www.theguardian.com/technology/2014/may/21/your-smartphones-best-app-battery-life-say-89`.
[8] N. Balasubramanian, A. Balasubramanian, and A. Venkataramani. Energy consumption in mobile phones: a measurement study and implications for network applications. In *Proc of IMC*, 2009.
[9] N. Ding, D. Wagner, X. Chen, A. Pathak, Y. C. Hu, and A. Rice. Characterizing and modeling the impact of wireless signal strength on smartphone battery drain. In *SIGMETRICS*, 2013.
[10] H. Falaki, D. Lymberopoulos, R. Mahajan, S. Kandula, and D. Estrin. A first look at traffic on smartphones. In *Proc. of IMC*, 2010.
[11] A. Garcia-Saavedra, P. Serrano, A. Banchs, and G. Bianchi. Energy consumption anatomy of 802.11 devices and its implication on modeling and design. In *CoNEXT*, 2012.
[12] J. Huang, F. Qian, A. Gerber, Z. M. Mao, S. Sen, and O. Spatscheck. A close examination of performance and power characteristics of 4g lte networks. In *Proc. of Mobisys*, 2012.
[13] J. Huang, F. Qian, Z. M. Mao, S. Sen, and O. Spatscheck. Screen-off traffic characterization and optimization in 3g/4g networks. In *IMC*, 2012.
[14] J. Huang, Q. Xu, B. Tiwana, Z. M. Mao, M. Zhang, and P. Bahl. Anatomizing application performance difference on smartphones. In *Proc. of Mobisys*, 2010.
[15] C.-Y. Li, C. Peng, S. Lu, and X. Wang. Energy-based rate adaptation for 802.11n. In *Proc. of ACM MobiCom*, 2012.
[16] R. Mittal, A. Kansal, and R. Chandra. Empowering developers to estimate app energy consumption. In *Proc. of ACM MobiCom*, 2012.

[17] A. Pathak, Y. C. Hu, and M. Zhang. Where is the energy spent inside my app? fine grained energy accounting on smartphones with eprof. In *Proc. of EuroSys*, 2012.
[18] F. Qian, Z. Wang, A. Gerber, Z. Mao, S. Sen, and O. Spatscheck. Profiling resource usage for mobile applications: a cross-layer approach. In *Proc. of Mobisys*, 2011.
[19] F. Qian, Z. Wang, A. Gerber, Z. M. Mao, S. Sen, and O. Spatscheck. Characterizing radio resource allocation for 3g networks. In *Proc. of IMC*, 2010.
[20] L. Ravindranath, J. Padhye, S. Agarwal, R. Mahajan, I. Obermiller, and S. Shayandeh. Appinsight: Mobile app performance monitoring in the wild. In *OSDI*, 2012.
[21] A. Shye, B. Scholbrock, and G. Memik. Into the wild: studying real user activity patterns to guide power optimizations for mobile architectures. In *MICRO*, 2009.
[22] J. Sommers and P. Barford. Cell vs. WiFi: On the performance of metro area mobile connections. In *IMC*, 2012.
[23] Q. Xu, J. Erman, A. Gerber, Z. Mao, J. Pang, and S. Venkataraman. Identifying diverse usage behaviors of smartphone apps. In *Proc. of IMC*, 2011.
[24] L. Zhang, B. Tiwana, Z. Qian, Z. Wang, R. Dick, Z. Mao, and L. Yang. Accurate Online Power Estimation and Automatic Battery Behavior Based Power Model Generation for Smartphones. In *Proc. of CODES+ISSS*, 2010.
[25] Y. Zhang, X. Wang, X. Liu, Y. Liu, L. Zhuang, and F. Zhao. Towards better cpu power management on multicore smartphones. In *Proc. of HotPower*, 2013.

APPENDIX

A. POWER MODELS FOR GALAXY S3/S4

We present the detailed power model of various phone components, derived by following the procedures described in §2.4.

CPU Power Model. In training the power model for Galaxy S3's dual-core CPU, we first ran CPU microbenchmarks while using the power meter to measure the power draw of the CPU under different frequencies with only core-0 turned on. We then repeated the process with both cores turned on [2]. Table 6 shows the CPU power draw at 100% CPU utilization for Galaxy S3 under a range of frequencies. Single-core results are shown with core-1 turned off.

In modeling the quad-core CPU on Galaxy S4, we followed the procedure in [25]. The power draw of the quad-core CPU is modeled as $P_{CPU} = P_{B,N_c} + \sum_i^{N_c} u_i \cdot P_\Delta(f_i)$, where P_{B,N_c} is the baseline CPU power with N_c enabled cores, $P_\Delta(f_i)$ is the power increment of core i at frequency f_i, and u_i is its utilization.

We first modeled the core-0 using the same method as with Galaxy S3. We then varied the number of cores online, but fix all online cores to the same frequency and 100% utilization. The increased power when turning on core-i is considered as the busy power for core-i at this frequency. Then we varied the frequency and repeat the process to obtain the busy power for each core at each frequency. For idle power, the procedure is the same except we kept the online cores idle instead of 100% busy. Table 7 shows the CPU power draw at 100% CPU utilization for Galaxy S4 under a range of frequencies with varying number of online cores.

To use the CPU model, we logged the frequencies of the each core as well as the utilization of each app active during the logging interval. In post-processing, we estimated the energy of each app over each interval based on the logged CPU frequency and the app's utilization, *i.e.,* as the power draw at that frequency under 100% utilization weighted by the app's actual utilization. Finally, we summed up the CPU energy consumed by that app in each interval to arrive at the total CPU energy consumption for the app.

[2] In running the benchmarks, we kept the screen display (a wallpaper) static with a fixed brightness level and subtracted the constant screen power which is easy to measure separately.

Table 6: Dual-core CPU power model for Galaxy S3, shown for 6 sample frequencies per core. The unit of CPU power is mW.

Core 0 (MHz)	Core 1 (MHz)						
	0	384	594	810	1026	1242	1512
384	296	744	766	818	873	977	1047
594	359	766	814	866	921	1036	1103
810	411	818	866	918	973	1080	1154
1026	455	873	921	977	1029	1136	1217
1242	555	981	1029	1084	1140	1199	1277
1512	633	1062	1106	1158	1221	1273	1351

Table 7: Galaxy S4 CPU power model for 3 sample frequencies with varying number of online cores. The power unit is mW.

	384MHz		1026 MHz		1890 MHz	
	P_{B,N_c}	$P_\Delta(f_i)$	P_{B,N_c}	$P_\Delta(f_i)$	P_{B,N_c}	$P_\Delta(f_i)$
1	86	207	86	438	86	1358
2	269	70	363	228	647	811
3	351	72	464	239	917	891
4	472	75	577	243	1205	962

Screen Power Model. Galaxy S3 and S4 phones have AMOLED screens, and thus in principle the screen power model should have two triggers: the brightness, and the content displayed on the screen. However, logging the content will impose unacceptable performance overhead. Further, we compared screen power of 10 popular apps and games under typical brightness settings and found the screen power differ by less than 18.5% for different displayed contents. This is much lower than the 45.5% to 77.0% screen power draw difference between the lowest and highest brightness levels on the two devices (fixing the displayed content). For these two reasons, we strike a balance between model accuracy and logging overhead by deriving a screen model solely based on the brightness using the following method: we used a set of wallpapers with various color tones, ranging from the darkest (pure black) to the brightest (pure white), and for each wallpaper we measured the screen power draw under each brightness level. Finally, for each brightness level, we used the average power draw across all wallpapers as the screen power under this brightness value.

Table 8 shows the screen power draw for Galaxy S3 and S4 for 6 sample brightness levels. S4 draws more screen power than S3 due to its larger screen size and higher resolution.

Table 8: Galaxy S3 and S4 screen power for 6 sample brightness levels.

Brightness	0	51	102	153	204	255
Power on S3 (mW)	417	452	484	511	542	573
Power on S4 (mW)	507	562	616	671	725	780

GPU Power Model. The GPUs on both Galaxy S3 and S4 have three power states: Active, Nap and Idle, and can be in four different frequencies. Thus the GPU power draw in different power state and frequency combinations differ. In GPU power modeling, we ran GPU microbenchmarks to generate workload and in the meanwhile measure the power draw using the power meter. The measured power consists of three parts: CPU power, GPU power and screen power. Hence we logged the frequency and utilization of CPUs, the frequency and state of GPU, as well as the brightness of the screen. In post-processing, we first isolated the power draw of GPU by subtracting the CPU and screen power (calculated by the CPU and screen power models) from the total power, and then calculated the average GPU power draw under each frequency and state combination to obtain the GPU power model. Table 9 shows the GPU power draw for Galaxy S3 and S4 under each frequency and state. The power of Idle state is always 0 hence not shown.

To use the GPU power model, we logged the duration of each GPU frequency and state combination every 1 second, and pre-

Table 9: Galaxy S3 and S4 GPU power model.

Galaxy S3				
Frequency (MHz)	128	200	300	400
Active power (mA)	729	975	1217	1482
Nap power (mA)	78	0	0	78
Galaxy S4				
Frequency (MHz)	128	200	320	450
Active power (mW)	293	398	562	1034
Nap power (mW)	0	0	0	164

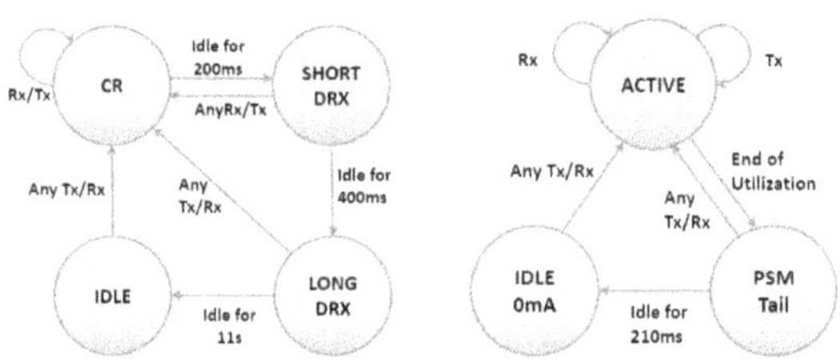

(a) LTE (b) WiFi

Figure 17: WiFi and LTE state machines for Galaxy S3 and S4.

dicted the GPU power draw of each interval based on the GPU model.

LTE, 3G, and WiFi Power Models. The LTE interface on smartphones has four power states. The power states and their transitions are shown in Figure 17(a): (1) *IDLE:* The interface is in idle states when the User Equipment (UE) does not send or receive any data. The interface consumes little power under the IDLE state, and periodically wakes up to check whether there are incoming data buffered at the network. (2) *CR:* When the UE sends or receives any data, the interface enters the Continuous Reception (CR) state and consumes high power. (3) *Short DRX:* After the UE finishes data transfer and becomes idle for 200ms, the interface will enter the Short DRX state, during which the interface consumes little power but wakes up frequently to check for incoming traffic. (3) *Long DRX:* The interface enters the Long DRX state after staying in Short DRX for 400 ms without receiving any data. Long DRX is similar to Short DRX except that the wakeup interval becomes longer. Note in the power model in Table 10 we refer the periodical spikes during Short DRX and Long DRX state as Short DRX and Long DRX, respectively, and refer the low base periods between spikes as LTE tail base, as shown in Figure 18, which plots the LTE power states on Galaxy S3 during a 100KB download under good signal strength (-90dBm). Finally, if the UE stays in Long DRX for 11 seconds without receiving any data, the interface will return to the IDLE state; otherwise, any data sending or receiving in Short DRX or Long DRX states will trigger it to enter the CR state.

The 3G interface has three RRC states: IDLE, FACH and DCH, as well as transition states between RRC states. We refer readers to [19] and [18] for a comprehensive discussion about the 3G states and transition rules.

The WiFi interface also has four power states: Tx, Rx, Tail, and Idle, as shown in Figure 17(b). The interface is in the Idle state when there is no traffic, and will enter the Tx (Rx) state when it starts sending (receiving) data. After data transfer, the interface will stay in the Tail state for 210 ms before it returns to the Idle state. The interface consumes very little power in the Idle state, moderate power in the Tail state, and high power in the Tx and Rx states.

For WiFi, 3G, and LTE interfaces, the power draw and duration at each state and state transitions are affected by the wireless signal strength [9]. We followed the procedure described in §2.4 to derive all the parameters in the power state machines for the WiFi, 3G, and LTE interfaces for Galaxy S3 and S4 phones. The parameters are shown in Table 10. We note the Tx/Rx power generally increases with weaker signal strength, but can decrease when the signal strength is extremely weak, at which point the throughput is significantly lower.

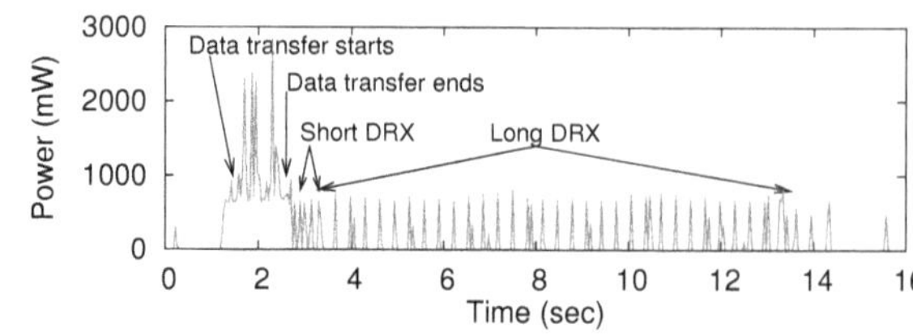

Figure 18: LTE Power states on Galaxy S3

We note the power models for these two phones differ from that in [12] conducted about three years ago. For example, while the LTE base has a similar duration of 11 seconds, the tail base power is down from about 1000 mW on the HTC phone used by [12] to zero in our measurement. An author of [12] has confirmed with us that they now also observe close to zero tail base power in their LTE measurements. Thus this difference from [12] is likely due to the newer LTE deployment.

Table 10: Parameters of signal-strength-aware power models for WiFi and LTE on Galaxy S3 and S4. The power unit is mW.

WiFi						
RSSI (dBm)	Galaxy S3			Galaxy S4		
	Tx	Rx	Tail	Tx	Rx	Tail
-50	564	396	242	654	451	289
-60	596	422	242	723	528	289
-70	641	431	242	1019	592	289
-80	704	400	242	1113	633	289
-85	702	382	242	892	514	289
The duration of WiFi tail for both phones is 210 ms.						

Galaxy S3 3G			
	promotion	DCH tail	FACH tail
-85	836mW, 1.6s	783mW, 3.3s	486mW, 6.7s
-95	836mW, 1.6s	1034mW, 3.3s	486mW, 6.7s
-105	836mW, 1.6s	1224mW, 3.3s	486mW, 6.7s

Galaxy S4 3G			
	promotion	DCH tail	FACH tail
-85	647mW, 2.1s	577mW, 3.3s	332mW, 1.7s
-95	663mW, 2.1s	679mW, 3.3s	390mW, 1.7s
-105	807mW, 2.2s	722mW, 3.3s	390mW, 1.7s

	Galaxy S3 3G		Galaxy S4 3G	
RSSI (dBm)	Tx (mW)	Rx (mW)	Tx (mW)	Rx (mW)
-85	1414	1300	667	843
-95	1737	1718	835	1043
-105	2280	2060	1772	1545

Galaxy S3 LTE			
	Power (mW)	Duration (ms)	Periodicity (ms)
LTE promotion	1200	200	N/A
Short DRX	788	41	100
Long DRX	788	45	320
LTE tail base	61	11000	N/A
DRX in IDLE	570	32	1280

Galaxy S4 LTE			
	Power (mW)	Duration (ms)	Periodicity (ms)
LTE promotion	1326	200	N/A
Short DRX	N/A	N/A	N/A
Long DRX	585	30	320
LTE tail base	69	11000	N/A
DRX in IDLE	452	24	1280

	S3 LTE		S4 LTE	
RSRP (dBm)	Tx (mW)	Rx (mW)	Tx (mW)	Rx (mW)
-85	1218	1085	1177	938
-95	1683	1264	1849	1110
-105	1840	1271	1699	1140

Newer Is Sometimes Better: An Evaluation of NFSv4.1

Ming Chen,[1] Dean Hildebrand,[2] Geoff Kuenning,[3]
mchen@cs.stonybrook.edu, dhildeb@us.ibm.com, geoff@cs.hmc.edu
Soujanya Shankaranarayana,[1] Bharat Singh,[1] and Erez Zadok[1]
{soshankarana, bhasingh, ezk}@cs.stonybrook.edu
[1]Stony Brook University, [2]IBM Research—Almaden, and [3]Harvey Mudd College

ABSTRACT

The popular Network File System (NFS) protocol is 30 years old. The latest version, NFSv4, is more than ten years old but has only recently gained stability and acceptance. NFSv4 is vastly different from its predecessors: it offers a stateful server, strong security, scalability/WAN features, and callbacks, among other things. Yet NFSv4's efficacy and ability to meet its stated design goals had not been thoroughly studied until now. This paper compares NFSv4.1's performance with NFSv3 using a wide range of micro- and macro-benchmarks on a testbed configured to exercise the core protocol features. We (1) tested NFSv4's unique features, such as delegations and statefulness; (2) evaluated performance comprehensively with different numbers of threads and clients, and different network latencies and TCP/IP features; (3) found, fixed, and reported several problems in Linux's NFSv4.1 implementation, which helped improve performance by up to 11×; and (4) discovered, analyzed, and explained several counter-intuitive results. Depending on the workload, NFSv4.1 was up to 67% slower than NFSv3 in a low-latency network, but exceeded NFSv3's performance by up to 2.9× in a high-latency environment. Moreover, NFSv4.1 outperformed NFSv3 by up to 172× when delegations were used.

Categories and Subject Descriptors

C.4 [**Performance of Systems**]: Performance Attributes

General Terms

Measurement, Performance

Keywords

NFSv4, Network File Systems

1. INTRODUCTION

Since its introduction, the Network File System (NFS) protocol has become a highly popular network-storage solution. Over 90% of enterprise storage capacity is served by network-based storage, and NFS represents a significant proportion of that total [28, 31].

SIGMETRICS'15, June 15–19, 2015, Portland, OR, USA.

ACM 978-1-4503-3486-0/15/06 ...$15.00.
http://dx.doi.org/10.1145/2745844.2745845.

Faster networks, the proliferation of virtualization, and the rise of cloud computing all contribute to continued increases in NFS deployments [1].

The continuous development and evolution of NFS has been critical to its success. Following NFSv2 (which we will refer to as V2 for brevity), NFSv3 (V3) added TCP support, 64-bit file sizes and offsets, asynchronous COMMITs, and performance features such as READDIRPLUS. NFSv4.0 (V4.0), the first minor version of NFSv4 (V4), had many improvements over V3, including (1) easier deployment with one single well-known port (2049) that handles all operations including file locking, quota management, and mounting; (2) stronger security using RPCSEC_GSS [25]; (3) more advanced client-side caching using delegations, which allow the cache to be used without lengthy revalidation; and (4) better operation coalescing via COMPOUND procedures. NFSv4.1 (V4.1), the latest minor version, further adds Exactly Once Semantics (EOS) so that retransmitted non-idempotent operations are handled correctly, and pNFS, which allows direct client access to multiple data servers and thus greatly improves performance and scalability [13, 25].

V4.1 became ready for production deployment only a couple of years ago [9, 20]. Because it is new and complex, V4.1 is less understood than older versions; we did not find any comprehensive evaluation of either V4.0 or V4.1 in the literature. (V4.0's RFC is 275 pages long, whereas V4.1's RFC is 617 pages long.) However, before adopting V4.1 for production, it is important to understand how it behaves in realistic environments. To this end, we thoroughly evaluated Linux's V4.1 implementation by comparing it to V3, the still-popular older version [20], in a wide range of environments using representative workloads.

This paper has four contributions: **(1)** a comprehensive comparison of the performance of V3 and V4.1 in low- and high-latency networks, using a wide variety of micro- and macro-workloads; **(2)** insightful performance analysis that sheds light on how underlying system components (networking, RPC, and local file systems) influence NFS's performance; **(3)** a deep analysis of the performance effect of V4.1's unique features (statefulness, sessions, delegations, etc.) in its Linux implementation; and **(4)** fixes to Linux's V4.1 implementation that improve its performance by up to 11×.

Some of our key findings are:

- How to tune V4.1 and V3 to reach up to 1177MB/s aggregate throughput in 10GbE networks with 0.2–40ms latency, while ensuring fairness among multiple NFS clients.
- When we increase the number of benchmarking threads to 2560, V4.1 achieves only 0.3× the performance of V3 in a low-latency network, but is 2.9× better with high latency.
- When reading small files, V4.1's delegations can improve performance up to 172× compared to V3, and can send 29× fewer NFS requests in a file-locking workload;

The rest of this paper is organized as follows. Section 2 describes our benchmarking methodology. Sections 3 and 4 discuss the results of data- and metadata-intensive workloads, respectively. Section 5 explores NFSv4's delegations. Section 6 examines macro-workloads using Filebench. Section 7 overviews related work. We conclude in Section 8, and discuss this study's limitations and future work in Section 9.

2. METHODOLOGY

Experimental Setup.

We used six identical Dell PowerEdge R710 machines for this study. Each has a six-core Intel Xeon X5650 2.66GHz CPU, 64GB of RAM, and an Intel 82599EB 10GbE NIC. We configured five machines as NFS clients and one as the NFS server. On the server, we installed eight Intel DC S3700 200GB SSDs in a RAID-0 configuration with 64KB stripes, using a Dell PERC 6/i RAID controller with a 256MB battery-backed write-back cache. The storage configuration was able to achieve read throughputs of up to 860MB/s. We chose these high speed 10GbE NICs and SSDs to avoid being bottlenecked by the network or the storage. Our initial experiments showed that even a single client could easily overwhelm a 1GbE network; similarly, a server provisioned with HDDs or even RAID-0 across several HDDs quickly became overloaded. We believe that NFS servers' hardware and network must be configured to scale well and that our chosen configuration represents modern servers; it reached 98.7% of the 10GbE NICs' maximum network bandwidth, allowing us to focus on the NFS protocol's performance rather than hardware limits.

All machines ran CentOS 7.0.1406 with a vanilla 3.14.17 Linux kernel. Both the OS and the kernel were the latest stable versions at the time we began this study. We chose CentOS because it is a freely available version of Red Hat Enterprise Linux, which is often used in enterprise environments. We manually ensured that all machines had identical BIOS settings. We connected the six machines using a Dell PowerConnect 8024F 24-port 10GbE switch. We enabled jumbo frames and set the Ethernet MTU to 9000 bytes. We also enabled TCP Segmentation Offload to leverage the offloading feature of our NIC and to reduce CPU overhead. We measured a round-trip time (RTT) of 0.2ms between two machines using `ping` and a raw TCP throughput of 9.88Gb/s using `iperf`.

Many parameters can affect NFS performance, including the file system used on the server, its format and mount options, network parameters, NFS and RPC parameters, export options, and client mount options. Unless noted otherwise, we did not change any default OS parameters. We used the default `ext4` file system, with default settings, for the RAID-0 NFS data volume, and chose Linux's in-kernel NFS server implementation. We exported the volume with default options, ensuring that `sync` was set so that writes were faithfully committed to stable storage as requested by clients. We used the default RPC settings, except that `tcp_slot_table_entries` was set to 128 to ensure the client could send and receive enough data to fill the network. We used 32 NFSD threads, and our testing found that increasing that value had a negligible impact on performance because the CPU and SSDs were rarely the bottleneck. On the clients, we used the default mount options, with the `rsize` and `wsize` set to 1MB, and the `actimeo` (attribute cache timeout) set to 60 seconds. Because our study focuses on the performance of NFS, in our experiments we used the default security settings, which do not use RPCSEC_GSS or Kerberos and thus do not introduce additional overheads.

Benchmarks and Workloads.

We developed a benchmarking framework named *Benchmaster*, which can launch workloads on multiple clients concurrently. To verify that Benchmaster can launch time-aligned workloads, we measured the time difference by NTP-synchronizing client clocks and then launching a program that simply writes the current time to a local file. We ran this test 1000 times and found an average delta of 235ms and a maximum of 432ms. This variation is negligible compared to the 5-minute running time of our benchmarks.

Benchmaster also periodically collects system statistics using tools such as `iostat` and `vmstat`, and by reading `procfs` entries such as `/proc/self/mountstats`. The `mountstats` file provides particularly useful details of each individual NFS procedure, including counts of requests, the number of timeouts, bytes sent and received, accumulated RPC queueing time, and accumulated RPC round-trip time. It also contains RPC transport-level information such as the number of RPC socket sends and receives, the average request count on the wire, etc.

We ran our tests long enough to ensure stable results, usually 5 minutes. We repeated each test at least three times, and computed the 95% confidence interval for the mean using the Student's t-distribution. Unless otherwise noted, we plot the mean of all runs' results, with the half-widths of the confidence intervals shown as error bars. We focused on system throughput and varied the number of threads in our benchmarking programs in our experiments. Changing the thread count allowed us to (1) infer system response time from single-thread results, (2) test system scalability by gradually increasing the number of threads, and (3) measure the maximum system throughput by using many threads.

To evaluate NFS performance over short- and long-distance networks, we injected delays ranging from 1ms to 40ms using `netem` at the NFS clients side. We measured 40ms to be the average latency of Internet communications within New York State. We measured New York-to-California latencies of about 100ms, but we do not report results using such lengthy delays because many experiments took too long just to initialize. For brevity, we refer to the network without extra delay as "zero-delay," and the network with $n$ms injected delay as "$n$ms-delay" in the rest of this paper.

We benchmarked four kinds of workloads:

1. Data-intensive micro-workloads that test the ability of NFS to maximize network and storage bandwidth (Section 3);
2. Metadata-intensive micro-workloads that exercise NFS's handling of file metadata and small messages (Section 4);
3. Micro-workloads that evaluate delegations, which are V4's new client-side caching mechanism (Section 5); and
4. Complex macro-workloads that represent real-world applications (Section 6).

3. DATA-INTENSIVE WORKLOADS

This section discusses four data-intensive micro-workloads that operate on one large file: random read, sequential read, random write, and sequential write.

3.1 Random Read

We begin with a workload where five NFS clients randomly read a 20GB file with a given I/O size. We compared the performance of V3 and V4.1 under a wide range of parameter settings including different numbers of benchmarking threads per client (1–16), different I/O sizes (4KB–1MB), and different network delays (0–40ms). We ensured that all experiments started with the same cache states by re-mounting the NFS directory and dropping the OS's page cache before each experiment. For all combinations of thread count, I/O size, and network delay, V4.1 and V3 performed equally well because these workloads were exercising the network and storage bandwidth rather than the differences between the two NFS protocols.

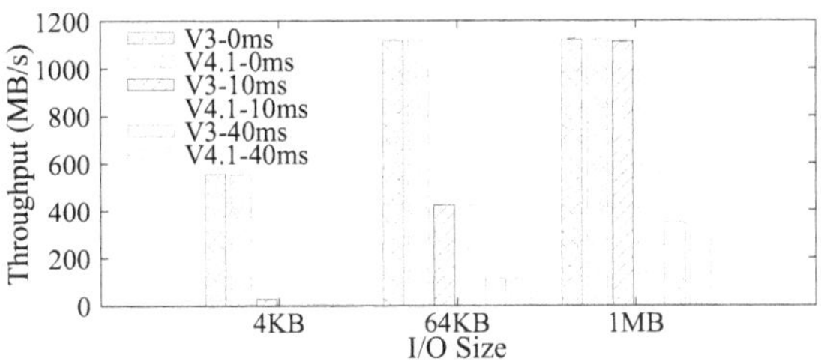

Figure 1: Random-read throughput with 16 threads and different network delays (varying I/O size).

We found that increasing the number of threads and the I/O size always improved a client's throughput. We also found that network delays had a significant impact on throughput, especially for smaller I/O sizes. As shown in Figure 1, a delay of 10ms reduced the throughput by 20× for 4KB I/Os, but by only 2.6× for 64KB ones, and did not make a difference for 1MB I/Os. The throughputs in Figure 1 were averaged over the 5-minute experiment run, which can be divided into two phases demarcated by the time when the NFS server finally cached the entire 20GB file. NFS's throughput was bottlenecked by the SSDs in the first phase, and by the network in the second. The large throughput drop for 4KB I/Os (20×) was because the 10ms delay lowered the request rate far enough that the first phase did not finish within 5 minutes. But with larger I/Os, even with 10ms network delay the NFS server was able to cache the entire 20GB during the run. Note that the storage stack performed better with larger I/Os: the throughput of our SSD RAID is 75.5MB/s with 4KB I/Os, but 285MB/s with 64KB I/Os (measured using direct I/O and 16 threads), largely thanks to the SSDs' inherent internal parallelism.

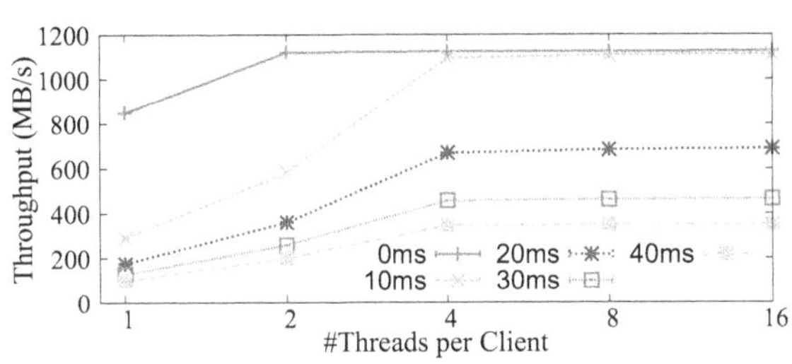

Figure 2: Random-read throughput with 1MB I/O size, default 2MB TCP maximum buffer size, and different network delays (varying the number of threads per client).

However, when we increased the network delay further, from 10ms to 40ms, we could not saturate the 10GbE network (Figure 2) even if we added more threads and used larger I/O sizes. As shown in Figure 2, the curves for 20ms, 30ms, and 40ms reached a limit at 4 threads. We found that this limit was caused by the NFS server's maximum TCP buffer sizes (`rmem_max` and `wmem_max` size), which restricted TCP's congestion window (i.e., the amount of data on the wire). To saturate the network, the `rmem_max` and `wmem_max` sizes must be larger than the network's bandwidth-delay product. After we changed those values from their default of 2MB to 32MB (larger than $\frac{10Gb/s \times 40ms}{5}$ where 5 is the number of clients), we achieved a maximum throughput of 1120MB/s when using 8 or more threads in the 20ms- to 40ms-delay networks. These experiments show that we can come close to the maximum network bandwidth for data-intensive workloads by tuning the TCP buffer size, I/O size, and the number of threads for both V3 and V4.1. To avoid being limited by the maximum TCP buffer size, we used 32MB for `rmem_max` and `wmem_max` for all machines and experiments in the rest of this paper.

3.2 Sequential Read

We next turn to an NFS sequential-read workload, where five NFS clients repeatedly scanned a 20GB file from start to end using an I/O size of 1MB. For this workload, V3 and V4.1 performed equally well: both achieved a maximum aggregate throughput of 1177MB/s. However, we frequently observed a *winner-loser pattern* among the clients, for both V3 and V4.1, exhibiting the following three traits: (1) the clients formed two clusters, one with high throughput (winners), and the other with low throughput (losers); (2) often, the winners' throughput was approximately double that of the losers; and (3) no client was consistently a winner or a loser, and a winner in one experiment might became a loser in another.

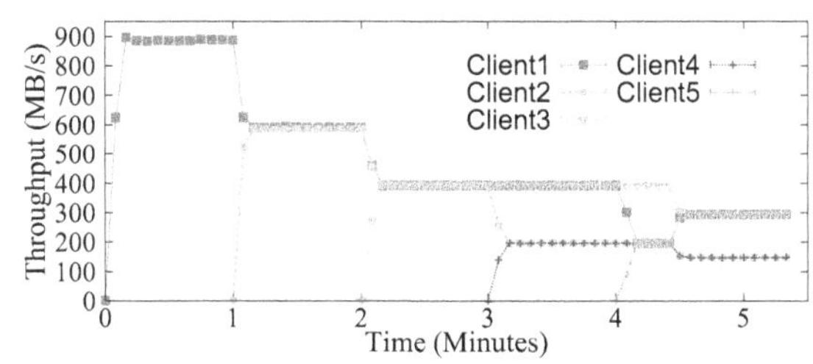

Figure 3: Sequential-read throughputs of individual clients when they were launched one after the other at an interval of one minute. Results of one run of experiments.

The winner-loser pattern was unexpected given that all the five clients had the same hardware, software, and settings, and were performing the same operations. Initially, we suspected that the pattern was caused by the order in which the clients launched the workload. To test that hypothesis, we repeated the experiment but launched the clients in a controlled order, one additional client every minute. However, the results disproved any correlation between experiment launch order and the winners. Figure 3 shows that Client2 started second but ended up as a loser, whereas Client5 started last but became a winner. Figure 3 also shows that the winners had about twice the throughput of the losers. We repeated this experiment multiple times and found no correlation between a client's start order and its chance of being a winner or loser.

By tracing the server's networking stack, we discovered that the winner-loser pattern is closely related to the server's use of physical queues in its network interface card (NIC). Every NIC has a physical transmit queue (`tx-queue`) holding outbound packets, and a physical receive queue (`rx-queue`) tracking empty buffers for inbound packets [24]. Many modern NICs have multiple sets of `tx-queues` and `rx-queues` to allow networking to scale with the number of CPU cores (each queue can be configured to interrupt a specific core), and to facilitate better NIC virtualization [24]. Linux uses hashing to decide which `tx-queue` to use for each outbound packet. However, not all packets are hashed; instead, each TCP socket has a field recording the `tx-queue` the last packet was forwarded to. If a socket has any existing packets in the recorded `tx-queue`, its next packet is also placed in that queue. This approach allows TCP to avoid generating out-of-order packets by placing packet n on a long queue and $n+1$ on a shorter one. However, a side effect is that for highly active TCP flows that always have outbound packets in the queue, the hashing is effectively done per-flow rather than per-packet. (On the other hand, if the socket has no packets in the recorded `tx-queue`, its next packet is re-hashed, probably to a new `tx-queue`.)

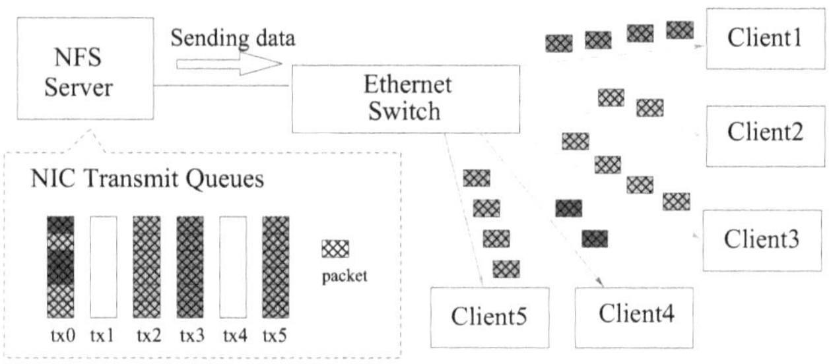

Figure 4: Illustration of Hash-Cast.

The winner-loser pattern is caused by uneven hashing of TCP flows to `tx-queues`. In our particular experiments, the server had five flows (one per client) and a NIC configured with six `tx-queues`. If two of the flows were hashed into one `tx-queue` and the rest went into three separate `tx-queues`, then the two flows sharing a `tx-queue` got half the throughput of the other three because all `tx-queues` were transmitting data at the same rate. We call this phenomenon—hashing unevenness causing a winner-loser pattern of throughput—*Hash-Cast*, which is illustrated in Figure 4.

Hash-Cast explains the performance anomalies illustrated in Figure 3. First, Client1, Client2, and Client3 were hashed into `tx3`, `tx0`, and `tx2`, respectively. Then, Client4 was hashed into `tx0`, which Client2 was already using. Later, Client5 was hashed into `tx3`, which Client1 was already using. However, at 270 seconds, Client5's `tx-queue` drained and it was rehashed into `tx5`. At the experiment's end, Client1, Client3, and Client5 were using `tx3`, `tx2`, and `tx5`, respectively, while Client2 and Client4 shared `tx0`. Hash-Cast also explains why the losers usually got half the throughputs of the winners: the {0,0,1,1,1,2} distribution is the most likely hashing result (we calculated its probability as roughly 69%).

To eliminate hashing unfairness, we evaluated the use of a single `tx-queue`. Unfortunately, we still observed an unfair throughput distribution across clients because of complicated networking algorithms such as *TSO Automatic Sizing*, which can form feedback loops that keep slow TCP flows always slow [10]. To resolve this issue, we further configured `tc qdisc` to use Stochastic Fair Queueing (SFQ), which achieves fairness by hashing flows to many software queues and sends packets from those queues in a round-robin manner [21]. Most importantly, SFQ used 127 software queues so that hash collisions were much less probable compared to using only 6 queues. To further alleviate the effect of collisions, we set SFQ's hashing perturbation rate to 10 seconds using `tc qdisc`, so that the mapping from TCP flows to software queues changed every 10 seconds.

Note that using a single `tx-queue` with SFQ did not reduce the aggregate network throughput compared to using multiple `tx-queues` without SFQ. We measured only negligible performance differences between these two configurations. We found that many of Linux's queuing disciplines assume a single `tx-queue` and could not be configured to use multiple ones. Thus, it might be desirable to use just one `tx-queue` in many systems, not just NFS servers. To ensure fairness among clients, for the remainder of experiments in this paper we used SFQ with a single `tx-queue`. The random-read results shown in Section 3.1 also used SFQ.

3.3 Random Write

The random-write workload is the same as the random-read one discussed in Section 3.1 except that the clients were writing data instead of reading. Each client had a number of threads that repeatedly wrote a specified amount (I/O size) of data at random offsets in a pre-allocated 20GB file. All writes were in-place and did not change the file size. We opened the file with `O_SYNC` set, to ensure that the clients write data back to the NFS server instead of just caching it locally. This setup is similar to many I/O workloads in virtualized environments [28], which use NFS heavily.

We varied the I/O size from 4KB to 1MB, the number of threads from 1 to 16, and the injected network delay from 0ms to 10ms. We ran the experiments long enough to ensure that the working sets, including in the 4KB I/O case, were at least 10 times larger than our RAID controller's cache size. As expected, larger I/O sizes and more threads led to higher throughputs, and longer network delays reduced throughput. V4.1 and V3 performed comparably, with V4.1 slightly worse (2% on average) in the zero-delay network.

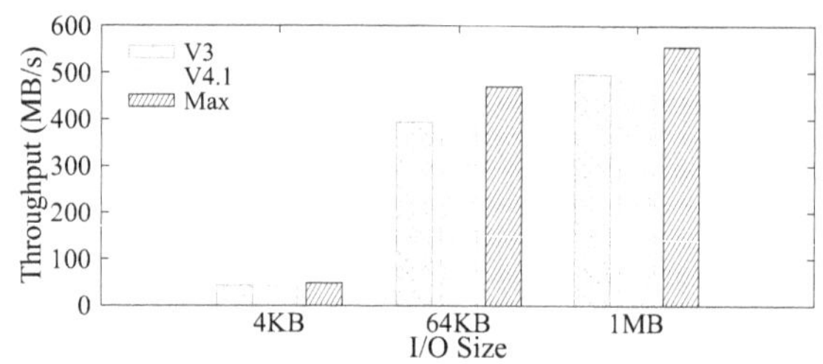

Figure 5: Random-write throughput in a zero-delay network.

Figure 5 shows the random-write throughput when we varied the I/O size in the zero-delay network. V4.1 and V3 achieved around the same throughput, but both were significantly slower than the maximum performance of our SSD RAID (measured on the server side without NFS). Neither V4.1 nor V3 achieved the maximum throughput even with more threads. We initially suspected that the lower throughputs were caused by the network, but the throughput did not improve when we repeated the experiment directly on the NFS server over the loopback device. Instead, we found the culprit to be the `O_SYNC` flag, which has different semantics in `ext4` than in NFS. The POSIX semantics of `O_SYNC` require all meta-data updates to be synchronously written to disk. On Linux's local file systems, however, `O_SYNC` is implemented so that only the actual file data and the meta-data directly needed to retrieve that data are written synchronously; other meta-data remains buffered. Since our workloads used only in-place writes, which updated the file's modification time but not the block mapping, writing an `ext4` file did not update meta-data. In contrast, the NFS implementation more strictly adheres to POSIX, which mandates that the server commit both the written data and "all file system metadata" to stable storage before returning results. Therefore, we observed many meta-data updates in NFS, but not in `ext4`. The overhead of those extra updates was aggravated by `ext4`'s journaling of meta-data changes on the server side. The extra updates and the journaling introduced numerous extra I/Os, causing NFS's throughput to be significantly lower than the RAID-0's maximum (measured without NFS). This finding highlights the importance of understanding the effects of the NFS server's implementation and the underlying file system that it exports.

We also tried the experiments without setting `O_SYNC`, which generated a bursty workload to the NFS server. Clients initially realized high throughput (over 1GB/s) since all data was buffered in their caches. Once the number of dirty pages passed a threshold, the throughput dropped to near zero as the clients began flushing those pages to the server; this process took up to 3 minutes depending on the I/O size. After that, the write throughput became high again, until caches filled—and the bursty pattern then repeated.

3.4 Sequential Write

We also benchmarked sequential-write workloads, where each client had a single thread writing sequentially to the 20GB file. V4.1 and V3 again had the same performance. However, the single-threaded sequential-write throughputs were lower than the corresponding multi-threaded random-write throughputs because our all-SSD storage backend favors multi-threaded I/O accesses due to the SSD's internal parallelism [2]. For sequential writes, the O_SYNC behavior we discussed in Section 3.3 had an even stronger effect if the backend storage used HDDs, because the small disk writes generated by the meta-data updates and the associated journaling broke the sequentiality of NFS's writes to disk. We measured a 50% slowdown caused by this effect when we used HDDs for our storage backend instead of SSDs.

4. METADATA-INTENSIVE WORKLOADS

The data-intensive workloads discussed so far are more sensitive to network and I/O bandwidth than to latency. This section focuses on meta-data-intensive workloads, which are critical to NFS's overall performance because of the popularity of uses such as shared home directories, where common workloads like software development and document processing involve many small- to medium-sized files. We discuss three micro-workloads that exercise NFS's meta-data operations by operating on a large number of small files: file reads, file creations, and directory listings.

4.1 Read Small Files

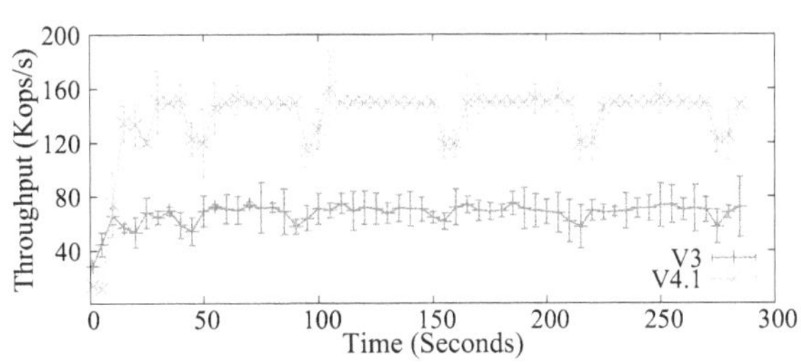

Figure 6: Throughput of reading small files with one thread in a zero-delay network.

We pre-allocated 10,000 4KB files on the NFS server. Figure 6 shows the results of the 5 clients randomly reading entire files repeatedly for 5 minutes. The throughputs of both V3 and V4.1 increased quickly during the first 10 seconds and then stabilized once the clients had read and cached all files. V4.1 started slower than V3, but outperformed V3 by 2× after their throughputs stabilized. We observed that V4.1 made 8.3× fewer NFS requests than V3 did. The single operation that caused this difference was GETATTR, which accounted for 95% of all the requests performed by V3. These GETATTRs were being used by the V3 clients to revalidate their client-side cache. However, V4.1 rarely made any requests once its throughput had stabilized. Further investigation revealed that this was due to V4.1's delegation mechanism, which allows client-side caches to be used without revalidation. We discuss and evaluate V4's delegations in greater detail in Section 5.

To investigate read performance with fewer caching effects, we used a 10ms network delay to increase the time it would take to cache all of the files. With this delay, the clients did not finish reading all of the files during the same 5-minute experiment. We observed that the client's throughput dropped to under 94 ops/s for V3 and under 56 ops/s for V4.1. Note that each V4.1 client made an average of 243 NFS requests per second, whereas each V3 client made only 196, which is counter-intuitive given that V4.1 had lower throughput. The reason for V4.1's lower throughput is its more verbose stateful nature: 40% of V4.1's requests are state-maintaining requests (e.g., OPENs and CLOSEs in this case), rather than READs. State-maintaining requests do not contribute to throughput, and since most files were not cached, V4.1's delegations could not help reduce the number of stateful requests.

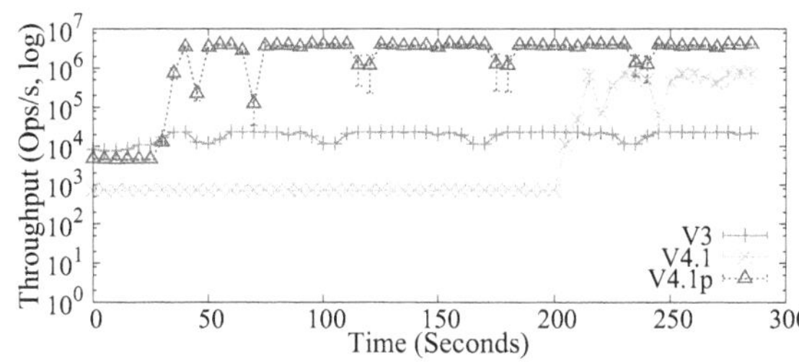

Figure 7: Throughput of reading small files with 16 threads in a 10ms-delay network ($\log_{10}$).

To compensate for the lower throughput due to the 10ms network delay, we increased the number of threads on each client, and then repeated the experiment. Figure 7 shows the throughput results (log scale). With 16 threads per client V3's throughput (the red line) started at around 8100 ops/s and quickly increased to 55,800 ops/s. After that, operations were served by the client-side cache; only GETATTR requests were made for cache revalidation. V4.1's throughput (the green curve) started at only 723 ops/s, which is eleven times slower than that of V3. It took 200 seconds for V4.1 to cache all files; then V4.1 overtook V3, and afterwards performed 25× faster thanks to delegations. V4.1 also made 71% fewer requests per second than V3; this reversed the trend from the no-latency-added single-thread case (Figure 6), where V4.1 had lower throughput but made more requests.

To understand this behavior, we reviewed the mountstat data for the V4.1 tests. We found that the average RPC queuing time of V4.1's OPEN and CLOSE requests was as long as 223ms, while that average queuing time of all V4.1's other requests (ACCESS, GETATTR, LOOKUP, and READ) was shorter than 0.03ms. (The RPC queuing time is the time between when an RPC is initialized and when it begins transmitting over the wire.) This means that some OPENs and CLOSEs waited over 200ms in a client-side queue before the client started to transmit them.

To diagnose the long delays, we used Systemtap to instrument all the rpc_wait_queues in Linux's NFS client kernel module and found the culprit to be an rpc_wait_queue for seqid, which is an argument to OPEN and CLOSE requests [25]; it was used by V4.0 clients to notify the server of changes in client-side states. V4.0 requests that needed to change the seqid were fully serialized by this wait queue. The problem is exacerbated by the fact that once entered into this queue, a request is not dequeued until it receives the server's reply. However, seqid is obsolete in V4.1: the latest standard [25] explicitly states that "The 'seqid' field of the request is not used in NFSv4.1, but it MAY be any value and the server MUST ignore it."

We fixed the long queuing time for `seqid` by avoiding the queue entirely. (We have submitted a patch to the kernel mailing list.) For V4.0, `seqid` is still used and our patch does not change its behavior. We repeated the experiments with these changes; the new results are shown as the blue curve in Figure 7. V4.1's performance improved by more than 6× (from 723 ops/s to 4655 ops/s). V4.1 finished reading all the files within 35 seconds, and thereafter stabilized at a throughput 172× higher than that of V3 (thanks to delegations). In addition to the higher throughput, V4.1's average response time was shorter than that of V3, also because of delegations. For brevity, we refer to the patched NFSv4.1 as V4.1p in following discussions.

We noted a periodic performance drop every 60 seconds in Figures 6 and 7, which corresponds to the `actimeo` mount option. When this timer expires, client-cached metadata must again be retrieved from the server, temporarily lowering throughput.

4.2 File Creation

We demonstrated above that client-side caching, especially delegations, can greatly reduce the number of NFS meta-data requests when reading small files. To exercise NFS's meta-data operations more, we now turn to a file-creation workload, where client-side caching is less effective. We exported one NFS directory for each of the five clients, and instructed each client to create 10,000 files of a given size in its dedicated directory, as fast as possible.

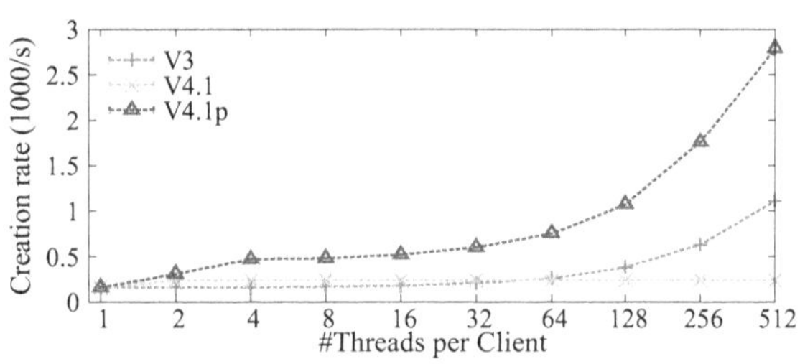

Figure 8: Rate of creating empty files in a 10ms-delay network.

Figure 8 shows the speed of creating empty files in the 10ms-delay network. To test scalability, we varied the number of threads per client from 1 to 512. V4.1 started at the same speed as V3 when there was only one thread per client. Between 2–32 threads, V4.1 outperformed V3 by 1.1–1.5×, and V4.1p (NFSv4.1 with our patch) outperformed V3 by 1.9–2.9×. Above 32 threads, however, V4.1 became 1.1–4.6× *slower* than V3, whereas V4.1p was 2.5–2.9× *faster* than V3.

As shown in Figure 8, when the number of threads per client increased from 1 to 16, V3 sped up by only 12.5%, V4.1 by 50%, and V4.1p by 225%. In terms of scalability (1–16 threads), V3 scaled poorly, with an average performance boost of merely 3% each power-of-two step in the thread count. V4.1 scaled slightly better, with an average 10% boost per step. But, because of the `seqid` synchronizing bottleneck explained in Section 4.1, its performance did not improve at all once the thread count increased beyond two. With the `seqid` problem fixed, V4.1p scaled much better, with an average boost of 34% per step. With 16–512 threads, V3's scalability improved significantly, and it achieved a high average performance boost of 44% per step; V4.1p also scaled well with an average boost of 40% per step.

V4.1p always outperformed the original V4.1, by up to 11.6× with 512 threads. Therefore, for the rest of this paper, we only report figures for V4.1p, unless otherwise noted.

In the 10ms-delay network, the rates of creating empty, 4KB, and 16KB files differed by less than 2% when there were more than 4 threads, and by less than 27% with fewer threads; thus, they all had the same trends. As shown in Figure 8, depending on the number of threads, V4.1p created small files 1.9–2.9× faster than V3 did. To understand why, we analyzed the `mountstats` data and found that the two versions differed significantly in the number of outstanding NFS requests (i.e., requests sent but not yet replied to). We show the average number of outstanding NFS requests in Figure 9, which closely resembles Figure 8 in overall shape. This suggests that V4.1p performed faster than V3 because the V4.1p clients sent more requests to the server at one time. We examined the client code and discovered that V3 clients use synchronous RPC calls (rpc_call_sync) to create files, whereas V4.1p clients use asynchronous calls (rpc_call_async) that go through a work queue (nfsiod_workqueue). We believe that the asynchronous calls are the reason why V4.1p had more outstanding requests: the long network delay allowed multiple asynchronous calls to accumulate in the work queue and be sent out in batch, allowing networking algorithms such as TCP Nagle to efficiently coalesce multiple RPC messages. Sending fewer but larger messages is faster than sending many small ones, so V4.1p achieved higher rates. Our analysis was confirmed by the `mountstats` data, which showed that V4.1p's OPEN requests had significantly longer queuing times (up to 30×) on the client side than V3's CREATEs. (V3 uses CREATEs to create files whereas V4.1p uses OPENs.) Because V3's server is stateless, all its mutating operations have to be synchronous; otherwise a server crash might lose data. V4, however, is stateful and can perform mutating operations asynchronously because it can restore states properly in case of server crashes [22].

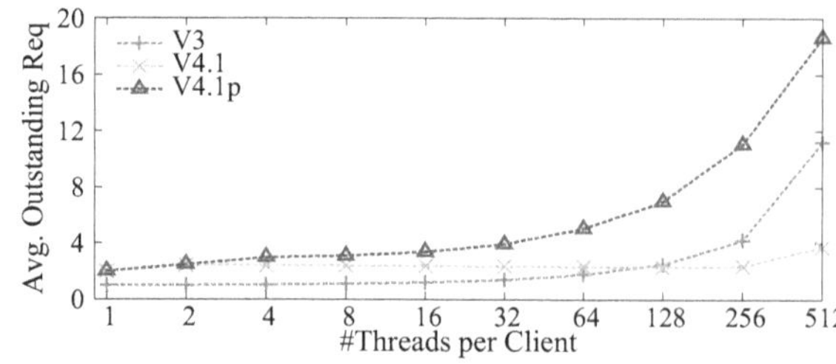

Figure 9: Average number of outstanding requests when creating empty files in a 10ms-delay network.

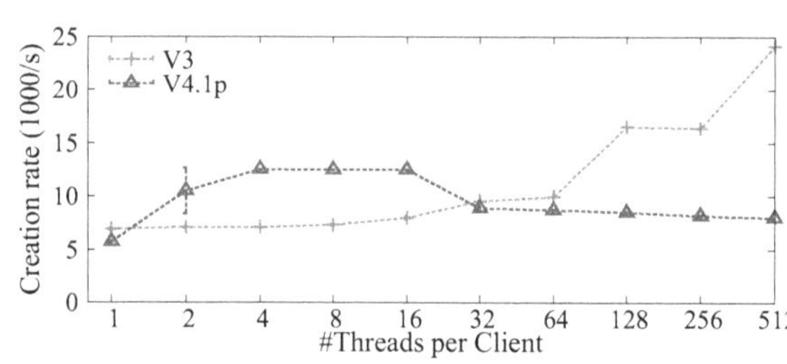

Figure 10: Rate of creating empty files in a zero-delay network.

In the zero-delay network, there was not a consistent winner between the two NFS versions (Figure 10). Depending on the number of threads, V4.1p varied from 1.76× faster to 3× slower than V3. In terms of scalability, V3's speed increased slowly when we began adding threads, but jumped quickly between 64 and 512 threads. In contrast, V4.1p's speed improved quickly at the initial stage, but plateaued and then dropped when we used more than 4 threads.

To understand why, we looked into the `mountstats` data, and found that the corresponding graph (not shown) of the average number of outstanding requests closely resembles Figure 10. It again suggests that the lower speed was the result of a client sending requests rather slowly. With further analysis, we found that V4.1p's performance drop after 32 threads was caused by high contention for session slots, which are V4.1p's unique resources the server allocates to clients. Each session slot allows one request; if a client runs out of slots (i.e., has reached the maximum number of concurrent requests the server allows), it has to wait until one becomes available, which happens when the client receives a reply for any of its outstanding requests. We instrumented the client kernel module and collected the waiting time on the session slots. As shown in Figure 11, waiting began at 32 threads, which is also where V4.1p's performance began dropping (Figure 10). Note that with 512 threads, the average waiting time is 2500ms, or 12,500× the 0.2ms round-trip time. (The 10ms-delay experiment also showed waiting for session slots, but the wait time was short compared to the network RTT and thus had a smaller effect on performance.)

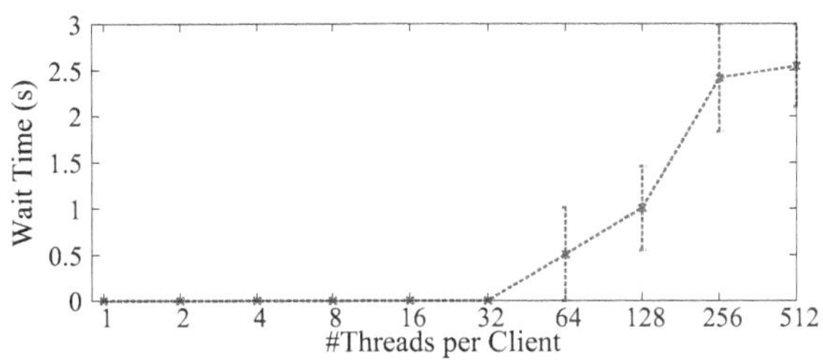

Figure 11: Average waiting time for V4.1p's session slots of ten experimental runs. Error bars are standard deviations.

We note that Figure 11 had high standard deviations above 32 threads per client. This behavior results from typical non-real-time scheduling artifacts in Linux, where some threads can win and be scheduled first, while others wait longer. Even when we ran the same experiment 10 times, standard deviations did not decrease, suggesting a non-Gaussian, multi-modal distribution [27]. In addition to V4.1p's higher wait time in this figure, the high standard deviation means that it would be harder to enforce SLAs with V4.1p for highly-concurrent applications.

With 2–16 threads (Figure 10), V4.1p's performance advantage over V3 was because of V4.1p's asynchronous calls (the same as explained above); V4.1p's OPENs had around 4× longer queuing time, which let multiple requests accumulate and be sent out in batch. This queuing time was not caused by the lack of available session slots (Figure 11). This was verified by evaluating the use of a single thread, in which case V4.1p performed 17% slower than V3 because V4.1p's OPEN requests are more complex and took longer to process than V3's CREATE (see Section 4.3).

One possible solution to V4.1p's session-slot bottleneck is to enlarge the number of server-side slots to match the client's needs. However, slots consume resources: for example, the server must then increase its *duplicate request cache* (DRC) size to maintain its *exactly once semantics* (EOS). Increasing the DRC size can be expensive, because the DRC has to be persistent and is possibly saved in NVRAM. V3 does not have this issue because it does not provide EOS, and does not guarantee that it will handle retransmitted non-idempotent operations correctly. Consequently, V3 outperformed V4.1p when there were more than 64 threads (Figure 10).

4.3 Directory Listing

We now turn to another common meta-data-intensive workload: listing directories. We used Filebench's directory-listing workload, which operates on a pre-allocated NFS directory tree that contains 50,000 empty files and has a mean directory width of 5. Each client ran one Filebench instance, which repeatedly picks a random subdirectory in the tree and lists its contents.

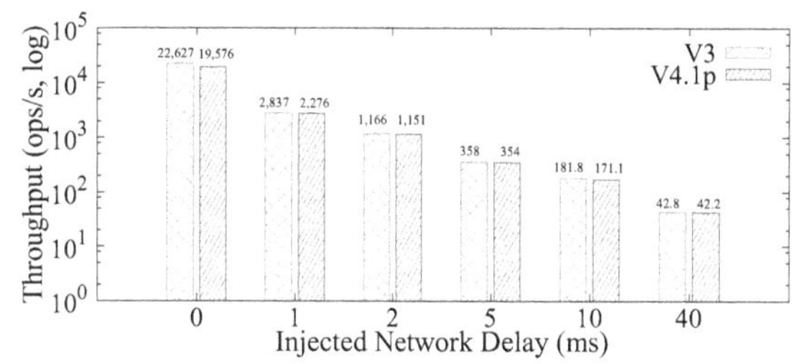

Figure 12: Directory listing throughput ($\log_{10}$).

This workload is read-only, and showed behavior similar to that of reading small files (Section 4.1) in that its performance depended heavily on client-side caching. Once all content was cached, the only NFS requests were for cache revalidations. Figure 12 (log scale) shows the throughput of single-threaded directory listing in networks with different delays. In general, V4.1p performed slightly worse than V3. The biggest difference was in the zero-delay network, where V4.1p was 15% slower. `mountstats` showed that V4.1p's requests had longer round-trip times, which implies that the server processed those requests slower than V3: 10% slower for READDIR, 27% for GETATTR, 33% for ACCESS, and 36% for LOOKUP. This result is predictable because the V4.1p protocol, which is stateful and has more features (EOS, delegations, etc.), is substantially more complex than V3. As we increased the network delay, the processing time of V4.1p became less important: V4.1p's performance was within 94–99% of V3.

With 16 threads, V4.1p's throughput was 95–101% of V3's. Note that V4.1p's asynchronous RPC calls did not influence this workload much because most of this workload's requests did not mutate states. Only the state-mutating V4.1p requests are asynchronous: OPEN, CLOSE, LOCK, and LOCKU. (WRITE is also asynchronous, but this workload does not have any.)

5. NFSV4 DELEGATIONS

In this section, we discuss delegations, an advanced client-side caching mechanism that is a key new feature of NFSv4. Caching is essential to good performance in any system, but in distributed systems like NFS it gives rise to consistency problems. V2 and V3 explicitly ignored strict consistency [7, p. 10], but supported a limited form of validation via the GETATTR operation. In practice, clients validate their cache contents frequently, causing extra server load and adding significant delay in high-latency networks.

In V4, the cost of cache validation is reduced by letting a server *delegate* a file to a particular client for a limited time, allowing accesses to proceed at local speed. While holding the delegation, a client need not revalidate its attributes or contents. If any other clients want to perform conflicting operations, the server can recall the delegation using *callbacks* via a server-to-client back-channel connection. Delegations are based on the observation that file sharing is infrequent [25] and rarely concurrent [15]. Thus, they can boost performance most of the time, but can also hurt performance in the presence of concurrent and conflicting file sharing.

Delegations have two types: *open delegations* of files, and *directory delegations*. The former comes in either "read" or "write" variants. We will focus on read delegations of regular files because they are the simplest and most common type—and are also the only delegation type currently supported in the Linux kernel [11].

5.1 Granting a Delegation

An open delegation is granted when a client opens a file with an appropriate flag. However, clients must not assume that a delegation will be granted, because that choice is up to the server. If a delegation is rejected, the server can explain its decision via flags in the open reply (e.g., lock contention, unsupported delegation type). Even if a delegation is granted, the server is free to recall it at any time via the back channel. Recalling a delegation may involve multiple clients and multiple messages, which may lead to considerable delay. Thus, the decision to grant the delegation might be complex. However, because Linux currently supports only file-read delegations, it uses a simpler decision model. The delegation is granted if three conditions are met: (1) the back channel is working, (2) the client is opening the file with `O_RDONLY`, and (3) the file is not currently open for write by any client.

During our initial experiments we did not observe any delegations even when all three conditions held. We traced the kernel using `SystemTap` and discovered that the Linux NFS server's implementation of delegations was outdated: it did not recognize new delegation flags introduced by NFSv4.1. The effect was that if an NFS client got the filehandle of a file before the client opened the file (e.g., using `stat`), no delegation was granted. We fixed the problem with a kernel patch, which has been accepted into the mainline Linux kernel.

5.2 Delegation Performance: Locked Reads

We previously showed the benefit of delegations in Figure 7, where delegations helped V4.1p read small files 172× faster than V3. This improvement is due to the elimination of cache revalidation traffic; no communication with the server (GETATTRs) is needed to serve reads from cache. Nevertheless, delegations can improve performance even further in workloads with file locking. To quantify the benefits, we repeated the delegation experiment performed by Gulati [12] but scaled it up. We pre-allocated 1000 4KB files in a shared NFS directory and then mounted it on the five clients. Each client repeatedly opened each of the files in the shared NFS directory, locked it, read the entire file, and then unlocked it. (Locking the file is a technique used to ensure an atomic read.) After ten repetitions the client moved to the next file.

Operation	NFSv3	NFSv4.1 deleg. off	NFSv4.1 deleg. on
OPEN	0	10,001	1000
READ	10,000	10,000	1000
CLOSE	0	10,001	1000
ACCESS	10,003	9003	3
GETATTR	19,003	19,002	1
LOCK	10,000	10,000	0
LOCKU	10,000	10,000	0
LOOKUP	1002	2	2
FREE_STATEID	0	10,000	0
TOTAL	**60,008**	**88,009**	**3009**

Table 1: NFS operations performed by each client for NFSv3 and NFSv4.1 (delegations on and off). Each NFSv4.1 operation represents a compound procedure. For clarity, we omit trivial operations (e.g., PUTFH) in compounds. NFSv3's LOCK and LOCKU come from the Network Lock Manager (NLM).

Table 1 shows the number of operations performed by V3 and by V4.1p with and without delegation. Only V4.1p shows OPENs and CLOSEs because only V4 is stateful. When delegations were on, V4.1p used only 1000 OPENs even though each client opened each file ten times. This is because each client obtained a delegation on the first OPEN; the following nine were performed locally. Note that in Table 1, without a delegation (for V3 and V4.1p with delegations off), each application read incurred an expensive NFS READ operation even though the same reads were repeated ten times. Repeated reads were not served from the client-side cache because of file locking, which forces the client to revalidate the data.

Another problem is caused by the timestamp granularity on the NFS server. Traditionally, NFS provides close-to-open cache consistency. Timestamps are updated at the server when a file is closed, and any client subsequently opening the same file revalidates its local cache by checking its attributes with the server. If the locally-saved timestamp of the file is out of date, the client's cache of the file is invalidated. Unfortunately, some NFS servers offer only one-second granularity, which is too coarse for modern systems; clients could miss intermediate changes made by other clients within one second. In this situation, NFS locking provides stronger cache coherency by first checking the server's timestamp granularity. If the granularity is finer than one microsecond, the client revalidates the cache with GETATTR; otherwise, the client invalidates the cache. Since the Linux in-kernel server uses a one-second granularity, each read operation incurs a READ RPC request because the preceding LOCK has invalidated the client's local cache.

Invalidating an entire cached file can be expensive, since NFS is often used to store large files such as virtual disk images [28], media files, etc. The problem is worsened by two factors: (1) invalidation happens even when the client is simply acquiring read (not write) locks, and (2) a file's entire cache contents are invalidated even if the lock only applies to a single byte. In contrast, the NFS client with delegation was able to satisfy nine of the ten repeated READs from the page cache. There was no need to revalidate the cache at all because its validity was guaranteed by the delegation.

Another major difference among the columns in Table 1 was the number of GETATTRs. In the absence of delegation, GETATTRs were used for two purposes: to revalidate the cache upon file open, and to update file meta-data upon read. The latter GETATTRs were needed because the locking preceding the read invalidated both the data and meta-data caches for the locked file. A potential optimization for V4.1p would be to have the client append a GETATTR to the LOCK in the same compound, and let the server piggyback file attributes in its reply. This could save 10,000 GETATTR RPCs.

The remaining differences between the experiments with and without delegations were due to locking. A LOCK/LOCKU pair is sent to the server when the client does not have a delegation. Conversely, no NFS communication is needed for locking when a delegation exists. For V4.1p with delegations off, one FREE_STATEID follows each LOCKU to free the resource (stateid) used by the lock at the server. (A potential optimization would be to append the FREE_STATEID operation to the same compound procedure that includes LOCKU; this could save another 10,000 RPCs.)

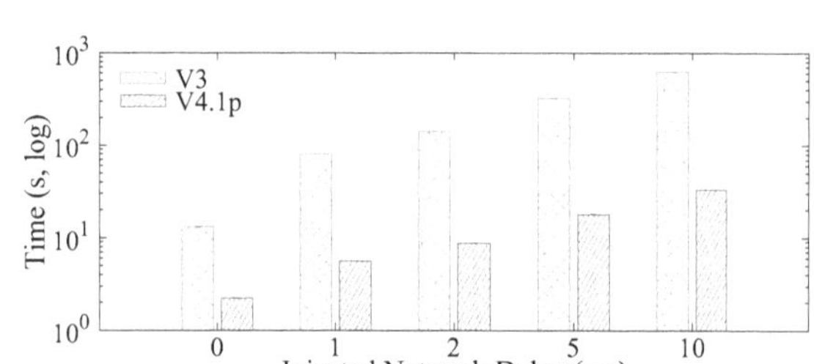

Figure 13: Running time of the locked-reads experiment ($\log_{10}$). Lower is better.

In total, delegations cut the number of V4.1p operations by over 29× (from 88K to 3K). This enabled the original stateful and "chattier" V4.1p (with extra OPEN, CLOSE, and FREE_STATEID calls) to finish the same workload using only 5% of the requests used by V3. In terms of data volume, V3 sent 3.8MB and received 43.7MB, whereas V4.1p with delegation sent 0.6MB and received 4.5MB. Delegation helped V4.1p reduce the outgoing traffic by 6.3× and the incoming traffic by 9.7×. As seen in Figure 13, these reductions translate to a 6–19× speedup in networks with 0–10ms latency.

5.3 Delegation Recall Impact

To evaluate the overhead of conflicting delegations, we created two groups of NFS clients: the Delegation Group (DG) grabs and holds NFS delegations on 1000 files by opening them with the `O_RDONLY` flag, while the Recall Group (RG), recalls those delegations by opening the same files with `O_RDWR`. To test scalability, we varied the number of RG clients from one to four. For n clients in the DG, an RG open generated n recalls because each DG client's delegation had to be recalled separately.

We compared the cases when the DG clients were and were not holding delegations. Each DG client needed two operations to respond to a recall: a DELEGRETURN to return the delegation, and an OPEN to re-open the file (since the delegation was no longer valid).

For the RG client, the presence of a delegation incurred one additional NFS OPEN per file. The first OPEN failed, returning an `NFS4ERR_DELAY` error to tell the client to try again later because the server needed to recall outstanding delegations. The second open was sent as a retry and succeeded.

The running time of the experiment varied dramatically, from 0.2 seconds in the no-delegation case to 100 seconds with delegation. This 500× delay was introduced by the RG client, which failed in the first OPEN and retried it after a timeout. The initial timeout length is hard-coded to 100ms in the client kernel module (`NFS4_POLL_RETRY_MIN` in the Linux source code), and is doubled every time the retry fails. This long timeout was the dominating factor in the experiment's running time.

To test delegation recall in networks with longer latencies, we repeated the experiment after injecting network delays from 1–10ms. Under those conditions, the experiment's running time increased from 100s to 120s. With 10ms of extra network latency, the running time was still dominated by the client's retry timeout. However, when we increased the number of clients in DG from one to four, the total running time did not change. This suggests the delegation recall works well when there are several clients holding conflicting delegations at the same time.

We believe that a long initial timeout of 100ms is questionable considering that most SLAs specify a latency of 10–100ms [3]. Also, because Linux does not support write delegations, Linux NFS clients do not have any dirty data (of delegated files) to write back to the server, and thus should be able to return delegations quickly. We believe it would be better to start with a much shorter timeout; if that turns out to be too small, the client will back-off quickly anyway since the timeout increases exponentially.

6. MACRO-WORKLOADS

We now turn to macro-workloads that mix data and meta-data operations. These are more complex than micro-workloads, but also more closely match the real world. Our study used Filebench's File Server, Web Server, and Mail Server workloads [14].

6.1 The File Server Workload

The File Server workload includes opens, creates, reads, writes, appends, closes, stats, and deletes. All dirty data is written back to the NFS server on close to enforce NFS's close-to-open semantics. We created one Filebench instance for each client and ran each experiment for 5 minutes. We used the File Server workload's default settings: each instance had 50 threads operating on 10,000 files (in a dedicated NFS directory) with an average file size of 128KB, with the sizes chosen using Filebench's gamma function [29].

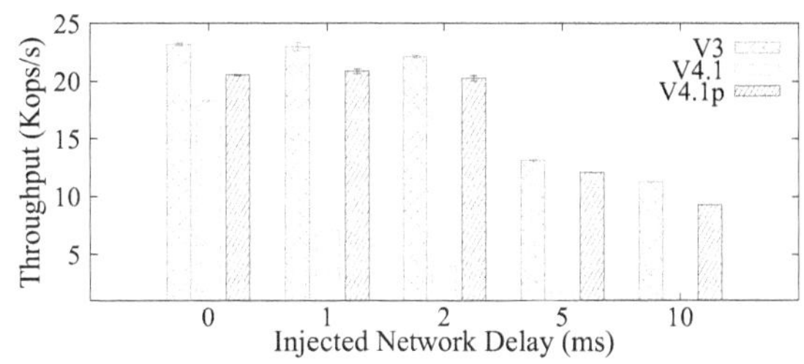

Figure 14: File Server throughput (varying network delay)

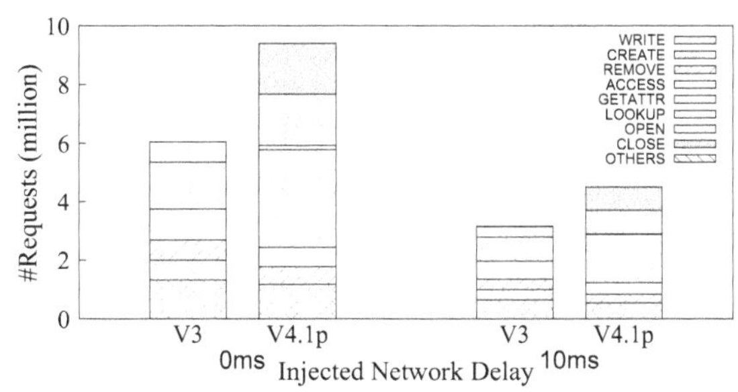

Figure 15: Number of NFS requests made by the File Server

As shown in Figure 14, V4.1p had lower throughput than V3. Without any injected network delay, V4.1p's throughput was 12% lower because V4.1p is stateful and more talkative. To maintain state, V4.1p did 3.5 million OPENs and CLOSEs (Figure 15), which was equivalent to 58% of all V3's requests. Note that 0.6 million of the OPENs not only maintained states, but also created files. Without considering OPEN and CLOSE, V4.1p and V3 made roughly the same number of requests: V4.1p sent 106% more GETATTRs than V3 did, but no CREATEs and 78% fewer LOOKUPs.

V4's verbosity hurts its performance, especially in high-latency networks. We observed the same problems in other workloads such as small-file reading (Section 4.1), where V4 was 40% slower than V3 with a single thread and a 10ms-delay network. Verbosity is the result of V4's stateful nature, and the V4 designers were aware of the issue. To reduce verbosity, V4 provides compound procedures, which pack multiple NFS operations into one message. However, compounds have not been implemented effectively in Linux (and other OSes): most contain only 2–4 often-trivial operations (e.g., SEQUENCE, PUTFH, and GETFH); and applications currently have no ability to generate their own compounds. We believe that implementing effective compounds is difficult for two reasons: (1) The POSIX API dictates a synchronous programming model: issue one system call, wait, check the result, and only then issue the next call. (2) Without transaction support, failure handling in compounds with many operations is fairly difficult.

In this File Server workload, even though V4.1p made a total of 56% more requests than V3, V4.1p was only 12% slower because its asynchronous calls allowed 40–95% more outstanding requests (as explained in Section 4.2). When we injected delay into the network (Figure 14), V4.1p continued to perform slower than V3, by 8–18% depending on the delay. V4.1p's delegation mechanism did not help for the File Server workload because it contains mostly writes, and most reads were cached (also Linux does not currently support write delegations).

Figure 14 also includes the unpatched V4.1. As we increased the network delay, V4.1p performed increasingly better than V4.1, eventually reaching a 10.5× throughput improvement. We conclude that our patch helps V4.1's performance in both micro- and macro-workloads, especially as network delays increase.

6.2 The Web Server Workload

Filebench's Web Server workload emulates servicing HTTP requests: 100 threads repeatedly operate on 1000 files, in a dedicated directory per client, representing HTML documents with a mean size of 16KB. The workload reads 10 randomly-selected files in their entirety, and then appends 16KB to a log file that is shared among all threads, causing contention. We ran one Web Server instance on each of the five NFS clients.

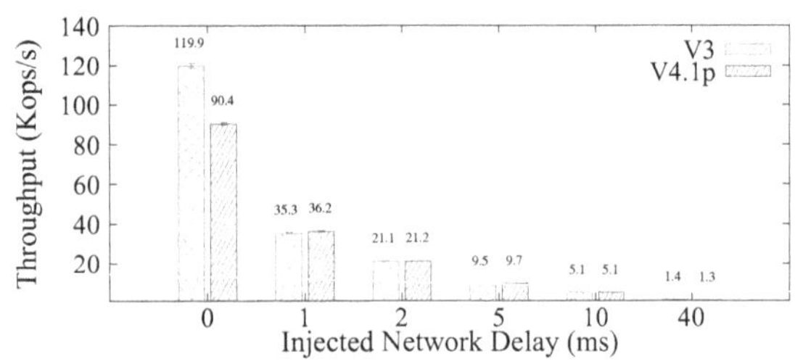

Figure 16: Web Server throughput (varying network delay).

Figure 16 shows the throughput with different network delays. V4.1p was 25% slower than V3 in the zero-delay network. The `mountstats` data showed that the average round-trip time (RTT) of V4.1p's requests was 19% greater than for V3. As the network delay increased, the RPC RTT became overshadowed by the delay, and V4.1p's performance became close to V3's and even slightly better (up to 2.6%). V4.1p's longer RTT was due to its complexity and longer processing time on the server side, as explained in Section 4.3. With longer network delays, V4.1p's performance picked up and matched V3's because of its use of asynchronous calls.

To test delegations, we changed the Filebench workload to specify that the HTML files are read-only, and confirmed that the change enabled delegations. In the zero-delay network, delegations reduced the number of V4.1p's `getattr` requests from over 8.7M to only 11K, and `opens` and `closes` from over 8.8M to about 10K. In summary, delegations cut the total number of all NFS requests by more than 10×. However, the substantial reduction in requests did not bring a corresponding performance boost: the throughput increased by only 3% in the zero-delay network, and actually decreased by 8% in the 1ms-delay situation. We were able to identify the problem as the writes to the log file. With delegations, each Web Server thread finished the first 10 reads from the client-side cache without any network communication, but then was blocked at the last write operation.

To characterize the bottleneck, we varied the number of threads in the workload and repeated the experiments with delegations both on and off. Figure 17 shows that delegations improved V4.1p's single-threaded performance by 7.4×, from 18 to 137 Kops/s. As the thread count increased, the log write began to dominate and delegations' benefit decreased, eventually making no difference: and the two curves of V4.1p in Figure 17 converged. With delegations, V4.1p was 2.2× faster than V3 when using one thread. However, V4.1p began to slow down with 4 threads, whereas V3 sped up and did not slow down until the thread number increased to 64. The

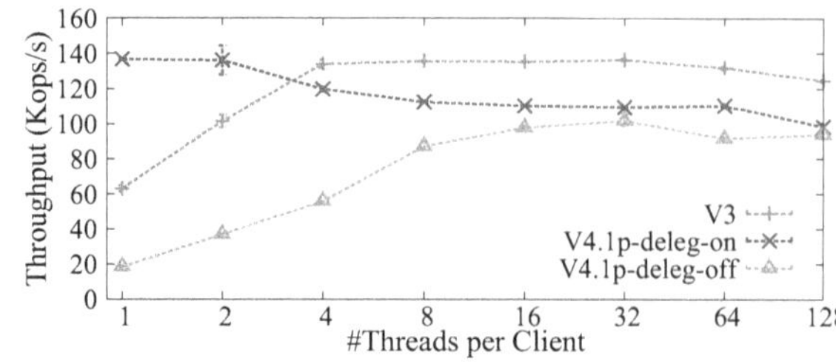

Figure 17: Web Server throughput in the zero-delay network (varying thread count per client).

eventual slowdown of both V3 and V4.1p was because the system became overloaded when the log-writing bottleneck was hit. However, V4.1p hit the bottleneck with fewer threads than V3 did because V4.1p, with delegations, only performed repeated WRITEs, whereas V3 performed ten GETATTRs (for cache revalidation) before each WRITE. With more than 32 threads, V4.1p's performance was also hurt by waiting for session slots (see Section 4.2).

This Web Server macro-workload demonstrated how the power of V4.1p's delegations can be limited by the absence of write delegations in the current version of Linux. Any real-world application that is not purely read-only might quickly bottleneck on writes even though read delegations can eliminate most NFS read and revalidation operations. However, write delegations will not help if all clients are writing to a single file, such as a common log.

6.3 The Mail Server Workload

Filebench's Mail Server workload mimics `mbox`-style e-mail activities, including compose, receive, read, and delete. Each Mail Server instance has 16 threads that repeat the following sets of operations on 1000 files in a flat directory: (1) create, write, fsync, and close a file (compose); (2) open, read, append, fsync, and close a file (receive); (3) open, read, and close a file (read); (4) delete a file (delete). The initial average file size was 16KB, but that could increase if appends were performed. We created a dedicated NFS directory for each NFS client, and launched one Mail Server instance per client. We tested different numbers of NFS clients, in addition to different network delays.

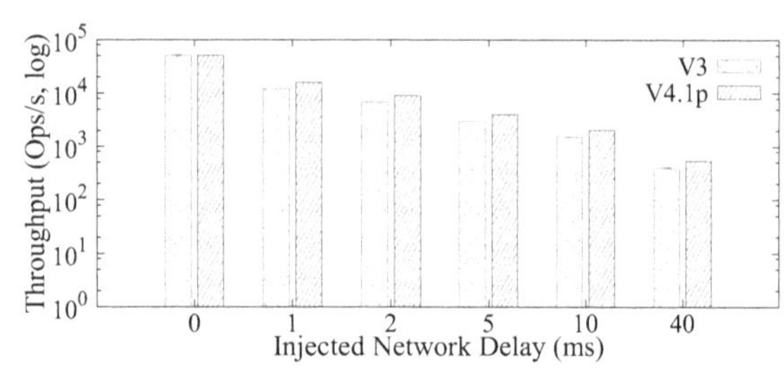

Figure 18: Mail Server throughput (varying network delay)

Figure 18 (note the log Y scale) presents the Mail Server throughput with different network delays. Without delay, V4.1p and V3 had the same throughput; with 1–40ms delay, V4.1p was 1.3–1.4× faster. Three factors affected V4.1p's performance: (1) V4.1p made more NFS requests for the same amount of work (see Section 6.1); and (2) V4.1p's operations were more complex and had longer RPC round-trip times (see Section 4.3); but (3) V4.1p made many asynchronous RPC calls and helped the networking algorithms coalesce RPC messages (see Section 4.1). Although the first two factors hurt V4.1p's performance, the third more than compensated for them. Increasing the network delay did not change factor (1), but diminished the effect of (2) as the delay gradually came to dominate the RPC RTT. Longer network delays also magnified the benefits of factor (3) because longer round trips were mitigated by coalescing requests. Thus, V4.1p increasingly outperformed V3 (1.3–1.4×) as the delay grew. V4.1p's read delegations did not help in this workload because most of its activities write files (reads are largely cached). This again shows the potential benefit of write delegations, even though Linux does not currently support them.

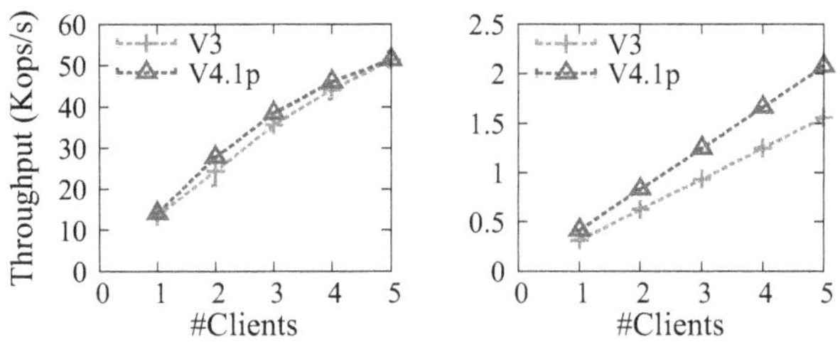

(a) No network delay (b) 10ms network delay

Figure 19: Mail Server throughput (varying client count)

Figure 19 shows the aggregate throughput of the Mail Server workload with different numbers of NFS clients in the zero- and 10ms-delay networks. With zero delay, the aggregate throughput increased linearly from 1 to 3 clients, but then slowed because the NFS server became heavily loaded. An injected network delay of 10ms significantly reduced the NFS request rate: the server's load was much lighter, and although the aggregate throughput was lower, it increased linearly with the number of clients.

7. RELATED WORK

NFS versions 2 and 3 are popular and have been widely deployed and studied. Wittle and Keith designed the LADDIS NFS workload and measured NFS's response time and throughput under various loads [30]. Based on LADDIS, the SPECsfs suites were designed to benchmark and compare the performance of different NFS server implementations [26]. Martin and Culler [19] studied NFS's behavior on high performance networks. They found that NFS servers were most sensitive to processor overhead, but insensitive to network bandwidth due to the dominant effect of small metadata operations. Ellard and Seltzer designed a simple sequential-read workload to benchmark and improve NFS's readahead algorithm [8]; they also studied several complex NFS benchmarking issues including the ZCAV effect, disks' I/O reordering, the unfairness of disk scheduling algorithms, and differences between NFS over TCP vs. UDP. Boumenot conducted a detailed study of NFS performance problems [6] in Linux, and found that the low throughput of Linux NFS was caused not by processor, disk, or network performance limits, but by the NFS implementation's sensitivity to network latency and lack of concurrency. Lever et al. introduced a new sequential-write benchmark and used it to measure and improve the write performance of Linux's NFS client [16].

Most prior studies [6, 8, 16, 19, 26, 30] were about V2 and V3. NFS version 4, the latest NFS major version, is dramatically different from previous versions, and is far less studied in the literature. Prior work on V4 focuses almost exclusively on V4.0, which is quite different than V4.1 due to the introduction of sessions, Exactly Once Semantics (EOS), and pNFS. Harrington et al. summarized major NFS contributors' efforts in testing the correctness and performance of Linux's V4.0 [4] implementation. Radkov et al. compared the performance of a prototype version of V4.0 and iSCSI in IP-networked storage [23]. Martin [18] compared the file operation performance between Linux V3 and V4.0; Kustarz [14] evaluated the performance of Solaris's V4.0 implementation and compared it with V3. However, Martin and Kustarz studied only V4.0's basic file operations without exercising unique features such as statefulness and delegations. Hildebrand and Honeyman explored the scalability of storage systems using pNFS, an important part of V4.1. Eshel et al. [17] used V4.1 and pNFS to build Panache, a clustered file system disk cache that shields applications from WAN latency and outages while using shared cloud storage.

Only a handful of authors have studied the delegation mechanisms provided by NFSv4. Batsakis and Burns extended V4.0's delegation model to improve the performance and recoverability of NFS in computing clusters [5]. Gulati et al. built a V4.0 cache proxy, also using delegations, to improve NFS's performance in WANs [12]. However, both of these studies were concerned more with enhancing NFS's delegations to design new systems rather than evaluating the impact of standard delegations on performance. Although Panache is based on V4.1, it revalidated its cache using the traditional method of checking timestamps of file objects instead of using delegations.

As the latest minor version of V4, V4.1's Linux implementation is still evolving [11]. To the best of our knowledge there are no existing, comprehensive performance studies of Linux's NFSv4.1 implementation that cover its advanced features such as statefulness, sessions, and delegations.

8. CONCLUSIONS

We have presented a comprehensive benchmarking study of Linux's NFSv4.1 implementation. Our study found that: **(1)** V4.1's read delegations can effectively avoid cache revalidation and help it perform up to 172× faster than V3. **(2)** Read delegations alone, however, are not enough to significantly improve the overall performance of realistic macro-workloads because V4.1 might still be bottlenecked by write operations. Therefore, we believe that write delegations are needed to maximize the benefits of delegations. **(3)** Moreover, delegations should be avoided in workloads that share data, since conflicts can incur a delay of at least 100ms. **(4)** We found that V4.1's stateful nature makes it more talkative than V3, which hurts V4.1's performance and makes it slower in low-latency networks (e.g., LANs). Also, V4.1's compound procedures, which were designed to help the problem, are not in practice effective. **(5)** However, in high-latency networks (e.g., WANs), V4.1's performed comparably to and even better than V3's since V4.1's statefulness permits higher concurrency through asynchronous RPC calls. For highly threaded workloads, however, V4.1 can be bottlenecked by the number of session slots. **(6)** We also showed that NFS's interactions with the networking and storage subsystems are complex, and system parameters should be tuned carefully to achieve high NFS throughput. **(7)** We identified a Hash-Cast networking problem that causes unfairness among NFS clients, and presented a solution. **(8)** Lastly, we made improvements to Linux's V4.1 implementation that boost its performance by up to 11×.

9. LIMITATIONS AND FUTURE WORK

This work has two limitations that can be addressed in the future: **(1)** Most of our workloads did not share files among clients. Because sharing is infrequent in the real world [25], it is critical that any sharing be representative. One solution would be to replay multi-client NFS traces from real workloads, but this task is challenging in a distributed environment. **(2)** Our WAN emulation using `netem` was simple, and did not consider harsh packet loss, intricate delays, or complete outages in real networks.

Lastly, we believe that V4.1's compound procedures hold much promise but are woefully underutilized. We plan to implement more advanced compounds, such as transactional NFS compounds that can coalesce many operations and execute them atomically on the server. With transactional compounds, programmers, instead of waiting and then checking the status of each operation, can perform many operations at once and use exception handlers to deal with failures. Such a design could greatly simplify programming and improve performance at the same time.

Acknowledgments

We thank the anonymous SIGMETRICS reviewers for their valuable comments. We also thank Lakshay Akula, Vasily Tarasov, Arun Olappamanna Vasudevan, and Ksenia Zakirova for their help in this study. This work was made possible in part thanks to NSF awards CNS-1223239, CNS-1251137, and CNS-1302246.

10. REFERENCES

[1] A. Bessani and R. Mendes and T. Oliveira and N. Neves and M. Correia and M. Pasin and P. Verissimo. SCFS: A Shared Cloud-backed File System. In *USENIX ATC 14*, pages 169–180. USENIX, 2014.

[2] N. Agrawal, V. Prabhakaran, T. Wobber, J. Davis, M. Manasse, and R. Panigraphy. Design tradeoffs for SSD performance. In *Proceedings of the USENIX Annual Technical Conference*, pages 57–70, Boston, MA, June 2008.

[3] M. Alizadeh, A. Greenberg, D. Maltz, J. Padhye, P. Patel, B. Prabhakar, S. Sengupta, and M. Sridharan. Data Center TCP. In *Proceedings of the ACM SIGCOMM 2010 Conference*, pages 63–74, 2010.

[4] B. Harrington, A. Charbon, T. Reix, V. Roqueta, J. B. Fields, T. Myklebust, and S. Jayaraman. NFSv4 test project. In *Linux Simposium*, pages 115–134, 2006.

[5] A. Batsakis and R. Burns. Cluster delegation: High-performance, fault-tolerant data sharing in NFS. In *Proceedings of the 14th IEEE International Symposium on High Performance Distributed Computing*. IEEE, July 2005.

[6] Christopher M. Boumenot. The performance of a Linux NFS implementation. Master's thesis, Worcester Polytechnic Institute, May 2002.

[7] B. Callaghan, B. Pawlowski, and P. Staubach. NFS Version 3 Protocol Specification. Technical Report RFC 1813, Network Working Group, June 1995.

[8] D. Ellard and M. Seltzer. NFS tricks and benchmarking traps. In *Proceedings of the Annual USENIX Technical Conference, FREENIX Track*, pages 101–114, San Antonio, TX, June 2003. USENIX Association.

[9] Sorin Faibish. NFSv4.1 and pNFS ready for prime time deployment, 2011.

[10] John Fastabend and Eric Dumazet. [BUG?] ixgbe: only num_online_cpus() of the tx queues are enabled, 2014. `http://comments.gmane.org/gmane.linux.network/307532`.

[11] Bruce Fields. NFSv4.1 server implementation. `http://goo.gl/vAqR0M`.

[12] A. Gulati, M. Naik, and R. Tewari. Nache: Design and Implementation of a Caching Proxy for NFSv4. In *Proceedings of the Fifth USENIX Conference on File and Storage Technologies (FAST '07)*, pages 199–214, San Jose, CA, February 2007. USENIX Association.

[13] D. Hildebrand and P. Honeyman. Exporting storage systems in a scalable manner with pNFS. In *Proceedings of MSST*, Monterey, CA, 2005. IEEE.

[14] Eric Kustarz. Using Filebench to evaluate Solaris NFSv4, 2005. NAS conference talk.

[15] A. W. Leung, S. Pasupathy, G. Goodson, and E. L. Miller. Measurement and analysis of large-scale network file system workloads. In *Proceedings of the USENIX Annual Technical Conference*, pages 213–226, Boston, MA, June 2008.

[16] C. Lever and P. Honeyman. Linux NFS Client Write Performance. In *Proceedings of the Annual USENIX Technical Conference, FREENIX Track*, pages 29–40, Monterey, CA, June 2002. USENIX Association.

[17] M. Eshel and R. Haskin and D. Hildebrand and M. Naik and F. Schmuck and R. Tewari. Panache: A Parallel File System Cache for Global File Access. In *FAST*, pages 155–168. USENIX, 2010.

[18] Ben Martin. Benchmarking NFSv3 vs. NFSv4 file operation performance, 2008. Linux.com.

[19] R. Martin and D. Culler. NFS Sensitivity to High Performance Networks. In *Proceedings of SIGMETRICS*. ACM, 1999.

[20] Alex McDonald. The background to NFSv4.1. *;login: The USENIX Magazine*, 37(1):28–35, February 2012.

[21] Paul E. McKenney. Stochastic fairness queueing. In *INFOCOM'90*, pages 733–740. IEEE, 1990.

[22] Trond Myklebust. File creation speedups for NFSv4.2, 2010.

[23] P. Radkov, L. Yin, P. Goyal, P. Sarkar, and P. Shenoy. A performance comparison of NFS and iSCSI for IP-networked storage. In *Proceedings of the USENIX Conference on File and Storage Technologies (FAST)*, pages 101–114, San Francisco, CA, March/April 2004. USENIX Association.

[24] Scott Rixner. Network virtualization: Breaking the performance barrier. *Queue*, 6(1):37:36–37:ff, Jan 2008.

[25] S. Shepler and M. Eisler and D. Noveck. NFS Version 4 Minor Version 1 Protocol. Technical Report RFC 5661, Network Working Group, January 2010.

[26] SPEC. SPECsfs2008. `www.spec.org/sfs2008`, 2008.

[27] V. Tarasov, S. Bhanage, E. Zadok, and M. Seltzer. Benchmarking File System Benchmarking: It *IS* Rocket Science. In *Proceedings of HotOS XIII:The 13th USENIX Workshop on Hot Topics in Operating Systems*, Napa, CA, May 2011.

[28] Vasily Tarasov, Dean Hildebrand, Geoff Kuenning, and Erez Zadok. Virtual machine workloads: The case for new benchmarks for NAS. In *Proceedings of the USENIX Conference on File and Storage Technologies (FAST)*, San Jose, CA, February 2013. USENIX Association.

[29] A. W. Wilson. Operation and implementation of random variables in Filebench.

[30] M. Wittle and B. E. Keith. LADDIS: The next generation in NFS file server benchmarking. In *Proceedings of the Summer USENIX Technical Conference*, pages 111–128, Cincinnati, OH, June 1993. USENIX Association.

[31] N. Yezhkova, L. Conner, R. Villars, and B. Woo. *Worldwide enterprise storage systems 2010–2014 forecast: recovery, efficiency, and digitization shaping customer requirements for storage systems.* IDC, May 2010. IDC #223234.

A Large-Scale Study of Flash Memory Failures in the Field

Justin Meza
Carnegie Mellon University
meza@cmu.edu

Qiang Wu
Facebook, Inc.
qwu@fb.com

Sanjeev Kumar
Facebook, Inc.
skumar@fb.com

Onur Mutlu
Carnegie Mellon University
onur@cmu.edu

ABSTRACT

Servers use flash memory based solid state drives (SSDs) as a high-performance alternative to hard disk drives to store persistent data. Unfortunately, recent increases in flash density have also brought about decreases in chip-level reliability. In a data center environment, flash-based SSD failures can lead to downtime and, in the worst case, data loss. As a result, it is important to understand flash memory reliability characteristics over flash lifetime in a realistic production data center environment running modern applications and system software.

This paper presents the first large-scale study of flash-based SSD reliability in the field. We analyze data collected across a majority of flash-based solid state drives at Facebook data centers over nearly four years and many millions of operational hours in order to understand failure properties and trends of flash-based SSDs. Our study considers a variety of SSD characteristics, including: the amount of data written to and read from flash chips; how data is mapped within the SSD address space; the amount of data copied, erased, and discarded by the flash controller; and flash board temperature and bus power.

Based on our field analysis of how flash memory errors manifest when running modern workloads on modern SSDs, this paper is the first to make several major observations: (1) *SSD* failure rates do *not* increase monotonically with *flash chip* wear; instead they go through several distinct periods corresponding to how failures emerge and are subsequently detected, (2) the effects of read disturbance errors are *not* prevalent in the field, (3) sparse logical data layout across an SSD's physical address space (e.g., non-contiguous data), as measured by the amount of metadata required to track logical address translations stored in an SSD-internal DRAM buffer, can greatly affect SSD failure rate, (4) higher temperatures lead to higher failure rates, but techniques that throttle SSD operation appear to greatly *reduce* the negative reliability impact of higher temperatures, and (5) data written by the operating system to flash-based SSDs does *not* always accurately indicate the amount of wear induced on flash cells due to optimizations in the SSD controller and buffering employed in the system software. We hope that the findings of this first large-scale flash memory reliability study can inspire others to develop other publicly-available analyses and novel flash reliability solutions.

SIGMETRICS'15, June 15–19, 2015, Portland, OR, USA.
ACM 978-1-4503-3486-0/15/06.
http://dx.doi.org/10.1145/2745844.2745848.

Categories and Subject Descriptors

B.3.4. [**Hardware**]: Memory Structures—*Reliability, Testing, and Fault-Tolerance*

Keywords

flash memory; reliability; warehouse-scale data centers

1. INTRODUCTION

Servers use flash memory for persistent storage due to the low access latency of flash chips compared to hard disk drives. Historically, flash capacity has lagged behind hard disk drive capacity, limiting the use of flash memory. In the past decade, however, advances in NAND flash memory technology have increased flash capacity by more than 1000×. This rapid increase in flash capacity has brought both an increase in flash memory use and a decrease in flash memory reliability. For example, the number of times that a cell can be reliably programmed and erased before wearing out and failing dropped from 10,000 times for 50 nm cells to only 2,000 times for 20 nm cells [28]. This trend is expected to continue for newer generations of flash memory. Therefore, if we want to improve the operational lifetime and reliability of flash memory-based devices, we must first fully understand their failure characteristics.

In the past, a large body of prior work examined the failure characteristics of flash cells in controlled environments using small numbers e.g., tens) of raw flash chips (e.g., [36, 23, 21, 27, 22, 25, 16, 33, 14, 5, 18, 4, 24, 40, 41, 26, 31, 30, 37, 6, 11, 10, 7, 13, 9, 8, 12, 20]). This work quantified a variety of flash cell failure modes and formed the basis of the community's understanding of flash cell reliability. Yet prior work was limited in its analysis because these studies: (1) were conducted on small numbers of raw flash chips accessed in adversarial manners over short amounts of time, (2) did not examine failures when using real applications running on modern servers and instead used synthetic access patterns, and (3) did not account for the storage software stack that real applications need to go through to access flash memories. Such conditions assumed in these prior studies are substantially different from those experienced by flash-based SSDs in large-scale installations in the field. In such large-scale systems: (1) real applications access flash-based SSDs in different ways over a time span of *years*, (2) applications access SSDs via the storage software stack, which employs various amounts of buffering and hence affects the access pattern seen by the flash chips, (3) flash-based SSDs employ aggressive techniques to reduce device wear and to correct errors, (4) factors in platform design, including how many SSDs are present in a node, can affect the access patterns to SSDs, (5) there can be significant variation in reliability due to the existence of a very large number of SSDs and flash chips. All of these real-world conditions present in large-scale systems likely influence the observed reliability characteristics and trends of flash-based SSDs.

Our goal is to understand the nature of flash-based solid state drive failures in the field. To this end, we provide the *first comprehensive study of flash memory reliability trends in a large-scale production data center environment.* Our study is based on data collected from a majority of flash-based SSDs in Facebook's server fleet, with operational lifetimes extending over nearly four years and comprising many millions of device-days of usage. We analyze SSDs of different capacities and data transfer technologies, with a focus on understanding how various *internal factors* (i.e., those related to how the device operates) and *external factors* (i.e., those related to the environment the SSD operates in) affect flash-based SSD reliability.

Our main contribution is a rigorous characterization of the reliability trends of flash-based SSDs in the field. We observe several reliability trends for flash-based SSDs that have not been discussed before in prior works:

1. Flash-based SSDs do *not* fail at a monotonically increasing rate with wear. They instead go through *several* distinct reliability periods corresponding to how failures emerge and are subsequently detected. Unlike the monotonically-increasing failure trends for *individual flash chips* [6, 12, 20], across a large number of *flash-based SSDs* we observe *early detection*, *early failure*, *usable life*, and *wearout* periods, whose failure rates can vary by up to 81.7%.
2. Read disturbance errors (i.e., errors caused in neighboring pages due to a read [11, 8]) are *not* prevalent in the field. SSDs that have read the most data do not show a statistically significant increase in failure rates.
3. Sparse logical data layout across an SSD's physical address space (e.g., non-contiguous data), as measured by the amount of SSD-internal DRAM buffer usage for flash translation layer metadata, greatly affects device failure rate. In addition, dense logical data layout (e.g., contiguous data) with adversarial access patterns (e.g., small, sparse writes) also negatively affects SSD reliability.
4. Higher temperatures lead to higher failure rates, but techniques used in modern SSDs that throttle SSD operation (and, consequently, the amount of data written to flash chips) appear to greatly reduce the reliability impact of higher temperatures by reducing access rates to the raw flash chips.
5. The amount of data written by the operating system to *an SSD* is not the same as the amount of data that is eventually written to flash *cells*. This is due to system-level buffering and wear reduction techniques employed in the storage software stack and the SSDs. It is important that system-level flash reliability studies account for these effects.

2. BACKGROUND AND METHODOLOGY

2.1 Server Flash Device Architecture

We examine a set of flash-based SSDs similar to those employed commonly in server hardware and available from companies such as Fusion-io, Hitachi, Intel, OCZ, Seagate, and Virident. These SSDs connect to the server using the PCI Express (PCIe) bus. The SSD controller coordinates the transfer of data to and from the host and performs various functions designed to improve the performance and reliability of flash memory. Figure 1 provides an illustration of the architecture of a server SSD.

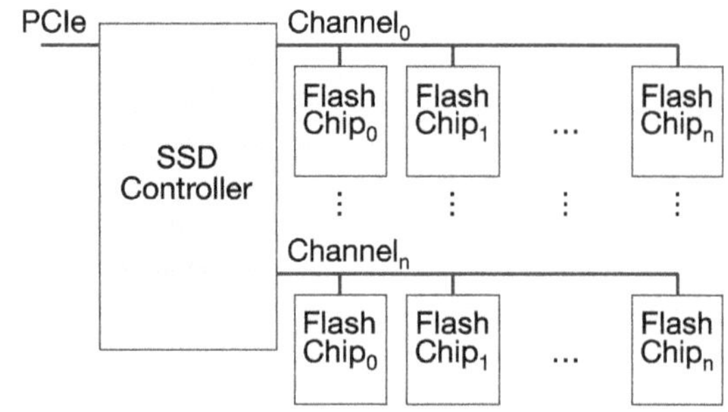

Figure 1: Server SSD architecture.

In order to achieve high bandwidth and low access latency – despite potentially long chip read and write latencies – these SSDs typically employ many channels that can be operated in parallel, with a number of chips connected to each channel. By mapping data across the channels, multiple channels can provide data in parallel, helping to ensure that the SSD can service data at close to the bandwidth of the PCIe connection.

In addition to orchestrating flash chip access, the SSD controller logic also plays a role in managing the reliability of the flash memory chips. Since flash cells wear out after a certain number of writes, SSD controllers must perform *wear leveling* in order to distribute cell wear more evenly across the cells in each flash chip. To do this, the SSD controller determines when and where pages of flash data should be erased or copied and maintains a mapping of logical addresses to physical locations, known as the flash translation layer (FTL) [15]. FTL data is stored in a DRAM buffer and is managed by the SSD controller. When blocks of flash cells are deemed unreliable for further use, the SSD controller *discards* them to avoid the risk of encountering an uncorrectable error on them.

2.2 Flash Errors and Their Handling

As prior works have shown in controlled environments, the repeated wear caused by reading and writing data from/to flash cells degrades their reliability over time, leading to relatively high error rates [36, 23, 21, 27, 22, 25, 16, 33, 14, 5, 18, 4, 24, 40, 41, 26, 31, 30, 37, 6, 10, 7, 9, 8, 12, 20]. To protect against such errors, additional data is stored in each channel to maintain various error correcting codes (ECC) computed over data in in the channel. These codes must be sufficiently strong to protect against the errors that may occur in flash chips over time.

The SSD controller is responsible for using the ECC information to detect errors in the flash chips. Such flash controllers typically use a progressive approach to error correction: *small errors* (on the order of bits per KB of data) are quickly corrected using logic in the SSD controller while *large errors* (on the order of >10's of bits per KB) are corrected using more complex controller logic or with assistance from a driver running on the host. Thus, large errors that may be uncorrectable from an SSD's perspective, may be correctable from the system's perspective. For example, during the course of a read operation, if the SSD controller is unable to correct the errors in a particular chunk of data, the data and the ECC information is sent to the host machine where a driver uses the host machine's CPU to perform more complex error cor-

Platform	SSDs	PCIe	Per SSD					
			Capacity	Age (years)	Data written	Data read	UBER
A	1	v1, ×4	720 GB	2.4 ± 1.0	27.2 TB	23.8 TB	5.2×10^{-10}
B	2				48.5 TB	45.1 TB	2.6×10^{-9}
C	1	v2, ×4	1.2 TB	1.6 ± 0.9	37.8 TB	43.4 TB	1.5×10^{-10}
D	2				18.9 TB	30.6 TB	5.7×10^{-11}
E	1		3.2 TB	0.5 ± 0.5	23.9 TB	51.1 TB	5.1×10^{-11}
F	2				14.8 TB	18.2 TB	1.8×10^{-10}

Table 1: The platforms examined in our study. PCIe technology is denoted by vX, ×Y where X = version and Y = number of lanes. Data was collected over the entire age of the SSDs. Data written and data read are to/from the physical storage over an SSD's lifetime. UBER = uncorrectable bit error rate (Section 3.2).

rection and forwards the result to the host's OS. Errors that are not correctable by the driver result in data loss.[1]

Our SSDs allow us to collect information only on large errors that are uncorrectable by the SSD but correctable by the host. For this reason, our results are in terms of such SSD-uncorrectable but host-correctable errors, and when we refer to *uncorrectable errors* we mean these type of errors. We refer to the occurrence of such uncorrectable errors in an SSD as an *SSD failure.*

2.3 The Systems

We examined the majority of flash-based SSDs in Facebook's server fleet, which have operational lifetimes extending over nearly four years and comprising many millions of SSD-days of usage. Data was collected over the lifetime of the SSDs. We found it useful to separate the SSDs based on the type of *platform* an SSD was used in. We define a platform as a combination of the device capacity used in the system, the PCIe technology used, and the number of SSDs in the system. Table 1 characterizes the platforms we examine in our study.

We examined a range of high-capacity multi-level cell (MLC) flash-based SSDs with capacities of 720 GB, 1.2 TB, and 3.2 TB. The technologies we examined spanned two generations of PCIe, versions 1 and 2. Some of the systems in the fleet employed one SSD while others employed two. Platforms A and B contain SSDs with around two or more years of operation and represent 16.6% of the SSDs examined; Platforms C and D contain SSDs with around one to two years of operation and represent 50.6% of the SSDs examined; and Platforms E and F contain SSDs with around half a year of operation and represent around 22.8% of the SSDs examined.

2.4 Measurement Methodology

The flash devices in our fleet contain registers that keep track of statistics related to SSD operation (e.g., number of bytes read, number of bytes written, number of uncorrectable errors). These registers are similar to, but distinct from, the standardized SMART data stored by some SSDs to monitor their reliability characteristics [3]. The values in these registers can be queried by the host machine. We use a collector script to retrieve the raw values from the SSD and parse them into a form that can be curated in a Hive [38] table. This process is done in real time every hour.

The scale of the systems we analyzed and the amount of data being collected posed challenges for analysis. To process the many millions of SSD-days of information, we used a cluster of machines to perform a parallelized aggregation of the data stored in Hive using MapReduce jobs in order to get a set of lifetime statistics for each of the SSDs we analyzed. We then processed this summary data in R [2] to collect our results.

[1]We do not examine the rate of data loss in this work.

2.5 Analytical Methodology

Our infrastructure allows us to examine a *snapshot* of SSD data at a point in time (i.e., our infrastructure *does not* store *timeseries* information for the many SSDs in the fleet). This limits our analysis to the behavior of the fleet of SSDs at a point in time (for our study, we focus on a snapshot of SSD data taken during November 2014). Fortunately, the number of SSDs we examine and the diversity of their characteristics allow us to examine how reliability trends change with various characteristics. When we analyze an SSD characteristic (e.g., the amount of data written to an SSD), we group SSDs into buckets based on their value for that characteristic in the snapshot and plot the failure rate for SSDs in each bucket.

For example, if an SSD s is placed in a bucket for N TB of data written, it is *not* also placed in the bucket for $(N-k)$ TB of data written (even though at some point in its life it did have only $(N-k)$ TB of data written). When performing bucketing, we round the value of an SSD's characteristic to the nearest bucket and we eliminate buckets that contain less than 0.1% of the SSDs analyzed to have a statistically significant sample of SSDs for our measurements. In order to express the confidence of our observations across buckets that contain different numbers of servers, we show the 95th percentile confidence interval for all of our data (using a binomial distribution when considering failure rates). We measure SSD failure rate for each bucket in terms of the fraction of SSDs that have had an uncorrectable error compared to the total number of SSDs in that bucket.

3. BASELINE STATISTICS

We will first focus on the overall error rate and error distribution among the SSDs in the platforms we analyze and then examine correlations between different failure events.

3.1 Bit Error Rate

The bit error rate (BER) of an SSD is the rate at which errors occur relative to the amount of information that is transmitted from/to the SSD. BER can be used to gauge the reliability of data transmission across a medium. We measure the uncorrectable bit error rate (UBER) from the SSD as:

$$UBER = \frac{Uncorrectable\ errors}{Bits\ accessed}$$

For flash-based SSDs, UBER is an important reliability metric that is related to the SSD lifetime. SSDs with high UBERs are expected to have more failed cells and encounter more (severe) errors that may potentially go undetected and corrupt data than SSDs with low UBERs. Recent work by Grupp et al. examined the BER of *raw* MLC flash chips (without performing error correction in the flash controller) in a controlled environment [20]. They found the raw BER to vary from 1×10^{-1} for the least reliable flash chips down to 1×10^{-8} for the most reliable, with most chips having a BER in the 1×10^{-6} to 1×10^{-8} range. Their study did *not* analyze the effects of the use of chips *in SSDs under real workloads and system software*.

Table 1 shows the UBER of the platforms that we examine. We find that for flash-based SSDs used in servers, the UBER ranges from 2.6×10^{-9} to 5.1×10^{-11}. While we expect that the UBER of the SSDs that we measure (which correct small errors, perform wear leveling, and are not at the end of their rated life but still being used in a production environment) should be less than the raw chip BER in Grupp et al.'s study (which did not correct any errors in the flash controller, exercised flash chips until the end of their rated life, and accessed flash chips in an adversarial manner), we find that in some cases the BERs were within around one order of magnitude of each other. For example, the UBER of Platform B in our study, 2.6×10^{-9}, comes close to the lower end of the raw chip BER range reported in prior work, 1×10^{-8}.

Thus, we observe that in flash-based SSDs that employ error correction for small errors and wear leveling, the UBER ranges from around 1/10 to 1/1000× the raw BER of similar flash chips examined in prior work [20]. This is likely due to the fact that our flash-based SSDs correct small errors, perform wear leveling, and are not at the end of their rated life. As a result, the error rate we see is smaller than the error rate the previous study observed.

As shown by the SSD UBER, the effects of uncorrectable errors are noticeable across the SSDs that we examine. We next turn to understanding how errors are distributed among a population of SSDs and how failures occur within SSDs.

3.2 SSD Failure Rate and Error Count

Figure 2 (top) shows the SSD incidence failure rate within each platform – the fraction of SSDs in each platform that have reported at least one uncorrectable error. We find that SSD failures are relatively common events with between 4.2% and 34.1% of the SSDs in the platforms we examine reporting uncorrectable errors. Interestingly, the failure rate is much lower for Platforms C and E despite their comparable amounts of data written and read (cf. Table 1). This suggests that there are differences in the failure process among platforms. We analyze which factors play a role in determining the occurrence of uncorrectable errors in Sections 4 and 5.

Figure 2 (bottom) shows the average yearly uncorrectable error rate among SSDs within the different platforms – the sum of errors that occurred on all servers within a platform over 12 months ending in November 2014 divided by the number of servers in the platform. The yearly rates of uncorrectable errors on the SSDs we examined range from 15,128 for Platform D to 978,806 for Platform B. The older Platforms A and B have a higher error rate than the younger Platforms C through F, suggesting that the incidence of uncorrectable errors increases as SSDs are utilized more. We will examine this relationship further in Section 4.

Platform B has a much higher average yearly rate of uncorrectable errors (978,806) compared to the other platforms (the second highest amount, for Platform A, is 106,678). We find that this is due to a small number of SSDs having a much

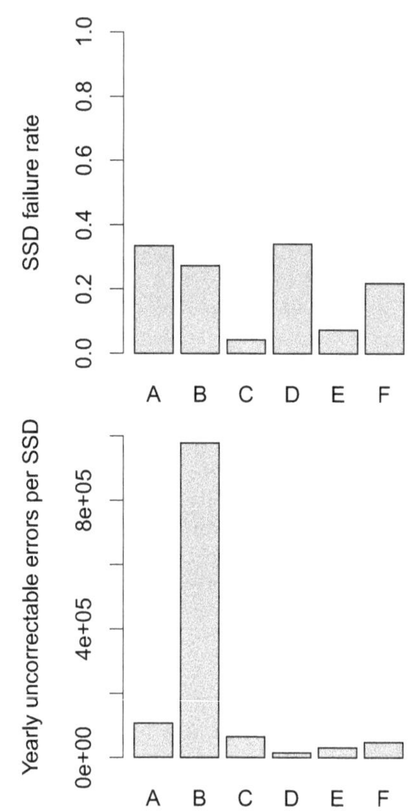

Figure 2: The failure rate (top) and average yearly uncorrectable errors per SSD (bottom), among SSDs within each platform.

higher number of errors in that platform: Figure 3 quantifies the distribution of errors among SSDs in each platform. The x axis is the normalized SSD number within the platform, with SSDs sorted based on the number of errors they have had over their lifetime. The y axis plots the number of errors for a given SSD in log scale. For every platform, we observe that the top 10% of SSDs with the most errors have over 80% of all uncorrectable errors seen for that platform. For Platforms B, C, E, and F, the distribution is even more skewed, with 10% of SSDs with errors making up over 95% of all observed uncorrectable errors. We also find that the distribution of number of errors among SSDs in a platform is similar to that of a Weibull distribution with a shape parameter of 0.3 and scale parameter of 5×10^3. The solid black line on Figure 3 plots this distribution.

An explanation for the relatively large differences in errors per machine could be that error events are correlated. Examining the data shows that this is indeed the case: during a recent two weeks, 99.8% of the SSDs that had an error during the first week also had an error during the second week. We therefore conclude that an SSD that has had an error in the past is highly likely to continue to have errors in the future. With this in mind, we next turn to understanding the correlation between errors occurring on both devices in the two-SSD systems we examine.

3.3 Correlations Between Different SSDs

Given that some of the platforms we examine have two flash-based SSDs, we are interested in understanding if the likeli-

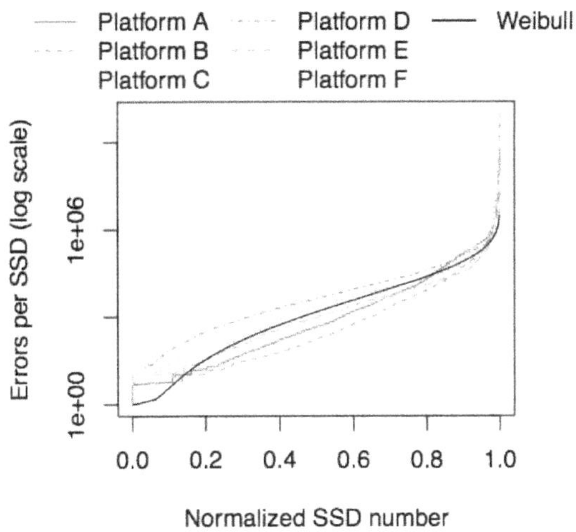

Figure 3: The distribution of uncorrectable error count across SSDs. The total number of errors per SSD is highly skewed, with a small fraction of SSDs accounting for a majority of the errors. The solid dark line plots a Weibull distribution that resembles the error trends.

hood of one SSD failing is affected by the other SSD failing. To examine this, we computed the conditional probability of both SSDs failing given that one SSD failed. We compute the conditional probability by dividing the number of systems in which both SSDs failed over their lifetime by the number of systems in which at least one SSD failed over its lifetime.

We find that the conditional probability of both SSDs failing given one SSD has failed is 42.2% for Platform B, 59.9% for Platform D, and 39.8% for Platform F. For comparison, if there were no correlation between SSD failures in the same machine and failures were uniformly distributed among SSDs, we would expect the conditional probability of both devices failing given that one SSD already failed to be similar to the uncorrectable error rate. For example, if one SSD in a server in Platform B fails, and that failure has no influence on the other SSD in the same server failing, the probability of the other SSD failing should be the same as the first SSD failing, 27.3%.

Instead, we find that one SSD failing in a machine *does* increase the probability of the other SSD failing (by 14.9% for Platform B, 25.8% for Platform D, and 17.8% for Platform F). This suggests that operational conditions related to the platform that SSDs are in contribute to the SSD failure trends we observe.

These baseline statistics we have examined raise questions about SSD failure in the field. For example, *how do workload-dependent characteristics (such as the amount of data written or read) affect failure rates? What role does the SSD controller play in SSD failure?* and *How do external factors (such as temperature) affect SSD failure trends?* We seek to answer these questions by examining how a variety of *internal* and *external* characteristics affect SSD failure trends, in Sections 4 and 5.

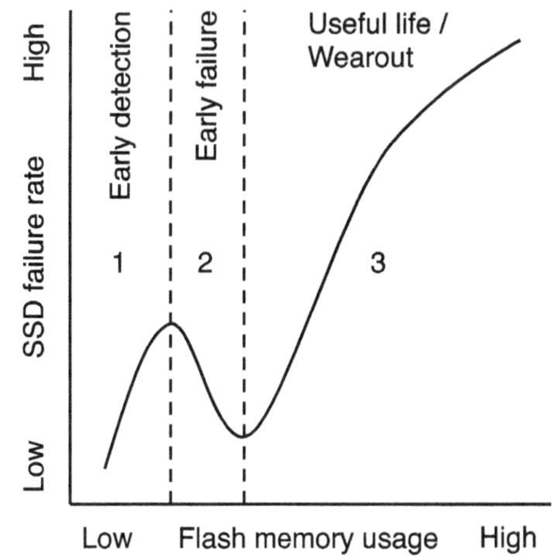

Figure 4: SSD lifecycle failure pattern. SSDs fail at different rates during several distinct periods throughout their lifetime (measured by usage)

4. THE ROLE OF INTERNAL FACTORS

We examine next how factors related to the *internals of the flash chips and the SSD controller* affect uncorrectable errors over an SSD's lifetime. We examine the effects of writing data to flash cells, reading data from flash cells, copying and erasing data, discarding unusable blocks, and the SSD-internal DRAM buffer usage.

4.1 Data Written to Flash Cells

Due to the physical properties that govern them, flash cels have been shown to become less reliable the more times their contents are *programmed and erased*, i.e., *P/E cycles* the flash cell has endured (we refer the reader to [6], which provides a good summary of flash cell operation and characteristics). Several recent works have quantified the effects of P/E cycles on various error mechanisms in small sets of recent flash chips (e.g., [6, 7, 8, 9, 10, 11, 12, 13, 20]). The effects of P/E cycles on flash reliability are important to understand because they can be exacerbated in higher capacity MLC chips commonly used in flash-based SSDs.

In order to examine the effect of P/E cycles on flash reliability, we consider the amount of data *written directly to flash cells* over each SSD's lifetime. Our framework allows us to measure this value, which more accurately portrays flash memory usage over its lifetime compared to software-level writes. Note that software-level writes (i.e., write requests sent by software to the storage device) do *not* directly get exposed to the flash cells due to layers of buffering in the storage software stack (we will examine their effects in Section 5.3).

Prior reliability studies on hard disk drives in the field (e.g., [35]) observed a trend with respect to writes, called the *bathtub curve.* The bathtub curve is so named because of its shape with respect to device failure rate over time: devices initially experience a high failure rate during an early failure period, followed by a low rate of failure during the useful life period, and ultimately a high failure rate once again during their wearout period. In the SSDs we examine, we notice an additional period *before* the early failure period that we call the *early detection period.* During the early detection period, which occurs when SSDs are young (measured by data written directly to flash cells), cells are read, programmed, and erased, and unreliable cells are identified by the SSD controller, resulting in an initially high failure rate among devices. Figure 4 pictorially illustrates the lifecycle failure pattern we observe, which is quantified by Figure 5.

Figure 5 plots how the failure rate of SSDs varies with the amount of data written to the flash cells. We have grouped the platforms based on the individual capacity of their SSDs. Notice that across most platforms, the failure rate is low when little data is written to flash cells. It then increases at first (corresponding to the early detection period, region 1 in the figures), and decreases next (corresponding to the early failure period, region 2 in the figures). Finally, the error rate generally increases for the remainder of the SSD's lifetime (corresponding to the useful life and wearout periods, region 3 in the figures). An obvious outlier for this trend is Platform C – in Section 5, we observe that some *external* characteristics of this platform lead to its atypical lifecycle failure pattern.

Note that different platforms are in different stages in their lifecycle depending on the amount of data written to flash cells. For example, SSDs in Platforms D and F, which have the least amount of data written to flash cells on average, are mainly in the early detection or early failure periods. On the other hand, SSDs in older Platforms A and B, which have more data written to flash cells, span all stages of the lifecycle failure pattern (depicted in Figure 4). For SSDs in Platform A, we observe up to an 81.7% difference between the failure rates of SSDs in the early detection period and SSDs in the wearout period of the lifecycle.

As explained before and as depicted in Figure 4, the lifecycle failure rates we observe with the amount of data written to flash cells does *not* follow the conventional bathtub curve. In particular, the new *early detection period* we observe across the large number of devices leads us to investigate why this "early detection period" behavior exists. Recall that the early detection period refers to failure rate increasing early in lifetime (i.e., when a small amount of data is written to the SSD). After the early detection period, failure rate starts decreasing.

We hypothesize that this non-monotonic error rate behavior during and after the early detection period can be accounted for by a *two-pool* model of flash blocks: one pool of blocks, called the *weaker pool*, consists of cells whose error rate increases much faster than the other pool of blocks, called the *stronger pool*. The weaker pool quickly generates uncorrectable errors (leading to increasing failure rates observed in the early detection period as these blocks keep failing). The cells comprising this pool ultimately fail and are taken out of use early by the SSD controller. As the blocks in the weaker pool are exhausted, the overall error rate starts decreasing (as we observe *after* the end of what we call the *early detection period*) and it continues to decrease until the more durable blocks in the stronger pool start to wear out due to typical use.

We notice a general increase in the duration of the lifecycle periods (in terms of data written) for SSDs with larger capacities. For example, while the early detection period ends after around 3 TB of data written for 720 GB and 1.2TB SSDs (in Platforms A, B, C, and D), it ends after around 10 TB of data written for 3.2 TB SSDs (in Platforms E and F). Similarly, the early failure period ends after around 15 TB of data written for 720 GB SSDs (in Platforms A and B), 28 TB for 1.2 TB SSDs (in Platforms C and D), and 75 TB for 3.2 TB SSDs (in Platforms E and F). This is likely due to the more flexibility a higher-capacity SSD has in reducing wear across a larger number of flash cells.

4.2 Data Read from Flash Cells

Similar to *data written*, our framework allows us to measure the amount of *data directly read from flash cells* over each SSD's lifetime. Prior works in controlled environments have shown that errors can be induced due to read-based access patterns [5, 32, 6, 8]. We are interested in understanding how prevalent this effect is across the SSDs we examine.

Figure 6 plots how failure rate of SSDs varies with the amount of data read from flash cells. For most platforms (i.e., A, B, C, and F), the failure rate trends we see in Figure 6 are similar to those we observed in Figure 5. We find this similarity when the *average* amount of data written to flash cells by SSDs in a platform is more than the *average* amount of data read from the flash cells. Platforms A, B, C, and F show this behavior.[2]

[2]Though Platform B has a set of SSDs with a large amount of data read, the *average* amount of data read across all SSDs in this platform is less than the *average* amount of data written.

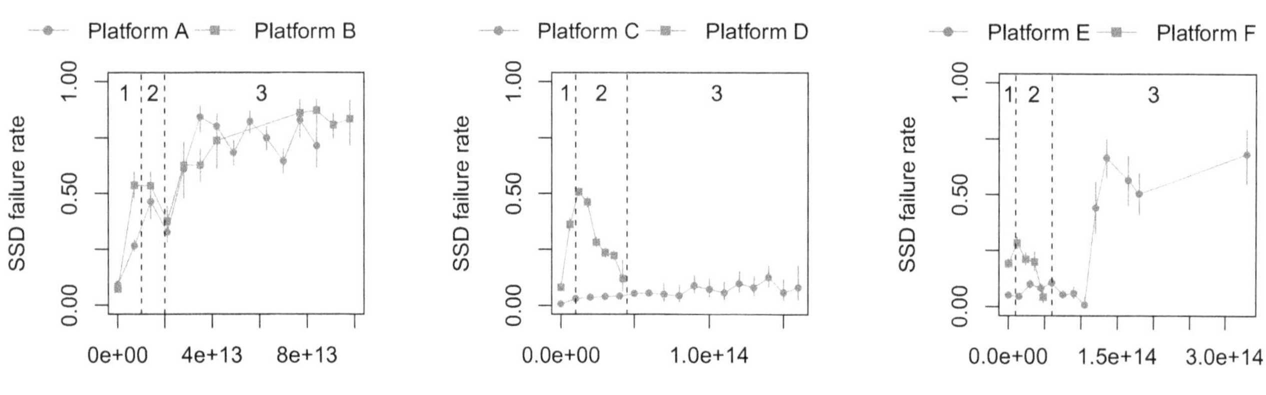

Figure 5: SSD failure rate vs. the amount of data written to flash cells. SSDs go through several distinct phases throughout their life: increasing failure rates during early detection of less reliable cells (1), decreasing failure rates during early cell failure and subsequent removal (2), and eventually increasing error rates during cell wearout (3).

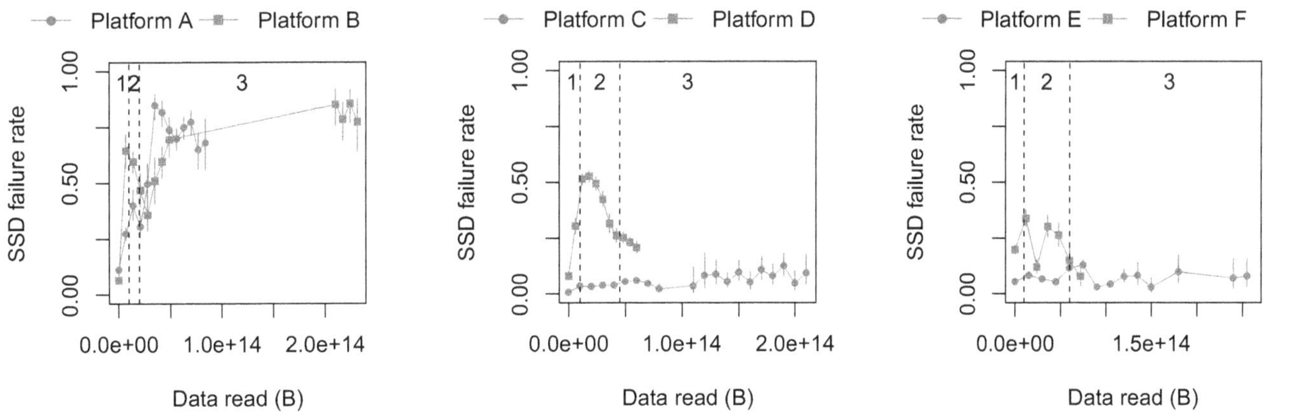

Figure 6: SSD failure rate vs. the amount of data read from flash cells. SSDs in Platform E, where over twice as much data is read from flash cells as written to flash cells, do not show failures dependent on the amount of data read from flash cells.

In Platform D, where more data is read from flash cells than written to flash cells (30.6 TB versus 18.9 TB, on average), we notice error trends associated with the early detection and early failure periods. Unfortunately, even though devices in Platform D may be prime candidates for observing the occurrence of read disturbance errors (because more data is read from flash cells than written to flash cells), the effects of early detection and early failure appear to dominate the types of errors observed on this platform.

In Platform E, however, over twice as much data is read from flash cells as written to flash cells (51.1 TB versus 23.9 TB on average). In addition, unlike Platform D, devices in Platform E display a diverse amount of utilization. Under these conditions, we *do not* observe a statistically significant difference in the failure rate between SSDs that have read the most amount of data versus those that have read the least amount of data. This suggests that the effect of read-induced errors in the SSDs we examine is not predominant compared to other effects such as write-induced errors. This corroborates prior flash cell analysis that showed that most errors occur due to retention effects and not read disturbance [32, 11, 12].

4.3 Block Erases

Before new data can be written to a page in flash memory, the entire block needs to be first erased.[3] Each erase wears out the block as shown in previous works [32, 11, 12]. Our infrastructure tracks the average number of blocks erased when an SSD controller performs *garbage collection*. Garbage collection occurs in the background and erases blocks to ensure that there is enough available space to write new data. The basic steps involved in garbage collection are: (1) selecting blocks to erase (e.g., blocks with many unused pages), (2) copying pages from the selected block to a free area, and (3) erasing the selected block [29]. While we do not have statistics on how frequently garbage collection is performed, we examine the *number of erases per garbage collection period* metric as an indicator of the average amount of erasing that occurs within each SSD.

We examined the relationship between the number of erases performed versus the failure rate (not plotted). Across the SSDs we examine, we find that the failure trends in terms of erases are correlated with the trends in terms of data written (shown in Figure 5). This behavior reflects the typical operation of garbage collection in SSD controllers: As more data is written, wear must be leveled across the flash cells within an SSD, requiring more blocks to be erased and more pages to be copied to different locations (an effect we analyze next).

[3]Flash pages (around 8 KB in size) compose each flash block. A flash block is around 128 × 8 KB flash pages.

4.4 Page Copies

As data is written to flash-based SSDs, pages are copied to free areas during garbage collection in order to free up blocks with unused data to be erased and to more evenly level wear across the flash chips. Our infrastructure measures the number of pages copied across an SSD's lifetime.

We examined the relationship between the number of pages copied versus SSD failure rate (not plotted). Since the page copying process is used to free up space to write data and also to balance the wear due to writes, its operation is largely dictated by the amount of data written to an SSD. Accordingly, we observe similar SSD failure rate trends with the number of copied pages (not plotted) as we observed with the amount of data written to flash cells (shown in Figure 5).

4.5 Discarded Blocks

Blocks are discarded by the SSD controller when they are deemed unreliable for further use. Discarding blocks affects the usable lifetime of a flash-based SSD by reducing the amount of over-provisioned capacity of the SSD. At the same time, discarding blocks has the potential to reduce the amount of errors generated by an SSD, by preventing unreliable cells from being accessed. Understanding the reliability effects of discarding blocks is important, as this process is the main defense that SSD controllers have against failed cells and is also a major impediment for SSD lifetime.

Figure 7 plots the SSD failure rate versus number of discarded blocks over the SSD's lifetime. For SSDs in most platforms, we observe an initially decreasing trend in SSD failure rate with respect to the number of blocks discarded followed by an increasing and then finally decreasing failure rate trend.

We attribute the initially high SSD failure rate when few blocks have been discarded to the two-pool model of flash cell failure discussed in Section 4.1. In this case, the weaker pool of flash blocks (corresponding to weak blocks that fail

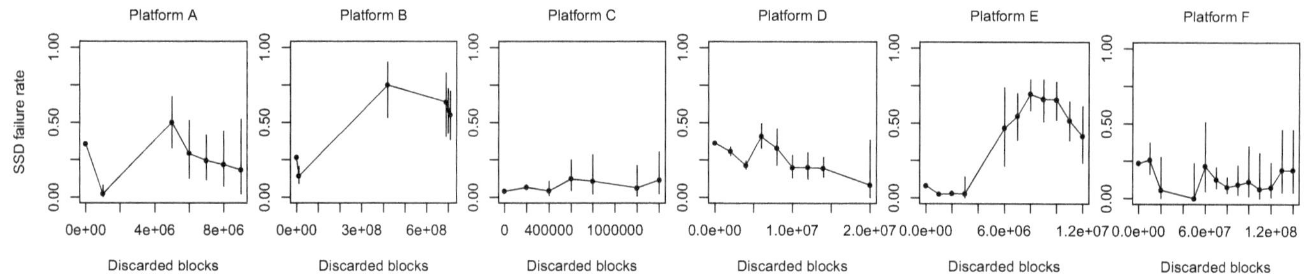

Figure 7: SSD failure rate vs. the number of discarded blocks. We find that (1) failure rate is relatively high among SSDs that have discarded few blocks (far left of plots), (2) some SSDs seem to effectively mask failures by discarding blocks (initial decrease in failure rates), and (3) discarding a large amount of blocks is indicative of higher failure rates (toward the right of plots).

early) cause errors before they can be discarded by the SSD controller, causing an initially high SSD failure rate. On the other hand, the stronger pool of flash blocks (which fail due to gradual wearout over time) contribute to the subsequent decrease in SSD failure rate. Some SSDs that have discarded a large number of blocks have high error rates (e.g., Platforms A, B, and E), indicating that discarding a large number of blocks is a good indicator of the likelihood of SSD failure.

We further examined the devices with the largest number of discarded blocks and found that the number of blocks that are discarded is *not* correlated with the amount of data written to or read from flash cells (examined in Sections 4.1 and 4.2). In other words, we observe SSDs of both low *and* high usage across their lifetime (measured by flash cell reads and writes) that have discarded large amounts of blocks and have high failure rates. This suggests that the relationship between discarded blocks and failure rate is to some extent intrinsic to the SSD. Thus, some SSDs, despite discarding many blocks, continue to encounter uncorrectable errors at a much higher rate than their peers.

4.6 DRAM Buffer Usage

Flash-based SSDs use internal DRAM to provide buffer space for SSD controller metadata or for data to be written to the flash chips. The SSDs we examine use the internal DRAM buffer space only to store metadata related to the flash translation layer mapping for logical addresses to physical addresses. This allows the SSD controller to locate data on an SSD quickly, reducing the performance impact of address translation.

The SSDs we examine use the DRAM buffer *less* when data is *densely allocated* (e.g., contiguous data) and use the DRAM buffer *more* when data is *sparsely allocated* (e.g., non-contiguous data). As an illustrative example, using an SSD to read from a *large* file would lead to a contiguous allocation of data on the SSD and a *small* DRAM buffer usage (due to a small number of mappings that need to be tracked in the FTL). On the other hand, using an SSD to read from and write to many *small* files would lead to many non-contiguous allocations of data on the SSD and a *large* DRAM buffer usage (due to a large number of mappings that need to be tracked in the FTL).

Examining DRAM buffer usage can therefore provide an indication of how system data allocation behavior affects flash reliability. To capture the DRAM buffer usage of SSDs, we examine the average amount of DRAM buffer space used over two recent weeks of SSD operation, sampled at one hour intervals.

Figure 8 plots the failure rate for SSDs that use different amounts of DRAM buffer space on average. For some platforms (A, B, and D), we observe that as more DRAM buffer space is used, SSD failure rate increases. Such a trend indicates that some systems that allocate data more sparsely have higher failure rates. Such behavior is potentially due to the fact that sparse data allocation can correspond to access patterns that write small amounts of non-contiguous data, causing the SSD controller to more frequently erase and copy data compared to writing contiguous data.

While Platform C does not appear to be sensitive to DRAM buffer usage, Platforms E and F demonstrate a trend of higher error rates at lower DRAM buffer usage. We attribute this behavior to a separate pattern of write behavior that we hypothesize these SSDs are subjected to. In these platforms, we believe that the SSDs allocate large, contiguous regions of data (resulting in low DRAM buffer usage) but write to them sparsely but intensely (leading to cell wearout). This could occur, for example, when frequently updating small fields in a large, contiguously-allocated data structure.

Interestingly, we observe similar failure behavior with DRAM buffer usage at the *application level* (Figure 9). We examine six of the largest distributions of applications on Platform B: Graph Search is a distributed graph search service; Batch Processor executes long-running asynchronous jobs; Key–Value Store stores persistent mappings of keys to values; Load Balancer is a programmable traffic routing framework; Distributed Key–Value Store is like a Key–Value Store with strong reliability, availability, and consistency guarantees; and Flash Cache is a cache for data with a large working set and low access frequency [19]. Applications across SSDs have increasing failure rates with increasing DRAM buffer usage (sparse data mappings) and in some cases have increases in failure rates at lower DRAM buffer usage (dense data mappings, e.g., Batch Processor and Flash Cache).

We conclude that small, sparse writes negatively affect SSD failure rates the most for sparse data mappings (e.g., non-contiguous data). But failures are also noticeable for dense data mappings (e.g., contiguous data). Given this behavior, we believe that there is the potential for developing more effective techniques to handle the adversarial access pattern of small, sparse writes.

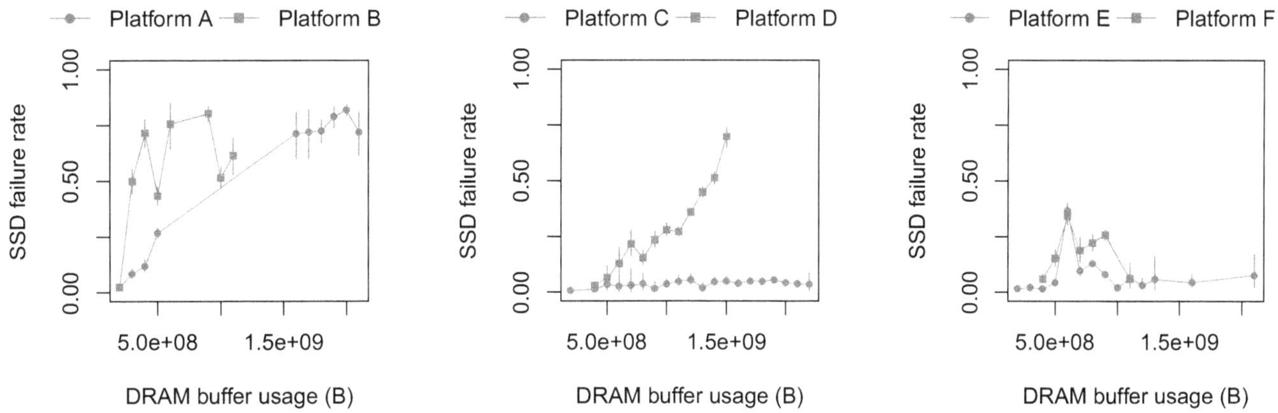

Figure 8: SSD failure rate vs. DRAM buffer usage. Sparse data mappings (e.g., non-contiguous data, indicated by high DRAM buffer usage to store flash translation layer metadata) negatively affect SSD reliability the most (Platforms A, B, and D). Additionally, some dense data mappings (e.g., contiguous data in Platforms E and F) also negatively affect SSD reliability, likely due to the effect of small, sparse writes.

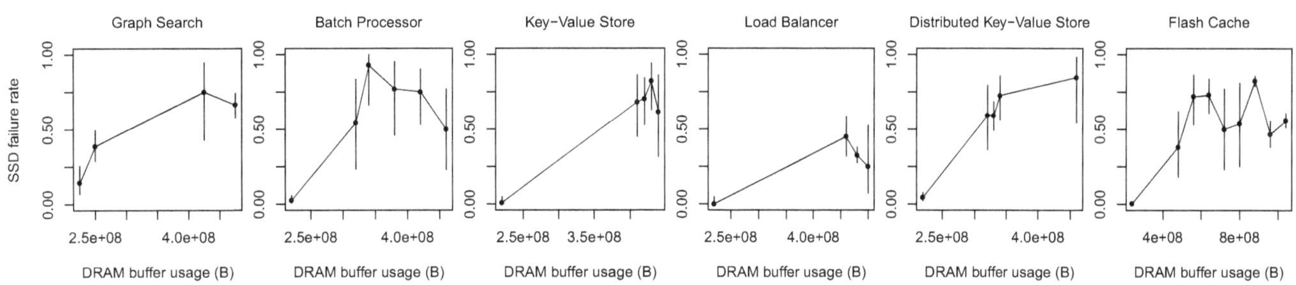

Figure 9: SSD failure rate vs. DRAM buffer usage across six applications that run on Platform B. We observe similar DRAM buffer effects to Figure 8, even among SSDs running the same application.

5. THE ROLE OF EXTERNAL FACTORS

We next examine how factors external to the SSD influence the errors observed over an SSD's lifetime. We examine the effects of temperature, PCIe bus power, and system-level writes reported by the OS.

5.1 Temperature

It is commonly assumed that higher temperature negatively affects the operation of flash-based SSDs. In flash *cells*, higher temperatures have been shown to cause cells to age more quickly due to the temperature-activated Arrhenius effect [39]. Temperature-dependent effects are especially important to understand for flash-based SSDs in order to make adequate data center provisioning and cooling decisions. To examine the effects of temperature, we used temperature measurements from temperature sensors embedded on the SSD cards, which provide a more accurate portrayal of the temperature of flash cells than temperature sensors at the server or rack level.

Figure 10 plots the failure rate for SSDs that have various average operating temperatures. We find that at an operating temperature range of 30 to 40°C, SSDs across server platforms see similar failure rates or slight increases in failure rates as temperature increases.

Outside of this range (at temperatures of 40°C and higher), we find that SSDs fall into one of three categories with respect to their reliability trends vs. temperature: (1) temperature-sensitive with increasing failure rate (Platforms A and B), (2) less temperature-sensitive (Platforms C and E), and (3) temperature-sensitive with decreasing failure rate (Platforms D and F). There are two factors that may affect the trends we observe with respect to SSD temperature.

One potential factor when analyzing the effects of temperature is the operation of the SSD controller in response to changes in temperature. The SSD controllers in some of the SSDs we examine attempt to ensure that SSDs do not exceed certain temperature thresholds (starting around 80°C). Similar to techniques employed in processors to reduce the amount of processor activity in order to keep the processor within a certain temperature range, our SSDs attempt to change their behavior (e.g., reduce the frequency of SSD access or, in the extreme case, shut down the SSD) in order not to exceed temperature thresholds.

A second potential factor is the thermal characteristics of the machines in each platform. The existence of two SSDs in a machine (in Platforms B, D, and F) compared to one SSD in a machine may (1) increase the thermal capacity of the machine (causing its SSDs to reach higher temperatures more quickly and increase the work required to cool the SSDs) and (2) potentially reduce airflow to the components, prolonging the effects of high temperatures when they occur.

One hypothesis is that temperature-sensitive SSDs with increasing error rates, such as Platforms A and B, may not employ as aggressive temperature reduction techniques as other platforms. While we cannot directly measure the actions the SSD controllers take in response to temperature events, we examined an event that can be correlated with temperature

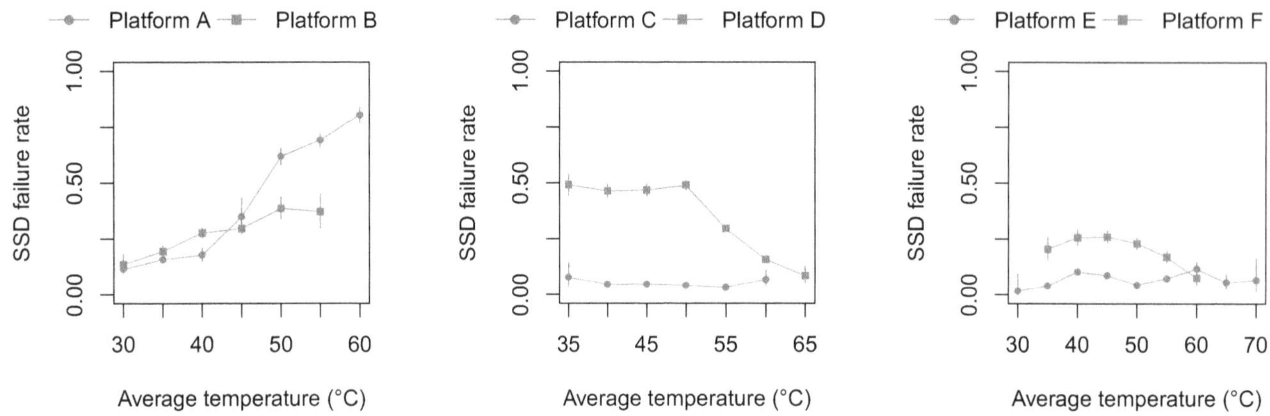

Figure 10: SSD failure rate vs. temperature. Operational temperatures of 30 to 40°C generally show increasing failure rates. Failure trends at and above 40°C follow three distinct failure rate patterns: increasing, not sensitive, and decreasing.

reduction: whether or not an SSD has throttled its operation in order to reduce its power consumption. Performing a large number of writes to an SSD consumes power and increases the temperature of the SSD. Figure 11 plots, for each temperature, the fraction of machines that have ever been throttled. Examining this figure confirms that Platforms A and B, where no machines or few machines have been throttled, exhibit behavior that is typical for SSDs without much preventative action against temperature increases. In these platforms, as temperature increases, failure rate of SSDs increases.

In contrast to Platforms A and B, Platforms C and E, which are less temperature-sensitive, throttle their SSDs more aggressively across a range of temperatures. From Figure 10 we can see that throttled SSDs have lower failure rates (in Platforms C and E) compared to SSDs that are throttled less or not throttled at all (Platforms A and B). We attribute the relatively low SSD failure rate for Platforms C and E we have observed in our measurements to the very aggressive throttling that occurs for SSDs in these two platforms. Such throttling could potentially reduce performance, though we are not able to examine this effect.

SSDs in Platforms D and F employ a relatively low amount of throttling (Figure 11), but exhibit the counter-intuitive trend of decreasing failure rate with increased temperature. Recall from Section 4.1 that these SSDs are predominantly in their early detection and early failure periods and so the failure rates for most SSDs in these platforms are relatively high compared to their peers in Platforms C and E. It is likely that a combination of power throttling and some other form of temperature-dependent throttling employed by the SSD controller that we are not able to measure is responsible for reducing the failure rate among the SSDs in Platforms D and F as temperature increases.

5.2 Bus Power Consumption

According to the PCIe standard, the nominal bus power consumption for the PCIe ×4 SSDs that we analyze is 10 W (regardless of PCIe version 1 or 2). Our infrastructure allows us to measure the average amount of power consumed on the PCIe bus by SSDs. As power consumption in servers can lead to increased electricity use for operation and cooling in data centers, we are interested in understanding the role that SSD power draw plays with respect to errors.

Figure 12 plots the failure rate for SSDs that operate at different average amounts of bus power consumption. Recall that Platforms A and B use PCIe v1 and that Platforms C through F use PCIe v2. We make three observations about the operation of these SSDs. First, PCIe v2 SSDs (Platforms C through F) support twice the bandwidth of PCIe v1 SSDs (Platforms A and B) by operating at twice the frequency, leading to around twice the amount of power consumed between the two sets of SSDs: SSDs supporting PCIe v1 operate in the range of 4 to 7.5 W and SSDs supporting PCIe v2 operate in the range of 8 to 14.5 W. Second, we find that the bus power that SSDs consume can vary over a range of around 2× between the SSDs that consume the least bus power and

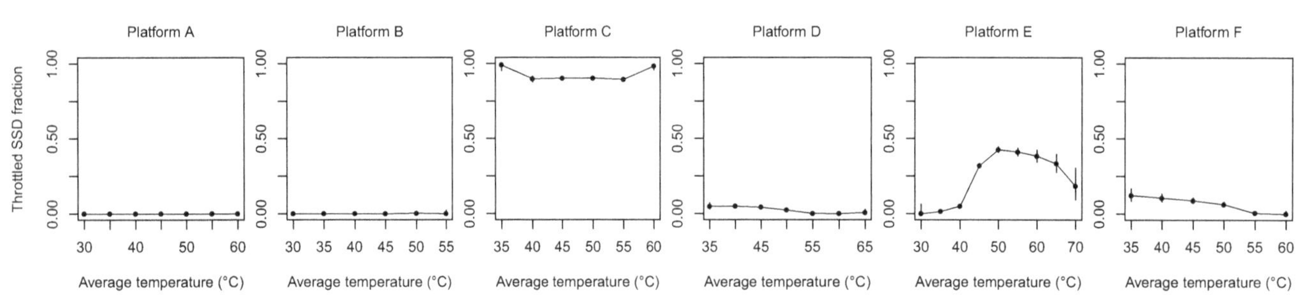

Figure 11: Fraction of SSDs ever throttled vs. SSD temperature. While SSDs in some platforms are never throttled (A and B), others are throttled more aggressively (C and E).

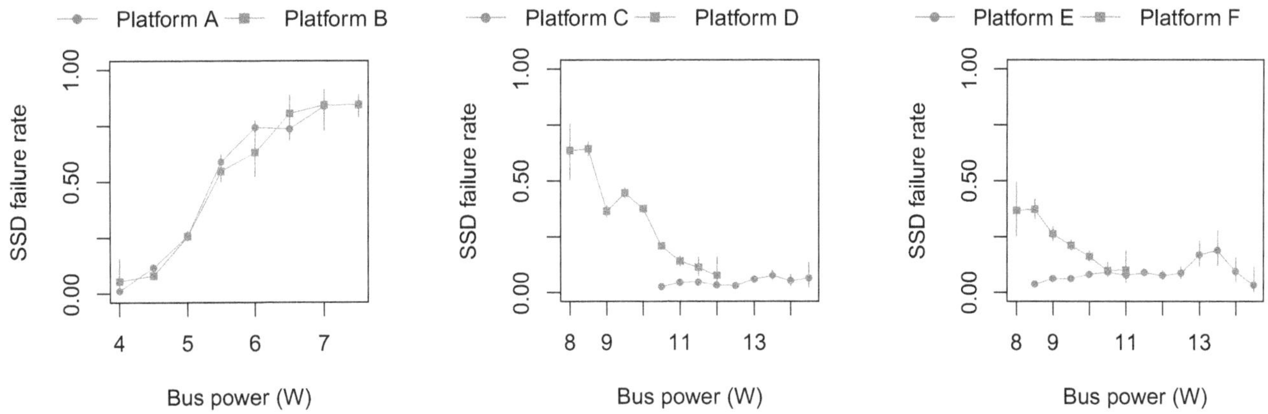

Figure 12: SSD failure rate vs. bus power consumption. PCIe v2 SSDs (Platforms C through F) consume more bus power than PCIe v1 SSDs (Platforms A and B) due to their higher frequency. Bus power consumption range (1) spans up to around 2× for SSDs within a platform (e.g., Platform B) and (2) is typically different from the nominal PCIe bus power of 10 W.

those that consume the most within a platform. Third, we find that PCIe v2 SSDs in systems that use two SSDs (Platforms D and F) tend to consume lower bus power compared to PCIe v2 SSDs in systems that use one SSD (Platforms C and E). This may be due to SSD access being distributed between the two SSDs. Note, however, that the *total* bus power consumption of a two-SSD system is larger than a single-SSD system.

With regard to failure rates, we observe that the trends for bus power consumption are correlated with those of average temperature. We believe that the higher bus power consumption is due to more data being transmitted and more data being transmitted requires more power to read or write from the SSD, which in turn increases the SSD temperature. One interesting result of this correlation is that techniques that aim to reduce SSD temperature in the absence of precise temperature sensors may be able to use bus power consumption as a proxy.

5.3 Data Written by the System Software

While we have shown that the amount of data that is written to flash cells has a direct effect on flash-based SSD lifetime, it is less clear what effect *system-level writes* reported by the OS (i.e., writes initiated by the system software on behalf of user programs or the file system) have on SSD error characteristics. Note that not all data written by system software may get written to flash chips due to system-level buffering. However, the reduction of writes performed by the system software is often used as a figure of merit in techniques that evaluate flash reliability in lieu of modeling the wear reduction techniques present in SSDs. Therefore, we are interested in examining whether or not different amounts of writes performed by the system software lead to different error characteristics in SSDs.

To this end, we measured the number of sectors (512 B in size) modified by the OS on behalf of the applications running on our machines over their lifetime, which we refer to as *data written by the system software*. Figure 13 plots the failure rate for SSDs where the OS has written different numbers of sectors over their lifetime.

In general, we observe that the total amount of data written by the system software is correlated with increased failure rates (following similar trends as the SSD lifecycle from Figure 4). There is one important caveat: some systems where a large amount of data has been written by the system software, have lower failure rates. This can be seen, for example, in Platforms A, B, and F: while there is a general trend toward higher SSD failure rates with larger amounts of data written by the system software for other platforms, the SSDs in Platforms A, B, and F can have lower failure rates with larger amounts of data written by the system software. We believe that this is due to the fact that systems that write more data may be able to benefit more from system-level buffering (e.g., the OS page cache) along with techniques employed by the SSD controller to reduce the amount of wear on flash cells (e.g., data encoding schemes that help reduce the number of program or erase operations).

To confirm this trend, Figure 14 plots the amount of data *actually written to the flash chips* compared to the amount of data *the system software reported as having written*. SSDs in Platforms B and F clearly show that writing more data at the system software-level does *not* always imply physically writing more data to flash chips. In fact, writing more data at the system software level may actually offer the system software more opportunities to *coalesce* data in system-level buffers before writing it to the flash cells, resulting in smaller numbers of actual writes to the flash chips. This observation suggests that work concerned with improving flash reliability *must* consider the effects of buffering across the system when evaluating different techniques.

6. LIMITATIONS AND POTENTIAL CONFOUNDING FACTORS

Workload changes due to SSD failure. In order to make systems more resilient to SSD failures, data replication is employed at the software level in some workloads. Such replication stores multiple copies of data (e.g., three copies) across different servers. In the event that data on one SSD becomes unavailable (e.g., due to an SSD failure), a copy of data can still be readily accessible.

In Section 3.3, we examined the correlation between SSD failures *within* the same server. Note that, with replication, an SSD failure will not shift the workload to the other SSD in the same server, as replicated copies are spread out among

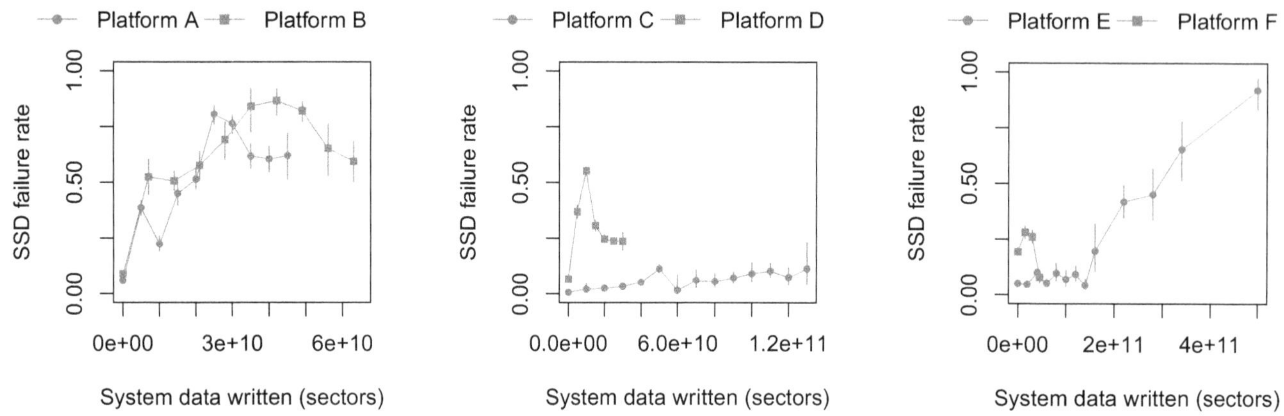

Figure 13: SSD failure rate vs. system data written by the system software. Interestingly, the amount of data written by the system software is not always an accurate indication of the amount of wear induced in an SSD, as seen in Platforms A and B, where more data written by the system software can correspond to lower failure rates.

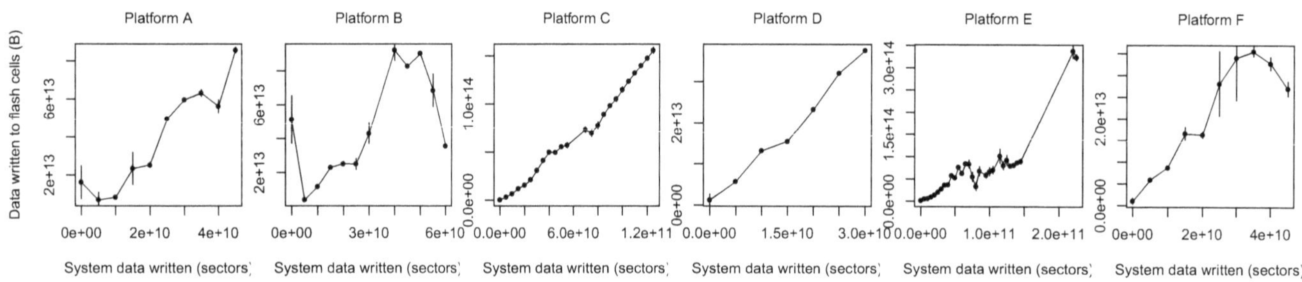

Figure 14: Actual data written to flash *cells* vs. data the OS reported as having been written. Due to buffering present in the system software (e.g., the page cache), the amount of data written by the system software does not always correspond to the amount of data written to the SSD (e.g., in Platforms A, B, and F).

different servers. Replication will, however, increase the utilization of other SSDs that contain copies of data. As such, correlation between SSD failures in *different* servers may exist, though we do not examine such effects in this work.

Performance effects. We also did not examine how the performance of a system was affected by the rate of uncorrectable errors on its SSDs and whether this made machines with SSDs reporting errors less effective at executing their workload.

SSD and flash chip access patterns. Our data collection infrastructure did not allow us to collect detailed access traces to the SSDs and flash chips we examined. This posed challenges for understanding the underlying causes of error behavior. While we examined the aggregate behavior of SSDs (e.g., amount of data written/read to/from flash chips in Sections 4.1 and 4.2) in order to gain insight into potential underlying access pattern trends, we believe that further SSD and flash chip access pattern analysis is needed to fully understand the underlying causes of the reliability trends we have identified.

Error correction scheme. The SSDs we examined used one viable strategy for error correction. Data uncorrectable by the SSD is forwarded to the host for repair. We note that such an error correction scheme may *not* be employed on other SSDs (and may not even be possible for some SSDs, such as those that use the NVMe interface [1]). While our results are still representative of the types of uncorrectable errors that such SSDs face, we believe that it will be beneficial for future studies to examine the effects of different error correction schemes in SSDs.

SSD data loss and repair. Recall from Section 2.2 that when an error is not correctable by an SSD, it is forwarded for repair to the host that the SSD is connected to. When the host cannot repair an error, data loss ensues. We did not examine the rate of data loss in the systems we evaluated. Nor did we examine the rate of SSD replacement. However, we believe that such an analysis (potentially combined with various error correction schemes, as mentioned above) would be very useful to perform in future work.

As we also mentioned in Section 2.2, the amount of errors the SSDs we examined can tolerate without the assistance of the host is on the order of bits per KB of data (similar to data reported in [17]). However, we do not have visibility into the error correction schemes employed on the host for larger amounts of errors (>10's of bits per KB of data).

7. RELATED WORK

To our knowledge, this paper provides the first comprehensive study of flash-based SSD reliability trends in the field. Prior flash memory reliability studies focused on flash *chip* reliability and evaluated only *a small number* of flash chips in *controlled* environments.

The closest related work, by Grupp et al. [20], examined the cost, performance, capacity, and reliability trends of flash memory in the context of a prototypical server flash storage device similar in architecture to SSDs deployed in data centers (Figure 1). Based on their study, the authors project several challenges for the adoption of flash in a server context. One drawback of the reliability results presented in [20] is that the experiments were performed in a controlled environment, under synthetic workloads, while modeling only the latency – but not the function – of the SSD controller on a small number (45) of flash chips.

A recent work by Ouyang et al. [34] performed a study of programmable SSD controllers at a large-scale web services company, Baidu. While this work examined flash-based SSDs in the field, it did not analyze the reliability characteristics of SSDs and instead focused on bandwidth, capacity, and cost.

Several studies examined flash chips in controlled environments in order to understand their error characteristics. Our study is orthogonal to these works. Early analysis of flash circuitry identified flash reliability trends attributed to program disturbance due to tunneling effects and hot-electron injection [36, 23, 21, 27, 22], quantum-level noise effects [25, 16], erratic tunneling [33, 14], data-retention and read disturbance [5, 18, 4], and detrapping-induced retention effects [24, 40, 41, 26, 31, 30, 37]. A series of works by Cai et al. [6, 11, 10, 7, 9, 13, 8, 12] identified patterns of errors for more recent MLC flash *chips* and proposed techniques to help mitigate their effects. These studies can help identify (and mitigate) the trends in flash error patterns at the raw chip level. However, it is unclear from these studies to what extent *flash-based SSDs* in the field running real workloads and real system software over a long time may exhibit such error patterns (and how to ensure the reliability of such SSDs). For example, compared to prior chip-level studies, we find that *SSD* failure rates do *not* increase monotonically with *flash chip* wear; that read disturbance errors are *not* prevalent in the field; that the data layout across an SSD's physical address space has an effect on SSD failure rate; that SSD controller throttling techniques can help mitigate temperature-induced errors; and that optimizations in the SSD controllers and buffering employed in the system software reduces the amount of data written to flash chips. These differences from prior studies can be attributed to our holistic study of flash errors when running on real SSD controllers, under real system software, and with real data center workloads.

8. SUMMARY AND CONCLUSIONS

We performed an extensive analysis of the effects of various factors on flash-based SSD reliability across a majority of the SSDs employed at Facebook, running production data center workloads. We analyze a variety of internal and external characteristics of SSDs and examine how these characteristics affect the trends for uncorrectable errors. To conclude, we briefly summarize the key observations from our study and discuss their implications for SSD and system design.

Observation 1: *We observe that SSDs go through several distinct failure periods – early detection, early failure, usable life, and wearout – during their lifecycle, corresponding to the amount of data written to flash chips.*

Due to pools of flash blocks with different reliability characteristics, failure rate in a population does *not* monotonically increase with respect to amount of data written to flash chips. This is unlike the failure rate trends seen in raw flash chips. We suggest that techniques should be designed to help reduce or tolerate errors *throughout SSD lifecycle*. For example, additional error correction *at the beginning of an SSD's life* could help reduce the failure rates we see during the *early detection* period.

Observation 2: *We find that the effect of read disturbance errors is not a predominant source of errors in the SSDs we examine.*

While prior work has shown that such errors can occur under certain access patterns in controlled environments [5, 32, 6, 8], we do *not* observe this effect across the SSDs we examine. This corroborates prior work which showed that the effect of retention errors in flash cells dominate error rate compared to read disturbance [32, 6]. It may be beneficial to perform a more detailed study of the effect of these types of errors in flash-based SSDs used in servers.

Observation 3: *Sparse data layout across an SSD's physical address space (e.g., non-contiguously allocated data) leads to high SSD failure rates; dense data layout (e.g., contiguous data) can also negatively impact reliability under certain conditions, likely due to adversarial access patterns.*

Further research into flash write coalescing policies with information from the system level may help improve SSD reliability. For example, information about write access patterns from the operating system could potentially inform SSD controllers of non-contiguous data that is accessed very frequently, which may be one type of access pattern that adversely affects SSD reliability and is a candidate for storing in a separate write buffer.

Observation 4: *Higher temperatures lead to increased failure rates, but do so most noticeably for SSDs that do not employ throttling techniques.*

In general, we find techniques like *throttling*, which may be employed to reduce SSD temperature, to be effective at reducing the failure rate of SSDs. We also find that SSD temperature is correlated with the power used to transmit data across the PCIe bus, which can potentially be used as a proxy for temperature in the absence of SSD temperature sensors.

Observation 5: *The amount of data reported to be written by the system software can overstate the amount of data actually written to flash chips, due to system-level buffering and wear reduction techniques.*

Techniques that simply reduce the *rate* of software-level writes may not reduce the failure rate of SSDs. Studies seeking to model the effects of reducing software-level writes on flash reliability should also consider how other aspects of SSD operation, such as system-level buffering and SSD controller wear leveling, affect the *actual* amount of data written to SSDs.

Conclusions. We hope that our new observations, with real workloads and real systems from the field, can aid in (1) understanding the effects of different factors, including system software, applications, and SSD controllers on flash memory reliability, (2) the design of more reliable flash architectures and systems, and (3) improving the evaluation methodologies for future flash memory reliability studies.

9. ACKNOWLEDGMENTS

We thank the anonymous reviewers for their insightful comments. This work is supported in part by Samsung and the Intel Science and Technology Center for Cloud Computing, as well as NSF grants 0953246, 1065112, 1212962, and 1320531.

10. REFERENCES

[1] NVM Express Specification. `http://www.nvmexpress.org/specifications/`.

[2] The R Project for Statistical Computing. `http://www.r-project.org/`.

[3] American National Standards Institute. AT Attachment 8 – ATA/ATAPI Command Set. `http://www.t13.org/documents/uploadeddocuments/docs2008/d1699r6a-ata8-acs.pdf`, 2008.

[4] H. Belgal, N. Righos, I. Kalastirsky, et al. A New Reliability Model for Post-Cycling Charge Retention of Flash Memories. IRPS, 2002.

[5] A. Brand, K. Wu, S. Pan, et al. Novel Read Disturb Failure Mechanism Induced By Flash Cycling. IRPS, 1993.

[6] Y. Cai, E. F. Haratsch, O. Mutlu, et al. Error Patterns in MLC NAND Flash Memory: Measurement, Characterization, and Analysis. In *DATE*, 2012.

[7] Y. Cai, E. F. Haratsch, O. Mutlu, et al. Threshold Voltage Distribution in MLC NAND Flash Memory: Characterization, Analysis, and Modeling. In *DATE*, 2013.

[8] Y. Cai, Y. Luo, S. Ghose, et al. Read Disturb Errors in MLC NAND Flash Memory: Characterization and Mitigation. In *DSN*, 2015.

[9] Y. Cai, Y. Luo, E. F. Haratsch, et al. Data Retention in MLC NAND Flash Memory: Characterization, Optimization and Recovery. In *HPCA*, 2015.

[10] Y. Cai, O. Mutlu, E. F. Haratsch, et al. Program Interference in MLC NAND Flash Memory: Characterization, Modeling, and Mitigation. In *ICCD*, 2013.

[11] Y. Cai, G. Yalcin, O. Mutlu, et al. Flash Correct-and-Refresh: Retention-Aware Error Management for Increased Flash Memory Lifetime. In *ICCD*, 2012.

[12] Y. Cai, G. Yalcin, O. Mutlu, et al. Error Analysis and Retention-Aware Error Management for NAND Flash Memory. *ITJ*, 2013.

[13] Y. Cai, G. Yalcin, O. Mutlu, et al. Neighbor-Cell Assisted Error Correction for MLC NAND Flash Memories. In *SIGMETRICS*, 2014.

[14] A. Chimenton and P. Olivo. Erratic Erase in Flash Memories – Part I: Basic Experimental and Statistical Characterization. *IEEE Trans. Elect. Dev.*, 50(4), 2003.

[15] T.-S. Chung, D.-J. Park, S. Park, et al. A survey of flash translation layer. *J. Sys. Arch.*, 55, 2009.

[16] C. Compagnoni, A. Spinelli, R. Gusmeroli, et al. First Evidence for Injection Statistics Accuracy Limitations in NAND Flash Constant-Current Fowler-Nordheim Programming. IEDM Tech Dig., 2007.

[17] J. Cooke. The Inconvenient Truths of NAND Flash Memory. In *Flash Memory Summit*, 2007.

[18] R. Degraeve, F. Schuler, B. Kaczer, et al. Analytical Percolation Model for Predicting Anomalous Charge Loss in Flash Memories. *IEEE Trans. Elect. Dev.*, 51(9), 2004.

[19] A. Gartrell, M. Srinivasan, B. Alger, et al. McDipper: A Key-Value Cache for Flash Storage. `https://www.facebook.com/notes/10151347090423920`, 2013.

[20] L. M. Grupp, J. D. Davis, and S. Swanson. The Bleak Future of NAND Flash Memory. In *FAST*, 2012.

[21] S. Hur, J. Lee, M. Park, et al. Effective Program Inhibition Beyond 90nm NAND Flash Memories. NVSM, 2004.

[22] S. Joo, H. Yang, K. Noh, et al. Abnormal Disturbance Mechanism of Sub-100 nm NAND Flash Memory. *Japanese J. Applied Physics*, 45(8A), 2006.

[23] T. Jung, Y. Choi, K. Suh, et al. A 3.3V 128Mb Multi-Level NAND Flash Memory for Mass Storage Applications. ISSCC, 1996.

[24] M. Kato, N. Miyamoto, H. Kume, et al. Read-Disturb Degradation Mechanism Due to Electron Trapping in the Tunnel Oxide for Low-Voltage Flash Memories. IEDM, 1994.

[25] H. Kurata, K. Otsuga, A. Kotabe, et al. The Impact of Random Telegraph Signals on the Scaling of Multilevel Flash Memories. VLSI, 2006.

[26] J. Lee, J. Choi, D. Park, et al. Degradation of Tunnel Oxide by FN Current Stress and Its Effects on Data Retention Characteristics of 90-nm NAND Flash Memory. IRPS, 2003.

[27] J. Lee, C. Lee, M. Lee, et al. A New Program Disturbance Phenomenon in NAND Flash Memory by Source/Drain Hot-Electrons Generated by GIDL Current. NVSM, 2006.

[28] A. Maislos. A New Era in Embedded Flash Memory, 2011. Presentation at Flash Memory Summit.

[29] Micron. Garbage Collection in Single-Level Cell NAND Flash Memory. Technical report, 2011.

[30] N. Mielke, H. Belgal, A. Fazio, et al. Recovery Effects in the Distributed Cycling of Flash Memories. IRPS, 2006.

[31] N. Mielke, H. Belgal, I. Kalastirsky, et al. Flash EEPROM Threshold Instabilities due to Charge Trapping During Program/Erase Cycling. *IEEE Trans. Dev. and Mat. Reliability*, 2(3), 2004.

[32] N. Mielke, T. Marquart, N. Wu, et al. Bit Error Rate in NAND Flash Memories. In *IRPS*, 2008.

[33] T. Ong, A. Fazio, N. Mielke, et al. Erratic Erase in ETOX^{TM} Flash Memory Array. VLSI, 1993.

[34] J. Ouyang, S. Lin, S. Jiang, et al. SDF: Software-Defined Flash for Web-Scale Internet Storage Systems. ASPLOS, 2014.

[35] B. Schroeder and G. A. Gibson. Disk Failures in the Real World: What Does an MTTF of 1,000,000 Hours Mean to You? In *FAST*, 2007.

[36] K. Suh, B. Suh, Y. Lim, et al. A 3.3 V 32 Mb NAND Flash Memory with Incremental Step Pulse Programming Scheme. *IEEE JSSC*, 30(11), 1995.

[37] K. Takeuchi, S. Satoh, T. Tanaka, et al. A Negative Vth Cell Architecture for Highly Scalable, Excellently Noise-Immune, and Highly Reliable NAND Flash Memories. *IEEE JSSC*, 34(5), 1995.

[38] A. Thusoo, J. Sen Sarma, N. Jain, et al. Hive – A Petabyte Scale Data Warehouse Using Hadoop. In *ICDE*, 2010.

[39] M. Xu, C. Tan, and L. MingFu. Extended Arrhenius Law of Time-to-Breakdown of Ultrathin Gate Oxides. *Applied Physics Letters*, 82(15), 2003.

[40] R. Yamada, Y. Mori, Y. Okuyama, et al. Analysis of Detrap Current Due to Oxide Traps to Improve Flash Memory Retention. IRPS, 2000.

[41] R. Yamada, T. Sekiguchi, Y. Okuyama, et al. A Novel Analysis Method of Threshold Voltage Shift Due to Detrap in a Multi-Level Flash Memory. VLSI, 2001.

Online Convex Optimization Using Predictions*

Niangjun Chen†, Anish Agarwal†, Adam Wierman†,
Siddharth Barman†, Lachlan L. H. Andrew‡
†California Institute of Technology, Pasadena, CA, USA,
E-mail: {ncchen,aagarwal,adamw,sid.barman} @caltech.edu
‡Monash University, Australia, E-mail: lachlan.andrew@monash.edu

ABSTRACT

Making use of predictions is a crucial, but under-explored, area of online algorithms. This paper studies a class of online optimization problems where we have external noisy predictions available. We propose a stochastic prediction error model that generalizes prior models in the learning and stochastic control communities, incorporates correlation among prediction errors, and captures the fact that predictions improve as time passes. We prove that achieving sublinear regret and constant competitive ratio for online algorithms requires the use of an unbounded prediction window in adversarial settings, but that under more realistic stochastic prediction error models it is possible to use Averaging Fixed Horizon Control (AFHC) to simultaneously achieve sublinear regret and constant competitive ratio in expectation using only a constant-sized prediction window. Furthermore, we show that the performance of AFHC is tightly concentrated around its mean.

Categories and Subject Descriptors

F.2.0 [**Analysis of Algorithms and Problem Complexity**]: General

General Terms

Algorithms, Performance, Theory

1. INTRODUCTION

Making use of predictions about the future is a crucial, but under-explored, area of online algorithms. In this paper, we use online convex optimization to illustrate the insights that can be gained from incorporating a general, realistic model of prediction noise into the analysis of online algorithms.

Online convex optimization. In an online convex optimization (OCO) problem, a learner interacts with an environment in a sequence of rounds. In round t the learner chooses an action x_t from a convex decision/action space G, and then the environment reveals a convex cost function c_t and the learner pays cost $c_t(x_t)$. An algorithm's goal is to minimize total cost over a (long) horizon T.

OCO has a rich theory and a wide range of important applications. In computer science, it is most associated with the so-called k-experts problem, an online learning problem where in each round t the algorithm chooses one of k possible actions, viewed as following the advice of one of k "experts".

However, OCO is being increasingly broadly applied and, recently has become prominent in networking and cloud computing applications, including the design of dynamic capacity planning, load shifting and demand response for data centers [25, 29, 30, 31, 35], geographical load balancing of internet-scale systems [28, 42], electrical vehicle charging [16, 25], video streaming [21, 22] and thermal management of systems-on-chip [46, 47].

In typical applications of online convex optimization in networking and cloud computing there is an additional cost in each round, termed a "switching cost", that captures the cost of changing actions during a round. Specifically, the cost is $c_t(x_t)+ \| x_t - x_{t-1} \|$, where $\| \cdot \|$ is a norm (often the one-norm). This additional term makes the online problem more challenging since the optimal choice in a round then depends on future cost functions. These "smoothed" online convex optimization problems have received considerable attention in the context of networking and cloud computing applications, e.g., [28, 29, 30, 31, 32], and are also relevant for many more traditional online convex optimization applications where, in reality, there is a cost associated with a change in action, e.g., portfolio management. *We focus on smoothed online convex optimization problems.*

A mismatch between theory and practice. As OCO algorithms make their way into networking and cloud computing applications, it is increasingly clear that there is a mismatch between the pessimistic results provided by the theoretical analysis (which is typically adversarial) and the near-optimal performance observed in practice.

Concretely, two main performance metrics have been studied in the literature: *regret*, defined as the difference between the cost of the algorithm and the cost of the offline optimal static solution, and the *competitive ratio*, defined as the maximum ratio between the cost of the algorithm and the cost of the offline optimal (dynamic) solution.

Within the *machine learning community*, regret has been heavily studied [20, 45, 49] and there are many simple algorithms that provide provably sublinear regret (also called "no regret"). For example, online gradient descent achieves $O(\sqrt{T})$-regret [49], even when there are switching costs [4]. In contrast, the *online algorithms community* considers a more general class of problems called "metrical task systems" (MTS) and focuses on competitive ratio [7, 8, 29]. Most results in this literature are "negative", e.g., when c_t are ar-

*This work is partially supported by the NSF through CNS-1319820, EPAS-1307794, CNS-0846025, CCF-1101470 and the ARC through DP130101378.

SIGMETRICS'15, June 15–19, 2015, Portland, OR, USA.

http://dx.doi.org/10.1145/2745844.2745854.

bitrary, the competitive ratio grows without bound as the number of states in the decision space grows [8]. Exceptions to such negative results come only when structure is imposed on either the cost functions or the decision space, e.g., when the decision space is *one-dimensional* it is possible for an online algorithm to have a constant competitive ratio, e.g., [29]. However, *even in this simple setting no algorithms performs well for both competitive ratio and regret.* No online algorithm can have sublinear regret and a constant competitive ratio, even if the decision space is one-dimensional and cost functions are linear [4].

In contrast to the pessimism of the analytic work, applications in networking and cloud computing have shown that OCO algorithms can significantly outperform the static optimum while nearly matching the performance of the dynamic optimal, i.e., simultaneously do well for regret and the competitive ratio. Examples include dynamic capacity management of a single data center [2, 29] and geographical load balancing across multiple data centers [28, 35, 36].

It is tempting to attribute this discrepancy to the fact that practical workloads are not adversarial. However, a more important factor is that, in reality, *algorithms can exploit relatively accurate predictions about the future*, such as diurnal variations [5, 19, 31]. But a more important contrast between the theory and application is simply that, in reality, *predictions about the future are available and accurate, and thus play a crucial role in the algorithms.*

Incorporating predictions. It is no surprise that predictions are crucial to online algorithms in practice. In OCO, knowledge about future cost functions is valuable, even when noisy. However, despite the importance of predictions, we do not understand how prediction noise affects the performance (and design) of online convex optimization algorithms.

This is not due to a lack of effort. Most papers that apply OCO algorithms to networking and cloud computing applications study the impact of prediction noise, e.g., [1, 3, 31, 35]. Typically, these consider numerical simulations where i.i.d. noise terms with different levels of variability are added to the parameter being predicted, e.g., [18, 40]. While this is a valuable first step, it does not provide any *guarantees* about the performance of the algorithm with realistic prediction errors (which tend to be correlated, since an overestimate in one period is likely followed by another overestimate) and further does not help inform the *design* of algorithms that can effectively use predictions.

Though most work on predictions has been simulation based, there has also been significant work done seeking analytic guarantees. This literature can be categorized into:

(i) *Worst-case models* of prediction error typically assume that there exists a lookahead window ω such that within that window, prediction is near-perfect (*too optimistic*), and outside that window the workload is adversarial (*too pessimistic*), e.g., [8, 29, 28, 32, 12].

(ii) *Simple stochastic models* of prediction error typically consider i.i.d. errors, e.g., [10, 31, 30]. Although this is analytically appealing, it ignores important features of prediction errors, as described in the next section.

(iii) *Detailed stochastic models* of specific predictors applied for specific signal models, such as [48, 38, 39, 23]. This leads to less pessimistic results, but the guarantees, and the algorithms themselves, become *too fragile* to assumptions on the system evolution.

Contributions of this paper. First, *we introduce a general colored noise model for studying prediction errors in online convex optimization problems.* The model captures three important features of real predictors: (i) it allows for arbitrary correlations in prediction errors (e.g., both short and long range correlations); (ii) the quality of predictions decreases the further in the future we try to look ahead; and (iii) predictions about the future are updated as time passes. Further, it strikes a middle ground between the worst-case and stochastic approaches. In particular, it does not make any assumptions about an underlying stochastic process or the design of the predictor. Instead, it only makes (weak) assumptions about the stochastic form of the error of the predictor; these assumptions are satisfied by many common stochastic models, e.g., the prediction error of standard Weiner filters [44] and Kalman filters [24]. Importantly, by being agnostic to the underlying stochastic process, the model allows worst-case analysis with respect to the realization of the underlying cost functions.

Second, using this model, *we show that a simple algorithm, Averaging Fixed Horizon Control (AFHC) [28], simultaneously achieves sublinear regret and a constant competitive ratio in expectation using very limited prediction*, i.e., a prediction window of size $O(1)$, in nearly all situations when it is feasible for an online algorithm to do so (Theorem 2). Further, we show that the performance of AFHC is tightly concentrated around its mean (Theorem 10). Thus, AFHC extracts the asymptotically optimal value from predictions. Additionally, our results inform the choice of the optimal prediction window size. (For ease of presentation, both Theorems 9 and 10 are stated and proven for the specific case of online LASSO – see Section 2 – but the proof technique can be generalized in a straightforward way.)

Importantly, Theorem 5 highlights that the dominant factor impacting whether the prediction window should be long or short in AFHC is not the variance of the noise, but rather the correlation structure of the noise. For example, if prediction errors are i.i.d. then it is optimal for AFHC to look ahead as far as possible (i.e., T) regardless of the variance, but if prediction errors have strong short-range dependencies then the optimal prediction window is constant sized regardless of the variance.

Previously, AFHC had only been analyzed in the adversarial model [29], and our results are in stark contrast to the pessimism of prior work. To highlight this, we prove that in the "easiest" adversarial model (where predictions are exact within the prediction window), no online algorithm can achieve sublinear regret *and* a constant competitive ratio when using a prediction window of constant size (Theorem 1). This contrast emphasizes the value of moving to a more realistic stochastic model of prediction error.

2. ONLINE CONVEX OPTIMIZATION WITH SWITCHING COSTS

Throughout this paper we consider online convex optimization problems with switching costs, i.e., "smoothed" online convex optimization (SOCO) problems.

2.1 Problem Formulation

The standard formulation of an online optimization problem with switching costs considers a convex decision/action space $G \subset \mathbb{R}^n$ and a sequence of cost functions $\{c_1, c_2, \ldots\}$, where each $c_t : G \to \mathbb{R}^+$ is convex. At time t, the online algorithm first chooses an action, which is a vector $x_t \in G$, the environment chooses a cost function c_t from a set $\mathcal{C}$, and the algorithm pays a stage cost $c_t(x_t)$ and a switching cost $\beta||x_t - x_{t-1}||$ where $\beta \in (\mathbb{R}^+)$. Thus, the total cost of the online algorithm is defined to be

$$\text{cost}(ALG) = \mathbb{E}_x\left[\sum_{t=1}^{T} c_t(x_t) + \beta||x_t - x_{t-1}||\right], \quad (1)$$

where $x_1, \ldots, x_T$ are the actions chosen by the algorithm, ALG. Without loss of generality, assume the initial action $x_0 = 0$, the expectation is over any randomness used by the algorithm, and $||\cdot||$ is a seminorm on $\mathbb{R}^n$.

Typically, a number of assumptions about the action space G and the cost functions c_t are made to allow positive results to be derived. In particular, the action set G is often assumed to be closed, nonempty, and bounded, where by bounded we mean that there exists $D \in \mathbb{R}$ such that for all $x, y \in G$, $||x - y|| \leq D$. Further, the cost functions c_t are assumed to have a uniformly bounded subgradient, i.e., there exists $N \in \mathbb{R}^+$ such that, for all $x \in G$, $||\nabla c_t(x)|| \leq N$.

Since our focus in this paper is on predictions, we consider a variation of the above with *parameterized* cost functions $c_t(x_t; y_t)$, where the parameter y_t is the focus of prediction. Further, except when considering worst-case predictions, we adopt a specific form of c_t for concreteness. We focus on a tracking problem where the online algorithm is trying to do a "smooth" tracking of y_t and pays a least square penalty each round.

$$\text{cost}(ALG) = \mathbb{E}_x\left[\sum_{t=1}^{T} \frac{1}{2}||y_t - Kx_t||_2^2 + \beta||x_t - x_{t-1}||_1.\right], \tag{2}$$

where the target $y_t \in \mathbb{R}^m$, and $K \in \mathbb{R}^{m\times n}$ is a (known) linear map that transforms the control variable into the space of the tracking target. Let $K^\dagger$ be the Moore-Penrose pseudoinverse of K.

We focus on this form because it represents an online version of the LASSO (Least Absolute Shrinkage and Selection Operator) formulation, which is widely studied in a variety of contexts, e.g., see [13, 14, 15, 41] and the references therein. Typically in LASSO the one-norm regularizer is used to induce sparsity in the solution. In our case, this corresponds to specifying that a good solution does not change too much, i.e., $x_t - x_{t-1} \neq 0$ is infrequent. Importantly, the focus on LASSO, i.e., the two-norm loss function and one-norm regularizer, is simply for concreteness and ease of presentation. Our proof technique generalizes (at the expense of length and complexity).

We assume that K^TK is invertible and that the static optimal solution to (2) is positive. Neither of these is particularly restrictive. If K has full column rank then K^TK is invertible. This is a reasonable, for example, when the dimensionality of the action space G is small relative to the output space. Note that typically K is designed, and so it can be chosen to ensure these assumptions are satisfied. Additionally if K is invertible, then it no longer appears in the results provided.

Finally, it is important to highlight a few contrasts between the cost function in (2) and the typical assumptions in the online convex optimization literature. First, note that the feasible action set $G = \mathbb{R}^n$ is unbounded. Second, note that gradient of c_t can be arbitrarily large when y_t and Kx_t are far apart. Thus, both of these are relaxed compared to what is typically studied in the online convex optimization literature. We show in Section 5 that, we can have sublinear regret even in this relaxed setting.

2.2 Performance Metrics

The performance of online algorithms for SOCO problems is typically evaluated via two performance metrics: *regret* and the *competitive ratio*. Regret is the dominant choice in the machine learning community and competitive ratio is the dominant choice in the online algorithms community. The key difference between these measures is whether they compare the performance of the online algorithm to the offline optimal static solution or the offline optimal dynamic solution. Specifically, the optimal offline *static* solution, is[1]

$$STA = \operatorname*{argmin}_{x\in G} \sum_{t=1}^{T} c_t(x) + \beta||x||, \tag{3}$$

and the optimal *dynamic* solution is

$$OPT = \operatorname*{argmin}_{(x_1,\ldots,x_T)\in G^T} \sum_{t=1}^{T} c_t(x_t) + \beta||(x_t - x_{t-1})||. \tag{4}$$

DEFINITION 1. *The **regret** of an online algorithm, ALG, is less than $\rho(T)$ if the following holds:*

$$\sup_{(c_1,\ldots,c_T)\in\mathcal{C}^T} \text{cost}(ALG) - \text{cost}(STA) \leq \rho(T). \tag{5}$$

DEFINITION 2. *An online algorithm ALG is said to be $\rho(T)$-**competitive** if the following holds:*

$$\sup_{(c^1,\ldots,c^T)\in\mathcal{C}^T} \frac{\text{cost}(ALG)}{\text{cost}(OPT)} \leq \rho(T) \tag{6}$$

The goals are typically to find algorithms with a (small) constant competitive ratio ("constant-competitive") and to find online algorithms with sublinear regret, i.e., an algorithm ALG that has regret $\rho(T)$ bounded above by some $\hat{\rho}(T) \in o(T)$; note that $\rho(T)$ may be negative if the concept we seek to learn varies dynamically. Sublinear regret is also called "no-regret", since the time-average loss of the online algorithm goes to zero as T grows.

2.3 Background

To this point, there are large literatures studying both the designs of no-regret algorithms and the design of constant-competitive algorithms. However, in general, these results tell a pessimistic story.

In particular, on a positive note, it is possible to design simple, no-regret algorithms, e.g., *online gradient descent* (OGD) based algorithms [49, 20] and *Online Newton Step and Follow the Approximate Leader* algorithms [20]. (Note that the classical setting does not consider switching costs; however, [4] shows that similar regret bounds can be obtained when switching costs are considered.)

However, when one considers the competitive ratio, results are much less optimistic. Historically, results about competitive ratio have considered weaker assumptions, i.e., the cost functions c_t and the action set G can be nonconvex, and the switching cost is an arbitrary metric $d(x_t, x_{t-1})$ rather than a seminorm $||x_t - x_{t-1}||$. The weakened assumptions, together with the tougher offline target for comparison, leads to the fact that most results are "negative". For example, [8] has shown that any deterministic algorithm must be $\Omega(n)$-competitive given metric decision space of size n. Furthermore, [7] has shown that any randomized algorithm must be $\Omega(\sqrt{\log n/\log\log n})$-competitive. To this point, positive results are only known in very special cases. For example, [29] shows that, when G is a one dimensional normed space, there exists a deterministic online algorithm that is 3-competitive.

Results become even more pessimistic when one asks for algorithms that perform well for both competitive ratio and regret. Note that performing well for both measures is particularly desirable for many networking and cloud computing

[1]One switching cost is incurred due to the fact that we enforce $x_0 = 0$.

applications where it is necessary to both argue that a dynamic control algorithm provides benefits over a static control algorithm (sublinear regret) and is near optimal (competitive ratio). However, a recent result in [4] highlights that such as goal is impossible: even when the setting is restricted to a one dimensional normed space with linear cost functions no online algorithm can simultaneously achieve sublinear regret and constant competitive ratio [2].

3. MODELING PREDICTION ERROR

The adversarial model underlying most prior work on online convex optimization has led to results that tend to be pessimistic; however, in reality, *algorithms can often use predictions about future cost functions in order to perform well.*

Knowing information about future cost functions is clearly valuable for smoothed online convex optimization problems, since it allows you to better justify whether it is worth it to incur a switching cost during the current stage. Thus, it is not surprising that predictions have proven valuable in practice for such problems.

Given the value of predictions in practice, it is not surprising that there have been numerous attempts to incorporate models of prediction error into the analysis of online algorithms. We briefly expand upon the worst-case and stochastic approaches described in the introduction to motivate our approach, which is an integration of the two.

Worst-case models. Worst-case models of prediction error tend to assume that there exists a lookahead window, w, such that within that window, a perfect (or near-perfect, e.g., error bounded by ε) prediction is available. Then, outside of that window the workload is adversarial. A specific example is that, for any t the online algorithm knows $y_t, \ldots, y_{t+w}$ precisely, while $y_{t+w+1}, \ldots$ are adversarial.

Clearly, such models are both *too optimistic* about the the predictions used and *too pessimistic* about what is outside the prediction window. The result is that algorithms designed using such models tend to be too trusting of short term predictions and too wary of unknown fluctuations outside of the prediction window. Further, such models tend to underestimate the value of predictions for algorithm performance. To illustrate this, we establish the following theorem.

THEOREM 1. *For any constant $\gamma > 0$ and any online algorithm A (deterministic or randomized) with constant lookahead w, either the competitive ratio of the algorithm is at least γ or its regret, is $\Omega(T)$. Here T is the number of cost functions in an instance.*

The above theorem focuses on the "easiest" worst-case model, i.e., where the algorithm is allowed perfect lookahead for w steps. Even in this case, an online algorithm must have super-constant lookahead in order to simultaneously have sublinear regret and a constant competitive ratio. Further, the proof (given in Appendix A.1) highlights that this holds even in the scalar setting with linear cost functions. Thus, worst-case models are *overly pessimistic* about the value of prediction.

Stochastic models. Stochastic models tend to come in two forms: (i) i.i.d. models or (ii) detailed models of stochastic processes and specific predictors for those processes.

In the first case, for reasons of tractability, prediction errors are simply assumed to be i.i.d. mean zero random variables. While such an assumption is clearly analytically appealing, it is also quite simplistic and ignores many important features of prediction errors. For example, in reality, predictions have increasing error the further in time we look ahead due to correlation of predictions errors in nearby points in time. Further, predictions tend to be updated or refined as time passes. These fundamental characteristics of predictions cannot be captured by the i.i.d. model.

In the second case, which is common in control theory, a specific stochastic model for the underlying process is assumed and then an optimal predictor (filter) is derived. Examples here include the derivation of Weiner filters and Kalaman filters for the prediction of wide-sense stationary processes and linear dynamical systems respectively, see [23]. While such approaches avoid the pessimism of the worst-case viewpoint, they instead tend to be fragile to the underlying modeling assumptions. In particular, an online algorithm designed to use a particular filter based on a particular stochastic model lacks the robustness to be used in settings where the underlying assumptions are not valid.

3.1 A General Prediction Model

A key contribution of this paper is the development of a model for studying predictions that provides a middle ground between the worst-case and the stochastic viewpoints. The model we propose below seeks a middle ground by not making any assumption on the underlying stochastic process or the design of the predictor, but instead making assumptions only on the form of the error of the predictor. Thus, it is agnostic to the predictor and can be used in worst-case analysis with respect to the realization of the underlying cost functions.

Further, the model captures three important features of real predictors: (i) it allows for correlations in prediction errors (both short range and long range); (ii) the quality of predictions decreases the further in the future we try to look ahead; and (iii) predictions about the future are refined as time passes.

Concretely, throughout this paper we model prediction error via the following equation:

$$y_t = y_{t|\tau} + \sum_{s=\tau+1}^{t} f(t-s)e(s). \tag{7}$$

Here, $y_{t|\tau}$ is the prediction of y_t made at time $\tau < t$. Thus, $y_t - y_{t|\tau}$ is the prediction error, and is specified by the summation in (7). In particular, the prediction error is modeled as a weighted linear combination of per-step noise terms, $e(s)$ with weights $f(t-s)$ for some deterministic impulse function f. The key assumptions of the model are that $e(s)$ are i.i.d. with mean zero and positive definite covariance R_e; and that f satisfies $f(0) = I$ and $f(t) = 0$ for $t < 0$. Note that, as the examples below illustrate, it is common for the impulse function to decay as $f(s) \sim 1/s^{\alpha}$. As we will see later, this simple model is flexible enough to capture the prediction error that arise from classical filters on time series, and it can represent all forms of stationary prediction error by using appropriate forms of f.

Some intuition for the form of the model can be obtained by expanding the summation in (7). In particular, note that for $\tau = t-1$ we have

$$y_t - y_{t|t-1} = f(0)e(t) = e(t), \tag{8}$$

which highlights why we refer to $e(t)$ as the per-step noise.

Further, expanding the summation further gives

$$y_t - y_{t|\tau} = f(0)e(t) + f(1)e(t-1) + \ldots + f(t-\tau-1)e(\tau+1). \tag{9}$$

[2]Note that this impossibility is not the result of the regret being additive and the competitive ratio being multiplicative, as [4] proves the parallel result for competitive difference, which is an additive comparison to the dynamic optimal.

Note that the first term is the one-step prediction error $y_t - y_{t|t-1}$; the first two terms make up the two-step prediction error $y_t - y_{t|t-2}$; and so on. This highlights that predictions in the model have increasing noise as one looks further ahead in time and that predictions are refined as time goes forward.

Additionally, note that the form of (9) highlights that the impulse function f captures the degree of short-term/long-term correlation in prediction errors. Specifically, the form of $f(t)$ determines how important the error t steps in the past is for the prediction. Since we assume no structural form for f, complex correlation structures are possible.

Naturally, the form of the correlation structure plays a crucial role in the performance results we prove. But, the detailed structure is not important, only its effect on the aggregate variance. Specifically, the impact of the correlation structure on performance is captured through the following two definitions, which play a prominent role in our analysis. First, for any $w > 0$, let $||f_w||^2$ be the two norm of prediction error covariance over $(w+1)$ steps of prediction, i.e.,

$$||f_w||^2 = \mathrm{tr}(\mathbb{E}[\delta y_w \delta y_w^T]) = \mathrm{tr}(R_e \sum_{s=0}^{w} f(s)^T f(s)), \tag{10}$$

where $\delta y_w^T = y_{t+w} - y_{t+w|t-1} = \sum_{s=t}^{t+w} f(t+w-s)e(s)$. The derivation of (10) is found in the proof of Theorem 5.

Second, let $F(w)$ be the two norm square of the projected cumulative prediction error covariance, i.e.,

$$F(w) = \sum_{t=0}^{w} \mathbb{E}||KK^{\dagger}\delta y_w||^2 = \mathrm{tr}(R_e \sum_{s=0}^{w}(w-s+1)f(s)^T KK^{\dagger} f(s)). \tag{11}$$

Note that $KK^{\dagger}$ is the orthogonal projector onto the range space of K. Hence it is natural that the definitions are over the induced norm of $KK^{\dagger}$ since any action chosen from the space F can only be mapped to the range space of K i.e. no algorithm, online or offline, can track the portion of y that falls in the null space of K.

Finally, unraveling the summation all the way to time zero highlights that the process y_t can be viewed as a random deviation around the predictions made at time zero, $y_{t|0} := \hat{y}_t$, which are specified externally to the model:

$$y_t = \hat{y}_t + \sum_{s=1}^{t} f(t-s)e(s). \tag{12}$$

This highlights that an instance of the online convex optimization problem can be specified via either the process y_t or via the initial predictions $\hat{y}_t$, and then the random noise from the model determines the other. We discuss this more when defining the notions of regret and competitive ratio we study in this paper in Section 3.3.

3.2 Examples

While the form of the prediction error in the model may seem mysterious, it is quite general, and includes many of the traditional models as special cases. For example, to recover the worst-case prediction model one can set, $\forall t, e(t) = 0$ and $\hat{y}_{t'}$ as unknown $\forall t' > t + w$ and then take the worst case over $\hat{y}$. Similarly, a common approach in robust control is to set $f(t) = \begin{cases} I, & t = 0; \\ 0, & t \neq 0 \end{cases}$, $|e(s)| < D, \forall s$ and then consider the worst case over e.

Additionally, strong motivation for it can be obtained by studying the predictors for common stochastic processes. In particular, the form of (7) matches the prediction error of standard Weiner filters [44] and Kalman filters [24], etc. To highlight this, we include a few brief examples below.

EXAMPLE 1 (WIENER FILTER). *Let $\{y_t\}_{t=0}^T$ be a wide-sense stationary stochastic process with $\mathbb{E}[y_t] = \hat{y}_t$, and covariance $\mathbb{E}[(y_i - \hat{y}_i)(y_j - \hat{y}_j)^T] = R_y(i-j)$, i.e., the covariance matrix $R_y > 0$ of $y = [y_1\ y_2\ \ldots y_T]^T$ is a Toeplitz matrix. The corresponding $e(s)$ in the Wiener filter for the process is called the "innovation process" and can be computed via the Wiener-Hopf technique [23]. Using the innovation process $e(s)$, the optimal causal linear prediction is*

$$y_{t|\tau} = \hat{y}_t + \sum_{s=1}^{\tau} \langle y_t, e(s)\rangle ||e(s)||^{-2} e(s),$$

and so the correlation function $f(s)$ as defined in (7) is

$$f(s) = \langle y_s, e(0)\rangle ||e(0)||^{-2} = R_y(s)R_e^{-1}, \tag{13}$$

which yields

$$||f_w||^2 = \frac{1}{R_e}\sum_{s=0}^{w} R_y(s)^2 \text{ and } F(w) = \frac{1}{R_e}\sum_{s=0}^{w}(w-s+1)R_y(s)^2.$$

EXAMPLE 2 (KALMAN FILTER). *Consider a stationary dynamical system described by the hidden state space model*

$$x'_{t+1} = Ax'_t + Bu_t, \quad y_t = Cx'_t + v_t.$$

where the $\{u_t, v_t, x_0\}$ are $m\times 1, p\times 1$, and $n\times 1$-dimensional random variables such that

$$\left\langle \begin{bmatrix} u_i \\ v_j \\ x_0 \end{bmatrix}, \begin{bmatrix} u_i \\ v_j \\ x_0 \\ 1 \end{bmatrix} \right\rangle = \begin{bmatrix} Q\delta_{ij} & S\delta_{ij} & 0 & 0 \\ S^*\delta_{ij} & R\delta_{ij} & 0 & 0 \\ 0 & 0 & \Pi_0 & 0 \end{bmatrix}.$$

The Kalman filter for this process yields the optimal causal linear estimator $y_{t|\tau} = K[y_1^T, \ldots, y_\tau^T]^T$ such that $y_{t|\tau} = \arg\min \mathbb{E}_\tau ||y_t - K'[y_1^T, \ldots, y_\tau^T]^T||^2$. When t is large and the system reaches steady state, the optimal prediction is given in the following recursive form [23]:

$$x'_{t+1|t} = Ax'_{t|t-1} + K_p e(t),\ y_{0|-1} = 0,\ e(0) = y_0,$$
$$e(t) = y_t - Cx'_{t|t-1},$$

where $K_p = (APC^* + BS)R_e^{-1}$, is the Kalman gain, and $R_e = R + CPC^*$ is the covariance of the innovation process e_t, and P solves

$$P = APA^* + CQC^* - K_p R_e K_p^*.$$

This yields the predictions

$$y_{t|\tau} = \sum_{s=1}^{\tau}\langle y_t, e(s)\rangle R_e^{-1} e(s)$$
$$= \sum_{s=1}^{\tau} CA^{t-s-1}(APC^* + BS)R_e^{-1} e(s).$$

Thus, for stationary Kalman filter, the prediction error correlation function is

$$f(s) = CA^{s-1}(APC^* + BS)R_e^{-1} = CA^{s-1}K_p, \tag{14}$$

which yields

$$||f_w||^2 = \sum_{s=0}^{w} \mathrm{tr}(R_e(CA^{s-1}K_p)^T KK^{\dagger}(CA^{s-1}K_p)) \text{ and}$$

$$F(w) = \sum_{s=0}^{w}(w-s+1)\mathrm{tr}(R_e(CA^{s-1}K_p)^T KK^{\dagger}(CA^{s-1}K_p)).$$

3.3 Performance Metrics

A key feature of the prediction model described above is that it provides a general stochastic model for prediction errors while not imposing any particular underlying stochastic process or predictor. Thus, it generalizes a variety of stochastic models while allowing worst-case analysis.

More specifically, when studying online algorithms using the prediction model above, one could either specify the instance via y_t and then use the form of (7) to give random predictions about the instance to the algorithm or, one could specify the instance using $\hat{y} := y_{t|0}$ and then let the y_t be randomly revealed using the form of (12). Note that, of the two interpretations, the second is preferable for analysis, and thus we state our theorems using it.

In particular, our setup can be interpreted as allowing an adversary to specify the instance via the initial (time 0) predictions $\hat{y}$, and then using the prediction error model to determine the instance y_t. We then take the worst-case over $\hat{y}$. This corresponds to having an adversary with a "shaky hand" or, alternatively, letting the adversary specify the instance but forcing them to also provide unbiased initial predictions.

In this context, we study the following notions of (expected) regret and (expected) competitive ratio, where the expectation is over the realization of the prediction noise e and the measures consider the worst-case specification of the instance $\hat{y}$.

DEFINITION 3. *We say an online algorithm ALG, has (expected)* ***regret*** *at most $\rho(T)$ if*

$$\sup_{\hat{y}} \mathbb{E}_e[\text{cost}(ALG) - \text{cost}(STA)] \leq \rho(T). \tag{15}$$

DEFINITION 4. *We say an online algorithm ALG is $\rho(T)$-* ***competitive*** *(in expectation) if*

$$\sup_{\hat{y}} \frac{\mathbb{E}_e[\text{cost}(ALG)]}{\mathbb{E}_e[\text{cost}(OPT)]} \leq \rho(T). \tag{16}$$

Our proofs bound the competitive ratio through an analysis of the competitive difference, which is defined as follows.

DEFINITION 5. *We say an online algorithm ALG has (expected)* ***competitive difference*** *at most $\rho(T)$ if*

$$\sup_{\hat{y}} \mathbb{E}_e\left[\text{cost}(ALG) - \text{cost}(OPT)\right] \leq \rho(T). \tag{17}$$

Note that these expectations are with respect to the prediction noise, $(e(t))_{t=1}^T$, and so cost(OPT) is also random. Note also that when cost$(OPT) \in \Omega(\rho(T))$ and ALG has competitive difference at most $\rho(T)$, then the algorithm has a constant (bounded) competitive ratio.

4. AVERAGING FIXED HORIZON CONTROL

A wide variety of algorithms have been proposed for online convex optimization problems. Given the focus of this paper on predictions, the most natural choice of an algorithm to consider is Receding Horizon Control (RHC), a.k.a., Model Predictive Control (MPC).

There is a large literature in control theory that studies RHC/MPC algorithms, e.g., [17, 33] and the references therein; and thus RHC is a popular choice for online optimization problems when predictions are available, e.g., [6, 43, 26, 11]. However, recent results have highlighted that while RHC can perform well for one-dimensional smoothed online optimization problems, it does not perform well (in the worst case) outside of the one-dimension case. Specifically, the competitive ratio of RHC with perfect lookahead w is $1+O(1/w)$ in the one-dimensional setting, but is $1+\Omega(1)$ outside of this setting, i.e., the competitive ratio does not decrease to 1 as the prediction window w increases [28].

In contrast, a promising new algorithm, Averaging Fixed Horizon Control (AFHC) proposed by [28] in the context of geographical load balancing maintains good performance in high-dimensional settings, i.e., maintains a competitive ratio of $1 + O(1/w)$[3]. Thus, in this paper, we focus on AFHC. Our results highlight that AFHC extracts the asymptotically optimal value from predictions, and so validates this choice.

As the name implies, AFHC averages the choices made by Fixed Horizon Control (FHC) algorithms. In particular, AFHC with prediction window size $(w + 1)$ averages the actions of $(w + 1)$ FHC algorithms.

ALGORITHM 1 (FIXED HORIZON CONTROL). *Let $\Omega_k = \{i : i \equiv k \mod (w+1)\} \cap [-w, T]$ for $k = 0, \ldots, w$. Then $FHC^{(k)}(w+1)$, the kth FHC algorithm is defined in the following manner. At timeslot $\tau \in \Omega_k$ (i.e., before c_τ is revealed), choose actions $x^{(k)}_{FHC,t}$ for $t = \tau, \ldots \tau + w$ as follows: If $t \leq 0$, $x^{(k)}_{FHC,t} = 0$. Otherwise, let $x_{\tau-1} = x^{(k)}_{FHC,\tau-1}$, and let $(x^{(k)}_{FHC,t})_{t=\tau}^{\tau+w}$ be the vector that solves*

$$\min_{x_\tau,\ldots,x_{\tau+w}} \sum_{t=\tau}^{\tau+w} \hat{c}_t(x_t) + \beta||(x_t - x_{t-1})||$$

where $\hat{c}_t(\cdot)$ is the prediction of the future cost $c_t(\cdot)$ for $t = \tau, \ldots, \tau + w$.

Note that in the classical OCO with $(w + 1)$-lookahead setting, $\hat{c}_t(\cdot)$ is exactly equal to the true cost $c(\cdot)$. Each FHC$^{(k)}(w+1)$ can be seen as a length $(w+1)$ fixed horizon control starting at position k. Given $(w + 1)$ versions of FHC, AFHC is defined as the following:

ALGORITHM 2 (AVERAGING FIXED HORIZON CONTROL). *At timeslot $t \in 1, ..., T$, $AFHC(w + 1)$ sets*

$$x_{AFHC,t} = \frac{1}{w+1} \sum_{k=0}^{w} x^{(k)}_{FHC,t}. \tag{18}$$

5. AVERAGE-CASE ANALYSIS

We first consider the average-case performance of AFHC (in this section), and then consider distributional analysis (in Section 6). We focus on the tracking problem in (2) for concreteness and conciseness, though our proof techniques generalize. Note that, unless otherwise specified, we use $||\cdot|| = ||\cdot||_2$.

Our main result shows that AFHC can simultaneously achieve sublinear regret and a constant competitive ratio using only a *constant-sized* prediction window in nearly all cases that it is feasible for an online algorithm to do so. This is in stark contrast with Theorem 1 for the worst-case prediction model.

THEOREM 2. *Let w be a constant. AFHC(w+1) is constant-competitive whenever $\inf_{\hat{y}} \mathbb{E}_e[OPT] = \Omega(T)$ and has sublinear regret whenever $\inf_{\hat{y}} \mathbb{E}_e[STA] \geq \alpha_1 T - o(T)$, for $\alpha_1 = 4V + 8B^2$, where*

$$V = \frac{\beta||K^\dagger||_1||f_w|| + 3\beta^2||(K^TK)^{-1}\mathbb{1}|| + F(w)/2}{w+1} \tag{19}$$

$$B = \beta||(K^T)^\dagger\mathbb{1}||. \tag{20}$$

[3] Note that this result assumes that the action set is bounded, i.e., for all feasible action x, y, there exists $D > 0$, such that $||x - y|| < D$, and that there exists $e_0 > 0$, s.t. $c_t(0) \geq e_0, \forall t$. The results we prove in this paper make neither of these assumptions.

and $||M||_1$ denotes the induced 1-norm of a matrix M

Theorem 2 imposes bounds on the expected costs of the dynamic and static optimal in order to guarantee a constant competitive ratio and sublinear regret. These bounds come about as a result of the noise in predictions. In particular, prediction noise makes it impossible for an online algorithm to achieve sublinear expected cost, and thus makes it infeasible for an online algorithm to compete with dynamic and static optimal solutions that perform too well. This is made formal in Theorems 3 and 4, which are proven in Appendix B. Recall that R_e is the covariance of an estimation error vector, $e(t)$.

THEOREM 3. *Any online algorithm ALG that chooses x_t using only (i) internal randomness independent of $e(\cdot)$ and (ii) predictions made up until time t, has expected cost $\mathbb{E}_e[\text{cost}(ALG)] \geq \alpha_2 T + o(T)$, where $\alpha_2 = \frac{1}{2}||R_e^{1/2}||^2_{KK^\dagger}$.*

THEOREM 4. *Consider an online algorithm ALG such that $\mathbb{E}_e[\text{cost}(ALG)] \in o(T)$. The actions, x_t, of ALG can be used to produce one-step predictions $y'_{t|t-1}$, such that mean square of the one-step prediction error is smaller than that for $y_{t|t-1}$, i.e., $\mathbb{E}_e||y_t - y'_{t|t-1}||^2 \leq \mathbb{E}_e||y_t - y_{t|t-1}||^2$, for all but sublinearly many t.*

Theorem 3 implies that it is impossible for any online algorithm that uses extra information (e.g., randomness) independent of the prediction noise to be constant competitive if $\mathbb{E}_e[\text{cost}(OPT)] = o(T)$ or to have sublinear regret if $\mathbb{E}_e[\text{cost}(STA)] \leq (\alpha_2 - \varepsilon)T + o(T)$, for $\varepsilon > 0$.

Further, Theorem 4 states that if an online algorithm does somehow obtain asymptotically smaller cost than possible using only randomness independent of the prediction error, then it must be using more information about future y_t than is available from the predictions. This means that the algorithm can be used to build a better predictor.

Thus, the consequence of Theorems 3 and 4 is the observation that the condition in Theorem 2 for the competitive ratio is tight and the condition in Theorem 2 for regret is tight up to a constant factor, i.e., α_1 versus α_2. (Attempting to prove matching bounds here is an interesting, but very challenging, open question.)

In the remainder of the section, we outline the analysis needed to obtain Theorem 2, which is proven by combining Theorem 5 bounding the competitive difference of AFHC and Theorem 9 bounding the regret of AFHC. The analysis exposes the importance of the correlation in prediction errors for tasks such as determining the optimal prediction window size for AFHC. Specifically, the window size that minimizes the performance bounds we derive is determined not by the quality of predictions, but rather by how quickly error correlates, i.e., by $||f_\omega||^2$.

Proof of Theorem 2

The first step in our proof of Theorem 2 is to bound the competitive difference of AFHC. This immediately yields a bound on the competitive ratio and, since it is additive, it can easily be adapted to bound regret as well.

The main result in our analysis of competitive difference is the following. This is the key both to bounding the competitive ratio and regret.

THEOREM 5. *The competitive difference of $AFHC(w+1)$ is $O(T)$ and bounded by:*

$$\sup_{\hat{y}} \mathbb{E}_e[\text{cost}(AFHC) - \text{cost}(OPT)] \leq VT \tag{21}$$

where V is given by (19)

Theorem 5 implies that the competitive ratio of $AFHC$ is bounded by a constant when $\text{cost}(OPT) \in \Omega(T)$.

The following corollary of Theorem 5 is obtained by minimizing V with respect to w.

COROLLARY 6. *For $AFHC$, the prediction window size that minimizes the bound in Theorem 5 on competitive difference is a finite constant (independent of T) if $F(T) \in \omega(T)$ and is T if there is i.i.d noise*[4].

The intuition behind this result is that if the prediction model causes noise to correlate rapidly, then a prediction for a time step too far into the future will be so noisy that it would be best to ignore it when choosing an action under AFHC. However, if the prediction model is nearly independent, then it is optimal for AFHC to look over the entire time horizon, T, since there is little risk from aggregating predictions. Importantly, notice that the quality (variance) of the predictions is not determinant, only the correlation.

Theorem 5 is proven using the following lemma (proven in the appendix) by taking expectation over noise.

LEMMA 7. *The cost of $AFHC(w+1)$ for any realization of y_t satisfies*

$$\text{cost}(AFHC) - \text{cost}(OPT) \leq$$

$$\frac{1}{w+1}\sum_{k=0}^{w}\sum_{\tau\in\Omega_k}\left(\beta||x^*_{\tau-1} - x^{(k)}_{\tau-1}||_1 + \sum_{t=\tau}^{\tau+w}\frac{1}{2}||y_t - y_{t|\tau-1}||^2_{KK^\dagger}\right).$$

Next, we use the analysis of the competitive difference in order to characterize the regret of AFHC. In particular, to bound the regret we simply need a bound on the gap between the dynamic and static optimal solutions.

LEMMA 8. *The suboptimality of the offline static optimal solution STA can be bounded below on each sample path by*

$$\text{cost}(STA) - \text{cost}(OPT)$$
$$\geq \frac{1}{2}\left(\sqrt{\sum_{t=1}^{T}||y_t - \bar{y}||^2_{KK^\dagger}} - 2B\sqrt{T}\right)^2 - 2B^2T - C$$

where $\bar{y} = \frac{\sum_{t=1}^T y_t}{T}$, $B = \beta||(K^T)^\dagger \mathbb{1}||_2$ and $C = \frac{\beta^2 \mathbb{1}^T(K^TK)^{-1}\mathbb{1}}{2T}$.

Note that the bound above is in terms of $||(y_t - \bar{y})||^2_{KK^\dagger}$, which can be interpreted as a measure of the variability y_t. Specifically, it is the projection of the variation onto the range space of K.

Combining Theorem 5 with Lemma 8 gives a bound on the regret of AFHC, proven in Appendix B.

THEOREM 9. *AHFC has sublinear expected regret if*

$$\inf_{\hat{y}} \mathbb{E}_e \sum_{t=1}^{T} ||KK^\dagger(y_t - \bar{y})||^2 \geq (8V + 16B^2)T,$$

where V and B are defined in (19) *and* (20).

Finally, we make the observation that, for all instances of y:

$$\begin{aligned}
\text{cost}(STA) &= \frac{1}{2}\sum_{t=1}^{T}||y_t - K_x||^2 + \beta||x||_1 \\
&\geq \frac{1}{2}\sum_{t=1}^{T}||(I - KK^\dagger)y_t + KK^\dagger y_t - Kx||^2 \\
&= \frac{1}{2}\sum_{t=1}^{T}||(I - KK^\dagger)y_t||^2 + \frac{1}{2}||KK^\dagger y_t - Kx||^2 \\
&\geq \frac{1}{2}||KK^\dagger(y_t - \bar{y})||^2.
\end{aligned}$$

Hence by Theorem 9, we have the condition of the Theorem.

[4]Specifically $f(0) = I, f(t) = 0 \forall t > 0$

6. CONCENTRATION BOUNDS

The previous section shows that AFHC performs well in expectation, but it is also important to understand the distribution of the cost under AFHC. In this section, we show that, with a mild additional assumption on the prediction error $e(t)$, the event when there is a large deviation from the expected performance bound proven in Theorem 5 decays exponentially fast.

The intuitive idea behind the result is the observation that the competitive difference of AFHC is a function of the uncorrelated prediction error $e(1),\dots,e(T)$ that does not put too much emphasis on any one of the random variables $e(t)$. This type of function normally has sharp concentration around its mean because the effect of each $e(t)$ tends to cancel out.

For simplicity of presentation, we state and prove the concentration result for AFHC for the one dimensional tracking cost function

$$\frac{1}{2}\sum_{t=1}^{T}(y_t - x_t)^2 + \beta|x_t - x_{t-1}|.$$

In this case, $R_e = \sigma^2$, and the correlation function $f : \mathbb{N} \to R$ is a scalar valued function. The results can all be generalized to the multidimensional setting.

Additionally, for simplicity of presentation, we assume (for this section only) that $\{e(t)\}_{t=1}^{T}$ are uniformly bounded, i.e., $\exists \epsilon > 0$, s.t. $\forall t$, $|e(t)| < \epsilon$. Note that, with additional effort, the boundedness assumption can be relaxed to the case of $e(t)$ being subgaussian, i.e., $\mathbb{E}[\exp(e(t)^2/\epsilon^2)] \le 2$, for some $\epsilon > 0$.[5]

To state the theorem formally, let VT be the upper bound of the expected competitive difference of $AFHC$ in (21). Given $\{\hat{y}_t\}_{t=1}^{T}$, the competitive difference of $AFHC$ is a random variable that is a function of the prediction error $e(t)$. The following theorem shows that the probability that the cost of $AFHC$ exceeds that of OPT by much more than the expected value VT decays rapidly.

THEOREM 10. *The probability that the competitive difference of $AFHC$ exceeds VT is exponentially small, i.e., for any $u > 0$:*

$$\begin{aligned}
&\mathbb{P}(\text{cost}(AFHC) - \text{cost}(OPT) > VT + u)\\
\le&\exp\left(\frac{-u^2}{8\epsilon^2\frac{\beta^2 T}{(w+1)\sigma^2}||f_w||^2}\right) + \exp\left(\frac{-u^2}{16\epsilon^2\lambda(2\frac{T}{w+1}F(w)+u)}\right)\\
\le&2\exp\left(\frac{-u^2}{a+bu}\right),
\end{aligned}$$

where $||f_w||^2 = (\sum_{t=0}^{w}|f(t)|^2)$, the parameter λ of concentration

$$\lambda \le \sum_{t=0}^{w}(w-t)f(t)^2 = \frac{1}{\sigma^2}F(w),$$

and $a = 8\epsilon^2[T/(w+1)]\max(\frac{\beta^2}{\sigma^2}||f_w||^2, 4\lambda F(w))$, $b = 16\epsilon^2\lambda$.

The theorem implies that the tail of the competitive difference of $AFHC$ has a Bernstein type bound. The bound decays much faster than the normal large deviation bounds obtained by bounding moments, i.e., Markov Inequality or Chebyshev Inequality. This is done by more detailed analysis of the structure of the competitive difference of $AFHC$ as a function of $e = (e(1),\dots,e(T))^T$.

Note that smaller values of a and b in Theorem 10 imply a sharper tail bound. We can see that smaller $||f_w||$ and smaller $F(w)$ implies the tail bound decays faster. Since higher prediction error correlation implies higher $||f_w||$ and $F(w)$, Theorem 10 quantifies the intuitive idea that, the performance of AFHC concentrates more tightly around its mean when the prediction error is less correlated.

Proof of Theorem 10

To prove Theorem 10, we start by decomposing the bound in Lemma 7. In particular, Lemma 7 gives

$$\text{cost}(AFHC) - \text{cost}(OPT) \le g_1 + g_2 \tag{22}$$

where

$$g_1 = \frac{1}{w+1}\sum_{k=0}^{w}\sum_{\tau\in\Omega_k}\beta|x^*_{\tau-1} - x^{(k)}_{\tau-1}|,$$

represents loss due to the switching cost, and

$$g_2 = \frac{1}{w+1}\sum_{k=0}^{w}\sum_{\tau\in\Omega_k}\sum_{t=\tau}^{\tau+w}\frac{1}{2}(y_t - y_{t|\tau-1})^2,$$

represents the loss due to the prediction error.

Let $V_1 = \frac{3\beta^2 T}{w+1} + \frac{\beta T}{w+1}||f_w||_2$, and $V_2 = \frac{T}{2(w+1)}F(w)$. Note that $VT = V_1 + V_2$. Then, by (22),

$$\begin{aligned}
&\mathbb{P}(\text{cost}(AFHC) - \text{cost}(OPT) > u + VT)\\
&\le \mathbb{P}(g_1 > u/2 + V_1 \text{ or } g_2 > u/2 + V_2)\\
&\le \mathbb{P}(g_1 > u/2 + V_1) + \mathbb{P}(g_2 > u/2 + V_2). \qquad (23)
\end{aligned}$$

Thus, it suffices to prove concentration bounds for the loss due to switching cost, g_1, and the loss due to prediction error, g_2, deviating from V_1 and V_2 respectively. This is done in the following. The idea is to first prove that g_1 and g_2 are functions of $e = (e(1),\dots,e(T))^T$ that are not "too sensitive" to any of the elements of e, and then apply the method of bounded difference [34] and Log-Sobolev inequality [27]. Combining (23) with Lemmas 11 and 15 below will complete the proof of Theorem 10.

Bounding the loss due to switching cost. This section establishes the following bound on the loss due to switching:

LEMMA 11. *The loss due to switching cost has a sub-Gaussian tail: for any $u > 0$,*

$$\mathbb{P}(g_1 > u + V_1) \le \exp\left(\frac{-u^2}{2\epsilon^2\beta^2\frac{T}{w+1}(||f_w||)^2}\right). \tag{24}$$

To prove Lemma 11, we introduce two lemmas. Firstly, we use the first order optimality condition to bound g_1 above by a linear function of $e = (e(1),\dots,e(T))^T$ using the following lemma proved in the Appendix.

LEMMA 12. *The loss due to switching cost can be bounded above by*

$$g_1 \le \frac{3\beta^2 T}{w+1} + \frac{\beta}{w+1}\sum_{k=0}^{w}\sum_{\tau\in\Omega_k}\left|\sum_{s=1\vee(\tau-w-2)}^{\tau-1} f(\tau-1-s)e(s)\right| \tag{25}$$

Let $g_1'(e)$ be the second term of g_1. Note that the only randomness in the upper bound (25) comes from g_1'.

[5]This involves more computation and worse constants in the concentration bounds. Interested readers are referred to Theorem 12 and the following remark of [9] for a way to generalize the concentration bound for the switching cost (Lemma 11), and Theorem 1.1 of [37] for a way to generalize the concentration bound for prediction error (Lemma 15).

LEMMA 13. *The expectation of $g_1'(e)$ is bounded above by*

$$\mathbb{E}_e g_1'(e) \leq \frac{\beta T}{w+1} ||f_w||_2.$$

With Lemma 13, we can reduce (24) to proving a concentration bound on $g_1'(e)$, since

$$\mathbb{P}(g_1 > u + V_1) \leq \mathbb{P}(g_1' - \mathbb{E}g_1'(e) \leq u). \quad (26)$$

To prove concentration of $g_1'(e)$, which is a function of a collection of independent random variables, we use the method of bounded difference, i.e., we bound the difference of $g_1'(e)$ where one component of e is replaced by an identically-distributed copy. Specifically, we use the following lemma, the one-sided version of one due to McDiarmid:

LEMMA 14 ([34], LEMMA 1.2). *Let $X = (X_1, \ldots, X_n)$ be independent random variables and Y be the random variable $f(X_1, \ldots, X_n)$, where function f satisfies*

$$|f(x) - f(x_k')| \leq c_k$$

whenever x and x_k' differ in the kth coordinate. Then for any $t > 0$,

$$\mathbb{P}(Y - \mathbb{E}Y > t) \leq \exp\left(\frac{-2t^2}{\sum_{k=1}^n c_k^2}\right).$$

PROOF OF LEMMA 11. Let $e = (e(1), \ldots, e(T))^T$, and $e_k' = (e(1), \ldots, e'(k), \ldots, e(T))^T$ be formed by replacing $e(k)$ with an independent and identically distributed copy $e'(k)$. Then

$$|g_1(e) - g_1(e_k')| \leq \frac{1}{w+1}\beta \sum_{m=0}^{w} |f(m)(e(k) - e'(k))|$$
$$\leq \frac{2}{w+1}\epsilon\beta \sum_{m=0}^{w} |f(m)| =: c_k.$$

Hence

$$\sum_{k=1}^{T} c_k^2 = \frac{4\epsilon^2\beta^2 T}{(w+1)^2}\left(\sum_{m=0}^{w} |f(m)|\right)^2 \leq 4\epsilon^2\beta^2 \frac{T}{(w+1)\sigma^2}||f_w||^2.$$

By Lemma 14,

$$\mathbb{P}(g_1'(e) - \mathbb{E}g_1'(e) > u) \leq \exp\left(\frac{-u^2}{2\epsilon^2\beta^2 \frac{T}{(w+1)\sigma^2}(||f_w||)^2}\right).$$

Substituting this into (26) and (24) finishes the proof. □

Bounding the loss due to prediction error. In this section we prove the following concentration result for the loss due to correlated prediction error.

LEMMA 15. *The loss due to prediction error has Berstein type tail: for any $u > 0$,*

$$\mathbb{P}(g_2 > u + V_2) \leq \exp\left(\frac{-u^2}{8\epsilon^2\lambda(\frac{T}{w+1}F(w) + u)}\right). \quad (27)$$

To prove Lemma 15, we characterize g_2 as a convex function of e in Lemma 16. We then show that this is a *self-bounding* function. Combining convexity and self-bounding property of g_2, Lemma 17 makes use of the convex Log-Sobolev inequality to prove concentration of g_2.

LEMMA 16. *The expectation of g_2 is $\mathbb{E}g_2 = V_2$, and g_2 is a convex quadratic form of e. Specifically, there exists a matrix $A \in \mathbb{R}^{T\times T}$, such that $g_2 = \frac{1}{2}||Ae||^2$. Furthermore, the spectral radius of λ of AA^T satisfies $\lambda \leq F(w)$.*

Hence, (27) is equivalent to a concentration result of g_2:

$$\mathbb{P}(g_2 > V_2 + u) = \mathbb{P}(g_2 - \mathbb{E}g_2 > u).$$

The method of bounded difference used in the previous section is not good for a quadratic function of e because the uniform bound of $|g_2(e) - g_2(e_k')|$ is too large since

$$|g_2(e) - g_2(e_k')| = \frac{1}{2}|(e - e'(k))^T A^T A(e + e'(k))|,$$

where the $(e + e'(k))$ term has T non-zero entries and a uniform upper bound of this will be in $\Omega(T)$. Instead, we use the fact that the quadratic form is self-bounding. Let $h(e) = g_2(e) - \mathbb{E}g_2(e)$. Then

$$||\nabla h(e)||^2 = ||A^T Ae||^2 = (Ae)^T(AA^T)(Ae)$$
$$\leq \lambda(Ae)^T(Ae) = 2\lambda[h(e) + \mathbb{E}V_2].$$

We now introduce the concentration bound for a self-bounding function of a collection of random variables. The proof uses the convex Log-Sobolev inequality [27].

LEMMA 17. *Let $f : \mathbb{R}^n \to \mathbb{R}$ be convex and random variable X be supported on $[-d/2, d/2]^n$. If $\mathbb{E}[f(X)] = 0$ and f satisfies the self-bounding property*

$$||\nabla f||^2 \leq af + b, \quad (28)$$

for $a, b > 0$, then the tail of $f(X)$ can be bounded as

$$\mathbb{P}\{f(X) > t\} \leq \exp\left(\frac{-t^2}{d^2(2b + at)}\right). \quad (29)$$

Now to complete the proof of Lemma 15, apply Lemma 17 to the random variable $Z = h(e)$ to obtain

$$\mathbb{P}\{g_2 - \mathbb{E}g_2 > u\} \leq \exp\left(-\frac{u^2}{8\lambda_{\max}\epsilon^2(2V_2 + u)}\right)$$

for $t > 0$, i.e.,

$$\mathbb{P}\{g_2 > u + v_2\} \leq \exp\left(-\frac{u^2}{8\lambda_{\max}\epsilon^2(2V_2 + t)}\right)$$
$$= \exp\left(\frac{-u^2}{8\epsilon^2\lambda(\frac{T}{w+1}F(w) + u)}\right).$$

7. CONCLUDING REMARKS

Making use of predictions about the future is a crucial, but under-explored, area of online algorithms. In this paper, we have introduced a general colored noise model for studying predictions. This model captures a range of important phenomena for prediction errors including, general correlation structures, prediction noise that increases with the prediction horizon, and refinement of predictions as time passes. Further it allows for worst-case analysis of online algorithms in the context of stochastic prediction errors.

To illustrate the insights that can be gained from incorporating a general model of prediction noise into online algorithms, we have focused on online optimization problems with switching costs, specifically, an online LASSO formulation. Our results highlight that a simple online algorithm, AFHC, can simultaneously achieve a constant competitive ratio and a sublinear regret in expectation in nearly any situation where it is feasible for an online algorithm to do so. Further, we show that the cost of AFHC is tightly concentrated around its mean.

We view this paper as a first step toward understanding the role of predictions in the design of online optimization algorithms and, more generally, the design of online algorithms. In particular, while we have focused on a particular, promising algorithm, AFHC, it is quite interesting to ask if it is possible to design online algorithms that outperform AFHC. We have proven that AFHC uses the asymptotically minimal amount of predictions to achieve constant competitive ratio and sublinear regret; however, the cost of other algorithms may be lower if they can use the predictions more efficiently.

In addition to studying the performance of algorithms other than AFHC, it would also be interesting to generalize the prediction model further, e.g., by considering non-stationary processes or heterogeneous $e(t)$.

8. REFERENCES

[1] M. A. Adnan, R. Sugihara, and R. K. Gupta. Energy efficient geographical load balancing via dynamic deferral of workload. In *IEEE Int. Conf. Cloud Computing (CLOUD)*, pages 188–195, 2012.

[2] H. Amur, J. Cipar, V. Gupta, G. R. Ganger, M. A. Kozuch, and K. Schwan. Robust and flexible power-proportional storage. In *Proc. ACM Symp. Cloud computing*, pages 217–228, 2010.

[3] G. Ananthanarayanan, A. Ghodsi, S. Shenker, and I. Stoica. Effective straggler mitigation: Attack of the clones. In *Proc. NSDI*, volume 13, pages 185–198, 2013.

[4] L. Andrew, S. Barman, K. Ligett, M. Lin, A. Meyerson, A. Roytman, and A. Wierman. A tale of two metrics: Simultaneous bounds on competitiveness and regret. In *Conf. on Learning Theory (COLT)*, pages 741–763, 2013.

[5] M. F. Arlitt and C. L. Williamson. Web server workload characterization: The search for invariants. In *Proc. ACM SIGMETRICS*, pages 126–137, 1996.

[6] A. Bemporad and M. Morari. Robust model predictive control: A survey. In *Robustness in identification and control*, pages 207–226. Springer, 1999.

[7] A. Blum, H. Karloff, Y. Rabani, and M. Saks. A decomposition theorem and bounds for randomized server problems. In *Proc. Symp. Found. Comp. Sci. (FOCS)*, pages 197–207, Oct 1992.

[8] A. Borodin, N. Linial, and M. E. Saks. An optimal on-line algorithm for metrical task system. *J. ACM*, 39(4):745–763, 1992.

[9] S. Boucheron, G. Lugosi, and O. Bousquet. Concentration inequalities. In *Advanced Lectures on Machine Learning*, pages 208–240. Springer, 2004.

[10] S. Boyd, M. Mueller, B. OÕDonoghue, and Y. Wang. Performance bounds and suboptimal policies for multi-period investment. *Foundations and Trends in Optimization*, 1(1):1–69, 2012.

[11] E. F. Camacho and C. B. Alba. *Model predictive control.* Springer, 2013.

[12] J. Camacho, Y. Zhang, M. Chen, and D. Chiu. Balance your bids before your bits: The economics of geographic load-balancing. *Proc. of ACM e-Energy*, 2014.

[13] E. J. Candès, Y. Plan, et al. Near-ideal model selection by $\ell 1$ minimization. *Ann. Stat.*, 37(5A):2145–2177, 2009.

[14] V. Chandrasekaran, B. Recht, P. A. Parrilo, and A. S. Willsky. The convex geometry of linear inverse problems. *Foundations of Computational Mathematics*, 12(6):805–849, 2012.

[15] M. A. Figueiredo, R. D. Nowak, and S. J. Wright. Gradient projection for sparse reconstruction: Application to compressed sensing and other inverse problems. *IEEE J. Sel. Topics Signal Processing*, 1(4):586–597, 2007.

[16] L. Gan, U. Topcu, and S. Low. Optimal decentralized protocol for electric vehicle charging. *IEEE Transactions on Power Systems*, 28(2):940–951, 2013.

[17] C. E. Garcia, D. M. Prett, and M. Morari. Model predictive control: theory and practice—a survey. *Automatica*, 25(3):335–348, 1989.

[18] D. Gmach, J. Rolia, C. Bash, Y. Chen, T. Christian, A. Shah, R. Sharma, and Z. Wang. Capacity planning and power management to exploit sustainable energy. In *Proc. IEEE Int. Conf. Network and Service Management (CNSM)*, pages 96–103, 2010.

[19] D. Gmach, J. Rolia, L. Cherkasova, and A. Kemper. Workload analysis and demand prediction of enterprise data center applications. In *Proc. IEEE Int. Symp. Workload Characterization*, IISWC '07, pages 171–180. IEEE Computer Society, 2007.

[20] E. Hazan, A. Agarwal, and S. Kale. Logarithmic regret algorithms for online convex optimization. *Machine Learning*, 69(2-3):169–192, 2007.

[21] V. Joseph and G. de Veciana. Variability aware network utility maximization. *arXiv preprint arXiv:1111.3728*, 2011.

[22] V. Joseph and G. de Veciana. Jointly optimizing multi-user rate adaptation for video transport over wireless systems: Mean-fairness-variability tradeoffs. In *Proc. IEEE INFOCOM*, pages 567–575, 2012.

[23] T. Kailath, A. H. Sayed, and B. Hassibi. *Linear estimation.* Prentice-Hall, Inc., 2000.

[24] R. E. Kalman. A new approach to linear filtering and prediction problems. *J. Fluids Engineering*, 82(1):35–45, 1960.

[25] S.-J. Kim and G. B. Giannakis. Real-time electricity pricing for demand response using online convex optimization. In *IEEE Innovative Smart Grid Tech. Conf. (ISGT)*, pages 1–5, 2014.

[26] D. Kusic, J. O. Kephart, J. E. Hanson, N. Kandasamy, and G. Jiang. Power and performance management of virtualized computing environments via lookahead control. *Cluster computing*, 12(1):1–15, 2009.

[27] M. Ledoux. Concentration of measure and logarithmic Sobolev inequalities. In *Seminaire de probabilites XXXIII*, pages 120–216. Springer, 1999.

[28] M. Lin, Z. Liu, A. Wierman, and L. L. Andrew. Online algorithms for geographical load balancing. In *Int. Green Computing Conference (IGCC)*, pages 1–10. IEEE, 2012.

[29] M. Lin, A. Wierman, L. Andrew, and E. Thereska. Dynamic right-sizing for power-proportional data centers. *IEEE/ACM Trans. Networking*, 21(5):1378–1391, Oct 2013.

[30] Z. Liu, I. Liu, S. Low, and A. Wierman. Pricing data center demand response. In *Proc. ACM Sigmetrics*, 2014.

[31] Z. Liu, A. Wierman, Y. Chen, B. Razon, and N. Chen. Data center demand response: Avoiding the coincident peak via workload shifting and local generation. *Performance Evaluation*, 70(10):770–791, 2013.

[32] L. Lu, J. Tu, C.-K. Chau, M. Chen, and X. Lin. Online energy generation scheduling for microgrids with intermittent energy sources and co-generation. In *Proc. ACM SIGMETRICS*, pages 53–66, 2013.

[33] D. Q. Mayne, J. B. Rawlings, C. V. Rao, and P. O. Scokaert. Constrained model predictive control: Stability and optimality. *Automatica*, 36(6):789–814, 2000.

[34] C. McDiarmid. On the method of bounded differences. *Surveys in combinatorics*, 141(1):148–188, 1989.

[35] B. Narayanaswamy, V. K. Garg, and T. Jayram. Online optimization for the smart (micro) grid. In *Proc. ACM Int. Conf. on Future Energy Systems*, page 19, 2012.

[36] A. Qureshi, R. Weber, H. Balakrishnan, J. Guttag, and B. Maggs. Cutting the electric bill for internet-scale systems. *ACM SIGCOMM Computer Communication Review*, 39(4):123–134, 2009.

[37] M. Rudelson and R. Vershynin. Hanson-Wright inequality and sub-Gaussian concentration. *Electron. Commun. Probab.*, 18(82):1–9, 2013.

[38] A. P. Sage and J. L. Melsa. Estimation theory with applications to communications and control. Technical report, DTIC Document, 1971.

[39] S. Sastry and M. Bodson. *Adaptive control: stability, convergence and robustness.* Courier Dover Publications, 2011.

[40] E. Thereska, A. Donnelly, and D. Narayanan. Sierra: a power-proportional, distributed storage system. *Microsoft Research, Cambridge, UK, Tech. Rep. MSR-TR-2009-153*, 2009.

[41] R. Tibshirani. Regression shrinkage and selection via the LASSO. *J. Royal Stat. Soc. Ser. B*, pages 267–288, 1996.

[42] H. Wang, J. Huang, X. Lin, and H. Mohsenian-Rad. Exploring smart grid and data center interactions for electric power load balancing. *ACM SIGMETRICS Performance Evaluation Review*, 41(3):89–94, 2014.

[43] X. Wang and M. Chen. Cluster-level feedback power control for performance optimization. In *High Performance Computer Architecture*, pages 101–110. IEEE, 2008.

[44] N. Wiener. *Extrapolation, interpolation, and smoothing of stationary time series*, volume 2. MIT press, Cambridge, MA, 1949.

[45] L. Xiao. Dual averaging methods for regularized stochastic learning and online optimization. *J. Machine Learning Research*, 11:2543–2596, 2010.

[46] F. Zanini, D. Atienza, L. Benini, and G. De Micheli. Multicore thermal management with model predictive control. In *Proc. IEEE. European Conf. Circuit Theory and Design (ECCTD)*, pages 711–714, 2009.

[47] F. Zanini, D. Atienza, G. De Micheli, and S. P. Boyd. Online convex optimization-based algorithm for thermal management of MPSoCs. In *Proc. ACM Great Lakes Symp. VLSI*, pages 203–208, 2010.

[48] X. Y. Zhou and D. Li. Continuous-time mean-variance portfolio selection: A stochastic LQ framework. *Applied Mathematics & Optimization*, 42(1):19–33, 2000.
[49] M. Zinkevich. Online convex programming and generalized infinitesimal gradient ascent. In *Proc. Int. Conf. Machine Learning (ICML)*, pages 928–936. AAAI Press, 2003.

APPENDIX

A. PROOFS FOR SECTION 3

A.1 Proof of Theorem 1

For a contradiction, assume that there exists an algorithm $\mathcal{A}'$ that achieves constant competitive ratio *and* sublinear regret with constant lookahead. We can use algorithm $\mathcal{A}'$ to obtain another online algorithm $\mathcal{A}$ that achieves constant competitive ratio *and* sublinear regret *without* lookahead. This contradicts Theorem 4 of [4], and we get the claim.

Consider an instance $\{c_1, c_2, \ldots, c_T\}$ without lookahead. We simply "pad" the input with ℓ copies of the zero function $\mathbf{0}$ if $\mathcal{A}'$ has a lookahead of ℓ. That is the input to $\mathcal{A}'$ is: $c_1, \mathbf{0}, \ldots, \mathbf{0}, c_2, \mathbf{0}, \ldots, \mathbf{0}, c_3, \mathbf{0}, \ldots$

We simulate $\mathcal{A}'$ and set the tth action of $\mathcal{A}$ equal to the $((t-1)(\ell+1)+1)$th action of $\mathcal{A}'$. Note that the optimal values of the padded instance are equal to the optimal values of the given instance. Also, by construction, $\text{cost}(\mathcal{A}) \leq \text{cost}(\mathcal{A}')$. Therefore, if $\mathcal{A}'$ achieves constant competitive ratio *and* sublinear regret then so does $\mathcal{A}$, and the claim follows.

B. PROOFS FOR SECTION 5

B.1 Proof of Theorem 3

PROOF. Let $(x_{ALG,t})_{t=1}^T$ be the solution produced by online algorithm ALG. Then

$$\begin{aligned}\text{cost}(ALG) \geq& \frac{1}{2}\sum_{t=1}^T ||y_t - Kx_{ALG,t}||^2\\ =&\frac{1}{2}\sum_{t=1}^T ||(I-KK^\dagger)y_t||^2 + ||KK^\dagger y_t - Kx_{ALG,t}||^2,\end{aligned}$$

by the identity $(I - KK^\dagger)K = 0$. Let $\epsilon_t = x_{ALG,t} - K^\dagger y_{t|t-1}$, i.e., $\epsilon_t = x_{ALG,t} - K^\dagger(y_{t|0} - \sum_{s=1}^{t-1} f(t-s)e(s))$. Since all predictions made up until t can be expressed in terms of $y_{\cdot|0}$ and $e(\tau)$ for $\tau < t$, which are independent of $e(t)$, and all other information (internal randomness) available to ALG is independent of $e(t)$ by assumption, ϵ_t is independent of $e(t)$. It follows that

$$\begin{aligned}&\mathbb{E}_e[\text{cost}(ALG)] \geq \mathbb{E}_e[||KK^\dagger y_t - K(K^\dagger y_{t|t-1} + \epsilon_t)||^2]\\ =&\frac{1}{2}\sum_{t=1}^T \mathbb{E}_{e\setminus e(t)}\mathbb{E}_{e(t)|e\setminus e(t)}||KK^\dagger e(t)^T - K\epsilon_t||^2 \qquad (30)\\ =&\frac{1}{2}\sum_{t=1}^T \mathbb{E}_{e\setminus e(t)}(||R_e^{1/2}||^2_{KK^\dagger} + ||(\mathbb{E}_{e(t)}\epsilon_t\epsilon_t^T)^{1/2}||^2_{K^TK})\\ \geq&\frac{T}{2}||R_e^{1/2}||^2_{KK^\dagger},\end{aligned}$$

where the first equality uses the identity $(I - KK^\dagger)K = 0$, and the second uses the independence of ϵ_t and $e(t)$. □

B.2 Proof of Theorem 4

By Theorem 3, if $\mathbb{E}[\text{cost}(ALG)] \in o(T)$, there must be some t such that ϵ_t is not independent of $e(t)$. By expanding the square term in (30) and noting it is nonnegative:

$$\mathbb{E}[e(t)^TK\epsilon_t] \leq \frac{1}{2}||R_e^{1/2}||^2_{KK^\dagger,F} + \frac{1}{2}||(\mathbb{E}\epsilon_t\epsilon_t^T)^{1/2}||^2_{K^TK,F}.$$

Each nonzero $\mathbb{E}[e(t)^TK\epsilon_t]$ can at most make one term in (30) zero, since there are T terms in (30) that are each lower bounded by $\frac{1}{2}||R_e^{1/2}||^2$, and by assumption $\mathbb{E}[\text{cost}(ALG)]$ is sublinear. There can be at most a sublinear number of t such that $\mathbb{E}[e(t)^TK\epsilon_t] = 0$.

For every other t, we must have $\mathbb{E}[e(t)^TK\epsilon_t] > 0$. Let $l_t = \mathbb{E}[e(t)^TK\epsilon_t] > 0$, and $a_t = ||(\mathbb{E}\epsilon_t\epsilon_t^T)^{1/2}||^2_{KK^T,F} > 0$.

Hence, at time t, the algorithm can produce prediction $y'_{t|t-1} = y_{t|t-1} + \frac{1}{w_t}K\epsilon_t$, where the coefficient w_t is chosen later. Then the one step prediction error variance:

$$\begin{aligned}\mathbb{E}||y_t - y'_{t|t-1}||^2 &= \mathbb{E}||e(t) - \frac{1}{w_t}K\epsilon_t||^2\\ &= ||R_e^{1/2}||^2_F - \frac{2}{w_t}l_t + \frac{1}{w_t^2}a_t.\end{aligned}$$

Pick any $w_t > a_t/2l_t$. Then $\mathbb{E}||y_t - y'_{t|t-1}||^2 < ||R_e^{1/2}||^2_F = \mathbb{E}||y_t - y_{t|t-1}||^2$. Hence ALG can produce better one-step prediction for all but sublinearly many t.

B.3 Proof of Lemma 7

To prove Lemma 7, we use the following Lemma.

LEMMA 18. *The competitive difference of FHC with fixed $(w+1)$-lookahead for any realization is given by*

$$\begin{aligned}\text{cost}(FHC^{(k)}) \leq& \text{cost}(OPT) + \sum_{\tau\in\Omega_k}\beta||(x^*_{\tau-1} - x^{(k)}_{\tau-1})||_1\\ &+ \frac{1}{2}\sum_{\tau\in\Omega_k}\sum_{t=\tau}^{\tau+w}||KK^\dagger(y_t - y_{t|\tau-1})||^2.\end{aligned}$$

where x_t^* is the action chosen by the dynamic offline optimal.

PROOF OF LEMMA 7. Note that $\text{cost}(FHC^{(k)})$ is convex. The result then follows with a straightforward application of Jensen's inequality to Lemma 18. By the definition of $AFHC$, we have the following inequality:

$$\text{cost}(AFHC) \leq \frac{1}{w+1}\sum_{k=0}^{w}\text{cost}(FHC^{(k)})$$

By substituting the expression for $\text{cost}(FHC^{(k)})$ into the equation above and simplifying, we get the desired result. □

Before we prove Lemma 18, we first introduce a new algorithm we term $OPEN$. This algorithm runs an open loop control over the entire time horizon, T. Specifically, it chooses actions x_t, for $t \in 1, \ldots, T$, that solves the following optimization problem:

$$\min \frac{1}{2}\sum_{t=1}^T (y_{t|0} - Kx_t)^2 + \beta||(x_t - x_{t-1})||_1$$

$FHC^{(k)}$ can be seen as starting at $x^k_{FHC,\tau-1}$, using prediction $y_{\cdot|\tau-1}$, and running $OPEN$ from τ to $\tau + w$. Then repeating with updated prediction $y_{\cdot|\tau+\omega}$. We first prove the following Lemma characterizing the performance of $OPEN$.

LEMMA 19. *Competitive difference of $OPEN$ over a time horizon, T, is given by*

$$\text{cost}(OPEN) - \text{cost}(OPT) \leq \sum_{t=1}^T \frac{1}{2}||\hat{y}_t - y_t||^2_{KK^\dagger}$$

PROOF. Recall that the specific OCO we are studying is

$$\min_x \sum_{t=1}^T \frac{1}{2}||y_t - Kx_t||^2 + \beta||(x_t - x_{t-1})||_1 \qquad (31)$$

where $x_t \in \mathbb{R}^n$, $y_t \in \mathbb{R}^m$, $K \in \mathbb{R}^{m\times n}$ and the switching cost, $\beta \in \mathbb{R}_+$.

We first derive the dual of (31) by linearizing the l_1 norm which leads to the following equivalent expression of the objective above:

$$\min_{x,z} \frac{1}{2}\sum_{t=1}^{T} ||y_t - Kx_t||^2 + \beta \mathbb{1}^T z_t$$
$$\text{s.t.} \quad z_t \geq x_t - x_{t-1}, z_t \geq x_{t-1} - x_t, \quad \forall t.$$

Hence the Lagrangian is

$$L(x,z;\bar{\lambda},\underline{\lambda}) = \frac{1}{2}\sum_{t=1}^{T} ||y_t - Kx_t||^2 + \langle \bar{\lambda}_t - \underline{\lambda}_t, x_t - x_{t-1}\rangle + \langle \beta\mathbb{1} - (\bar{\lambda}_t + \underline{\lambda}_t), z_t\rangle.$$

where we take $\lambda_{T+1} = 0$ and $x_0 = 0$.

Let $\lambda_t = \bar{\lambda}_t - \underline{\lambda}_t$ and $w_t = \bar{\lambda}_t + \underline{\lambda}_t$. Dual feasibility requires $w_t \leq \beta\mathbb{1}, \forall t$, which implies $-\beta\mathbb{1} \leq \lambda_t \leq \beta\mathbb{1}, \forall t$. Dual feasibility also requires $\langle \beta\mathbb{1} - w_t, z_t\rangle = 0, \forall t$.

Now by defining $s_t = \lambda_t - \lambda_{t+1}$ and equating the derivative with respect to x_t to zero, the primal and dual optimal x_t^*, s_t^* must satisfy $K^TKx_t^* = K^Ty_t - s_t^*$.

Note by premultiplying the equation above by x_t^{*T}, we have $\langle x_t^*, s_t^*\rangle = \langle Kx_t^*, y_t\rangle - ||Kx_t^*||^2$. If instead we premultiply the same equation by $(K^T)^\dagger$, we have after some simplification that $Kx_t^* = (KK^\dagger)y_t - (K^T)^\dagger s_t^*$. We can now simplify the expression for the optimal value of the objective by using the above two equations:

$$\text{cost}(OPT) = \sum_{t=1}^{T} \frac{1}{2}||y_t - Kx_t^*||^2 + \langle x_t^*, s_t^*\rangle$$
$$= \sum_{t=1}^{T} \frac{1}{2}||y_t||^2 - \frac{1}{2}||KK^\dagger y_t - (K^T)^\dagger s_t^*||^2 \tag{32}$$

Observe that (32) implies s_t^* minimizes the following expression $\sum_{t=1}^{T} ||KK^\dagger y_t - (K^T)^\dagger s_t^*||^2$ over the constraint set $\mathcal{S} = \{s_t | s_t = \lambda_t - \lambda_{t+1}, -\beta\mathbb{1} \leq \lambda_t \leq \beta\mathbb{1} \text{ for } 1 \leq t \leq T, \lambda_{T+1} = 0\}$.

$$\text{cost}(OPEN) - \text{cost}(OPT) = p(\hat{x}; y) - p(x; y)$$
$$= p(\hat{x}; \hat{y}) - p(x; y) + p(\hat{x}; y) - p(\hat{x}; \hat{y}_t)$$
$$= \sum_{t=1}^{T} \frac{1}{2}||\hat{y}_t||^2 - \frac{1}{2}||K\hat{x}_t||^2 - \frac{1}{2}||y_t||^2 + \frac{1}{2}||Kx_t^*||^2 + \frac{1}{2}||y_t - K\hat{x}_t||^2 - \frac{1}{2}||\hat{y}_t - K\hat{x}_t||^2$$

Expanding the quadratic terms, using the property of the pseudo-inverse that $K^\dagger KK^\dagger = K^\dagger$, and using the fact that $Kx_t^* = KK^\dagger y_t - (K^T)^\dagger s_t^*$, we have

$$\text{cost}(OPEN) - \text{cost}(OPT)$$
$$= \sum_{t=1}^{T} \frac{1}{2}\left(||KK^\dagger y_t - (K^T)^\dagger s_t^*||^2 - ||(KK^\dagger y_t - (K^T)^\dagger \hat{s}_t)||^2\right) + \frac{1}{2}\left(||\hat{y}_t - y_t||^2 - ||(I - KK^\dagger)(\hat{y}_t - y_t)||^2\right)$$
$$\leq \sum_{t=1}^{T} \frac{1}{2}||\hat{y}_t - y_t||^2 - \frac{1}{2}||(I - KK^\dagger)(\hat{y}_t - y_t)||^2$$
$$= \sum_{t=1}^{T} \frac{1}{2}||KK^\dagger(\hat{y}_t - y_t)||^2.$$

where the first inequality is because of the characterization of s_t^* following (32). □

PROOF OF LEMMA 18. The proof is a straightforward application of Lemma 19. Summing the cost of $OPEN$ for all $\tau \in \Omega_k$ and noting that the switching cost term satisfying the triangle inequality gives us the desired result. □

B.4 Proof of Theorem 5

We first define the sub-optimality of the open loop algorithm over expectation of the noise. $\mathbb{E}[||(y_t - \hat{y}_t)||^2_{KK^\dagger}]$ is the expectation of the projection of the prediction error $t+1$ time steps away onto the range space of K, given by:

$$\mathbb{E}[||(y_t - \hat{y}_t)||^2_{KK^\dagger}] = \mathbb{E}||\sum_{s=1}^{t} KK^\dagger(f(t-s)e(s))||^2$$
$$= \mathbb{E}[\sum_{s_1=1}^{t}\sum_{s_2=1}^{t} e(s_1)^T f(t-s_1)^T (KK^\dagger)^T (KK^\dagger) f(t-s_2) e(s_2)]$$
$$= \text{tr}(\sum_{s_1=1}^{t}\sum_{s_2=1}^{t} f(t-s_1)^T (KK^\dagger)(KK^\dagger) f(t-s_2) \mathbb{E}[e(s_2)e(s_1)^T])$$
$$= \sum_{s=0}^{t-1} \text{tr}(f(s)^T (KK^\dagger) f(s) R_e),$$

where the last line is because $\mathbb{E}[e(s_1)e(s_2)^T] = 0$ for all $s_1 \neq s_2$, and $KK^\dagger K = K$. Note that this implies $||f_{t-1}||^2 = \sum_{s=0}^{t-1} \text{tr}(f(s)^T f(s) R_e)$. We now write the expected suboptimality of the open loop algorithm as

$$\mathbb{E}[\text{cost}(OPEN) - \text{cost}(OPT)] \leq \sum_{t=1}^{T} \frac{1}{2}\mathbb{E}[||y_t - \hat{y}_t||^2_{KK^\dagger}]$$
$$= \frac{1}{2}\sum_{s=0}^{T-1}\sum_{t=s}^{T-1} \text{tr}(f(s)^T KK^\dagger f(s) R_e)$$
$$= \frac{1}{2}\sum_{s=0}^{T-1} (T-s)\text{tr}(f(s)^T KK^\dagger f(s) R_e) = F(T-1)$$

where the first equality is by rearranging the summation.

Now we take expectation of the expression we have in Lemma 7. Taking expectation of the second penalty term (prediction error term), we have:

$$\frac{1}{w+1}\sum_{k=0}^{w}\sum_{\tau\in\Omega_k}\sum_{t=\tau}^{\tau+w} \mathbb{E}\frac{1}{2}||(KK^\dagger)(y_t - y_{t|\tau-1})||^2$$
$$= \frac{1}{2(w+1)}\sum_{k=0}^{w}\sum_{\tau\in\Omega_k} F(w) = \frac{T}{2(w+1)}F(w)$$

We now need to bound the first penalty term (switching cost term). By taking the subgradient with respect to x_t and by optimality we have $\forall t = 1, \ldots, T$

$$0 \in K^T(Kx_t^* - y_t) + \beta\partial||(x_t^* - x_{t-1}^*)||_1 + \beta\partial||(x_{t+1}^* - x_t^*)||_1$$
$$\Rightarrow x_t^* \in [(K^TK)^{-1}(K^Ty_t - 2\beta\mathbb{1}), (K^TK)^{-1}(K^Ty_t + 2\beta\mathbb{1})]$$

where the implication is because the sub-gradient of a 1-norm function $||\cdot||_1$ is between $-\mathbb{1}$ to $\mathbb{1}$.

Similarly, since $x_{\tau-1}^{(k)}$ is the last action taken over a FHC horizon, we have that for all $\tau \in \Omega_k$,

$$x_{\tau-1}^{(k)} \in [(K^TK)^{-1}(K^Ty_{\tau-1|\tau-w-2} - \beta\mathbb{1}), (K^TK)^{-1}(K^Ty_{\tau-1|\tau-w-2} + \beta\mathbb{1})]$$

Taking expectation of one of the switching cost term and upper bounding with triangle inequality:

$$\begin{aligned}&\mathbb{E}\left|\left|(x^*_{\tau-1} - x^{(k)}_{\tau-1})\right|\right|_1 \\ \leq& ||K^\dagger||_1\mathbb{E}||y_{\tau-1} - y_{\tau-1|\tau-2-w}||_1 + 3\beta||(K^TK)^{-1}\mathbb{1}||_1 \\ \leq& ||K^\dagger||_1||f_w|| + 3\beta||(K^TK)^{-1}\mathbb{1}||_1 \end{aligned} \quad (33)$$

where the first inequality is by the definition of induced norm, the second inequality is due to concavity of the square-root function and Jensen's inequality. Summing (33) over k and τ, we have the expectation of the switching cost term. Adding the expectation of both penalty terms (loss due to prediction error and loss due to switching cost) together, we get the desired result.

B.5 Proof of Lemma 8

We first characterize cost(STA):

$$\text{cost}(STA) = \min_x \frac{1}{2}\sum_{t=1}^T ||y_t - Kx||_2^2 + \beta\mathbb{1}^Tx$$

By first order conditions, we have the optimal static solution $x = K^\dagger\bar{y} - \frac{\beta}{T}(K^TK)^{-1}\mathbb{1}$. Substituting this to cost(STA) and simplifying, we have:

$$\begin{aligned}cost(STA) =& \frac{1}{2}\sum_{t=1}^T\left(||(I-KK^\dagger)y_t||_2^2 + ||KK^\dagger(y_t-\bar{y})||_2^2\right) \\ &- \frac{\beta^2\mathbb{1}^T(K^TK)^{-1}\mathbb{1}}{2T} + \beta\mathbb{1}^TK^\dagger\bar{y}\end{aligned}$$

Let $C = \frac{\beta^2\mathbb{1}^T(K^TK)^{-1}\mathbb{1}}{2T}$. Subtracting cost$(OPT)$ in (32) from the above, we have cost(STA) − cost(OPT) equals:

$$\begin{aligned}&\frac{1}{2}\sum_{t=1}^T(||KK^\dagger(y_t-\bar{y})||_2^2 - ||KK^\dagger y_t||_2^2 + ||KK^\dagger y_t - (K^T)^\dagger s_t^*||_2^2) \\ &+ \beta\mathbb{1}^TK^\dagger\bar{y} - C \\ =& \frac{1}{2}\sum_{t=1}^T\left(||KK^\dagger(y_t-\bar{y}) - (K^T)^\dagger s_t^*||_2^2\right) + \langle K^\dagger\bar{y}, \beta\mathbb{1} - \lambda_1\rangle - C \\ \geq& \frac{1}{2}\sum_{t=1}^T\left(||KK^\dagger(y_t-\bar{y}) - (K^T)^\dagger s_t^*||_2^2\right) - C\end{aligned}$$

The first equality is by expanding the square terms and noting $s_t = \lambda_t - \lambda_{t+1}$. The last inequality is because $-\beta\mathbb{1} \leq \lambda_t \leq \beta\mathbb{1}$ and $\beta\mathbb{1}^TK^\dagger\bar{y}$ being positive by assumption that the optimal static solution is positive. Now we bound the first term of the inequality above:

$$\begin{aligned}&\frac{1}{2}\sum_{t=1}^T\left(||KK^\dagger(y_t-\bar{y}) - (K^T)^\dagger s_t^*||_2^2\right) \\ \geq& \frac{1}{2}\sum_{t=1}^T\left(||KK^\dagger(y_t-\bar{y})||^2\right) - \sum_{t=1}^T\langle KK^\dagger(y_t-\bar{y}), (K^T)^\dagger s_t^*\rangle \\ \geq& \frac{1}{2}\sum_{t=1}^T\left(||KK^\dagger(y_t-\bar{y})||^2\right) - 2\beta\sum_{t=1}^T||KK^\dagger(y_t-\bar{y})||\,||(K^T)^\dagger\mathbb{1}|| \\ \geq& \frac{1}{2}\sum_{t=1}^T\left(||KK^\dagger(y_t-\bar{y})||^2\right) - 2B\sqrt{T\sum_{t=1}^T||(KK^\dagger)(y_t-\bar{y})||^2}\end{aligned}$$

where $B = \beta||(K^T)^\dagger\mathbb{1}||_2$.

By subtracting C from the expression above and completing the sqaure, we have the desired result.

B.6 Proof of Theorem 9

Using the results of Lemma 8, taking expectation and applying Jensen's inequality, we have:

$$\begin{aligned}&\mathbb{E}_e\left[\text{cost}(STA) - \text{cost}(OPT)\right] \\ \geq& \mathbb{E}_e\left[\frac{1}{2}\sum_{t=1}^T||KK^\dagger(y_t-\bar{y})||^2 - 2B\sqrt{T\sum_{t=1}^T||(KK^\dagger)(y_t-\bar{y})||^2} - C\right] \\ \geq& \frac{1}{2}\left(\sqrt{\mathbb{E}_e\sum_{t=1}^T(||KK^\dagger(y_t-\bar{y})||^2)} - 2B\sqrt{T}\right)^2 - 2B^2T - C.\end{aligned}$$

Hence by Theorem 5, the regret of $AFHC$ is

$$\begin{aligned}&\sup_{\hat{y}}\left(\mathbb{E}_e[\text{cost}(AFHC) - \text{cost}(OPT) + \text{cost}(OPT) - \text{cost}(STA)]\right) \\ \leq& VT + 2B^2T + C - \frac{1}{2}\inf_{\hat{y}}\left(\sqrt{\mathbb{E}_e\sum_{t=1}^T||(y_t-\bar{y})||^2_{KK^\dagger}} - 2B\sqrt{T}\right)^2.\end{aligned}$$

Let $S(T) = \mathbb{E}_e\sum_{t=1}^T||y_t - \bar{y}||^2_{KK^\dagger}$. By the above, to prove $AFHC$ has sublinear regret, it is sufficient that

$$VT + 2B^2T - \frac{1}{2}\inf_{\hat{y}}(\sqrt{S(T)} - 2B\sqrt{T})^2 < g(T) \quad (34)$$

for some sublinear $g(T)$. By the hypothesis of Theorem 9, we have $\inf_{\hat{y}} S(T) \geq (8A + 16B^2)T$.
Then, $S(T) \geq (\sqrt{2VT + 4B^2T} + 2B\sqrt{T})^2$, and (34) holds since $VT + 2B^2T - \frac{1}{2}\inf_{\hat{y}}(\sqrt{S(T)} - 2B\sqrt{T})^2 \leq VT + 2B^2T - \frac{1}{2}\left(\sqrt{2VT + 4B^2T}\right)^2 = 0$.

C. PROOFS FOR SECTION 6

C.1 Proof of Lemma 12

By the triangle inequality, we have

$$\begin{aligned}g_1 =& \frac{1}{w+1}\sum_{k=0}^w\sum_{\tau\in\Omega_k}\beta|x^*_{\tau-1} - x^{(k)}_{\tau-1}| \\ \leq& \frac{1}{w+1}\sum_{k=0}^w\sum_{\tau\in\Omega_k}\beta\Big(|x^*_{\tau-1} - y_{\tau-1}| + |y_{\tau-1} - y_{\tau-1|\tau-w-2}| \\ &+ |y_{\tau-1|\tau-w-2} - x^{(k)}_{\tau-1}|\Big).\end{aligned}$$

By first order optimality condition, we have $x^*_{\tau-1} \in \{y_{\tau-1} - 2\beta, y_{\tau-1} + 2\beta\}$, and $x^{(k)}_{\tau-1} \in \{y_{\tau-1|\tau-w-2} - \beta, y_{\tau-1|\tau-w-2} + \beta\}$. Hence, by the prediction model,

$$g_1 \leq \frac{3\beta^2T}{w+1} + \frac{\beta}{w+1}\sum_{k=0}^w\sum_{\tau\in\Omega_k}\left|\sum_{s=1\vee(\tau-w-2)}^{\tau-1}f(\tau-1-s)e(s)\right|$$

C.2 Proof of Lemma 13

Note that by Lemma 12, we have

$$\begin{aligned}\mathbb{E}g_1'(e) \leq& \frac{\beta}{w+1}\sum_{k=0}^w\sum_{\tau\in\Omega_k}\mathbb{E}\left|\sum_{s=1\vee(\tau-w-2)}^{\tau-1}f(\tau-1-s)e(s)\right| \\ \leq& \frac{\beta}{w+1}\sum_{k=0}^w\sum_{\tau\in\Omega_k}\sqrt{\sigma^2\sum_{s=0}^w f^2(s)} = \frac{\beta T}{w+1}||f_w||^2.\end{aligned}$$

where the second inequality is by Jensen's inequality and taking expectation.

C.3 Proof of Lemma 16

By definition of g_2 and unraveling the prediction model, we have

$$g_2 = \frac{1}{w+1}\sum_{k=0}^{w}\sum_{\tau\in\Omega_k}\sum_{t=\tau}^{\tau+w}\frac{1}{2}(y_t - y_{t|\tau-1})^2$$
$$= \frac{1}{w+1}\sum_{k=0}^{w}\sum_{\tau\in\Omega_k}\sum_{t=\tau}^{\tau+w}\frac{1}{2}(\sum_{s=\tau}^{t} f(t-s)e(s))^2.$$

Writing it in matrix form, it is not hard to see that

$$g_2 = \frac{1}{w+1}\sum_{k=0}^{w}\frac{1}{2}||A_k e||^2,$$

where A_k has the block diagonal structure given by

$$A_k = \text{diag}(A_k^1, A_k^2, \ldots, A_k^2, A_k^3),^6 \tag{35}$$

and there are the types of submatrices in A_k given by, for $i = 1, 2, 3$:

$$A_k^i = \begin{pmatrix} f(0) & 0 & \cdots & 0 \\ f(1) & f(0) & \cdots & 0 \\ \vdots & \vdots & \ddots & \vdots \\ f(v_i) & f(v_{i-1}) & \cdots & f(0) \end{pmatrix},$$

where $v_1 = k-2$ if $k \geq 2$ and $v_1 = k+w-1$ otherwise. $v_2 = w$, $v_3 = (T-k+1) \mod (w+1)$. Note that in fact, the matrix A_k^2 is the same for all k. Hence, we have

$$g_2 = \frac{1}{2}e^T(\frac{1}{w+1}\sum_{k=0}^{w}A_k^T A_k)e = \frac{1}{2}||Ae||^2,$$

where we define A to be such that $A^T A = \frac{1}{w+1}\sum_{k=0}^{w}A_k^T A_k$, this can be done because the right-hand side is positive semidefinite, since A_k is lower triangular. The last equality is because all A_l^2 has the same structure. Let λ be the maximum eigenvalue of AA^T, which can be expressed by

$$\lambda = \max_{||x||=1} x^T AA^T x$$
$$= \frac{1}{w+1}\max_{||x||=1}\sum_{k=0}^{w}x^T A_k A_k^T x \leq \frac{1}{w+1}\sum_{k=0}^{w}\lambda_k,$$

where λ_k is the maximum eigenvalue of $A_k A_k^T$. Note that A_k has a block diagonal structure, hence $A_k A_k^T$ also has block diagonal structure, and if we divide the vector $x = (x_1, x_2, \ldots, x_m)$ into sub-vectors of appropriate dimension, then by the block diagonal nature of $A_k A_k^T$, we have

$$x^T A_k A_k^T x = x_1^T A_k^1 {A_k^1}^T x_1 + x_2^T A_k^2 {A_k^2}^T x_2 + \ldots + x_{m-1}^T A_k^2 {A_k^2}^T x_{m-1} + x_m^T A_k^3 {A_k^3}^T x_m.$$

Hence, if we denote the maximum eigenvalues of λ_k^i as the maximum eigenvalue of the matrix $A_k^i {A_k^i}^T$, then we have

$$\lambda_k = \max_x \frac{x^T A_k A_k^T x}{x^T x}$$
$$= \max_{x_1,\ldots,x_m}\frac{x_1^T A_k^1 {A_k^1}^T x_1 + x_2^T A_k^2 {A_k^2}^T x_2 + \ldots + x_m^T A_k^3 {A_k^3}^T x_m}{x_1^T x_1 + \ldots + x_m^T x_m}$$
$$\leq \max_{x_1,\ldots,x_m}\frac{\max(\lambda_k^1, \lambda_k^2, \lambda_k^3)\cdot(x_1^T x_1 + \ldots + x_m^T x_m)}{x_1^T x_1 + \ldots + x_m^T x_m}$$
$$\leq \max(\lambda_k^1, \lambda_k^2, \lambda_k^3),$$

where λ_k^i is the maximum eigenvalue of A_k^i for $i \in \{1, 2, 3\}$. As $A_k^i {A_k^i}^T$ are all positive semidefinite, we can bound the maximum eigenvalue by trace, and note that A_k^1 and A_k^3 are submatrix of A_k^2, we have

$$\lambda_k \leq \max(\lambda_k^1, \lambda_k^2, \lambda_k^3) \leq \text{tr}(A_k^2 {A_k^2}^T) = \frac{1}{\sigma^2}F(w).$$

[6] The submatrix A_k^2 is repeated $\left\lfloor \frac{T-k+1}{\omega+1} \right\rfloor$ times in A_k for $k \geq 2$, and $\left\lfloor \frac{T-k-\omega}{\omega+1} \right\rfloor$ times for otherwise.

C.4 Proof of Lemma 17

To prove the lemma, we use the following variant of Log-Sobolev inequality

LEMMA 20 (THEOREM 3.2, [27]). *Let $f : \mathbb{R}^n \to \mathbb{R}$ be convex, and random variable X be supported on $[-d/2, d/2]^n$, then*

$$\mathbb{E}[\exp(f(X))f(X)] - \mathbb{E}[\exp(f(X))]\log\mathbb{E}[\exp(f(X))]$$
$$\leq \frac{d^2}{2}\mathbb{E}[\exp(f(X))||\nabla f(X)||^2].$$

We will use Lemma 20 to prove Lemma 17. Denote the moment generating function of $f(X)$ by

$$m(\theta) := \mathbb{E}e^{\theta f(X)}, \qquad \theta > 0.$$

The function $\theta f : \mathbb{R}^n \to \mathbb{R}$ is convex, and therefore it follows from Lemma 20 that

$$\mathbb{E}\left[e^{\theta f}\theta f\right] - \mathbb{E}\left[e^{\theta f}\right]\ln\mathbb{E}\left[e^{\theta f}\right] \leq \frac{d^2}{2}\mathbb{E}\left[e^{\theta f}||\theta\nabla f||^2\right],$$
$$\theta m'(\theta) - m(\theta)\ln m(\theta) \leq \frac{1}{2}\theta^2 d^2\mathbb{E}[e^{\theta f}||\nabla f||^2].$$

By to the self-bounding property (28),

$$\theta m'(\theta) - m(\theta)\ln m(\theta) \leq \frac{1}{2}\theta^2 d^2\mathbb{E}[e^{\theta f(X)}(af(X)+b)]$$
$$= \frac{1}{2}\theta^2 d^2\left[am'(\theta) + bm(\theta)\right].$$

Since $m(\theta) > 0$, dividing by $\theta^2 m(\theta)$ gives

$$\frac{d}{d\theta}\left[\left(\frac{1}{\theta} - \frac{ad^2}{2}\right)\ln m(\theta)\right] \leq \frac{bd^2}{2}. \tag{36}$$

Since $m(0) = 1$ and $m'(0) = \mathbb{E}f(X) = 0$, we have

$$\lim_{\theta\to 0^+}\left(\frac{1}{\theta} - \frac{ad^2}{2}\right)\ln m(\theta) = 0,$$

and therefore integrating both sides of (36) from 0 to s gives

$$\left(\frac{1}{s} - \frac{ad^2}{2}\right)\ln m(s) \leq \frac{1}{2}bd^2 s, \tag{37}$$

for $s \geq 0$. We can bound the tail probability $\mathbb{P}\{f > t\}$ with the control (37) over the moment generating function $m(s)$. In particular,

$$\mathbb{P}\{f(X) > t\} = \mathbb{P}\left\{e^{sf(X)} > e^{st}\right\} \leq e^{-st}\mathbb{E}\left[e^{sf(X)}\right]$$
$$= \exp[-st + \ln m(s)]$$
$$\leq \exp\left[-st + \frac{bd^2 s^2}{2 - asd^2}\right],$$

for $s \in [0, 2/(ad^2)]$. Choose $s = t/(bd^2 + ad^2 t/2)$ to get

$$\mathbb{P}\{f(X) > t\} \leq \exp\left(\frac{-t^2}{d^2(2b + at)}\right).$$

Reliable Multiple-choice Iterative Algorithm for Crowdsourcing Systems

Donghyeon Lee
Seoul National University
Seoul, Korea
donghyeon@snu.ac.kr

Joonyoung Kim
Seoul National University
Seoul, Korea
kimjymcl@snu.ac.kr

Hyunmin Lee
Seoul National University
Seoul, Korea
kakamin0@snu.ac.kr

Kyomin Jung
Seoul National University
Seoul, Korea
kjung@snu.ac.kr

ABSTRACT

The appearance of web-based crowdsourcing systems gives a promising solution to exploiting the wisdom of crowds efficiently in a short time with a relatively low budget. Despite their efficiency, crowdsourcing systems have an inherent problem in that responses from workers can be unreliable since workers are low-paid and have low responsibility. Although simple majority voting can be a solution, various research studies have sought to aggregate noisy responses to obtain greater reliability in results through effective techniques such as Expectation-Maximization (EM) based algorithms. While EM-based algorithms get the limelight in crowdsourcing systems due to their useful inference techniques, Karger et al. [8, 9] made a significant breakthrough by proposing a novel iterative algorithm based on the idea of low-rank matrix approximations and the message passing technique. They showed that the performance of their iterative algorithm is order-optimal, which outperforms majority voting and EM-based algorithms. However, their algorithm is not always applicable in practice since it can only be applied to binary-choice questions. Recently, they devised an inference algorithm for multi-class labeling [10], which splits each task into a bunch of binary-choice questions and exploits their existing algorithm. However, it has difficulty in combining into real crowdsourcing systems since it over-exploits redundancy in that each split question should be queried in multiple times to obtain reliable results.

In this paper, we design an iterative algorithm to infer true answers for multiple-choice questions, which can be directly applied to real crowdsourcing systems. Our algorithm can also be applicable to short-answer questions as well. We analyze the performance of our algorithm, and prove that the error bound decays exponentially. Through extensive experiments, we verify that our algorithm outperforms majority voting and EM-based algorithm in accuracy.

SIGMETRICS'15, June 15–19, 2015, Portland, OR, USA.

http://dx.doi.org/10.1145/2745844.2745871.

Categories and Subject Descriptors

G.3 [**Probability and Statistics**]: Statistical Computing; F.2 [**Analysis of Algorithms and Problem Complexity**]: Miscellaneous

General Terms

Algorithms, Performance

Keywords

Crowdsourcing; Resource Allocation; Multiple-choice; Iterative Learning

1. INTRODUCTION

Crowdsourcing has become one of the cornerstones of research in the development of human computation-based intelligence systems. New web-based services such as Amazon Mechanical Turk have arisen and become popular, as they can provide ideal solutions, gathering enormous responses from widespread crowds in a short time with a relatively low budget [13, 14]. For example, ImageNet, a large-scale image database, was a successful project that exploited the idea of crowdsourcing to label 3.2 million images hierarchically [3].

Despite the innovative framework of crowdsourcing systems, responses from workers can be unreliable [7, 12, 17, 18], since workers hired by crowdsourcing systems are low-paid and have low responsibility. Therefore, extensive works have been proceeded to find reliable solutions that infer the true answers from noisy responses. One natural method for aggregating responses is majority voting. But due to its simplicity, Expectation-Maximization (EM)-based algorithms have become popular. Since EM-based algorithms can deal with inference problems with latent variables and unknown model parameters, researchers applied the EM algorithm to proper graphical models for crowdsourcing systems, and showed that their results generally outperform those of majority voting [16, 20, 21]. Recently, Karger et al. [8, 9] made a significant breakthrough by proposing a novel iterative algorithm based on the idea of low-rank matrix approximations and the message passing technique. They showed that the performance of their iterative algorithm is order-optimal, which outperforms majority voting and EM-based algorithms.

Major research studies in this field have concentrated on cases with binary answers, yes (+1) or no (-1) [9, 21]. One example of such a binary case would be when workers have to determine whether a given image is suitable for children. However, real crowdsourced data posted on Amazon Mechanical Turk usually consists of multiple-choice questions and short-answer questions, so more general inference techniques should be employed.

In this paper, we focus on a more general structure for crowdsourcing systems that can be applied to multiple-choice questions. Note that we consider multiple-choice questions in which all choices are independent from each other. Independent multiple choices differ from linearly ordered choices which are commonly used in rating systems. For example, classifying types of cancers in patients is appropriate for an independent multiple-choice case, whereas determining the stage of a specific cancer of a patient is adequate for a linearly ordered choices case. We are currently focusing on the former case, which has greater applicability in D-ary classification problems. Moreover, we do not make a restriction on variation in the number of choices for each multiple-choice question. In addition, we suggest a method to transform short-answer questions into several multiple-choice questions so that our algorithm can be applied.

Our algorithm iteratively computes relative reliability of each worker in a novel way, where relative reliability is exploited as a weight of the worker's responses. Our algorithm also gets reliable results rapidly with small error compared to majority voting or EM-based algorithms. One of our main contributions is the performance guarantee of our algorithm by proving that the error bound of our algorithm decays exponentially. An interesting aspect of the error bound is its dependency on the negative entropy of workers in a perspective on information theory. Naturally, it is reasonable to assume that the true answers can be revealed by how much information there is in the workers' responses. We verify the performance of our algorithm through numerical experiments on various cases, which is close to that of oracle estimator. We also verify that our algorithm can infer relative reliability of workers almost correctly by experiments

Moreover, we addressed a strategy to gain responses with greater reliability from diligent workers in an adaptive manner. In this strategy, some pilot tasks chosen from whole tasks can be exploited to assess the expertise of the crowds. Note that we consider pilot tasks that differ from golden standard units. The relative reliability of workers can be estimated through given pilot tasks by applying our algorithm. In other words, we can initially assess workers' reliability with a small number of tasks, even if their true answers are unknown. Since the relative reliability of workers are estimated by managing the number of tasks each worker is given, we can expect to get responses with greater reliability for the same budget in an efficient way. Since our algorithm generally converges rapidly, our work can be combined to the context of online learning, which is more realistic setting for crowdsourcing systems.

The paper is organized as follows: We discuss related work in Section 1.1. In Section 2, we make a setup, and we describe our algorithm to infer the true answers for multiple-choice questions in Section 3. Then, we look into some applications in Section 4 and provide performance guarantees for our algorithm in Section 5. In Section 6, we present comparative results through numerical experiments, and we draw conclusions in Section 7.

1.1 Related Work

A common, intuitive strategy for aggregating responses is majority voting, which is widely used in real life due to its simplicity. However, in crowdsourcing systems, this simple inference technique has several limitations, since it assumes all workers have an equal level of expertise, and it gives the same weight to all responses. In general, there are unreliable workers such as novices or free money collectors, and even adversarial workers can be shown, so majority voting has obvious weak points when workers are unreliable [17].

There have been various approaches to trying to improve the reliability of results from unreliable responses. Two key ideas are introducing latent variables and estimating results by an iterative algorithm known as the EM algorithm. Dawid and Skene [2] exploited these ideas when they developed a simple probabilistic model using confusion matrices for each labeler as latent variables. They proposed an iterative algorithm based on EM to infer ground truth from unreliable responses.

Since the EM algorithm has an effective procedure to evaluate missing or hidden data and performs quite well, this model has been generalized and extended by several researchers. The GLAD model [21] combines the implicit characteristics of tasks and workers. Responses from workers are determined by several factors, such as the difficulty of the task, the expertise of the labeler, and the true label. The EM-based model can operate flexibly on various cases by introducing extra latent variables, which can be represented as the natural properties of tasks and workers [20]. Another variant proposed by Raykar et al. [16] considers a proper classifier for crowdsourcing systems, and aims to learn the classifier and the ground truth together.

Despite its popularity, there are some arguments in existing EM algorithms. The main thing is lack of intensive analysis about performance guarantees since their performance is only empirically evaluated in most cases. Another point is that inference techniques based on EM algorithms are not scalable. If the data size increases, EM-based algorithms become inefficient and degenerate, because their time and space requirements grow exponentially. Moreover, designing model-based EM algorithms with greater complexity leads to the introduction of an increased number of latent variables and model parameters. Apart from the computational complexity problem, the performance of EM-based algorithms could degenerate due to the initialization problem, even though it is designed to be a more complex model. Alternative approaches have been suggested by Karger et al. [8] in the context of spectral methods that use low-rank matrix approximations. They treated the data matrix A which involves workers' responses perturbed by a random noise. The true answers can be approximated by a rank-1 matrix, of which the singular vector reflects the correct answer of the tasks. When the spectral radius of the signal matrix outweighs the spectral radius of the random noise matrix, the correct answers can be extracted by the singular vector of the data matrix A. Using the power iteration method, the top singular vector can be obtained more efficiently compared to the computation complexity of EM-based algorithms.

They also proposed a novel iterative learning algorithm [9] that learns the likelihood of candidate answers and the reliability of workers. It is inspired by the standard *Belief Propagation* (BP) algorithm, which approximates the maximal marginal distribution of variables. This message passing algorithm achieves almost the same results as the previous spectral method, but they provide novel analysis techniques such as *Density Evolution* in coding theory to improve the error bound more tightly, which decays exponentially. Although they did not assume any prior knowledge, Liu et al. [15] shows that choosing a suitable prior can improve the performance via a Bayesian approach.

Recently, Karger et al. [10] focused on multi-class labeling based on their existing novel algorithms, but their strategy for multi-class labeling is well suited to the linearly ordered choices, not independent multiple choices. By converting each multiple-choice question into a bunch of binary-choice questions, they could exploit the existing algorithms to determine true answers of multiple-choice questions. Although this strategy can be extended to independent multiple choices, it overexploits redundancy since each task should be split and queried in multiple times to obtain reliable results. Furthermore, in real crowdsourcing systems, it is natural that workers solve intact multiple-choice questions rather than split binary-choice questions. Therefore it has difficulty in combining into real crowdsourcing systems.

On top of the problem inferring the true answers, proper adaptive strategies are developed to utilize reliable workers when they are reusable. [4, 5, 6, 22] showed that the performance can be significantly improved through exploration/exploitation approaches.

2. SETUP

In this section, we define some variables and notations for problem formulation. Consider a set of m tasks, each of which can be a multiple-choice question that only has one correct answer. The number of choices for task i is denoted D_i. All tasks are distributed to several workers through a proper task allocation strategy.

Suppose that n workers participate to perform m tasks. We consider a probabilistic model to generate responses when workers face tasks. We assume that a worker j is parameterized by a latent variable $p_j \in [0,1]$, which represents the probability of getting a correct answer. In other words, each worker gives the correct answer with a probability p_j and the wrong answer with probability $1-p_j$ in the decision-making process. When a worker gives a wrong answer, we can assume that the worker has chosen one of distractors uniformly at random, so the probability of each wrong choice is $\frac{1-p_j}{D_i-1}$. It is reasonable that this latent variable p_j refers to the reliability of the worker, since it captures the ability or diligence of the worker.

In the response process, when a worker j solves an assigned task i, we define the submitted response $\vec{A}^{ij}$ in vector form. The response is represented as a D_i-dimensional binary unit vector $\vec{A}^{ij}$, having 1-of-D_i representation in which the element indicating the chosen answer is equal to 1 and all other elements are equal to 0. The values of A_d^{ij} therefore satisfy $A_d^{ij} \in \{0,1\}$ and $\sum_d A_d^{ij} = 1$ where A_d^{ij} is the dth component of the response $\vec{A}^{ij}$. For example, when there are three choices, the possible answer forms are $(1,0,0)$, $(0,1,0)$, and $(0,0,1)$. Our goal is to determine the correct answer for each task by querying and aggregating all the responses from the workers.

3. ALGORITHM

In this section, we propose our multiple-iterative algorithm with a minimum number of assignments. In advance, using random regular bipartite graph-generating model, we emulate a real crowdsourcing system scenario. Then, the message update rules of our iterative algorithm are explained. In addition, we propose the generalized iterative algorithm for general setting such as a adaptive strategy.

3.1 Task Allocation

To design a graph model for a crowdsourcing system, we use a bipartite graph which consists of two types of node sets. m tasks are defined as the set of nodes $[m]$ at the left side of the graph, and n workers are defined as the set of nodes $[n]$ at the right side respectively. Each edge represents an assignment between a task and a worker and this is determined according to the task assignment method. For simplicity, the ith task and the jth worker are denoted as i and j respectively. Given a bipartite graph $G = \{[m] \cup [n], E\}$ representing the allocation graph between tasks and workers, we connect the edge (i,j) if task i is assigned to worker j. We decide the task node degree l in proportion to the resources we can spend. In addition, the worker node degree r is determined by the work capacity that an individual worker can manage. Since we recruit workers through open-call, the (l,r) regular bipartite graph is adequate for our setting. To generate a (l,r) random regular bipartite graph such that $ml = nr$, we bring a simple random construction model known as the *pairing model*(This is also called a configuration model in [9]). In fact, any arbitrary bipartite graph instance can be used for task allocation. However, we will use the *pairing model* which generates a random bipartite graph with a local tree-like property. Using this property, we prove the tight error bounds of our algorithm in Section 5.3.

3.2 Multiple Iterative Algorithm

In this section, we describe the basic operations of our algorithm and the process of inferring true answers. For each edge (i,j), the response is denoted as $\vec{A}^{ij} \in U = \{\vec{e}_u | u \in [1:D_i]\}$ which consists of D dimensional binary unit vectors all of whose components are 0 or 1. To extract the true answers from the unreliable responses of workers, we propose an iterative algorithm for multiple-choice questions.

Our algorithm generates two types of messages between task nodes and worker nodes. The first type is the task message $\vec{x}_{i\to j}$, which is denoted as a D_i dimensional vector. Each component of this vector corresponds to the likelihood meaning the possibility being a true answer. The second type is a worker message $y_{j\to i}$ which specifies the reliable worker j. Since these worker messages are strongly correlated with the reliability p_j, our algorithm can assess relative reliability. Hence, we will empirically verify the correlation between $\{y_{j\to i}\}$ and $\{p_j\}$ in section 6. The initial messages of our iterative algorithm are sampled independently from the *Gaussian* distribution with unit mean and variance, i.e., $y_{j\to i}^{(0)} \sim \mathcal{N}(1,1)$. Unlike EM-based algorithms [2, 21], our approach is not sensitive to initial conditions as long as the consensus of the group of workers is positively biased. Now, we define the adjacent set of task i as ∂i and similarly the adjacent set of worker j is defined as ∂j. Then, at the kth it-

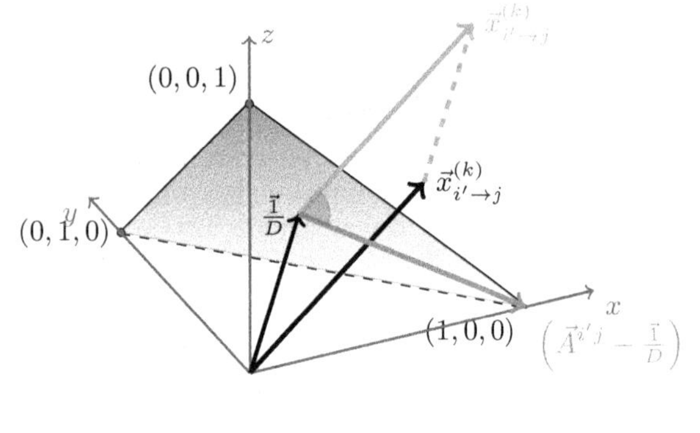

Figure 1: Description of a task message $\vec{x}^{(k)}_{i'\to j}$ and a response vector $\vec{A}^{i'j}$, in the message vector space when $\vec{A}^{i'j} = (1, 0, 0)$ and $D_{i'} = 3$.

eration, both messages are updated using the following rules:

$$\vec{x}^{(k)}_{i\to j} = \sum_{j'\in\partial i\backslash j} \vec{A}^{ij'} y^{(k-1)}_{j'\to i}, \qquad \forall(i,j) \in E \quad (1)$$

$$y^{(k)}_{j\to i} = \sum_{i'\in\partial j\backslash i} \left(\vec{A}^{i'j} - \frac{\vec{1}}{D}\right) \cdot \vec{x}^{(k-1)}_{i'\to j}, \qquad \forall(i,j) \in E \quad (2)$$

At the task message update process shown in (1), our algorithm gives weight to the answer according to the reliability of a worker. At the worker message update process shown in (2), it gives greater reliability to a worker who strongly follows consensus of other workers.

Figure 1 describes two vectors in the message vector space. As shown above, $(\vec{A}^{i'j} - \frac{\vec{1}}{D})$ represents the difference between response of worker j for task i' and the random answer $\frac{\vec{1}}{D}$. Also, $\vec{x}^{(k-1)}_{i'\to j}$ means the weighted sum of responses of other workers who have solved the task i'. Thus, the inner product of these two vectors in (2) can assess the similarity between the response of worker j for the task i' and sum of those of other workers who have solved the task i'. A larger positive similarity value of the two vectors means that worker j is more reliable. Meanwhile, the negative value specifies that the worker j does not follow the consensus of other workers and our algorithm regards the worker j as unreliable. Specially, when $\vec{x}^{(k-1)}_{i'\to j}$ and $(\vec{A}^{i'j} - \frac{\vec{1}}{D})$ are orthogonal for fixed task i', the inner product of two vector is close to zero. This means that $\vec{x}^{(k-1)}_{i'\to j}$ does not contribute to the message of the worker j. Then, $y^{(k)}_{j\to i}$ is defined as the sum of the inner product from each task message except for that of task i, representing the relative reliability of the worker j. Returning to (1), $\vec{x}^{(k)}_{i\to j}$ is determined by the weighted voting of workers who have solved task i, except for the message from the worker j. The worker j' contributes to the response $\vec{A}^{ij'}$ as much as the weight value $y^{(k-1)}_{j'\to i}$. Thus, $\vec{x}^{(k)}_{i\to j}$ is defined as the sum of $\vec{A}^{ij'} y^{(k-1)}_{j'\to i}$ which represents the estimated true answer for the task i. The following describes the pseudo code of our algorithm.

The maximum number of iterations k_{max} is analyzed in section 5.2. In practice, a dozen of iterations is sufficient for the convergence of our algorithm. After k_{max} iterations, our algorithm makes the final estimate vector $\vec{x}_i$ of a task i,

Algorithm 1 Multiple Iterative Algorithm

```
Input: E, {A^{ij}}_{(i,j)∈E}, k_max
Output: Estimation ∀i ∈ [m], t̂_i ∈ {e_{u_i} | u_i ∈ [1 : D]}
For ∀(i,j) ∈ E do
    Initialize y^{(0)}_{j→i} with random Z_ij ~ N(1,1);
For k = 1,2...,k_max do
    For ∀(i,j) ∈ E do x^{(k)}_{i→j} ← Σ_{j'∈∂i\j} A^{ij'} y^{(k-1)}_{j'→i};
    For ∀(i,j) ∈ E do y^{(k)}_{j→i} ← Σ_{i'∈∂j\i} (A^{i'j} − 1/D) · x^{(k-1)}_{i'→j};
For ∀j ∈ [n] do y_j ← Σ_{i∈∂j} (A^{ij} − 1/D) · x^{(k_max−1)}_{i→j};
For ∀i ∈ [m] do x_i ← Σ_{j∈∂i} A^{ij} y^{(k_max−1)}_{j→i};
Estimate vector t̂_i = e_{u_i}   where u_i = arg max_d(x_i)
```

and each component of the vector represents the possibility of being the true answer. Our algorithm infers the true answer by choosing u_i that has the maximum component among final likelihoods of $\vec{x}_i$. Then, our algorithm outputs the estimate of the true answer denoted as a unit vector, $\vec{e}_{u_i}$.

3.3 Task Allocation for General Setting

In the previous section, we proposed our iterative algorithm for a bipartite graph according to the *pairing model*. However, the number of workers allocated to each task can differ in cases that are more general. That must bring about the variation of the number of tasks that each worker solves. Hence, we consider a general bipartite graph with various node degrees. To apply our algorithm in this scenario, the update rules of both messages should be slightly changed in terms of the task node degree l_i and the worker node degree r_j. For a task message $\vec{x}^{(k)}_{i\to j}$, we divide each message value by the task node degree $(l_i - 1)$ so that tasks with different degrees receive the similar effect from worker nodes. In other words, dividing by $(l_i - 1)$ equalizes the task message values. Likewise, a worker message $y^{(k)}_{j\to i}$ is divided by the worker node degree $(r_j - 1)$ for general setting.

In addition to the generalization of the degree profile, we consider the various number of choices for each task (For example $\forall i \in [m]$, $D_i \in \{2, 3, 4\}$). In practice, the number of choice for each task can differ from one another and our Algorithm 2 can cope with this variation. The following describes the pseudo code of our generalized algorithm.

Algorithm 2 Generalized Multiple Iterative Algorithm

```
Input: E, {A^{ij}}_{(i,j)∈E}, k_max
Output: Estimation ∀i ∈ [m], t̂_i ∈ {e_{u_i} | u_i ∈ [1 : D_i]}
For ∀(i,j) ∈ E do
    Initialize y^{(0)}_{j→i} with random Z_ij ~ N(1,1);
For k = 1,2...,k_max do
    For ∀(i,j) ∈ E do x^{(k)}_{i→j} ← Σ_{j'∈∂i\j} (1/(l_i−1)) A^{ij'} y^{(k-1)}_{j'→i};
    For ∀(i,j) ∈ E do
        y^{(k)}_{j→i} ← Σ_{i'∈∂j\i} (1/(r_j−1)) (A^{i'j} − 1/D_{i'}) · x^{(k-1)}_{i'→j};
For ∀j ∈ [n] do
    y_j ← Σ_{i∈∂j} (1/(r_j−1)) (A^{ij} − 1/D_i) · x^{(k_max−1)}_{i→j};
For ∀i ∈ [m] do x_i ← Σ_{j∈∂i} (1/(l_i−1)) A^{ij} y^{(k_max−1)}_{j→i};
Estimate vector t̂_i = e_{u_i}   where u_i = arg max_d(x_i)
```

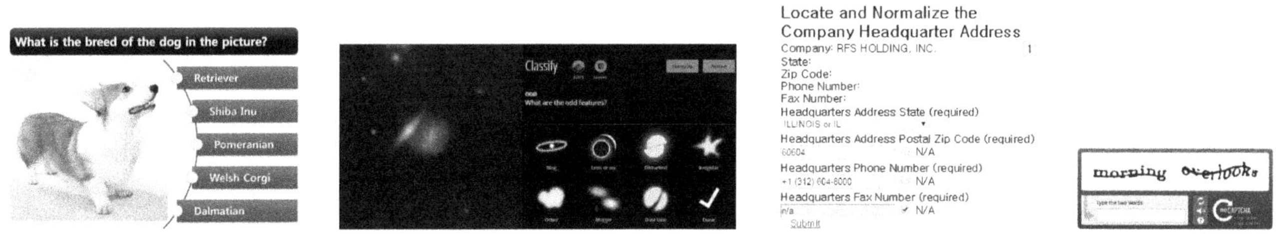

(a) An independent multiple-choice question: Determining the breed of a dog.

(b) GalaxyZoo project: classifying galaxies according to their shapes.

(c) A real task in Amazon Mechanical Turk: Filling up address information of a given company.

(d) reCAPTCHA: Typing words for spam protection and a book digitization project.

Figure 2: Examples of multiple-choice questions.

Adaptive task allocation method. One of significant points of our algorithm is that worker's relative reliability can be assessed in the course of its iterations. If we use this property, the performance of inferring the true answer can be improved further. Consider the adaptive strategy as an improvement method using the above property. First, a small portion of the tasks is used to infer the reliability of each worker using the iterative algorithm. Then, we select partial workers who have higher worker values to message and let them solve all of the remaining tasks. Although this method gives a larger burden to workers who are more reliable, the total number of edges is maintained. In section 6, the adaptive task allocation method will be explained in detail and we will verify some of the gains of this method through several experiments.

4. APPLICATIONS

We described an algorithmic solution to crowdsourcing systems for multiple-choice questions in the previous section, and we now look into some applications that our algorithm can treat. As we can see in crowdsourcing systems like Amazon Mechanical Turk, tasks are distributed in the form of multiple-choice questions and short-answer questions like entering zip-code. Although previous algorithms like [9, 21] have shown remarkable results in binary cases, a merit of our algorithm is that outstanding results can even be achieved on multiple-choice and short-answer questions that real tasks usually contain. Furthermore, a remarkable characteristic of our model is that the number of choices can vary for each question. This flexibility makes our model more applicable for real crowdsourced data. In this section, we describe some applications in detail that can apply our algorithm.

Labeling or tagging images is a common usage of exploiting crowdsourcing systems, and shows successful results in practice [3]. One of such example is classifying species or breeds of dogs in the images illustrated in Figure 2(a). Such tasks are very tough for machines, and even humans who have no background knowledge of dogs. These tasks are suitable for crowdsourcing materials and have multiple choices that are directly applicable to our algorithm.

Another application of labeling tasks is Galaxy Zoo, one of the well known projects using the wisdom of crowds (cf. Figure 2(b)). Galaxy Zoo has distributed over 300,000 images of galaxies to crowds for classification by their shape. Any volunteer with no prior knowledge can visit the website, where they are presented with an image of a galaxy and instructions of labeling manner. Then they answer a series of questions about the visual form of the galaxy, like whether it has arms or a bulge. Each step consists of multiple-choice questions, and the number of choices varies for each question. Since our algorithm is flexible for the number of choices, the responses of Galaxy Zoo can be easily aggregated using our algorithm.

For short-answer questions, it is hard to aggregate workers' responses in general, because their responses can vary. Our algorithm can settle this problem with the idea of transforming short-answer questions into several multiple-choice questions. When the length of the response to a short-answer question is fixed, short-answer questions can be split into several smaller tasks by considering each character of a response. In other words, each character is treated as one *microtask* in short-answer questions. For example, consider the task of entering a fixed-length answer such as a zip code like 97232. It can be treated as five microtasks, and each of the characters has 10 possible answers, from 0 to 9. Note that in each microtask, we only consider the number of choices as much as the number of candidate answers. For example, if candidate answers for a microtask are "4", "7", and "9", then we set the number of choices to three for this microtask. In addition, we can decide a set of candidate answers as all gathered responses simply, or only responses of top-K likelihood effectively.

Next, we consider when the length of the response varies. We can make another small task that determines the true length of the response and then we can discard the answers whose length is determined as a minor option. In summary, every short-answer question can be decomposed to several microtasks by considering each character of the answer and its length. Characters of the response and its length are transformed into small microtasks, and each microtask is considered a multiple-choice question. Thus, by applying our algorithm, responses to these short-answer questions can be easily aggregated. For a real task in Amazon Mechanical Turk, as illustrated in Figure 2(c), entering zip codes or phone numbers is an example of short-answer questions.

Another popular crowdsourcing application for short-answer questions is reCAPTCHA [19] illustrated in Figure 2(d). In its original version, CAPTCHA was first introduced to distinguish automatic bots by typing some characters correctly in a given image. It was extended to reCAPTCHA which digitalizes some hard phrases that Optical Character Recognition (OCR) techniques cannot recognize. In this case, the length of responses can vary, so a small task determining the length of response is necessary, as we mentioned. Although discarding the rest of the responses can be viewed as a waste, it is a tolerable loss, since the length of the responses is generally consistent. In addition, we need discuss the number of tasks r, each worker is given. In reCAPTCHA, we can only assign one entering task to each worker, while our algorithm needs sufficient number of tasks for each worker to ensure reliable inference. However, since we split each worker's response into several microtasks, the task size problem is naturally solved.

Another special application of our algorithm is as an adaptive task allocation strategy, since it explicitly computes the relative reliability of the workers, even with no prior knowledge of the worker distribution. If we design a proper adaptive strategy for crowdsourcing systems, we can boost its performance from the perspective of quality control of workers. The best workers can be recruited and exploited to resolve more questions. It can be viewed as a method for finding experts from crowds or filtering out workers who just spam for rewards; therefore, we can exploit reliable workers efficiently under the same budget through an adaptive task allocation strategy. We will examine such an adaptive strategy in the experiment section.

5. ANALYSIS OF ALGORITHMS

In this section, we provide proof for the performance guarantee of Algorithm 1. In *Theorem 1*, we show that the error bound depends on task degree l and the quality of the workers. More precisely, we show that an upper bound on the probability of error decays exponentially. From this section, we assume that $D_i = D$ for all $i \in [n]$.

5.1 Quality of workers

Let $\vec{v}_j$ denote the confusion vector of each worker j. Each component of the vector means the probability that a worker chooses the corresponding choice for a response. For a fixed task i with true answer $\hat{t}_{u_i} \in U$, the confusion vector $\vec{v}_j$ of worker j is defined as follows:

$$v_{jd} = \begin{cases} p_j & \text{if } \hat{t}_{u_i} = \vec{e}_d \\ \frac{1-p_j}{D-1} & \text{otherwise} \end{cases}$$

From an information theoretical perspective, the quality of workers can be defined as negative entropy with an offset and using the above confusion vector, we can define the quality of workers as

$$q = \mathbb{E}\Big[H(p) - \bar{p}\log(\hat{D}) + \log(D)\Big], \tag{3}$$

where $H(p) = p\log p + \bar{p}\log\bar{p}, \quad \bar{p} = 1-p, \quad \hat{D} = D-1.$

According to the quality of each worker, we can divide the workers into three types. At the extreme, workers with a quality close to zero make arbitrary responses. Since, we cannot obtain any information from them, let us define them as "Non-informative workers." At the other extreme, workers with the a quality close to one make almost true answers and we call them "Reliable workers." Lastly, there are workers who make wrong answers on purpose and affect the crowdsourcing system badly; they can be regarded as "Malicious workers." In our algorithm, since the worker message value y_j is related to the quality, workers with negative y_j, positive y_j and y_j close to zero correspond to "Reliable workers," "Malicious workers," and "Non-informative workers," respectively.

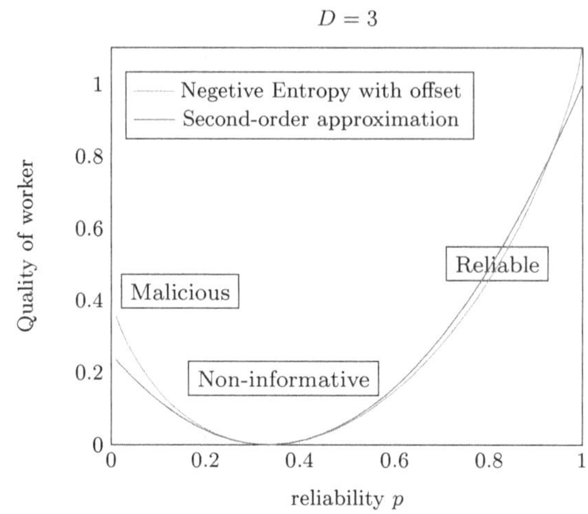

Figure 3: Comparison of the quality between negative entropy with offset and second-order polynomial approximation.

Although the quality of workers theoretically follows negative entropy, we found that a second-order polynomial approximation is sufficient for our analysis as described in Figure 3. As the dimension of the tasks increase, the approximation deviates from the real quality. Nevertheless, second-order approximation fits well to the real quality in the acceptable dimension case that our algorithm targets.

$$q \simeq \tilde{q}_1 = \mathbb{E}\Big[\Big(\frac{D}{D-1}\Big)^2\Big(p_j - \frac{1}{D}\Big)^2\Big] \tag{4}$$

For simplicity, we will use this approximated quality in the following sections. There is one more necessary assumption about worker distribution that workers give the correct answers on average rather than random or adversarial answers, so that $E[p_j] > \dfrac{1}{D}$. Given only workers' responses, any inference algorithms analogize the true answers from the general or popular choices of crowds. Consider an extreme case in which everyone gives adversarial answers in a binary classification task; no algorithm can correctly infer the reliability of the crowd. Hence, the assumption $E[p_j] > \dfrac{1}{D}$ is a natural necessary.

5.2 Bound on the Average Error Probability

From now on, let $\hat{l} \equiv l-1$, $\hat{r} \equiv r-1$, and the average quality of workers is defined as $q = \mathbb{E}[(\frac{D}{D-1})^2(p_j - \frac{1}{D})^2]$. Also, σ_k^2 denotes the effective variance in the *sub-Gaussian* tail of the task message distribution after k iterations.

$$\sigma_k^2 \equiv \frac{2q}{\mu^2 T^{k-1}} + \Big(\frac{D}{D-1}\Big)^2\Big(3 + \frac{1}{8q\hat{r}}\Big)\Big[\frac{1-1/T^{k-1}}{1-1/T}\Big], \tag{5}$$

where $T = \dfrac{(D-1)^2}{(D^2-D-1)}q^2\hat{l}\hat{r}.$

THEOREM 1. *For fixed $l > 1$ and $r > 1$, assume that m tasks are assigned to n workers according to a random (l, r)-regular bipartite graph according to the pairing model. If the distribution of the reliability satisfies $\mu \equiv \mathbb{E}[\frac{D}{D-1}(p_j - \frac{1}{D})] > 0$ and $T > 1$, then for any $t \in \{e_i\}^m$, the estimate after k iterations of the iterative algorithm achieves*

$$\frac{1}{m}\sum_{i=1}^{m}\mathbb{P}(t_i \neq \hat{t}_i^{(k)}) \leqslant (D-1)e^{-lq/(2\sigma_k^2)} + \frac{3lr}{m}(\hat{l}\hat{r})^{2k-2}. \quad (6)$$

The second term of the equation is the upper bound of probability that the graph dose not have a local tree-like structure and it can be quite small as long as we treat a large number of tasks. Therefore, the dominant factor of the upper bound is the first exponential term. As shown in (5), $T = 1$ is the crucial condition and we can satisfy $T > 1$ by using a sufficiently larger l or r. Then, with $T > 1$, σ_k^2 converges to a finite limit σ_∞^2, and we have

$$\sigma_\infty^2 = \left(3 + \frac{1}{8q\hat{r}}\right)\left(\frac{T}{T-1}\right). \quad (7)$$

Thus, the bounds of the first term of (6) does not depend on the number of tasks m or the number of iterations k. The following corollary describes an upper bound that only depends on l, q, σ_∞^2, and D.

COROLLARY 1. *Under the hypotheses of Theorem 1, there exists $m_0 = 3lre^{lq/4\sigma_\infty^2}(\hat{l}\hat{r})^{2(k-1)}$ and $k_0 = 1+(\log(q/\mu^2)/\log T)$ such that*

$$\frac{1}{m}\sum_{i=1}^{m}\mathbb{P}(t_i \neq \hat{t}_i^{(k)}) \leqslant De^{-lq/(4\sigma_\infty^2)}, \quad (8)$$

for all $k \geqslant k_0$ and for all $m \geqslant m_0$.

PROOF. First, we will show that $\sigma_k^2 \leqslant 2\sigma_\infty^2$ for $k \geqslant 1 + (\log(q/\mu^2)/\log T)$. Since $T > 1$, as per our assumption, $\sigma_k^2 = (2q/\mu^2 T^{k-1}) + (\frac{D}{D-1})^2(3 + 1/8q\hat{r})\frac{1-1/T^{k-1}}{T-1} \leqslant 2 + \sigma_\infty^2 \leqslant \sigma_\infty^2 + \sigma_\infty^2 \leqslant 2\sigma_\infty^2$. Therefore, the first term of (6) is bounded like $(D-1)e^{-lq/2\sigma_k^2} \leqslant (D-1)e^{-lq/4\sigma_\infty^2}$. Next, it is sufficient to set $m \geqslant 3lre^{lq/4\sigma_\infty^2}(\hat{l}\hat{r})^{2(k-1)}$ to ensure $\frac{3lr}{m}(\hat{l}\hat{r})^{2k-2} \leqslant e^{-lq/(4\sigma_\infty^2)}$. □

From *corollary 1*, we obtained that the required number of iterations k_0, is small in that it is the only logarithmic in l,r,q,μ and D. On the other hand, although the required number of entire tasks m_0, is very large in *corollary 1*, the experimental result in section 6 shows that the performance of error exhibits exponential decay as stated in (8).

Now, if we assume that there are no limitation on worker degree r and $T \geqslant 2$, we can find $\sigma_\infty^2 \leqslant 2(3 + 1/8q\hat{r})$. Then, for all $r \geqslant 1 + 1/8q$, as similar with the [11], we get the following bound:

$$\frac{1}{m}\sum_{i=1}^{m}\mathbb{P}(t_i \neq \hat{t}_i^{(k)}) \leqslant De^{-lq/32}. \quad (9)$$

Also, we can check the following corollary in terms of the number of queries per task l to achieve a target accuracy. Hence, we get the following corollary.

COROLLARY 2. *Using the task assignment scheme according to pairing model with $r \geqslant 1 + 1/8q$ and the iterative algorithm, it is sufficient to query $(32/q)log(D/\epsilon)$ times per task to guarantee that the error bound is at most ϵ for any $\epsilon \leqslant 1/2$ and for all $m \geqslant m_0$.*

5.3 Proof of the Theorem 1

The proof is roughly composed of three parts. First, the second term at the right-hand side of (6) is proved using its local tree-like property. Second, the remaining term of the right-hand side of (6) is verified using *Chernoff bound* in the assumption that the estimates of the task message follow *sub-Gaussian* distribution. Lastly, we prove that the assumption of the second part is true within certain parameters. To apply *density evolution* with multi-dimensional vector form is difficult in that the cross term of each components are generated. Therefore our proof can be differentiated from binary setting in [11].

Without a loss of generality, it is possible to assume that the true answer of each task, for any $i \in [m]$, $t_i = \vec{e}_1$. Let $\hat{t}_i^{(k)}$ denote the estimated answer of task i defined in section 5.2. If we draw a task $\mathbf{I}$, uniformly at random from the task set, the average probability of error can be denoted as

$$\frac{1}{m}\sum_{i\in[m]}\mathbb{P}(t_i \neq \hat{t}_i^{(k)}) = \mathbb{P}(t_\mathbf{I} \neq \hat{t}_\mathbf{I}^{(k)}), \quad (10)$$

Let $\mathrm{G}_{\mathbf{I},k}$ denote a subgraph of G that consists of all the nodes whose distance from the node '$\mathbf{I}$' is at most k. After k iterations, the local graph with root '$\mathbf{I}$' is $\mathrm{G}_{\mathbf{I},2k-1}$, since the update process operates twice for each iteration. To take advantage of *density evolution*, the full independence of each branch is needed. Thus, we bound the probability of error with two terms, one that represents the probability that subgraph $\mathrm{G}_{\mathbf{I},2k-1}$ is not a tree and the other, which represents the probability that $\mathrm{G}_{\mathbf{I},2k-1}$ is a tree with a wrong answer.

$$\begin{aligned}\mathbb{P}(t_\mathbf{I} \neq \hat{t}_\mathbf{I}^{(k)}) &\leqslant \mathbb{P}(\mathrm{G}_{\mathbf{I},2k-1} \text{ is not a tree }) \\ &+ \mathbb{P}(\mathrm{G}_{\mathbf{I},2k-1} \text{ is a tree and } t_\mathbf{I} \neq \hat{t}_\mathbf{I}^{(k)}). \quad (11)\end{aligned}$$

The following lemma bounds the first term and proves that the probability that a local subgraph is not a tree vanishes as m grows. A proof of Lemma 1 is provided [11] (cf. *Karger, Oh and Shah* 2011, section 3.2).

LEMMA 1. *From a random (l,r)-regular bipartite graph generated according to the pairing model,*

$$\mathbb{P}(\mathrm{G}_{\mathbf{I},2k-1} \textit{ is not a tree }) \leqslant \left(\hat{l}\hat{r}\right)^{(2k-2)}\frac{3lr}{m}.$$

From the result of Lemma 1, we can concentrate directly on the second term of (11) and define the pairwise difference of task messages as $\tilde{\mathbf{x}}_d^{(k)} = \mathbf{x}_1^{(k)} - \mathbf{x}_d^{(k)}$ for $^\forall d \in [2:D]$.

$$\begin{aligned}\mathbb{P}(t_\mathbf{I} \neq \hat{t}_\mathbf{I}^{(k)} | \mathrm{G}_{\mathbf{I},k} \text{ is a tree}) &\leqslant \mathbb{P}(\cup_{d=2}^{D}\{\tilde{x}_\mathbf{I}^{(k)} \leqslant 0\} | \mathrm{G}_{\mathbf{I},k} \text{ is a tree}) \\ &\leqslant \mathbb{P}(\cup_{d=2}^{D}\{\tilde{x}_\mathbf{I} \leqslant 0\}).\end{aligned}$$

To obtain a tight upper bound on $\mathbb{P}(\cup_{d=2}^{D}\{\hat{\mathbf{x}}_d^{(k)} \leqslant 0\})$ of our iterative algorithm, we assume that $\tilde{\mathbf{x}}_d^{(k)}$ follow *sub-Gaussian* distribution for any $d \in [2:D]$ and prove these in section 5.4. Then, *Chernoff bound* is applied to the independent message branches and this brings us the tight bound of our algorithm. A random variable $\mathbf{z}$ with mean m is said to be *sub-Gaussian* with parameter $\tilde{\sigma}$ if for any $\lambda \in \mathbb{R}$ the following inequality holds:

$$\mathbb{E}[e^{\lambda \mathbf{z}}] \leqslant e^{m\lambda + (1/2)\tilde{\sigma}^2\lambda^2}. \quad (12)$$

We will first show that for $^\forall d \in [2:D]$, $\tilde{\mathbf{x}}_d^{(k)}$ is *sub-Gaussian* with mean m_k and parameter $\tilde{\sigma}_k^2$ for specific region of λ, precisely for $|\lambda| \leqslant 1/(2m_{k-1}\hat{r})$. Now we define

$$m_k \equiv \mu\hat{l}U^{k-1}, \quad ^\forall k \in \mathbb{N}$$

$$\tilde{\sigma}_k^2 \equiv 2\hat{l}S^{k-1} + [\mu^2\hat{l}^2\hat{r}(3q^2\hat{l}\hat{r} + \hat{l}/8)]U^{2k-4}\left[\frac{1-(1/T)^{k-1}}{1-(1/T)}\right],$$

$$\text{where } U = \frac{D-1}{D}q\hat{l}\hat{r}, \quad S = \frac{D^2-D-1}{D^2}\hat{l}\hat{r}$$

$$T = \frac{U^2}{S} = \frac{(D-1)^2}{D^2-D-1}q^2\hat{l}\hat{r}$$

then

$$\mathbb{E}[e^{\lambda\tilde{\mathbf{x}}_d^{(k)}}] \leqslant e^{m_k\lambda + (1/2)\tilde{\sigma}_k^2\lambda^2}. \tag{13}$$

The locally tree-like property of a sparse random graph provides the distributional independence among incoming messages, that is $\mathbb{E}[e^{\lambda\hat{\mathbf{x}}_d^{(k)}}] = \mathbb{E}[e^{\lambda\tilde{\mathbf{x}}_d^{(k)}}]^{(l/\hat{l})}$. Thus, $\hat{\mathbf{x}}_d^{(k)}$ satisfies $\mathbb{E}[e^{\lambda\hat{\mathbf{x}}_d^{(k)}}] \leqslant e^{(l/\hat{l})m_k\lambda + ((l/2\hat{l}))\tilde{\sigma}_k^2\lambda^2}$ for all $d \in [2:D]$. Because of full independence of each branch, we can apply *Chernoff bound* with $\lambda = -m_k/(\tilde{\sigma_k^2})$, and then we obtain

$$\mathbb{P}(\hat{\mathbf{x}}_d^{(k)} \leqslant 0) \leqslant \mathbb{E}[e^{\lambda\hat{\mathbf{x}}_d^{(k)}}] \leqslant e^{-lm_k^2/(2\hat{l}\tilde{\sigma}_k^2)}. \tag{14}$$

$$\begin{aligned}\mathbb{P}(\cup_{d=2}^D\{\hat{\mathbf{x}}_d^{(k)} \leqslant 0\}) &\leqslant \sum_{d=2}^D \mathbb{P}(\hat{\mathbf{x}}_d^{(k)} \leqslant 0) \\ &\leqslant (D-1)e^{-lm_k^2/(2\hat{l}\tilde{\sigma}_k^2)}. \end{aligned} \tag{15}$$

Since $m_k m_{k-1}/(\tilde{\sigma}_k^2) \leqslant 1/(3\hat{r})$, we can easily check $|\lambda| \leqslant 1/(2m_{k-1}\hat{r})$. This finalizes the *Proof of the Theorem 1*.

5.4 Proof of Sub-Gaussianity

Now we prove that for all $d \in [2:D]$, $\tilde{\mathbf{x}}_d^{(k)}$ is *sub-Gaussian* with some m_k and $\tilde{\sigma}_k^2$. Recurrence relation of the evolution of the MGFs(moment generating functions) on $\tilde{\mathbf{x}}_d$ and $\mathbf{y_p}$ are stated as

$$\begin{aligned}\mathbb{E}[e^{\lambda\tilde{\mathbf{x}}_d^{(k)}}] &= \Big(\mathbb{E}_{\mathbf{p}}\Big[\mathbf{p}\mathbb{E}\Big[e^{\lambda\mathbf{y}_p^{(k-1)}}|\mathbf{p}\Big] + \frac{\bar{\mathbf{p}}}{D-1}\mathbb{E}\Big[e^{-\lambda\mathbf{y}_p^{(k-1)}}|\mathbf{p}\Big] \\ &\quad + \frac{\bar{\mathbf{p}}}{D-1}(D-2)\Big]\Big)^{\hat{l}},\end{aligned} \tag{16}$$

$$\begin{aligned}\mathbb{E}[e^{\lambda\mathbf{y}_p^{(k)}}] &= \Big(p\mathbb{E}\Big[e^{\lambda(\frac{1}{D}\sum_{d=2}^D\tilde{\mathbf{x}}_d^{(k)})}\Big] \\ &\quad + \frac{\bar{p}}{D-1}\sum_{j=2}^D\mathbb{E}\Big[e^{\lambda(-\tilde{\mathbf{x}}_j^{(k)} + \frac{1}{D}\sum_{d=2}^D\tilde{\mathbf{x}}_d^{(k)})}\Big]\Big)^{\hat{r}},\end{aligned} \tag{17}$$

where $\bar{p} = 1-p$ and $\bar{\mathbf{p}} = 1-\mathbf{p}$.

Using above MGFs and *mathematical induction*, we can prove that $\tilde{\mathbf{x}}_d^{(k)}$ are *sub-Gaussian*, for all $d \in [2:D]$.

First, for $k=1$, we prove that all of $\tilde{\mathbf{x}}_d^{(1)}$ are *sub-Gaussian* random variables with mean $m_1 = \mu\tilde{l}$ and variance $\tilde{\sigma}_1^2 = 2\tilde{l}$, where $\mu \equiv \mathbb{E}[\frac{D}{D-1}(p_j - \frac{1}{D})]$. Using *Gaussian* initialization of $\mathbf{y}_p \sim \mathcal{N}(1,1)$, we obtain $\mathbb{E}[e^{\lambda\mathbf{y}_p^{(0)}}] = e^{\lambda+(1/2)\lambda^2}$ regardless of p. Substituting this into equation (13), we have

$$\begin{aligned}\mathbb{E}[e^{\lambda\tilde{\mathbf{x}}_d^{(1)}}] &= \Big(\mathbb{E}_{\mathbf{p}}\Big[\mathbf{p}e^{\lambda+(1/2)\lambda^2} + \Big(\frac{1-\mathbf{p}}{D-1}\Big)e^{-\lambda+(1/2)\lambda^2} \\ &\quad + \Big(\frac{1-\mathbf{p}}{D-1}\Big)(D-2)\Big]\Big)^{\hat{l}} \\ &\leqslant \Big(\mathbb{E}[a]e^{\lambda} + \Big(\mathbb{E}[\bar{a}]e^{-\lambda}\Big)^{\hat{l}}e^{(1/2)\hat{l}\lambda^2} \\ &\leqslant e^{(\mu\lambda+\lambda^2)\hat{l}},\end{aligned} \tag{18}$$

$$\text{where} \quad a = \frac{Dp+D-2}{2(D-1)}, \quad \bar{a} = 1-a = \frac{D(1-p)}{2(D-1)}$$

where the first inequality follows from the fact that $2 \leqslant e^{\lambda} + e^{-\lambda}$ for any $\lambda \in \mathbb{R}$, and the second inequality follows from that

$$be^z + (1-b)e^{-z} \leqslant e^{(2b-1)z+(1/2)z^2}, \tag{19}$$

for any $z \in \mathbb{R}$ and $b \in [0,1]$ (cf. *Alon and Spencer* 2008, Lemma A.1.5) [1].

From k^{th} inductive hypothesis, we have $\mathbb{E}[e^{\lambda\tilde{\mathbf{x}}_d^{(k)}}] \leqslant e^{m_k\lambda+(1/2)\tilde{\sigma}_k^2\lambda^2}$ for $|\lambda| \leqslant 1/(2m_{k-1}\hat{r})$. Now, we will show $\mathbb{E}[e^{\lambda\tilde{\mathbf{x}}_d^{(k+1)}}] \leqslant e^{m_{k+1}\lambda+(1/2)\tilde{\sigma}_{k+1}^2\lambda^2}$ for $|\lambda| \leqslant 1/(2m_k\hat{r})$. In advance, substituting (19) into (17), we have

LEMMA 2. *For any* $|\lambda| \leqslant 1/(2m_k\hat{r})$ *and* $p \in [0,1]$, *we get*

$$\mathbb{E}[e^{\lambda\mathbf{y}_p^{(k)}}] \leqslant \Big[\Big(pe^{(1/2)m_k\lambda} + \bar{p}e^{-(1/2)m_k\lambda}\Big)\Big]^{\hat{r}} \cdot e^{(\frac{D-2}{2D})\hat{r}m_k\lambda + (\frac{D^2-D-1}{D^2})\hat{r}\tilde{\sigma}_k^2\lambda^2}.$$

Similar to (18)'s process, from (16), we get

$$\mathbb{E}[e^{\lambda\tilde{\mathbf{x}}_d^{(k+1)}}] \leqslant \mathbb{E}_{\mathbf{p}}\Big(a\mathbb{E}\Big[e^{\lambda\mathbf{y}_p^{(k)}}\Big] + \bar{a}\mathbb{E}\Big[e^{-\lambda\mathbf{y}_p^{(k)}}\Big]\Big)^{\hat{l}}.$$

with $2 \leqslant e^{\lambda} + e^{-\lambda}$ for any $\lambda \in \mathbb{R}$.
Substituting the result of Lemma 2 into the above inequality provides

$$\begin{aligned}\mathbb{E}[e^{\lambda\tilde{\mathbf{x}}_d^{(k+1)}}] &\leqslant \mathbb{E}_{\mathbf{p}}\Big[a\Big(\mathbf{p}e^{(1/2)m_k\lambda} + \bar{\mathbf{p}}e^{-(1/2)m_k\lambda}\Big)^{\hat{r}} \\ &\quad + \bar{a}\Big(\mathbf{p}e^{(1/2)m_k\lambda} + \bar{\mathbf{p}}e^{-(1/2)m_k\lambda}\Big)^{\hat{r}}\Big]^{\hat{l}} \\ &\quad \cdot e^{(\frac{D-2}{2D})\hat{l}\hat{r}m_k\lambda + (\frac{D^2-D-1}{D^2})\hat{l}\hat{r}\tilde{\sigma}_k^2\lambda^2}.\end{aligned} \tag{20}$$

Now we are left to bound (20) using following Lemma 3.

LEMMA 3. *For any* $|z| \leqslant 1/(2\hat{r})$ *and* $p \in [0,1]$, *we get*

$$\mathbb{E}_{\mathbf{p}}\Big[a\Big(\mathbf{p}e^{\frac{D-1}{D}z} + \bar{\mathbf{p}}e^{-\frac{1}{D}z}\Big) + \bar{a}\Big(\mathbf{p}e^{-\frac{D-1}{D}z} + \bar{\mathbf{p}}e^{\frac{1}{D}z}\Big)\Big]^{\hat{r}} \leqslant e^{\frac{D-1}{D}q\hat{r}z + \left(\frac{3}{2}q\hat{r}+\frac{1}{8}\right)\hat{r}z^2}.$$

Applying this to (20) gives

$$\mathbb{E}[e^{\lambda\tilde{\mathbf{x}}_d^{(k+1)}}] \leqslant e^{\frac{D-1}{D}q\hat{l}\hat{r}m_k\lambda + \left[\left(\frac{3}{2}q\hat{r}+\frac{1}{8}\right)m_k^2 + \left(\frac{D^2-D-1}{D^2}\right)\tilde{\sigma}_k^2\right]\hat{l}\hat{r}},$$

for $|\lambda| \leqslant 1/(2m_k\hat{r})$.

From the result of *mathematical induction*, we can obtain the recurrence relations of two parameters of the *sub-Gaussians*

$$m_{k+1} = \Big[\frac{D-1}{D} q\hat{l}\hat{r}\Big] m_k,$$

$$\tilde{\sigma}_{k+1}^2 = \Big[\Big(\frac{3}{2}q\hat{r} + \frac{1}{8}\Big)m_k^2 + \Big(\frac{D^2-D-1}{D^2}\Big)\tilde{\sigma}_k^2\Big]\hat{l}\hat{r},$$

with $\frac{D-1}{D}q\hat{l}\hat{r} \geqslant 1$, where m_k is increasing geometric series. Thus, the above recursions hold for $|\lambda| \leqslant 1/(2m_k\hat{r})$ and we get

$$m_k = \mu\hat{l}\Big[\frac{D-1}{D}q\hat{l}\hat{r}\Big]^{k-1},$$

for all $k \in \mathbb{N}$. Substituting m_k into $\tilde{\sigma}_k^2$, we obtain

$$\tilde{\sigma}_k^2 = a\tilde{\sigma}_{k-1}^2 + bc^{k-2}, \tag{21}$$

where

$$a = \frac{D^2-D-1}{D^2}\hat{l}\hat{r}, \quad b = \mu^2\hat{l}^3\hat{r}\big(\frac{3}{2}q\hat{r}+\frac{1}{8}\big) \quad c = \Big[\frac{D-1}{D}q\hat{l}\hat{r}\Big]^2$$

For $T \neq 1$, This type of recurrence relation can be represented as the following closed formula.

$$\tilde{\sigma}_k^2 = \tilde{\sigma}_1^2 a^{k-1} + bc^{k-2}\Big[\frac{1-(a/c)^{k-1}}{1-(a/c)}\Big]. \tag{22}$$

This finishes the proof of (13).

Proof of Lemma 2. In the $k+1^{th}$ inductive step of *mathematical induction*, we assume that $\mathbb{E}[e^{\lambda\tilde{\mathbf{x}}_d^{(k)}}] \leqslant e^{m_k\lambda+(1/2)\tilde{\sigma}_k^2\lambda^2}$ for any $d \in [2:D]$ with $|\lambda| \leqslant 1/(2m_{k-1}\hat{r})$. In other words, all of $\tilde{\mathbf{x}}_d^{(k)}$ follow *sub-Gaussian* distribution with parameters m_k and $\tilde{\sigma}_k^2$. From (17), each component at the right-hand side can be represented as the product of several combinations of $[e^{\lambda\tilde{\mathbf{x}}_d^{(k)}}]$ and the product of variables means a linear combination in the exponential field. Using *hölder's inequality*, we prove that the linear transformation of *sub-Gaussian* random variables follows also *sub-Gaussian* distribution with some parameters. Moreover, these parameters are determined by D, mean m_k and variance $\tilde{\sigma}_k^2$ of each *sub-Gaussian* $\tilde{\mathbf{x}}_d^{(k)}$. Applying *h"older's inequality* to (17), the first term at the right-hand side of (17) gives

$$\mathbb{E}\Big[e^{\lambda(\frac{1}{D}\sum_{d=2}^{D}\tilde{\mathbf{x}}_d^{(k)})}\Big] \leqslant \prod_{d=2}^{D}\Big[\mathbb{E}\Big(e^{\lambda(1/D)\tilde{\mathbf{x}}_d^{(k)}}\Big)^{D-1}\Big]^{\frac{1}{D-1}}$$

$$\leqslant e^{(\frac{D-1}{D})m_k\lambda+(\frac{D-1}{2D^2})\tilde{\sigma}_k^2\lambda^2}.$$

For the second term at the right-hand side of (17), we have

$$\mathbb{E}\Big[e^{\lambda(-\tilde{\mathbf{x}}_j^{(k)}+\frac{1}{D}\sum_{d=2}^{D}\tilde{\mathbf{x}}_d^{(k)})}\Big] \leqslant \mathbb{E}\Big[e^{-\lambda(\frac{D-1}{D})\tilde{\mathbf{x}}_j^{(k)}}\Big]$$

$$\cdot \prod_{d=2,d\neq j}^{D}\Big[\mathbb{E}\Big(e^{\lambda(1/D)\tilde{\mathbf{x}}_d^{(k)}}\Big)^{D-1}\Big]^{\frac{1}{D-1}}$$

$$\leqslant e^{(-\frac{1}{D})m_k\lambda+(\frac{D^2-D-1}{2D^2})\tilde{\sigma}_k^2\lambda^2}.$$

Getting these two results together finishes the proof of Lemma 2.

Proof of Lemma 3. From (19), we get

$$\Big(\mathbf{p}e^{\frac{D-1}{D}z} + \bar{\mathbf{p}}e^{-\frac{1}{D}z}\Big) \leqslant e^{(\mathbf{p}-\frac{1}{D})z+\frac{1}{8}z^2}.$$

Applying this result to the original formula, we have

$$\mathbb{E}_{\mathbf{p}}\Big[a\Big(\mathbf{p}e^{\frac{D-1}{D}z} + \bar{\mathbf{p}}e^{-\frac{1}{D}z}\Big) + \bar{a}\Big(\mathbf{p}e^{-\frac{D-1}{D}z} + \bar{\mathbf{p}}e^{\frac{1}{D}z}\Big)\Big]^{\hat{r}}$$

$$\leqslant \mathbb{E}\Big[e^{\frac{D}{D-1}(\mathbf{p}-\frac{1}{D})\hat{r}z+\frac{1}{2}(\mathbf{p}-\frac{1}{D})^2\hat{r}^2z^2}\Big]\cdot e^{\frac{1}{8}\hat{r}z^2}.$$

In this point, we bring the fact that $e^a \leqslant 1+a+0.63a^2$ for $|a| \leqslant 5/8$

$$\mathbb{E}\Big[e^{\frac{D}{D-1}(\mathbf{p}-\frac{1}{D})\hat{r}z+\frac{1}{2}(\mathbf{p}-\frac{1}{D})^2\hat{r}^2z^2}\Big]$$

$$\leqslant \mathbb{E}\Big[1+\Big(\frac{D-1}{D}\Big)q\hat{r}z + \frac{1}{2}\Big(\frac{D-1}{D}\Big)^2 q\hat{r}^2z^2$$

$$+0.63\Big\{\Big(\frac{D-1}{D}\Big)q\hat{r}z + \frac{1}{2}\Big(\frac{D-1}{D}\Big)^2 q\hat{r}^2z^2\Big\}^2\Big]$$

$$\leqslant 1+\Big(\frac{D-1}{D}\Big)q\hat{r}z + \frac{3}{2}\Big(\frac{D-1}{D}\Big)^2 q\hat{r}^2z^2$$

$$\leqslant e^{\big(\frac{D-1}{D}\big)q\hat{r}z+\frac{3}{2}q\hat{r}^2z^2},$$

for $|z| \leqslant 1/(2\hat{r})$ and $D \leqslant 2$.

Phase Transition. As shown in (22), the performance of our algorithm is only bounded when the condition $T > 1$ is satisfied. Meanwhile, with $T < 1$, $\tilde{\sigma}_k^2$ which means the variance of the $\tilde{\mathbf{x}}_d^{(k)}$ diverges as the number of iteration k increases. In this case, our performance guarantee is no longer valid and the performance becomes worse compared to other algorithms such as EM and majority voting. Note that except for extreme case such as when using very low quality workers and the deficient assignments, $T > 1$ is easily satisfied and our performance guarantee is valid. In section 6, we will verify the existence of this critical point at $T = 1$ through several experiments with different conditions.

$$\frac{a}{c} = \frac{(D-1)^2}{(D^2-D-1)}q^2\hat{l}\hat{r} = T.$$

6. EXPERIMENTS

In this section, we verify the performance of the *multiple iterative algorithm* discussed in the previous sections with different sets of simulations. First, we check that the error of the iterative algorithm exhibits exponential decay as l increases or q increases. In addition, we show that our algorithm achieves a better performance than that of the majority voting and EM approach above a phase transition of $T = 1$. Next simulation investigates the linear relationship between y_j value and the ratio of $the\ number\ of\ correct\ answers$ to r_j for each worker. Then, we do experiments on the adaptive scenario by varying the proportion of pilot tasks and selected reliable workers. Finally, we do simulations on the experiments introduced above with a task set consisting of various D values.

Comparison with other algorithms. To show the competitiveness of our algorithm, we ran our *multiple iterative algorithm*, majority voting, and the EM approach for 2000 tasks and 2000 workers with fixed D = 2, 3, 4, and 5 (Figure 4 and Figure 5). The performance of the oracle estimator

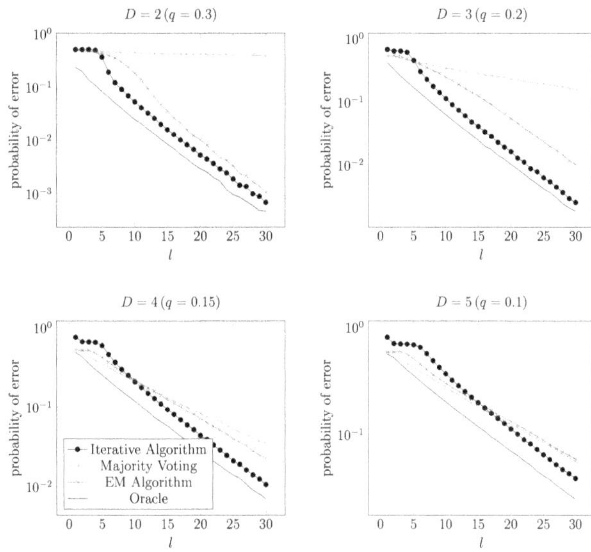

Figure 4: Comparisons of probabilities of error between different algorithms varying l values ($m = n = 2000$, $l = r$).

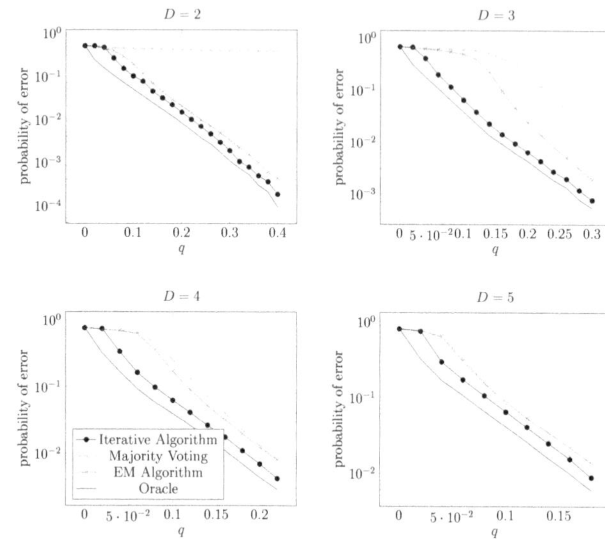

Figure 5: Comparisons of probabilities of error between different algorithms varying q values ($m = n = 2000$, $l = r = 25$).

is also presented as a lower bound and the EM algorithm is implemented with Dawid and Skene's method [2]. In Figure 4, we can check that the probability of error decays exponentially as l increases, and is lower than that of the majority voting and EM approach above the phase transition $T = 1$. In addition, in Figure 5, we find the probabilities of error decays as q increases.

We expect a phase transition at $T = \frac{(D-1)^2}{(D^2-D-1)} q^2 \hat{l}\hat{r} = 1$ or $l = 1 + \sqrt{\frac{(D^2-D-1)}{(D-1)^2}\frac{1}{q}}$ when $l = r$ according to our theorem. With this, we can expect transitions to happen around $l = 4.33$ for $D = 2 (q = 0.3)$, $l = 6.59$ for $D = 3 (q = 0.2)$, $l = 8.37$ for $D = 4 (q = 0.15)$, and $l = 11.89$ for $D = 5 (q = 0.1)$. From the experiments in Figure 4, we see that iterative algorithm starts to perform better than majority voting around $l = 5, 6, 10, 18$ for each D. Note that these values are very similar with the theoretical values. It follows from the fact the error of our method increases with k when $T < 1$ as stated in Section 5. As can clearly be seen from the simulation results, we can check that the l values required for achieving $T > 1$ are not large. For example, if we consider dealing with short-answer questions like reCAPTCHA which is introduced in Section 4, carrying off the required $r (= l)$ is accomplished easily since each alphabet is considered as a separate question.

Adaptive Scenario. The inference of workers' relative reliability in the course of iterations is one of the algorithm's most important aspects. Now, we define $\hat{p_j}$ for each worker j as following:

$$\hat{p_j} = \frac{the\, number\, of\, correct\, answers}{r_j}.$$

After k_{max} iterations, we can find reliable workers by the value of worker message y_j since this value is proportional to $\hat{p_j}$, which is influenced by p_j. Relative reliability y_j is calculated by the following equation in Algorithm 1.

$$y_j \leftarrow \sum_{i \in \partial j} \left(\vec{A}^{ij} - \frac{\vec{1}}{D} \right) \cdot \vec{x}_{i \to j}^{(k_{max}-1)}$$

Figure 6 shows that there are strong correlations between y_j and $\hat{p_j}$. In one simulation, the correlation coefficients[1] between y_j and $\hat{p_j}$ are measured as 0.993, 0.989, 0.968, 0.938 for each $D = 2$, 3, 4, and 5, which are significantly large values. We can also check that the line passes approximately the point of $(\frac{1}{D}, 0)$, which represents a non-informative worker's reliability, as expected in Section 5.

One of the utilizations of this correlation property is the *adaptive scenario*, which extracts more reliable workers from the crowds after the inference of pilot tasks, and lets them solve the remaining tasks. We can improve the performance of our algorithm further with the scenario. The strategy consists of two steps in detail. In the first step, we use $m' = \alpha m$ pilot tasks to infer the relative reliability of workers using the iterative algorithm.

$$m' = \alpha m, n' = n$$
$$l' = l, r' = \alpha r$$

In the second step, we select βn workers who have higher $|y_j|$ values after the first step, and each worker solves $\frac{m-m'}{\beta m} r$ tasks out of the remaining $m - m'$ tasks. We sort them out with higher $|y_j|$ values since we can gain less information from workers who have lower $|y_j|$ values, which means that their reliability is closer to $1/D$ than those of the others (Figure 6 and Figure 3).

$$m'' = m - m', n'' = \beta n$$
$$l'' = l, r'' = \frac{m - m'}{\beta m} r$$

[1]Pearson product-moment correlation coefficient(PPMCC) is used for evaluation.

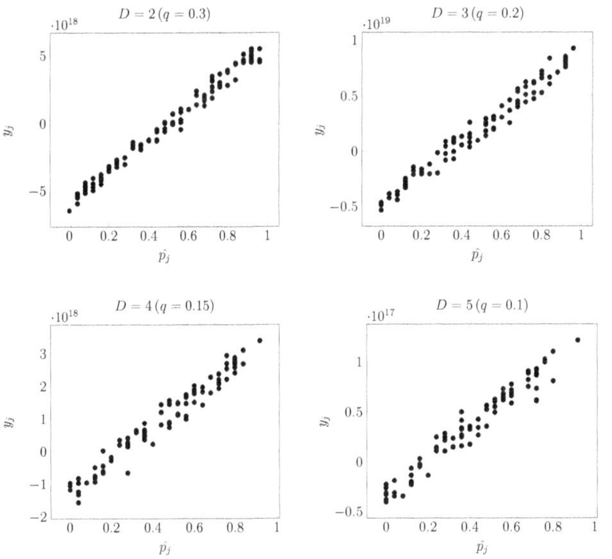

Figure 6: Relationship between y_j and $\hat{p_j}$ ($m = n = 2000$, $k = 10$).

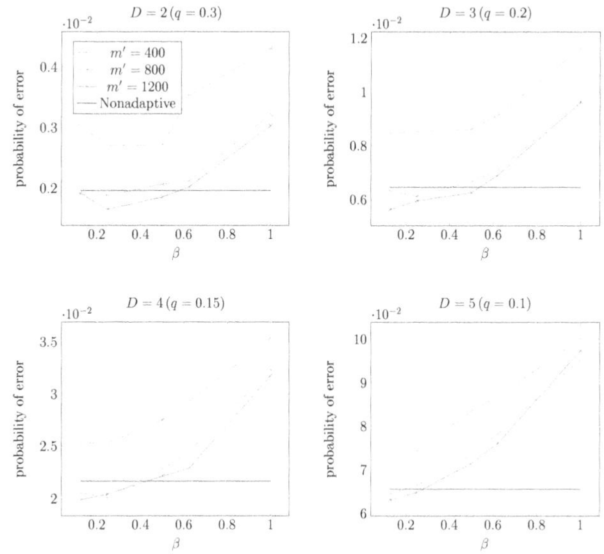

Figure 7: Adaptive Scenario ($m = n = 2000$, $l = 25$).

To show the performance improvements when using the adaptive scenario, we perform experiments with several (m', β) sets. Figure 7 shows that the probability of error is smaller than for the non-adaptive scenario when proper m' and β are used. Specifically, as β decreases, the error tends to decrease since fewer, but more reliable, workers then solve the rest of the questions. However, we have to consider each worker's inherent capacity[2] when choosing an appropriate β. With limited capacity, we cannot use an unreasonably low β, since it places too high a burden on each worker. In addition, we have to take enough m' pilot tasks to guarantee the accuracy of the relative reliability, which are inferred in the first step.

Simulations on a set of various D values. To show the performance of the *generalized multiple iterative algorithm*, we do simulations on a task set consisting of various D values with Algorithm 2. In detail, we repeat the same experiments with a question set composed in $1:1:1$ ratios of tasks which D are 2, 3, 4 respectively. Then, we have to investigate for the general case that q is calculated with the following equation.

$$q = \mathbb{E}[q_j] = \mathbb{E}\left[\left(\frac{D_i}{D_i - 1}\right)^2 \left(p_{ij} - \frac{1}{D_i}\right)^2\right]$$

We define q_j as an individual quality of the worker j. To perform simulations and to analyze the results, we have to make an assumption that a worker with individual quality q_j solves question with a reliability p_{ij} for each D_i. We can check that the same tendencies found in previous simulations also appear in Figure 8. There is also the strong correlation between y_j and $\hat{p_j}$ as 0.960. This result is notable in that in the real world, there are many more cases where questions have varying number of choices than fixed ones.

[2]The number of possible questions that each worker can manage to solve in one transaction.

7. CONCLUSION

We have proposed an iterative algorithm that can handle multiple-choice and short-answer questions which are general types of questions in real crowdsourcing systems. Especially for short-answer questions, we provide a method of transforming original tasks into several microtasks. Therefore, we give a general solution for real crowdsourcing systems to infer the correct answers from unreliable responses. From the performance analysis of our algorithm, we have proved that an upper bound on the probability of error decays exponentially and we have verified that our algorithm outperforms majority voting and EM-based algorithm through numerical experiments.

For the future works, our work can be combined to the context of online learning, or we can think of another model for multiple-choice questions that have multiple correct answers, not just one correct answer.

Acknowledgments

This research was in parts funded by Basic Science Research Program through the National Research Foundation of Korea (NRF) funded by the Ministry of Science, ICT & Future Planning (2012R1A1A1014965), and in parts funded by the Brain Korea 21 Plus Project in 2015. This work was also supported by Automation and System Research Institute (ASRI), SNU, and Institute of New Media and Communications (INMC), SNU.

8. REFERENCES

[1] N. Alon and J. H. Spencer. *The probabilistic method.* John Wiley & Sons, Hoboken, NJ, 2008.

[2] A. P. Dawid and A. M. Skene. Maximum likelihood estimation of observer error-rates using the em algorithm. *Applied statistics*, pages 20–28, 1979.

[3] J. Deng, W. Dong, R. Socher, L.-J. Li, K. Li, and L. Fei-Fei. Imagenet: A large-scale hierarchical image database. In *Computer Vision and Pattern*

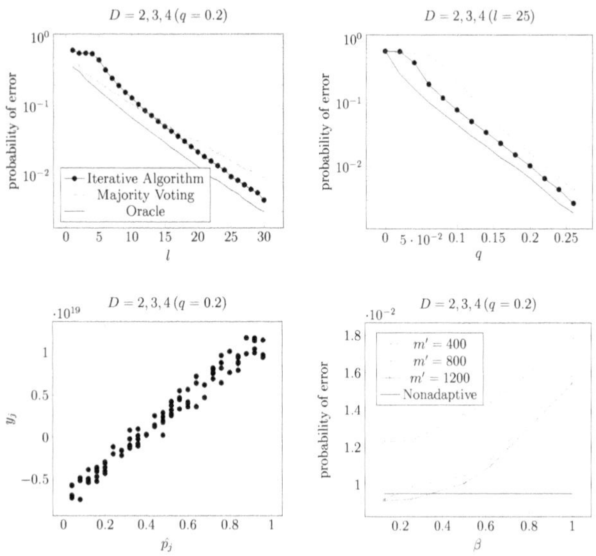

Figure 8: Simulations on a set of various D values ($m = n = 2000\,(D = 2 : 666\,/\,D = 3 : 667\,/\,D = 4 : 668)$).

Recognition, 2009. CVPR 2009. IEEE Conference on, pages 248–255. IEEE, 2009.

[4] P. Donmez, J. G. Carbonell, and J. Schneider. Efficiently learning the accuracy of labeling sources for selective sampling. In *Proceedings of the 15th ACM SIGKDD international conference on Knowledge discovery and data mining*, pages 259–268. ACM, 2009.

[5] S. Ertekin, H. Hirsh, and C. Rudin. Approximating the wisdom of the crowd. In *Proceedings of the Workshop on Computational Social Science and the Wisdom of Crowds*, 2011.

[6] C.-J. Ho, S. Jabbari, and J. W. Vaughan. Adaptive task assignment for crowdsourced classification. In *Proceedings of the 30th International Conference on Machine Learning (ICML-13)*, pages 534–542, 2013.

[7] P. G. Ipeirotis, F. Provost, and J. Wang. Quality management on amazon mechanical turk. In *Proceedings of the ACM SIGKDD workshop on human computation*, pages 64–67. ACM, 2010.

[8] D. R. Karger, S. Oh, and D. Shah. Budget-optimal crowdsourcing using low-rank matrix approximations. In *Communication, Control, and Computing (Allerton), 2011 49th Annual Allerton Conference on*, pages 284–291. IEEE, 2011.

[9] D. R. Karger, S. Oh, and D. Shah. Iterative learning for reliable crowdsourcing systems. In *Advances in neural information processing systems*, pages 1953–1961, 2011.

[10] D. R. Karger, S. Oh, and D. Shah. Efficient crowdsourcing for multi-class labeling. In *Proceedings of the ACM SIGMETRICS/international conference on Measurement and modeling of computer systems*, pages 81–92. ACM, 2013.

[11] D. R. Karger, S. Oh, and D. Shah. Budget-Optimal Task Allocation for Reliable Crowdsourcing Systems. *Operations Research*, 62(1):1–24, Feb. 2014.

[12] G. Kazai, J. Kamps, and N. Milic-Frayling. An analysis of human factors and label accuracy in crowdsourcing relevance judgments. *Information retrieval*, 16(2):138–178, 2013.

[13] A. Kittur, E. H. Chi, and B. Suh. Crowdsourcing user studies with mechanical turk. In *Proceedings of the SIGCHI conference on human factors in computing systems*, pages 453–456. ACM, 2008.

[14] C. J. Lintott, K. Schawinski, A. Slosar, K. Land, S. Bamford, D. Thomas, M. J. Raddick, R. C. Nichol, A. Szalay, D. Andreescu, et al. Galaxy zoo: morphologies derived from visual inspection of galaxies from the sloan digital sky survey. *Monthly Notices of the Royal Astronomical Society*, 389(3):1179–1189, 2008.

[15] Q. Liu, J. Peng, and A. Ihler. Variational inference for crowdsourcing. In *Advances in Neural Information Processing Systems*, pages 692–700, 2012.

[16] V. C. Raykar, S. Yu, L. H. Zhao, G. H. Valadez, C. Florin, L. Bogoni, and L. Moy. Learning from crowds. *The Journal of Machine Learning Research*, 11:1297–1322, 2010.

[17] V. S. Sheng, F. Provost, and P. G. Ipeirotis. Get another label? improving data quality and data mining using multiple, noisy labelers. In *Proceedings of the 14th ACM SIGKDD international conference on Knowledge discovery and data mining*, pages 614–622. ACM, 2008.

[18] R. Snow, B. O'Connor, D. Jurafsky, and A. Y. Ng. Cheap and fast—but is it good?: evaluating non-expert annotations for natural language tasks. In *Proceedings of the conference on empirical methods in natural language processing*, pages 254–263. Association for Computational Linguistics, 2008.

[19] L. Von Ahn, B. Maurer, C. McMillen, D. Abraham, and M. Blum. recaptcha: Human-based character recognition via web security measures. *Science*, 321(5895):1465–1468, 2008.

[20] P. Welinder, S. Branson, P. Perona, and S. J. Belongie. The multidimensional wisdom of crowds. In *Advances in neural information processing systems*, pages 2424–2432, 2010.

[21] J. Whitehill, T.-f. Wu, J. Bergsma, J. R. Movellan, and P. L. Ruvolo. Whose vote should count more: Optimal integration of labels from labelers of unknown expertise. In *Advances in neural information processing systems*, pages 2035–2043, 2009.

[22] Y. Zheng, S. Scott, and K. Deng. Active learning from multiple noisy labelers with varied costs. In *Data Mining (ICDM), 2010 IEEE 10th International Conference on*, pages 639–648. IEEE, 2010.

An Online Learning Approach to Improving the Quality of Crowd-Sourcing

Yang Liu, Mingyan Liu
Department of Electrical Engineering and Computer Science
University of Michigan, Ann Arbor
Email: {youngliu,mingyan}@eecs.umich.edu

ABSTRACT

We consider a crowd-sourcing problem where in the process of labeling massive datasets, multiple labelers with unknown annotation quality must be selected to perform the labeling task for each incoming data sample or task, with the results aggregated using for example simple or weighted majority voting rule. In this paper we approach this labeler selection problem in an online learning framework, whereby the quality of the labeling outcome by a specific set of labelers is estimated so that the learning algorithm over time learns to use the most effective combinations of labelers. This type of online learning in some sense falls under the family of multi-armed bandit (MAB) problems, but with a distinct feature not commonly seen: since the data is unlabeled to begin with and the labelers' quality is unknown, their labeling outcome (or reward in the MAB context) cannot be directly verified; it can only be estimated against the crowd and known probabilistically. We design an efficient online algorithm LS_OL using a simple majority voting rule that can differentiate high- and low-quality labelers over time, and is shown to have a regret (w.r.t. always using the optimal set of labelers) of $O(\log^2 T)$ uniformly in time under mild assumptions on the collective quality of the crowd, thus regret free in the average sense. We discuss performance improvement by using a more sophisticated majority voting rule, and show how to detect and filter out "bad" (dishonest, malicious or very incompetent) labelers to further enhance the quality of crowd-sourcing. Extension to the case when a labeler's quality is task-type dependent is also discussed using techniques from the literature on continuous arms. We present numerical results using both simulation and a real dataset on a set of images labeled by Amazon Mechanic Turks (AMT).

Categories and Subject Descriptors

F.1.2 [**Modes of Computation**]: Online computation; I.2.6 [**Artificial Intelligence**]: Learning; H.2.8 [**Database Applications**]: Data mining

SIGMETRICS'15, June 15–19, 2015, Portland, OR, USA.

http://dx.doi.org/10.1145/2745844.2745874.

General Terms

Algorithm, Theory, Experimentation

Keywords

Crowd-sourcing, online learning, quality control

1. INTRODUCTION

Machine learning techniques often rely on correctly labeled data for purposes such as building classifiers; this is particularly true for supervised discriminative learning. As shown in [19,22], the quality of labels can significantly impact the quality of the trained classifier and in turn the system performance. Semi-supervised learning methods, e.g. [5,15,25] have been proposed to circumvent the need for labeled data or lower the requirement on the size of labeled data; nonetheless, many state-of-the-art machine learning systems such as those used for pattern recognition continue to rely heavily on supervised learning, which necessitates cleanly labeled data. At the same time, advances in instrumentation and miniaturization, combined with frameworks like participatory sensing, rush in enormous quantities of unlabeled data.

Against this backdrop, crowd-sourcing has emerged as a viable and often favored solution as evidenced by the popularity of the Amazon Mechanical Turk (AMT) system. Prime examples include a number of recent efforts on collecting large-scale labeled image datasets, such as ImageNet [7] and LabelMe [21]. The concept of crowd-sourcing has also been studied in contexts other than processing large amounts of unlabeled data, see e.g., user-generated map [10], opinion/information diffusion [9], and event monitoring [6] in large, decentralized systems.

Its many advantages notwithstanding, the biggest problem with crowd-sourcing is quality control: as shown in several previous studies [12, 22], if labelers (e.g., AMTs) are not selected carefully the resulting labels can be very noisy, due to reasons such as varying degrees of competence, individual biases, and sometimes irresponsible behavior. At the same time, the cost in having a large amount of data labeled (payment to the labelers) is non-trivial. This makes it important to look into ways of improving the quality of the crowd-sourcing process and the quality of the results generated by the labelers.

In this paper we approach the labeler selection problem in an online learning framework, whereby the labeling quality of the labelers is estimated as tasks are assigned and performed, so that an algorithm over time learns to use the more effective combinations of labelers for arriving tasks. This problem in some sense can be cast as a multi-armed bandit (MAB) problem, see e.g., [4, 16, 23]. Within such a framework, the objective is to select the best of a set of choices (or "arms") by repeatedly sampling different choices (referred to as *exploration*), and their empirical quality is subsequently used to control how often a choice is used (referred to as *exploitation*). However, there are two distinct features that set our problem apart from the existing literature in bandit problems. Firstly, since the data is unlabeled to begin with and the labelers' quality is unknown, a particular choice of labelers leads to unknown quality of their labeling outcome (mapped to the "reward" of selecting a choice in the MAB context). Whereas this reward is assumed to be known instantaneously following a selection in the MAB problem, in our model this remains unknown and at best can only be estimated with a certain error probability. This poses significant technical challenge compared to a standard MAB problem. Secondly, to avoid having to deal with a combinatorial number of arms, it is desirable to learn and estimate each individual labeler's quality separately (as opposed to estimating the quality of different combinations of labelers). The optimal selection of labelers then depends on individual qualities as well as how the labeling outcome is computed using individual labels. In this study we will consider both a simple majority voting rule as well as a weighted majority voting rule and derive the respective optimal selection of labelers given their estimated quality.

Due to its online nature, our algorithm can be used in real time, processing tasks as they arrive. Our algorithm thus has the advantage of performing quality assessment and adapting to better labeler selections as tasks arrive. This is a desirable feature because generating and processing large datasets can incur significant cost and delay, so the ability to improve labeler selection on the fly (rather than waiting till the end) can result in substantial cost savings and improvement in processing quality. Below we review the literature most relevant to the study presented in this paper in addition to the MAB literature cited above.

Within the context of learning and differentiating labelers' expertise in crowd-sourcing systems, a number of studies have looked into offline algorithms. For instance, in [8], methods are proposed to eliminate irrelevant users from a set of user-generated dataset; in this case the elimination is done as post-processing to clean up the data since the data has already been labeled by the labelers (tasks have been performed). In [13] an iterative algorithm is proposed that infers labeling quality using a process similar to belief propagation and it is shown that label aggregation based on this method outperforms simple majority voting. Another example is the family of matrix factorization or matrix completion based methods, see e.g., [24], where labeler selection is implicitly done through the numerical process of finding the best recommendation for a participant. Again this is done after the labeling has already been done for all data by all (or almost all) labelers. This type of approaches is more appropriate when used in a recommendation system where data and user-generated labels already exist in large quantities.

Recent study [14] has examined the fundamental trade-off between labeling accuracy and redundancy in task assignment in crowd-sourcing systems. In particular, it is shown that a labeling accuracy of $1-\varepsilon$ for each task can be achieved with a per-task assignment redundancy no more than $O(K/q \cdot \log(K/\varepsilon))$; thus more redundancy can be traded for more accurate outcome. In [14] the task assignment is done in a one-shot fashion (thus non-adaptive) rather than sequentially with each task arrival as considered in our paper, thus the result is more applicable to offline settings similar to those cited in the previous paragraph.

Within online solutions, the concept of active learning has been quite intensively studied, where the labelers are guided to make the labeling process more efficient. Examples include [12], which uses a Bayesian framework to actively assign unlabeled data based on past observations on labeling outcomes, and [18], which uses a probabilistic model to estimate the labelers' expertise. However, most studies on active learning require either an oracle to verify the correctness of the finished tasks which in practice does not exist, or ground-truth feedback from indirect but relevant experiments (see e.g., [12]). Similarly, existing work on using online learning for task assignment also typically assumes the availability of ground truth (as in MAB problems). For instance, in [11] online learning is applied to sequential task assignment but ground-truth of the task performance is used to estimate the performer's quality.

Our work differs from the above as we do not require an oracle or the availability of ground-truth; we instead impose a mild assumption on the collective quality of the crowd (without which crowd-sourcing would be useless and would not have existed). Secondly, our framework allows us to obtain performance bounds on the proposed algorithm in the form of regret with respect to the optimal strategy that always uses the best set of labelers; this type of performance guarantee is lacking in most of the work cited above. Last but not least, our algorithm is broadly applicable to generic crowd-sourcing task assignments rather than being designed for specific type of tasks or data.

Our main contributions are summarized as follows.

1. We design an online learning algorithm to estimate the quality of labelers in a crowd-sourcing setting without ground-truth information but with mild assumptions on the quality of the crowd as a whole, and show that it is able to learn the optimal set of labelers under both simple and weighted majority voting rules and attains no-regret performance guarantees (w.r.t. always using the optimal set of labelers).

2. We similarly provide regret bounds on the cost of this learning algorithm w.r.t. always using the optimal set of labelers.

3. We show how our model and results can be extended to the case where the quality of a labeler may be task-type dependent, as well as a simple procedure to quickly detect and filter out "bad" (dishonest, malicious or incompetent) labelers to further enhance the quality of crowd-sourcing.

4. Our validation includes both simulation and the use of a real-world AMT dataset.

The remainder of the paper is organized as follows. We formulate our problem in Section 2. In Sections 3 and 4 we introduce our learning algorithm along with regret analysis under a simple majority and weighted majority voting rule, respectively. We extend our model to the case where labelers' expertise may be task-dependent in Section 5. Numerical experiments are presented in Section 6. Section 7 concludes the paper.

2. PROBLEM FORMULATION AND PRELIMINARIES

2.1 The crowd-sourcing model

We begin by introducing the following major components of the crowd-sourcing system we consider.

1. *User.* There is a single user with a sequence of tasks (unlabeled data) to be performed/labeled. Our proposed online learning algorithm is to be employed by the user in making labeler selections. Throughout our discussion the terms *task* and *unlabeled data* will be used interchangeably.

2. *Labeler.* There are a total of M labelers, each may be selected to perform a labeling task for a piece of unlabeled data.

The set of labelers is denoted by $\mathcal{M} = \{1, 2, ..., M\}$. A labeler i produces the true label for each assigned task with probability p_i independent of the task; a more sophisticated task-dependent version is discussed in Section 5. This will also be referred to as the quality or accuracy of this labeler. We will assume no two labelers are exactly the same, i.e., $p_i \neq p_j, \forall i \neq j$ and we consider non-trivial cases with $0 < p_i < 1, \forall i$. These quantities are unknown to the user a priori. We will also assume that the accuracy of the collection of labelers satisfies $\bar{p} := \sum_{i=1}^{M} \frac{p_i}{M} > \frac{1}{2}$, and that $M > \frac{\log 2}{2(\bar{p}-1/2)^2}$. The justification and implication of these assumptions are discussed in more detail in Section 2.3.

Our learning system works in discrete time steps $t = 1, 2, ..., T$. At time t, a task $k \in \mathcal{K}$ arrives to be labeled, where $\mathcal{K}$ could be either a finite or infinite set. For simplicity of presentation, we will assume that a single task arrives at each time, and that the labeling outcome is binary: 1 or 0; however, both assumptions can be fairly easily relaxed[1]. For task k, the user selects a subset $S_t \subseteq \mathcal{M}$ to label it. The label generated by labeler $i \in S_t$ for data k at time t is denoted by $L_i(t)$.

The set of labels $\{L_i(t)\}_{i \in S_t}$ generated by the selected labelers then need to be combined to produce a single label for the data; this is often referred to as the information aggregation phase. Since we have no prior knowledge on the labelers' accuracy, we will first apply the simple majority voting rule over the set of labels; later we will also examine a more sophisticated weighted majority voting rule. Mathematically, the majority voting rule at time t leads to the following label output:

$$L^*(t) = \text{argmax}_{l \in \{0,1\}} \sum_{i \in S_t} I_{L_i(t)=l} , \tag{1}$$

with ties (i.e., $\sum_{i \in S_t} I_{L_i(t)=0} = \sum_{i \in S_t} I_{L_i(t)=1}$, where I denotes the indicator function) broken randomly.

Denote by $\pi(S_t)$ the probability of obtaining the correct label following the simple majority rule above, and we have:

$$\pi(S_t) = \underbrace{\sum_{S: S \subseteq S_t, |S| \geq \lceil \frac{|S_t|+1}{2} \rceil} \prod_{i \in S} p_i \cdot \prod_{j \in S_t \setminus S} (1 - p_j)}_{\text{Majority wins}} + \underbrace{\frac{\sum_{S: S \subseteq S_t, |S| = \frac{|S_t|}{2}} \prod_{i \in S} p_i \cdot \prod_{j \in S_t \setminus S} (1 - p_j)}{2}}_{\text{Ties broken equally likely}} . \tag{2}$$

Denote by c_i a normalized cost/payment per task to labeler i and consider the following linear cost function

$$\mathcal{C}(S) = \sum_{i \in S} c_i, \; S \subseteq \mathcal{M} . \tag{3}$$

Extensions of our analysis to other forms of cost functions are feasible though with more cumbersome notations. Denote

$$S^* = \text{argmax}_{S \subseteq \mathcal{M}} \pi(S) , \tag{4}$$

thus S^* is the optimal selection of labelers given each individual's accuracy. We also refer to $\pi(S)$ as the utility for selecting the set of labelers S and denote it equivalently as $U(S)$. $\mathcal{C}(S^*)$ will be referred to as the necessary cost per task. In most crowd-sourcing systems the main goal is to obtain high quality labels while the cost accrued is a secondary issue. For completeness, however, we will also analyze the tradeoff between the two. Therefore we shall adopt two objectives when designing an efficient online algorithm: choosing the best set of labelers while keeping the cost low.

It should be noted that one can also combine labeling accuracy and cost to form a single objective function, such as $\pi(S) - \mathcal{C}(S)$. The resulting analysis is quite similar to and can be easily reproduced from that presented in this paper .

[1]Indeed in our experiment shown later in Section 6, our algorithm is applied to a non-binary multi-label case.

2.2 Off-line optimal selection of labelers

Before addressing the learning problem, we will first take a look at how to efficiently derive the optimal selection S^* given accuracy probabilities $\{p_i\}_{i \in \mathcal{M}}$. This will be a crucial step repeatedly invoked by the learning procedure we develop next, to determine the set of labelers to use given a set of *estimated* accuracy probabilities.

The optimal selection is a function of the values $\{p_i\}_{i \in \mathcal{M}}$ and the aggregation rule used to compute the final label. While there is a combinatorial number of possible selections, the next two results combined lead to a very simple and linear-complexity procedure in finding the optimal S^*.

THEOREM 1. *Under the simple majority vote rule, the optimal number of labelers $s^* = |S^*|$ must be an odd number.*

THEOREM 2. *The optimal set S^* is monotonic, i.e., if we have $i \in S^*$ and $j \notin S^*$ then we must have $p_i > p_j$.*

Proofs of the above two theorems can be found in the appendices. Using these results, given a set of accuracy probabilities the optimal selection under the majority vote rule consists of the top s^* (an odd number) labelers with the highest quality; thus we only need to compute s^*, which has a linear complexity of $O(M/2)$. A set that consists of the highest m labelers will henceforth be referred to as a *m-monotonic set*, and denoted as $S^m \subseteq \mathcal{M}$.

2.3 The lack of ground truth

As mentioned, a key difference between our model and many other studies on crowd-sourcing as well as the basic framework of MAB problems is that we lack ground-truth in our system; we elaborate on this below. In a standard MAB setting, when a player (the user in our scenario) selects a set of arms (labelers) to activate, she immediately finds out the rewards associated with those selected arms. This information allows the player to collect statistics on each arm (e.g., sample mean rewards) which is then used in her future selection decisions. In our scenario, the user sees the labels generated by each selected labeler, but does not know which ones are true. In this sense the user does not find out about her reward immediately after a decision; she can only do so probabilistically over a period of time through additional estimation devices. This constitutes the main conceptual and technical difference between our problem and the standard MAB problem.

Given the lack of ground-truth, the crowd-sourcing system is only useful if the average labeler is more or less trustworthy. For instance, if a majority of the labelers produce the wrong label most of the time, unbeknownst to the user, then the system is effectively useless, i.e., the user has no way to tell whether she could trust the outcome so she might as well abandon the system. It is therefore reasonable to have some trustworthiness assumption in place. Accordingly, we have assumed that $\bar{p} = \sum_{i=1}^{M} \frac{p_i}{M} > 0.5$, i.e., the average labeling quality is higher than 0.5 or a random guess; this is a common assumption in the crowd-sourcing literature (see e.g., [8]). Note that this is a fairly mild assumption: not all labelers need to have accuracy $p_i > 0.5$ or near 0.5; some labeler may have arbitrarily low quality (~ 0) as long as it is in the minority.

Denote by X_i a binomial random variable with parameter p_i to model labeler i's outcome on a given task: $X_i = 1$ if her label is correct and 0 otherwise. Using Chernoff Hoeffding's inequality we have

$$P(\frac{\sum_{i=1}^{M} X_i}{M} > 1/2) = 1 - P(\frac{\sum_{i=1}^{M} X_i}{M} \leq 1/2)$$
$$= 1 - P(\frac{\sum_{i=1}^{M} X_i}{M} - \bar{p} \leq 1/2 - \bar{p})$$
$$\geq 1 - e^{-2M\cdot(\bar{p}-1/2)^2} .$$

Define $a_{\min} := P(\frac{\sum_{i=1}^{M} X_i}{M} > 1/2)$; this is the probability that a simple majority vote over the M labelers is correct. Therefore, if $\bar{p} > 1/2$ and further $M > \frac{\log 2}{2(\bar{p}-1/2)^2}$, then $1 - e^{-2M\cdot(\bar{p}-1/2)^2} > 1/2$, meaning a simple majority vote would be correct most of the time. Throughout the paper we will assume both these conditions are true. It also follows that we have:

$$P(\frac{\sum_{i \in S^*} X_i}{s^*} > 1/2) \geq P(\frac{\sum_{i=1}^{M} X_i}{M} > 1/2),$$

where the inequality is due to the definition of the optimal set S^*.

3. LEARNING THE OPTIMAL LABELER SELECTION

In this section we present an online learning algorithm LS_OL that over time learns each labeler's accuracy, which it then uses to compute an estimated optimal set of labelers using the properties given in the previous section.

3.1 An online learning algorithm LS_OL

The algorithm consists of two types of time steps, exploration and exploitation, as is common to online learning. However, the design of the exploration step is complicated by the additional estimation needs due to the lack of ground-truth revelation. Specifically, a set of tasks will be designated as "testers" and may be repeatedly assigned to the same labeler in order to obtain consistent results used for estimating her label quality. This can be done in one of two ways depending on the nature of the tasks. For tasks like survey questions (e.g. those with multiple choices), a labeler may indeed be prompted to answer the same question (or equivalent variants with alternative wording) multiple times, usually not in succession, during the survey process. This is a common technique used by survey designers for quality control by testing whether a participant answers questions randomly or consistently, whether a participant is losing attention over time, and so on, see e.g., [20]. For tasks like labeling images, a labeler may be given identical images repeatedly or each time with small, added iid noise.

With the above in mind, the algorithm conceptually proceeds as follows. A condition is checked to determine whether the algorithm should explore or exploit in a given time step. If it is to exploit, then the algorithm selects the best set of labelers based on current quality estimates to label the arriving task. If it is to explore, then the algorithm will either assign an old task (an existing tester) or the new arriving task (which then becomes a tester) to the entire set of labelers $\mathscr{M}$ depending on whether all existing testers have been labeled enough number of times. Because of the need to repeatedly assign an old task, some new tasks will not be immediately assigned (those arriving during an exploration step while an old task remains under-labeled). These tasks will simply be given a random label (e.g., with error probability 1/2) but their numbers are limited by the frequency of an exploration step ($\sim \log^2 T$), as we shall detail later.

Before proceeding to a more precise description of the algorithm, a few additional notions are in order. Denote the n-th label outcome (via majority vote over M labelers in exploration) for task k by $y_k(n)$. Denote by $y_k^*(N)$ the label obtained using majority rule over the N label outcomes $y_k(1), y_k(2), \cdots, y_k(N)$:

$$y_k^*(N) = \begin{cases} 1, & \frac{\sum_{n=1}^{N} I_{y_k(n)=1}}{N} > 0.5 \\ 0, & \text{otherwise} \end{cases} , \qquad (5)$$

with ties broken randomly. It is this majority label after N tests on a tester task k that will be used to analyze different labeler's performance. A tester task is always assigned to all labelers for labeling. Following our earlier assumption that the repeated assignments of the same task use identical and independent variants of the task, we will also take the repeated outcomes $y_k(1), y_k(2), \cdots, y_k(N)$ to be independent and statistically identical.

Denote by $E(t)$ the set of tasks assigned to the M labelers during exploration steps up to time t. For each task $k \in E(t)$ denote by $\hat{N}_k(t)$ the number of times k has been assigned. Consider the following random variable defined at each time t:

$$\mathscr{O}(t) = I_{|E(t)| \leq D_1(t) \text{ or } \exists k \in E(t) \text{ s.t. } \hat{N}_k(t) \leq D_2(t)} ,$$

where

$$D_1(t) = \frac{1}{(\frac{1}{\max_{m:m \text{ odd}} m\cdot n(S^m)} - \alpha)^2 \cdot \varepsilon^2} \cdot \log t ,$$
$$D_2(t) = \frac{1}{(a_{\min} - 0.5)^2} \cdot \log t ,$$

and $n(S^m)$ is the number of all possible majority subsets (for example when $|S^m| = 5$, $n(S^m)$ is the number of all possible subset of size being at least 3) of S^m, ε a bounded constant, and α a positive constant such that $\alpha < \frac{1}{\max_{m:m \text{ odd}} m\cdot n(S^m)}$. Note that $\mathscr{O}(t)$ captures the event when either an insufficient number of tester tasks have been assigned under exploration or some tester task has been assigned insufficient number of times in exploration.

Our online algorithm for labeler selection is formally stated in Figure 1. The LS_OL algorithm can either go on indefinitely or terminate at some time T. As we show below the performance bound on this algorithm holds uniformly in time so it does not matter when it terminates.

3.2 Main results

The standard metric for evaluating an online algorithm in the MAB literature is *regret*, the difference between the performance of an algorithm and that of a reference algorithm which often assumes foresight or hindsight. The most commonly used is the *weak regret* measure with respect to the best single-action policy assuming a priori knowledge of the underlying statistics. In our problem context, this means to compare our algorithm to the one that always uses the optimal selection S^*. It follows that this weak regret, up to time T, is given by

$$R(T) = T \cdot U(S^*) - \sum_{t=1}^{T} U(S_t) ,$$
$$R_{\mathscr{C}}(T) = \sum_{t=1}^{T} \mathscr{C}(S_t) - T \cdot \mathscr{C}(S^*) ,$$

where S_t is the selection made at time t by our algorithm; if t happens to be an exploration step then $S_t = \mathscr{M}$ and $U(S_t)$ is either 1/2 due to random guess of an arriving task that is not labeled, or $a_{\min}$ when a tester task is labeled for the first time. $R(T)$ and $R_{\mathscr{C}}(T)$ respectively capture the regret of the learning algorithm in perfor-

Online Labeler Selection: LS_OL

1: Initialization at $t = 0$: Initialize the estimated accuracy $\{\tilde{p}_i\}_{i\in\mathcal{M}}$ to some value in $[0,1]$; denote the initialization task as k, set $E(t) = \{k\}$ and $\hat{N}_k(t) = 1$.

2: At time t a new task arrives: If $\mathcal{O}(t) = 1$, the algorithm explores.

2.1: If there is no task $k \in E(t)$ such that $\hat{N}_k(t) \le D_2(t)$, then assign the new task to $\mathcal{M}$ and update $E(t)$ to include it and denote it by k; if there is such a task, randomly select one of them, denoted by k, to $\mathcal{M}$. $\hat{N}_k(t) := \hat{N}_k(t) + 1$; obtain the label $y_k(\hat{N}_k(t))$;

2.2: Update $y_k^*(\hat{N}_k(t))$ (using the alternate indicator function notation $I(\cdot)$):

$$y_k^*(\hat{N}_k(t)) = I(\frac{\sum_{\hat{t}=1}^{\hat{N}_k(t)} y_k(\hat{t})}{\hat{N}_k(t)} > 0.5) .$$

2.3: Update labelers' accuracy estimate $\forall i \in \mathcal{M}$:

$$\tilde{p}_i = \frac{\sum_{k\in E(t), k \text{ arrives at time } \hat{t}} I(L_i(\hat{t}) = y_k^*(\hat{N}_k(t)))}{|E(t)|} .$$

3: Else if $\mathcal{O}(t) = 0$, the algorithm exploits and computes:

$$S_t = \text{argmax}_m \tilde{U}(S^m) = \text{argmax}_{S\subseteq\mathcal{M}} \tilde{\pi}(S) ,$$

which is solved using the linear search property, but with the current estimates $\{\tilde{p}_i\}$ rather than the true quantities $\{p_i\}$, resulting in estimated utility $\tilde{U}()$ and $\tilde{\pi}()$. Assign the new task to those in S_t.

4: Set $t = t+1$ and go to Step 2.

Figure 1: Description of LS_OL

mance and in cost. Define:

$$\Delta_{\max} = \max_{S\neq S^*} U(S^*) - U(S),\ \delta_{\max} = \max_{i\neq j} |p_i - p_j| ,$$
$$\Delta_{\min} = \min_{S\neq S^*} U(S^*) - U(S),\ \delta_{\min} = \min_{i\neq j} |p_i - p_j| .$$

ε is a constant such that $\varepsilon < \min\{\frac{\Delta_{\min}}{2}, \frac{\delta_{\min}}{2}\}$. For analysis we assume $U(S^i) \neq U(S^j)$ if $i \neq j$[2]. Define the sequence $\{\beta_n\}$: $\beta_n = \sum_{t=1}^{\infty} \frac{1}{t^n}$. Our main theorem is stated as follows.

THEOREM 3. *The regret can be bounded uniformly in time:*

$$R(T) \le \frac{U(S^*)}{(\frac{1}{\max_{m:m \text{ odd}} m\cdot n(S^m)} - \alpha)^2 \cdot \varepsilon^2 \cdot (a_{\min} - 0.5)^2} \cdot \log^2(T)$$
$$+ \Delta_{\max}(2\sum_{\substack{m=1\\ m \text{ odd}}}^{M} m\cdot n(S^m) + M)\cdot(2\beta_2 + \frac{1}{\alpha\cdot\varepsilon}\beta_{2-z}) , \quad (6)$$

$$R_{\mathcal{C}}(T) \le \frac{\sum_{i\notin S^*} c_i}{(\frac{1}{\max_{m:m \text{ odd}} m\cdot n(S^m)} - \alpha)^2 \cdot \varepsilon^2} \cdot \log T$$
$$+ \frac{\sum_{i\in\mathcal{M}} c_i}{(\frac{1}{\max_{m:m \text{ odd}} m\cdot n(S^m)} - \alpha)^2 \cdot \varepsilon^2 \cdot (a_{\min} - 0.5)^2} \cdot \log^2(T)$$
$$+ (M - |S^*|)\cdot(2\sum_{\substack{m=1\\ m \text{ odd}}}^{M} m\cdot n(S^m) + M)\cdot(2\beta_2 + \frac{1}{\alpha\cdot\varepsilon}\beta_{2-z}) , \quad (7)$$

where $0 < z < 1$ is a positive constant.

First note that the regret is nearly logarithmic in T and therefore it has zero average regret as $T \to \infty$; such an algorithm is often referred to as a zero-regret algorithm. Secondly the regret bound is inversely related to the minimum accuracy of the crowd (through $a_{\min}$). This is to be expected: with higher accuracy (a larger $a_{\min}$) of the crowd, crowd-sourcing generates ground-truth outputs with higher probability and thus the learning process could be accelerated. Finally, the bound also depends on $\max_m m\cdot n(S^m)$ which is roughly on the order of $O(\frac{2^m\sqrt{m}}{\sqrt{2\pi}})$.

3.3 Regret analysis of LS_OL

We now outline key steps in the proof of the above theorem. This involves a sequence of lemmas; the proofs of most can be found in the appendices. There are a few that we omit for brevity; in those cases sketches are provided.

Step 1: We begin by noting that the regret consists of that arising from the exploration phase and from the exploitation phase, denoted by $R_e(T)$ and $R_x(T)$, respectively:

$$R(T) = E[R_e(T)] + E[R_x(T)] .$$

The following result bounds the first element of the regret.

LEMMA 1. *The regret up to time T from the exploration phase can be bounded as follows:*

$$E[R_e(T)] \le U(S^*)\cdot(D_1(T)\cdot D_2(T)) . \quad (8)$$

We see the regret depends on the exploration parameters as product. This is because for tasks arriving in exploration steps, we assign it at least $D_2(T)$ times to the labelers; each time when re-assignment occurs, a new arriving task is given a random label while under an optimal scheme each missed new task means a utility of $U(S^*)$.

Step 2: We now bound the regret arising from the exploitation phase as a function of the number of times the algorithm uses a sub-optimal selection when the ordering of the labelers is correct, and the number of times the estimates of the labelers' accuracy result in a wrong ordering. The proof of the lemma below is omitted as it is fairly straightforward.

LEMMA 2. *For the regret from exploitation we have:*

$$E[R_x(T)] \le \Delta_{\max}\left(E[\sum_{t=1}^{T}(\mathcal{E}_1(t) + \mathcal{E}_2(t))]\right) . \quad (9)$$

Here $\mathcal{E}_1(t) = I_{S_t\neq S^*}$, conditioned on correct ordering of labelers, counts the event when a sub-optimal section (other than S^*) was used at time t based on the current estimates $\{\tilde{p}_i\}$. $\mathcal{E}_2(t)$ counts the event when at time t the set $\mathcal{M}$ is sorted in the wrong order because of erroneous estimates $\{\tilde{p}_i\}$.

Step 3: We proceed to bound the two terms in (9) separately. In this part of the analysis we only consider those times t when the algorithm exploits.

[2]This can be precisely established when $p_i \neq p_j, \forall i \neq j$.

LEMMA 3. *At time t we have:*

$$E[\mathscr{E}_1(t)] \leq \sum_{\substack{m=1 \\ m\ odd}}^{M} m \cdot n(S^m) \cdot (\frac{2}{t^2} + \frac{1}{\alpha \cdot \varepsilon \cdot t^{2-z}}) . \quad (10)$$

The idea behind the above lemma is to use a union bound over all possible events where the wrong set is chosen when the ordering of the labelers is correct according to their true accuracy.

LEMMA 4. *At time t we have:*

$$E[\mathscr{E}_2(t)] \leq M(\frac{2}{t^2} + \frac{1}{\alpha \cdot \varepsilon \cdot t^{2-z}}) . \quad (11)$$

Step 4: Summing up all above results and rearranging terms lead to the theorem. Specifically,

$$\begin{aligned} E[R_x(T)] &\leq \Delta_{\max} \sum_{\substack{m=1 \\ m\ \text{odd}}}^{M} 2 \sum_{t=1}^{T} m \cdot n(S^m) \cdot (\frac{2}{t^2} + \frac{1}{\alpha \cdot \varepsilon \cdot t^{2-z}}) \\ &+ \Delta_{\max} \cdot M \cdot \sum_{t=1}^{T} (\frac{2}{t^2} + \frac{1}{\alpha \cdot \varepsilon \cdot t^{2-z}}) \\ &\leq 2 \cdot \Delta_{\max} \sum_{\substack{m=1 \\ m\ \text{odd}}}^{M} m \cdot n(S^m) \cdot \sum_{t=1}^{\infty} (\frac{2}{t^2} + \frac{1}{\alpha \cdot \varepsilon \cdot t^{2-z}}) \\ &+ \Delta_{\max} \cdot M \cdot \sum_{t=1}^{\infty} (\frac{2}{t^2} + \frac{1}{\alpha \cdot \varepsilon \cdot t^{2-z}}) \\ &= \Delta_{\max} (2 \cdot \sum_{\substack{m=1 \\ m\ \text{odd}}}^{M} m \cdot n(S^m) + M) \cdot (2\beta_2 + \frac{1}{\alpha \cdot \varepsilon} \beta_{2-z}) . \end{aligned}$$

Since $\beta_{2-z} < \infty$ for $z < 1$, we have bounded the exploitation regret by a constant. Summing over all terms in $E[R_e(T)]$ and $E[R_x(T)]$ we obtain the main theorem.

3.4 Cost analysis of LS_OL

We now analyze the cost regret. Following similar analysis we first note that it can be calculated separately for the exploration and exploitation steps. For *exploration* steps we know the cost regret is bounded by

$$\sum_{i \notin S^*} c_i \cdot D_1(T) + \sum_{i \in \mathscr{M}} c_i \cdot D_1(T) \cdot (D_2(T) - 1)$$

where the second term is due to the fact for all costs associated with task re-assignments are treated as additional costs.

For *exploitation* steps the additional cost is upper-bounded by

$$(M - |S^*|) \cdot E[\sum_{t=1}^{T} (\mathscr{E}_1(t) + \mathscr{E}_2(t))] .$$

Using earlier results we know the cost regret $R_{\mathscr{C}}(T)$ will be similar to $R(T)$ with both terms bounded by either a log term or a constant. Plugging in $D_1(T), D_2(T), E[\sum_{t=1}^{T} (\mathscr{E}_2(t)], E[\sum_{t=1}^{T} \mathscr{E}_2(t)]$ we establish the regret for $R_{\mathscr{C}}(T)$ as claimed in our main result.

3.5 Discussion

We end this section with a discussion on how to relax a number of assumptions adopted in our analytical framework.

3.5.1 *IID re-assignments*

The first concerns the re-assignment of the same task (or iid copies of the same task) and the assumption that the labeling outcome each time is independent. In the case where iid copies are available, this assumption is justified. In the case when the exact same task must be re-assigned, enforcing a delay between successive re-assignments can make this assumption more realistic. Suppose the algorithm imposes a random delay τ_k, a positive random variable uniformly upper-bounded by $\tau_k \leq \tau_{\max}, \forall k$. Then following similar analysis we can show the regret is at most $\tau_{\max}$ times larger, i.e., it can be bounded by $\tau_{\max} \cdot R(T)$, where $R(T)$ is as defined in Eqn.(6).

3.5.2 *Prior knowledge on several constants*

The second assumption concerns the selection of constant ε by the algorithm and the analysis which requires knowledge on $\Delta_{\min}$ and $\delta_{\min}$. This assumption however can be removed by using a decreasing sequence ε_t. This is a standard technique that has been commonly used in the online learning literature, see e.g., [3,17,23]. Specifically, let

$$\varepsilon_t = \frac{1}{\log^{\eta}(t)}, \text{ for some } \eta > 0 .$$

Replace $\log(t)$ with $\log^{1+2\eta}(t)$ in $D_1(t)$ and $D_2(t)$ it can be shown that $\exists T_0$ s.t. : $\varepsilon_{T_0} < \varepsilon$. Thus the regret associated with using an imperfect ε_t is bounded by $\sum_{t=1}^{T_0} 2\varepsilon_t = \sum_{t=1}^{T_0} \frac{2}{\log^{\eta} t} = C_{T_0}$, a constant.

3.5.3 *Detecting bad/incompetent labelers*

The last assumption we discuss concerns the quality of the set of labelers, assumed to satisfy the condition $\min\{a_{\min}, \bar{p}\} > 0.5$. Recall the bounds were derived based on this assumption and are indeed functions of $a_{\min}$. While in this discussion we will not seek to relax this assumption, below we describe a simple "vetting" procedure that can be easily incorporated into the LS_OL algorithm to quickly detect and filter out outliner labelers so that over the remaining labelers we can achieve higher values of $a_{\min}$ and $\bar{p}$, and consequently a better bound. The procedure keeps count of the number of times a labeler differs from the majority opinion during the exploration steps, then over time we can safely eliminate those with high counts.

The justification behind this procedure is as follows. Let random variable $Z_i(t)$ denote whether labeler i agrees with the majority vote in labeling a task in a given assignment in exploration step t: $Z_i(t) = 1$ if they disagree and 0 otherwise. Then

$$\begin{aligned} P(Z_i(t) = 1) &= (1 - p_i) \cdot \pi(\mathscr{M}) + p_i \cdot (1 - \pi(\mathscr{M})) \\ &= \pi(\mathscr{M}) + p_i \cdot (1 - 2\pi(\mathscr{M})) , \end{aligned} \quad (12)$$

where recall $\pi(\mathscr{M})$ is the probability the majority vote is correct. Under the same assumption $a_{\min} > 1/2$ we have $\pi(\mathscr{M}) > 1/2$, and it follows that $P(Z_i(t) = 1)$ is decreasing in p_i, i.e., the more accurate a labeler is, the less likely she is going to disagree with the majority vote, as intuition would suggest. It further follows that for $p_i > p_j$ we have

$$\varepsilon_{ij} := E[Z_i(t) - Z_j(t)] < 0 .$$

Similarly, if we consider the disagreement counts over N assignments, $\sum_{t=1}^{N} Z_j(t)$, then for $p_i > p_j$ we have

$$\begin{aligned} &P(\sum_{t=1}^{N} Z_i(t) < \sum_{t=1}^{N} Z_j(t)) \\ &= P(\frac{\sum_{t=1}^{N} (Z_i(t) - Z_j(t))}{N} < 0) \\ &= P(\frac{\sum_{t=1}^{N} (Z_i(t) - Z_j(t))}{N} - \varepsilon_{ij} < -\varepsilon_{ij}) \\ &\geq 1 - e^{-2\varepsilon_{ij}^2 N} . \end{aligned} \quad (13)$$

That is, if the number of assignments N is on the order of $\log T/\varepsilon_{ij}^2$, then the above probability approaches 1, which bounds the likelihood that labeler i (higher quality) will have fewer number of disagreements than labeler j. Therefore if we rank and order the labelers in decreasing order of their accumulated disagreement counts then the worst labeler is going to be at the top of the list with increasing probability (approaching 1). If we eliminate the worst performer, then we improve $a_{\min}$ which leads to better bounds as shown in Eqn. (6) and Eqn. (7). Compared to the exploration steps detailed earlier where in order to differentiate labelers' expertise (by estimating p_i) $O(\log^2 T)$ assignments are needed, here we only need $O(\log T)$ assignments, a much faster process. In practice, we could decide to remove the worst labeler when the probability of not making an error (per Eqn. (13)) exceeds a certain threshold.

4. WEIGHTED MAJORITY VOTE AND ITS REGRET

The crowd-sourced labeling performance could be improved by employing more sophisticated majority voting mechanism. Specifically, under our online learning algorithm LS_OL, statistics over each labeler's expertise could be collected with significant confidence; this enables a weighted majority voting mechanism. In this section we analyze the regret of a similar learning algorithm using weighted majority voting.

4.1 Weighted Majority Voting

We start with defining the weights. At time t, after observing labels produced by the labelers, we can optimally (*a posteriori*) determine the mostly likely label of the task by solving the following:

$$\mathrm{argmax}_{l\in\{0,1\}} P(L^*(t) = l | L_1(t), ..., L_M(t)) . \quad (14)$$

Suppose at time t the true label for task k is 1. Then we have,

$$\begin{aligned} &P(L^*(t) = 1 | L_1(t), ..., L_M(t)) \\ &= \frac{P(L_1(t), ..., L_M(t), L^*(t) = 1)}{P((L_1(t), ..., L_M(t))} \\ &= \frac{P(L_1(t), ..., L_M(t) | L^*(t) = 1) \cdot P(L^*(t) = 1)}{P((L_1(t), ..., L_M(t))} \\ &= \frac{P(L^*(t) = 1)}{P((L_1(t), ..., L_M(t))} \cdot \prod_{i:L_i(t)=1} p_i \cdot \prod_{i:L_i(t)=0} (1-p_i) . \end{aligned}$$

And similarly we have

$$\begin{aligned} &P(L^*(t) = 0 | L_1(t), ..., L_M(t)) \\ &= \frac{P(L^*(t) = 0)}{P((L_1(t), ..., L_M(t))} \cdot \prod_{i:L_i(t)=0} p_i \cdot \prod_{i:L_i(t)=1} (1-p_i) . \end{aligned}$$

Following standard hypothesis testing procedure and assuming equal priors $P(L^*(t) = 1) = P(L^*(t) = 0)$, a true label of 1 can be correctly produced if

$$\prod_{i:L_i(t)=1} p_i \cdot \prod_{i:L_i(t)=0} (1-p_i) > \prod_{i:L_i(t)=0} p_i \cdot \prod_{i:L_i(t)=1} (1-p_i) .$$

with ties broken randomly and equally likely. Take $\log(\cdot)$ on both sides and the above condition reduces to

$$\sum_{i:L_i(t)=1} \log \frac{p_i}{1-p_i} > \sum_{j:L_j(t)=0} \log \frac{p_j}{1-p_j} .$$

Indeed if $p_1 = ... = p_M$ the above reduces to $|\{i : L_i(t) = 1\}| > |\{i : L_i(t) = 0\}|$ which is exactly the simple majority rule. Under the weighted majority vote, each labeler i's decision is modulated by weight $\log \frac{p_i}{1-p_i}$. When $p_i > 0.5$, the weight $\log \frac{p_i}{1-p_i} > 0$, which may be viewed as an opinion that adds value; when $p_i < 0.5$, the weight $\log \frac{p_i}{1-p_i} < 0$, an opinion that actually hurts; when $p_i = 0.5$ the weight is zero, an opinion that does not count as it mounts to a random guess. The above constitutes the weighted majority vote rule we shall use in a revised learning algorithm and the regret analysis that follow.

Before proceeding to the regret analysis, we again first characterize the optimal labeler set selection assuming known labelers' accuracy. In this case the odd-number selection property no longer holds, but thanks to the monotonicity of $\log \frac{p_i}{1-p_i}$ in p_i we have the same monotonicity property in the optimal set and a linear-complexity solution space.

THEOREM 4. *Under the weighted majority vote and assuming $p_i \geq 0.5, \forall i$, the optimal set S^* is monotonic, i.e., if we have $i \in S^*$ and $j \notin S^*$ then we must have $p_i > p_j$.*

The assumption of all $p_i \geq 0.5$ is for simplicity in presentation, because a labeler with $p_i < 0.5$ is equivalent to another with $p_i := 1 - p_i$ by flipping its label.

4.2 Main results

We now analyze the performance of a similar learning algorithm using weighted majority vote. The algorithm LS_OL is modified as follows. Denote by

$$W(S) = \sum_{i\in S} \log \frac{p_i}{1-p_i}, \ \forall S \subseteq \mathscr{M} , \quad (15)$$

and $\tilde{W}$ its estimated version when using estimated accuracies $\tilde{p}_i$. Denote by $\delta_{\min}^W = \min_{S\neq S', W(S)\neq W(S')} |W(S) - W(S')|$ and let $\varepsilon < \delta_{\min}^W/2$. At time t (assuming in exploitation), the algorithm selects the estimated optimal set S_t. These labelers then return their labels that divide them into two subsets, say S (with one label) and its complement $S_t \backslash S$ (with the other label). If $\tilde{W}(S) \geq \tilde{W}(S_t\backslash S) + \varepsilon$, we will call S the majority set and take its label as the voting outcome. If $|\tilde{W}(S) - \tilde{W}(S_t\backslash S)| < \varepsilon$, we will call them equal sets and randomly select one of the labels as the voting outcome. Intuitively ε serves as a tolerance that helps to remove the error due to inaccurate estimations. In addition, the constant $D_1(t)$ is revised to the follow:

$$D_1(t) = \left(\frac{1}{\max_m \max\{4C\cdot m, m\cdot n(S^m)\}} - \alpha\right)^2 \cdot \varepsilon^2 \cdot \log t,$$

where C is a constant satisfying

$$C > \max_i \max\{\frac{1+\varepsilon/4}{p_i}, \frac{1-\varepsilon/4}{1-p_i}, \frac{\varepsilon/4}{p_i}, \frac{\varepsilon/4}{1-p_i}\} .$$

With above modifications in mind, we omit the detailed algorithm description for a concise presentation. We have the following theorem on the regret of this revised algorithm ($R_{\mathscr{C}}(T)$ has a very similar format and its detail is omitted).

THEOREM 5. *The regret under weighted majority vote can be bounded uniformly in time:*

$$\begin{aligned} R(T) \leq &\frac{U(S^*)}{\left(\frac{1}{\max_m \max\{4C\cdot m, m\cdot n(S^m)\}} - \alpha\right)^2 \cdot \varepsilon^2 \cdot (a_{\min} - 0.5)^2} \log^2 T \\ &+ \Delta_{\max}(2 \cdot \sum_{m=1}^{M} m\cdot n(S^m) + M + \frac{M^2}{2}) \cdot (2\beta_2 + \frac{1}{\alpha\cdot\varepsilon}\beta_{2-z}) . \end{aligned}$$

Again the regret is on the order of $O(\log^2 T)$ in time. It has a larger constant compared to that under simple majority vote. However, the weighted majority vote has a better optimal solution, i.e., we are converging slightly slower to a however better target. Meanwhile note that by using weighted majority vote on the testers, $a_{\min}$ can be also be potentially increased which leads to a better upper bound.

The proof of this theorem is omitted for brevity and because most of it is similar to the case of simple majority vote. There is however one main difference: under the weighted majority vote there is additional error in computing the weighted majority vote. Whereas under simple majority we simply find the majority set by counting the number of votes, under weighted majority the calculation of the majority set is dependent on the estimated weights $\log \frac{\tilde{p}_i}{1-\tilde{p}_i}$ which inherits errors in $\{\tilde{p}_i\}$. This additional error, associated with bounding the error of getting

$$\tilde{W}(\hat{S}) - \tilde{W}(S \backslash \hat{S}) < \varepsilon, \text{ when } W(\hat{S}) > W(S \backslash \hat{S})$$

and

$$\tilde{W}(\hat{S}) - \tilde{W}(S \backslash \hat{S}) \geq \varepsilon, \text{ when } W(\hat{S}) = W(S \backslash \hat{S})$$

for $\hat{S} \subseteq S \subseteq \mathscr{M}$, can be separately bounded using similar methods as shown in the simple majority vote case (bounding estimation error with a sufficiently large number of samples) and can again be factored into the overall bound. This is summarized in the following lemma.

LEMMA 5. *At time t, for set $\hat{S} \subseteq S \subseteq \mathscr{M}$ and its complement $S \backslash \hat{S}$, if $W(\hat{S}) > W(S \backslash \hat{S})$, then at an exploitation step t, $\forall\, 0 < z < 1$,*

$$P(\tilde{W}(\hat{S}) - \tilde{W}(S \backslash \hat{S}) < \varepsilon) \leq |S| \cdot \left(\frac{2}{t^2} + \frac{1}{\alpha \cdot \varepsilon \cdot t^{2-z}}\right).$$

Moreover, if $W(\hat{S}) = W(S \backslash \hat{S})$, then

$$P(|\tilde{W}(\hat{S}) - \tilde{W}(S \backslash \hat{S})| > \varepsilon) \leq |S| \cdot \left(\frac{2}{t^2} + \frac{1}{\alpha \cdot \varepsilon \cdot t^{2-z}}\right).$$

The rest of the proof can be found in the appendices.

5. LABELERS WITH DIFFERENT TYPES OF TASKS

We now discuss an extension where labelers' difference in their quality in labeling varies according to different types of data samples/tasks. For example, some are more proficient with labeling image data while some may be better at annotating audio data. In this case we can use contextual information to capture these differences, where a specific context refers to a different data/task type. There are two cases of interest from a technical point of view: when the space of all context information is finite, and when this space is infinite. We will denote a specific context by w and the set of all contexts as $\mathscr{W}$.

In the case of discrete context, $|\mathscr{W}| < \infty$ and we can apply the same algorithm to learn, for each combination $\{i, w\}_{i \in \mathscr{M}, w \in \mathscr{W}}$, the pairwise labeler-context accuracy. This extension is rather straightforward except for a longer exploration phase. In fact, since exploration is needed for each labeler i under each possible context w, we may expect the regret to be $|\mathscr{W}|$ times larger compared to the previous $R(T)$. This indeed can be more precisely established using the same methodology.

The case of continuous context information is more challenging, but can be dealt with using the technique introduced in [2] for bandit problems with a continuum of arms. The main idea is to divide the infinite context information space into a finite but increasing number of subsets. For instance, if we model the context information space as $\mathscr{W} = [0, 1]$ then we can divide this unit interval into $v(t)$ sub-intervals:

$$[0, \frac{1}{v(t)}], \ldots, [\frac{v(t)-1}{v(t)}, 1],$$

with $v(t)$ being an increasing sequence of t. Denote these intervals as $B_i(t), i = 1, 2 \ldots, v(t)$, which become more and more fine-grained with increasing t and increasing $v(t)$.

Given these intervals the learning algorithm works as follows. At time t, for each interval $B_i(t)$ we compute the estimated optimal set of labelers by calculating the estimated utility of all subsets of labelers, and this is done over the entire interval $B_i(t)$ (contexts within $B_i(t)$ are viewed as a bundle). If at time t we have context $w_i \in B_i(t)$ then this estimated optimal set is used. The regret of this procedure consists of two parts. The first part is due to selecting a sub-optimal set of labelers for $B_i(t)$ (owing to incorrect estimates of the labelers' accuracy). This part of the regret is bounded by $O(1/t^2)$. The second part of the regret arises from the fact that even if we compute the correct optimal set for interval $B_i(t)$, it may not be optimal for the specific context $w_t \in B_i(t)$. However, when $B_i(t)$ becomes sufficiently small, and under a uniform Lipschitz condition we can bound this part of the regret as well.

Taken together, if we revise the condition for entering the exploration phase (constants $D_1(t)$ and $D_2(t)$) to grow on the order of $O(t^z \log t)$ instead of $\log t$, for some constant $0 < z < 1$, then the regret $R(T)$ in this case is on the order of $T^z \log T$; thus it remains sub-linear and therefore has a zero average regret, but this is worse than the log bound we can obtain in other cases.

We omit all technical details since they are rather direct extensions combining our earlier results with the literatures on continuous arms.

6. NUMERICAL EXPERIMENT

In this section we validate the proposed algorithms with a few examples using both simulation and real data.

6.1 Simulation study

Our first setup consists of $M = 5$ labelers, whose quality $\{p_i\}$ are randomly and uniformly generated to satisfy a preset $a_{\min}$ as follows: select $\{p_i\}$ randomly between $[a_{\min}, 1]$. Note that this is a simplification because not all $\{p_i\}$ need to be above $a_{\min}$ for the requirement to hold. An example of these are shown in Table 1 (for $a_{\min} = 0.6$) but remain unknown to the labelers. A task arrives at each time t. We assume a unit labeling cost $c = 0.02$. The experiments are run for a period of $T = 2{,}000$ time units (2,000 tasks in total). The results shown below are the average over 100 runs. Denote by G_1, G_2 the *exploration constants* concerning the two constants (in $D_1(t)$ and $D_2(t)$) that control the exploration part of the learning. G_1, G_2 are set to be sufficiently large based on the other parameters:

	L_1	L_2	L_3	L_4	L_5
p_i	0.763	0.781	0.625	0.783	0.727

Table 1: An example of the simulation setup.

$$(G_1, G_2) = \left(\frac{1}{\left(\frac{1}{\max_{m: m \text{ odd}} m \cdot n(S^m)} - \alpha\right)^2 \cdot \varepsilon^2}, \frac{1}{(a_{\min} - 0.5)^2}\right).$$

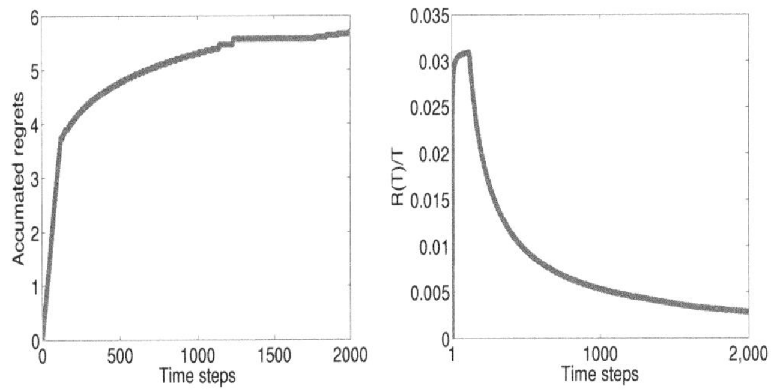

(a) Accumulative regret (b) Average regret $R(T)/T$

Figure 2: Regret of the LS_OL algorithm.

We first show the accumulative and average regret under the simple majority vote rule in Figure 2. From the set of figures we observe a logarithmic increase of accumulated regret and correspondingly a sub-linear decrease for its average over time. The cost regret $R_{\mathscr{C}}(T)$ has a very similar trend as mentioned earlier (recall the regret terms of $R_{\mathscr{C}}(T)$ align well with the those in $R(T)$) and is thus not show here. We then compare the performance of our labeler selection to the naive crowd-sourcing algorithm, by taking a simple majority vote over the whole set of labelers each time. This is plotted in Figure 3 in terms of the average reward over time. There is a clear performance improvement after an initialization period (where exploration happens).

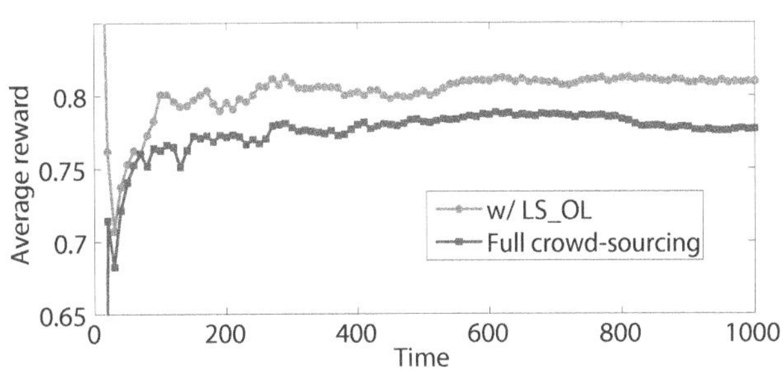

Figure 3: Performance comparison: online labeler selection v.s. full crowd-sourcing (majority vote)

In addition to the logarithmic growth, we are interested in how the performance is affected by the inaccuracy of the crowd expertise. These results are shown in Figure 4. We observe the effect of different choices of $a_{\min} = 0.6, 0.7, 0.8$. As expected, we see when $a_{\min}$ is small, the verification process of the labels takes more samples to become accurate. Therefore in the process more error is introduced in the estimation of the labelers' qualities, which results in slower convergence.

We next compare the performance between simple majority vote and weighted majority vote (both with LS_OL). One example trace of accumulated reward comparison is shown in Figure 5; the advantage of weighted majority vote can be seen clearly. We then repeat the set of experiments and average the results over 500 runs; the comparison is shown in Table 2 under different number of candidate labelers (all of their labeling qualities are uniformly generated).

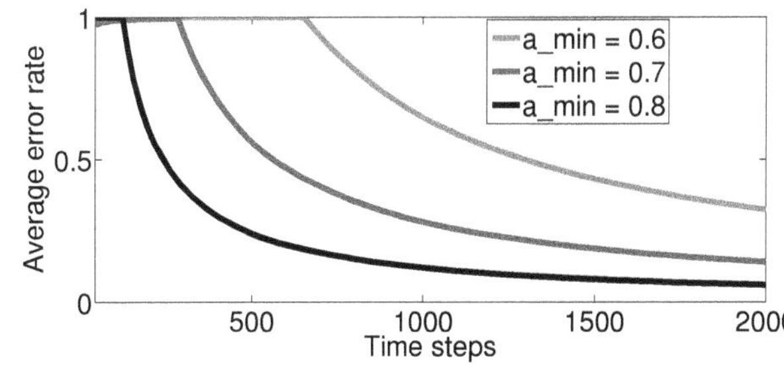

Figure 4: Effect of $a_{\min}$: higher $a_{\min}$ leads to much better performance.

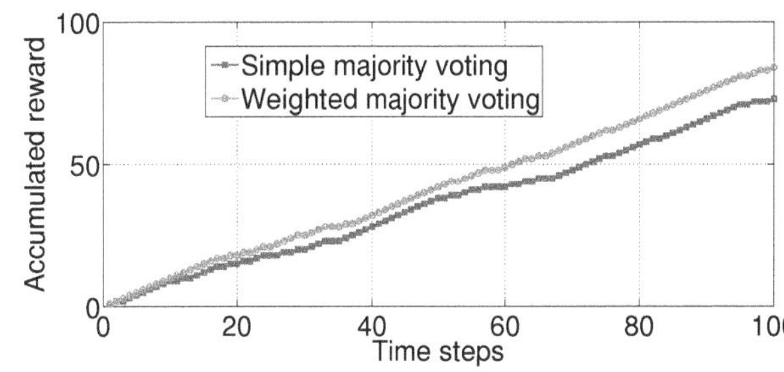

Figure 5: Comparing weighted and simple majority voting within LS_OL.

M	5	10	15	20
Full crowd-sourcing (majority vote)	0.5154	0.5686	0.7000	0.7997
Majority vote w/ LS_OL	0.8320	0.9186	0.9434	0.9820
Weighted majority vote w/ LS_OL	**0.8726**	**0.9393**	**0.9641**	**0.9890**

Table 2: Average reward per labeler: there is a clear gap between with and without using LS_OL.

6.2 Study on a real AMT dataset

We also apply our algorithm to a dataset shared at [1]. This dataset contains 1,000 images each labeled by the same set of 5 AMTs. The labels are on the scale from 0 to 4 indicating how many scenes are seen from each image, such as field, airport, animal, etc. A label of 0 implies no scene can be discerned. Besides the ratings from the AMTs, there is a second dataset from [1] summarizing keywords for scenes of each image. We also analyze this second dataset and count the number of unique descriptors for each image and use this count as the ground-truth, to which the results from AMT are compared.

We start with showing the number of disagreements each AMT has with the group over the 1000 images. The total numbers of disagreement of the 5 AMTs are shown in Table 3, while Figure 6 shows the cumulative disagreement over the set of images ordered by their numerical indices in the database. It is quite clear that AMT 5 shows significant and consistent disagreement with the rest. AMT 3 comes next while AMTs 1, 2, and 4 are clearly more in general agreement.

	AMT1	AMT2	AMT3	AMT4	AMT5
# of disagreement	348	353	376	338	441

Table 3: Total number of disagreement each AMT has.

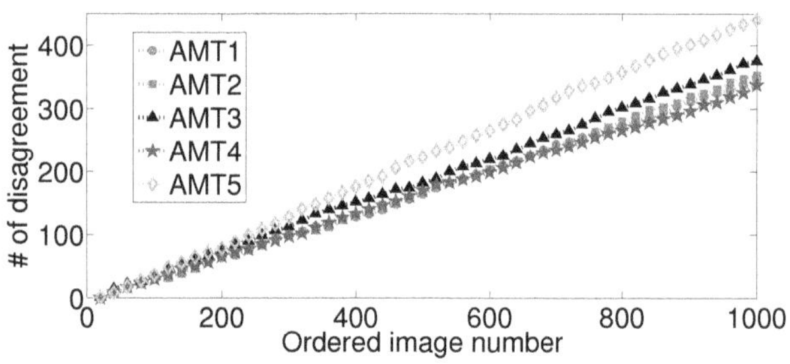

Figure 6: Cumulated number of disagreements.

The images are not in sequential order, as the original experiment was not done in an online fashion. To test our algorithm, we will continue to use their numerical indices to order them as if they arrived sequentially in time and feed them into our algorithm. By doing so we essentially test the performance of conducting this type of labeling tasks online whereby the administrator of the tasks can dynamically alter task assignments to obtain better results.

In this experiment we use LS_OL with majority vote and with the addition of the detection and filtering procedure discussed in Section 3.5.3, which is specified to eliminate the worst labeler after a certain number of steps such that the error in the rank ordering is less than 0.1. The algorithm otherwise runs as described earlier. Indeed we see this happen around step 90, as highlighted in Figure 7 along with a comparison to using the full crowd-sourcing method with majority vote. The algorithm also eventually correctly estimates the best set to consist of AMTs 1, 2, and 4. All images' labeling error as compared to the ground-truth at the end of this process is shown as a CDF (error distribution over the images) in Figure 8; note the errors are discrete due to the discrete labels. It is also worth noting that under our algorithm the cost is much lower because AMT 5 was soon eliminated, while AMT 3 was only used very infrequently once the correct estimate has been achieved.

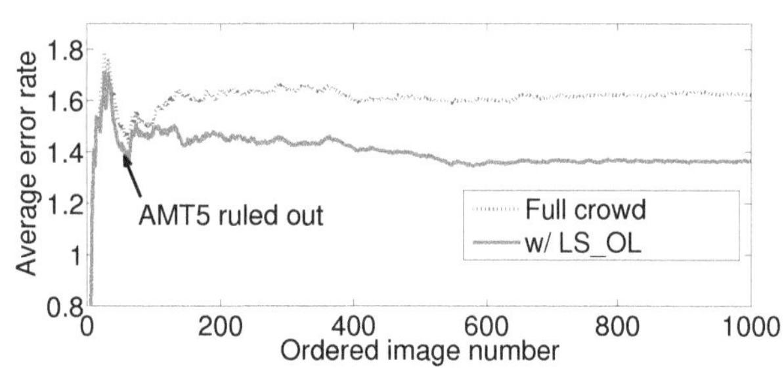

Figure 7: Average error comparison: online labeler selection v.s. full crowd-sourcing.

7. CONCLUSION

To our best knowledge, this is the first work formalizing and addressing the issue of learning labelers' quality in an online fashion for the crowd-sourcing problem and proposing solutions with performance guarantee. We developed and analyzed an online learning algorithm that can differentiate high and low quality labelers over time and select the best set for labeling tasks with $O(\log^2 T)$ regret uniform in time. In addition, we showed how performance could be further improved by utilizing more sophisticated voting techniques. We discussed the applicability of our algorithm to more general cases where labelers' quality varies with contextually different tasks and how to detect and remove malicious labelers when there is a lack of ground-truth. We validate our results via both synthetic and real world AMT data.

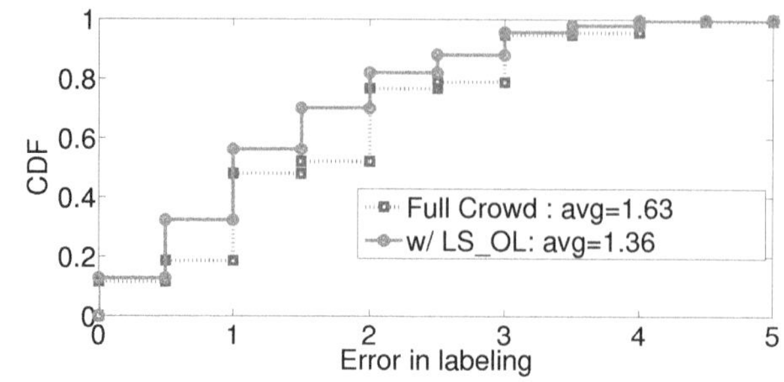

Figure 8: Labeling error distribution comparison.

Acknowledgment

This work is partially supported by the NSF under grant CNS-1422211 and DHS under grant HSHQDC-13-C-B0015.

8. REFERENCES

[1] AMT dataset. http://tamaraberg.com/importanceDataset/.

[2] AGRAWAL, R. The Continuum-Armed Bandit Problem. *SIAM journal on control and optimization 33*, 6 (1995), 1926–1951.

[3] ANANDKUMAR, A., MICHAEL, N., TANG, A. K., AND SWAMI, A. Distributed algorithms for learning and cognitive medium access with logarithmic regret. *Selected Areas in Communications, IEEE Journal on 29*, 4 (2011), 731–745.

[4] AUER, P., CESA-BIANCHI, N., AND FISCHER, P. Finite-time Analysis of the Multiarmed Bandit Problem. *Mach. Learn. 47* (May 2002), 235–256.

[5] CHAPELLE, O., SINDHWANI, V., AND KEERTHI, S. S. Optimization Techniques for Semi-supervised Support Vector Machines. *The Journal of Machine Learning Research 9* (2008), 203–233.

[6] CHOFFNES, D. R., BUSTAMANTE, F. E., AND GE, Z. Crowdsourcing Service-level Network Event Monitoring. *SIGCOMM Comput. Commun. Rev. 40*, 4 (Aug. 2010), 387–398.

[7] DENG, J., DONG, W., SOCHER, R., LI, L.-J., LI, K., AND FEI-FEI, L. ImageNet: A Large-Scale Hierarchical Image Database.

[8] GHOSH, A., KALE, S., AND MCAFEE, P. Who moderates the moderators?: Crowdsourcing abuse detection in user-generated content. In *Proceedings of the 12th ACM Conference on Electronic Commerce* (New York, NY, USA, 2011), EC '11, ACM, pp. 167–176.

[9] GUILLE, A., HACID, H., FAVRE, C., AND ZIGHED, D. A. Information diffusion in online social networks: A survey. *ACM SIGMOD Record 42*, 2 (2013), 17–28.

[10] HAKLAY, M., AND WEBER, P. Openstreetmap: User-generated Street Maps. *Pervasive Computing, IEEE 7*, 4 (2008), 12–18.

[11] HO, C.-J., AND VAUGHAN, J. W. Online task assignment in crowdsourcing markets. In *AAAI'12* (2012), pp. -1–1.

[12] HUA, G., LONG, C., YANG, M., AND GAO, Y. Collaborative Active Learning of a Kernel Machine

Ensemble for Recognition. In *Computer Vision (ICCV), 2013 IEEE International Conference on* (2013), IEEE, pp. 1209–1216.

[13] KARGER, D. R., OH, S., AND SHAH, D. Iterative learning for reliable crowdsourcing systems. In *Advances in neural information processing systems* (2011), pp. 1953–1961.

[14] KARGER, D. R., OH, S., AND SHAH, D. Efficient crowdsourcing for multi-class labeling. In *ACM SIGMETRICS Performance Evaluation Review* (2013), vol. 41, ACM, pp. 81–92.

[15] KULIS, B., BASU, S., DHILLON, I., AND MOONEY, R. Semi-supervised Graph Clustering: a Kernel Approach. *Machine learning 74*, 1 (2009), 1–22.

[16] LAI, T. L., AND ROBBINS, H. Asymptotically Efficient Adaptive Allocation Rules. *Advances in Applied Mathematics 6* (1985), 4–22.

[17] LIU, H., LIU, K., AND ZHAO, Q. Learning in a changing world: Non-bayesian restless multi-armed bandit. Tech. rep., DTIC Document, 2010.

[18] LONG, C., HUA, G., AND KAPOOR, A. Active Visual Recognition with Expertise Estimation in Crowdsourcing. In *Computer Vision (ICCV), 2013 IEEE International Conference on* (2013), IEEE, pp. 3000–3007.

[19] NATARAJAN, N., DHILLON, I., RAVIKUMAR, P., AND TEWARI, A. Learning with Noisy Labels. In *Advances in Neural Information Processing Systems* (2013), pp. 1196–1204.

[20] REA, L. M., AND PARKER, R. A. *Designing and conducting survey research: A comprehensive guide*. John Wiley & Sons, 2012.

[21] RUSSELL, B. C., TORRALBA, A., MURPHY, K. P., AND FREEMAN, W. T. LabelMe: A Database and Web-Based Tool for Image Annotation. *Int. J. Comput. Vision 77*, 1-3 (May 2008), 157–173.

[22] SHENG, V. S., PROVOST, F., AND IPEIROTIS, P. G. Get Another Label? Improving Data Quality and Data Mining Using Multiple, Noisy Labelers. In *Proceedings of the 14th ACM SIGKDD international conference on Knowledge discovery and data mining* (2008), ACM, pp. 614–622.

[23] TEKIN, C., AND LIU, M. Online Learning of Rested and Restless Bandits. *Information Theory, IEEE Transactions on 58*, 8 (2012), 5588–5611.

[24] ZHONG, E., FAN, W., AND YANG, Q. Contextual collaborative filtering via hierarchical matrix factorization. In *SDM'12* (2012), pp. 744–755.

[25] ZHU, X., AND GOLDBERG, A. B. *Introduction to Semi-Supervised Learning*. Synthesis Lectures on Artificial Intelligence and Machine Learning.

Appendices

Proof of Theorem 1

We prove by contradiction. Suppose m is even and we order all selected users by their labeling capability in descending order $p_1 \geq \ldots \geq p_m$. We now prove

$$\pi(p_1, \ldots, p_{m-1}) \geq \pi(p_1, \ldots, p_m) \tag{16}$$

Consider the following. By adding p_m, the gain for $\pi(p_1, \ldots, p_{m-1})$ is $\frac{p_m \cdot P(T_1)}{2}$, where

$$T_1 = \{\# \text{ of correct labels} = \# \text{ of wrong labels} - 1\}.$$

That is, only when the number of correct labels is exactly the same as the number of wrong labels less one does adding a m-th correct label change the outcome of the majority vote (in this case there is a tie so the label changes with probability $1/2$); when the former number is smaller or bigger, adding one more vote does not change the results. On the other hand, the loss is $\frac{(1-p_m)\cdot P(T_2)}{2}$, where

$$T_2 = \{\# \text{ of correct labels} = \# \text{ of wrong labels} + 1\}.$$

We now compare $p_m \cdot P(T_1)$ and $(1-p_m) \cdot P(T_2)$. Within the set T_2, each event is of the form where some labeler i gives the correct label while the rest are half correct and half wrong. Denote this event by ω_i and by ω_{-i} the event that the rest of the labels (given by those other than i) are half right and half wrong. Note for each ω_i there is a corresponding event $\hat{\omega}_i \in T_1$ where i gives the wrong labels while the rest are half correct and half wrong. Since $p_i \geq p_m$ we have

$$(1-p_m) \cdot p_i \cdot P(\omega_{-i}) \geq p_m \cdot (1-p_i) \cdot P(\omega_{-i}) \,. \tag{17}$$

At the same time, $P(\omega_i) = p_i \cdot P(\omega_{-i}), P(\hat{\omega}_i) = (1-p_i) \cdot P(\omega_{-i})$, i.e., $(1-p_m) \cdot P(\omega_i) \geq p_m \cdot P(\hat{\omega}_i)$. This is true for all ω_i. Therefore we have

$$\begin{aligned}
&(1-p_m) \cdot P(T_2) \\
&= (1-p_m) \cdot P(\cup_i \, \omega_i) \\
&= \sum_{\omega_i} (1-p_m) \cdot P(\omega_i) \\
&\geq \sum_{\hat{\omega}_i} p_m \cdot P(\hat{\omega}_i) = p_m \cdot P(T_1)
\end{aligned} \tag{18}$$

Therefore we have proved $\pi(p_1, \ldots, p_{m-1}) \geq \pi(p_1, \ldots, p_m)$. Moreover

$$\begin{aligned}
&U(\{1,2,\ldots,m-1\}) - U(\{1,2,\ldots,m\}) \\
&= \pi(p_1, \ldots, p_{m-1}) - \pi(p_1, \ldots, p_m) > 0.
\end{aligned} \tag{19}$$

Therefore a selection of an even number of labelers can always be improved by removing the least accurate labeler, resulting in an odd number of labelers in the selection.

Proof of Theorem 2

Consider a m-set S. Suppose there is a $i \notin S$ and a $j \in S$ such that $p_i > p_j$. Then the probability of making a correct annotation is given by

$$\begin{aligned}
&P_S(\# \text{ of correct labels} > \# \text{ of wrong labels}) \\
&= p_j \cdot P(T_1) + (1-p_j) \cdot P(T_2)
\end{aligned}$$

where

$$T_1 = \{\# \text{ correct label} > \# \text{ wrong label} - 1 \text{ in } S \backslash j\} \tag{20}$$

$$T_2 = \{\# \text{ correct label} > \# \text{ wrong label} + 1 \text{ in } S \backslash j\} \tag{21}$$

Now replace j with i and denote $\hat{S} = S \backslash j \cup \{i\}$ we have

$$\begin{aligned}
&P_{\hat{S}}(\# \text{ of correct labels} > \# \text{ of wrong labels}) \\
&= p_i \cdot P(T_1) + (1-p_i) \cdot P(T_2) \,.
\end{aligned}$$

It follows that

$$P_{\hat{S}} - P_S = (p_i - p_j) \cdot (P(T_1) - P(T_2)) \,. \tag{22}$$

If an event $\omega \in T_2$ we must also have $\omega \in T_1$, thus we have $T_2 \subset T_1$; therefore $P(T_1) - P(T_2) > 0$, and we conclude that $P_{\hat{S}} - P_S > 0$, completing the proof.

Proof of Lemma 1

Denote by $n(T)$ the number of times an exploration phase has been activated up to time T. Since for labeler i there is at most $D_1(T)\cdot D_2(T)$ number of exploration phases, we have

$$n(T)=\sum_{i=1}^{T} I_{\text{at least one task in exploration phase at } t}$$
$$\le \sum_{k=1}^{D_1(t)}\sum_{i=1}^{T} I_{\text{task } k \text{ in reassignment phase at } t} \le D_1(T)\cdot D_2(T)\,,$$

where the first inequality comes from union bound. Then

$$E[R_e(T)] \le U(S^*)\cdot n(T) = U(S^*)\cdot (D_1(T)\cdot D_2(T))\,.$$

Proof of Lemma 3

Firstly notice via union bound we have the following bound at any time t:

$$E[\mathscr{E}_1(t)] \le \sum_{\substack{m=1\\ m \text{ odd}}}^{M} P(\tilde{U}(S^m)\ge \tilde{U}(S^*))\,. \tag{23}$$

Now consider each term in the above summation $P(\tilde{U}(S^m)\ge \tilde{U}(S^*))$. We will use the following fact to bound it.

LEMMA 6. *The probability of using a sub-optimal selection S^m is bounded as follows,*

$$P(\tilde{U}(S^m)\ge\tilde{U}(S^*)) \le P(\tilde{U}(S^m) > U(S^m)+\varepsilon) + P(\tilde{U}(S^*) < U(S^*)-\varepsilon)\,, \tag{24}$$

and for $S\in\{S^m,S^*\}$ we have

$$P(|\tilde{U}(S)-U(S)|>\varepsilon) \le n(S)\cdot \sum_{i\in S} P(|\tilde{p}_i-p_i| > \frac{\varepsilon}{n(S)\cdot|S|})\,. \tag{25}$$

We shall now use the above lemma; its own proof is given later in this appendix.

Consider each term $P(|\tilde{p}_i-p_i|>\frac{\varepsilon}{n(S)\cdot|S|})$ in the lemma

$$\begin{aligned}
&P(|\tilde{p}_i-p_i|>\frac{\varepsilon}{n(S)\cdot|S|})\\
&=\underbrace{P(|\tilde{p}_i-p_i|>\frac{\varepsilon}{n(S)\cdot|S|}\,|\,\frac{\sum_{k:k\in E(t)} I_{y_k^*=0}}{|E(t)|}\le\frac{\alpha\cdot\varepsilon}{t^z})}_{\textbf{Term 1}}\\
&\cdot P(\frac{\sum_{k:k\in E(t)} I_{y_k^*=0}}{|E(t)|}\le\frac{\alpha\cdot\varepsilon}{t^z})\\
&+P(|\tilde{p}_i-p_i|>\frac{\varepsilon}{n(S)\cdot|S|}\,|\,\frac{\sum_{k:k\in E(t)} I_{y_k^*=0}}{|E(t)|}>\frac{\alpha\cdot\varepsilon}{t^z})\\
&\underbrace{\cdot P(\frac{\sum_{k:k\in E(t)} I_{y_k^*=0}}{|E(t)|}>\frac{\alpha\cdot\varepsilon}{t^z})}_{\textbf{Term 2}}
\end{aligned} \tag{26}$$

where $0<z<1$ is a constant. This is different from the classical learning problem in the sense we need to deal with extra errors associated with imperfect feedbacks. The first term takes care of the event when the sum of error is lower than certain threshold while the second term captures the other case.

For **Term 1** the conditional probability is bounded as follows:

$$\begin{aligned}
&P(|\tilde{p}_i-p_i|>\frac{\varepsilon}{n(S)\cdot|S|}\,|\,\frac{\sum_{k:k\in E(t)} I_{y_k^*=0}}{|E(t)|}\le\frac{\alpha\cdot\varepsilon}{t^z})\\
&\le P(|\tilde{p}_i-p_i|>(\frac{1}{n(S)\cdot|S|}-\frac{\alpha}{t^z})\cdot\varepsilon)\\
&\le 2\cdot e^{-2((\frac{1}{n(S)\cdot|S|}-\frac{\alpha}{t^z})\cdot\varepsilon)^2\cdot D_1(t)}\le\frac{2}{t^2}\,,
\end{aligned} \tag{27}$$

since $D_1(t)=\frac{1}{(\frac{1}{n(S)\cdot|S|}-\alpha)^2\cdot\varepsilon^2}\cdot\log t$. Consider **Term 2**,

$$\begin{aligned}
P(\frac{\sum_{k:k\in E(t)} I_{y_k^*=0}}{|E(t)|}>\frac{\alpha\cdot\varepsilon}{t^z}) &\le \frac{E[\frac{\sum_{k:k\in E(t)} I_{y_k^*=0}}{|E(t)|}]}{\frac{\alpha\cdot\varepsilon}{t^z}}\\
&=\frac{\frac{\sum_{k:k\in E(t)} E[I_{y_k^*=0}]}{|E(t)|}}{\frac{\alpha\cdot\varepsilon}{t^z}}\,,
\end{aligned} \tag{28}$$

by the Markov inequality. Note more strict bound could be obtained via other bounding techniques. Consider each term in the summation

$$\begin{aligned}
E[I_{y_k^*=0}] &= P(y_k^*=0)\\
&=P(\sum_{n=1}^{\hat{N}_k(t)} I_{y_k(n)}>0.5\cdot\hat{N}_k(t))\\
&\le e^{-2(a_{\min}-0.5)^2\cdot\hat{N}_k(t)}\le\frac{1}{t^2}\,,
\end{aligned}$$

where $\hat{N}_k(t)$ is the number of feedbacks received for task k up-to time t; the inequality is due to the fact that $\hat{N}_k(t)\ge D_2(t)\ge 1/(a_{\min}-0.5)^2\log t$. This means that for each labeler, it has performed on at least $D_1(T)$ tasks, and each task must have at least $D_2(T)$ testing results available.

Consequently we have

$$P(\frac{\sum_{k\in E(t)} I_{y_k^*=0}}{|E(t)|}>\frac{\alpha\cdot\varepsilon}{t^z})\le\frac{1/t^2}{\alpha\cdot\varepsilon/t^z}=\frac{1}{\alpha\cdot\varepsilon\cdot t^{2-z}}\,.$$

The other two terms in the summation are bounded by 1 since they are probability measures. Summing up, we have

$$P(|\tilde{U}(S)-U(S)|>\varepsilon)\le n(S)\cdot|S|\cdot(\frac{2}{t^2}+\frac{1}{\alpha\cdot\varepsilon\cdot t^{2-z}})\,. \tag{29}$$

Summing over S^m, m odd completes the proof.

Proof of Lemma 4

We have the following fact:

$$\begin{aligned}
E[\mathscr{E}_2(t)] &\le P(\cup_{i\in\mathscr{M}}|\tilde{p}_i-p_i|>\varepsilon)\\
&\le\sum_{i\in\mathscr{M}} P(|\tilde{p}_i-p_i|>\varepsilon)\,.
\end{aligned}$$

This is because if $|\tilde{p}_i-p_i|\le\varepsilon, \forall i$ then we must have for $p_i>p_j$,

$$\tilde{p}_i-\tilde{p}_j\ge p_i-\varepsilon-p_j-\varepsilon>0,$$

which means there is no error in ordering. Similarly as above we have

$$P(|\tilde{p}_i-p_i|>\varepsilon)\le\frac{2}{t^2}+\frac{1}{\alpha\cdot\varepsilon\cdot t^{2-z}}\,. \tag{30}$$

Therefore,

$$E[\mathscr{E}_2(t)]\le M(\frac{2}{t^2}+\frac{1}{\alpha\cdot\varepsilon\cdot t^{2-z}})\,. \tag{31}$$

Proof of Lemma 6

We first bound the inequality in Eqn.(24). To see why this inequality is true, consider the following fact

$$\{\omega : \tilde{U}(S^m) \geq \tilde{U}(S^*)\} \subseteq$$
$$\{\omega : \tilde{U}(S^m) > U(S^m) + \varepsilon\} \cup \{\omega : \tilde{U}(S^*) < U(S^*) - \varepsilon\} , \quad (32)$$

since if $\tilde{U}(S^m) \leq U(S^m) + \varepsilon$, $\tilde{U}(S^*) \geq U(S^*) - \varepsilon$, we then have

$$\tilde{U}(S^m) - \tilde{U}(S^*) \leq U(S^m) + \varepsilon - U(S^*) + \varepsilon$$
$$\leq -\Delta_{\min} + 2\varepsilon < -\Delta_{\min} + \Delta_{\min} = 0 ,$$

which contradicts the fact that $\tilde{U}(S^m) \geq \tilde{U}(S^*)$. Thus

$$P(\tilde{U}(S^m) \geq \tilde{U}(S^*)) \leq P(\tilde{U}(S^m) > U(S^m) + \varepsilon)$$
$$+ P(\tilde{U}(S^*) < U(S^*) + \varepsilon) ,$$

by the union bound. The bounding effort then reduces to bounding each of above probabilities. Note that for any set S, plug in $U(S)$ we have

$$|\tilde{U}(S) - U(S)| = |\sum_{S':S' \subseteq S,\, |S'| \geq \lceil \frac{|S|}{2} \rceil} (\prod_{i \in S'} \tilde{p}_i \prod_{S \backslash S'} (1 - \tilde{p}_j))$$
$$- \prod_{i \in S'} p_i \prod_{S \backslash S'} (1 - p_j))| . \quad (33)$$

Therefore

$$P(|\tilde{U}(S) - U(S)| > \varepsilon) = P(\sum_{S':S' \subseteq S,\, |S'| \geq \lceil \frac{|S|}{2} \rceil} |\prod_{i \in S'} \tilde{p}_i \prod_{S \backslash S'} (1 - \tilde{p}_j)$$
$$- \prod_{i \in S'} p_i \prod_{S \backslash S'} (1 - p_j)| > \varepsilon)$$
$$\leq \sum_{S':S' \subseteq S,\, |S'| \geq \lceil \frac{|S|}{2} \rceil} P(|\prod_{i \in S'} \tilde{p}_i \prod_{S \backslash S'} (1 - \tilde{p}_j)$$
$$- \prod_{i \in S'} p_i \prod_{S \backslash S'} (1 - p_j)| > \frac{\varepsilon}{n(S)}) ,$$

where the last inequality comes from the union bound. We further use the following results (which can be proved separately but the proof is omitted) to separate the above product terms into summations.

LEMMA 7. *For $k \geq 1$ and two sequences $\{l_i\}_{i=1}^m$ and $\{q_i\}_{i=1}^m$ and $0 \leq l_i, q_i \leq 1, \forall i = 1, ..., k.$, we have*

$$|\prod_{i=1}^m l_i - \prod_{j=1}^m q_j| \leq \sum_{i=1}^m |l_i - q_i| . \quad (34)$$

Using this result, we have

$$|\prod_{i \in S'} \tilde{p}_i \prod_{j \in S \backslash S'} (1 - \tilde{p}_j) - \prod_{i \in S'} p_i \prod_{j \in S \backslash S'} (1 - p_j)|$$
$$\leq \sum_{i \in S'} |\tilde{p}_i - p_i| + \sum_{j \in S \backslash S'} |(1 - \tilde{p}_j) - (1 - p_j)|$$
$$= \sum_{i \in S} |\tilde{p}_i - p_i| .$$

Therefore using the union bound we have

$$P(|\prod_{i \in S'} \tilde{p}_i \prod_{S \backslash S'} (1 - \tilde{p}_j) - \prod_{i \in S'} p_i \prod_{S \backslash S'} (1 - p_j)| > \frac{\varepsilon}{n(S)})$$
$$\leq \sum_{i \in S} P(|\tilde{p}_i - p_i| > \frac{\varepsilon}{n(S) \cdot |S|}) .$$

Therefore summing up all of the above we have

$$P(|\tilde{U}(S) - U(S)| > \varepsilon)$$
$$\leq \sum_{S':S' \subseteq S,\, |S'| \geq \lceil \frac{|S|}{2} \rceil} \sum_{i \in S} P(|\tilde{p}_i - p_i| > \frac{\varepsilon}{n(S) \cdot |S|})$$
$$= n(S) \cdot \sum_{i \in S} P(|\tilde{p}_i - p_i| > \frac{\varepsilon}{n(S) \cdot |S|}) . \quad (35)$$

Proof of Theorem 4

We prove this by contradiction. Suppose there exists a pair (i, j), $i \in S, j \notin S$ such that $p_i < p_j$. We discuss the following cases. First of all as we already noted we have $\log \frac{p_i}{1-p_i} < \log \frac{p_j}{1-p_j}$. Consider the following fact the probability for correct labeling is given by

$$P_c = p_i \cdot P(T_1) + (1 - p_i) \cdot P(T_2) + \frac{P(T_3)}{2} , \quad (36)$$

where

$$T_1 = \{\sum_{u \in S_c} \log \frac{p_u}{1 - p_u} > \sum_{e \in S_w} \log \frac{p_e}{1 - p_e} - \log \frac{p_i}{1 - p_i}\} ,$$
$$T_2 = \{\sum_{u \in S_c} \log \frac{p_u}{1 - p_u} > \sum_{e \in S_w} \log \frac{p_e}{1 - p_e} + \log \frac{p_i}{1 - p_i}\} ,$$

and

$$T_3 = \{\text{A tie occurs}\}, \quad (37)$$

where $S_c \neq S_w$ and $S_c \cup S_w = \mathscr{M} - \{i\}$, indicating the set of correct and wrong labelers respectively. Essentially the first two events correspond to cases when there is a majority group (including and excluding i respectively) and T_3 corresponds to the case when there is a tie.

Changing p_i to p_j since

$$P(T_1^j) \geq P(T_1),\ P(T_2) \geq P(T_2^j) ,$$

if $p_i > 0.5$, where $T_q^j, q \in \{1,2\}$ correspond to $T_q, q \in \{1,2\}$ by replacing i with j. And we have

$$p_j \cdot P(T_1^j) + (1 - p_j) \cdot P(T_2^j)$$
$$- p_i \cdot P(T_1) - (1 - p_i) \cdot P(T_2)$$
$$\geq (p_j - p_i) \cdot (P(T_1) - P(T_2)) \geq 0 .$$

For T_3 consider the case p_i is in S_c. Then changing p_i to p_j will break the equilibrium and the probability of a correct output will become

$$p_j \cdot P(S_c) \cdot P(S_w) > p_i \cdot P(S_c) \cdot P(S_w) = \frac{P(T_3)}{2} , \quad (38)$$

where $P(S_c), P(S_w)$ correspond to the probabilities from the correct and wrong labelers, i.e.,

$$P(S_c) = \sum_{u \in S_c} p_u,\ P(S_w) = \sum_{e \in S_w} (1 - p_e) , \quad (39)$$

and the last inequality comes from the fact that in the equal case the probabilities of the label being either 0 or 1 are equivalent with each other.

Proof of Lemma 5

First of all we have

$$P(\tilde{W}(\hat{S}) - \tilde{W}(S \backslash \hat{S}) < \varepsilon) \leq P(\tilde{W}(\hat{S}) - W(\hat{S}) < -\varepsilon/2)$$
$$+ P(\tilde{W}(S \backslash \hat{S}) - W(S \backslash \hat{S}) > \varepsilon/2) .$$

This is because otherwise if

$$\tilde{W}(\hat{S}) - W(\hat{S}) \geq -\varepsilon/2,$$
$$\tilde{W}(S\backslash\hat{S}) - W(S\backslash\hat{S}) < \varepsilon/2\,,$$

we have

$$\tilde{W}(\hat{S}) - \tilde{W}(S\backslash\hat{S}) \geq W(\hat{S}) - W(S\backslash\hat{S}) - \varepsilon \geq \varepsilon\,, \quad (40)$$

which gives us a contradiction.

Consider each term above we have,

$$\begin{aligned}
&P(\tilde{W}(\hat{S}) - W(\hat{S}) < -\varepsilon/2)\\
&\leq \sum_{i\in\hat{S}} P(|\log\frac{\tilde{p}_i}{1-\tilde{p}_i} - \log\frac{p_i}{1-p_i}| > \frac{\varepsilon}{2|\hat{S}|})\\
&\leq \sum_{i\in\hat{S}} P(|\log\frac{\tilde{p}_i}{1-\tilde{p}_i} - \log\frac{p_i}{1-p_i}| > \frac{\varepsilon}{2|\hat{S}|}||\tilde{p}_i - p_i| \geq \frac{\varepsilon}{4C|\hat{S}|})\\
&\quad \cdot P(|\tilde{p}_i - p_i| \geq \frac{\varepsilon}{4C|\hat{S}|}) +\\
&\sum_{i\in\hat{S}} P(|\log\frac{\tilde{p}_i}{1-\tilde{p}_i} - \log\frac{p_i}{1-p_i}| \geq \frac{\varepsilon}{2|\hat{S}|}||\tilde{p}_i - p_i| < \frac{\varepsilon}{4C|\hat{S}|})\\
&\quad \cdot P(|\tilde{p}_i - p_i| < \frac{\varepsilon}{4C|\hat{S}|})\\
&\leq \sum_{i\in S} P(|\tilde{p}_i - p_i| \geq \frac{\varepsilon}{4C|\hat{S}|}) \leq |\hat{S}|(\frac{2}{t^2} + \frac{1}{\alpha\cdot\varepsilon\cdot t^{2-z}})\,.
\end{aligned}$$

Since

$$D_1(t) \geq 1/(\frac{1}{\max_m 4C\cdot m} - \alpha)\log t,\ \alpha < \frac{1}{\max_m 4C\cdot m}\,,$$

as well as the fact that when $|\tilde{p}_i - p_i| \leq \frac{\varepsilon}{4C|\hat{S}|}$ and

$$C > \max_i \max\{\frac{1+\varepsilon/4}{p_i}, \frac{1-\varepsilon/4}{1-p_i}, \frac{\varepsilon/4}{p_i}, \frac{\varepsilon/4}{1-p_i}\}\,,$$

we have

$$|\log\frac{\tilde{p}_i}{1-\tilde{p}_i} - \log\frac{p_i}{1-p_i}| \leq 2C\cdot|\tilde{p}_i - p_i| < \frac{\varepsilon}{2|\hat{S}|}\,,$$

where we have used the following results.

LEMMA 8. *With $\tilde{p}_i, p_i$ bounded away from 0 and 1 we have,*

$$|\log\frac{\tilde{p}_i}{1-\tilde{p}_i} - \log\frac{p_i}{1-p_i}| \leq 2C\cdot|\tilde{p}_i - p_i|\,, \quad (41)$$

where C is a constant satisfying,

$$C > \max_i \max\{\frac{1}{p_i}, \frac{1}{\tilde{p}_i}, \frac{1}{1-p_i}, \frac{1}{1-\tilde{p}_i}\}. \quad (42)$$

Similarly we have

$$P(\tilde{W}(S\backslash\hat{S}) - W(S\backslash\hat{S}) > \varepsilon/2) \leq |S\backslash\hat{S}|(\frac{2}{t^2} + \frac{1}{\alpha\cdot\varepsilon\cdot t^{2-z}})\,.$$

Combine above we have

$$P(\tilde{W}(\hat{S})) - \tilde{W}(S\backslash\hat{S}) < \varepsilon) \leq |S|\cdot(\frac{2}{t^2} + \frac{1}{\alpha\cdot\varepsilon\cdot t^{2-z}})\,.$$

For the other case when $W(\hat{S}) = W(S\backslash\hat{S})$ we have,

$$\begin{aligned}
P(|\tilde{W}(\hat{S}) - \tilde{W}(S\backslash\hat{S})| > \varepsilon) &\leq P(|\tilde{W}(\hat{S}) - W(\hat{S})| \geq \varepsilon/2)\\
&+ P(|\tilde{W}(S\backslash\hat{S}) - W(S\backslash\hat{S})| \geq \varepsilon/2)\\
&\leq |S|\cdot(\frac{2}{t^2} + \frac{1}{\alpha\cdot\varepsilon\cdot t^{2-z}})\,,
\end{aligned} \quad (43)$$

where the second inequality is established similarly as in the first case.

Proof of Lemma 7

We prove the claim by induction. Notice when $m=1$ the inequality holds trivially. When $m=2$ we have

$$\begin{aligned}
&|l_1\cdot l_2 - q_1\cdot q_2|\\
&= |(l_1-q_1)\cdot\frac{l_2+q_2}{2} + (l_2-q_2)\cdot\frac{l_1+q_1}{2}|\\
&\leq |(l_1-q_1)\cdot\frac{l_2+q_2}{2}| + |(l_2-q_2)\cdot\frac{l_1+q_1}{2}|\\
&= |l_1-q_1|\cdot|\frac{l_2+q_2}{2}| + |l_2-q_2|\cdot|\frac{l_1+q_1}{2}|\\
&\leq |l_1-q_1| + |l_2-q_2|\,.
\end{aligned} \quad (44)$$

The last inequality used the fact

$$|\frac{l_1+q_1}{2}| \leq 1,\quad |\frac{l_2+q_2}{2}| \leq 1\,.$$

Suppose the inequality holds for m.

$$\begin{aligned}
&|\prod_{i=1}^{m+1} l_i - \prod_{j=1}^{m+1} q_j| = |\prod_{i=1}^{m} l_i\cdot l_{m+1} - \prod_{j=1}^{m} q_j\cdot q_{m+1}|\\
&\leq |\prod_{i=1}^{m} l_i - \prod_{j=1}^{m} q_j| + |l_{m+1} - q_{m+1}|\\
&\leq \sum_{i=1}^{m+1} |l_i - q_i|\,,
\end{aligned} \quad (45)$$

where the second inequality comes from the induction basis for $m=2$, since

$$0 \leq \prod_{i=1}^{m} l_i, \prod_{j=1}^{m} q_j \leq 1\,,$$

and the last inequality uses the induction hypothesis.

Proof of Lemma 8

Observe the following facts:

$$\begin{aligned}
&|\log\frac{\tilde{p}_i}{1-\tilde{p}_i} - \log\frac{p_i}{1-p_i}|\\
&= |\log\tilde{p}_i - \log p_i + \log(1-p_i) - \log(1-\tilde{p}_i)|\\
&\leq |\log\tilde{p}_i - \log p_i| + |\log(1-p_i) - \log(1-\tilde{p}_i)|\\
&\leq 2C|\tilde{p}_i - p_i|\,,
\end{aligned} \quad (46)$$

since all four terms are bounded from 0 and the last inequality comes from classical inequality of $\log(\cdot)$ functions.

Learning to Rank: Regret Lower Bounds and Efficient Algorithms

Richard Combes
Centrale-Supelec,L2S
Gif-sur-Yvette, France
richard.combes@supelec.fr

Stefan Magureanu, Alexandre Proutière, Cyrille Laroche
KTH, Royal Institute of Technology
Stockholm, Sweden
{magur,alepro,laroche}@kth.se

ABSTRACT

Algorithms for learning to rank Web documents, display ads, or other types of items constitute a fundamental component of search engines and more generally of online services. In such systems, when a user makes a request or visits a web page, an ordered list of items (e.g. documents or ads) is displayed; the user scans this list in order, and clicks on the first relevant item if any. When the user clicks on an item, the reward collected by the system typically decreases with the position of the item in the displayed list. The main challenge in the design of sequential list selection algorithms stems from the fact that the probabilities with which the user clicks on the various items are unknown and need to be learned. We formulate the design of such algorithms as a stochastic bandit optimization problem. This problem differs from the classical bandit framework: (1) the type of feedback received by the system depends on the actual relevance of the various items in the displayed list (if the user clicks on the last item, we know that none of the previous items in the list are relevant); (2) there are inherent correlations between the average relevance of the items (e.g. the user may be interested in a specific topic only). We assume that items are categorized according to their topic and that users are clustered, so that users of the same cluster are interested in the same topic. We investigate several scenarios depending on the available side-information on the user before selecting the displayed list: (a) we first treat the case where the topic the user is interested in is known when she places a request; (b) we then study the case where the user cluster is known but the mapping between user clusters and topics is unknown. For both scenarios, we derive regret lower bounds and devise algorithms that approach these fundamental limits.

Categories and Subject Descriptors

I.2.6 [**Computing Methodologies**]: Learning; G.3 [**Mathematics of Computing**]: Probability and Statistics

Keywords

search engines; ad-display optimization; multi-armed bandits; learning

SIGMETRICS'15 June 15 - 19, 2015, Portland, OR, USA

ACM 978-1-4503-3486-0/15/06 ...$15.00.
http://dx.doi.org/10.1145/2745844.2745852.

1. INTRODUCTION

In this paper, we address the problem of learning to rank a set of items based on user feedback. Specifically, we consider a service, where users repeatedly issue queries (e.g. a text string). There are N items, and given the query, a decision maker picks an ordered subset or list of items of size L to be presented to the user. The user examines the items of the list in order, and clicks on the first item she is interested in. The goal for the decision maker is to maximize the number of clicks (over a fixed time horizon, i.e., for a fixed number of queries), and to present the most relevant items in the first slots or positions in the list. The probability for a user to click on an item is unknown to the decision maker initially, and must be learned in an on-line manner, through trial and error. The problem of learning to rank is fundamental in the design of several online services such as search engines [1], ad-display systems [2] and video-on-demand services where the presented items are webpages, ads, and movies, respectively.

The main challenge in the design of learning-to-rank algorithms stems from the prohibitively high number of possible decisions: there are $N!/(N-L)!$ possible lists and typically, we may have more than 1000 items and 10 slots. Hence even trying each decision once can be too costly and inefficient. Fortunately, when selecting a list of items, the decision maker may leverage useful side-information about both the user and her query. For instance, in search engines, the decision maker may be aware of her gender, age, location, etc., and could also infer from her query the type of documents she is interested in (i.e., the topic of her query), which in turn may significantly prune the set of items to choose from. Formally, we assume that the set of items can be categorized into K different disjoint groups, each group corresponding to a given *topic*. Similarly, users are clustered into K classes, such that a class-k user is interested in items in group $h(k)$ only (h is a 1-to-1 mapping from the user classes to the groups of items). This structure simplifies the problem. Two main issues remain however. 1) Even though we could know the class k of the user issuing the query as well as the group of items of interest $h(k)$, we still need to select in that group the L most relevant items. 2) The topic of the query could remain unclear. For example, the query "jaguar" in a search engine may correspond to several topics, for instance a car manufacturer, an animal or a petascale supercomputer. In this case, it seems appropriate to select items from several groups to make sure that at least one item in the list is relevant. This feature is referred to as *diversity principle* in the literature [3]. Another important and final feature of the problem stems from the nature of the decisions: The reward, e.g. the probability that there exists a relevant item in the displayed list, typically exhibits *diminishing returns*, e.g., it can be a submodular function of the set of displayed items [4].

We propose a model that captures both the diversity principle and the diminishing return property, and formalize the problem of designing online learning-to-rank algorithms as a stochastic structured Multi-Armed Bandit (MAB) problem. Stochastic MAB problems [5,6] constitute the most fundamental sequential decision problems with an exploration vs. exploitation trade-off. In such problems, the decision maker selects an arm (here a list of items) in each round, and observes a realization of the corresponding unknown reward distribution. Each decision is based on past decisions and observed rewards. The objective is to maximize the expected cumulative reward over some time horizon by balancing exploitation (arms with higher observed rewards should be selected often) and exploration (all arms should be explored to learn their average rewards). Equivalently, the performance of a decision rule or algorithm can be measured through its expected *regret*, defined as the gap between the expected reward achieved by the algorithm and that achieved by an Oracle algorithm always selecting the best arm. Our MAB problem differs from the classical bandit framework in several ways. First, the type of feedback received by the system depends on the actual relevance of the various items in the displayed list. For example, if the user clicks on the last item, we know that none of the previous items in the list are relevant. Conversely, if the user clicks on the first item, we do not get any feedback for the subsequent items in the list. Then, the rewards of two lists containing a common item are not independent.

There has recently been an important effort to tackle structured MAB problems similar to ours, refer to Section 2 for a survey of existing results. The design of previously proposed learning-to-rank algorithms has been based on heuristics, and these algorithms seem like reasonable solutions to the problem. In contrast, here, our aim is to devise algorithms with provably minimum regret. Our contributions are as follows:

(i) We first investigate the case where the topic of the user query is known. We derive problem-specific regret lower bounds satisfied by *any* algorithm. We also propose PIE (Parsimonious Item Exploration), an algorithm whose regret matches our lower bound, and scales as $O(N_{h(k)}\log(T))$ when applied to queries of class-k users. Here N_k denotes the number of items in the group $h(k)$, and T denotes the time horizon, i.e., the number of queries. The exploration of apparently suboptimal items under PIE is *parsimonious*, as these items are explored only in a single position of the list.

(ii) We then handle the case where the class of the user issuing the query is known, but the group of items she is interested in is not (i.e., the mapping h is unknown). For this scenario, we propose PIE-C (where "C" stands for "Clustered"), an algorithm that efficiently learns the mapping h, and in turn, exhibits the same regret guarantees as PIE, i.e., as if the mapping h was known initially. In fact, we establish that learning the topic of interest for each user class incurs a constant regret (i.e., that does not scale with the time horizon T).

(iii) Finally, we illustrate the performance of PIE and PIE-C using numerical experiments. To this aim, we use both artificially generated data and real-world data extracted from the MovieLens dataset. In all cases, our algorithms outperform existing algorithms.

2. RELATED WORK

Learning to rank relevant contents has attracted a lot of attention in recent years with an increasing trend of modeling the problem as a MAB with semi-bandit feedback. Most of existing models for search engines do not introduce a sufficiently strong structure to allow for the design of efficient algorithms. For example, in [3,4,7–9], the authors hardly impose any structure in their model. Indeed, they consider scenarios where the random variables representing the relevance of the various items are arbitrarily correlated, and even sometimes depart from the stochastic setting by considering adversarial item relevances. The only important structure that these work consider relates to the diminishing return property, and they typically assume that the reward is just a submodular function of the subset of displayed items, see e.g. [4]. As a consequence, the regret guarantees that can be achieved in the corresponding MAB problems (e.g. submodular bandit problems) are weak; a regret with sublinear scaling in the time horizon cannot be achieved. For instance, in submodular bandits, and its variants, the regret has to be defined by considering, as a benchmark, the performance of the best offline polynomial-time algorithm whose approximation ratio is $1-1/e$ [10] unless $NP \subset DTIME(n^{\log\log(n)})$, which indeed implies that the true regret scales linearly with time. In absence of strong structure, one cannot hope to develop algorithms that learn to rank items in a reasonable time. We believe that our model by its additional and natural clustered structure is more appropriate, and in turn, allows us to devise efficient algorithms, i.e., algorithms whose regret scales as $\log(T)$ as the time horizon T grows large.

In [11], Kholi et al. present an analysis close to ours. There, each user is represented by a binary vector in $\{0,1\}^N$ indicating the relevance of the various items to that user, and users are assumed to arrive according to an i.i.d. process with unknown distribution D. They first assume that the relevances of the different items are independent, similar to our setting, and propose a UCB1-based algorithm whose regret provably scales as $O(NL\log(T))$. UCB1 is unfortunately suboptimal, and as we show in this paper, one may devise algorithms with regret scaling as $O(N\log(T))$ in this setting. Then, to extend their results to more general distributions D (allowing for arbitrary correlations among items), the authors of [11] leverage a recent and elegant result from [12] to establish that a regret guarantee scaling as $(1-1/e)T$.

In [13], Slivkins et al. investigate a scenario where items are represented by vectors in a metric space, and assume that their relevance probabilities are Lipschitz continuous. While this model captures the positive correlation between similar items, it does not account for negative correlations between topics. For example, if a user issues the query "jaguar", and if she is not interested in cars, it means that most likely her query concerns the animal.

There has been over the last decade an important research effort towards the understanding of structured MAB problems, see [14] for a recent survey. By structure, we mean that the reward as a function of the arm has some specific properties. Various structures have been investigated in the literature, e.g., Lipschitz [15–18], linear [19], convex [20]. The structure of the MAB problem corresponding to the design of learning-to-rank algorithms is different, and to our knowledge, this paper proposes the first solution (regret lower bounds, and asymptotically optimal algorithms) to this problem.

3. SYSTEM MODEL

3.1 Users, Items, and Side-information

Our model captures the two important properties of online services mentioned in the introduction, namely the diversity principle and the diminishing return property. Let $\mathcal{N}=\{1,..,N\}$ be a set of items (news, articles, files, etc.). Time proceeds in rounds. In each round, a user makes a query and in response to this query, the decision maker has to select from $\mathcal{N}$ an ordered list of L items. We denote by $\mathcal{U}=\{u\subset\mathcal{N}: u=\{u_1,..,u_L\}, u_i\in\mathcal{N}, u_i\neq u_j \text{ if } i\neq j\}$ the set of all possible decisions. The user scans the selected list in order, and stops as soon as she identifies a relevant item. In round n, the relevance of items to the user is captured by a random vector $X(n) = (X_i(n), i \in \mathcal{N}) \in \{0,1\}^N$, where for any item i, $X_i(n) = 1$ if and only if it is relevant.

Item / User classification. We assume that the set $\mathcal{N}$ is partioned into K disjoint groups $\mathcal{N}_1, \dots, \mathcal{N}_K$ of respective cardinalities $N_1, \dots, N_K$. For example, in the case of a query "jaguar", we could consider three groups, corresponding to items related to the animal, the car brand, or a super-computer. This partition of the various items corresponds to the possible broad *topics* of user queries. Similarly, we categorize users into K different classes, and denote by $h(k)$ the index of the topic of interest for class-k users, i.e., the query of class-k users concern items in $\mathcal{N}_{h(k)}$. The mapping h could be known or not as discussed below. Denote by $k(n)$ the class of the user making the query in round n. $(k(n), n \geq 1)$ are i.i.d. random variables with distribution $\phi = (\phi_1, \dots, \phi_K)$ where $\phi_k = \mathbb{P}[k(n) = k] > 0$. Now, given $k(n) = k$, $(X_i(n), i \in \mathcal{N})$ are independent. Let $\theta_{ki} = \mathbb{P}[X_i(n) = 1 | k(n) = k]$ denote the probability that item i is relevant to class-k users. As already noticed in [9], the above independence assumption captures the diminishing return property. Indeed, given $k(n) = k$, if u is the set of displayed items, the probability that the user finds at least one relevant item in u is $1 - \prod_{i=1}^{L}(1 - \theta_{ku_i})$, which is a submodular function of u (hence with diminishing return).

Observe that the set of users is not specified in our model. We assume that there is an infinite pool of users, that the class of the user issuing a query in round n is drawn from distribution ϕ, and that this user does not issue any query in subsequent rounds. In particular, we cannot learn the class of users from observations. This contrasts with the model proposed in [21], where the set of users is finite, and hence the decision maker can learn the classes of the various users when they repeatedly place queries.

Diversity principle. To capture the diversity principle in our model, we assume that when a user makes a query, she is interested in a single topic only, i.e., in items within a single group $\mathcal{N}_{h(k)}$ only. More precisely, we assume that for all $k, \ell \in [K] := \{1, \dots, K\}$:

$$\max_{i \in \mathcal{N}_\ell} \theta_{ki} \begin{cases} < \delta & \text{if } \ell \neq h(k), \\ > \Delta & \text{if } \ell = h(k), \end{cases} \tag{1}$$

for some fixed $0 < \delta < \Delta < 1$. Typically, we assume that there is an item that is highly relevant to users of a given class, so that e.g., $\Delta > 1/2$. When in round n, the topic $h(k(n))$ is not known, items of various types should be explored and displayed in the L slots so that the chance of displaying a relevant item is maximized. In other words, (1) captures the diversity principle.

Side-information and Feedback. In round n, under decision rule π, an ordered list of L items is displayed. This decision depends on past observations and some side information, i.e., in round n, the decision rule π maps $((u^\pi(s), f(s), i(s), s < n), i(n))$ to a decision in $\mathcal{U}$, where $u^\pi(s)$, $f(s)$, and $i(s)$ denote the list selected under π, the received feedback, and the side information in round s, respectively.

Feedback: In round n, if the ordered list $u = (u_1, \dots, u_L)$ is displayed, the decision maker is informed about the first relevant item in the list, i.e., $f(n) = \min\{i \leq L : X_{u_i}(n) = 1\}$. By convention, $f(n) = 0$ if none of the displayed items is relevant. This type of feedback is often referred to as *semi-bandit* feedback in the bandit literature.

Side-information: we model different types of systems depending on the information available to the decision maker about the user placing the query. For example, when a user issues a query, one could infer from her age, gender, location, and other attributes the topic of her query. In such a case, the decision maker knows, before displaying the list of items, the topic of the query, i.e., in round n, $i(n) = h(k(n))$. Alternatively, the decision maker could know the user class (which could be extracted from users' interactions in a social network) but not the topic of her query, i.e., $i(n) = k(n)$. In this case, the mapping h remains unknown.

3.2 Rewards and Regret

To formulate our objectives, we specify the reward of the system when presenting a given ordered list, and introduce the notion of regret which we will aim at minimizing.

The reward is assumed to be a decreasing function of the position of the first relevant of its items, e.g., in search engines, it is preferable to display the most relevant item first. The reward function is denoted by $r(\cdot)$, i.e., the reward is $r(\ell)$ where ℓ denotes the position of the first relevant item in the list. In absence of relevant item, no reward is collected. Without loss of generality, we assume that rewards are in $[0, 1]$.

In view of our assumptions, the expected reward when presenting an ordered list u to a class-k user is:

$$\mu_\theta(u, k) := \sum_{l=1}^{L} r(l) \theta_{ku_l} \prod_{i=1}^{l-1} (1 - \theta_{ku_i}),$$

where $\theta := (\theta_{ki}, k \in [K], i \in \mathcal{N})$ captures the statistical properties of the system.

The performance of a decision rule π is characterised through the notion of regret which compares the performance of an Oracle algorithm aware of the parameter θ to that of the decision rule π up to a given time horizon T (in rounds). The way regret is defined depends on the available side-information. To simplify the presentation and the results, we make the two following assumptions:
(A1) In each group of items, there are at least L items that are relevant with a probability greater than δ. In particular, $N_k \geq L$ for all $k \in [K]$.
(A2) The number of groups K is larger than the number of slots L.
Under these two assumptions, the performance of an Oracle algorithm can be expressed in a simple way. It depends however on the available side-information.

Known topic: When in each round n, the topic $h(k(n))$ is known, the best decision in this round consists in displaying the L most relevant items of group $\mathcal{N}_{h(k(n))}$. For any user class k, and $\ell = h(k)$, for all $i \in [N]$, i_ℓ denotes the item in $\mathcal{N}_\ell$ with the i-th highest relevance: $\theta_{k1_\ell} \geq \theta_{k2_\ell} \geq \dots \geq \theta_{kN_\ell}$. The list maximizing the expected reward given that the user class is $k(n) = k$ is $u^{\star,k} := (1_{h(k)}, \dots, L_{h(k)})$. Thus, the expected reward under the Oracle algorithm is:

$$\mu^\star_{1,\theta} := \sum_{k \in [K]} \phi_k \mu_\theta(u^{\star,k}, k),$$

and the regret under algorithm π up to round T is defined as:

$$R^\pi_\theta(T) := T\mu^\star_{1,\theta} - \mathbb{E}\left[\sum_{n=1}^{T} \mu_\theta(u^\pi(n), k(n))\right].$$

To simplify the presentation, we assume that given a user class k, the optimal list is unique, i.e., for any $u \neq u^{\star,k}$, $\mu_\theta(u,k) < \mu_\theta(u^{\star,k}, k)$.

Known user class, and unknown topic: In this case, since the Oracle algorithm is aware of the parameter θ, it is also aware of the mapping h. Thus, the regret of algorithm π is the same as in the previous case, i.e., up to time T, the regret is $R^\pi_\theta(T)$.

Our objective is to devise efficient sequential list selection algorithms in both scenarios, when the topic of successive queries are known, and when only the class of the user issuing the query is known.

4. A SINGLE GROUP OF ITEMS AND USERS

In this section, we study the case where $K = 1$, i.e., there is a single class of user and a single group of item. Even with $K = 1$, our bandit problem remains challenging, due the non-linear reward structure and the reward-specific feedback. To design efficient algorithms, we need to determine *how many* and *where* apparently sub-optimal items should be included for exploration in the displayed list.

When $K = 1$, we can drop the indexes k and $h(k)$. To simplify the notation, we replace $\theta_{ki_{h(k)}}$ by θ_i for all $i \in [N]$. More precisely, we have N items, and users are statistically identical, i.e., θ_i denotes the probability that item i is relevant. Let $\theta = (\theta_1, \dots, \theta_N)$ and w.l.o.g. the items are ordered so that $\theta_1 \geq \theta_2 \geq \dots \geq \theta_N$. We denote by $u^\star = (1, \dots, L)$ the list with maximum expected reward, $\mu_\theta^\star$. The regret of policy π up to round T is then $R_\theta^\pi(T) = T\mu_\theta^\star - \mathbb{E}[\sum_{n=1}^T \mu_\theta(u^\pi(n))]$, where $\mu_\theta(u)$ is the expected reward of list u.

4.1 Regret Lower Bound

We first derive a generic regret lower bound valid for any decreasing reward function $r(\cdot)$. This lower bound will be made more explicit for particular choices of reward functions. We define *uniformly good* algorithms as in [22]. A uniformly good algorithm π satisfies $R_\theta^\pi(T) = o(T^a)$ for all parameters θ and all $a > 0$. Later, it will become clear that such algorithms exist, and therefore we only restrict our attention to the set of such algorithms. We denote by $I(a, b)$ the Kullback-Leibler divergence between two Bernoulli distributions of respective means a and b, i.e., $I(a, b) = a\log(a/b) + (1 - a)\log((1 - a)/(1 - b))$. We further define $\mathcal{U}(i) = \{u \in \mathcal{U} : i \in u\}$, the set of lists in $\mathcal{U}$ that include the item with the i-th highest relevance. Finally, for any list u, and any item $i \in u$, we denote by $p_i(u)$ the position of i in u.

THEOREM 1. *For any uniformly good algorithm π, we have:*

$$\lim\inf_{T\to\infty} \frac{R^\pi(T)}{\log(T)} \geq c(\theta), \tag{2}$$

where $c(\theta)$ is the minimal value of the objective function in the following optimization problem (P_θ):

$$\inf_{c_u \geq 0, u \in \mathcal{U}} \sum_{u \in \mathcal{U}} c_u(\mu_\theta^\star - \mu_\theta(u)) \tag{3}$$

$$\text{s.t.} \sum_{u \in \mathcal{U}(i)} c_u I(\theta_i, \theta_L) \prod_{s < p_i(u)} (1 - \theta_{u_s}) \geq 1, \forall i > L.$$

The solution of the optimization problem (P_θ) has a natural interpretation. For any $u \in \mathcal{U}$, c_u represents the expected number of times the list u should be displayed using an algorithm minimizing the regret. More precisely, u should be displayed $c_u \log(T)$ times asymptotically when the time horizon T grows large. Theorem 1 and its above interpretation are applications of the theory of controlled Markov chains with unknown transition kernel developed in [23]. Next we specify the solution of (P_θ) for two particular classes of reward functions. Define for $i < L$, $\Delta_i = r(i) - r(i+1)$, and $\Delta_L = r(L)$.

1) Reward functions such that: $\Delta_i \geq \Delta_L > 0$ for all $i < L$. This assumption on the reward function seems natural in the context of search engines where the rewards obtained from items presented first are high and rapidly decrease as the position of the item increases.

PROPOSITION 1. *Assume that $\Delta_i \geq \Delta_L > 0$ for $i < L$. Then for all $u \in \mathcal{U}$ such that $u \neq u^\star$, the coefficient c_u corresponding to the solution of (P_θ) satisfies: If for some $i > L$, $u = (1, \dots, L - 1, i)$,*

$$c_u = \frac{1}{I(\theta_i, \theta_L) \prod_{j<L}(1 - \theta_j)},$$

else $c_u = 0$. Hence, we have:

$$c(\theta) = \Delta_L \sum_{i=L+1}^N \frac{\theta_L - \theta_i}{I(\theta_i, \theta_L)}.$$

The above proposition states that very few lists from $\mathcal{U}_k$ should be explored $\Theta(\log(T))$ times. These lists include the $(L - 1)$ most relevant items in the $(L-1)$ first slots, and an item that is not within the L most relevant items in the last slot. In other words, an optimal algorithm should include only one sub-optimal item in the list when it explores, and this item should be placed last. This observation will simplify the design of asymptotically optimal algorithms – although of course, initially, the decision maker does not know the $(L - 1)$ most relevant items. Note that the minimum regret scales as $(N - L)\log(T)$; this indicates that optimal algorithms should really exploit the reward and feedback structures.

2) Reward functions such that: $\Delta_i = 0$ for all $i < L$, and $\Delta_L > 0$. This scenario may be appropriate in the case of display ads, where the reward obtained when a user clicks does not depend on the position of the ad on the webpage.

PROPOSITION 2. *Assume that $\Delta_i = 0$ for all $i < L$, and $\Delta_L > 0$. Then for all $u \in \mathcal{U}$ such that $u \neq u^\star$, the coefficient c_u corresponding to the solution of (P_θ) satisfies:*
If for some $i > L$, $u = (i, 1, \dots, L - 1)$,

$$c_u = \frac{1}{I(\theta_i, \theta_L)},$$

Else $c_u = 0$. Hence, we have:

$$c(\theta) = \Delta_L \prod_{j<L}(1 - \theta_j) \sum_{i=L+1}^N \frac{(\theta_L - \theta_i)}{I(\theta_i, \theta_L)}.$$

Again the above proposition states that very few lists should be explored $\Theta(\log(T))$ times. These lists are those containing the $(L - 1)$ most relevant items in the $(L - 1)$ last positions, and an item that is not within the L most relevant items in the first position. In other words, the exploration of items is performed in the first position. Observe that as in the previous case, the minimum regret scales as $(N - L)\log(T)$.

3) General Reward Function. An explicit expression for the lower bound $c(\theta)$ for general reward function is more challenging to derive. However, we suspect that the lists u such that $c_u > 0$ are $w_l^i = (1, \dots, (l - 1), i, l, \dots, (L - 1))$ for some $i > L$. In other words, only one suboptimal item, (i.e., for $i > L$, the i-th most relevant item) is explored at a time, and we should explore i in the l-th position. To determine this position, we make the following heuristic reasoning. Let us fix the number of times i is explored. Given this fixed exploration rate, we select position l that induces the smallest regret. Let us assume that i is explored in slot l. When the list w_l^i is displayed, the probability p_l that i is actually explored is: $p_l = \prod_{j=1}^{l-1}(1 - \theta_j)$. The average number of times i is actually explored when placed in position l is proportional to $1/p_l$. Hence the position $\text{oes}(i)$ where i should be placed should satisfy:

$$\text{oes}(i) \in \arg\min_{l \leq L} f(\theta, w_l^i), \tag{4}$$

where $f(\theta, w_l^i) = \frac{\mu_\theta^\star - \mu_\theta(w_l^i)}{p_l}$. Let $w^i = w^i_{\text{oes}(i)}$. If the argmin in (4) is realized for different positions, we break ties arbitrarily. We state the following conjecture.

For any decreasing reward function $r(\cdot)$, and for $u \in \mathcal{U}$, the coefficient c_u in the solution of (P_θ) has the following form:

$$c_u = \begin{cases} \frac{1}{I(\theta_i, \theta_L) p_{\text{oes}(i)}} & \text{if } u = w^i \text{ for some } i > L, \\ 0 & \text{otherwise.} \end{cases}$$

Observe that the conjecture holds in Cases 1) and 2). In the former, it is optimal to place any suboptimal item i ($i > L$) in the last slot, in which case $p_{\text{oes}(i)} = \prod_{j=1}^{L-1}(1-\theta_j)$. In the latter, it is optimal to place any suboptimal item i in the first slot, in which case $p_{\text{oes}(i)} = 1$.

4.2 Optimal Algorithms

Next we present asymptotically optimal sequential list selection algorithms, i.e., their limiting regret (as T grows large) matches the lower bound derived above. To describe our algorithms, we need to introduce the following definitions. Let $u(n)$ be the list selected in round n, and let $p_i(n)$ denote the position at which item i is shown if $i \in u(n)$, and $p_i(n) = 0$ otherwise. Recall that a sample of θ_i is obtained if and only if $i \in u(n)$ and $X_{i'}(n) = 0$ for all $i' \in \{u_1(n), ..., u_{p_i(n)-1}\}$. Define

$$o_i(n) := \mathbf{1}\left\{i \in u(n), \forall l' < p_i(n), X_{u_{l'}(n)}(n) = 0\right\}.$$

Then we get a sample from θ_i in round n iff $o_i(n) = 1$. Let $t_i(n) := \sum_{n' \le n} o_i(n')$ be the number of samples obtained for θ_i up to round n. The corresponding empirical mean is:

$$\hat{\theta}_i(n) = \frac{1}{t_i(n)} \sum_{n' \le n} o_i(n') X_i(n')$$

if $t_i(n) > 0$ and $\hat{\theta}_i(n) = 0$ otherwise. We also define $c_i(n)$ as the number of times that a list containing i has been selected up to round n: $c_i(n) := \sum_{n' \le n} \mathbf{1}\{i \in u(n')\}$. Let $j(n) = (j_1(n), ..., j_N(n))$ be the indices of the items with empirical means sorted in decreasing order, so that:

$$\hat{\theta}_{j_1(n)}(n) \ge \hat{\theta}_{j_2(n)}(n) \ge ... \ge \hat{\theta}_{j_N(n)}(n)$$

We assume that ties are broken arbitrarily. Define the list of L "leaders" at time n as $\mathcal{L}(n) = (j_1(n), ..., j_L(n))$. The algorithms we propose use the indexes used by the KL-UCB algorithm, known to be optimal in classical MAB problems [24]. The KL-UCB index $b_i(n)$ of item i in round n is:

$$b_i(n) = \max\{q \in [0,1] : t_i(n) I(\hat{\theta}_i(n), q) \le f(n)\},$$

where $f(n) = \log(n) + 4\log(\log(n))$. Let:

$$\mathcal{B}(n) := \{i \notin \mathcal{L}(n) : b_i(n) \ge \hat{\theta}_{j_L(n)}(n)\}.$$

be the set of items which are not in the set of leaders, and whose index are larger than the empirical mean of item $j_L(n)$. Intuitively, $\mathcal{B}(n)$ includes items which are potentially better than the worst current leader. For $1 \le i \le N$, define decision:

$$U_i^l(n) = (j_1(n), ..., j_{l-1}(n), i, j_l(n), ..., j_{L-1}(n)).$$

$U_i^l(n)$ is the list obtained by considering the $L-1$ first items of $\mathcal{L}(n)$, and by placing item i at position l. We are now ready to present our algorithms. The latter, referred to as PIE(l), are parametrized by $l \in \{1, \ldots, L\}$, the position where the exploration is performed. In round n, PIE(l) proceeds as follows:

(i) if $\mathcal{B}(n)$ is empty, then the leader is selected: $u(n) = \mathcal{L}(n)$;

(ii) otherwise, we select $u(n) = \mathcal{L}(n)$ with probability $1/2$, and $u(n) = U^l_{i(n)}(n)$ with probability $1/2$, where $i(n)$ is chosen from $\mathcal{B}(n)$ uniformly at random.

Algorithm PIE(l)

Init: $\mathcal{B}(1) = \emptyset$, $\hat{\theta}_i(1) = 0 = b_i(1)\ \forall i$, $\mathcal{L}(1) = \{1, \ldots, L\}$
For $n \ge 1$:
If $\mathcal{B}(n) = \emptyset$, select $\mathcal{L}(n)$
Else w.p.1/2, select $\mathcal{L}(n)$, w.p. select $U_I^l(n)$, $I \in \mathcal{B}(n)$ unif. distributed
Compute: $\mathcal{B}(n+1)$, $\mathcal{L}(n+1)$, and $\hat{\theta}_i(n+1)$, $b_i(n+1)$, $\forall i$

Refer to pseudo-code of PIE(l) for a formal description. Note that the PIE(l) algorithm has low computational complexity. It can be easily checked that it requires at each round $O(N + L\log(N))$ operations. In the following theorem, we provide a finite-time regret upper bound of the PIE(l) algorithm. Introduce $\eta = \prod_{i=1}^{L-1}(1-\theta_i)^{-1}$ and recall that $p_l = \prod_{i'<l}(1-\theta_{i'})$ and $u^{i,l} = (1, \ldots, (l-1), i, (l+1), \ldots, (L-1))$ for all $i > l$.

THEOREM 2. *Under algorithm π=PIE(l), for all $T \ge 1$ and, all $\epsilon > 0$ and all $0 < \delta < \delta_0 = \min_{i<N}(\theta_i - \theta_{i+1})/2$, the regret under π satifies:*

$$R^\pi(T) = f(T) c^{PIE(l)}(\theta, \delta) + C(\theta, \delta, \epsilon),$$

where

$$c^{PIE(l)}(\theta, \delta) = p_l^{-1} \sum_{i=L+1}^{N} \frac{\mu(u^\star) - \mu(u^{i,l})}{I(\theta_i + \delta, \theta_L - \delta)},$$

$$C(\theta, \delta, \epsilon) = 2N\eta[(5 + 8NL)\eta + (3 + 2L)\delta^{-2}] + 15L + (N-L)p_l^{-1}\left[\epsilon^{-2}p_l^{-1} + \delta^{-2}(1-\epsilon)^{-1}\right].$$

As a consequence:

$$\limsup_{T\to\infty} \frac{R^\pi(T)}{\log(T)} \le c^{PIE(l)}(\theta) := \sum_{i=L+1}^{N} \frac{\mu(u^\star) - \mu(u^{i,l})}{\prod_{i'<l}(1-\theta_{i'}) I(\theta_i, \theta_L)}.$$

A direct consequence of the above theorem is that PIE(L) and PIE(1) are asymptotically optimal in Case 1) (convex decreasing reward functions) and Case 2) (constant rewards), respectively. Indeed, one can easily check that for example $c^{\text{PIE}(L)}(\theta) = c(\theta)$ in Case 1).

4.3 Proofs: Lower Bounds

4.3.1 *Proof of Theorem 1*

The result is a consequence of the theory of controlled Markov chain with unknown transition rates [23]. We apply the formalism of [23] as follows. The state space of the Markov chain is $\mathcal{X} = \{0, 1, .., L\}$, and the state will capture the feedback obtained from the previous decision, i.e., $x = 0$ means that no item in the list is relevant, and $x = i$ means that the first relevant item is in position i. The set of control actions is the set of lists $\mathcal{U}$. The transition probability from state x to state y given that the chosen list is u is $p(x, y; u, \theta)$ where

$$p(x, y; u, \theta) = p(y; u, \theta) = \begin{cases} \prod_{s=1}^{L}(1-\theta_{u_s}) \text{ if } y = 0, \\ \theta_{u_y} \prod_{s=1}^{y-1}(1-\theta_{u_s}) \text{ if } y \in \{1, .., L\}. \end{cases}$$

The reward associated to the state x and the control action u is denoted by $g(x, u)$, and here we have $g(x, u) = r(x)$. Finally, the set of control laws is $\mathcal{G} = \mathcal{U}$. The expected reward under the control law u is $\mu_\theta(u)$. Next we apply Theorem 1 in [23]. To this aim, we first introduce the KL divergence between two parameters $\lambda \in [0, 1]^N$ and θ under control law u as:

$$I^u(\lambda, \theta) = \sum_{s=1}^{L} \theta_{u_s} \left[\prod_{i=1}^{s-1}(1-\theta_{u_i})\right] \log\left(\frac{\theta_{u_s}\prod_{i=1}^{s-1}(1-\theta_{u_i})}{\lambda_{u_s}\prod_{i=1}^{s-1}(1-\lambda_{u_i})}\right) + \left[\prod_{i=1}^{s}(1-\theta_{u_i})\right] \log\left(\frac{\prod_{i=1}^{s}(1-\theta_{u_i})}{\prod_{i=1}^{s}(1-\lambda_{u_i})}\right),$$

which can be rewritten as:

$$I^u(\theta, \lambda) = \sum_{i=1}^{L} I(\theta_{u_i}, \lambda_{u_i}) \prod_{s=1}^{i-1}(1-\theta_{u_s}).$$

Let us further introduce the set of *bad* parameters $B(\theta)$ as:

$$B(\theta) = \{\lambda \in [0, 1]^N : I^{u^\star}(\theta, \lambda) = 0 \text{ and } \exists u \neq u^\star, \mu_\lambda(u) > \mu_\theta^\star\},$$

where $\mu_\lambda(u)$ denotes the expected reward of decision u under parameter λ. By definition, if $\lambda \in B(\theta)$, there is $i > L$ such that $\lambda_i > \theta_L$. Thus we can decompose $B(\theta)$ into the union of sets $B_i(\theta) = \{\lambda \in B(\theta), \lambda_i > \theta_L\}$ over $i \in \{L+1, .., N\}$. By Theorem 1 in [23], we have, for any uniformly good algorithm π:

$$\liminf_{T\to\infty} \frac{R^\pi(T)}{\log(T)} \geq c(\theta),$$

where

$$c(\theta) = \inf_{c_u \geq 0, u \in \mathcal{U}} \sum_{u \neq u^\star} c_u(\mu_\theta^* - \mu_\theta(u))$$
$$\text{s. t. } \forall i > L, \inf_{\lambda \in B_i(\theta)} \sum_{u \neq u^\star} c_u I^u(\theta, \lambda) \geq 1.$$

By definition of $B_i(\theta)$, if $\lambda \in B_i(\theta)$, then $\lambda_i > \theta_L$. It can easy seen that $\inf_{\lambda \in B_i(\theta)} I^u(\theta, \lambda)$ is achieved for some parameter $\lambda^\star$ such that $\lambda_i^\star = \theta_L$ and $\lambda_j^\star = \theta_j$ for $j \neq i$ and hence:

$$\inf_{\lambda \in B_i(\theta)} I^u(\theta, \lambda) = \sum_{u \in \mathcal{U}(i)} c_u \prod_{s < p_i(u)} (1-\theta_{u_s}) I(\theta_i, \theta_L) \geq 1.$$

This completes the proof. □

4.3.2 *Proof of Proposition 1*

For $i > L$, we define v^i the list such that $v_j^i = j$ for $j < l$, and $v_L^i = i$. According to Proposition 1, these lists only should be explored under an optimal algorithm. Let $c = \{c_u : u \neq u^\star\}$ be a solution of the LP introduced in Theorem 1. We prove by contradiction that $c_u > 0$ implies that there exists $i > l$ such that $u = v^i$. Assume $\exists u \neq u^\star$ such that $c_u > 0$ and $u \neq v^i, \forall i > L$. We propose a new set of coefficients $c' = \{c'_u : u \neq u^\star\}$ such the value of objective function $c'(\theta)$ of the LP under c' is less than under c. We use the following notation: $c_{w,i} = c_v \frac{\prod_{s<i}(1-\theta_{w_s})}{\prod_{s<L}(1-\theta_s)}$ for any $w \in \mathcal{U}$. Recall that $p_i(w)$ is the position of i in w. Now introduce c' such that for all $u \neq u^\star$:

$$c'_w = \begin{cases} 0 & \text{if } w = u, \\ c_w + c_{u,p_i(u)} & \text{if } \exists i > L \text{ such that } w = v^i, \\ c_w & \text{otherwise.} \end{cases}$$

We show that c' yields a strictly lower value of the objective function in the LP of Theorem 1 than c, a contradiction. Denote by $c(\theta)$ and $c'(\theta)$ the value of the objective function of the LP under c and c', respectively. We have:

$$c(\theta) - c'(\theta) = c_u(\mu_\theta^* - \mu_\theta(u)) - \sum_{i: u_i > L} c_{u,i}(\mu_\theta^* - \mu_\theta(v^{u_i})).$$

It is easy to check that: $\mu_\theta(u) = r(1) - \sum_{l=1}^{L} \Delta_l \prod_{s \leq l}(1-\theta_{u_s})$. Therefore $\mu_\theta^* - \mu_\theta(u) = \sum_{i=1}^{L} \Delta_i(\prod_{s\leq i}(1-\theta_{u_s}) - \prod_{s \leq i}(1-\theta_s))$. Since $\Delta_L = r(L)$, we have:

$$\mu_\theta^* - \mu_\theta(u) - \sum_{i:u_i>L} \frac{\prod_{s<i}(1-\theta_{u_j})}{\prod_{s<L}(1-\theta_j)}(\mu_\theta^* - \mu_\theta(v^{u_i})) =$$
$$\sum_{i=1}^{L} \Delta_i(\prod_{s\leq i}(1-\theta_{u_s}) - \prod_{s\leq i}(1-\theta_s)) - \sum_{i:u_i>L} \Delta_L \prod_{s<i}(1-\theta_{u_s})(\theta_L - \theta_{u_i}).$$

Let $i \leq L$ such that $u_i > L$. We have:

$$\Delta_i(\prod_{s\leq i}(1-\theta_{u_s}) - \prod_{s\leq i}(1-\theta_s)) - \Delta_L \prod_{s<i}(1-\theta_{u_s})(\theta_L - \theta_{u_i})$$
$$\geq \Delta_i(\prod_{s<i}(1-\theta_{u_s})(1-\theta_L) - \prod_{s\leq i}(1-\theta_s)) > 0.$$

We deduce:

$$c_u(\mu_\theta^* - \mu_\theta(u)) > \sum_{\substack{i \\ u_i > L}} c_{u,i}(\mu_\theta^* - \mu_\theta(v^{u_i})).$$

And hence, $c'(\theta) < c(\theta)$. We have shown that in c the solution of the LP involved in Theorem 1, $c_u > 0$ iff $\exists i > l$: $u = v^i$. Now we can easily solve the LP in light of this result, and show that the c_u's are of the form as stated in Proposition 1. The proof of Proposition 2 is similar. □

4.4 Proof: Regret Upper bound for PIE(l)

4.4.1 *Preliminaries*

Before analyzing the regret of PIE(l), we state and prove Lemma 1. The latter shows that, under algorithm PIE(l), the set of rounds at which either
(i) the set of leaders is different from the optimal decision, or
(ii) the empirical mean of one of the leaders deviates from its expectation by more than a fixed quantity $\delta > 0$,
has finite size (in expectation). Note that (i) and (ii) are not mutually exclusive. The upper bound provided by Lemma 1 is explicit as a function of the parameters $(\theta_i)_i$ and δ.

LEMMA 1. *Define* $\delta_0 = \min_{i<N}(\theta_i - \theta_{i+1})/2$ *and* $\eta = \prod_{i=1}^{L-1}(1-\theta_i)^{-1}$. *Let* $0 < \delta < \delta_0$ *and define the following sets of rounds:*

$$\mathcal{A} = \{n \geq 1 : \mathcal{L}(n) \neq u^\star\},$$
$$\mathcal{D} = \{n \geq 1 : \exists i \in \mathcal{L}(n) : |\hat{\theta}_i(n) - \theta_i| \geq \delta\}.$$

and $\mathcal{C} = \mathcal{A} \cup \mathcal{D}$. *Under algorithm PIE(l), for all* $0 < \delta < \delta_0$ *we have:*

$$\mathbb{E}[|\mathcal{C}|] \leq 2N\eta[(5+8NL)\eta + (3+2L)\delta^{-2}] + 15L.$$

Proof. Fix $\delta < \delta_0$ throughout the proof. Our goal is to upper bound the expected size of $\mathcal{C}$. To do so, we decompose $\mathcal{C}$ in an appropriate manner. We introduce the following sets of instants:

$$\mathcal{E} = \{n \geq 1 : \exists i \in \{1,...,L\} : b_i(n) \leq \theta_i\}$$
$$\mathcal{G} = \{n \geq 1 : n \in \mathcal{A} \setminus (\mathcal{D} \cup \mathcal{E}), \exists i \in \{1,...,L\} \setminus \mathcal{L}(n) : |\hat{\theta}_i(n) - \theta_i| \geq \delta\}.$$

We first check that $\mathcal{C} \subset \mathcal{D} \cup \mathcal{E} \cup \mathcal{G}$. Since $\mathcal{C} = \mathcal{A} \cup \mathcal{D}$, it is sufficient to prove that $\mathcal{A} \subset (\mathcal{D} \cup \mathcal{E} \cup \mathcal{G})$. Let $n \in \mathcal{A} \setminus (\mathcal{D} \cup \mathcal{E})$. Let $i, i' \in \mathcal{L}(n)$, with $i < i'$. Since $n \notin \mathcal{D}$ we have $|\hat{\theta}_i(n) - \theta_i| \leq \delta$, $|\hat{\theta}_{i'}(n) - \theta_{i'}| \leq \delta$, and $\delta \leq (\theta_i - \theta_{i'})/2$, therefore $\hat{\theta}_i(n) \geq \hat{\theta}_{i'}(n)$. This proves that $(j_1(n), ..., j_L(n))$ is an increasing sequence. We have that $j_L(n) > L$, otherwise we have $(j_1(n), ..., j_L(n)) = (1, 2, ..., L)$ hence $\mathcal{L}(n) = u^\star$ and $n \notin \mathcal{A}$, a contradiction. Since $j_L(n) > L$ there exists $i \leq L$ such that $i \notin \mathcal{L}(n)$. Let us now prove by contradiction that $|\hat{\theta}_i(n) - \theta_i| \geq \delta$. Assume that $|\hat{\theta}_i(n) - \theta_i| \leq \delta$, then we have $|\hat{\theta}_{j_L(n)}(n) - \theta_{j_L(n)}| \leq \delta$ (since $j_L(n) \in \mathcal{L}(n)$ and $n \notin \mathcal{D}$) so that $\hat{\theta}_i(n) > \hat{\theta}_{j_L(n)}(n)$. In turn this would imply that $i \in \mathcal{L}(n)$ which is a contradiction. Finally we have proven that $n \in \mathcal{A} \setminus (\mathcal{D} \cup \mathcal{E})$ implies $n \in \mathcal{G}$. Hence $\mathcal{C} \subset \mathcal{D} \cup \mathcal{E} \cup \mathcal{G}$, and by a union bound:

$$\mathbb{E}[|\mathcal{C}|] \leq \mathbb{E}[|\mathcal{D}|] + \mathbb{E}[|\mathcal{E}|] + \mathbb{E}[|\mathcal{G}|].$$

Next we prove the following inequalities:
(a) $\mathbb{E}[|\mathcal{D}|] \leq 2N\eta\left[10\eta + 3\delta^{-2}\right]$;
(b) $\mathbb{E}[|\mathcal{E}|] \leq 15L$;
(c) $\mathbb{E}[|\mathcal{G}|] \leq 4NL\eta\left[4\eta + \delta^{-2}\right]$.

Inequality (a): We further decompose $\mathcal{D}$ as $\mathcal{D} = \cup_{i=1}^{N}(\mathcal{D}_{i,1} \cup \mathcal{D}_{i,2})$, with:

$$\mathcal{D}_{i,1} = \{n \geq 1 : i \in \mathcal{L}(n), j_L(n) \neq i, |\hat{\theta}_i(n) - \theta_i| \geq \delta\}$$
$$\mathcal{D}_{i,2} = \{n \geq 1 : i \in \mathcal{L}(n), j_L(n) = i, |\hat{\theta}_i(n) - \theta_i| \geq \delta\}$$

In other words, $\mathcal{D}_{i,1}$ is the set of rounds at which i is not the L-th leader, so that if $n \in \mathcal{D}_{i,1}$ then i will be included in $u(n)$. $\mathcal{D}_{i,2}$ is the set of instants at which i is the L-th leader, so that if $n \in \mathcal{D}_{i,2}$, then either i or $i(n)$ will be included in $u(n)$.

First let $n \in \mathcal{D}_{i,1}$. Then we have $i \in u(n)$ by definition of the algorithm. Hence $\mathbb{E}[o_i(n)|n \in \mathcal{D}_{i,1}] \geq \eta^{-1}$. Furthermore, for all n, $\mathbf{1}\{n \in \mathcal{D}_{i,1}\}$ is $\mathcal{F}_{n-1}$ measurable ($\mathcal{F}_{n-1}$ the σ-algebra generated by $u(s)$ and the corresponding feedback for $s \leq n-1$). Therefore we can apply the second statement of Lemma 5, presented in Appendix (with $H := \mathcal{D}_{i,1}$, $c := \eta^{-1}$) to obtain: $\mathbb{E}[|\mathcal{D}_{i,1}|] \leq 2\eta\left[2\eta + \delta^{-2}\right]$.

Next let $n \in \mathcal{D}_{i,2}$. Then we have that $i \in u(n)$ with probability at least $1/2$ by definition of the algorithm, so that $\mathbb{E}[o_i(n)|n \in \mathcal{D}_{i,2}] \geq \eta^{-1}/2$. Also $\mathbf{1}\{n \in \mathcal{D}_{i,2}\}$ is $\mathcal{F}_{n-1}$ measurable. Hence applying the second statement of Lemma 5 (with $H \equiv \mathcal{D}_{i,2}$, $c \equiv \eta^{-1}/2$) we obtain: $\mathbb{E}[|\mathcal{D}_{i,2}|] \leq 4\eta\left[4\eta + \delta^{-2}\right]$.

Applying a union bound over $1 \leq i \leq N$, we get:

$$\mathbb{E}[|\mathcal{D}|] \leq \sum_{i=1}^{N} \mathbb{E}[|\mathcal{D}_{i,1}|] + \mathbb{E}[|\mathcal{D}_{i,2}|] \leq 2N\eta\left[10\eta + 3\delta^{-2}\right].$$

Inequality (b): Decompose $\mathcal{E}$ as $\mathcal{E} = \cup_{i=1}^{L}\mathcal{E}_i$ where

$$\mathcal{E}_i = \{n \geq 1 : b_i(n) \leq \theta_i\}.$$

Applying Lemma 6 we obtain that $\mathbb{E}[|\mathcal{E}_i|] \leq 15$ for all i, so that:

$$\mathbb{E}[|\mathcal{E}|] \leq \sum_{i=1}^{L} \mathbb{E}[|\mathcal{E}_i|] \leq 15L.$$

Inequality (c): Decompose $\mathcal{G}$ as $\mathcal{G} = \cup_{i=1}^{L}\mathcal{G}_i$ where

$$\mathcal{G}_i = \{n \geq 1 : n \in \mathcal{A} \setminus (\mathcal{D} \cup \mathcal{E}), i \notin \mathcal{L}(n), |\hat{\theta}_i(n) - \theta_i| \geq \delta\}.$$

For a given $i \leq L$, $\mathcal{G}_i$ is the set of rounds at which i is not one of the leaders, and is not accurately estimated. Let $n \in \mathcal{G}_i$. Since $i \notin \mathcal{L}(n)$, we must have $j_L(n) > L$. In turn, since $n \notin \mathcal{D}$ we have $|\hat{\theta}_{j_L(n)}(n) - \theta_{j_L(n)}| \leq \delta$, so that

$$\hat{\theta}_{j_L(n)}(n) \leq \theta_{j_L(n)} + \delta \leq \theta_{L+1} + \delta \leq (\theta_{L+1} + \theta_L)/2.$$

Furthermore, since $n \notin \mathcal{E}$ and $1 \leq i \leq L$, we have $b_i(n) \geq \theta_i \geq \theta_L \geq (\theta_{L+1} + \theta_L)/2 \geq \hat{\theta}_{j_L(n)}(n)$. This implies that $i \in \mathcal{B}(n)$. Since $i(n)$ has uniform distribution over $\mathcal{B}(n)$, we have that $i(n) = i$ with probability at least $1/N$. We have that for all n, $\mathbf{1}\{n \in \mathcal{G}_i\}$ is $\mathcal{F}_{n-1}$ measurable. Further, $\mathbb{E}[o_i(n)|n \in \mathcal{G}_i] \geq \eta^{-1}/(2N)$. So we can apply Lemma 5 (with $H \equiv \mathcal{G}_i$ and $c \equiv \eta^{-1}/(2N)$) to yield: $\mathbb{E}[|\mathcal{G}_i|] \leq 4N\eta\left[4N\eta + \delta^{-2}\right]$

Using a union bound over $1 \leq i \leq L$, we obtain:

$$\mathbb{E}[|\mathcal{G}|] \leq \sum_{i=1}^{L} \mathbb{E}[|\mathcal{G}_i|] \leq 4NL\eta\left[4N\eta + \delta^{-2}\right].$$

Putting inequalities (a), (b) and (c) together, we obtain the announced result:

$$\mathbb{E}[|\mathcal{C}|] \leq \mathbb{E}[|\mathcal{D}|] + \mathbb{E}[|\mathcal{E}|] + \mathbb{E}[|\mathcal{G}|]$$
$$\leq 2N\eta[(5+8NL)\eta + (3+2L)\delta^{-2}] + 15L,$$

which concludes the proof. □

4.4.2 Proof of Theorem 2

We decompose the regret by distinguishing rounds in $\mathcal{C}$ (as defined in the statement of Lemma 1), and other rounds. For all $i > L$, we define the sets of instants between 1 and T at which $n \notin \mathcal{C}$ and decision $u^{i,l}$ is selected (recall that $u^{i,l} = (1, \ldots, (l-1), i, (l+1), \ldots, (L-1))$):

$$\mathcal{K}_i = \{1 \leq n \leq T : n \notin \mathcal{C}, \mathcal{L}(n) = u^\star, u(n) = u^{i,l}\}.$$

By design of the algorithm, when $n \notin \mathcal{C}$, the leader is the optimal decision, and so the only sub-optimal decisions that can be selected are $\{u^{L+1,l}, ..., u^{N,l}\}$. Hence the set of instants at which a suboptimal decision is selected verifies:

$$\{1 \leq n \leq T : u(n) \neq u^\star\} \subset \mathcal{C} \cup (\cup_{i=L+1}^{N}\mathcal{K}_i).$$

Since $\mu(u^\star) - \mu(u) \leq 1$ for all u, we obtain the upper bound:

$$R^\pi(T) \leq \mathbb{E}[|\mathcal{C}|] + \sum_{i=L+1}^{N}\left[\mu(u^\star) - \mu(u^{i,l})\right]\mathbb{E}[|\mathcal{K}_i|].$$

By Lemma 1, we have:

$$\mathbb{E}[|\mathcal{C}|] \leq 2N\eta[(5+8NL)\eta + (3+2L)\delta^{-2}] + 15L.$$

Hence, to complete the proof, it is sufficient to prove that, for all $i \geq L+1$, all $\epsilon > 0$ and all $0 < \delta < \theta_L - \theta_{L+1}$, we have:

$$\mathbb{E}[|\mathcal{K}_i|] \leq p_l^{-1} \frac{f(T)}{(1-\epsilon) I(\theta_i + \delta, \theta_L - \delta)} + p_l^{-1}\left[p_l^{-1}\epsilon^{-2} + \delta^{-2}(1-\epsilon)^{-1}\right]. \quad (5)$$

Define the number of rounds in $\mathcal{K}_i$ before round n: $k_i(n) = \sum_{n' \leq n} \mathbf{1}\{n' \in \mathcal{K}_i\}$. Fix $\epsilon > 0$, define $t_0 = f(T)/I(\theta_i + \delta, \theta_L - \delta)$, and define the following subsets of $\mathcal{K}_i$:

$$\mathcal{K}_{i,1} = \left\{ n \in \mathcal{K}_i : t_i(n) \leq p_l(1-\epsilon)k_i(n) \text{ or } |\hat{\theta}_i(n) - \theta_i| \geq \delta \right\},$$
$$\mathcal{K}_{i,2} = \{ n \in \mathcal{K}_i : t_0 \leq p_l(1-\epsilon)k_i(n) \}.$$

Namely, $\mathcal{K}_{i,1}$ is the set of rounds in $\mathcal{K}_i$ where either item i has been sampled (we recall that i is sampled iff all items presented before i where not relevant) less than $p_l(1-\epsilon)k_i(n)$ times or and its empirical mean deviates from its expectation by more than δ. $\mathcal{K}_{i,2}$ is the number of instants in $\mathcal{K}_i$ where $p_l(1-\epsilon)k_i(n)$ is smaller than t_0, i.e $\mathcal{K}_{i,2}$ is the set of the first $t_0 p_l^{-1}(1-\epsilon)^{-1}$ instants of $\mathcal{K}_i$.

Let us prove that $\mathcal{K}_i \subset \mathcal{K}_{i,1} \cup \mathcal{K}_{i,2}$. We proceed by contradiction: Consider $n \in \mathcal{K}_i \setminus (\mathcal{K}_{i,1} \cup \mathcal{K}_{i,2})$. We prove that we have both (a) $t_i(n) \geq t_0$ and (b) $b_i(n) \geq \theta_L - \delta$. Since $n \notin \mathcal{K}_{i,1}$ we have that $t_i(n) \geq p^{-1}(1-\epsilon)k_i(n)$ and since $n \notin \mathcal{K}_{i,2}$ we have $p_l(1-\epsilon)k_i(n) \geq t_0$. So (a) holds. By definition of the algorithm, we have that $i \in \mathcal{B}(n)$, so that $b_i(n) \geq \hat{\theta}_{j_L(n)}(n)$. Furthermore, since $n \in \mathcal{K}_i$ we have that $n \notin \mathcal{C}$, so that $j_L(n) = L$, and $|\hat{\theta}_L(n) - \theta_L| \leq \delta$. In turn, this implies $b_i(n) \geq \hat{\theta}_{j_L(n)}(n) = \hat{\theta}_L(n) \geq \theta_L - \delta$ so (b) holds as well. Combining (a) and (b) with the definition of $b_i(n)$:

$$t_0 I(\hat{\theta}_i(n), \theta_L - \delta) \leq t_i(n) I(\hat{\theta}_i(n), \theta_L - \delta) \leq f(n) \leq f(T),$$

and thus: $I(\hat{\theta}_i(n), \theta_L - \delta) \leq I(\theta_i - \delta, \theta_L - \delta)$, which proves that $|\hat{\theta}_i(n) - \theta_i| \geq \delta$ using the fact that the function $x \mapsto I(x,y)$ is decreasing for $0 \leq x \leq y$. Hence $n \in \mathcal{K}_{i,1}$ which is a contradiction since we assumed that $n \in \mathcal{K}_i \setminus (\mathcal{K}_{i,1} \cup \mathcal{K}_{i,2})$. Hence $\mathcal{K}_i \subset \mathcal{K}_{i,1} \cup \mathcal{K}_{i,2}$ as announced. We now provide upper bounds on the expected sizes of $\mathcal{K}_{i,1}$ and $\mathcal{K}_{i,2}$.

Set $\mathcal{K}_{i,1}$: Since $n \in \mathcal{K}_{i,1} \subset \mathcal{K}_i$ implies $u(n) = u^{i,l}$ we have that $\mathbb{E}[o_i(n) | n \in \mathcal{K}_{i,1}] = p_l$. Applying Corollary 1 presented in Appendix (with $H \equiv \mathcal{K}_{i,1}$ and $c \equiv p_l$) we obtain:

$$\mathbb{E}[|\mathcal{K}_{i,1}|] \leq p_l^{-1}\left[p_l^{-1}\epsilon^{-2} + \delta^{-2}(1-\epsilon)^{-1}\right].$$

Set $\mathcal{K}_{i,2}$: Since $n \in \mathcal{K}_{i,2}$ implies that $k_i(n) \leq t_0 p_l^{-1}(1-\epsilon)^{-1}$ and that $k_i(n)$ is incremented at n, we have that:

$$\mathbb{E}[|\mathcal{K}_{i,2}|] \leq t_0 p_l^{-1}(1-\epsilon)^{-1}.$$

Putting it all together we obtain the desired bound (5) on the expected size of $\mathcal{K}_i$, which concludes the proof of the first statement of Theorem 2. The second statement of the theorem is obtained by taking the limit $T \to \infty$ and then $\delta \to 0$. □

5. KNOWN TOPIC

In the remaining of the paper, we consider $K > 1$ groups of users and items, and switch back to the notations introduced in Section 3. In this section, we consider the scenario where in each round n, the topic of the request is known, i.e., the decision maker is informed about $h(k(n))$ before selecting the items to be displayed. In such a scenario, the problem of the design of sequential list selection algorithms can be decomposed into K independent bandit problems, one for each topic. Indeed in view of Assumption (A1), when the topic of the request is $h(k)$, any algorithm should present, in the list, items from $\mathcal{N}_{h(k)}$ only. The K independent MAB problems are instances of the problems considered in the previous section. As a consequence, we can apply the analysis of Section 4, and immediately deduce regret lower bounds and asymptotically optimal algorithms. Optimal algorithms are obtained by just running K independent PIE(l) algorithms, one for each topic. We refer to as $K\times$PIE(l) the resulting global algorithm.

Define $\mathcal{U}_k$ as the set of lists containing items from $\mathcal{N}_{h(k)}$ only, i.e., $\mathcal{U}_k := \{u \in \mathcal{U} : \forall s \in [L], u_s \in \mathcal{N}_{h(k)}\}$. We denote by $\mathcal{U}_k(i) = \{u \in \mathcal{U}_k : i_{h(k)} \in u\}$, the set of lists in $\mathcal{U}_k$ that include the item $i_{h(k)}$ with the i-th highest relevance in $\mathcal{N}_{h(k)}$. Finally, for $u \in \mathcal{U}_k(i)$, we refer to as $p_i(u)$ as the position of $i_{h(k)}$ in the list u. The following theorem is a direct consequence of Theorem 1.

THEOREM 3. *Let $\theta \in [0,1]^{K\times N}$. For any uniformly good algorithm π, we have:*

$$\liminf_{T\to\infty} \frac{R^\pi(T)}{\log(T)} \geq \sum_{k\in[K]} c_k(\theta), \quad (6)$$

where for any $k \in [K]$, $c_k(\theta)$ is the minimal value of the objective function in the following optimization problem $(P_{\theta,k})$:

$$\inf_{c_u \geq 0, u \in \mathcal{U}_k} \sum_{u\in\mathcal{U}_k} c_u(\mu_\theta^{\star,k} - \mu_\theta(u,k)) \quad (7)$$
$$\text{s.t.} \sum_{u\in\mathcal{U}_k(i)} c_u \prod_{s<p_i(u)} (1-\theta_{ku_s}) I(\theta_{ki_{h(k)}}, \theta_{kL_{h(k)}}) \geq 1,$$
$$\forall i > L.$$

The LPs $(P_{\theta,k})$ are similar to (P_θ) presented in Theorem 1, and enjoy the same simplifications (see Propositions 1 and 2) when the reward function has the specific structure of Case 1) or 2). Observe that the regret lower bound does not depend on the proportions of queries made by users of the various classes (remember that we assumed that $\phi_k > 0$ for all $k \in [K]$) – this is simply due to the facts that over the time horizon T, we roughly have $\phi_k T$ queries generated by class-k users, and that the regret incurred for class-k users is $c_k(\theta)\log(\phi_k T) \approx c_k(\theta)\log(T)$.

The next theorem is a direct consequence of Theorem 2, and states that $K\times$PIE(L) and $K\times$PIE(1) are asymptotically optimal in Cases 1) and 2), respectively.

THEOREM 4. *Assume that the reward function has the specific structure described in Case 1) (resp. 2)). Under algorithm $\pi = K\times$PIE(L) (resp. $\pi = K\times$PIE(1)), we have for all θ:*

$$\limsup_{T\to\infty} \frac{R^\pi(T)}{\log(T)} \leq \sum_{k\in[K]} c_k(\theta).$$

6. KNOWN USER-CLASS AND UNKNOWN TOPIC

In this section, we address the problem with $K > 1$ groups of users and items, and where in each round n, the decision maker is aware of the class of the user issuing the query, but does not know the mapping h, i.e., initially, the decision maker does not know which topic the users of the various classes are interested in. Of course, this scenario is more challenging than the one where, before selecting a list of items, the decision maker is informed on the topic $h(k(n))$, and hence, the regret lower bound described in Theorem 3 is still valid.

Next we devise a sequential list selection algorithm that learns the mapping h very rapidly. More precisely, we prove that its asymptotic regret satisfies the same regret upper bound as those

Algorithm PIE-C(l, d)

Init: $\hat{\theta}_{ki}(1) = 0, \forall i, k$

For $n \geq 1$**:**

Get the class $k(n)$ of the user issuing the query, and compute $C(n) = \{h \in [K] : \max_{i \in \mathcal{N}_h} \hat{\theta}_{k(n)i}(n) \geq d\}$

If $C(n) = \emptyset$, select $u(n) \in \mathcal{U}$ uniformly at random

Else Select group $\hat{h}(n)$ uniformly at random from $C(n)$ and run PIE(l) on $\mathcal{N}_{\hat{h}(n)}$

Compute: $\hat{\theta}_{ki}(n+1), \forall i, k$

derived for $K\times$PIE(l) when the topic is known, which means that the fact that the mapping h is unknown incurs a sub-logarithmic regret. Thus, our algorithm is asymptotically optimal since its regret upper bound matches the lower bound derived in Theorem 3.

6.1 Optimal Algorithms

To describe our algorithms, we introduce the following notations. Let $u(n)$ be the list selected in round n, and let $p_i(n)$ denote the position at which item i is shown if $i \in u(n)$, and $p_i(n) = 0$ otherwise. Let $X_{ki}(n) \in \{0, 1\}$ denote the relevance of item i when presented to a class-k user in round n. Define

$$o_{ki}(n) := \mathbf{1}\left\{k(n) = k, i \in u(n), \forall l' < p_i(n), X_{ku_{l'}(n)}(n) = 0\right\}$$

the event indicating whether a query of a class-k user arrives in round n and this user scans item i. Then we get a sample from θ_{ki} in round n iff $o_i(n) = 1$. Let $t_{ki}(n) := \sum_{n' \leq n} o_{ki}(n')$ be the number of samples obtained, up to round n, for θ_{ki}. The corresponding empirical mean is:

$$\hat{\theta}_{ki}(n) = \frac{1}{t_{ki}(n)} \sum_{n' \leq n} o_{ki}(n') X_{ki}(n')$$

if $t_{ki}(n) > 0$ and $\hat{\theta}_{ki}(n) = 0$ otherwise. The KL-UCB index $b_{ki}(n)$ of item i when presented to a class-k user in round n is:

$$b_{ki}(n) = \max\{q \in [0, 1] : t_{ki}(n) I(\hat{\theta}_{ki}(n), q) \leq f(n)\},$$

where $f(n) = \log(n) + 4\log(\log(n))$. Finally, for any user class k and topic h, we define $j_{kh}(n) = (j_{kh,1}(n), ..., j_{kh,N_h}(n))$, the items of $\mathcal{N}_h$ with empirical means sorted in decreasing order for users of class k in round n. Namely:

$$\hat{\theta}_{kj_{kh,1}(n)}(n) \geq \hat{\theta}_{kj_{kh,2}(n)}(n) \geq ... \geq \hat{\theta}_{kj_{kh,N_h}(n)}(n)$$

and $j_{kh,i}(n) \in \mathcal{N}_h$ for all k, h, and i.

The PIE-C(l, d) Algorithm. The algorithm is parametrized by $l \in [L]$ which indicates the position in which apparently sub-optimal items are explored, and by d, a real number chosen strictly between δ and Δ. To implement such an algorithm, we do not need to know the maximum expected relevance δ of items of uninteresting topics, nor the lower bound Δ of the highest relevance of items whose topic corresponds to that of the query. We just need to know a number d in between.

In round n, PIE-C(l, d) maintains an estimator $\hat{h}(n)$ of the topic $h(k(n))$ requested by the user, and it proceeds as follows. Given the user-class $k(n)$, we first identify the set of *admissible* topics $C(n)$:

$$C(n) = \{h \in [K] : \max_{i \in \mathcal{N}_h} \hat{\theta}_{k(n)i}(n) \geq d\}.$$

This set corresponds to the topics that according to our observations up to round n, could be the topic requested by the class-$k(n)$ user.

(i) If $C(n) = \emptyset$, $\hat{h}(n) = -1$ (we don't know what the topic is), and we select $u(n)$ uniformly at random over the set of possible decisions $\mathcal{U}$;

(ii) If $C(n) \neq \emptyset$,

- Select $\hat{h}(n) \in C(n)$ uniformly at random;
- Define leaders at time n: $\mathcal{L}(n)$ lists in order the L items in $\mathcal{N}_{\hat{h}(n)}$ with largest empirical means,

$$\mathcal{L}(n) = (j_{k(n)\hat{h}(n),1}(n), ..., j_{k(n)\hat{h}(n),L}(n));$$

- Define the possible decisions $U_i(n)$ for all $i \in \mathcal{N}_{\hat{h}(n)} \setminus \mathcal{L}(n)$ obtained by replacing in $\mathcal{L}(n)$ the l-th item by i;
- Define

$$\mathcal{B}(n) = \{i \in \mathcal{N}_{\hat{h}(n)} \setminus \mathcal{L}(n) : b_{k(n)i}(n) \geq \hat{\theta}_{j_{k(n)\hat{h}(n),L}(n)}(n)\};$$

- (a) If $\mathcal{B}(n) = \emptyset$, select the list $\mathcal{L}(n)$, and (b) If $\mathcal{B}(n) \neq \emptyset$, choose $i(n)$ uniformly at random in $\mathcal{B}(n)$ and select either $\mathcal{L}(n)$ with probability $1/2$ or decision $U_{i(n)}(n)$ with probability $1/2$.

Note that when $\hat{h}(n)$ is believed to estimate $h(k(n))$ accurately (i.e., when $C(n) \neq \emptyset$), then the algorithm mimics the $K\times$PIE(l) algorithm. Refer to the pseudocode of PIE-C(l, d) for a formal description. The following theorem states that PIE-C(l, d) exhibits the same asymptotic regret as the optimal algorithms when the topic of each request is known.

THEOREM 5. *Assume that the reward function has the specific structure described in Case 1) (resp. 2)). For all $\delta < d < \Delta$, under the algorithm π =PIE-C(L, d) (resp. π =PIE-C($1, d$)), we have for all θ:*

$$\lim\sup_{T \to \infty} \frac{R^\pi(T)}{\log(T)} \leq \sum_{k \in [K]} c_k(\theta).$$

6.2 Proof: Regret Upper Bound for PIE-C(l, d)

The proof of Theorem 5 consists in showing that the set of rounds at which the estimation of the topic $h(k(n))$ of the request fails is finite in expectation. As already mentioned, when the estimation is correct the algorithm behaves like $K\times$PIE(l), and the analysis of its regret in such rounds in the same as that under $K\times$PIE(l). Hence, we just need to control the size of the following set of rounds:

$$\mathcal{M} = \{n \geq 1 : \hat{h}(n) \neq h(k(n))\}.$$

LEMMA 2. *Under algorithm PIE-C(l,d) we have:*

$$\mathbb{E}[|\mathcal{M}|] \leq 2KN\left[2(N+1) + (d-\delta)^{-2} + (\Delta - d)^{-2}\right]$$

The above bound is minimized by setting $d = (\Delta + \delta)/2$, in which case:

$$\mathbb{E}[|\mathcal{M}|] \leq 4KN\left[N + 1 + 4(\Delta - \delta)^{-2}\right]$$

Proof. For all k, we define the most popular item for class-k users: $i_k^\star = \arg\max_i \theta_{ki}$. We decompose $\mathcal{M}$ by introducing the following sets:

$$\mathcal{M}_k = \{n \in \mathcal{M}, k(n) = k\},$$
$$\mathcal{M}_{k,-1} = \{n \in \mathcal{M}_k, \hat{h}(n) = -1, |\hat{\theta}_{ki_k^\star}(n) - \theta_{ki_k^\star}| \geq \Delta - d\},$$
$$\mathcal{M}_{k,i} = \{n \in \mathcal{M}_k, i = u_1(n), |\hat{\theta}_{ki}(n) - \theta_{ki}| \geq d - \delta\}.$$

$\mathcal{M}_{k,-1}$ is the set of rounds at which a user of class k makes a request, the set of admissible topics for class k users is empty $C(n)$, and $\theta_{ki_k^\star}$ is badly estimated. $\mathcal{M}_{k,i}$ is the set of rounds at which a user of class k makes a request, item $i \notin \mathcal{N}_{h(k)}$ is presented in the first slot (note that i is not interesting to that user) and θ_{ki} is badly estimated. We have that: $\mathcal{M} = \cup_{k=1}^{K} \mathcal{M}_k$ since $k(n) \in \{1, ..., K\}$.

We prove that for all k: $\mathcal{M}_k \subset \mathcal{M}_{k,-1} \cup (\cup_{i \notin \mathcal{N}_{h(k)}} \mathcal{M}_{k,i})$. Consider $n \in \mathcal{M}_k$, so that $k(n) = k$ and $\hat{h}(n) \neq h(k)$. We distinguish two cases:

(i) If $\hat{h}(n) = -1$, then $C(n) = \emptyset$. So $h(k) \notin C(n)$, and by definition of $C(n)$, this implies that $\max_{i \in \mathcal{N}_{h(k)}} \hat{\theta}_{ki}(n) \leq d$. Since $i_k^\star \in \mathcal{N}_{h(k)}$ we have $\hat{\theta}_{ki_k^\star}(n) \leq d$. Since $i_k^\star = \arg\max_i \theta_{ki}$, we have $\theta_{k,i_k^\star} \geq \Delta$. Hence we have that both $\hat{\theta}_{ki_k^\star}(n) \leq d$ and $\theta_{ki_k^\star} \geq \Delta$, so we have $|\hat{\theta}_{ki_k^\star}(n) - \theta_{ki_k^\star}| \geq \Delta - d$ and therefore $n \in \mathcal{M}_{k,-1}$.

(ii) If $\hat{h}(n) \notin \{h(k), -1\}$, then by design of the algorithm $u(n) \subset \{1, ..., N\} \setminus \mathcal{N}_{h(k)}$ since $\{\mathcal{N}_1, ..., \mathcal{N}_K\}$ forms a partition of $\{1, ..., N\}$. Hence there exists $i \notin \mathcal{N}_{h(k)}$ such that $u_1(n) = i$. By design of the algorithm, since $u_1(n) = i$, we have $\hat{\theta}_{ki}(n) = \arg\max_{i' \in \mathcal{N}_{\hat{h}(n)}} \hat{\theta}_{ki'}(n)$ and $\arg\max_{i' \in \mathcal{N}_{\hat{h}(n)}} \hat{\theta}_{ki'}(n) \geq d$ since $\hat{h}(n) \in C(n)$. Therefore $\hat{\theta}_{ki}(n) \geq d$ and we know that $\theta_{ki} \leq \delta$ since $i \notin \mathcal{N}_{h(k)}$, so that $|\hat{\theta}_{ki}(n) - \theta_{ki}| \geq d - \delta$. Summarizing, $\hat{h}(n) \notin \{h(k), -1\}$ implies that there exists $i \notin \mathcal{N}_{h(k)}$ such that $u_1(n) = i$ and $|\hat{\theta}_{ki}(n) - \theta_{ki}| \geq d - \delta$, therefore $n \in \cup_{i \notin \mathcal{N}_{h(k)}} \mathcal{M}_{k,i}$.

Hence we have proven, as announced, that $\mathcal{M}_k \subset \mathcal{M}_{k,-1} \cup_{i \notin \mathcal{N}_{h(k)}} \mathcal{M}_{k,i}$. We now upper bound the expected sizes of sets $\mathcal{M}_{k,-1}$ and $\mathcal{M}_{k,i}$.

Set $\mathcal{M}_{k,-1}$: When $n \in \mathcal{M}_{k,-1}$, $u(n)$ is uniformly distributed over the set of possible decisions $\mathcal{U}$, so that $\mathbb{P}[u_1(n) = i_k^\star | n \in \mathcal{M}_{k,-1}] = 1/N$. In turn, this implies that $\mathbb{E}[o_{ki_k^\star}(n) | n \in \mathcal{M}_{k,-1}] = 1/N$. Appying Lemma 5, second statement (with $H \equiv \mathcal{M}_{k,-1}$, $c \equiv 1$ and $\delta \equiv \Delta - d$), we obtain:

$$\mathbb{E}[|\mathcal{M}_{k,-1}|] \leq 2N \left[2N + (\Delta - d)^{-2}\right].$$

Set $\mathcal{M}_{k,i}$: When $n \in \mathcal{M}_{k,i}$, we have that $u_1(n) = i$ and $k(n) = k$ so that $\mathbb{E}[o_{k,i}(n) | n \in \mathcal{M}_{k,i}] = 1$. Applying Lemma 5, second statement (with $H \equiv \mathcal{M}_{k,i}$, $c \equiv 1$ and $\delta \equiv d - \delta$), we obtain:

$$\mathbb{E}[|\mathcal{M}_{k,i}|] \leq 2 \left[2 + (d - \delta)^{-2}\right].$$

Using a union bound we have:

$$\begin{aligned}\mathbb{E}[|\mathcal{M}_{k,-1}|] &\leq \mathbb{E}[|\mathcal{M}_{k,-1}|] + \sum_{i \notin \mathcal{N}_{h(k)}} \mathbb{E}[|\mathcal{M}_{k,i}|] \\ &\leq 2N \left[2N + (\Delta - d)^{-2}\right] + 2N \left[2 + (d - \delta)^{-2}\right] \\ &= 2N \left[2(N+1) + (d - \delta)^{-2} + (\Delta - d)^{-2}\right],\end{aligned}$$

and summing over $k \in \{1, ..., K\}$ we obtain the announced result:

$$\begin{aligned}\mathbb{E}[|\mathcal{M}|] &= \sum_{k=1}^{K} \mathbb{E}[|\mathcal{M}_k|] \\ &\leq 2KN \left[2(N+1) + (d - \delta)^{-2} + (\Delta - d)^{-2}\right],\end{aligned}$$

which concludes the proof. □

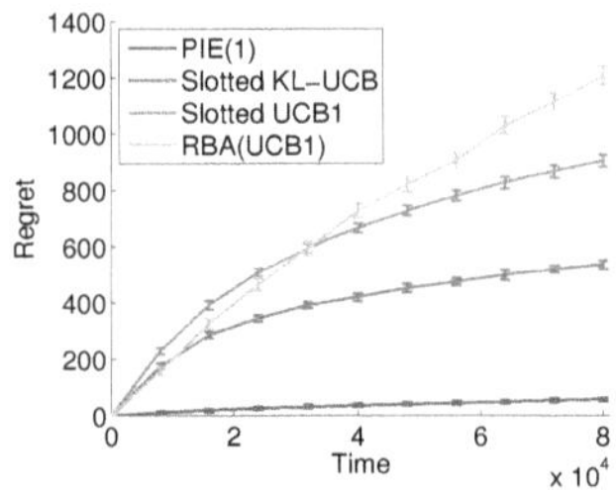

(a) Case 2: $\forall l$, $r(l) = 1$.

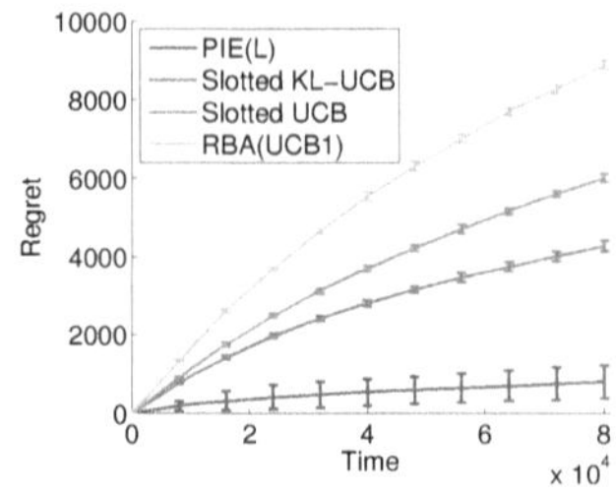

(b) Case 1: $\forall l$, $r(l) = 2^{1-l}$.

Figure 1: Performance of PIE(1) / PIE(L) and other UCB-based algorithms. A single group of items and users. Error bars represent the standard deviation.

7. NUMERICAL EXPERIMENTS

In this section, we evaluate the practical performance of our algorithms using both artificially generated and real-world data[1].

7.1 Artificial Data

We first evaluate the PIE and PIE-C algorithms in the scenarios presented in Sections 4, 5, and 6. In these scenarios, the algorithms are optimal and hence they should outperform any other algorithm.

A Single group of users / items. First we assume there exists only one relevant topic ($K = 1$) consisting of $N = 800$ items. We consider $L = 10$ and evaluate the performance of the algorithms over the arrival of $T = 8 \times 10^4$ user queries. The parameter θ is artificially generated as follows:

$$\theta_i = 0.55 \times (1 - (i-1)/(N-1)).$$

In Figure 1(a), we consider the reward to be $r(l) = 1$ for $l \in \{1, ..., L\}$ while in Figure 1(b), we assume the reward decreases geometrically with the slot ($r(l) = 2^{1-l}$, $l \in \{1, ..., L\}$). Under these assumptions, PIE(1) and PIE(L) respectively are asymptotically optimal according to Theorem 2. We compare their performance to that of Slotted UCB, Slotted KL-UCB algorithms, and RBA (Ranked Bandit Algorithm) proposed in [7] and [11]. In Slotted UCB (resp. KL-UCB), the L items with the largest UCB (resp. KL-UCB) indexes are displayed, whereas RBA runs L independent bandit algorithms, one for each slot. In particular, for all items k, the bandit algorithm assigned to slot l can only access the observations obtained from k when k was played in slot l (RBA attempts to learn an item's so-called *marginal utility* for each slot). Observe that PIE significantly outperforms all other algorithms.

Multiple groups of users / items. Next, we consider $K = 5$ groups of users and items, and $N = 4,000$ items. We assume all groups are of equal size so that $\phi_k = 1/K$ for all k. There are N/K items in each group. We define $j(i,k) = (i - h(k)N/K)$, and generate the parameter θ as follows:

$$\theta_{ki} = \begin{cases} 0.55 \times (1 - (j(i,k) - 1)/(N-1)) & \text{if } i \in \mathcal{N}_{h(k)}, \\ 0.05 & \text{otherwise.} \end{cases}$$

Figure 2 presents the performance of $5 \times$PIE(1) (referred to as PIE(1) in the figure) when the decision maker knows the mapping between user classes and topics $h(\cdot)$, and that of PIE-C(1,0.5) when $h(\cdot)$ is unknown. Figure 2 corroborates the theoretical result of Theorem 5: The performance loss due to the need to learn the mapping $h(\cdot)$ is rather limited, especially the time horizon grows large.

[1]We use the Movielens10M dataset, available at http://grouplens.org/datasets/movielens/

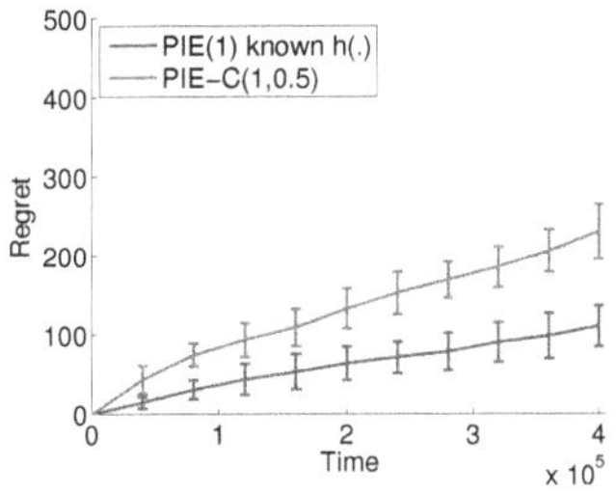

Figure 2: Performance of PIE(1) and PIE-C(1,d). $K = 5$ groups of users and items. Case 2: $\forall l, r(l) = 1$.

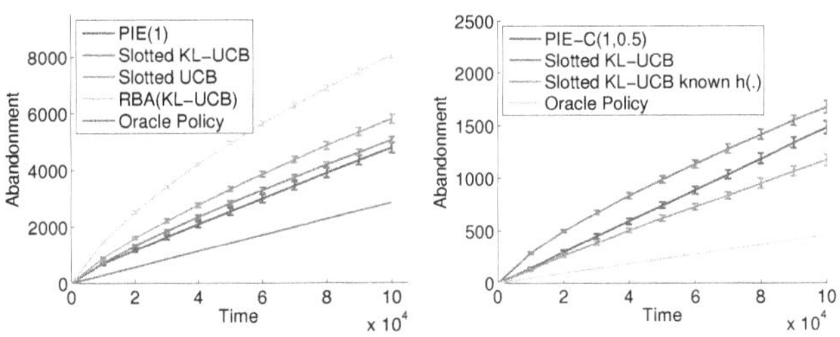

(a) $K = 1$ topic.

(b) $K = 4$ topics.

Figure 3: Performance of PIE(1) and PIE-C(1, d) on real world data.

7.2 Real-world Data

We further investigate the performance of our algorithms on real-world systems. We use the Movielens dataset which contains the ratings given by users to a large set of movies. The dataset is a large matrix $X = (X_{a,m})$ where $X_{a,m} \in \{0, 1, ..., 5\}$ is the rating given by user a to movie m. The highest rating is 5, the lowest is 1, and 0 denotes an absence of rating, as most users did not watch the whole set of movies. From matrix X, we created a binary matrix Y such that $Y_{a,m} = 0$ if $X_{a,m} < 4$ and $Y_{a,m} = 1$ otherwise. We say that movie m is *interesting* to user a iff $Y_{a,m} = 1$.

We first selected the 100 most popular movies with less than 13,000 ratings (to avoid movies with good ratings for a large majority of users) and the 61,357 users who rated at least one of those movies. We extracted the corresponding sub-matrix of Y. To cluster the users and the movies, we use the classical spectral method. We extracted the 4 largest singular values of Y and their corresponding singular vectors $\gamma_i, i \in \{1, 2, 3, 4\}$. We then assigned each user a to the cluster $k = \text{argmax}_i\, Y_a \cdot \gamma_i$, where Y_a is the a-th line of matrix Y. We performed a similar classification of movies.

In Figure 3(a), we consider class-1 users, and compare the performance of algorithms already considered in Subsection 7.1, Scenario 1. The simulation proceeds as follows: in round n, we draw a class-1 user, denoted by $a(n)$, uniformly at random. The considered algorithm chooses an action $u(n)$, if $u(n)$ contains an interesting movie i for user $a(n)$, i.e., $Y_{a(n)i} = 1$, the system collects a unit reward, otherwise the reward is 0. We emulate the semi-bandit feedback by assuming the algorithm is informed about uninteresting movies j, i.e., $Y_{a(n)j} = 0$, placed above i in the list of $L = 10$ movies. Here the performance of the algorithm is quantified through the notion of *abandonment*, as introduced in [7]. The abandonment is the number of rounds in which no interesting movies are displayed. As a benchmark, we use an Oracle policy that displays the L most popular movies for users of class 1 in every round. Note that we use abandonment as a performance metric rather than the regret, because the optimal policy is hard to compute given the fact that the ratings offered by a user to different movies are not always independent in our data set. Again, PIE outperforms the Slotted variants of UCB and KL-UCB which in turn significantly outperform RBA(KL-UCB). In fact, the cost of learning in PIE (compared to the Oracle policy is limited): the abandonment under PIE does not exceed twice that of the Oracle policy. Note that the performance gain under PIE compared to Slotted KL-UCB is much higher in our artificial data simulations. We believe that this may be firstly due to the inaccuracy of our model when used against this particular data-set, and secondly due to the fact that the gain under PIE increases with the number of items N.

In Figure 3(b), we consider $K = 4$ groups, each topic consisting of 25 items. Again, the performance of PIE-C algorithm is not too far from that of the Oracle policy. PIE-C is compared to Slotted KL-UCB and a Slotted KL-UCB aware of the groups and of the mapping $h(\cdot)$. The former just ignores the group structure and runs as if there were a single group only, whereas the latter consists in K parallel and independent instances of Slotted KL-UCB, one for each user class k and item group $h(k)$. PIE-C outperforms Slotted KL-UCB, and its performance is similar to that of Slotted KL-UCB with known mapping $h(\cdot)$. Again this indicates that PIE-C rapidly learns the mapping $h(\cdot)$.

8. CONCLUSION

In this paper, we investigated the design of learning-to-rank algorithms for online systems, such as search engines and ad-display systems. We proposed PIE and PIE-C, two asymptotically optimal algorithms that rapidly learn users' preferences, and the most relevant items to be listed in response to user queries. These two algorithms are devised assuming that users and items are clustered, and that the decision maker knows the class of the user issuing the query. It would be interesting to further extend these algorithms to scenarios where the classes of the various users are initially unknown. The paper also presents a preliminary performance evaluation of our algorithms. In future work, we will further investigate the way our algorithms perform against various kinds of real-world dataset, including hopefully real traces extracted from search engines, such as google or bing.

9. ACKNOWLEDGEMENTS

Research supported by SSF, VR and ERC grant 308267.

10. REFERENCES

[1] C. Burges, T. Shaked, E. Renshaw, A. Lazier, M. Deeds, N. Hamilton, and G. Hullender, "Learning to rank using gradient descent," in *Proc. of ICML*, 2005.

[2] S. Pandey, D. Agarwal, D. Chakrabarti, and V. Josifovski, "Bandits for taxonomies: A model based approach," in *Proc. of SIAM SDM*, 2007.

[3] F. Radlinski and T. Joachims, "Active exploration for learning rankings from clickthrough data," in *Proc. of ACM SIGKDD*, 2007.

[4] M. J. Streeter, D. Golovin, and A. Krause, "Online learning of assignments." in *Proc. of NIPS*, 2009.

[5] H. Robbins, "Some aspects of the sequential design of experiments," *Bulletin of the American Mathematical Society*, vol. 58, no. 5, pp. 527–535, 1952.

[6] J. Gittins, *Bandit Processes and Dynamic Allocation Indices*. John Wiley, 1989.

[7] F. Radlinski, R. Kleinberg, and T. Joachims, "Learning diverse rankings with multi-armed bandits," in *Proc. of ICML*, 2008.

[8] Y. Yue and T. Joachims, "Interactively optimizing information retrieval systems as a dueling bandits problem," in *Proc. of ICML*, 2009.

[9] Y. Yue and C. Guestrin, "Linear submodular bandits and their application to diversified retrieval," in *Proc. of NIPS*, 2011.

[10] S. Khuller, A. Moss, and J. S. Naor, "The budgeted maximum coverage problem," *Inf. Process. Lett.*, vol. 70, no. 1, pp. 39–45, Apr. 1999.

[11] P. Kohli, M. Salek, and G. Stoddard, "A fast bandit algorithm for recommendations to users with heterogeneous tastes," in *Proc. of AAAI*, 2013.

[12] S. Agrawal, Y. Ding, A. Saberi, and Y. Ye, "Correlation robust stochastic optimization," in *Proc. of ACM SODA*, 2010.

[13] A. Slivkins, F. Radlinski, and S. Gollapudi, "Ranked bandits in metric spaces: learning optimally diverse rankings over large document collections," *Journal of Machine Learning Research*, 2013.

[14] S. Bubeck and N. Cesa-Bianchi, "Regret analysis of stochastic and nonstochastic multi-armed bandit problems," *Foundations and Trends in Machine Learning*, vol. 5, no. 1, pp. 1–122, 2012.

[15] R. Agrawal, "The continuum-armed bandit problem," *SIAM J. Control and Optimization*, vol. 33, no. 6, pp. 1926–1951, 1995.

[16] R. Kleinberg, A. Slivkins, and E. Upfal, "Multi-armed bandits in metric spaces," in *Proc. of STOC*, 2008.

[17] S. Bubeck, R. Munos, G. Stoltz, and C. Szepesvári, "Online optimization in x-armed bandits," in *Proc. of NIPS*, 2008.

[18] S. Magureanu, R. Combes, and A. Proutiere, "Lipschitz bandits: Regret lower bound and optimal algorithms," in *Proc. of COLT*, 2014.

[19] V. Dani, T. P. Hayes, and S. M. Kakade, "Stochastic linear optimization under bandit feedback," in *Proc. of COLT*, 2008.

[20] A. Flaxman, A. T. Kalai, and H. B. McMahan, "Online convex optimization in the bandit setting: gradient descent without a gradient," in *Proc. of ACM SODA*, 2005.

[21] L. Bui, R. Johari, and S. Mannor, "Clustered bandits," *http://arxiv.org/abs/1206.4169*, 2012.

[22] T. L. Lai and H. Robbins, "Asymptotically efficient adaptive allocation rules," *Advances in Applied Mathematics*, vol. 6, no. 1, pp. 4–2, 1985.

[23] T. L. Graves and T. L. Lai, "Asymptotically efficient adaptive choice of control laws in controlled markov chains," *SIAM Journal on Control and Optimization*, vol. 35, no. 3, pp. 715–743, 1997.

[24] A. Garivier and O. Cappé, "The KL-UCB algorithm for bounded stochastic bandits and beyond," in *Proc. of COLT*, 2011.

[25] R. Combes and A. Proutiere, "Unimodal bandits: Regret lower bounds and optimal algorithms," in *Proc. of ICML, http://arxiv.org/abs/1405.5096*, 2014.

APPENDIX

A. SUPPORTING LEMMAS FOR THE PROOF OF THEOREM 2

Lemma 3 allows to control the fluctuations of the estimate $\hat{\theta}_i(n)$ evaluated at a random time ϕ. We assume that ϕ is a stopping time, and that the number of rounds before ϕ where a decision containing i has been taken is greater than a number s. This result is instrumental in analyzing the finite time regret of algorithms (such as ours) that take decisions based on the estimates $\hat{\theta}_i(n)$. Lemma 3 is a consequence of Lemma 4, which is reproduced here for completeness.

LEMMA 3. *Let $\{Z_t\}_{t\in\mathbb{Z}}$ be a sequence of independent random variables with values in $[0,1]$. Define $\mathcal{F}_n$ the σ-algebra generated by $\{Z_t\}_{t\le n}$ and the filtration $\mathcal{F}=(\mathcal{F}_n)_{n\in\mathbb{Z}}$. Consider $s\in\mathbb{N}$, $n_0\in\mathbb{Z}$ and $T\ge n_0$. We define $S_n=\sum_{t=n_0}^{n} B_t(Z_t-\mathbb{E}[Z_t])$, where $B_t\in\{0,1\}$ is a $\mathcal{F}_{t-1}$-measurable random variable. Further consider that for all t, almost surely we have $B_t\ge \bar{B}_t C_t$, where both $\bar{B}_t$ and C_t are $\{0,1\}$ -valued, $\mathcal{F}_{t-1}$-measurable random variables, such that for all t: $\mathbb{P}[C_t=1]\ge c>0$.*

Further define $t_n=\sum_{t=n_0}^{n} B_t$ and $c_n=\sum_{t=n_0}^{n}\bar{B}_t$. Define $\phi\in\{n_0,\dots,T+1\}$ a $\mathcal{F}$-stopping time such that either $c_\phi\ge s$ or $\phi=T+1$.

Then for all $\epsilon>0$ we have that:

$$\mathbb{P}[S_\phi\ge t_\phi\delta\ ,\ \phi\le T]\le e^{-2s\epsilon^2c^2}+e^{-2c(1-\epsilon)s\delta^2}.$$

As a consequence:

$$\mathbb{P}[|S_\phi|\ge t_\phi\delta\ ,\ \phi\le T]\le 2(e^{-2s\epsilon^2c^2}+e^{-2c(1-\epsilon)s\delta^2}).$$

Proof. We prove the first statement, as the second statement follows by symmetry.

When event $S_\phi\ge t_\phi\delta$ occurs, we have either that (a) $t_\phi\le c(1-\epsilon)c_\phi$ or (b) $S_\phi\ge t_\phi\delta$ and $t_\phi\ge c(1-\epsilon)c_\phi\ge c(1-\epsilon)s$. In case (a), if $\phi\le T$, we have:

$$\sum_{t=n_0}^{n}\bar{B}_tC_t\le\sum_{t=n_0}^{n}B_t=t_\phi\le c(1-\epsilon)c_\phi=c(1-\epsilon)\sum_{t=n_0}^{\phi}\bar{B}_t,$$

and therefore:

$$\sum_{t=n_0}^{\phi}\bar{B}_tC_t\le c(1-\epsilon)\sum_{t=n_0}^{\phi}\bar{B}_t$$

$$\sum_{t=n_0}^{\phi}\bar{B}_t(C_t-c)\le -c\epsilon\sum_{t=n_0}^{\phi}\bar{B}_t$$

$$\sum_{t=n_0}^{\phi}\bar{B}_t(C_t-\mathbb{E}[C_t])\le -c\epsilon\sum_{t=n_0}^{\phi}\bar{B}_t.$$

where the last inequality holds because $\mathbb{E}[C_t]\ge c$ for all t. We may now apply Lemma 4 (with $Z_t\equiv C_t$, $B_t\equiv\bar{B}_t$, and $\delta\equiv c\epsilon$) to obtain:

$$\begin{aligned}&\mathbb{P}[t_\phi\le c(1-\epsilon)c_\phi\ ,\ \phi\le T]\\&\le\mathbb{P}\left[\sum_{t=n_0}^{\phi}\bar{B}_t(C_t-\mathbb{E}[C_t])\le -c\epsilon\sum_{t=n_0}^{\phi}\bar{B}_t\ ,\ \phi\le T\right]\\&\le e^{-2s\epsilon^2c^2}.\end{aligned}$$

In case (b), define another stopping time ϕ', such that $\phi'=\phi$ if $t_\phi\ge c(1-\epsilon)c_\phi$ and $\phi'=T+1$ otherwise. Note that ϕ' is indeed a stopping time. We apply Lemma 4 a second time (with $\phi\equiv\phi'$, $s\equiv c(1-\epsilon)s$) to obtain:

$$\begin{aligned}&\mathbb{P}[S_\phi\ge t_\phi\delta\ ,\ t_\phi\ge c(1-\epsilon)c_\phi\ ,\ \phi\le T]\\&=\mathbb{P}\left[S_{\phi'}\ge t_{\phi'}\delta\ ,\ \phi'\le T\right]\le e^{-2c(1-\epsilon)s\delta^2}.\end{aligned}$$

Summing the inequalities obtained in cases (a) and (b), we prove the announced result:

$$\mathbb{P}[S_\phi\ge t_\phi\delta\ ,\ \phi\le T]\le e^{-2s\epsilon^2c^2}+e^{-2c(1-\epsilon)s\delta^2}.$$

which concludes the proof. □

LEMMA 4. *([25]) Let $\{Z_t\}_{t\in\mathbb{Z}}$ be a sequence of independent random variables with values in $[0,1]$. Define $\mathcal{F}_n$ the σ-algebra generated by $\{Z_t\}_{t\le n}$ and the filtration $\mathcal{F}=(\mathcal{F}_n)_{n\in\mathbb{Z}}$. Consider $s\in\mathbb{N}$, $n_0\in\mathbb{Z}$ and $T\ge n_0$. We define $S_n=\sum_{t=n_0}^{n}B_t(Z_t-\mathbb{E}[Z_t])$, where $B_t\in\{0,1\}$ is a $\mathcal{F}_{t-1}$-measurable random variable. Further define $t_n=\sum_{t=n_0}^{n}B_t$. Define $\phi\in\{n_0,\dots,T+1\}$ a $\mathcal{F}$-stopping time such that either $t_\phi\ge s$ or $\phi=T+1$.*

Then we have that:

$$\mathbb{P}[S_\phi\ge t_\phi\delta\ ,\ \phi\le T]\le\exp(-2s\delta^2).$$

As a consequence:

$$\mathbb{P}[|S_\phi|\ge t_\phi\delta\ ,\ \phi\le T]\le 2\exp(-2s\delta^2).$$

Lemma 5 is a consequence of Lemma 3, and allows to upper bound the size of random sets of rounds where decisions containing i have been sampled and the empirical mean $\hat{\theta}_i(n)$ deviates from its expectation by more than a fixed amount $\delta>0$.

LEMMA 5. *Let us fix $c>0$ and $1\le i\le N$. Consider a random set of rounds $H\subset\mathbb{N}$, such that, for all n, $\mathbf{1}\{n\in H\}$ is $\mathcal{F}_{n-1}$ measurable. Further assume for all n we have: $\mathbb{E}[o_i(n)|n\in H]\ge c>0$. Consider a random set $\Lambda=\cup_{s\ge1}\{\tau_s\}\subset\mathbb{N}$, where for all s, τ_s is a stopping time such that $\sum_{n=1}^{\tau_s}\mathbf{1}\{n\in H\}\ge s$.*

Then for all i and $\epsilon>0$ and $\delta>0$ we have that:

$$\sum_{n\ge0}\mathbb{P}[n\in\Lambda,|\hat{\theta}_i(n)-\theta_i|\ge\delta]\le c^{-1}\left[\frac{1}{\epsilon^2c}+\frac{1}{\delta^2(1-\epsilon)}\right].$$

As a consequence:

$$\sum_{n\ge0}\mathbb{P}[n\in\Lambda,|\hat{\theta}_i(n)-\theta_i|\ge\delta]\le 2c^{-1}\left[2c^{-1}+\delta^{-2}\right].$$

Proof. Fix $T<\infty$ and s. Apply Lemma 3 (with $Z_t\equiv X_i(t)$, $B_t\equiv o_i(n)$, $\bar{B}_t\equiv\mathbf{1}\{n\in H\}$, C_t a Bernoulli variable with parameter $\mathbb{E}[o_i(n)|n\in H]$ which is conditionally independent of $\mathbf{1}\{n\in H\}$) to obtain:

$$\mathbb{P}[|\hat{\theta}_i(\tau_s)-\theta_i|\ge\delta,\tau_s\le T]\le 2(e^{-2s\epsilon^2c^2}+e^{-2c(1-\epsilon)s\delta^2}).$$

Using a union bound over s, for all $\epsilon>0$ we get:

$$\begin{aligned}\sum_{n\le T}\mathbb{P}[n\in\Lambda,|\hat{\theta}_i(n)-\theta_i|\ge\delta]&\le\sum_{s\ge1}\mathbb{P}[|\hat{\theta}_i(\tau_s)-\theta_i|\ge\delta,\tau_s\le T]\\&\le\sum_{s\ge1}2(e^{-2s\epsilon^2c^2}+e^{-2c(1-\epsilon)s\delta^2})\\&\le\frac{1}{\epsilon^2c^2}+\frac{1}{c(1-\epsilon)\delta^2}\\&=c^{-1}\left[\frac{1}{\epsilon^2c}+\frac{1}{\delta^2(1-\epsilon)}\right],\end{aligned}$$

where we have used the following inequality twice $\sum_{s\ge1}e^{-sw}\le\int_0^{+\infty}e^{-sw}ds=1/w$, valid for all $w>0$. Since the above inequality holds for all T, and its r.h.s. does not depend on T we conclude that:

$$\sum_{n\geq 1} \mathbb{P}[n \in \Lambda, |\hat{\theta}_i(n) - \theta_i| \geq \delta] \leq c^{-1} \left[\frac{1}{\epsilon^2 c} + \frac{1}{\delta^2(1-\epsilon)} \right],$$

which concludes the proof of the first statement.

The second statement is obtained by setting $\epsilon = 1/2$. □

COROLLARY 1. *Consider $c > 0$ and $1 \leq i \leq N$ fixed. Consider a random set of instants $H \subset \mathbb{N}$, such that, for all n, $\mathbf{1}\{n \in H\}$ is $\mathcal{F}_{n-1}$ measurable. Further assume for all n we have: $\mathbb{E}[o_i(n)|n \in H] \geq c > 0$. Define $h_i(n) = \sum_{n' \leq n} \mathbf{1}\{n' \in H\}$. Consider $\epsilon > 0$ and $\delta > 0$ and define the set:*

$$\mathcal{H} = \left\{ n \in H : \left(t_i(n) \leq (1-\epsilon) h_i(n) \right) \vee \left(|\hat{\theta}_i(n) - \theta_i| \geq \delta \right) \right\}$$

Then we have:

$$\mathbb{E}[|\mathcal{H}|] \leq c^{-1} \left[c^{-1} \epsilon^{-2} + \delta^{-2} (1-\epsilon)^{-1} \right].$$

Proof. Straightforward from the proof of Lemma 5 with $\Lambda = H$. □

Lemma 6 is a straightforward consequence of Theorem 10 in [24], and states that the expected number of times the index of a given item i underestimates its true value is finite, and upper bounded by a constant that does not depend on the parameters $(\theta_i)_i$.

LEMMA 6. *([24]) Define:*

$$b_i(n) = \max\{q \in [0,1] : t_i(n) I(\hat{\theta}_i(n), q) \leq f(n)\},$$

with $f(n) = \log(n) + 4\log(\log(n))$.

There exists a constant C_0 independent of $(\theta_i)_i$ such that for all i we have:

$$\sum_{n\geq 0} \mathbb{P}[b_i(n) < \theta_i] \leq C_0.$$

In particular one has $C_0 \leq 2e \sum_{n\geq 1} \lceil f(n) \log(n) \rceil e^{-f(n)} \leq 15$.

Bandits with Budgets: Regret Lower Bounds and Optimal Algorithms

Richard Combes
Centrale-Supelec, L2S
Gif-sur-Yvette, France
richard.combes@supelec.fr

Chong Jiang
Electrical and Computer Engineering
University of Illinois at Urbana-Champaign, USA
chongjiang@gmail.com

Rayadurgam Srikant
Electrical and Computer Engineering
University of Illinois at Urbana-Champaign, USA
rsrikant@illinois.edu

ABSTRACT

We investigate multi-armed bandits with budgets, a natural model for ad-display optimization encountered in search engines. We provide asymptotic regret lower bounds satisfied by any algorithm, and propose algorithms which match those lower bounds. We consider different types of budgets: scenarios where the advertiser has a fixed budget over a time horizon, and scenarios where the amount of money that is available to spend is incremented in each time slot. Further, we consider two different pricing models, one in which an advertiser is charged for each time her ad is shown (i.e., for each impression) and one in which the advertiser is charged only if a user clicks on the ad. For all of these cases, we show that it is possible to achieve $O(\log(T))$ regret. For both the cost-per-impression and cost-per-click models, with a fixed budget, we provide regret lower bounds that apply to any uniformly good algorithm. Further, we show that B-KL-UCB, a natural variant of KL-UCB, is asymptotically optimal for these cases. Numerical experiments (based on a real-world data set) further suggest that B-KL-UCB also has the same or better finite-time performance when compared to various previously proposed (UCB-like) algorithms, which is important when applying such algorithms to a real-world problem.

Categories and Subject Descriptors

I.2.6 [**Computing Methodologies**]: Learning; G.3 [**Mathematics of Computing**]: Probability and Statistics

Keywords

ad-display optimization; search engines; multi-armed bandits; learning; budgets; UCB; KL-UCB

1. INTRODUCTION

The multi-armed bandit (MAB) involves an decision maker who samples from several statistical populations with unknown distributions (also called "arms"), with the goal of maximizing the cumulative sum of drawn samples (called the "rewards"). The objective is to minimize the *regret*, which is the difference between the sum of rewards obtained by a given sampling strategy, and that of the best sampling strategy if the distribution of each arm were known. The number of arms can be finite (discrete bandits), countably infinite (infinite-armed bandits) or uncountably infinite (continuous bandits). MABs are stylized models for sequential decision problems with uncertainty, featuring in particular the so-called "exploration-exploitation" trade-off. MABs have been an active subject of research since the 30's, [24], [21].

For discrete bandits with uncorrelated arms, a notable result is [20], showing that in the asymptotic regime $T \to \infty$ (with T denoting the time horizon), there exists a regret lower bound for any algorithm that achieves $O(\log(T))$ regret for any input distribution, and provides an algorithm whose regret matches this lower bound. Further research has provided computationally simple, asymptotically optimal algorithms [19], [12], [16], with good finite-time behaviour.

More recent research has focused on so-called structured MABs, where the unknown parameters of the problem (say the expected values of the arms) have a certain structure and lie in some set known to the decision maker. The goal is to quantify the performance gain due to a given type of structure, and both regret lower bounds and asymptotically optimal algorithms have been proposed for certain structures. Structured MABs are interesting because they naturally arise in the design of computer systems (at large), for instance: wireless networks [9], shortest-path routing [13], search engines [23] and ad-display optimization [22].

For discrete bandits several structures have been studied: unimodal [7], combinatorial [5], arms with lower bounded differences [4] to name but a few. Continuous bandits are by definition bandits with correlated arms, since the expected reward (as a function of the arm) is assumed to be continuous. Many natural structures have been considered, including: Lipshitz continuous [17], unimodal [28], strongly convex [10].

In this paper we study the problem of discrete MABs with budgets, where the number of times a given arm may be selected is upper bounded by a number called the budget. The budget of an arm need not be deterministic: it may be a random variable, and may depend on the sample path (the successive rewards of arms). MABs with budgets are a natural model for ad-display optimization (e.g., Google Ad-Words). Given a search query, several advertisers would like to display an ad and the search engine must choose which ad to display. The chosen ad is displayed to a user (this is termed an impression) who may or may not click on it. The corresponding advertiser is charged either when her ad is shown (cost-per-impression), or clicked (cost-per-click). Each advertiser has a maximal amount of money she can spend, so that any ad cannot be displayed infinitely many times. Uncertainty is due to the fact

SIGMETRICS'15 June 15 - 19, 2015, Portland, OR, USA

ACM 978-1-4503-3486-0/15/06 ...$15.00.
http://dx.doi.org/10.1145/2745844.2745847.

that the probability for a given ad to be clicked (also known as the click-through-rate or CTR) is unknown and must be learnt.

Our model is a generalization of the models considered in [22],[14]. We will consider three cases:

- Cost-Per-Impression (CPI): an arm may be played a deterministic number of times
- Cost-Per-Click (CPC): an arm may be played until its accumulated reward is above a deterministic number
- General budgets: the maximal number of plays of an arm is an arbitrary non-decreasing function of time, and may depend on the sample path

It is noted that the general budgets assumption allows for feedback. This is well-suited for ad-display optimization because in practice advertisers may change their future budget allocations based on the historical (sample path) click-through-rates.

Our contribution

(a) For general budgets, we demonstrate that B-KL-UCB, a natural variant of KL-UCB, achieves $O(\log(T))$ regret, improving the results of [2], [22] which give an upper bound of $O(\sqrt{T})$. The proof uses a coupling argument, showing that, when we consider an arbitrary algorithm π and the optimal algorithm $\pi^\star$ run on the same sample path, at any given time, the expected value of the best arm available to π is higher than that available to $\pi^\star$. This induces a type of majorization order that allows us to prove the result.

(b) Next we consider the CPC and CPI case where the budget of each arm is a linear function of the time horizon, and we prove asymptotic (when the time horizon goes to infinity) regret lower bounds satisfied by any algorithm achieving $O(\log(T))$ regret regardless of problem parameters. The technique for proving the lower bound is different than the one introduced by Lai and Robbins in the seminal paper [20], and uses an inequality of [27] by reducing the problem to a single classical hypothesis test at the end of the time horizon. This technique might be useful beyond the scope of this article, as it renders the proofs significantly shorter than the original one proposed by Lai and Robbins.

(c) We provide finite-time regret upper bounds for B-KL-UCB. As a consequence, we prove that B-KL-UCB is asymptotically optimal in the CPI case, as well as in the CPC case if a simple separation assumption on the budgets is satisfied (which would most likely be the case in practice). For instance the set of budget vectors that do not satisfy this condition has Lebesgue measure zero.

(d) We assess the finite-time performance of B-KL-UCB using numerical experiments. The simulation parameters (number of advertisers and CTRs) are extracted from a publicly available data set [1]. We confirm the intuition provided by our theoretical results that B-KL-UCB works significantly better than UCB-type algorithms based on Hoeffding's inequality (such as the ones proposed in [14, 22]) which do not take into account the variance of the rewards, and lower bound the Kullback-Leibler (KL) divergence by twice the square distance (Pinsker's inequality). Indeed, in practice the values of the arms are small (most popular ads have a CTR of 2% or less), hence have low variance when they are modeled as Bernoulli random variables. An algorithm which is a heuristic modification of the PD-BwK algorithm proposed in [2] performs similarly to B-KL-UCB in simulations, although it lacks a corresponding problem-dependent regret bound and additionally requires knowledge of the time horizon.

Related Work

First, for arbitrarily large budgets, the problem reduces to the classical multi-armed bandit problem [20], and B-KL-UCB reduces to KL-UCB, which is known to be asymptotically optimal for that problem. The regret lower bounds also reduce to the classical one from [20]. Also, one can notice that bandits with budgets are an instance of sleeping bandits [18], which are bandit problems where not all arms may be selected at a given time. However, in [18], the available arms are chosen by an oblivious adversary, so that arms available at a given time are arbitrary but *may not depend on the arms selected previously*. Hence there is no straightforward extension of [18] to our setting. A different but related setting is that of bandits with a single knapsack constraint, considered in [25, 26]. Namely, all arms may be played until a weighted sum (with known weights) of the number of draws of each arms exceeds a known constant. The crucial difference is that in this model the optimal policy draws *a single arm* (maximizing the ratio between its expected reward and its weight), while in our setting the optimal policy (in general) plays several arms.

Another related problem is the knapsack bandit studied in [2]. There are several constraints on the weighted sum of rewards obtained on the different arms. Any arm might be selected, until one of the constraints is violated, and then the problem stops. There is a similarity between knapsack bandits and bandits with budgets (explored in the simulations section). However the results of [2] are quite different from ours: [2] considers minimax regret (for a given T, the regret on the worst problem instance, which in general depends on T), while we study problem-dependent regret, where a fixed instance is considered and we study the regret as T goes to infinity (as in [20]). Specifically, the authors obtain a minimax regret of $O(\sqrt{T})$ (up to multiplicative logarithmic terms). It is also noted that the algorithms in [2] rely on knowledge of T, whereas our algorithm does not.

The rest of the paper is organized as follows: in section 2 we define the model considered for bandits with budgets. In section 3 we prove that the optimal policy for each of the models considered here is the greedy policy (i.e. the one which plays the available arm with the highest expected value). In section 4 we provide lower bounds on the regret of any uniformly good algorithm in the CPI and CPC case. In section 5 we provide regret upper bounds for algorithm B-KL-UCB and demonstrate its asymptotic optimality in the CPI and CPC cases. In section 6 we assess the finite time performance of B-KL-UCB and its competitors by numerical experiments. Section 7 concludes the paper. For ease of reading, proofs and intermediate results are found in section 10. Some additional intermediate results are found in the appendix.

2. THE MODEL

We consider a bandit problem with a finite number of arms $K \geq 1$ and time horizon $T \geq 0$. Time is discrete, at time $n \in \{1, ..., T\}$ a decision maker is provided with a set of allowed arms $A(n) \subset \{1, ..., K\}$, and selects an arm $k(n) \in A(n)$. Then she receives a reward $X_{k(n)}(t_{k(n)}(n))$, where $t_k(n)$ is the number of times arm k has been selected between time 1 and n. We assume that the rewards $(X_k(i))_{1 \leq k \leq K, i \geq 0}$ are independent, and that $X_k(i)$ is a Bernoulli random variable with parameter μ_k. We define $S_k(t) = \sum_{i=1}^{t} X_k(i)$ to be the accumulated rewards obtained from arm k after selecting it t times. We denote by $\mu = (\mu_1, \ldots, \mu_K) \in [0,1]^K$ the parameters of the problem. We assume that there exists functions $n \mapsto c_k(n)$ called budgets, so that the allowed set of arms can be written as: $A(n) = \{1 \leq k \leq K : t_k(n) \leq c_k(n)\}$. It is noted that $c_k(n)$ is not assumed to be deterministic and is possibly sample path dependent. We call sample path dependent any quantity that depends on the rewards $(X_k(i))_{1 \leq k \leq K, i \geq 0}$.

We will consider three possible models for the availability of arms:

- Cost-per-impression (CPI): $c_k(n) = Tc_k$ for all $n \leq T$ with $c_k \geq 0$ a constant.
- Cost-per-click (CPC): $c_k(n) = \tau_k$ for all $n \leq T$, where $\tau_k = \min\{t : S_k(t) \geq Tc_k\}$ and $c_k \geq 0$ a constant.
- General budgets: $n \mapsto c_k(n)$ an increasing, possibly sample path dependent function.

We denote by $\mathcal{F}_n$ the σ-algebra generated by

$$\{A(1), \ldots, A(n+1), X_{k(1)}(t_{k(1)}(1)), \ldots, X_{k(n)}(t_{k(n)}(n))\}.$$

We consider adaptive policies, so that $k(n)$ is $\mathcal{F}_{n-1}$ measurable for all n. We denote by Π the set of adaptive policies. When the decision rule considered is not clear from a context we denote it with a superscript, for instance $k^{\pi}(n)$ is the arm selected at time n by policy $\pi \in \Pi$. We define $\pi^\star$ to be the oracle policy (which knows μ) and maximizes the expected accumulated sum of rewards: $\sum_{k=1}^{K} \mu_k \mathbb{E}[t_k^{\pi^\star}(T)]$. We further define the *regret* of decision rule π by:

$$R^{\pi}(T) = \sum_{k=1}^{K} \mu_k \mathbb{E}[t_k^{\pi^\star}(T)] - \sum_{k=1}^{K} \mu_k \mathbb{E}[t_k^{\pi}(T)].$$

The regret of policy π is the loss in accumulated reward due to the the fact that parameters μ are unknown to π. We say that policy π is uniformly good if, for all problem instances, $R^{\pi}(T) = O(\log(T))$ when $T \to \infty$.

In this article we present our results when rewards are Bernoulli distributed, mainly for simplicity and due to the fact that the model originates from ad-display optimization where rewards (click / no click) are indeed Bernoulli distributed. However, it should be clear that the regret upper bounds apply without modification to any bounded reward distribution in $[0,1]$. Furthermore, both upper and lower bounds hold for rewards in a one-dimensional exponential family, (provided that they are sub-Gaussian), by replacing the Bernoulli KL divergence with the appropriate divergence measure. For instance, for Gaussian rewards with known variance, our results hold where the KL divergence is taken equal to the square distance divided by twice the variance. See the discussion in [12] for additional clarification.

3. PRELIMINARY RESULTS

3.1 Some notations

We assume that the arms are indexed such that $\mu_1 > \ldots > \mu_K$. For both the CPI and CPC cases we define $c = (c_1, \ldots, c_K)$ to be the budget vector. We define $I(p,q) = p\log(\frac{p}{q}) + (1-p)\log(\frac{1-p}{1-q})$ to be the KL divergence between Bernoulli distributions of parameters p and q. We use the convention that the value of an empty sum is zero, so that $\sum_{k'=1}^{0} \cdots = 0$.

3.1.1 CPI case

In the CPI case we define $k^\star = \min\{k : \sum_{k'=1}^{k} c_{k'} \geq 1\}$ to be the last arm played by a greedy policy with knowledge of the μ_k's, which would play the arms in increasing order (until their respective budgets are exhausted). We define the fraction of time that such a policy would play arm $k^\star$: $\overline{c} = 1 - \sum_{k'=1}^{k^\star - 1} c_{k'}$. It is noted that $\overline{c} > 0$, and that $\overline{c} = 1$ if $k^\star = 1$.

3.1.2 CPC case

Consider the CPC case. We recall the definition of τ_k, $\tau_k = \min\{t : S_k(t) \geq Tc_k\}$ which is the number of plays of arm k until Tc_k successes are realized. We define the random variable $\tilde{k}$ to be the last arm played by a policy which would play the arms in increasing order (until their respective budgets are exhausted):

$$\tilde{k} = \begin{cases} \min\{k : \sum_{k'=1}^{k} \tau_{k'} \geq T\}, & \text{if } \sum_{k=1}^{K} \tau_k \geq T \\ K, & \text{otherwise} \end{cases}.$$

We define the random variable $\overline{\tau}$ to be the number of plays of arm $\tilde{k}$: $\overline{\tau} = T - \sum_{k=1}^{\tilde{k}-1} \tau_k$. It is noted that $\overline{\tau} = T$ if $\tilde{k} = 1$.

We will relate these random quantities to the deterministic quantities obtained by taking expectations over sample paths. That is, we define $d_k = c_k / \mu_k$, the expected fraction of time that arm k could possibly be played, so that a CPI model with budgets of Td_k emulates this CPC model with budgets of Tc_k. We then define $k^\star = \min\{k : \sum_{k'=1}^{k} d_{k'} \geq 1\}$, the last arm played by the greedy policy with knowledge of the μ_k's, modulo the randomness in the budgets. It is noted that the definition of $k^\star$ is not the same for CPI and CPC. Finally, we define $\overline{d} = 1 - \sum_{k=1}^{k^\star - 1} d_k$, the fraction of time that such a policy would play arm $k^\star$.

3.1.3 High probability events

We use the following convention throughout the remainder of the article: For a given event $\mathcal{A}$, we say that $\mathcal{A}$ occurs with high probability (w.h.p.) iff there exists a function $p_{\mathcal{A}}(\mu, c)$ such that for all T: $1 - \mathbb{P}[\mathcal{A}] \leq p_{\mathcal{A}}(\mu, c) T^{-1}$. Also we say that $\mathcal{A}$ occurs with small probability if its complement occurs w.h.p. It is noted that any event that occurs with small probability incurs only a *constant regret*. Denote by $r(T)$ the regret of a sample path, and consider $\mathcal{A}$ an event that occurs w.h.p., then, since $r(T) \leq T$:

$$\begin{aligned} R^{\pi}(T) = \mathbb{E}[r(T)] &= \mathbb{E}[r(T)\mathbf{1}\{\mathcal{A}\}] + \mathbb{E}[r(T)\mathbf{1}\{\mathcal{A}^c\})] \\ &\leq \mathbb{E}[r(T)\mathbf{1}\{\mathcal{A}\}] + p_{\mathcal{A}}(\mu, c). \end{aligned}$$

Hence given an event $\mathcal{A}$ which occurs with small probability, when analysing the regret of algorithms, one may simply ignore any sample path on which $\mathcal{A}$ occurs, at the expense of a constant regret term.

3.2 Optimal policy

In the case of general budgets, calculating the expected reward of the optimal policy is not completely straightforward. This is due to the fact that the set of available arms $A(n)$ is a random variable, and depends on the arms selected at instants $\{1, \ldots, n-1\}$ as well as the rewards $(X_k(i))_{1 \leq k \leq K, i \geq 0}$.

Define $\hat{\pi}$ to be the (greedy) policy which plays the arms in increasing order until their budgets are exhausted, i.e., $k^{\hat{\pi}}(n) = \min A^{\hat{\pi}}(n)$. It turns out that in the general budgets case (so in the CPI and CPC cases as well), we have that $\pi^\star = \hat{\pi}$ from which we can characterize the value of $\pi^\star$.

PROPOSITION 1. *For general budgets, we have that $\pi^\star = \hat{\pi}$, i.e. the greedy policy is optimal.*

In the CPI case, the reward of $\pi^\star$ is $\overline{R}T$ with:

$$\overline{R} = \sum_{k=1}^{k^\star - 1} c_k \mu_k + \overline{c} \mu_{k^\star}.$$

In the CPC case the expected accumulated reward of $\pi^\star$ is:

$$\mathbb{E}[\mu_{\tilde{k}} \overline{\tau} + \sum_{k=1}^{\tilde{k}-1} \mu_k \tau_k].$$

4. REGRET LOWER BOUNDS

To simplify the regret lower and upper bounds we define $\Delta = \min_{k \neq k'} |\mu_k - \mu_{k'}|$. For $0 < \epsilon < \Delta$ we define:

$$\delta_k^\epsilon = \sum_{k' > k} \frac{\mu_k - \mu_{k'}}{I(\mu_{k'} + \epsilon, \mu_k)}.$$

with the convention that $\delta_k = \delta_k^0$.

Theorems 4.1 and 4.2 give lower bounds on the regret of *any* uniformly good algorithm.

THEOREM 4.1. *Consider the CPI case. For any uniformly good policy $\pi \in \Pi$, we have that for all $k > k^\star$:*

$$\lim_{T \to \infty} \inf \frac{\mathbb{E}[t_k^\pi(T)]}{\log(T)} \geq \frac{1}{I(\mu_k, \mu_{k^\star})}.$$

By corollary the regret satisfies the lower bound:

$$\lim_{T \to \infty} \inf \frac{R^\pi(T)}{\log(T)} \geq \delta_{k^\star}$$

THEOREM 4.2. *Consider the CPC case. For any uniformly good policy $\pi \in \Pi$, we have that for all $k > k^\star$:*

$$\lim_{T \to \infty} \inf \frac{\mathbb{E}[t_k^\pi(T)]}{\log(T)} \geq \frac{1}{I(\mu_k, \mu_{k^\star})}.$$

By corollary the regret satisfies the lower bound:

$$\lim_{T \to \infty} \inf \frac{R^\pi(T)}{\log(T)} \geq \delta_{k^\star}$$

For both the CPI and CPC cases, it is noted that arms $k \leq k^\star$ do not contribute to the regret lower bound, and that the minimal number of times an arm $k > k^\star$ may be played depends only on its expected value and the value of $\mu_{k^\star}$. In fact it is as if arms below $k^\star$ do not matter at all for our analysis. This will be made clear in light of the matching upper bounds derived in section 5. Furthermore, note that when the budgets are large enough, (for instance by setting $c_1 = 1$ in the CPI case, and letting $c_1 \to \infty$ in the CPC case), we have that $k^\star = 1$, so that Theorems 4.1 and 4.2 reduce to the well known result of Lai and Robbins [20].

The proof technique is similar to that of [4, 3, 6], and uses a reduction to a hypothesis test between two point hypotheses (a Neyman-Pearson test). However, the way in which we choose our hypothesis test is able to precisely recover the Lai and Robbins lower bound in [20], whereas the results in [4] do not do so. In particular, consider a given uniformly good algorithm π and two parameters μ and λ such that π must have a different behaviour under μ and λ. Say π plays a certain arm $O(T)$ times under λ, but only $O(\log(T))$ times under μ. Then we argue that the algorithm must be a hypothesis test with risk $O(T^{-1})$ between hypotheses $H_0 = \{\mu\}$ and $H_1 = \{\lambda\}$. Of course the original proof [20] used such an argument, but involved some manipulations of likelihood ratios, whereas we use an inequality of [27] which reduces these calculations to essentially a single line. Also note that, contrary to [4], we do not treat the arms played at times $n \in \{1, ..., T\}$ as a series of tests, but simply argue that the number of times each arm has been sampled by the end of the time horizon $(t_1(T), ..., t_K(T))$ can be used as a test statistic.

Finally, it should be noted that both Theorems 4.1 and 4.2 are still valid when the rewards are not Bernoulli, and instead belong to a parametric family of distributions for which one can define the KL divergence. In that case one may simply replace the Bernoulli KL divergence $I(\cdot, \cdot)$ by the relevant divergence measure, e.g., for Gaussian rewards with fixed variance one may replace $I(\cdot, \cdot)$ by the square distance divided by twice the variance.

5. REGRET UPPER BOUNDS

In this section we analyse the regret of B-KL-UCB, an algorithm which is asymptotically optimal (in most cases of interest), i.e., its regret matches the lower bounds given in section 4. It is a natural extension of KL-UCB [12] proposed for bandits with independent arms, which reaches the Lai-Robbins bound [20].

We define the empirical reward of arm k at time n: $\hat{\mu}_k(n) = S_k(t_k(n))/t_k(n)$ if $t_k(n) > 0$ and $\hat{\mu}_k(n) = 0$ otherwise. We introduce the (KL-UCB) index of arm k at time n:

$$b_k(n) = \sup\{q \in [\hat{\mu}_k(n), 1] : t_k(n) I(\hat{\mu}_k(n), q) \leq f(n)\},$$

with $f(n) = \log(n) + 3\log(\log(n))$. The B-KL-UCB algorithm is the rule that picks the *available arm* with largest index:

Algorithm 1 B-KL-UCB

for $n = 1, 2, \ldots, T$ **do**
  pull arm $k(n) = \arg\max_{k \in A(n)} b_k(n)$
end for

5.1 General budgets

Theorem 5.1 proves that B-KL-UCB achieves $O(\log(T))$ regret in the general budgets case. This in particular proves that in the gradual budget case considered in [14] (where $c_k(n)$ is deterministic and proportional to n), we also have $O(\log(T))$ regret, which is an improvement on the $O(\sqrt{T})$ upper bound derived in [14].

The proof is based on the following coupling argument: we show that if π = B-KL-UCB and the optimal policy $\pi^\star$ are run on the same sample path, then we have that, at all time instants n, $\min A^\pi(n) \leq \min A^{\pi^\star}(n)$. Hence either $k^\pi(n) \leq k^{\pi^\star}(n)$, which incurs no regret, or we have that $k^\pi(n) > k^{\pi^\star}(n) \geq \min A^{\pi^\star}(n) \geq \min A^\pi(n)$, which happens only $O(\log(T))$ times. We derive and use Lemma 10.3, an intermediate result shown in appendix. Lemma 10.3 enables us to deal with bandit problems where the available set of arms is a stochastic process and might depend on the past decisions, hence we believe it could be useful beyond the scope of this article, to analyse problems such as sleeping bandits [18] and knapsack bandits [2].

THEOREM 5.1. *Consider general budgets. Under policy π = B-KL-UCB, for all $0 < \epsilon < \Delta$ the regret admits the upper bound:*

$$R^\pi(T) \leq f(T) \sum_{k=2}^{K} \frac{\mu_1 - \mu_k}{I(\mu_k + \epsilon, \mu_{k-1})} + CK(\log(\log(T)) + \epsilon^{-2}).$$

with $C > 0$ a constant independent of μ, c and ϵ.

5.2 CPI case

Theorem 5.2, gives a finite-time regret upper bound for B-KL-UCB in the CPI case, from which we can deduce that B-KL-UCB is asymptotically optimal.

THEOREM 5.2. *(i) Under policy π = B-KL-UCB, for all $0 < \epsilon < \Delta$ the regret admits the upper bound:*

$$R^\pi(T) \leq f(T)\delta_{k^\star}^\epsilon + CK(\log(\log(T)) + \epsilon^{-2}) + C_0(c, \mu).$$

with $C > 0$ a constant independent of μ, c and ϵ, and $C_0(c, \mu) > 0$ a function independent of T and ϵ.

(ii) By corollary:

$$\lim_{T \to \infty} \sup \frac{R^\pi(T)}{\log(T)} \leq \delta_{k^\star},$$

i.e., B-KL-UCB is asymptotically optimal.

REMARK 1. *Note that Theorem 5.2 is not simply a specialization of Theorem 5.1 to the the CPI case, as the coefficients of $f(T)$ are different in the two cases. In particular, there is no proxy for $k^\star$ in the general budget case, whereas we exploit the existence of $k^\star$ to tighten the upper bound in Theorem 5.2.*

5.3 CPC case

Theorem 5.3, gives a finite-time regret upper bound for B-KL-UCB in the CPC case, from which we can deduce that B-KL-UCB is asymptotically optimal. In the derived regret upper bound, the dominant term (the multiplicative term in front of the $\log(T)$) is a convex combination of $\delta_{k^\star}$ and $\delta_{k^\star+1}$. By Theorem 5.2, those quantities represent the asymptotic regret in the CPI case where the last played arm by $\tilde{\pi}$ is $k^\star$ and $k^\star + 1$ respectively. Furthermore if we add the separation assumption $\sum_{k=1}^{k^\star} d_k > 1$, then the asymptotic regret is that of the CPI case. Since the regret lower bound of theorem 4.2 is met by the upper bound, B-KL-UCB is asymptotically optimal.

The proof of Theorem 5.3 involves upper bounding the number of times a sub-optimal arm might be played, and we do so by decomposing this number based on the expected value of the best arm available (i.e $\min A(n)$). As in the general budgets case, Lemma 10.3 is instrumental here. The proof is completed by studying the concentration of τ_k and $\tilde{k}$ and $\overline{\tau}$, based on classical concentration inequalities.

THEOREM 5.3. *(i) Under policy π = B-KL-UCB, there exists $\alpha(T) \in [0, 1]$ such that, for all $0 < \epsilon < \Delta$ the regret admits the upper bound:*

$$R^\pi(T) \leq f(T)\left[\alpha(T)\delta^\epsilon_{k^\star} + (1-\alpha(T))\delta^\epsilon_{k^\star+1}\right] + CK(\log(\log(T)) + \epsilon^{-2}) + C_1(c,\mu),$$

with $C > 0$ a constant independent of μ, c and ϵ, and $C_1(c, \mu) > 0$ a function independent of T and ϵ.

(ii) By corollary:

$$\limsup_{T\to\infty} \frac{R^\pi(T)}{\log(T)} \leq \max(\delta_{k^\star}, \delta_{k^\star+1}).$$

(iii) If $\sum_{k=1}^{k^\star} d_k > 1$ we have $\alpha(T) \to_{T\to\infty} 1$ so that

$$\limsup_{T\to\infty} \frac{R^\pi(T)}{\log(T)} \leq \delta_{k^\star},$$

i.e., B-KL-UCB is asymptotically optimal.

6. NUMERICAL EXPERIMENTS

6.1 Data set and simulation parameters

We now compare the finite-time performance of B-KL-UCB with that of previously proposed algorithms. The simulation parameters, namely the values of K (the number of arms) and μ (the vector of reward probabilities), are extracted from a publicly available data set [1]. The data set describes user queries and displayed ads for a popular search engine, over the course of one day.

For our purposes, this dataset is a set of keywords, each containing a set of ads. Each ad has been subject to some number of impressions, a fraction of which have resulted in clicks. These simulations will use the empirical CTRs based on a keyword from this dataset. Since the number of ad impressions in the dataset is heavily skewed, using the click-through rate of an ad with only a few impressions would be prone to quantization effects (e.g., many arms with CTRs of exactly $\frac{1}{2}, \frac{1}{3}, \dots$), so we first prune away any ad with fewer than 100 impressions. The histogram of click-through rates is shown in Figure 1. Indeed, the CTRs tend to be small. We filter the keywords present in the data set, and select those which contain at least 3 ads, 10^5 total impressions across those ads, and an overall click-through rate (total number of clicks divided by total number of impressions) of at least 1%. We chose keyword id #158 in the dataset, which we will refer to as keyword β. We then set K to be the number of different ads that have been displayed when β was requested, and for $1 \leq k \leq K$, we estimate μ_k by the empirical click probability for k, that is the number of clicks on k divided by the number of impressions for k. We obtain $K = 28$, and the values of $\mu_1, ..., \mu_K$ are shown in Figure 2 and Table 1.

Please note that the data is anonymized, so that each keyword and each ad is represented as a number, from which it is not possible to retrieve the actual query or the identity of the advertiser. The values of the budgets c are not available, so in the simulations to follow, we extract from the data only the K and μ of keyword β, and assign an equal budget to every arm. The budget is used as a parameter in our simulations, since it is unknown.

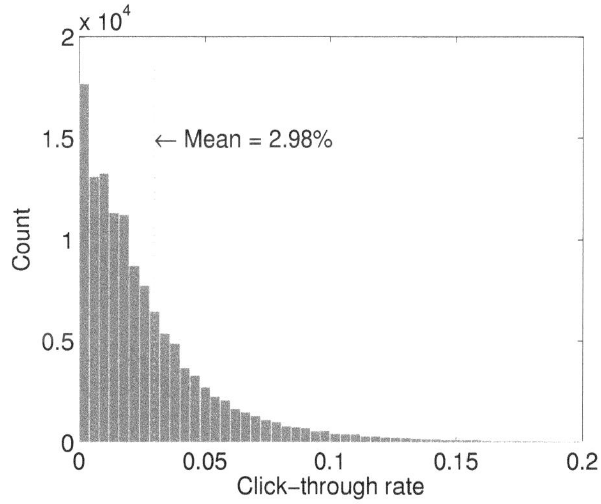

Figure 1: Histogram of CTRs for all ads with $\geq$ 100 impressions, from the KDD Cup dataset.

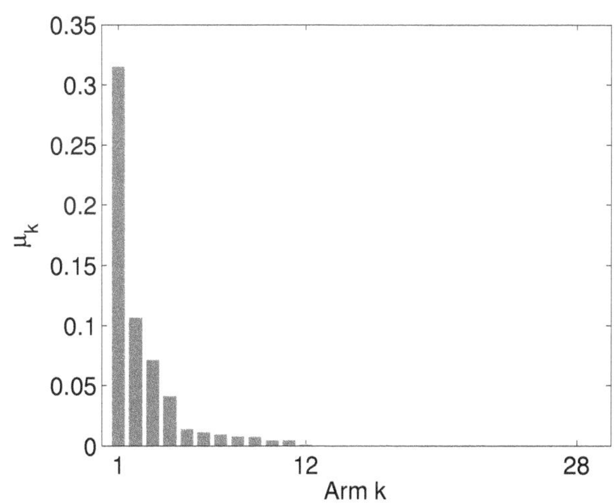

Figure 2: Plot of μ_k vs. k for the 28 ads with keyword β.

0.3153	0.1070	0.0716	0.0417	0.0144	0.0118
0.0099	0.0082	0.0081	0.0050	0.0049	0.0013

Table 1: List of the 12 non-zero entries in μ for keyword β.

6.2 Competing algorithms

We assess the performance of several algorithms identified as follows:

- B-KL-UCB: The algorithm proposed in this article.
- B-UCB1: The algorithms proposed in [14], [22]. It is noted that the two algorithms are not identical, but are nearly so. Roughly, those algorithms behave the same as B-KL-UCB except that the KL-UCB index $b_k(n)$ is replaced by the UCB index $\hat{\mu}_k(n) + \sqrt{2\log(n)/t_k(n)}$. Since they give the same performance, we only show the performance of one of them in the interest of readability.
- Balance-BwK (Balance Bandits with Knapsacks): an adaptation of the first algorithm proposed in [2] to bandits with budgets.
- PD-BwK (Primal Dual Bandits with Knapsacks): an adaptation of the second algorithm proposed in [2] to bandits with budgets.

In the knapsack bandit problem studied in [2], there are multiple resources and each arm consumes some combination thereof. The problem terminates when any one of the resources is exhausted. This is somewhat similar to our problem, where each arm's budget can be thought of as a resource. However, in our problem, even if the budget for one of the arms is exhausted, we can continue to play the other arms. Thus, while the algorithms in [2] do not directly apply to our model, nevertheless we attempt to modify those algorithms to fit our model and study how well they perform compared to our algorithm. In particular, the Balance-BwK and PD-BwK algorithms we consider here are tuned versions of the original algorithms proposed in [2], which take into account the additional structure. Namely, there are fewer unknown parameters in a problem instance of bandits with budgets than in bandits with knapsacks, e.g. resource k is known a priori to be consumed only when arm k is played. For completeness we provide a full description, including pseudo-code, of the tuned versions of Balance-BwK and PD-BwK in subsection 6.4.

6.3 Numerical results

The regret of each studied algorithm is calculated by averaging its sample path regret over 4000 independent runs.

First, we investigate the regret $R^{\pi}(T)$ as a function of the arm budgets (which determine $k^{\star}$). We fix a time horizon of $T = 1000K = 28000$. We consider uniform budgets so that for all k and n, $c_k(n) = cT$ where c is a parameter. We calculate the regret as a function of c.

Recall that for large budgets, the problem reduces to the classical bandit problem (and $k^{\star} = 1$). As budgets decrease, $k^{\star}$ transitions to $2, 3, \ldots, K$. We plot the regret of the various algorithms as we change the budget, in Figure 3 for the CPI model and in Figure 4 for the CPC model. These results show B-KL-UCB out-performs the other three algorithms across the entire range of $k^{\star}$, although our variant of PD-BwK stays a close second.

Next, we investigate the regret $R^{\pi}(T)$ as a function of the time horizon T. In order to fix $k^{\star}$ while letting time progress, the budgets must grow linearly with time. Instead of restarting the simulation with different budgets and time horizons, for simplicity of

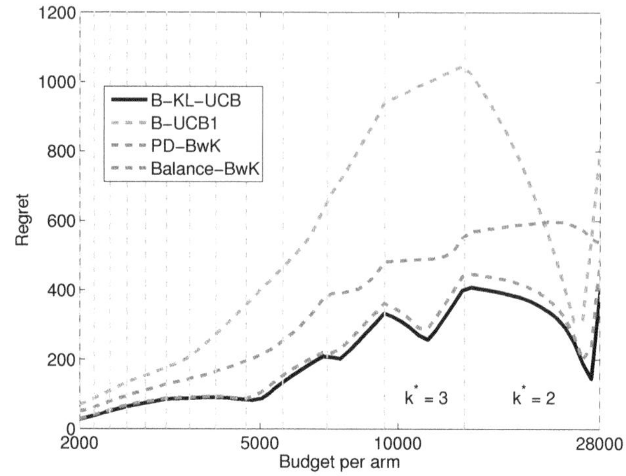

Figure 3: Plot of regret at time $T = 28000$ vs. the budget Tc given to each arm, under the CPI model. The dotted vertical lines demarcate $k^{\star}$ transitions.

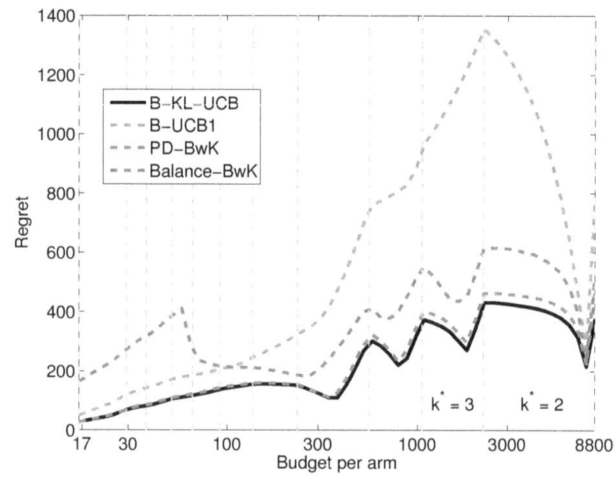

Figure 4: Plot of regret at time $T = 28000$ vs. the budget Tc given to each arm, under the CPC model. The dotted vertical lines demarcate $k^{\star}$ transitions.

simulation we use incremental budgets (by replacing Tc_k with nc_k in the RHS of the CPI and CPC definitions of $c_k(n)$, which removes all dependence on T) and a fixed $T = 10^6$. For the CPI model, we present two plots where $k^{\star} = 6$; in Figure 5, $\sum_{k=1}^{k^{\star}} c_k = 1$, and in Figure 6, $\sum_{k=1}^{k^{\star}} c_k > 1$. Similarly, for the CPC model, we again set $k^{\star} = 6$ and show two plots; in Figure 7, $\sum_{k=1}^{k^{\star}} d_k = 1$, and in Figure 8, $\sum_{k=1}^{k^{\star}} d_k > 1$. The results confirm that B-KL-UCB and PD-BwK again out-perform the other two algorithms, with very similar regrets. Furthermore, despite our upper bound for the regret not being tight in the $\sum_{k=1}^{k^{\star}} d_k = 1$ case, empirically we do not see any degradation in performance, suggesting that perhaps B-KL-UCB is optimal even when the separation assumption is violated. It should be noted that B-KL-UCB performs at least as well as both of the modified BwK algorithms, even though the BwK algorithms require knowledge of the time horizon T and B-KL-UCB does not.

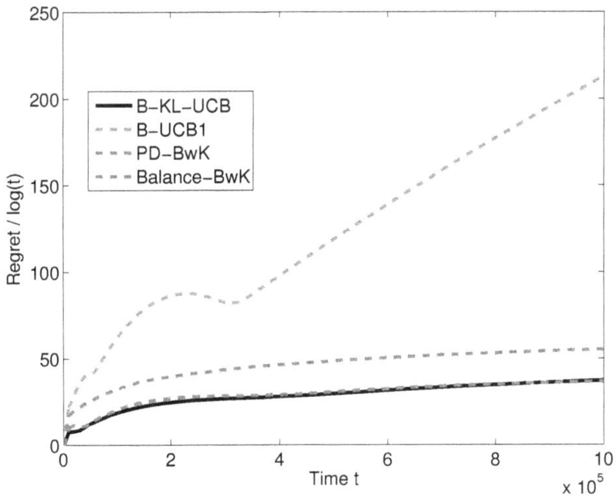

Figure 5: Plot of regret vs. time, with $k^\star = 6$ and $\sum_{k=1}^{k^\star} c_k = 1$, under the CPI model. Each arm is given the same incremental budget per timestep of $1/6$.

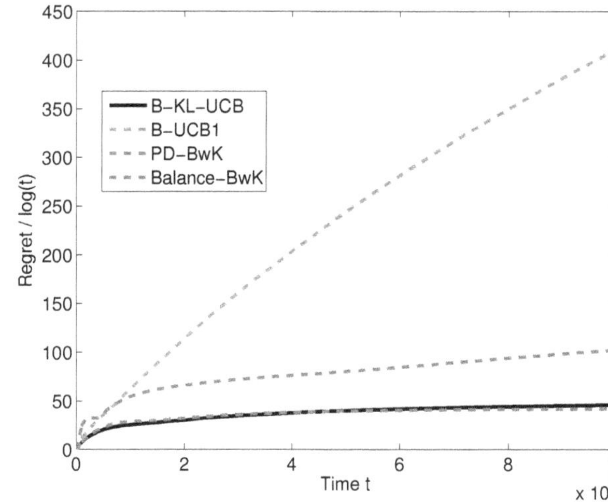

Figure 7: Plot of regret vs. time, with $k^\star = 6$ and $\sum_{k=1}^{k^\star} d_k = 1$, under the CPC model. Each arm is given the same incremental budget per timestep of 0.00489.

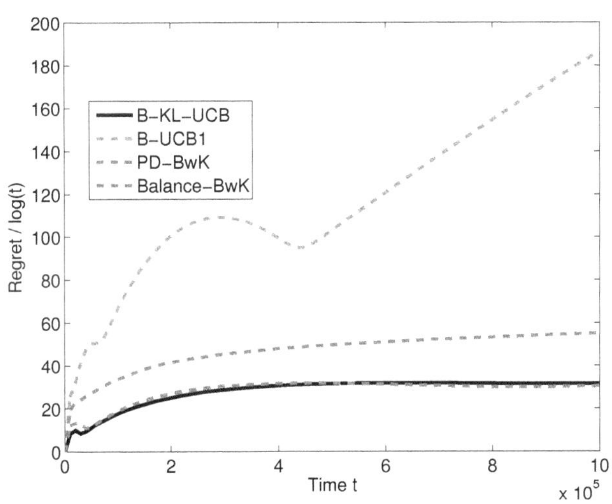

Figure 6: Plot of regret vs. time, with $k^\star = 6$ and $\sum_{k=1}^{k^\star} c_k > 1$, under the CPI model. Each arm is given the same incremental budget per timestep of $1/5.5$.

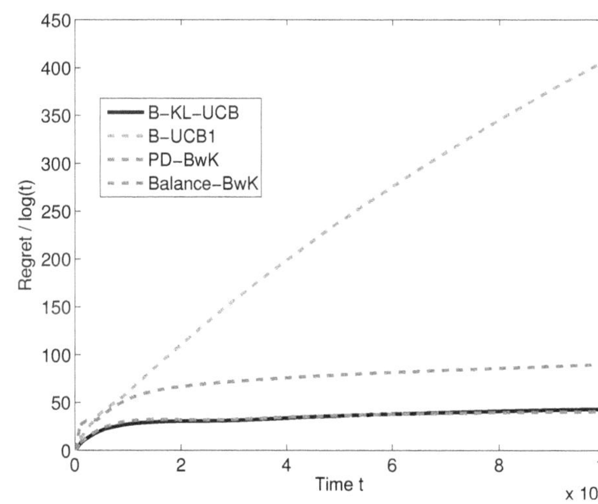

Figure 8: Plot of regret vs. time, with $k^\star = 6$ and $\sum_{k=1}^{k^\star} d_k > 1$, under the CPC model. Each arm is given the same incremental budget per timestep of 0.006.

6.4 BwK algorithms

For both BwK algorithms, we use the so-called confidence radius of an arm

$$\text{rad}(\nu, N) = \sqrt{\frac{C_{rad}\nu}{N}} + \frac{C_{rad}}{N},$$

where $C_{rad} = \log(TK(K+1))$, ν stands for the current estimate of the expected reward from the arm, and N stands for the number of times that the arm has been played so far. We will also assume the budgets are fixed at the start, so that $n \mapsto c_k(n)$ is a constant.

The idea behind Balance BwK is to ensure that the budgets of the best arms are simultaneously exhausted at T. However, this is not possible since the μ_k's are unknown; therefore, we attempt to exhaust the budgets simultaneously using the current confidence-bound adjusted estimates of the μ_k's. Specifically, we divide time into phases of K time slots each, and we do the following at each the beginning of each phase:

(i) Based on the current estimates of the rewards of the arms, we identify the set of best arms, which collectively have enough budget to be the only arms played. During this process, we also compute an estimate of the number of times each of these arms can be played over the time horizon.

(ii) The probability of playing an arm is simply this estimated number of times it can be played, divided by T.

Now we provide more details about the above computation. To compute $\mathcal{D}$, first we sort the arms (by decreasing order) based on their index $u_k(n)$, settling ties arbitrarily. Next, we iterate through this list, assigning probability mass $\dfrac{c_k}{L_{n,k}}$ to $\mathcal{D}_k$. We do so until we have accumulated probability 1. If the budget of all arms has been exhausted, assign any remaining probability to the virtual arm with 0 reward and 0 consumption.

The idea behind PD-BwK is to think of each arm's total budget as a resource, each with a fictitious "price", internal to the algorithm. Initially, all of the prices are equal, but as arms are played,

Algorithm 2 Balance-BwK

for each phase $p = 0, 1, 2, \ldots$ **do**
  for each arm $k = 1, \ldots, K$ **do**
    compute UCB estimate for the reward vector,
    $u_{n,k} = \min\{\hat{\mu}_k(n) + \mathrm{rad}(\hat{\mu}_k(n), t_k(n)), 1\}$
    if model is CPI **then**
      resource consumption vector is known a priori, $L_{n,k} = 1$
    else if model is CPC **then**
      compute LCB estimate for the resource consumption vector,
      $L_{n,k} = \max\{\hat{\mu}_k(n) - \mathrm{rad}(\hat{\mu}_k(n), t_k(n)), 0\}$
    end if
  end for
  compute a distribution $\mathcal{D}$ over arms, described in detail below

  for $t = 1, \ldots, K$ **do**
    choose an arm k as an independent sample from $\mathcal{D}$
    if k has enough budget remaining **then**
      pull k
    else
      pull the virtual arm with 0 reward
    end if
    halt if time horizon is met
  end for
end for

their remaining budgets (resources) decrease. As each resource becomes more scarce, we respond by multiplicatively increase its price. Additionally, since there is a finite time horizon, the remaining number of time steps is also a resource, with its own price that increases every time step. We then define the "cost" of playing arm k to be the expected total price of all resources consumed: the price of resource k multiplied by the expected consumption of resource k, plus the price of time (multiplied by one, the number of time steps that will be consumed). If we knew the μ_k's, a greedy policy approach would be to always play the arm that maximized the expected reward divided by the expected cost. However, since the μ_k's are unknown, we replace these deterministic quantities (expected consumption of resource k, expected reward from playing arm k) by their confidence-bound adjusted estimates. For the CPI model, we can simplify this and replace the expected consumption of resource k by 1, since it is known a priori that each play of an arm reduces the remaining budget by exactly 1. We note that the way in which prices are increased has to be carefully chosen, and is a function of the time horizon T. As an implementation detail, we actually track the logarithm of the prices and use the corresponding additive update rule, in order to improve numerical stability.

7. CONCLUSION

In this work we have investigated bandits with budgets, which are a natural model for ad-display optimization encountered in search engines. We use the same approach as in the study of the classical bandit: we provide asymptotic regret lower bounds satisfied by any algorithm, and propose algorithms which match those lower bounds. For general budgets we have shown that it is possible to achieve $O(\log(T))$ regret. For CPI and CPC budgets we have provided regret lower bounds that apply to any uniformly good algorithm. Further, we have shown that B-KL-UCB, a natural variant of KL-UCB, is asymptotically optimal. Numerical experiments (based on a real-world data set) further suggest that B-KL-UCB outperforms previously proposed UCB-like algorithms (by a significant margin), so that designing asymptotically optimal algorithms is not purely a theoretical pursuit and yields schemes with good finite-time performance. This is of interest when applying those algorithms to practical problems such as ad-display optimization.

Algorithm 3 PD-BwK

set $\epsilon = \sqrt{\log(K+1)/B}$, where $B = \min\{T, \min_k Tc_k\}$
in the first K rounds, pull each arm once
initialize the price vector, $v_1 = \mathbf{1}_{K+1}$
for $n = K+1, \ldots, T$ **do**
  for each arm $k = 1, \ldots, K$ **do**
    compute UCB estimate for the reward vector,
    $u_{n,k} = \min\{\hat{\mu}_k(n) + \mathrm{rad}(\hat{\mu}_k(n), t_k(n)), 1\}$
    if model is CPI **then**
      resource consumption vector is known a priori, $L_{n,k} = 1$
    else if model is CPC **then**
      compute LCB estimate for the resource consumption vector,
      $L_{n,k} = \max\{\hat{\mu}_k(n) - \mathrm{rad}(\hat{\mu}_k(n), t_k(n)), 0\}$
    end if
  end for
  $y_n = v_n / \left(\mathbf{1}^T v_n\right)$
  pull arm $j \in \arg\min_{k \in \{1,\ldots,K\}} \left\{ \frac{y_{K+1} + y_k L_{n,k}}{u_{n,k}} \right\}$
  $v_{n+1,j} = v_{n,j} \cdot (1+\epsilon)^{L_{n,j}}$
  $v_{n+1,K+1} = v_{n,K+1} \cdot (1+\epsilon)$
end for

8. ACKNOWLEDGEMENTS

This research was partially supported by AFOSR Grant FA 9550-10-1-0573.

9. REFERENCES

[1] Kdd cup challenge. https://www.kddcup2012.org/c/kddcup2012-track2.

[2] A. Badanidiyuru, R. Kleinberg, and A. Slivkins. Bandits with knapsacks. In *Proc. of FOCS*, 2013.

[3] J. Broder and P. Rusmevichientong. Dynamic pricing under a general parametric choice model. *Operations Research*, 60(4):965–980, 2012.

[4] S. Bubeck, V. Perchet, and P. Rigollet. Bounded regret in stochastic multi-armed bandits. In *Proc. of COLT*, 2013.

[5] N. Cesa-Bianchi and G. Lugosi. Combinatorial bandits. *J. Comput. Syst. Sci.*, 78(5):1404–1422, 2012.

[6] S. S. Chandramouli. Multi armed bandit problem: some insights. Accessed: 2013-09-26.

[7] R. Combes and A. Proutiere. Unimodal bandits: Regret lower bounds and optimal algorithms. In *Proc. of ICML*, 2014.

[8] R. Combes and A. Proutiere. Unimodal bandits: Regret lower bounds and optimal algorithms. Technical Report, http://arxiv.org/abs/1405.5096, 2014.

[9] R. Combes, A. Proutiere, D. Yun, J. Ok, and Y. Yi. Optimal rate sampling in 802.11 systems. In *Proc. of IEEE INFOCOM*, 2014.

[10] E. W. Cope. Regret and convergence bounds for a class of continuum-armed bandit problems. *IEEE Trans. Automat. Contr.*, 54(6):1243–1253, 2009.

[11] A. Garivier. Informational confidence bounds for self-normalized averages and applications. In *Proc. of ITW*, 2013.

[12] A. Garivier and O. Cappé. The KL-UCB algorithm for bounded stochastic bandits and beyond. In *Proc. of COLT*, 2011.

[13] A. Gyorgy, T. Linder, G. Lugosi, and G. Ottucsak. The on-line shortest path problem under partial monitoring. *Journal of Machine Learning Research*, 2007.

[14] C. Jiang and R. Srikant. Bandits with budgets. In *Proc. of CDC*, 2013.

[15] T. Kailath. The divergence and bhattacharyya distance measures in signal selection. *IEEE Trans. Communications*, 15(1):52 – 60, February 1967.

[16] E. Kaufmann, N. Korda, and R. Munos. Thompson sampling: An asymptotically optimal finite-time analysis. In *Proc. of ALT*, 2012.

[17] R. Kleinberg. Nearly tight bounds for the continuum-armed bandit problem. In *Proc. of NIPS*, 2004.

[18] R. Kleinberg, A. Niculescu-Mizil, and Y. Sharma. Regret bounds for sleeping experts and bandits. In *Proc. of COLT*, 2008.

[19] T. Lai. Adaptive treatment allocation and the multi-armed bandit problem. *The Annals of Statistics*, 15(3):1091–1114, 09 1987.

[20] T. Lai and H. Robbins. Asymptotically efficient adaptive allocation rules. *Advances in Applied Mathematics*, 6(1):4–2, 1985.

[21] H. Robbins. Some aspects of the sequential design of experiments. *Bulletin of the American Mathematical Society*, 58(5):527–535, 1952.

[22] A. Slivkins. Dynamic ad allocation: Bandits with budgets. http://arxiv.org/abs/1306.0155, 2013.

[23] A. Slivkins, F. Radlinski, and S. Gollapudi. Ranked bandits in metric spaces: learning diverse rankings over large document collections. *Journal of Machine Learning Research*, 2013.

[24] W. R. Thompson. On the likelihood that one unknown probability exceeds another in view of the evidence of two samples. *Biometrika*, 25(3-4):285–294, 1933.

[25] L. Tran-Thanh, A. Chapman, E. M. de Cote, A. Rogers, and N. R. Jennings. Epsilon-first policies for budget-limited multi-armed bandits. In *Proc. of AAAI*, 2010.

[26] L. Tran-Thanh, A. Chapman, A. Rogers, and N. R. Jennings. Knapsack based optimal policies for budget-limited multi-armed bandits. In *Proc. of AAAI*, 2012.

[27] A. B. Tsybakov. *Introduction to non-parametric estimation*. Springer, 2008.

[28] J. Yu and S. Mannor. Unimodal bandits. In *Proc. of ICML*, 2011.

10. PROOFS

10.1 Ordering lemma

We define the ordered majorization property: given x and y in $\mathbb{R}^K$, we write $x \lesssim y$ iff $\sum_{k=1}^K x_k = \sum_{k=1}^K y_k$ and for all k: $\sum_{k'=1}^k x_{k'} \leq \sum_{k'=1}^k y_{k'}$. In fact, if x and y are taken as elements of the simplex of $\mathbb{R}^K$ (so that they represent probability distributions on $\{1,\dots,K\}$), the ordered majorization property is equivalent to the strong stochastic order (ordering of c.d.f's). Also, consider $a \in \mathbb{R}^K$ with $k \mapsto a_k$ non-increasing, then we have that $x \lesssim y$ implies: $\sum_{k=1}^K a_n x_n \leq \sum_{k=1}^K a_n y_n$.

The result of Lemma 10.1 states that if the greedy policy $\hat{\pi}$ and an arbitrary policy π are run on the same sample path, then vectors $t^\pi(n) = (t_1^\pi(n),\dots,t_1^\pi(n))$ and $t^{\pi^\star}(n) = (t_1^{\hat{\pi}}(n),\dots,t_1^{\hat{\pi}}(n))$ satisfy $t^\pi(n) \lesssim t^{\hat{\pi}}(n)$ at all time instants n. This ordering property has two non-trivial consequences: (i) it allows us to show that the greedy policy is in fact the optimal policy for general budgets (including the CPI and CPC case), and (ii) it constitutes the crux of our regret upper bound in the case of general budgets. Once again we believe that this is a general property in bandit problems (such as sleeping bandits) where the set of available arms is time-varying and might depend on the sample paths, so that Lemma 10.1 could be useful in analyzing those problems as well, although we have not explored that possibility here.

LEMMA 10.1. *Consider an arbitrary policy π and the greedy policy $\hat{\pi}$, then one has $t^\pi(n) \lesssim t^{\hat{\pi}}(n)$ a.s. for all $n \geq 1$.*

Proof. We proceed by induction. Clearly $t^\pi(0) = (0,0,\dots,0) \lesssim t^{\hat{\pi}}(0)$. Define $n' = \max\{n : t^\pi(n) \lesssim t^{\hat{\pi}}(n)\}$, and assume that $n' < \infty$. Since $t^\pi(n'+1) \lesssim t^{\hat{\pi}}(n'+1)$ is false, we must have $\min A^\pi(n'+1) > \min A^{\hat{\pi}}(n'+1)$. Define $k = \min A^\pi(n'+1)$, so we must have:

$$\sum_{k'=1}^k t_{k'}^\pi(n'+1) > \sum_{k'=1}^k t_{k'}^{\hat{\pi}}(n'+1),$$

which implies that there exists $k' \leq k$ such that $t_{k'}^\pi(n'+1) > t_{k'}^{\hat{\pi}}(n'+1)$, so that $k' \in A^{\hat{\pi}}(n'+1)$. By definition $\hat{\pi}$ selects the arm $\min A^{\hat{\pi}}(n'+1) \leq k' \leq k$, which is a contradiction. Hence such an $n' < \infty$ does not exist, which proves the result. □

10.2 Proof of Proposition 1

Proof. Consider any policy π such that $k^\pi(n)$ is $\mathcal{F}_{n-1}$ measurable. Define $Y_n^\pi = X_{k^\pi(n)}(t_{k^\pi(n)}(n))$ the reward observed at time n and define $M_n^\pi = \sum_{t=1}^n Y_n^\pi - \sum_{k=1}^K \mu_k t_k^\pi(n)$. Then $(M_n^\pi)_n$ is a martingale:

$$M_{n+1}^\pi = M_n^\pi + \sum_{k=1}^K \mathbf{1}\{k^\pi(n) = k\}(Y_n^\pi - \mu_k)$$

$$\mathbb{E}[M_{n+1}^\pi | \mathcal{F}_n] = M_n^\pi + \sum_{k=1}^K \mathbf{1}\{k^\pi(n) = k\}(\mu_k - \mu_k) = M_n^\pi.$$

so that $\mathbb{E}[M_T^\pi] = \mathbb{E}[M_0^\pi] = 0$. Hence the expected reward of π can be written as:

$$\mathbb{E}[r^\pi(T)] = \sum_{k=1}^K \mu_k \mathbb{E}[t_k^\pi(T)].$$

Using Lemma 10.1 , one has $t^\pi(T) \lesssim t^{\hat{\pi}}(T)$ a.s. Since $k \to \mu_k$ is decreasing we have:

$$\sum_{k=1}^K \mu_k t_k^\pi(T) \leq \sum_{k=1}^K \mu_k t_k^{\hat{\pi}}(T) \text{ a.s.}$$

Taking expectations we obtain that $\mathbb{E}[r^\pi(T)] \leq \mathbb{E}[r^{\hat{\pi}}(T)]$. Since the above reasoning is true for all policies we have proven that $\hat{\pi}$ is the optimal policy which concludes the proof. □

10.3 Lower bounds: intermediate results

The following results are instrumental for establishing our regret lower bounds. Lemma 10.2 is an inequality derived in [27] (first noted in [15]), which relates the risk of a hypothesis test between two point hypotheses to the KL divergence between them. Here P and Q represent the two probability distributions corresponding to the two point hypotheses, and the test is taken to be $\mathbf{1}\{\mathcal{A}\}$ with $\mathcal{A}$ an arbitrary event.

LEMMA 10.2 ([27]). *Consider two probability measures P and Q, both absolutely continuous with respect to a given measure. Denote by $KL(P||Q)$ the Kullback Leiber divergence between P and Q. Then for any event $\mathcal{A}$ we have:*

$$P(\mathcal{A}) + Q(\mathcal{A}^c) \geq (1/2)\exp\{-\min(KL(P||Q), KL(Q||P))\}$$

We will be considering change of measure arguments, and in order to avoid confusion, for a given parameter μ we denote by $\mathbb{P}_\mu$ and $\mathbb{E}_\mu$ the probability and expectation under μ. Given an algorithm π running on some parametric bandit, Proposition 2 allows us to calculate the KL divergence of the rewards observed by π, if π were run on the same bandit problem with parameters μ and λ.

PROPOSITION 2. *Consider a bandit problem where the reward of each arm lies in some parametric family, and denote $I(\cdot,\cdot)$ the corresponding KL divergence. Consider a given algorithm π and a given time horizon T. Denote by $Y^T = (Y(1), ..., Y(T))$ with $Y(n) = X_{k^\pi(n)}(t_k^\pi(n))$ the reward from the arm drawn at time n. Consider two parameters μ and λ, and define P and Q to be the distributions of Y^T under parameters μ and λ respectively. Then one has:*

$$KL(P||Q) = \sum_{k=1}^{K} \mathbb{E}_\mu[t_k^\pi(T)] I(\mu_k, \lambda_k).$$

Proof. The proof follows from a straightforward conditioning argument. □

Proposition 3 enables us to lower bound the regret of a given sample path based on the difference on the number of times arm k is selected by the optimal policy and a given policy π:

PROPOSITION 3. *For all $1 \leq k \leq K$ and all policies π we have the following inequality:*

$$\sum_{k'=1}^{K} \mu_k(t_{k'}^{\pi^\star}(T) - t_{k'}^{\pi}(T)) \geq |t_k^{\pi^\star}(T) - t_k^\pi(T)|\Delta.$$

with $\Delta = \min_{1\leq k' \leq K-1}(\mu_{k'} - \mu_{k'+1}) > 0$.

Proof. This holds as a straightforward consequence of majorization. □

10.4 Proof of Theorem 4.1

Consider a fixed uniformly good policy π. Consider $k > k^\star$ fixed, $\epsilon > 0$ fixed and define parameter λ, with $\lambda_k = \mu_{k^\star} + \epsilon$, and $\lambda_{k'} = \mu_{k'}$, $k' \neq k$. Define $\tilde{c} = \min(c_k, \bar{c})$, and the event $\mathcal{A} = \{t_k^\pi(T) \geq T\tilde{c}/2\}$. Denote by $Y^T = (Y(1), ..., Y(T))$ with $Y(n) = X_{k^\pi(n)}(t_k^\pi(n))$ the reward from the arm drawn at time n. Define P and Q the distributions of Y^T under parameters μ and λ respectively. From Proposition 2 we have:

$$KL(P||Q) = \sum_{k=1}^{K} \mathbb{E}_\mu[t_k^\pi(T)] I(\mu_k, \lambda_k) = \mathbb{E}_\mu[t_k^\pi(T)] I(\mu_k, \mu_{k^\star} + \epsilon).$$

Notice that $\mathbf{1}\{\mathcal{A}\}$ is a function of Y^T, and apply Lemma 10.2:

$$\begin{aligned} P(\mathcal{A}) + Q(\mathcal{A}^c) &\geq (1/2)\exp[-\min(KL(P||Q), KL(Q||P))] \\ &\geq (1/2)\exp[-KL(P||Q)], \end{aligned}$$

so by taking logarithms:

$$\mathbb{E}_\mu[t_k^\pi(T)] I(\mu_k, \mu_{k^\star} + \epsilon) \geq -\log(2) - \log(P(\mathcal{A}) + Q(\mathcal{A}^c)). \quad (1)$$

Let us now upper bound $P(\mathcal{A})$ and $Q(\mathcal{A}^c)$. Under parameter μ we have $t_k^{\pi^\star}(T) = 0$, and under λ we have $t_k^{\pi^\star}(T) = T\tilde{c}$. Applying Proposition 3 we lower bound the sample path regret as follows:

$$\begin{aligned} r(T) &\geq \Delta t_k^\pi(T)\mathbf{1}\{\mathcal{A}\} && \mathbb{P}_\mu\text{- a.s.} \\ r(T) &\geq \epsilon|\tilde{c} - t_k^\pi(T)|\mathbf{1}\{\mathcal{A}^c\} && \mathbb{P}_\lambda\text{- a.s.} \end{aligned}$$

We apply Proposition 3 twice, once under parameter μ, and another time under parameter λ (in this case Δ equals ϵ). When $\mathcal{A}$ occurs, $t_k^\pi(T) \geq T\tilde{c}/2$, and when $\mathcal{A}^c$ occurs, $|\tilde{c} - t_k^\pi(T)| \geq T\tilde{c}/2$, so taking expectations:

$$\begin{aligned} \mathbb{E}_\mu[r(T)] &\geq \Delta T(\tilde{c}/2)P(\mathcal{A}) \\ \mathbb{E}_\lambda[r(T)] &\geq \epsilon T(\tilde{c}/2)Q(\mathcal{A}^c) \end{aligned}$$

Since π is uniformly good, $\mathbb{E}_\mu[r(T)]$ and $\mathbb{E}_\lambda[r(T)]$ must be $O(\log(T))$ so $P(\mathcal{A})$ and $Q(\mathcal{A}^c)$ are $O(T^{-1}\log(T))$. In turn $-\log(P(\mathcal{A}) + Q(\mathcal{A}^c)) \sim_{T\to\infty} \log(T)$ and replacing in (1) we have that:

$$\liminf_{T\to\infty} \frac{\mathbb{E}_\mu[t_k^\pi(T)]}{\log(T)} \geq \frac{1}{I(\mu_k, \mu_{k^\star} + \epsilon)}.$$

The reasoning above is valid for any $\epsilon > 0$, letting $\epsilon \to 0$ in the above equation gives the announced result.

□

10.5 Proof of Theorem 4.2

We proceed as in the proof of Theorem 4.1. Consider a fixed uniformly good policy π. Consider $k > k^\star$ fixed, $\epsilon > 0$ fixed and define parameter λ, with $\lambda_k = \mu_{k^\star} + \epsilon$, and $\lambda_{k'} = \mu_{k'}$, $k' \neq k$.

Define $\tilde{d} = \min(d_k, \bar{d})$, and the event:

$$\mathcal{B} = \cup_{k=1}^{K}\{|Td_k - \tau_k| \leq T\tilde{d}/(4K)\}.$$

From Lemma B.1 (to be proved in the next section), $\mathcal{B}$ occurs w.h.p. (under both $\mathbb{P}_\mu$ and $\mathbb{P}_\lambda$). On all sample paths where $\mathcal{B}$ occurs we have the following inequalities:

$$\begin{aligned} T - \sum_{k=1}^{k^\star-1} \tau_k &\geq T(\bar{d} - \tilde{d}/4) \geq 3T\tilde{d}/4, \\ T - \sum_{k=1}^{k^\star} \tau_k &\leq T(1 - \sum_{k=1}^{k^\star} d_k + \tilde{d}/4) \leq T\tilde{d}/4, \\ \tau_k &\geq T(d_k - \tilde{d}/(4K)) \geq 3T\tilde{d}/4. \end{aligned}$$

Define the event $\mathcal{A} = \{t_k^\pi(T) \geq T\tilde{d}/2\}$. Denote by $Y^T = (Y(1), ..., Y(T))$ with $Y(n) = X_{k^\pi(n)}(t_k^\pi(n))$ the reward from the arm drawn at time n. Define P and Q the distributions of Y^T under parameters μ and λ respectively. From Proposition 2 we have:

$$KL(P||Q) = \sum_{k=1}^{K} \mathbb{E}_\mu[t_k^\pi(T)] I(\mu_k, \lambda_k) = \mathbb{E}_\mu[t_k^\pi(T)] I(\mu_k, \mu_{k^\star} + \epsilon).$$

Notice that $\mathbf{1}\{\mathcal{A}\}$ is a function of Y^T, and apply Lemma 10.2:

$$\begin{aligned} P(\mathcal{A}) + Q(\mathcal{A}^c) &\geq (1/2)\exp[-\min(KL(P||Q), KL(Q||P))] \\ &\geq (1/2)\exp[-KL(P||Q)], \end{aligned}$$

so by taking logarithms:

$$\mathbb{E}_\mu[t_k^\pi(T)] I(\mu_k, \mu_{k^\star} + \epsilon) \geq -\log(2) - \log(P(\mathcal{A}) + Q(\mathcal{A}^c)). \quad (2)$$

Let us now upper bound $P(\mathcal{A})$ and $Q(\mathcal{A}^c)$. First it is noted that

$$\begin{aligned} P(\mathcal{A}) &= P(\mathcal{A} \cap \mathcal{B}) + P(\mathcal{A} \cap \mathcal{B}^c) \leq P(\mathcal{A} \cap \mathcal{B}) + P(\mathcal{B}^c) \\ &= P(\mathcal{A} \cap \mathcal{B}) + O(T^{-1}). \end{aligned}$$

since $\mathcal{B}$ occurs w.h.p. By the same reasoning, $Q(\mathcal{A}^c) \leq Q(\mathcal{A}^c \cap \mathcal{B}) + O(T^{-1})$, so we can restrict our attention to the events $\mathcal{A} \cap \mathcal{B}$ and $\mathcal{A}^c \cap \mathcal{B}$.

Applying Proposition 3 we lower bound the sample path regret as follows:

$$r(T) \geq \Delta |t_k^{\pi^\star}(T) - t_k^{\pi}(T)| \mathbf{1}\{\mathcal{A} \cap \mathcal{B}\} \qquad \mathbb{P}_\mu\text{- a.s.}$$
$$r(T) \geq \epsilon |t_k^{\pi^\star}(T) - t_k^{\pi}(T)| \mathbf{1}\{\mathcal{A}^c \cap \mathcal{B}\} \qquad \mathbb{P}_\lambda\text{- a.s.}$$

Under parameter μ, when event $\mathcal{A} \cap \mathcal{B}$ occurs, we have $t_k^{\pi^\star}(T) \leq T - \sum_{k=1}^{k^\star} \tau_k \leq T\tilde{d}/4$ and $t_k^{\pi}(T) \geq T\tilde{d}/2$. Similarly, under λ, when event $\mathcal{A}^c \cap \mathcal{B}$ occurs, we have $t_k^{\pi^\star}(T) \geq \min(\tau_k, T - \sum_{k=1}^{k^\star-1} \tau_k) \geq 3T\tilde{d}/4$, and $t_k^{\pi}(T) \leq T\tilde{d}/2$. Replacing in the above inequalities and taking expectations we get:

$$\mathbb{E}_\mu[r(T)] \geq \Delta T(\tilde{d}/4) P(\mathcal{A} \cap \mathcal{B}),$$
$$\mathbb{E}_\lambda[r(T)] \geq \epsilon T(\tilde{d}/4) Q(\mathcal{A}^c \cap \mathcal{B}).$$

Since π is uniformly good, both $\mathbb{E}_\mu[r(T)]$ and $\mathbb{E}_\lambda[r(T)]$ are $O(\log(T))$, so that $P(\mathcal{A} \cap \mathcal{B})$ and $Q(\mathcal{A}^c \cap \mathcal{B})$ are $O(T^{-1}\log(T))$. In turn $-\log(P(\mathcal{A}) + Q(\mathcal{A}^c)) \sim_{T\to\infty} \log(T)$ and replacing in (1) we have that:

$$\liminf_{T\to\infty} \frac{\mathbb{E}_\mu[t_k^{\pi}(T)]}{\log(T)} \geq \frac{1}{I(\mu_k, \mu_{k^\star} + \epsilon)}.$$

Since the reasoning above is valid for any $\epsilon > 0$, letting $\epsilon \to 0$ in the above equation gives the announced result.

□

10.6 Proof of Theorem 5.1

Proof. Consider $0 < \epsilon < \Delta$ fixed. Define $d(n) = \mu_{k^{\pi^\star}(n)} - \mu_{k^{\pi}(n)}$, and write the sample path regret as: $r(T) = \sum_{n=1}^{T} d(n)$. Consider a time instant n such that $d(n) > 0$. Then $1 \leq k^{\pi^\star}(n) < k^{\pi}(n)$ and $d(n) \leq \mu_1 - \mu_{k^{\pi}(n)}$, so that:

$$r(T) \leq \sum_{k\geq 2}^{K} (\mu_1 - \mu_k)|B_k|, \tag{3}$$

with $B_k = \{n \leq T : k^{\pi}(n) = k, k^{\pi^\star}(n) \leq k-1\}$. Consider $n \in B_k$. From Lemma 10.1, we have that: $t^{\pi}(n) \lesssim t^{\pi^\star}(n)$, which implies that $\min A^{\pi}(n) \leq \min A^{\pi^\star}(n) = k^{\pi^\star}(n) \leq k-1$. Therefore we have $\min A^{\pi}(n) \leq k-1$, so that applying Lemma 10.3 we obtain:

$$\mathbb{E}[|B_k|] \leq \frac{f(T)}{I(\mu_k + \epsilon, \mu_{k-1})} + \epsilon^{-2} + C\log(\log(T)).$$

Taking expectations and replacing in (3) we get the announced result:

$$R^{\pi}(T) \leq f(T) \sum_{k\geq 2} \frac{\mu_1 - \mu_k}{I(\mu_k + \epsilon, \mu_{k-1})} + K(\epsilon^{-2} + C\log(\log(T)))$$

which concludes the proof.

□

10.7 Proof of Theorem 5.2

Proof. Recall that for the optimal policy we have: $t_k(T) = c_k T$ for $k < k^\star$, $t_{k^\star}(T) = \bar{c}T$, and $t_k(T) = 0$ for $k > k^\star$. Therefore the regret of a sample path is:

$$r(T) = \bar{c}T\mu_{k^\star} + \sum_{k=1}^{k^\star-1} c_k T \mu_k - \sum_{k=1}^{K} \mu_k t_k(T).$$

Using statement (i) of Lemma B.3, we have that $t_k(T) = c_k T$ for $k < k^\star$ w.h.p., therefore $t_{k^\star}(T) = \bar{c}T - \sum_{k>k^\star} t_k(T)$ and:

$$r(T) = \bar{c}T\mu_{k^\star} - \sum_{k\geq k^\star} \mu_k t_k(T) = \sum_{k>k^\star} (\mu_{k^\star} - \mu_k) t_k(T) \text{ w.h.p.}$$

Taking expectations:

$$R^{\pi}(T) \leq \sum_{k>k^\star} (\mu_{k^\star} - \mu_k)\mathbb{E}[t_k(T)] + O(1). \tag{4}$$

Since $\sum_{k=1}^{k^\star-1} c_k T + \bar{c}T = T$, we have that $\max_{1\leq n\leq T}(\min A(n)) = k^\star$. Hence applying Lemma 10.3, for all $k > k^\star$ we have:

$$\mathbb{E}[t_k(T)] \leq \frac{f(T)}{I(\mu_k + \epsilon, \mu_{k^\star})} + C(\log(\log(T)) + \epsilon^{-2}).$$

with C a constant. Replacing in (4) we obtain the announced result:

$$R^{\pi}(T) \leq f(T) \sum_{k>k^\star} \frac{\mu_{k^\star} - \mu_k}{I(\mu_k + \epsilon, \mu_{k'})} + KC(\log(\log(T)) + \epsilon^{-2}),$$
$$= f(T)\delta_{k^\star}^{\epsilon} + KC(\log(\log(T)) + \epsilon^{-2}).$$

which concludes the proof.

□

10.8 Proof of Theorem 5.3

Proof.

First statement

From Lemma B.2 we have $\tilde{k} \in \{k^\star, k^\star + 1\}$ w.h.p. Define the following events:

$$\mathcal{A} = \{\tilde{k} = k^\star\},$$
$$\mathcal{B} = \{\tilde{k} = k^\star + 1, t_{k^\star}(T) = \tau_{k^\star}\},$$
$$\mathcal{C} = \{\tilde{k} = k^\star + 1, t_{k^\star}(T) < \tau_{k^\star}\}.$$

We decompose the regret according to the occurence of $\mathcal{A}$, $\mathcal{B}$ or $\mathcal{C}$.

Regret of sample paths in $\mathcal{A}$

First, consider a sample path in $\mathcal{A}$. Define $\tilde{\tau} = T - \sum_{k=1}^{k^\star-1} \tau_k$. It is noted that $\tilde{\tau} \geq 0$. The regret of such a sample path is:

$$r(T) = \tilde{\tau}\mu_{k^\star} + \sum_{k<k^\star} \tau_k \mu_k - \sum_{k=1}^{K} t_k(T)\mu_k.$$

Using statement (ii) of Lemma B.3 we have $t_k(T) = \tau_k$ for all $k < k^\star$, therefore $t_{k^\star}(T) = \tilde{\tau} - \sum_{k>k^\star} t_k(T)$ so that the regret is:

$$r(T) = \sum_{k>k^\star} t_k(T)(\mu_{k^\star} - \mu_k).$$

Since $\tilde{k} = k^\star$ we have that $\max_{1\leq n\leq T}(\min A(n)) = k^\star$. Taking expectations and applying Lemma 10.3:

$$\mathbb{E}[r(T)\mathbf{1}\{\mathcal{A}\}]$$
$$\leq \mathbb{P}[\mathcal{A}] f(T)\delta_{k^\star}^{\epsilon} + CK(\log(\log(T)) + \epsilon^{-2})$$

with C a constant.

Regret of sample paths in $\mathcal{B}$

Consider a sample path in $\mathcal{B}$. Define $\tilde{\tau} = T - \sum_{k=1}^{k^\star} \tau_k$. The regret is:

$$r(T) = \tilde{\tau}\mu_{k^\star+1} + \sum_{k\leq k^\star} \tau_k \mu_k - \sum_{k=1}^{K} t_k(T)\mu_k.$$

By the definition of $\mathcal{B}$ we have $t_{k^\star}(T) = \tau_{k^\star}$ and using statement (ii) of Lemma B.3 we have $t_k(T) = \tau_k$ for all $k < k^\star$. Therefore $t_{k^\star+1}(T) = \tilde{\tau} - \sum_{k>k^\star+1} t_k(T)$ and the regret is:

$$r(T) = \sum_{k>k^\star+1} t_k(T)(\mu_{k^\star+1} - \mu_k).$$

Since $\tilde{k} = k^\star + 1$ we have that $\max_{1\leq n\leq T}(\min A(n)) = k^\star + 1$. Taking expectations and applying Lemma 10.3:

$$\begin{aligned}
&\mathbb{E}[r(T)\mathbf{1}\{\mathcal{B}\}] \\
&\leq \sum_{k>k^\star+1} \mathbb{E}[t_k(T)\mathbf{1}\{\mathcal{B}\}](\mu_{k^\star+1} - \mu_k), \\
&\leq \sum_{k>k^\star+1} \frac{\mathbb{P}[\mathcal{B}](\mu_{k^\star+1} - \mu_k)f(T)}{I(\mu_k+\epsilon, \mu_{k^\star+1})} + \epsilon^{-2} + C\log(\log(T)) \\
&= \mathbb{P}[\mathcal{B}]f(T)\delta^{\epsilon}_{k^\star+1} + CK(\log(\log(T)) + \epsilon^{-2})
\end{aligned}$$

Regret of sample paths in $\mathcal{C}$

Finally consider sample paths in $\mathcal{C}$. Define $\tilde{\tau} = T - \sum_{k=1}^{k^\star} \tau_k$. The regret is:

$$r(T) = \tilde{\tau}\mu_{k^\star+1} + \sum_{k\leq k^\star} \tau_k\mu_k - \sum_{k=1}^{K} t_k(T)\mu_k.$$

Using statement (ii) of Lemma B.3 we have $t_k(T) = \tau_k$ for all $k < k^\star$. Therefore $t_{k^\star}(T) = \tilde{\tau} + \tau_{k^\star} - \sum_{k>k^\star} t_k(T)$. The regret is:

$$\begin{aligned}
r(T) &= \tilde{\tau}\mu_{k^\star+1} + \tau_{k^\star}\mu_{k^\star} - \left(\mu_{k^\star}t_{k^\star}(T) + \sum_{k>k^\star} t_k(T)\mu_k\right) \\
&= \tilde{\tau}\mu_{k^\star+1} + \tau_{k^\star}\mu_{k^\star} - \\
&\quad \left(\mu_{k^\star}(\tilde{\tau} + \tau_{k^\star} - \sum_{k>k^\star} t_k(T)) + \sum_{k>k^\star} t_k(T)\mu_k\right) \\
&= (\mu_{k^\star+1} - \mu_{k^\star})\tilde{\tau} + \sum_{k>k^\star} t_k(T)(\mu_{k^\star} - \mu_k).
\end{aligned}$$

Using the fact that $\mu_{k^\star+1} - \mu_{k^\star} < 0$ we have the upper bound:

$$r(T) \leq \sum_{k>k^\star} t_k(T)(\mu_{k^\star} - \mu_k).$$

Since $t_{k^\star}(T) < \tau_{k^\star}$ we have that $\max_{1\leq n\leq T}(\min A(n)) = k^\star$. Taking expectations and applying Lemma 10.3:

$$\begin{aligned}
\mathbb{E}[r(T)\mathbf{1}\{\mathcal{C}\}] &\leq \sum_{k>k^\star} \mathbb{E}[t_k(T)\mathbf{1}\{\mathcal{C}\}](\mu_{k^\star} - \mu_k), \\
&\leq \sum_{k>k^\star} \frac{\mathbb{P}[\mathcal{C}](\mu_{k^\star} - \mu_k)f(T)}{I(\mu_k+\epsilon, \mu_{k^\star})} + \epsilon^{-2} + C\log(\log(T)) \\
&= \mathbb{P}[\mathcal{C}]f(T)\delta^{\epsilon}_{k^\star} + CK(\log(\log(T)) + \epsilon^{-2})
\end{aligned}$$

Therefore, defining $\alpha(T) = \mathbb{P}[\mathcal{A}] + \mathbb{P}[\mathcal{C}]$ and noting that $\mathbb{P}[\mathcal{A}] + \mathbb{P}[\mathcal{B}] + \mathbb{P}[\mathcal{C}] \leq 1$ so that $\mathbb{P}[\mathcal{B}] \leq 1 - \alpha(T)$, we obtain the announced result:

$$\begin{aligned}
R^\pi(T) \leq & f(T)(\alpha(T)\delta^{\epsilon}_{k^\star} + (1-\alpha(T))\delta^{\epsilon}_{k^\star+1}) \\
& + 3CK(\log(\log(T)) + \epsilon^{-2}).
\end{aligned}$$

which proves the first statement of the theorem.

Second statement

Using Lemma B.1, we have that if $\sum_{k=1}^{k^\star} d_k > 1$, then $\sum_{k=1}^{k^\star} \tau_k > 1$ w.h.p, so that $\tilde{k} = k^\star$ w.h.p. Hence $\mathbb{P}[\mathcal{B}] \to_{T\to\infty} 0$ and $\mathbb{P}[\mathcal{C}] \to_{T\to\infty} 0$, and letting $T \to \infty$ in the first statement of the theorem yields the second statement.

□

10.9 Upper bounds: an intermediate result

LEMMA 10.3. *Consider arbitrary budgets. For any policy π, and $k > k'$, define the set of instants:*

$$B^{\pi}_{k,k'} = \{n : k(n) = k, \max_{1\leq n\leq T}(\min A^\pi(n)) \leq k'\}.$$

and consider any event $\mathcal{A}$. Then under policy B-KL-UCB, for all $0 < \epsilon < \mu_{k'} - \mu_k$ we have:

$$\mathbb{E}\left[|B_{k,k'}|\mathbf{1}\{\mathcal{A}\}\right] \leq \mathbb{P}[\mathcal{A}]\frac{f(T)}{I(\mu_k+\epsilon, \mu_{k'})} + \epsilon^{-2} + CK\log(\log(T)),$$

with $C > 0$ a constant.

Proof.

Consider k, k', ϵ and $\mathcal{A}$ fixed. Define $t_0 = \frac{f(T)}{I(\mu_k+\epsilon,\mu_{k'})}$. Decompose $B_{k,k'}$ as:

$$\begin{aligned}
B_{k,k',1} &= \{n \in B_{k,k'}, t_k(n) \leq t_0\} && \text{(i)} \\
B_2 &= \cup_{k''}\tilde{B}_{k'',2},\ \tilde{B}_{k'',2} = \{n \leq T : b_{k''}(n) < \mu_{k''}\} && \text{(ii)} \\
B_{k,k',3} &= \{n \in B_{k,k'} \setminus B_2, t_k(n) > t_0\}. && \text{(iii)}
\end{aligned}$$

and $B_{k,k'} \subset B_{k,k',1} \cup B_2 \cup B_{k,k',3}$.

(i) At each $n \in B_{k,k',1}$, $t_k(n)$ is incremented and $t_k(n) \leq t_0$, so $|B_{k,k',1}| \leq t_0$ surely.

(ii) From Lemma A.1, we have $\mathbb{E}[|\tilde{B}_{k'',2}|] \leq O(\log(\log(T)))$ for all k'', so $\mathbb{E}[|B_2|] \leq O(K\log(\log(T)))$ by union bound.

(iii) Consider $n \in B_{k,k',3}$. We are going to prove that we have $|\hat{\mu}_k(n) - \mu_k| \geq \epsilon$. First if $\hat{\mu}_k(n) \geq \mu_{k'}$ we have $|\hat{\mu}_k(n) - \mu_k| \geq \epsilon$ trivially since $\epsilon < \mu_{k'} - \mu_k$. Now assume that $\hat{\mu}_k(n) < \mu_{k'}$. We have that $k(n) = k$ and there exists $k'' \leq k'$ such that $k'' \in A(n)$ since

$$\min A(n) \leq \max_{1\leq n\leq T}(\min A(n)) \leq k'.$$

Hence $b_k(n) \geq b_{k''}(n) \geq \mu_{k''} \geq \mu_{k'}$ since $n \notin B_2$. Furthermore, $t_k(n) \geq t_0$. By the definition of $b_k(n)$, this implies:

$$\begin{aligned}
t_k(n)I(\hat{\mu}_k(n), \mu_{k'}) &\leq f(T) \\
t_0 I(\hat{\mu}_k(n), \mu_{k'}) &\leq f(T) \\
I(\hat{\mu}_k(n), \mu_{k'}) &\leq I(\mu_k+\epsilon, \mu_{k'})
\end{aligned}$$

By monotonicity of the KL-divergence, this implies $|\hat{\mu}_k(n) - \mu_k| \geq \epsilon$ in this case as well. We have proven that:

$$B_{k,k',3} \subset \{n : k(n) = k, |\hat{\mu}_k(n) - \mu_k| \geq \epsilon\}.$$

so that $\mathbb{E}[|B_{k,k',3}|] \leq \epsilon^{-2}$ using [8][Lemma B.2].

Putting it all together:

$$\begin{aligned}
&\mathbb{E}[|B_{k,k'}|\mathbf{1}\{\mathcal{A}\}] \\
\leq &\mathbb{E}[|B_{k,k',1}|\mathbf{1}\{\mathcal{A}\}] + \mathbb{E}[|B_2|\mathbf{1}\{\mathcal{A}\}] + \mathbb{E}[|B_{k,k',3}|\mathbf{1}\{\mathcal{A}\}] \\
\leq &\mathbb{E}[t_0\mathbf{1}\{\mathcal{A}\}] + \mathbb{E}[|B_2|] + \mathbb{E}[|B_{k,k',3}|] \\
\leq &t_0\mathbb{P}[\mathcal{A}] + O(K\log(\log(T))) + \epsilon^{-2},
\end{aligned}$$

which proves the announced result.

□

APPENDIX

A. CONCENTRATION INEQUALITY

The following concentration inequality derived in [11] is instrumental here.

LEMMA A.1 ([11]). *Consider $\{X(n)\}_{n\geq 1}$ i.i.d. Bernoulli with parameter μ. Define $S_t = (1/t)\sum_{n=1}^{t} X(n)$, then for all $\delta > 0$ we have that:*

$$\mathbb{P}[\sup_{1\leq t\leq T} tI(S_t,\mu) \geq \delta] \leq 2e\lceil \delta \log(T)\rceil e^{-\delta}.$$

By Pinsker's inequality, $I(p,q) \geq 2(p-q)^2$ so that for all $\delta \geq 0$:

$$\mathbb{P}[\sup_{1\leq t\leq T} \sqrt{t}|S_t - \mu| \geq \delta] \leq 4e\lceil \delta^2 \log(T)\rceil e^{-2\delta^2}.$$

B. UPPER BOUNDS: TECHNICAL RESULTS

We present some lemmas which are instrumental for the regret analysis of B-KL-UCB in the three cases of interest.

LEMMA B.1. *For all k and $\epsilon > 0$, we have:*

$$\tau_k/T \in [d_k - \epsilon, d_k + \epsilon] \text{ w.h.p.}$$

Proof. We have to prove that $\mathbb{P}[\tau_k/T \notin [d_k - \epsilon, d_k + \epsilon]] = O(T^{-1})$. Using a union bound:

$$\mathbb{P}[\tau_k/T \notin [d_k-\epsilon, d_k+\epsilon]] \leq \mathbb{P}[\tau_k \leq T(d_k-\epsilon)] + \mathbb{P}[\tau_k \geq T(d_k+\epsilon)]. \quad (5)$$

Consider the first term in the r.h.s. of (5). The event $\tau_k \leq T(d_k-\epsilon)$ implies:

$$\sum_{i=1}^{T(d_k-\epsilon)} X_k(i) \geq Tc_k,$$

$$\sum_{i=1}^{T(d_k-\epsilon)} (X_k(i)-\mu_k) \geq Tc_k - T(d_k-\epsilon)\mu_k = T\epsilon\mu_k.$$

Applying Hoeffding's inequality we obtain:

$$\mathbb{P}\left[\sum_{i=1}^{T(d_k-\epsilon)} (X_k(i)-\mu_k) \geq T\epsilon\mu_k\right] \leq \exp\left(-\frac{2T\epsilon^2\mu_k^2}{d_k-\epsilon}\right).$$

Consider the second term in the r.h.s. of (5). The event $\tau_k \geq T(d_k+\epsilon)$ implies:

$$\sum_{i=1}^{T(d_k+\epsilon)} X_k(i) \leq Tc_k,$$

$$\sum_{i=1}^{T(d_k+\epsilon)} (X_k(i)-\mu_k) \leq Tc_k - T(d_k+\epsilon)\mu_k = -T\epsilon\mu_k.$$

Applying Hoeffding's inequality again we obtain:

$$\mathbb{P}\left[\sum_{i=1}^{T(d_k+\epsilon)} (X_k(i)-\mu_k) \leq -T\epsilon\mu_k\right] \leq \exp\left(-\frac{2T\epsilon^2\mu_k^2}{d_k+\epsilon}\right).$$

Therefore:

$$\mathbb{P}[\tau_k/T \notin [d_k-\epsilon, d_k+\epsilon]] \leq \exp\left(-\frac{2T\epsilon^2\mu_k^2}{d_k-\epsilon}\right) + \exp\left(-\frac{2T\epsilon^2\mu_k^2}{d_k+\epsilon}\right) = O(T^{-1})$$

so $\tau_k/T \in [d_k-\epsilon, d_k+\epsilon]$ w.h.p., which is the announced result. □

LEMMA B.2. *In the CPC case, we have $\tilde{k} \in \{k^\star, k^\star+1\}$ w.h.p.*

Proof. Define $\overline{d} = 1 - \sum_{k=1}^{k^\star-1} d_k$. By the definition of $k^\star$, $\overline{d} > 0$. Applying Lemma B.1 with $\epsilon = \overline{d}/(K+1)$, we have:

$$\sum_{k=1}^{k^\star-1} \tau_k \leq T\sum_{k=1}^{k^\star-1}(d_k + \overline{d}/(K+1))$$
$$= T(1-\overline{d}+\overline{d}(k^\star-1)/(K+1)) < T \text{ w.h.p.}$$

so $\tilde{k} \geq k^\star$ w.h.p.

If $k^\star = K$, then $\tilde{k} \leq k^\star + 1$ trivially. Otherwise, by the same reasoning, define $\underline{d} = (\sum_{k=1}^{k^\star+1} d_k) - 1$. By the definition of $k^\star$, $\underline{d} > 0$. Applying Lemma B.1 with $\epsilon = \underline{d}/(K+1)$, we have:

$$\sum_{k=1}^{k^\star+1} \tau_k \geq T\sum_{k=1}^{k^\star+1}(d_k - \underline{d}/(K+1))$$
$$= T(1+\underline{d}-\underline{d}(k^\star+1)/(K+1)) > T \text{ w.h.p.}$$

so $\tilde{k} \leq k^\star + 1$ w.h.p.

Therefore $\tilde{k} \in \{k^\star, k^\star+1\}$ w.h.p. which concludes the proof. □

LEMMA B.3. *Consider algorithm B-KL-UCB.*

(i) In the CPI case, for all $k < k^\star$ we have $t_k(T) = c_k T$ w.h.p.

(ii) In the CPC case, for all $k < k^\star$ we have $t_k(T) = \tau_k$ w.h.p.

Proof.

First consider the CPC case. Consider $k < k^\star$ fixed, and consider the event $\mathcal{A} = \{t_k(T) < \tau_k\}$. Consider $k' > k$. Using Lemma A.1 (first statement) with $\delta = f(T)$ we have that for all $1 \leq n \leq T$: $b_k(n) \geq \mu_k$ w.h.p. Using Lemma A.1 (second statement) with $\delta = 2\log(T)$ we have that:

$$\hat{\mu}_{k'}(n) \leq \mu_{k'} + \sqrt{2\log(T)/t_k(n)} \text{ w.h.p.}$$

Using Pinsker's inequality:

$$b_{k'}(n) \leq \hat{\mu}_{k'}(n) + \sqrt{\frac{2\log(T)}{t_{k'}(n)}},$$

so that:

$$b_{k'}(n) \leq \mu_{k'} + \sqrt{\frac{8\log(T)}{t_{k'}(n)}} \text{ w.h.p.}$$

Since k' is only selected at instants n such that $b_{k'}(n) \geq b_k(n)$, this implies that:

$$t_{k'}(T) \leq \frac{8\log(T)}{(\mu_k-\mu_{k'})^2} \text{ w.h.p.} \quad (6)$$

Define $\overline{d} = \sum_{k'=1}^{k^\star-1} d_{k'}$. We have $\overline{d} < 1$ by the definition of $k^\star$. If $t_k(T) < \tau_k$, from Lemma B.1, we have that $\sum_{k'=1}^{k^\star-1}\tau_{k'} \leq T(1+\overline{d})/2$ w.h.p. Using (6) we obtain that:

$$T = \sum_{k'=1}^{K} t_{k'}(T) \leq \sum_{k'\leq k}\tau_{k'} + \sum_{k'>k} t_{k'}(T)$$
$$\leq \sum_{k'=1}^{k^\star-1}\tau_{k'} + \sum_{k'>k} t_{k'}(T) \leq \frac{T(1+\overline{d})}{2} + O(\log(T)) < T \text{ w.h.p.}$$

for large T, a contradiction (recall that $\overline{d} < 1$ so that $(1+\overline{d})/2 < 1$). Therefore $\mathcal{A}$ occurs with small probability, and for all $k < k^\star$, $t_k(T) = \tau_k$ w.h.p., which concludes the proof.

The proof in the CPI case follows from the same argument.

Social Network Monetization via Sponsored Viral Marketing

Parinya Chalermsook*
Max-Planck-Institut für Informatik, Saarbrücken, Germany
parinya@mpi-inf.mpg.de

Atish Das Sarma
eBay Research Labs, eBay Inc., San Jose, USA
atish.dassarma@gmail.com

Ashwin Lall
Denison University, Granville, Ohio, USA
lalla@denison.edu

Danupon Nanongkai†
KTH Royal Institute of Technology, Sweden
danupon@gmail.com

ABSTRACT

Viral marketing is a powerful tool for online advertising and sales because it exploits the influence people have on one another. While this marketing technique has been beneficial for advertisers, it has not been shown how the social network *providers* such as Facebook and Twitter can benefit from it. In this paper, we initiate the study of *sponsored viral marketing* where a social network provider that has complete knowledge of its network is hired by several advertisers to provide viral marketing. Each advertiser has its own advertising budget and a fixed amount they are willing to pay for each user that adopts their product or shares their ads. The goal of the social network provider is to gain the most revenue from the advertisers. Since the products or ads from different advertisers may compete with each other in getting users' attention, and advertisers pay differently per share and have different budgets, it is very important that the social network providers start the "seeds" of the viral marketing of each product at the right places in order to gain the most benefit.

We study both when advertisers have limited and unlimited budgets. In the unlimited budget setting, we give a *tight* approximation algorithm for the above task: we present a polynomial-time $O(\log n)$-approximation algorithm for maximizing the expected revenue, where n is the number of nodes (i.e., users) in the social network, and show that no polynomial-time $O(\log^{1-\epsilon} n)$-approximation algorithm exists, unless $\mathsf{NP} \subseteq \mathsf{DTIME}(n^{\text{poly} \log n})$. In the limited budget setting, we show that it is hopeless to solve the problem (even approximately): unless $\mathsf{P} = \mathsf{NP}$, there is no polynomial-time $O(n^{1-\epsilon})$-approximation algorithm. We perform experiments on several data sets to compare our provable algorithms to several heuristic baselines.

Categories and Subject Descriptors

F.2.2 [**Analysis of Algorithms and Problem Complexity**]: Nonnumerical Algorithms and Problems—*Computations on discrete structures*; G.2.2 [**Discrete Mathematics**]: Graph Theory—*Graph algorithms*

General Terms

Algorithms, Theory

Keywords

social networks, approximation algorithms

1. INTRODUCTION

Online advertising has become the main source of revenue for many companies which provide free services over the Internet, such as Google Search, Facebook, YouTube and Flickr. Since HotWire sold the first banner ads in 1994, online advertising has evolved into many forms and techniques. Some of these techniques, such as Google's *sponsored search*, have benefited their developers tremendously. In this paper, we propose and study a new form of adversing, which could potentially benefit social network providers such as Facebook and Twitter. We call it *sponsored viral marketing*.

We are motivated by the current situation where big social network providers such as Facebook continue to explore various different approaches for monetization. According to the research company eMarketer[1], the current main source of revenue for Facebook is from the *display ads* market where Facebook can use the demographic information from the profiles of hundreds of millions of its users to target the ads directly to them. However, many recent data and reports (e.g. [17, 18, 33]) suggest that it is not clear how much advantage Facebook has over other internet companies which

*Work partially done while at IDSIA, Lugano, Switzerland. Supported by the Swiss National Science Foundation project 200020_144491/1 and by Hasler Foundation Grant 11099.

†Part of this work was done while this author was at Nanyang Technological University, Singapore, and University of Vienna, Austria

[1] http://www.emarketer.com/newsroom/index.php/google-display-ad-leader/

SIGMETRICS'15, June 15–19, 2015, Portland, OR, USA.

http://dx.doi.org/10.1145/2745844.2745853.

can also collect user information in many other ways, like Google, in this market. For a definitive competitive advantage that goes beyond exploiting just user information, one needs to explore new monetization schemes that better exploit the strength and distinguishing features of social networks.

In this paper, rather than leveraging users' demographic information, we aim at exploiting the *word-of-mouth effects* uniquely provided by social networks: people tend to trust their friends' recommendations more than other advertising channels. Even with all the data that social network providers have about each of their users, social influence can be even more reliable in influencing a person's online purchasing behavior. Much research work has been undertaken recently in finding ways to capitalize on this observation (e.g. [3,5,15,28,29,31,36]). There has also been much effort in exploiting this feature by both social network providers and marketers. For example, Facebook used to have *Beacon* as part of its advertisement system to send data from external websites to its website; e.g., if a user buys a movie ticket on Fandango, Facebook would publish the purchase to her friends, presumably increasing their likelihood of watching the movie as well. More recently, Facebook has introduced *Sponsored Stories Ads*: if a user engages with a business's page, app, or event, the business can pay Facebook to highlight this activity to her friends. While there is some evidence that this type of advertising is more effective than display ads (e.g. [16]), it tends to degrade users' comfort with the social network and has led to several lawsuits as the information is usually published without users' consent.

Another way to exploit the word-of-mouth effect is *viral marketing*. This strategy is used by many advertising companies to exploit existing social networks by encouraging users to share product information with their friends, e.g. by offering a discount for each friend adopting the product. The fact that this strategy lets users share their information at will helps avoid degrading users' experiences. It, however, makes this strategy trickier to use: Since information is not forced to spread, there is a chance that, if the strategy is not implemented well, the product information might not spread as widely as it might have otherwise. This difficulty, which exists even when there is one product, has led to an active area of research namely *influence propagation* (e.g. [3, 5, 15, 28, 29, 31, 36]). The situation becomes much more difficult when there are many independent advertising companies competing for users' attention.

In this paper, we study the opportunity of social network providers to generate revenue from advertising companies who want to employ viral marketing in the presence of competition. The viral marketing services provided by the social network providers give many advantages to advertising companies. For example, the social network providers have much more information about their social networks and thus they can employ viral marketing campaigns more efficiently than the independent companies might. More importantly, social network providers can avoid unnecessary competition since they know information being shared in their networks and can organize several viral marketing campaigns from different advertising companies in a *centralized* manner.

Consider, for example, a situation where a phone company wants to advertise its cell phone on a social network. It is willing to give away some free phones (called *seeds*) to some users who express their interest. The hope is that these users will recommend the phone to their friends who, in turn, might buy the phone and recommend it further. There are many existing algorithms that the company can employ (e.g. [28]). However, the company might not be able to do this efficiently by itself. One reason is that it might not have so much information about the social network. Moreover, the company might not be able to measure the effectiveness of its campaign since it cannot track users' behavior in the social network. Further, there might be many other phone companies who want to do the same task. Since the phone companies know nothing about other companies or their approaches, they might end up giving free phones to the same group of people, leading to unnecessarily fierce competition (since most users will buy at most one phone) and sub-optimal revenue for everyone.

Instead, the phone companies might delegate the task of running their campaigns to the social network itself. For each phone sold in the social network, the company pays the social network provider a *commission* (perhaps based on the profit margin of the company). One clear advantage of this approach is that the provider has a better knowledge of the social network structure; so, it might be able to run the viral marketing campaigns more efficiently. Moreover, the social network provider might encourage users to buy phones through its website (e.g. by giving discounts) so that the effectiveness of the campaigns can be measured. More importantly, the social network provider might be able to help companies avoid unnecessary competition; e.g., it might give phones from different companies to users in different locations or social groups. Similarly, this model can be used for many other commodities, from movie tickets to laptops.

In some situations, the spread of the products or ads might not correspond directly to income of the advertising companies. For example, companies might want to promote their new fan page or spread movie trailers. In these situations, companies may impose *budgets* on their campaigns as the maximum amount of money they will pay the social network provider. Since the social network provider has no way to restrict the spread of the product across the network, the advertising company only agrees to pay per user until its advertising budget has been exhausted. This has the effect of making the problem more interesting because otherwise the advertising company which is willing to pay the most per user may dominate over the other advertising companies. We consider both the cases of limited and unlimited budgets.

In this paper, we initiate the study of how a social network provider can *maximize its expected revenue* in the above situation. To model the spread of the products based on friend recommendations, we use a generalization of the *independent cascade model* that was proposed in [22] and popularized in [28]. Unlike most models in the past that consider only a single advertising company, we assume that there are a number of competing advertising companies. Having multiple advertising companies makes the problem considerably more interesting.

The challenge of this problem is to choose the seeds (e.g., free phones) of different campaigns to the right group of users to ensure that many users will adopt these campaigns while campaigns do not interfere with each others' spread too much. Moreover, since different companies might offer different commissions and impose different budgets, it is important to make sure that campaigns from companies that pay more are spread more. This precludes the possibility of optimizing total revenue by simply maximizing the revenue of each advertising company independently.

Our problem is a generalization of the classic problem considered by Kempe et. al. [28] in that ours reduces to it in the case of a single advertising company. As a result, it is straightforward to see that their NP-hardness proof applies to our problem, and their algorithm applies to our problem for the case of a single advertising company. The most significant generalization in our paper is that our goal is to maximize the social network provider's revenue from multiple competing advertising companies.

The main contributions of this paper are as follows:

- We formulate the expected revenue maximization problem via influence propagation in online social networks from the perspective of the social network provider in the presence of multiple competing advertising entities with varying constraints.
- We show a simple polynomial-time $O(\log n)$-approximation algorithm for this problem in the unlimited budget case, where n is the size of the social network.
- We show that the above algorithm is *almost tight* in the sense that, for any $\epsilon > 0$, there is no polynomial-time algorithm that has an approximation ratio of $O(\log^{1-\epsilon} n)$ unless $\mathsf{NP} \subseteq \mathsf{DTIME}(n^{\text{poly} \log n})$. Since the latter is highly improbable, our abovementioned algorithm is likely the optimal solution for this problem.
- In the limited budget setting, the problem turns out to be very hard to approximate in the sense that there is no $O(n^{1-\epsilon})$ approximation algorithm for any $\epsilon > 0$, unless $\mathsf{P} = \mathsf{NP}$. Hence, it is very unlikely that a reasonable algorithm exists for this problem.
- We perform extensive experiment evaluation on several data sets. We test our algorithms and heuristics along various dimensions and show detailed comparative benefits of our techniques.

Organization. The rest of this paper is laid out as follows. Section 2 defines the terms and notation used in this paper and formalizes the problem. Our proposed approximation algorithms and their guarantees are presented in Section 3, and the corresponding hardness lower bound results are presented in Section 4. Section 5 shows the efficacy of our algorithms using real social network data. In Section 6 we discuss the related work most relevant to us. Finally, we state our conclusions and discuss future work in Section 7.

2. DEFINITIONS

We model the social network by a weighted directed graph $G = (V, E, w)$ with n nodes. Each node corresponds to a user in the social network, and each directed edge (u, v) with weight $w(u, v) \in [0, 1]$ represents the fact that user u can influence user v with probability $w(u, v)$. The spread of product adoption across the social network follows the independent cascade model [22]. That is, the spreading process works in *rounds* as follows. If node u adopts product i at time t, then each neighbor v of u that has not adopted any product in a previous round puts product i into her *consideration set* at time $t + 1$ with probability $w(u, v)$. Note that there might be multiple copies of i in the consideration set; this could happen when more than one neighbor of v adopts product i in the previous round. User v will pick a product from her consideration set to adopt based on her preference ordering $\preceq_v$ over the products, breaking ties randomly. Since the social network provider does not know $\preceq_v$, our algorithm will not assume this knowledge as well—its existence is assumed to make the model well-defined.

We consider the problem of advertising products from m advertisers on the network. Each advertiser i is defined by a quadruple (k_i, p_i, B_i, S_i) where k_i is the number of products the advertiser is willing to give away for free to "seed" the network, p_i is the commission the advertiser pays for each product adoption, B_i is the total budget for the advertiser, and $S_i \subseteq V(G)$ is the set of nodes that we can seed with the advertiser's product (i.e., the set of users willing to use advertiser i's product for free). Our goal is to place seeds for each advertiser i on k_i nodes so as to maximize the expected revenue of the social network owner, as explained below. We note that many seeds could be put on a single node; however, only one seed (i.e. the one that the node prefers the most) will be adopted by such a node. (For example, if we give two phones to a user, she will likely to use only one of them.)

Suppose $\mathcal{T} = \{T_i \subseteq S_i \mid |T_i| \leq k_i\}_{i=1}^m$ is a valid solution to the problem $(G, \mathcal{C})$ where $\mathcal{C} = \{C_i\}_{i=1}^m = \{(k_i, p_i, B_i, S_i)\}_{i=1}^m$. The expected revenue associated with this solution is computed as follows. For each product i, let n_i be a random variable denoting the number of nodes that adopts i after the spreading process is complete. Then, the expected revenue of the social network is

$$\mathrm{rev}(G, \mathcal{C}, \mathcal{T}) = E[\sum_{i=1}^{m} \min(p_i n_i, B_i)] = \sum_{i=1}^{m} E[\min(p_i n_i, B_i)].$$

Our objective, given the problem input $(G, \mathcal{C})$, is to identify seeds of nodes in such a way that this expected revenue is maximized. More precisely, we want to compute a set of seeds whose expected revenue is as close as possible to $\mathsf{OPT}(G, \mathcal{C})$, the maximum value of $\mathrm{rev}(G, \mathcal{C}, \mathcal{T}')$ among all possible $\mathcal{T}' = \{T_i' \subseteq S_i \mid |T_i'| \leq k_i\}_{i=1}^m$.

3. APPROXIMATION ALGORITHM FOR UNLIMITED BUDGET SETTING

In this section we present an $O(\log n)$-approximation algorithm for the sponsored viral marketing problem when each company C_i has unlimited budget $B_i = \infty$. Notice that this is still an interesting problem since only the budget is removed and the objective is still to maximize the expected revenue which operates on the *commission* values of p_i. Our algorithm crucially relies on the fact that the *uniform commission* case of the problem, i.e. when all companies offer the same commission per user (p_i), can be approximated within a constant factor. This is done by adapting an algorithm for the *submodular function maximization problem with a matroid constraint* [9, 19] to this setting. We will explain this in Section 3.1. Then, in Section 3.2, we will show how to transform the general case (i.e., non-uniform commission) to the uniform commission case, paying an extra cost of $O(\log n)$ in the approximation factor.

3.1 Uniform Commission Case

First, let us formally define the instances of the *uniform commission* case of the problem. We say that an instance $(G, \mathcal{C})$ is uniform if there is a number p' such that for all company $C_i \in \mathcal{C}$, we have $p_i = p'$. We show later that in this case, the revenue function $\mathrm{rev}(G, \mathcal{C}, \cdot)$ turns out to be a submodular function with respect to the solution set $\mathcal{T}$, thus allowing us to use the theory of submodular optimization to solve the problem.

Maximizing a Monotone Submodular Function subject to a Partition Matroid Constraint. Consider the following problem. We are given a ground set X of n elements and a function $f : 2^X \to \mathbb{R}_+$ that is *monotone non-decreasing submodular* where we say that f is *submodular* if $f(A \cup B) + f(A \cap B) \leq f(A) + f(B)$ for all $A, B \subseteq X$ and *monotone non-decreasing* if $f(A) \leq f(B)$ for all $A \subseteq B$. Since describing f explicitly (i.e. values of $f(S)$ for all possible sets $S \subseteq X$) can be computationally expensive, we are interested in the *approximate value oracle* model; i.e., there is a polynomial-time algorithm (called an oracle) with parameter $\gamma \geq 1$ that takes a set $S \subseteq X$ as an input and computes the function $\tilde{f}(S)$ such that $f(S)/\gamma \leq \tilde{f}(S) \leq \gamma f(S)$. In the *monotone submodular function maximization problem*, we are given an integer c and want to find a set $S \subseteq X$ such that $|S| \leq c$ and $f(S)$ is maximized.

In this paper, we use the generalization of the above problem where we have an additional restriction on the set S we want to find. This restriction is called the *partition matroid constraint*. In this case, X is partitioned into ℓ disjoint sets $X_1, X_2, \ldots, X_\ell$ where each X_i has associated integer c_i, so the problem instance can be specified by a triple $(X = \bigcup_{i=1}^m X_i, \{c_i\}_{i=1}^m, f)$. Our goal is to find a set $S \subseteq X$ such that $|S \cap X_i| \leq c_i$, for all i, and $f(S)$ is maximized. Observe that this problem generalizes the previous problem since the previous problem corresponds to the setting where $\ell = 1$, $X_1 = X$ and $c_1 = c$.

The problem of maximizing a monotone submodular function subject to a partition matroid constraint is a special case of the problem of maximizing a monotone submodular function subject to an *arbitrary* matroid constraint[2]. The latter problem has been extensively studied, and many constant-approximation algorithms have been previously discovered (e.g. [9, 19]). In particular, the tight $\frac{1}{1-1/e}$-approximation algorithm based on pipage rounding and continuous greedy process techniques was presented by Calinescu et al. [10]. Another algorithm which is simpler and computationally more efficient is the greedy 2-approximation algorithm by Fisher, Nemhauser, and Wolsey [19]. We will use the latter algorithm in this paper due to its simplicity and efficiency. This algorithm simply starts with the empty set, and repeatedly adds an element that maximizes marginal gain, while maintaining the partition matroid constraint as an invariant. See Algorithm 1 for details.

Fisher et al. [19] analyzed the greedy algorithm when $\tilde{f}(S) = f(S)$ and showed that this algorithm is a 2-approximation algorithm. Calinescu et al. [9] analyzed the algorithm when $\tilde{f}$ is an approximate oracle (more importantly, they generalized the result of [19] to *p-systems*). We need an approximate-value-oracle version of this result which follows from [9], as stated below.

LEMMA 1. *([9, 19]) For a non-negative, monotone submodular function f, let S be a set obtained from Algorithm 1. Let $\tilde{f}$ and $\gamma \geq 1$ be such that $f(S)/\gamma \leq \tilde{f}(S) \leq \gamma f(S)$ for all $S \subseteq X$. Let S^* be a set that maximizes the value of f over all sets satisfying the partition matroid constraint. Then, $f(S) \geq f(S^*)/2\gamma$; in other words, set S gives a 2γ-approximation.*

[2]We do not define the general matroid constraint here, since it is more complicated and not needed in this paper.

Algorithm 1 Greedy 2γ-approximation algorithm for submodular maximization subject to a partition matroid constraint

Input: Ground set $X = \bigcup_i X_i$, constraints $\{c_i\}$ and an oracle computing function $\tilde{f}$ where $\tilde{f}(S) \in (\frac{1}{\gamma} f(S), \gamma f(S))$ for all $S \subseteq X$
Output: Set $S \subseteq X$ such that $f(S) \geq (\max_{S'} f(S'))/(2\gamma)$.

```
S = ∅, A = ∅.
repeat
    A = {e | ∀i : |(S ∪ {e}) ∩ X_i| ≤ c_i}
    if A ≠ ∅ then
        e = argmax_{e'∈A} f̃(S ∪ {e'})
        S = S ∪ {e}
    end if
until A = ∅
return S
```

Algorithm for Uniform Commission Case. We convert an instance $(G, \mathcal{C})$ of our sponsored viral marketing problem into instance $(X, \{c_i\}_{i=1}^m, f)$ of the function maximization problem as follows. For each company $C_i \in \mathcal{C}$, we create $X_i = \{(i, u) \mid u \in S_i\}$ and let $c_i = k_i$. We then let the ground set be $X = \bigcup_i X_i$. Consider a function $f : 2^X \to \mathbb{R}_+$ where $f(S) = \text{rev}(G, \mathcal{C}, \mathcal{T})$ where $\mathcal{T} = \{T_i\}_{i=1}^m$ is defined by $T_i = \{u : (i, u) \in S\}$. In other words, $f(S)$ captures the expected revenue we get when we place seeds of company C_i on all nodes u such that $(i, u) \in S$. Also note that a set S satisfies the partition matroid constraint (i.e., $|S \cap X_i| \leq c_i$ for all i) if and only if the corresponding set $\mathcal{T}$ satisfies the constraint of the sponsored viral marketing problem (i.e., we put at most k_i seeds of company i on nodes in S_i). This leads us to the following simple observation.

OBSERVATION 2. $\mathsf{OPT}(G, \mathcal{C}) = \max_{S:(\forall i)|S \cap X_i| \leq c_i} f(S)$. *Moreover, any set $S \subseteq X$ that satisfies the partition matroid constraint can be transformed into a solution $\mathcal{T}$ of the sponsored viral marketing problem such that $f(X) = \text{rev}(G, \mathcal{C}, \mathcal{T})$.*

Thus, if we can compute an α-approximate solution to the problem of maximizing $f(S)$ with the partition matroid constraint above, we will immediately get an α-approximate solution for the sponsored viral marketing problem as well. The key in solving this function maximization problem is the fact that our function f is monotone non-decreasing submodular.

To show this, observe that since every company has the same commission, say p, and an unlimited budget, the revenue we get depends solely on the number of nodes that adopt *any* product; it does not matter so much (in terms of the revenue we get) which product each node adopts in the end. To be precise, let $\sigma(S)$ be the expected number of nodes adopting *any* product when we put the seeds on nodes in $\bigcup_{T_i \in \mathcal{T}} T_i$ where $\mathcal{T}$ is as defined above. Then, the expected revenue that we will get is $f(S) = p\sigma(S)$. Thus, in order to show that function f is monotone non-decreasing submodular, it is enough to show that the function σ is monotone non-decreasing submodular. Note that function σ is nothing but the expected number of nodes that adopt some product when we place seeds on nodes in $\bigcup_{T_i \in \mathcal{T}} T_i$ (it does not matter which companies these seeds belong to). This is the quantity we want to maximize in the problem of maximizing the spread of influence through a social network, which is already shown to be monotone non-decreasing submodular [28]! This allows us to conclude that f is submodular as well.

The above observation also allows us to construct an oracle for computing f: As done in [28], we put seeds of a single product on nodes in $\bigcup_{T_i \in \mathcal{T}} T_i$ and simulate the diffusion process to count the number of nodes that adopt the product. By repeating this polynomial number of times, we are able to obtain $\tilde{\sigma}(S)$ that is an arbitrarily close approximation to $\sigma(S)$, with high probability. Using $\tilde{f}(S) = p\tilde{\sigma}(S)$, we get $\tilde{f}(S)$ that is an arbitrarily close approximation to $f(S)$ as well. Then, we can use Algorithm 1 to obtain a 2γ-approximation of the optimal solution of the sponsored viral marketing problem in the case of uniform commission.

3.2 General Case

Algorithm 2 $O(\log n)$-Approximation Algorithm

Input: Social network G with unknown user preferences (over products) and set $\mathcal{C} = \{C_i\}_{i=1}^m$ of m companies where each company C_i is a quadruple (k_i, p_i, B_i, S_i).

Output: Set of seeds $\mathcal{T} = \{T_i \subset S_i \mid |T_i| \leq k_i\}$ such that $\text{rev}(G, \mathcal{C}, \mathcal{T}) = \Omega(\mathsf{OPT}(G, \mathcal{C})/\log n)$.

1: For any i, define $p'_i = 2^j$ where j is such that $2^j \leq p_i < 2^{j+1}$. Let $C'_i = (k_i, p'_i, B_i, S_i)$ and $\mathcal{C}' = \{C'_i\}_{i=1}^m$.
2: For all j, let $\mathcal{C}'_j = \{C'_i \mid p'_i = 2^j\}$.
3: For all j, compute the solution $\mathcal{T}'_j$ of the instance $(G, \mathcal{C}'_j)$ (using an arbitrary user preference) such that $\text{rev}(G, \mathcal{C}'_j, \mathcal{T}'_j) = \Omega(\mathsf{OPT}(G, \mathcal{C}'_j))$ using the algorithm for the uniform commission case presented in Section 3.1.
4: **return** $\mathcal{T}'_j$ with maximum value of $\text{rev}(G, \mathcal{C}'_j, \mathcal{T}'_j)$ among all possible j.

Our simple $O(\log n)$ approximation algorithm is outlined in Algorithm 2. The algorithm first rounds each company's commission down to the nearest power of two and partitions them into groups based on their approximate commissions: For each company $C_i \in \mathcal{C}$ with commission p_i, the algorithm rounds p_i down to p'_i as shown in Line 1. We use C'_i to denote the same company C_i with the rounded commission p'_i. Then, the algorithm partitions $\mathcal{C}'$ into $\mathcal{C}'_j$ as in Line 2. Observe that all companies in $\mathcal{C}'_j$, for all j, have the same commission. This allows us to compute $\text{rev}(G, \mathcal{C}'_j, \mathcal{T}'_j)$ for all j using the algorithm for the uniform commission case, as shown in Line 3. We then simply return the solution that gives us the most revenue. Note that our algorithm can be made slightly more efficient by considering only j between $j^* - 2\log n$ and j^* where $j^* = \lfloor \log_2(\max_i p'_i) \rfloor$. This fact will be clear in the analysis. It might seem counterintuitive that our algorithm only focuses on collecting the revenue from one commission group, but we show in the next section that this algorithm gives essentially the best possible approximation guarantee (so trying to collect revenues from different commission groups will not help.) We now analyze the algorithm.

THEOREM 3. *Algorithm 2 is returns a solution $\mathcal{T}'_j$ such that $\text{rev}(G, \mathcal{C}', \mathcal{T}'_j) = \Omega(\mathsf{OPT}(G, \mathcal{C})/\log n)$. In other words, it is $O(\log n)$-approximation.*

The theorem states that the seeds assigned by the algorithm result in an expected revenue that is at least a $\Omega(\frac{1}{\log n})$ fraction of the expected revenue of an *optimal* placement of seeds for all advertisers. This essentially suggests that the presented algorithm, while very simple, efficient and easy to implement, is actually very good at choosing from exponentially many possibilities of seeds for every advertiser and make assignments in a manner that helps maximize the social networks' revenue. A good comparison is to observe that if the advertisers operated independently, this could potentially result in a hugely negative competition that not only affected their own revenues but resulted in an arbitrarily large (depending on the number of advertisers) factor of loss to the social network. In the subsequent section, we will also show that our algorihm in fact performs *best possible* from a computational complexity standpoint.

The rest of this section is devoted to proving Theorem 3. First, we note that changing the commission of each company C_i from p_i to p'_i does not change the revenue we get from any solution too much. This is simply because $p'_i \geq p_i/2$ for all i. We thus have the following lemma.

LEMMA 4. *For any solution $\mathcal{T}$ of the sponsored viral marketing problem,* $\text{rev}(G, \mathcal{C}, \mathcal{T}) \geq \text{rev}(G, \mathcal{C}', \mathcal{T}) \geq \text{rev}(G, \mathcal{C}, \mathcal{T})/2$. *Consequently,* $\mathsf{OPT}(G, \mathcal{C}, f) \geq \mathsf{OPT}(G, \mathcal{C}', f) \geq \mathsf{OPT}(G, \mathcal{C}, f)/2$.

Let j^* be the minimum integer j such that $p'_i \leq 2^j$ for all i, i.e., $j^* = \log_2(\max_i p'_i)$. Let $\mathcal{C}'' = \cup_{j^* - 2\log n \leq j \leq j^*} \mathcal{C}'_j$; i.e., $\mathcal{C}''$ contains only the companies having "large" commission and ignores the rest of the companies. We show this does not lose us too much revenue.

LEMMA 5. $\mathsf{OPT}(G, \mathcal{C}'') \geq \mathsf{OPT}(G, \mathcal{C}')/2$

PROOF. Let $p'_{\max} = 2^{j^*}$ (or, equivalently, $p'_{\max} = \max_i p'_i$) and $w_{\max} = \max_{e \in E(G)} w(e)$. Note that

$$\mathsf{OPT}(G, \mathcal{C}') \geq p'_{\max} w_{\max}$$

since we can get a revenue of $p'_{\max} w_{\max}$ by placing a seed of the company with commission $p'_{\max}$ on a node u where u is such that there is an edge uv with $w(uv) = w_{\max}$.

Note further that the revenue we can get from any company in $\mathcal{C}' \setminus \mathcal{C}''$ when we place a seed on a node u is at most $\sum_{v \in V(G)} w(uv) \frac{p'_{\max}}{2n^2} \leq \frac{\mathsf{OPT}(G, \mathcal{C})}{2n}$ since every company in $\mathcal{C}' \setminus \mathcal{C}''$ has commission at most

$$p'_{\max}/2^{2\log n + 1} = p_{\max}/2n^2.$$

Thus, the expected total revenue we get from companies in $\mathcal{C}' \setminus \mathcal{C}''$ is at most $\mathsf{OPT}(G, \mathcal{C}')/2$. In other words,

$$\mathsf{OPT}(G, \mathcal{C}') - \mathsf{OPT}(G, \mathcal{C}'') \leq \mathsf{OPT}(G, \mathcal{C}')/2.$$

The lemma follows. □

Finally, we use the fact that $\mathcal{C}''$ consists of companies having $O(\log n)$ different values of commission to show the following simple lemma.

LEMMA 6. $\max_{j^* - 2\log n \leq j \leq j^*} \mathsf{OPT}(G, \mathcal{C}'_j) = \Omega(\frac{\mathsf{OPT}(G, \mathcal{C}'')}{\log n})$.

PROOF. Since $\mathcal{C}'' = \bigcup_{j^* - 2\log n \leq j \leq j^*} \mathcal{C}'_j$, we have that

$$\mathsf{OPT}(G, \mathcal{C}'') \leq \sum_{j^* - 2\log n \leq j \leq j^*} \mathsf{OPT}(G, \mathcal{C}'_j).$$

Thus, there exists j such that $\mathsf{OPT}(G, \mathcal{C}'_j) \geq \frac{\mathsf{OPT}(G, \mathcal{C}'')}{2\log n + 1}$. □

Combining all above lemmas, we have that (recall that $\mathcal{T}'_j$ is the solution returned by Algorithm 2)

$$\begin{aligned} \text{rev}(G, \mathcal{C}, \mathcal{T}'_j) &\geq \text{rev}(G, \mathcal{C}', \mathcal{T}'_j) \\ &= \Omega\left(\max_{j^*-2\log n \leq j \leq j^*} \mathsf{OPT}(G, \mathcal{C}'_j)\right) \\ &= \Omega\left(\frac{\mathsf{OPT}(G, \mathcal{C}'')}{\log n}\right) \\ &= \Omega\left(\frac{\mathsf{OPT}(G, \mathcal{C}')}{\log n}\right) \\ &= \Omega\left(\frac{\mathsf{OPT}(G, \mathcal{C})}{\log n}\right). \end{aligned}$$

This completes the proof of Theorem 3.

4. HARDNESS OF APPROXIMATION

In this section, we prove our hardness results. The $\Omega(n^{1-\epsilon})$ hardness of approximating the limited-budget case is proven in Section 4.1. We prove $\Omega(\log^{1-\epsilon} n)$ hardness for the unlimited budget setting in Section 4.2.

4.1 Limited Budget Setting

Our reduction starts from the Donation Center Location problem (DCL), introduced by Huang and Svitkina [27]. In DCL, we are given a bipartite graph $G = (A \cup L, E)$ where A is a collection of *agents* and L is a collection of *centers*. $V(G)$ is the number of vertices in G. Each center $\ell \in L$ has limited capacity $c_\ell \in \mathbb{Z}_+$ that represents the maximum number of agents that can be served, and each vertex $a \in A$ has strictly ordered preference ranking $\preceq_a$ of its neighbors in L. Our objective is to compute a triple (A', L', σ) where $L' \subseteq L$ is a set of centers to open, $A' \subseteq A$, and assignment $\sigma : A' \to L'$ such that: (1) The number of agents assigned to any center ℓ is at most c_ℓ, i.e. $|\{a \in A' : \sigma(a) = \ell\}| \leq c_\ell$ and (2) Each $a \in A'$ is assigned to its highest ranked neighbor in L'. We are interested in finding such a triple while maximizing $|A'|$. Our starting point is the following hardness of approximation result due to Chalermsook, Laekhanukit, and Nanongkai [12].

THEOREM 7. *[12] For any positive number $\epsilon > 0$, unless* $\mathsf{NP} = \mathsf{ZPP}$, *it is hard to approximate* DCL *to within a factor of* $|V(G)|^{1-\epsilon}$.

Now we show an approximation-preserving reduction from DCL to the sponsored viral marketing problem, i.e. given an instance of DCL, we construct an instance of sponsored viral marketing problem such that the value of the optimal solution in the latter problem is the same as that of the former.

Construction. Given an instance $G = (A \cup L, E)$ of DCL, we create an instance $(G', \mathcal{C}' = \{(k_i, p_i, B_i, S_i)\}_{i=1}^m)$ as follows. The graph G' is a directed bipartite graph $G' = (A \cup L, E')$ on the same sets of vertices and edges. The only difference is that we turn the graph into directed graph: There is a directed edge $\ell a \in E'$ if and only if $\ell a \in E$. The weight of every edge is $w_{\ell a} = 1$. For each $\ell \in L$, we have a company $\mathsf{comp}(\ell)$ with $k_{\mathsf{comp}(\ell)} = 1$, $p_{\mathsf{comp}(\ell)} = 1$, $B_{\mathsf{comp}(\ell)} = c_\ell$, and $S_{\mathsf{comp}(\ell)} = \{\ell\}$. Each node $a \in A$ has the preference $\preceq'_a$ over products $\{\mathsf{comp}(\ell)\}_{\ell \in L}$ in a way that is consistent with its ranking over ℓ, i.e. $\mathsf{comp}(\ell) \preceq'_a \mathsf{comp}(\ell')$ if and only if $\ell \preceq_a \ell'$. This completes the description of our reduction.

Analysis. Let OPT and OPT' denote the optimal revenue of the DCL instance and our instance respectively. We argue that $\mathsf{OPT} = \mathsf{OPT}'$. First, to show that $\mathsf{OPT} \leq \mathsf{OPT}'$, consider any solution (L', A', σ) of DCL. For each node $\ell \in L'$, we put the seed of company $\mathsf{comp}(\ell)$ at node ℓ. We argue that the total profit made from this strategy is $|A'|$: Consider each node $a \in A'$ who sees the seeds at nodes $\{\ell : \ell a \in E'\}$. It must be the case that $\mathsf{comp}(\sigma(a))$ is among the products a considers and must be highest w.r.t. the rank $\preceq'_a$, so we can get the revenue of 1 from a. It is easy to check that each company has enough budget, since for each ℓ, we know that $|\{a : \sigma(a) = \ell\}| \leq c_\ell$.

Now we argue that $\mathsf{OPT}' \leq \mathsf{OPT}$. Let $L' \subseteq L$ be a subset of vertices on which the seeds are placed and $A' \subseteq A$ be the set of nodes that contribute to the total profit. Define $\sigma : A' \to L'$ by setting $\sigma(a)$ to be the node $\ell \in L'$ such that product $\mathsf{comp}(\ell)$ is bought by a. It is easy to check (using the arguments similar to that in the previous paragraph) that (L', A', σ) is a feasible solution for DCL instance, thus implying that $\mathsf{OPT}' \leq \mathsf{OPT}$. We have thus shown the following theorem.

THEOREM 8. *Let $\epsilon > 0$ be sufficiently small constant. Unless* $\mathsf{NP} = \mathsf{ZPP}$, *there is no $n^{1-\epsilon}$ approximation algorithm for sponsored viral marketing problem in the limited budget setting.*

This result essentially says that the problem of identifying good seed sets to maximize expected revenue for the social network is computationally intractable when advertisers operate under limited budgets. This still does not preclude, from a practical standpoint, an algorithm that conceivably does very well in practice in allocating seeds. Also notice that while we prove the computational intractability of the problem from the social network provider's revenue maximization standpoint, it is important to note that (and perhaps can be deferred to future for a concrete result in this direction) the social network provider presumably can do a significantly better job of maximize profit than individual advertisers may do independently. Our objective compares against the optimal solution from the network's standpoint which is a stringent comparison. More likely if independent advertisers operate in isolation in marketing currently, they are resulting in unnecessarily revenue-detracting competition.

4.2 Unlimited Budget Setting

To prove the hardness of approximation in this setting, we make a connection between our problem and UNIT-DEMAND MIN-BUYING PRICING (UDP-MIN). In the UDP-MIN problem, we are given a collection of items $\mathcal{I}$ and consumers $\mathcal{C}$, where each consumer $C \in \mathcal{C}$ is associated with budget B_C and a subset of items $S_C \subseteq \mathcal{I}$ she is interested in purchasing. Once the price function $p : \mathcal{I} \to \mathbb{R}_+$ is fixed, each consumer C buys the cheapest item in S_C if $\min_{I \in S_C} p(I) \leq B_C$ (in which case, we earn a revenue of $\min_{I \in S_C} p(I)$ from consumer C); otherwise, the consumer buys nothing (in which case, our revenue from this consumer is zero). The objective of the problem is to compute the price function that maximizes the total revenue.

We remark the distinction in the terms we use. If we talk about the items in the pricing problem, we refer to them as *items*, while we refer to those in our problem as *products/ companies*. We need the following theorem which shows the hardness of approximation for UDP-MIN.

THEOREM 9. *[11] For any $\epsilon > 0$, it is hard to approximate* UDP-MIN *to within a factor of* $\log^{1-\epsilon}(|\mathcal{C}|+|\mathcal{I}|)$, *unless* NP *has a quasi-polynomial time algorithm.*

Construction. Consider an instance $(\mathcal{C}, \mathcal{I})$ of UDP-MIN. Denote by $\mathcal{B} = \{B_C\}_{C\in\mathcal{C}}$ the set of all possible consumers' budgets. We create an instance $(G', \mathcal{C}' = \{C'_i\}_{i=1}^m)$ as follows. First the graph $G' = (U \cup V, E)$ is bipartite. Edges are always directed from vertices in U to those in V. For each item $I \in \mathcal{I}$, for each possible budget $B \in \mathcal{B}$, we have a vertex $u(I, B)$ in set U, so the total number of vertices in U is

$$|U| = |\mathcal{B}||\mathcal{I}| \leq |\mathcal{C}||\mathcal{I}|.$$

Now for each consumer $C \in \mathcal{C}$, we have a vertex $v(C)$, so $|V| = |\mathcal{C}|$. There is an edge connecting $u(I, B)v(C) \in E$ if and only if $I \in S_C$ and $B_C \leq B$. Finally, each edge e in the graph has weight $w(e) = 1$. This completes the description of graph G'.

Now we define the companies and their parameters. For each item $I \in \mathcal{I}$, for each possible budget $B \in \mathcal{B}$, we have a company/product $\mathsf{comp}(I, B)$ with the following parameters: the number of seeds $k'_{\mathsf{comp}(I,B)} = 1$, the price $p'_{\mathsf{comp}(I,B)} = B$, and the node set $S_{\mathsf{comp}(I,B)} = \{u(I, B)\}$; recall that the budget of each company is ∞ in this setting. Each node $v(C) \in V$ has the ranking $\preceq_{v(C)}$ of companies $\{\mathsf{comp}(I, B)\}$ based on the values of B, i.e. $\mathsf{comp}(I, B) \preceq_{v(C)} \mathsf{comp}(I', B')$ if and only if $B > B'$. This completes our construction. See Figures 1 and 2 for illustration.

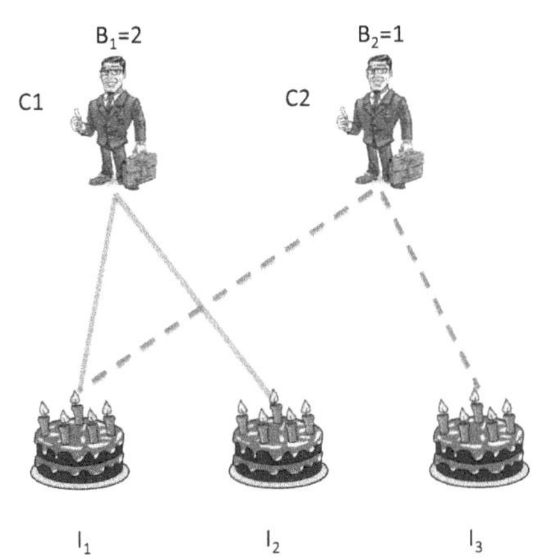

Figure 1: An instance of UDP-MIN. An edge between consumer and item shows that the consumer is interested in that item.

Analysis. Let OPT and OPT$'$ denote the optimal revenue of the pricing instance $(\mathcal{C}, \mathcal{I})$ and our instance $(G', \mathcal{C}')$ respectively. We will argue that OPT $=$ OPT$'$.

To show OPT $\leq$ OPT$'$, consider an optimal price function $p^* : \mathcal{I} \rightarrow \mathbb{R}_+$. Observe that any optimal price function must have $p^*(I) \in \mathcal{B}$ for all $I \in \mathcal{I}$: Otherwise, suppose that

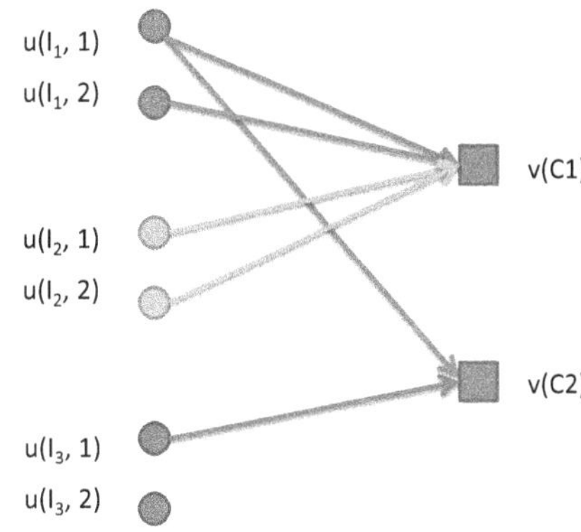

Figure 2: The graph G' obtained from the reduction.

$B' < p^*(I) < B$ for some $B', B \in \mathcal{B}$ that are consecutive in values. We could have increased $p^*(I)$ to B because any consumer C who can afford I will still be able to afford it with the new price. Let $\mathcal{C}^* \subseteq \mathcal{C}$ be the set of consumers who contribute to the value of OPT, i.e. consumers who made purchases. For each consumer $C \in \mathcal{C}^*$, let $\sigma(C) \in S_C$ denote the item with minimum price $p^*(I)$ in S_C. This is the item that consumer C purchases.

Our strategy to collect revenue is as follows: For each $I \in \mathcal{I}$, each company $\mathsf{comp}(I, p^*(I))$ puts its seed at $u(I, p^*(I))$. The seeds of other companies are not placed anywhere. Now consider each node $v(C)$ for $C \in \mathcal{C}^*$ and let $I^* = \sigma(C)$. It suffices to argue that the revenue we get from this node is $p^*(I^*)$. Notice that there is an edge $u(I^*, p^*(I^*))v(C) \in E$, so node $v(C)$ adopts product $\mathsf{comp}(I^*, p^*(I^*))$. Since $I \in S_C$ if and only if $v(C)$ adopts $\mathsf{comp}(I, p(I))$, it must be the case that $\mathsf{comp}(I^*, p^*(I^*))$ is ranked highest w.r.t. $\preceq_{v(C)}$ (because the price $p^*(I^*)$ is lowest). This means that node $v(C)$ picks $\mathsf{comp}(I^*, p^*(I^*))$ and therefore pays the price of $p^*(I^*)$.

Next, we prove that OPT$'$ $\leq$ OPT. Let $\mathcal{C}^* \subseteq \mathcal{C}'$ be the set of companies who placed the seeds in the optimal strategy. We partition $\mathcal{C}^*$ into $\mathcal{C}^* = \bigcup_{I\in\mathcal{I}} \mathcal{C}^*_I$ where $\mathcal{C}^*_I$ contains the companies of the form $\mathsf{comp}(I, B)$ for some B.

CLAIM 10. *For any $I \in \mathcal{I}$, we can assume without loss of generality that $|\mathcal{C}^*_I| \in \{0, 1\}$.*

PROOF. Assume that there are $B, B' \in \mathcal{B}$ such that both $\mathsf{comp}(I, B)$ and $\mathsf{comp}(I, B')$ belong to $\mathcal{C}^*_I$ such that $B < B'$. We argue that no node $v(C)$ buys $u(I, B')$ which allows us to remove the seed at $u(I, B')$ while preserving the revenue. Assume otherwise that some $v(C)$ bought $u(I, B')$. From the construction, there must also be an edge $u(I, B)v(C)$ and $u(I, B') \prec_{v(C)} u(I, B)$. This is impossible because $v(C)$ would have preferred to buy $u(I, B)$ instead. □

The above claim allows us to "recover" the price function p^* for $(\mathcal{C}, \mathcal{I})$ that collects the same revenue. We set the price $p^*(I) = \infty$ if $|\mathcal{C}^*_I| = 0$; otherwise, we set $p^*(I) = B$ where $\mathsf{comp}(I, B) \in \mathcal{C}^*_I$. Now, let $V^* \subseteq V$ be the subset of nodes that contribute to the value of OPT'. For each consumer C such that $v(C) \in V^*$, let $\mathsf{comp}(I^*, B^*)$ be the product chosen by $v(C)$, so node $v(C)$ contributes B^* to the value of OPT. We argue that consumer C also pays the value of B^* with respect to the price p^*. This will conclude the proof.

Assume to the contrary that, in the pricing instance $(\mathcal{C}, \mathcal{I})$, consumer C buys some item $\tilde{I}$ with $p^*(\tilde{I}) < B^*$. This implies that $u(\tilde{I}, p^*(\tilde{I}))v(C) \in E$, and that $\mathsf{comp}(I^*, B^*) \prec_{v(C)} \mathsf{comp}(\tilde{I}, p^*(\tilde{I}))$. Hence, $\mathsf{comp}(\tilde{I}, p^*(\tilde{I}))$ would have been bought instead of $\mathsf{comp}(I^*, B^*)$.

Gap Analysis. Notice that the size of the instance is $|V(G')| \leq |\mathcal{C}||\mathcal{I}|$, so the hardness gap $\log^{1-\epsilon}(|\mathcal{C}| + |\mathcal{I}|)$ translates to $\Omega(\log^{1-\epsilon}|V(G')|)$ as desired. We conclude by stating our result formally.

THEOREM 11. *Let $\epsilon > 0$ be any sufficiently small constant. Then, unless $\mathsf{NP} \subseteq \mathsf{DTIME}(n^{\text{poly}\log n})$, there is no $\log^{1-\epsilon} n$ approximation algorithm for sponsored viral marketing problem even when each advitiser has unlimited budget.*

Notice that this result proves the *near*-optimality of our algorithm presented in the previous section.

5. EXPERIMENTAL EVALUATION

We experimentally tested our algorithms against several heuristic baselines via simulations. In addition to Algorithm 2 from Section 3, we introduce a heuristic extension of this algorithm. The point of this section is to empirically show that a coordinated strategy by the social network provider will always outperform uncoordinated advertisers. All the simulations in this section were run on real social network data. All the code was written in C and run on an Intel Core 2 Duo running Ubuntu 12.04.2.

We ran our simulations on social networks made available by the Stanford Network Analysis Project (SNAP)[3]. More specifically, we used a Slasdot user directed network collected in April 2009 (82168 nodes, 948464 edges), a DBLP coauthorship dataset (317080 nodes, 1049866 edges), and a directed Epinions who-trusts-whom social network (75879 nodes, 508837 edges).

Recall that Algorithm 2 identifies the highest tier of commissions and assigns seeds only to them. It is indeed sometimes better to omit the low commission advertisers as they may decrease overall revenue by taking away nodes from higher commission advertisers. In the case that large parts of the network are not influenced (e.g., if the propagation probability is low), however, it is better to include these lower commission advertisers as they do not interfere. Additionally, there are business reasons why they should not be neglected. Motivated by this, we introduce a heuristic version of our algorithm (Algorithm 2H, described below) to avoid this issue.

We compared the following algorithms:

- **Algorithm 2** is the algorithm from Section 3.
- **Random** assigns seeds uniformly at random (included as a baseline).
- **GreedyEach** is the result when each advertiser picks seeds independently of each of the others.

[3]https://snap.stanford.edu

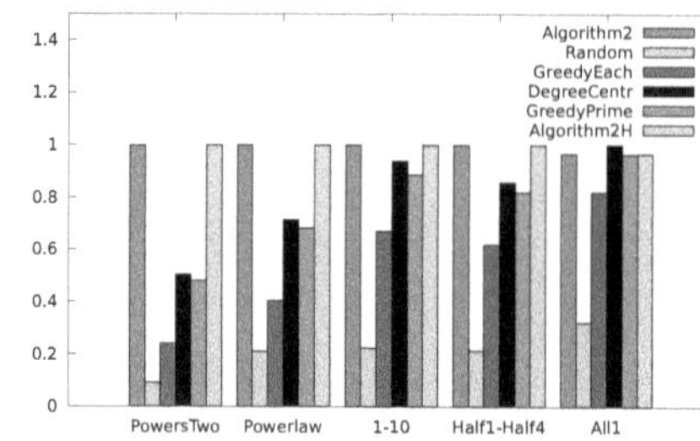

(a) Slashdot

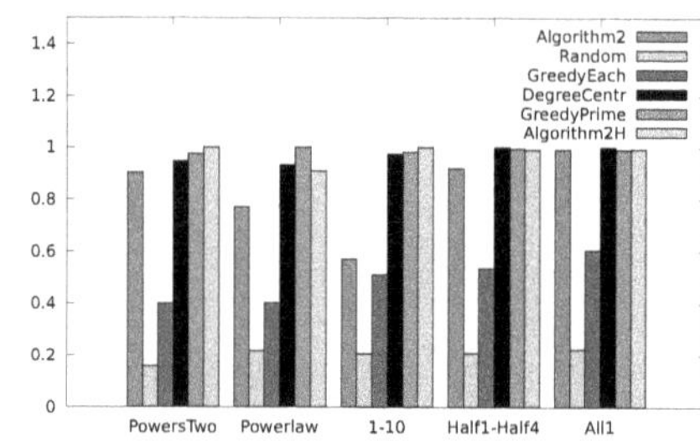

(b) DBLP

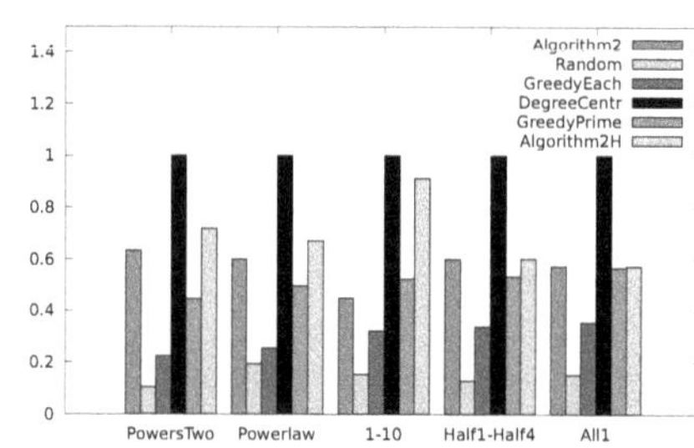

(c) Epinion

Figure 3: Relative performance of algorithms with different commission (p) distributions. (Note: the revenues for each distribution have been normalized by the best algorithm to make all of them fit the same scale.)

- **DegreeCentrality** is a heuristic in which the highest degree nodes are used as seeds. The higher commission advertisers are assigned the higher degree nodes.
- **GreedyPrime** computes the greedy solution for all the advertiser's seeds assuming equal commissions and then assigns these nodes to the advertisers in non-increasing order of commission.
- **Algorithm 2H** is a heuristic version of Algorithm 2. It adds unassigned seeds from Algorithm 2 to the highest degree unassigned nodes and returns the better of this solution and that of Algorithm 2 (thus the performance of Algorithm 2H will never be worse than that of Algorithm 2).

Note that the **GreedyEach** algorithm is the most likely algorithm used by uncoordinated advertisers. We will show that the other algorithms (except Random) outperform this one empirically with many different parameter settings.

In the runs of each of the greedy algorithms, the revenue was estimated using 100 runs of simulation. Using more runs

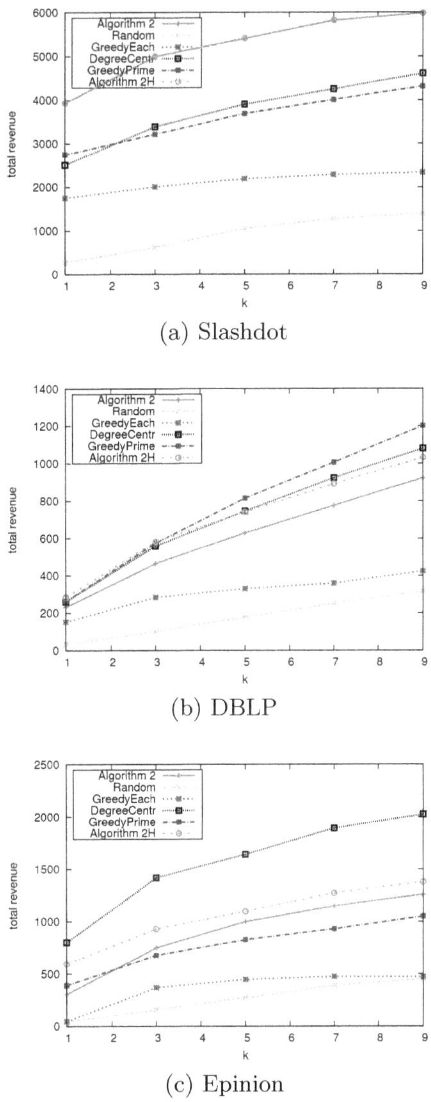

(a) Slashdot

(b) DBLP

(c) Epinion

Figure 4: Varying the number of seeds per advertiser (k) on all data sets

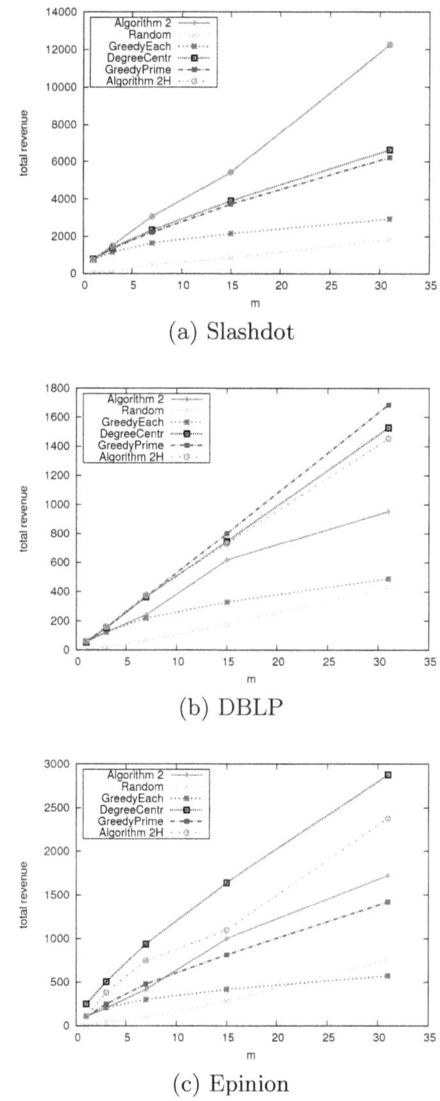

(a) Slashdot

(b) DBLP

(c) Epinion

Figure 5: Varying the number advertiser (m) on all data sets

did not significantly change the results. The final evaluation of each algorithm was performed with 10,000 runs of simulation. All the values in the following graphs are the means of ten independent runs of each algorithm.

Since our algorithm divides advertisers into tiers by commission, we first studied the effect of the advertiser commission distribution on the performance of each of the above algorithms. In particular, we tried the following distributions:

- PowersTwo: $1, 2^1, 2^2, \ldots, 2^9$
- PowerLaw: $1, 1, 1, 1, 1, 1, 1, 1, 2, 2, 2, 2, 4, 4, 8$
- 1-10: $1, 2, 3, \ldots, 10$
- Half1Half4: 5 1's, 5 4's
- All1: 10 1's

From Figure 3, we can see that Algorithm 2H was best or close to best for all distributions in Slashdot and DBLP. For the Epinions dataset, the degree centrality heuristic was consistently the best. The connectivity of this network is such that using high degree nodes works better for it than the greedy method.

For the remaining experiments, we set default values and varied parameters one-by-one to see the effect this would have on the performance of the algorithms. Unless otherwise stated, all the following results used a uniform propagation probability of $P = 0.01$ (1%), fifteen advertisers with commissions distributed by a power law as described above ($m = 15$), and $k = 5$ seeds per advertiser.

Figure 4 shows the effect of varying the number of seeds per advertiser (k). In the case of the Slashdot data set, Algorithm 2 performs the best. The DBLP dataset shows a case in which the heuristic performs better since it spreads unseeded advertiser on unreached parts of the network. As in the previous figure, the degree centrality heuristic is best on the Epinions data. Similar results can be observed when varying the number of advertisers (m) in Figure 5.

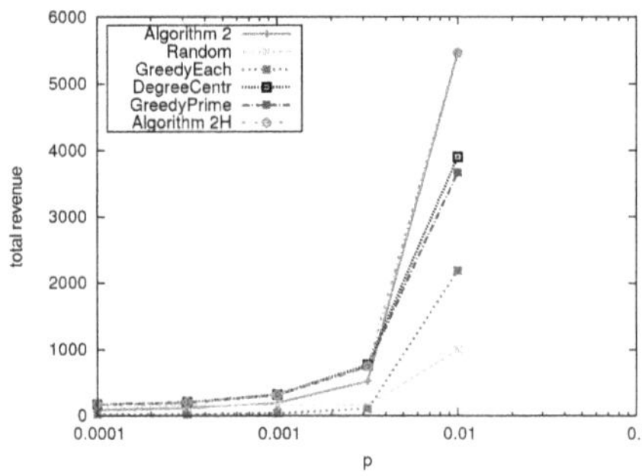

(a) Slashdot

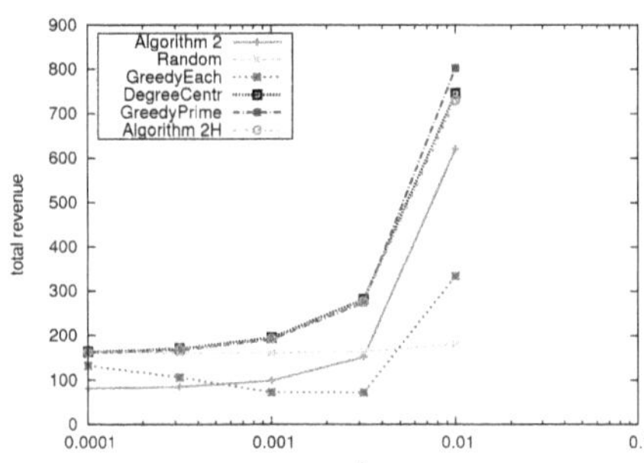

(b) DBLP

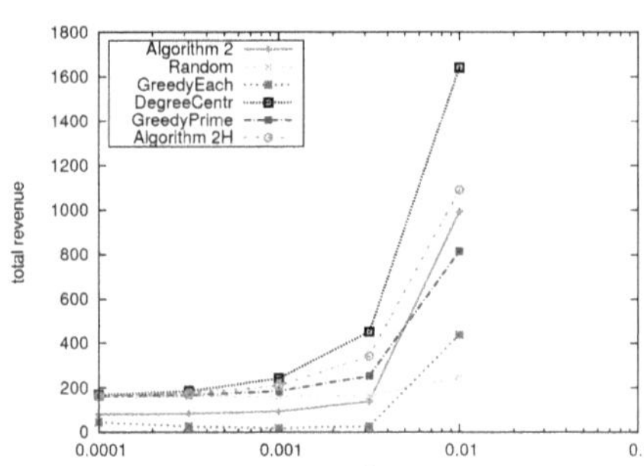

(c) Epinion

Figure 6: Varying the propagation probability (P) on all data sets

When we vary the propagation probability in Figure 6, the advantage of Algorithm 2H over Algorithm 2 becomes apparent. For very low probabilities, there are parts of the social network that advertisers are not reaching and it makes sense to seed these with the low commission advertisers. Hence, we see Algorithm 2H outperform Algorithm 2 in most cases. However, when the probability rises to the extent that most of the network is being influenced, Algorithm 2 rapidly catches up.

Note that in all cases our algorithms greatly outperform GreedyEach, the result when all the advertisers greedily assign their seeds in an uncoordinated manner. This demonstrates the advantage of a coordinated strategy by the social network owner over uncoordinated efforts by the advertisers.

6. RELATED WORK

There is a large body of work studying the correlation of activity among friends in online communities; see examples in [20, 32, 34]. Most are forms of diffusion research, built on the premise that user engagement is contagious. As such, a user is more likely to adopt new products or behaviors if her friends do so [4, 29]; and large cascades of behavior can be triggered by the actions of a few individuals [20, 32].

A number of theoretical models have been developed to model influence cascades [14, 30]. In the context of social networks, the threshold model [24] and the independent cascade model [22] are widely applied. The seminal work of Kempe et al. [28] includes the general cascade model which forms the basis of our work. There has also been a long line of work on viral marketing starting from [15, 31].

The concept of competition in influence maximization has also been studied extensively in recent years. A paper that adopts a follower's perspective, by Carnes et al. [10], considers an advertiser trying to maximize influence when a competing technology is already present. An extension of the threshold models under the competitive setting was studied by Borodin et al. [7] and another model was proposed by Bharathi et al. [5]. In more recent work, He et al. [26] consider the setting where an advertiser wants to *block* the influence of a competitor. Another recent paper that considers competition and how to defeat it in an adversarial setting is due to Shirazipourazad et al. [35].

Goyal-Kearns [23] study competitive contagion in networks and explore equilibria and price of anarchy. Tzoumas et al. [37] study questions around the existence of pure strategy Nash equilibria by focusing on 2-player competitive diffusion games. More recently Goldberg-Liu [21] provide approximation algorithms for finding the smallest set of nodes that can trigger a cascade that results in every node in the graph adopting the technology.

Datta et al. [13] consider viral marketing with multiple products with a profit maximization setting that is similar to ours. They study the problem of selecting seed nodes for multiple products to maximize the overall influence. Like us, they have a maximum budget for each product and have a certain set of allowed seeds corresponding to each product. Their work differs from ours in two fundamental ways: (1) they consider a non-competitive setting in the sense that each node can get influenced by multiple products and end up adopting more than one; and (2) they enforce a hard constraint on each node on how many different products may choose it as a seed. Notice that our problem is far more general given that we consider a competitive model with individual users having their preferences across products. A very recent work on similar lines is due to Borodin et al. [6]. Their setting is similar to us in that there are competitive agents such as advertisers who want to spread their ads or products on the network, and a centralized social network owner who wishes to optimize total influence (or social welfare). However, they consider the game theoretic problem where each advertiser has a true demand on number of seeds they would like to instantiate and the social network owner want to design mechanisms where each agent is incentivized to reveal their true demand. There have been several other papers as well in general influence maximization type questions and we list some other recent ones here [1, 2, 8, 25].

7. CONCLUSIONS

As several companies fight for the attention of users in the social context to leverage influence spread, competition for the same users on similar products becomes inevitable. A natural question that arises in this framework is how do the social network advertisement managers reconcile all these conflicting objectives from various companies, while maximizing their profits, by taking advantage of users' influence on one another. In this paper, we explore a very generic framework that takes the social network's viewpoint with the goal of revenue maximization. The holistic theoretical study here captures the motivation, algorithmic techniques, as well as the boundaries or limits of this framework. Specifically, in the case of unlimited budgets, we show a polynomial time $O(\log n)$ approximation algorithm for maximizing the expected revenue and further prove that no polynomial time approximation algorithm exists, assuming $\mathsf{NP} \not\subseteq \mathsf{DTIME}(n^{\text{poly}\log n})$, with a guarantee of $O(\log^{1-\epsilon} n)$. In the limited budget setting, the problem appears intractable as we show that no $O(n^{1-\epsilon})$-approximation algorithm exists under the assumption that $\mathsf{P} \neq \mathsf{NP}$. In terms of experimental evaluation, we tested our techniques against several baseline heuristics and demonstrated that a coordinated strategy by the social network operator will vastly outperform an uncoordinated strategy by the advertisers.

From an overall motivational standpoint, several directions remain to be explored. It would be interesting to extend our work to a setting where advertisers' demands can be admitted online, as often in practice new advertisers, budgets, and products arrive in a continuous manner, without a clean notion of timesteps or rounds. Further, the associated budgets could be changing with time and/or may need to be handled across various data centers. Another orthogonal yet very important consideration is that in a real social network, often one can only learn approximate edge influence probabilities with varying degrees of accuracy, and these may even change with time.

There also remain specific theoretical open questions to be addressed and we mention two here. First, recall that in our case the preference function $\preceq_v$ of each node is random. That is, if there are many products in the consideration set at the same time, each user picks the product in a random fashion. The hardness result however does not apply to this case. Secondly, if the seeds of each company could be placed at any node, the hardness result would not apply. Conceivably there may be a good approximation algorithm even in the limited budget setting.

8. REFERENCES

[1] D. Agrawal, C. Budak, and A. El Abbadi. Information diffusion in social networks: observing and affecting what society cares about. In *CIKM*, pages 2609–2610, 2011.

[2] D. Agrawal, C. Budak, and A. El Abbadi. Information diffusion in social networks: Observing and influencing societal interests. *PVLDB*, 4(12):1512–1513, 2011.

[3] A. Anagnostopoulos, R. Kumar, and M. Mahdian. Influence and correlation in social networks. In *KDD'08*.

[4] L. Backstrom, D. Huttenlocher, J. Kleinberg, and X. Lan. Group formation in large social networks: membership, growth, and evolution. In *KDD '06*.

[5] S. Bharathi, D. Kempe, and M. Salek. Competitive influence maximization in social networks. In *WINE*, 2007.

[6] A. Borodin, M. Braverman, B. Lucier, and J. Oren. Strategyproof mechanisms for competitive influence in networks. In *WWW*, 2013.

[7] A. Borodin, Y. Filmus, and J. Oren. Threshold models for competitive influence in social networks. In *WINE*, 2010.

[8] C. Budak, D. Agrawal, and A. El Abbadi. Limiting the spread of misinformation in social networks. In *WWW*, pages 665–674, 2011.

[9] G. Călinescu, C. Chekuri, M. Pál, and J. Vondrák. Maximizing a monotone submodular function subject to a matroid constraint. *SIAM J. Comput.*, 40(6):1740–1766, 2011. Also in IPCO'07 and STOC'08.

[10] T. Carnes, C. Nagarajan, S. M. Wild, and A. van Zuylen. Maximizing influence in a competitive social network: a follower's perspective. In *ICEC*, pages 351–360, 2007.

[11] P. Chalermsook, J. Chuzhoy, S. Kannan, and S. Khanna. Improved hardness results for profit maximization pricing problems with unlimited supply. In *APPROX-RANDOM*, pages 73–84, 2012.

[12] P. Chalermsook, B. Laekhanukit, and D. Nanongkai. Graph products revisited: Tight approximation hardness of induced matching, poset dimension, and more. In *SODA*, 2013.

[13] S. Datta, A. Majumder, and N. Shrivastava. Viral marketing for multiple products. In *ICDM*, 2010.

[14] P. S. Dodds and D. J. Watts. A generalized model of social and biological contagion. *Journal of Theoretical Biology*, 2005.

[15] P. Domingos and M. Richardson. Mining the network value of customers. In *KDD*, pages 57–66, 2001.

[16] J. Edwards. Chart: Facebook's sponsored stories are way more effective than display ads. *Business Insider*, 2012.

[17] A. Efrati. Google expected to surpass facebook in display-ad sales. *The Wall Street Journal*, 2012.

[18] S. Fiegerman. Google will overtake facebook in u.s. display ad revenue this year [report]. *Mashable Business*, 2012.

[19] M. Fisher, G. Nemhauser, and L. Wolsey. An analysis of approximations for maximizing submodular set functions-II. In M. Balinski and A. Hoffman, editors, *Polyhedral Combinatorics*, volume 8 of *Mathematical Programming Studies*, pages 73–87. Springer Berlin Heidelberg, 1978.

[20] M. Gladwell. *The Tipping Point: How Little Things Can Make a Big Difference*. 2002.

[21] S. Goldberg and Z. Liu. The diffusion of networking technology. In *SODA*, 2013.

[22] J. Goldenberg, B. Libai, and E. Muller. Talk of the Network: A Complex Systems Look at the Underlying Process of Word-of-Mouth. *Marketing Letters*, 2001.

[23] S. Goyal and M. Kearns. Competitive contagion in networks. In *STOC*, pages 759–774, 2012.

[24] M. Granovetter. Threshold Models of Collective Behavior. *The American Journal of Sociology*, 1978.

[25] J. D. Hartline, V. S. Mirrokni, and M. Sundararajan. Optimal marketing strategies over social networks. In *WWW*, pages 189–198, 2008.

[26] X. He, G. Song, W. Chen, and Q. Jiang. Influence blocking maximization in social networks under the competitive linear threshold model. In *SDM*, pages 463–474, 2012.

[27] C.-C. Huang and Z. Svitkina. Donation center location problem. In *FSTTCS*, pages 227–238, 2009.

[28] D. Kempe, J. Kleinberg, and E. Tardos. Maximizing the spread of influence through a social network. In *KDD'03*.

[29] J. Leskovec, L. A. Adamic, and B. A. Huberman. The dynamics of viral marketing. *ACM Trans. Web*, 2007.

[30] M. E. J. Newman. Spread of epidemic disease on networks. *Physical Review E*, 2002.

[31] M. Richardson and P. Domingos. Mining knowledge-sharing sites for viral marketing. In *KDD*, pages 61–70, 2002.

[32] E. M. Rogers. *Diffusion of Innovations*. Simon and Schuster, 2003.

[33] M. Rogowsky. Will facebook generate more revenue than google? *Quora*, 2012.

[34] D. M. Romero, B. Meeder, and J. Kleinberg. Differences in the mechanics of information diffusion. In *WWW '11*.

[35] S. Shirazipourazad, B. Bogard, H. Vachhani, A. Sen, and P. Horn. Influence propagation in adversarial setting: how to defeat competition with least amount of investment. In *CIKM*, 2012.

[36] S. Simon and K. R. Apt. Choosing products in social networks. In *WINE*, 2012.

[37] V. Tzoumas, C. Amanatidis, and E. Markakis. A game-theoretic analysis of a competitive diffusion process over social networks. In *WINE*, 2012.

Spy vs. Spy: Rumor Source Obfuscation

Giulia Fanti
University of California, Berkeley
fanti@berkeley.edu

Peter Kairouz
University of Illinois at Urbana-Champaign
kairouz2@illinois.edu

Sewoong Oh
University of Illinois at Urbana-Champaign
swoh@illinois.edu

Pramod Viswanath
University of Illinois at Urbana-Champaign
pramodv@illinois.edu

ABSTRACT

Anonymous messaging platforms, such as Secret, Yik Yak, and Whisper, have emerged as important social media for sharing one's thoughts without the fear of being judged by friends, family, or the public. Further, such anonymous platforms are crucial in nations with authoritarian governments; the right to free expression and sometimes the personal safety of the author of the message depend on anonymity. Whether for fear of judgment or personal endangerment, it is crucial to keep anonymous the identity of the user who initially posted a sensitive message. In this paper, we consider an adversary who observes a snapshot of the spread of a message at a certain time. Recent advances in rumor source detection shows that the existing messaging protocols are vulnerable against such an adversary. We introduce a novel messaging protocol, which we call adaptive diffusion, and show that it spreads the messages fast and achieves a perfect obfuscation of the source when the underlying contact network is an infinite regular tree: all users with the message are nearly equally likely to have been the origin of the message. Experiments on a sampled Facebook network show that it effectively hides the location of the source even when the graph is finite, irregular and has cycles.

Categories and Subject Descriptors

G.2.2 [**Graph Theory**]: Network problems, Graph algorithms

Keywords

Anonymous Social Media; Rumor Spreading; Privacy

1. INTRODUCTION

Microblogging platforms form a core aspect of the fabric of the present Internet; popular examples include Twitter and Facebook. Users propagate short messages (texts, images, videos) through the platform via local friendship links. The forwarding of messages often occurs through built-in mechanisms that rely on user input, such as clicking "like" or "share" with regards to a particular post. Brevity of message, fluidity of user interface, and trusted party communication combine to make these microblogging platforms a major communication mode of modern times. There has been tremendous recent interest in the privacy implications of these platforms, as evidenced by the explosive growth of *anonymous microblogging* platforms, like Secret[1] [1], Whisper [2], and Yik Yak [3]. These platforms enable users to share messages with friends without leaking the message author's identity. In such applications, it is crucial to hide the identity of the user who initially posted the message.

Existing anonymous messaging services store both messages and authorship information on centralized servers, which makes them vulnerable to government subpoenas, hacking, or direct company access. A more robust solution would be to store this information in a distributed fashion; each node would know only its own friends, and message authorship information would never be transmitted to any party. Distributed systems are more robust to monitoring due to lack of central points of failure. However, even under distributed architectures, simple anonymous messaging protocols (such as those used by commercial anonymous microblogging apps) are still vulnerable against an adversary with side information, as proved in recent advances in rumor source detection. In this work, we study in depth a basic building block of the messaging protocol that would underpin truly anonymous microblogging platform – *broadcasting a single message on a contact network with the goal of obfuscating the source* under strong adversarial conditions. Specifically, we consider contact networks that represent a social graph among users of the service.

A natural strategy for preventing source identification by an adversary would be to spread the message as fast as possible; with reliable connection to infrastructure like the Internet, this could be in principle done nearly instantaneously. If all users receive the message instantaneously, any user is equally likely to have been the source. However, this strategy is not available in many of the key real-life scenarios we are considering. For instance, in social networks, messages

[1]Since the first writing of this paper, Secret shut down. However, we believe this is not due to lack of demand for anonymous messaging platforms, as other similar platforms are seeing widespread success.

SIGMETRICS'15, June 15–19, 2015, Portland, OR, USA.

http://dx.doi.org/10.1145/2745844.2745866.

are spread based on users approving the message via liking, sharing or retweeting (to enable social filtering and also to avoid spamming) – this scenario naturally has inherent random delays associated with when the user happens to encounter the message and whether or not she decides to "like" the message. Indeed, standard models of rumor spreading in networks explicitly model such random delays via a *diffusion* process: messages are spread independently over different edges with a fixed probability of spreading (discrete time model) or an exponential time to spread (continuous time model).

Related work. Anonymous communication has been a popular research topic for decades. For instance, anonymous point-to-point communication allows a sender to communicate with a receiver without the receiver learning the sender's identity. A great deal of successful work has emerged in this area, including Tor [8], Freenet [5], Free Haven [7], and Tarzan [10]. In contrast to this body of work, we address the problem of anonymously *broadcasting* a message over an underlying contact network (e.g., a social network). Anonymous broadcast communication has been most studied in context of the dining cryptographers' (DC) problem. We diverge from the vast literature on this topic [4, 6, 11, 12, 23] in approach and formulation. We consider statistical spreading models rather than cryptographic encodings, accommodate computationally unbounded adversaries, and consider arbitrary network structures rather than a fully connected network.

Within the realm of statistical message spreading models, the problem of detecting the origin of an epidemic or the source of a rumor has been studied under the *diffusion* model. Recent advances in [20, 19, 24, 18, 9, 13, 25, 17, 16, 14, 15] show that it is possible to identify the source within a few hops with high probability. Drawing an analogy to epidemics, we refer to a person who has received the message as 'infected' and the act of passing the message as 'spreading the infection'. Consider an adversary who has access to the underlying *contact network* of friendship links and the snapshot of infected nodes at a certain time. The problem of locating a rumor source, first posed in [20], naturally corresponds to graph-centrality-based inference algorithms: for a continuous time model, [20, 19] used the rumor centrality measure to correctly identify the source after time T (with probability converging to a positive number for large d-regular and random trees, and with probability proportional to $1/\sqrt{T}$ for lines). The probability of identifying the source increases even further when multiple infections from the same source are observed [24]. With multiple sources of infections, spectral methods have been proposed for estimating the number of sources and the set of source nodes in [18, 9]. When infected nodes are allowed to recover as in the susceptible-infected-recovered (SIR) model, Jordan centrality was proposed in [13, 25] to estimate the source. In [25], it is shown that the Jordan center is still within a bounded hop distance from the true source with high probability, independent of the number of infected nodes. Under natural and diffusion-based message spreading – as seen in almost every content-sharing platform today – an adversary with some side-information can identify the rumor source with high confidence. We overcome this vulnerability by asking the reverse question: can we design messaging protocols that spread fast while protecting the anonymity of the source?

Model. We focus on anonymous microblogging built atop an underlying contact network, such as a network of phone contacts or Facebook friends. In such systems, the designer has some control over the spreading rate, by introducing artificial delays on top of the usual random delays due to users' approval of the messages. We model this physical setup as a discrete-time system, where any individual receiving a message approves it immediately at the next timestep, at which point the protocol determines how much delay to introduce before sending the message to each of her uninfected neighbors. Given this control, the system designer wishes to design a spreading protocol that makes inference on the source of the message difficult. The assumption that all nodes are willing to approve and pass the message is not new. Such assumptions are common in the analysis of rumor spreading [20, 19, 25], and our deviation from those standard models is that we are operating in discrete time and approvals are immediate.

Adversary. Following the adversarial model assumed in prior work on rumor source detection [20, 19, 25], we assume the adversary knows the whole underlying contact network and, at a certain time, it observes a snapshot of the state of all the nodes, i.e. who has received the message thus far. This adversary is strong in the sense that it sees the whole contact network as well as every node's state, but it is also limited in the sense that the adversary is not aware of when (or from whom) a particular node received the message. This model captures an adversary that is able to indirectly observe the contents of users' devices without actively compromising the devices; for instance, if the message in question contains the time and location of a protest, then the adversary learns a snapshot of the infection at a given point in time by observing who attends the protest. This adversarial model also captures an adversary that is able to monitor the network state more closely, but only at a high cost. As such, it cannot afford to continuously monitor state. We design a new anonymous messaging protocol, which we call *adaptive diffusion*, that is inherently distributed and provides strong anonymity guarantees under this adversarial model. We discuss other plausible adversarial models in Section 5.

Spreading. At time $t = 0$, a single user $v^* \in V$ starts to spread a message on a contact network $G = (V, E)$ where users and contacts are represented by nodes and edges, respectively. Upon receiving the message, a node can send the message to any of its neighbors. We assume a discrete-time system and model the delays due to user approval and intermittent network access via a deterministic delay of one time unit. Therefore, a message always propagates with a delay of at least one time unit. Our goal is to introduce appropriate random delays into the system in order to obfuscate the identity of the source v^*. After T timesteps, let $V_T \subseteq V$, G_T, and $N_T \triangleq |V_T|$ denote the set of infected nodes, the subgraph of G containing only V_T, and the number of infected nodes, respectively. At a certain time T, an adversary observes the infected subgraph G_T and produces an estimate $\hat{v}$ of the source v^* of the message (with probability of detection $P_D = \mathbb{P}(\hat{v} = v^*)$). Since the adversary is assumed to not have any prior information on which node is likely to be the source, we use the maximum likelihood estimator

$$\hat{v}_{\text{ML}} = \arg\max_{v \in G_T} \mathbb{P}(G_T|v). \quad (1)$$

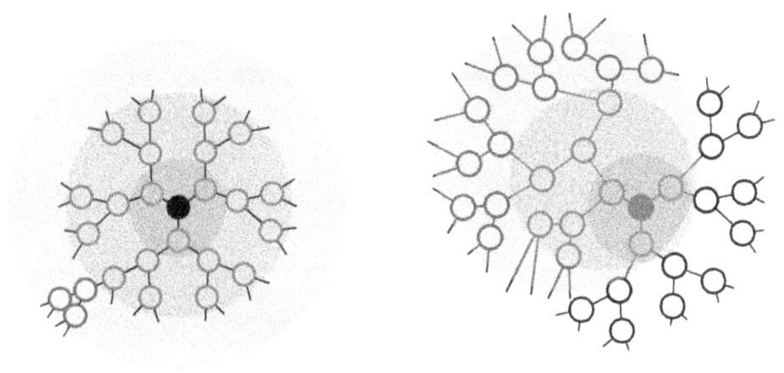

Figure 1: Illustration of a spread of infection when spreading immediately (left) and under the adaptive diffusion (right).

We wish to achieve the following performance metrics.

(*a*) We say a protocol has an *order-optimal rate of spread* if the expected time for the message to reach n nodes scales linearly compared to the time required by the fastest spreading protocol.

(*b*) We say a protocol achieves a *perfect obfuscation* if the probability of source detection for the maximum likelihood estimator conditioned on n nodes being infected is bounded by

$$\mathbb{P}(\,\hat{v}_{\rm ML} = v^* | N_T = n\,) \quad = \quad \frac{1}{n} + o\Big(\frac{1}{n}\Big)\,. \qquad (2)$$

Key insights. Figure 1 (left) illustrates an example of the spread when the message is propagated immediately upon reception. The source is indicated by a solid circle. This scheme spreads the message fast but the source is trivially identified as the center of the infected subgraph if the contact network is an infinite tree. This is true independent of the infection size. Even if we introduce some randomness at each node, the source will still be identified within a few hops. This is due to the fact that the source is close to some notion of the center of the infected subgraph [20, 25].

Since we do not know *a priori* when the adversary is going to attack, the main challenge is to ensure that the source is equally likely to be anywhere in the infection at *any given time*. Figure 1 (right) illustrates the main idea of our approach: we intentionally break the symmetry around the source. This is achieved by combining two insights illustrated in the two warm-up examples in Section 2. The first insight is that nodes farther away from the source should spread the infection faster. The second insight is that the spread should be coordinated in order to maintain a symmetric structure centered around a 'virtual source' node. This leads to the source node being anywhere in the infected subgraph with equal probability.

Contributions. We introduce a novel messaging protocol, which we call *adaptive diffusion*, with provable author anonymity guarantees against strong adversaries. Our protocol is inherently distributed and spreads messages fast, i.e., the time it takes adaptive diffusion to reach n users is at most twice the time it takes the fastest spreading scheme which immediately passes the message to all its neighbors.

We further prove that adaptive diffusion provides perfect obfuscation of the source when applied to regular tree contact networks. The source hides perfectly within all infected users, i.e., the likelihood of an infected user being the source of the infection is equal among all infected users. For a more general class of graphs which can be finite, irregular and have cycles, we provide results of numerical experiments on real-world social networks and synthetic networks showing that the protocol hides the source at nearly the best possible level of obfuscation.

Organization. The remainder of this paper is organized as follows. To warm up, we introduce, in Section 2, two messaging protocols customized for lines and trees. Combining the key insights of these two approaches, we introduce, in Section 3, a new messaging protocol called *adaptive diffusion* and analyze its performance theoretically and empirically, in Section 4. Section 5 discusses limitations and future work.

2. WARM-UP EXAMPLES

In this section, we discuss two special contact networks as warm-up examples: a line and a regular tree with degree larger than two. We provide two fully-distributed, customized messaging protocols, one for each case, and show that these protocols spread messages quickly while effectively hiding the source. However, these protocols fail to protect the identity of the source when applied to a broader class of contact networks. In particular, the "Line Protocol", which is developed for line contact networks, reveals the source with high probability when applied to a regular tree with degree larger than two. Similarly, the "Tree Protocol", developed for regular tree contact networks with degree greater than two, reveals the source with high probability when applied to a line. In Section 3, we introduce a novel messaging protocol, which we call *adaptive diffusion*, that combines the key ideas behind the two approaches presented in this section.

2.1 Spreading on a line

Given a contact network of an infinite line, consider the following deterministic spreading protocol. At time $t = 1$, the source node infects its left and right neighbors. At $t \geq 2$, the leftmost and rightmost infected nodes spread the message to their uninfected neighbors. Thus, the message spreads one hop to the left and one hop to the right of the true source at each timestep. This scheme spreads as fast as possible, infecting $N_T = 2T + 1$ nodes at time T, but the source is trivially identified as the center of the infection.

Adding a little bit of randomness can significantly decrease the probability of detection. Consider a discrete-time *random diffusion* model with a parameter $p \in (0, 1)$ where at each time t, an infected node infects its uninfected neighbor with probability p. Using the analysis from [20] where the continuous time version of this protocol was studied, we can show that this protocol spreads fast, infecting $\mathbb{E}[N_T] = 2pT + 1$ nodes on average at time T. Further, the probability of source detection $P_D = \mathbb{P}(\hat{v}_{\rm ML} = v^*)$ for the maximum likelihood estimator scales as $1/\sqrt{p(1-p)T}$. With $p = 1/2$ for example, this gives a simple messaging protocol with a probability of source detection vanishing at a rate of $1/\sqrt{T}$.

In what follows, we show that with an appropriate choice of *time-dependent* randomness, we can achieve almost perfect source obfuscation without sacrificing the spreading rate. The key insight is to add randomness such that all the infected nodes are (almost) equally likely to have been the origin of the infection (see Figure 2 and Equation (6)). This can be achieved by adaptively choosing the spreading rate such that *the farther away the infection is from the source the more likely it is to spread.* We now apply this insight to design precisely how fast the spread should be for each infected node at any timestep. A node v is designed to infect a neighbor at time $t \in \{1, 2, \ldots\}$ with probability

$$p_{v,t} \quad \triangleq \quad \frac{\delta_H(v, v^*) + 1}{t+1}\,, \tag{3}$$

where $\delta_H(v, v^*)$ is the hop distance between an infected node v at the boundary of infection and the source v^*. The details of this spreading model are summarized in Protocol 3 (Line Protocol).

The next proposition shows that this protocol achieves the two main goals of an anonymous messaging protocol: order-optimal spreading rate and close-to-perfect obfuscation.

PROPOSITION 2.1. *Suppose that the underlying contact network G is an infinite line, and one node v^* in G starts to spread a message according to Protocol 3 (Line Protocol) at time $t = 0$. At a certain time $T \geq 0$ an adversary estimates the location of the source v^* using the maximum likelihood estimator $\hat{v}_{\mathrm{ML}}$ defined in Equation (1). The following properties hold for the Line Protocol:*

(*a*) *the expected number of infected nodes at time T is $\mathbb{E}[N_T] = T + 1$;*

(*b*) *the probability of source detection at time T is upper bounded by*

$$\mathbb{P}(\hat{v}_{\mathrm{ML}} = v^*) \quad \leq \quad \frac{2T+1}{(T+1)^2}\,; \text{ and} \tag{4}$$

(*c*) *the expected hop-distance between the true source v^* and its estimate $\hat{v}_{\mathrm{ML}}$ is lower bounded by*

$$\mathbb{E}[\delta_H(v^*, \hat{v}_{\mathrm{ML}})] \quad \geq \quad \frac{T^3}{9(T+1)^2}\,. \tag{5}$$

The proof of the above proposition can be found in Appendix B. Compared to the (fastest-spreading) deterministic spreading model with a spreading rate of $N_T = 2T + 1$, The Line Protocol is slower by a factor of 2. This type of constant-factor loss in the spreading rate is inevitable: the only way to deviate from the deterministic spreading model is to introduce appropriate delays. The probability of detection is $2/\mathbb{E}[N_T] + o(1/\mathbb{E}[N_T])$, which is almost perfect obfuscation up to a factor of 2. Further, the expected distance of the true source from the ML source estimate scales linearly with the size of the infection $\mathbb{E}[N_T]$, which is the best separation one can hope to achieve.

To illustrate the power of the Line Protocol, we consider a fixed T and a finite ring graph of size larger than $2T + 1$, and compare the protocol to a simple random diffusion. If the source v^* is chosen uniformly at random on the ring and its message is spread according to the Line Protocol, then the probability of the source being detected given a set of infected nodes V_T is

$$\mathbb{P}(v^* = k \,|\, V_T) \quad = \quad \frac{1}{|V_T|} + O\Big(\frac{1}{|V_T|^2}\Big)\,, \tag{6}$$

for all $k \in V_T$ and $|V_T| \leq 2T + 1$. This follows from the exact computation of the posterior distribution, which can be found at the end of Appendix B. For an example with $|V_T| = 101$, Figure 2 illustrates how the Line Protocol flattens the posterior distribution compared to the random diffusion model. When messages are sent according to the random diffusion model, the source can only hide in the central part, which has width $O(\sqrt{T})$, leading to a probability of source detection on the order of $1/\sqrt{T}$ [20].

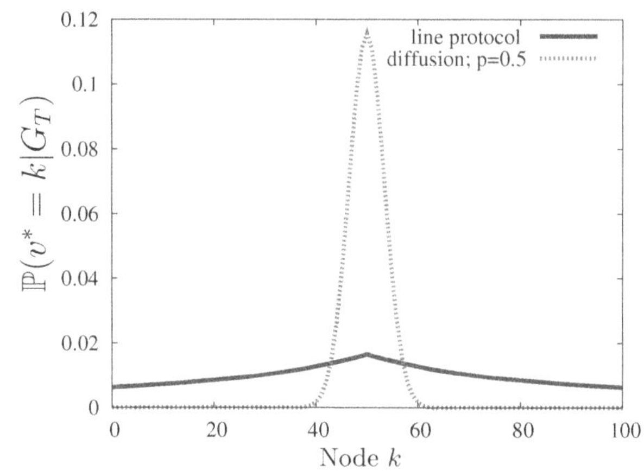

Figure 2: The Line Protocol has a close-to-uniform posterior distribution $\mathbb{P}(v^* = k \,|\, V_T = \{1, \ldots, 101\})$.

On an infinite line, the Line Protocol provides maximum protection, since the probability of detection scales as $1/\mathbb{E}[N_T]$ for any T. When the Line Protocol is applied to regular trees with degree larger than two, the infected subgraph contains exponentially many paths starting at v^* of length close to T. In such cases, the Jordan center (i.e., the node with the smallest maximum distance to every other node in the graph) matches the source with positive probability, as shown in Figure 3 for different d-regular trees.

2.2 Spreading on a regular tree

Consider the case when the underlying contact network is an infinite d-regular tree with d larger than two. Analogous to the line network, the fastest spreading protocol infects all the uninfected neighbors at each timestep. This spreads fast, infecting $N_T = 1 + d((d-1)^T - 1)/(d-2)$ nodes at time T, but the source is trivially identified as the center of the infected subtree. In this case, the infected subtree is a balanced regular tree where all leaves are at equal depth from the source.

Now consider a random diffusion model. At each timestep, each uninfected neighbor of an infected node is independently infected with probability p. In this case, $\mathbb{E}[N_T] = 1 + pd((d-1)^T - 1)/(d-2)$, and it was shown in [20] that the probability of correct detection for the maximum likelihood estimator of the rumor source is $\mathbb{P}(\hat{v}_{\mathrm{ML}} = v^*) \geq C_d$ for some positive constant C_d that only depends on the degree d. Hence, the source is only hidden in a constant number of nodes close to the center, even when the total number of infected nodes is arbitrarily large.

We now present a protocol that spreads the message fast ($N_T = O((d-1)^{T/2})$) and hides the source within a constant fraction of the infected nodes ($\mathbb{P}(\hat{v}_{\mathrm{ML}} = v^*) = O(1/N_T)$). This protocol keeps the infected subtree balanced: at any time t, all the leaves of the infected subtree are at the same hop distance from its center. Further, as we will see next, the leaves of the infected subtree are equally likely to have been

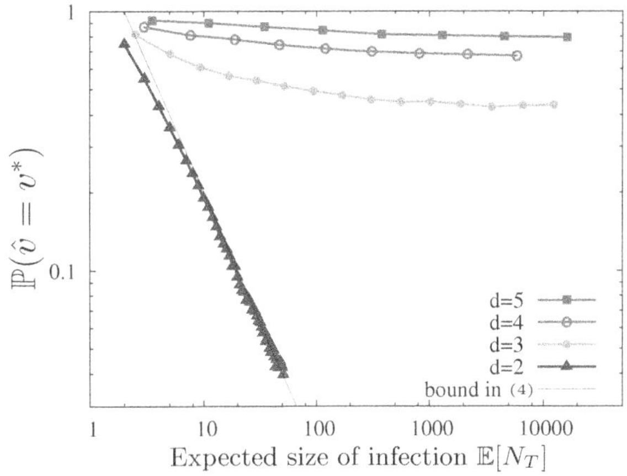

Figure 3: Detection probability versus the average size of infection on regular trees using Jordan center estimator, which is the ML estimate in case of a line ($d = 2$). For $d > 2$, the source is easily detected.

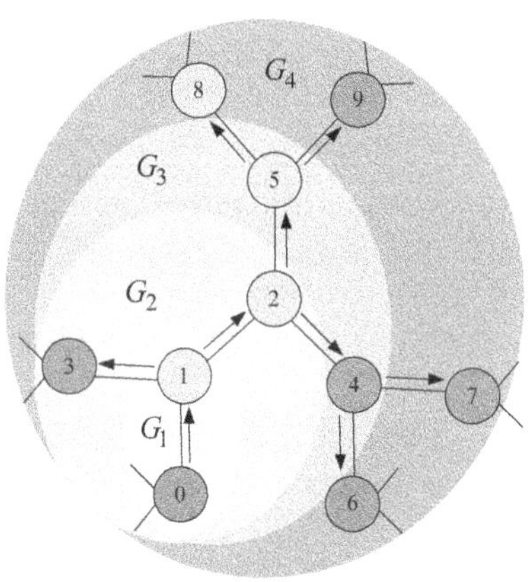

Figure 4: Spreading on a tree. The red node is the message source. Yellow nodes denote nodes that have been, are, or will be the center of the infected subtree.

the source. Figure 4 illustrates how this protocol spreads a message on a regular tree of degree 3. At $t = 1$, node 0 (the message author) infects one of its neighbors (node 1 in this example) uniformly at random. Node 1 will be referred to as the virtual source at $t = 1$. The virtual source at time t is the center of the infected subtree at time $2t$. At $t = 2$, node 1 infects all its uninfected neighbors, making the infected subgraph G_2 a balanced tree with node 1 at the center. Among the uninfected neighbors of node 1, one node is chosen to be the new virtual source (node 2 in the example). The message then spreads to the uninfected neighbors of node 2 at time $t = 3$, and then to their neighbors at time $t = 4$ making G_4 a balanced tree with node 2 at the center. Notice that any given time t, all leaves are equally likely to have been the source. This follows form the symmetric structure of G_t. The distributed implementation of this spreading algorithm is given in Protocol 4 (Tree Protocol).

The Tree Protocol ensures that the source can hide among the leaf nodes of the infected subtree, i.e. all leaves are equally likely to have been the source. Since a significant fraction of the infected nodes are at the leaf, this protocol achieves an almost *perfect obfuscation*.

PROPOSITION 2.2. *Suppose that the underlying contact network G is an infinite d-regular tree with $d > 2$, and one node v^* in G starts to spread a message according to Protocol 4 (Tree Protocol) at time $t = 0$. At a certain time $T \geq 1$ an adversary estimates the location of the source v^* using the maximum likelihood estimator $\hat{v}_{\text{ML}}$. Then the following properties hold for the Tree Protocol:*

(*a*) *the number of infected nodes at time $T \geq 1$ is at least*

$$N_T \;\geq\; \frac{(d-1)^{(T+1)/2}}{d-2}\;; \tag{7}$$

(*b*) *the probability of source detection for the maximum likelihood estimator at time T is*

$$\mathbb{P}(\hat{v}_{\text{ML}} = v^*) \;=\; \frac{d-1}{2+(d-2)N_T}\;;\; \textit{and} \tag{8}$$

(*c*) *the expected hop-distance between the true source v^* and its estimate $\hat{v}$ is lower bounded by*

$$\mathbb{E}[\delta_H(v^*, \hat{v}_{\text{ML}})] \;\geq\; \frac{T}{2}\,. \tag{9}$$

The proof of the above proposition can be found in Appendix C. Equation (7) shows that the spreading rate of the Tree Protocol is $O((d-1)^{T/2})$, which is slower than the deterministic spreading model that infects $O((d-1)^T)$ nodes at time T. This is inevitable, as we explained in relation to the Line Protocol.

Although this protocol spreads fast and provides an almost perfect obfuscation on a tree with degree larger than two, it fails when the contact network is a line. There are only two leaves in a line, so at any given time T, the source can be detected with probability 1/2, independent of the size of the infected subgraph. Another drawback of this approach, is that even in the long run, not every node receives the message. For instance, the neighbors of the source node that are not chosen in the first step are never infected. In the following section, we address these issues and propose a new messaging protocol that combines the key ideas of both spreading models presented in this section.

3. ADAPTIVE DIFFUSION

Section 2 showed that by changing the infection rate and direction based on state variables, the source can hide from the adversary. In particular, the messaging protocols presented in Sections 2.1 and 2.2 provide provable anonymity guarantees for line graphs and d-regular trees with $d > 2$, respectively. However, the Line Protocol fails to protect the source on graphs with larger degree. Similarly, the Tree Protocol fails to protect the source on a line and does not pass the message to some of the nodes. To overcome these challenges, we use ideas from the Line Protocol (nodes farther away from the source spread message faster) and from the Tree Protocol (keep the infected subgraph balanced and keep the source closer to the leaves) to design a protocol that achieves perfect obfuscation and spreads fast on all regular trees, including lines. We call this protocol *adaptive diffusion* to emphasize the fact that unlike diffusion, the protocol adapts the infection rate and direction as a function of time.

We step through the intuition of the adaptive diffusion spreading model with an example, partially illustrated in

Figure 5. Suppose that the underlying contact network is an infinite d-regular tree. As illustrated in Figure 5, we ensure that the infected subgraph G_t at any even timestep $t \in \{2, 4, \ldots\}$ is a balanced tree of depth $t/2$, i.e. the hop distance from any leaf to the root (or the center of the graph) is $t/2$. We call the root node of G_t the "virtual source" at time t, and denote it by v_t. We use $v_0 = v^*$ to denote the true source. To keep the regular structure at even timesteps, we use the odd timesteps to transition from one regular subtree G_t to another one G_{t+2} with depth incremented by one.

Figure 5 illustrates two sample evolutions of infection, as per adaptive diffusion. The source $v^* = 0$ starts the infection at $t = 0$. At time $t = 1$, node 0 infects node 1 and passes the virtual source token to it, i.e. $v_2 = 1$ (we only define virtual sources for even timesteps). At time $t = 1$, node 1 infects its uninfected neighbors, nodes 2 and 3. Notice that it requires two timesteps to infect nodes $\{1, 2, 3\}$ in order to spread infection to G_2, which is a balanced tree of depth 1 rooted at node $v_2 = 1$. At time $t = 3$, the adaptive diffusion protocol has two choices, either to pass the virtual source token to one of node 1's neighbors that is not a previous virtual source, for example node 2 (Figure 5 left), or to keep the virtual source at node 1 (Figure 5 right). In the former case, it again takes two timesteps to spread infection to G_4, which is a balanced tree of depth 2 rooted at node $v_4 = 2$. In the latter case, only one timestep is required, but we add a unit time delay to be consistent with the previous case. Hence, $G_3 = G_4$ which is a balanced tree of depth 2 rooted at node $v_4 = 1$. This random infection process can be defined as a time-inhomogeneous (time-dependent) Markov chain over the state defined by the location of the current virtual source $\{v_t\}_{t \in \{0,2,4,\ldots\}}$.

By the symmetry of the underlying contact network (which we assume is an infinite d-regular tree) and the fact that the next virtual source is chosen uniformly at random among the neighbors of the current virtual source, it is sufficient to consider a Markov chain over the hop distance between the true source v^* and v_t, the virtual source at time t. Therefore, we design a Markov chain over the state

$$h_t \quad = \quad \delta_H(v^*, v_t) \,,$$

for even t. Figure 5 shows an example with $(h_2, h_4) = (1, 2)$ on the left and $(h_2, h_4) = (1, 1)$ on the right.

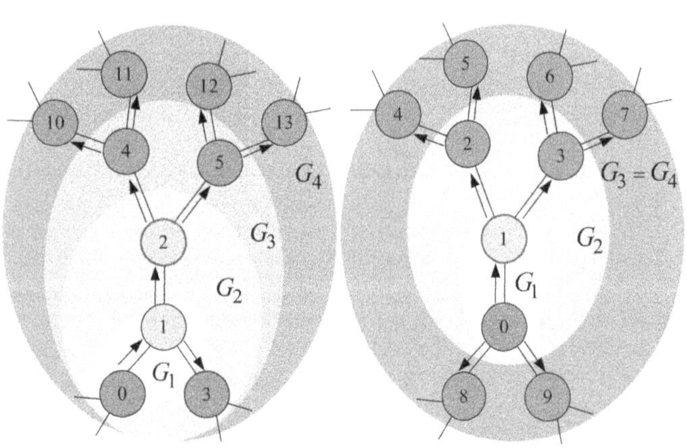

Figure 5: Adaptive diffusion over regular trees. Yellow nodes indicate the set of virtual sources (past and present), and for $T = 4$, the virtual source node is outlined in red.

At every even timestep, the protocol randomly determines whether to keep the virtual source token ($h_{t+2} = h_t$) or to pass it ($h_{t+2} = h_t + 1$). Using ideas from Section 2.1, we will construct an time-inhomogeneous Markov chain over $\{h_t\}_{t \in \{2,4,6,\ldots\}}$ by choosing appropriate transition probabilities as a function of time t and current state h_t. For an even t, we denote this probability by

$$\alpha_d(t, h) \;\triangleq\; \mathbb{P}\big(h_{t+2} = h_t | h_t = h\big) \,, \qquad (10)$$

where the subscript d denotes the degree of the underlying contact network. For the running example, at $t = 2$, the virtual source remains at the current node (right) with probability $\alpha_3(2, 1)$, or passes the virtual source to a neighbor with probability $1 - \alpha_3(2, 1)$ (left). The parameters $\alpha_d(t, h)$ fully describe the transition probability of the Markov chain defined over $h_t \in \{1, 2, \ldots, t/2\}$. Let $p^{(t)} = [p_h^{(t)}]_{h \in \{1,\ldots,t/2\}}$ denote the distribution of the state of the Markov chain at time t, i.e. $p_h^{(t)} = \mathbb{P}(h_t = h)$. The state transition can be represented as the following $((t/2) + 1) \times (t/2)$ dimensional column stochastic matrices:

$$p^{(t+2)} = \begin{bmatrix} \alpha_d(t,1) & & & \\ 1 - \alpha_d(t,1) & \alpha_d(t,2) & & \\ & 1 - \alpha_d(t,2) & \ddots & \\ & & \ddots & \alpha_d(t, t/2) \\ & & & 1 - \alpha_d(t, t/2) \end{bmatrix} p^{(t)} \,.$$

We treat h_t as strictly positive, because at time $t = 0$, when $h_0 = 0$, the virtual source is always passed. Thus, $h_t \geq 1$ afterwards. We design the the parameters $\alpha_d(t, h)$ to achieve perfect hiding. Precisely, at all even t, we desire $p^{(t)}$ to be

$$p^{(t)} = \frac{d-2}{(d-1)^{t/2} - 1} \begin{bmatrix} 1 \\ (d-1) \\ \vdots \\ (d-1)^{t/2-1} \end{bmatrix} \in \mathbb{R}^{t/2} \,, \qquad (11)$$

for $d > 2$ and for $d = 2$, $p^{(t)} = (2/t)\mathbf{1}_{t/2}$ where $\mathbf{1}_{t/2}$ is all ones vector in $\mathbb{R}^{t/2}$. There are $d(d-1)^{h-1}$ nodes at distance h from the virtual source, and by symmetry all of them are equally likely to have been the source:

$$\begin{aligned} \mathbb{P}(G_T | v^*, \delta_H(v^*, v_t) = h) \;&=\; \frac{1}{d(d-1)^{h-1}} p_h^{(t)} \\ &=\; \frac{d-2}{d((d-1)^{t/2} - 1)} \,, \end{aligned}$$

for $d > 2$, which is independent of h. Hence, all the infected nodes (except for the virtual source) are equally likely to have been the source of the origin. This statement is made precise in Equation (14).

Together with the desired probability distribution in Equation (11), this gives a recursion over t and h for computing the appropriate $\alpha_d(t, h)$'s. After some algebra and an initial state $p^{(2)} = 1$, we get that the following choice ensures the desired Equation (11):

$$\alpha_d(t, h) = \begin{cases} \frac{(d-1)^{t/2-h+1} - 1}{(d-1)^{t/2+1} - 1} & \text{if } d > 2 \\ \frac{t-2h+2}{t+2} & \text{if } d = 2 \end{cases} \qquad (12)$$

With this choice of parameters, we show that adaptive diffusion spreads fast, infecting $N_t = O((d-1)^{t/2})$ nodes at time t and each of the nodes except for the virtual source is equally likely to have been the source.

THEOREM 3.1. *Suppose the contact network is a d-regular tree with $d \geq 2$, and one node v^* in G starts to spread a message according to Protocol 1 at time $t = 0$. At a certain time $T \geq 0$ an adversary estimates the location of the source v^* using the maximum likelihood estimator $\hat{v}_{\mathrm{ML}}$. The following properties hold for Protocol 1:*

(a) *the number of infected nodes at time T is*

$$N_T \geq \begin{cases} \frac{2(d-1)^{(T+1)/2}-d}{(d-2)} + 1 & \text{if } d > 2 \\ T+1 & \text{if } d = 2 \end{cases} \quad (13)$$

(b) *the probability of source detection for the maximum likelihood estimator at time T is*

$$\mathbb{P}(\hat{v}_{\mathrm{ML}} = v^*) \leq \begin{cases} \frac{d-2}{2(d-1)^{(T+1)/2}-d} & \text{if } d > 2 \\ (1/T) & \text{if } d = 2 \end{cases} \quad (14)$$

(c) *the expected hop-distance between the true source v^* and its estimate $\hat{v}_{\mathrm{ML}}$ under maximum likelihood estimation is lower bounded by*

$$\mathbb{E}[d(\hat{v}_{\mathrm{ML}}, v^*)] \geq \frac{d-1}{d}\frac{T}{2}. \quad (15)$$

Protocol 1 describes the details of the implementation of adaptive diffusion. The first three steps are always the same. At time $t = 1$, the rumor source v^* selects, uniformly at random, one of its neighbors to be the virtual source v_2 and passes the message to it. Next at $t = 2$, the new virtual source v_2 infects all its uninfected neighbors forming G_2 (see Figure 5). Then node v_2 chooses to either keep the virtual source token with probability $\alpha_d(2, 1)$ or to pass it along.

If v_2 chooses to remain the virtual source i.e., $v_4 = v_2$, it passes 'infection messages' to all the leaf nodes in the infected subtree, telling each leaf to infect all its uninfected neighbors. Since the virtual source is not connected to the leaf nodes in the infected subtree, these infection messages get relayed by the interior nodes of the subtree. This leads to N_t messages getting passed in total (we assume this happens instantaneously). These messages cause the rumor to spread symmetrically in all directions at $t = 3$. At $t = 4$, no more spreading occurs.

If v_2 does *not* choose to remain the virtual source, it passes the virtual source token to a randomly chosen neighbor v_4, excluding the previous virtual source (in this example, v_0). Thus, if the virtual source moves, it moves away from the true source by one hop. Once v_4 receives the virtual source token, it sends out infection messages. However, these messages do not get passed back in the direction of the previous virtual source. This causes the infection to spread asymmetrically over only one subtree of the infected graph (G_3 in left panel of Figure 5). In the subsequent timestep ($t = 4$), the virtual source remains fixed and passes the same infection messages again. After this second round of asymmetric spreading, the infected graph is once again symmetric about the virtual source v_4 (G_4 in left panel of Figure 5).

Although adaptive diffusion obfuscates the source on infinite regular trees, real world contact networks have cycles, and degrees are irregular, and the size is finite. We study how adaptive diffusion works under more realistic contact networks.

Protocol 1 Adaptive Diffusion

Require: contact network $G = (V, E)$, source v^*, time T, degree d
Ensure: set of infected nodes V_T

$V_0 \leftarrow \{v^*\}$, $h \leftarrow 0$, $v_0 \leftarrow v^*$
v^* selects one of its neighbors u at random
$V_1 \leftarrow V_0 \cup \{u\}$, $h \leftarrow 1$, $v_1 \leftarrow u$
let $N(u)$ represent u's neighbors
$V_2 \leftarrow V_1 \cup N(u) \setminus \{v^*\}$, $v_2 \leftarrow v_1$
$t \leftarrow 3$
for $t \leq T$ **do**
  v_{t-1} selects a random variable $X \sim U(0, 1)$
  if $X \leq \alpha_d(t-1, h)$ **then**
    for all $v \in N(v_{t-1})$ **do**
      Infection Message(G,v_{t-1},v,G_t)
  else
    v_{t-1} randomly selects $u \in N(v_{t-1}) \setminus \{v_{t-2}\}$
    $h \leftarrow h + 1$
    $v_t \leftarrow u$
    for all $v \in N(v_t) \setminus \{v_{t-1}\}$ **do**
      Infection Message(G,v_t,v,V_t)
      if $t + 1 > T$ **then**
        break
      Infection Message(G,v_t,v,V_t)
  $t \leftarrow t + 2$
procedure INFECTION MESSAGE(G,u,v,V_t)
  if $v \in V_t$ **then**
    for all $w \in N(v) \setminus \{u\}$ **do**
      Infection Message(G,v,w,G_t)
  else
    $V_t \leftarrow V_{t-2} \cup \{v\}$

4. GENERAL CONTACT NETWORKS

We study adaptive diffusion on general networks when the underlying graph is cyclic, irregular, and finite.

4.1 Irregular tree networks

We first consider tree networks with potentially different degrees at the vertices. Although the degrees are irregular, we still apply adaptive diffusion with $\alpha_{d_0}(t, h)$'s chosen for a specific d_0 that might be mismatched with the graph due to degree irregularities. There are a few challenges in this degree-mismatched adaptive diffusion. First, finding the maximum likelihood estimate of the source is not immediate, due to degree irregularities. Second, it is not clear *a priori* which choice of d_0 is good. We first show an efficient message-passing algorithm for computing the maximum likelihood source estimate. Using this estimate, we illustrate through simulations how adaptive diffusion performs and show that the detection probability is not too sensitive to the choice of d_0 as long as d_0 is above a threshold that depends on the degree distribution.

Efficient ML estimation. To keep the discussion simple, we assume that T is even. The same approach can be naturally extended to odd T. Since the spreading pattern in adaptive diffusion is entirely deterministic given the sequence of virtual sources at each timestep, computing the likelihood $\mathbb{P}(G_T|v^* = v)$ is equivalent to computing the probability of the virtual source moving from v to v_T over T timesteps. On trees, there is only one path from v to v_T and since we do not allow the virtual source to "backtrack", we only need to compute the probability of every virtual source sequence $(v_0, v_2, \ldots, v_T)$ that meets the constraint $v_0 = v$. Due to the Markov property exhibited by adaptive diffusion, we have $\mathbb{P}(G_T|\{(v_t, h_t)\}_{t\in\{2,4,\ldots,T\}}) = \prod_{\substack{t<T-1 \\ t \text{ even}}} \mathbb{P}(v_{t+2}|v_t, h_t)$, where $h_t = \delta_H(v_0, v_t)$. For t even, $\mathbb{P}(v_{t+2}|v_t, h_t) = \alpha_d(t, h_t)$ if $v_t = v_{t+2}$ and $\frac{1-\alpha_d(t,h_t)}{\deg(v_t)-1}$ otherwise. Here $\deg(v_t)$ denotes the degree of node v_t in G. Given a virtual source trajectory $\mathcal{P} = (v_0, v_2, \ldots, v_T)$, let $\mathcal{J}_\mathcal{P} = (j_1, \ldots, j_{\delta_H(v_0,v_T)})$ denote the timesteps at which a new virtual source is introduced, with $1 \leq j_i \leq T$. It always holds that $j_1 = 2$ because after $t = 0$, the true source chooses a new virtual source and $v_2 \neq v_0$. If the virtual source at $t = 2$ were to keep the token exactly once after receiving it (so $v_2 = v_4$), then $j_2 = 6$, and so forth. To find the likelihood of a node being the true source, we sum over *all* such trajectories

$$\mathbb{P}(G_T|v_0) = \sum_{\mathcal{J}_\mathcal{P}:\mathcal{P}\in\mathcal{S}(v_0,v_T,T)} \underbrace{\frac{1}{\deg(v_0)} \prod_{k=1}^{\delta_H(v_0,v_T)-1} \frac{1}{\deg(v_{j_k})-1}}_{A_{v_0}} \times$$
$$\underbrace{\prod_{\substack{t<T \\ t \text{ even}}} \left(\mathbb{1}_{\{t+2\notin\mathcal{J}_\mathcal{P}\}}\alpha_d(t,h_t) + \mathbb{1}_{\{t+2\in\mathcal{J}_\mathcal{P}\}}(1-\alpha_d(t,h_t))\right)}_{B_{v_0}}, \quad (16)$$

where $\mathbb{1}$ is the indicator function and $S(v_0, v_T, T) = \{\mathcal{P} : \mathcal{P} = (v_0, v_2, \ldots, v_T)$ is a valid trajectory of the virtual source$\}$. Intuitively, part A_{v_0} of the above expression is the probability of choosing the set of virtual sources specified by $\mathcal{P}$, and part B_{v_0} is the probability of keeping or passing the virtual source token at the specified timesteps. Equation (16) holds for both regular and irregular trees. Since the path between two nodes in a tree is unique, and part A_{v_0} is (approximately) the product of node degrees in that path, A_{v_0} is identical for all trajectories $\mathcal{P}$. Pulling A_{v_0} out of the summation, we wish to compute the summation over all valid paths $\mathcal{P}$ of part B_{v_0} (for ease of exposition, we will use B_{v_0} to refer to this whole summation). Although there are combinatorially many valid paths, we can simplify the formula in Equation (16) for the particular choice of $\alpha_d(t, h)$'s defined in (12).

PROPOSITION 4.1. *Suppose that the underlying contact network $\tilde{G}$ is an infinite tree with degree of each node larger than one. One node $\tilde{v}^*$ in $\tilde{G}$ starts to spread a message at time $t = 0$ according to Protocol 1 with the choice of $d = d_0$. At a certain even time $T \geq 0$, the maximum likelihood estimate of $\tilde{v}^*$ given a snapshot of the infected subtree $\tilde{G}_T$ is*

$$\arg\max_{v\in\tilde{G}_T\setminus\tilde{v}_T} \frac{d_0}{\deg(v)} \prod_{v'\in p(\tilde{v}_T,v)\setminus\{\tilde{v}_T,v\}} \frac{d_0-1}{\deg(v')-1} \quad (17)$$

where $\tilde{v}_T$ is the (Jordan) center of the infected subtree $\tilde{G}_T$, $p(\tilde{v}_T, v)$ is the unique path from $\tilde{v}_T$ to v, and $\deg(v')$ is the degree of node v'.

To understand this proposition, consider Figure 6, which was spread using adaptive diffusion (Protocol 1) with a choice of $d_0 = 2$. Then Equation (17) can be computed easily for each node, giving $[1/2, 1, 0, 1, 2/3, 1/2, 1/2, 1/4]$ for nodes $[1, 2, 3, 4, 5, 6, 7, 8]$, respectively. Hence, nodes 2 and 4 are most likely. Intuitively, nodes whose path to the center have small degrees are more likely. However, if we repeat this estimation assuming $d_0 = 4$, then Equation (17) gives $[3, 2, 0, 2, 4/3, 3, 3, 3/2]$. In this case, nodes 1, 6, and 7 are most likely. When d_0 is large, adaptive diffusion tends to place the source closer to the leaves of the infected subtree, so leaf nodes are more likely to have been the source.

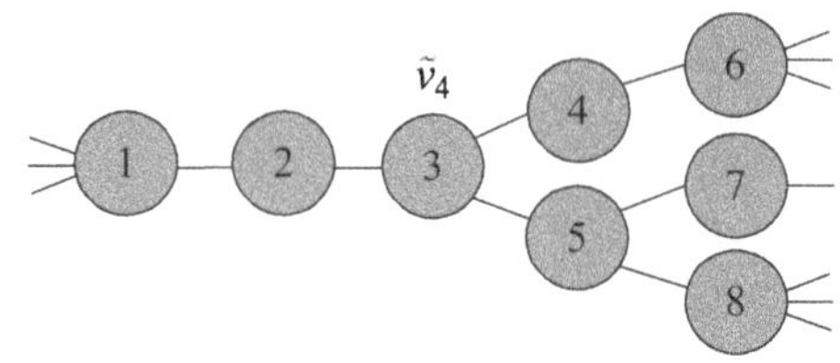

Figure 6: Irregular tree $\tilde{G}_4$ with virtual source $\tilde{v}_4$.

PROOF OF PROPOSITION 4.1. We first make two observations: (*a*) Over regular trees, $\mathbb{P}(G_T|u) = \mathbb{P}(G_T|w)$ for any $u \neq w \in G_T$, even if they are different distances from the virtual souce. (*b*) Part B_{v_0} is identical for regular and irregular graphs, as long as the distance from the candidate source node to v_T is the same in both, and the same d_0 is used to compute $\alpha_{d_0}(t, h)$. That is, let $\tilde{G}_T$ denote an infected subtree over an *irregular* tree network, with virtual source $\tilde{v}_T$, and G_T will denote a *regular* infected subtree with virtual source v_T. For candidate sources $\tilde{v}_0 \in \tilde{G}_T$ and $v_0 \in G_T$, if $\delta_H(\tilde{v}_T, \tilde{v}_0) = \delta_H(v_T, v_0) = h$, then $B_{v_0} = B_{\tilde{v}_0}$. So to find the likelihood of $\tilde{v}_0 \in \tilde{G}_T$, we can solve for $B_{\tilde{v}_0}$ using the likelihood of $v_0 \in G_T$, and compute $A_{\tilde{v}_0}$ using the degree information of every node in the infected, irregular subgraph.

To solve for $B_{\tilde{v}_0}$, note that over regular graphs, $A_v = 1/(d_0\,(d_0-1)^{\delta_H(v,v_T)-1})$, where d_0 is the degree of the regular graph. If G is a regular tree, Equation (16) still applies. Critically, for regular trees, the $\alpha_{d_0}(t, h)$'s are designed such that the likelihood of each node being the true source is equal. Hence,

$$\mathbb{P}(G_T|v_0) = \underbrace{\frac{1}{d_0(d_0-1)^{\delta_H(v_0,v_T)-1}}}_{A_{v_0}} \times B_{v_0}\,, \quad (18)$$

is a constant that does not depend on v_0. This gives $B_{v_0} \propto (d_0-1)^{\delta_H(v_T,v_0)}$. From observation (*b*), we have that $B_{\tilde{v}_0} = B_{v_0}$. Thus we get that for a $\tilde{v}_0 \in \tilde{G}_T \setminus \{\tilde{v}_T\}$,

$$\begin{aligned}\mathbb{P}(\tilde{G}_T|\tilde{v}_0) &= A_{\tilde{v}_0}\, B_{\tilde{v}_0} \\ &\propto \frac{(d_0-1)^{\delta_H(\tilde{v}_T,\tilde{v}_0)}}{\deg(\tilde{v}_0)\prod_{\tilde{v}'\in p(\tilde{v}_T,\tilde{v}_0)\setminus\{\tilde{v}_0,\tilde{v}_T\}}(\deg(\tilde{v}')-1)}\end{aligned}$$

After scaling appropriately and noting that $|p(\tilde{v}_T, \tilde{v}_0)| = \delta_H(\tilde{v}_T, \tilde{v}_0) + 1$, this gives the formula in Equation (17). □

Implementation and numerical simulations. We provide an efficient message passing algorithm for computing the ML estimate in Equation (17), which is naturally distributed. We then use this estimator to simulate message spreading for random irregular trees and show that when d_0 exceeds a threshold (determined by the degree distribution), obfuscation is not too sensitive to the choice of d_0.

$A_{\tilde{v}_0}$ can be computed efficiently for irregular graphs with a simple message-passing algorithm. In this algorithm, each

Algorithm 2 ML estimator of (17)

Input: infected network $\tilde{G}_T = (\tilde{V}_T, \tilde{E}_T)$, virtual source $\tilde{v}_T$, time T, the spreading model parameter d_0
Output: $\text{argmax}_{\tilde{v} \in \tilde{V}_T} \mathbb{P}(\tilde{G}_T | \tilde{v}^* = \tilde{v})$
$P_{\tilde{v}} \triangleq \mathbb{P}(\tilde{G}_T | \tilde{v}^* = \tilde{v})$.
$P_{\tilde{v}_T} \leftarrow 0$
$A_{\tilde{v}} \leftarrow 1$ for $\tilde{v} \in \tilde{V}_T \setminus \{\tilde{v}_T\}$
$A_{\tilde{v}_T} \leftarrow 0$
$A \leftarrow$ Degree Message(G_T, $\tilde{v}_T$, $\tilde{v}_T$, A)
$\mathbb{P}(G_T | v_{leaf}) \leftarrow \frac{1}{d_0(d_0-1)^{T/2-1}} \prod_{\substack{t<T \\ t \text{ even}}} (1 - \alpha_{d_0}(t, \frac{t}{2}))\}$
for all $\tilde{v} \in \tilde{V}_T \setminus \{\tilde{v}_T\}$ **do**
  $h \leftarrow \delta_H(\tilde{v}, \tilde{v}_T)$
  $B_{\tilde{v}} \leftarrow \mathbb{P}(G_T | v_{leaf}) \cdot d_0 \cdot (d_0 - 1)^{h-1}$
  $P_{\tilde{v}} \leftarrow A_{\tilde{v}} \cdot B_{\tilde{v}}$
return $\text{argmax}_{\tilde{v} \in \tilde{V}_T} P_{\tilde{v}}$
procedure DEGREE MESSAGE($\tilde{G}_T$, $\tilde{u}$, $\tilde{v}$, A)
  for all $\tilde{w} \in N(\tilde{v}) \setminus \{\tilde{u}\}$ **do**
    if $\tilde{v} = \tilde{u}$ **then**
      $A_{\tilde{w}} \leftarrow A_{\tilde{v}} / deg(\tilde{w})$
      Degree Message($\tilde{G}_T$, $\tilde{v}$, $\tilde{w}$, A)
    else
      if $\tilde{v}$ is not a leaf **then**
        $A_{\tilde{w}} \leftarrow A_{\tilde{v}} \cdot deg(\tilde{v}) / (deg(\tilde{w}) \cdot (deg(\tilde{v}) - 1))$
        Degree Message($\tilde{G}_T$, $\tilde{v}$, $\tilde{w}$, A)
  return A

node $\tilde{v}$ multiplies its degree information by a cumulative likelihood that gets passed from the virtual source to the leaves. Thus if there are $\tilde{N}_T$ infected nodes in $\tilde{G}_T$, then $A_{\tilde{v}_0}$ for every $\tilde{v}_0 \in \tilde{G}_T$ can be computed by passing $O(\tilde{N}_T)$ messages. This message-passing is outlined in procedure 'Degree Message' of Algorithm 2. For example, consider computing A_5 for the graph in Figure 6. The virtual source $\tilde{v}_T = 3$ starts by setting $A_2 = \frac{1}{2}$, $A_4 = \frac{1}{2}$, and $A_5 = \frac{1}{3}$. This gives A_5, but to compute other other values of $A_{\tilde{w}}$, the message passing continues. Each of the nodes $\tilde{v} \in N(3)$ in turn sets $A_{\tilde{w}}$ for *their* children $\tilde{w} \in N(\tilde{v})$; this is done by dividing $A_{\tilde{v}}$ by $deg(\tilde{w})$ and replacing the factor of $\frac{1}{deg(\tilde{v})}$ in $A_{\tilde{v}}$ with $\frac{1}{deg(\tilde{v}-1)}$. For example, node 5 would set $A_7 = \frac{A_5}{2} \cdot \frac{3}{2}$.This step is applied recursively until reaching the leaves.

As discussed earlier, $B_{\tilde{v}_0}$ only depends on d_0 and $\delta_H(\tilde{v}_T, \tilde{v}_0)$. If $v_{\text{leaf}} \in G_T$ is a leaf node and G is a regular tree, we get

$$\mathbb{P}(G_T | v_{\text{leaf}}) = \underbrace{\frac{1}{d_0(d_0-1)^{T/2-1}}}_{A_{v_{\text{leaf}}}} \underbrace{\prod_{\substack{t<T \\ t \text{ even}}} (1 - \alpha_{d_0}(t, \frac{t}{2}))}_{B_{v_{\text{leaf}}}}. \quad (19)$$

If $\tilde{v}_0$ is $h < T/2$ hops from $\tilde{v}_T$, then for node v_0 with $\delta_H(v_0, v_T) = h < T/2$ over a *regular* tree,

$$\mathbb{P}(G_T | v_0) = \mathbb{P}(G_T | v_{\text{leaf}}) = \frac{1}{d_0 \cdot (d_0 - 1)^{h-1}} B_{v_0}.$$

Finally, $B_{\tilde{v}_0} = B_{v_0}$. So to solve for B_5 in our example, we compute $\mathbb{P}(G_T | v_{leaf})$ for a 3-regular graph at time $T = 4$. This gives $\mathbb{P}(G_4 | v_{leaf}) = A_{v_{leaf}} \cdot B_{v_{leaf}} = \frac{1}{6} \cdot (1 - \alpha_3(2, 1)) = \frac{1}{9}$. Thus $B_5 = \mathbb{P}(G_4 | v_{leaf}) \cdot d_0 \cdot (d_0 - 1)^{h-1} = \mathbb{P}(G_4 | v_{leaf}) \cdot 3 \cdot (2)^0 = \frac{1}{3}$. This gives $\mathbb{P}(\tilde{G}_4 | 5) = A_5 \cdot B_5 = \frac{1}{9}$. The same can be done for other nodes in the graph to find the maximum likelihood source estimate.

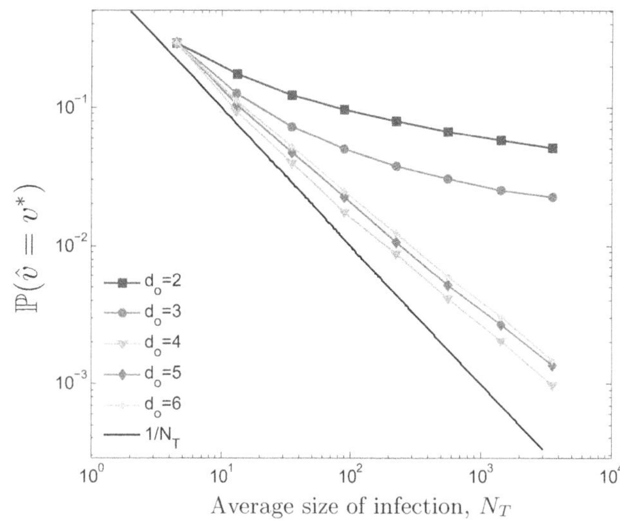

Figure 7: The probability of detection by the maximum likelihood estimator depends on the assumed degree d_0; the source cannot hide well below a threshold value of d_0.

We tested adaptive diffusion over random trees; each node's degree was drawn i.i.d. from a fixed distribution. Figure 7 illustrates simulation results for random trees in which each node has degree 3 or 4 with equal probability, averaged over 100,000 trials. By the law of large numbers, the number of nodes infected scales as $N_T = e^{T\mathbb{E}[\log(D-1)]} \sim 2.45^T$, where D represents the degree distribution of the underlying random irregular tree. The value of d_0 corresponds to a regular tree with size scaling as $(d_0 - 1)^T$. Hence, one can expect that for $d_0 - 1 < 2.45$, the source is likely to be in the center of the infection, and for $d_0 > 2.45$ the source is likely to be at the boundary of the infection. Since the number of nodes in the boundary is significantly larger than the number of nodes in the center, the detection probability is lower for $d_0 - 1 > 2.45$. This is illustrated in the figure, which matches our prediction. In general, $d_0 = 1 + \lceil e^{\mathbb{E}[\log(D-1)]} \rceil$ provides the best obfuscation, and it is robust for any value above that. In this plot, data points represent successive even timesteps; their uniform spacing implies the message is spreading exponentially quickly.

Figure 8 illustrates the probability of detection as a function of infection size while varying the degree distribution of the underlying tree. The notation $(3, 5) \Rightarrow (0.5, 0.5)$ in the legend indicates that each node in the tree has degree 3 or 5, each with probability 0.5. For each distribution tested, we chose d_0 to be the maximum degree of each degree distribution. The average size of infection scales as $N_T = e^{T\mathbb{E}[\log(D-1)]}$ as expected, whereas the probability of detection scales as $(d_{\min} - 1)^{-T} = 2^{-T}$, which is independent of the degree distribution. This suggests that adaptive diffusion fails to provide near-perfect obfuscation when the underlying graph is irregular, and the gap increases with the irregularity of the graph.

4.2 Real World Networks

To understand how adaptive diffusion fares in realistic scenarios that involve cycles, irregular degrees, and finite graph size, we ran the adaptive diffusion protocol over an underlying connectivity network of 10,000 Facebook users

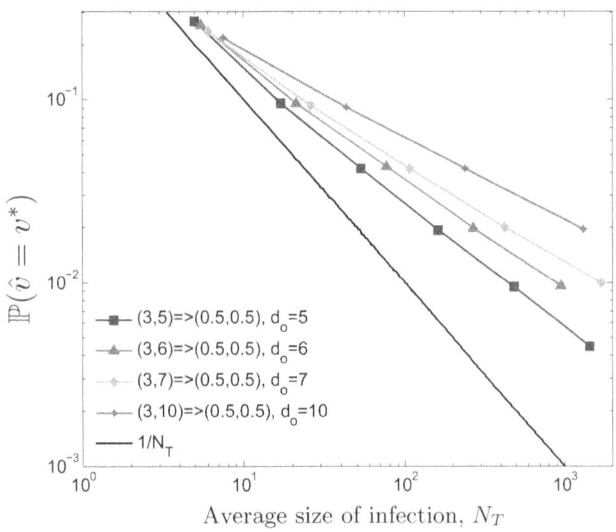

Figure 8: Adaptive diffusion no longer provides perfect obfuscation for highly irregular graphs.

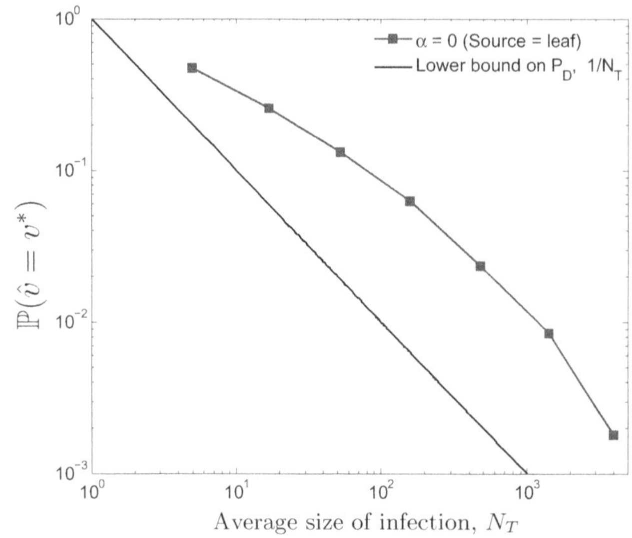

Figure 9: Near-ML probability of detection for the Facebook graph with adaptive diffusion.

in New Orleans circa 2009, as described by the Facebook WOSN dataset [22]. We eliminated all nodes with fewer than three friends (this approach is taken by several existing anonymous applications so users cannot guess which of their friends originated the message), which left us with a network of 9,502 users. Over this underlying network, we selected a node uniformly at random as the rumor source, and spread the message using adaptive diffusion setting with $d_0 = \infty$, which means that the virtual source is always passed to a new node. This choice is to make the ML source estimation faster, and other choices of d_0 could outperform this naive choice. To preserve the symmetry of our constructed trees as much as possible, we constrained each infected node to infect a maximum of three other nodes in each timestep. We also give the adversary access to the undirected infection *subtree* that explicitly identifies all pairs of nodes for which one node spread the infection to the other. This subtree is overlaid on the underlying contact network, which is not necessarily tree-structured. We demonstrate in simulation (Figure 9) that even with this strong side information, the adversary can only identify the true message source with low probability.

Using the naive method of enumerating every possible message trajectory, it is computationally expensive to find the exact ML source estimate since there are 2^T possible trajectories, depending on whether the virtual source stayed or moved at each timestep. If the true source is one of the leaves, we can closely approximate the ML estimate *among all leaf nodes*, using the same procedure as described in 4.1, with one small modification: in graphs with cycles, the term $(\deg(v_{j_k}) - 1)$ from equation (16) should be substituted with $(\deg_u(v_{j_k}) - 1)$, where $\deg_u(v_{j_k})$ denotes the number of uninfected neighbors of v_{j_k} at time j_k. Loops in the graph cause this value to be time-varying, and also dependent on the location of v_0, the candidate source. We did not approximate the ML estimate for non-leaves because the simplifications used in Section 4.1 to compute the likelihood no longer hold, leading to an exponential increase in the problem dimension.

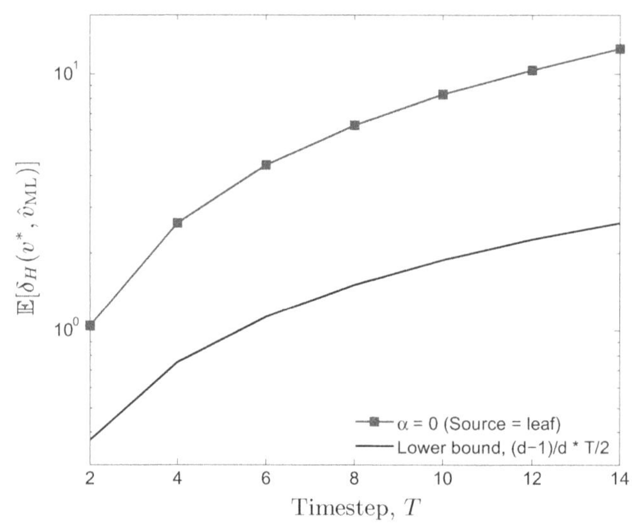

Figure 10: Hop distance between true source and estimated source over infection subtree for adaptive diffusion over the Facebook graph.

This approach is only an approximation of the ML estimate because the virtual source could move in a loop over the social graph (i.e., the same node could be the virtual source more than once, in nonadjacent timesteps).

On average, adaptive diffusion reached 96 percent of the network within 10 timesteps using $d_0 = 4$. We also computed the average distance of the true source from the estimated source *over the infected subtree* (Figure 10). We see that as time progresses, so does the hop distance of the estimated source from the true source. In social networks, nearly everyone is within a small number of hops (say, 6 hops [21]) from everyone else, so this computation is not as informative in this setting. However, it is relevant in location-based connectivity graphs, which can induce large hop distances between nodes.

5. DISCUSSION

Besides the adversarial model studied in this paper, anonymous messaging applications face challenges under alternative adversarial models that can occur in practice. Examples include (*a*) an adversary that corrupts a subset of network nodes through malware, bribery, or Sybil node creation in order to access metadata like message timing and sender identity; (*b*) an adversary that prevents nodes from following the messaging protocol (e.g., via malware); or (*c*) an adversarial network provider that monitor all network activity and analyzes this activity retroactively.

All these adversarial attacks increase the chance of source identification, which is a challenging problem for designing anonymous protocols. To a large extent, de-anonymization is an arms race in which there is always side information for an adversary to exploit. The point is to make that exploitation as expensive and difficult as possible, thereby preventing it from scaling. Within this arms race, anonymous spreading protocols ensure that adversaries cannot use message propagation patterns as a weapon.

6. ACKNOWLEDGMENTS

This work has been supported by the Army Research Office (ARO) contract W911NF-14-1-0220, and has greatly benefited from discussions with professor Kannan Ramchandran of University of California, Berkeley.

7. REFERENCES

[1] Secret. `https://www.secret.ly`.

[2] Whisper. `http://whisper.sh`.

[3] Yik yak. `http://www.yikyakapp.com/`.

[4] D. Chaum. The dining cryptographers problem: Unconditional sender and recipient untraceability. *Journal of cryptology*, 1(1), 1988.

[5] I. Clarke, O. Sandberg, B. Wiley, and T.W. Hong. Freenet: A distributed anonymous information storage and retrieval system. In *Designing Privacy Enhancing Technologies*. Springer, 2001.

[6] H. Corrigan-Gibbs and B. Ford. Dissent: accountable anonymous group messaging. In *Proc. CCS*. ACM, 2010.

[7] R. Dingledine, M.J. Freedman, and D. Molnar. The free haven project: Distributed anonymous storage service. In *Designing Privacy Enhancing Technologies*. Springer, 2001.

[8] R. Dingledine, N. Mathewson, and P. Syverson. Tor: The second-generation onion router. Technical report, DTIC Document, 2004.

[9] V. Fioriti and M. Chinnici. Predicting the sources of an outbreak with a spectral technique. *arXiv preprint arXiv:1211.2333*, 2012.

[10] M.J. Freedman and R. Morris. Tarzan: A peer-to-peer anonymizing network layer. In *Proc. CCS*. ACM, 2002.

[11] S. Goel, M. Robson, M. Polte, and E. Sirer. Herbivore: A scalable and efficient protocol for anonymous communication. Technical report, Cornell University, 2003.

[12] P. Golle and A. Juels. Dining cryptographers revisited. In *Advances in Cryptology-Eurocrypt 2004*. Springer, 2004.

[13] Wuqiong Luo, W Tay, and Mei Leng. How to identify an infection source with limited observations. 2013.

[14] E. A. Meirom, C. Milling, C. Caramanis, S. Mannor, A. Orda, and S. Shakkottai. Localized epidemic detection in networks with overwhelming noise. 2014.

[15] C. Milling, C. Caramanis, S. Mannor, and S. Shakkottai. On identifying the causative network of an epidemic. In *Allerton Conference*, pages 909–914, 2012.

[16] C. Milling, C. Caramanis, S. Mannor, and S. Shakkottai. Detecting epidemics using highly noisy data. In *MobiHoc*, pages 177–186, 2013.

[17] Chris Milling, Constantine Caramanis, Shie Mannor, and Sanjay Shakkottai. Network forensics: Random infection vs spreading epidemic. In *Proceedings of the 12th ACM SIGMETRICS/PERFORMANCE Joint International Conference on Measurement and Modeling of Computer Systems*, SIGMETRICS '12, pages 223–234, New York, NY, USA, 2012. ACM.

[18] B. A. Prakash, J. Vreeken, and C. Faloutsos. Spotting culprits in epidemics: How many and which ones? In *ICDM*, volume 12, pages 11–20, 2012.

[19] D. Shah and T. Zaman. Finding rumor sources on random graphs. *arXiv preprint arXiv:1110.6230*, 2011.

[20] D. Shah and T. Zaman. Rumors in a network: Who's the culprit? *Information Theory, IEEE Transactions on*, 57(8):5163–5181, Aug 2011.

[21] Johan Ugander, Brian Karrer, Lars Backstrom, and Cameron Marlow. The anatomy of the facebook social graph. *arXiv preprint arXiv:1111.4503*, 2011.

[22] Bimal Viswanath, Alan Mislove, Meeyoung Cha, and Krishna P. Gummadi. On the evolution of user interaction in facebook. In *Proceedings of the 2nd ACM SIGCOMM Workshop on Social Networks (WOSN'09)*, August 2009.

[23] L. von Ahn, A. Bortz, and N.J. Hopper. K-anonymous message transmission. In *Proc. CCS*. ACM, 2003.

[24] Zhaoxu Wang, Wenxiang Dong, Wenyi Zhang, and Chee Wei Tan. Rumor source detection with multiple observations: Fundamental limits and algorithms. 2014.

[25] K. Zhu and L. Ying. A robust information source estimator with sparse observations. *arXiv preprint arXiv:1309.4846*, 2013.

APPENDIX

A. LINE AND TREE PROTOCOLS

A.1 Line Protocol

Let the underlying contact network be an infinite line with $V = \{..., -1, 0, 1, 2, ...\}$ and $E = \{(i, i+1) : i \in \mathbb{Z}\}$. At time t, an infected node v at the boundary spreads the infection to its uninfected neighbor with probability $p_{v,t}$ given in Equation (3). 'Infection' means transmitting the message, the hop-distance of the node (incremented by one), and the current timestep since the start of the outbreak (incremented by one). Note that this protocol is naturally distributed.

A.2 Tree Protocol

At time $t = 0$, the source node v^* is initialized with $s_{1,v^*} = 1$ and $s_{2,v^*} = 0$. At time $t = 1$, v^* selects, uni-

Protocol 3 Spreading on a line

Require contact network $G = (V, E)$, source v^*, time T
Ensure: infected subgraph $G_T = (V_T, E_T)$
$V_0 \leftarrow \{v^*\}$
$\delta_H(v^* - 1, v^*) \leftarrow 1$ and $\delta_H(v^* + 1, v^*) \leftarrow 1$
$t \leftarrow 1$
for $t \leq T$ **do**
  $v \leftarrow$ rightmost node in V_t
  draw a random variable $X \sim U(0, 1)$
  if $X \leq (\delta_H(v, v^*) + 1)/(t + 1)$ **then**
    $V_t \leftarrow V_{t-1} \cup \{v + 1\}$
    $\delta_H(v + 1, v^*) \leftarrow \delta_H(v, v^*) + 1$
  $v \leftarrow$ leftmost node in V_t
  draw a random variable $Y \sim U(0, 1)$
  if $Y \leq (\delta_H(v, v^*) + 1)/(t + 1)$ **then**
    $V_t \leftarrow V_{t-1} \cup \{v - 1\}$
    $\delta_H(v - 1, v^*) \leftarrow \delta_H(v, v^*) + 1$
  $t \leftarrow t + 1$

Protocol 4 Spreading on a tree

Require contact network $G = (V, E)$, source v^*, time T
Ensure: infected subgraph $G_T = (V_T, E_T)$
$V_0 \leftarrow \{v^*\}$
$s_{1,v^*} \leftarrow 0$ and $s_{2,v^*} \leftarrow 0$
v^* selects one of its neighbors u at random
$V_1 \leftarrow V_0 \cup \{u\}$
$s_{1,u} \leftarrow 1$ and $s_{2,u} \leftarrow 1$
$t \leftarrow 2$
for $t \leq T$ **do**
  for all $v \in V_{t-1}$ with $s_{2,v} > 0$ **do**
    if $s_{1,v} = 1$ **then**
      v selects one of its uninfected neighbors u at random
      $V_t \leftarrow V_{t-1} \cup \{u\}$
      $s_{1,u} \leftarrow 1$ and $s_{2,u} \leftarrow s_{2,v} + 1$
      $s_{1,v} \leftarrow 0$
    else
      for all uninfected neighboring nodes w of v **do**
        $V_t \leftarrow V_{t-1} \cup \{w\}$
        $s_{1,w} \leftarrow 0$ and $s_{2,w} \leftarrow s_{2,v} - 1$
        $s_{2,v} \leftarrow 0$
  $t \leftarrow t + 1$

formly at random, one of its neighboring nodes (say node u) and passes the updated state variables $s_{1,u} = 1$ and $s_{2,u} = 1$ along with the message to u. The first state $s_{1,u} = 1$ indicates that node u is one of the 'virtual sources'. The second state $s_{2,u} = 1$ indicates that node u will eventually be at height 1 in the infected subtree. Afterwards, the protocol iterates the following procedures. Any infected node v that is not a future virtual source creates 'offsprings' that are not virtual sources ($s_{1,v'} = 0$) and have heights decreased by one ($s_{1,v'} = s_{1,v} - 1$). Any node v with height zero (i.e., $s_{2,v} = 0$) stops spreading the infection in order to ensure that v and the true source are at the same depth from the center of G_t for any t. An infected node v that is a future virtual source proceeds similarly, with one difference: it chooses one of its neighbors to be a virtual source with the second state incremented by one, i.e. $s_{2,v'} = s_{2,v} + 1$. Protocol 4 summarizes this process and Figure 4 illustrates that if the contact network is a regular tree, this process keeps the infected subtree balanced and regular, with the true source hiding among the leaves.

Figure 4 shows an example of this spreading algorithm. At time $t = 0$, node $v^* = 0$ starts spreading a rumor in the network. At $t = 1$, node 0 infects node 1 and sets $s_{1,1} = 1$ and $s_{2,1} = 1$. At $t = 2$, node 1 infects node 3 and sets $s_{1,3} = 0$ and $s_{2,3} = 0$. Node 1 also infects node 2 and sets $s_{1,2} = 1$ and $s_{2,2} = 2$. At $t = 3$, node 2 infects node 4 and sets $s_{1,4} = 0$ and $s_{2,4} = 1$. Node 2 also infects node 5 and sets $s_{1,5} = 1$ and $s_{2,5} = 3$. Observe that node 3 will not infect any of its neighbors because $s_{1,3} = 0$ and $s_{2,3} = 0$.

by sending a state information along with the message. Each infected node u keeps two state variables: a binary variable $s_{1,u} \in \{0, 1\}$ and a non-negative integer $s_{2,u} \in \{0, 1, 2, \ldots, t\}$. The binary state $s_{1,u}$ marks the future virtual sources of the infected subtree; if $s_{1,u} = 1$, then node u will be the Jordan center of the graph at some point in the future. The integer state $s_{2,u}$ keeps track of the eventual 'height' of node u in the infected subtree. In the example above, node 3 will always be at the leaf, so it has $s_{2,3} = 0$, where as node 9 is currently a leaf, but eventually will be at height 2 and has $s_{2,9} = 2$, since node 5 will be at some point a center of infected subtree of depth 3. These state variables are computed for each node when it is infected, and is constant over time.

B. PROOF OF PROPOSITION 2.1

Spreading rate. Consider the following time-dependent random walk on $\mathbb{N}_0 = \{0, 1, \ldots\}$. Let x_t be the position of a black dot at time t and assume that $x_0 = 0$. At time $t \geq 1$, the dot can either move to the right: $x_t = x_{t-1} + 1$ with probability $p(t, x_{t-1}) = (x_{t-1} + 1)/(t + 1)$; or stay where it is: $x_t = x_{t-1}$ with probability $q(t, x_{t-1}) = 1 - p(t, x_{t-1})$. We claim that $\mathbb{P}(x_T = k) = 1/(T + 1)$, for $k \in \{0, \ldots, T\}$. We will prove this by induction on T. Observe that for $T = 1$, $x_1 = x_0 + 1 = 1$ with probability $1/2$ and $x_1 = 0$ with probability $1/2$. Therefore, the claim is true for $T = 1$. Assume it is true for $T - 1$. At $t = T$,

$$\begin{aligned}
\mathbb{P}(x_T = 0) &= \mathbb{P}(x_{T-1} = 0)\left(1 - \frac{1}{T+1}\right) = \frac{1}{T+1} \\
\mathbb{P}(x_T = T) &= \mathbb{P}(x_{T-1} = T)\frac{T}{T+1} = \frac{1}{T+1} \\
\mathbb{P}(x_T = k) &= \mathbb{P}(x_{T-1} = k - 1)\frac{k}{T+1} + \\
&\quad \mathbb{P}(x_{T-1} = k)\left(1 - \frac{k+1}{T+1}\right) = \frac{1}{T+1},
\end{aligned}$$

for $k \in \{1, \ldots, T - 1\}$. Thus, the claim is true for any T.

Given v^* and T, consider an infected subgraph G_T generated by Protocol 3 (Line Protocol). G_T can be decomposed into two independent chains: the chain to the right of v^* represented by G_T^r and the chain to the left of v^* represented by G_T^l. Therefore, we can write $G_T = G_T^r \cup G_T^l \cup \{v^*\}$, where $|G_T^r|, |G_T^l| \in \{0, \ldots, T\}$. The Line Protocol spreads on each side of v^* according to the time-inhomogeneous random walk described above. Hence, $|G_T^r|$ and $|G_T^l|$ are independent and identically distributed, and $\mathbb{P}(|G_T^r| = k) = 1/(T + 1)$ for any $k \in \{0, \ldots, T\}$. The number of infected nodes $N_T = |G_T| = |G_T^r| + |G_T^l| + 1$ is the sum of two independent and uniformly distributed random variables. Thus, it is distributed according to the triangular distribution:

$$\mathbb{P}(N_T = k) = \frac{1}{(T+1)^2}\begin{cases} k, & k \le T+1, \\ 2(T+1)-k, & k \le 2T+1, \end{cases} \quad (20)$$

Probability of detection. Assume that the adversary observes an infected subgraph G_T of size $N_T = |G_T| = k$. Moreover, assume that the adversary knows T. Not knowing T will only lead to worse performance. If $k \le T+1$, then for any $v \in G_T$ assumed to be the rumor source, we have that $|G_T^r| = k_r$, $|G_T^l| = k - k_r - 1$ with $k_r \in \{0, 1, \dots, T\}$. Therefore, $\mathbb{P}(G_T|v) = \mathbb{P}(\{|G_T^r| = k_r\} \cap \{|G_T^l| = k - k_r - 1\}) = 1/(T+1)^2$. This means that all $v \in G_T$ are equally likely and the maximum likelihood algorithm would select one node $v \in G_T$ at random. Hence, the probability of detecting the true source $\mathbb{P}(\hat{v}_{ML} = v^*|G_T, v^*) = 1/(T+1)$ whenever $k \le T+1$. If $k > T+1$, then for some nodes $v \in G_T$, we have that $|G_T^r| = k_r$, $|G_T^l| = k - k_r - 1$ with $k_r > T$ or $|G_T^r| = k - k_r$, $|G_T^l| = k_l$ with $k_l > T$. These nodes could not have generated G_T in T timesteps and therefore $\mathbb{P}(G_T|v) = 0$ for all such nodes. The reader can verify that there are $2k - 2T$ many such nodes. For the other nodes, one can easily verify (similar to above) that $\mathbb{P}(G_T|v) = 1/(T+1)^2$. Therefore, the probability of detecting the true source $\mathbb{P}(\hat{v}_{ML} = v^*|G_T, v^*) = 1/(2T - k + 1)$ whenever $k > T+1$. Putting it all together, we get that

$$\begin{aligned} \mathbb{P}(\hat{v}_{ML} = v^*) &= \sum_{G_T} \mathbb{P}(\hat{v}_{ML} = v^*|G_T)\mathbb{P}(G_T|v^*) \\ &= \sum_{k=0}^{T} \frac{1}{k+1}\frac{k+1}{(T+1)^2} \\ &\quad + \sum_{T+1}^{2T} \frac{1}{2T-k+1}\frac{2T-k+1}{(T+1)^2} \\ &= \frac{2T+1}{(T+1)^2}. \end{aligned} \quad (21)$$

Finally, observe that $\mathbb{P}(\hat{v}_{ML} = v^*)$ is not a function of v^*.

We can use the above analysis to compute the exact posterior distribution of the Line Protocol when the underlying contact network is a finite ring. To put a prior on the source location, we fix the observation time T and consider a finite ring of size larger than $2T+1$. Assuming uniform prior for the source location on this finite ring, the next remark provides the posterior distribution of the source, given that we observe infected nodes $\{1, \dots, m\}$ for some integer $m \le 2T+1$.

REMARK B.1. *Let the infected nodes be $\{1, 2, \dots, m\}$, then*

$$\mathbb{P}(v^* = k|G_T) = \frac{1}{Z_m}\sum_{t=\max\{m-k,k-1\}}^{\infty} \frac{1}{(t+1)^2}\left(\frac{m+1}{(t+2)} - \frac{k(m-k+1)}{(t+2)^2}\right), \quad (22)$$

for all $k \in [m]$ where Z_m is the normalizing constant to ensure the probabilities sum to one.

PROOF OF REMARK B.1. Denote the m infected nodes by $\{1, \dots, m\}$, and let G^* denote the infected subgraph. Then, for $k \le (1+m)/2$,

$$\begin{aligned} &\mathbb{P}(\text{there exists a time } T \text{ such that } G_T = G^*|v^* = k) \quad (23) \\ &= \sum_{t=m-k}^{\infty} \mathbb{P}(G_t = G^* \text{ and } G_{t+1} \ne G^*|v^* = k) \quad (24) \\ &= \sum_{t=m-k}^{\infty} \frac{1}{(1+t)^2}\left(1 - \left(\frac{t+2-k}{t+2}\right)\left(\frac{t+2-(m-k+1)}{t+2}\right)\right), \quad (25) \end{aligned}$$

where the last line follows from Equation (20), where $\mathbb{P}(|G_T^l| = k-1) = 1/(T+1)$, $\mathbb{P}(|G_T^r| = m-k) = 1/(T+1)$, and $\mathbb{P}(\text{no infection at time } t+1|G_t = G^* \text{ and } v^* = k) = ((t+2-k)(t+1+k-m)/(t+2)^2)$. For $k \ge (1+m)/2$, we have a similar formula with summation starting from $k-1$. With the uniform prior on the finite ring, this proves Equation (22). □

C. PROOF OF PROPOSITION 2.2

First, under Protocol 4 (Tree Protocol), G_T is a complete $(d-1)$-ary tree (with the exception that the root has d children) of depth $T/2$ whenever T is even. G_T is made up of two complete $(d-1)$-ary trees of depth $(T-1)/2$ each with their roots connected by an edge whenever T is odd. Therefore, it follows that N_T is a deterministic function of T and is given by

$$N_T = \begin{cases} 1, & T = 0, \\ \frac{2(d-1)^{(T+1)/2}}{d-2} - \frac{2}{d-2}, & T \ge 1,\ T \text{ odd}, \\ \frac{d(d-1)^{T/2}}{d-2} - \frac{2}{d-2}, & T \ge 2,\ T \text{ even}; \end{cases} \quad (26)$$

The lower bound on N_T in Equation (7) follows immediately from the above expression.

For any given infected graph G_T, it can be verified that any non-leaf node could not have generated G_T under the Tree Protocol. In other words, $\mathbb{P}(G_T|v \text{ non-leaf node}) = 0$ and v could not have started the rumor. On the other hand, we claim that for any two leaf nodes $v_1, v_2 \in G_T$, we have that $\mathbb{P}(G_T|v_1) = \mathbb{P}(G_T|v_2) > 0$. This is true because for each leaf node $v \in G_T$, there exists a sequence of state values $\{s_{1,u}, s_{2,u}\}_{u \in G_T}$ that evolves according to the Tree Protocol with $s_{1,v} = 1$ and $s_{2,v} = 0$. Further, the regularity of the underlying graph G ensures that all these sequences are equally likely. Therefore, the probability of correct rumor source detection under the maximum likelihood algorithm is given by $\mathbb{P}_{ML}(T) = 1/N_{l,T}$, where $N_{l,T}$ represents the number of leaf nodes in G_T. It can be also shown that $N_{l,T}$ and N_T are related to each other by the following expression

$$N_{l,T} = \frac{(d-2)N_T + 2}{d-1}. \quad (27)$$

This proves expression for $\mathbb{P}(\hat{v}_{\mathrm{ML}} = v^*)$ given in (8).

Expected distance. For any $v^* \in G$ and any T, $\mathbb{E}[\delta_H(v^*, \hat{v}_{\mathrm{ML}})]$ is given by

$$\mathbb{E}[\delta_H(v^*, \hat{v}_{\mathrm{ML}})] = \sum_{v \in G}\sum_{G_T} \mathbb{P}(G_T|v^*)\mathbb{P}(\hat{v}_{\mathrm{ML}} = v)\delta_H(v^*, v). \quad (28)$$

As indicated above, no matter where the rumor starts from, G_T is a $(d-1)$-ary tree (with the exception that the root has d children) of depth $T/2$ whenever T is even. Moreover, $\hat{v}_{\mathrm{ML}} = v$ with probability $1/N_{l,T}$ for all v leaf nodes in G_T. Therefore, the above equation can be solved exactly to obtain the expression provided in the statement of the proposition.

D. PROOF OF THEOREM 3.1

Spreading rate. Once again, under Protocol 1, G_T is a complete $(d-1)$-ary tree (with the exception that the root has d children) of depth $T/2$ whenever T is even. Whenever T is odd, with probability $\alpha(T,h)$, G_T is again such a $(d-1)$-ary tree of depth $(T+1)/2$. With probability $1-\alpha(T,h)$, G_T is made up of two $(d-1)$-ary trees of depth $(T-1)/2$ each with their roots connected by an edge. Therefore, it follows that when $d>2$, N_T is given by

$$N_T = \begin{cases} 1, & T=0, \\ \frac{2(d-1)^{(T+1)/2}}{d-2} - \frac{2}{d-2}, & T\geq 1,\ T \text{ odd, w.p. } (1-\alpha)\ , \\ \frac{d(d-1)^{(T+1)/2}}{d-2} - \frac{2}{d-2}, & T\geq 1,\ T \text{ odd, w.p. } \alpha\ , \\ \frac{d(d-1)^{T/2}}{d-2} - \frac{2}{d-2}, & T\geq 2,\ T \text{ even }; \end{cases} \tag{29}$$

Similarly, when $d=2$, N_T can be expressed as follows:

$$N_T = \begin{cases} 1, & T=0, \\ T+1, & T\geq 1,\ T \text{ odd, w.p. } (1-\alpha)\ , \\ T+2, & T\geq 1,\ T \text{ odd, w.p. } \alpha\ , \\ T+2, & T\geq 2,\ T \text{ even }; \end{cases} \tag{30}$$

The lower bound on N_T in Equation (7) follows immediately from the above expressions.

Probability of detection. For any given infected graph G_T, the virtual source v_T cannot have been the source node, since the true source always passes the token at timestep $t=1$. So $\mathbb{P}(G_T|v=v_T)=0$. We claim that for any two nodes that are not the virtual source at time T, $u,w\in G_T$, $\mathbb{P}(G_T|u)=\mathbb{P}(G_T|w)>0$. This is true iff for any non-virtual-source node v, there exists a sequence of virtual sources $v_{i\,i=0}^{\,T}$ that evolves according to Protocol 1 with $v_0=v$ that results in the observed G_T, and for all $u,w\in G_T\setminus\{v_T\}$, this sequence has the same likelihood. In a tree, a unique path exists between any pair of nodes, so we can always find a valid path of virtual sources from a candidate node $u\in G_T\setminus\{v_T\}$ to v_T. We claim that any such path leads to the formation of the observed G_T. Due to regularity of G and the symmetry in G_T, for even T, $\mathbb{P}(G_T|v^{(1)})=\mathbb{P}(G_T|v^{(2)})$ for all $v^{(1)},v^{(2)}\in G_T$ with $\delta_H(v^{(1)},v_T)=\delta_H(v^{(2)},v_T)$. Moreover, recall that the $\alpha_d(t,h)$'s were designed to satisfy the distribution in Equation 11. Combining these two observations with the fact that we have $(d-1)^h$ infected nodes h-hops away from the virtual source, we get that for all $v^{(1)},v^{(2)}\in G_T\setminus\{v_T\}$, $\mathbb{P}(G_T|v^{(1)})=\mathbb{P}(G_T|v^{(2)})$. For odd T, if the virtual source remains the virtual source, then G_T stays symmetric about v_T, in which case the same result holds. If the virtual source passes the token, then G_T is perfectly symmetric about the edge connecting v_{T-1} and v_T. Since both nodes are virtual sources (former and present, respectively) and $T>1$, the adversary can infer that neither node was the true source. Since the two connected subtrees are symmetric and each node within a subtree has the same likelihood of being the source by construction (Equation 11), we get that for all $v^{(1)},v^{(2)}\in G_T\setminus\{v_T,v_{T-1}\}$, $\mathbb{P}(G_T|v^{(1)})=\mathbb{P}(G_T|v^{(2)})$. Thus at odd timesteps, $\mathbb{P}(\hat{v}_{ML}=v^*)\geq 1/(N_T-2)$.

Greedy-Bayes for Targeted News Dissemination

Laurent Massoulié
Microsoft Research-Inria Joint Centre
laurent.massoulie@inria.fr

Mesrob I. Ohannessian *
University of California, San Diego
mesrob@gmail.com

Alexandre Proutière
KTH Royal Institute of Technology
alepro@kth.se

ABSTRACT

This work addresses user targeting for news content delivery. Specifically, we wish to disseminate a fresh news content, whose topic is yet unknown, to all interested users, while "spamming" a minimum number of uninterested users. We formulate this as an online stochastic optimization problem that extends in several ways the classical multi-armed bandit problem.

We introduce GREEDY-BAYES, a policy with appealing robustness properties. We establish optimal scaling of a suitably defined regret measure in various scenarios of interest. To that end we develop an original proof technique based on martingale concentration inequalities. Numerical experiments show that GREEDY-BAYES improves upon Thompson sampling, the state-of-the-art algorithm for bandit problems.

Our analysis further implies that low regret can only be achieved if the assessment of content relevance for one user leverages feedback from users with widely distinct tastes. This impacts the design of efficient news dissemination platforms: existing systems typically do not leverage such negative feedback and could hence be improved upon with adequate extensions.

Categories and Subject Descriptors

H.3.3 [**Information Search and Retrieval**]: Information filtering—*recommender systems*; C.4 [**Performance of Systems**]: Modeling techniques

General Terms

Algorithms, Theory, Performance

Keywords

Robust News Delivery, Bayesian, Multi-Armed Bandit

*Work conducted when the author was at the Microsoft Research-Inria Joint Centre.

SIGMETRICS'15, June 15–19, 2015, Portland, OR, USA.

DOI: http://dx.doi.org/10.1145/2745844.2745868.

1. INTRODUCTION

Access to more personalized, better-targeted information, is a major challenge in a world of users with scarce attention resources and a plethora of information to choose from. Users' means to access news online can be broadly categorized as proceeding in a pull mode, when a user checks a news website, or in a push mode, as content is proactively pushed onto the user. For example, Google News corresponds to pull mode while Twitter corresponds to push mode.

Much research has been devoted to optimizing performance of pull-based news systems (see e.g. [14, 10]). There, the designer has no control over which user accesses the system, and simply strives to choose the most relevant news for that user, whoever she might be.

Push systems, especially those based on online social networks such as Facebook or Twitter, have also received considerable attention. They differ from pull systems notably as they operate on "fresh" news, that may not have been finely characterized yet. The main focus in this domain has been to characterize influential users and the way news may propagate "virally" through cascades of influence (see e.g. [11, 13]).

In contrast, little attention has been paid to understanding the fundamental limits on performance of news push systems, be they based on online social networks or not. We believe that such an understanding is needed, as it can lead to improved system designs, in particular when dealing with "fresh", yet uncategorized news. Furthermore it may shed light on the efficiency limitations and potential pitfalls for solutions based on online social networks.

Our contributions in this paper towards such an understanding are as follows:

(a) We propose a model to capture the performance of news push systems on fresh content. In this model, our objective is to disseminate a news content whose topic is unknown or difficult to identify, to all interested users, while "spamming" a minimum number of uninterested users. To this aim, we proceed sequentially and select one user at a time based on the feedback of previously exposed users. The design of such sequential user selection strategies is formulated as an online stochastic optimization problem, that extends the classical multi-armed bandit model in several ways: i) Arms, which reflect users onto whom to push a given news, can be accessed only once; ii) We aim to find the set of a posteriori interested users, rather than the "best arm"; iii) We must stop when remaining users dislike the content, so that the time horizon for decision making is not fixed a priori but instead has to be determined.

(b) We develop the so-called GREEDY-BAYES policy. It enjoys a distinguishing robustness property as it relies only on pseudo-Bayesian updates, based on a crude approximation of the true model parameters.

(c) We analyze the performance of GREEDY-BAYES and provide both general and specialized upper bounds on its regret. Analyses of classical bandit problems don't apply to the present setup. We therefore develop original proof techniques which may be of independent interest. They rely crucially on advanced concentration inequalities, namely the so-called Bernstein inequality for martingales.

(d) We corroborate these results with lower bounds, paralleling the general and specialized upper bounds, showing that our proposed approach is order-optimal.

Organization.

We present our model and the GREEDY-BAYES policy in Section 2. We give three types of regret upper bounds for GREEDY-BAYES. We first give in Section 3 a general regret upper bound in $O(\tau \log(n)/\delta^2)$, where n is the number of users, τ the number of topics, and δ a margin on the user preferences. We show that the variant THOMPSON-SAMPLING of our algorithm also exhibits such scaling. As shown in Section 5 any general regret upper bound must be of that order.

In Section 4 we provide refined regret upper bounds in $O(\tau/\delta^2)$ under an additional structural assumption. We then show that this bound can be lowered to $O(\log(\tau)/\delta^2)$ in a specific scenario with further additional structure. Both bounds are n-independent and illustrate that GREEDY-BAYES implicitly exploits the structure present in the problem.

In Section 5, we provide general regret lower bounds valid for any algorithm. These match the orders of our upper bounds in the three scenarios considered, thus establishing order-optimality of GREEDY-BAYES in the considered situations.

In Section 6, we report numerical experiments which confirm our theory and give empirical evidence that GREEDY-BAYES outperforms its variant THOMPSON-SAMPLING.

After reviewing related work in Section 7, we provide concluding remarks in Section 8.

2. MODEL AND POLICIES

2.1 Model and Objectives

Our model is as follows. We denote the sets of users and topics by $\mathcal{U}$ and $\mathcal{T}$, and we let $n := |\mathcal{U}|$ and $\tau := |\mathcal{T}|$ be the overall number of users and topics, respectively. Under a given topic $t \in \mathcal{T}$ of a content item, users independently determine whether they appreciate it or dislike it. We model this by independent Bernoulli random variables which we access only if the user is exposed to the content, and where the probability of user $u \in \mathcal{U}$ appreciating a content of topic $t \in \mathcal{T}$ is $p_{ut} \in [0, 1]$. The parameters p_{ut} are unknown. However, we assume that from previous exposures to various contents, we know whether a topic t is typically interesting for a user u, i.e., we know whether $p_{ut} > 1/2$. We consider the dissemination of a single news item, whose topic $\theta \in \mathcal{T}$ is unknown.

To model the dissemination process, we consider the set of sequential policies that proceed by selecting users $U^1, U^2, \cdots$ without replacement until either the set of users is exhausted or a stopping condition is reached. At step $i \geq 1$, we decide either to stop the dissemination or to expose the news to a yet unexposed user $U^i \in \mathcal{U}^i := \mathcal{U} \setminus \{U^1, \dots, U^{i-1}\}$. If user U^i is selected, we observe her appreciation X^i of the news item, where X^i is a Bernoulli r.v. with mean $p_{U^i\theta}$. The decision taken at step i is based on all previous decisions and observations, so that U^i is $\mathcal{G}^i$-measurable, where $\mathcal{G}^i := \sigma(U^1, X^1, \dots, U^{i-1}, X^{i-1})$. The step at which the dissemination terminates is denoted by I, a (random) stopping time with respect to the filtration $(\mathcal{G}^i, i \geq 1)$. We consider the set of policies that leverage the assumed side-information (whether $p_{ut} > 1/2$).

Our objective is to devise a sequential user selection policy under which most of the users interested in the news item are exposed, while not spamming too many uninterested users. To formalize this objective, we assume that (i) not exposing a user yields a reward equal to 0, (ii) selecting a user who appreciates (resp. does not appreciate) the news item brings a reward equal to +1 (resp. −1). We adopt this symmetric weighting to simplify the presentation, but everything could readily be generalized to differing weights, and even multiple grades of appreciation. The expected reward of selecting user u under topic t is thus $2p_{ut} - 1$. The total expected reward of a policy that selects users $U^1, \dots, U^{I-1}$ under the true topic θ can thus be written as: $\sum_{i=1}^{I-1} 2p_{U^i\theta} - 1$.

As in classical multi-armed bandit (MAB) problems, we quantify the performance of a policy through the notion of *regret* that compares its expected reward to that obtained by an "Oracle policy" aware of the true topic θ. The Oracle policy exposes only those users u with $p_{u\theta} > \frac{1}{2}$, thus achieving an expected reward: $\sum_{u\in\mathcal{U}} \max\{2p_{u\theta} - 1, 0\}$. Hence the regret of a policy selecting users $U^1, \dots, U^{I-1}$ under the true topic θ is:

$$C = \left(\sum_{u\in\mathcal{U}} \max\{2p_{u\theta} - 1, 0\}\right) - \left(\sum_{i=1}^{I-1} 2p_{U^i\theta} - 1\right).$$

To capture the stated goal of reaching as many interested users as possible, while not "spamming" those who are not interested, we decompose the regret into the following two types. First, we have the *missed opportunity* regret (the complement of the notion of *recall* in information retrieval):

$$C_0 = \sum_{u\in\mathcal{U}^I} \max\{0, 2p_{u\theta} - 1\}, \tag{1}$$

which represents the cumulative expected reward of appreciative users that the dissemination misses. Second, we have the *spamming* regret (the complement of the notion of *precision* in information retrieval):

$$C_1 = \sum_{u\in\mathcal{U}\setminus\mathcal{U}^I} \max\{0, 1 - 2p_{u\theta}\}, \tag{2}$$

which represents the cumulative expected penalty of non-appreciative users that the dissemination targets. It is easy to see that $C = C_0 + C_1$, and any efficient dissemination policy would need to balance these two types of regret.

Conventions: Throughout the paper, subscripts are reserved for users (for which we use letters u, U, $\mathcal{U}$) and topics (for which we use letters t, θ, T, $\mathcal{T}$). If two subscripts appear, the first refers to a user and the second to a topic. Selection steps are indicated by superscripts (for which we use letters i, j, I). Whenever we use sets as subscripts, it is understood that we take the union of all indexed elements. For example, $\mathcal{A}_\mathcal{B}$ means $\bigcup_{b\in\mathcal{B}} \mathcal{A}_b$.

2.2 The Greedy-Bayes Approach

To describe our policy, we introduce the following notations. For any topic t, and any user u:

$$g_{ut} := \mathbf{1}\{p_{ut} > 1/2\}.$$

Additionally, we let

$$\mathcal{T}_u := \{t \in \mathcal{T} : g_{ut} = 1\}$$

be all topics appreciated by user u, and conversely for a given t, we let

$$\mathcal{U}_t := \{u \in \mathcal{U} : g_{ut} = 1\}$$

be all users who appreciate the topic t.

The approach we propose proceeds as follows. We maintain a probability distribution $\nu^i = \{\nu^i(t)\}_{t\in\mathcal{T}}$ over $\mathcal{T}$ at each step $i \geq 1$. We initialize with $\nu_t^1 = 1/\tau$ uniformly over $\mathcal{T}$. At each step $i \geq 1$, if we decide not to terminate the dissemination, we select a user $U^i \in \mathcal{U}^i$ such that:

$$U^i \in \arg\max_{u\in\mathcal{U}^i} \nu^i(\mathcal{T}_u)\,, \tag{3}$$

where $\nu^i(\mathcal{T}_u) := \sum_{t\in\mathcal{T}} g_{ut}\nu^i(t)$. After observing X^i, we perform the following updates for all $t \in \mathcal{T}$:

$$\nu_t^{i+1} = \frac{\nu^i(t)\,[q_{U^it}X^i + (1-q_{U^it})(1-X^i)]}{\sum_{s\in\mathcal{T}} \nu_s^i[q_{U^is}X^i + (1-q_{U^is})(1-X^i)]}, \tag{4}$$

where, for an intensity parameter $r \in (0,1]$ to be specified, we define:

$$q_{ut} := \frac{1+r}{2}g_{ut} + \frac{1-r}{2}(1-g_{ut}). \tag{5}$$

It now remains to specify the stopping criterion, i.e., the step at which we decide to stop the dissemination. We stop it at step i if the probability distribution of ν^i puts very little mass on topics t in which the remaining users $u \in \mathcal{U}^i$ are interested. More precisely, for some large threshold A to be specified, we stop at step i if and only if:

$$\nu^i(\mathcal{T}_{\mathcal{U}^i}) \leq \frac{1}{A+1} \Leftrightarrow \frac{\nu^i(\mathcal{T}\setminus\mathcal{T}_{\mathcal{U}^i})}{1-\nu^i(\mathcal{T}\setminus\mathcal{T}_{\mathcal{U}^i})} \geq A. \tag{6}$$

We call the resulting algorithm Greedy-Bayes, in reference to the greedy selection process in (3) and to the (pseudo) Bayesian update of (4). A formal description of Greedy-Bayes is presented in its pseudo-code.

Algorithm Greedy-Bayes

1: **Input:** The $n \times \tau$ preference indicator matrix g; update intensity r; stopping threshold A.
2: **Initialization:**
   $q_{ut} \leftarrow \frac{1+r}{2}g_{ut} + \frac{1-r}{2}(1-g_{ut})$, $\forall u \in \mathcal{U}, t \in \mathcal{T}$.
   $\nu_t^1 \leftarrow 1/\tau$, $\forall t \in \mathcal{T}$.
3: **repeat**
4: **Selection step** i:
   $U^i \leftarrow \arg\max\left\{\sum_{t\in\mathcal{T}} g_{ut}\nu^i(t)\,, u \in \mathcal{U}^i\right\}$.
5: **Update step** i:
   $\nu_t^{i+1} \leftarrow \frac{\nu^i(t)[q_{U^it}X^i+(1-q_{U^it})(1-X^i)]}{\sum_{s\in\mathcal{T}}\nu_s^i[q_{U^is}X^i+(1-q_{U^is})(1-X^i)]}$, $\forall t \in \mathcal{T}$.
6: **Increment:**
   $i \leftarrow i+1$
7: **until** $\nu^i(\mathcal{T}_{\mathcal{U}^i}) \leq \frac{1}{A+1}$, and in particular if $\mathcal{U}^i = \emptyset$.
8: **Output:** $I, U^1, \cdots, U^{I-1}$ and $X^1, \cdots, X^{I-1}$.

It is important to note that the policy does not require knowledge of the precise values of the p_{ut}, and the knowledge of g_{ut} is enough. In this paper, we also consider a variant of Greedy-Bayes, where in the selection step, rather than averaging over topics, we sample a representative topic and evaluate rewards based on this sample. This places us in a context that is akin to Thompson Sampling in traditional MAB problems. The resulting policy is referred to as Thompson-Sampling. The only difference from Greedy-Bayes is that Step 4 is replaced with: Draw a sample topic T^i according to ν^i and choose any U^i such that $g_{uT^i} = 1$.

3. GENERIC REGRET UPPER BOUNDS

We now analyze the performance of Greedy-Bayes and Thompson-Sampling. Throughout the analysis, we assume that a δ-margin condition holds: there exists δ, $0 < \delta \leq \frac{1}{2}$ such that

$$p_{ut} \notin (\tfrac{1}{2}-\delta, \tfrac{1}{2}+\delta), \qquad \forall u \in \mathcal{U}, t \in \mathcal{T}.$$

The next theorem provides generic upper bounds for the regret achieved under either Greedy-Bayes or Thompson-Sampling.

Theorem 1. *Let $(p_{ut})_{u\in\mathcal{U},t\in\mathcal{T}}$ satisfy the δ-margin condition, and let the parameters satisfy $\delta \leq r \leq \frac{3}{2}\delta$ and $\log A \geq 20\log n + 8\log\tau$. Then, the expected regret $\mathbb{E}(C)$ is of the order of $O(\frac{\tau}{\delta^2}\log(n\tau))$, hence $O(\frac{\tau}{\delta^2}\log(n))$ when $\tau \leq n$, for both* Greedy-Bayes *and* Thompson-Sampling.

More precisely, the overall expected regret decomposes into a missed opportunity regret $\mathbb{E}(C_0)$ of order $o(1)$, and a spamming regret $\mathbb{E}(C_1)$ of order $O(\frac{\tau}{\delta^2}\log(n\tau))$.

Remark 1. *In our regret analysis, we actually control the number of interested users that the algorithm misses as well as the number of spammed users. The regret bounds are then obtained by noting that, always, $|2p_{ut}-1| \leq 1$.*

When we consider scenarios where p_{ut} can take only two values, namely $1/2 \pm \delta$, then it is easy to see that the upper bounds can be reduced by a factor $1/\delta$ since, in this case, $|2p_{ut}-1| = 2\delta$.

We prove Theorem 1 by controlling separately the spamming regret C_1 and the missed opportunity regret C_0, which we present respectively as Propositions 1 and 2 for Greedy-Bayes. We give the proof for Thompson-Sampling separately. The primary approach in these proofs is to characterize the interplay between the spam events and the concentration of ν^i on the true topic. To capture this, it turns out that basic Azuma-Hoeffding inequalities are not sufficient, since we need a finer scale-variance control. We use instead a stronger Bernstein-type martingale concentration inequality due to Freedman [8], which we quote here for convenience:

Theorem 2. *(Freedman [8]) Let $\xi_1, \xi_2 \ldots$ be a sequence of martingale differences with respect to some filtration $\{\mathcal{G}^i\}$ such that for some constant $a > 0$, $|\xi_j| \leq a$. Let $M^i := \xi_1 + \cdots + \xi_i$ be the corresponding martingale, and $\langle M\rangle^i$ its corresponding compensator defined as $\langle M\rangle^i = \sum_{j=1}^i \mathbb{E}(\xi_j^2|\mathcal{G}^{j-1})$. Then for a given finite stopping time I with respect to the filtration $\{\mathcal{G}^i\}$, for all $z, L > 0$, one has*

$$\mathbb{P}(\max_{i\leq I}|M^i| > z, \langle M\rangle_I \leq L) \leq 2\mathrm{e}^{-\frac{z^2}{2(L+az/3)}}.$$

3.1 Proof of Theorem 1 for Greedy-Bayes

3.1.1 Spamming Regret C_1

We first study the spamming regret C_1 defined in (2). We say that we have a "spam" event at step i if $g_{U^i\theta} = 0$ and let $Z^i \in \{0,1\}$ be the indicator of that event. Introduce:

$$R^i := \frac{\nu^i(\theta)}{\nu^i(\mathcal{T}_{\mathcal{U}^i\setminus\mathcal{U}_\theta})}$$
$$S^i := \log(R^i/R^{i-1}), \text{ with } S^1 := \log(R^1),$$

where $\mathcal{T}_{\mathcal{U}^i\setminus\mathcal{U}_\theta}$ contains topics appreciated by those remaining users who do not appreciate θ.

REMARK 2. *Quantity R^i conditions the occurrence of spam, and is therefore key to our analysis, as we now explain. If a user u_+ appreciative of θ remains in $\mathcal{U}^i$ and $R^i > 1$ then no spamming will occur under* GREEDY-BAYES. *Indeed, user u_+ will be preferred to any remaining user u_- not appreciative of θ, as $R^i > 1$ implies that*

$$\nu^i(\mathcal{T}_{u_+}) \geq \nu^i(\theta) \geq \nu^i(\mathcal{T}_{\mathcal{U}^i\setminus\mathcal{U}_\theta}) \geq \nu^i(\mathcal{T}_{u_-}).$$

If no appreciative user remains, i.e. $\mathcal{U}^i \setminus \mathcal{U}_\theta = \mathcal{U}^i$, and if $R^i > A$ then the stopping condition (6) will hold and no further spamming will occur. Indeed, condition $R^i > A$ implies that $\nu^i(\mathcal{T}_{\mathcal{U}^i}) < \nu^i(\theta)/A \leq 1/A$.

We now give a technical lemma which will be instrumental to controlling R^i.

LEMMA 1. *Let $\tilde{R}^i$ and $\tilde{S}^i$ be defined as follows*

$$\tilde{R}^i := \frac{\nu^i(\theta)}{\nu^i(\mathcal{T}_{\mathcal{U}^{i-1}\setminus\mathcal{U}_\theta})},$$
$$\tilde{S}^i := \log(\tilde{R}^i/R^{i-1}).$$

It holds that $\tilde{R}^i \leq R^i$ and $\tilde{S}^i \leq S^i$. Furthermore, the variables $\tilde{S}^i$ are bounded: $|\tilde{S}^i| \leq r' := \log\frac{1+r}{1-r}$. Let

$$\mathcal{T}_-^i := \mathcal{T}_{U^i} \text{ if } \theta \notin \mathcal{T}_{U^i},\ \mathcal{T}\setminus\mathcal{T}_{U^i} \text{ otherwise,}$$
$$Q^i := \frac{\nu^i(\mathcal{T}_-^i)}{\nu^i(\mathcal{T}_{\mathcal{U}^i\setminus\mathcal{U}_\theta})}.$$

Then, provided $r \leq \frac{3}{2}\delta$, under the δ-margin condition the following properties hold:

$$|\tilde{S}^{i+1}| \leq 8rQ^i, \quad (7)$$
$$\mathbb{E}(\tilde{S}^{i+1}|\mathcal{G}^i) \geq \delta r Q^i \geq \frac{\delta r Z^i}{\tau}. \quad (8)$$

PROOF. The claim of $\tilde{R}^i \leq R^i$ is due to the monotonicity (more elements) of $\mathcal{U}^{i-1}$ in the denominator, and the claim on $\tilde{S}^i$ follows directly. Now let $\delta' = |p_{U^i\theta} - 1/2|$. By the δ-margin assumption, $\delta' \geq \delta$. To reduce clutter, fix i and write $Q = Q^i$. The update rule of (4) determines the value of $\tilde{S}^{i+1}$ conditionally on $\mathcal{G}^i$ as a function of X^i. After some simplification, we obtain

$$\tilde{S}^{i+1} = \begin{cases} \log(\frac{1}{1-Q+Q(1-r)/(1+r)}) & \text{with prob. } \frac{1}{2}+\delta', \\ \log(\frac{1}{1-Q+Q(1+r)/(1-r)}) & \text{with prob. } \frac{1}{2}-\delta'. \end{cases}$$

Since $Q \in [0,1]$, we first deduce from this that $|\tilde{S}^i| \leq \log\frac{1+r}{1-r}$. By using the fact that $r \leq \frac{3}{2}\delta \leq \frac{3}{4}$ and approximations to the logarithm, including $\log(1+x) \leq x$, we further deduce that $|\tilde{S}^i| \leq 8rQ$. Taking conditional expectation yields

$$\begin{aligned}
\mathbb{E}(\tilde{S}^{i+1}|\mathcal{G}^i) &= -(\tfrac{1}{2}+\delta')\log(1-Q+Q\tfrac{1-r}{1+r}) \\
&\quad -(\tfrac{1}{2}-\delta')\log(1-Q+Q\tfrac{1+r}{1-r}) \\
&\geq -\log\Big(1-Q+(\tfrac{1}{2}+\delta')Q\tfrac{1-r}{1+r} \\
&\qquad +(\tfrac{1}{2}-\delta')Q\tfrac{1+r}{1-r}\Big) \\
&= -\log\left(1+\frac{2r^2-4\delta' r}{1-r^2}Q\right) \\
&\geq -\frac{2r^2-4\delta' r}{1-r^2}Q \geq -\frac{2r^2-4\delta r}{1-r^2}Q \\
&\geq \frac{4-2r/\delta}{1-r^2}\delta r Q \geq \delta r Q,
\end{aligned}$$

where we have used that $-\log(x)$ is convex, that $\log(1+x) \leq x$, that $\delta' \geq \delta$ by the δ-margin assumption, and that $r \leq \frac{3}{2}\delta$ by hypothesis.

It remains to show that $Q \geq Z^i/\tau$. To this end, first note that $Z^i = 1$ implies that $\mathcal{T}_-^i = \mathcal{T}_{U^i}$. Since the selection of U^i maximizes $\nu^i(\mathcal{T}_u)$, it thus follows that Q maximizes $\nu^i(\mathcal{T}_u)/\nu^i(\mathcal{T}_{\mathcal{U}^i\setminus\mathcal{U}_\theta})$. Since for all $t \in \mathcal{T}_{\mathcal{U}^i\setminus\mathcal{U}_\theta}$ there exists $u \in \mathcal{U}^i$ such that $t \in \mathcal{T}_u$, it follows that

$$\nu^i(t)/\nu^i(\mathcal{T}_{\mathcal{U}^i\setminus\mathcal{U}_\theta}) \leq \nu^i(\mathcal{T}_u)/\nu^i(\mathcal{T}_{\mathcal{U}^i\setminus\mathcal{U}_\theta}) \leq Q.$$

This entails that $Q < 1/\tau$ is impossible, as it would lead, after summing the previous inequality over $t \in \mathcal{T}_{\mathcal{U}^i\setminus\mathcal{U}_\theta}$ to the contradiction $1 < |\mathcal{T}_{\mathcal{U}^i\setminus\mathcal{U}_\theta}|/\tau \leq 1$, since there are at most τ elements in $\mathcal{T}_{\mathcal{U}^i\setminus\mathcal{U}_\theta}$. □

We now provide bounds on the expected spamming regret, $\mathbb{E}(C_1)$:

PROPOSITION 1. *Given parameters $r \leq \frac{3}{2}\delta$ and $A \geq 1$, the expected spamming regret $\mathbb{E}(C_1)$ of* GREEDY-BAYES *is no larger than $x + o(1)$ where*

$$x = \left(\tfrac{B\tau}{\delta^2}\left[3\log n + \log(1+\tfrac{B\tau}{\delta^2})\right]\right) \vee \left(\tfrac{2\tau}{\delta r}\log A\right),$$

for some large constant B (which we can set explicitly to $B = 1028$).

PROOF. Since C_1 is bounded by n, the desired result will hold if one can show that

$$\mathbb{P}(C_1 > x) = o(n^{-1}).$$

Note that C_1 is no larger than $\sum_j Z^j$, by bounding $|2p_{U^j\theta} - 1|$ by 1 for every spam event $Z^j = 1$. Thus $\mathbb{P}(C_1 > x)$ is no larger than

$$\mathbb{P}(\sum_{j=1}^{I} Z^j > x) = \sum_{i=1}^{n}\mathbb{P}(Z^i = 1, \sum_{j=1}^{i-1} Z^j = x).$$

The desired result will thus follow if for all $i = 1, \ldots, n$,

$$\mathbb{P}(Z^i = 1, \sum_{j=1}^{i-1} Z^j = x) = o(n^{-2}). \quad (9)$$

In preparation to using Theorem 2, let:

$$\xi_j := \tilde{S}^j - \mathbb{E}(\tilde{S}^j|\mathcal{G}^{j-1}),$$
$$H^i := \textstyle\sum_{j=1}^i \mathbb{E}(\tilde{S}^j|\mathcal{G}^{j-1}),$$
$$N^i := \textstyle\sum_{j=1}^i \tilde{S}^j - H^i.$$

Applying bounds (7) and (8) of Lemma 1, we have:

$$\begin{aligned} H^i &\geq \textstyle\sum_{j=1}^{i-1} \delta r Q^j, & (10)\\ \langle N\rangle^i &\leq 64r^2 \textstyle\sum_{j=1}^{i-1} Q^j, & (11)\\ \tau \textstyle\sum_{j=1}^{i-1} Q^j &\geq \textstyle\sum_{j=1}^{i-1} Z^j. & (12)\end{aligned}$$

Thus the quantity of interest in Equation (9) verifies

$$\mathbb{P}(Z^i = 1, \sum_{j=1}^{i-1} Z^j = x) \leq \sum_{\ell > x} \mathbb{P}(Z^i = 1, \lceil \tau \sum_{j=1}^{i-1} Q^j \rceil = \ell),$$

where we have used Inequality (12).

On the event $\{\lceil \tau \sum_{j=1}^{i} Q^j \rceil = \ell\}$, one has

$$\begin{aligned} H^i &\geq \tfrac{\delta r}{\tau}(\ell - 1),\\ \langle N\rangle^i &\leq 64\tfrac{r^2}{\tau}\ell. \end{aligned} \quad (13)$$

Moreover, under $Z^i = 1$, we necessarily have $R^i \leq A$, for otherwise either an appreciative user would be selected, or stopping would occur, as explained in Remark 2. Thus, as $\exp\left(\sum_{j=1}^{i} S^j\right) = R^i$ and since $\tilde{S}^j \leq S^j$ by Lemma 1, we that $N^i + H^i = \sum_{j=1}^{i} \tilde{S}^j \leq \sum_{j=1}^{i} S^j \leq \log(A)$ on $Z^i = 1$. Let

$$x_\ell := \tfrac{\delta r}{\tau}(\ell - 1) - \log A \geq \tfrac{\delta r}{2\tau}(\ell - 1), \quad (14)$$

where we have used the fact that $\ell - 1 \geq x \geq \frac{2\tau}{\delta r}\log A$, by hypothesis. Combined with Inequalities (13), this yields

$$\begin{aligned} &\mathbb{P}(Z^i = 1, \lceil \tau \textstyle\sum_{j=1}^{i} Q^j \rceil = \ell)\\ &\leq \mathbb{P}(|N^i| \geq x_\ell, \langle N\rangle^i \leq 64\tfrac{r^2}{\tau}\ell). \end{aligned}$$

Since $r \leq \frac{3}{2}\delta \leq \frac{3}{4}$, we have $|S^j| \leq \log\frac{1+r}{1-r} \leq 3r$ and thus $|\xi_j| \leq 6r$. We then invoke Bernstein's inequality of Theorem 2 with $a = 6r$ and $L = 64r^2\ell/\tau$, to upper bound this last probability by:

$$2\exp\left(-\frac{x_\ell}{2(a/3 + L/x_\ell)}\right) = 2\exp\left(-\frac{x_\ell}{4(r + 32\frac{r^2}{\tau}\ell/x_\ell)}\right).$$

Using $x_\ell \geq \frac{\delta r}{2\tau}(\ell - 1)$ from (14), the fact that $\frac{\ell}{\ell-1} \leq 2$ for $\ell > 1$, and that $\delta < \frac{1}{2}$, we further bound this by (letting $B = 1028$):

$$2\exp\left(-\frac{\frac{\delta}{2\tau}(\ell-1)}{4(1 + 128/\delta)}\right) \leq 2\exp\left(-\tfrac{\delta^2}{B\tau}(\ell - 1)\right).$$

It now readily follows that the quantity of interest in (9) can be bounded by:

$$\begin{aligned} &\sum_{\ell > x} 2\exp\left(-\tfrac{\delta^2}{B\tau}(\ell-1)\right) = 2\exp\left(-\tfrac{\delta^2}{B\tau}x\right)\frac{1}{1 - \exp\left(-\frac{\delta^2}{B\tau}\right)}\\ &\leq 2n^{-3}\frac{\left(1 + \frac{B\tau}{\delta^2}\right)^{-1}}{1 - \exp\left(-\frac{\delta^2}{B\tau}\right)} \leq 2n^{-3} = o(n^{-2}) \end{aligned}$$

where we have used the fact that:

$$x \geq \tfrac{B\tau}{\delta^2}\left[3\log n + \log(1 + \tfrac{B\tau}{\delta^2})\right],$$

and that $(1 + 1/y)(1 - e^{-y}) \geq 1$ for all $y > 0$. This concludes the proof. □

3.1.2 *Missed Opportunity Regret C_0*

We now study the missed opportunity regret, for which we introduce further notation that parallels the techniques presented so far. For $t \in \mathcal{T}$, we define:

$$\begin{aligned} &R_t^i := \tfrac{\nu^i(\theta)}{\nu^i(t)},\\ &S_t^i := \log\left(\tfrac{R_t^i}{R_t^{i-1}}\right), \qquad \text{with } S_t^1 := \log R_t^1 = 0\\ &Z_t^i := \mathbf{1}_{t \in \mathcal{T}_-^i} \equiv \mathbf{1}_{\theta \in \mathcal{T}_{U^i}, t \notin \mathcal{T}_{U^i}} + \mathbf{1}_{\theta \notin \mathcal{T}_{U^i}, t \in \mathcal{T}_{U^i}}, \end{aligned}$$

where $\mathcal{T}_-^i$ is as in Lemma 1.

Remark 3. *Quantity R_t^i critically conditions the missed opportunity cost and is thus key to our analysis. Specifically, if there are appreciative users remaining, i.e. $\theta \in \mathcal{T}_{\mathcal{U}^i}$, and we do stop, then there must exist $t \notin \mathcal{T}_{\mathcal{U}^i}$ such that $R_t^i \leq \frac{\tau}{A}$, i.e. $\nu^i(t) \geq \frac{A}{\tau}\nu^i(\theta)$. Indeed, otherwise if $\forall t \notin \mathcal{T}_{\mathcal{U}^i}$ we have $\nu^i(t) < \frac{A}{\tau}\nu^i(\theta)$, then $\nu^i(\mathcal{T} \setminus \mathcal{T}_{\mathcal{U}^i}) < A\nu^i(\theta) \leq A\nu^i(\mathcal{T}_{\mathcal{U}^i})$, which violates the stopping condition (6). This will be instrumental to bound the missed opportunity regret by controlling the probability of deviations of R_t^i.*

Lemma 2. *The random variable S_t^i is bounded, i.e. $|S_t^i| \leq r' := \log\frac{1+r}{1-r}$. It further satisfies*

$$\begin{aligned} \mathbb{E}(S_t^{i+1}|\mathcal{G}^i) &= r' Z_t^i |2p_{U^i\theta} - 1|\\ &\geq 2\delta r' Z_t^i, & (15)\\ Var(S_t^{i+1}|\mathcal{G}^i) &= (r')^2 Z_t^i[1 - (2p_{U^i\theta} - 1)^2]\\ &\leq (r')^2 Z_t^i. & (16)\end{aligned}$$

The proof trivially follows by noting that if $Z_t^i = 0$, $S_t^{i+1} = 0$, while if $Z_t^i = 1$, then conditionally on $\mathcal{G}^i$, $S_t^{i+1} = r'$ with probability $1/2 + \delta_i$ and $S_t^{i+1} = -r'$ with probability $1/2 - \delta_i$ where $\delta_i := |p_{U^i\theta} - 1/2|$.

We now control the missed opportunity regret C_0 through a suitable choice of parameter A in the stopping criterion (6):

Proposition 2. *Assume that A verifies*

$$\log(A/\tau) \geq 2(2r'/3 + r'/(2\delta))[3\log n + \log\tau]. \quad (17)$$

Then $\mathbb{E}C_0$ is $o(1)$ as $n \to \infty$. In particular, if $r \leq \frac{3}{2}\delta$, then it follows that (17) is satisfied by choosing $\log A \geq 20\log n + 8\log\tau$.

Proof. Let $\mathcal{E}$ be the event that the algorithm stops at a step I at which a remaining user $u \in \mathcal{U}^I$ is interested in topic θ, that is $\theta \in \mathcal{T}_u$. The result of the proposition will follow if $\mathbb{P}(\mathcal{E}) = o(n^{-1})$. By the argument in Remark 3, stopping when there are appreciative users implies there exists a user such that $R_t^I \leq \frac{\tau}{A}$. Therefore:

$$\begin{aligned} \mathbb{P}(\mathcal{E}) &= \sum_{i=1}^{n} \mathbb{P}(I = i, \theta \in \mathcal{T}_{\mathcal{U}^i})\\ &\leq \sum_{i=1}^{n} \mathbb{P}(I = i, \exists t \in \mathcal{T}_{\mathcal{U}^i} : R_t^i \leq \tfrac{\tau}{A})\\ &\leq n\tau \max_{i \leq n, t \in \mathcal{T}} \mathbb{P}(R_t^i \leq \tfrac{\tau}{A})\\ &\leq n^2\tau \max_{i \leq n, k \leq i, t \in \mathcal{T}} \mathbb{P}\Big(\sum_{j=1}^{i} Z_t^j = k, R_t^i \leq \tfrac{\tau}{A}\Big). \end{aligned}$$

Now fix t, and let $\xi_j = S_t^j - \mathbb{E}(S_t^j|\mathcal{G}^{j-1})$, and note that since $|S_t^j| \le r'$ it follows that $\xi_j \le 2r'$. Next introduce

$$\begin{aligned} G^i &:= \textstyle\sum_{j=1}^i \mathbb{E}(S_t^j|\mathcal{G}^{j-1}),\\ M^i &:= \textstyle\sum_{j=1}^i S_t^j - G^i, \text{ and}\\ \langle M\rangle^i &:= \textstyle\sum_{j=1}^i \mathrm{Var}(S_t^j|\mathcal{G}^{j-1}).\end{aligned}$$

We then have:

$$\begin{aligned}&\mathbb{P}(\sum_{j=1}^i Z_t^j = k, R_t^i \le \tau/A)\\ &\quad= \mathbb{P}(\sum_{j=1}^i Z_t^j = k, \sum_{j=1}^i S_t^j \le \log(\tau/A))\\ &\quad= \mathbb{P}(\sum_{j=1}^i Z_t^j = k, G^i + M^i \le \log(\tau/A)).\end{aligned}$$

By (15) and (16), when $\sum_{j=1}^i Z_t^j = k$, it holds that $G^i \ge 2\delta r'(k-1)^+$ and $\langle M\rangle^i \le r'^2 k$. Thus

$$\begin{aligned}&\mathbb{P}(\sum_{j=1}^i Z_t^j = k, G^i + M^i \le \log(\tau/A))\\ &\quad\le \mathbb{P}(M^i \le \log(\tau/A) - 2\delta r'(k-1)^+, \langle M\rangle^i \le r'^2 k).\end{aligned}$$

We can now apply the Bernstein's inequality of Theorem 2 with these ξ_j, using $a = 2r'$ and $L = r'^2 k$, to yield the following upper bound on the right-hand side of the above expression:

$$\exp\left(-\frac{(\log(A/\tau) + 2\delta r'(k-1)^+)}{2(2r'/3 + r'^2 k/[\log(A/\tau) + 2\delta r'(k-1)^+])}\right).$$

This expression will be less than $1/(n^3\tau)$ provided

$$\frac{(\log(\frac{A}{\tau}) + 2\delta r'(k-1)^+}{2(2\frac{r'}{3} + r'^2 k/[\log(\frac{A}{\tau}) + 2\delta r'(k-1)^+])} \ge \log(n^3\tau)$$

or equivalently

$$\begin{aligned}&\frac{\log(\frac{A}{\tau}) + 2\delta r'(k-1)^+}{2\log(n^3\tau)}\\ &\qquad\ge \left[2\frac{r'}{3} + \frac{r'^2 k}{\log(\frac{A}{\tau}) + 2\delta r'(k-1)^+}\right].\end{aligned}$$

By setting $k = 0$ in the left-hand side to minimize it, and $k \to \infty$ in the right-hand side to maximize it, we obtain that this property holds for all k provided

$$\log(\frac{A}{\tau}) \ge 2\log(n^3\tau)\left[2r'/3 + \frac{r'}{2\delta}\right],$$

and under this condition we therefore have that $\mathbb{P}(\mathcal{E}) = o(n^{-1})$, concluding the main proof. Under $r \le \frac{3}{2}\delta$, the claimed simplified expression follows by the fact that $r' = \log\frac{1+r}{1-r} \le 4\delta \le 2$. □

3.2 Proof of Theorem 1 for Thompson-Sampling

We now establish a similar upper bound for the regret incurred by the THOMPSON-SAMPLING variant of GREEDY-BAYES, as described in Section 2, thus completing the proof of Theorem 1.

PROPOSITION 3. *Under the assumptions made in Propositions 1 and 2, the regret under* THOMPSON-SAMPLING *is at most* $O(\tau\log n/\delta^2)$.

PROOF. The average missed opportunity regret, $\mathbb{E}(C_0)$ is $o(1)$ by the same analysis as that of GREEDY-BAYES. To control the spamming regret $\mathbb{E}(C_1)$ we distinguish spamming events according to the topic T^i that was sampled upon spamming. We shall establish an upper bound of $O(\log n/\delta^2)$ on the corresponding spamming regret for each possible value t of T^i, from which the result will follow by just summing these upper bounds.

Fix $t \ne \theta$ and write for some K to be specified:

$$\begin{aligned}\mathbb{E}C_1(t) &:= \mathbb{E}\textstyle\sum_{i=1}^I Z^i \mathbf{1}_{T^i=t}\\ &\le K + \sum_{k\ge K}\mathbb{P}(\sum_{i=1}^I Z^i\mathbf{1}_{T^i=t} > k)\\ &= K + \sum_{k\ge K, i>k}\mathbb{P}(Z^i\mathbf{1}_{T^i=t} = 1, \sum_{j=1}^{i-1} Z^j\mathbf{1}_{T^j=t} = k)\\ &\le K + \sum_{k\ge K, i>k, x>k}\mathbb{P}(Z^i\mathbf{1}_{T^i=t} = 1, \sum_{j=1}^{i-1} Z_t^j = x)\\ &\le K + \sum_{k\ge K, i>k, x>k}\mathbb{P}(T^i = t, \sum_{j=1}^{i-1} Z_t^j = x)\\ &= K + \sum_{k\ge K, i>k, x>k}\int_0^1 \mathbb{P}(\nu^i(t) > a, \sum_{j=1}^{i-1} Z_t^j = x)da\\ &\le K + \sum_{k\ge K, i>k, x>k}\int_0^1 \mathbb{P}(1/R_t^i > a, \sum_{j=1}^{i-1} Z_t^j = x)da.\end{aligned}$$

In the above we used the previously introduced variables Z_t^j and noticed that $Z_t^j \ge Z^j\mathbf{1}_{T^j=t}$. By making the change of variables $b = -\log a$, the previous integral reads

$$\int_0^\infty \mathbb{P}(S_t^i < b, \sum_{j=1}^{i-1} Z_t^j = x)e^{-b}db.$$

Arguing as in the proof of Proposition 2, we obtain the following upper bound for the probability in the last integral:

$$\begin{aligned}&\mathbb{P}(S_t^i < b, \sum_{j=1}^{i-1} Z_t^j = x)\\ &\quad\le \mathbb{P}(|M_i| \ge 2\delta r'x - b, \langle M\rangle_i \le r'^2 x)\\ &\quad\le 2\exp\left(-\frac{|2\delta r'x - b|}{2(r'/3 + r'^2 x/|2\delta r'x - b|}\right).\end{aligned}$$

For $b \le \delta r'x$, this is in turn no larger than $2\exp(-\delta^2 x/3)$. We eventually obtain

$$\int_0^\infty \mathbb{P}(S_t^i < b), \sum_{j=1}^{i-1} Z_t^j = x)e^{-b}db \le 2e^{-\delta^2 x/3} + e^{-\delta r' x}.$$

Plugging this back in our previous upper bound and noting that the sums over k, i, x involve each at most n terms, we get

$$\mathbb{E}C_1(t) \le K + n^3\left(2e^{-\delta^2 K/3} + e^{-\delta r' K}\right).$$

Choosing $K = \delta^{-1}\log n\max(10/\delta, 4/r')$, since $1/r' = O(1/\delta)$, this upper bound is indeed $O(\delta^{-2}\log n)$, which concludes the proof. □

4. IMPROVED UPPER BOUNDS

In this section, we establish improved regret upper bounds for GREEDY-BAYES in scenarios with additional structure (a similar result may hold for THOMPSON-SAMPLING, but this is not proven here.) We first analyze the spamming regret until the point when "good users" are exhausted, showing that it does not scale with n. We next show that when the sets of good users for distinct topics differ by a sufficient amount, then no further spamming regret is incurred. This yields an overall regret of order $O(\tau/\delta^2)$, as stated in Theorem 3. We then show that with further additional structure this upper bound can be reduced to $O(\log \tau/\delta^2)$.

4.1 Spamming While Good Users Remain

We now provide a tighter control of the number of spam events until all users in the "good" set $\mathcal{U}_\theta$ are exposed. Denote by I' the time step i at which one either stops or exposes the last user in $\mathcal{U}_\theta$. Let $C_1' := \sum_{i=1}^{I'} Z^i$ be the spamming regret up to time I'. We then have

PROPOSITION 4. *For GREEDY-BAYES, assuming $r \geq \delta$, the expected spamming regret up to time I' verifies*

$$\mathbb{E}C_1' \leq 52\frac{(\tau-1)}{\delta^2}. \tag{18}$$

PROOF. At each step $i \leq I'$ such that $Z^i = 1$, necessarily $\sum_{t\in\mathcal{T}_{Ui}} \nu_i^t \geq \nu_i^\theta$, for otherwise one of the users in $\mathcal{U}_\theta$ available up to I' would have been preferred and no spamming would have occurred. Thus

$$\begin{aligned}\mathbb{E}C_1' &\leq \mathbb{E}\sum_{i=1}^{I'} Z^i \sum_{t\neq\theta} Z_t^i \min(1, \tfrac{\nu^i(t)}{\nu^i(\theta)})\\ &= \sum_{t\neq\theta}\mathbb{E}\sum_{i=1}^{I'} Z^i Z_t^i \min(1, \tfrac{1}{R_t^i}).\end{aligned}$$

Fix then $t \in \mathcal{T}\setminus\{\theta\}$. Introduce for all $k \geq 1$ the stopping time I_k defined as

$$I_k := \inf\{i \geq 1 : \sum_{j=1}^{i} Z_t^j \geq k\}.$$

We then have the following upper bound

$$\mathbb{E}\sum_{i=1}^{I'} Z^i Z_t^i \min(1, \tfrac{1}{R_t^i}) \leq \sum_{k\geq 1}\mathbb{E}\min(1, \tfrac{1}{R_t^{I_k}}). \tag{19}$$

We now bound the terms in this last summation for any fixed $k \geq 1$. Recall that $\log R_t^i = M^i + G^i$. One readily has, for any fixed $K > 0$,

$$\begin{aligned}\mathbb{E}\min(1, \tfrac{1}{R_t^{I_k}}) &\leq \mathbb{P}(M^{I_k} + G^{I_k} \leq 0) + \mathrm{e}^{-K}\\ &\quad +\mathbb{E}(\tfrac{1}{R_t^{I_k}}\mathbf{1}_{0<M^{I_k}+G^{I_k}<K})\\ &\leq \mathbb{P}(M^{I_k} + G^{I_k} \leq 0) + 2\mathrm{e}^{-K}\\ &\quad + \int_0^K \mathrm{e}^{-u}\mathbb{P}(M^{I_k} + G^{I_k} < u)du,\end{aligned}$$

where we used an integration by parts. By definition of I_k, in view of Lemma 2, one has

$$\langle M\rangle^{I_k} \leq (r')^2(k-1),\ G^{I_k} \geq 2\delta r'(k-1).$$

Fix now $K = \delta r'(k-1)$. Then for all $u \in (0, K)$, one has

$$\begin{aligned}\mathbb{P}(M^{I_k} + G^{I_k} < u) &\leq \mathbb{P}\big(|M^{I_k}| \geq \delta r'(k-1),\\ &\qquad \langle M\rangle^{I_k} \leq (r')^2(k-1)\big)\\ &\leq 2\mathrm{e}^{-\frac{\delta r'(k-1)}{2(r'/3+r'/\delta)}}\\ &\leq 2\mathrm{e}^{-\delta^2(k-1)/3},\end{aligned}$$

where we used Bernstein's inequality and the fact that the increments of martingale M are bounded by r'. This yields

$$\begin{aligned}&\mathbb{E}\min(1, \tfrac{1}{R_t^{I_k}})\\ &\leq 2\mathrm{e}^{-\delta r'(k-1)} + 2(\delta r'(k-1)+1)\mathrm{e}^{-\delta^2(k-1)/3}.\end{aligned}$$

The sum over $k \geq 1$ of the right-hand side in the above expression equals

$$\frac{2}{1-\mathrm{e}^{-\delta r'}} + \frac{2}{1-\mathrm{e}^{-\delta^2/3}}\left(1 + \frac{\delta r'}{1-\mathrm{e}^{-\delta^2/3}}\right).$$

To simplify this expression, we use the inequality $1/(1-\mathrm{e}^{-x}) \leq 2x^{-1}$, valid for any $x \in [0,1]$. The last upper bound is then in turn no larger than $\frac{4}{\delta r'} + \frac{48}{\delta^2}$, itself at most $52/\delta^2$ as $r' \geq r$ and we assumed $r \geq \delta$. □

4.2 Topic Diversity and Constant Regret

We now introduce a structural condition on topic diversity which will imply an upper bound on regret that is independent of n. Specifically, we say that the topic θ is c-good if

$$\forall t \in \mathcal{T},\ t \neq \theta \Rightarrow |\mathcal{U}_\theta \setminus \mathcal{U}_t| \geq c\log n. \tag{20}$$

We then have the following result.

THEOREM 3. *Under the δ-margin condition, for $r \in [\delta, 3\delta/2]$ and stopping criterion A satisfying (17), if content θ is c-good where c satisfies*

$$c \geq \max\left(\frac{1}{\delta r'}\frac{\log(A\tau)}{\log n}, \frac{6\log(n\tau)}{\delta^2\log n}, \frac{10\log(1/\delta)}{\delta^2\log n}\right), \tag{21}$$

the regret of GREEDY-BAYES under true topic θ is $O(\tau/\delta^2)$.

Before giving the proof, note that if $\log A = 20\log n + 8\log\tau$ with equality in Theorem 3, and if $\tau \leq n$ and $\delta \geq 1/n$, then Condition (21) can be replaced with $c \geq 15/\delta^2$ (noting that $r' = \log\frac{1+r}{1-r} \geq 2r \geq 2\delta$, and that the first term dominates).

PROOF. The result will follow from Proposition 4 if the expected regret is dominated by the spamming regret incurred prior to exposing all users of $\mathcal{U}_\theta$. This in turn holds if with probability $1 - o(n^{-1})$ GREEDY-BAYES stops as soon as the last "good" user in $\mathcal{U}_\theta$ is exposed. It thus suffices to show that

$$\mathbb{P}(\exists t \neq \theta, R_t^{I'} \leq \tau A) = o(n^{-1}),$$

which holds if $\mathbb{P}(R_t^{I'} \leq \tau A) = o(n^{-1}/\tau)$ uniformly in $t \neq \theta$. Now observe that by the definition of I', and since θ is c-good, $\sum_{i=1}^{I'} Z_t^i \geq c\log n$, and

$$\begin{aligned}\mathbb{P}(R_t^{I'} \leq \tau A) &\leq \sum_{k\geq c\log n}\mathbb{P}\left(R_t^{I'} \leq \tau A, \sum_{i=1}^{I'} Z_t^i = k\right)\\ &\leq \sum_{k\geq c\log n-1}\mathbb{P}\left(|M^{I'}| \geq 2\delta r'k - \log(A\tau), \langle M\rangle^{I'} \leq r'^2 k\right)\\ &\leq \sum_{k\geq c\log n-1}\exp\left(-\frac{x_k}{\frac{4}{3}r' + 2x_k^{-1}r'^2k}\right),\end{aligned}$$

where we noted $x_k := 2\delta r'k - \log(A\tau)$, used the facts that the increments of M^i are bounded by $2r'$, on $\{\sum_{i=1}^{I'} Z_t^i = k\}$ necessarily $G^{I'} \geq 2\delta r'k$ and $\langle M\rangle^{I'} \leq r'^2 k$, and finally applied Bernstein's inequality.

Then, under Condition (21), stopping occurs at I' with probability $1 - o(n^{-1})$. Indeed, as $c \log n \geq \log(A\tau)/(\delta r')$, it holds that $x_k \geq \delta r' k$. The previous sum is thus no larger (owing to $\delta < 1/2$) than

$$\sum_{k \geq c \log n - 1} \exp\left(-\frac{3\delta^2 k}{8}\right) \leq n^{-3c\delta^2/8} O(\delta^{-2}).$$

The logarithm of this last expression reads $-\frac{3c\delta^2}{8} \log n - 2\log(\delta) + O(1)$. We obtain the desired comparison as this reads $-\log(n\tau) - \omega(1)$ by the last two conditions imposed on c in (21). □

4.3 Further Regret Reductions

To conclude this section, we show that the regret can be even lower than $O(\tau/\delta^2)$ when the matrix $\{g_{ut}\}$ exhibits a "nice" combinatorial structure. Specifically an upper bound on regret of GREEDY-BAYES in $O(\log \tau/\delta^2)$ will be established for the following example.

Users are organized in $2K$ groups that are indexed by $k \in \{1, \ldots, 2K\}$, each group comprising $n/(2K)$ identical users. There are $\tau = 2^K$ topics, indexed by $t = \{t_1, \ldots, t_K\} \in \{0,1\}^K$. The matrix p_{ut} is then specified as follows. Denoting by k the group to which user u belongs, when $k \leq K$ we assume that $p_{ut} = 1/2 + \delta$ if $t_k = 0$ and $p_{ut} = 1/2 - \delta$ otherwise. When $k > K$, we assume that $p_{ut} = 1/2 + \delta$ if $t_{k-K} = 1$ and $p_{ut} = 1/2 - \delta$ otherwise. We then have the following regret upper bound.

PROPOSITION 5. *Assume that $\delta^{-2} \log(\frac{\tau}{\delta^2}) = o(n/K)$ and $\delta^{-2} \log(n) = o(n/K)$. Then in the present scenario, the regret of* GREEDY-BAYES *with the usual stopping rule and choice of $r \in [\delta, 3\delta/2]$ is $O(\delta^{-2} \log \tau)$.*

The proof parallels that of Proposition 4, adapting its argument by the introduction of suitable stopping times, leveraging Lemma 1 and bounds on the quantities Q^i that stem from the combinatorial structure of the present example. We defer it to the Appendix for space reasons. Finally, note that Proposition 5 applies for instance when δ is fixed and $K \leq (\log n)^\beta$ for some bounded exponent $\beta > 0$.

5. REGRET LOWER BOUNDS

We now establish regret lower bounds. We first provide a generic lower bound, valid for an arbitrary choice of parameters $(p_{ut}, u \in \mathcal{U}, t \in \mathcal{T})$, which when specialized to specific choices p_{ut} implies regret scaling at least like $\Omega(\log n)$. We then provide refined lower bounds on specific examples where the regret does not scale with n and qualify there the dependency of regret on τ. Eventually, we show on three scenarios that our previous regret upper bounds for GREEDY-BAYES are order-optimal.

In what follows, for any $(a, b) \in [0, 1]$,

$$\mathcal{I}(a, b) = a \log(a/b) + (1 - a) \log((1 - a)/(1 - b))$$

is the Kullback-Leibler divergence between two Bernoulli distributions with respective means a and b. We will repeatedly use the fact that $\mathcal{I}(a, b) \leq (a - b)^2/(a(1 - a))$ [3]. For any two measures ζ and ζ', $KL(\zeta, \zeta')$ denotes the Kullback-Leibler divergence between ζ and ζ'. As changes of measure will be involved, we emphasize dependency on the true topic θ of probability measure $\mathbb{P}$ and corresponding expectation by denoting them $\mathbb{P}_\theta$ and $\mathbb{E}_\theta$ respectively.

5.1 Generic Lower Bounds

We denote by S^π the set of users selected under algorithm π. We define an algorithm π to be *ψ-uniformly good* if given the topic θ, we have:

$$(i)\ \mathbb{P}_\theta[S^\pi \cap \mathcal{U}_\theta \neq \mathcal{U}_\theta] = o(1/n),$$
$$(ii)\ \mathbb{P}_\theta[|S^\pi \setminus \mathcal{U}_\theta| \geq \psi(\delta, \tau, n)] = o(1/n),$$

for some function $\psi(\delta, \tau, n) > 0$. Note that in view of Theorem 1, and in particular the proof of Proposition 1, GREEDY-BAYES is ψ-uniformly good with $\psi(\delta, \tau, n) = \kappa \frac{\tau}{\delta^2} \log(n)$ for some constant $\kappa > 1$.

THEOREM 4. *Let θ denote the true topic. For any ψ-uniformly good algorithm π, we have: for all $t \neq \theta$, if*

$$\max(|\mathcal{U}_t \setminus \mathcal{U}_\theta|, |\mathcal{U}_\theta \setminus \mathcal{U}_t|) \geq \psi(\delta, \tau, n),$$

then for n large enough:

$$\mathbb{E}_\theta\left[\sum_{u \in S^\pi} \mathcal{I}(p_{u\theta}, p_{ut})\right] \geq \log(n). \tag{22}$$

PROOF. Let θ, t be two distinct topics in $\mathcal{T}$, π be any algorithm and $\mathcal{F}$ denote the σ-field of all the information accrued when the algorithm stops. Then for any event $A \in \mathcal{F}$ such that $0 < \mathbb{P}_\theta[A] < 1$:

$$\mathbb{E}_\theta\left[\sum_{u \in S^\pi} \mathcal{I}(p_{u\theta}, p_{ut})\right] \geq \mathcal{I}(\mathbb{P}_\theta[A], \mathbb{P}_t[A]). \tag{23}$$

This inequality is a simple extension of inequalities derived in [9, 5]. For completeness we present its proof after completing that of Theorem 4.

Let π be a ψ-uniformly good algorithm. We apply the above inequality for a particular event A. Let $A_1 = \{S^\pi \cap \mathcal{U}_\theta = \mathcal{U}_\theta\}$, $A_2 = \{|S^\pi \setminus \mathcal{U}_\theta| < \psi(\delta, \tau, n)\}$, and $A = A_1 \cap A_2$. We distinguish two cases:

(i) Assume that $|\mathcal{U}_t \setminus \mathcal{U}_\theta| \geq \psi(\delta, \tau, n)$. Since π is uniformly good, $\mathbb{P}_\theta[A] \to 1$ as $n \to \infty$. Further observe that $\mathbb{P}_t[A] = o(1/n)$ since $|S^\pi \setminus \mathcal{U}_\theta| < \psi(\delta, \tau, n)$ and hence $S^\pi \setminus \mathcal{U}_\theta$ cannot cover all elements of $\mathcal{U}_t$. We deduce that:

$$\mathcal{I}(\mathbb{P}_\theta[A], \mathbb{P}_t[A]) = \log\left(\frac{1}{\mathbb{P}_t[A]}\right)(1 + o(1)) \geq \log(n),$$

for n large enough.

(ii) The case $|\mathcal{U}_\theta \setminus \mathcal{U}_t| \geq \psi(\delta, \tau, n)$ is treated similarly. □

PROOF. (of (23)). Let $(Y_u, u \in \mathcal{U})$ be a set of binary random variables indicating for any $u \in \mathcal{U}$ whether user u is interested in the content item ($Y_u = 1$). As before, for time $i \leq n$, we let U^i denote the user selected under algorithm π. In the notation of Section 2, we have the correspondence $X^i = Y_{U^i}$. For every topic t, introduce the function

$$f_t(Y_u) = \begin{cases} p_{ut}, & \text{if } Y_u = 1, \\ 1 - p_{ut}, & \text{otherwise.} \end{cases}$$

Using the convention that beyond the stopping time we select a dummy user $U^i = 0 \notin \mathcal{U}$, we can write the log-likelihood ratio of the observations under π as:

$$L^\pi = \sum_{u \in \mathcal{U}} \sum_{i=1}^{n} 1_{U^i = u} \log \frac{f_\theta(Y_u)}{f_t(Y_u)}.$$

We have:

$$\mathbb{E}_\theta[L^\pi] = \mathbb{E}_\theta\left[\sum_{u \in S^\pi} \mathcal{I}(p_{u\theta}, p_{ut})\right].$$

Furthermore, for any $A \in \mathcal{F}$, a change of measure argument yields:

$$\mathbb{P}_t[A] = \mathbb{E}_\theta[1_A \exp(-L^\pi)] = \mathbb{P}_\theta[A]\mathbb{E}_\theta[\exp(-L^\pi)|A].$$

Now by Jensen's inequality

$$\mathbb{P}_t[A] \geq \mathbb{P}_\theta[A]\exp(-\mathbb{E}_\theta[L^\pi|A]),$$

so that $\mathbb{E}_\theta[L^\pi|A] \geq \log(\mathbb{P}_\theta[A]/\mathbb{P}_t[A])$. Applying the above analysis to A^c yields $\mathbb{E}_\theta[L^\pi|A^c] \geq \log(\mathbb{P}_\theta[A^c]/\mathbb{P}_t[A^c])$. Combining these results, we obtain:

$$\mathbb{E}_\theta[L^\pi] \geq \mathcal{I}(\mathbb{P}_\theta[A], \mathbb{P}_t[A]),$$

which establishes (23). □

Theorem 4 implies the following generic lower bound on the expected regret $\mathbb{E}_\theta[C_1^\pi]$ satisfied by any ψ-uniformly good algorithm π.

COROLLARY 1. *Let π be a ψ-uniformly good algorithm. Then for n large enough, $\mathbb{E}_\theta[C_1^\pi] \geq \tilde{C}_1(\delta, \tau, n)$ where $\tilde{C}_1(\delta,\tau,n)$ is the minimal value of the objective function in the following optimization problem:*

$$\begin{aligned} \text{minimize} \quad & \sum_{u \in \mathcal{U}\setminus\mathcal{U}_\theta} y_u(1-2p_{ut}) \\ \text{over} \quad & y_u \in [0,1], u \in \mathcal{U} \\ \text{such that} \quad & \forall t \in \mathcal{T},\ \textit{if}\ \max(|\mathcal{U}_t \setminus \mathcal{U}_\theta|, |\mathcal{U}_\theta \setminus \mathcal{U}_t|) \geq \psi(\delta,\tau,n) \\ & \quad \textit{then} \sum_{u\in\mathcal{U}} y_u \mathcal{I}(p_{u\theta}, p_{ut})] \geq \log(n). \end{aligned}$$

The above corollary is simply obtained by interpreting y_u as $\mathbb{P}_\theta[u \in S^\pi]$, and by remarking that

$$\mathbb{E}_\theta\left[\sum_{u\in S^\pi} \mathcal{I}(p_{u\theta}, p_{ut})\right] = \sum_{u\in\mathcal{U}} \mathbb{P}_\theta[u \in S^\pi]\mathcal{I}(p_{u\theta}, p_{ut})].$$

In fact, the solution $(y_u, u \in \mathcal{U}\setminus\mathcal{U}_\theta)$ of the above LP lower bounds the probabilities of selecting uninterested users under an optimal algorithm. This solution depends on the specific values of p_{ut}'s. We now use this regret lower bound to establish the order-optimality of our generic regret upper bound for GREEDY-BAYES and THOMPSON-SAMPLING in Theorem 1. To this aim, we introduce the following example.

Example 1: Assume that $\mathcal{U}_\theta = \emptyset$, and that there are $\tau - 1$ other groups such that for any $t \neq \theta$, $|\mathcal{U}_t| \geq \psi(\delta,\tau,n)$ and for any $t' \neq t$, $\mathcal{U}_t \cap \mathcal{U}_{t'} = \emptyset$. Here we choose $\psi(\delta,\tau,n) = \kappa\frac{\tau}{\delta^2}\log(n)$ for some large constant κ, so that ψ corresponds to the regret upper bound for GREEDY-BAYES established in Theorem 1. Assume further that p_{ut} can take two values only, $\frac{1}{2}-\delta$ and $\frac{1}{2}+\delta$, with $\delta < \frac{1}{4}$. Then

$$\mathcal{I}(p_{u\theta}, p_{ut}) = \begin{cases} \mathcal{I}(\frac{1}{2}-\delta, \frac{1}{2}+\delta) \leq 16\delta^2 & \text{if } t \in \mathcal{U}_t, \\ 0 & \text{otherwise} \end{cases}$$

so that for any ψ-uniformly good algorithm π and for n large enough, the constraints in Corollary 1 entail $\sum_{u\in\mathcal{U}_t} y_u \geq \frac{\log n}{16\delta^2}$. Summing over $t \neq \theta$, Corollary 1 yields $\mathbb{E}_\theta[C_1^\pi] \geq \frac{\tau}{8\delta}\log(n)$. Note that this regret lower bound matches, up to a multiplicative constant, the regret upper bound of Theorem 1 when strengthened to the case where $p_{ut} \in \{\frac{1}{2}-\delta, \frac{1}{2}+\delta\}$, see Remark 1.

5.2 Refined Lower Bounds

As shown in Section 4, GREEDY-BAYES exhibits constant regret in some cases. In these scenarios, since the generic lower bound of Corollary 1 does not take into consideration the added structure, it is uninformative. In other words, by maximizing the worst case expected regret over a smaller space of possibilities, lower bounds that are refined specifically for these cases become necessarily *lower*. This is the task that we undertake here. In particular, we obtain bounds that do not depend on n (constant regret), and match the regret upper bounds derived for GREEDY-BAYES.

Example 2. Consider a scenario with τ topics, such that for all t, $|\mathcal{U}_t|$ does not depend on t. One topic θ is designated, and all user sets of other topics $t, t' \neq \theta$ intersect that of θ at the same users, with the remainder mutually disjoint and of cardinality $c\log(n)$, satisfying (21). More precisely, we have $\mathcal{U}_t \cap \mathcal{U}_\theta = \mathcal{U}_{t'} \cap \mathcal{U}_\theta$, $|\mathcal{U}_t \setminus \mathcal{U}_\theta| = c\log(n)$, and $(\mathcal{U}_t \setminus \mathcal{U}_\theta) \cap (\mathcal{U}_{t'} \setminus \mathcal{U}_\theta) = \emptyset$. We further assume that for any t, $u \in \mathcal{U}_t$, $p_{ut} = 1/2+\delta$, and for $u \notin \mathcal{U}_t$, $p_{ut} = 1/2-\delta$. All topics are thus symmetric versus θ, and are c-good, so that the regret incurred under GREEDY-BAYES is $O(\tau/\delta)$ (see Remark 1). We show now that this scaling is optimal.

PROPOSITION 6. *Consider Example 2, and let π be an algorithm such that: $\mathbb{P}_\theta[S^\pi \cap \mathcal{U}_\theta \neq \mathcal{U}_\theta] = o(1/n)$. Then for any topic θ, $\mathbb{E}_\theta[C_1^\pi] \geq (\tau-1)/(64\delta)$ for n large enough.*

PROOF. Consider the topic θ and another topic t. We provide a lower bound on the expected regret under π, when the true topic is θ, incurred when selecting users in $F = \mathcal{U}_t \setminus \mathcal{U}_\theta$. Let us denote this regret by $C_1^\pi(F)$. Let $G = \mathcal{U}_\theta \setminus \mathcal{U}_t$, and let $C_1^\pi(G)$ denote the regret under π, when the true topic is t, incurred when selecting users in G. By symmetry, we have: $\mathbb{E}_\theta[C_1^\pi(F)] = \mathbb{E}_t[C_1^\pi(G)]$. We also have:

$$\mathbb{E}_\theta[C_1^\pi(F)] + \mathbb{E}_t[C_1^\pi(G)] = \delta\sum_{i=1}^{n}(\mathbb{P}_\theta[U^i \in F] + \mathbb{P}_t[U^i \in G]),$$

where by convention, after the algorithm π terminates, it selects a dummy user $U^i = 0 \notin \mathcal{U}$. Now assume that an *Oracle* reveals at the beginning that the topic is either θ or t. With this information, we can decrease the regrets $\mathbb{E}_\theta[C_1^\pi(F)]$ and $\mathbb{E}_t[C_1^\pi(G)]$ under π by first selecting all users in $\mathcal{U}_\theta \cap \mathcal{U}_t$, and then by selecting the users either in F or G in the same order as they appear under π. We further assume that when a user in F (resp. in G) is selected, the Oracle reveals to the decision maker the outcome of an arbitrary user in G (resp. F), although this user remains available for future selection. Note that the choice of this user in G (resp. F) does not matter, since the corresponding $p_{u\theta}$ and p_{ut} do not depend on u in Example 2.

As the Oracle provides more information, the regret of an optimal policy is hence decreased. Abusing notation, π refers to any algorithm under this modified setup. In what follows, we denote by i the time at which the i-th user in F or G is selected under algorithm π. Note that at time i, the information available consists of the outcomes $X = (X_1, X_1' \ldots, X_{i-1}, X_{i-1}')$ of the users selected in F and G, for non-primed and primed respectively. Denote by ζ_i^θ and ζ_i^t the distributions of these outcomes when the true topic is θ and t, respectively. We can then apply Lemma 4 in [4] (this inequality is classical in hypothesis testing theory [15], Chapter 2):

$$\mathbb{P}_\theta[U^i \in F] + \mathbb{P}_t[U^i \in G] \geq \tfrac{1}{2}\exp(-KL(\zeta_i^\theta, \zeta_i^t)). \quad (24)$$

Now we have:

$$KL(\zeta_i^\theta, \zeta_i^t) = (i-1)(\mathcal{I}(\tfrac{1}{2}+\delta, \tfrac{1}{2}-\delta) + \mathcal{I}(\tfrac{1}{2}-\delta, \tfrac{1}{2}+\delta)) \\ \leq 32(i-1)\delta^2.$$

We now sum (24) over time i. Note that before the algorithm terminates, if the topic is θ or t, then $c\log(n)$ users in $F \cup G$ have to be selected (this is due to the facts that $|\mathcal{U}_\theta \cap \mathcal{U}_t| = c\log(n)$ and that π is required to select all users interested in the true topic with high probability). Hence the sum contains at least $c\log(n)$ terms. In summary, we get, for n large enough:

$$\mathbb{E}_\theta[C_1^\pi(F)] = \tfrac{1}{2}(\mathbb{E}_\theta[C_1^\pi(F)] + \mathbb{E}_\theta[C_1^\pi(G)]) \\ \geq \frac{\delta}{2} \sum_{j=1}^{c\log(n)} \exp(-32j\delta^2) \geq \frac{1}{64\delta}.$$

Finally by symmetry, $\mathbb{E}_\theta[C_1^\pi] = (\tau-1)\mathbb{E}_\theta[C_1^\pi(F)]$, where we accumulate the regret due to the selection of all alternatives t other than θ. This is due to the fact that in Example 2, $(\mathcal{U}_t \setminus \mathcal{U}_\theta) \cap (\mathcal{U}_{t'} \setminus \mathcal{U}_\theta) = \emptyset$ for all $t \neq t'$ other than θ. Thus $\mathbb{E}_\theta[C_1^\pi] \geq \frac{\tau-1}{64\delta}$. □

Example 3. Consider the scenario presented in Section 4.3 for which, as we saw, GREEDY-BAYES admits a regret of at most $O(\log \tau/\delta^2)$.

PROPOSITION 7. *For the example of Section 4.3, let π be any algorithm such that: $\mathbb{P}_\theta[S^\pi \cap \mathcal{U}_\theta \neq \mathcal{U}_\theta] = o(1/n)$. Then for any topic θ, $\mathbb{E}_\theta[C_1^\pi] \geq \log(\tau)/(64\delta)$ for n large enough.*

PROOF. The proof is similar to that of Proposition 6. We select two topics θ and t such that $\mathcal{U}_\theta$ and $\mathcal{U}_t$ differs on one group of users only, and we show that $\mathbb{E}_\theta[C_1^\pi(F)] \leq 1/(64\delta)$. Now there are exactly K groups not covered by θ, and from there we deduce that $\mathbb{E}_\theta[C_1^\pi] \geq K/(64\delta) = \Omega(\log(\tau)/\delta)$. □

6. EXPERIMENTAL RESULTS

We now present numerical experiments to validate the theory and to gain further insight into the performance of both GREEDY-BAYES and THOMPSON-SAMPLING. We focus on two scenarios:

(1) Users are divided into $\tau - 1$ groups of $n/(\tau-1)$ users each, each appreciating exactly one topic. Let $\mathcal{U}_j$ denote group j, we have that for all $u \in \mathcal{U}_j$:

$$p_{ut} = \tfrac{1}{2} + (2 \times \mathbf{1}\{t = j\} - 1)\ \delta.$$

Furthermore topic τ is pure spam, $p_{u\tau} = \frac{1}{2} - \delta$.

(2) Users independently choose $\tau/2$ topics to like, and this uniformly at random. Again p_{ut} is restricted to lie in $\{\frac{1}{2}-\delta, \frac{1}{2}+\delta\}$.

The parameters we use for our policies are $r = \frac{3}{2}\delta$ and $\log A = \alpha(\log n + \log \tau)$, where $\alpha = 0.005$. The theory applies only for α of the order of 10 or more, but we found experimentally that the smaller values work better.

Scenario (1) is used to illustrate two phenomena. When the true topic is the pure spam topic $\theta = \tau$, we expect regret to scale in $\log n$ by Example 1 in Section 5. When the true topic is not spam, then we expect instead regret to be constant in n but to scale linearly in τ, by Example 2 in Section 5.

Scenario (2) is meant as a more realistic variant of Example 3 of Section 5, where instead of having homogeneous groups, each user independently selects good topics. There we expect regret to be bounded in n and to scale with $\log \tau$.

We simulate Scenario 1 with 2,500 Monte-Carlo samples, under two configurations. First, when the truth is pure spam, with $\delta = \frac{1}{3}$, $\tau = 30$ topics and n between 100 and 1,000 users. Second, when the truth is appreciated by a group, with $\delta = \frac{1}{3}$, $n = 2{,}000$ users and $\tau = 2$ to 20 topics, which places us squarely within the domain of Section 4 and Example 2 in Section 5.

The estimated expected regrets are shown in Figures 1 and 2, respectively. The light shaded area represents one standard deviation of the regret, whereas the darker shaded area gives a 95% confidence interval at each point of the estimated expected regret. The key observations are: the roughly logarithmic dependence on n for the pure spam topic as predicted by our general regret bounds, and the roughly linear dependence on τ for the non-spam topic, as anticipated by our refined regret bounds.

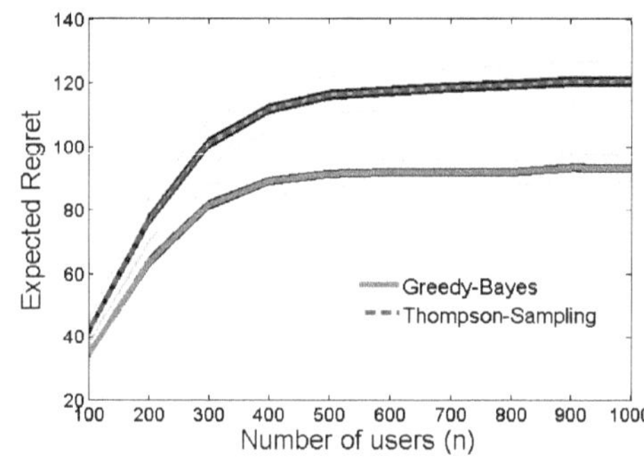

Figure 1: Scenario 1 with $\delta = \frac{1}{3}$, $\tau = 30$ topics and $n = 100$ to 1,000 users. We show the estimated expected regret with a 95% confidence interval (small dark-colored area) and one standard deviation of the regret (large light-colored area).

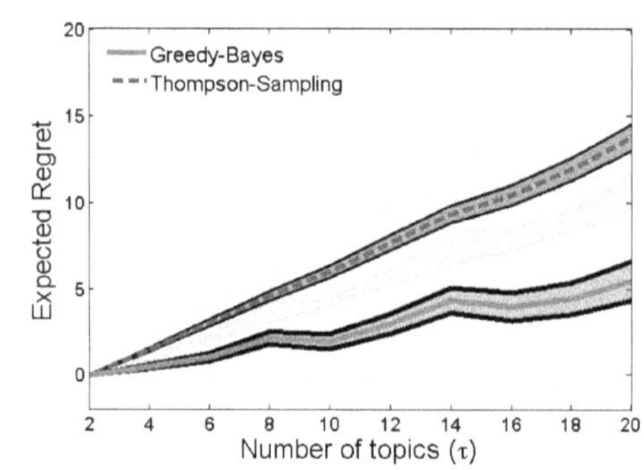

Figure 2: Scenario 1, the same experimental setup of Figure 1, but with $\delta = \frac{1}{3}$, $n = 2{,}000$ users, and $\tau = 2$ to 20 topics.

For Scenario 2 we also simulate 2,500 samples, under both n varying and τ varying. In Figure 3(a), we fix $\tau = 50$ and vary $n = 100$ to 2000. In Figure 3(b), we fix $n = 1{,}000$ and vary $\tau = 10$ to 100. In either case, $\delta = 0.2$. We observe that there is practically no regret growth with n, while there is growth with τ, but much slower than linear – possibly logarithmic. This is precisely the behavior described by the improved analysis of Section 4.3 and Proposition 7.

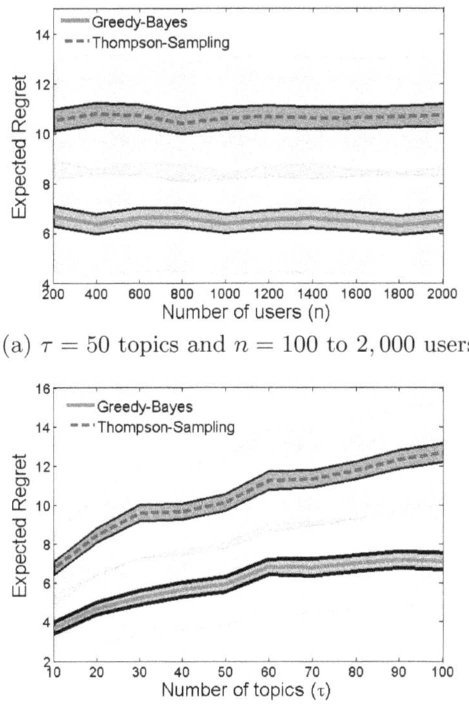

(a) $\tau = 50$ topics and $n = 100$ to $2,000$ users

(b) $n = 1,000$ users and $\tau = 10$ to 100 topics

Figure 3: Scenario 2, under the same experimental setup of Figures 1 and 2, with $\delta = 0.2$.

Beyond the verification of the various bounds, note that these numerical experiments shed light on the fact that GREEDY-BAYES has consistently lower regret than THOMPSON-SAMPLING, even if both are of the same order. Since all things, including stopping conditions, are the same between the two algorithms except for the selection rule, this suggests that the more conservative averaging of GREEDY-BAYES is preferable to the more noisy exploration of THOMPSON-SAMPLING. Beyond the present context, this may have implications more generally to sequential decision policies of such Bayesian nature.

7. RELATED WORK

Li et al. [14] and Kohli et al. [10] consider a news pull scenario where adequate news are to be proposed to a user who visits a given site. We consider the dual push problem of which users to send a fresh news to.

El-Arini et al [6] address how to select a small set of posts in the blogosphere to achieve an efficient coverage of the topics debated overall. They extend this formulation to include user personalization through user-specific weights in the coverage objective function. This corresponds to a scenario where knowledge about the news items is already available, in contrast with the setup we consider.

A rich literature studies how information propagates in social networks, in particular due to influence exerted between acquaintances [11, 13]. Enabling efficient and targeted dissemination of information is indeed one of the promises of online social networks. In this respect, our work establishes an interesting benchmark.

By characterizing the performance of a central controller and establishing that dissemination must leverage negative feedback, we point to limits of news dissemination over such networks. Indeed, propagation based only on positive influence would perform worse than if negative feedback is also leveraged.

Our problem formulation is related to Multi-Armed Bandit (MAB) problems [12] (see [3] for a survey) of which many variants have been studied. Key differences are as follows. In our setup, i) each arm (user) can be used only once, whereas in the MAB literature each arm is sampled sufficiently to learn its statistics. ii) Also we don't aim at finding the best arm, but at selecting a target set of good arms. iii) Finally we need to learn when to stop, again in contrast with the classical MAB setup.

The infinite bandit problem [1, 2] and to the secretary problem [7] are the closest formulations we know of, in that they require some form of stopping, but differ in aspects i) and ii).

8. CONCLUSION

Motivated by push-based news dissemination systems, we proposed a model of sequential user selection extending traditional multi-armed bandit problems. We introduced GREEDY-BAYES, a robust policy whose performance we proved to be order-optimal in several scenarios of interest. Our proof techniques may be of independent interest, e.g. to characterize the performance of Thompson Sampling.

It is tempting to conjecture that GREEDY-BAYES remains optimal over an even wider range, and we will investigate this in future work.

9. REFERENCES

[1] D. A. Berry, R. W. Chen, A. Zame, D. C. Heath, and L. A. Shepp. Bandit problems with infinitely many arms. *Annals of Statistics*, 25(5):2103–2116, 1997.

[2] T. Bonald and A. Proutiere. Two-threshold algorithms for the infinite-armed bandits with Bernoulli rewards. In *Advances in Neural Information Processing Systems 26*, pages 2184–2192. 2013.

[3] S. Bubeck and N. Cesa-Bianchi. Regret Analysis of Stochastic and Nonstochastic Multi-armed Bandit Problems. *Foundations and Trends in Machine Learning*, 5(1):1–122, 2012.

[4] S. Bubeck, V. Perchet, and P. Rigollet. Bounded regret in stochastic multi-armed bandits. *J. Mach. Learn. Res.*, 30:122–134, 2013.

[5] R. Combes and A. Proutiere. Unimodal Bandits without Smoothness. *CoRR*, abs/1406.7447, 2014.

[6] K. El-Arini, G. Veda, D. Shahaf, and C. Guestrin. Turning Down the Noise in the Blogosphere. In *ACM KDD*, pages 661–670, 2009.

[7] T. S. Ferguson. Who Solved the Secretary Problem? *Statistical Science*, 4(3):282–289, 08 1989.

[8] D. Freedman. On tail probabilities for martingales. *Annals of Probability*, 3:100–118, 1975.

[9] E. Kaufmann, O. Cappé, and A. Garivier. On the Complexity of Best Arm Identification in Multi-Armed Bandit Models. *ArXiv e-prints*, July 2014.

[10] P. Kohli, M. Salek, and G. Stoddard. A Fast Bandit Algorithm for Recommendations to Users with Heterogeneous Tastes. In *AAAI*, 2013.

[11] G. Kossinets, J. Kleinberg, and D. Watts. The structure of information pathways in a social communication network. In *ACM SIGKDD*, 2008.
[12] T. Lai and H. Robbins. Asymptotically efficient adaptive allocation rules. *Advances in Applied Mathematics*, 6(1):4–2, 1985.
[13] J. Leskovec, A. Singh, and J. Kleinberg. Patterns of influence in a recommendation network. In *Advances in Knowledge Discovery and Data Mining, LNCS*, pages 380–389. 2006.
[14] L. Li, W. Chu, J. Langford, and R. Schapire. A Contextual-Bandit Approach to Personalized News Article Recommendation. In *WWW*, pages 661–670, 2010.
[15] A. B. Tsybakov. *Introduction to Nonparametric Estimation.* Springer Publishing Company, Incorporated, 1st edition, 2008.

APPENDIX

Proof of Proposition 5

Let us first verify that the conditions of Theorem 3 apply. Note that for any two distinct topics θ, t, necessarily there is an index $k \leq K$ such that $t_k \neq \theta_k$. The user groups labeled k and $k+K$ hence have opposite preferences on topics θ and t, liking one and disliking the other. Thus each content θ is c-good with $c = n/(2K \log n)$. Condition (21) therefore holds because of the assumption $\delta^{-2} = o(n/(K \log n))$.

We now introduce the stopping time J which is the first time step at which we have spammed $n/2K$ users. It is readily seen that prior to J, whenever a spamming decision occurs under GREEDY-BAYES, necessarily the corresponding quantity Q^i as defined in Lemma 1 must be at least 1/2. Indeed prior to J, for any remaining good user, say a user belonging to group $k \leq K$, there is at least one user available in the corresponding group $K + k$. Denote by $\mathcal{T}_k$ the set of topics liked by group k. Since

$$\sum_{t \in \mathcal{T}_k} \nu_t^i + \sum_{t \in \mathcal{T}_k + K} \nu_t^i = 1,$$

for one of these two users the corresponding sum is at least 1/2. Thus, if spam occurs it must be that $Q^i \geq 1/2$.

Let us then introduce the stopping times J_m defined as

$$J_m := \inf\{i \geq 1 : \lceil 2 \sum_{j=1}^{i} Q^j \rceil \geq m\}.$$

Since for $i \leq J$, $Z^i \leq 2Q^i$, spamming events prior to J must occur at some stopping time J_m. Thus arguing as in the proof of Proposition 4

$$\begin{aligned}\mathbb{E}\textstyle\sum_{i=1}^{J} Z^i &\leq \textstyle\sum_{m \geq 1} \mathbb{P}(Z^{J_m} = 1; J_m \leq J) \\ &\leq \textstyle\sum_{m \geq 1} \mathbb{P}(R^{J_m} \leq 1; J_m \leq J) \\ &\leq \textstyle\sum_{m \geq 1} \mathbb{P}(\sum_{j=1}^{J_m} S^j \leq \log \tau; J_m \leq J)\end{aligned}$$

By J_m's definition, one has $m-4 < \sum_{j=1}^{J_m-1} 2Q^j < m$. Hence

$$\begin{aligned}\langle N \rangle^{J_m} &\leq 9r^2 m/2, \\ H^{J_m} &\geq \delta r \textstyle\sum_{j=1}^{J_m-1} Q^j \geq \delta r(m/2 - 2).\end{aligned}$$

Bernstein's inequality yields here

$$\begin{aligned}&\mathbb{P}(\textstyle\sum_{j=1}^{J_m} S^j \leq \log \tau; J_m \leq J) \\ &\leq \mathbb{P}\left(|N^{J_m}| \geq \delta r(\tfrac{m}{2} - 2) - \log \tau, \langle N \rangle^{J_m} \leq 9r^2 m/2\right) \\ &\leq 2\exp\left(-\frac{-x_m}{4r + 9r^2 m/x_m}\right),\end{aligned}$$

where we set $x_m := \delta r(m/2 - 2) - \log \tau$. We upper bound this probability by 1 for $m < 8 + 4\log \tau/(\delta r)$ and note for $m \geq 8 + 4 \log \tau/(\delta r)$ necessarily $x_m \geq \delta r m/4$. This yields

$$\mathbb{E}\sum_{i=1}^{J} Z^i \leq 8 + 4 \log \tau/(\delta r) + 2 \sum_{m \geq 1} e^{-\frac{-\delta m}{4(4+36/\delta)}}.$$

The sum is $O(\delta^{-2})$, hence the overall bound is $O(\log \tau/\delta^2)$.

It remains to find a bound of a lesser order on the expected number of spam events between the stopping times J and I'. To that end we further adapt the argument in the proof of Proposition 4. Specifically, on $J < I'$ one has

$$\frac{n}{2K} \leq \sum_{i=1}^{J} Z^j \leq 2 \sum_{i=1}^{J} Q^i,$$

and at further spam events the corresponding Q must increase by more than $1/\tau$. By changing and letting the stopping times I_k be defined as

$$I_k := \inf\{i \geq 1 : \lceil \tau \sum_{j=1}^{i} Q^j \rceil \geq k + (\tau/2)n/(2K)\},$$

we have

$$\begin{aligned}\mathbb{E}\textstyle\sum_{i=J+1}^{I'} Z^i &\leq \textstyle\sum_{k \geq 1} \mathbb{P}(Z^{I_k} = 1; I_k \leq I') \\ &\leq \textstyle\sum_{k \geq 1} \mathbb{P}(R^{I_k} \leq 1; I_k \leq I').\end{aligned}$$

We thus have $\mathbb{E}\sum_{i=J+1}^{I'} Z^i \leq \sum_{k \geq 1} \mathbb{P}(\sum_{j=1}^{I_k} S^j \leq \log \tau)$.

At the stopping time I_k one has, by I_k's definition, that

$$k - 2\tau + \frac{\tau}{2}\frac{n}{2K} < \sum_{j=1}^{I_k-1} \tau Q^j < k + \frac{\tau}{2}\frac{n}{2K},$$

and hence $\langle N \rangle^{I_k} \leq 9r^2[k/\tau + n/(4K)]$. Note further that

$$H^{I_k} \geq \delta r \sum_{j=1}^{I_k-1} Q^j \geq \delta r(k/\tau + n/(4K) - 2).$$

We thus find, by Bernstein's inequality, that

$$\begin{aligned}\mathbb{P}(\textstyle\sum_{j=1}^{I_k} S^j \leq \log \tau) &\leq \mathbb{P}\Big(|N^{I_k}| \geq \delta r(\tfrac{k}{\tau} + \tfrac{n}{4K} - 2) - \log \tau, \\ &\qquad \langle N \rangle^{I_k} \leq 9r^2 k/\tau + n/(4K)\Big) \\ &\leq 2\exp\left(-\frac{x_k}{4r + x_k^{-1} 18 r^2(\frac{k}{\tau} + \frac{n}{4K})}\right),\end{aligned}$$

where in the above we set $x_k = \delta r(k/\tau + n/(4K) - 2) - \log \tau$. Note that n/K is large compared to $\delta^{-2}\log \tau$, under the assumption that $\delta^{-2}\log(\tau\delta^{-2}) = o(n/K)$. The previous sum can thus be written as

$$\sum_{k \geq 0} 2\exp\left(-\Theta(\delta^2(k/\tau + n/K))\right) = \Theta(\tau\delta^{-2})e^{-\Theta(\delta^2 n/K)}.$$

This is $o(1)$ as we assume $\delta^{-2}\log(\tau\delta^{-2}) = o(n/K)$. □

DiskAccel: Accelerating Disk-Based Experiments by Representative Sampling

Mojtaba Tarihi*
tarihi@ce.sharif.edu

Hossein Asadi*†
asadi@sharif.edu

Hamid Sarbazi-Azad*‡
azad@sharif.edu

* Department of Computer Engineering, Sharif University of Technology, Tehran, Iran
† AICT Innovation Center, Sharif University of Technology, Tehran, Iran
‡ Institute for Research in Fundamental Sciences, Tehran, Iran

ABSTRACT

Disk traces are typically used to analyze real-life workloads and for replay-based evaluations. This approach benefits from capturing important details such as varying behavior patterns, bursty activity, and diurnal patterns of system activity, which are often missing from the behavior of workload synthesis tools. However, accurate capture of such details requires recording traces containing long durations of system activity, which are difficult to use for replay-based evaluation. One way of solving the problem of long storage trace duration is the use of disk simulators. While publicly available disk simulators can greatly accelerate experiments, they have not kept up with technological innovations in the field. The variety, complexity, and opaque nature of storage hardware make it very difficult to implement accurate simulators. The alternative, replaying the whole traces on real hardware, suffers from either long run-time or required manual reduction of experimental time, potentially at the cost of reduced accuracy. On the other hand, burstiness, autocorrelation, and complex spatio-temporal properties of storage workloads make the known methods of sampling workload traces less effective.

In this paper, we present a methodology called DiskAccel to efficiently select key intervals of a trace as representatives and to replay them to estimate the response time of the whole workload. Our methodology extracts a variety of spatial and temporal features from each interval and uses efficient data mining techniques to select the representative intervals. To verify the proposed methodology, we have implemented a tool capable of running whole traces or selective intervals on real hardware, warming up hardware state in an accelerated manner, and emulating request causality while minimizing request inter-arrival time error. Based on our experiments, DiskAccel manages to speed up disk replay by more than two orders of magnitude, while keeping average estimation error at 7.6%.

SIGMETRICS'15, June 15–19, 2015, Portland, OR, USA.

http://dx.doi.org/10.1145/2745844.2745856 .

1. INTRODUCTION

Storage devices are a key component of any computing environment for intermediate and long-term data storage. Apart from supporting the required capacity, they must meet performance demands at an acceptable cost. As a result, storage devices have long been the subject of many performance optimizations such as prefetching [8], request scheduling [57], caching [47, 23], layout optimizations [33], and hybrid storage [23, 37].

An integral part of designing a high-performance storage device is evaluation of algorithms, cache configurations, and/or other optimization techniques under study. Evaluating such design refinements requires accurate experimentation, which is often very time-consuming. Software-based simulators [6] provide repeatable and closely observable experimental setups without the need for real hardware. However, storage devices are opaque and contain many sophisticated algorithms. Although methodologies exist to automatically extract new device parameters [40], serious issues remain unresolved as shown by our previous experimental studies [49]. In particular, while storage simulators are generally sufficient for preliminary studies of algorithms, they in no way can be used for complete evaluation of algorithms and as such, use of real hardware is essential.

Input workloads, which should be replayed on real hardware, have a strong impact on experiments. These workloads either come from real machines or are generated by benchmarks and synthesis tools. Parameterizable software benchmarks are a popular source of evaluation workloads [20, 30, 9], but are not very representative of real-life workloads. Studies presented in [16, 21] show that while actual workloads are very bursty and exhibit diurnal patterns, widely used benchmarks cannot be configured for these properties. Worse yet, many benchmarks cannot even accurately control inter-arrival times despite its significant influence on performance [3, 27]. Benchmarks results are also influenced by host hardware; a faster processor can decrease I/O inter-arrival time and larger memory can greatly improve operating system caching.

Another obstacle for repeated experiments which can greatly hinder hardware-based experiments is the duration of storage traces ranging from hours to days and weeks. Previous studies have resorted to run traces as fast as possible [50], speed up inter-arrival time [51, 39], manually select portions of the trace [61, 14, 57], and manual selection along with speed-ups [60]. These methods either lack reproducibility or do not preserve key parameters of trace behavior.

Long experimentation times also hinder microprocessor

simulations. To alleviate this issue, two main schemes have been proposed which reduce workload size [13, 58]. These methods select certain workload intervals and use their measurements to project the performance of the whole workload. They also keep the state up to date by use of checkpoints or warm-ups. As a result, these schemes can provide accurate estimations while running only a fraction of the original workload which would have taken days or weeks to simulate in full. For I/O workloads, clustering was used in [15] to enhance trace synthesis. In [44], clustering was used to create a classification decision tree for use in controllers of *Solid-State Drives* (SSDs). CART models used in [53] can be used for performance projection and tree-based workload trimming. To the best of our knowledge, none of these works focus on accurate and replay-based reduction of I/O workloads.

In this paper, we present a methodology called DiskAccel that greatly accelerates trace-based storage evaluation on real hardware. DiskAccel employs traces recorded from real servers and uses a variety of properties to select a representative subset of the workload. This process does not use performance numbers obtained from other hardware devices so that the selection becomes independent of hardware. Although this methodology can also be employed with software simulators, due to concerns with accuracy issues noted above, we focus on using real hardware to maximize accuracy. As part of DiskAccel, we have developed a tool to replay the representative intervals on target hardware. Our tool avoids many pitfalls of trace-based experiments by (a) warm-up of hardware cache by replaying an appropriate number of preceding requests, (b) enforcing inter-request dependency by constructing dependency trees, and (c) accurate control of request arrival time by avoiding scheduling delays.

The process of selecting representative intervals divides each trace into multiple intervals, extracts a variety of features from each interval, and then performs clustering. The features used include address and time entropy, request randomness, seek time, and working set locality. We use a weighted variant of the K-Means clustering algorithm similar to [13], and select the point closest to the cluster centroid as the cluster representative. To perform experiments based on this sampling methodology, we have developed a tool to run the representative intervals with timing accuracy and disk state warm-up on real hardware[1]. To increase timing accuracy, we use busy-waiting and real-time Linux facilities [34] to minimize request inter-arrival time error. Warm-up selects requests leading up to the representative intervals such that their footprint is equal to the cache capacity of the target hardware. These requests are then run in an accelerated manner before running the representative interval. We also try to replicate the request dependency by controlling request arrival times in a closed-loop manner. More specifically, we treat read requests as being blocking and consider writes to be non-blocking. This heuristic is essential as almost every publicly existing traces lack essential high level information such as request flags and issuing thread and process identification (ID). To the best of our knowledge, this is the first attempt to present a methodology to accelerate replay-based I/O experiments while keeping error rates at a minimum. In addition, this is the first work which presents efficient warm-up technique for disk drives to speed up I/O experiments.

To validate DiskAccel, we use the *Microsoft Research Cambridge* (MSRC) workloads [28] to test our methodology against a wide variety of workloads. We perform clustering based on the extracted features and validate our methodology in two steps. First, we use the performance numbers embedded in the traces to compare the whole trace average response time against the weighted response time. This yields an average relative error of 3.6% error for all traces in [28] and a worst-case error of 12.1%. In the experiments, we perform full runs on 11 of the selected traces (each spanning approximately one week) with no acceleration on our hardware testbed to serve as a reference. We then compare the relative error of choosing representative intervals on these traces with the new performance results. This yields an average error of 6.5% and a maximum error of 13.6%. Finally, we perform partial runs on our hardware testbed with an average speed-up of 577x versus full one-week runs and compare the weighted response time against the average response time of the numbers yielded from full one-week runs. This yields an average and maximum relative errors of 7.6% and 17.2%, respectively.

In the following, we discuss the related work in Sec. 2. Our experimental methodology is explained in Sec. 3. Then, we present our methodology of reducing replay time in Sec. 4. Details of methodology for replaying traces is covered in Sec. 5. Next, we validate our methodology on a completely different hardware setup in Sec. 6. We conclude the paper in Sec. 7 and discuss the limitations and future directions of our work.

2. RELATED WORK

In this section, we first discuss previous methodologies in synthesis of storage workloads and point out their deficiencies. We then cover trace reduction methodologies used on storage and microprocessor traces and evaluate their usability in storage workloads. Finally, we discuss the use of real disks in storage benchmarking and highlight the important measures that must be taken to ensure high accuracy of performance measurements.

2.1 Trace Synthesis and Benchmarks

Storage traces capture a record of I/O requests sent to the storage subsystem over a period of time. In some scenarios, however, it is essential to scale a workload to the desired hardware configuration. This practice is particularly useful when measuring the maximum potential of underlying hardware or when trying to optimize software or storage subsystem parameters. This is where benchmarks excel the most as the users are able to tune various options and settings.

Benchmark programs attempt to generate a workload similar to a certain application. Benchmark tools such as Postmark [20], Bonnie++ [9], and Iozone [30] are publicly available and have been widely used to evaluate storage algorithms and architectures. However, I/O benchmarks have difficulties in replicating burstiness and auto-correlation [50] despite these behaviors being exhibited widely by I/O workloads [32, 21, 22]. It should also be noted that our proposed methodology can also be used on traces generated by such benchmarks to accelerate experiments.

Trace synthesis programs try to replicate key properties of workloads to yield a portable and tunable replacement

[1]This tool is available at: http://dsn.ce.sharif.edu/software

for traces. Such approaches include synthesizing traces using Binomial distribution [54, 14, 15] and multi-distribution fits [59] to approaches based on spatio-temporal entropy [52]. Trace shuffling and piece-wise synthesis of traces in [14] demonstrates that although long-range dependence is present, the use of sufficiently large time intervals diminishes its impact. Hence, short-range dependency can represent the inter-arrival times of each interval.

2.2 Trace Reduction

While real-world traces contain key spatio-temporal properties, their long duration must be addressed appropriately. In this section, previous works on reduction and compaction of storage and microprocessor traces will be covered.

Microprocessor simulations are essential for architecture explorations. While various software programs exist to simulate processor behavior at the required level, they tend to be as far as five- to six-orders of magnitude slower than real hardware [58]. This, coupled with a large volume of multi-billion instruction traces makes it very expensive to investigate architectural ideas without resorting to trace size reduction.

Two studies are well-known on the subject of sampling CPU traces, SMARTS [58], which performs systematic sampling of intervals for detailed simulation, and SimPoint [13], which uses per-interval feature extraction and clustering to pick representative intervals. Both studies report massive time savings with negligible error.

Systematic sampling in [58] relies upon assuming a normal distribution of response time in intervals. This expectation can easily be satisfied through the Central Limit Theorem, assuming intervals are numerous and independent. While this assumption does not hold for individual I/O requests, it does hold for request intervals as pointed out by [14]. In Sec. 4, we perform a viability study for using a similar solution for I/O traces.

SimPoint [13] uses clustering algorithms to group similar intervals and select representatives. In earlier releases of this work, intervals had a fixed number of instructions. Later on, variable length intervals were supported by common sequence matching. SimPoint takes advantage of availability of the binaries generating the trace to form much more descriptive and accurate feature vectors based on the code structure. In [24], different feature vectors for this tool were evaluated, of note is the use of accessed memory addresses as the sole source of features which yields poor results. Clustering is performed by a modified version of K-Means which supports weighting different points belonging to each interval. As K-Means needs K, the number of clusters, to be specified, *Bayesian Information Criterion* (BIC) [42] was used to choose the best clustering resulted by different values of K.

The study presented in [14] divides traces into fixed-duration intervals and shows that such divisions can be used and synthesized independent of the history with little impact on accuracy. This study was later used by [15] which extracts temporal information from these intervals and then performs clustering to pick representative intervals as the subject of synthesis. In [44], clustering was used as a step to find out which features can better distinguish key behavior classes. The features used are mostly spatial and the resulting classes specify the main behaviors exhibited, e.g., fully sequential, part-sequential, and part-random. The evaluation for clustering was a goodness of fit measure and the final result is a decision tree which can be used in an SSD controller to optimize for these behaviors. The authors found out that out of the different clustering algorithms, K-Means is the best choice.

A variety of features based on spatial and temporal properties of traces were extracted by [48] for each interval. Interval features were then subjected to a process termed deduplication by the authors to reduce the number of per-interval property sets. These properties were then used to generate benchmark configuration parameters to produce a behavior similar to that of the source trace.

2.3 Replaying I/O Traces

Workload traces offer an opportunity to evaluate hardware devices and algorithms in real-life scenarios. However, proper care must be taken to ensure that meaningful performance results are obtained.

Storage traces record I/O activity from computers where requests often depend on each other. While performing experiments, open-loop as opposed to closed-loop control of requests greatly affects experimental results [41]. Tools such as blktrace/blkparse [5] and fio [4] can perform closed-loop control in a multi-threaded manner provided that this information has been recorded in the trace. TBBT [60] and ROOT [55] try to infer inter-request relationship based on the higher level semantics of the syscalls and *Network File System* (NFS) layers, respectively. Both //TRACE [26] interferes with program activity to discover request dependencies. We cover this subject in Sec. 5.1.

When a certain inter-arrival time is chosen, it must be enforced with high accuracy. Anderson et al. [3] studied the effect of inter-arrival error or drift time on measurement accuracy from trace replay. They subsequently developed a replay tool which kept drift time to a maximum of $100\mu s$.

Another key detail that can affect trace replay results is the state of the storage subsystem, including disks and controller-level cache. To ensure that cache contents are valid for experiments, appropriate warm-up is necessary. For example, the authors in [25, 56] used a portion of a trace to perform warm-up. The latter also tried to match the warm-up of synthetic workloads to the size of hardware state. This will be further discussed in Sec. 5.2.

3. EXPERIMENTAL SETUP

Performance Measure. The performance measure used in this paper is the average request response time which is the time spent between sending a request to the I/O subsystem and receiving operation acknowledgement. Should the operation be blocking, response time indicates the amount of processing time wasted waiting for I/O and a major performance bottleneck for many use cases. In other words, we compare the reference average response time against response time projected by our subset of the workload to measure the accuracy of our methodology. We use *Weighted Response Time* (WRT) calculation to project performance of the whole workload. To compute WRT, as shown in Equation 1, we weight the selected representative intervals by the total number of requests represented by that interval. If we use WRT on the whole workload and assume each interval to only represent itself, the result is the reference average response time. Weighting emphasizes dense intervals over sparse intervals for calculating average request times. There

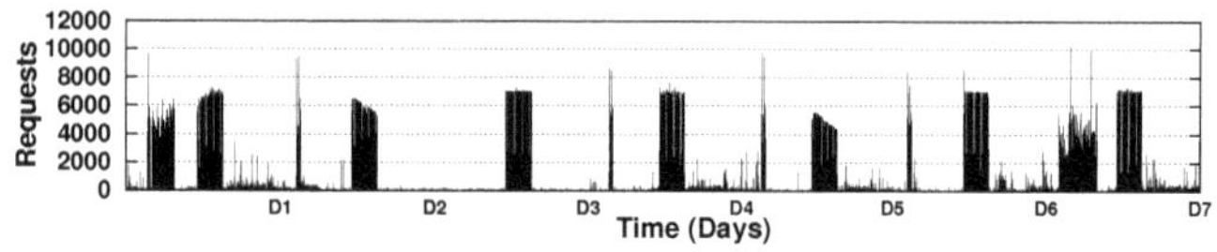

Figure 1: Average per-minute requests of usr_1 trace from [28] (Note the diurnal patterns).

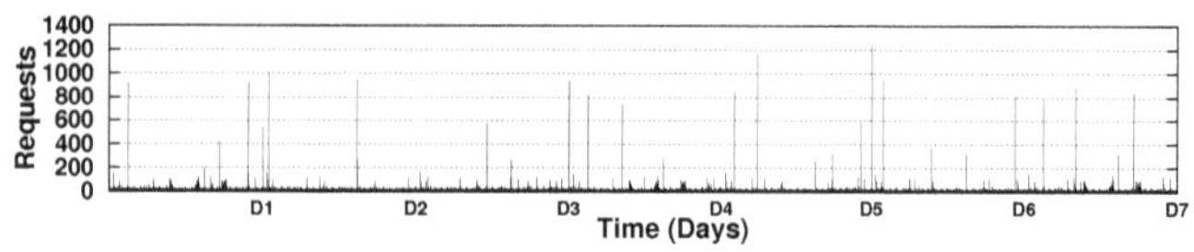

Figure 2: Average per-minute requests of rsrch_0 trace from [28] (Non-diurnal, very bursty, and having no well-defined patterns).

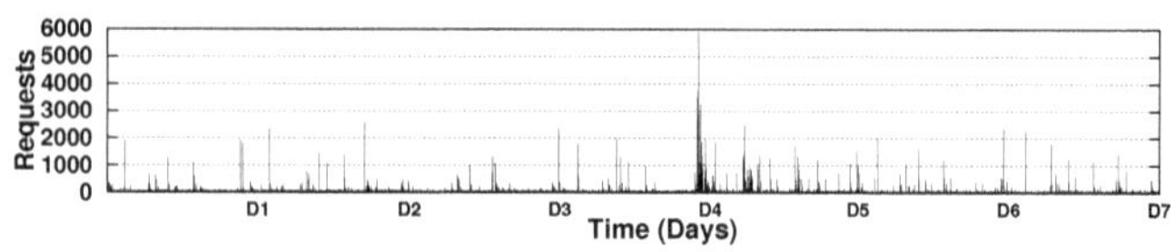

Figure 3: Average per-minute requests of hm_0 trace from [28] (Bursty, activity peaks on a certain day).

are two benefits to this choice. First, dense intervals contain more requests and represent more user activity. Second, the extra strain they put onto the hardware further increases the response time, affecting I/O performance even more [29].

$$RT_{average} = \frac{\sum\limits_{I \in Intervals} RT_{interval}(I) \times Count_{interval}(I)}{\sum\limits_{I \in Intervals} Count_{interval}(I)} \quad (1)$$

Workloads. We used 36 traces, referred to as the *Microsoft Research Cambridge* (MSRC) traces [28], which have been recorded from a variety of servers used for research, web development, terminal services, printing, hardware monitoring, and web proxy services. Each trace is approximately a week long and records requests to a single volume. These traces contain from a few hundred requests to well over a hundred million requests. Burstiness is present throughout and the long duration has allowed them to demonstrate diurnal and weekly patterns. This duration, however, is a serious challenge for replay on real hardware. We show the average per-minute requests for *usr_1*, *rsrch_0*, and *hm_0* in Figure 1, Figure 2, and Figure 3, respectively. It can be seen that these workloads are bursty and while *usr_1* (hosting user data) shows a clear diurnal pattern, the other two are much less predictable. In case of the *hm_0* workload which is used for hardware monitoring, the activity peaks on a single day. These three traces demonstrate the difficulty of representative tracing. To record diurnal and bursty patterns, it is necessary to record long periods of activity but such long traces make replaying difficult.

Testbed. We initially use the same response time numbers embedded on the original traces to test the first part of our methodology, but to fully validate our findings we developed a tool to (a) perform whole one-week runs of a selected number of traces to serve as new references, and (b) perform partial runs including only the representative intervals and compare their WRT against the newly obtained reference numbers. We replay the traces on identical 3.5" 5400RPM 500GB Seagate Momentus Disks of the same batch. We took a number of steps to prevent interferences with our experiments, (a) no file systems were mounted on the target drives and they were directly accessed via their device nodes (/dev/sdXX), (b) device nodes are opened with the O_DIRECT flag to prevent kernel caching on target drives, (c) we used the *RT_PREEMPT* real-time capability patch for Linux [34] and set top priority to the program, and (d) recorded trace data in memory and performed processing beforehand to prevent I/O blocking. The requests are sent with the Linux's Native Asynchronous I/O [12] which allows us to get the exact request finish times while being able to have multiple requests in flight. These enhancements, however, are not sufficient to minimize drift time and similar to [3] we had to use busy-waiting. This is because *usleep* and *nanosleep* calls must be avoided due to serious inaccuracies [36]. Switching to busy-waiting reduced average drift time by hundreds of microseconds even when the real-time patch was active.

Evaluation Steps. DiskAccel workflow can be seen in Figure 4. DiskAccel selects representative intervals via clustering and then runs them on a system. We took the following steps for evaluating DiskAccel:

1. First, we evaluate the accuracy of DiskAccel at picking representatives (Step 1 in Figure 5). We compare WRT of representative intervals against the whole workload average response time. WRT and average RT are both generated using the original response time values embedded in MSRC traces. In the latter two steps, we will exclusively use response times obtained from our own testbed.

2. To validate Step 1, we first replay a selected number of MSRC traces[2] in *whole* on our testbed at the original pace (one week) and use it as a reference instead of the original response time values. We then use the obtained response time values to validate our evaluation of selecting representatives (Step 2, Figure 5).

3. In Step 3 (Figure 5), we evaluate the accuracy of DiskAccel as a whole. The difference between this step and Step 2 is use of response time results from **partial** testbed runs instead of using whole trace response times used for calculating WRT. It must be noted that the reference average response time is still calculated using the whole, one-week runs similar to Step 2. Partial runs represents both stages of DiskAccel (a) picking representative intervals, evaluated in Step 1 and further validated in Step 2 and (b) replaying on our testbed, including warm-up.

4. TRACE SAMPLING

To reduce traces to a small number of representative intervals, our methodology first performs clustering to choose

[2]Due to the extensive time needed to run each MSRC trace at original speeds, we had to use a subset of these workloads to reduce experimentation time. We tried to pick a single trace from each class for this purpose: *hm_0*, *mds_1*, *prn_0*, *proj_4*, *prxy_0*, *rsrch_0*, *src1_2*, *ts_0*, *usr_2*, *wdev_0*, *web_2*.

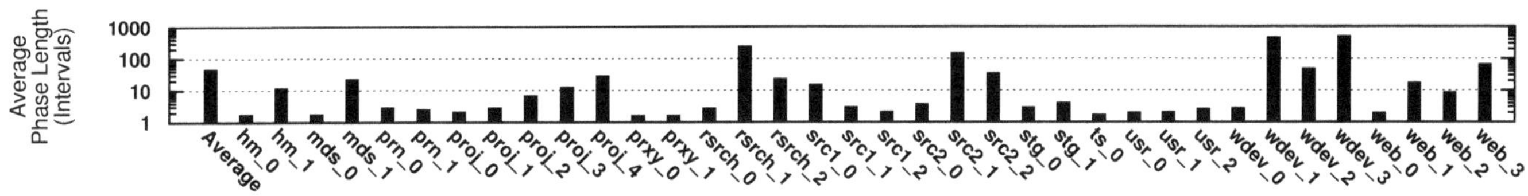

Figure 6: Average phase length across 10-second intervals (A phase is defined as a continuous stretch of intervals where variation between the response time of each two intervals is less than 10%.)

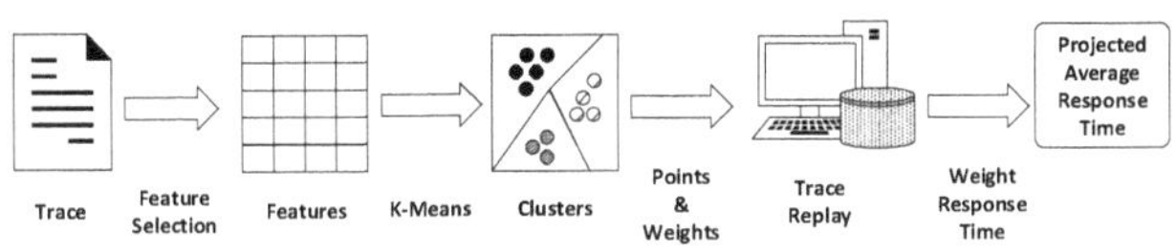

Figure 4: DiskAccel workflow.

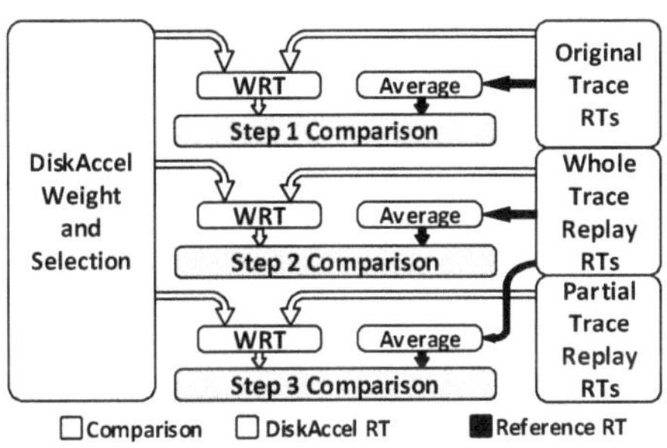

Figure 5: Evaluation steps (RT: Response Time, WRT: Weighted Response Time).

the representative intervals and then replays them while performing warm-up and enforcing request dependency. In this section, we focus on I/O traces and their difference with CPU traces. Then, a systematic sampling based on SMARTS [58] will be evaluated and its shortcomings will be demonstrated. Finally, we describe the process of clustering trace intervals and compare the accuracy and time reduction that can be achieved by choosing representative intervals.

4.1 I/O versus CPU Workloads

Before we engage in application of various sampling techniques, we demonstrate key differences of CPU traces in comparison to I/O traces. First of all, CPUs have much higher activity levels in comparison to I/O devices, meaning an I/O trace of the same activity is going to have much lower number of requests than that of the CPU traces. Second, I/O traces are very bursty [32, 21, 22] and the response time fluctuates wildly between request intervals, while in CPU traces *Cycles per Instruction* (CPI) remains constant for many different intervals [10]. Due to the bursty and sparse nature of storage workloads, unlike microprocessor based methodologies which divide traces into intervals based on the number of requests within them [58, 13], we divide each trace into intervals of a fixed duration.

Burstiness and auto-correlation of storage workloads [32, 21, 22] means that requests cannot be considered independently and any sampling must capture the temporal context of requests. The solution used by [14] was to use a duration-based division of I/O traces which captures temporal context and manages to greatly diminish the impact of long range dependence on performance. We group requests into 10-second intervals. There are a number of reasons behind this selection; first of all, the authors in [14] show that this interval duration diminishes the effect of long range dependence very well. Secondly, as will be demonstrated in Sec. 6.2, run-time of per-interval warm-ups dwarf that of the actual intervals being measured. Nevertheless, a week contains roughly sixty-thousand individual 10-second intervals, a number that allows low error and considerable speed-ups by our proposed methodology.

To demonstrate the difference between I/O and CPU trace behavior, we show the average duration of a "phase" in MSRC traces [28] in Figure 6. Similar to [13], we define a phase as a set of successive intervals where performance fluctuates by less than 10%. Based on the trace, the average phase length can vary from a single interval to multiple hours. It must be noted that long average phase length can also be caused by extreme sparsity, as is the case for the three most dense traces with less than 100 requests per hour on average. It is evident from these results that storage traces cannot be expected to have well-defined phases such as microprocessor traces. However, although I/O response time can affect processor CPI [17], the lack of phase behavior at the I/O request level does not mean that there is no phase behavior at the fine level of detail captured by microprocessor traces. I/O requests are removed from the details of microprocessor activity in such cases.

4.2 Systematic Sampling

In this section, we evaluate the effectiveness of using systematic sampling at representing the performance of the whole trace. SMARTS [58] determines the number of sampled intervals which must run in a detailed manner by using confidence intervals. It then uses systematic sampling with a fixed period to select these intervals and run them in a detailed manner. We evaluate the effectiveness of both these steps using MSRC traces [28] and conclude that this strategy is unsuitable for reducing storage traces.

Similar to SMARTS [58], we first determine the number of intervals using normal distribution confidence intervals. Figure 7 shows the total duration of requests that must be sampled in order to reach a maximum error margin of 15% with a confidence of 90%. This tolerance is much more relaxed than the work in [58] but we believe it is essential due to the bursty nature of storage workloads.

As can be seen from the results in Figure 7, some workloads can be significantly reduced. However, this does not extend to every workload and on average, *500 minutes* of pure replay time (sans the significant overhead of cache warm-up) is needed based on this method. These reductions, while significant, are still impractical for repetitive experiments. This method is also prone to over- and under-reporting the number of intervals. For example, *rsrch_0*, *wdev_1*, and *prxy_0* are reported to require less than *4 samples* but *hm_0* which contains less than 700 requests is reported to need over *27 minutes* of pure interval run-time.

As explained earlier, intervals in [58] are sampled by a fixed period. This requires the specification of a starting offset. This choice is much more challenging for storage workloads as they are bursty and lack well-defined phase behavior. For example, some starting offsets result in entirely empty set of samples for some traces. As noted earlier, this methodology may poorly estimate the number of required samples. To aid systematic sampling, two improvements were tested (a) the minimum number of samples is set to 30 to alleviate the issue of under-sampling (*Min30* versus *NoMin*) (b) since a starting offset is needed for systematic sampling, we choose the single run containing the most requests (*Single*) versus averaging the 10 most populated runs (*Avg10*). Please note that should we use the latter enhancement in practice, it results in 10x slower experiments.

It can be concluded from the experiments (Figure 8) that even with the above enhancements and when using the numbers embedded in the traces themselves, systematic sampling produces significant error. The *Single_30Min* which does not average multiple runs has significant error, even in workloads such as *proj_3*, *rsrch_1*, and *hm_1* where multiple hours worth of samples need to be taken. We attribute this high error to (a) lack of phase behavior in most traces (depicted in Figure 6) and (b) the burstiness of workloads which makes the choice of representative intervals challenging. This is in stark contrast with microprocessor instruction traces where phase behavior is far better defined [46]. We conclude that a guided sampling methodology based on the properties of request intervals is essential for higher accuracy of trace size reduction.

4.3 Feature Extraction and Data Mining

Shortcomings of systematic sampling show that a guided method of selecting representative intervals is essential for reaching higher accuracy. As it is not a good practice to use the performance numbers of a certain hardware configuration when trying to design a general methodology, we refrain from using response time results in clustering and only use these numbers to measure the accuracy of our methodology. Instead, we use properties such as trace request arrival time, address, and type to generate feature vectors for clustering.

Use of *Arrival Time Entropy* as a key property of trace behavior has been proposed in [54, 14, 52]; the latter work also uses address entropy to identify uneven accesses to disk locations. We use the multi-level aggregation scheme shown in Figure 9 which has been used in [54, 14, 15] to estimate the entropy of data points in continuous space. At each aggregation level, buckets have the same size and the next aggregation level is obtained by merging consecutive array buckets in pairs. At every level, a bucket is treated as an alphabet letter in discrete Shannon Entropy [45] calculations and the number of requests within it as the letter frequency.

We use this multi-level aggregation methodology to measure the time and address entropy. While time is continuous and can be divided easily, address is a discrete quantity. Thus, we use 512 bytes as the smallest unit, which is the common denominator of request addresses as it used to be disk sector size for a long time. For both entropy calcula-

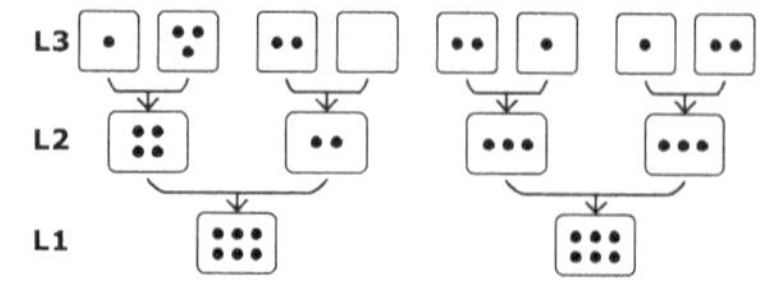

Figure 9: Using different aggregation levels for calculating entropy.

tions, we use 16 unique levels of aggregation which is higher than what was used in [14].

Arrival Time Entropy as described above, is an effective measure of workload burstiness and has been used in several studies [54, 14, 15]. Bursty behavior concentrates many requests in a compact period of time, skewing temporal distribution and reducing entropy. *Address-space entropy* translates to a higher spatial and temporal locality, which can greatly improve cache performance. *Working Set Locality* is defined as the ratio of total interval traffic to the number of unique sectors (working set) accessed in an interval. This measure was named "aggregation ratio" in [15].

We have conducted experiments with multiple features indicative of interval load. We use *Total Traffic*, *Average Request Size*, *Working Set Size*, and Interval *Request Count* as basic features. However, further discrimination between requests is necessary. Read and write requests have a different performance in I/O subsystems [17]. While writes can simply be satisfied by recording data in cache or non-volatile RAM, reads (or more specifically, read misses) should lead to immediate fetch of data, either from storage cache or media. As a result, read operations have a much more pronounced impact on system performance [17] and thus, it is likely beneficial for them to have a higher priority. As such, we also use *Read Ratio* as one of the main features.

Another key property of I/O workloads which affects both *Hard Disk Drives* (HDDs) and *Solid State Drives* (SSDs) is the randomness of I/O requests. Aside from poor cache performance, vastly different implementation details penalize random requests compared to sequential requests. Random accesses force HDDs to perform complex seeks, reducing performance. For SSDs, random accesses generate many more requests to the flash chips, reducing throughput. To recognize random requests, we use a queue-aware distance based scheme similar to what was used in [2]. In this classification, the distance of address of each new request is compared against the address of a number of recent requests. The minimum distance referred to as *Travel Distance* is compared against *Randomness Distance Threshold.*

If the travel distance exceeds this threshold, the request is classified as random. In this paper, this number of recent requests (queue depth) is taken to be 32 requests and Randomness Distance Threshold is 128KB, which seem to be the queue depth and read-ahead length of our surveyed disk drives. *Randomness Ratio* is the feature representing the fraction of random requests within an interval. We also use the sum of request Travel Distance and Average request Travel Distance, as *Total Travel Distance* and *Average Travel Distance* features, respectively. Table 1 shows the features investigated in this study for the construction of feature vectors along with the properties which we think are related to these features.

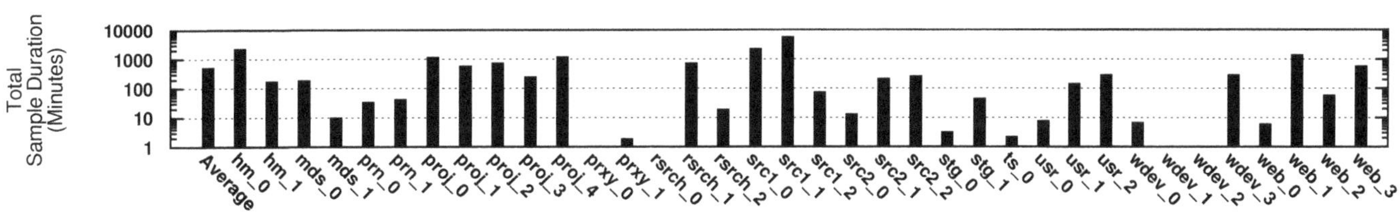

Figure 7: Total duration of intervals selected by confidence-based sampling with a maximum error of 15% and a confidence of 90%. The full duration of the traces is one week (~10000 minutes).

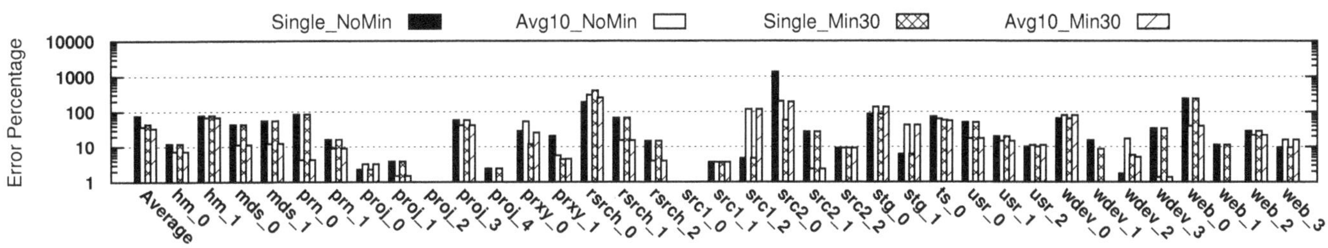

Figure 8: Error percentage of using a SMARTS-like [58] systematic sampling policy on 10-second intervals. AvgN averages the N runs with the highest total request count (Single = Avg1). MinK places a minimum bound of K on the sample count (NoMin = Min1).

4.4 Data Mining

Clustering algorithms group data points based on features similarities. Our aim at data mining, similar to SimPoint [13] is to, (a) group trace intervals into similar clusters and (b) choose a suitable representative for each cluster. We group features together to construct feature vectors as inputs of the clustering algorithm and use WRT error as a measure of accuracy.

As dense request intervals have much more impact on performance [29], the process of clustering and selecting representative intervals must take interval density into account. In other words, the process of clustering must support weighting data points. The authors in [1] conduct a study on weighted clustering where different data points may have different weights assigned. Based on their classification, K-Means is *weight-sensitive* and its clustering behavior is always affected by the repetition of points, noted by them as a naive method of applying weights to data points. SimPoint 3.0 [13] faces a similar challenge due to use of variable length intervals and augments K-Means with support for interval weighting.

We use a weighted variation of K-Means [7] which supports the application of weights to each individual data point. Before feeding the feature vectors to clustering, we perform preprocessing using [19] to center data on zero and set the variance to unity to improve the output of machine learning. We also had to specify K, the number of clusters, in K-Means. Our calculations of error show that the value of K has a great impact on response time estimation error. To select K, we have implemented BIC [42], based on the SimPoint 3.0 implementation in [13] which supports weights, as well as F_k from [31]. Both these methods use distortion and the number of clusters to determine the optimal number of clusters. Based on our experiments, BIC performs better and we omit the results of F_k here due to page limitation. In our methodology, we generate clusterings with K ranging from 2 to 50 with approximately sixty-thousand 10-second intervals as input and choose the clustering with the lowest BIC.

Table 1 shows the final set of features that were extracted for every interval with a short description of each feature. Depending on the selection of features, each interval is represented by a point with the features as its coordinates and the number of requests within it as the weight. Weighted K-Means is then performed on the data with different values of K, forming clusters and reporting the centroids. Intervals represented by points closest to cluster centroid are picked as the cluster representative. We use weighted response time of the representative intervals to measure the error in estimated response time compared to the weighted response time of all intervals. We weight the representative intervals by the total number of requests inside the cluster.

For simplicity, we have used a unified feature vector across all traces. We aim to improve upon this in our future work. The best feature vector for clustering data based on our experiments is *ArqWslRndAntEntTreAte*, which uses Average Request Size, Working Set Locality, Randomness, Address and Time Entropy, Total and Average (Queue-Based) Travel Distance as the feature vector. We choose this name based on the three-word short form in Table 1. Figure 10 shows WRT error by clustering using weighted K-means. Our results show an average and maximum error of 3.6% and 12.1% using the original response time in the traces themselves.

5. TRACE REPLAY

We presented details of our experiment testbed in Sec. 3. In this section, we explain the process of enforcing dependency and the methodology used for warm-up of state before each representative interval is run.

5.1 Enforcing Causality

A very important difference of replaying traces versus running programs is the fact that inter-arrival time of requests is partly influenced by the inter-arrival time of original hardware. This is caused by inter-request dependency in the

Table 1: List of features explored for clustering.

Feature Name	Short Form	Description	Related Property
Random Ratio	*Rnd*	Percentage of Queue-Based Random Requests (See [2])	Temporal and Spatial Locality
Read Ratio	*Rd*	Percentage of Read Requests	Read Frequency
Total Traffic	*Mss*	Sum of Request Sizes	Device Load
Total Request Count	*Cnt*	Total Number of Requests	Device Load
Address Entropy	*Ant*	Multi-level Address Shannon Entropy	Temporal and Spatial Locality
Arrival Time Entropy	*Ent*	Multi-level Arrival Time Shannon Entropy	Burstiness
Working Set	*Wst*	Sum of Unique Locations Accessed	Device Load, Temporal Locality
Working Set Locality	*Wsl*	Ratio of Total Traffic to Working Set	Temporal Locality
Average Request Size	*Arq*	Ratio of Total Traffic to Request Count	Device Load
Travel Distance	*Tre*	Queue-Based Request Offset Travel (See [2])	Spatial Locality, Seek Count
Average Travel Distance	*Ate*	Average Queue-Based Request Offset Travel (See [2])	Spatial Locality, Seek Count

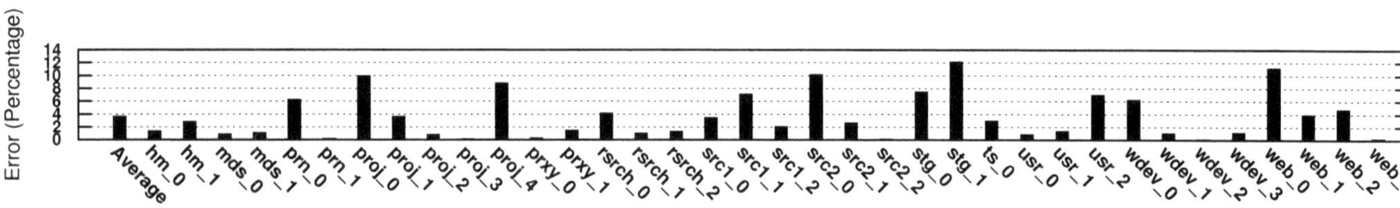

Figure 10: Per-trace WRT error of our chosen feature vector *ArqWslRndAntEntTreAte* with original response times (Step 1 in Figure 5).

original system activity. Ignoring this dependency is referred to as open-loop replaying which causes significant error [41], making closed-loop replays essential. However, most of traces available in public domain fail to record important semantic information and this information must be inferred based on the type and arrangement of requests.

Our replay tool replays traces in a closed-loop manner by constructing I/O request dependency trees. Consider the scenario in Figure 11; in the original replay, request A must finish before B is issued (Top). On the destination hardware, A may take considerably longer (Middle and Bottom). Open-loop replay (Middle) issues request B by Δ_{OL} units of time after A starts, even if it violates the dependency. In contrast, closed-loop replaying waits Δ_{CL} units of time *after* A is finished before sending request B. We believe this method better reflects the relationship between requests.

As noted earlier, enforcement of dependencies is much easier and accurate when detailed traces [55, 26] are present. These tools use rich information to enforce dependency as it was present in the original run. Most available public datasets such as the one used in our study [28] lack detailed information, especially those that record long periods of activity which is more representative. As a result, we have to make approximations of trace behavior for replays.

While it is possible to replay every request as blocking (i.e., controlled similar to A and B in Figure 11), we do not believe it represents real system behavior. Specifically, writes are normally cached by the operating system inside the main memory and are flushed to disk based on operating system behavior. While written data can be flushed to disk by calling *flush()* on Linux and *fcntl(F_FULLSYNC)* on Mac OS X [55], the study in [35] shows that a small percentage of reads are non-blocking and write behavior depends on the workload. As a result, out of the trace requests, we consider reads to be blocking and writes to be non-blocking. As a further support for this decision, it has been observed that

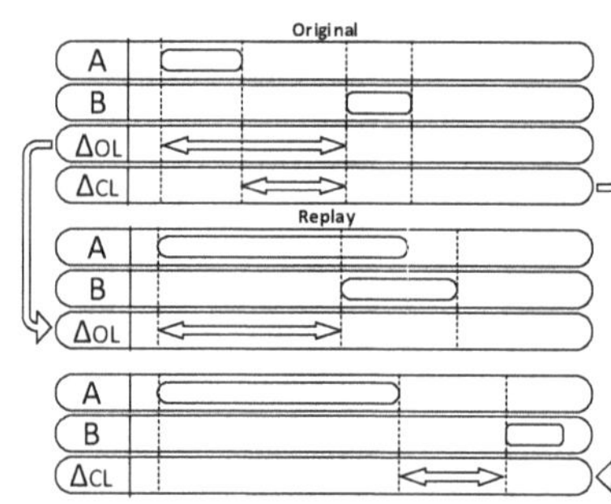

Figure 11: Comparison of open-loop (Middle) and closed-loop (Bottom) replays of a recorded workload (Top). Originally (Top), B depends on A and its start is Δ_{OL} and Δ_{CL} units of time after the start and finish time of A, respectively. On the destination, A takes longer than original and unlike the open-loop replay (Middle), close-loop (Bottom) replay avoids potential conflicts.

microprocessor CPI has a correlation with average I/O read request response time [17], but no such relation exists with average request time for combined read/write requests.

We propose a dependency policy such that in the absence of semantic information, read and write operations are assumed to be blocking and non-blocking, respectively. In other words, when calculating request arrival time in our replay tool we have three scenarios, (a) requests following a read requests conclusion will have their arrival time calculated based on its finish (Figure 11, bottom), (b) requests that arrive before a read concluding only depend on its arrival time (Figure 11, middle), and (c) requests that follow a write, whether it concludes or not depend on its arrival time (Figure 11, middle).

An example of this policy can be seen in Figure 12 which

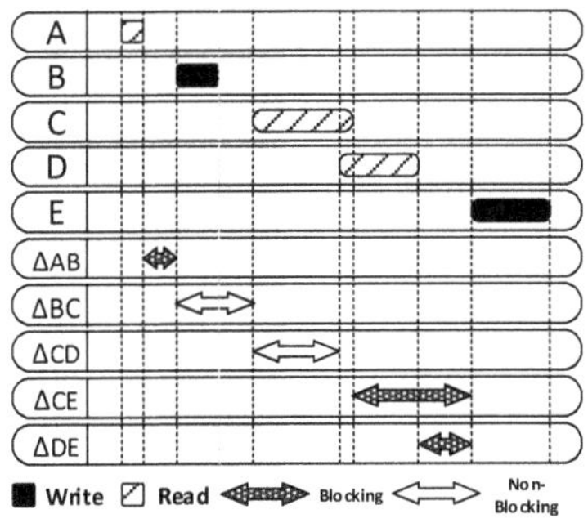

Figure 12: Inferring dependencies by treating reads as blocking and writes as non-blocking.

shows the arrival and finish time in the original trace. Dependencies are inferred based on arrival time and request type. A is a read and is finished before B starts. Thus, it falls under the first scenario and is blocking. B is a write and falls under the third scenario. In other words, we assume that after the program issues A and B, the wait time is only caused by CPU thinking time and not waiting on their results. Request D arrives before C is completed and falls under the second scenario. We assume CPU was actually thinking before issuing D as it did not need C to finish to get issued. Request E arrives after *both* C and D are finished and falls under the first scenario, where both Δ_{CE} and Δ_{DE} have to be preserved. In other words, $Arrival_E = max(Finish_C + \Delta_{CE}, Finish_D + \Delta_{DE})$ where $Arrival_E$ is the calculated arrival time and variables $Finish_C$ and $Finish_D$ describe the finishing time in our testbed. Enforcing both these delta times ensures that even if requests C and D are acknowledged in a different order than the original trace, the assumed constant processing time will be preserved. Since the introduction of *Native Command Queuing* (NCQ) to the Serial ATA standard, out of order acknowledgment should be assumed to be present in all modern storage hardware.

5.2 Accelerated Warm-up

As the goal of DiskAccel is to run storage traces with the greatest possible accuracy, the architectural state of the hardware must be warmed up appropriately. While restoration of architectural state can be performed via checkpoints [13], this capability is rarely available on real hardware. As a result, warm-up of the state should be performed by sending requests.

In [58], this is performed via a step called *Detailed Warm-up*, where a portion of the instruction trace preceding each selected interval is replayed. Between the end of a run and next detailed warm-up, instructions are emulated so the user visible state is always valid, but detailed warm-up should cover the whole architectural state. For I/O traces, an arbitrary portion of the traces has been used to warm up the state [25, 56].

To minimize run-time, we should reduce the time spent on warm-up. However, architectural state of storage subsystems is much larger than that of microprocessors. While current microprocessors have tens of megabytes of cache at most, cache size can be as large as 128MB for HDDs [43], 512MB for SSDs [38], and much more extensive caching is performed in enterprise storage systems.

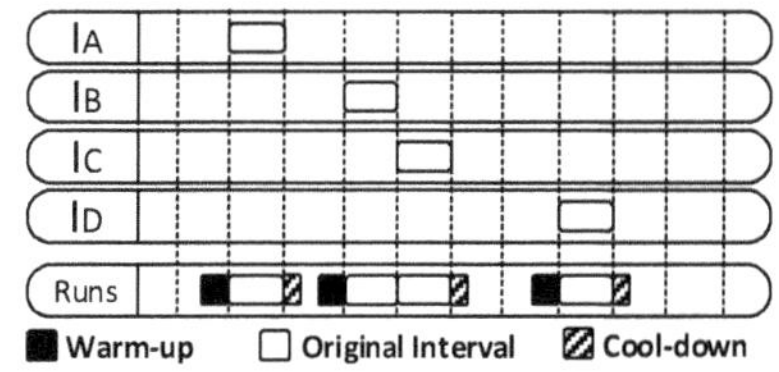

Figure 13: Runs generated (including warm-up and cool-down) for the representative intervals $I_A...I_D$. Since I_B and I_C are continuous, a singular run can perform measurements for both of them.

The warm-up process must select enough requests before each representative interval so the cache is warmed up. As hit ratio of workloads might be variable, we should care about the request footprint and not the sum of request sizes. To track request footprint, we use interval trees to track each unique accessed sector. We then move in backwards from the start of each representative interval and stop when the total capacity of unique disk locations reaches the capacity of the cache. Please note that due to operations such as read-ahead, much fewer requests must be selected to warm up the cache but we choose a pessimistic policy to ensure the accuracy of warm-up. After the last requests in a representative interval is issued, there is a possibility that requests exist that preceded the conclusion of these requests. To increase accuracy, after all requests in a representative interval are issued, we send requests that originally arrived before these requests finished. We refer to this as *cool-down* process.

A high level view of the replaying process for representative intervals can be seen in Figure 13. $I_A...I_D$ are the selected representative intervals and three runs have been generated for replaying them. The striped lines show the interval boundaries; each run is preceded by a warm-up and in its conclusion, a cool-down process is run. I_B and I_C are immediate neighbors and thus, I_B can act as warm-up for I_C and I_C can perform as a cool-down for I_B. This allows them to share the same run.

The warm-up behavior of our solution has important advantages: (a) if the device cache is so large that warm-up of multiple intervals overlaps, the runs are joined and warm-up time is reduced considerably, (b) if the workload is very dense, not all the requests between different representative intervals are run and only the required amount of warm-up is performed.

6. EXPERIMENTAL VALIDATION

As mentioned previously, we use a subset of MSRC [28] in the experiments. All these traces approximately span over a week and have been taken from a variety of servers. While these traces do include the response time of the original server, we use our implementation of a trace runner to (a) validate the results of the clustering process and (b) test the viability and accuracy of running representative trace intervals to estimate the original request response time. We will explain the results of these two experiments in the following subsections.

6.1 Cross-validation of Clustering

In the previous section, we used the response time of the original trace to measure the accuracy of our methodology

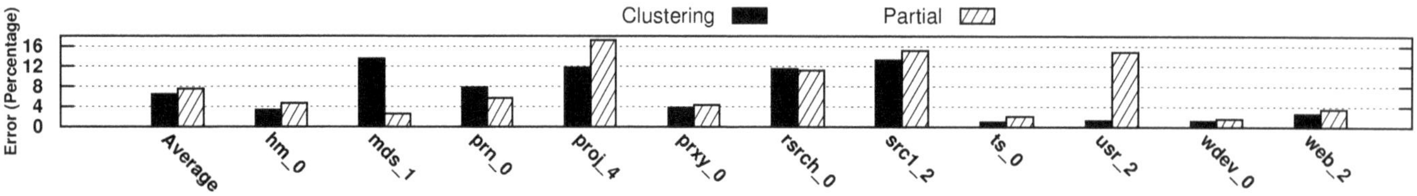

Figure 14: Per-trace WRT error of our chosen feature vector *ArqWslRndAntEntTreAte*, compared against the reference. The "clustering" statistic is the WRT error by clustering whole trace runs (Step 2 in Figure 5) and "partial" refers to the WRT error of partial trace runs (Step 3 in Figure 5). The reference for both cases is the average response time of a whole trace replay.

(Step 1 in Figure 5). To rule out the possibility of our learning methodology being overly tuned to the *Redundant Array of Independent Disks* (RAID) used on the original machines, we use our replay tool described in Sec. 3 to perform the replays on our testbed. Multiple identical and independent disks were used to perform concurrent experiments.

In Step 1 of Figure 5, we used the original response time values in the trace both as the reference and for calculating WRT. In Step 2, we repeat this comparison with different hardware. We use our replay tool to run the thread in full with no acceleration (requiring one week with each individual disk). The resulting response time values were used for calculating both the reference and WRT values yielding an average and maximum error of 6.5% and 13.6%, respectively. Detailed results can be seen in Figure 14 as "clustering" error bars. This error is comparable to those obtained from the original traces and demonstrates that our clustering methodology can successfully select representative intervals that are accurate across different hardware (Single SATA HDDs vs. RAID1 and RAID5 arrays [28]). In the next section, we conduct experiments to perform partial runs (Step 3 of Figure 5).

6.2 Running Representative Intervals

The actual process of DiskAccel only runs the representative intervals on the target hardware and uses WRT to estimate the response time of a complete run. To run each interval, hardware state must be similar to that of the original run at the start of a representative interval. To do so, key properties of the target hardware and list of representative intervals are given to our trace replaying tool.

In our tool, the warm-up of hardware state is performed by running a number of requests preceding each representative interval, so that the hardware cache has the same contents as the complete run. Warm-up requests are selected via an interval tree which ensures that requests are selected by their total footprint and not the sum of request sizes. To speed up the warm-up process, warm-up requests are run as fast as possible.

As cache size varies by different hardware, different number of requests must be sent for warm-up and user must supply cache size according to the hardware on which requests are replayed. Another user-supplied parameter is disk queue depth which is the number of requests that can be concurrently processed by storage hardware. If more requests than queue capacity are to be sent by the hardware, the trace replaying tool must block until at least one request is finished. Cache size and queue capacity for our disks are 8MB and 32 requests, respectively.

We replayed the representative intervals of the selected traces using our replaying tool, weighted each interval by the number of requests within its cluster and calculated WRT. The WRT error, reported by only replaying the representative intervals is reported in Figure 14. The average and maximum response time errors are 7.6% and 17.2%, respectively.

The main aim of the methodology introduced in this paper is to reduce the run-time for replay-based experiments. In Figure 15 we display (a) run-time of the whole trace, (b) partial runs with no accelerated warm-up, calculated based on the original trace arrival time (a lower bound as our testbed is slower), (c) run-time with accelerated warm-up measured on our testbed, and (d) pure run-time of representative intervals with no warm-up. The results show massive speed-ups (the graph is log-scale) compared to both the unaccelerated run and the full run-time with a 577 times reduction on average.

In short, DiskAccel can select representative intervals independent of the hardware configuration using a clustering process that must be run only once for each trace. DiskAccel needs about 20 minutes of run-time for partial runs (including warm-up) of a one-week trace. Our tool also manages to massively reduce run times while keeping average and maximum error across different hardware to a minimum.

6.3 Discussion

As noted in Figure 14, estimation error of our current methodology can be attributed to (a) the process of clustering and choice of representatives, and (b) partial replay and warm-up of state. Our clustering uses a constant feature vector for choosing representative intervals. While we tried alternative approaches such as *DBSCAN* [11] as well as augmenting K-Means with *Principal Component Analysis* (PCA) [18] (as implemented in [19]), we did not achieve better results. We plan to enhance our machine learning with suitable feature selection to improve the results. Based on our investigations, we believe that the error caused by partial runs is mainly caused by discrepencies in low-level behavior of HDD (i.e., cache flush after idleness). We hope to improve this behavior by controlling the timing of requests as the warm-up finishes.

7. CONCLUSION

In this paper, we introduced a methodology, called DiskAccel, to extract key properties of storage traces and use them to select representative intervals by employing the weighted K-Means algorithm. We also developed a tool to effectively run the representative intervals, fill the hardware cache for warm-up, and enforce request dependencies.

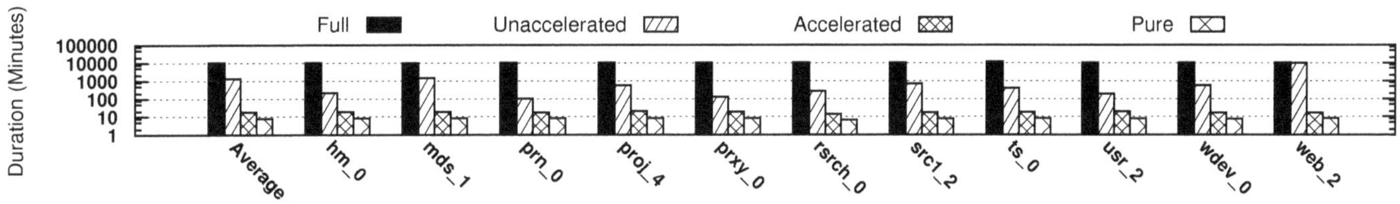

Figure 15: Run time durations of different modes, Whole trace (Full), Partial runs without accelerated warm-up (Unaccelerated), Partial runs with accelerated warm-up (Accelerated), and without warm-up (Pure).

We performed the evaluation of DiskAccel at three different steps. We began by evaluating the ability of the clustering process at accurate estimation of whole trace average response times; first, using the response times recorded in the original trace and then, using response times from replay of whole traces using our tool. We also used our replay tool to only run the representative intervals with the required warm-up in an accelerated manner. Our methodology managed to estimate the average response time by an average and maximum error of %7.6 and %17.2, respectively while speeding up the I/O experiments by 577 times on average.

As a future work, one can further improve the current solution so error and experimentation times could be further reduced. We also limited our study to a single hardware setup due to the time-consuming nature of gathering reference response times at the original rate. We would like to study the behavior of the proposed methodology for more diverse hardware setups, especially SSDs and hybrid hardware architectures in the future.

8. REFERENCES

[1] M. Ackerman, S. Ben-David, S. Branzei, and D. Loker. Weighted clustering. In *AAAI*, pages 858–863, 2012.

[2] I. Ahmad. Easy and Efficient Disk I/O Workload Characterization in VMware ESX Server. In *Proc. IISWC'07*, pages 149–158, Sept.

[3] E. Anderson, M. Kallahalla, M. Uysal, and R. Swaminathan. Buttress: A toolkit for flexible and high fidelity i/o benchmarking. In *Proc. FAST'04*, pages 4–4.

[4] J. Axboe. Fio-flexible io tester. `http://freecode.com/projects/fio`, 2008. [Online; accessed 1-August-2014].

[5] A. D. Brunelle. Block i/o layer tracing: blktrace, 2006.

[6] J. S. Bucy, J. Schindler, S. W. Schlosser, and G. R. Ganger. The disksim simulation environment version 4.0 reference manual (cmu-pdl-08-101). *Parallel Data Laboratory*, page 26, 2008.

[7] J. Burkardt. KMEANS - the K-Means Data Clustering Problem. `http://people.sc.fsu.edu/~jburkardt/m_src/kmeans/kmeans.html`, 2013. [Online; accessed 16-June-2014].

[8] P. Cao, E. W. Felten, A. R. Karlin, and K. Li. Implementation and performance of integrated application-controlled file caching, prefetching, and disk scheduling. *TOCS*, 14(4):311–343, 1996.

[9] R. Coker. Bonnie++. `http://www.coker.com.au/bonnie++/`, 2001. [Online; accessed 20-June-2014].

[10] A. S. Dhodapkar and J. E. Smith. Comparing program phase detection techniques. In *Proc. MICRO'03*, page 217.

[11] M. Ester, H. P. Kriegel, J. Sander, and X. Xu. A Density-Based Algorithm for Discovering Clusters in Large Spatial Databases with Noise. In E. Simoudis, J. Han, and U. Fayyad, editors, *Second International Conference on Knowledge Discovery and Data Mining*, pages 226–231. AAAI Press, 1996.

[12] Google. AIOUserGuide. `https://code.google.com/p/kernel/wiki/AIOUserGuide`, 2014. [Online; accessed 1-August-2014].

[13] G. Hamerly, E. Perelman, J. Lau, and B. Calder. Simpoint 3.0: Faster and more flexible program phase analysis. *JILP*, 7(4):1–28, 2005.

[14] B. Hong and T. M. Madhyastha. The relevance of long-range dependence in disk traffic and implications for trace synthesis. In *Proc. MSST'05*, pages 316–326.

[15] B. Hong, T. M. Madhyastha, and B. Zhang. Cluster-based input/output trace synthesis. In *Proc. IPCCC'05*, pages 91–98.

[16] W. W. Hsu, A. J. Smith, and H. C. Young. Characteristics of production database workloads and the tpc benchmarks. *IBM Systems Journal*, 40(3):781–802, 2001.

[17] B. Jacob, S. Ng, and D. Wang. *Memory Systems: Cache, DRAM, Disk*. 2010.

[18] I. Jolliffe. *Principal Component Analysis*. John Wiley & Sons, Ltd, 2005.

[19] E. Jones, T. Oliphant, P. Peterson, et al. SciPy: Open source scientific tools for Python. `http://www.scipy.org/`, 2001–. [Online; accessed 1-August-2014].

[20] J. Katcher. Postmark: A new file system benchmark. Technical report, Technical Report TR3022, Network Appliance, 1997. www.netapp.com/tech_library/3022.html, 1997.

[21] S. Kavalanekar, D. Narayanan, S. Sankar, E. Thereska, K. Vaid, and B. Worthington. Measuring database performance in online services: a trace-based approach. In *Performance Evaluation and Benchmarking*, pages 132–145. 2009.

[22] S. Kavalanekar, B. Worthington, Q. Zhang, and V. Sharda. Characterization of storage workload traces from production windows servers. In *Proc. IISWC'08*, pages 119–128.

[23] T. Kgil and T. Mudge. Flashcache: a nand flash memory file cache for low power web servers. In *Proc. CASES'06*, pages 103–112.

[24] J. Lau, S. Schoemackers, and B. Calder. Structures for phase classification. In *Proc. ISPASS'04*, pages 57–67.

[25] C. Maltzahn, K. J. Richardson, and D. Grunwald. Reducing the disk i/o of web proxy server caches. In *Proc. ATC'99*, pages 225–238.

[26] M. P. Mesnier, M. Wachs, R. R. Simbasivan, J. Lopez, J. Hendricks, G. R. Ganger, and D. R. O'Hallaron. //trace: Parallel trace replay with approximate causal events. In *Proc. FAST'07*.

[27] N. Mi, G. Casale, L. Cherkasova, and E. Smirni. Injecting realistic burstiness to a traditional client-server benchmark. In *Proc. ICAC'09*, pages 149–158.

[28] D. Narayanan, A. Donnelly, and A. Rowstron. Write off-loading: Practical power management for enterprise storage. *ACM ToS*, 4(3):10:1–10:23, Nov. 2008.

[29] D. Narayanan, A. Donnelly, E. Thereska, S. Elnikety, and A. Rowstron. Everest: Scaling down peak loads through i/o off-loading. In *Proc. OSDI'08*, December.

[30] W. D. Norcott and D. Capps. Iozone filesystem benchmark. `http://www.iozone.org/`, 2006. [Online; accessed 20-June-2014].

[31] D. T. Pham, S. S. Dimov, and C. Nguyen. Selection of k in k-means clustering. *Proceedings of the Institution of Mechanical Engineers, Part C: Journal of Mechanical Engineering Science*, 219(1):103–119, 2005.

[32] A. Riska and E. Riedel. Disk drive level workload characterization. In *Proc. ATC'06*, pages 97–102.

[33] M. Rosenblum and J. K. Ousterhout. The design and implementation of a log-structured file system. *TOCS*, 10(1):26–52, 1992.

[34] S. Rostedt and D. V. Hart. Internals of the rt patch. In *Proceedings of the Linux symposium*, 2007.

[35] C. Ruemmler and J. Wilkes. Unix disk access patterns. In *USENIX Winter*, volume 93, pages 405–420, 1993.

[36] R. Saikkonen. Linux i/o port programming mini - howto. `www.tldp.org/HOWTO/pdf/IO-Port-Programming.pdf`, 2000. [Online; accessed 19-November-2014].

[37] R. Salkhordeh, H. Asadi, and S. Ebrahimi. Operating system level data tiering using online workload characterization. *The Journal of Supercomputing*, 71(4):1534–1562, 2015.

[38] Samsung Corporation. *Samsung SSD 840 PRO Series*, August 2013. Rev. 1.2.

[39] P. Scheuermann, G. Weikum, and P. Zabback. Data partitioning and load balancing in parallel disk systems. *The VLDB Journal*, 7(1):48–66, 1998.

[40] J. Schindler and G. R. Ganger. Automated disk drive characterization (poster session). *SIGMETRICS Perform. Eval. Rev.*, 28(1):112–113, June 2000.

[41] B. Schroeder, A. Wierman, and M. Harchol-Balter. Open versus closed: A cautionary tale. In *Proc. NSDI'06*, pages 18–18, 2006.

[42] G. Schwarz. Estimating the dimension of a model. *The Annals of Statistics*, 6:461–464, 1978.

[43] Seagate Corporation. *Enterprise Capacity 3.5 HDD Data Sheet*, April 2014.

[44] B. Seo, S. Kang, J. Choi, J. Cha, Y. Won, and S. Yoon. Io workload characterization revisited: A data-mining approach. *IEEE TC*, 63(12):3026–3038, Dec 2014.

[45] C. E. Shannon. A note on the concept of entropy. *Bell System Tech. J*, 27:379–423, 1948.

[46] T. Sherwood, E. Perelman, G. Hamerly, and B. Calder. Automatically characterizing large scale program behavior. In *Proc. ASPLOS'02*, pages 45–57.

[47] A. J. Smith. Disk cache-miss ratio analysis and design considerations. *TOCS*, 3(3):161–203, 1985.

[48] V. Tarasov, S. Kumar, J. Ma, D. Hildebrand, A. Povzner, G. Kuenning, and E. Zadok. Extracting flexible, replayable models from large block traces. In *Proc. FAST'12*, pages 22–22, 2012.

[49] M. Tarihi. Serious problems using dixtrac extracted parameters. `https://sos.ece.cmu.edu/pipermail/disksim-users/2013-July/000821.html`, 2013. [Online; accessed 16-June-2014].

[50] A. Traeger, E. Zadok, N. Joukov, and C. P. Wright. A nine year study of file system and storage benchmarking. *ACM TOS*, 4(2):5, 2008.

[51] B. Trushkowsky, P. Bodík, A. Fox, M. J. Franklin, M. I. Jordan, and D. A. Patterson. The scads director: Scaling a distributed storage system under stringent performance requirements. In *Proc. FAST'11*, pages 12–12.

[52] M. Wang, A. Ailamaki, and C. Faloutsos. Capturing the spatio-temporal behavior of real traffic data. *Performance Evaluation*, 49(1):147–163, 2002.

[53] M. Wang, K. Au, A. Ailamaki, A. Brockwell, C. Faloutsos, and G. Ganger. Storage device performance prediction with cart models. In *Proc. MASCOTS'04*, pages 588–595, Oct.

[54] M. Wang, T. Madhyastha, N. H. Chan, S. Papadimitriou, and C. Faloutsos. Data mining meets performance evaluation: Fast algorithms for modeling bursty traffic. In *Proc. ICDE'02*, pages 507–516.

[55] Z. Weiss, T. Harter, A. C. Arpaci-Dusseau, and R. H. Arpaci-Dusseau. ROOT: Replaying Multithreaded Traces with Resource-Oriented Ordering. In *Proc. SOSP'13*, November 2013.

[56] T. M. Wong and J. Wilkes. My cache or yours? making storage more exclusive. In *Proc. ATEC'02*, pages 161–175, 2002.

[57] B. L. Worthington, G. R. Ganger, and Y. N. Patt. Scheduling algorithms for modern disk drives. *SIGMETRICS Perform. Eval. Rev.*, 22(1):241–251, may 1994.

[58] R. E. Wunderlich, T. F. Wenisch, B. Falsafi, and J. C. Hoe. SMARTS: Accelerating microarchitecture simulation via rigorous statistical sampling. In *Proc. ISCA'03*, pages 84–95.

[59] J. Zhang, A. Sivasubramaniam, H. Franke, N. Gautam, Y. Zhang, and S. Nagar. Synthesizing Representative I/O Workloads for TPC-H. In *Proc. HPCA'04*, pages 142–142, Feb.

[60] N. Zhu, J. Chen, T.-c. Chiueh, and D. Ellard. TBBT: Scalable and Accurate Trace Replay for File Server Evaluation. In *Proc. SIGMETRICS'05*, pages 392–393, 2005.

[61] Q. Zhu, Z. Chen, L. Tan, Y. Zhou, K. Keeton, and J. Wilkes. Hibernator: Helping disk arrays sleep through the winter. In *Proc. SOSP'05*, pages 177–190.

Combining Phase Identification and Statistic Modeling for Automated Parallel Benchmark Generation

Ye Jin
North Carolina State University
yjin6@ncsu.edu

Xiaosong Ma
Qatar Computing Research Institute
xma@qf.org.qa

Mingliang Liu*
Amazon.com, Inc.
mig@amazon.com

Qing Liu Jeremy Logan Norbert Podhorszki Jong Youl Choi Scott Klasky
Oak Ridge National Laboratory
{liuq, loganjs, pnorbert, choij, klasky}@ornl.gov

ABSTRACT

Parallel application benchmarks are indispensable for evaluating/optimizing HPC software and hardware. However, it is very challenging and costly to obtain high-fidelity benchmarks reflecting the scale and complexity of state-of-the-art parallel applications. Hand-extracted synthetic benchmarks are time- and labor-intensive to create. Real applications themselves, while offering most accurate performance evaluation, are expensive to compile, port, reconfigure, and often plainly inaccessible due to security or ownership concerns.

This work contributes APPRIME, a novel tool for trace-based automatic parallel benchmark generation. Taking as input standard communication-I/O traces of an application's execution, it couples accurate automatic phase identification with statistical regeneration of event parameters to create compact, portable, and to some degree reconfigurable parallel application benchmarks. Experiments with four NAS Parallel Benchmarks (NPB) and three real scientific simulation codes confirm the fidelity of APPRIME benchmarks. They retain the original applications' performance characteristics, in particular their relative performance across platforms. Also, the result benchmarks, already released online, are much more compact and easy-to-port compared to the original applications.

Categories and Subject Descriptors

C.4 [**Performance of Systems**]: Measurement techniques; Modeling techniques

General Terms

Measurement; Performance

*Work was performed as intern at Qatar Computing Research Institute, during PhD study at Tsinghua University.

SIGMETRICS'15, June 15–19, 2015, Portland, OR, USA.

http://dx.doi.org/10.1145/2745844.2745876.

Keywords

Benchmark generation; HPC applications; Traces; Markov Chain Model; Phase Identification; Asynchronous I/O

1. INTRODUCTION

Benchmarks play a critical role in evaluating hardware and software systems. Compared to CPU, database, and mobile test workloads, supercomputing benchmarks are especially challenging and costly to construct or acquire. With both the scale (in terms of problem size and parallelism) and the complexity of applications growing alongside machine sizes, kernel-based benchmarks such as the NPB suite [7] fail to portrait state-of-the-art applications (e.g., multi-physics codes). Meanwhile, hand extracted benchmarks based on real-world, large-scale applications (such as FLASHIO [19] and GTCBench [14]) are highly labor-intensive to create and cannot easily keep up with the evolution of their long-lived base applications.

To this end, recent research developed tools for automatic generation of communication benchmarks based on trace compression and replay [36, 40]. The automatically generated codes can keep up with the original application's evolution rather easily. However, replay-based benchmarks have several intrinsic drawbacks. They require the use of a specialized, compression-enabled tracing library and cannot leverage existing traces or standard tracing libraries. Also, they are driven by timestamp information collected in the original traces, making them more suitable for reproducing communication patterns rather than recreating comprehensive, platform-dependent parallel workloads encompassing the interplay among computation, communication, and I/O.

Meanwhile, there are also recent projects investigating the creation of reconfigurable benchmarks, to be discussed in more details in Section 5. However, such tools possess significant restrictions. The more general-purpose benchmark tools [11, 16] require users to "assemble" a synthetic benchmark from a limited number of key workload characteristics such as instruction mix and instruction-level parallelism. Skel [20], a parallel I/O benchmark creation tool, also requires users to clearly identify the begin and end points of periodic I/O phases. In addition, they are not designed to include computation or communication activities.

In this paper, we propose APPRIME, an automatic benchmark generation tool based on off-line statistical trace profile extraction. Given an iterative parallel simulation (the most common type of large-scale HPC applications), APPRIME takes as input the set of traces generated by parallel processes in one execution of this original application, and automatically generates as output *benchmark source code* with similar computation, communication, and I/O behavior. This result benchmark comes with a concise configuration file for users to set execution parameters, such as the number of timesteps and checkpoint frequency. Rather than only aiming at future parallel trace replay, APPRIME strives to "understand" (to some extent) an application and create a stand-alone benchmark that imitates its behavior.

Unlike trace-replay-based benchmark creation tools, APPRIME obtains information from traces but takes a "statistical view" of applications, where a benchmark should reproduce the distributions (in many aspects of parallel program behavior, from instruction composition, to relative ranks of communication partners, to file read/write sizes), rather than line-by-line repetition of traced events. On the other hand, it recognizes that parallel programs are usually tightly coupled SPMD codes, whose executions do not build on random events: activities across processes and across timestep iterations are highly correlated (if not identical). Therefore APPRIME takes a hybrid approach, with (1) automatic trace-based phase/timestep identification through string analysis, (2) Markov-Chain-based timestep behavior model to enable reconfigurable execution length, and (3) statistical regeneration of event parameters. This way, APPRIME retains the accurate event ordering for communication and I/O calls within each timestep, as well as the transitions between different types of timesteps (a phenomenon observed in our real application study). Meanwhile, it regenerates event parameters, plus the time gaps as *computation intervals* between each adjacent events, according to their value *distributions* observed from the traces. By distilling patterns, the end product APPRIME benchmarks are more flexible, portable, and human-comprehensible.

Note that APPRIME is intended to emulate the base application's behavior in *all three* major dimensions: computation, communication, and I/O. This paper presents our first step, a proof-of-concept prototype focusing on *re-producing communication and I/O activities.* The current prototype emulates computation in a rather simplistic manner, by sleep intervals with statistically generated durations. The reproduction of computation activities, planned as future work, is to be plugged in as a building block.

We evaluated our APPRIME prototype with iterative parallel simulations, including three large-scale, closed-source applications and four communication-heavy NAS Parallel Benchmarks. All three real applications are current top-tier resource consumers on Titan [3], the world's No.2 supercomputer. In addition, we verified with the owners/users of all other resource-intensive applications there (marked with * in Table 1) that APPRIME can adequately model their computation, communication and I/O activities. Table 1 summarizes the diverse application domain, execution scale, source availability, and APPRIME benchmark generation status of all applications we examined.

Our evaluation results verify that automatically generated APPRIME benchmarks are compact, portable, and able to accurately represent applications' performance characteristics. All of our generated benchmarks have been released online [1], while we plan to extend the effort to other closed-source applications in Table 1. The initial success also motivates our ongoing work on refining APPRIME with statistical computation workload regeneration, plus other extensions (see future work discussion in Section 6).

[1]Allocation indicates the product of the number of allocated nodes times the assumed total execution hours.

Name	Project domain	Typical prod. run scale (# of cores)	Open source	Current status
XGC*	Gyrokinetic	225,280	No	Done
GTS*	Gyrokinetic	262,144	No	Done
HFODD*	Nuclear	299,008	Yes	Confirmed applicable
AWP-ODC*	Wave propagation	223,074	No	Confirmed applicable
NAMD*	Molecular dynamics	1,000 - 20,000	No	Confirmed applicable
S3D*	Molecular physics	96,000 - 180,000	No	Confirmed applicable
BEC2	Unitary qubit	110,592	No	Done
QMC-Pack*	Electronic molecular	256 - 16,000	No	Confirmed applicable
Lammps*	Molecular dynamics	12,500 - 130,000	Yes	Confirmed applicable
SPEC-FEM3D*	Wave propagation	150 - 600	Yes	Confirmed applicable
NAS-BT	Tri-diagonal solver	N/A	Yes	Done
NAS-LU	Gauss-seidel solver	N/A	Yes	Done
NAS-CG	Conjugate gradient	N/A	Yes	Done
NAS-SP	SP-diagonal solver	N/A	Yes	Done

*: Applications with * are awarded with large allocations[1]through the DOE INCITE program [2].
All APPRIME generated benchmarks are released online [1].

Table 1: Applications evaluated, or examined as candidate, for APPrime benchmark generation

2. SAMPLE APPRIME USE CASES

For further motivation, we give two sample use cases that highlight the need for realistic, configurable, and compact parallel benchmark codes. While our approach is not library-specific, for convenience we limit our discussion to codes using the MPI communication library [12] for the rest of the paper, due to MPI's dominance in parallel scientific applications and its capability of performing both inter-node communication and parallel file I/O. Note that though we gave two specific use cases, a single or a set of APPRIME benchmark(s) can be published and used as general HPC benchmarks.

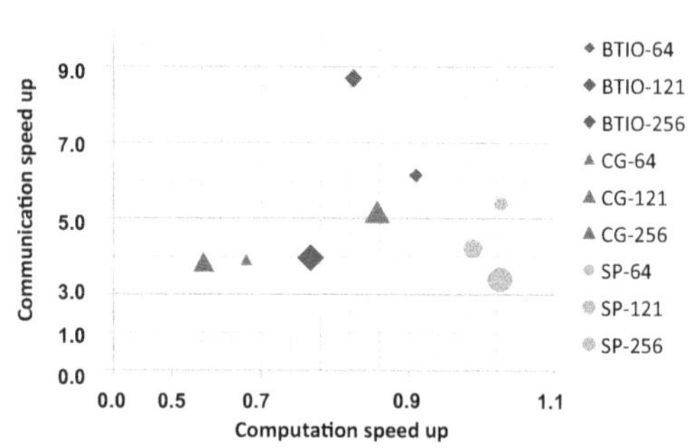

Figure 1: Sample cross-platform performance

Use Case 1: Cross-Platform Performance Estimation Application users constantly need to adopt new platforms (supercomputers, clusters, and clouds) as their applications outlive machines. Estimating cross-platform performance for real parallel applications, however, is highly challenging. Figure 1 illustrates this by plotting the relative performance of three real-world applications across our two tested platforms (to be described in detail later). Not only is the relative performance highly application-dependent, for the same application, the computation and communication dimensions (axes x and y) show very different time ratios, each of which further depends on the execution scale. Therefore, it is very difficult to "guess" a given application's performance on a new candidate platform, from either hardware/software parameters or published results for other programs, without actual porting and testing.

Unfortunately, for a scientist assessing candidate platforms for simulation A, it costs a significant amount of time *and* labor just to port the code to each candidate machine. For example, scientific applications typically depend on quite a few third-party libraries (such as Petsc and netCDF), which require non-trivial effort to acquire/install on each platform, not to mention adjusting codes or scripts to build the entire application. With APPRIME, the scientist can collect traces of one or more typical executions of A on its current platform. APPRIME takes such traces as input, and generates "fake" codes A' as benchmark, with complete MPI source code. A' performs fake computation and communicates (reads/writes) junk data, without relying on libraries beyond MPI. However, the computation, communication, and I/O patterns are all generated based on the original applications' traced behavior. Better, A' can be configured in a similar way as A, with users' changing parameters such as the number of iterations and frequency of periodic I/O operations, via the job submission script. A' therefore supports almost effortless porting while maintaining A's essential behavior, allowing cost-effective candidate machine evaluation.

Use Case 2: I/O Method and Sensitivity Assessment APPRIME can also help library and middle-ware developers assess their design or optimizations without involving real applications and their developers. For example, I/O library designers prefer to evaluate their product using real application codes, with given real I/O behaviors (I/O frequency, burstiness, size, and access patterns), as well as real interplay between I/O and computation/communication. The latter is particularly important when asynchronous operations are used. However, to obtain and to successfully build several state-of-the-art parallel simulations itself is a daunting task, let alone modification of unfamiliar, large source code to enable the use of new I/O libraries or interfaces. APPRIME allows I/O library designers to simply request execution traces from such applications, say B, C, and D, and again generates their fake counterparts B', C', and D', with highlighted (parallel) I/O calls. The designers can then apply their libraries or library updates to these benchmarks, validating their approaches with experiments and checking the impact of user-set configurations or internal parameters.

3. APPRIME DESIGN

We design our APPRIME prototype to validate the idea of generating accurate yet reconfigurable benchmark based on statistical summarized *profile* of traces, without retaining or replaying the original/compressed trace. Figure 2 illustrates the software architecture of APPRIME and its two-phase workflow: *trace profile extraction* (*extractor* for short in the rest of the paper) and *automatic configurable benchmark generation* (*generator*).

To construct a parallel parametric benchmark with APPRIME, users need to provide the following input: (1) a set of traces from one or more prior executions of the target application, (2) the number of timesteps executed in the traced run, and (3) the frequency of each type of periodic I/Os (such as checkpoint and result-snapshot output). Below we give more details on the design of the extractor and generator components, respectively.

3.1 Trace Profile Extraction

The APPRIME extractor automatically parses input per-process traces into multiple phases and identifies the main loop as well as other periodic I/O patterns. Its design is based on the observation that most iterative parallel applications have similar execution patterns in the form of $I(C^xW)^*F$ [41]. Here I and F are the one-time initialization and finalization phases, respectively. The iterative computation component contains C, the *timestep computation phase* (including communication activities involved in computation), and W, the *periodic I/O phase*.

While most parallel iterative simulations share the aforementioned common pattern, there are several issues complicating automatic phase recognition. First, there are often some degree of deviation from this pattern in recorded traces across different timesteps. For example, two of the seven applications we experimented with contain around 0.3% of communication events not fitting into the repetitive pattern. Such variance exists not only with operation event parameters, but also the count and ordering of events themselves. Second, there are often more than one periodic I/O phases, with each occurring in a different frequency: an application may capture one snapshot of intermediate results every 200 timesteps, plus one checkpoint every 1000 timesteps. In addition, real application traces may contain the execution records from a large number of processes (e.g., 100,000+ for production runs today), with each further containing many timesteps. Identifying the repetitive pattern both within and across processes at such scale requires efficient and scalable trace processing.

As to be discussed in the rest of this section, the first two challenges are addressed by further extending the iterative computation template. Here C is replaced by $C_{[0,\ a]}D^{0|1}C_{[b,\ |C|]}$, allowing rare but possible irregular D phases. Also, a user-supplied number of different I/O phases, W_i, are allowed, each occurring at its own *regular* interval. Given the total number of timesteps (number of times C was executed in the trace) and the I/O frequence for each W_i, APPRIME will generate benchmark that reproduces the interleaving pattern of C and all W_i phases, while discarding occurrences of the minor D detected. We address the third challenge with a new, fast string-based phase recognition algorithm, leveraging the extra knowledge of user-specified timestep counts and I/O frequencies, given as input to APPRIME.

3.1.1 Trace Parsing

APPRIME accepts traces produced by popular tracing libraries such as DUMPI [5] and ScalaTrace [22]. It is also

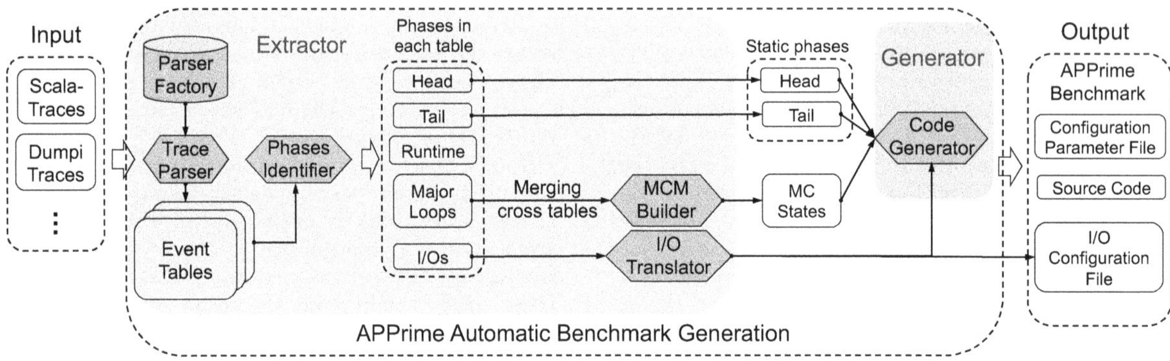

Figure 2: APPrime overall workflow. The left part is input, right part output. It has two phases, which are trace profile extractor and benchmark generator respectively.

fairly straightforward to extend our support to other tracing libraries. These traces typically contain sequences of library (MPI) calls, each with a list of parameter values, plus begin/end timestamps of the invocation.

APPRIME pre-processes such traces by parsing each record and then building per-process *event tables*. Figure 3 shows a sample event table segment along with the corresponding DUMPI trace. Each table row describes a traced MPI event, with attributes such as start/end time stamps, data type, etc. Note that with event timestamps, the untraced *computation intervals* are implicitly stored for each event. The *Phase ID* and *Phase type* fields, currently marked as "N/A", are to be filled by the Phase Identifier (Section 3.1.2).

There are a number of design considerations key to the efficiency of trace parsing: (1) tasks of parsing traces from different processes are mutually independent and therefore can be easily parallelized; (2) trace parsing is done via linear scan, accommodating APPRIME traces or event tables that are larger than memory size, by staging data to/from secondary storage; (3) an event table may appear sparse, with over 20 columns covering all MPI call parameter names, but is implemented using a compact delimited text format. For all our experiments with seven workloads, APPRIME generates per-process event tables with size always smaller than the original decompressed DUMPI trace, as summarized in Table 4.

3.1.2 Phase Identification

The extractor aims at identifying the aforementioned common structure from the input traces. It takes the per-process event tables as input, and fills the missing *Phase ID* and *Phase type* fields in these tables. At the end of this procedure, each event will be assigned a pair of phase ID and phase type that it is considered belonging to (e.g., "Phase ID of 3 and type of C" indicates "the 3rd iteration C phase"). Note that we do not further identify nested loops within the major computation loop, as APPRIME performs summary of communication and I/O operation distributions and regenerates benchmark with a statistical approach. Therefore the trace length, in terms of the number of events within a major iteration, is not a concern, as shown in Table 4.

The premise of APPRIME's automatic trace phase identification is that the application behaviors are deemed to be identical or highly similar across iterations. Admittedly, as mentioned earlier, we did observe *data-dependent* activities triggered by dynamic conditions (e.g. error checking/handling). But such deviation from the "regular" iteration behavior is quite small. We observe that the majority of large-scale applications (such as *all* of the top 15 resource consumers in Table 1) satisfy the following assumptions, making them eligible for APPRIME's fast, specialized phase identification algorithm:

Original ASCII DUMPI Trace

...

MPI_Bcast entering at walltime 102625.244058046, int count=1, MPI_Datatype datatype=4 (MPI_INT), int root=0, MPI_Comm comm=4 (user-defined-comm), MPI_Bcast returning at walltime 102625.2449640.

MPI_Barrier entering at walltime 102625.245683046, MPI_Comm comm=5 (user-defined-comm), MPI_Barrier returning at walltime 102625.2534360.

MPI_File_open entering at walltime 102627.269166046, MPI_Comm comm=5 (user-defined-comm), int amode=0 (CREATE), filename="simple.out", MPI_Info info=0 (MPI_INFO_NULL), MPI_File file=1 (user-file), MPI_File_open returning at walltime 102627.4391070.

...

Sample Joint Per-process Event Table of Communication and I/O Events

Computational intervals

MPI function name	Start	End	Data count	Root	Comm. rank	File access mode	Phase ID	Phase type	...
...	...	...	...	...	...	...	...	...	...
MPI_Bcast	...5.244	...5.245	1	0	4	N/A	N/A	N/A	...
MPI_Barrier	...5.246	...5.253	N/A	N/A	5	N/A	N/A	N/A	...
MPI_File_open	...7.269	...7.439	N/A	N/A	5	CREATE	N/A	N/A	...
...	...	...	...	...	...	...	...	...	...

Figure 3: Example of trace and event table segment

1. The iterative application's trace event sequence follows the extended two-level template proposed above.

2. The number of timesteps (i.e., the total count of C phase iterations) and frequencies of all periodic I/O (W_i) phases are known in advance.

3. The repeating C phases are identical, as well as all W_i of same frequency, in terms of communication and I/O event sequences (not necessarily parameter values), among different timesteps within each process.

4. D phases, if any, have the lowest occurrences compared to C or W_i phases, and each of them should be shorter than a single C phase and, in its entirety, not a subsequence of the C phase.

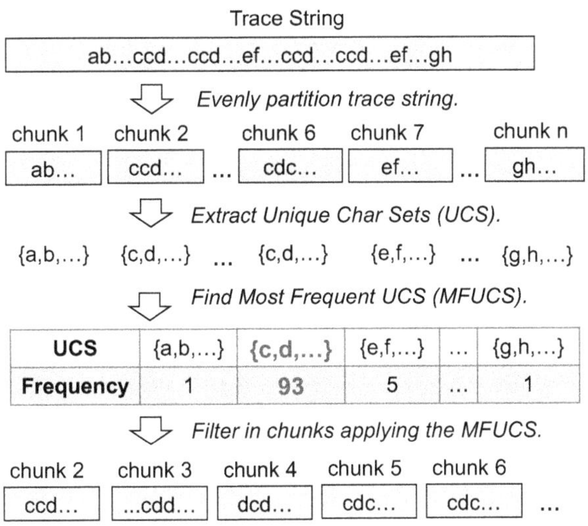

Figure 4: Using MFUCS to locate desired chunks

These assumptions hold for all real-world applications or benchmarks tested in this work. In particular, later in the paper Table 4 shows that the total length of D phases (in terms of event counts) is about 0.3% of the total execution. In the case that the relatively strong 4th assumption is indeed found to be invalid for a certain application, APPRIME employs a backup algorithm. It performs more general, yet much slower string pattern recognition, with a time complexity of $O(m^3)$, where m is the total trace length in event count. With either algorithm, there is no constraint on input trace length, allowing APPRIME to handle traces from production runs, whose typical iteration number and I/O frequency settings are given in Table 2 (application descriptions are given in Section 4.1).

App.	# Timesteps	Snapshot freq.	Checkpoint freq.
BEC2	100,000	1/500TS	1/20,000TS
XGC	100,000	1/500TS	1/10,000TS
GTS	30,000	1/200TS	1/4,000TS

Table 2: Sample production run settings of real applications

APPRIME first converts records stored in each *event table* into a compact trace string, retaining only the event names (communication and I/O function names). Each unique event name is mapped to a single character, based on the observation that typical applications use a small subset of MPI library routines [33]. This has been confirmed by our own observation: Table 4 shows that the seven applications tested use from 11 to 38 unique MPI functions. This step transforms the original phase detection to a string pattern matching problem, where each character in the trace string represents a traced event. Our goal is to find the substrings composing C and other recurring phases.

Our solution is inspired by a Coarse-to-Fine approach [24] proposed for efficient object detection in image processing. The main intuition is that (1) repetitions of C compose a major part of the string and (2) we know n, the exact number of C's repetition. Consequently, if we simply partition the trace string uniformly into n *chunks*, considering the non-C characters included, each chunk would be (slightly) longer than the actual C phase string. Further, we know that I and F occur only once, while W and D occur at a (much) lower frequency. By converting each chunk into a directed graph and searching for the most frequent one, we can identify *clean chunks* that contain only segments from the C phase.

Candidates for such clean chunks are quickly selected by computing the *Unique Character Set (UCS)* of each chunk, which is the vertex set of the graph, as illustrated in Figure 4. Here the UCS of $\{c, d, ...\}$ is found to be the most frequent (93 times), therefore all the chunks with this UCS are selected to perform more fine-grained analysis, such as direct edge set comparison, to identify the C substring that reappears (with "rotation" effect considered) most frequently.

Once the C phase string is found, APPRIME re-scans the entire trace string, identifying the remaining phases. Intuitively, the "head" preceding the first occurrence of C (first timestep) is marked as I, while the "tail" following the last timestep as F. Based on the given I/O frequency for each W_i, APPRIME examines the "gap strings" between the appropriate pair of adjacent C phase strings (e.g., if the frequency of a W_i is once per 50 timesteps, we will check between the 50th and the 51st timesteps). We apply a simple string matching algorithm here to identify the maximum common substring for each W_i. This is an iterative process starting with the most frequent I/O phase, as often such a phase is contained in the same gap string as a less frequent one, and needs to be removed for identifying the latter. All the characters not belonging to any C, I, F, or W phases are considered D phase events and ignored in the rest of APPRIME processing.

Considering the "rotation" effect of C substrings in "clean chunks", the worst-case time complexity of the phase identification step is $O(m^2/n)$, where the trace contains m events in n timesteps. In practice, phase identification makes a very small part of APPRIME's processing overhead, which is dominated by the I/O-heavy trace processing. Table 4 gives the total sequential processing time on a Core-2 Duo with 4GB memory laptop for generating each APPRIME benchmark in column "Time cost".

3.1.3 Event and Timestep State Summarization

By now, APPRIME has partitioned the trace into timesteps, with events assigned the appropriate phase type and phase ID information. The next step is to transform the linear sequence of events, with recurrent phases identified, into a compact structure that easily maps to loops, for subsequent benchmark code construction.

Recall that in our phase detection, we only looked at the event names, ignoring the event parameters. Since we made a strong assumption that each iteration of the C phase forms the *identical* series of events, we wondered whether these events also used identical parameter values (such as message sizes, peer ranks in point-to-point communication, and communicators). The answer is negative: from timestep to timestep, the parameter values do vary. This is logical considering that the sequence of events conform to the compile-time code sequence, while the parameter values are mostly assigned dynamically at runtime. An interesting finding is that these values form *clusters*, indicating the existence of a relatively small set of internal "timestep states", which are groups of timesteps having same or highly similar behaviors.

Such program behavior, confirmed across our tested set of applications and benchmarks, lends us more opportunities to summarize and reproduce variances in computation/communication patterns statistically. To create a concise, configurable benchmark that *approximates* the target application's behavior instead of replaying the specific execution traced, APPRIME performs such summarization in three dimensions: (1) detecting distinct timestep states, plus the transition probability between a pair of states, (2) replacing the actual event sequence with the *probability distribution* of events and event parameters within a timestep state, and (3) comparing and grouping the behavior of all processes.

Throughout the three dimensions, APPRIME' design needs to balance between accuracy and code's compactness/reconfigurability. A large number of program states or process groups, while more faithful to the original application, lead to verbose, "replay-style" codes. Below we present APPRIME' design choices in its multi-dimensional summarization.

Event Parameter Histogram Construction For event parameters, including the computational intervals, we take the standard solution of building histograms [38]: one per parameter per event, across all phase iterations. We found the majority of parameter fields in our test applications to be either constant or with normal distribution in value, so we apply Sturges's formula [30] to decide the bin number and bin width. With a few exceptions, such as GTS' point-to-point communication buffer sizes with bimodal distribution, we found Doane's formula [10] working well. APPRIME can be easily extended with more sophisticated histogram building techniques if necessary. After constructing such global histograms, we now replace the original values in the table with the associated bin's mean value.

Cross-process Event Table Merging Next, APPRIME merges similar event segments with the same phase rank across all per-process event tables. This procedure goes through all event tables, starting from that of process 1, merging them into the process 0 event table ("root table"), one after another. Recall that applications going through such summarization already passed the phase identification step, meeting expectations on matching C phase (as well as the number of C iterations) and matching W_i frequencies.

When merging the corresponding phases (segments in a pair of event tables with matching phase type and phase ID) from different processes, both segments' events may or may not match. In the former case, APPRIME merges corresponding events, for each of which creating a list of all distinct parameter values. In the latter case (e.g., when there are "aggregator" processes which act differently than its "ordinary" peers), APPRIME first merges the "matching events", starting from collective event pairs with matching parameters. Then APPRIME inserts remaining events into the "root table" between each two "matching events" following their original sequence. During this procedure, APPRIME stores each event's preceding *computational intervals* from all applicable processes in a 1D array.

Markov Chain Model Construction: Our final dimension in program behavior summarization is the timestep-to-timestep C phase event parameter variance, which we adopt Markov Chain (MC) [23] to model statistically. MC is a technique to model state transitions, where the next state depends only on the current state but not on the sequence of events preceding it. Most parallel simulations are iterative scientific simulations whose C phases possess this property. After further inspection of the attribute values in event tables among different C phases, we choose the following three key parameters as the metrics to group C phases into one *MC state*: (1) message (buffer) size, (2) rank of target communicating process, and (3) the communicator ID. The rest of most events' parameters values are found to be static across timesteps. Then the MC Builder assigns the result MC state with an unique state rank, as depicted in Figure 6. Finally, the MC Builder statistically computes the transition probability between each pair of states and stores the result in a probabilistic transition matrix.

With timestep states identified, the APPRIME MC Builder statistically calculates a per-process, per-timestep-state 1D histogram for each *computational intervals* ("bubbles" between adjacent traced events), to retain the state-specific computation duration distribution, see Figure 5. As to I/O, since periodic I/O calls are found to have static parameter values, APPRIME is able to summarize each type of W_i phases with only one state, which always transits to itself.

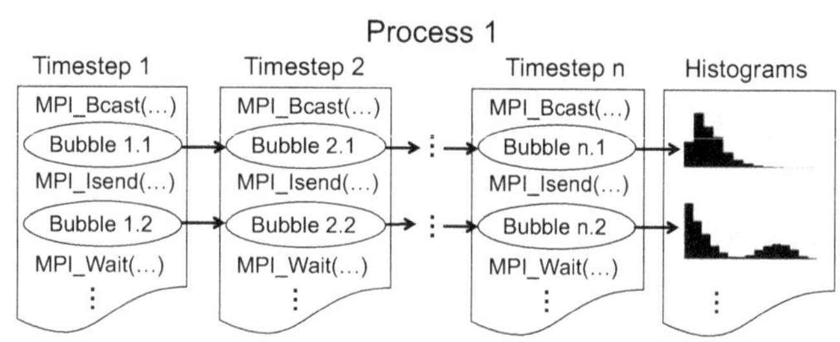

Figure 5: Profiling computation intervals (bubbles) across timesteps

Properly concatenated together, these models will guide the code generator to emit output benchmark codes. Note that while alternative tools, such as Hidden Markov Model (HMM) [25], may offer more powerful modeling, we consider MC sufficient based on scientific parallel applications' rather static behavior. In fact, the result MC models we obtained from applications are close to finite state machines.

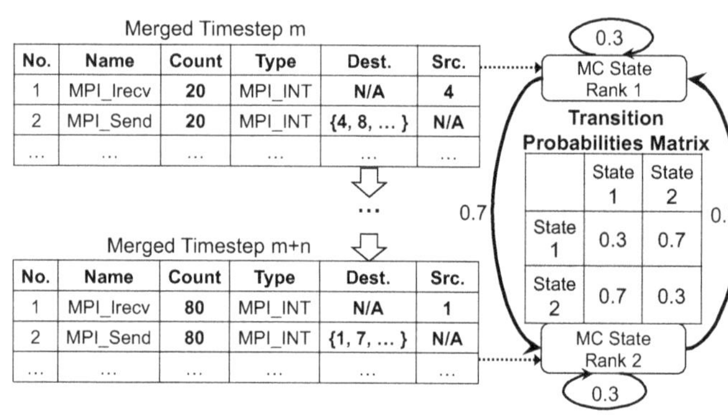

Figure 6: Converting timesteps (C phases) to MC states

3.2 Configurable Benchmark Generation

Given the event tables and transition matrices produced by the APPRIME extractor, finally the APPRIME generator

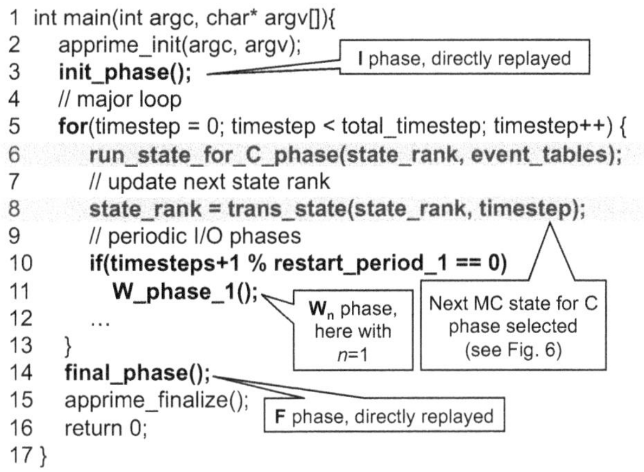

Figure 7: Code structure in main()

automatically constructs a source program that resembles the original application. Following the aforementioned template ($I(C^xW)^*F$), the generator creates the one-time static phases I and F, and most importantly, the iterative phase between the two, with reconfigurable parameters such as the number of timesteps and periodic I/O frequencies. Within this major loop, each iteration has one C phase recreating the behavior summarized by its corresponding MC state. Periodic I/O phases are inserted at appropriate frequencies.

Rather than replaying the exact sequence of timestep states recorded, the MC model constructed by the extractor allows the generator to dynamically select the next MC state to transit to at the end of each timestep, as shown in Figure 7.

Within each MC state, though, the generator deploys the more faithful direct replay strategy, transforming event table entries to respective communication or I/O calls, with corresponding recorded parameter values for each process. Note that identical values across processes have already been compressed in the merged event tables. Usually, values are represented as one dimensional array and each of its elements is for one process.

Between each pair of adjacent communication or I/O calls, APPRIME inserts a *computation interval*, whose length is generated statistically according to the 1D histogram array (as discussed in Section 3.1.3). This is done by inserting `usleep(duration)` calls, where `duration` is determined by randomly sampling the appropriate histogram. As the histograms capture inter-process latency variances, load imbalance is retained by recreating the "computation bubble" distribution across different processes. This is because: for most iterative parallel applications, every computation gap varies considerably across processes in the same timestep. For example, None Uniform Memory Access (NUMA) platforms such as Titan and Sith at ORNL, bring obvious underlying imbalance across processes. Meanwhile, total execution time of different timesteps for the same state possesses a negligible variation, as shown in Table 4.

The current APPRIME prototype ignores the captured D phases, though it is straightforward to reproduce statistically similar "noises" according to the traced events.

4. EVALUATION

We validate its major design choices and demonstrate the output benchmarks' effectiveness using the aforementioned use cases. For use case 1 (cross-platform performance assessment), we used the four most communication-intensive members (BTIO, SP, CG, and LU) of the NPB benchmark suite [7]. For use case 2 (I/O configuration evaluation), we started with three large real-world applications (all proprietary), whose developers/users are interested in exploring asynchronous I/O through data staging: the quantum turbulence code BEC2 [31] and two gyro-kinetic particle simulations: XGC [26] and GTS [35].

In this section, we evaluate our APPRIME prototype, implemented in over $16K$ lines of Java code. Our tests used two platforms of Oak Ridge Leadership Computing Facility (OLCF) supercomputer/clusters. Table 3 lists their major configurations.

Name	# of nodes	Cores per node	Mem. per node	OS	File system
Titan	18,688	16	32GB	Cray xk7	Lustre
Sith	40	32	64GB	Linux	Lustre

Table 3: Tested platforms

A major focus of our evaluation is *accuracy*, measuring the similarity in behavior between the original application A and the APPRIME benchmark A', potentially across multiple platforms. We examined not only the overall performance, but also the breakdown of time spent on computation, communication, and I/O. In addition, we checked whether the inter-processes load imbalance and overall performance variance in A is retained in A'. Each test run three times and we report the average, with error bars indicating standard deviation. All traces are collected with the SST DUMPI library [17].

4.1 Summary of Application Trace Characteristics

Before presenting results, we first give information on our seven test workloads. Table 4 summarizes key statistics collected in APPRIME's step-by-step trace processing. For each application, we list statistics from two sample executions, with 64 and 256 processes respectively. All NAS benchmarks use the D-class problem size.

We make the following observations. (1) With only 256 processes, parallel application runs produce sizable traces (1.1GB to 51.3GB). The size of event tables are smaller, but stays quite stable relative to the original trace size (around 70%). (2) APPRIME's compact string representation of event name sequence produces per-process strings under 100KB in most cases, enabling efficient phase recognition. (3) As reported by a previous study [33], each application uses a rather small subset of MPI functions (11 to 38 unique MPI routines). (4) Each NPB benchmark has only one C phase state, creating homogeneous timesteps. In contrast, both of the two gyrokinetic simulations (XGC and GTS) have two states. (5) The same applications also contain small portions of noise (D phases), which is not found in other applications or benchmarks we tested. They account for 0.1% and 0.3% of traced events respectively and appear safe to ignore in our benchmark creation. (6) At the end of its trace processing, APPRIME significantly reduces the traces into compact profiles for code generation (average 7.4MB, median 3.5MB). Note that the profile size only

App	# of procs	# of TSs	Trace size§	Table size§	# events in one state	String size	# unique funcs	# of states	D%*	TSV% ¶	Profile size
BTIO	64	250	832 MB	584 MB	183	44.4 KB	16	1	0%	2.1%	2.2 MB
BTIO	256	250	7.02 GB	4.75 GB	266	91.5 KB	16	1	0%	4.3%	8.1 MB
CG	64	100	1.42 GB	1.00 GB	789	77.8 KB	11	1	0%	1.5%	3.4 MB
CG	256	100	7.51 GB	5.50 GB	1478	101.2 KB	11	1	0%	1.8%	11 MB
SP	64	500	1.44 GB	960 MB	139	68.1 KB	15	1	0%	1.4%	1.4 MB
SP	256	500	11.7 GB	7.43 GB	278	138 KB	15	1	0%	3.5%	6.1 MB
LU	64	300	18 GB	12.3 GB	1604	471 KB	11	1	0%	2.3%	11.3 MB
LU	256	300	75 GB	51.3 GB	1604	471 KB	11	1	0%	3.8%	44.2 MB
BEC2	64	100	142 MB	101 MB	74	7.5 KB	14	1	0%	1.8%	1.1 MB
BEC2	256	200	1.08 GB	800 MB	74	14.7 KB	14	1	0%	2.7%	3.6 MB
XGC	64	100	262 MB	243 MB	73	11.5 KB	28	2	0.1%	4.3%	0.98 KB
XGC	256	200	2.1 GB	1.64 GB	103	15.3 KB	28	2	0.1%	5.8%	1.4 MB
GTS	64	50	213 MB	137 MB	391	11.6 KB	38	2	0.3%	5.6%	1.9 MB
GTS	256	100	1.83 GB	1.15 GB	391	24.9 KB	38	2	0.3%	5.9%	7.2 MB

†: timestep §: total *: percentage of traced events identified as D phases ¶: average relative time variation among timesteps within one execution on Sith

Table 4: All seven applications' executions and trace features, their A' benchmarks are released online [1].

grows with the execution scale but not with the number of timesteps.

4.2 Justification of Methodology

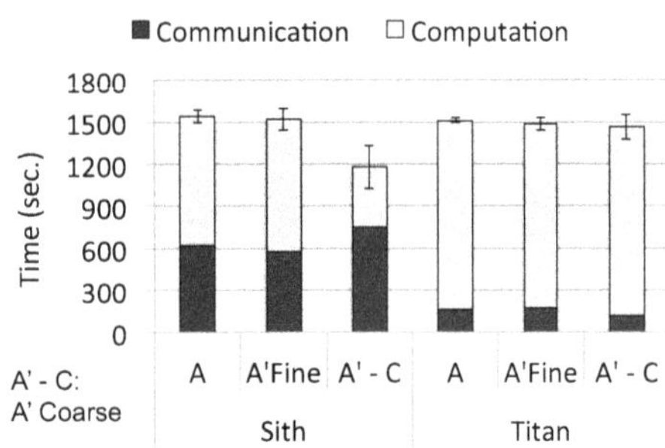

Figure 8: Performance accuracy: coarse-grained vs. fine-grained benchmark generation of BEC2

Next, we validate APPRIME's design, by answering the following questions:

1. Do we really need to identify individual (and potentially heterogeneous) timesteps in parallel simulations? Since we take a statistical approach and the number of timesteps is known, what difference will it make if we simply partition the overall traces by the timestep number?
2. Does the distribution-based code generation introduce variance not belonging to the original application?
3. Can APPRIME produce significantly more compact benchmarks compared to the original applications?
4. For applications with heterogeneous timesteps (in communication behavior), how soon can we recognize these states?

To answer the first question, we constructed a coarser-granularity alternative to the standard APPRIME approach. It statistically summarizes traces using lightweight profiling (our implementation uses mpiP [34]), collecting per process high-level statistical information for each MPI function called in the application. Similarly, the *computational intervals* are profiled at a coarser granule, for each type of (MPI) event, instead of identifying the accurate C phase event sequences and profiling at the per-event level as in

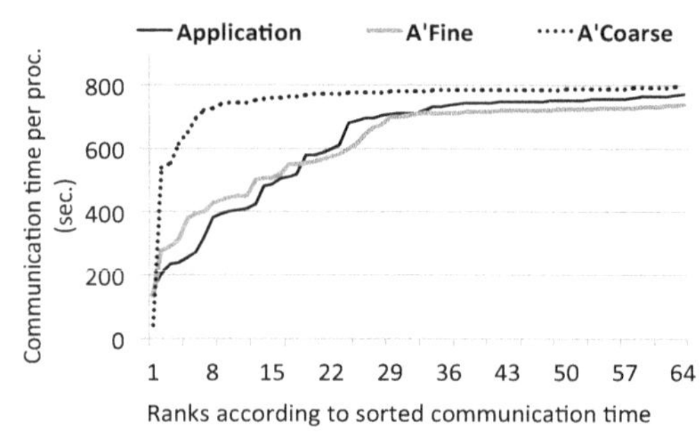

Figure 9: Captured inter-process latency variances by SP on Sith

the standard approach. The coarse-grained benchmark for application A, which we label A' *Coarse* (as opposed to A' *Fine* for the standard output), is created by partitioning the event profiled uniformly into the known timestep counts and generating event sequence and parameter values according to the profiled distribution. Special care is taken to handle calls such as MPI_Isend, MPI_Irecv, and MPI_Waitall as atomic event groups, to avoid deadlocks.

Figure 8 reports the computation-communication time breakdown on both test platforms. A in this case is the NAS SP application, which we find to contain a fair level of load variance across processes. As can be seen in Figure 8, the A' *Coarse* benchmark has significantly lower fidelity than A' *Fine*, which stays close to A in overall computation / communication time on both platforms. In addition, A' *Coarse* produces significantly larger execution time variance on Sith. As to be seen in Figure 10, standard APPRIME's randomized bin selection gives very small room for generating extra variances, while the coarse-grained version allows much more dynamic behavior at runtime.

Figure 9 further zooms into the communication load balance behavior. We sort the total measured communication time among the 64 processes, creating three monotonically growing curves for A, A' *Fine*, and A' *Coarse*, respectively. The A' *Coarse* curve closely traces the A curve, demonstrating its capability of recreating not only the overall execution time, but also the communication overhead distribution. The A' *Coarse* curve, on the other hand, misses some

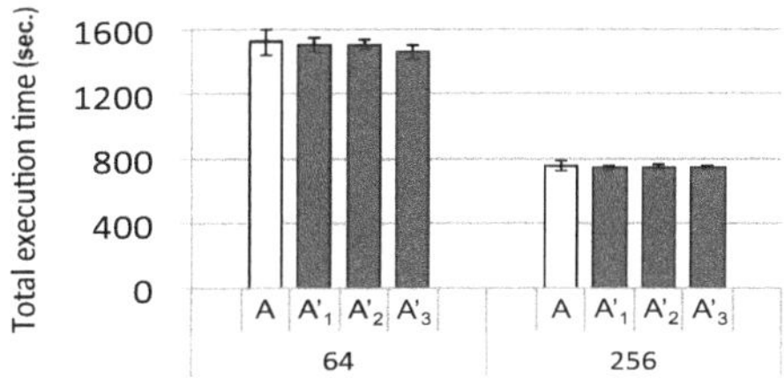

Figure 10: BEC2's APPrime benchmark performance consistency

of the skewed communication workload assignment and produces a more "balanced" curve. This and the previous set of results illustrate that simply relying on the high-level event occurrence and parameter distribution is not able to generate high-fidelity benchmarks.

Next, to answer the 2nd question, we examined the impact of APPRIME's randomized bin selection when performing distribution-guided benchmark code generation. Figure 10 illustrates the result using the BEC2 application, where we show the performance (plus performance variance) of the original application A, and three versions of APPRIME benchmarks (A'_1, A'_2, and A'_3) using three different random number generation seeds. The results confirm that the benchmarks do not incur additional variances. Actually, the A' benchmarks show smaller performance variance compared to A, due to that they are all derived from the same instance of traced executions. Hopefully this limitation can be eliminated when we add real computation workload generation into APPRIME.

App	Lines of code		Max # of	Min # of
	A	A'	TS tested	TS required
BEC2	1.5K	856	1000	1
XGC	93.7K	7.7K	1000	36
GTS	178.4K	13.7K	200	2

Table 5: Statistics regarding timestep state identification, including the minimum number of timesteps required to capture all states

Table 5 answers the last two questions, by giving the size (in lines of code) of the three real applications and their APPRIME counterparts, plus information on timestep state recognition. While the code size reduction is modest (less than half) for the already compact BEC2, there is a more than 10-fold reduction for both XGC and GTS. The generated code is in standard C and does not rely on libraries other than MPI or ADIOS I/O. As a result, the APPRIME benchmarks are very easy to port. In comparison, the original applications take a graduate student author experienced with parallel programs $8-24$ working hours to port even to a library-rich platform.

For XGC and GTS, each with two timestep states identified, the state set "convergence" happens rather early. According to Table 5, their second timestep states are discovered at the 36th and 2nd timestep respectively. We also executed all three real applications using their production run length given in Table 2: 1000 timesteps for BEC and XGC, and 200 timesteps for GTS, with no new timestep states discovered. This confirms our finding from interacting with scientists that the set of timestep behaviors is rather small and can be identified by running a short "prefix" of the application. To further verify the "predictability" of small APPRIME tracing runs, Figure 11 shows the effectiveness of using a relatively short tracing run (100 timesteps for BEC2 and XGC, 50 for GTS) to generate APPRIME benchmarks. The APPRIME benchmarks are shown to stay consistent with the original applications, even with runs much longer than traced ones.

4.3 Use Case Evaluation

4.3.1 Results: Cross-Platform Relative Performance

We assessed APPRIME benchmarks' capability of retaining the original applications' relative performance across our two test platforms, Sith and Titan. Figure 12 gives all three phases (computation, communication and I/O) time cost and the total execution time's variation of the four NAS benchmarks tested, along with that of the corresponding APPRIME benchmarks.

Considering their different compute capability, we collected input traces for the original applications *on each platform* and generated the platform-specific *computational interval* distributions. Note that this handling does not live up to our use case objective (to avoid porting applications) and is meant to be fixed by adding real compute activity regeneration, as discussed in Section 6. Therefore, the assessment focus is on the cross-platform fidelity of the synthetic communication and I/O workloads. APPRIME benchmarks are shown in Figure 12 to closely match the original applications' relative behavior across applications, job scales, and platforms.

In addition, we verified that all the APPRIME benchmarks after the four NAS benchmarks produce *identical* event name sequences as the original applications do. By automatically creating benchmarks highly faithful to the original application, yet without disclosing original programs (either source or executable), APPRIME can help users quickly assess the capability of different platform choices for their target workloads.

4.3.2 Results: Asynchronous I/O Configuration Assessment

In this section, we demonstrate that APPRIME benchmarks are able to help in examine the impact of different I/O methods, or even specific I/O settings. Our experiments

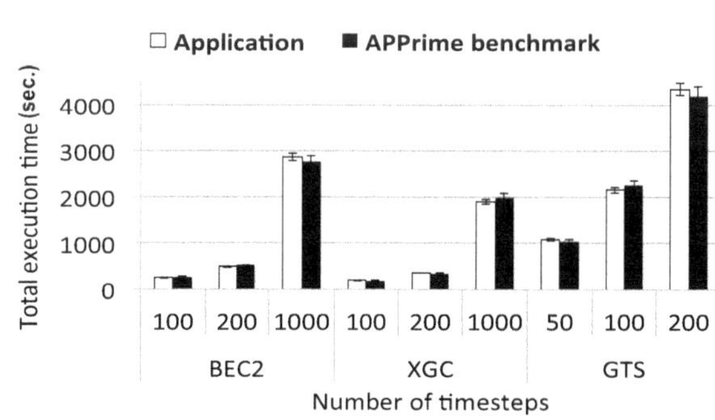

Figure 11: Performance accuracy of APPrime benchmarks in long executions, with short traced runs for training

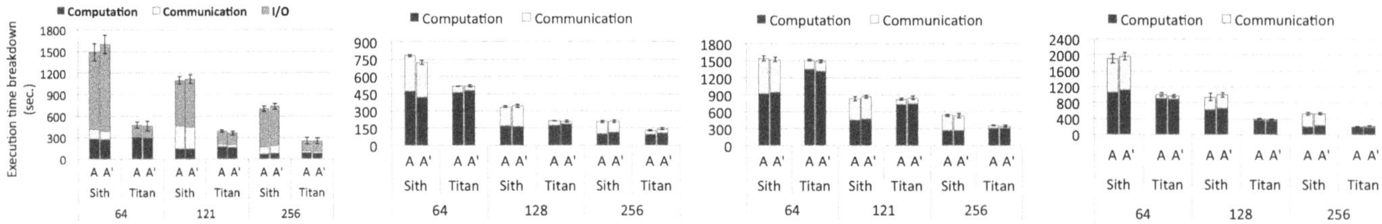

(a) BTIO (b) CG (c) SP (d) LU

Figure 12: Computation, communication and I/O phases time of selected NAS benchmarks on two platforms

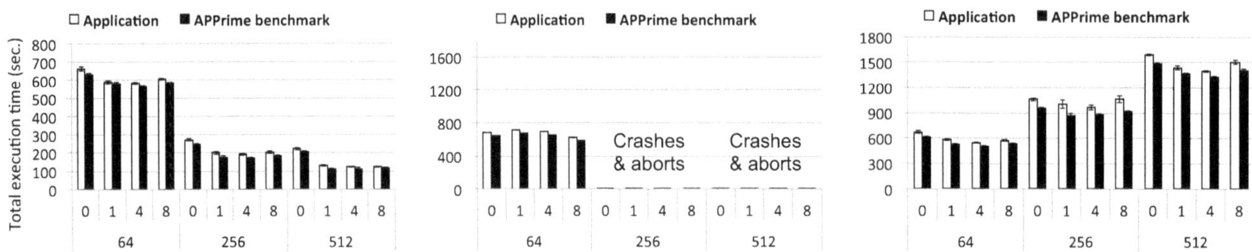

(a) BEC2 (b) GTS (c) XGC

Figure 13: Total execution time with different numbers of asynchronous I/O staging processes

compared the behavior of our three real-world applications along with their APPRIME counterparts, by enabling asynchronous I/O (data staging) via the ADIOS parallel I/O library [4]. In such async-I/O is adopted, the periodic output content will be collected by a small group of *staging nodes*, who write the data to the parallel file system while the compute processes resume their computation.

Figure 13 gives the execution time of BEC2, GTS, and XGC applications, with three different execution scales and four staging process settings. "0 staging process" indicates that synchronous I/O is used. As APPRIME retains the original configuration file of the application and reproduce the automatically identified I/O phases, the I/O settings can be configured in the same way as for the original applications. The results show that (1) the total execution time of APPRIME benchmarks remain faithful to the original applications, and (2) the relative impact of using different number of staging processes is corrected reflected by the APPRIME benchmarks. For example, the APPRIME benchmark runs correctly reveal that for BEC2, asynchronous I/O brings significant saving to the overall execution time, especially with larger-scale runs, while deploying more than one staging process does not bring much incremental benefit. As another example, for XGC APPRIME runs properly indicate that adopting 4 staging processes appear to be the configuration sweet point.

Note that GTS crashes when performing I/O with ADIOS in 256- and 512-process runs. After consulting the ADIOS team, we suspect the reason to be a problem with the application's I/O call arguments. To verify that APPRIME is able to reproduce such crashes, we generated the APPRIME benchmark with traces from an execution with I/O turned off, and inserted the I/O phase using the Skel tool [20] using the same GTS I/O configuration file. The benchmark, at both 256 and 512 scales, also aborted with errors during checkpoint output.

Finally, we also verified that the APPRIME benchmarks' reconfigurability in adjusting the periodic I/O frequency. Again they accurately reflect the original application's performance behavior (result chart omitted due to space limit).

5. RELATED WORK

Tracing and Profiling Communication trace collection and analysis tools (*e.g.*, [5, 29, 18, 21, 22]), plus postmortem trace replay tools (*e.g.*, [8, 15]), have been widely used to understand and to optimize large-scale HPC applications. To address the large size of parallel execution traces, several compression tools [40, 39, 22, 43] present in-situ lossless or lossy trace compression. Profiling tools [13, 34, 6] take a relatively light-weight approach by summarizing aggregate or statistical information of parallel job executions. APPRIME builds on trace collection and analysis, with the goal of understanding and simulating the *application* itself (rather than its certain executions) as stand-alone, portable, and to some extent configurable benchmark code.

Trace-based Application Analysis Given traces from executions of different scales, ScalaExtrap [37] successfully identifies and extrapolates communication topologies, though with several constraints (requiring certain patterns such as stencil/mesh manner point-to-point communication). Currently APPRIME does not support automatic problem size or job size scaling, but it can potentially leverage similar approaches to extrapolate application behavior observed at different scales. By taking a statistical approach, such extrapolation can be applied to communication, computation, and I/O in a consistent way. However, the current strict and accurate event recreating per timestep might need to be relaxed.

There also exists trace analysis work on phase identification, *e.g.*, by applying signal processing techniques [9]. The authors demonstrated that the proposed tool reduced trace size effectively, but was not able to correctly identify HPC applications' iterative structures. Other automatic techniques like Stranger for PHP [42] usually have strict constraints on the input string regarding grammar and language. The lack of fixed alphabetic or consistent iterative structure across different applications, as well as noise phases, motivates us to design our own algorithm for trace-based parallel iterative programs' phase recognition.

Benchmark Generation It is widely recognized (and confirmed by this study) that these benchmarks cannot fully keep up with state-of-the-art parallel applications in terms of problem size, execution scale, or behavior complexity. Existing automatic generation techniques, such as BenchMaker [11, 16] and HBench [27], also use statistical models to characterize the original applications using metrics like instruction set, memory access stride, and cache miss rate. With APPRIME, we couple statistical modeling (for generating parameter values such as buffer sizes, computation intervals, and communication partners) with accurate event sequence matching and re-creation, to build highly realistic and somewhat configurable parallel benchmarks. At the same time, there is prior work on benchmark extraction based on compressed communication trace, in particular ScalaBenGen [36]. However, it focuses on communication behavior recreation, requires in-house trace format, and generates benchmarks with hardcoded number of timestep and I/O frequencies and methods. Therefore we did not evaluate it in our experiments for comparison. The performance fidelity of APPRIME is similar to that reported by ScalaBenGen. Meanwhile, APPRIME captures the more high-level timestep phases (rather than loops heuristically identified at runtime), tolerates heterogeneous timestep behaviors, and works with standard trace collection tools as well as existing traces.

Finally, compiler-assisted source code reduction (such as slicing) [28, 44, 32] offers an alternative approach to generating benchmark. As discussed by other researchers [36], such static techniques have significant disadvantages even for creating communication-only benchmarks. For example, they rely on the availability of *all* source codes of the application and its dependent libraries. Skel [20] automatically generates skeletal I/O applications with ADIOS API from an abstraction of simulation I/O parameters. Compared to these reduction-based and specialized code skeletons, APPRIME aims at generating comprehensive, generic application benchmarks by analyzing and recreating the original applications' dynamic behavior.

6. CONCLUSION AND FUTURE WORK

This paper presents APPRIME, a tool that intelligently distills the behavior profile of parallel, iterative applications from execution traces and automatically generates compact, portable benchmark codes. APPRIME takes a hybrid approach that couples fine-grained communication and I/O event sequence matching (for automatic timestep recognition) and statistical event modeling (for event parameter and computation interval regeneration). Through our experiments with macro-benchmarks and real-world large applications, we have verified that APPRIME generates compact, portable benchmarks that retain the original applications' performance characteristics across multiple execution scales and platforms. Our study also indicates that today's applications possess complex behaviors (such as heterogeneous timesteps) not portrayed in popular parallel benchmarks such as the NPB NAS suite.

Based on the validation results reported in this paper, our on-going work is investigating ways to regenerate synthetic computation activities simulating real-application workloads. This can be viewed as a recursive step within APPRIME, where we "zooms into" the computation intervals and statistically regenerate integer/floating-point computation instructions, memory access operations, instruction level parallelism, and thread level parallelism.

7. ACKNOWLEDGMENT

We thank the anonymous reviewers for their valuable comments and suggestions. The work is facilitated by QCRI's internship program. It is also partially supported by research grants at involved institutes: NSF awards CCF-0937908, CCF-0937690, and CNS-1318564 (NCSU), DOE Office of Science, Office of Advanced Scientific Computing Research, SciDAC program, and Oak Ridge Leadership Computing Facility (ORNL), and the National High-Tech Research and Development Plan (863 project) 2012AA01A302 and NSFC project 61472201 (Tsinghua University).

8. REFERENCES

[1] APPrime Website. http://www.apprimecodes.org/.

[2] DOE INCITE. http://www.doeleadershipcomputing.org/awards/.

[3] OLCF Titan. https://www.olcf.ornl.gov/titan/.

[4] H. Abbasi, M. Wolf, G. Eisenhauer, S. Klasky, K. Schwan, and F. Zheng. DataStager: Scalable Data Staging Services for Petascale Applications. In *Cluster Computing*, 2010.

[5] H. Adalsteinsson, S. Cranford, D. A. Evensky, J. P. Kenny, J. Mayo, A. Pinar, and C. L. Janssen. A Simulator for Large-Scale Parallel Computer Architectures. In *International Journal of Distributed Systems and Technologies*, 2010.

[6] L. Adhianto, S. Banerjee, M. Fagan, M. Krentel, G. Marin, J. Mellor-Crummey, and N. R. Tallent. Hpctoolkit: Tools for performance analysis of optimized parallel programs. *Concurrency and Computation: Practice and Experience*, 2010.

[7] D. H. Bailey, E. Barszcz, J. T. Barton, D. S. Browning, R. L. Carter, L. Dagum, R. A. Fatoohi, P. O. Frederickson, T. A. Lasinski, R. S. Schreiber, H. D. Simon, V. Venkatakrishnan, and S. K. Weeratunga. The nas parallel benchmark: Summary and preliminary results. In *Supercomputing*, pages 158–165, New York, NY, USA, 1991.

[8] H. Brunst, H.-C. Hoppe, W. E. Nagel, and M. Winkler. Performance Optimization for Large Scale Computing: The Scalable VAMPIR Approach. In *International Conference on Computational Science*, 2001.

[9] M. Casas, R. M. Badia, and J. Labarta. Automatic Phase Detection and Structure Extraction of MPI Applications. *International Journal of High Performance Computing Applications*, 2010.

[10] D. P. Doane. Aesthetic Frequency Classifications. *The American Statistician*, 1976.

[11] J. Dujmović. Automatic Generation of Benchmark and Test Workloads. In *WOSP/SIPEW*, 2010.

[12] E. Gabriel, G. E. Fagg, G. Bosilca, T. Angskun, J. J. Dongarra, J. M. Squyres, V. Sahay, P. Kambadur, B. Barrett, A. Lumsdaine, R. H. Castain, D. J. Daniel, R. L. Graham, and T. S. Woodall. Open MPI: Goals, concept, and design of a next generation MPI implementation. In *11th European PVM/MPI Users' Group Meeting*, pages 97–104, Budapest, Hungary, September 2004.

[13] M. Geimer, F. Wolf, B. J. N. Wylie, E. Ábrahám, D. Becker, and B. Mohr. The Scalasca Performance Toolset Architecture. In *Concurrency and Computation: Practice and Experience*, 2010.

[14] GTC2link. GTC-benchmark in NERSC-8 suite, 2013.

[15] C. L. Janssen, H. Adalsteinsson, and J. P. Kenny. Using Simulation to Design Extremescale Applications and Architectures: Programming Model Exploration. *ACM SIGMETRICS*, 2011.

[16] A. M. Joshi, L. Eeckhout, and L. K. John. The Return of Synthetic Benchmarks. In *SPEC Benchmark Workshop*, 2008.

[17] J. P. Kenny, G. Hendry, B. Allan, and D. Zhang. Dumpi: The mpi profiler from the sst simulator suite. `https://bitbucket.org/jpkenny/dumpi`, 2011.

[18] A. Knupfer, R. Brendel, H. Brunst, H. Mix, and W. Nagel. Introducing the Open Trace Format (OTF). In V. Alexandrov, G. Albada, P. Sloot, and J. Dongarra, editors, *International Conference on Computational Science*, 2006.

[19] R. Latham, C. Daley, W. keng Liao, K. Gao, R. Ross, A. Dubey, and A. Choudhary. A case study for scientific i/o: improving the flash astrophysics code. *CSD*, 5(1):015001, 2012.

[20] J. Logan, S. Klasky, H. Abbasi, Q. Liu, G. Ostrouchov, M. Parashar, N. Podhorszki, Y. Tian, and M. Wolf. Understanding I/O Performance Using I/O Skeletal Applications. In *Euro-Par*, 2012.

[21] M. Noeth, F. Mueller, M. Schulz, and B. de Supinski. Scalable compression and replay of communication traces in massively parallel environments. In *IPDPS*, 2007.

[22] M. Noeth, P. Ratn, F. Mueller, M. Schulz, and B. R. de Supinski. ScalaTrace: Scalable Compression and Replay of Communication Traces for High-Performance Computing. *J. Parallel Distrib. Comput.*, 2009.

[23] F. Pachet, P. Roy, and G. Barbieri. Finite-length Markov Processes with Constraints. In *IJCAI*, 2011.

[24] M. Pedersoli, A. Vedaldi, and J. Gonzalez. A coarse-to-fine approach for fast deformable object detection. In *Computer Vision and Pattern Recognition*, pages 1353–1360, 2011.

[25] L. R. Rabiner and B. H. Juang. An introduction to hidden Markov models. *ASSP Magazine*, pages 4–15, January 1986.

[26] S. Ku, C. S. Chang, and P. H. Diamond. Full-f Gyrokinetic Particle Simulation of Centrally Heated Global ITG Turbulence from Magnetic Axis to Edge Pedestal Top in A Realistic Tokamak Geometry. *Nuclear Fusion*, 2009.

[27] M. Seltzer, D. Krinsky, K. Smith, and X. Zhang. The Case for Application-Specific Benchmarking. In *Hot Topics in Operating Systems*, 1999.

[28] S. Shao, A. K. Jones, and R. Melhem. A Compiler-based Communication Analysis Approach for Multiprocessor Systems. In *IPDPS*, 2006.

[29] S. Shende and A. D. Malony. TAU: The tau parallel performance system. *International Journal of High Performance Computing Applications*, 20(2), 2006.

[30] H. A. Sturges. The Choice of a Class Interval. *Journal of the American Statistical Association*, 1926.

[31] G. Vahala, M. Soe, B. Zhang, J. Yepez, L. Vahala, J. Carter, and S. Ziegeler. Unitary Qubit Lattice Simulations of Multiscale Phenomena in Quantum Turbulence. In *Supercomputing*, 2011.

[32] L. Van Ertvelde and L. Eeckhout. Dispersing Proprietary Applications as Benchmarks Through Code Mutation. *ACM SIGOPS OSR*, 2008.

[33] J. Vetter and F. Mueller. Communication characteristics of large-scale scientific applications for contemporary cluster architectures. In *IPDPS*, 2002.

[34] J. S. Vetter and M. O. McCracken. Statistical Scalability Analysis of Communication Operations in Distributed Applications. *ACM SIGPLAN*, 2001.

[35] W. X. Wang and Z. Lin and W. M. Tang and W. W. Lee and S. Ethier and J. L. V. Lewandowski and G. Rewoldt and T. S. Hahm and J. Manickam. Gyro-kinetic Simulation of Global Turbulent Transport Properties in Tokamak Experiments. *Physics of Plasmas*, 2006.

[36] X. Wu, V. Deshpande, and F. Mueller. ScalaBenchGen: Auto-Generation of Communication Benchmarks Traces. In *IPDPS*, 2012.

[37] X. Wu and F. Mueller. ScalaExtrap: Trace-based Communication Extrapolation for SPMD Programs. In *ACM PPoPP*, 2011.

[38] X. Wu, K. Vijayakumar, F. Mueller, X. Ma, and P. Roth. Probabilistic communication and i/o tracing with deterministic replay at scale. In *ICPP*, 2011.

[39] Q. Xu and J. Subhlok. Construction and Evaluation of Coordinated Performance Skeletons. In *HiPC*, 2008.

[40] Q. Xu, J. Subhlok, R. Zheng, and S. Voss. Logicalization of Communication Traces from Parallel Execution. In *IISWC*, 2009.

[41] L. T. Yang, X. Ma, and F. Mueller. Cross-Platform Performance Prediction of Parallel Applications Using Partial Execution. In *Supercomputing*, 2005.

[42] F. Yu, M. Alkhalaf, and T. Bultan. Stranger: An Automata-Based String Analysis Tool for PHP. In J. Esparza and R. Majumdar, editors, *Lecture Notes in Computer Science*. 2010.

[43] J. Zhai, J. Hu, X. Tang, X. Ma, and W. Chen. Cypress: Combining static and dynamic analysis for top-down communication trace compression. In *Supercomputing*, 2014.

[44] J. Zhai, T. Sheng, J. He, W. Chen, and W. Zheng. FACT: Fast Communication Trace Collection for Parallel Applications Through Program Slicing. In *Supercomputing*, 2009.

Power of d Choices for Large-Scale Bin Packing: A Loss Model

Qiaomin Xie, Xiaobo Dong, Yi Lu and Rayadurgam Srikant
University of Illinois at Urbana-Champaign
Urbana, IL 61801, USA
{qxie3,dong6,yilu4,rsrikant}@illinois.edu

ABSTRACT

We consider a system of N parallel servers, where each server consists of B units of a resource. Jobs arrive at this system according to a Poisson process, and each job stays in the system for an exponentially distributed amount of time. Each job may request different units of the resource from the system. The goal is to understand how to route arriving jobs to the servers to minimize the probability that an arriving job does not find the required amount of resource at the server, i.e., the goal is to minimize blocking probability. The motivation for this problem arises from the design of cloud computing systems in which the jobs are virtual machines (VMs) that request resources such as memory from a large pool of servers. In this paper, we consider power-of-d-choices routing, where a job is routed to the server with the largest amount of available resource among $d \geq 2$ randomly chosen servers. We consider a fluid model that corresponds to the limit as N goes to infinity and provide an explicit upper bound for the equilibrium blocking probability. We show that the upper bound exhibits different behavior as B goes to infinity depending on the relationship between the total traffic intensity λ and B. In particular, if $(B-\lambda)/\sqrt{\lambda} \to \alpha$, the upper bound is doubly exponential in $\sqrt{\lambda}$ and if $(B-\lambda)/\log_d \lambda \to \beta$, $\beta > 1$, the upper bound is exponential in λ. Simulation results show that the blocking probability, even for small B, exhibits qualitatively different behavior in the two traffic regimes. This is in contrast with the result for random routing, where the blocking probability scales as $O(1/\sqrt{\lambda})$ even if $(B-\lambda)/\sqrt{\lambda} \to \alpha$.

Categories and Subject Descriptors

G.3 [**Probability and Statistics**]: Stochastic processes, Queueing theory

General Terms

Algorithms, Theory, Performance

SIGMETRICS'15, June 15–19, 2015, Portland, OR, USA.

http://dx.doi.org/10.1145/2745844.2745849.

Keywords

Randomized Algorithms; Loss Model; Resource Allocation; Virtual Machine Assignment; Fluid Limit Analysis

1. INTRODUCTION

We consider a system of N parallel homogeneous servers. Each server has B units of a resource. There are J different types of jobs. Jobs of type j arrive at the system according to a rate-$N\lambda_j$ Poisson process, and each type-j job requires b_j units of resource and stays in the system for an exponentially distributed amount of time with mean 1. Let $\lambda = \sum_{j=1}^{J} \lambda_j b_j$ denote the total traffic intensity.

Each arriving job is routed to a server according to a routing policy and requires zero-delay service. If the selected server has sufficient resource to accommodate the arriving job, the job will be processed immediately. Otherwise the job is blocked, i.e., it leaves the system immediately without being served. The goal is to understand how to route arriving jobs to the servers to minimize the probability that an arriving job does not find the required amount of resource at the server, i.e., to minimize blocking probability.

For each server m, let $n_{j,m}(t)$ denote the number of type-j jobs that the server is serving at time t. We use

$$\mathbf{n}_m(t) = (n_{1,m}(t), n_{2,m}(t), ..., n_{J,m}(t))$$

to denote the state of server m. Note that $\mathbf{n}_m$ is feasible only if server m has enough resource to accommodate all these jobs. That is,

$$\sum_{j=1}^{J} n_{j,m} b_j \leq B.$$

The model is motivated by the design of cloud computing systems in which the jobs are virtual machines (VMs) that request resources from a large pool of servers. Some examples of cloud computing systems are Amazon EC2 system [1], Google's AppEngine [3] and Microsoft's Azure [5]. Users submit requests for resource in the form of virtual machines (VMs). Each request specifies the amount of physical resources it needs in terms of processor power, memory, I/O bandwidth, disk, etc.

The resource allocation problem for VMs is a stochastic bin-packing problem [6, 9], but with VMs terminating after an application has completed. This motivates our model with jobs arriving and departing the system, which was first considered in [15] and is referred to as a *service* model in [26]. When a user submits VM requests in a cloud computing system, any request that is not immediately fulfilled is typically rejected [5]. This motivates us to consider a loss model and its blocking probability, in contrast to the models in [15, 26].

In our model, we consider one-dimensional packing constraint for the requests of resources. While VM requests can be modelled as multi-dimensional bin-packing, it has been observed that memory is the dominating bottleneck [11]. Due to the large size of a cloud computing system, we consider asymptotic blocking probability as $N \to \infty$.

We consider the power-of-d-choices routing algorithm for this system. An arriving job is routed to the server with the largest amount of available resource among $d \geq 2$ randomly chosen servers. When none of the chosen servers has enough resource to accommodate the job, it is rejected. In this paper, we focus on the fluid limit as $N \to \infty$ and the asymptotic blocking probability. To the best of our knowledge, this is the first work of studying power-of-d-choices routing algorithm in a loss model with packing constraints.

1.1 Related Work

VMs packing problem. Some recent work model the VMs allocation as stochastic bin packing with item departures [11, 17], and focus on improving resource utilization with different packing algorithms. Some other recent work study this problem with different performance objectives, including maximizing system throughput [15], minimizing heavy-traffic queue lengths [16], and minimizing the total energy consumption [29]. In this paper, we are interested in zero-delay service, i.e., a VM is served immediately upon arrival. The recent works in [24, 26, 25] also study zero-delay service. However, their performance objective is to minimize the number of servers occupied, which is different from ours. In particular, they consider the case of infinite number of servers, while we consider finite number of servers and study the blocking probability in the limit as the number of servers goes to infinity.

The Power-of-d-choices algorithm. Azar et. al. [4] were the first to analyze randomized load balancing schemes using balls-and-bins model. Another line of work focus on the queueing systems, [18, 19, 28, 8, 10, 14, 20, 31]. In particular, a supermarket model has been used widely to analyze the randomized load balancing schemes. Vvedenskaya et.al. [28] and Mitzenmacher [18] showed that when each arriving job is assigned to the shortest $d \geq 2$ randomly chosen queues, the equilibrium queue sizes decay doubly exponentially in the limit as the number of servers goes to infinity. This is a substantial improvement over the $d = 1$ case, where the queue size decays exponentially. While the work in [27] does not address power-of-d choices routing directly, similar analytical techniques have been used there to study the impact of resource pooling in large server farms. However, to the best of our knowledge, the performance of the power-of-d-choices algorithm ($d \geq 2$) for a loss model has not been studied previously. Related work has also been done in parallel with our work in [21]

1.2 Organization of the Paper

The rest of the paper is organized as follows. Section 1.3 introduces the notation used in this paper. Section 2 states the precise model and main results. The proofs of these main results will be deferred to later sections. We first study the loss model under the power-of-d-choices algorithm ($d \geq 2$) for the case when jobs are homogeneous, i.e., all jobs are of the same type, in Section 3-5. Section 3 justifies the use of fluid approximation of sufficiently large finite systems. Section 4 develops an upper bound for the stationary point of the fluid model. Section 5 analyzes the blocking probability in two different limiting regimes. We then extend our analysis to the case with heterogeneous jobs based on an independence ansatz in Section 6.

1.3 Notation

We will use bold letters to denote vectors in $\mathbb{R}^B$ or $\mathbb{N}^J$ or $\mathbb{N}^{J\times N}$, and ordinary letters for scalars. Dot product in the vector spaces $\mathbb{R}^J$ is denoted by $\langle \mathbf{x}, \mathbf{y} \rangle$.

Let $\mathbb{N}_+$ be the set of non-negative integers. The following notations will be used throughout the paper:

$$\begin{aligned}
\mathcal{C} &\triangleq \left\{ \mathbf{n} \in \mathbb{N}_+^J : \sum_{j=1}^{J} n_j b_j \leq B \right\}, \\
\mathcal{Q}^{(N)} &\triangleq \left\{ \mathbf{Q} = \{\mathbf{n}_1, \mathbf{n}_2, ..., \mathbf{n}_N\} : \mathbf{n}_m \in \mathcal{C}, \forall m = 1, 2, ..., N \right\}, \\
\mathcal{S} &\triangleq \left\{ \mathbf{s} \in [0,1]^{B+1} : 1 = s_0 \geq s_1 \geq ... \geq s_B \geq 0 \right\}, \\
\mathcal{S}^{(N)} &\triangleq \left\{ \mathbf{s} \in \mathcal{S} : s_i = \frac{K_i}{N}, \text{ for some } K_i \in \mathbb{N}_+, \forall i \right\}, \\
\mathcal{P} &\triangleq \left\{ \mathbf{p} \in \mathbb{R}^{|\mathcal{C}|} : \sum_{i=1}^{|\mathcal{C}|} p_i = 1,\ p_i \geq 0,\ \forall i \right\}.
\end{aligned}$$

And we will use the following notation for asymptotic comparisons; here f and g are positive functions:

1. $f(x) \lesssim g(x)$ for $f(x) = \mathcal{O}(g(x))$, and $f(x) \gtrsim g(x)$ for $f(x) = \Omega(g(x))$.
2. $f(x) \sim g(x)$ for $\lim_{x\to\infty} \frac{f(x)}{g(x)} = 1$.

2. PROBLEM STATEMENT AND MAIN RESULTS

We briefly recap the model that was stated in the introduction. We consider a system with N servers, each of which has B units of a resource, such as CPU, memory, etc. This system is accessed by J different types of jobs, where each type of job is characterized by the number of units of resource that it demands. Jobs of type j arrive according to a Poisson process of rate $N\lambda_j$, each type-j job requests b_j units of the resource, and each job stays in the system for an exponentially distributed amount of time with mean 1. We use $\mathbf{b} = (b_1, b_2, ..., b_J)$ to denote the vector of resource units required by different job types. The arrival processes of the different job types and the job holding times are all independent of each other. We consider two cases separately, $J = 1$ which we call the *homogeneous job* case and $J > 1$ which we call the *heterogeneous job* case. In the homogeneous case, we assume without loss of generality that $b_1 = 1$, i.e., all jobs require one unit of resource.

Our goal is to study the blocking probability of the power-of-d-choices routing: under this routing scheme, upon each job arrival, d servers are selected uniformly at random and the job is routed to the least loaded of the servers (the one with the least amount of resource used). If none of the selected servers has sufficient amount of resource, then the arriving job is blocked and lost. The performance in the case $d = 1$ is fundamentally different from the cases where $d > 1$. Therefore, we study these two cases separately. In the case of $d = 1$, since we are routing an arrival to a randomly selected server, we will call this scheme *the random routing* scheme. We will reserve the use of the term *power-of-d-choices* routing to the case where $d > 1$.

Next, we present the main results of the paper, for the homogeneous job case first followed by the heterogeneous job case.

2.1 Homogeneous Jobs

Before we present our main results, we introduce some notation. Consider a system with N servers. Let $S_k^{(N)}(t)$ denote the fraction of servers with at least k jobs in service at time t. We use $\boldsymbol{\pi}^{(N)} = (\pi_0^{(N)}, \pi_1^{(N)}, ..., \pi_B^{(N)})$ to denote the equilibrium distribution of $\mathbf{S}^{(N)}(t) = \{S_i^{(N)}(t)\}_{i=0}^B$. We will approximate $\boldsymbol{\pi}^{(N)}$ by the stationary state of the following fluid model in a manner which will be made precise later.

DEFINITION 1. *(Fluid Model). Given any initial condition $\mathbf{s}^0 \in \mathcal{S}$, a function $\mathbf{s}(t) : [0, \infty) \to \mathcal{S}$ is said to be a solution to the fluid model if:*

1. $\mathbf{s}(0) = \mathbf{s}^0$;
2. $s_0(t) = 1$ *for any* $t \geq 0$;
3. $\mathbf{s}(t)$ *satisfies the following differential equations for any* $t \geq 0$:

$$\frac{ds_k(t)}{dt} = \begin{cases} \lambda(s_{k-1}^d - s_k^d) - k(s_k - s_{k+1}), & 1 \leq k \leq B-1 \\ \lambda(s_{B-1}^d - s_B^d) - Bs_B, & k = B \end{cases} \tag{1}$$

Equation (1) can be written as

$$\dot{\mathbf{s}}(t) = \mathbf{F}(\mathbf{s}),$$

where

$$F_k(\mathbf{s}) = \begin{cases} \lambda(s_{k-1}^d - s_k^d) - k(s_k - s_{k+1}), & 1 \leq k \leq B-1 \\ \lambda(s_{B-1}^d - s_B^d) - Bs_B, & k = B \end{cases}$$

The k-th function $F_k(\mathbf{s})$ is the drift of s_k at point $\mathbf{s}(t)$. The stationary point of the differential equation (1), denoted by $\boldsymbol{\pi}$, satisfies

$$\mathbf{F}(\boldsymbol{\pi}) = \mathbf{0}. \tag{2}$$

The following theorem presents the main convergence result (in the limit $N \to \infty$) for the homogeneous job case.

THEOREM 1. *The fluid model has a unique stationary distribution $\boldsymbol{\pi}$ and the sequence of stationary distribution $\boldsymbol{\pi}^{(N)}$ converges weakly to $\delta_{\boldsymbol{\pi}}$, which is the Dirac measure concentrated on $\boldsymbol{\pi}$. That is,*

$$\lim_{N \to \infty} \boldsymbol{\pi}^{(N)} = \delta_{\boldsymbol{\pi}}, \text{ in distribution.}$$

Due to the convergence result above and due to the Poisson nature of the arrival process, π_B^d is a good approximation to the blocking probability experienced by arriving jobs, denoted by $P_b^{(N)}$, in a system with N servers. This is due to the fact that, in the limit as $N \to \infty$, the servers become independent. However, that is not directly established in the convergence theorem above. But it can be argued as follows: using Little's law, we have

$$N\lambda(1 - P_b^{(N)}) = N \sum_{k=1}^{B} \pi_k^{(N)}.$$

Summing $F_k(\boldsymbol{\pi}) = 0$ over $1 \leq k \leq B$ yields

$$\lambda(1 - \pi_B^d) = \sum_{k=1}^{B} \pi_k.$$

Let $P_b = \pi_B^d$. From Theorem 1, we can approximate $P_b^{(N)}$ by P_b when N is sufficiently large.

While $\boldsymbol{\pi}$ can be computed recursively from Eq. (2), we provide a closed-form expression which provides an upper bound on π_B for all values of λ and B for the case $d \geq 2$. This upper bound is useful later to understand the striking performance difference between the cases $d = 1$ and $d > 1$.

THEOREM 2. *(Upper bound) Let $\boldsymbol{\pi}$ denote the stationary point of the fluid model. Define $\{\bar{\pi}_k\}_{k=0}^B$ as follows:*

$$\bar{\pi}_k = \begin{cases} 1, & 0 \leq k \leq i_0 + 1 \\ \dfrac{\lambda^{\frac{d^{k-i_0-1}-1}{d-1}}}{(k-1)(k-2)^{d^1} \cdots (i_0+1)^{d^{k-i_0-2}}}, & i_0 + 1 < k \leq B \end{cases} \tag{3}$$

where $i_0 = \lfloor \lambda \rfloor$.

Then $\bar{\boldsymbol{\pi}}$ is an upper bound for $\boldsymbol{\pi}$, i.e., for any $0 \leq k \leq B$,

$$\bar{\pi}_k \geq \pi_k.$$

Note that in the case $d = 1$, since we are randomly selecting a server, by the property of Poisson processes, the blocking probability is given by the well-known Erlang-B formula for $M/M/B/B$ systems:

$$\mathcal{B}(B, \lambda) = \frac{\lambda^B / B!}{\sum_{k=0}^{B} (\lambda^k / k!)}. \tag{4}$$

Comparing equations (3) and (4), we can see that the blocking probability goes to zero faster in the case of $d \geq 2$, compared to that for $d = 1$.

To further provide insight into the blocking probability P_b in the case of $d \geq 2$, we consider two limiting regimes: (i) $\frac{B-\lambda}{\sqrt{\lambda}} \to \alpha$ as $B \to \infty$ and (ii) $\frac{B-\lambda}{\log_d \lambda} \to \beta$ as $B \to \infty$. We call the former the heavy-traffic regime and the latter the critically-loaded regime. The heavy-traffic has been studied extensively in the context of $M/M/B/B$ and $G/G/B/B$ systems [7, 30, 23].

THEOREM 3. *Let $\lambda < B$ and $\frac{\lambda}{B} \to 1$ as $B \to \infty$, then*

$$\pi_B \lesssim (e^{-\frac{c^2}{2}})^{\frac{(B-\lambda)^2}{\lambda}} d^{(1-c)(B-\lambda)-1}, \tag{5}$$

where c is an arbitrary constant satisfying $0 < c < 1$.

In particular,

1. *If $\frac{B-\lambda}{\sqrt{\lambda}} \to \alpha$ as $B \to \infty$, where $\alpha > 0$, then*

$$\log_d \log \frac{1}{P_b} \gtrsim ((1-c)\alpha + o(1))\sqrt{\lambda}.$$

That is, the blocking probability decays doubly exponentially in $\sqrt{\lambda}$.

2. *If $\frac{B-\lambda}{\log_d \lambda} \to \beta$ as $B \to \infty$, where $\beta > 1$, then there exists a constant $\gamma = (1-c)\beta - 1 > 0$ such that*

$$\log \frac{1}{P_b} \gtrsim \lambda^{\gamma + o(1)}.$$

That is, the blocking probability decays exponentially in λ^γ.

Remark. Theorem 3 shows that the fluid limit of the equilibrium blocking probability is dominated by an asymptotic upper bound, which exhibits very different behavior depending on the relationship between λ and B as B goes to infinity. In particular, if $\frac{B-\lambda}{\sqrt{\lambda}} \to \alpha$, the upper bound is doubly exponential in $\sqrt{\lambda}$ and if $\frac{B-\lambda}{\log \lambda} \to \beta$, $\beta > 1$, the upper bound is exponential in λ^η. This is in contrast with the result for random routing, where the blocking probability scales as $O(\frac{1}{\sqrt{\lambda}})$ even if $\frac{B-\lambda}{\sqrt{\lambda}} \to \alpha$.

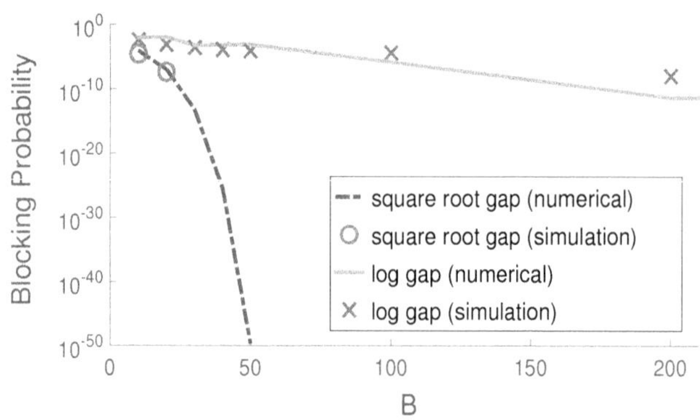

Figure 1: Blocking probability for the power-of-two-choices algorithm with different load gap. Line curves are obtained by solving Eq. (2) numerically. Markers are from simulations with $N = 1000$.

Numerical Results: Figure 1 shows the blocking probability for the power-of-two-choices algorithm with $B - \lambda = \sqrt{\lambda}$ and $B - \lambda = 2\log\lambda$, both by solving Eq. (2) numerically and by simulating a finite system with $N = 1000$. Note that the y-axis is in log scale. We can see that even for small B, the blocking probability P_b exhibits qualitatively different behavior in these two regions: with $\log\lambda$ load gap, P_b decays exponentially; while for $\sqrt{\lambda}$ load gap, P_b decays much faster. For $B = 30$, P_b is of order 10^{-15} with $\sqrt{\lambda}$ load gap. It requires very long simulation time in order to observe blocking event. We simulated around 10^{10} arrivals and no job blocking was observed for $B \geq 30$.

To extend the results in this section to the heterogeneous job case, we present a well-known alternative viewpoint of the derivation of $\boldsymbol{\pi}$. Suppose we assume that, in steady-state, the servers become independent of each other and due to symmetry, the number of jobs in each server is given by $\boldsymbol{\pi}$. In this case, let us focus on a particular server, say server 1, and write down the Markov chain corresponding to the number of jobs in the server. To describe the transition rate of this Markov chain, suppose that the server has k jobs currently in service. Then, the arrival rate of jobs to this server (call it q_k) is $N\lambda$ times the probability that an arriving job selects this server. It is easy that q_k is given by

$$q_k = N\lambda \cdot \frac{d}{N}\left(\sum_{i=1}^{d} \frac{1}{i}\binom{d-1}{i-1}(\pi_k^{(N)} - \pi_{k+1}^{(N)})^{i-1}(\pi_{k+1}^{(N)})^{d-i}\right),$$

which in the limit as $N \to \infty$ becomes

$$q_k = \lambda\left(\frac{\pi_k^d - \pi_{k+1}^d}{\pi_k - \pi_{k+1}}\right).$$

Thus, the Markov chain can be represented by the transition diagram in Figure 2. It is now easy to see that the steady-state distribution of this Markov chain is given by Eq. (2). This independence ansantz will be used in the next section to derive blocking probability results for the heterogeneous job case.

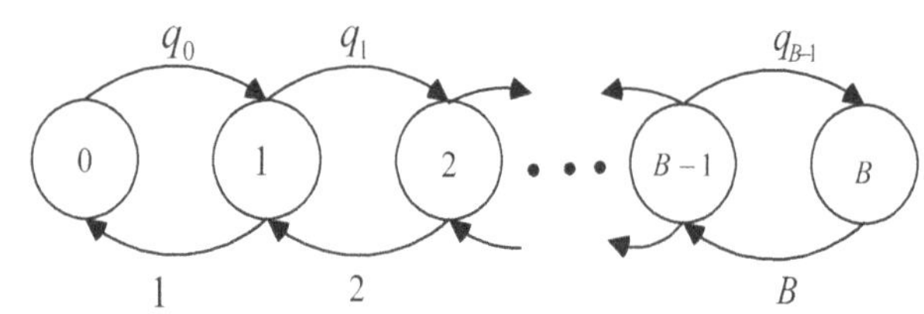

Figure 2: State-transition-rate diagram for server 1 with B units of resource and homogeneous job arrivals.

2.2 Heterogeneous Jobs

We use the independence ansatz in the previous subsection as follows. Consider a particular server, say server 1, and let $\mathbf{n} = (n_1, ..., n_J)$ be the number of jobs of different types in this server. Let $\{p_\mathbf{n}\}_{\mathbf{n}\in\mathcal{C}}$ denote the asymptotic equilibrium distribution for server 1. Then $p_\mathbf{n}$ is also the asymptotic fraction of servers in state $\mathbf{n}$.

Under the asymptotic independence assumption, the arrival process of type j jobs to server 1 is a state-dependent Poisson process with rate $\lambda_j(\mathbf{n})$, which is given by

$$\lambda_j(\mathbf{n}) = \lambda_j\left(\sum_{i=1}^{d}\binom{d}{i}E_\mathbf{n}^{i-1}G_\mathbf{n}^{d-i}\right), \quad (6)$$

where

$$E_\mathbf{n} = \sum_{\substack{\hat{\mathbf{n}}\in\mathcal{C}\\ \langle\hat{\mathbf{n}},\mathbf{b}\rangle = \langle\mathbf{n},\mathbf{b}\rangle}} p_{\hat{\mathbf{n}}}, \quad G_\mathbf{n} = \sum_{\substack{\mathbf{n}'\in\mathcal{C}\\ \langle\mathbf{n}',\mathbf{b}\rangle > \langle\mathbf{n},\mathbf{b}\rangle}} p_{\mathbf{n}'}.$$

Let $B_j = \lfloor \frac{B}{b_j} \rfloor$ denote the maximum number of type-j jobs that a server can serve simultaneously. In the case of two job types, the Markov chain is shown in Figure 3. However, it is difficult to analyze the equilibrium distribution of this Markov and obtain a simple expression for the blocking probability. Therefore, we study a one-dimensional recursion as in [12] and [22].

THEOREM 4. *The tail distribution $\mathbf{r}$ of the number of occupied resource units satisfies the following equation for any $k = 0, 1, ..., B$:*

$$\sum_{j=1}^{J}\lambda_j b_j(r_{k-b_j}^d - r_{k-b_j+1}^d) = k(r_k - r_{k+1}), \quad (7)$$

where $r_x = 1$ for any $x \leq 0$ and $r_{B+1} = 0$.

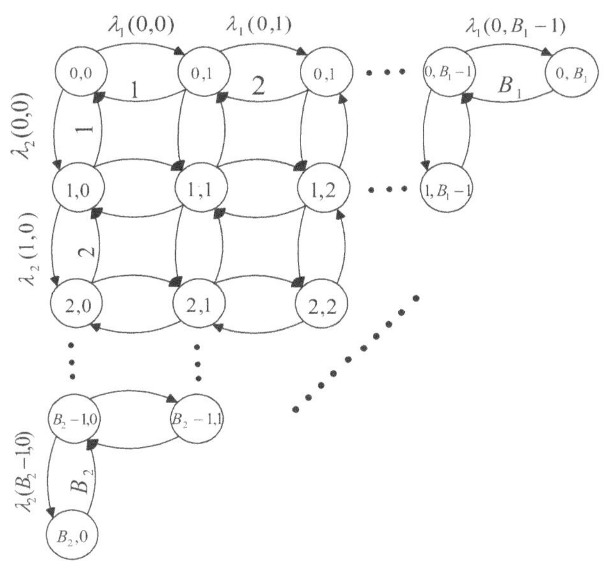

Figure 3: State-transition-rate diagram for server 1 with B units of resource and two types of jobs arrivals.

As for the blocking probability, we obtain analogous results as for homogeneous jobs. Let $b = \max_{j=1,\dots,J} b_j$, and denote the blocking probability for jobs of type j by P_{b_j}. We have the following theorem.

THEOREM 5. *Let $\lambda < B$ and $\frac{\lambda}{B} \to 1$ as $B \to \infty$,*

$$r_{B-b+1} \lesssim (e^{-\frac{c^2}{2}})^{\frac{(B-\lambda)^2}{b\lambda} d^{(1-c)(\frac{B-\lambda}{b})-1}}, \tag{8}$$

where c is an arbitrary constant satisfying $0 < c < 1$.
In particular,

1. *If $\frac{B-\lambda}{\sqrt{\lambda}} \to \alpha$ as $B \to \infty$, where $\alpha > 0$, then*

$$\log_d \log \frac{1}{P_{b_j}} \gtrsim ((1-c)\frac{\alpha}{b} + o(1))\sqrt{\lambda},$$

$\forall j \in \{1, 2, ..., J\}$. *That is, for any type of jobs, the blocking probability decays doubly exponentially in $\sqrt{\lambda}$.*

2. *If $\frac{B-\lambda}{\log_d \lambda} \to \beta$ as $B \to \infty$, where $\beta > b$, then there exists a constant $\eta = (1-c)\frac{\beta}{b} - 1 > 0$ such that*

$$\log \frac{1}{P_{b_j}} \gtrsim \lambda^{\eta + o(1)},$$

$\forall j \in \{1, 2, ..., J\}$. *That is, for any type of jobs, the blocking probability decays exponentially in λ^η.*

The results in this section are derived under the independence ansatz. The existing technique to establish asymptotic independence depends on monotonicity, which does not hold for our problem. Although we do not have the tools to prove the ansatz without monotonicity, we believe that it is true in terms of the random nature of power-of-d-choices algorithm. Alternatively, one can use the fluid approximation: first show convergence of the stochastic system to a differential equation, then show that the differential equation has a unique stationary point to which it converges starting from any initial condition, and finally prove certain tightness results. We have done all of this for the homogeneous case in the next section. In the heterogeneous case, we only have partial results: we can prove convergence to a differential equation and also show that the equation (7) is one of the stationary points of the differential equation. The rest of the steps need to be verified.

3. CONVERGENCE RESULTS FOR THE HOMOGENEOUS CASE

In this section, we focus on the convergence results that justify the approximation of the sample paths $\mathbf{S}^{(N)}(t)$ of sufficiently large systems using the solution $\mathbf{s}(t)$ to the fluid model. Before showing the convergence results rigorously, we introduce some notation for system state and provide some interpretation of the fluid model defined in Section 2.1.

3.1 Preliminaries

Fix the number of servers N. With homogeneous jobs, system state can be represented by $\mathbf{Q}^{(N)}(t) = (n_1^{(N)}(t), n_2^{(N)}(t), ..., n_N^{(N)}(t))$, where $n_m^{(N)}(t)$ is the number of jobs in server m at time t. Under the Poisson arrivals and i.i.d exponential service time assumption, the process $\{\mathbf{Q}^{(N)}(t), t \geq 0\}$ is Markov with state space $\mathcal{Q}^{(N)}$. Note that $0 \leq n_m^{(N)}(t) \leq B$ as each server can accommodate at most B jobs simultaneously. Define

$$S_k^{(N)}(t) = \frac{1}{N} \sum_{i=1}^{(N)} \mathbb{I}_{[k,B]}(n_i^{(N)}(t)), \ \forall k \in \{0, 1, 2, ..., B\},$$

where $S_k^{(N)}(t)$ represents the fraction of servers with at least k jobs in service. Note that $S_0^{(N)}(t) = 1$ for all t. Since the system is fully symmetric, the evolution of the system can be described by the process $\{\mathbf{S}^{(N)}(t), t \geq 0\}$, which is also Markov. Moreover, the system is stable for any $\lambda \geq 0$, as the amount of resource at each server is finite and there is no extra waiting room for arrivals. Hence the Markov process $\{\mathbf{S}^{(N)}(t), t \geq 0\}$ is positive recurrent. We use $\boldsymbol{\pi}^{(N)} = (\pi_0^{(N)}, \pi_1^{(N)}, ..., \pi_B^{(N)})$ to denote its equilibrium distribution.

Explanation for the drift of $s_k(t)$ in Eq. (1): Consider a system with N servers. We will identify the expected change in the fraction of servers with at least k jobs in service over a small period of time of length dt.

(I). The first term corresponds to the change caused by the arrivals. When an arriving job is assigned to a server with $k-1$ jobs, $S_k^{(N)}$ increases by $\frac{1}{N}$. Observe that the number of servers with at least j jobs for $j \neq k$, does not change. Thus $S_k^{(N)}$ is increased by $\frac{1}{N}$ if only if an arriving job joins a server with $k-1$ jobs. Note that the probability that all d sampled servers have at least $k-1$ jobs is s_{k-1}^d. The difference $s_{k-1}^d - s_k^d$ is the probability that at least one of the sampled servers has $k-1$ jobs. With total arrival rate $N\lambda$, the increment for $S_k^{(N)}$ during this time period due to arrival is hence $dt \times N\lambda \times \frac{1}{N} \times (s_{k-1}^d - s_k^d) = \lambda(s_{k-1}^d - s_k^d)dt$.

(II). The second term corresponds to the decrease due to the completion of jobs. The argument is similar to that of the first term.

3.2 Convergence Results

We first provide an overview of the convergence results:

First we prove some properties of the fluid model. We will show that there exists a unique solution $\boldsymbol{\pi}$ to the differential equations (1) which is stationary with respect to t, i.e., $\mathbf{F}(\boldsymbol{\pi}) = \mathbf{0}$ (Lemma 1). Moreover, given any finite initial condition, the solution to the fluid equation is unique and converges to the stationary solution as $t \to \infty$ (Lemma 2).

The second step is to show that as $N \to \infty$, the evolution of process $\mathbf{S}^{(N)}(t)$ converges uniformly, over any finite time interval, to the unique solution of the fluid model (Lemma 5). The result is derived by applying Kurtz's theorem ([13, 18]) for density dependent jump Markov processes.

The last step is to prove that the sequence of the steady-state distribution of $\mathbf{S}^{(N)}(t)$ (denoted by $\boldsymbol{\pi}^{(N)}$), concentrates at the unique stationary distribution of the fluid model ($\boldsymbol{\pi}$) as $N \to \infty$ (Theorem 1).

LEMMA 1. *There exists a unique solution $\boldsymbol{\pi} \in \mathcal{S}$ of the differential equation (1) that is invariant with respect to t, i.e.,* $\mathbf{F}(\boldsymbol{\pi}) = \mathbf{0}$.

We defer the full proof of Lemma 1 to the appendix and provide an outline below.

Proof outline of Lemma 1

Existence: The stationary solution $\boldsymbol{\pi}$ satisfies the equation $\mathbf{F}(\boldsymbol{\pi}) = \mathbf{0}$. We construct a continuous mapping $\mathbf{G} : \mathcal{S} \to \mathcal{S}$, such that a fixed point of $\mathbf{G}$ is a solution to $\mathbf{F}(\boldsymbol{\pi}) = \mathbf{0}$. By Brouwer Fixed Point Theorem, $\mathbf{G}$ has at least one fixed point, i.e., there exists $\boldsymbol{\pi} \in \mathcal{S}$ such that $\mathbf{F}(\boldsymbol{\pi}) = \mathbf{0}$.

Uniqueness: We prove the uniqueness of stationary solution by contradiction and induction. First we show that if there exist two stationary solutions $\boldsymbol{\pi}$ and $\hat{\boldsymbol{\pi}}$ satisfying $\pi_B = \hat{\pi}_B$, then $\pi_k = \hat{\pi}_k$ for any k. Therefore if there exist two different solutions $\boldsymbol{\pi}$ and $\hat{\boldsymbol{\pi}}$, $\pi_B \neq \hat{\pi}_B$. Assume $\pi_B < \hat{\pi}_B$, by induction, we can show that $\pi_k < \hat{\pi}_k$ for any $k = 0, 1, ..., B$, which contradicts with the fact that $\pi_0 = \hat{\pi}_0 = 1$.

LEMMA 2. *Given any initial condition $\mathbf{s}^0 \in \mathcal{S}$,*

1. *the fluid model has a unique solution $\mathbf{s}(\mathbf{s}^0, t)$ in $\mathcal{S}$,*
2. *as $t \to \infty$, the solution $\mathbf{s}(\mathbf{s}^0, t)$ converges to the unique stationary solution $\boldsymbol{\pi}$.*

We need the following lemmas to prove Lemma 2. The proofs of Lemma 3-4 are provided in the appendix.

LEMMA 3. *Let $\bar{\mathbf{s}}(t)$ and $\mathbf{s}(t)$ be the solutions to differential equations (1) with initial condition $\bar{\mathbf{s}}^0$ and $\mathbf{s}^0$ respectively. If $\bar{s}_k^0 \le s_k^0$ for $k = 1, 2, ..., B$, then $\bar{s}_k(t) \le s_k(t)$ for any $t \ge 0$.*

LEMMA 4. *Let $\psi(t) = \sum_{k=0}^{B} |s_k(t) - \pi_k|$, where $\mathbf{s}(t)$ is the solution to differential equations (1) with initial condition $\mathbf{s}^0$ satisfying $s_k^0 \ge \pi_k$ for any k (or $s_k^0 \le \pi_k$ for any k), then $\psi(t)$ converges to 0 as $t \to \infty$.*

Proof of Lemma 2: Item 1 follows by the arguments in Theorem 1.(a) of [28].

For any initial values $\mathbf{s}^0 \in \mathcal{S}$, define two initial conditions $\mathbf{s}^u$ and $\mathbf{s}^l$: $s_k^u = \max\{s_k^0, \pi_k\}$, $s_k^l = \min\{s_k^0, \pi_k\}$ for any k. Let $\mathbf{s}^u(t)$ and $\mathbf{s}^l(t)$ denote the solutions with initial conditions $\mathbf{s}^u$ and $\mathbf{s}^l$ respectively. From Lemma 3, we have $s_k^u(t) \ge \pi_k \ge s_k^l(t)$ for all t and any k. Thus it is sufficient to show that $\lim_{t\to\infty} |\mathbf{s}^u(t) - \pi| = \lim_{t\to\infty} |\mathbf{s}^l(t) - \pi| = 0$, where $|\cdot|$ is l_1 norm. The result follows directly from Lemma 4. ∎

LEMMA 5. *Consider a sequence of systems with the number of servers N increasing to infinity. Fix any $T > 0$. If the sequence of initial system state $\{\mathbf{S}^{(N)}(0)\}_{N=1}^{\infty}$ concentrates on some $\mathbf{s}^0 \in \mathcal{S}$ as $N \to \infty$, then*

$$\lim_{N\to\infty} \sup_{t\in[0,T]} |\mathbf{S}^{(N)}(t) - \mathbf{s}(\mathbf{s}^0, t)| = 0 \quad a.s. \tag{9}$$

where $\mathbf{s}(\mathbf{s}^0, t)$ is the solution to the differential equation (1) given initial condition $\mathbf{s}^0$.

The following lemma is used to prove Lemma 5.

LEMMA 6. *The drift function $\mathbf{F}(\mathbf{s})$ is Lipschitz, i.e., there exits a constant $M > 0$ such that for any $\mathbf{x}, \mathbf{y} \in \mathcal{S}$,*

$$|\mathbf{F}(\mathbf{x}) - \mathbf{F}(\mathbf{y})| \le M|\mathbf{x} - \mathbf{y}|,$$

where $|\cdot|$ is l_1 norm.

Proof of Lemma 5: We prove this lemma by Kurtz's theorem [13].

(a). It is easy to check that $\{\mathbf{S}^{(N)}(t), t \ge 0\}$ is a density dependent jump Markov process with state space $\mathcal{S}^{(N)}$.

(b). When the system is in state $\mathbf{s}$, the possible transitions is given by $\mathcal{L} = \{\pm\mathbf{e}_k : 1 \le k \le B\}$, where $\mathbf{e}_k$ are vectors with only the $k-$th element equal to $1/N$ and all other elements zero. The transition rates are given by $q_{\mathbf{s},\mathbf{s}+\mathbf{l}}^{(N)} = N\beta_{\mathbf{l}}(\mathbf{s})$, where $\beta_{\mathbf{e}_k}(\mathbf{s}) = \lambda(s_{k-1}^d - s_k^d)$ and $\beta_{-\mathbf{e}_k}(\mathbf{s}) = k(s_k - s_{k+1})$. Therefore the rate at which jumps occur is bounded above by $\lambda + B$ everywhere.

(c). Lemma 6 states that the differential equation for the limiting deterministic process satisfies the Lipschitz condition.

Then the result follows by Kurtz's Theorem. ∎

Proof of Theorem 1:

We will use $\Rightarrow$ for weak convergence throughout the proof.

Note that set $\mathcal{S}$ is compact. By a corollary of Prokhorov's Theorem, for any subsequence of $\{N\}$, there exists a subsubsequence $\{N_k\}$ such that $\boldsymbol{\pi}^{(N_k)}$ converges weakly to some probability distribution $\bar{\boldsymbol{\pi}}$. By the Skorokhod's representation theorem, there exist a sequence of random vector $\{\mathbf{X}^{(N_k)}\}$ and a random vector $\bar{\mathbf{X}}$ such that

$$\mathbf{X}^{(N_k)} \stackrel{d}{=} \boldsymbol{\pi}^{(N_k)} \quad \bar{\mathbf{X}} \stackrel{d}{=} \bar{\boldsymbol{\pi}},$$

and

$$\mathbf{X}^{(N_k)} \xrightarrow{a.s.} \bar{\mathbf{X}} \text{ as } k \to \infty.$$

Let $\mathbf{S}^{(N_k)}(0) = \mathbf{X}^{(N_k)}$, i.e., start the system with N_k servers at an initial condition specified by its stationary distribution. We use $\bar{\mathbf{S}}(t)$ to denote the random state of the dynamic system with initial condition $\bar{\mathbf{X}}$.

We have the following claim (proven in the appendix):

Claim 1: For any $t \ge 0$,

$$\mathbf{S}^{(N_k)}(t) \Rightarrow \bar{\mathbf{S}}(t) \text{ as } k \to \infty.$$

Then the result follows from the arguments in Theorem 5.1 of [2]. ■

Remark. Lemma 5 and Theorem 1 state that the behavior of sufficiently large systems can be approximated by that of the deterministic infinite system, which is described by a system of differential equations defined in Eq. (1).

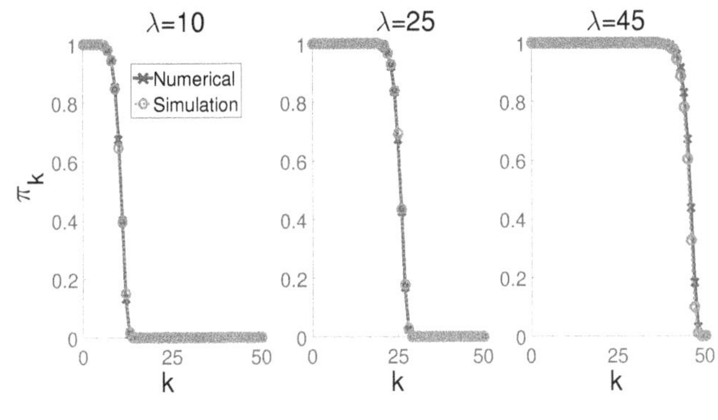

Figure 4: Equilibrium tail distribution for the power-of-two-choices algorithm with $B = 50$ at three different loads. The values for the stationary point are obtained numerically by solving Eq. (2). Simulation results are from a finite system with $N = 500$.

Numerical Result. Figure 4 shows the equilibrium tail distributions of the number of jobs at a server under the power-of-two-choices algorithm with $B = 50$ at three different loads, both by solving Eq. (2) numerically and by simulating a finite system with $N = 500$. We can see that the coincidence of the empirical distribution with the stationary point is almost exact. That is, values of the stationary point in the large system limit predict that of a finite system very well.

4. AN UPPER-BOUND FOR THE HOMOGENEOUS CASE

Unlike the supermarket model operating under the power-of-d-choices policy [18, 28], there is no explicit expression for the stationary point $\boldsymbol{\pi}$ of the loss model. We establish an explicit upper-bound for $\boldsymbol{\pi}$. Observe that the proposed upper-bound $\bar{\boldsymbol{\pi}}$ (defined in Eq. (3)) can be expressed by a recursive formula as follows:

$$\bar{\pi}_k = \begin{cases} 1, & 0 \le k \le i_0 + 1 \\ \frac{\lambda}{k-1}\bar{\pi}_{k-1}^d, & i_0 + 1 < k \le B \end{cases}$$

where $i_0 = \lfloor \lambda \rfloor$.

Proof of Theorem 2: We complete the proof in two steps.

(i) First we show that $\pi_k \le \frac{\lambda}{k}\pi_{k-1}^d$ for $1 \le k \le B$ by backward induction. The inequality holds for $k = B$:

$$\pi_B - \frac{\lambda}{B}\pi_{B-1}^d = -\frac{\lambda}{B}\pi_B^d \le 0.$$

Assume that $\pi_{k+1} \le \frac{\lambda}{k+1}\pi_k^d$ hold for $k + 1 \le B$. Then

$$\pi_k - \frac{\lambda}{k}\pi_{k-1}^d = \pi_{k+1} - \frac{\lambda}{k}\pi_k^d \le \pi_{k+1} - \frac{\lambda}{k+1}\pi_k^d \le 0.$$

Hence $\pi_k \le \frac{\lambda}{k}\pi_{k-1}^d$, $\forall k = 1, 2, ..., B$.

(ii) Next we prove the theorem by induction.

For any $k \le i_0 + 1$, $\bar{\pi}_k = 1 \ge \pi_k$.

Assume that $\bar{\pi}_k \ge \pi_k$ hold for some $k \ge i_0 + 1$. Then

$$\bar{\pi}_{k+1} = \frac{\lambda}{k}\bar{\pi}_k^d \ge \frac{\lambda}{k}\pi_k^d \ge \frac{\lambda}{k}\pi_k^d + \pi_k - \frac{\lambda}{k}\pi_{k-1}^d = \pi_{k+1},$$

where the first inequality comes from the assumption and the second one follows by the property of $\boldsymbol{\pi}$ we just proved. ■

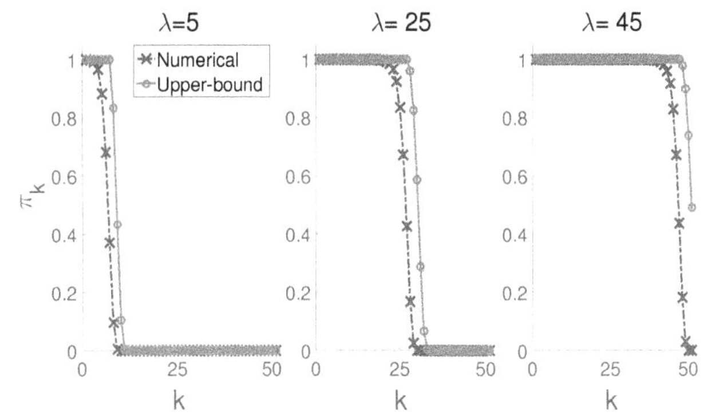

Figure 5: An upper bound for the stationary point.

Figure 5 compares the equilibrium tail distribution of the stationary point and the proposed distribution $\bar{\boldsymbol{\pi}}$ with $B = 50$ at three different loads. We can see that the upper bound always holds. Moreover, the proposed distribution characterizes the steep slope of the stationary point, i.e., π_k decreases drastically from 1 to 0 at some k.

Since the performance measure of primary interest is the blocking probability P_b, we are interested in the tightness of the upper-bound blocking probability.

$\rho = \lambda/B$	Fluid limit	Upper-bound
0.6	0	0
0.8	0	4.508×10^{-27}
0.84	0.0000	7.003×10^{-7}
0.88	1.873×10^{-25}	0.0426
0.9	5.229×10^{-13}	0.2419
0.92	8.240×10^{-7}	0.5535
0.94	7.854×10^{-4}	0.8122

Table 1: The blocking probability for the power-of-two-choices policy with $B = 50$ at different load.

Table 1 compares the upper-bound blocking probability and values of the stationary fluid limit under the power-of-two-choices policy with $B = 50$ at different loads. The values given by the upper-bound are quite close to that of the stationary fluid limit at low to medium load. With B fixed, as the load increases towards 1, the gap increases. We have seen that the proposed upper-bound resembles a shift of the stationary fluid limit from Fig. 5. At high load, the upper-bound shifts too much that the resulting bound for blocking probability becomes loose. However, if we fix the load $\rho = \frac{\lambda}{B}$ for the system, we can see that the upper-bound blocking probability $\bar{\pi}_B^d$ decays to 0 as B increases. This implies that the upper-bound becomes tight for sufficiently large B.

5. PROOF OF THEOREM 3

We devote this section to the proof of Theorem 3. We begin by proving the following lemma.

LEMMA 7. *Let $\lambda < B$ and $\frac{\lambda}{B} \to 1$ as $B \to \infty$. If $\frac{k}{B-\lambda} \to \theta$ as $B \to \infty$, where θ is a constant satisfying $0 \le \theta < 1$, then*

$$\frac{\lambda^{B-i_0-k} \cdot i_0!}{(B-k)!} \sim e^{-\frac{(1-\theta)^2(B-\lambda)^2}{2\lambda}}, \qquad (10)$$

where $i_0 = \lfloor \lambda \rfloor$.

Proof. By Stirling's formula, we have

$$\begin{aligned} &\frac{\lambda^{B-i_0-k} \cdot i_0!}{(B-k)!} \\ \sim\ & \lambda^{B-i_0-k} \frac{\sqrt{2\pi i_0} \cdot (\frac{i_0}{e})^{i_0}}{\sqrt{2\pi(B-k)} \cdot (\frac{B-k}{e})^{B-k}} \\ \sim\ & \sqrt{\frac{i_0}{B-k}} \cdot e^{B-k-\lambda} \left(\frac{\lambda}{B-k}\right)^{\lambda} \cdot \left(\frac{\lambda}{B-k}\right)^{B-k-\lambda} \\ \sim\ & e^{B-k-\lambda} \left(\frac{\lambda}{B-k}\right)^{\lambda} \cdot \left(\frac{\lambda}{B-k}\right)^{B-k-\lambda} \qquad (11) \end{aligned}$$

Define $\Delta = B - \lambda$. Note that $\lambda/\Delta \to \infty$ as $B \to \infty$. And $(B-k-\lambda) \sim (1-\theta)\Delta$. Then we have

$$\begin{aligned} \left(\frac{\lambda}{B-k}\right)^{B-k-\lambda} &\sim \left(\frac{\lambda}{\lambda + (1-\theta)\Delta}\right)^{(1-\theta)\Delta} \\ &\sim \left(1 + \frac{(1-\theta)\Delta}{\lambda}\right)^{-(1-\theta)\Delta} \\ &\sim \left[\left(1 + \frac{(1-\theta)}{\lambda/\Delta}\right)^{-\lambda/\Delta}\right]^{-(1-\theta)\frac{\Delta^2}{\lambda}} \\ &\sim e^{-(1-\theta)^2\frac{\Delta^2}{\lambda}} \qquad (12) \end{aligned}$$

Now consider the first two terms in Eq. (11).

$$\begin{aligned} &\log\left(e^{B-k-\lambda}\left(\frac{\lambda}{B-k}\right)^{\lambda}\right) \\ \sim\ & (1-\theta)\Delta - \lambda \log\left(1 + \frac{(1-\theta)\Delta}{\lambda}\right) \\ \sim\ & (1-\theta)\Delta - \lambda\left(\frac{(1-\theta)\Delta}{\lambda} - \frac{1}{2}\left(\frac{(1-\theta)\Delta}{\lambda}\right)^2 + o(\lambda)\right) \\ \sim\ & \frac{(1-\theta)^2\Delta^2}{2\lambda} + o(1) \end{aligned}$$

That is,

$$e^{B-k-\lambda}\left(\frac{\lambda}{B-k}\right)^{\lambda} \sim e^{\frac{(1-\theta)^2\Delta^2}{2\lambda}} \qquad (13)$$

Equations (12)-(13) yield the asymptotic approximation in Eq. (10). ■

Proof of Theorem 3:
From Theorem 2, it is sufficient to show that the upper bound $\bar{\pi}_B$ defined in (3) satisfies Eq. (5). We establish this result using Lemma 7.

We can write $\bar{\pi}_B$ as

$$\begin{aligned} \bar{\pi}_B =\ & \left(\frac{\lambda^{B-i_0-1} \cdot i_0!}{(B-1)!}\right) \cdot \left(\frac{\lambda^{B-i_0-2} \cdot i_0!}{(B-2)!}\right)^{(d-1)\cdot d^0} \\ & \cdot \left(\frac{\lambda^{B-i_0-3} \cdot i_0!}{(B-3)!}\right)^{(d-1)d} \cdots \left(\frac{\lambda \cdot i_0!}{(i_0+1)!}\right)^{(d-1)d^{B-i_0-3}} \qquad (14) \end{aligned}$$

Note that each term within the bracket in Eq.(14) is no greater than 1. We can obtain an upper bound for $\bar{\pi}_B$ by discarding some terms in Eq. (14). In particular, consider keeping the first m terms, where $m = (1-c)(B-\lambda)$, c is an arbitrary constant satisfying $0 < c < 1$. From Lemma 7, each term we keep here can be approximated by using Eq (10). Define $\Delta = B - \lambda$. Then we have

$$\begin{aligned} \bar{\pi}_B \le\ & \left(\frac{\lambda^{B-i_0-1} \cdot i_0!}{(B-1)!}\right) \cdot \left(\frac{\lambda^{B-i_0-2} \cdot i_0!}{(B-2)!}\right)^{(d-1)d^0} \\ & \cdots \left(\frac{\lambda^{B-i_0-m} \cdot i_0!}{(B-m)!}\right)^{(d-1)d^{m-2}} \\ \sim\ & e^{-\frac{\Delta^2}{2\lambda}\left[(1-\frac{1}{\Delta})^2 + (1-\frac{2}{\Delta})^2\cdot(d-1) + \cdots + (1-\frac{m}{\Delta})^2\cdot(d-1)d^{m-2}\right]} \\ \lesssim\ & e^{-\frac{c^2\Delta^2}{2\lambda}\cdot d^{m-1}} \\ =\ & \left(e^{-\frac{c^2}{2}}\right)^{\frac{\Delta^2}{\lambda}\cdot d^{(1-c)\Delta - 1}}. \end{aligned}$$

We complete the proof for Eq. (5). As discussed in Section 2.1, we have $P_b = \pi_B^d$. Thus,

$$P_b \lesssim \left(e^{-\frac{c^2}{2}}\right)^{\frac{\Delta^2}{\lambda}\cdot d^{(1-c)\Delta}}$$

Now we can study the blocking probability with various load gap by analyzing the exponent $\frac{c^2}{2}\frac{\Delta^2}{\lambda} \cdot d^{(1-c)\Delta}$.

1. $\frac{B-\lambda}{\sqrt{\lambda}} \to \alpha$: we have:

$$\begin{aligned} &\log_d \log \frac{1}{P_b} \\ \gtrsim\ & 2\log_d \Delta - \log_d \lambda + \log_d \frac{c^2}{2} + (1-c)\Delta \\ \sim\ & ((1-c)\alpha + o(1))\sqrt{\lambda}. \end{aligned}$$

2. $\frac{B-\lambda}{\log_d \lambda} \to \beta$: As $\beta > 1$ and $0 < c < 1$ is an arbitrary constant, we can select c to make $\gamma = (1-c)\beta - 1 > 0$. Then we have:

$$\begin{aligned} &\log_d \log \frac{1}{P_b} \\ \gtrsim\ & ((1-c)\beta - 1)\log_d \lambda + 2\log_d \log \lambda + o(1) \\ \sim\ & (\gamma + o(1))\log_d \lambda. \end{aligned}$$

Hence

$$\log \frac{1}{P_b} \gtrsim \lambda^{\gamma + o(1)}.$$

■

6. HETEROGENEOUS JOBS

In this section, we focus on the heterogeneous job case. In particular, we will employ the ansatz in [8], which asserts that in equilibrium, any finite set of queues in a randomized load balancing system become asymptotically independent as the number of queues goes to infinity. This will allows us to derive the equilibrium distribution by studying a single server, which has state-dependent Poisson arrivals.

6.1 Independence Ansatz

The asymptotic independence for a supermarket model operating under the power-of-d policy with exponentially distributed service time was established by Graham [10] using the propagation of chaos approach. And the independence ansatz for general service time distributions was demonstrated in [8]. A key step of the existing approaches involves standard coupling to establish a monotonicity property for the supermarket model, which is essential to proving the independence ansatz. The monotonicity property states that there exists a coupling such that the evolution of a system with any non-zero initial condition stochastically dominates the evolution of the same system with the all-zeros initial condition. The monotonicity argument is used to demonstrate uniform convergence, i.e., the distance between the two evolutions of the system monotonically decreases with time. This ensures convergence of the system under the arbitrary initial condition to the limiting equilibrium distribution.

We found that it is difficult to establish the independence ansatz using such approach as the loss model with the power-of-d policy does not satisfy the monotonicity property. Consider two copies $\mathbf{X}_1(\cdot)$ and $\mathbf{X}_2(\cdot)$ of the loss model under the power-of-d policy. And assume element-wise dominance of $\mathbf{X}_1(\cdot)$ over $\mathbf{X}_2(\cdot)$. With exponential service times, departures of the two systems can always be coupled. Problem comes from blocking for arrivals. As an arrival is blocked when it is assigned to a server with insufficient resource, it is possible that jobs are blocked in the heavier-loaded system $\mathbf{X}_1(\cdot)$ while enter the lighter-loaded system $\mathbf{X}_2(\cdot)$. This might break the dominance. Therefore monotonicity does not hold for the loss model by standard coupling.

Justification of the independence ansatz for our model remains to be done. However, we believe that it is true considering the randomized nature of power-of-d algorithms. In this following section, we derive some interesting results under the independence ansatz.

6.2 Equilibrium Distribution for A Single Queue

We assume asymptotic independence for the loss model with the power-of-d algorithm. Consider server 1 (by symmetry, any server) in the large N limit. Under the asymptotic independence assumption, the arrival process of type j jobs to server 1 is a state-dependent Poisson process with rate $\lambda_j(\mathbf{n})$, which is given in Eq. (6).

We can explain Eq (6) as follows: Assume that server 1 is of state $\mathbf{n}$. When a type j job arrives at the system, it will join server 1 *only if* server 1 is chosen and the state $\mathbf{n}'$ of any other selected server satisfies the condition $\langle \mathbf{n}', \mathbf{b}\rangle \geq \langle \mathbf{n}, \mathbf{b}\rangle$, i.e., server 1 has the largest amount of available resource. Note that server 1 is selected as one of the d sampled servers with probability $\frac{\binom{N-1}{d-1}}{\binom{N}{d}} = \frac{d}{N}$. Consider the case where $i-1$ out of the other $d-1$ selected servers have the same amount of available resource, $i \in \{1, 2, ..., d\}$. Such an event happens with probability $\binom{d-1}{i-1} E_{\mathbf{n}}^{i-1} G_{\mathbf{n}}^{d-i}$, where $E_{\mathbf{n}}$ ($G_{\mathbf{n}}$) represents the fraction of servers with the same (larger) amount of resource occupied. As ties are broken randomly, server 1 is selected with probability $\frac{1}{i}$. Hence the probability that the arrival is routed to server 1 is given by

$$\sum_{i=1}^{d} \frac{d}{N} \cdot \frac{1}{i} \cdot \binom{d-1}{i-1} E_{\mathbf{n}}^{i-1} G_{\mathbf{n}}^{d-i} = \frac{1}{N} \sum_{i=1}^{d} \binom{d}{i} E_{\mathbf{n}}^{i-1} G_{\mathbf{n}}^{d-i}.$$

Multiplying this probability by the arrival rate of type j jobs and letting $N \to \infty$ yield Eq. (6).

Note that queue 1 is a birth-death process with state-dependent arrival and departure rates. The global balance equation is given by:

$$\left[\sum_{j=1}^{J} n_j \delta_j^-(\mathbf{n}) + \sum_{j=1}^{J} \lambda_j(\mathbf{n}) \delta_j^+(\mathbf{n})\right] p_{\mathbf{n}}$$
$$= \sum_{j=1}^{J} \lambda_j(\mathbf{n}_j^-) \delta_j^-(\mathbf{n}) p_{\mathbf{n}_j^-} + \sum_{j=1}^{J} (n_j + 1) \delta_j^+(\mathbf{n}) p_{\mathbf{n}_j^+}, \quad (15)$$

where

$$\mathbf{n}_j^+ = (n_1, n_2, ..., n_{j-1}, n_j + 1, n_{j+1}, ..., n_J),$$
$$\mathbf{n}_j^- = (n_1, n_2, ..., n_{j-1}, n_j - 1, n_{j+1}, ..., n_J),$$
$$\delta_j^+(\mathbf{n}) = \begin{cases} 1, & \text{if } \mathbf{n}_j^+ \in \mathcal{C} \\ 0, & \text{otherwise} \end{cases}$$
$$\delta_j^-(\mathbf{n}) = \begin{cases} 1, & \text{if } \mathbf{n}_j^- \in \mathcal{C} \\ 0, & \text{otherwise} \end{cases}$$

Moreover, the local balance equation is given by

$$\lambda_j(\mathbf{n}_j^-) \delta_j^-(\mathbf{n}) p_{\mathbf{n}_j^-} = n_j \delta_j^-(\mathbf{n}) p_{\mathbf{n}}, \quad (16)$$
$$\forall j \in \{1, 2, ..., J\}, \forall \mathbf{n} \in \mathcal{C}.$$

Remark. We notice that if the local balance equations are satisfied, the global balance equations are satisfied. However, we have not established that the global balance equations have a unique solution. This is normally true for queueing systems where the arrival rate is fixed; however, since the derivation here follows from the independence ansantz, the arrival rate depends on $\mathbf{p}$. Thus, establishing the uniqueness of the solution to Eq. (15) remains to be done.

6.3 One-dimensional Recursion

We are interested in the probability P_{b_j} that an arriving job of type j is blocked. Note that

$$P_{b_j} = \left(\sum_{\mathbf{n} \in \mathcal{T}_j^+} p_{\mathbf{n}}\right)^d, \quad (17)$$

where $\mathcal{T}_j^+ = \{\mathbf{n} \in \mathcal{C} : \mathbf{n}_j^+ \notin \mathcal{C}\}$.

The underlying high dimension of the state $\mathbf{n}$ makes it difficult to obtain the equilibrium distribution from Eq. (16). In order to quantify the blocking probability, we will use Kaufman-Roberts recursion [12, 22] to establish a one-dimensional recursion, regardless of the dimensionality of jobs types (Theorem 4). The key idea is to pay attention to the random variable $R(\mathbf{n}) = \sum_{j=1}^{J} n_j b_j$, which denote the amount of occupied resource. We use $\mathbf{r}$ to represent the tail distribution of $R(\mathbf{n})$, i.e.,

$$r_k = \Pr[R \geq k] = \sum_{\mathbf{n} \in \mathcal{C}: \langle \mathbf{n}, \mathbf{b} \rangle \geq k} p_{\mathbf{n}}, \text{ for } k = 0, 1, ..., B.$$

Note that r_k is also the asymptotic *fraction* of servers having at least k units of resource occupied. For ease of exposition, throughout this section, we define $r_x = 1$ for any $x \le 0$, and $r_{B+1} = 0$.

In order to prove Theorem 4, we need the following lemma.

LEMMA 8. *For any $j \in \mathcal{J}$, and $k \in \{0, 1, ..., B\}$,*

$$\lambda_j (r^d_{k-b_j} - r^d_{k-b_j+1}) = \mathbb{E}[n_j | \langle \mathbf{n}, \mathbf{b} \rangle = k] (r_k - r_{k+1}), \quad (18)$$

where $r_x = 1$ for any $x \le 0$ and $r_{B+1} = 0$.

Proof. Equation (16) can be written as :

$$\lambda_j(\mathbf{n}_j^-)\gamma_j(\mathbf{n}) p_{\mathbf{n}_j^-} = n_j p_{\mathbf{n}}, \quad (19)$$

where

$$\gamma_j(\mathbf{n}) = \begin{cases} 1 & \text{if } n_j \ge 1 \\ 0 & \text{if } n_j = 0 \end{cases}$$

For any $k \in \{0, 1, ..., B\}$, define $\mathcal{D}_k = \{\mathbf{n} \in \mathcal{C} : k = \sum_{j=1}^J n_j b_j\}$. Note that for any $\mathbf{n} \in \mathcal{D}_k$,

$$E_{\mathbf{n}} = r_k - r_{k+1}, \; G_{\mathbf{n}} = r_{k+1}.$$

Hence $\lambda_j(\mathbf{n})$ depends on $k = \langle \mathbf{n}, \mathbf{b} \rangle$ only.

Summing Eq. (19) over the set $\mathcal{D}_k$, we have

$$\sum_{\mathbf{n} \in \mathcal{D}_k} \lambda_j(\mathbf{n}_j^-)\gamma_j(\mathbf{n}) p_{\mathbf{n}_j^-} = \sum_{\mathbf{n} \in \mathcal{D}_k} n_j p_{\mathbf{n}}. \quad (20)$$

Consider the left-hand-side (LHS) of (20).

$$\begin{aligned} LHS &= \sum_{\mathbf{n} \in \mathcal{D}_k} \lambda_j(\mathbf{n}_j^-)\gamma_j(\mathbf{n}) p_{\mathbf{n}_j^-} \\ &= \lambda_j \sum_{\mathbf{n} \in \mathcal{D}_k} \left(\sum_{i=1}^d \binom{d}{i} E^{i-1}_{\mathbf{n}_j^-} G^{d-i}_{\mathbf{n}_j^-} \right) \gamma_j(\mathbf{n}) p_{\mathbf{n}_j^-} \\ &= \lambda_j \sum_{\mathbf{n} \in \mathcal{D}_k \cap \{\mathbf{n}: n_j \ge 1\}} \left(\sum_{i=1}^d \binom{d}{i} E^{i-1}_{\mathbf{n}_j^-} G^{d-i}_{\mathbf{n}_j^-} \right) p_{\mathbf{n}_j^-}. \end{aligned}$$

Note that

$$\begin{aligned} &\mathcal{D}_k \cap \{\mathbf{n} : n_j \ge 1\} \\ = &\left\{ \mathbf{n} \in \mathcal{C} : \sum_{i \ne j} n_i b_i + (n_j - 1) b_j = k - b_j, n_j \ge 1 \right\}. \end{aligned}$$

Let $\hat{\mathbf{n}} = \mathbf{n}_j^-$. Then

$$LHS = \lambda_j \sum_{\hat{\mathbf{n}} \in \mathcal{D}_{k-b_j}} \left(\sum_{i=1}^d \binom{d}{i} E^{i-1}_{\hat{\mathbf{n}}} G^{d-i}_{\hat{\mathbf{n}}} \right) p_{\hat{\mathbf{n}}}$$

$$\begin{aligned} &= \lambda_j \left(\sum_{i=1}^d \binom{d}{i} (r_{k-b_j} - r_{k-b_j+1})^{i-1} r^{d-i}_{k-b_j+1} \right) \sum_{\hat{\mathbf{n}} \in \mathcal{D}_{k-b_j}} p_{\hat{\mathbf{n}}} \\ &= \lambda_j \left(\sum_{i=1}^d \binom{d}{i} (r_{k-b_j} - r_{k-b_j+1})^{i} r^{d-i}_{k-b_j+1} \right) \\ &= \lambda_j (r^d_{k-b_j} - r^d_{k-b_j+1}). \end{aligned} \quad (21)$$

The right-hand side (RHS) of (20) can be written as

$$\begin{aligned} RHS &= \sum_{\mathbf{n} \in \mathcal{D}_k} n_j \frac{p_{\mathbf{n}}}{\mathbb{P}[\{\mathbf{n} : \langle \mathbf{n}, \mathbf{b} \rangle = k\}]} \mathbb{P}[\{\mathbf{n} : \langle \mathbf{n}, \mathbf{b} \rangle = k\}] \\ &= \sum_{\mathbf{n} \in \mathcal{D}_k} n_j \mathbb{P}[\mathbf{n} | \langle \mathbf{n}, \mathbf{b} \rangle = k] (r_k - r_{k+1}) \\ &= \mathbb{E}[n_j | \langle \mathbf{n}, \mathbf{b} \rangle = k] (r_k - r_{k+1}). \end{aligned} \quad (22)$$

Equation (18) follows from Eq. (21) and (22). ∎

Proof of Theorem 4: Multiplying Eq. (18) by b_j on both side and summing over j yields

$$\begin{aligned} &\sum_{j=1}^J \lambda_j b_j (r^d_{k-b_j} - r^d_{k-b_j+1}) \\ &= \sum_{j=1}^J b_j \mathbb{E}[n_j | k] (r_k - r_{k+1}) \\ &= \mathbb{E}\left[\sum_{j=1}^J b_j n_j | k \right] (r_k - r_{k+1}) \\ &= k (r_k - r_{k+1}) \end{aligned}$$

∎

Remark. We can write the blocking probability for jobs of type j as

$$P_{b_j} = \left(\sum_{\mathbf{n} \in \mathcal{C} : \langle \mathbf{n}, \mathbf{b} \rangle > B - b_j} p_{\mathbf{n}} \right)^d = r^d_{B-b_j+1}.$$

By solving Eq. (7), we can obtain P_{b_j} immediately. Compared with the formula (17), the one-dimensional recursion brings a significant reduction in computation.

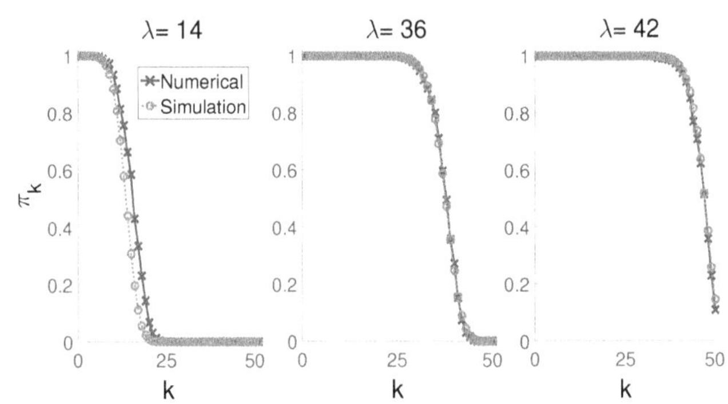

Figure 6: Equilibrium distribution of the number of occupied resource units for the power-of-two-choices algorithm with $B = 50$ and three types of jobs, where $\mathbf{b} = (1, 2, 4)$ and $\lambda_j = \lambda/7$. The values for the stationary point are obtained numerically by solving Eq. (7). Simulation results are from a finite system with $N = 1000$.

Numerical Results. Figure 6 compares the empirical distribution from simulation of a finite system with $N = 1000$ with the stationary point at three different loads. Simulation results coincide with the stationary point very well, which also verifies the validness of independence ansatz.

6.4 Upper Bound

We first establish an upper bound for the tail distribution $\mathbf{r}$ of the number of occupied resource units. Let $\lambda = \sum_{j=1}^J \lambda_j b_j$ be the total traffic intensity. We have the following theorem.

THEOREM 6. *Define* $\{\bar{r}_k\}_{k=0}^B$ *as follows:*

$$\bar{r}_k = \begin{cases} 1, & 0 \le k \le k_0 + 1 \\ \frac{1}{k-1} \sum_{j=1}^{J} \lambda_j b_j \bar{r}^d_{k-b_j}, & k_0 + 1 < k \le B \end{cases} \quad (23)$$

where $k_0 = \lfloor \lambda \rfloor$, $\bar{r}_x = 1$ *for any* $x \le 0$ *and* $\bar{r}_{B+1} = 0$.

Let $\{r_k\}_{k=0}^B$ *denote the solution to Eq (7). Then for any* $k = 0, 1, ..., B$,

$$\bar{r}_k \ge r_k.$$

Proof of Theorem 6 is essentially the same as that of Theorem 2.

LEMMA 9. *Define* $\{\tilde{r}_k\}_{k=0}^B$ *as follows:*

$$\tilde{r}_k = \begin{cases} 1, & 0 \le k < b(k_0' + 2) \\ \frac{\lambda}{(m-1)b} \tilde{r}^d_{k-b}, & mb \le k < (m+1)b,\ k \le B, \\ & m \in \mathbb{N} \text{ and } k_0' + 1 < m \le \frac{B}{b} \end{cases} \quad (24)$$

where $b = \max_{j=1,...,J} b_j$, *and* $k_0' = \lfloor \frac{\lambda}{b} \rfloor$

Then $\tilde{\mathbf{r}}$ *gives an upper bound for* $\bar{\mathbf{r}}$, *i.e., for any* $k = 0, 1, ..., B$,

$$\tilde{r}_k \ge \bar{r}_k.$$

The following corollary follows immediately by Theorem 6 and Lemma 9.

COROLLARY 1. $\tilde{\mathbf{r}}$ *is an upper bound for* $\mathbf{r}$, *i.e.,*

$$\tilde{r}_k \ge r_k, \forall k = 0, 1, ..., B.$$

Remark. Although the upper bound $\tilde{\mathbf{r}}$ has no explicit expression, the recursion is straightforward and no further iterative calculation is needed here. Lemma 9 provides a further upper bound on $\bar{\mathbf{r}}$ which is used in the analysis of the blocking probability in the heavy-traffic and critically-loaded traffic regimes (Theorem 5).

6.5 Proof Outline of Theorem 5

Proof outline of Theorem 5:

Note that $b = \max_{j=1,...,J} b_j$. By the monotonicity of the tail distribution $\{r_k\}_{k=0}^B$, the blocking probability P_{b_j} for type j jobs ($\forall j \in \{1, 2, ..., J\}$) satisfies

$$P_{b_j} = r^d_{B-b_j+1} \le r^d_{B-b+1} \le \tilde{r}^d_{B-b+1}.$$

Hence it is sufficient to show that the upper-bound $\tilde{r}_{B-b+1}$ satisfies (8).

From the definition of $\tilde{\mathbf{r}}$, we can see that $\{\tilde{r}_k\}_{k=0}^B$ consists of consecutive subsequences of size b, where elements in each subsequence have the same value. That is, $\forall k \in [mb, (m+1)b)$, $m \in \mathbb{N}$, $\tilde{r}_k = \tilde{r}_{mb}$. To analyze its asymptotic behavior, we consider the subsequence $\{\tilde{r}_{mb}\}_{m \in \mathbb{N}}$. Define the scaled arrival rate $\lambda' = \lambda/b$, and resource units $B' = \lfloor B/b \rfloor$. Then the recursion of $\{\tilde{r}_{mb}\}_{m=0}^{B'}$ is the same as $\bar{\pi}$ with arrival rate λ' and B' units of resource.

By following the proof for Theorem 3, we can establish the asymptotic behavior of $\tilde{r}_{B'b}$ in large B' limit, which gives Eq. (8). The analysis for the two limiting regimes is the same as that in Theorem 3.

Remark. Theorem 5 states that for the general case with multiple types of jobs, the blocking probability for jobs of any type under the power-of-d algorithm has exactly the same asymptotic behavior as that of homogeneous job case.

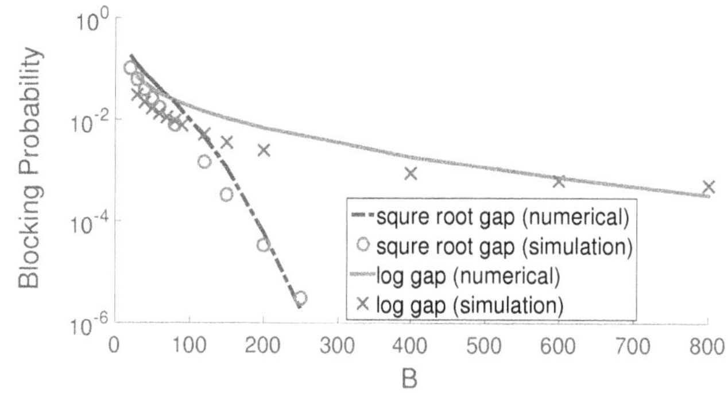

Figure 7: Blocking probability for the power-of-two-choices algorithm with different load gap. There are three types of jobs with $\mathbf{b} = (1, 2, 4)$. Line curves are obtained by solving Eq. (7) numerically. Markers are from simulations with $N = 1000$.

Numerical Results. We simulate a system of $N = 1000$ servers under the power-of-two-choices algorithm with different load gap. We consider three types of jobs with same arrival rate, i.e., $\lambda_1 = \lambda_2 = \lambda_3$, and $\mathbf{b} = (1, 2, 4)$. For each B, we simulate this system with different load gap $B - \lambda = \sqrt{\lambda}$ and $B - \lambda = 2 \log \lambda$, where $\lambda = \sum_j \lambda_j b_j$ is the total traffic intensity. Figure 7 compares the blocking probability for jobs that require the maximum amount of resource, i.e., type 3 jobs, with different load gap, both by solving Eq. (7) numerically and by simulation. Note that the y-axis is in log scale. Observe that the blocking probability for jobs of type 3 exhibits similar behavior as that of the homogeneous job case (Fig. 1). That is, P_{b_3} decays exponentially with $\log \lambda$ load gap, while it decays much faster with $\sqrt{\lambda}$ load gap. Similar behavior can be observed for the blocking probability of the other two types of jobs.

7. CONCLUSION AND FUTURE WORK

This paper considered a loss model for the VM assignment problem in a cloud system. The overall goal is to study how to route arriving jobs to the servers in order to minimize the probability that an arriving job does not find the required number of resources in the system. Using the fluid model approach, we showed that when arrivals are routed to the least utilized of $d \ge 2$ randomly selected servers, the blocking probability decays exponentially or doubly exponentially. This is a substantial improvement over the random policy. In addition, we developed an explicit upper-bound for the stationary fluid limit. The analysis of the upper-bound revealed significant insight into the asymptotic behavior of large systems with the power-of-d-choices ($d \ge 2$) algorithm.

We have seen that for a fixed B, the gap between the proposed upper-bound and the stationary fluid limit increases with the load. For future work, we are interested in characterizing the gap and establishing an approximation with higher accuracy. Some of current model assumptions could be relaxed to make the model closer to the real system, including the assumption of exponential service times and the constraint on the one-dimensionality of requested resources.

8. ACKNOWLEDGMENT

Qiaomin Xie and Yi Lu were supported by NSF grant CNS-1150080. The work of Xiaobo Dong and R. Srikant was supported in part by NSF Grant ECCS-1202065 and ARO MURI W911NF-12-1-0385. We thank Prof. Ravi Mazumdar for pointing out a gap in the proof of Lemma 1 in an earlier version of the paper.

9. REFERENCES

[1] Amazon EC2. `http://aws.amazon.com/ec2/`.

[2] V. Anantharam and M. Benchekroun. A technique for computing sojourn times in large networks of interacting queues. *Probability in the Engineering and Informational Sciences*, 7(04):441–464, 1993.

[3] Google App Engine. `https://cloud.google.com/appengine/docs?csw=1`.

[4] Y. Azar, A. Z. Broder, A. R. Karlin, and E. Upfal. Balanced allocations. *SIAM J. Comput.*, 29(1):180–200, Sept. 1999.

[5] Azure. `http://azure.microsoft.com/en-us/`.

[6] N. Bansal, A. Caprara, and M. Sviridenko. A new approximation method for set covering problems, with applications to multidimensional bin packing. *SIAM Journal on Computing*, 39(4):1256–1278, 2010.

[7] A. A. Borovkov. *Stochastic Processes in Queueing Theory.* Springer, 1976.

[8] M. Bramson, Y. Lu, and B. Prabhakar. Asymptotic independence of queues under randomized load balancing. *Queueing Systems*, 71(3):247–292, 2012.

[9] J. Csirik, D. S. Johnson, C. Kenyon, J. B. Orlin, P. W. Shor, and R. R. Weber. On the sum-of-squares algorithm for bin packing. *J. ACM*, 53(1):1–65, Jan. 2006.

[10] C. Graham. Chaoticity on path space for a queueing network with selection of the shortest queue among several. *Journal of Applied Probability*, 37(1):198–211, 2000.

[11] V. Gupta and A. Radovanovic. Online stochastic bin packing, 2012.

[12] J. Kaufman. Blocking in a shared resource environment. *Communications, IEEE Transactions on*, 29(10):1474–1481, Oct 1981.

[13] T. G. Kurtz. *Approximation of Population Processes.* Society for Industrial and Applied Mathematics, 1981.

[14] M. Luczak and C. McDiarmid. On the maximum queue length in the supermarket model. *The Annals of Probability*, 34(2):493–527, 2006.

[15] S. Maguluri, R. Srikant, and L. Ying. Stochastic models of load balancing and scheduling in cloud computing clusters. In *Proc. of IEEE INFOCOM*, pages 702–710, Mar 2012.

[16] S. T. Maguluri, R. Srikant, and L. Ying. Heavy traffic optimal resource allocation algorithms for cloud computing clusters. In *Proc. of the 24th International Teletraffic Congress*, pages 25:1–25:8, 2012.

[17] X. Meng, V. Pappas, and L. Zhang. Improving the scalability of data center networks with traffic-aware virtual machine placement. In *Proc. of IEEE INFOCOM*, pages 1154–1162, Piscataway, NJ, USA, 2010.

[18] M. Mitzenmacher. *The power of two choices in randomized load balancing.* PhD thesis, UC Berkeley, 1996.

[19] M. Mitzenmacher. Studying balanced allocations with differential equations. *Combinatorics, Probability and Computing*, 8(5):473–482, Sept. 1999.

[20] A. Mukhopadhyay and R. R. Mazumdar. Analysis of load balancing in large heterogeneous processor sharing systems. ArXiv preprint arXiv:1311.5806, 2013.

[21] A. Mukhopadhyay, R. R. Mazumdar, and F. Guillemin. Static versus dynamic user assignment to cloud resources. 2015.

[22] J. W. Roberts. A service system with heterogeneous user requirement. In G. Pujolle, editor, *Performance of Data Communications Systems and Their Applications*, 1981.

[23] R. Srikant and W. Whitt. Simulation run lengths to estimate blocking probabilities. *ACM Trans. Model. Comput. Simul.*, 6(1):7–52, Jan. 1996.

[24] A. L. Stolyar. An infinite server system with general packing constraints. ArXiv preprint arXiv:1205.4271, 2012.

[25] A. L. Stolyar and Y. Zhong. An infinite server system with general packing constraints: Asymptotic optimality of a greedy randomized algorithm. In *Proc. 53th Annu. Allerton Conf. Commun., Control Comput.*, pages 575–582, Oct 2013.

[26] A. L. Stolyar and Y. Zhong. A large-scale service system with packing constraints: Minimizing the number of occupied servers. *SIGMETRICS Perform. Eval. Rev.*, 41(1):41–52, June 2013.

[27] J. N. Tsitsiklis and K. Xu. On the power of (even a little) resource pooling. *Stochastic Systems*, 2(1):1–66, 2012.

[28] N. D. Vvedenskaya, R. L. Dobrushin, and F. I. Karpelevich. Queueing system with selection of the shortest of two queues: An asymptotic approach. *Probl. Peredachi Inf.*, 32(1):20–34, 1996.

[29] L. Wang, F. Zhang, A. V. Vasilakos, C. Hou, and Z. Liu. Joint virtual machine assignment and traffic engineering for green data center networks. *SIGMETRICS Perform. Eval. Rev.*, 41(3):107–112, Jan. 2014.

[30] W. Whitt. Heavy-traffic approximations for service systems with blocking. *AT&T Bell Laboratories Technical Journal*, 63(5):689–708, 1984.

[31] L. Ying, R. Srikant, and X. Kang. The power of slightly more than one sample in randomized load balancing. In *Proc. of IEEE INFOCOM*, 2015.

Appendix

Proof of Lemma 1

The case $\lambda = 0$ is trivial with a unique stationary solution $\boldsymbol{\pi} = (1, \underbrace{0, 0, ..., 0}_{B})$. We focus on the case $\lambda > 0$.

Existence: For ease of exposition, throughout the proof we define $x_{B+1} = 0$ for any $\mathbf{x} \in \mathcal{S}$.

Step 1. Define $\mathbf{G}(\mathbf{x})$, $\forall \mathbf{x} \in \mathcal{S}$.

For any $\mathbf{x} \in \mathcal{S}$, let $\mathbf{G}(\mathbf{x}) = (G_0(\mathbf{x}), G_1(\mathbf{x}), ..., G_B(\mathbf{x}))$, where $G_0(\mathbf{x}) = 1$, and $\forall k = 1, 2, ..., B$, $G_k(\mathbf{x}) \geq 0$ satisfies

$$\lambda G_k^d(\mathbf{x}) + kG_k(\mathbf{x}) - \lambda x_{k-1}^d - kx_{k+1} = 0. \tag{25}$$

We will show that $\mathbf{G}$ is uniquely determined by $\mathbf{x}$. Consider a sequence of functions $\{H_k(y_k)\}_{k=1}^B$, where

$$H_k(y_k) = \lambda y_k^d + ky_k - \lambda x_{k-1}^d - kx_{k+1}.$$

Since $\mathbf{x} \in \mathcal{S}$,

$$H_k(x_{k-1}) = kx_{k-1} - kx_{k+1} \geq 0,$$
$$H_k(x_{k+1}) = \lambda x_{k+1}^d - \lambda x_{k-1}^d \leq 0.$$

Note that $H_k(y_k)$ is strictly increasing in $y_k \in [0, \infty)$. Hence there exists a unique $y_k^* > 0$ such that $H_k(y_k^*) = 0$. By the definition of G_k in (25), $H_k(G_k) = 0$. Hence $G_k = y_k^*$ is determined by $\mathbf{x}$ uniquely, and

$$x_{k+1} \leq G_k(\mathbf{x}) \leq x_{k-1}. \tag{26}$$

Step 2. Show that $\mathbf{G}(\cdot)$ is mapping $\mathcal{S}$ into $\mathcal{S}$.

We will verify that $\forall \mathbf{x} \in \mathcal{S}$, $\mathbf{G}(\mathbf{x}) \in \mathcal{S}$, i.e., $1 = G_0(\mathbf{x}) \geq G_1(\mathbf{x}) \geq ... \geq G_B(\mathbf{x}) \geq 0$. For any $\mathbf{x} \in \mathcal{S}$, inequality in (26) ensures that $G_k \in [0, 1]$ for all k. To prove that $G_k \geq G_{k+1}$, consider a function

$$\varphi_k(z) = \lambda z^d + kz,$$

which is strictly increasing in $[0, 1]$. Hence it is sufficient to show that $\varphi_k(G_k) \geq \varphi_k(G_{k+1})$.

$$\begin{aligned}
& \varphi_k(G_k) - \varphi_k(G_{k+1}) \\
= \;& \lambda G_k^d + kG_k - \lambda G_{k+1}^d - (k+1)G_{k+1} + G_{k+1} \\
\overset{(a)}{=} \;& \lambda x_{k-1}^d + kx_{k+1} - \lambda x_k^d - (k+1)x_{k+2} + G_{k+1} \\
= \;& \lambda(x_{k-1}^d - x_k^d) + k(x_{k+1} - x_{k+2}) + G_{k+1} - x_{k+2} \\
\overset{(b)}{\geq} \;& G_{k+1} - \pi_{k+2} \\
\overset{(c)}{\geq} \;& 0,
\end{aligned}$$

where the equality (a) comes from the definition of G_k, G_{k+1} in (25), and the inequality (b) follows by the fact that $\mathbf{x} \in \mathcal{S}$, and the inequality (c) results from the property of G_k in (26).

Therefore $\mathbf{G}(\mathbf{x}) \in \mathcal{S}$.

Step 3. Show that $\mathbf{G}(\cdot)$ is continuous.

Consider any point $\mathbf{x} \in \mathcal{S}$. For every $\epsilon > 0$, set $\delta = \frac{\epsilon}{\lambda d+1}$. Let $\mathbf{y}$ be any point in $\mathcal{S}$ such that $|\mathbf{x} - \mathbf{y}| < \delta$. By the definition of $\mathbf{G}(\cdot)$, $\forall k = 1, 2, ..., B$,

$$\begin{aligned}
& \lambda(G_k^d(\mathbf{x}) - G_k^d(\mathbf{y})) + k(G_k(\mathbf{x}) - G_k(\mathbf{y})) \\
= \;& (G_k(\mathbf{x}) - G_k(\mathbf{y})) \left(\lambda \sum_{i=0}^{d-1} G_k^{d-1-i}(\mathbf{x}) G_k^i(\mathbf{y}) + k \right) \\
= \;& \lambda(x_{k-1}^d - y_{k-1}^d) + k(x_{k+1} - y_{k+1}) \\
= \;& \lambda(x_{k-1} - y_{k-1}) \left(\sum_{i=0}^{d-1} x_{k-1}^{d-1-i} y_{k-1}^i \right) + k(x_{k+1} - y_{k+1})
\end{aligned}$$

Then we have

$$\begin{aligned}
& |G_k(\mathbf{x}) - G_k(\mathbf{y})| \\
= \;& \frac{\left|\lambda(x_{k-1} - y_{k-1}) \left(\sum_{i=0}^{d-1} x_{k-1}^{d-1-i} y_{k-1}^i \right) + k(x_{k+1} - y_{k+1})\right|}{\lambda \sum_{i=0}^{d-1} G_k^{d-1-i}(\mathbf{x}) G_k^i(\mathbf{y}) + k} \\
\leq \;& \frac{\lambda d|x_{k-1} - y_{k-1}| + k|(x_{k+1} - y_{k+1})|}{k} \\
\leq \;& \lambda d|x_{k-1} - y_{k-1}| + |(x_{k+1} - y_{k+1})|,
\end{aligned}$$

which implies that

$$\begin{aligned}
& |\mathbf{G}(\mathbf{x}) - \mathbf{G}(\mathbf{y})| \\
= \;& \sum_{k=0}^{B} |G_k(\mathbf{x}) - G_k(\mathbf{y})| \\
\leq \;& \sum_{k=1}^{B} (\lambda d|x_{k-1} - y_{k-1}| + |(x_{k+1} - y_{k+1})|) \\
\leq \;& (\lambda d + 1) \sum_{k=0}^{B} |x_k - y_k| \\
< \;& (\lambda d + 1)\delta \\
= \;& \epsilon.
\end{aligned}$$

Therefore $\mathbf{G}$ is continuous at any point $\mathbf{x} \in \mathcal{S}$.

Step 4. Show that a fixed point of $\mathbf{G}$ in $\mathcal{S}$ is a stationary point.

Note that set $\mathbf{S}$ is compact and convex. Step 1-3 ensures that there exists a fixed point of $\mathbf{G}$ in $\mathcal{S}$, denoted by $\hat{\mathbf{x}}$. That is, $\hat{\mathbf{x}} = \mathbf{G}(\hat{\mathbf{x}})$. From the definition of $\mathbf{G}$ in (25), we have

$$F_k(\hat{\mathbf{x}}) = \lambda \hat{x}_k^d + k\hat{x}_k - \lambda \hat{x}_{k-1}^d - k\hat{x}_{k+1} = 0.$$

That is, $\hat{\mathbf{x}}$ is a stationary point.

Uniqueness: We prove the uniqueness of stationary solution by contradiction.

Assume that there exists two different solutions $\boldsymbol{\pi}$ and $\hat{\boldsymbol{\pi}}$. We claim that $\pi_B \neq \hat{\pi}_B$. Otherwise, we have

$$\pi_{B-1} = \sqrt[d]{\pi_B^d + \frac{B}{\lambda}\pi_B} = \hat{\pi}_{B-1}.$$

Note that

$$\pi_k = \sqrt[d]{\pi_{k+1}^d + \frac{k+1}{\lambda}(\pi_{k+1} - \pi_{k+2})}.$$

Hence by induction, we can show that $\pi_k = \hat{\pi}_k$ for any $k = 0, 1, ..., B$.

Consider the case that $\pi_B < \hat{\pi}_B$. Similarly, we can establish that $\pi_k < \hat{\pi}_k$ for any $k = 0, 1, ..., B$ by induction. Therefore, $\pi_0 < \hat{\pi}_0$, which contradicts with the fact that $\pi_0 = \hat{\pi}_0 = 1$. This completes the proof for the uniqueness. ∎

Proof of Lemma 3

Due to continuous dependence of a solution on the initial values, it is sufficient to show that if $\bar{s}_k^0 < s_k^0$ for any $k \geq 1$,

$\bar{s}_k(t) \le s_k(t)$ for all $t \ge 0$ and any k. Assume that strict inequalities hold for $t < t_1$ and are broken at $t = t_1$. Consider two cases:

(i) $\bar{s}_k(t_1) = s_k(t_1)$ for any k.
The uniqueness of solution ensures that $\bar{s}_k(t) = s_k(t)$ for all $t \ge t_1$ and any k. Hence the claim holds.

(ii) $\exists k^* \ge 1$ such that $\bar{s}_{k^*}(t_1) < s_{k^*}(t_1)$.
Then there exists $k \ge 1$ such that $\bar{s}_k(t_1) = s_k(t_1)$, and at least of one following conditions hold: $\bar{s}_{k-1}(t_1) < s_{k-1}(t_1)$, $\bar{s}_{k+1}(t_1) < s_{k+1}(t_1)$. If $k < B$, we have

$$\begin{aligned}\frac{d\bar{s}_k}{dt}(t_1) - \frac{ds_k}{dt}(t_1) &= \lambda(\bar{s}_{k-1}^d - s_{k-1}^d) + k(\bar{s}_{k+1} - s_{k+1}) \\ &\quad -\lambda(\bar{s}_k^d - s_k^d) - k(\bar{s}_k - s_k) \\ &< 0,\end{aligned}$$

where the inequality comes from the definition of k. Similarly, we can verify that $\frac{d\bar{s}_k}{dt}(t_1) - \frac{ds_k}{dt}(t_1) < 0$ if $k = B$.
Since $\bar{\mathbf{s}}(t)$ and $\mathbf{s}(t)$ are continuous functions of t, there exists $t_0 < t_1$ such that $\bar{s}_k(t_0) < s_k(t_0)$ and

$$\frac{d\bar{s}_k}{dt}(t) - \frac{ds_k}{dt}(t) < 0$$

for any $t \in (t_0, t_1)$. Thus

$$\bar{s}_k(t_1) - s_k(t_1) = \bar{s}_k(t_0) - s_k(t_0) + \int_{t_0}^{t_1} \left(\frac{d\bar{s}_k}{dt}(t) - \frac{ds_k}{dt}(t)\right) dt < 0,$$

which contradicts with the assumption that $\bar{s}_k(t_1) = s_k(t_1)$. ∎

Proof for Lemma 4

We will show that $d\psi(t)/dt \le -\psi$. Then $\psi(t) \le \psi(0)e^{-t}$, which implies that $\psi(t)$ converges to 0 exponentially fast.
Consider the case where $s_k^0 \ge \pi_k$ for any k. From Lemma 4, $s_k(t) \ge \pi_k$ for any $t \ge 0, \forall k \in \{0, 1, ..., B\}$. We can rewrite $\psi(t)$ as $\psi(t) = \sum_{k=0}^{B}(s_k(t) - \pi_k)$. Since $\mathbf{F}(\boldsymbol{\pi}) = \mathbf{0}$, $\dot{\mathbf{s}} = \mathbf{F}(\mathbf{s})$, we have

$$\begin{aligned}\frac{d\psi(t)}{dt} &= \sum_{k=0}^{B} \frac{ds_k(t)}{dt} \\ &= \sum_{k=1}^{B} F_k(\mathbf{s}(t)) - \sum_{k=1}^{B} F_k(\boldsymbol{\pi}) \\ &= \left(\lambda(s_0^d(t) - s_B^d(t)) - \sum_{k=1}^{B} s_k(t)\right) \\ &\quad - \left(\lambda(\pi_0^d - \pi_B^d) - \sum_{k=1}^{B} \pi_k\right) \\ &= -\lambda(s_B^d(t) - \pi_B^d) - \psi(t) \\ &\le -\psi(t),\end{aligned}$$

where the last inequality follows by the fact that $s_B^d(t) \ge \pi_B^d$.
The other case where $s_k^0 \le \pi_k$ for any k can be proved similarly. ∎

Proof of Lemma 6

Since $\mathbf{x}, \mathbf{y} \in \mathcal{S}$, for any $0 \le k \le B$

$$0 \le x_k \le 1, \ 0 \le y_k \le 1.$$

Then we have:

$$\begin{aligned}&|\mathbf{F}(\mathbf{x}) - \mathbf{F}(\mathbf{y})| \\ =& \sum_{k=1}^{B-1} |\lambda(x_{k-1}^d - x_k^d) - k(x_k - x_{k+1}) \\ & -\lambda(y_{k-1}^d - y_k^d) + k(y_k - y_{k+1})| \\ & +|\lambda(x_{B-1}^d - x_B^d) - Bx_B - \lambda(y_{B-1}^d - y_B^d) + By_B| \\ \le& \ 2\sum_{k=0}^{B} k|x_k - y_k| + 2\sum_{k=0}^{B} \lambda|x_k^d - y_k^d| \\ \le& \ 2B\sum_{k=0}^{B} |x_k - y_k| + 2\lambda \sum_{k=0}^{B}\left(|x_k - y_k| \sum_{i=0}^{d-1} x_k^{d-1-i} y_k^i\right) \\ \le& \ 2(B + d\lambda)\sum_{k=0}^{B} |x_k - y_k| \\ =& \ M|\mathbf{x} - \mathbf{y}|,\end{aligned}$$

where $M = 2(B + d\lambda)$. ∎

Proof of Claim 1

From Lemma 5, we have

$$\mathbf{S}^{(N_k)}(t) \Rightarrow \bar{\mathbf{S}}(t) \text{ as } k \to \infty.$$

By the definition of weak convergence, for a bounded continuous function f,

$$\mathbb{E}\left[f(\mathbf{S}^{(N_k)}(t))|\mathbf{S}^{(N_k)}(0)\right] \overset{n\to\infty}{\longrightarrow} \mathbb{E}\left[f(\bar{\mathbf{S}}(t))|\bar{\mathbf{S}}(0)\right],$$

if $\mathbf{S}^{(N_k)}(0) \to \bar{\mathbf{S}}(0)$ as $k \to \infty$.
As $\mathbf{S}^{(N_k)}(0) = \mathbf{X}^{(N_k)}$ and $\bar{\mathbf{S}}(0) = \bar{\mathbf{X}}$, by Skorokhod's representation theorem,

$$\mathbf{S}^{(N_k)}(0) \to \bar{\mathbf{S}}(0).$$

Define

$$\mathbf{Y}_k = \mathbb{E}\left[f(\mathbf{S}^{(N_k)}(t))|\mathbf{X}^{(N_k)}\right], \quad \mathbf{Y} = \mathbb{E}\left[f(\bar{\mathbf{S}}(t))|\bar{\mathbf{X}}\right].$$

Since f is bounded, $\mathbf{Y}_k$ and $\mathbf{Y}$ are bounded. By the bounded convergence theorem, we have

$$\mathbb{E}[\mathbf{Y}_k] \to \mathbb{E}[\mathbf{Y}].$$

This holds for all bounded, continuous f. Thus again by the definition of weak convergence,

$$\mathbf{S}^{(N_k)}(t) \Rightarrow \bar{\mathbf{S}}(t) \text{ as } k \to \infty$$

. ∎

Computable Bounds in Fork-Join Queueing Systems

Amr Rizk
University of Warwick

Felix Poloczek
University of Warwick / TU Berlin

Florin Ciucu
University of Warwick

ABSTRACT

In a Fork-Join (FJ) queueing system an upstream fork station splits incoming jobs into N tasks to be further processed by N parallel servers, each with its own queue; the response time of one job is determined, at a downstream join station, by the maximum of the corresponding tasks' response times. This queueing system is useful to the modelling of multi-service systems subject to synchronization constraints, such as MapReduce clusters or multipath routing. Despite their apparent simplicity, FJ systems are hard to analyze.

This paper provides the first *computable* stochastic bounds on the waiting and response time distributions in FJ systems. We consider four practical scenarios by combining 1a) renewal and 1b) non-renewal arrivals, and 2a) non-blocking and 2b) blocking servers. In the case of non-blocking servers we prove that delays scale as $\mathcal{O}(\log N)$, a law which is known for first moments under renewal input only. In the case of blocking servers, we prove that the same factor of $\log N$ dictates the stability region of the system. Simulation results indicate that our bounds are tight, especially at high utilizations, in all four scenarios. A remarkable insight gained from our results is that, at moderate to high utilizations, multipath routing "*makes sense*" from a queueing perspective for two paths only, i.e., response times drop the most when $N = 2$; the technical explanation is that the resequencing (delay) price starts to quickly dominate the tempting gain due to multipath transmissions.

Categories and Subject Descriptors

C.4 [**Computer Systems Organization**]: Performance of Systems; G.3 [**Mathematics of Computing**]: Probability and Statistics

Keywords

Fork-Join queue; Performance evaluation; Parallel systems; MapReduce; Multipath

SIGMETRICS'15, June 15–19, 2015, Portland, OR, USA.

ACM 978-1-4503-3486-0/15/06 ...$15.00.
http://dx.doi.org/10.1145/2745844.2745859.

1. INTRODUCTION

The performance analysis of Fork-Join (FJ) systems received new momentum with the recent wide-scale deployment of large-scale data processing that was enabled through emerging frameworks such as MapReduce [12]. The main idea behind these big data analysis frameworks is an elegant divide and conquer strategy with various degrees of freedom in the implementation. The open-source implementation of MapReduce, known as Hadoop [37], is deployed in numerous production clusters, e.g., Facebook and Yahoo [20].

The basic operation of MapReduce is depicted in Figure 1. In the *map phase*, a job is split into multiple tasks that are mapped to different workers (servers). Once a specific subset of these tasks finish their executions, the corresponding *reduce phase* starts by processing the combined output from all the corresponding tasks. In other words, the reduce phase is subject to a fundamental synchronization constraint on the finishing times of all involved tasks.

A natural way to model one reduce phase operation is by a *basic* FJ queueing system with N servers. Jobs, i.e., the input unit of work in MapReduce systems, arrive according to some point process. Each job is split into N (map) tasks (or *splits*, in the MapReduce terminology), which are simultaneously sent to the N servers. At each server, each task requires a random service time, capturing the variable task execution times on different servers in the map phase. A job leaves the FJ system when all of its tasks are served; this constraint corresponds to the specification that the reduce phase starts no sooner than when all of its map tasks complete their executions.

Concerning the execution of tasks belonging to different jobs on the same server, there are two operational modes. In the *non-blocking* mode, the servers are workconserving in the sense that tasks immediately start their executions once the previous tasks finish theirs. In the *blocking* mode, the mapped tasks of a job simultaneously start their executions, i.e., servers can be idle when their corresponding queues are not empty. The non-blocking execution mode prevails in MapReduce due to its conceivable efficiency, whereas the blocking execution mode is employed when the `jobtracker` (the node coordinating and scheduling jobs) waits for all machines to be ready to synchronize the configuration files before mapping a new job; in Hadoop, this can be enforced through the coordination service `zookeeper` [37].

In this paper we analyze the performance of the FJ queueing model in four practical scenarios by considering two broad arrival classes (driven by either renewal or non-renewal processes) and the two operational modes described above.

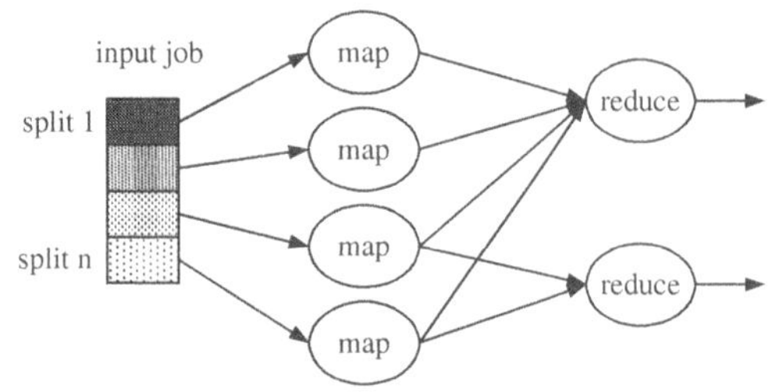

Figure 1: Schematic illustration of the basic operation of MapReduce.

The key contribution, to the best of our knowledge, are the first non-asymptotic and computable stochastic bounds on the waiting and response time distributions in the most relevant scenario, i.e., non-renewal (Markov modulated) job arrivals and the non-blocking operational mode. Under all scenarios, the bounds are numerically tight especially at high utilizations. This inherent tightness is due to a suitable martingale representation of the underlying queueing system, an approach which was conceived in [23] for the analysis of GI/GI/1 queues, and which was recently extended to address multi-class queues with non-renewal arrivals [11, 29]. The simplicity of the obtained stochastic bounds enables the derivation of scaling laws, e.g., delays in FJ systems scale as $\mathcal{O}(\log N)$ in the number of parallel servers N, for both renewal and non-renewal arrivals, in the non-blocking mode; more severe delay degradations hold in the blocking mode, and, moreover, the stability region depends on the same fundamental factor of $\log N$.

In addition to the direct applicability to the dimensioning of MapReduce clusters, there are other relevant types of parallel and distributed systems such as production or supply networks. In particular, by slightly modifying the basic FJ system corresponding to MapReduce, the resulting model suits the analysis of window-based transmission protocols over multipath routing. By making several simplifying assumptions such as ignoring the details of specific protocols (e.g., multipath TCP), we can provide a fundamental understanding of multipath routing from a queueing perspective. Concretely, we demonstrate that sending a flow of packets over two paths, instead of one, does generally reduce the steady-state response times. The surprising result is that by sending the flow over more than two paths, the steady-state response times start to increase. The technical explanation for such a rather counterintuitive result is that the $\log N$ resequencing price at the destination quickly dominates the tempting gain in the queueing waiting time due to multipath transmissions.

The rest of the paper is structured as follows. We first discuss related work on FJ systems and related applications. Then we analyze both non-blocking and blocking FJ systems with renewal input in Section 3, and with non-renewal input in Section 4. In Section 5 we apply the obtained results on the steady-state response time distributions to the analysis of multipath routing from a queueing perspective. Brief conclusions are presented in Section 6.

2. RELATED WORK

We first review analytical results on FJ systems, and then results related to the two application case studies considered in this paper, i.e., MapReduce and multipath routing.

The significance of the Fork-Join queueing model stems from its natural ability to capture the behavior of many parallel service systems. The performance of FJ queueing systems has been subject of multiple studies such as [4, 26, 35, 21, 24, 5, 7]. In particular, [4] notes that an exact performance evaluation of general FJ systems is remarkably hard due to the synchronization constraints on the input and output streams. More precisely, a major difficulty lies in finding an exact closed form expression for the joint steady-state workload distribution for the FJ queueing system. However, a number of results exist given certain constraints on the FJ system. The authors of [14] provide the stationary joint workload distribution for a two-server FJ system under Poisson arrivals and independent exponential service times. For the general case of more than two parallel servers there exists a number of works that provide approximations [26, 35, 24, 25] and bounds [4, 5] for certain performance metrics of the FJ system. Given renewal arrivals, [5] significantly improves the lower bounds from [4] in the case of heterogeneous phase-type servers using a matrix-geometric algorithmic method. The authors of [24] provide an approximation of the sojourn time distribution in a renewal driven FJ system consisting of multiple G/M/1 nodes. They show that the approximation error diminishes at extremal utilizations. Refined approximations for the mean sojourn time in two-server FJ systems that take the first two moments of the service time distribution are given in [21]; numerical evidence is further provided on the quality of the approximation for different service time distributions.

The closest related work to ours is [4], which provides computable lower and upper bounds on the expected response time in FJ systems under renewal assumptions with Poisson arrivals and exponential service times; the underlying idea is to artificially construct a more tractable system, yet subject to stochastic ordering relative to the original one. Our corresponding first order upper bound recovers the $\mathcal{O}(\log N)$ asymptotic behavior of the one from [4], and also reported in [26] in the context of an approximation; numerically, our bound is slightly worse than the one from [4] due to our main focus on computing bounds on the whole distribution (first order bounds are secondarily obtained by integration). Moreover, we show that the $\mathcal{O}(\log N)$ scaling law also holds in the case of Markov modulated arrivals. In a parallel work [22] to ours, the authors adopt a network calculus approach to derive stochastic bounds in a non-blocking FJ system, under a strong assumption on the input; for related constructions of such arrival models see [18].

Concerning concrete applications of FJ systems, in particular MapReduce, there are several empirical and analytical studies analyzing its performance. For instance, [39, 2] aim to improve the system performance via empirically adjusting its numerous and highly complex parameters. The targeted performance metric in these studies is the job response time, which is in fact an integral part of the business model of MapReduce based query systems such as [27] and time priced computing clouds such as Amazon's EC2 [1]. For an overview on works that optimize the performance of MapReduce systems see the survey article [28]. Using a similar idea as in [4], the authors of [32] derive asymptotic results on the response time distribution in the case of renewal arrivals; such results are further used to understand the impact of different scheduling models in the reduce phase of MapReduce. Using the model from [32] the work in [33] provides approximations for the number of jobs in a tandem system consisting of a map queue and a reduce queue in the heavy traffic regime. The work in [36] derives approximations of the mean response time in MapReduce systems using a mean value analysis technique and a closed FJ queueing system model from [34].

Concerning multipath routing, the works [3, 17] provided ground for multiple studies on different formulations of the underlying resequencing delay problem, e.g., [16, 38]. Factorization methods were used in [3] to analyze the disordering delay and the delay of resequencing algorithms, while the authors of [17] conduct a queueing theoretic analysis of an M/G/∞ queue receiving a stream of numbered customers. In [16, 38] the multipath routing model comprises Bernoulli thinning of Poisson arrivals over N parallel queueing stations followed by a resequencing buffer. The work in [16] provides asymptotics on the conditional probability of the resequencing delay conditioned on the end-to-end delay for different service time distributions. For $N = 2$ and exponential interarrival and service times, [38] derives a large deviations result on the resequencing queue size. Our work differs from these works in that we consider a model of the basic operation of window-based transmission protocols over multipath routing, motivated by the emerging application of multipath TCP [30]. We point out, however, that we do not model the specific operation of any particular multipath transmission protocol. Instead, we analyze a generic multipath transmission protocol under simplifying assumptions, in order to provide a theoretical understanding of the overall response times comprised of both queueing and resequencing delays.

Relative to the existing literature, our key theoretical contribution is to provide *computable* and non-asymptotic bounds on the *distributions* of the steady-state waiting and response times under both *renewal* and *non-renewal* input in FJ systems. The consideration of non-renewal input is particularly relevant, given recent observations that job arrivals are subject to temporal correlations in production clusters. For instance, [10, 19] report that job, respectively, flow arrival traces in clusters running MapReduce exhibit various degrees of burstiness.

3. FJ SYSTEMS WITH RENEWAL INPUT

We consider a FJ queueing system as depicted in Figure 2. Jobs arrive at the input queue of the FJ system according to some point process with interarrival times t_i between the i and $i+1$ jobs. Each job i is split into N tasks that are mapped through a bijection to N servers. A task of job i that is serviced by some server n requires a random service time $x_{n,i}$. A job leaves the system when all of its tasks finish their executions, i.e., there is an underlying synchronization constraint on the output of the system. We assume that the families $\{t_i\}$ and $\{x_{n,i}\}$ are independent.

In the sequel we differentiate between two cases, i.e., *a*) non-blocking and *b*) blocking servers. The first case corresponds to workconserving servers, i.e., a server starts servicing a task of the next job (if available) immediately upon finishing the current task. In the latter case, a server that finishes servicing a task is blocked until the corresponding job leaves the system, i.e., until the last task of the current job completes its execution. This can be regarded as an additional synchronization constraint on the input of the system, i.e., all tasks of a job start receiving service simultaneously. We will next analyze *a*) and *b*) for renewal arrivals.

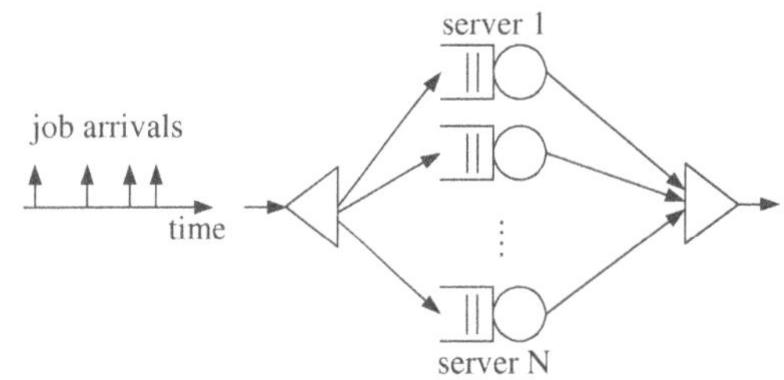

Figure 2: A schematic Fork-Join queueing system with N parallel servers. An arriving job is split into N tasks, one for each server. A job leaves the FJ system when all of its tasks are served. An arriving job is considered waiting until the service of the last of its tasks starts, i.e., when the previous job departs the system.

3.1 Non-Blocking Systems

Consider an arrival flow of jobs with renewal interarrival times t_i, and assume that the waiting time of the first job is $w_1 = 0$. Given N parallel servers, the *waiting time* w_j of the jth job is defined as

$$w_j = \max\left\{0, \max_{1\le k\le j-1}\left\{\max_{n\in[1,N]}\left\{\sum_{i=1}^{k} x_{n,j-i} - \sum_{i=1}^{k} t_{j-i}\right\}\right\}\right\}, \tag{1}$$

for all $j \ge 2$, where $x_{n,j}$ is the service time required by the task of job j that is mapped to server n. We count a job as waiting until its last task starts receiving service. Similarly, the *response times* of jobs, i.e., the times until the last corresponding tasks have finished their executions, are defined as $r_1 = \max_n x_{n,1}$ for the first job, and for $j \ge 2$ as

$$r_j = \max_{0\le k\le j-1}\left\{\max_{n\in[1,N]}\left\{\sum_{i=0}^{k} x_{n,j-i} - \sum_{i=1}^{k} t_{j-i}\right\}\right\}, \tag{2}$$

where by convention $\sum_{i=1}^{0} t_i = 0$; for brevity, we will denote $\max_n := \max_{n\in[1,N]}$.

We assume that the task service times $x_{n,j}$ are independent and identically distributed (iid). The stability condition for the FJ queueing system is given as $\mathsf{E}[x_{1,1}] < \mathsf{E}[t_1]$. By stationarity and reversibility of the iid processes $x_{n,j}$ and t_j, there exists a distribution of the steady-state waiting time w and steady-state response time r, respectively, which have the representations

$$w =_{\mathcal{D}} \max_{k\ge 0}\left\{\max_{n}\left\{\sum_{i=1}^{k} x_{n,i} - \sum_{i=1}^{k} t_i\right\}\right\} \tag{3}$$

and

$$r =_{\mathcal{D}} \max_{k\ge 0}\left\{\max_{n}\left\{\sum_{i=0}^{k} x_{n,i} - \sum_{i=1}^{k} t_i\right\}\right\}, \tag{4}$$

respectively. Here, $=_{\mathcal{D}}$ denotes equality in distribution. Note that the only difference in (3) and (4) is that for the latter the sum over the $x_{n,i}$ starts at $i = 0$ rather than at $i = 1$.

The following theorem provides stochastic upper bounds on w and r. The corresponding proof will rely on submartingale constructions and the Optional Sampling Theorem (see Lemma 6 in the Appendix).

THEOREM 1. (RENEWALS, NON-BLOCKING) *Given a FJ system with N parallel non-blocking servers that is fed by renewal job arrivals with interarrivals t_j. If the task service times $x_{n,j}$ are iid, then the steady-state waiting and response times w and r are bounded by*

$$\mathsf{P}[w \geq \sigma] \leq Ne^{-\theta_{nb}\sigma} \tag{5}$$

$$\mathsf{P}[r \geq \sigma] \leq N\mathsf{E}\left[e^{\theta_{nb}x_{1,1}}\right]e^{-\theta_{nb}\sigma} , \tag{6}$$

where θ_{nb} (with the subscript 'nb' standing for non-blocking) is the (positive) solution of

$$\mathsf{E}\left[e^{\theta x_{1,1}}\right]\mathsf{E}\left[e^{-\theta t_1}\right] = 1 . \tag{7}$$

We remark that the stability condition $\mathsf{E}[x_{1,1}] < \mathsf{E}[t_1]$ guarantees the existence of a positive solution in (7) (see also [29]).

PROOF. Consider the waiting time w. We first prove that for each $n \in [1, N]$ the process

$$z_n(k) = e^{\theta_{nb}\sum_{i=1}^{k}(x_{n,i}-t_i)}$$

is a martingale with respect to the filtration

$$\mathcal{F}_k := \sigma\{x_{n,m}, t_m \mid m \leq k, n \in [1, N]\} .$$

The independence assumption of $x_{n,j}$ and t_j implies that

$$\begin{aligned}
\mathsf{E}[z_n(k) \mid \mathcal{F}_{k-1}] &= \mathsf{E}\left[e^{\theta_{nb}\sum_{i=1}^{k}(x_{n,i}-t_i)} \,\middle|\, \mathcal{F}_{k-1}\right] \\
&= \mathsf{E}\left[e^{\theta_{nb}(x_{n,k}-t_k)}\right]e^{\theta_{nb}\sum_{i=1}^{k-1}(x_{n,i}-t_i)} \\
&= e^{\theta_{nb}\sum_{i=1}^{k-1}(x_{n,i}-t_i)} \\
&= z_n(k-1) , \qquad (8)
\end{aligned}$$

under the condition on θ_{nb} from the theorem. Moreover, $z_n(k)$ is obviously integrable by the condition on θ_{nb} from the theorem, completing thus the proof for the martingale property.

Next we prove that the process

$$z(k) = \max_n z_n(k) \tag{9}$$

is a submartingale w.r.t. $\mathcal{F}_k$. Given the martingale property of each of the z_n and the monotonicity of the conditional expectation we can write for $j \in [1, N]$:

$$\mathsf{E}\left[\max_n z_n(k) \,\middle|\, \mathcal{F}_{k-1}\right] \geq \mathsf{E}[z_j(k) \mid \mathcal{F}_{k-1}] = z_j(k-1) ,$$

where the inequality stems from $\max_n z_n(k) \geq z_j(k)$ for $j \in [1, N]$ a.s., whereas the subsequent equality stems from the martingale property (8) for $z_n(k)$ for all $n \in [1, N]$. Hence we can write

$$\mathsf{E}[z(k) \mid \mathcal{F}_{k-1}] \geq \max_n z_n(k-1) = z(k-1) , \tag{10}$$

which proves the submartingale property.

To derive a bound on the steady-state waiting time distribution, let $\sigma > 0$ and define the stopping time

$$K := \inf\left\{k \geq 0 \,\middle|\, \max_n \sum_{i=1}^{k}(x_{n,i} - t_i) \geq \sigma\right\} , \tag{11}$$

which is also the first point in time k where $z(k) \geq e^{\theta_{nb}\sigma}$. Note that with the representation of w from (3):

$$\{K < \infty\} = \{w \geq \sigma\} .$$

Now, using the Optional Sampling Theorem (see Lemma 6 from the Appendix) for submartingales with $k \geq 1$:

$$\begin{aligned}
N &= \sum_{n\in[1,N]} \mathsf{E}\left[e^{\theta_{nb}\sum_{i=1}^{k}(x_{n,i}-t_i)}\right] \\
&\geq \mathsf{E}\left[\max_n e^{\theta_{nb}\sum_{i=1}^{k}(x_{n,i}-t_i)}\right] \qquad (12) \\
&= \mathsf{E}[z(k)] \geq \mathsf{E}[z(K \wedge k)] \geq \mathsf{E}[z(K)1_{K<k}] \\
&\geq e^{\theta_{nb}\sigma}\mathsf{P}[K < k] ,
\end{aligned}$$

where we used the condition on θ_{nb} from the theorem in the first line, the union bound in the second line, and the submartingale property in the third line. In the last line we used the definition of the stopping time K; note that we use the notation $K \wedge n := \min\{K, n\}$. The proof completes by letting $k \to \infty$.

For the response time r, define the processes

$$\tilde{z}_n(k) = e^{\theta_{nb}\left(\sum_{i=0}^{k}x_{n,i} - \sum_{i=1}^{k}t_i\right)} ,$$

which differs from the z_n only in the range of the sum of the service times $x_{n,i}$. Then we proceed as for the derivation of the bound on the waiting time w. The only difference in the derivation is that inequality (12) translates to

$$N\mathsf{E}\left[e^{\theta_{nb}x_{1,1}}\right] \geq \mathsf{E}\left[\max_n e^{\theta_{nb}\left(\sum_{i=0}^{k}x_{n,i} - \sum_{i=1}^{k}t_i\right)}\right] .$$

□

Fixing the right hand sides in (5) and (6) to ε, we find that the corresponding quantiles on the waiting and response times grow with the number of parallel servers N as $\mathcal{O}(\log N)$, a law which was already demonstrated in the special case of Poisson arrival and exponential service times, and for first moments, in [26], and more generally in [4]. This scaling result is essential for dimensioning FJ systems such as MapReduce computing clusters, as it explains the impact of a MapReduce server pool size N on the job waiting/response times.

We note that the bound in Theorem 1 can be computed for different arrival and service time distributions as long as the MGF (moment generating function) and Laplace transform from (7) are computable. Given a scenario where the job interarrival process and the task size distributions in a MapReduce cluster are not known a priori, estimates of the corresponding MGF and Laplace transforms can be obtained using recorded traces, e.g., using the method from [15].

Next we illustrate two immediate applications of Theorem 1.

Example 1: Exponentially distributed interarrival and service times

Consider that the interarrival times t_i and service times $x_{n,i}$ are exponentially distributed with parameters λ and μ, respectively; note that when $N = 1$ the system corresponds to the M/M/1 queue. The corresponding stability condition becomes $\mu > \lambda$. Using Theorem 1, the bounds on the steady-state waiting and response time distributions are

$$\mathsf{P}[w \geq \sigma] \leq Ne^{-(\mu-\lambda)\sigma} \tag{13}$$

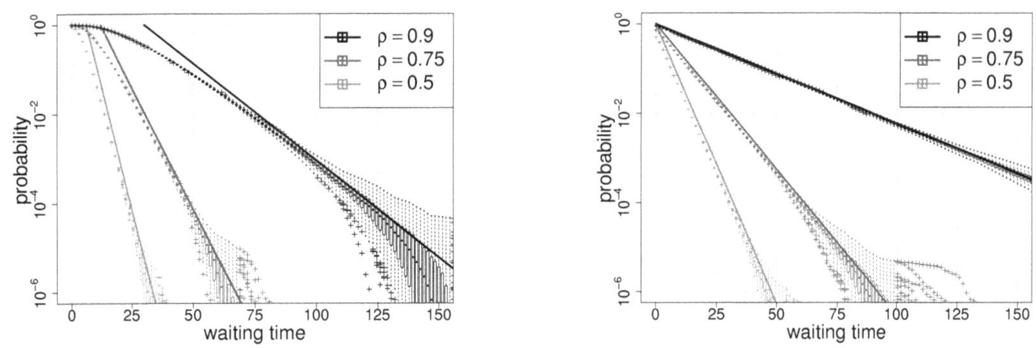

(a) Non-Blocking

(b) Blocking

Figure 3: Bounds on the waiting time distributions vs. simulations (renewal input): (a) the non-blocking case (13) and (b) the blocking case (22). The system parameters are $N = 20$, $\mu = 1$, and three utilization levels $\rho = \{0.9, 0.75, 0.5\}$ (from top to bottom). Simulations include 100 runs, each accounting for 10^7 slots.

and

$$\mathsf{P}[r \geq \sigma] \leq \frac{N}{\rho} e^{-(\mu-\lambda)\sigma} , \tag{14}$$

where the exponential decay rate $\mu - \lambda$ follows by solving $\frac{\mu}{\mu-\theta}\frac{\lambda}{\lambda+\theta} = 1$, i.e., the instantiation of (7).

Next we briefly compare our results to the existing bound on the mean response time from [4], given as

$$\mathsf{E}[r] \leq \frac{1}{\mu-\lambda}\sum_{n=1}^{N}\frac{1}{n} . \tag{15}$$

By integrating the tail of (14) we obtain the following upper bound on the mean response time

$$\mathsf{E}[r] \leq \frac{\log(N/\rho)+1}{\mu-\lambda} .$$

Compared to (15), our bound exhibits the same $\log N$ scaling law but is numerically slightly looser; asymptotically in N, the ratio between the two bounds converges to one. A key technical reason for obtaining a looser bound is that we mainly focus on deriving bounds on distributions; through integration, the numerical discrepancies accumulate.

For the numerical illustration of the tightness of the bounds on the waiting time distributions from (13) we refer to Figure 3.(a); the numerical parameters and simulation details are included in the caption.

Example 2: Exponentially distributed interarrival times and constant service times

We now consider the case of iid exponentially distributed interarrival times t_i with parameter λ, and deterministic service times $x_{n,i} = 1/\mu$, for all $i \geq 0$ and $n \in [1, N]$; note that when $N = 1$ the system corresponds to the M/D/1 queue.

The condition on the asymptotic decay rate θ_{nb} from Theorem 1 becomes

$$\frac{\lambda}{\lambda+\theta_{nb}} = e^{-\frac{\theta_{nb}}{\mu}} ,$$

which can be numerically solved; upper bounds on the waiting and response time distributions follow then immediately from Theorem 1.

3.2 Blocking Systems

Here we consider a blocking FJ queueing system, i.e., the start of each job is synchronized amongst all servers. We maintain the iid assumptions on the interarrival times t_i and service times $x_{n,i}$. The waiting time and response time for the jth job can then be written as

$$w_j = \max\left\{0, \max_{1\leq k\leq j-1}\left\{\sum_{i=1}^{k}\max_n x_{n,j-i} - \sum_{i=1}^{k} t_{j-i}\right\}\right\}$$

$$r_j = \max_{0\leq k\leq j-1}\left\{\sum_{i=0}^{k}\max_n x_{n,j-i} - \sum_{i=1}^{k} t_{j-i}\right\} .$$

Note that the only difference to (1) and (2) is that the maximum over the number of servers now occurs inside the sum.

It is evident that the blocking system is more conservative than the non-blocking system in the sense that the waiting time distribution of the non-blocking system is dominated by the waiting time distribution of the blocking system. Moreover, the stability region for the blocking system, given by $\mathsf{E}[t_1] > \mathsf{E}[\max_n x_{n,1}]$, is included in the stability region of the corresponding non-blocking system (i.e., $\mathsf{E}[t_1] > \mathsf{E}[x_{1,1}]$).

Analogously to (3), the steady-state waiting and response times w and r have now the representations

$$w =_{\mathcal{D}} \max_{k\geq 0}\left\{\sum_{i=1}^{k}\max_n x_{n,i} - \sum_{i=1}^{k} t_i\right\} \tag{16}$$

$$r =_{\mathcal{D}} \max_{k\geq 0}\left\{\sum_{i=0}^{k}\max_n x_{n,i} - \sum_{i=1}^{k} t_i\right\} . \tag{17}$$

The following theorem provides upper bounds on w and r.

THEOREM 2. (RENEWALS, BLOCKING) *Given a FJ queueing system with N parallel blocking servers that is fed by renewal job arrivals with interarrivals t_j and iid task service times $x_{n,j}$. The distributions of the steady-state waiting and response times are bounded by*

$$\begin{aligned} \mathsf{P}[w \geq \sigma] &\leq e^{-\theta_b \sigma} \\ \mathsf{P}[r \geq \sigma] &\leq \mathsf{E}\left[e^{\theta_b x_{1,1}}\right] e^{-\theta_b \sigma} , \end{aligned} \tag{18}$$

where θ_b (with the subscript 'b' standing for blocking) is the (positive) solution of

$$\mathsf{E}\left[e^{\theta \max_n x_{n,1}}\right] \mathsf{E}\left[e^{-\theta t_1}\right] = 1 \ . \qquad (19)$$

Before giving the proof we note that, in general, (19) can be numerically solved. Moreover, for small values of N, θ_b can be analytically solved.

PROOF. Consider the waiting time w. We proceed similarly as in the proof of Theorem 1. Letting $\mathcal{F}_k$ as above, we first prove that the process

$$y(k) = e^{\theta_b \sum_{i=1}^{k} (\max_n x_{n,i} - t_i)}$$

is a martingale w.r.t. $\mathcal{F}_k$ using a technique from [23]. We write

$$\begin{aligned}
\mathsf{E}\left[y(k) \mid \mathcal{F}_{k-1}\right] &= \mathsf{E}\left[e^{\theta_b \sum_{i=1}^{k} (\max_n x_{n,i} - t_i)} \,\Big|\, \mathcal{F}_{k-1}\right] \\
&= e^{\theta_b \sum_{i=1}^{k-1} (\max_n x_{n,i} - t_i)} \mathsf{E}\left[e^{\theta_b (\max_n x_{n,k} - t_k)}\right] \\
&= e^{\theta_b \sum_{i=1}^{k-1} (\max_n x_{n,i} - t_i)} \\
&= y(k-1) \ ,
\end{aligned}$$

where we used the independence and renewal assumptions for $x_{n,i}$ and t_i in the second line, and finally the condition on θ_b from (19).

In the next step we apply the Optional Sampling Theorem (37) to derive the bound from the theorem. We first define the stopping time K by

$$K := \inf\left\{ k \geq 0 \,\Bigg|\, \sum_{i=1}^{k} \left(\max_n x_{n,i} - t_i\right) \geq \sigma \right\} \ . \qquad (20)$$

Recall that $\mathsf{P}[K < \infty] = \mathsf{P}[w \geq \sigma]$. We can next write for every $k \in \mathbb{N}$

$$\begin{aligned}
1 &= \mathsf{E}\left[y(0)\right] \\
&= \mathsf{E}\left[y(K \wedge k)\right] \\
&\geq \mathsf{E}\left[y(K \wedge k) 1_{K<k}\right] \\
&= \mathsf{E}\left[e^{\theta_b \sum_{i=1}^{K} (\max_n x_{n,i} - t_i)} 1_{K<k}\right] \\
&\geq e^{\theta_b \sigma} \mathsf{P}\left[K < k\right] \ .
\end{aligned}$$

Taking $k \to \infty$ completes the proof. The proof for the response time r is analogous. □

Example 3: Exponentially distributed interarrival and service times

Consider interarrival and service times t_i and $x_{n,i}$ that are exponentially distributed with parameters λ and μ, respectively. In [31] it was shown that

$$\max_n L_n =_{\mathcal{D}} \sum_{n=1}^{N} \frac{L_n}{n}$$

for iid exponentially distributed random variables L_n, so that the stability condition $\mathsf{E}[t_1] > \mathsf{E}[\max_n x_{n,1}]$ becomes

$$\frac{1}{\lambda} > \frac{1}{\mu} \sum_{n=1}^{N} \frac{1}{n} \ . \qquad (21)$$

By applying Theorem 2, the bounds on the steady-state waiting and response time distributions are

$$\mathsf{P}\left[w \geq \sigma\right] \leq e^{-\theta_b \sigma} \qquad (22)$$

and

$$\mathsf{P}\left[r \geq \sigma\right] \leq \frac{\mu}{\mu - \theta_b} e^{-\theta_b \sigma} \ ,$$

where θ_b can be numerically solved from the condition

$$\prod_{n=1}^{N} \frac{n\mu}{n\mu - \theta_b} \frac{\lambda}{\lambda + \theta_b} = 1 \ .$$

For quick numerical illustrations we refer back to Figure 3.(b).

The interesting observation is that the stability condition from (21) depends on the number of servers N. In particular, as the right hand side grows in $\log N$, the system becomes unstable (i.e., waiting times are infinite) for sufficiently large N. This shows that the optional blocking mode from Hadoop should be judiciously enabled.

Example 4: Exponentially distributed interarrival and constant times

If the service times are deterministic, i.e., $x_{n,i} = 1/\mu$ for all $i \geq 0$ and $n \in [1, N]$, the representations of w and r from (16) and (17) match their non-blocking counterparts from (3) and (4) and hence the corresponding stability regions and stochastic bounds are equal to those from Example 2.

4. FJ SYSTEMS WITH NON-RENEWAL INPUT

In this section we consider the more realistic case of FJ queueing systems with non-renewal job arrivals. This model is particularly relevant given the empirical evidence that clusters running MapReduce exhibit various degrees of burstiness in the input [10, 19]. Moreover, numerous studies have demonstrated the burstiness of Internet traces, which can be regarded in particular as the input to multipath routing.

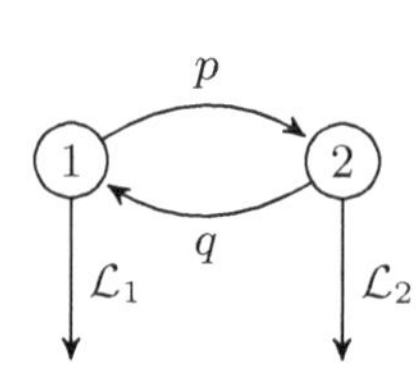

Figure 4: Markov modulating chain c_k for the job interarrival times.

We model the interarrival times t_i using a Markov modulated process. Concretely, consider a two-state modulating Markov chain c_k, as depicted in Figure 4, with a transition matrix T given by

$$T = \begin{pmatrix} 1-p & p \\ q & 1-q \end{pmatrix} \ , \qquad (23)$$

for some values $0 < p, q < 1$. In state $i \in \{1, 2\}$ the interarrival times are given by iid random variables L_i with distribution $\mathcal{L}_i$. Without loss of generality we assume that L_1 is stochastically smaller than L_2, i.e.,

$$\mathsf{P}\left[L_1 \geq t\right] \leq \mathsf{P}\left[L_2 \geq t\right] \ ,$$

for any $t \geq 0$. Additionally, we assume that the Markov chain c_k satisfies the burstiness condition

$$p < 1 - q \ , \qquad (24)$$

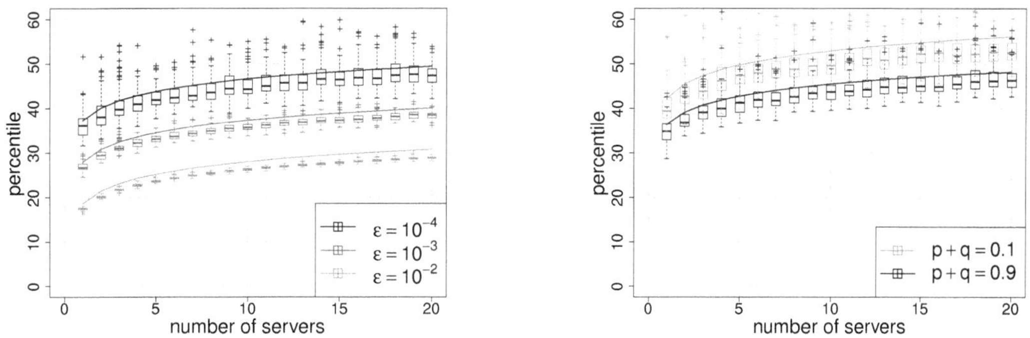

(a) Impact of ε

(b) Impact of the burstiness factor $p+q$

Figure 5: The $\mathcal{O}(\log N)$ scaling of waiting time percentiles w^ε for Markov modulated input (the non-blocking case (25)). The system parameters are $\mu = 1$, $\lambda_2 = 0.9$, $\rho = 0.75$ (in both (a) and (b)) $p = 0.1$, $q = 0.4$ (in (a)), three violation probabilities ε (in (a)), $\varepsilon = 10^{-4}$ and only two burstiness parameters $p+q$ (in (b)) (for visual convenience). Simulations include 100 runs, each accounting for 10^7 slots.

i.e., the probability of jumping to a different state is less than the probability of staying in the same state.

Subsequent derivations will exploit the following exponential transform of the transition matrix T defined as

$$T_\theta := \begin{pmatrix} (1-p)\,\mathsf{E}\left[e^{-\theta L_1}\right] & p\ \ \mathsf{E}\left[e^{-\theta L_2}\right] \\ q\ \ \mathsf{E}\left[e^{-\theta L_1}\right] & (1-q)\,\mathsf{E}\left[e^{-\theta L_2}\right] \end{pmatrix} ,$$

for some $\theta > 0$. Let $\Lambda(\theta)$ denote the maximal positive eigenvalue of T_θ, and the vector $h = (h(1), h(2))$ denote a corresponding eigenvector. By the Perron-Frobenius Theorem, $\Lambda(\theta)$ is equal to the spectral radius of T_θ such that h can be chosen with strictly positive components.

As in the case of renewal arrivals, we will next analyze both non-blocking and blocking FJ systems.

4.1 Non-Blocking Systems

We first analyze a non-blocking FJ system fed with arrivals that are modulated by a stationary Markov chain as in Figure 4. We assume that the task service times $x_{n,j}$ are iid and that the families $\{t_i\}$ and $\{x_{n,i}\}$ are independent. Note that both the definition of w_j from (1) and the representation of the steady-state waiting time w in (3) remain valid, due to stationarity and reversibility; the same holds for the response times.

The next theorem provides upper bounds on the steady-state waiting and response time distributions in the non-blocking scenario with Markov modulated interarrivals.

THEOREM 3. (NON-RENEWALS, NON-BLOCKING) *Given a FJ queueing system with N parallel non-blocking servers, Markov modulated job interarrivals t_j according to the Markov chain depicted in Figure 4 with transition matrix (23), and iid task service times $x_{n,j}$. The steady-state waiting and response time distributions are bounded by*

$$\mathsf{P}[w \geq \sigma] \;\leq\; N e^{-\theta_{nb}\sigma} \qquad (25)$$

$$\mathsf{P}[r \geq \sigma] \;\leq\; N\,\mathsf{E}\left[e^{\theta_{nb} x_{1,1}}\right] e^{-\theta_{nb}\sigma} , \qquad (26)$$

where θ_{nb} is the (positive) solution of

$$\mathsf{E}\left[e^{\theta x_{1,1}}\right]\Lambda(\theta) = 1 .$$

(Recall that $\Lambda(\theta)$ was defined as a spectral radius.)

We remark that the existence of a positive solution θ_{nb} is guaranteed by the Perron-Frobenius Theorem, see, e.g., [29].

PROOF. Consider the filtration

$$\mathcal{F}_k := \sigma\left\{x_{n,m}, t_m, c_m \,|\, m \leq k, n \in [1,N]\right\} ,$$

that includes information about the state c_k of the Markov chain. Now, we construct the process $z(k)$ as

$$\begin{aligned} z(k) &= h(c_k) e^{\theta_{nb}\left(\max_n \sum_{i=1}^k x_{n,i} - \sum_{i=1}^k t_i\right)} \\ &= \left(e^{\theta_{nb}\left(\max_n \sum_{i=1}^k x_{n,i} - kD\right)}\right)\left(h(c_k) e^{\theta_{nb}\left(kD - \sum_{i=1}^k t_i\right)}\right) \end{aligned} \qquad (27)$$

with the deterministic parameter

$$D := \theta_{nb}^{-1} \log\left(\mathsf{E}\left[e^{\theta_{nb} x_{1,1}}\right]\right) .$$

Note the similarity of $z(k)$ to (9) except for the additional function h. Roughly, the function h captures the correlation structure of the non-renewal interarrival time process.

Next we show that both terms of (27) are submartingales. In the first step we note that by the definition of D:

$$\mathsf{E}\left[e^{\theta_{nb}\left(\sum_{i=1}^k x_{n,i} - kD\right)} \,\middle|\, \mathcal{F}_{k-1}\right] = e^{\theta_{nb}\left(\sum_{i=1}^{k-1} x_{n,i} - (k-1)D\right)} ,$$

hence, following the line of argument in (10) the left factor of (27), which accounts for the additional $\max_n$, is a submartingale. The second step is similar to the derivations in [9, 13]. First, note that

$$\begin{aligned} \mathsf{E}\left[h(c_k) e^{\theta_{nb}(D - t_k)} \,\middle|\, \mathcal{F}_{k-1}\right] &= e^{\theta_{nb} D} T_{\theta_{nb}} h(c_{k-1}) \\ &= e^{\theta_{nb} D} \Lambda(\theta_{nb}) h(c_{k-1}) \\ &= h(c_{k-1}) , \end{aligned} \qquad (28)$$

where the last line is due to the definitions of D and θ_{nb}. Now, multiplying both sides of (28) by $e^{\theta_{nb}\left((k-1)D - \sum_{i=1}^{k-1} t_i\right)}$ proves the martingale and hence the submartingale property of the right factor in (27). As the process $z(k)$ is a product of two independent submartingales, it is a submartingale itself w.r.t. $\mathcal{F}_k$.

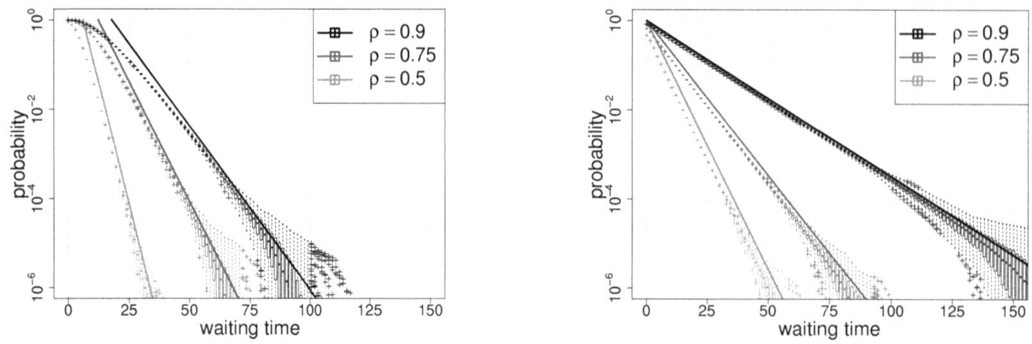

(a) Non-Blocking (b) Blocking

Figure 6: Bounds on the waiting time distributions vs. simulations (non-renewal input): (a) the non-blocking case (25) and (b) the blocking case (31). The parameters are $N = 20, \mu = 1, p = 0.1, q = 0.4, \lambda_1 \in \{0.4, 0.72, 0.72\}$ and $\lambda_2 \in \{0.9, 0.9, 1.62\}$ leading to utilizations $\rho \in \{0.5, 0.75, 0.9\}$. Simulations include 100 runs, each accounting for 10^7 slots.

Next we derive a bound on the steady-state waiting time distribution using the Optional Stopping Theorem. Here we use the stopping time K defined in (11). Recall that $\mathsf{P}[K < \infty] = \mathsf{P}[w \geq \sigma]$. On the one hand we can write for every $k \in \mathbb{N}$

$$\begin{aligned} \mathsf{E}[z(k)] &\geq \mathsf{E}[z(K \wedge k)] \\ &\geq \mathsf{E}[z(K \wedge k) 1_{K<k}] \\ &= \mathsf{E}\left[\max_n h(c_K) e^{\theta_{nb}\left(\sum_{i=1}^K x_{n,i} - \sum_{i=1}^K t_i\right)} 1_{K<k}\right] \\ &\geq e^{\theta_{nb}\sigma} \mathsf{E}[h(c_K) 1_{K<k}] \\ &= e^{\theta_{nb}\sigma} \mathsf{E}[h(c_K) \mid K < k] \, \mathsf{P}[K < k] \ . \end{aligned} \quad (29)$$

On the other hand we can upper bound the term

$$\begin{aligned} \mathsf{E}[z(k)] &= \mathsf{E}\left[\max_n e^{\theta_{nb}\left(\sum_{i=1}^k x_{n,i} - kD\right)}\right] \mathsf{E}\left[h(c_k) e^{\theta_{nb}\left(kD - \sum_{i=1}^k t_i\right)}\right] \\ &\leq N \mathsf{E}[h(c_1)] \ . \end{aligned}$$

Letting $k \to \infty$ in (29) leads to

$$\mathsf{P}[K < \infty] \leq \frac{\mathsf{E}[h(c_1)]}{\mathsf{E}[h(c_K) \mid K < \infty]} N e^{-\theta_{nb}\sigma} \ . \quad (30)$$

In Lemma 7 it is shown that the distribution of the random variable $(c_K \mid K < k)$ is stochastically smaller than the stationary distribution of the Markov chain. Given the burstiness condition in (24) and that the function h is monotonically decreasing [8], we can further upper bound the prefactor in (30) as

$$\frac{\mathsf{E}[h(c_1)]}{\mathsf{E}[h(c_K) \mid K < \infty]} \leq 1 \ ,$$

which completes the proof. The proof for the response time r is analogous. □

Remark: Note that, if the burstiness condition (24) is not fulfilled then we can still upper bound the prefactor in (30) using the trivial upper bound

$$\frac{\mathsf{E}[h(c_1)]}{\mathsf{E}[h(c_K) \mid K < \infty]} \leq \frac{\mathsf{E}[h(c_1)]}{\min_k h(c_k)} \ .$$

Figure 5 displays the bounds on the waiting time percentiles w^ε, for various violation probabilities ε, in the FJ system with non-renewal input. The bounds closely match the corresponding simulation results, shown as box-plots, while also exhibiting the $\mathcal{O}(\log N)$ scaling behavior (which can be also derived from both (25) and (26), as in Section 3).

4.2 Blocking Systems

Now we turn to the blocking variant of the FJ system that is fed by the same non-renewal arrivals as in the previous section. Without loss of generality we consider exponential distributions $\mathcal{L}_m$ for $m \in [1, 2]$. The main result is:

THEOREM 4. (NON-RENEWALS, BLOCKING) *Given a FJ system with N blocking servers, Markov modulated job interarrivals t_j, and iid task service times $x_{n,j}$. The steady-state waiting and response time distributions are bounded by*

$$\begin{aligned} \mathsf{P}[w \geq \sigma] &\leq e^{-\theta_b \sigma} \\ \mathsf{P}[r \geq \sigma] &\leq \mathsf{E}\left[e^{\theta_b x_{1,1}}\right] e^{-\theta_b \sigma} \ , \end{aligned} \quad (31)$$

where θ_b is the (positive) solution of

$$\mathsf{E}\left[e^{\theta \max_n x_{n,1}}\right] \Lambda(\theta) = 1 \ .$$

We remark that the positive solution for θ_b is guaranteed under the stronger stability condition $\mathsf{E}[t_1] > \mathsf{E}[\max_n x_{n,1}]$ and the Perron-Frobenius Theorem.

PROOF. Let $D := \theta_b^{-1} \log \mathsf{E}\left[e^{\theta_b \max_n x_{n,1}}\right]$ and define the process y by:

$$\begin{aligned} y(k) &= h(c_k) e^{\theta_b\left(\sum_{i=1}^k \max_n x_{n,i} - \sum_{i=1}^k t_i\right)} \\ &= \left(e^{\theta_b\left(\sum_{i=1}^k \max_n x_{n,i} - kD\right)}\right)\left(h(c_k) e^{\theta_b\left(kD - \sum_{i=1}^k t_i\right)}\right) \ . \end{aligned}$$

Similarly to the proofs of Theorem 2 and Theorem 3 one can show that both the first and second factor of y are martingales, and hence y is a martingale. We use the stopping time K in (20) and write

$$\begin{aligned} \mathsf{E}[h(c_1)] &= \mathsf{E}[y(0)] \\ &\geq \mathsf{E}[y(K \wedge k)] \\ &\geq \mathsf{E}[y(K \wedge k) 1_{K<k}] \\ &= \mathsf{E}\left[e^{\theta_b\left(\sum_{i=1}^K \max_n x_{n,i} - \sum_{i=1}^K t_i\right)} h(c_K) 1_{K<k}\right] \\ &\geq e^{\theta_b \sigma} \mathsf{E}[h(c_K) \mid K < \infty] \, \mathsf{P}[K < k] \ . \end{aligned}$$

Taking $k \to \infty$ we obtain the bound

$$\mathsf{P}[K < \infty] \le \frac{\mathsf{E}[h(c_1)]}{\mathsf{E}[h(c_K) \mid K < \infty]} e^{-\theta_b \sigma} \le e^{-\theta_b \sigma} ,$$

where we used Lemma 7 for the last inequality. The proof for r is analogous. □

A close comparison of the waiting time bound in the non-renewal case (31) to the corresponding bound in the renewal case (18) reveals that the decay factors θ_b depend on similar conditions, whereby the MGF of the interarrival times in (18) is replaced by the spectral radius of the modulating Markov chain in (31). Moreover, given the ergodicity of the underlying Markov chain, the blocking system with non-renewal input is subject to the same degrading stability region (in $\log N$) as in the renewal case (recall (21)).

For quick numerical illustrations of the tightness of the bounds on the waiting time distributions in both the non-blocking and blocking cases we refer to Figure 6.

So far we have contributed stochastic bounds on the steady-state waiting and response time distributions in FJ systems fed with either renewal and non-renewal job arrivals. The key technical insight was that the stochastic bounds in the non-blocking model grow as $\mathcal{O}(\log N)$ in the number of parallel servers N under non-renewal arrivals, which extends a known result for renewal arrivals [26, 4]. The same fundamental factor of $\log N$ was shown to drive the stability region in the blocking model. A concrete application follows next.

5. APPLICATION TO WINDOW-BASED PROTOCOLS OVER MULTIPATH ROUTING

In this section we slightly adapt and use the non-blocking FJ queueing system from Section 3.1 to analyze the performance of a *generic* window-based transmission protocol over multipath routing. While this problem has attracted much interest lately with the emergence of multipath TCP [30], it is subject to a major difficulty due to the likely overtaking of packets on different paths. Consequently, packets have to additionally wait for a *resequencing delay*, which directly corresponds to the synchronization constraint in FJ systems. We note that the employed FJ non-blocking model is subject to a convenient simplification, i.e., each path is modelled by a single server/queue only.

As depicted in Figure 7, we consider an arrival flow containing l batches of N packets, with $l \in \mathbb{N}$, at the fork node A. In practice, a *packet* as denoted here may represent an entire train of consecutive datagrams. The incoming packets are sent over multiple paths to the destination node B, where they need to be eventually reordered. We assume that the batch size corresponds to the transmission window size of the protocol, such that one packet traverses a single path only. For example, the first path transmits the packets $\{1, N+1, 2N+1, \dots\}$, i.e., packets are distributed in a round-robin fashion over the N paths. We also assume that packets on each path are delivered in a (locally-)FIFO order, i.e., there is no overtaking on the same path.

In analogy to Section 3.1, we consider a batch waiting until its last packet starts being transmitted. When the transmission of the last packet of batch j begins, the previous batch has already been received, i.e., all packets of the batch $j-1$ are *in order* at node B.

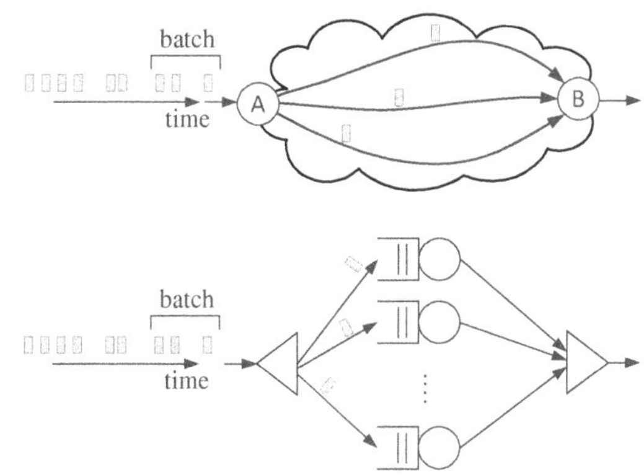

Figure 7: A schematic description of the window-based transmission over multipath routing; each path is modelled as a single server/queue.

We are interested in the response times of the batches, which are upper bounded by the largest response time of the packets therein. The arrival time of a batch is defined as the latest arrival time of the packets therein, i.e., when the batch is entirely received. Formally, the response time of batch $j \in \{lN+1 \mid l \in \mathbb{N}\}$ can be given by slightly modifying (2), i.e.,

$$r_j = \max_{0 \le k \le j-1} \left\{ \max_n \left\{ \sum_{i=0}^{k} x_{n,j-i} - \sum_{i=1}^{k} t_{n,j-i} \right\} \right\} .$$

The corresponding steady-state response time has the modified representation

$$r =_{\mathcal{D}} \max_{k \ge 0} \left\{ \max_n \left\{ \sum_{i=0}^{k} x_{n,i} - \sum_{i=1}^{k} t_{n,i} \right\} \right\} .$$

The modifications account for the fact that the packets of each batch are asynchronously transmitted on the corresponding paths (instead, in the basic FJ systems, the tasks of each job are simultaneously mapped). In terms of notations, the $t_{n,i}$'s now denote the interarrival times of the packets transmitted over the same path n, whereas $x_{n,i}$'s are iid and denote the transmission time of packet i over path n; as an example, when the arrival flow at node A is Poisson, $t_{n,i}$ has an Erlang E_N distribution for all n and i.

We next analyze the performance of the considered multipath routing for both renewal and non-renewal input.

Renewal Arrivals

Consider first the scenario with renewal interarrival times. Similarly to Section 3.1 we bound the distribution of the steady-state response time r using a submartingale in the time domain $j \in \{lN+1 | l \in \mathbb{N}\}$. Following the same steps as in Theorem 1, the process

$$z_n(k) = e^{\theta\left(\sum_{i=0}^{k} x_{n,i} - \sum_{i=1}^{k} t_{n,i}\right)}$$

is a martingale under the condition

$$\mathsf{E}\left[e^{\theta x_{1,1}}\right] \mathsf{E}\left[e^{-\theta t_{1,1}}\right] = 1 ,$$

where we used the filtration

$$\mathcal{F}_k := \sigma\{x_{n,m}, t_{n,m} | m \le k, n \in [1, N]\} .$$

Note that $\mathsf{E}\left[e^{-\theta t_{1,1}}\right]$ denotes the Laplace transform of the interarrival times of packets transmitted over each path. The proof that $\max_n z_n(k)$ is a submartingale follows a similar argument as in (10). Hence, we can bound the distribution of the steady-state response time as

$$\mathsf{P}\left[r \geq \sigma\right] \quad \leq \quad N\mathsf{E}\left[e^{\theta x_{1,1}}\right] e^{-\theta\sigma} \ , \qquad (32)$$

with the condition on θ from above.

Non-Renewal Arrivals

Next, consider a scenario with non-renewal interarrival times t_i of the packets arriving at the fork node A in Figure 7, as described in Section 4. On every path $n \in [1, N]$ the interarrivals are given by a sub-chain $(c_{n,k})_k$ that is driven by the N-step transition matrix $T^N = (\alpha_{i,j})_{i,j}$ for T given in (23). Similarly as in the proof of Theorem 3, we will use an exponential transform $(T^N)_\theta$ of the transition matrix that describes each path n, i.e.,

$$(T^N)_\theta := \begin{pmatrix} \alpha_{1,1}\beta_1 & \alpha_{1,2}\beta_2 \\ \alpha_{2,1}\beta_1 & \alpha_{2,2}\beta_2 \end{pmatrix} ,$$

with $\alpha_{i,j}$ defined above and β_1, β_2 being the elements of a vector β of conditional Laplace transforms of N consecutive interarrival times t_i. The vector β is given by

$$\beta := \begin{pmatrix} \beta_1 \\ \beta_2 \end{pmatrix} = \begin{pmatrix} \mathsf{E}\left[e^{-\theta \sum_{i=1}^{N} t_i} \,\middle|\, c_1 = 1\right] \\ \\ \mathsf{E}\left[e^{-\theta \sum_{i=1}^{N} t_i} \,\middle|\, c_1 = 2\right] \end{pmatrix} ,$$

and can be computed given the transition matrix T from (23) via an exponential row transform [9] (Example 7.2.7) denoted by

$$\tilde{T}_\theta := \begin{pmatrix} (1-p)\mathsf{E}\left[e^{-\theta L_1}\right] & p\mathsf{E}\left[e^{-\theta L_1}\right] \\ \\ q\mathsf{E}\left[e^{-\theta L_2}\right] & (1-q)\mathsf{E}\left[e^{-\theta L_2}\right] \end{pmatrix} ,$$

yielding $\beta = (\tilde{T}_\theta)^N \begin{pmatrix} 1 \\ 1 \end{pmatrix}$.

Denote $\Lambda(\theta)$ and $h = (h(1), h(2))$ as the maximal positive eigenvalue of the matrix $(T^N)_\theta$ and the corresponding right eigenvector, respectively. Mimicking the proof of Theorem 3, one can show for every path n that the process

$$z_n(k) = h(c_{n,k}) e^{\theta\left(\max_n \sum_{i=0}^{k} x_{n,i} - \sum_{i=1}^{k} t_{n,i}\right)}$$

is a martingale under the condition on (positive) θ

$$\mathsf{E}\left[e^{\theta x_{1,1}}\right] \Lambda(\theta) = 1 \ . \qquad (33)$$

Given the martingale representation of the processes $z_n(k)$ for every path n, the process

$$z(k) = \max_n z_n(k)$$

is a submartingale following the line of argument in (10). We can now use (30) and the remark at the end of Section 4.1 to bound the distribution of the steady-state response time r as

$$\mathsf{P}\left[r \geq \sigma\right] \leq \frac{\mathsf{E}\left[h(c_{1,1})\right]}{h(2)} N\mathsf{E}\left[e^{\theta x_{1,1}}\right] e^{-\theta\sigma} \ , \qquad (34)$$

where we also used that h is monotonically decreasing and θ as defined in (33).

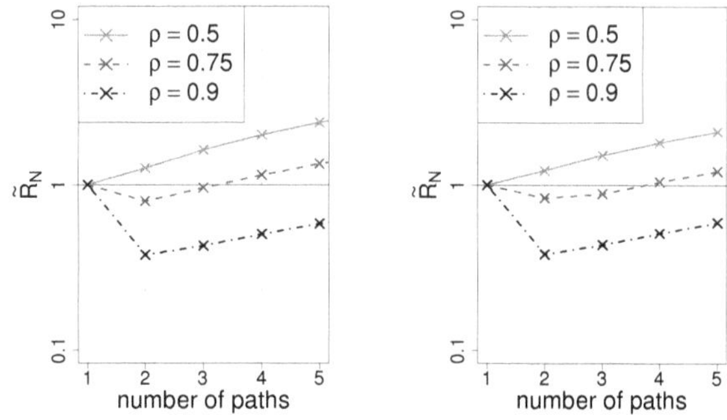

(a) Renewal (b) Non-renewal

Figure 8: Multipath routing reduces the average batch response time when $\tilde{R}_N < 1$; smaller $\tilde{R}_N$ corresponds to larger reductions. Baseline parameter $\mu = 1$ and non-renewal parameters: $p = 0.1, q = 0.4$, $\lambda_1 = \{0.39, 0.7, 0.88\}, \lambda_2 = 0.95$, yielding the utilizations $\rho = \{0.5, 0.75, 0.9\}$ (from top to bottom).

As a direct application of the obtained stochastic bounds (i.e., (32) and (34)), consider the problem of optimizing the number of parallel paths N subject to the batch delay (accounting for both queueing and resequencing delays). More concretely, we are interested in the number of paths N minimizing the overall average batch delay. Note that the path utilization changes with N as

$$\rho = \frac{\lambda}{N\mu} ,$$

since each path only receives $\frac{1}{N}$ of the input. In other words, the packets on each path are delivered much faster with increasing N, but they are subject to the additional resequencing delay (which increases as $\log N$ as shown in Section 3.1).

To visualize the impact of increasing N on the average batch response times we use the ratio

$$\tilde{R}_N := \frac{E\left[r_N\right]}{E\left[r_1\right]} ,$$

where, with abuse of notation, $E\left[r_N\right]$ denotes a bound on the average batch response time for some N, and $E\left[r_1\right]$ denotes the corresponding baseline bound for $N = 1$; both bounds are obtained by integrating either (32) or (34) for the renewal and the non-renewal case, respectively.

In the renewal case, with exponentially distributed interarrival times with parameter λ, and homogenous paths/servers where the service times are exponentially distributed with parameter μ, we obtain

$$\tilde{R}_N = \left(\frac{\log(N\mu/(\mu-\theta)) + 1}{\log(1/\rho) + 1}\right)\left(\frac{\mu - \lambda}{\theta}\right) , \qquad (35)$$

where θ is the solution of

$$\frac{\mu}{\mu - \theta}\left(\frac{\lambda}{\lambda + \theta}\right)^N = 1 \ .$$

In the non-renewal case we obtain the same expression for $\tilde{R}_N$ as in (35) except for the additional prefactor $\frac{\mathsf{E}[h(c_1(1))]}{h(2)}$ prior to N; moreover, θ is the implicit solution from (33).

Figure 8 illustrates $\tilde{R}_N$ as a function of N for several utilization levels ρ for both renewal (a) and non-renewal (b) input; recall that the utilization on each path is $\frac{\rho}{N}$. In both cases, the fundamental observation is that at small utilizations (i.e., roughly when $\rho \leq 0.5$), multipath routing increases the response times. In turn, at higher utilizations, response times benefit from multipath routing but only for 2 paths. While this result may appear as counterintuitive, the technical explanation (in (a)) is that the waiting time in the underlying $E_N/M/1$ queue quickly converges to $\frac{1}{\mu}$, whereas the resequencing delay grows as $\log N$; in other words, the gain in the queueing delay due to multipath routing is quickly dominated by the resequencing delay price.

6. CONCLUSIONS

In this paper we have provided the first computable and non-asymptotic bounds on the waiting and response time distributions in Fork-Join queueing systems. We have analyzed four practical scenarios comprising of either workconserving or non-workconserving servers, which are fed by either renewal or non-renewal arrivals. In the case of workconserving servers, we have shown that delays scale as $\mathcal{O}(\log N)$ in the number of parallel servers N, extending a related scaling result from renewal to non-renewal input. In turn, in the case of non-workconserving servers, we have shown that the same fundamental factor of $\log N$ determines the system's stability region. Given their inherent tightness, our results can be directly applied to the dimensioning of Fork-Join systems such as MapReduce clusters and multipath routing. A highlight of our study is that multipath routing is reasonable from a queueing perspective for two routing paths only.

Acknowledgement

This work was partially funded by the DFG grant Ci 195/1-1.

7. REFERENCES

[1] Amazon Elastic Compute Cloud EC2. `http://aws.amazon.com/ec2`.
[2] S. Babu. Towards automatic optimization of MapReduce programs. In *Proc. of ACM SoCC*, pages 137–142, 2010.
[3] F. Baccelli, E. Gelenbe, and B. Plateau. An end-to-end approach to the resequencing problem. *J. ACM*, 31(3):474–485, June 1984.
[4] F. Baccelli, A. M. Makowski, and A. Shwartz. The Fork-Join queue and related systems with synchronization constraints: Stochastic ordering and computable bounds. *Adv. in Appl. Probab.*, 21(3):629–660, Sept. 1989.
[5] S. Balsamo, L. Donatiello, and N. M. Van Dijk. Bound performance models of heterogeneous parallel processing systems. *IEEE Trans. Parallel Distrib. Syst.*, 9(10):1041–1056, Oct. 1998.
[6] P. Billingsley. *Probability and Measure*. Wiley, 3rd edition, 1995.
[7] O. Boxma, G. Koole, and Z. Liu. Queueing-theoretic solution methods for models of parallel and distributed systems. In *Proc. of Performance Evaluation of Parallel and Distributed Systems. CWI Tract 105*, pages 1–24, 1994.
[8] E. Buffet and N. G. Duffield. Exponential upper bounds via martingales for multiplexers with Markovian arrivals. *J. Appl. Probab.*, 31(4):1049–1060, Dec. 1994.
[9] C. Chang. *Performance Guarantees in Communication Networks*. Springer, 2000.
[10] Y. Chen, S. Alspaugh, and R. Katz. Interactive analytical processing in big data systems: A cross-industry study of mapreduce workloads. *Proc. VLDB Endow.*, 5(12):1802–1813, Aug. 2012.
[11] F. Ciucu, F. Poloczek, and J. Schmitt. Sharp per-flow delay bounds for bursty arrivals: The case of FIFO, SP, and EDF scheduling. In *Proc. of IEEE INFOCOM*, pages 1896–1904, April 2014.
[12] J. Dean and S. Ghemawat. MapReduce: Simplified data processing on large clusters. *Commun. ACM*, 51(1):107–113, Jan. 2008.
[13] N. Duffield. Exponential bounds for queues with Markovian arrivals. *Queueing Syst.*, 17(3–4):413–430, Sept. 1994.
[14] L. Flatto and S. Hahn. Two parallel queues created by arrivals with two demands I. *SIAM J. Appl. Math.*, 44(5):1041–1053, Oct. 1984.
[15] R. J. Gibbens. Traffic characterisation and effective bandwidths for broadband network traces. *J. R. Stat. Soc. Ser. B. Stat. Methodol.*, 1996.
[16] Y. Han and A. Makowski. Resequencing delays under multipath routing - Asymptotics in a simple queueing model. In *Proc. of IEEE INFOCOM*, pages 1–12, April 2006.
[17] G. Harrus and B. Plateau. Queueing analysis of a reordering issue. *IEEE Trans. Softw. Eng.*, 8(2):113–123, Mar. 1982.
[18] Y. Jiang and Y. Liu. *Stochastic Network Calculus*. Springer, 2008.
[19] S. Kandula, S. Sengupta, A. Greenberg, P. Patel, and R. Chaiken. The nature of data center traffic: Measurements & analysis. In *Proc. of ACM IMC*, pages 202–208, 2009.
[20] S. Kavulya, J. Tan, R. Gandhi, and P. Narasimhan. An analysis of traces from a production MapReduce cluster. In *Proc. of IEEE/ACM CCGRID*, pages 94–103, May 2010.
[21] B. Kemper and M. Mandjes. Mean sojourn times in two-queue Fork-Join systems: Bounds and approximations. *OR Spectr.*, 34(3):723–742, July 2012.
[22] G. Kesidis, B. Urgaonkar, Y. Shan, S. Kamarava, and J. Liebeherr. Network calculus for parallel processing. *CoRR*, abs/1409.0820, 2014.
[23] J. F. C. Kingman. Inequalities in the theory of queues. *J. R. Stat. Soc. Ser. B. Stat. Methodol.*, 32(1):102–110, 1970.
[24] S.-S. Ko and R. F. Serfozo. Sojourn times in G/M/1 Fork-Join networks. *Naval Res. Logist.*, 55(5):432–443, May 2008.
[25] A. S. Lebrecht and W. J. Knottenbelt. Response time approximations in Fork-Join queues. In *Proc. of UKPEW*, July 2007.
[26] R. Nelson and A. Tantawi. Approximate analysis of Fork/Join synchronization in parallel queues. *IEEE Trans. Computers*, 37(6):739–743, June 1988.

[27] R. Pike, S. Dorward, R. Griesemer, and S. Quinlan. Interpreting the data: Parallel analysis with Sawzall. *Sci. Program.*, 13(4):277–298, Oct. 2005.

[28] I. Polato, R. Ré, A. Goldman, and F. Kon. A comprehensive view of Hadoop research - a systematic literature review. *J. Netw. Comput. Appl.*, 46(0):1 – 25, Nov. 2014.

[29] F. Poloczek and F. Ciucu. Scheduling analysis with martingales. *Perform. Evaluation*, 79:56–72, Sept. 2014.

[30] C. Raiciu, S. Barre, C. Pluntke, A. Greenhalgh, D. Wischik, and M. Handley. Improving datacenter performance and robustness with multipath TCP. *SIGCOMM Comput. Commun. Rev.*, 41(4):266–277, Aug. 2011.

[31] A. Rényi. On the theory of order statistics. *Acta Mathematica Academiae Scientiarum Hungarica*, 4(3–4):191–231, 1953.

[32] J. Tan, X. Meng, and L. Zhang. Delay tails in MapReduce scheduling. *SIGMETRICS Perform. Eval. Rev.*, 40(1):5–16, June 2012.

[33] J. Tan, Y. Wang, W. Yu, and L. Zhang. Non-work-conserving effects in MapReduce: Diffusion limit and criticality. *SIGMETRICS Perform. Eval. Rev.*, 42(1):181–192, June 2014.

[34] E. Varki. Mean value technique for closed Fork-Join networks. *SIGMETRICS Perform. Eval. Rev.*, 27(1):103–112, May 1999.

[35] S. Varma and A. M. Makowski. Interpolation approximations for symmetric Fork-Join queues. *Perform. Eval.*, 20(1–3):245–265, May 1994.

[36] E. Vianna, G. Comarela, T. Pontes, J. Almeida, V. Almeida, K. Wilkinson, H. Kuno, and U. Dayal. Analytical performance models for MapReduce workloads. *Int. J. Parallel Prog.*, 41(4):495–525, Aug. 2013.

[37] T. White. *Hadoop: The Definitive Guide*. O'Reilly Media, Inc., 1st edition, 2009.

[38] Y. Xia and D. Tse. On the large deviation of resequencing queue size: 2-M/M/1 case. *IEEE Trans. Inf. Theory*, 54(9):4107–4118, Sept. 2008.

[39] M. Zaharia, A. Konwinski, A. D. Joseph, R. Katz, and I. Stoica. Improving MapReduce performance in heterogeneous environments. In *Proc. of USENIX OSDI*, pages 29–42, Dec. 2008.

APPENDIX

We assume throughout the paper that all probabilistic objects are defined on a common filtered probability space $(\Omega, \mathcal{A}, (\mathcal{F}_n)_n, \mathsf{P})$. All processes $(X_n)_n$ are assumed to be *adapted*, i.e., for each $n \geq 0$, the random variable X_n is $\mathcal{F}_n$-measurable.

DEFINITION 5. (MARTINGALE) *An integrable process* $(X_n)_n$ *is a* martingale *if and only if for each* $n \geq 1$

$$\mathsf{E}[X_n \mid \mathcal{F}_{n-1}] = X_{n-1} \ . \tag{36}$$

Further, X *is said to be a sub-(super-)martingale if in (36) we have* $\geq$ $(\leq)$ *instead of equality.*

The key property of (sub, super)-martingales that we use in this paper is described by the following lemma:

LEMMA 6. (OPTIONAL SAMPLING THEOREM) *Let* $(X_n)_n$ *be a martingale, and* K *a bounded stopping time, i.e.,* $K \leq n$ *a.s. for some* $n \geq 0$ *and* $\{K = k\} \in \mathcal{F}_k$ *for all* $k \leq n$*. Then*

$$\mathsf{E}[X_0] = \mathsf{E}[X_K] = \mathsf{E}[X_n] \ . \tag{37}$$

If X *is a sub-(super-)martingale, the equality sign in (37) is replaced by* $\leq$ $(\geq)$.

PROOF. See, e.g., [6]. □

Note that for *any* (possibly unbounded) stopping time K, the stopping time $K \wedge n$ is always bounded. We use Lemma 6 with the stopping times $K \wedge n$ in the proofs of Theorems 1 – 4.

LEMMA 7. *Let* c_k *be the Markov chain from Figure 4 and* K *be the stopping time from (11). Then the distribution of* $(c_K \mid K < \infty)$ *is stochastically smaller than the steady-state distribution of* c_k*, i.e.,*

$$\mathsf{P}[c_K = 2 \mid K < \infty] \leq \mathsf{P}[c_1 = 2] \ ,$$

or, equivalently,

$$\mathsf{E}[h(c_K) \mid K < \infty] \geq \mathsf{E}[h(c_k)] \ ,$$

for all monotonically decreasing functions h *on* $\{1, 2\}$.

PROOF. Using Bayes' rule and the stationarity of the process c_k, it holds:

$$\begin{aligned}\mathsf{P}[c_K = 2 \mid K < \infty] &= \sum_{k=1}^{\infty} \mathsf{P}[c_k = 2 \mid K = k]\, \mathsf{P}[K = k] \\ &= \sum_{k=1}^{\infty} \mathsf{P}[K = k \mid c_k = 2]\, \mathsf{P}[c_k = 2] \\ &= \mathsf{P}[c_1 = 2] \sum_{k=1}^{\infty} \mathsf{P}[K = k \mid c_k = 2] \ .\end{aligned}$$

Since L_1 is stochastically smaller than L_2, we have for any $k \geq 1$

$$\begin{aligned}&\mathbb{P}[K = k \mid c_k = 2] \\ &= \mathsf{P}\left[t_k \leq \max_n \sum_{i=1}^{k} x_{n,i} - \sum_{i=1}^{k-1} t_i - \sigma, \max_n \sum_{i=1}^{k-1} (x_{n,i} - t_i) < \sigma \,\middle|\, c_k = 2\right] \\ &\leq \mathsf{P}\left[t_k \leq \max_n \sum_{i=1}^{k} x_{n,i} - \sum_{i=1}^{k-1} t_i - \sigma, \max_n \sum_{i=1}^{k-1} (x_{n,i} - t_i) < \sigma\right] \\ &= \mathsf{P}[K = k] \ .\end{aligned}$$

Hence $\sum_{k=1}^{\infty} \mathsf{P}[K = k \mid c_k = 2] \leq 1$, which completes the proof. □

Reducing Latency via Redundant Requests: Exact Analysis

Kristen Gardner
School of Computer Science
Carnegie Mellon University
ksgardne@cs.cmu.edu

Samuel Zbarsky
Dept. of Mathematics
Carnegie Mellon University
szbarsky@andrew.cmu.edu

Sherwin Doroudi
Tepper School of Business
Carnegie Mellon University
sdoroudi@andrew.cmu.edu

Mor Harchol-Balter
School of Computer Science
Carnegie Mellon University
harchol@cs.cmu.edu

Esa Hyytiä
Dept. of Communications and Networking
Aalto University
esa.hyytia@aalto.fi

Alan Scheller-Wolf
Tepper School of Business
Carnegie Mellon University
awolf@andrew.cmu.edu

ABSTRACT

Recent computer systems research has proposed using redundant requests to reduce latency. The idea is to run a request on multiple servers and wait for the *first* completion (discarding all remaining copies of the request). However there is no exact analysis of systems with redundancy.

This paper presents the first exact analysis of systems with redundancy. We allow for any number of classes of redundant requests, any number of classes of non-redundant requests, any degree of redundancy, and any number of heterogeneous servers. In all cases we derive the limiting distribution on the state of the system.

In small (two or three server) systems, we derive simple forms for the distribution of response time of both the redundant classes and non-redundant classes, and we quantify the "gain" to redundant classes and "pain" to non-redundant classes caused by redundancy. We find some surprising results. First, the response time of a fully redundant class follows a simple Exponential distribution and that of the non-redundant class follows a Generalized Hyperexponential. Second, fully redundant classes are "immune" to any pain caused by other classes becoming redundant.

We also compare redundancy with other approaches for reducing latency, such as optimal probabilistic splitting of a class among servers (Opt-Split) and Join-the-Shortest-Queue (JSQ) routing of a class. We find that, in many cases, redundancy outperforms JSQ and Opt-Split with respect to overall response time, making it an attractive solution.

Categories and Subject Descriptors

G.3 [**Mathematics of Computing**]: Probability and Statistics—*Queueing theory; Markov processes*

SIGMETRICS'15, June 15 - 19, 2015, Portland, OR, USA.

http://dx.doi.org/10.1145/2745844.2745873.

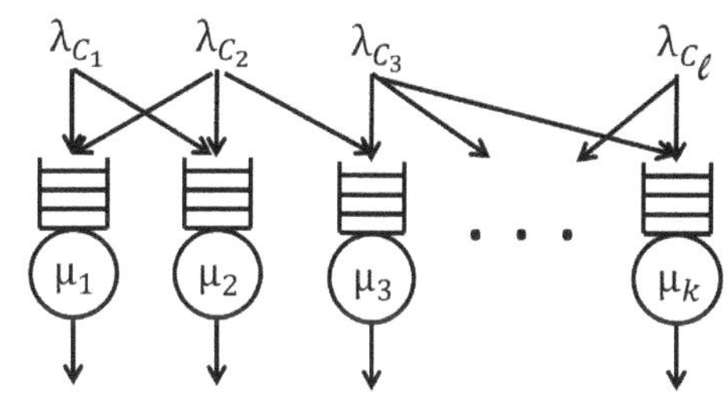

Figure 1: The general redundancy model. Each server j provides service at rate μ_j. Each class of jobs C_i arrives to the system as a Poisson process with rate λ_{C_i} and joins the queue at <u>all</u> servers in $S_{C_i} = \{j \mid \text{server } j \text{ can serve class } C_i\}$.

Keywords

Redundancy; Markov chain analysis

1. INTRODUCTION

Reducing latency has always been a primary concern for computer systems designers. Recent papers have proposed a new approach to reducing latency in multi-server systems: using *redundant requests* [2, 9, 33]. The motivation behind this approach comes from the observation that response times at servers can be highly variable [11, 33]. Two servers in the same system often differ in their current loads, their network congestion, and the configuration of their storage systems. Even if both servers are idle, the same request might experience a far lower service time at one server than another because the disk seek time could be much lower at one server than another (seek times often dominate service times [18]). The solution is to send the same request to the queues at multiple servers simultaneously (i.e., redundantly). When any copy of the request completes service, all remaining copies of the request are killed.

Using redundant requests is not free. First, data must be replicated among the set of servers to which the copies must be sent. Furthermore, using redundant requests adds to the system load. Nonetheless, using redundant requests has been shown to vastly improve latency in distributed systems, e.g., Google's BigTable service shows a 20-fold improvement in tail latency by using redundant requests [11].

Unfortunately, there is almost no work analyzing the benefits of redundant requests. Even a two-server system with one redundant class and one non-redundant class has not been analyzed. The first attempts to analyze systems with redundancy are as recent as 2014, but this work derives only bounds and approximations [20].

Redundant requests require a new queueing paradigm: there is no longer a single copy of each job, and redundant copies disappear instantly as soon as one copy completes. While redundant jobs bear some resemblance to fork-join systems, the two models are actually quite different because all copies must complete service in a fork-join system, whereas a redundant job only needs one copy to complete. Likewise, while redundant jobs bear some resemblance to coupled-processor systems, they differ in that the redundant copies can occupy multiple servers even when these servers have non-empty queues. Likewise, redundant jobs are not the same as flexible servers (see Section 2 for more details).

The state space required to capture systems with redundant jobs is very complex. It is not enough to know the number of jobs in each queue, or even the number of jobs of each class (redundant or non-redundant) within each queue. Rather, one needs to track the exact position and type of every job in every queue, so that one knows which jobs to delete when a copy of a redundant job completes service.

This paper provides the first closed form exact analysis of redundant queues. We derive the limiting distribution of the full queue state as well as (in some cases) the distribution of response time of each class of jobs. Our analysis assumes Exponential service times and Poisson arrivals. Our result applies to systems with any number of queues, k, any number of classes of jobs, ℓ, and any redundancy structure (see Figure 1). A *class* of jobs is associated with a set of servers that hold replicated data; the jobs of a class can be run on any of the servers associated with the class.

We also investigate how the approach of redundant requests compares to other common approaches for job assignment. For example, how does making m redundant copies of each request compare with optimally probabilistically splitting load among m queues (Opt-Split), or with joining the shortest of m queues (JSQ)? Furthermore, while redundancy may benefit the redundant class, what is the response time penalty to the other jobs in the system? Do other approaches create less of a penalty? Finally, if one class of jobs creates redundant copies, does that class suffer when others "join the redundancy game" and start creating redundant copies of their jobs as well?

We first investigate these questions in the context of three simple models, shown in Figure 2. In the $\mathbb{N}$ model (Figure 2(a)), there are two arrival streams of jobs, each with its own server. However, one class is redundant at both servers. The $\mathbb{N}$ model illuminates the response time benefit to the redundant class and the pain to the non-redundant class. We derive the exact distribution of response time for both classes, and explore what happens when the non-redundant class decides that it too wants to become redundant. In the $\mathbb{W}$ model (Figure 2(b)), we imagine that we have a stable system, where each server is serving its own stream of jobs, when a new stream of jobs arrives which can be processed at either server. We ask how to best deal with this new stream: redundancy, splitting, or dispatching to the shortest queue? We then turn to the $\mathbb{M}$ model (Figure 2(c)), where there is a "shared server," which can be used by all request streams. We ask how best to use this shared resource.

After exploring these questions for small systems, we turn to issues of scale, investigating scaled versions of the $\mathbb{N}$, $\mathbb{W}$, and $\mathbb{M}$ models. We use our exact closed form limiting distribution to derive the response time distribution for a fully redundant class in any size system.

The remainder of this paper is organized as follows. In Section 2, we describe related work and how it differs from the present work. In Section 3, we formalize our model and state our main theorem for the general system. In Sections 4, 5, and 6, we discuss detailed results for the $\mathbb{N}$, $\mathbb{M}$, and $\mathbb{W}$ models. Section 7 addresses how these models scale as the number of servers increases. In Section 8, we conclude.

2. PRIOR WORK

In this section, we review several models that are related to redundant requests. All of these models differ from ours in critical ways that change both the mathematical techniques available to analyze the system, and the results obtained. Nonetheless, we hope that the results in this paper might shed some light on the problems below, many of which are notoriously difficult.

Coupled Processor/Cycle Stealing

In a *coupled processor* system, there are two servers and two classes of jobs, A and B. Server 1 works on class A jobs in FCFS order, and server 2 works on class B jobs in FCFS order. However, if there are only jobs of one class in the system, the servers "couple" to serve that class at a faster rate: unlike in the redundancy model, class A jobs only get to use server 2 when the system is empty of B's (and vice-versa). Generating functions for the stationary distribution of the queue lengths in a two-server system with Exponential service times were derived in [12, 23], but this required solving complicated boundary value problems and provided little intuition for the performance of the systems. The stationary distribution of the workload in the two-server system was derived in [10] using a similar approach. In [17], a power-series approach was used to numerically compute the queue-length stationary distribution in systems with more than two servers under Exponential service times. Much of the remaining work on coupled processor models involves deriving bounds and asymptotic results (for example, [6]).

In the donor-beneficiary model (one-way cycle stealing), only one class of jobs (the beneficiary) receives access to both servers, typically only when no jobs of the other class are present. In addition, if there is only one beneficiary job present, one server must idle (the servers do not "couple"). The donor-beneficiary model has been studied, in approximation, in a variety of settings [16, 26]. However, it differs from the redundancy model because a job is never in service at more than one server, and because donor jobs often have full preemptive priority at their server.

Fork-Join

Another related model is the *fork-join* system, in which each job that enters a system with k servers splits into k pieces, one of which goes to each server. The job is considered complete only when all k pieces have completed service. This is different from the redundancy model because only one redundant request needs to finish service in the redundancy

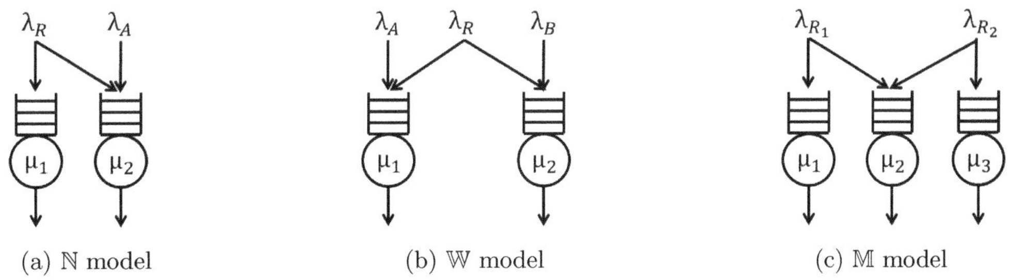

Figure 2: (a) The $\mathbb{N}$ model. Class A jobs join the queue at server 2 only, while class R jobs are redundant at both servers. (b) The $\mathbb{W}$ model. Class A jobs join the queue at server 1 only, class B jobs join the queue at server 2 only, and class R jobs are redundant at both servers. (c) The $\mathbb{M}$ model. Class R_1 jobs are redundant at servers 1 and 2, and class R_2 jobs are redundant at servers 2 and 3.

model. Furthermore, a fork-join job sends work to all k servers, whereas a redundant job of class C_i only sends copies to the servers in S_{C_i}, where S_{C_i} is a subset of the k servers. The fork-join model is known to be very difficult to analyze. Many papers have derived bounds and approximations for such a system (for example, [3, 4, 22, 25, 35]). Exact analysis remains an open problem except for the two-server case [13, 14]; see [8] for a more detailed overview.

Flexible Server Systems

A third related model is the *flexible server* system, in which each class of jobs has its own queue, and each server can serve some subset of classes. The design and performance of flexible server systems has been studied in [5, 29, 30, 31]. In a flexible server system, traditionally, when a server becomes available, it *chooses* the queue from which to take its next job according to some policy. By contrast in redundancy systems, each server has its own FCFS queue and jobs are routed to a subset of servers upon arrival. The key difference between flexible server systems and redundancy systems is that redundant jobs may be served by multiple servers simultaneously, whereas in a flexible server system, each job may be processed by only one server.

A special case of the flexible server system uses the following policy. When a server becomes available, it chooses the job that arrived earliest from among the jobs it can serve. This policy is similar to the redundant system because each server works in FCFS order among the jobs it can serve. However, there are no redundant jobs in this flexible server system; jobs cannot be *in service* at two servers at once. For this model, under a specific routing assumption when an arriving job sees multiple idle servers, the stationary distribution that satisfies the balance equations is given [32, 1]. Our redundancy model requires no such routing assumption, because arriving redundant jobs enter service at *all* idle servers. Finally, mean response times are lower in a redundant system than in an FCFS flexible server system; our exact analysis allows us to quantify this performance gap.

Redundancy Models

Recently, in 2012, the (n, k, r) system was proposed [27], where there are n servers, and each job sends a request to $k \le n$ of these servers. When $r \le k$ requests complete, the job is considered finished. If we view the k requests as k "redundant" copies of a job, the problem can be seen as similar to ours, although in our model, jobs can only be redundant at specific subsets of servers. Various bounds and approximations have been derived for the (n, k, r) model [19, 20, 27], and the optimal value of k has been determined for different system loads and costs of deleting extra redundant requests [28]. Additionally, other variants have been proposed where a job might wait before issuing redundant requests [34]. Unfortunately, the only exact analysis of the (n, k, r) system is for a highly simplified model in which each server is actually an M/M/∞ queue, so there is no queueing [19].

In the special case $r = 1$, which mostly closely matches our model, approximations have been found assuming that the queues are independent [33]. The optimal degree of replication and service discipline also has been studied [24].

3. MODEL

We consider a system with k servers, denoted $1, 2, \ldots, k$, and ℓ classes of jobs, denoted $C_1, C_2, \ldots, C_\ell$. (see Figure 1). The service time at server j is distributed Exponentially with rate μ_j for all $1 \le j \le k$, and each server processes the jobs in its queue in FCFS order. Each class of jobs C_i arrives to the system as a Poisson process with rate λ_{C_i}, and replicates itself by joining the queue at some fixed subset of the servers $S_{C_i} = \{j \mid \text{server } j \text{ can serve class } C_i\}$. Jobs in class C_i cannot join the queue at any server $j \notin S_{C_i}$. A job may be in service at multiple servers at the same time; if a job is in service at both servers i and j, it receives service at combined rate $\mu_i + \mu_j$.

Looking at Figure 1, it is difficult to figure out an appropriate state space. One might think that you could track the number of jobs of class at each queue, but this state space is missing information about which specific jobs are in multiple queues. Furthermore, servers are not independent, and job classes are not independent, so typical product-form type state spaces and solutions are unlikely to work.

The key insight that allows us to model this system is that we can view the system as having a single central queue in which all jobs wait in the order that they arrived (see Figure 3). Each server processes jobs from this central queue in FCFS order, skipping over those jobs it cannot serve. For example, in Figure 3, server 3 will skip over job $A^{(1)}$ and move to job $B^{(1)}$ when choosing its next job. We can write the state of the system as $(c_n, c_{n-1}, \ldots, c_1)$, where there are n jobs in the system, and c_i is the class of the ith job in this central queue; c_1 is the class of the job at the head of the queue, which is also in service at all servers in S_{C_1}.

Theorem 1. *The limiting probability of being in state* $(c_n,\ c_{n-1}, \ldots,\ c_1)$ *is*

$$\pi_{(c_n,\ldots,c_1)} = C \prod_{i=1}^{n} \frac{\lambda_{c_i}}{\sum\limits_{m \in \bigcup\limits_{j \leq i} S_{c_j}} \mu_m},$$

where C *is a normalizing constant.*

Proof. See Appendix. □

Although $\pi_{(c_n,\ c_{n-1},\ldots,\ c_1)}$ looks like a product-form solution, it is not; we cannot write the limiting probabilities as a product of independent marginal per-server terms, or as a product of independent marginal per-class terms. In fact, the form is quite unusual, as illustrated in Example 1.

Example 1. *Consider the system shown in Figure 3. Here, the current state is* $(B,\ B,\ A)$*, where the head of the queue is at the right, job* $A^{(1)}$ *is currently in service at servers 1 and 2, and job* $B^{(1)}$ *is currently in service at server 3. From Theorem 1, the limiting probability of this state is*

$$\pi_{(B,B,A)} = C \frac{\lambda_A}{\mu_1 + \mu_2} \left(\frac{\lambda_B}{\mu_1 + \mu_2 + \mu_3} \right)^2.$$

Corollary 1. *The general system with redundant requests is stable when* $\forall\ \mathcal{C} \subseteq \{C_1, \ldots, C_\ell\}$,

$$\sum_{C \in \mathcal{C}} \lambda_C < \sum_{m \in \bigcup\limits_{C \in \mathcal{C}} S_C} \mu_m. \tag{1}$$

Proof. All limiting probabilities $\pi_{(c_n,\ldots,\ c_1)}$ from Theorem 1 are in $(0,1)$ when $\forall\ \mathcal{C} \subseteq \{C_1, \ldots, C_\ell\}$, (1) holds. □

In Sections 4, 5, and 6, we use the result of Theorem 1 to study the $\mathbb{N}$, $\mathbb{W}$, and $\mathbb{M}$ models, defined below.

$\mathbb{N}$ Model

The $\mathbb{N}$ model is the simplest non-trivial example of a redundancy system where there are both redundant and non-redundant classes. In an $\mathbb{N}$ model there are two servers running at rates μ_1 and μ_2 and two classes of jobs (see Figure 2(a)). Class A jobs are non-redundant; they arrive with rate λ_A and join the queue at server 2 only ($S_A = \{2\}$). Class R jobs are redundant; they arrive with rate λ_R and join the queue at both servers ($S_R = \{1,\ 2\}$).

$\mathbb{W}$ Model

Consider a two-server, two-class system in which each class of jobs has its own dedicated server (no redundancy). Now suppose that a third class of jobs enters the system and chooses to be redundant at both servers. The $\mathbb{W}$ model helps us understand how the presence of this redundant class affects the existing non-redundant classes. In a $\mathbb{W}$ model, there are two servers running at rates μ_1 and μ_2 and three classes of jobs (see Figure 2(b)). Class A jobs arrive with rate λ_A and are served at server 1 only ($S_A = \{1\}$), class B jobs arrive with rate λ_B and are served at server 2 only ($S_B = \{2\}$), and class R jobs arrive with rate λ_R and may be served at both servers ($S_R = \{1,\ 2\}$).

$\mathbb{M}$ Model

Again consider the two-server, two-class system in which each class of jobs has its own dedicated server. Suppose

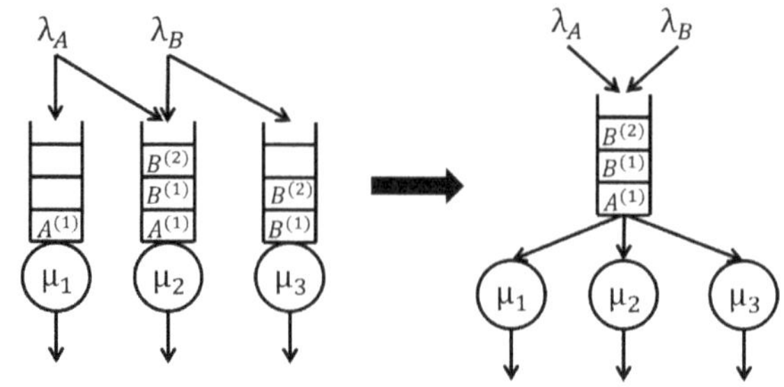

Figure 3: Let A and B be two job classes, where $A^{(i)}$ is the ith arrival of class A. We can view the general redundancy system (left) as having a single central queue from which each server works in FCFS order, skipping over those jobs it cannot serve (right). The central queue is an interleaving of the individual servers' queues, where each job appears only once, and appears in the order it arrived

that a new server is added to the system and all jobs issue redundant requests at this server. The $\mathbb{M}$ model helps us understand how best to use the new server. In an $\mathbb{M}$ model, there are three servers with rates μ_1, μ_2, and μ_3 and two job classes (see Figure 2(c)). Class R_1 jobs arrive with rate λ_{R_1} and join the queue at servers 1 and 2 ($S_{R_1} = \{1,\ 2\}$), and class R_2 jobs arrive with rate λ_{R_2} and have $S_{R_2} = \{2,\ 3\}$).

4. $\mathbb{N}$ MODEL

We first turn our attention to the $\mathbb{N}$ model (Figure 2(a)). An immediate consequence of Theorem 1 is Lemma 1, which gives the limiting distribution of the $\mathbb{N}$ model.

Lemma 1. *In the* $\mathbb{N}$ *model, the limiting probability of being in state* $(c_n,\ c_{n-1}, \ldots,\ c_1)$ *is:*

$$\pi_{(c_n,\ldots,c_1)} = C_{\mathbb{N}} \left(\frac{\lambda_A}{\mu_2} \right)^{a_0} \left(\frac{\lambda_R}{\mu_1 + \mu_2} \right)^{r} \left(\frac{\lambda_A}{\mu_1 + \mu_2} \right)^{a_1},$$

where a_0 *is the number of class* A *jobs before the first class* R *job,* a_1 *is the number of class* A *jobs after the first class* R *job,* r *is the total number of class* R *jobs in the queue, and* $C_{\mathbb{N}} = \frac{(\mu_2 - \lambda_A)(\mu_1 + \mu_2 - \lambda_A - \lambda_R)}{\mu_2(\mu_1 + \mu_2 - \lambda_A)}$ *is a normalizing constant.*

We use this result to find (Theorem 2) that for the redundant class (class R), response time is Exponentially distributed, which is pleasantly surprising because the system is not an M/M/1. Specifically, the distribution of response time is the same as that in an M/M/1, where the arrival rate is λ_R and the service rate is $\mu' = \mu_1 + \mu_2 - \lambda_A$. Note that μ' can be viewed as giving the R jobs the full μ_1, and the *portion* of μ_2 that is not appropriated for the class A jobs ($\mu_2 - \lambda_A$). Equivalently, this is the response time in an M/M/1 with arrival rate $\lambda_A + \lambda_R$ and service rate $\mu_1 + \mu_2$.[1]

Theorem 2. *In the* $\mathbb{N}$ *model,*

1. *The number of class* R *jobs in the system,* N_R*, is distributed* Geometric$(1 - \rho) - 1$*, where* $\rho = \frac{\lambda_R}{\mu_1 + \mu_2 - \lambda_A}$.

[1]This is counterintuitive because as we will see in Lemma 3, the distribution of response time for class R does not depend on whether class A is redundant or non-redundant.

2. *The response time of class R jobs, T_R, is distributed* $\text{Exp}(\mu_1 + \mu_2 - \lambda_A - \lambda_R)$.

PROOF. This is a special case of the more general result in Theorem 10, which is proved in Appendix B. □

In Theorem 3, we find that the response time for the non-redundant class, T_A, follows a Generalized Hyperexponential distribution[2]. We can view the mean response time of class A jobs as that of an M/M/1 with arrival rate λ_A and service rate μ_2, plus a penalty term that captures the extent to which the redundant jobs hurt the A's (Equation 3).

THEOREM 3. *In the N model,*

1. *The number of class A jobs in the system, N_A, has p.m.f.*

$$\Pr\{N_A = n_A\} = \zeta_{\mathbb{N}1}\left(\frac{\lambda_A}{\mu_2}\right)^{n_A} + \zeta_{\mathbb{N}2}\left(\frac{\lambda_A}{\mu_1 + \mu_2 - \lambda_R}\right)^{n_A} \quad (2)$$

where

$$\zeta_{\mathbb{N}1} = C_{\mathbb{N}}\left(\frac{\mu_1}{\mu_1 - \lambda_R}\right),$$

$$\zeta_{\mathbb{N}2} = C_{\mathbb{N}}\left(\frac{\lambda_R}{\mu_1 + \mu_2 - \lambda_R} - \frac{\lambda_R}{\mu_1 - \lambda_R}\right),$$

and $C_{\mathbb{N}}$ is as in Lemma 1.

2. *The distribution of response time of class A jobs is*

$$T_A \sim H_2(\nu_{\mathbb{N}1}, \nu_{\mathbb{N}2}, \omega_{\mathbb{N}}),$$

where

$$\nu_{\mathbb{N}1} = \mu_2 - \lambda_A$$
$$\nu_{\mathbb{N}2} = \mu_1 + \mu_2 - \lambda_A - \lambda_R$$
$$\nu_{\mathbb{N}3} = \mu_1 + \mu_2 - \lambda_A$$
$$\omega_{\mathbb{N}} = \frac{\lambda_R \nu_{\mathbb{N}1}}{(\mu_1 - \lambda_R)\nu_{\mathbb{N}3}}.$$

The expected response time of class A jobs is

$$\mathbb{E}[T_A] = \underbrace{\frac{1}{\nu_{\mathbb{N}1}}}_{\text{M/M/1}} + \underbrace{\frac{1}{\nu_{\mathbb{N}2}} - \frac{1}{\nu_{\mathbb{N}3}}}_{\text{penalty}}. \quad (3)$$

PROOF. Deferred to the end of the section. □

Figure 4 compares mean response time before class R jobs become redundant (each class sees its own independent M/M/1), and after class R jobs become redundant. We hold $\mu_1 = \mu_2 = 1$ and vary the load by increasing $\lambda_R = \lambda_A$. We find redundancy helps class R jobs by a factor of two (Figure 4(a)), but can hurt class A by up to 50% (Figure 4(b)).

In Lemma 3, we ask what happens if class A jobs decide they too should be redundant. That is, all jobs can be served at both servers - the system is *fully redundant*. This transforms the system into an M/M/1 with arrival rate $\lambda_A + \lambda_R$ and service rate $\mu_1 + \mu_2$ (Lemma 2). Surprisingly, class R is *immune* to pain when class A also becomes redundant: as Lemma 3 shows, the distribution of response time for class R is the same before and after class A becomes redundant. Of course, when the A's become redundant, they receive the benefit of having two servers.

[2]A Generalized Hyperexponential, $H_2(\nu_1, \nu_2, \omega)$ is defined as the weighted mixture of two Exponentials with rates ν_1 and ν_2, where the first Exponential is given weight $1+\omega$ and the second is given weight $-\omega$. Note that ω can be any real number; it need not be a probability [7].

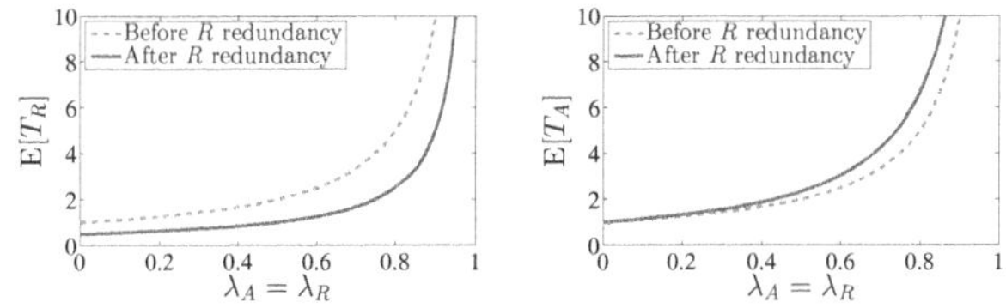

(a) Class R (b) Class A

Figure 4: Comparing mean response time before and after class R becomes redundant when $\mu_1 = \mu_2 = 1$ and $\lambda_A = \lambda_R$ for (a) class R, and (b) class A. The mean response time for the overall system is the weighted average of these two classes.

LEMMA 2. *The fully redundant system, in which all jobs issue redundant requests at both servers, is equivalent to an M/M/1 with arrival rate $\lambda_A + \lambda_R$ and service rate $\mu_1 + \mu_2$.*

PROOF. Deferred to the end of the section. □

LEMMA 3. *With respect to response time, both classes of jobs do at least as well in the fully redundant model as in the* $\mathbb{N}$ *model. In particular,*

1. $\mathbb{E}[T_A]^{\text{Fully Redundant}} \leq \mathbb{E}[T_A]^{\text{Redundant}}$

2. $T_R^{\text{Fully Redundant}} \stackrel{d}{=} T_R^{\text{Redundant}}$.

PROOF. Deferred to the end of the section. □

Going back to the $\mathbb{N}$ model with only one redundant class, redundancy clearly helps the redundant class considerably. But there are alternative latency-reducing strategies. For example, each redundant class could optimally probabilistically split jobs among all allowable servers (Opt-Split), or join the shortest queue among allowable servers (JSQ).

In Figure 5, we compare these other options for the $\mathbb{N}$ model, where the mean response times under Opt-Split are derived analytically (Definition 1), but JSQ is simulated. We find that, for the redundant class R, redundancy beats JSQ, which beats Opt-Split. Redundancy often is not much better than JSQ, yet they can differ by a factor of 2, depending on the load of class R and the relative server speeds.

Surprisingly, the non-redundant class A often prefers redundancy of the other class to Opt-Split or JSQ. This is because the non-redundant class wants the redundant class to spend as little time as possible blocking the A jobs at server 2, and redundancy helps with this.

Note that under Opt-Split we see an inflection point in mean response time for both class R and class A. For example, in Figures 5(a) and (b), there is an inflection point at $\lambda_R = 0.6$, when $\lambda_R = \lambda_A$. This phase change occurs because when $\lambda_R < \lambda_A$, no class R jobs go to server 2 under Opt-Split, but when $\lambda_R > \lambda_A$ the R's compete with the A's. Also observe that $\mathbb{E}[T]$ is not monotonically increasing; this is because as λ_R increases, the redundant class contributes more to the weighted average.

From the overall system's perspective, redundancy is always preferable to Opt-Split and JSQ because it optimizes overall server utilization.

When $\mu_1 = \mu_2$, even when non-redundant jobs prefer Opt-Split, redundancy is never more than 50% worse than Opt-Split for the non-redundant jobs (Theorem 4).

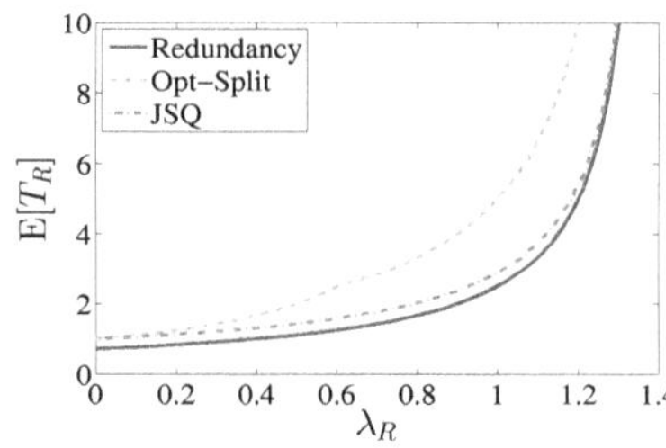

(a) $\mathbb{E}[T_R]$ when $\mu_1 = \mu_2$

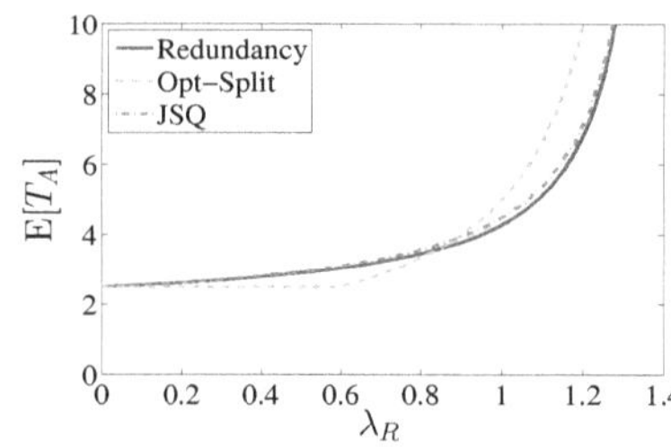

(b) $\mathbb{E}[T_A]$ when $\mu_1 = \mu_2$

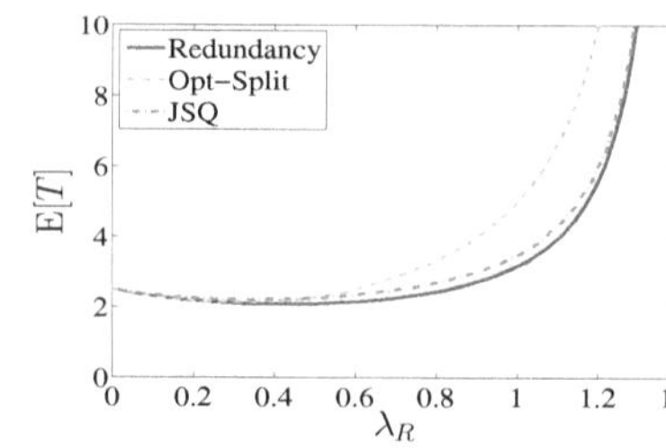

(c) $\mathbb{E}[T]$ when $\mu_1 = \mu_2$

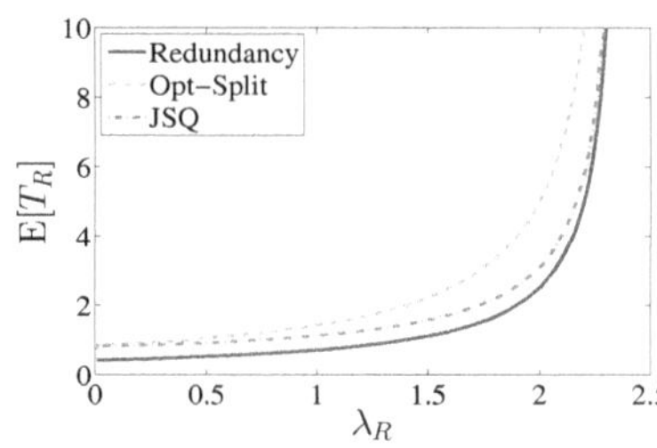

(d) $\mathbb{E}[T_R]$ when $2\mu_1 = \mu_2$

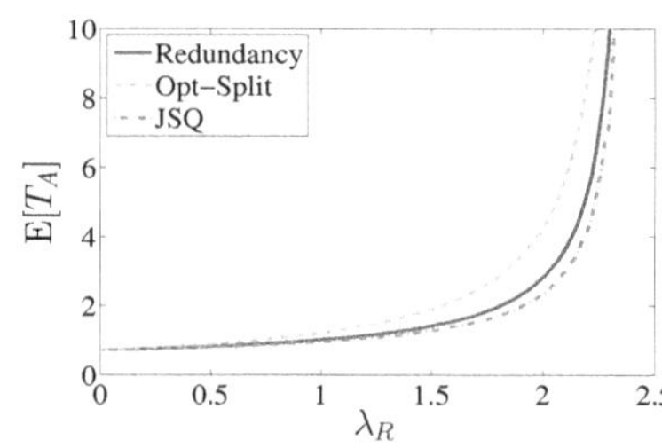

(e) $\mathbb{E}[T_A]$ when $2\mu_1 = \mu_2$

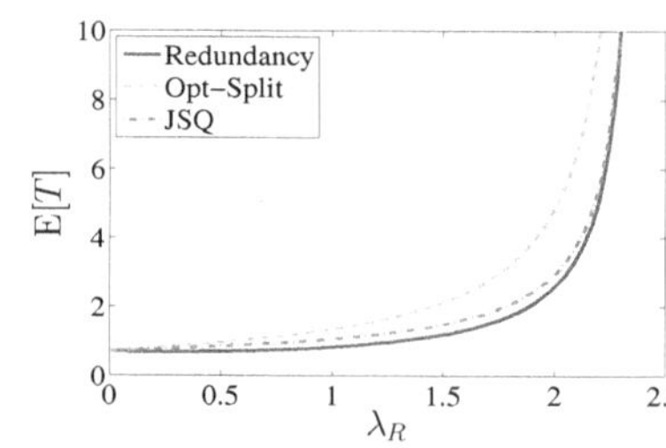

(f) $\mathbb{E}[T]$ when $2\mu_1 = \mu_2$

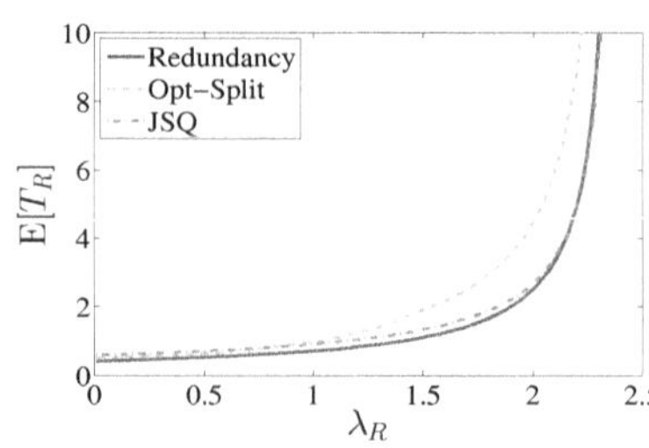

(g) $\mathbb{E}[T_R]$ when $\mu_1 = 2\mu_2$

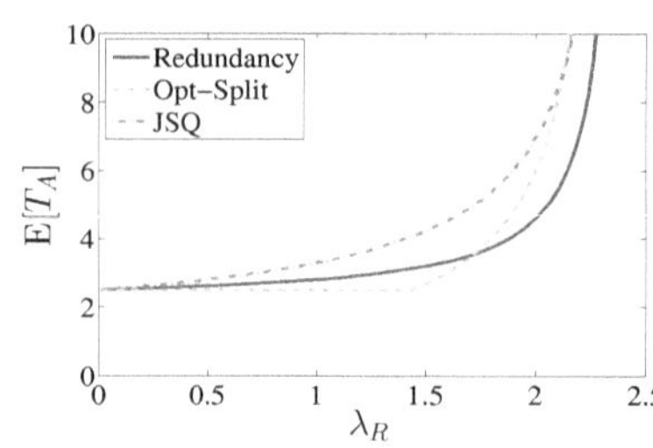

(h) $\mathbb{E}[T_A]$ when $\mu_1 = 2\mu_2$

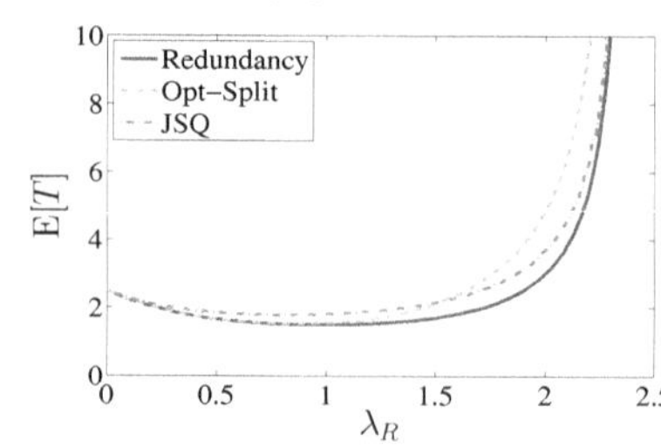

(i) $\mathbb{E}[T]$ when $\mu_1 = 2\mu_2$

Figure 5: Comparing redundancy (solid blue), Opt-Split (dashed green), and JSQ (dashed red) for the $\mathbb{N}$ model as λ_R increases with λ_A= 0.6. We plot mean response time for the redundant *R* class (left column), the non-redundant *A* class (middle column), and the overall system (right column). Rows represent different ratios of server speeds.

DEFINITION 1. *Under Opt-Split, p fraction of class R jobs go to server 2, and $1-p$ fraction go to server 1, where p is chosen to minimize $\mathbb{E}[T]$. The mean response times for class R jobs, class A jobs, and the system are respectively:*

$$\mathbb{E}[T_R]^{\text{Opt-Split}} = \frac{1-p}{\mu_1-(1-p)\lambda_R} + \frac{p}{\mu_2-\lambda_A-p\lambda_R}$$

$$\mathbb{E}[T_A]^{\text{Opt-Split}} = \frac{1}{\mu_2-\lambda_A-p\lambda_R}$$

$$\mathbb{E}[T]^{\text{Opt-Split}} = \frac{\lambda_A}{\lambda_A+\lambda_R}\mathbb{E}[T_A]^{\text{Opt-Split}} + \frac{\lambda_R}{\lambda_A+\lambda_R}\mathbb{E}[T_R]^{\text{Opt-Split}}.$$

THEOREM 4. *If $\mu_1 = \mu_2$, then the following are true:*

1. $\frac{1}{2} \leq \frac{\mathbb{E}[T_R]^{\text{Redundant}}}{\mathbb{E}[T_R]^{\text{Opt-Split}}} \leq 1$.
   If $\lambda_R > \lambda_A$, then $\frac{\mathbb{E}[T_R]^{\text{Redundant}}}{\mathbb{E}[T_R]^{\text{Opt-Split}}} = \frac{1}{2}$.
2. $\frac{\mathbb{E}[T_A]^{\text{Redundant}}}{\mathbb{E}[T_A]^{\text{Opt-Split}}} \leq \frac{3}{2}$.
3. $\frac{1}{2} \leq \frac{\mathbb{E}[T]^{\text{Redundant}}}{\mathbb{E}[T]^{\text{Opt-Split}}} \leq 1$.

PROOF. Deferred to the end of the section. $\square$

4.1 Proofs for $\mathbb{N}$ Model

PROOF. **[Theorem 3]** We first consider the case $n_A = 0$.

$$\Pr\{N_A = 0\} = C\sum_{i=0}^{\infty}\left(\frac{\lambda_R}{\mu_1+\mu_2}\right)^i = C\frac{\mu_1+\mu_2}{\mu_1+\mu_2-\lambda_R}.$$

For $n_A > 0$, we compute $\Pr\{N_A = n_A\}$ by summing over all values of r, and all values of a_0 and a_1 so that $a_0 + a_1 = n_A$:

$$\Pr\{N_A = n_A\} = C\beta_A^{n_A} + \sum_{a_0=0}^{n_A}\sum_{r=1}^{\infty} C\beta_A^{a_0}\alpha_R^r\alpha_A^{n_A-a_0}\binom{n_A-a_0+r-1}{n_A-a_0},$$

where $\beta_A = \frac{\lambda_A}{\mu_2}$, $\alpha_A = \frac{\lambda_A}{\mu_1+\mu_2}$, and $\alpha_R = \frac{\lambda_R}{\mu_1+\mu_2}$, which after some simplification yields the result in (2). We omit the details due to space considerations; for the full proof, see the associated technical report [15].

We now obtain the Laplace transform of the response time for class A jobs, $\widetilde{T}_A(s)$, via distributional Little's Law [21]. First, we find the z-transform of the number of class A jobs in the system, $\widehat{N}_A(z)$:

$$\widehat{N}_A(z) = \sum_{i=0}^{\infty}\Pr\{N_A = i\}z^i$$

$$= \zeta_{N1} \sum_{i=0}^{\infty} \left(\frac{\lambda_A}{\mu_2}\right)^i z^i + \zeta_{N2} \sum_{i=0}^{\infty} \left(\frac{\lambda_A}{\mu_1 + \mu_2 - \lambda_R}\right)^i z^i$$

$$= \frac{\zeta_{N1}\mu_2}{\mu_2 - \lambda_A z} + \frac{\zeta_{N2}(\mu_1 + \mu_2 - \lambda_R)}{\mu_1 + \mu_2 - \lambda_R - \lambda_A z}.$$

Observe that class A jobs depart the system in the same order in which they arrive, so A_{T_A}, the number of class A arrivals during a class A response time, is equivalent to N_A, the number of class A jobs seen by an A departure. Then since $\widehat{A}_{T_A}(z) = \widetilde{T}_A(\lambda_A - \lambda_A z)$, we have:

$$\widetilde{T}_A(\lambda_A - \lambda_A z) = \widehat{N}_A(z)$$

$$= \frac{\zeta_{N1}\mu_2}{\mu_2 - \lambda_A z} + \frac{\zeta_{N2}(\mu_1 + \mu_2 - \lambda_R)}{\mu_1 + \mu_2 - \lambda_R - \lambda_A z}.$$

Let $s = \lambda_A - \lambda_A z$, so $z = 1 - \frac{s}{\lambda_A}$. Then we have

$$\widetilde{T}_A(s) = \frac{\zeta_{N1}\mu_2}{\mu_2 - \lambda_A(1 - \frac{s}{\lambda_A})} + \frac{\zeta_{N2}(\mu_1 + \mu_2 - \lambda_R)}{\mu_1 + \mu_2 - \lambda_R - \lambda_A(1 - \frac{s}{\lambda_A})}$$

$$= (1 + \omega_N)\frac{\nu_{N1}}{\nu_{N1} + s} - \omega_N \frac{\nu_{N2}}{\nu_{N2} + s}.$$

This is the transform of a Generalized Hyperexponential distribution, $H_2(\nu_{N1}, \nu_{N2}, \omega_N)$. Finally,

$$\mathbb{E}[T_A] = -\widetilde{T}'_A(s)|_{s=0}$$

$$= -\left[(1 + \omega_N)\frac{-\nu_{N1}}{(\nu_{N1} + s)^2} + \omega_N \frac{\nu_{N2}}{(\nu_{N2} + s)^2}\right]\Bigg|_{s=0}$$

$$= \frac{1}{\nu_{N1}} + \frac{1}{\nu_{N2}} - \frac{1}{\nu_{N3}}. \quad \square$$

PROOF. **[Lemma 2]** In the fully redundant model, all jobs enter the FCFS queue at both servers and depart from both servers immediately upon completion at either server. This is exactly an M/M/1 with arrival rate $\lambda_A + \lambda_B$ and service rate $\mu_1 + \mu_2$. $\square$

PROOF. **[Lemma 3]** From Theorem 2, in the $\mathbb{N}$ model, $T_R \sim \text{Exp}(\mu_1 + \mu_2 - \lambda_A - \lambda_B)$, which is the response time distribution in an M/M/1 with arrival rate $\lambda_A + \lambda_R$ and service rate $\mu_2 + \mu_2$. From Theorem 3, in the $\mathbb{N}$ model,

$$\mathbb{E}[T_A] = \frac{1}{\mu_1 + \mu_2 - \lambda_A - \lambda_R} + \frac{1}{\mu_2 - \lambda_A} - \frac{1}{\mu_1 + \mu_2 - \lambda_A},$$

which is at least the mean response time in an M/M/1 with arrival rate $\lambda_A + \lambda_R$ and service rate $\mu_1 + \mu_2$ since $\frac{1}{\mu_2 - \lambda_A} - \frac{1}{\mu_1 + \mu_2 - \lambda_A}$ is nonnegative. $\square$

PROOF. **[Theorem 4]** Definition 1 gives us $\mathbb{E}[T_R]^{\text{Opt-Split}}$, $\mathbb{E}[T_A]^{\text{Opt-Split}}$, and $\mathbb{E}[T]^{\text{Opt-Split}}$. We know $\mathbb{E}[T_A]^{\text{Redundant}}$ from Theorem 3. Theorem 2 tells us that

$$T_R^{\text{Redundant}} \sim \text{Exp}(\mu_1 + \mu_2 - \lambda_A - \lambda_R),$$

so we know that $\mathbb{E}[T_R]^{\text{Redundant}} = \frac{1}{\mu_1 + \mu_2 - \lambda_A - \lambda_R}$. Finally,

$$\mathbb{E}[T]^{\text{Redundant}} = \frac{\lambda_R}{\lambda_A + \lambda_R}\mathbb{E}[T_R]^{\text{Redundant}} + \frac{\lambda_A}{\lambda_A + \lambda_R}\mathbb{E}[T_A]^{\text{Redundant}}.$$

Thus, $\frac{\mathbb{E}[T_R]^{\text{Redundant}}}{\mathbb{E}[T_R]^{\text{Opt-Split}}}$, $\frac{\mathbb{E}[T_A]^{\text{Redundant}}}{\mathbb{E}[T_A]^{\text{Opt-Split}}}$, and $\frac{\mathbb{E}[T]^{\text{Redundant}}}{\mathbb{E}[T]^{\text{Opt-Split}}}$, and the desired results follow after some minor algebra. $\square$

5. $\mathbb{W}$ MODEL

We now consider the $\mathbb{W}$ model (see Figure 2(b)). The $\mathbb{W}$ model has two non-redundant classes, A and B, each with its own server. A third class, R, enters the system and issues redundant requests at both servers. We study how this redundant class affects the performance of the system.

An immediate consequence of Theorem 1 is Lemma 4, which gives the limiting distribution of the $\mathbb{W}$ model.

LEMMA 4. *In the $\mathbb{W}$ model, the limiting probability of being in state $(c_n, c_{n-1}, \ldots, c_1)$ depends on c_1, as follows:*

$$\pi_{(c_n,\ldots,A)} = C_{\mathbb{W}} \left(\frac{\lambda_A}{\mu_1}\right)^{a_0} \left(\frac{\lambda_A}{\mu_1 + \mu_2}\right)^{a_1} \left(\frac{\lambda_B}{\mu_1 + \mu_2}\right)^{b_1} \left(\frac{\lambda_R}{\mu_1 + \mu_2}\right)^{r}$$

$$\pi_{(c_n,\ldots,B)} = C_{\mathbb{W}} \left(\frac{\lambda_B}{\mu_2}\right)^{b_0} \left(\frac{\lambda_A}{\mu_1 + \mu_2}\right)^{a_1} \left(\frac{\lambda_B}{\mu_1 + \mu_2}\right)^{b_1} \left(\frac{\lambda_R}{\mu_1 + \mu_2}\right)^{r}$$

$$\pi_{(c_n,\ldots,R)} = C_{\mathbb{W}} \left(\frac{\lambda_A}{\mu_1 + \mu_2}\right)^{a_1} \left(\frac{\lambda_B}{\mu_1 + \mu_2}\right)^{b_1} \left(\frac{\lambda_R}{\mu_1 + \mu_2}\right)^{r},$$

where a_0 is the number of class A jobs before the first class B or R job, b_0 is the number of class B jobs before the first class A or R job, a_1 (respectively, b_1) is the number of class A (class B) jobs after the first job of class R or B (A), r is the total number of class R jobs, and

$$C_{\mathbb{W}} = \frac{(\mu_1 - \lambda_A)(\mu_2 - \lambda_B)(\mu_1 + \mu_2 - \lambda_A - \lambda_B - \lambda_R)}{\mu_1\mu_2(\mu_1 + \mu_2 - \lambda_A - \lambda_B)}$$

is a normalizing constant.

Like in the $\mathbb{N}$ model, the redundant class (class R) has an Exponentially distributed response time (Theorem 5). This is again surprising because the system is not an M/M/1. Nonetheless, the response time for the redundant class is stochastically equivalent to the response time in an M/M/1 with arrival rate λ_R and service rate $\mu' = \mu_1 + \mu_2 - \lambda_A - \lambda_B$. We can interpret μ' as the remaining service capacity in the system after λ_A and λ_B have been apportioned to classes A and B respectively. Alternatively, we can view the response time for the redundant class as that in an M/M/1 with arrival rate $\lambda_A + \lambda_B + \lambda_R$ and service rate $\mu_1 + \mu_2$.

THEOREM 5. *In the $\mathbb{W}$ model,*

1. *The number of class R jobs in the system, N_R, is distributed* Geometric$(1-\rho)-1$, *where* $\rho = \frac{\lambda_R}{\mu_1+\mu_2-\lambda_A-\lambda_B}$.
2. *The response time of class R jobs, T_R, is distributed* $\text{Exp}(\mu_1 + \mu_2 - \lambda_A - \lambda_B - \lambda_R)$.

PROOF. The proof follows the same approach as that of Theorem 10, and is omitted. $\square$

In Theorem 6, we derive the distribution of response time for the non-redundant class A (class B is symmetric). Again like in the $\mathbb{N}$ model, we find that T_A follows a Generalized Hyperexponential distribution. In addition, the mean response time of class A (or class B) jobs can be interpreted as that in an M/M/1 with arrival rate λ_A and service rate μ_1, plus a penalty term that captures the extent to which the redundant class hurts the A's (or B's) (Equation 4). Surprisingly, this penalty is the same for class A and class B even if they have different loads: the pain caused by the redundant class is shared equally among the non-redundant classes.

THEOREM 6. *In the $\mathbb{W}$ model,*

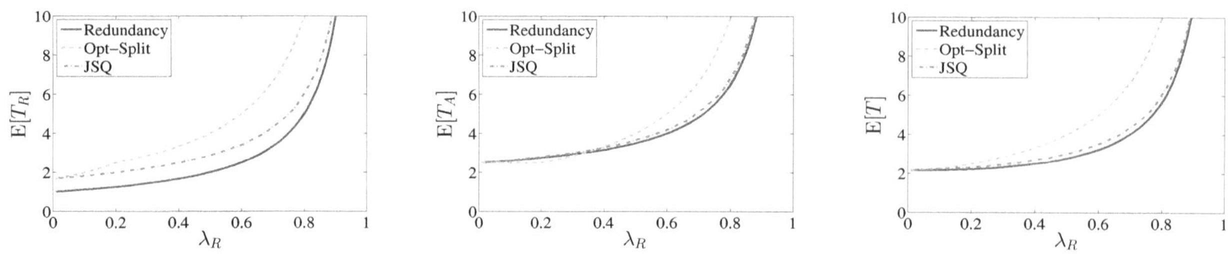

(a) $\mathbb{E}[T_R]$ (b) $\mathbb{E}[T_A]$ (c) $\mathbb{E}[T]$

Figure 6: Comparing redundancy (solid blue), Opt-Split (dashed green), and JSQ (dashed red) for the $\mathbb{W}$ model as λ_R increases, for $\mu_1 = \mu_2 = 1$, $\lambda_A = 0.6$, and $\lambda_B = 0.4$. Lines shown include mean response time for (a) class R, (b) class A, and (c) the system. Results for other values of μ_1 and μ_2 are similar.

1. *The number of class A jobs in the system, N_A, has p.m.f.*

$$\Pr\{N_A = n_A\} = \zeta_{\mathbb{W}1}\left(\frac{\lambda_A}{\mu_1}\right)^{n_A} + \zeta_{\mathbb{W}2}\left(\frac{\lambda_A}{\mu_1+\mu_2-\lambda_B-\lambda_R}\right)^{n_A},$$

where

$$\zeta_{\mathbb{W}1} = \frac{(\mu_1-\lambda_A)(\mu_2-\lambda_B)(\mu_1+\mu_2-\lambda_A-\lambda_B-\lambda_R)}{\mu_1(\mu_2-\lambda_B-\lambda_R)(\mu_1+\mu_2-\lambda_A-\lambda_B)}$$

$$\zeta_{\mathbb{W}2} = \frac{-\lambda_R(\mu_1-\lambda_A)(\mu_1+\mu_2-\lambda_A-\lambda_B-\lambda_R)}{(\mu_2-\lambda_B-\lambda_R)(\mu_1+\mu_2-\lambda_A-\lambda_B)}.$$

2. *The distribution of response time of class A jobs is*

$$T_A \sim H_2(\nu_{\mathbb{W}1}, \nu_{\mathbb{W}2}, \omega_{\mathbb{W}}),$$

where

$$\nu_{\mathbb{W}1} = \mu_1 - \lambda_A$$
$$\nu_{\mathbb{W}2} = \mu_1+\mu_2-\lambda_A-\lambda_B-\lambda_R$$
$$\omega_{\mathbb{W}} = \frac{(\mu_2-\lambda_B)\nu_{\mathbb{W}2}}{(\mu_2-\lambda_B-\lambda_R)\nu_{\mathbb{W}3}}.$$

The mean response time of class A jobs is

$$\mathbb{E}[T_A] = \underbrace{\frac{1}{\nu_{\mathbb{W}1}}}_{\text{M/M/1}} + \underbrace{\frac{1}{\nu_{\mathbb{W}2}} - \frac{1}{\nu_{\mathbb{W}3}}}_{\text{penalty}}, \quad (4)$$

where

$$\nu_{\mathbb{W}3} = \mu_1+\mu_2-\lambda_A-\lambda_B.$$

PROOF. The proof follows the same approach as that of Theorem 3, and is omitted. □

The introduction of a new redundant class clearly hurts the existing non-redundant classes, because the new redundant jobs compete for service with the non-redundant jobs. We now ask what would happen if class R chose which queue(s) to join according to some alternative policy, for example, Opt-Split or JSQ.

In Figure 6, we compare these options, where the mean response time under Opt-Split is derived analytically (Definition 2), but JSQ is simulated. We find that for the redundant class, redundancy outperforms JSQ, which in turn outperforms Opt-Split (Figure 6(a)).

For the non-redundant classes (Figure 6(b)), mean response time is often lower under redundancy than under Opt-Split or JSQ, particularly under higher loads of redundant jobs. This is because even though a larger number of R jobs compete with class A at server 1, some of these R jobs depart the system without ever using server 1 (they complete service at server 2 before entering service at server 1), and some of these R jobs receive service on both servers at once, thus departing the system faster. As in the $\mathbb{N}$ model, redundancy is always better for the overall system (Figure 6(c)).

When the servers are homogeneous, in the few cases in which mean response time of class A or B is lower under Opt-Split than under redundancy, we show that redundancy is never more than 50% worse for the A or B jobs.

DEFINITION 2. *Under Opt-Split, p fraction of class R jobs go to server 1, and $1-p$ fraction go to server 2, where p is chosen to minimize $\mathbb{E}[T]$. The mean response times for class R jobs, class A jobs, and the overall system are:*

$$\mathbb{E}[T_R]^{\text{Opt-Split}} = \frac{p}{\mu_1-\lambda_A-p\lambda_R} + \frac{1-p}{\mu_2-\lambda_B-(1-p)\lambda_R}$$

$$\mathbb{E}[T_A]^{\text{Opt-Split}} = \frac{1}{\mu_1-\lambda_A-p\lambda_R}$$

$$\mathbb{E}[T]^{\text{Opt-Split}} = \frac{\lambda_A}{\lambda_A+\lambda_B+\lambda_R}\mathbb{E}[T_A]^{\text{Opt-Split}} + \frac{\lambda_B}{\lambda_A+\lambda_B+\lambda_R}\mathbb{E}[T_B]^{\text{Opt-Split}} + \frac{\lambda_R}{\lambda_A+\lambda_B+\lambda_R}\mathbb{E}[T_R]^{\text{Opt-Split}}.$$

The mean response time for class B is symmetric to that of class A.

THEOREM 7. *If $\mu_1 = \mu_2$, then the following are true:*

1. $\frac{1}{2} \le \frac{\mathbb{E}[T_R]^{\text{Redundant}}}{\mathbb{E}[T_R]^{\text{Opt-Split}}} \le 1.$
   If $\lambda_R \ge |\lambda_A - \lambda_B|$, then $\frac{\mathbb{E}[T_R]^{\text{Redundant}}}{\mathbb{E}[T_R]^{\text{Opt-Split}}} = \frac{1}{2}.$

2. $\frac{1}{2} \le \frac{\mathbb{E}[T_A]^{\text{Redundant}}}{\mathbb{E}[T_A]^{\text{Opt-Split}}} \le \frac{3}{2}.$

3. $\frac{1}{2} \le \frac{\mathbb{E}[T]^{\text{Redundant}}}{\mathbb{E}[T]^{\text{Opt-Split}}} \le 1.$

PROOF. We have $\mathbb{E}[T_R]^{\text{Opt-Split}}$, $\mathbb{E}[T_A]^{\text{Opt-Split}}$, and $\mathbb{E}[T]^{\text{Opt-Split}}$ from Definition 2. We also know $\mathbb{E}[T_A]^{\text{Redundant}}$ from Theorem 6. Theorem 5 tells us that

$$T_R^{\text{Redundant}} \sim \text{Exp}(\mu_1+\mu_2-\lambda_A-\lambda_B-\lambda_R),$$

so

$$\mathbb{E}[T_R]^{\text{Redundant}} = \frac{1}{\mu_1 + \mu_2 - \lambda_A - \lambda_B - \lambda_R}.$$

Finally,

$$\begin{aligned}\mathbb{E}[T]^{\text{Redundant}} &= \frac{\lambda_R}{\lambda_A + \lambda_B + \lambda_R}\mathbb{E}[T_R]^{\text{Redundant}} \\ &+ \frac{\lambda_A}{\lambda_A + \lambda_B + \lambda_R}\mathbb{E}[T_A]^{\text{Redundant}} \\ &+ \frac{\lambda_B}{\lambda_A + \lambda_B + \lambda_R}\mathbb{E}[T_B]^{\text{Redundant}}.\end{aligned}$$

We use these expressions to find $\frac{\mathbb{E}[T_R]^{\text{Redundant}}}{\mathbb{E}[T_R]^{\text{Opt-Split}}}$, $\frac{\mathbb{E}[T_A]^{\text{Redundant}}}{\mathbb{E}[T_A]^{\text{Opt-Split}}}$, and $\frac{\mathbb{E}[T]^{\text{Redundant}}}{\mathbb{E}[T]^{\text{Opt-Split}}}$, and the desired results follow after some minor algebra. □

6. $\mathbb{M}$ MODEL

Finally, we consider the $\mathbb{M}$ model (Figure 2(c)). Unlike the $\mathbb{N}$ and $\mathbb{W}$ models, there are two redundant classes in an $\mathbb{M}$ model, classes R_1 and R_2. We study how to best use a shared server to which both classes issue redundant requests. For convenience, throughout the remainder of this section we use the notation

$$\begin{aligned}\mu_{1,2,3} &= \mu_1 + \mu_2 + \mu_3 \\ \mu_{1,2} &= \mu_1 + \mu_2 \\ \mu_{2,3} &= \mu_2 + \mu_3.\end{aligned}$$

An immediate consequence of Theorem 1 is Lemma 5, which gives the limiting distribution of the $\mathbb{M}$ model.

LEMMA 5. *In the $\mathbb{M}$ model, the limiting probability of being in state $(c_n, c_{n-1}, \ldots, c_1)$ depends on c_1, as follows:*

$$\pi_{(c_n,\ldots,R_1)} = C_{\mathbb{M}}\left(\frac{\lambda_{R_1}}{\mu_{1,2}}\right)^{r_{1,0}}\left(\frac{\lambda_{R_1}}{\mu_{1,2,3}}\right)^{r_{1,1}}\left(\frac{\lambda_{R_2}}{\mu_{1,2,3}}\right)^{r_{2,1}}$$

$$\pi_{(c_n,\ldots,R_2)} = C_{\mathbb{M}}\left(\frac{\lambda_{R_2}}{\mu_{2,3}}\right)^{r_{2,0}}\left(\frac{\lambda_{R_1}}{\mu_{1,2,3}}\right)^{r_{1,1}}\left(\frac{\lambda_{R_2}}{\mu_{1,2,3}}\right)^{r_{2,1}}$$

where $r_{1,0}$ (respectively, $r_{2,0}$) is the number of class R_1 (R_2) jobs before the first class R_2 (R_1) job, $r_{1,1}$ (respectively, $r_{2,1}$) is the number of class R_1 (R_2) jobs after the first R_2 (R_1) job, and

$$C_{\mathbb{M}} = \frac{(\mu_{1,2} - \lambda_{R_1})(\mu_{1,2,3} - \lambda_{R_1} - \lambda_{R_2})(\mu_{2,3} - \lambda_{R_2})}{\mu_{1,2}\mu_{2,3}(\mu_{1,2,3} - \lambda_{R_1} - \lambda_{R_2}) + \lambda_{R_1}\lambda_{R_2}\mu_2}$$

is a normalizing constant.

In Theorem 8, we derive the distribution of response time for class R_1 (class R_2 is symmetric). The response time for class R_1 follows a Generalized Hyperexponential distribution.

Note that in the $\mathbb{N}$ and $\mathbb{W}$ models, the redundant class had Exponentially distributed response time and the response time distribution for *non-redundant* classes was a Generalized Hyperexponential, whereas in the $\mathbb{M}$ model, the *redundant* class has a Generalized Hyperexponential response time distribution. We hypothesize that the response time distribution is related to the degree of redundancy: fully redundant classes see Exponentially distributed response time, and partially redundant or non-redundant classes see Generalized Hyperexponentially distributed response times.

THEOREM 8. *In the $\mathbb{M}$ model,*

1. *The number of class R_1 jobs, N_{R_1} has p.m.f.*

$$\Pr\{N_{R_1} = n\} = \zeta_{\mathbb{M}1}\left(\frac{\lambda_{R_1}}{\mu_{1,2}}\right)^n + \zeta_{\mathbb{M}2}\left(\frac{\lambda_{R_1}}{\mu_{1,2,3} - \lambda_{R_2}}\right)^n,$$

where

$$\zeta_{\mathbb{M}1} = C_{\mathbb{M}}\frac{\mu_3}{\mu_3 - \lambda_{R_2}}$$

$$\zeta_{\mathbb{M}2} = C_{\mathbb{M}}\left(\frac{\lambda_{R_2}}{\mu_{2,3} - \lambda_{R_2}} - \frac{\lambda_{R_1}}{\mu_{1,2,3} - \lambda_{R_2}}\right).$$

2. *The distribution of response time of class R_1 jobs is*

$$T_{R_1} \sim H_2(\nu_{\mathbb{M}1}, \nu_{\mathbb{M}2}, \omega_{\mathbb{M}}),$$

where

$$\begin{aligned}\nu_{\mathbb{M}1} &= \mu_{1,2} - \lambda_{R_1} \\ \nu_{\mathbb{M}2} &= \mu_{1,2,3} - \lambda_{R_1} - \lambda_{R_2} \\ \omega_{\mathbb{M}} &= \zeta_{\mathbb{M}1}\frac{\mu_{1,2}}{\mu_{1,2} - \lambda_{R_1}}\end{aligned}$$

PROOF. The proof follows the same approach as that of Theorem 3, and is omitted. □

Both classes obviously benefit from issuing redundant requests on a shared server rather than each class having a single dedicated server. However, one might wonder whether mean response time could be further reduced by using some other policy, like Opt-Split or JSQ, instead of redundancy. In Figure 7 we investigate the relative performance of these alternative policies. Mean response time under Opt-Split is derived analytically (Definition 3); JSQ is simulated.

DEFINITION 3. *Under Opt-Split, p fraction of class R_1 jobs go to server 2, and $1-p$ fraction go to server 1, and q fraction of class R_2 jobs go to server 2, and $1-q$ fraction go to server 3. We choose p and q to minimize the overall mean response time, given by*

$$\begin{aligned}\mathbb{E}[T]^{\text{Opt-Split}} &= \frac{(1-p)\lambda_{R_1}}{\lambda_{R_1} + \lambda_{R_2}} \cdot \frac{1}{\mu_1 - (1-p)\lambda_{R_1}} \\ &+ \frac{p\lambda_{R_1} + q\lambda_{R_2}}{\lambda_{R_1} + \lambda_{R_2}} \cdot \frac{1}{\mu_2 - p\lambda_{R_1} - q\lambda_{R_2}} \\ &+ \frac{(1-q)\lambda_{R_2}}{\lambda_{R_1} + \lambda_{R_2}} \cdot \frac{1}{\mu_3 - (1-q)\lambda_{R_2}}.\end{aligned}$$

In all cases, redundancy outperforms both Opt-Split and JSQ. For homogeneous servers (Figure 7(a)), mean response time under JSQ approaches that under redundancy at high load, but at low load, redundancy is better by a factor of 2. For heterogeneous servers (Figure 7(b)), as the service rate of the shared server increases, mean response time under Opt-Split approaches that under redundancy (Theorem 9), but JSQ is worse by a factor of 2. As the system is symmetric, the response times of the individual classes are the same as that of the overall system, and thus are not shown.

We analytically prove performance bounds for the $\mathbb{M}$ model:

THEOREM 9. *In the $\mathbb{M}$ model, for any μ_1, μ_2, μ_3, λ_{R_1}, and λ_{R_2} such that the system is stable,*

1. *If $\mu_1 = \mu_2 = \mu_3$ and $\lambda_{R_1} = \lambda_{R_2}$, $\frac{1}{3} \leq \frac{\mathbb{E}[T]^{\text{Redundant}}}{\mathbb{E}[T]^{\text{Opt-Split}}} \leq \frac{1}{2}$.*

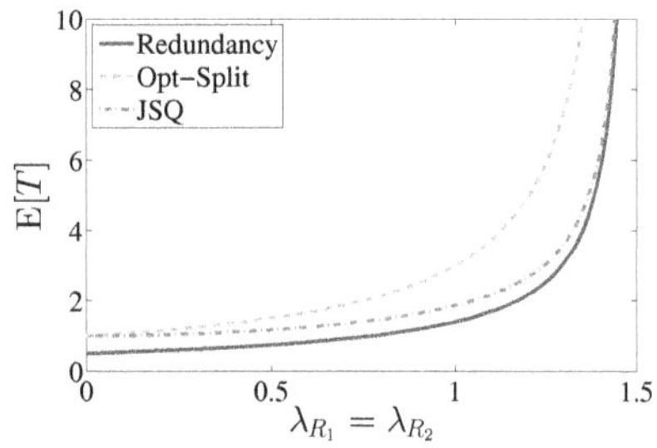

(a) $\mu_1 = \mu_2 = \mu_3 = 1$

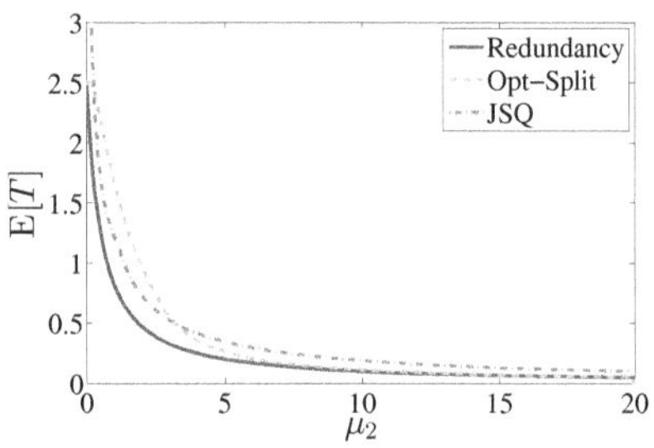

(b) $\mu_1 = \mu_3 = 1$, $\lambda_{R_1} = \lambda_{R_2} = 0.6$.

Figure 7: Comparing redundancy, Opt-Split, and JSQ for the $\mathbb{M}$ model. Lines shown include mean response time for the overall system under redundancy (solid blue), Opt-Split (dashed green), and JSQ with tiebreaking in favor of the faster server (dashed red). Mean response time as a function of (a) increasing $\lambda_{R_1} = \lambda_{R_2}$, (b) increasing μ_2.

2. $\lim_{\mu_2 \to \infty} \frac{\mathbb{E}[T]^{\text{Redundant}}}{\mathbb{E}[T]^{\text{Opt-Split}}} = 1.$

3. $\frac{\mathbb{E}[T]^{\text{Redundant}}}{\mathbb{E}[T]^{\text{Opt-Split}}} \leq 1.$

PROOF. We know $\mathbb{E}[T]^{\text{Opt-Split}}$ from Definition 3, and

$$\mathbb{E}[T]^{\text{Redundant}} = \frac{\lambda_{R_1}}{\lambda_{R_1} + \lambda_{R_2}} \mathbb{E}[T_{R_1}]^{\text{Redundant}} + \frac{\lambda_{R_2}}{\lambda_{R_1} + \lambda_{R_2}} \mathbb{E}[T_{R_2}]^{\text{Redundant}},$$

where we know $\mathbb{E}[T_{R_1}]^{\text{Redundant}}$ and $\mathbb{E}[T_{R_2}]^{\text{Redundant}}$ from Theorem 8. We can then write $\frac{\mathbb{E}[T]^{\text{Redundant}}}{\mathbb{E}[T]^{\text{Opt-Split}}}$, and the desired results follow after some minor algebra. □

7. SCALE

Thus far, we only have considered systems with two servers (the $\mathbb{N}$ and $\mathbb{W}$ models) and three servers (the $\mathbb{M}$ model). We now turn our attention to the question of scale.

The scaled $\mathbb{N}$, $\mathbb{W}$, and $\mathbb{M}$ models are shown in Figure 8. In the scaled $\mathbb{N}$ model, there are k servers and k classes of jobs (see Figure 8(a)). Class R jobs replicate at all servers, while jobs from class C_i join only the queue at server i for $2 \leq i \leq k$. The scaled $\mathbb{W}$ model is similar; there are k servers and $k+1$ classes of jobs, with class R replicating at all servers, and class C_i going only to server i, $1 \leq i \leq k$ (see Figure 8(b)). In the scaled $\mathbb{M}$ model, each class R_i, $1 \leq i < k$, joins the queue at its own dedicated server and at a single server shared by all classes (see Figure 8(c)).

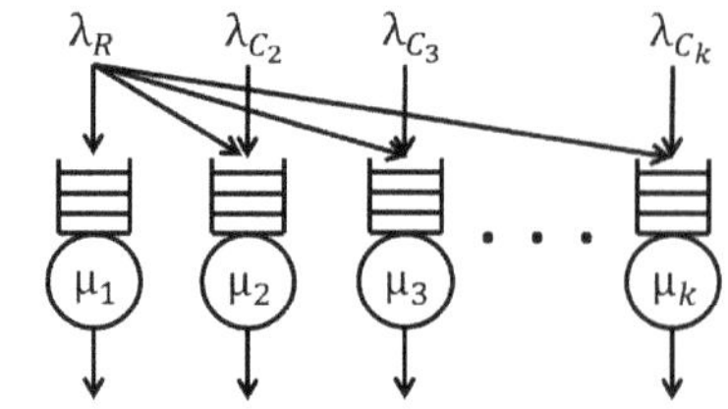

(a) Scaled $\mathbb{N}$ model

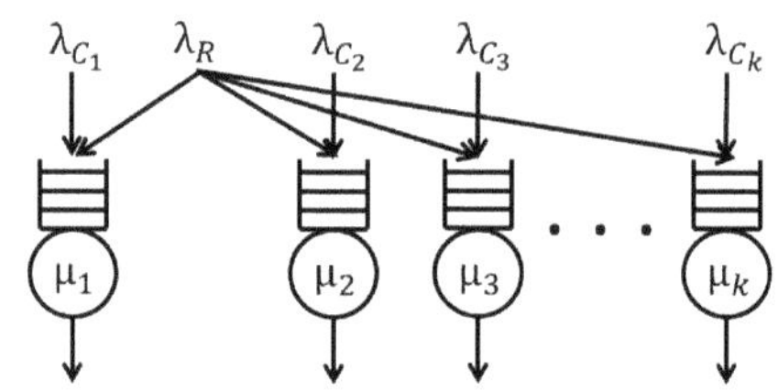

(b) Scaled $\mathbb{W}$ model

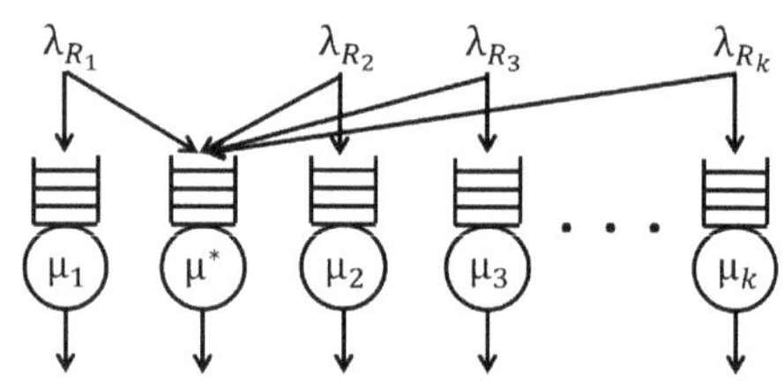

(c) Scaled $\mathbb{M}$ model

Figure 8: Scaled versions of (a) the $\mathbb{N}$ model, (b) the $\mathbb{W}$ model, and (c) the $\mathbb{M}$ model.

The limiting probabilities derived in Theorem 1 for the general redundancy system apply to the scaled $\mathbb{N}$, $\mathbb{W}$, and $\mathbb{M}$ models. In Theorem 10, we use this result to find that in both the scaled $\mathbb{N}$ and $\mathbb{W}$ models, response time for class R is Exponentially distributed, extending the results of Theorem 2 and Theorem 5 respectively.

THEOREM 10.

1. In the scaled $\mathbb{N}$ model, the distribution of the number of class R jobs in the system is

$$N_R \sim \text{Geometric}\left(1 - \frac{\lambda_R}{\sum_{i=1}^k \mu_i - \sum_{i=2}^k \lambda_i}\right) - 1,$$

and the distribution of the response time of class R jobs is

$$T_R \sim \text{Exp}\left(\sum_{i=1}^k \mu_i - \sum_{i=2}^k \lambda_i - \lambda_R\right).$$

2. In the scaled $\mathbb{W}$ model, the distribution of the number of class R jobs in the system is

$$N_R \sim \text{Geometric}\left(1 - \frac{\lambda_R}{\sum_{i=1}^k \mu_i - \sum_{i=1}^k \lambda_i}\right) - 1,$$

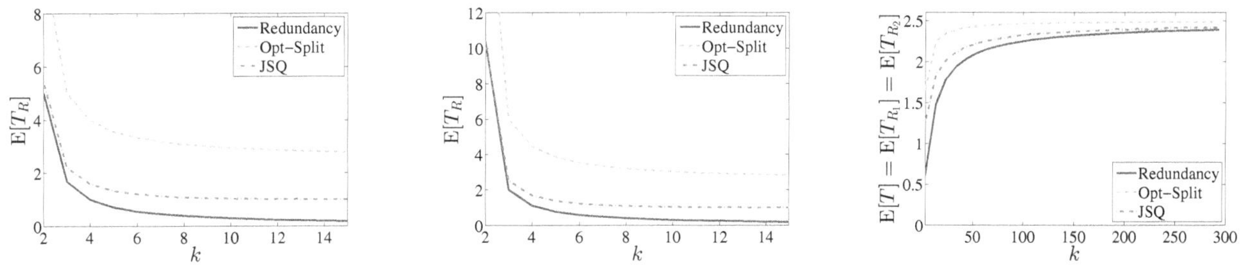

(a) Scaled $\mathbb{N}$ (b) Scaled $\mathbb{W}$ (c) Scaled $\mathbb{M}$

Figure 9: Comparing $\mathbb{E}[\mathbf{T}_R]$ under redundancy (solid blue), Opt-Split (dashed green), and JSQ (dashed red) in scaled systems with homogeneous servers, all with rate 1. (a) The scaled $\mathbb{N}$ model with $\lambda_{C_i}= 0.6$ for all non-redundant classes, and $\lambda_R= 1.2$. (b) The scaled $\mathbb{W}$ model with $\lambda_{C_i}= 0.6$ for all non-redundant classes, and $\lambda_R= 0.7$. (c) The scaled $\mathbb{M}$ model with $\lambda_{R_i}= 0.6$ for all classes.

and the distribution of the response time of class R jobs is

$$T_R \sim \text{Exp}\left(\sum_{i=1}^{k} \mu_i - \sum_{i=1}^{k} \lambda_i - \lambda_R\right).$$

PROOF. See Appendix. □

For the $\mathbb{M}$ model and for the non-redundant classes in the $\mathbb{N}$ and $\mathbb{W}$ models, the result from Theorem 1 does not easily yield a closed form expression in the scaled models. The results discussed in the remainder of this section for these classes are obtained via simulation.

For the two-server $\mathbb{N}$ and $\mathbb{W}$ models, we saw that the redundant class had lower mean response time under redundancy than under both JSQ and Opt-Split, but often JSQ was very close to redundancy. Here, for scaled models, we investigate whether redundancy enjoys a greater advantage over JSQ and Opt-Split as the number of servers increases.

Indeed, we find that the redundant class sees a much greater benefit under redundancy than under Opt-Split and JSQ as k increases for the scaled $\mathbb{N}$ and $\mathbb{W}$ models (see Figures 9(a) and (b)). In fact, as k increases, the benefit grows unboundedly because when a class R job enters a system with high k, it tends to see many idle servers. Under Opt-Split, this job may not be routed to one of the the idle servers. Under JSQ, the job goes to a *single* idle server i and receives mean response time $\frac{1}{\mu_i}$. Under redundancy, the job gets to use *all* of the idle servers, thereby receiving mean response time $\frac{1}{\sum_i \mu_i}$.

In the two-server $\mathbb{N}$ and $\mathbb{W}$ models, we saw that the benefit that class R received from redundancy came at a cost to the non-redundant class A. In the scaled $\mathbb{N}$ and $\mathbb{W}$ models, this cost approaches 0 because the pain caused by the redundant class is spread among all non-redundant classes, so the effect on any one of these classes is minimal; the response time for each non-redundant class C_i approaches that of an M/M/1 with arrival rate λ_{C_i} and service rate μ_i.

In the three-server version of the $\mathbb{M}$ model (Section 6), we saw that redundancy significantly outperformed Opt-Split and JSQ. In Figure 9(c), we look at the relative performance of the three policies as k increases. In the scaled $\mathbb{M}$ model, at low k, redundancy indeed gives a lower mean response time than Opt-Split and JSQ. However, as k increases, response time becomes the same under all three policies. As the load on the shared server becomes high, no class benefits from this server; each class experiences an independent M/M/1. Convergence to k independent M/M/1 queues is slow; for example, at $k = 200$, redundancy still provides a 5% lower mean response time than independent M/M/1 queues.

8. CONCLUSION

In this paper we study a multi-server system with *redundant requests*. In such a system, each job that arrives joins the queue at some subset of the servers and departs the system as soon as it completes service at one of these servers. While recent empirical work in computer systems has demonstrated that redundant requests can greatly reduce response time, theoretical analysis of systems with redundancy has proved challenging.

We present the first exact analysis of systems with redundancy, deriving the limiting distribution of the queue state. Our state space is very complex and furthermore yields a non-product form, and non-obvious, limiting distribution. Nonetheless, we find very clean, simple results for response time distributions for both redundant and non-redundant classes in small systems. For large systems, we derive the response time distribution of a fully redundant class. Many of our results are counterintuitive:

1. The redundant class experiences a response time distribution identical to that in an M/M/1, even though the system is not an M/M/1 ($\mathbb{N}$ and $\mathbb{W}$ models).
2. Once a class is fully redundant, it is *immune* to additional classes becoming redundant: the distribution of its response time does not change ($\mathbb{N}$ and $\mathbb{W}$ model).
3. The non-redundant class often prefers the other class to be redundant as opposed to routing the other class according to Opt-Split or JSQ ($\mathbb{N}$ and $\mathbb{W}$ models).
4. Given two classes of jobs, A and B, each with its own queue, if a class R is redundant at both queues, the pain caused to class A is equal to that caused to class B, even though A's and B's respective arrival rates and service rates may be different ($\mathbb{W}$ model).
5. When multiple classes share a single server, redundancy can improve mean response time relative to Opt-Split and JSQ by a factor of 2 ($\mathbb{M}$ model).
6. As the number of servers increases, redundancy gives an even greater benefit to the redundant class while

causing less pain to the non-redundant classes (scaled $\mathbb{N}$ and scaled $\mathbb{W}$ models).

The redundancy system is closely related to many other queueing models for which exact analysis has long been elusive: Coupled processor systems, fork-join systems, and systems with flexible servers all bear a resemblance to redundancy systems in that they all involve jobs that can be processed by multiple servers. The specific mechanism that determines which jobs run on which servers, and whether jobs can run simultaneously on multiple servers, varies between models, but all of these models share the underlying theme of flexibility. We hope that the new analysis presented in this paper will provide insights on how to analyze these other difficult systems.

Acknowledgments

This material is based upon work supported by the National Science Foundation Graduate Research Fellowship under Grant No. DGE-1252522; was funded by NSF-CMMI-1334194 and NSF-CSR-1116282, by the Intel Science and Technology Center for Cloud Computing, and by a Google Faculty Research Award 2015/16; and has been supported by the Academy of Finland in TOP-Energy project (grant no. 268992).

9. REFERENCES

[1] I. Adan and G. Weiss. A skill based parallel service system under FCFS-ALIS - steady state, overloads, and abandonments. *Stochastic Systems*, 4(1):250–299, 2014.

[2] G. Ananthanarayanan, A. Ghodsi, S. Shenker, and I. Stoica. Effective straggler mitigation: Attack of the clones. In *NSDI*, pages 185–198, April 2013.

[3] F. Baccelli and A. Makowski. Simple computable bounds for the fork-join queue. Technical Report RR-0394, Inria, 1985.

[4] F. Baccelli, A. M. Makowski, and A. Shwartz. The fork-join queue and related systems with synchronization constraints: Stochastic ordering and computable bounds. *Advances in Applied Probability*, 21:629–660, 1989.

[5] A. Bassamboo, R. S. Randhawa, and J. A. V. Mieghem. A little flexibility is all you need: On the value of flexible resources in queueing systems. *Operations Research*, 60:1423–1435, 2012.

[6] S. Borst, O. Boxma, and M. V. Uitert. The asymptotic workload behavior of two coupled queues. *Queueing Systems*, 43(1-2):81–102, January 2003.

[7] R. F. Botta, C. M. Harris, and W. G. Marchal. Characterizations of generalized hyperexponential distribution functions. *Communications in Statistics, Stochastic Models*, 3(1):115–148, 1987.

[8] O. Boxma, G. Koole, and Z. Liu. Queueing-theoretic solution methods for models of parallel and distributed systems. In *Performance Evaluation of Parallel and Distributed Systems Solution Methods. CWI Tract 105 & 106*, pages 1–24, 1994.

[9] H. Casanova. Benefits and drawbacks of redundant batch requests. *Journal of Grid Computing*, 5(2):235–250, February 2007.

[10] J. W. Cohen and O. J. Boxma. *Boundary Value Problems in Queueing System Analysis*. North-Holland Publishing Company, 1983.

[11] J. Dean and L. A. Barroso. The tail at scale. *Communications of the ACM*, 56(2):74–80, February 2013.

[12] G. Fayolle and R. Iasnogorodski. Two coupled processors: The reduction to a Riemann-Hilbert problem. *Zeitschrift fur Wahrscheinlichkeitstheorie und vervandte Gebiete*, 47(3):325–351, 1979.

[13] L. Flatto. Two parallel queues created by arrivals with two demands II. *SIAM Journal on Applied Mathematics*, 45(5):1159–1166, October 1985.

[14] L. Flatto and S. Hahn. Two parallel queues created by arrivals with two demands I. *SIAM Journal on Applied Mathematics*, 44(5):250–255, October 1984.

[15] K. Gardner, S. Zbarsky, S. Doroudi, M. Harchol-Balter, E. Hyytiä, and A. Scheller-Wolf. Queueing with redundant requests: First exact analysis. Technical Report CMU-CS-14-143R, January 2015.

[16] M. Harchol-Balter, C. Li, T. Osogami, A. Scheller-Wolf, and M. Squillante. Cycle stealing under immediate dispatch task assignment. In *Annual Symposium on Parallel Algorithms and Architectures*, pages 274–285, June 2003.

[17] G. Hooghiemstra, M. Keane, and S. V. de Ree. Power series for stationary distributions of coupled processor models. *SIAM Journal on Applied Mathematics*, 48(5):861–878, October 1988.

[18] H. Huang, W. Hung, and K. G. Shin. FS2: dynamic data replication in free disk space for improving disk performance and energy consumption. In *Proc. of SOSP'05*, pages 263–276, December 2005.

[19] G. Joshi, Y. Liu, and E. Soljanin. Coding for fast content download. In *Allerton Conference'12*, pages 326–333, 2012.

[20] G. Joshi, Y. Liu, and E. Soljanin. On the delay-storage trade-off in content download from coded distributed storage systems. *IEEE Journal on Selected Areas in Communications*, 32(5):989–997, May 2014.

[21] J. Keilson and L. Servi. A distributional form of Little's Law. *Operations Research Letters*, 7(5):223–227, 1988.

[22] C. Kim and A. K. Agrawala. Analysis of the fork-join queue. *IEEE Transactions on Computers*, 38(2):1041–1053, February 1989.

[23] A. G. Konheim, I. Meilijson, and A. Melkman. Processor-sharing of two parallel lines. *Journal of Applied Probability*, 18(4):952–956, December 1981.

[24] G. Koole and R. Righter. Resource allocation in grid computing. *Journal of Scheduling*, 11:163–173, 2009.

[25] R. Nelson and A. N. Tantawi. Approximate analysis of fork/join synchronization in parallel queues. *IEEE Transactions on Computers*, 37(6):739–743, 1988.

[26] T. Osogami, M. Harchol-Balter, and A. Scheller-Wolf. Analysis of cycle stealing with switching times and thresholds. In *SIGMETRICS*, pages 184–195, June 2003.

[27] N. B. Shah, K. Lee, and K. Ramchandran. The MDS queue: Analysing latency performance of codes and redundant requests. Technical Report arXiv:1211.5405, November 2012.

[28] N. B. Shah, K. Lee, and K. Ramchandran. When do redundant requests reduce latency? Technical Report arXiv:1311.2851, June 2013.

[29] A. L. Stolyar and T. Tezcan. Control of systems with flexible multi-server pools: a shadow routing approach. *Queueing Systems*, 66:1–51, 2010.

[30] J. Tsitsiklis and K. Xu. On the power of (even a little) resource pooling. *Stochastic Systems*, 2:1–66, 2012.

[31] J. Tsitsiklis and K. Xu. Queueing system topologies with limited flexibility. In *SIGMETRICS*, 2013.

[32] J. Visschers, I. Adan, and G. Weiss. A product form solution to a system with multi-type jobs and multi-type servers. *Queueing Systems*, 70:269–298, 2012.

[33] A. Vulimiri, P. B. Godfrey, R. Mittal, J. Sherry, S. Ratnasamy, and S. Shenker. Low latency via redundancy. In *CoNEXT*, pages 283–294, December 2013.

[34] D. Wang, G. Joshi, and G. Wornell. Efficient task replication for fast response times in parallel computation. Technical Report arXiv:1404.1328, April 2014.

[35] C. Xia, Z. Liu, D. Towsley, and M. Lelarge. Scalability of fork/join queueing networks with blocking. In *SIGMETRICS*, pages 133–144, June 2007.

APPENDIX

A. PROOF OF THEOREM 1

THEOREM 1. *The limiting probability of being in state* $(c_n, c_{n-1}, \ldots, c_1)$ *is*

$$\pi_{(c_n,\ldots,c_1)} = C\prod_{i=1}^{n} \frac{\lambda_{c_i}}{\sum\limits_{m\in \bigcup\limits_{j\le i} S_{c_j}} \mu_m},$$

where C *is a normalizing constant.*

PROOF. We begin by writing local balance equations for our states. The local balance equations are:

$$\begin{aligned} A &\equiv \text{Rate entering state } (c_n,\ldots, c_1) \text{ due to an arrival} \\ &= \text{Rate leaving state } (c_n,\ldots, c_1) \text{ due to a departure} \equiv A' \end{aligned}$$

$$\begin{aligned} B_c &\equiv \text{Rate entering state } (c_n,\ldots, c_1) \text{ due to a departure of class } c \\ &= \text{Rate leaving state } (c_n,\ldots, c_1) \text{ due to an arrival of class } c \equiv B'_c. \end{aligned}$$

For an empty system, the state is (). It is not possible to enter state () due to an arrival or to leave due to a departure, so we only have one local balance equation of the form $B_c = B'_c$:

$$\pi_{()}\lambda_c = \pi_{(c)} \sum_{m\in S_c} \mu_m. \tag{5}$$

For any other state $(c_n, c_{n-1}, \ldots, c_1)$, we have local balance equations of the form:

$$A = \pi_{(c_{n-1},\ldots,c_1)}\lambda_{c_n} = \pi_{(c_n,\ldots,c_1)} \sum_{m\in\bigcup_{j\le n} S_{c_j}} \mu_m = A' \tag{6}$$

$$\begin{aligned} B_c &= \sum_{i=0}^{n} \sum_{\substack{m\in S_c,\\ m\notin S_{c_j},\\ 1\le j\le i}} \pi_{(c_n,\ldots,c_{i+1},c,c_i,\ldots,c_1)}\mu_m \\ &= \pi_{(c_n,\ldots,c_1)}\lambda_c = B'_c. \end{aligned} \tag{7}$$

We guess the following form for $\pi_{(c_n,\ldots,c_1)}$:

$$\pi_{(c_n,\ldots,c_1)} = C\prod_{i=1}^{n} \frac{\lambda_{c_i}}{\sum\limits_{m\in \bigcup\limits_{j\le i} S_{c_j}} \mu_m}. \tag{8}$$

We will prove inductively that our guess satisfies the balance equations. The base case is state (). Substituting the guess from (8) into the left-hand side of (5), we get:

$$\begin{aligned} \pi_{(c)} \sum_{m\in S_c} \mu_m &= C\frac{\lambda_c}{\sum\limits_{m\in S_c}\mu_m} \sum_{m\in S_c} \mu_m \\ &= C\lambda_c \\ &= \pi_{()}\lambda_c, \end{aligned}$$

which is exactly the right-hand side of (5).

Now, assume that (6) and (7) hold for some $n-1 \ge 0$. We will show that both hold for n.

1. $\mathbf{A} = \mathbf{A'}$. From (6), we have:

$$\begin{aligned} A = \pi_{(c_{n-1},\ldots,c_1)}\lambda_{c_n} &= C\prod_{i=1}^{n-1} \frac{\lambda_{c_i}}{\sum\limits_{m\in \bigcup\limits_{j\le i} S_{c_j}} \mu_m}\lambda_{c_n} \\ &= \pi_{(c_n,\ldots,c_1)}\frac{\sum_{m\in \bigcup\limits_{j\le n} S_{c_j}} \mu_m}{\lambda_{c_n}}\lambda_{c_n} \\ &= \pi_{(c_n,\ldots,c_1)} \sum_{m\in \bigcup\limits_{j\le n} S_{c_j}} \mu_m = A'. \end{aligned}$$

2. $\mathbf{B_c} = \mathbf{B'_c}$. From (7), we have:

$$\begin{aligned} B_c &= \sum_{i=0}^{n} \sum_{\substack{m\in S_c,\\ m\notin S_{c_j},\\ 1\le j\le i}} \pi_{(c_n,\ldots,c_{i+1},c,c_i,\ldots,c_1)}\mu_m \\ &= \sum_{i=0}^{n-1} \sum_{m\in S_c\setminus \bigcup\limits_{j\le i} S_{c_j}} \pi_{(c_n,\ldots,c_{i+1},c,c_i,\ldots,c_1)}\mu_m \\ &\quad + \sum_{m\in S_c\setminus \bigcup\limits_{j\le n} S_{c_j}} \pi_{(c,c_n,\ldots,c_1)}\mu_m \\ &= \sum_{i=0}^{n-1} \sum_{m\in S_c\setminus \bigcup\limits_{j\le i} S_{c_j}} \frac{\lambda_{c_n}\pi_{(c_{n-1},\ldots,c_{i+1},c,c_i,\ldots,c_1)}}{\sum_{t\in \bigcup\limits_{j\le n} S_{c_j}\cup S_c}\mu_t}\mu_m \\ &\quad + C\frac{\lambda_c\sum_{m\in S_c\setminus \bigcup\limits_{j\le n} S_{c_j}}\mu_m}{\sum_{m\in \bigcup\limits_{j\le n} S_{c_j}\cup S_c}\mu_m}\prod_{i=1}^{n} \frac{\lambda_{c_i}}{\sum\limits_{m\in \bigcup\limits_{j\le i} S_{c_j}} \mu_m} \\ &= \frac{\lambda_{c_n}}{\sum\limits_{m\in \bigcup\limits_{j\le n} S_{c_j}\cup S_c}\mu_m} \sum_{i=0}^{n-1} \sum_{m\in S_c\setminus \bigcup\limits_{j\le i} S_{c_j}} \pi_{(c_{n-1},\ldots,c_{i+1},c,c_i,\ldots,c_1)}\mu_m \\ &\quad + \lambda_c\pi_{(c_n,\ldots,c_1)}\frac{\sum_{m\in S_c\setminus \bigcup\limits_{j\le n} S_{c_j}}\mu_m}{\sum_{m\in \bigcup\limits_{j\le n} S_{c_j}\cup S_c}\mu_m} \\ &= \frac{\lambda_{c_n}}{\sum_{m\in\bigcup_{j\le n} S_{c_j}\cup S_c}\mu_m}\pi_{(c_{n-1},\ldots,c_1)}\lambda_c \end{aligned}$$

$$+ \lambda_c \pi_{(c_n,\ldots,c_1)} \frac{\sum_{m \in S_c \setminus \bigcup_{j \le n} S_{c_j}} \mu_m}{\sum_{m \in \bigcup_{j \le n} S_{c_j} \cup S_c} \mu_m}$$

$$= C\lambda_c \frac{\lambda_{c_n}}{\sum_{m \in \bigcup_{j \le n} S_{c_j} \cup S_c} \mu_m} \prod_{i=1}^{n-1} \frac{\lambda_{c_i}}{\sum_{m \in \bigcup_{j \le i} S_{c_j}} \mu_m}$$

$$+ \lambda_c \pi_{(c_n,\ldots,c_1)} \frac{\sum_{m \in S_c \setminus \bigcup_{j \le n} S_{c_j}} \mu_m}{\sum_{m \in \bigcup_{j \le n} S_{c_j} \cup S_c} \mu_m}$$

$$= \lambda_c \pi_{(c_n,\ldots,c_1)} \frac{\sum_{m \in \bigcup_{j \le n} S_{c_j}} \mu_m}{\sum_{m \in \bigcup_{j \le n} S_{c_j} \cup S_c} \mu_m}$$

$$+ \lambda_c \pi_{(c_n,\ldots,c_1)} \frac{\sum_{m \in S_c \setminus \bigcup_{j \le n} S_{c_j}} \mu_m}{\sum_{m \in \bigcup_{j \le n} S_{c_j} \cup S_c} \mu_m}$$

$$= \lambda_c \pi_{(c_n,\ldots,c_1)} = B'_c.$$

Hence the local balance equations hold for all n, and so the guess for the limiting probabilities from (8) is correct. □

B. PROOF OF THEOREM 10

THEOREM 10.

1. *In the scaled* $\mathbb{N}$ *model, the distribution of the number of class* R *jobs in the system is*

$$N_R \sim \text{Geometric}\left(1 - \frac{\lambda_R}{\sum_{i=1}^k \mu_i - \sum_{i=2}^k \lambda_i}\right) - 1,$$

and the distribution of the response time of class R *jobs is*

$$T_R \sim \text{Exp}\left(\sum_{i=1}^k \mu_i - \sum_{i=2}^k \lambda_i - \lambda_R\right).$$

2. *In the scaled* $\mathbb{W}$ *model, the distribution of the number of class* R *jobs in the system is*

$$N_R \sim \text{Geometric}\left(1 - \frac{\lambda_R}{\sum_{i=1}^k \mu_i - \sum_{i=1}^k \lambda_i}\right) - 1,$$

and the distribution of the response time of class R *jobs is*

$$T_R \sim \text{Exp}\left(\sum_{i=1}^k \mu_i - \sum_{i=1}^k \lambda_i - \lambda_R\right).$$

PROOF. To find $\Pr\{N_R = n_R\}$, we will consider the non-R jobs in the queue as being split into two pieces: the non-R jobs before the first R in the queue, and the non-R jobs after the first R in the queue. We sum over all possible lengths of these two pieces, and all possible classes of these non-R jobs. Let x_0 be the number of non-R jobs before the first R in the queue, and let x_1 be the number of non-R jobs after the first R in the queue. Then we have:

$$\Pr\{N_R = n_R\} = \sum_{x_0=0}^{\infty} \sum_{x_1=0}^{\infty} C\eta_R^{n_R} X_0 \binom{x_1 + n_R - 1}{x_1} \prod_{\substack{j \ge x_0 \\ c_j \ne R}} X_1$$

$$= C\eta_R^{n_R} \left(\sum_{x_0=0}^{\infty} X_0\right) \left(\sum_{x_1=0}^{\infty} X_1^{x_1} \binom{x_1 + n_R - 1}{x_1}\right),$$

where

$$\eta_R = \frac{\lambda_R}{\sum_{m=1}^k \mu_m},$$

$$X_0 = \prod_{j=1}^{x_0} \frac{\sum_{c_i \ne R} \lambda_{c_i}}{\sum_{m \in \bigcup_{t \le j} S_t} \mu_m},$$

$$X_1 = \frac{\sum_{c_i \ne R} \lambda_{c_i}}{\sum_{m=1}^k \mu_m}.$$

The sums in the numerators of X_0 and X_1 take into account all of the possible combinations of classes making up the x_0 and x_1 jobs, respectively.

Now let $C_1 = \sum_{x_0=0}^{\infty} X_0$ (note that this is a constant with respect to n_R). Using the identity $\sum_{i=0}^{\infty} p^i \binom{i+n-1}{i} = \left(\frac{1}{1-p}\right)^n$ for $|p| < 1$, we have:

$$\Pr\{N_R = n_R\} = CC_1 \eta_R^{n_R} \left(\frac{1}{1 - \frac{\sum_{c_i \ne R} \lambda_{c_i}}{\sum_m \mu_m}}\right)^{n_R}$$

$$= CC_1 \left(\frac{\lambda_R}{\sum_m \mu_m - \sum_{c_i \ne R} \lambda_{c_i}}\right)^{n_R}.$$

Using the normalization equation

$$\sum_{n_R=0}^{\infty} \Pr\{N_R = n_R\} = 1,$$

we find

$$CC_1 = 1 - \frac{\lambda_R}{\sum_m \mu_m - \sum_{c_i \ne R} \lambda_{c_i}}.$$

Hence $N_R \sim \text{Geometric}(1 - \frac{\lambda_R}{\sum_m \mu_m - \sum_{c_i \ne R} \lambda_{c_i}}) - 1$.

Next, we obtain the Laplace transform of the response time for class R jobs, $\widetilde{T}_R(s)$, via distributional Little's Law. First, we consider the z-transform of the number of class-R Poisson arrivals during T, $\widehat{A}_{T_R}(z) = \widetilde{T}_R(\lambda_R - \lambda_R z)$. Class R jobs depart the system in the same order in which they arrive, so A_{T_R} is equivalent to N_R, the number of jobs seen by an R departure. Hence

$$\widetilde{T}_R(\lambda_R - \lambda_R z) = \widehat{N}_R(z).$$

We know that N_R is distributed Geometric$(p) - 1$, where $p = 1 - \frac{\lambda_R}{\sum_m \mu_m - \sum_{c_i \ne R} \lambda_{c_i}}$. Hence we have

$$\widetilde{T}_R(\lambda_R - \lambda_R z) = \widehat{N}_R(z) = \frac{p}{1 - z(1-p)}.$$

Let $s = \lambda_R - \lambda_R z$, so that $z = 1 - s/\lambda_R$. Then we have

$$\widetilde{T}_R(s) = \frac{p}{1 - (1 - \frac{s}{\lambda_R})(1-p)},$$

which after some simplification gives

$$\widetilde{T}_R(s) = \frac{\sum_m \mu_m - \sum_{c_i \ne R} \lambda_{c_i} - \lambda_R}{\sum_m \mu_m - \sum_{c_i \ne R} \lambda_{c_i} - \lambda_R + s}.$$

Hence $T_R \sim \text{Exp}(\sum_m \mu_m - \sum_{c_i \ne R} \lambda_{c_i} - \lambda_R)$.

The derivation for the $\mathbb{W}$ model is very similar, and is omitted here. □

Joint Cyber and Physical Attacks on Power Grids: Graph Theoretical Approaches for Information Recovery

Saleh Soltan
Electrical Engineering
Columbia University
New York, NY
saleh@ee.columbia.edu

Mihalis Yannakakis
Computer Science
Columbia University
New York, NY
mihalis@cs.columbia.edu

Gil Zussman
Electrical Engineering
Columbia University
New York, NY
gil@ee.columbia.edu

ABSTRACT

Recent events demonstrated the vulnerability of power grids to cyber attacks and to physical attacks. Therefore, we focus on *joint cyber and physical attacks* and develop methods to retrieve the grid state information following such an attack. We consider a model in which an adversary attacks a zone by physically disconnecting some of its power lines and blocking the information flow from the zone to the grid's control center. We use tools from linear algebra and graph theory and leverage the properties of the power flow DC approximation to develop methods for information recovery. *Using information observed outside the attacked zone, these methods recover information about the disconnected lines and the phase angles at the buses.* We identify *sufficient conditions on the zone structure* and *constraints on the attack characteristics* such that these methods can recover the information. We also show that it is NP-hard to find an approximate solution to the problem of partitioning the power grid into the minimum number of attack-resilient zones. However, since power grids can often be represented by planar graphs, we develop a *constant approximation partitioning algorithm for these graphs*. Finally, we numerically study the relationships between the grid's resilience and its structural properties, and demonstrate the partitioning algorithm on real power grids. The results can provide insights into the design of a secure control network for the smart grid.

Categories and Subject Descriptors

C.4 [**Performance of Systems**]: Reliability, availability, and serviceability; G.2.2 [**Discrete Mathematics**]: Graph Theory—*Graph algorithms, Network problems*

Keywords

Power Grids; Cyber Attacks; Physical Attacks; Information Recovery; Graph Theory; Algorithms

SIGMETRICS'15, June 15–19, 2015, Portland, OR, USA.

ACM 978-1-4503-3486-0/15/06 ...$15.00.
http://dx.doi.org/10.1145/2745844.2745846.

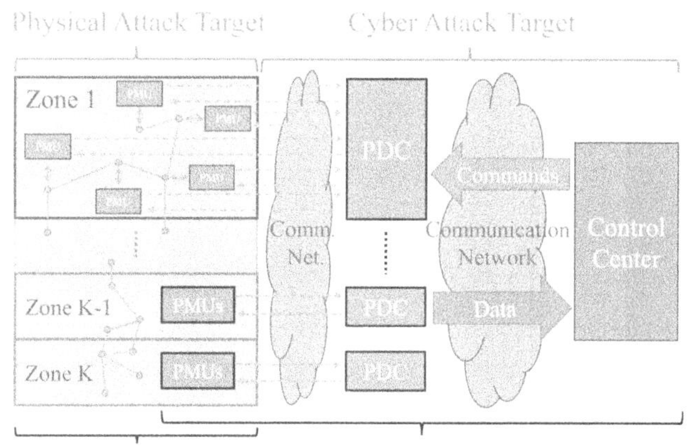

Figure 1: Components of the power grid and potential attacks: physical attacks target the physical infrastructure (lines, substations, etc.); Cyber attacks target the SCADA system – an adversary can disallow the information from the PMUs within the zone to reach the control center.

1. INTRODUCTION

Power grids are vulnerable to cyber attacks [7] and to physical attacks (e.g., the Apr. 2014 attack on a California substation [6]). These attacks may cause large-scale failures, initiate cascades (e.g., [3–5]), and have devastating effects on almost every aspect of modern life. As illustrated in Fig. 1, two main components of the power grid are (i) the physical infrastructure of the power transmission system (power lines, substations, power stations), and (ii) the Supervisory Control and Data Acquisition (SCADA) system responsible for monitoring and controlling the grid (we refer to it as the *control network*). Physical attacks target the former while cyber attacks target the latter.

The effects of a physical attack can be mitigated, if the control center has accurate understanding of its impacts and acts quickly to compensate for failures. However, if physical attacks are accompanied by cyber attacks that make information about the status of the attacked zones unavailable, the control center cannot take effective action. Hence, in this paper *we focus on developing methods for recovering the information about the status of the power grid following a joint cyber and physical attack as well as on studying the resilience of different topologies and the resilience to different attacks.*

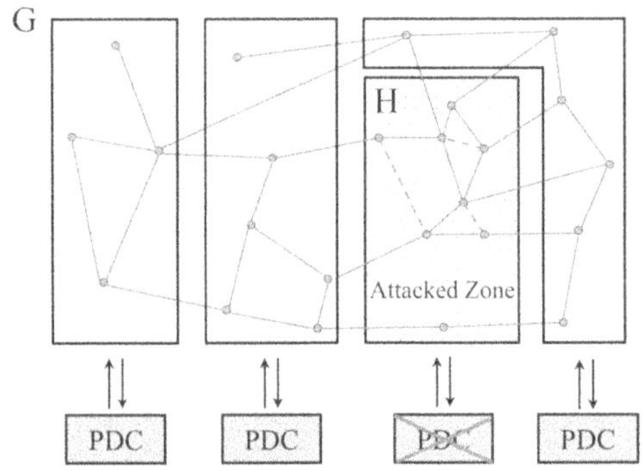

Figure 2: G is the power grid graph and H is an induced subgraph of G that represents the attacked zone. An adversary attacks a zone by disconnecting some of its power lines (red dashed lines) and disallowing the information from the PMUs within the zone to reach the control center.

We consider the linearized *direct-current (DC) power flow model*[1], a practical relaxation of the alternating-current (AC) model. We also use a simplified version of the *control network model* of [28] that includes Phasor Measurement Units (PMU), Phasor Data Concentrators (PDC), and a control center (see Fig. 1). We define a *zone* as a set of buses (nodes), power lines (edges), PMUs, and an associated PDC. We consider an attack on a zone that disconnects some edges within the zone (physical attack), and disallows the information from the PMUs within the zone to reach the control center (cyber attack). An adversary can perform the cyber attack by, for example, disabling the zone's associated PDC. Alternatively, the communication network between the PMUs and the PDC or between the PDC and the control center can be attacked.

As illustrated in Fig. 2, as a result of an attack, some lines get disconnected, and the phase angles and the status of the lines within the *attacked zone* $H = (V_H, E_H)$ become unavailable. Our objective is to recover the phase angles and detect the disconnected lines by using the information available outside of the attacked zone.

The idea underlying many of our results is that power flows are governed by the laws of physics, where a failure changes line flows and nodes' phase angles all over the power grid [40]. We show that based on this physical property, it is possible to estimate the state in the attacked zone using the information available outside of the zone. Specifically, we use the matrix representation of the DC equations and the notion of *admittance matrix*, and apply matrix analysis and graph theoretical tools to *develop methods for retrieving the information from the attacked zone*.

We present *necessary and sufficient conditions on the structure of a zone such that our methods are guaranteed to recover the information*. We prove that if there is a *matching* between the nodes inside and outside the attacked zone that covers the inside nodes (V_H), then the phase angles of the nodes in the attacked zone are recoverable by solving a set of linear equations of size $|V_H|$. We also prove that if H is *acyclic*, then the disconnected lines in H are detectable by solving a set of linear equations of size $|E_H|$. Moreover, we show that if H is *planar*, under some constraints, the disconnected lines are detectable by solving a Linear Programming (LP) problem.

We develop another method to simultaneously recover the phase angles and detect disconnected lines by solving a single LP problem. We show that if there is a *partial matching* between the nodes inside and outside of H, and H is *planar*, then under certain constraints on the attack (i.e., on the disconnected lines), this method is guaranteed to recover the information. Based on these results, we present the Post-Attack Recovery and Detection (PARD) Algorithm.

We study the problem of partitioning the power grid into the minimum number of attack-resilient zones (i.e., zones in which the information can be recovered by the methods mentioned above). We show that this problem is not approximable to within $n^{1-\epsilon}$ for all $\epsilon > 0$, unless P=NP. However, since power grids can often be represented by planar graphs, we introduce the Zone Selection (ZS) Algorithm and show that it provides a constant approximation ratio for these graphs. This algorithm can be used for designing a more secure control network for smart grids.

Finally, we present numerical results to assess the relationship between the structural properties of the power grid and its resilience to joint attacks and to demonstrate the operation of the ZS Algorithm on several power grids.

The main contributions of this paper are three fold. We use matrix analysis and graph theoretical tools to: (i) develop methods to recover the phase angles and detect the disconnected lines after a joint cyber and physical attack, (ii) find graph classes for which these methods are guaranteed to recover the information, (iii) develop an algorithm for partitioning the power grid into attack-resilient zones.

This paper is organized as follows. Section 2 reviews related work. Section 3 describes the models and reviews graph theoretical terms. In Section 4, we focus on information recovery and in Section 5, we study the grid partitioning problem. Section 6 provides numerical results and Section 7 provides concluding remarks and directions for future work. Most of the proofs appear in Appendix B.

2. RELATED WORK

The vulnerability of general networks to attacks was thoroughly studied in the past (e.g., [8,31,36] and references therein). Specifically, attacks and failures in power grids were studied using probabilistic failure propagation models (e.g., [18,20,47], and references therein) as well as using deterministic DC power flows [12,14,22,32,40]. Malicious data attacks on the power grid control network were also studied [21,30,33,44]. However, to the best of our knowledge, none of the previous works considered power grid vulnerability to joint cyber and physical attacks.

In Section 4, we study the problem of recovering the phase angles and detecting disconnected edges after a joint cyber and physical attack. It is related to the problem of line outages identification from changes in phase angles that was studied in [42,43]. However, these studies were limited to at most two line failures. The problem of line failure identification in an internal system using the information from an external system was studied in [49], which only provided a heuristic algorithm that was evaluated for only one or two line failures.

In Section 5, we study the problem of partitioning the power grid into the minimum number of attack-resilient zones. This problem is similar to the PMU placement problems

[1]The DC model is commonly used in large-scale contingency analysis of power grids [14,15,37,49].

studied in [29,35,48]. Recently, this problem has attracted a lot of attention in India after the major blackouts of 2013 [29]. In [48] the problem of PMU placement for line outage detection was studied. However, none of the previous works considered the problem of PMU placement from the security point of view and when both the PDC/PMUs and the physical network can be attacked.

In Section 5, we reduce the attack-resilient zone partitioning problem to the problem of partitioning a graph into subgraphs such that each subgraph is (i) acyclic, and (ii) there is a matching between nodes inside and outside the subgraph that covers all the subgraph nodes. This problem is closely related to the problems of *vertex arboricity* (which is known to be NP-hard to be determined [26, p.193]) and *k-matching cover* of a graph (which can be found in $O(n^3)$ time [45]). However, to the best of our knowledge, the joint problem was not studied before.

Since the power grid and its robustness have drawn a lot of recent attention, several performance evaluation tools were used successfully to analyze power grids (e.g., [25, 27, 34], and references therein). This paper continues this line of work, using tools from linear algebra and graph theory.

3. MODEL AND DEFINITIONS

3.1 DC Power Flow Model

We adopt the linearized (or DC) power flow model, which is widely used as an approximation for the non-linear AC power flow model [11]. In particular, we follow [13–15] and represent the power grid by a connected undirected graph $G = (V, E)$ where $V = \{1, 2, \ldots, n\}$ and $E = \{e_1, \ldots, e_m\}$ are the set of nodes and edges corresponding to the buses and transmission lines, respectively. Each edge e_i is a set of two nodes $e_i = \{u, v\}$. p_v is the active power *supply* ($p_v > 0$) or *demand* ($p_v < 0$) at node $v \in V$ (for a *neutral node* $p_v = 0$). We assume *pure reactive* lines, implying that each edge $\{u, v\} \in E$ is characterized by its *reactance* $r_{uv} = r_{vu}$.

Given the power supply/demand vector $\vec{p} \in \mathbb{R}^{|V| \times 1}$ and the reactance values, a *power flow* is a solution $\mathbf{P} \in \mathbb{R}^{|V| \times |V|}$ and $\vec{\theta} \in \mathbb{R}^{|V| \times 1}$ of:

$$\sum_{v \in N(u)} p_{uv} = p_u, \ \forall\ u \in V \tag{1}$$

$$\theta_u - \theta_v - r_{uv} p_{uv} = 0, \ \forall\ \{u, v\} \in E \tag{2}$$

where $N(u)$ is the set of neighbors of node u, p_{uv} is the power flow from node u to node v, and θ_u is the phase angle of node u. Eq. (1) guarantees (classical) flow conservation and (2) captures the dependency of the flow on the reactance values and phase angles. Additionally, (2) implies that $p_{uv} = -p_{vu}$. When the total supply equals the total demand in each connected component of G, (1)-(2) has a unique solution [15, lemma 1.1].[2] Eq.(1)-(2) are equivalent to the following matrix equation:

$$\mathbf{A}\vec{\theta} = \vec{p} \tag{3}$$

[2]The uniqueness is in the values of p_{uv}s rather than θ_us (shifting all θ_us by equal amounts does not violate (2)).

where $\mathbf{A} \in \mathbb{R}^{|V| \times |V|}$ is the *admittance matrix* of G,[3] defined as follows:

$$a_{uv} = \begin{cases} 0 & \text{if } u \neq v \text{ and } \{u, v\} \notin E, \\ -1/r_{uv} & \text{if } u \neq v \text{ and } \{u, v\} \in E, \\ -\sum_{w \in N(u)} a_{uw} & \text{if } u = v. \end{cases}$$

Note that in power grids nodes can be connected by multiple edges, and therefore, if there are k multiple edges between nodes u and v, $a_{uv} = -\sum_{i=1}^{k} 1/r_{uv_i}$. Once $\vec{\theta}$ is computed, the flows, p_{uv}, can be obtained from (2).

Notation. Throughout this paper we use bold uppercase characters to denote matrices (e.g., $\mathbf{A}$), italic uppercase characters to denote sets (e.g., V), and italic lowercase characters and overline arrow to denote column vectors (e.g., $\vec{\theta}$). For a matrix $\mathbf{Q}$, q_{ij} denotes its $(i, j)^{\text{th}}$ entry. For a column vector $\vec{y}$, $\vec{y}^t$ denote its transpose, y_i denotes its ith entry, $\|\vec{y}\|_1 := \sum_{i=1}^{n} |y_i|$ is its l_1-norm, and $\text{supp}(\vec{y}) := \{i | y_i \neq 0\}$ is its support.

3.2 Control Network

We use the simplified version of the model described in [28] to model the SCADA system to which we refer as the control network. Fig. 1 illusterates the components of the control network. We assume that there is a Phasor Measurement Unit (PMU) at each node of G. The PMU at node i reports the phase angle θ_i as well as the status of the edges (either *operational* or *failed*) adjacent to node i. Phasor Data Concentrators (PDC) gather the data collected by PMUs. The data gathered by PDCs is sent to a control center which monitors and controls the entire grid. A *zone* is a subgraph induced by a subset of nodes with a single associated PDC.

3.3 Attack Model

We study attacks on power grids that affect both the physical infrastructure and the control network. We assume that an adversary attacks a zone by: (i) disconnecting some edges within the attacked zone (physical attack), and (ii) disallowing the information from the PMUs within the zone to reach the control center (cyber attack). An adversary can perform the cyber attack by, for example, disabling the zone's associated PDC. Alternatively, the communication network between the PMUs and the PDC or between the PDC and the control center can be attacked. We assume that disconnecting edges within a zone does not make G disconnected.

Fig. 2 shows an example of an attack on the zone represented by H. Due to the attack, some edges are disconnected (we refer to these edges as *failed edges*) and the phase angles and the status of the edges within the *attacked zone* become unavailable. We denote the set of failed edges in zone H by $F \subseteq E_H$. Upon failure, the edges are removed from the graph and the flows are redistributed according to (1)-(2).

Notation. Throughout this paper, we denote an attacked zone by $H = (V_H, E_H)$. Without loss of generality we assume that the indices are such that $V_H = \{1, 2, \ldots, |V_H|\}$ and $E_H = \{e_1, e_2, \ldots, e_{|E_H|}\}$. We denote the complement of the zone H by $\bar{H} = G \backslash H$. If X, Y are two subgraphs of G, $\mathbf{A}_{X|Y}$ and $\mathbf{A}_{V_X|V_Y}$ both denote the submatrix of the admittance matrix of G with rows from V_X and columns from V_Y. For instance, $\mathbf{A}$ can be written in any of the following

[3]When $r_{uv} = 1\ \forall \{u, v\} \in E$, the admittance matrix $\mathbf{A}$ is the *Laplacian matrix* of the graph.

Table 1: Summary of notation.

Notation	Description
$G = (V, E)$	The graph representing the power grid
$\mathbf{A}$	Admittance matrix of G
$\vec{\theta}$	Vector of the phase angles of the nodes in G
H	A subgraph of G representing the attacked zone
F	Set of failed edges due to an attack
$\mathbf{D}$	Incidence matrix of G
$\bigcirc'$	The value of $\bigcirc$ after an attack
$\bar{\bigcirc}$	The complement of $\bigcirc$
$\bigcirc^*$	The dual of $\bigcirc$

forms,

$$\mathbf{A} = \begin{bmatrix} \mathbf{A}_{H|H} & \mathbf{A}_{H|\bar{H}} \\ \mathbf{A}_{\bar{H}|H} & \mathbf{A}_{\bar{H}|\bar{H}} \end{bmatrix}, \mathbf{A} = \begin{bmatrix} \mathbf{A}_{G|H} & \mathbf{A}_{G|\bar{H}} \end{bmatrix}, \mathbf{A} = \begin{bmatrix} \mathbf{A}_{H|G} \\ \mathbf{A}_{\bar{H}|G} \end{bmatrix}.$$

We use the very same notation for the vectors. For instance $\vec{\theta}_H$ and $\vec{\theta}_{\bar{H}}$ are the vectors of phase angle of the nodes in H and $\bar{H}$, respectively. We use the prime symbol ($'$) to denote the values after an attack. For instance, G', $\mathbf{A}'$, and $\vec{\theta}'$ are used to represent the graph, the admittance matrix of the graph, and the phase angles of the nodes after an attack.

3.4 Graph Theoretical Terms

In this paper, we use several graph theoretical terms and theorems, most of which are reviewed in Appendix A. We briefly review some of the important definitions in this subsection. Most of the definitions are borrowed from [16].

Subgraphs, Cuts, and Cycles: Let X and Y be subsets of the nodes of a graph G. $G[X]$ denotes the subgraph of G *induced* by X. We denote by $E[X, Y]$ the set of edges of G with one end in X and the other end in Y. We denote the complement of a set X by $\bar{X} = V \backslash X$. The *coboundary* of X is the set $E[X, \bar{X}]$ and is denoted by $\partial(X)$. $\partial(v)$ denotes the coboundary of $X = \{v\}$. $G[X, \bar{X}]$ denotes the subgraph of G induced by the edges from $E[X, \bar{X}]$. We say that $Q \subseteq E$ is *G-separable*, if there are pairwise edge-disjoint cycles $C_q (q \in Q)$, such that $\forall q \in Q, q \in C_q$ [39].

Planar Graphs: A graph G is *planar*, if it can be drawn in the plane so that its edges intersect only at their ends. A planar graph G partitions the rest of the plane into a number of edgewise-connected open sets called the *faces* of G.

Given a planar graph G, its dual graph G^* is defined as follows. Corresponding to each face c of G there is a node c^* of G^*, and corresponding to each edge e of G there is an edge e^* of G^*. Two nodes c_1^* and c_2^* are joined by the edge e^* in G^*, if and only if their corresponding faces c_1 and c_2 are separated by the edge e in G. It is easy to see that the dual G^* of a planar graph G is itself a planar graph [16].

Incidence Matrix: Suppose we assign an arbitrary orientation to the edges of G. We denote the set of oriented edges by $\mathcal{E} = \{\epsilon_1, \epsilon_2, \ldots, \epsilon_m\}$. The (node-edge) *incidence matrix* of G is denoted by $\mathbf{D} \in \{-1, 0, 1\}^{|V| \times |E|}$ and defined as follows,

$$d_{ij} = \begin{cases} 0 & \text{if } \epsilon_j \text{ is not incident to node } i, \\ 1 & \text{if } \epsilon_j \text{ is coming out of node } i, \\ -1 & \text{if } \epsilon_j \text{ is going into node } i. \end{cases}$$

When we use the incidence matrix, we assume an arbitrary orientation for the edges unless we mention an specific orientation. $\mathbf{D}_H \in \{-1, 0, 1\}^{|V_H| \times |E_H|}$ is the submatrix of $\mathbf{D}$ with rows from V_H and columns from E_H.

4. ATTACK ANALYSIS

In this section, we study the effects of an attack and provide analytical methods for recovering the phase angles and detecting failed edges in the attacked zone H. We find conditions on the structural properties of a zone and constraints on the failed edges for which these methods successfully recover the phase angles and detect the failed edges. These conditions depend on the connections between V_H and $\bar{V}_H$ as well as the inner connections of the nodes in H. Therefore, we refer to them as *external* and *internal* conditions on H, respectively. Finally, based on the methods, we present the Post-Attack Recovery and Detection (PARD) Algorithm. Table 2 summarizes the results regarding the resilience of a zone based on its internal and external conditions, and the constraints on the set of failed edges F.

In this section, when we describe our methods, we assume that there are no edges $\{i, j\} \in E_H$ for which $\theta_i' = \theta_j'$ (we refer to these edges as *null-edges*). Following (2), a null-edge does not carry any flow. Thus, we cannot detect the status of those edges since they cannot be distinguished from failed edges. However, we can detect the null-edges and treat them separately (we consider this in the PARD Algorithm).

4.1 Recovery of Phase Angles

In this subsection, we introduce a method to recover the phase angles of the nodes in an attacked zone H. We provide sufficient conditions on $G[V_H, \bar{V}_H]$ such that the method recovers the phase angles of the nodes in V_H successfully. As we mentioned, since these conditions depend only on the connections between V_H and $\bar{V}_H$, we refer to them as the *external conditions* on H.

The following lemma is the first step towards designing the method for recovering the phase angles and for detecting the failed edges (see Subsection 4.2).

LEMMA 1. $\text{supp}(\mathbf{A}(\vec{\theta} - \vec{\theta}')) \subseteq V_H$.

PROOF. Suppose $F = \{e_{i_1}, e_{i_2}, \ldots, e_{i_k}\} \subseteq E_H$ are the edges that are disconnected from the grid after the attack on the zone H. Define the column vectors $\vec{x_1}, \vec{x_2} \ldots \vec{x_k} \in \{-1, 0, 1\}^n$ associated with the failed edges as follows. If $e_{i_j} = \{s_j, t_j\}$ then $\vec{x_j}$ is 1 in its $s_j{}^{th}$ entry, -1 in its t_j^{th} entry, and 0 everywhere else. It is easy to see that $\mathbf{A}'$ is related to $\mathbf{A}$ as $\mathbf{A}' = \mathbf{A} - \sum_{j=1}^{k} a_{s_j t_j} \vec{x_j} \vec{x_j}^t$. Since the graph G does not get disconnected after an attack, the flow equations in G' are $\mathbf{A}'\vec{\theta}' = \vec{p}$. On the other hand, $\mathbf{A}\vec{\theta} = \vec{p}$, therefore $\mathbf{A}\vec{\theta} - \mathbf{A}'\vec{\theta}' = 0$. Thus,

$$0 = \mathbf{A}\vec{\theta} - \mathbf{A}'\vec{\theta}' = \mathbf{A}\vec{\theta} - \mathbf{A}\vec{\theta}' + \sum_{j=1}^{k} a_{s_j t_j} \vec{x_j} \vec{x_j}^t \vec{\theta}'$$

$$\Rightarrow \mathbf{A}(\vec{\theta} - \vec{\theta}') = -\sum_{j=1}^{k} a_{s_j t_j} \vec{x_j} \vec{x_j}^t \vec{\theta}'$$

$$\Rightarrow \text{supp}(\mathbf{A}(\vec{\theta} - \vec{\theta}')) \subseteq \bigcup_{i=1}^{k} \text{supp}(\vec{x_j} \vec{x_j}^t \vec{\theta}') \subseteq \bigcup_{i=1}^{k} \{s_j, t_j\}$$

$$\Rightarrow \text{supp}(\mathbf{A}(\vec{\theta} - \vec{\theta}')) \subseteq \bigcup_{i=1}^{k} \{s_j, t_j\} \subseteq V_H. \quad \square$$

One of the immediate results of Lemma 1 is the following corollary. This corollary gives a true statement about $\vec{\theta}'$ (recall that $\vec{\theta}'$ is partly unknown). It states that $\vec{\theta}'$ is in the solution space of the matrix equation (4).

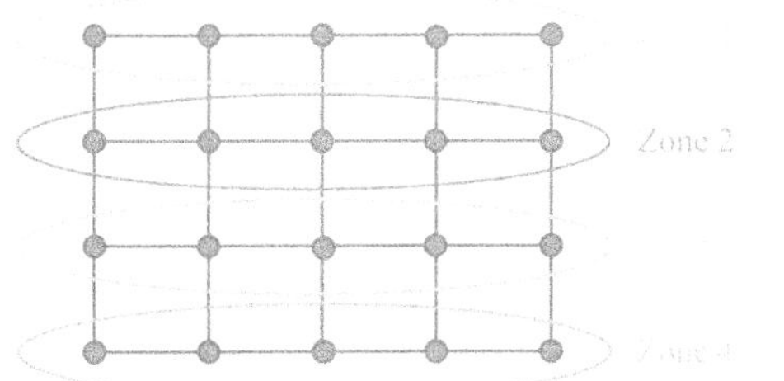

Figure 3: An example of a graph and set of zones such that each zone is both well-supported and acyclic.

COROLLARY 1. $\mathbf{A}_{H|G}(\vec{\theta} - \vec{\theta}') = 0.$ (4)

We find sufficient conditions such that the solution $\vec{\theta}'_H$ to (4) is unique (given $\vec{\theta}$ and $\vec{\theta}'_{\bar{H}}$), and consequently $\vec{\theta}'_H$ can be recovered after any attack on H. We first define a *well-supported* zone.

Definition 1. A zone H is called *well-supported*, if $\vec{\theta}'_H$ can be recovered after any attack on H.

Using Corollary 1, the following theorem gives sufficient condition for a zone H to be *well-supported.*

THEOREM 1. *A zone H is* well-supported, *if $\mathbf{A}_{\bar{H}|H}$ has linearly independent columns.*

PROOF. From Corollary 1 we know that $\mathbf{A}_{\bar{H}|G}(\vec{\theta} - \vec{\theta}') = 0$, therefore $\mathbf{A}_{\bar{H}|H}\vec{\theta}'_H = \mathbf{A}_{\bar{H}|\bar{H}}(\vec{\theta}_{\bar{H}} - \vec{\theta}'_{\bar{H}}) + \mathbf{A}_{\bar{H}|H}\vec{\theta}_H$. The only unknown in this equation is $\vec{\theta}'_H$. Now since $\mathbf{A}_{\bar{H}|H}$ has linearly independent columns, this equation has a unique solution $\vec{\theta}'_H$ which can be computed in polynomial time. Thus, $\vec{\theta}'_H$ can be recovered in this case and zone H is well-supported. □

It can be seen that the sufficient condition in Theorem 1 depends on the reactance values. However, the following corollary relaxes the condition in Theorem 1. It shows that if $G[V_H, \bar{V}_H]$ has a matching that covers V_H, then for almost any reactance values for the edges in $E[V_H, \bar{V}_H]$, H is *well-supported.* The idea is that the set of reactance values for the edges in $E[V_H, \bar{V}_H]$ for which $\mathbf{A}_{\bar{H}|H}$ does not have linearly independent columns is a measure zero set in the real space [38].

COROLLARY 2. *If there is a matching in $G[V_H, \bar{V}_H]$ that covers V_H, then H is* well-supported *almost surely.*[4]

In reality, since the reactance values are derived by the physical properties of the lines, we expect that these values are relatively random around a mean value. Thus, following Corollary 2, the existence of a matching that covers every node in V_H is enough for a zone to be well-supported (see Fig. 3 for an example of a graph in which every node in a zone is covered by a matching). Hence, in the following sections we consider the existence of a matching as a sufficient external condition on H to be well-supported.

4.2 Detecting Failed Edges

In this subsection, we assume that after an attack, the phase angles are recovered using the method in Subsection 4.1 (i.e., by solving (4)). We introduce methods to detect the failed edges using $\vec{\theta}'$. We provide sufficient conditions on H such that these methods detect the failed edges successfully. As we mentioned, since these conditions depend only on the connections between the nodes in H, we refer to them as *internal conditions* on H.

[4]In probability theory, one says that an event happens almost surely, if it happens with probability one.

The following Lemma is the foundation for our approach to find the failed edges. It limits the set of failed edges to the solution space of the matrix equation (5). It can be considered as the complement of Corollary 1.

LEMMA 2. *There exists a vector $\vec{x} \in \mathbb{R}^{|E_H|}$ such that* $\text{supp}(\vec{x}) = \{i | e_i \in F\}$ *and*

$$\mathbf{D}_H\vec{x} = \mathbf{A}_{H|G}(\vec{\theta} - \vec{\theta}'). \quad (5)$$

PROOF. We use the notation that we used in proof of Lemma 1. Recall from the proof of Lemma 1 that $\mathbf{A}(\vec{\theta} - \vec{\theta}') = -\sum_{j=1}^{k} a_{s_j t_j} \vec{x}_j \vec{x}_j{}^t \vec{\theta}'$. It is easy to see that if $\vec{d}_1, \vec{d}_2, \ldots, \vec{d}_m$ are the columns of the incidence matrix $\mathbf{D}$, then $\forall j (1 \leqslant j \leqslant k)$, there exists $b_j \in \mathbb{R}$ such that $b_j \vec{d}_{i_j} = -a_{s_j t_j} \vec{x}_j \vec{x}_j{}^t \vec{\theta}'$. Therefore, $\mathbf{A}(\vec{\theta} - \vec{\theta}') = \sum_{j=1}^{k} b_j \vec{d}_{i_j}$. Thus, if we define $\vec{y} \in \mathbb{R}^m$ such that $\forall e_{i_j} \in F, y_{i_j} = b_j$ and 0 elsewhere, then $\mathbf{A}(\vec{\theta} - \vec{\theta}') = \mathbf{D}\vec{y}$ and $\text{supp}(\vec{y}) \subseteq \{i_1, i_2, \ldots, i_k\}$. However, from the Corollary 1 we know that $\mathbf{A}_{\bar{H}|G}(\vec{\theta} - \vec{\theta}') = 0$. Moreover, since $F \subseteq E_H$, $\vec{y}_{\bar{H}} = 0$. Thus, we can restrict the equation only to the components of the zone H, which means that $\mathbf{A}_{H|G}(\vec{\theta} - \vec{\theta}') = \mathbf{D}_H \vec{y}_H$. Now it is easy to see that since we assumed that no null-edges are in F, all the b_is are nonzero and $\text{supp}(\vec{y}_H) = \{i_1, i_2, \ldots, i_k\}$. Therefore, $\vec{x} = \vec{y}_H$ is a solution to (5) and $\text{supp}(\vec{x}) = \{i | e_i \in F\}$. □

Lemma 2 provides important information regarding the failed edges. It states that there exists a solution $\vec{x}$ to (5) such that $\text{supp}(\vec{x})$ reveals the set of failed edges. However, the solution to (5) may not be unique. The Lemma below provides a necessary and sufficient condition on H such that the solution to (5) is unique.

LEMMA 3. *The solution to (5) is unique and* $\text{supp}(\vec{x}) = \{i | e_i \in F\}$, *if and only if H is acyclic.*

According to Lemma 3 the set of failed edges for any attack can be detected, if and only if H is acyclic. Fig. 3 shows an example of a graph and set of zones such that each zone is both well-supported and acyclic (case I in Table 2).

Although Lemma 3 requires H to be an acyclic graph in order for the solution of (5) to be unique, by setting some constraints on the failed edges F, we provide a method to detect the failed edges in broader class of graphs. The underlying idea is that the set of failed edges is expected to be relatively sparse compared to the overall set of edges within a zone. Thus, we are interested in the solutions of (5) that are relatively sparse. The l_0-norm should be used to capture the sparseness of a vector. However, since minimizing l_0-norm is a combinatorial problem in general cases, we prefer to use l_1-norm which is known to be a good approximation of the l_0-norm. Thus, we consider the following minimization problem,

$$\min \|\vec{x}\|_1 \text{ s.t. } \mathbf{D}_H\vec{x} = \mathbf{A}_{H|G}(\vec{\theta} - \vec{\theta}'). \quad (6)$$

Notice that (6) is still linear and can be solved using Linear Programming. Moreover, when the solution to (6) also appears to be sparse, which is usually the case in the considered scenario, there are very fast algorithms to solve it [23].

The Lemma below states that by solving (6), the failed edges can be detected in more cases than by solving (5). The idea that we use in proof of Lemma 4 is the core idea in proofs of Theorems 2 and 3, as well. Namely, the null

Table 2: Summary of the results in Section 4. The external/internal conditions on the structural properties of a zone H such that after an attack with certain constraints, the phase angles can be recovered and the failed edges can be detected by solving (8). Matching and partial matching refer to matchings in $G[V_H, \bar{V}_H]$ that cover V_H and $V_H \backslash (V_H^{\text{in}} \cup V_H^{\text{out}})$, respectively.

Case	External conditions	Internal conditions	Attack constraints	Resilience	Results
I	Matching	Acyclic	None	attack-resilient	Corollary 2/Lemma 3
II	Matching	Planar	$\forall$ cycle C, $\lvert C \cap F\rvert < \lvert C \backslash F\rvert$ F^* is H^*-separable	weakly-attack-resilient	Corollary 2/Theorem 2
III	Partial matching	Acyclic	$\forall v \in V_H^{\text{in}}$, $\lvert\partial(v) \cap F\rvert < \lvert\partial(v) \backslash F\rvert$	weakly-attack-resilient	Lemmas 3,6/Corollary 5
IV	Partial matching	Planar No cycle contains an inner-connected-node	$\forall$ cycle C, $\lvert C \cap F\rvert < \lvert C \backslash F\rvert$ $\forall v \in V_H^{\text{in}}$, $\lvert\partial(v) \cap F\rvert < \lvert\partial(v) \backslash F\rvert$ F^* is H^*-separable	weakly-attack-resilient	Theorem 3/Corollary 5

space of D_H is in one-to-one correspondence with the cycle space of the graph H. Therefore, there are graph theoretical interpretations to the solution space of (5). Hence, by using tools from graph theory and linear algebra, we find the solution to (5) with the minimum l_1-norm.

LEMMA 4. *If H is a cycle and $|E_H \cap F| < |E_H \backslash F|$, the solution to (6) is unique and* $\text{supp}(\vec{x}) = \{i | e_i \in F\}$.

PROOF. Here without loss of generality, we assume that $\mathbf{D}_H$ is the incidence matrix of H when edges of H has been oriented clockwise. Since H is connected, it is known that $\text{rank}(\mathbf{D}_H) = |V_H| - 1$ [9, Theorem 2.2]. Therefore, $\dim(\text{Null}(\mathbf{D}_H)) = 1$. Suppose $\vec{c} \in \mathbb{R}^{|E_H|}$ is the all one vector. It is easy to see that $\mathbf{D}_H \vec{c} = 0$. Since $\dim(\text{Null}(\mathbf{D}_H)) = 1$, $\vec{c}$ is the basis for the null space of $\mathbf{D}$. Suppose $\vec{x}$ is a solution to (5) such that $\text{supp}(\vec{x}) = \{i | e_i \in F\}$ (from Lemma 2 we know that such a solution exists). To prove that $\vec{x}$ is the unique solution for (6), we only need to prove that $\forall c \in \mathbb{R} \backslash \{0\}$, $\|\vec{x}\|_1 < \|\vec{x} - c\vec{e}\|_1$. Without loss of generality we can assume that $x_1, x_2, \ldots, x_k$ are the nonzero elements of $\vec{x}$, in which $k = |F|$. From the assumption we know that $|E_H \cap F| < |E_H \backslash F|$, therefore $k < |E_H|/2$. Hence, we have

$$\begin{aligned}\|\vec{x} - c\vec{e}\|_1 &= \sum_{i=1}^{k} |x_i - c| + (|E_H| - k)|c| \\ &= \sum_{i=1}^{k} (|x_i - c| + |c|) + (|E_H| - 2k)|c| \\ &\geqslant \sum_{i=1}^{k} |x_i| + (|E_H| - 2k)|c| > \sum_{i=1}^{k} |x_i| = \|\vec{x}\|_1.\end{aligned}$$

Thus, the solution to (6) is unique. □

COROLLARY 3. *If all the cycles in H are edge-disjoint and for any cycle C in H, $|C \cap F| < |C \backslash F|$, then the solution to (6) is unique and* $\text{supp}(\vec{x}) = \{i | e_i \in F\}$.

The following Theorem extends the idea in the proof of Lemma 4 and provides sufficient conditions for failed edges in a planar graph H to be detected by solving (6) (recall from subsection 3.4 that H^* is the dual of the planar graph H and F^* is the dual of the set of failed edges).

THEOREM 2. *In a planar graph H, the solution to (6) is unique and* $\text{supp}(\vec{x}) = \{i | e_i \in F\}$, *if the following conditions hold:* (i) *for any cycle C in H, $|C \cap F| < |C \backslash F|$, and* (ii) *$F^*$ is H^*-separable.*

Fig. 4 shows an example of a zone H for which the set of failed edges can be detected by solving (6) based on Theorem 2 (case II in Table 2).

The Corollary below states that in planar bipartite graphs, condition (ii) in Theorem 2 immediately holds, if condition (i) holds.

COROLLARY 4. *In a planar bipartite graph H, the solution to (6) is unique and* $\text{supp}(\vec{x}) = \{i | e_i \in F\}$, *if for any cycle C in H, $|C \cap F| < |C \backslash F|$.*

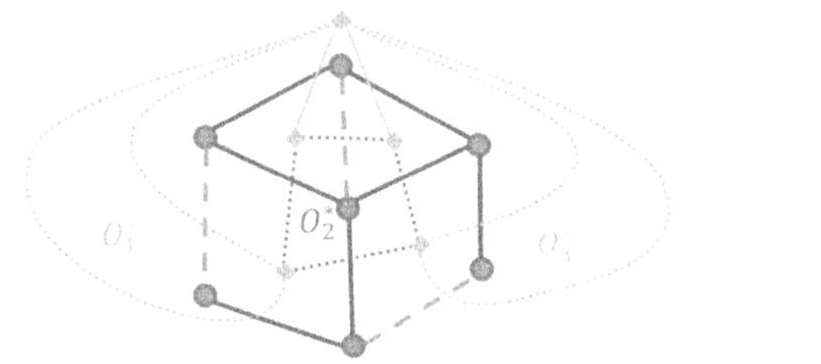

Figure 4: An example of a zone H and a set of failed edges (shown by red dashed lines) that can be detected by solving (6) based on Theorem 2. The diamond orange nodes are the nodes of the dual graph H^*. As can be seen, the dual of the failed edges can be covered by three edge disjoint cycles O_1^*, O_2^*, O_3^* (shown by dotted lines) in H^*. Thus, as Theorem 2 requires, F^* is H^*-separable.

Theorem 2 and Corollary 4 are important since power grids are usually considered to be planar. For instance, lattice graphs are planar bipartite.

4.3 Simultaneous Phase Angles Recovery and Failed Edges Detection

In Subsection 4.1 we showed that the phase angles of the zone H are recoverable, if there is a matching in $G[V_H, \bar{V}_H]$ that covers V_H. However, in reality, this condition might be very difficult and costly to maintain (i.e., it may require to increase the number of zones). Therefore, in this subsection, using similar ideas as in subsection 4.2, we relax the external conditions on H.

The key idea which is summarized in the following Lemma, is to combine Corollary 1 and Lemma 2.

LEMMA 5. *There exist vectors $\vec{x} \in \mathbb{R}^{|E_H|}$ and $\vec{\delta}_H \in \mathbb{R}^{|V_H|}$ such that* $\text{supp}(\vec{x}) = \{i | e_i \in F\}$, $\vec{\delta}_H = \vec{\theta}_H - \vec{\theta}'_H$, *and*

$$\begin{aligned}\mathbf{D}_H \vec{x} &= \mathbf{A}_{H|H} \vec{\delta}_H + \mathbf{A}_{H|\bar{H}} \vec{\delta}_{\bar{H}} \\ \mathbf{A}_{\bar{H}|H} \vec{\delta}_H &+ \mathbf{A}_{\bar{H}|\bar{H}} \vec{\delta}_{\bar{H}} = 0\end{aligned} \qquad (7)$$

where $\vec{\delta}_{\bar{H}} = \vec{\theta}_{\bar{H}} - \vec{\theta}'_{\bar{H}}$ and is known.

From Subsections 4.1 and 4.2 we know that the solution to (7) is unique, if and only if H is acyclic and $\mathbf{A}_{H|H}$ has linearly independent columns. Therefore, to deal with cases for which $\mathbf{A}_{H|H}$ does not have linearly independent columns, we consider a similar optimization problem as in (6) but with more constraints. For this reason, as we mentioned in Subsection 4.2, since the set of failed edges is expected to be relatively sparse compared to the overall set of edges, we consider the following optimization problem.

$$\begin{aligned}&\min \|\vec{x}\|_1 \text{ s.t.} \\ &\mathbf{D}_H \vec{x} = \mathbf{A}_{H|H} \vec{\delta}_H + \mathbf{A}_{H|\bar{H}} \vec{\delta}_{\bar{H}} \\ &\mathbf{A}_{\bar{H}|H} \vec{\delta}_H + \mathbf{A}_{\bar{H}|\bar{H}} \vec{\delta}_{\bar{H}} = 0.\end{aligned} \qquad (8)$$

The following Lemma states that if there is an independent set of nodes in H with no neighbors in $\bar{H}$, then under some conditions on F, we can recover F and $\vec{\theta}'_H$ by solving (8) even when $\mathbf{A}_{\bar{H}|H}$ does not have linearly independent columns (case III in Table 2). First, we define *inner-connected* nodes.

Definition 2. A node $v \in V_H$ is called *H-inner-connected* if $N(v) \subseteq V_H$. It is called *H-outer-connected* if $N(v) \subseteq V_{\bar{H}}$. We denote the set of *$H$-inner-connected* and *$H$-outer-connected* nodes by V_H^{in} and V_H^{out}, respectively.

LEMMA 6. *Suppose H-inner-connected nodes form an independent set. If H is acyclic,* $\text{rank}(\boldsymbol{A}_{\bar{H}|H}) = |V_H| - |V_H^{in}|$, *and $\forall v \in V_H^{in}, |\partial(v) \cap F| < |\partial(v) \backslash F|$, then the solution $\vec{x}, \vec{\delta}$ to (8) is unique. Moreover,* $\text{supp}(\vec{x}) = \{i | e_i \in F\}$ *and* $\vec{\delta}_H = \vec{\theta}_H - \vec{\theta}'_H$.

PROOF. The idea of the proof is very similar to the proof of Lemma 4. Suppose $\vec{x}, \vec{\delta}_H$ is the solution to (7) such that $\text{supp}(\vec{x}) = \{i | e_i \in F\}$ and $\vec{\delta}_H = \vec{\theta}_H - \vec{\theta}'_H$. From Lemma 5 we know that such a solution exists. We show that this solution is the unique solution to (8) in this setting.

Without loss of generality in addition to assuming $V_H = \{1, 2, 3, \ldots, |V_H|\}$ and $E_H = \{e_1, e_2, \ldots, e_{|E_H|}\}$, we can assume the labeling of the nodes in G is such that $V_H^{\text{in}} = \{1, 2, \ldots, t\}$ is the set of H-inner-connected nodes. Suppose $\vec{\alpha}_1, \vec{\alpha}_2, \ldots, \vec{\alpha}_t \in \mathbb{R}^{|V_H|}$ are the coordinate vectors, in other words $\vec{\alpha}_i$ is 1 at its ith entry and 0 everywhere else. It is easy to see that $\forall i \in V_H^{\text{in}} : A_{\bar{H}|H}\vec{\alpha}_i = 0$. On the other hand, since $\text{rank}(\mathbf{A}_{\bar{H}|H}) = |V_H| - t$ and $\vec{\alpha}_i$s are linearly independent, $\vec{\alpha}_1, \vec{\alpha}_2, \ldots, \vec{\alpha}_t$ form a basis for $\text{Null}(\mathbf{A}_{\bar{H}|H})$.

Assume $\mathbf{D}_H$ is the incidence matrix of H when its edges are oriented such that for each $i \in V_H^{\text{in}}$, the edges are coming out of i. Now suppose $\vec{z}$ is another solution to (8), it is easy to see that $\mathbf{D}_H(\vec{z} - \vec{x}) = \mathbf{A}_{H|H}\vec{\alpha}$ for a vector $\vec{\alpha} \in \text{Null}(\mathbf{A}_{\bar{H}|H})$. Since $\vec{\alpha} \in \text{Null}(\mathbf{A}_{\bar{H}|H})$, there are unique coefficients $c_1, c_2, \ldots, c_t \in \mathbb{R}$ such that $\vec{\alpha} = c_1\vec{\alpha}_1 + c_2\vec{\alpha}_2 + \cdots + c_t\vec{\alpha}_t$. Thus,

$$\begin{aligned}\mathbf{D}_H(\vec{z} - \vec{x}) &= \mathbf{A}_{H|H}\vec{\alpha} = \mathbf{A}_{H|H}(c_1\vec{\alpha}_1 + c_2\vec{\alpha}_2 + \cdots + c_t\vec{\alpha}_t) \\ &= c_1\mathbf{A}_{H|H}\vec{\alpha}_1 + c_2\mathbf{A}_{H|H}\vec{\alpha}_2 + \cdots + c_t\mathbf{A}_{H|H}\vec{\alpha}_t.\end{aligned}$$

Suppose $\vec{d}_j$ is the column associated with edge e_j in D_H. Notice that for each $i \in V_H^{\text{in}}$, $\partial(i) \subseteq E_H$. Therefore, $\forall i \in V_H^{\text{in}}$ and $\forall e_j \in \partial(i)$, $\vec{d}_j$ is a column of $\mathbf{D}_H$. It is easy to see that for any $i \in V_H^{\text{in}}$, $\sum_{j: e_j \in \partial(i)} \vec{d}_j = \mathbf{A}_{H|H}\vec{\alpha}_i$. If for any $i \in V_H^{\text{in}}$ we define vector $\vec{b}_i \in \{0, 1\}^{|E_H|}$ as follows,

$$b_{ij} := \begin{cases} 1 & \text{if } e_j \in \partial(i) \\ 0 & \text{otherwise,} \end{cases}$$

then $\mathbf{D}_H\vec{b}_i = \mathbf{A}_{H|H}\vec{\alpha}_i$ for any $i \in V_H^{\text{in}}$. Thus,

$$\begin{aligned}&\mathbf{D}_H(c_1\vec{b}_1 + \cdots + c_t\vec{b}_t) = c_1\mathbf{A}_{H|H}\vec{\alpha}_1 + \cdots + c_t\mathbf{A}_{H|H}\vec{\alpha}_t \\ &\quad \Rightarrow \mathbf{D}_H(\vec{z} - \vec{x}) = \mathbf{D}_H(c_1\vec{b}_1 + c_2\vec{b}_2 + \cdots + c_t\vec{b}_t).\end{aligned}$$

Now since H is acyclic, $\mathbf{D}_H$ has linearly independent columns. Thus, from the equation above we can conclude that,

$$\begin{aligned}&\vec{z} - \vec{x} = c_1\vec{b}_1 + c_2\vec{b}_2 + \cdots + c_t\vec{b}_t \\ &\Rightarrow \vec{z} = \vec{x} + c_1\vec{b}_1 + c_2\vec{b}_2 + \cdots + c_t\vec{b}_t.\end{aligned}$$

Using equation above, we show that $\|\vec{z}\|_1 > \|\vec{x}\|_1$ unless $c_1 = c_2 = \cdots = c_t = 0$. First, notice that since V_H^{in} is an independent set, $\forall i \neq j \in V_H^{\text{in}}$, $\partial(i) \cap \partial(j) = \emptyset$. Suppose $\forall i \in V_H^{\text{in}}, |\partial(i) \cap F| = k_i$, we have

$$\begin{aligned}\|\vec{z}\|_1 &= \|\vec{x} + c_1\vec{b}_1 + c_2\vec{b}_2 + \cdots + c_t\vec{b}_t\|_1 \\ &= \sum_{i \in V_H^{\text{in}}}\Big((|\partial(i)| - k_i)|c_i| + \sum_{j \in F \cap \partial(i)} |x_j + c_i|\Big) + \sum_{i \in F \backslash \partial(V_H^{\text{in}})} |x_i| \\ &= \sum_{i \in V_H^{\text{in}}}\Big((|\partial(i)| - 2k_i)|c_i| + \sum_{j \in F \cap \partial(i)}(|x_j + c_i| + |c_i|)\Big) + \sum_{i \in F \backslash \partial(V_H^{\text{in}})} |x_i| \\ &\leqslant \sum_{i \in V_H^{\text{in}}}\Big((|\partial(i)| - 2k_i)|c_i| + \sum_{j \in F \cap \partial(i)} |x_j|\Big) + \sum_{i \in F \backslash \partial(V_H^{\text{in}})} |x_i| \\ &\leqslant \sum_{i \in V_H^{\text{in}}}((|\partial(i)| - 2k_i)|c_i|) + \sum_{i \in V_H^{\text{in}}} \sum_{j \in F \cap \partial(i)} |x_j| + \sum_{i \in F \backslash \partial(V_H^{\text{in}})} |x_i| \\ &\leqslant \sum_{i \in V_H^{\text{in}}}((|\partial(i)| - 2k_i)|c_i|) + \|\vec{x}\|_1.\end{aligned}$$

Now, since from the assumptions $\forall i \in V_H^{\text{in}}, k_i < |\partial(i)|/2$, it is easy to see that $\sum_{i \in V_H^{\text{in}}}((\partial(i) - 2k_i)|c_i|) + \|\vec{x}\|_1 < \|\vec{z}\|_1$, unless $c_1 = c_2 = \cdots = c_t = 0$. Since $\vec{z}$ is a solution to (8), we should have $c_1 = c_2 = \cdots = c_t = 0$, and $\vec{z} = \vec{x}$. Thus, $\vec{x}$ is the unique solution to (8) and $\text{supp}(\vec{x}) = \{i | e_i \in F\}$. From the proof, it is easy to see that $\vec{\delta}_H$ is also unique. □

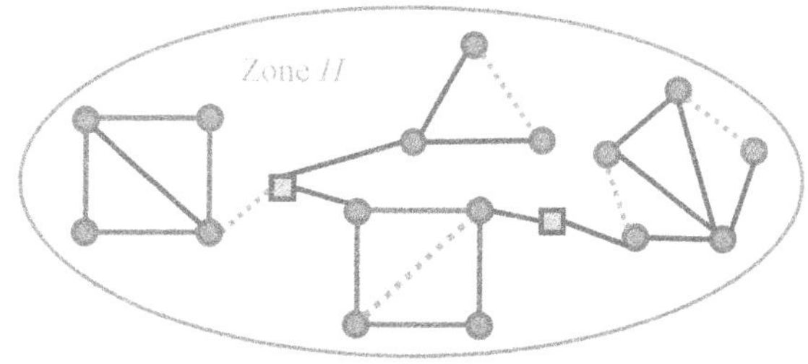

Figure 5: An example of a zone H and an attack such that the phase angles can be recovered and the failed edges can be detected by solving (8) based on Theorem 3. The squared green nodes are the H-inner-connected nodes. The failed edges are shown by red dashed edges.

To generalize Lemma 6, first let us consider cases in which H contains H-outer-connected nodes. The Lemma below shows that the value of δ for these nodes is unique.

LEMMA 7. *If v is H-outer-connected and $\vec{\delta}_H$ is a solution to (7), then δ_v is unique and equal to $\delta_v = 1/d(v)\sum_{u \in N(v)} \delta_u$, where $d(v)$ is the degree of node v.*

In the following theorem, we generalize Lemma 6. This theorem combines Lemma 6 and Theorem 2, and provides a broader class of graphs in which solving (8) recovers phase angles and detects the failed edges after an attack.

THEOREM 3. *In a planar graph H, the solution $\vec{x}, \vec{\delta}_H$ to (8) is unique with* $\text{supp}(\vec{x}) = \{i | e_i \in F\}$ *and* $\vec{\delta}_H = \vec{\theta}_H - \vec{\theta}'_H$, *if the following conditions hold:* (i) $\forall v \in V_H^{\text{in}}$, $|\partial(v) \cap F| < |\partial(v) \backslash F|$, (ii) *for any cycle C in H,* $|C \cap F| < |C \backslash F|$, (iii) *$F^*$ is H^*-separable,* (iv) *in $\boldsymbol{A}_{\bar{H}|H}$, columns associated with nodes that are neither H-inner-connected nor H-outer-connected are linearly independent,* (v) *no cycle in H contains a H-inner-connected node, and* (vi) *H-inner-connected nodes form an independent set.*

Note that when H is well-supported, there are no H-inner-connected or H-outer-connected nodes. Thus, conditions (i), (iv), (v), and (vi) immediately hold and Theorem 3 reduces to Theorem 2.

Algorithm 1 - Post-Attack Recovery & Detection (PARD)

Input: A connected graph G, phase angles before the attack $\vec{\theta}$, and partial phase angles after the attack $\vec{\theta}'_H$.

1: Detect the attacked zone H by checking for missing data.
2: Compute $\vec{x}, \vec{\delta}_H$ the solution to (8) by Linear Programming.
3: Compute $\vec{\theta}'_H = \vec{\theta}_H - \vec{\delta}_H$.
4: Compute $F = \{e_i | i \in \text{supp}(\vec{x})\}$.
5: Detect the set of null-edges that appear after the attack as $N = \{\{i,j\} \in E_H | \theta'_i = \theta'_j\}$.
6: **return** N, F, $\vec{\theta}'_H$.

Fig. 5 shows an example of a zone H and an attack such that the phase angles can be recovered and the failed edges can be detected by solving (8) using Theorem 3 (case IV in Table 2). As it can be seen, this theorem covers a broad set of graphs and attacks for which we can recover the phase angles and detect the failed edges. Notice that here, with similar argument as in Corollary 2 we can replace condition (iv) in Theorem 3 with a simpler matching condition as follows.

COROLLARY 5. *If there is a matching in $G[V_H, \bar{V}_H]$ that covers $V_H \backslash (V_H^{\text{in}} \cup V_H^{\text{out}})$, then condition* (iv) *in Theorem 3 holds almost surely.*

To conclude, we define the *attack-resilient* and *weakly-attack-resilient* notions to summarize the resilience of a zone to joint cyber and physical attacks.

Definition 3. A zone H is called *attack-resilient*, if it is both well-supported and acyclic.

Definition 4. A zone H is called *weakly-attack-resilient*, if $\vec{\theta}'_H$ and F can be uniquely found after a constrained attack on the zone H by solving (8).

It is easy to see that an attack-resilient zone is also weakly-attack-resilient.

4.4 Post-Attack Recovery and Detection Algorithm

In this subsection, we present the Post-Attack Recovery and Detection (PARD) Algorithm for recovering the phase angles and detecting the failed edges after an attack on a zone H. Based on the results provided in previous subsections, if zone H is weakly-attack-resilient, the PARD Algorithm will recover the phase angles and detect the failed edges after a constrained attack.

Notice that if there are some failed edges but no data is missing, then from the data that is gathered by the PDCs from the PMUs, all the information regarding the status of the lines and phase angles is available and there is no need for the algorithm. Thus, as the first step, the PARD Algorithm detects the attacked zone H by checking the missing data (line 1). Then, it solves (8) by Linear Programming to obtain $\vec{x}, \vec{\delta}_H$. If H is weakly-attack-resilient, from the results in previous subsections, we know that $\vec{x}, \vec{\delta}_H$ are unique, $\vec{\theta}'_H = \vec{\theta}_H - \vec{\delta}_H$ (line 3), and $F = \{e_i | i \in \text{supp}(\vec{x})\}$ (line 4). Finally, using $\vec{\theta}'$ computed in previous line, the PARD Algorithm detects the set of null-edges N (line 5), and returns N, F, and $\vec{\theta}'_H$.

5. ZONE SELECTION ALGORITHM

In this section we use the results from Section 4 to provide an algorithm for partitioning the power grid into the minimum number of attack-resilient zones. From Lemma 3 and

Algorithm 2 - 3-Acyclic Partition of Planar (3APP)

Input: A non-empty planar graph G.

Find a node $v \in V$ such that $\deg(v) \leqslant 5$.
if $G \backslash v = \varnothing$ **then** set $Q_1 = Q_2 = Q_3 = \varnothing$.
else Find 3-partition of $G \backslash v$ using 3APP Algorithm as Q_1, Q_2, Q_3.
Add v to the partition that $|N(v) \cap Q_i|$ is minimum.
return Q_1, Q_2, Q_3.

Corollary 2, for a zone H to be attack-resilient, it is sufficient that H is acyclic and there is a matching in $G[V_H, \bar{V}_H]$ that covers every node in V_H. Fig. 3 shows an example of a partitioning such that each zone is attack-resilient. Thus, we define a *matched-forest* partition of a graph G as follows.

Definition 5. A *matched-forest* partition of a graph G into $H_1, H_2, \ldots, H_k$ is a partition such that for any i, H_i is acyclic and $G[V_{H_i}, \bar{V}_{H_i}]$ has a matching that covers V_{H_i}.

The problem of finding a matched-forest partition of G is closely related to two previously known problems of *vertex arboricity* and *k-matching cover* of a graph. The vertex arboricity $a(G)$ of a graph G is the minimum number of subsets into which the nodes of G can be partitioned so that each subset induces an acyclic graph. It is known that determining $a(G)$ is NP-hard [26, p.193].

A k-matching cover of a graph G is a union of k matchings of G which covers V. The matching cover number of G, denoted by $mc(G)$, is the minimum number k such that G has a k-matching cover. An optimal matching cover of a graph on n nodes can be found in $O(n^3)$ time [45].

Using these results, we study the time complexity of the *minimum matched-forest* partition problem.[5] The following Lemma shows that it is hard to find the minimum matched-forest partition of a graph.

LEMMA 8. *The problem of finding the minimum matched-forest partition of a graph G is NP-hard.*

Moreover, we show that finding the minimum matched-forest partition is even hard to approximate. We use the well-known result by Zuckerman [51] that for all $\epsilon > 0$, it is NP-hard to approximate *chromatic number* to within $n^{1-\epsilon}$.

LEMMA 9. *For all $\epsilon > 0$, it is NP-hard to approximate the minimum matched-forest partition of a graph G to within $n^{1-\epsilon}$.*

Despite these hardness results, we provide the polynomial-time Zone Selection (ZS) Algorithm to find a matched-forest partition of a graph. We prove that the ZS Algorithm provides a constant approximation for the minimum matched-forest partition of a graph G when G is planar.

Before describing the ZS Algorithm in detail, we first describe an algorithm that is used in the ZS Algorithm, when G is planar. It is known that for a planar graph G, $a(G) \leqslant 3$ [19]. Based on the proof provided in [19], we introduce a recursive 3-Acyclic Partition of Planar (3APP) Algorithm. The Lemma below shows the correctness of this Algorithm.

LEMMA 10. *The 3APP Algorithm partitions the nodes of a planar graph G into 3 subsets such that each subset induces an acyclic graph.*

[5]To the best of our knowledge, this is the first time that the problem is studied.

Algorithm 3 - Zone Selection (ZS)

Input: A connected graph G.

1: Find an optimal matching cover $M_1, M_2, \ldots, M_t$ of G [45].
2: For each M_i, separate the matched nodes into two set of nodes V_{2i-1}, V_{2i} such that $\forall \{v, u\} \in M$, $v \in V_{2i-1}$ and $u \in V_{2i}$.
3: For any $1 \leqslant i \leqslant 2t$, $Q_i = V_i \backslash \bigcup_{j=1}^{i-1} Q_j$.
4: **for** each Q_i **do**
5:   **if** $G[Q_i]$ is acyclic **then continue**
6:   **if** $G[Q_i]$ is a planar graph **then**
7:     Use 3APP Algorithm to partition $G[Q_i]$.
8:   **else**
9:     Use any greedy algorithm to partition $G[Q_i]$ into acyclic subgraphs.
10: Name the resulted partitions $P_1, \ldots, P_k$.
11: **return** $P_1, \ldots, P_k$.

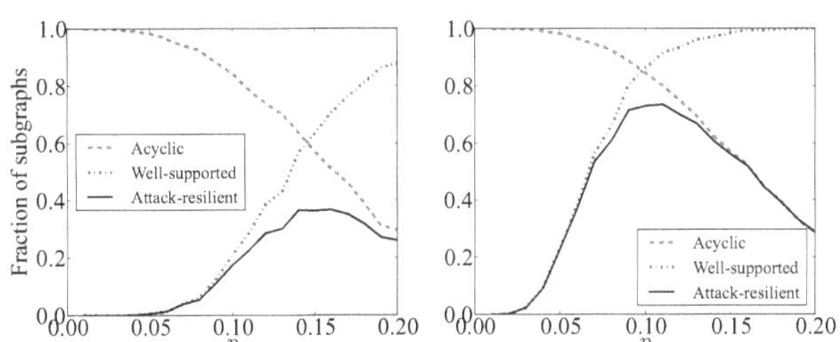

(a) $n = 30$ (b) $n = 50$

Figure 6: The relationships between the number of edges in random graphs (or equivalently p), and the fraction of induced subgraphs that form well-supported and acyclic zones of size $|V_H| = 10$. For each p, 100 random graphs were generated and in each graph, 100 subgraphs were chosen randomly.

We now present the ZS Algorithm. The ZS Algorithm first finds an optimal matching cover $M_1, M_2, \ldots, M_t$ of G using an $O(n^3)$ algorithm introduced in [45] (line 1). Then, in lines 2 and 3, it uses this matching cover to partition V into $Q_1, Q_2, \ldots, Q_{2t}$. It is easy to see that for each Q_i, $M_{\lceil i/2 \rceil} \cap E[Q_i, \bar{Q}_i]$ is the matching in $G[Q_i, \bar{Q}_i]$ that covers nodes in Q_i. Then, in order to satisfy the acyclicity condition on the partitions, it partitions Q_is that do not induce an acyclic graph, into subsets so that each subset induces an acyclic graph. When $G[Q_i]$ is a planar graph, it uses 3APP Algorithm to partition $G[Q_i]$. When it is not, it uses any *greedy algorithm* to do so. Thus, the resulted partition $P_1, P_2, \ldots, P_k$ satisfies the conditions of a matched-forest partition.

The lemma below states that when G is planar, the ZS Algorithm provides a constant approximation of the optimal matched-forest partition. We demonstrate the results obtained by the algorithm in the following section.

LEMMA 11. *If G is planar, the ZS Algorithm provides a 6-approximation of the minimum* matched-forest *partition of G in $O(n^3)$.*

6. NUMERICAL RESULTS

In this section, we (i) numerically study the relationship between the structural properties of a grid and its resilience to joint cyber and physical attacks, and (ii) demonstrate the results obtained by the ZS Algorithm in several known power grid networks.

To assess the relationship between the structural properties of a grid and its resilience to attacks, we quantify the resilience by the fraction of the node induced subgraphs of G that form attack-resilient zones. Recall from Section 4 that a zone H is attack-resilient, if it is well-supported and acyclic. We first study the relationships between the number of edges and the fraction of induced subgraphs that form well-supported, acyclic, and attack-resilient zones. These relationships can be best demonstrated in *random graphs* [24], since by increasing p (the probability that two nodes are connected), the total number of edges increases.

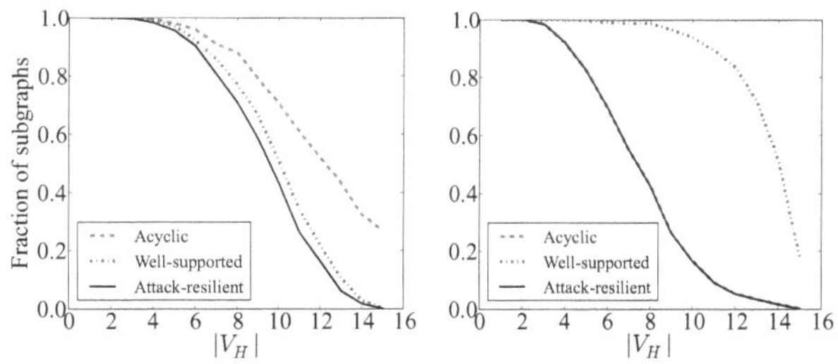

(a) $n = 30, m = 56$ (b) $n = 30, m = 104$

Figure 7: The relationship between the size of the zone $|V_H|$ in scale-free graphs, and the fraction of induced subgraphs that form well-supported and acyclic zones of size $|V_H|$. For each case, 1000 subgraphs were chosen randomly.

We generated random graphs with $n = 30$ and $n = 50$ nodes with various p values. For each p, we generated 100 random graphs and in each graph randomly selected 100 subgraphs of size 10. We then computed the fraction of subgraphs that form well-supported, acyclic, and attack-resilient zones. As can be seen in Fig. 6, as p increases, the fraction of subgraphs that form acyclic zones decreases and the fraction that form well-supported zones increases. In Fig. 6(a), when $p \approx 0.14$ these two fractions are equal and the fraction of attack-resilient subgraph is maximized. As can be seen in Fig. 6(b), the value of p for which these two fractions are equal (i.e., the fraction of attack-resilient subgraphs is maximized) decreases as n increases.

We also illustrate the relationships between the size of the zone $|V_H|$ and the fraction of induced subgraphs that form well-supported, acyclic, and attack-resilient zones. It is known that *scale-free graphs* are relatively good representatives of power grid networks [10], and therefore, we focus here on such graphs. Fig. 7 shows the relationships in scale-free graphs with $n = 30$ nodes and $m = 56$ or 104 edges. As can be seen in 7(a), as the size of the zone increases, the fraction of zones that are well-supported decreases faster than the fraction of zones that are acyclic. Thus, the well-supportedness is the restricting factor for attack-resilience. However, this trend is different in 7(b). Since the graph has more edges, as the size of the zone increases, the fraction of zones that are acyclic decreases faster than the fraction of zones that are well-supported. Here, the acyclicity is the restricting factor.

Overall, these results show that the structure of the grid plays an important role in its resilience and should be considered when designing a control network.[6]

[6]Clearly, random and scale free graphs do not model power grids perfectly. However, we used them to gain insight into the relations between structural properties and resilience. In future work, we will study more realistic network topologies [41].

Table 3: Number of partitions into which the ZS Algorithm divides different networks.

Network	Nodes	Edges	Partitions
IEEE 14-Bus	14	20	2
IEEE 30-Bus	30	41	2
IEEE 118-Bus	118	179	5
IEEE 300-Bus	300	409	14
Polish grid	3120	3684	10
Colorado state grid	662	864	6
Western interconnection	13135	16860	9

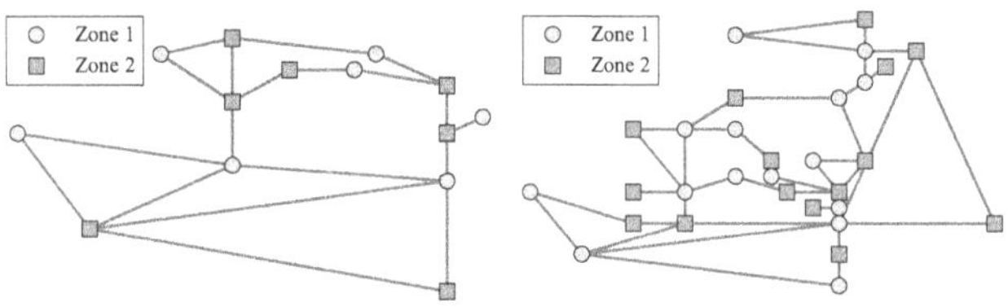

(a) IEEE 14 bus (b) IEEE 30 bus

Figure 8: Partitioning of the IEEE 14 and IEEE 30 bus systems into 2 attack resilient zones (using the ZS Algorithm).

We now demonstrate results obtained by the ZS Algorithm in several known power networks. Table 3 lists the considered grids and number of resulting partitions. For example, Fig. 8 shows the partitions obtained by ZS Algorithm in the IEEE 14-Bus and 30-Bus benchmark systems [2]. As can be seen, in both cases the graphs can be partitioned into two attack-resilient zones. We also evaluated the ZS Algorithm on the IEEE 118 and 300-bus systems, the Polish grid (available with MATPOWER [50]), the Colorado state grid, and the U.S. Western Interconnection network.[7] For example, the 6 zones into which the Colorado grid is partitioned appear in Fig. 9. Recall form Section 5 that when G is planar, the ZS Algorithm is a 6-approximation algorithm for the minimum matched-forest problem. However, as can be seen from the examples above, in practice, it partitions the networks into few zones.

We note that the ZS Algorithm does not take the geographical constraints into account. Thus, when partitioning very large networks such as the Western Interconnection (see Fig. 10), the nodes in the same partition may be geographically distant from each other. This is impractical, since the PMUs from the same zone should send the data to a single PDC. However, it is easy to see that if a zone is attack-resilient, any of its subgraphs is also attack-resilient. Therefore, the partitions obtained by the ZS Algorithm can be further divided into smaller zones based on geographical constraints (e.g., into zones within different states in Fig. 10). This approach does not result in an optimal partitioning. Hence, obtaining an efficient partitioning with geographical constraints is a subject of future work.

7. CONCLUSION

We studied joint cyber and physical attacks on power grids. We developed methods to recover information about the phase angles of the nodes and the disconnected edges, using only the information available from outside of the attacked zone. We identified graph structures and constraints on the disconnected edges for which these methods are guaranteed to recover the state information. Moreover, we showed that the problem of partitioning the grid into the minimum number of attack-resilient zones is not approximable to within $n^{1-\epsilon}$ for all $\epsilon > 0$ unless P=NP. However, for planar graphs, we developed an approximation algorithm for the partitioning problem. Finally, we illustrated via numerical results the relationship between the structural properties of the power grid and its resilience to joint attacks as well as the operation of the partitioning algorithm.

This is one of the first steps towards understanding the vulnerabilities of power grids to joint cyber and physical attacks and developing methods to mitigate their effects. Hence, there are still many open problems. In particular, we plan to generalize Theorems 2 and 3 to a broader class of graphs. Moreover, we will develop algorithms to partition the grid into weakly-attack-resilient zones while taking into account geographical constraints and constraints on the number and positions of the PDCs. Finally, we will study the interdependencies between cascading failures in power grids and its control network when the control network faces sophisticated cyber attacks.

[7]The data of the Western Interconnection (and of Colorado) was obtained from the Platts Geographic Information System (GIS) [1].

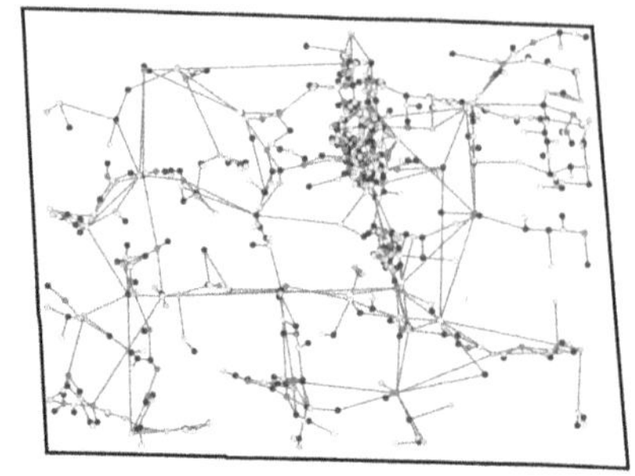

Figure 9: Partitioning of the Colorado state grid into 6 attack-resilient zones (using the ZS Algorithm). Nodes with the same color are in the same zone.

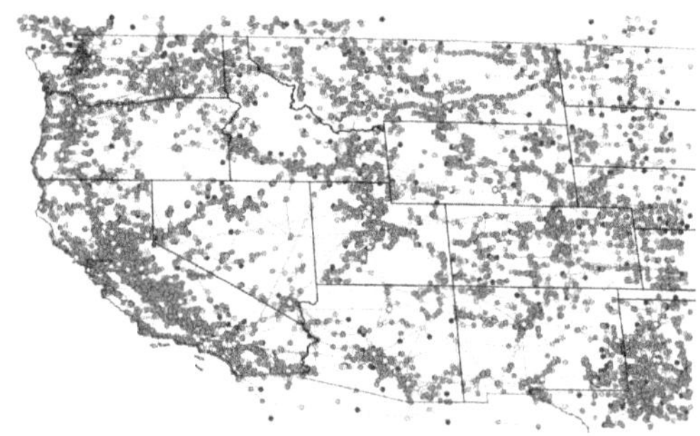

Figure 10: Partitioning of the U.S. Western Interconnection into 9 attack-resilient zones (using the ZS Algorithm). Nodes with the same color are in the same zone.

Acknowledgement

This work was supported in part by CIAN NSF ERC under grant EEC-0812072, the People Programme (Marie Curie Actions) of the European Unions Seventh Framework Programme (FP7/2007-2013) under REA grant agreement no. [PIIF-GA-2013-629740].11, NSF under grant CCF-1320654, and DTRA grant HDTRA1-13-1-0021. We thank Meric Uzunoglu and Andrey Bernstein for their help with processing the WI data.

8. REFERENCES

[1] Platts GIS Data. http://www.platts.com/Products/gisdata.

[2] Power systems test case archive. Available at: http://www.ee.washington.edu/research/pstca/.

[3] U.S.-Canada Power System Outage Task Force. Report on the August 14, 2003 blackout in the United States and Canada: Causes and recommendations. 2004.

[4] Report of the enquiry committee on grid disturbance in Northern region on 30th July 2012 and in Northern, Eastern and North-Eastern region on 31st July 2012, Aug. 2012.

[5] The Federal Energy Regulatory Comission (FERC) and the North American Electric Reliability Corporation (NERC). Arizona-Southern California Outages on September 8, 2011. 2012.

[6] Assault on California power station raises alarm on potential for terrorism. Source: http://goo.gl/RiuhI1, 2014.

[7] Cybersecurity and the North American electric grid: New policy approaches to address an evolving threat. Source: http://goo.gl/WgUbPI, 2014.

[8] R. Albert, H. Jeong, and A.-L. Barabási. Error and attack tolerance of complex networks. *Nature*, 406(6794):378–382, 2000.

[9] R. Bapat. *Graphs and matrices*. Springer, 2010.

[10] A.-L. Barabási and R. Albert. Emergence of scaling in random networks. *Science*, 286(5439):509–512, 1999.

[11] A. R. Bergen and V. Vittal. *Power Systems Analysis*. Prentice-Hall, 1999.

[12] A. Bernstein, D. Bienstock, D. Hay, M. Uzunoglu, and G. Zussman. Sensitivity analysis of the power grid vulnerability to large-scale cascading failures. *ACM SIGMETRICS Perform. Eval. Rev.*, 40(3):33–37, 2012.

[13] A. Bernstein, D. Bienstock, D. Hay, M. Uzunoglu, and G. Zussman. Power grid vulnerability to geographically correlated failures - analysis and control implications. In *Proc. IEEE INFOCOM'14*, Apr. 2014.

[14] D. Bienstock. Optimal control of cascading power grid failures. *Proc. IEEE CDC-ECC*, Dec. 2011.

[15] D. Bienstock and A. Verma. The $N-k$ problem in power grids: New models, formulations, and numerical experiments. *SIAM J. Optimiz.*, 20(5):2352–2380, 2010.

[16] J. A. Bondy and U. Murty. Graph theory, volume 244 of graduate texts in mathematics, 2008.

[17] J. A. Bondy and U. S. R. Murty. *Graph theory with applications*. Macmillan London, 1976.

[18] S. Buldyrev, R. Parshani, G. Paul, H. Stanley, and S. Havlin. Catastrophic cascade of failures in interdependent networks. *Nature*, 464(7291):1025–1028, 2010.

[19] G. Chartrand, D. Geller, and S. Hedetniemi. Graphs with forbidden subgraphs. *J. Combin. Theory Ser. B*, 10(1):12–41, 1971.

[20] D. P. Chassin and C. Posse. Evaluating North American electric grid reliability using the Barabási–Albert network model. *Phys. A*, 355(2-4):667 – 677, 2005.

[21] G. Dán and H. Sandberg. Stealth attacks and protection schemes for state estimators in power systems. In *Proc. IEEE SmartGridComm'10*, 2010.

[22] I. Dobson, B. Carreras, V. Lynch, and D. Newman. Complex systems analysis of series of blackouts: cascading failure, critical points, and self-organization. *Chaos*, 17(2):026103, 2007.

[23] D. Donoho and Y. Tsaig. Fast solution of l1-norm minimization problems when the solution may be sparse, 2006. *Preprint at http://statweb.stanford.edu/~donoho/Reports/2006/kstep-20061005.pdf.*

[24] P. Erdős and A. Rényi. On random graphs. *Publicationes Mathematicae Debrecen*, 6:290–297, 1959.

[25] L. Gan, A. Wierman, U. Topcu, N. Chen, and S. H. Low. Real-time deferrable load control: handling the uncertainties of renewable generation. In *Proc. ACM e-Energy'13*, May 2013.

[26] M. R. Garey and D. S. Johnson. Computers and intractability: a guide to the theory of np-completeness. 1979.

[27] Y. Ghiassi-Farrokhfal, S. Keshav, C. Rosenberg, and F. Ciucu. Firming solar power. In *Proc. ACM SIGMETRICS'13 (poster description)*, June 2013.

[28] Y.-F. Huang, S. Werner, J. Huang, N. Kashyap, and V. Gupta. State estimation in electric power grids: Meeting new challenges presented by the requirements of the future grid. *IEEE Signal Process. Mag.*, 29(5):33–43, 2012.

[29] K. Khandeparkar, P. Patre, S. Jain, K. Ramamritham, and R. Gupta. Efficient PMU data dissemination in smart grid. In *Proc. ACM e-Energy'14 (poster description)*, June 2014.

[30] J. Kim and L. Tong. On topology attack of a smart grid: undetectable attacks and countermeasures. *IEEE J. Sel. Areas Commun*, 31(7):1294–1305, 2013.

[31] J. Kleinberg, M. Sandler, and A. Slivkins. Network failure detection and graph connectivity. In *Proc. ACM-SIAM SODA'04*, Jan. 2004.

[32] J. Liu, C. H. Xia, N. B. Shroff, and H. D. Sherali. Distributed optimal load shedding for disaster recovery in smart electric power grids: A second-order approach. In *Proc. ACM SIGMETRICS'14 (poster description)*, June 2014.

[33] Y. Liu, P. Ning, and M. K. Reiter. False data injection attacks against state estimation in electric power grids. *ACM Trans. Inf. Syst. Secur.*, 14(1):13, 2011.

[34] L. Lu, J. Tu, C.-K. Chau, M. Chen, and X. Lin. Online energy generation scheduling for microgrids with intermittent energy sources and co-generation. In *Proc. ACM SIGMETRICS'13*, June 2013.

[35] N. M. Manousakis, G. N. Korres, and P. S. Georgilakis. Taxonomy of PMU placement methodologies. *IEEE Trans. Power Syst.*, 27(2):1070–1077, 2012.

[36] C. Phillips. The network inhibition problem. In *Proc. ACM STOC'93*, May 1993.

[37] A. Pinar, J. Meza, V. Donde, and B. Lesieutre. Optimization strategies for the vulnerability analysis of the electric power grid. *SIAM J. Optimiz.*, 20(4):1786–1810, 2010.

[38] W. Rudin. *Real and complex analysis*. Tata McGraw-Hill Education, 1987.
[39] P. D. Seymour. On odd cuts and plane multicommodity flows. *P. Lond. Math. Soc.*, 3(1):178–192, 1981.
[40] S. Soltan, D. Mazauric, and G. Zussman. Cascading failures in power grids – analysis and algorithms. In *Proc. ACM e-Energy'14*, June 2014.
[41] S. Soltan and G. Zussman. A statistical method for synthetic power grid generation based on the U.S. Western Interconnection. Abstract presented at *SIAM NS'15*, May 2015.
[42] J. E. Tate and T. J. Overbye. Line outage detection using phasor angle measurements. *IEEE Trans. Power Syst.*, 23(4):1644–1652, 2008.
[43] J. E. Tate and T. J. Overbye. Double line outage detection using phasor angle measurements. In *Proc. IEEE PES'09*, July 2009.
[44] O. Vukovic, K. C. Sou, G. Dán, and H. Sandberg. Network-layer protection schemes against stealth attacks on state estimators in power systems. In *Proc. IEEE SmartGridComm'11*, 2011.
[45] X. Wang, X. Song, and J. Yuan. On matching cover of graphs. *Math. Program.*, 147(1-2):499–518, 2014.
[46] D. B. West et al. *Introduction to graph theory*, volume 2. Prentice hall Upper Saddle River, 2001.
[47] H. Xiao and E. M. Yeh. Cascading link failure in the power grid: A percolation-based analysis. In *Proc. IEEE Int. Work. on Smart Grid Commun.*, June 2011.
[48] Y. Zhao, A. Goldsmith, and H. V. Poor. On PMU location selection for line outage detection in wide-area transmission networks. In *Proc. IEEE PES'12*, July 2012.
[49] H. Zhu and G. B. Giannakis. Sparse overcomplete representations for efficient identification of power line outages. *IEEE Trans. Power Syst.*, 27(4):2215–2224, 2012.
[50] R. D. Zimmerman, C. E. Murillo-Sánchez, and R. J. Thomas. Matpower: Steady-state operations, planning, and analysis tools for power systems research and education. *IEEE Trans. Power Syst.*, 26(1):12–19, 2011.
[51] D. Zuckerman. Linear degree extractors and the inapproximability of max clique and chromatic number. In *Proc. ACM STOC'06*, May 2006.

APPENDIX

A. PRELIMINARIES

In this appendix we provide some of the known theorems and definitions used in the proofs.

A *bond* of a graph is a minimal nonempty edge cut, that is, a nonempty edge cut none of whose nonempty proper subsets is an edge cut.

A graph in which each node has even degree is called an *even* graph. A *circuit* is the union of edge-disjoint *cycles*. It is easy to see that a *cycle* is also a *circuit*.

THEOREM A.1 (THEOREM 5.2 [39]). *Let $G = (V, E)$ be a planar Eulerian graph, and let $F \subseteq E$. Then the following are equivalent:* (i) *F is G-separable,* (ii) *for each bond D, $|D \cap F| \leqslant |D - F|$.*

THEOREM A.2 (THEOREM 10.16 [17]). *Let G be a connected planar graph, and let G^* be a planar dual of G.* (i) *If C is a cycle of G, then C^* is a bond of G^*.* (ii) *If B is a bond of G, then B^* is a cycle of G^*.*

THEOREM A.3 (THEOREM 6.1.16 [46]). *The followings are equivalent for a planar graph G,* (i) *G is bipartite,* (ii) *every face of G has even length, and* (iii) *the dual graph G^* is Eulerian.*

THEOREM A.4 (EULER'S FORMULA [16]). *For any planar graph G with n nodes, m edges, r faces, and c connected components, the following formula holds, $n + r - m = c$.*

LEMMA A.1 (COROLLARY 2.16 [16]). *The symmetric difference of two even subgraphs is an even subgraph.*

B. PROOFS

PROOF OF COROLLARY 2. Suppose $M = (U, V_H)$ is the matching for $G[V_H, \bar{V}_H]$ that covers V_H, and suppose $U \subseteq \bar{V}_H$ are the matched nodes which are in $\bar{V}_H$. Since M is the matching in $G[V_H, \bar{V}_H]$ that covers H, thus $|U| = |V_H|$. Regarding Theorem 1, to show that H is well-supported almost surely, we need to show that the columns of the matrix $\mathbf{A}_{\bar{H}|H}$ are linearly independent almost surely. For this reason, we show that $\det(\mathbf{A}_{U|V_H}) \neq 0$ almost surely. $\det(\mathbf{A}_{U|V_H})$ can be considered as a polynomial of the nonzero entries of the admittance matrix using Leibniz formula. Now assume $U = \{u_1, u_2, \ldots, u_{|V_H|}\}$ are matched to $V_H = \{v_1, v_2, \ldots, v_{|V_H|}\}$ in order. It can be seen that $\prod_{i=1}^{|V_H|} a_{u_i v_i}$ is a term with nonzero coefficient in $\det(\mathbf{A}_{U|V_H})$. Therefore, $\det(\mathbf{A}_{U|V_H})$ is not a zero polynomial in terms of its nonzero entries. Now since the set of reactance values for the edges in $E[V_H, \bar{V}_H]$ such that $\det(\mathbf{A}_{U|V_H}) = 0$ is a measure zero set in the real space, thus $\det(\mathbf{A}_{U|V_H}) \neq 0$ almost surely. □

PROOF OF LEMMA 3. It is easy to see that the solution to (5) is unique if and only if $\mathbf{D}_H$ has linearly independent columns. It is known that $\text{rank}(\mathbf{D}_H) = |V_H| - c$ in which c is the number of connected components of H [9, Theorem 2.3]. Therefore, $\mathbf{D}_H$ has linearly independent columns if and only if each connected component of $\mathbf{D}_H$ is a tree, which means that $\mathbf{D}_H$ should be acyclic. □

PROOF OF THEOREM 2. Recall that we can assume $V_H = \{1, 2, \ldots, |V_H|\}$ and $E_H = \{e_1, e_2, \ldots, e_{|E_H|}\}$. We assign an arbitrary orientation to the edges of H and fix the embedding of H on the plane. We show the set of oriented edges by $\mathcal{E}_{\mathcal{H}} = \{\epsilon_1, \epsilon_2, \ldots, \epsilon_{|E_H|}\}$. Suppose H has r faces and $C_1, C_2, \ldots, C_r$ are the cycles that surrounded those faces. For each cycle C_i, define vector $\vec{c_i} \in \{-1, 0, 1\}^{|E_H|}$ as follows,

$$c_{ij} = \begin{cases} 0 & \text{if } \epsilon_j \notin C_i, \\ 1 & \text{if } \epsilon_j \in C_i \text{ and } \epsilon_j \text{ traverse } C_i \text{ clockwise}, \\ -1 & \text{if } \epsilon_j \in C_i \text{ and } \epsilon_j \text{ traverse } C_i \text{ counterclockwise}. \end{cases}$$

It is easy to see that $\forall i, \mathbf{D}_H \vec{c_i} = 0$. Therefore, $\vec{c_i} \in \text{Null}(\mathbf{D})$. On the other hand it is easy to see that $\vec{c_i}$s are linearly independent. If c is the number of connected components of H, then $\dim(\text{Null}(\mathbf{D})) = |E_H| - |V_H| + c$ which from *Euler's formula* is equal to r. Thus, $\vec{c_i}$s form a basis for the null space of the incidence matrix $\mathbf{D}$. Now suppose $\vec{x}$ is the solution to (5) such that $\text{supp}(\vec{x}) = \{i | e_i \in F\}$ (from Lemma 2 we know that such a solution exists). We need to prove that for any $\vec{z} = \vec{x} + y_1\vec{c_1} + \cdots + y_r\vec{c_r}$, $\|\vec{z}\|_1 \leqslant \|\vec{x}\|_1$ iff

$y_1 = y_2 = \cdots = y_r = 0$. Please notice that since $\vec{c_i}$s are the cycles associated with the faces of the planar graph H, each edge e_j appears in at most two cycles C_t and C_s. Thus, the entries of $\vec{z}$, z_js are in one of the following forms, (i) $z_j = 0$, (ii) $z_j = x_j$, (iii) $z_j = x_j \pm y_t$, (iv) $z_j = x_j \pm (y_t - y_s)$, or (v) $z_j = \pm(y_t - y_s)$.

First, we show that $\|\vec{z}\|_1 \geqslant \|\vec{x}\|_1$. Suppose $F = \{e_{i_1}, e_{i_2}, \ldots, e_{i_k}\}$. From the assumption, we know that F^* is H^*-separable. Thus, there are pairwise edge-disjoint cycles $O^*_j (1 \leqslant j \leqslant k)$ in H^*, such that $\forall e_{i_j} \in F, e^*_{i_j} \in O^*_j$. For each $j (1 \leqslant j \leqslant k)$ define $N_O(j) = \{p | e^*_p \in O^*_j\}$. From the definitions it is easy to see that $\forall p, q (1 \leqslant p \neq q \leqslant k), N_O(p) \cap N_O(q) = \varnothing$. Thus, $\|\vec{z}\|_1 \geqslant \sum_{j=1}^{k} \sum_{p \in N_O(j)} |z_p|$. On the other hand, from the triangle inequality, it is easy to see that for all $1 \leqslant j \leqslant k$, $\sum_{p \in N_O(j)} |z_p| \geqslant |x_{i_j}|$. Thus, $\|\vec{z}\|_1 \geqslant \sum_{j=1}^{k} \sum_{p \in N_O(j)} |z_p| \geqslant \sum_{j=1}^{k} |x_{i_j}| = \|\vec{x}\|_1$.

Now we show that $\|\vec{z}\|_1 = \|\vec{x}\|_1$ is not possible unless $y_1 = y_2 = \cdots = y_r = 0$. If $\{j_1, j_2, \ldots, j_t\}$ are the indices for which $y_{j_1} = y_{j_2} = \cdots = y_{j_t} = w$, then $y_{j_1}\vec{c_{j_1}} + \cdots + y_{j_t}\vec{c_{j_t}} = w\vec{c''}$ for which from Lemma A.1, $\vec{c''}$ is the vector associated with the circuit $C'' = C_{j_1} \Delta C_{j_2} \Delta \ldots \Delta C_{j_t}$ (Δ is the symmetric difference). Therefore we can rewrite $\vec{z}$ as $\vec{x} + w_1\vec{c''_1} + w_2\vec{c''_2} + \cdots + w_q\vec{c''_q}$ for which $w_1 > w_2 > \cdots > w_q$. If $q = 0$, then there is nothing left to prove. If $q = 1$, then it can be easily concluded from Lemma 4 that it is not possible to have $\|\vec{z}\|_1 = \|\vec{x}\|_1$ unless $w_1 = 0 \Rightarrow y_1 = y_2 = \cdots = y_r = 0$. Now assume $q > 1$, from what we showed previously, we know that in order to have $\|\vec{z}\|_1 = \|\vec{x}\|_1$, we should have $\|\vec{z}\|_1 = \sum_{j=1}^{k} \sum_{p \in N_O(j)} |z_p| = \sum_{j=1}^{k} |x_{i_j}| = \|\vec{x}\|_1$. Equality $\|\vec{z}\|_1 = \sum_{j=1}^{k} \sum_{p \in N_O(j)} |z_p|$ shows that $\text{supp}(\vec{z}) \subseteq \bigcup_{j=1}^{k} N_O(j)$. Equality $\sum_{j=1}^{k} \sum_{p \in N_O(j)} |z_p| = \sum_{j=1}^{k} |x_{i_j}|$ shows that w_1 should appear in $\|\vec{z}\|_1$, half of the time positive and half of the time negative. However, since w_1 has the largest value, it appears always as $w_1 - w_i$ in the instances like $|w_1 - w_i|$. Now from assumption we know that $|\text{supp}(\vec{x}) \cap C''_1| < |C''_1|/2$. Thus, there are more than $|C''_1|/2$ instances like $|w_1 - w_i|$ or $|w_1|$ in $\|\vec{z}\|_1$. Therefore, it is not possible that w_1 appears half of the time positive and half of the time negative in $\|\vec{z}\|_1$, which shows that if $q > 1$ then $\|\vec{z}\|_1 \neq \|\vec{x}\|_1$. Thus, the proof is complete. □

Proof of Corollary 4. H is bipartite, therefore from Theorem A.3, H^* is Eulerian. For any C in H, $|C \cap F| < |C \backslash F|$, therefore from Theorem A.2 for any bond C^* in H^*, $|C^* \cap F^*| < |C^* \backslash F^*|$. Combining these two, from Theorem A.1 we can conclude that F^* is H^*-separable. Thus, we can simply apply Theorem 2. □

Proof of Lemma 5. From Corollary 1 we know that $\vec{\delta}_H = \vec{\theta}_H - \vec{\theta}'_H$ is a solution to $\mathbf{A}_{\bar{H}|H}\vec{\delta}_H + \mathbf{A}_{\bar{H}|\bar{H}}\vec{\delta}_{\bar{H}} = 0$. Now if $\vec{\delta} = \vec{\theta} - \vec{\theta}'$, from Lemma 2 we know that there exists a vector $\vec{x} \in \mathbb{R}^{|E_H|}$ such that $\text{supp}(\vec{x}) = \{i | e_i \in F\}$ and $\mathbf{D}_H\vec{x} = \mathbf{A}_{H|H}\vec{\delta}_H + \mathbf{A}_{H|\bar{H}}\vec{\delta}_{\bar{H}}$. Thus, the proof is complete. □

Proof of Lemma 7. First, notice that since v is H-outer-connected, $N(v) \subseteq V_H$. Thus, $\delta_v = 1/d(v) \sum_{u \in N(v)} \delta_u$ implies that δ_v is unique. Now, let us compute the vth entry of the vectors on the both side of the equation $\mathbf{D}_H\vec{x} = \mathbf{A}_{H|H}\vec{\delta}_H + \mathbf{A}_{H|\bar{H}}\vec{\delta}_{\bar{H}}$. Since v is H-outer-connected, the vth row of $\mathbf{D}_H$ is a zero vector. Thus, $(\mathbf{D}_H\vec{x})_v = 0$ for any $\vec{x}$. It is also easy to see that $(\mathbf{A}_{H|H}\vec{\delta}_H)_v = \delta_v d(v)$ and $(A_{H|\bar{H}}\vec{\delta}_{\bar{H}})_v = -\sum_{u \in N(v)} \delta_u$. Since $(\mathbf{D}_H\vec{x})_v = (\mathbf{A}_{H|H}\vec{\delta}_H)_v + (A_{H|\bar{H}}\vec{\delta}_{\bar{H}})_v$, we can conclude that $\delta_v = 1/d(v) \sum_{u \in N(v)} \delta_u$. Thus, the proof is complete. □

Proof of Theorem 3. First, using Lemma 7, since the phase angles for the H-outer-connected nodes can be computed uniquely, without loss of generality and for simplicity, we can assume that H does not contain any H-outer-connected nodes. Suppose $\vec{c}_1, \ldots \vec{c}_r$ are the vectors associated with the faces in H as we defined in the proof of Theorem 2. Suppose $\vec{b}_1, \ldots, \vec{b}_t$ are the vectors associated with the coboundry of the H-inner-connected nodes as we defined in the proof of Lemma 6. All we need to prove is that if $\vec{x}$ is the solution to (7) such that $\text{supp}(\vec{x}) = \{i | e_i \in F\}$ then for any solution $\vec{z}$ for (7), $\|\vec{z}\|_1 > \|\vec{x} + y_1\vec{c}_1 + \cdots + y_r\vec{c}_1 + w_1\vec{b}_1 + \cdots + w_t\vec{b}_t\|_1$ unless $y_1 = \cdots = y_r = w_1 = \cdots = w_t = 0$. The rest of the proof is exactly similar to proofs of Lemma 6 and Theorem 2. The key is Condition (v) implies that the cycles ($\vec{c}_i$s) and coboundries ($\vec{b}_i$s) are edge disjoint. Thus, since all the conditions for Lemma 6 and Theorem 2 also hold here, with exactly the same approach as in the proofs of Lemma 6 and Theorem 2 we can conclude this Theorem. □

Proof of Lemma 8. We show that finding the minimum matched-forest partition is at least as hard as vertex arboricity. Suppose $G = (V, E)$ is given and we are interested in $a(G)$. We build a new graph $\hat{G} = (\hat{V}, \hat{E})$ by getting a copy of graph G, $G'' = (V'', E'')$ and connect every node in G to its counterpart in G''. Thus, $\hat{V} = V \cup V''$ and $\hat{E} = E \cup E'' \cup \{\{v_i, v''_i\} | v_i \in V\}$. We prove that $\hat{G}$ has a matched-forest partition of size k if and only if $a(G) \leqslant k$. First, let us assume $\hat{G}$ has a matched-forest partition of size k, namely $\hat{H}_1, \hat{H}_2, \ldots, \hat{H}_k$. Since subgraphs induced by $\hat{H}_1, \hat{H}_2, \ldots, \hat{H}_k$ in $\hat{G}$ are acyclic and partition $\hat{V}$, it is easy to see that subgraphs induced by $\hat{H}_1 \cap V, \hat{H}_2 \cap V, \ldots, \hat{H}_k \cap V$ in G are acyclic and partition V. Thus, $a(G) \leqslant k$. Now, let us assume $a(G) \leqslant k$. There should exists a partition of nodes of G into subsets $H_1, H_2, \ldots, H_k$ such that each subset induces an acyclic graph. Assume $H''_1, H''_2, \ldots, H''_k$ are the counterparts of these subsets in G''. For any $i, 1 \leqslant i \leqslant k-1$ define $\hat{H}_i = H_i \cup H''_{i+1}$, and $\hat{H}_k = H_k \cup H''_1$. It is easy to see that $\hat{H}_1, \hat{H}_2, \ldots, \hat{H}_k$ is a matched-forest partition of size k for $\hat{G}$. Thus, we proved that $\hat{G}$ has a matched-forest partition of size k if and only if $a(G) \leqslant k$. It means that the minimum matched-forest partition of $\hat{G}$ is equal to $a(G)$, which shows that the minimum matched-forest partition is at least as hard as vertex arboricity and therefore it is NP-hard. □

Proof of Lemma 9. For a graph G, assume $\chi(G)$ is its chromatic number. Since each color gives an independent set of G, induced subgraph by the nodes with the same color is acyclic with no edges. Thus, it is easy to see that $a(G) \leqslant \chi(G)$. Suppose there is an α-approximation algorithm for the minimum matched-forest problem. Define $\hat{G}$ as in proof of Lemma 8. Assume this algorithm partitions $\hat{G}$ into k subsets. From the proof of Lemma 8, it is easy to see that $k \leqslant \alpha a(G)$. On the other hand, since each acyclic graph has the chromatic number of at most 2, this algorithm gives the $2k$ coloring of graph G. However, $2k \leqslant 2\alpha a(G) \leqslant 2\alpha\chi(G)$. Thus, this algorithm gives a 2α-approximation of the chromatic number of G. However, the result by Zuckerman [51] states that for all $\epsilon > 0$, it is NP-hard to approximate chromatic number to within $n^{1-\epsilon}$. Therefore, for all $\epsilon > 0$, it is NP-hard to approximate the minimum matched-forest problem to within $n^{1-\epsilon}$ as well. □

Proof of Lemma 10. It is known that every planar graph has a node of degree less than or equal to 5 [46]. Therefore, line 1 of the algorithm can always find v. At line 4, recursively we know that subgraphs induced by Q_1, Q_2, Q_3 in $G\backslash v$ are acyclic. Now since $\deg(v) \leqslant 5$, there exists a partition such that $|N(v) \cap Q_i| \leqslant 1$. Without loss of generality we can assume that $|N(v) \cap Q_1| \leqslant 1$. Hence, adding v to Q_1 does not produces any cycles. Thus, subgraphs induced by $Q_1 \cup \{v\}, Q_2, Q_3$ in G are acyclic. □

PROOF OF LEMMA 11. Suppose OPT is the minimum number of matched-forest partitions of G and OPT_m is the number of optimal matching cover of G. Since for any subset V_H in the partition of $G = (V, E)$ into matched-forest partitions there exists a matching that covers V_H, we can cover V with OPT matchings. Thus, $OPT_m \leqslant OPT$. Now since G is planar, ZS Algorithm uses $3APP$ to partition Q_is into atmost 3 subsets. Hence, if k is the number of subsets returned by ZS Algorithm then $k \leqslant 3 \times 2 \times OPT_m \leqslant 6 \times OPT$. Thus, ZS Algorithm provides a 6-approximation of the minimum *matched-forest* partition of G.

As for the running time, ZS algorithm takes $O(n^3)$ time to find the optimal matching cover of G and $O(|Q_i|)$ to partition Q_i. Now since $k \leqslant n$ and $|Q_i| \leqslant n$, line 4 does not take more than $O(n^2)$. Thus, the total running time is $O(n^3)$. □

Impact of Fairness and Heterogeneity on Delays in Large-scale Content Delivery Networks

Virag Shah
The University of Texas at Austin
Texas, USA
virag@utexas.edu

Gustavo de Veciana
The University of Texas at Austin
Texas, USA
gustavo@ece.utexas.edu

ABSTRACT

We consider multi-class queueing systems where the per class service rates depend on the network state, fairness criterion, and is constrained to be in a symmetric polymatroid capacity region. We develop new comparison results leading to explicit bounds on the mean service time under various fairness criteria and possibly heterogeneous loads. We then study large-scale systems with growing numbers of service classes n (e.g., files), heterogenous servers m and polymatroid capacity resulting from a random bipartite graph modeling service availability (e.g., placement of files across servers). This models, for example, a large scale content delivery network (CDN) supporting parallel servicing of a download request. For an appropriate asymptotic regime, we show that the system's capacity region is uniformly close to a symmetric polymatroid – i.e., heterogeneity in servers' capacity and file placement disappears.

Combining our comparison results and the asymptotic 'symmetry' in large systems, we study performance robustness to heterogeneity in per class loads and fairness criteria. Roughly, if each class can be served by $c_n = \omega(\log n)$ servers, the load per class does not exceed $\theta_n = o\left(\min(\frac{n}{\log n}, c_n)\right)$, and average server utilization is bounded by $\gamma < 1$, then mean delay satisfies the following bound:

$$E[D^{(n)}] \leq K \frac{\theta_n}{c_n} \frac{1}{\gamma} \log\left(\frac{1}{1-\gamma}\right),$$

where K is a constant. Thus, large, randomly configured CDNs with a logarithmic number of file copies are robust to substantial load and server heterogeneities for a class of fairness criteria.

Categories and Subject Descriptors

C.4 [**Computer Systems Organization**]: Performance of Systems—*Modeling techniques*; G.2 [**Probability and Statistics**]: Queueing theory; H.2.4 [**Information Systems**]: Systems—*Concurrency*

SIGMETRICS'15, June 15–19, 2015, Portland, OR, USA.

http://dx.doi.org/10.1145/2745844.2745857.

General Terms

Performance, Theory

Keywords

Delays; queuing system; content delivery networks; content placement; parallel downloads; bipartite graphs; robustness; fairness; asymptotics

1. INTRODUCTION

In many shared network systems service rate is allocated to ongoing jobs based on a fairness criterion, e.g., α-fair (αF) (including max-min and proportional fair) as well as Balanced fair (BF), and other Greedy criteria [24]. When the network loads are stochastic a key open question is how the choice of fairness and network design will impact user perceived performance, e.g., job delays, as well as the sensitivity of performance to heterogeneity in network resources and traffic loads. Motivated by this challenge in this paper we take a step towards understanding these issues by investigating performance bounds for an interesting class of stochastic networks with symmetric polymatroid capacity under various fairness criteria.

The second question driving this paper is whether large scale systems can be designed to be inherently robust to heterogeneity and at what cost? Specifically we consider a centralized content delivery infrastructure where a collection of servers store and deliver large files, e.g., scientific datasets/visualization, 3D videos, software updates, other immersive technologies, and are aimed at doing so with small delays. Such centralized infrastructure could, for example, be part of a larger distributed content delivery network (CDN), where requests not currently available at distributed sites are forwarded to the centralized infrastructure which in turn delivers the files to the remote sites and/or users. There has been substantial recent interest in understanding basic design questions for these systems including, see e.g. [10, 14, 20, 23] and references therein: How should the number of file copies scale with the demand? What kinds of hierarchical caching policies are most suitable? How to best optimize storage/backhaul costs for unpredictable time-varying demands? Our focus is on CDNs that permit parallel file downloads from multiple servers – akin to peer-to-peer systems. In principle, with an appropriate degree of storage redundancy, one can achieve much better peak service rates, exploit diversity in service paths, produce robustness to failures, and provide better sharing of pooled server resources.

Intuitively when such systems have sufficient redundancy they will exhibit performance which is robust to limited heterogeneity in demands and server capacity, as well as to the fairness criterion driving resource allocation. Such systems might also circumvent the need for, and overheads (such as backhaul, state update, etc) associated with, dynamic caching. If this is the case, CDNs enabling parallel servicing of individual download requests could be more scalable and robust to serving popular content.

Our Contributions and Organization: The contributions of this paper are threefold, each of independent interest, and collectively, providing a significant step forward over what is known in the current literature.

a.) *Performance bounds:* In Sections 3-4 we consider a class of systems with symmetric polymatroid capacity for which we develop several rate allocation monotonicity properties which translate to performance comparisons amongst fairness policies, and eventually give explicit bounds on mean delays. Specifically we show that under homogeneous loads the mean delay achieved by Greedy and αF rate allocations are bounded by that of BF allocation which is computable. We then extend this upper bound to the case when the load is heterogeneous but 'majorized by a symmetric load'.

b.) *Uniform symmetry in large systems:* In Section 5 we consider a bipartite graph where nodes represent n job classes (files) and m servers with potentially heterogenous service capacity. The graph edges capture the ability of servers to serve the jobs in the given classes. If jobs can be concurrently served by multiple servers then the system's service capacity region is a polymatroid. We show that for appropriately scaled large system where the edge set is chosen at random (random file placement) the capacity region is uniformly close to a *symmetric* polymatroid.

c.) *Performance robustness in large systems:* By combining these two results, in Section 6 we provide a simple performance bound for large-scale content delivery systems. The bound exhibits performance robustness in such systems with respect to variations in total system load, heterogeneity in load across the classes, heterogeneity in server capacities, for α-fair based resource allocation. Specifically it establishes a clear link between the degree of content replication and permissible demand heterogeneity while ensuring performance scalability.

We have endeavored to provide as complete results as possible, and have deferred details to the appendix. Section 7 concludes the paper.

Related work: There is a substantial amount of related work. Yet the link between fairness in resource allocation and job delays in stochastic networks is poorly understood. The only fairness criterion for which explicit expressions or bounds are known is the Balanced Fair rate allocation [3] which generalizes the notion of 'insensitivity' of the processor sharing discipline in $M/G/1$ queuing system. Under balanced fairness, an explicit expression for mean delay was obtained in [5, 6] for a class of wireline networks, namely, those with line and tree topologies. Also, a performance bound for arbitrary polytope capacity region and arbitrary load was provided in [1]. Similarly [11] developed bounds for stochastic networks where flows can be split over multiple paths. These bounds and expressions are either too specific or too loose. In [22] we developed an expression for the mean delay for systems with polymatroid capacity and arbitrary loads under Balanced Fair rate allocations. Unfortunately the result has exponential computational complexity in general. However the symmetric case has low complexity, a fact we use in the sequel.

Balanced fair rate allocation is defined recursively and is difficult to implement. α-fair rate allocations [13, 19] which are based on maximizing a concave sum utility function over the system's capacity region – this includes proportional and max-min fair allocations, are more amenable to implementation [12, 15]. However, the only known explicit performance results for stochastic networks under such fairness criteria are for systems where proportional fair is equivalent to balanced fair [3, 17]. In [2], performance relationship under balanced and proportional fairness for several systems where they are not equivalent was studied through numerical computations, and were found to be relatively close in several scenarios.

In this paper we focus on a class of stochastic networks that can be characterized by a polymatroid capacity region. Such systems have also been considered in [22, 24]. For example, the work in [24] shows that when such systems are symmetric with respect to load and capacity, a greedy rate allocation is delay optimal. However, the result is brittle to asymmetries. We provide more details on greedy and other rate allocations in Section 3.

In summary when it comes to fairness criteria and stochastic network performance there is a gap between what is implementable and what is analyzable. One of the goals of this paper is to provide comparison results which address this gap, with particular focus on addressing user-performance in large-scale CDN systems prevalent today. In this setting the two works closest to this paper are [23] and [22]. Both adopt a natural model for a CDN-like system based on a bipartite graph which captures the availability of files at servers to support the file-download requests. They show that if the graph is chosen at random and scaled appropriately then user performance is robust to load heterogeneity. The authors in [23] consider a service model where each request can be served by a single server without preemption – recall we consider systems allowing parallel downloads. The flexibility of our service model leads to a significantly improved mean delay bound and the resulting robustness. For example, upon availability of c_n servers for each class, the maximum per-class load allowed in [23] is $o\left(\sqrt{\frac{c_n}{\log n}}\right)$ which is significantly lower than our limit of $o\left(\min(\frac{n}{\log n}, c_n)\right)$. Also in our work we are able to address the role of fairness criteria and robustness to heterogeneity in server capacities.

While our service model is similar to that in [22], our work in this paper is different in several respects. Firstly, in [22] we focused on mean delays only for Balanced fair resource allocation whereas in this paper we directly study the impact of fairness criteria on users' delays. Secondly, we consider here a different scaling regime where the number of job classes (files) n grows proportionally to the number of servers m. In our earlier work the system was by design symmetric whereas in this paper we establish the asymptotic symmetry. Thirdly, in this paper we establish new results on robustness to limited heterogeneity in file demands, server capacity and α-fairness criteria by providing a uniform bound on delays.

2. SYSTEM MODEL

Our system consists of a set F of n classes. Jobs for class $i \in F$ arrive as an independent Poisson process of rate λ_i. Let $\boldsymbol{\lambda} = (\lambda_i : i \in F)$. Service requirements of jobs are i.i.d exponential with mean ν. Let $\boldsymbol{\rho} = (\rho_i : i \in F)$, where $\rho_i = \lambda_i \nu$ denotes the load associated with class i.

Let $q_i(t)$ denote the *set* of ongoing jobs of class i at time t, i.e., jobs which have arrived but have not completed service, and $\mathbf{q}(t) = (q_i(t) : i \in F)$. Let $\mathbf{x}(t) = (x_i(t) : i \in F)$, where $x_i(t) \triangleq |q_i(t)|$, i.e., $\mathbf{x}(t)$ captures the number of ongoing jobs in each class.

We refer to $\mathbf{x}(t)$ as the state of the system at time t. Let $\mathbf{X}(t)$ correspond to the random vector describing the state of the system at time t. We refer to the random process $(\mathbf{X}(t) : t \geq 0)$ as the state process. For any $\mathbf{x}(t)$, let $A_{\mathbf{x}(t)}$ denote the set of active classes, i.e., the classes with at least one ongoing job.

Service Model: For any $v \in q_i(t)$, let $b_v(t)$ be the rate at which job v is served at time t. The vector $\mathbf{b}(t) = (b_v(t) : v \in \cup_i q_i(t))$ represents the rates assigned to ongoing jobs at time t. Within each class we assume that each job is allocated equal rate, i.e., $b_v(t) = b_u(t)$ for each $u, v \in q_i(t)$. If job v arrives at time t_v^a and has service requirement η_v, then it departs at time t_v^d such that $\eta_v = \int_{t_v^a}^{t_v^d} b_v(t)dt$. Thus, $t_v^d - t_v^a$ is the delay for job v.

Further, let $r_i(\mathbf{x}')$ be the total rate at which class i jobs are served at time t when $\mathbf{x}(t) = \mathbf{x}'$, i.e., at any time t, $r_i(\mathbf{x}(t)) = \sum_{v \in q_i(t)} b_v(t)$. Let $\mathbf{r}(\mathbf{x}') = (r_i(\mathbf{x}') : i \in F)$. We call the vector function $\mathbf{r}(.)$ the *rate allocation*. Note that the rate allocation at any time t depends only on the $\mathbf{x}(t)$ and thus can not depend on the residual file sizes of ongoing jobs.

Polymatroid Capacity Region: We shall consider systems where rate allocation $\mathbf{r}(\mathbf{x})$ for each $\mathbf{x}$ are constrained to be within a polymatroid capacity region $\mathcal{C}$.

Definition 1. *We say that $\mathcal{C}$ is a* **polymatroid** *if it takes the following form:*

$$\mathcal{C} = \left\{ \mathbf{r} \geq \mathbf{0} : \sum_{i \in A} r_i \leq \mu(A),\ \forall A \subset F \right\},$$

where $\mu(.)$ is a set function which satisfies the following properties:
1) Normalized: $\mu(\emptyset) = 0$.
2) Monotonic: if $A \subset B$, $\mu(A) \leq \mu(B)$.
3) Submodular: for all $A, B \subset F$,

$$\mu(A) + \mu(B) \geq \mu(A \cup B) + \mu(A \cap B).$$

The function $\mu(.)$ is called a **rank function**.

Polymatroids and submodular functions are well studied in literature, see e.g., [9, 21].

Definition 2. *A polymatroid $\mathcal{C}$ is a* **symmetric polymatroid** *if its rank function $\mu(.)$ satisfies the following property: for each $A \subset F$, we have $\mu(A) = h(|A|)$, where $h : \mathbb{Z}_+ \to \mathbb{R}_+$ is a non-decreasing concave function.*

For a given $\mathbf{x}$, we say $\mathbf{r}(\mathbf{x})$ is feasible if $\mathbf{r}(\mathbf{x}) \in \mathcal{C}$; when this is true for all $\mathbf{x}$, we say that the rate allocation $\mathbf{r}(.)$ is feasible. We call $\mathcal{C}$ the capacity region of the system. Symmetric polymatroid capacity regions appear in several systems, for example, Gaussian symmetric multi-access channels [24]. Further, we will see in Section 5 that certain types of large content delivery networks have approximately symmetric polymatroid capacity regions.

Polymatroid capacity regions $\mathcal{C}$ have a special property that for any $\mathbf{r} \in \mathcal{C}$, there exists $\mathbf{r}' \geq \mathbf{r}$ such that $\mathbf{r}' \in \mathcal{D} \triangleq \{\mathbf{r} \in \mathcal{C} : \sum_{i \in F} r_i = \mu(F)\}$ [9, 21]. Also, as evident from the definition, for any $A \subset F$ the set $\{\mathbf{r} \in \mathcal{C} : r_i = 0, \forall i \notin A\}$ is also a polymatroid, with a rank function which is the restriction of $\mu(.)$ to subsets of A.

Further, we let

$$\hat{\mathcal{C}} \triangleq \left\{ \boldsymbol{\rho}' \geq \mathbf{0} : \sum_{i \in A} \rho_i' < \mu(A),\ \forall A \subset F \right\}, \quad (1)$$

and will see, $\hat{\mathcal{C}}$ is the set of loads which are stabilizable for appropriate rate allocation policies.

Notation for ordering and majorization: In the sequel, we will rely on notation for ordering and majorization which we introduce below.

Let I be a finite arbitrary index set. Consider an arbitrary vector $\mathbf{z} = (z_i : i \in I)$. We let $z_{[1]} \geq z_{[2]} \geq \ldots, z_{[|I|]}$ denote the components of $\mathbf{z}$ in decreasing order. We let $|\mathbf{z}|$ denote $\sum_{i \in I} |z_i|$. We let $\mathbf{e}_i$ denote a vector with 1 at the ith coordinate and 0 elsewhere.

For vectors $\mathbf{z}$ and $\mathbf{z}'$ such that $z_i \leq z_i'$ for each $i \in I$, we write $\mathbf{z} \leq \mathbf{z}'$ and say that $\mathbf{z}$ is *dominated* by $\mathbf{z}'$.

Below we define *majorization* $(\prec)$ which describes how 'balanced' a vector is as compared to another vector. In words, by $\mathbf{z} \prec \mathbf{z}'$ we mean that $\mathbf{z}$ is 'more balanced' than $\mathbf{z}'$ but they have the same sum. By $\mathbf{z} \prec_w \mathbf{z}'$ we mean that $\mathbf{z}$ is 'more balanced' and has lower sum than $\mathbf{z}'$. Similarly, by $\mathbf{z} \prec^w \mathbf{z}'$ we mean that $\mathbf{z}$ is 'more balanced' and has larger sum than $\mathbf{z}'$.

Definition 3. *For vectors $\mathbf{z}$ and $\mathbf{z}'$ such that $|\mathbf{z}| = |\mathbf{z}'|$ and $\sum_{l=1}^{k} z_{[l]} \leq \sum_{l=1}^{k} z_{[l]}'$ for each $k \in \{1, 2, \ldots, |I|\}$, we say $\mathbf{z}$ is* majorized *by $\mathbf{z}'$, and denote this as $\mathbf{z} \prec \mathbf{z}'$.*

If we have $\sum_{l=1}^{k} z_{[l]} \leq \sum_{l=1}^{k} z_{[l]}'$ for each $k \in \{1, 2, \ldots, |I|\}$, we say $\mathbf{z}$ is weak-majorized from below *by $\mathbf{z}'$, and denote this as $\mathbf{z} \prec_w \mathbf{z}'$.*

Similarly, if we have $\sum_{l=0}^{k} z_{[|I|-l]} \geq \sum_{l=1}^{k} z_{[|I|-l]}'$ for each $k \in \{0, 1, \ldots, |I|-1\}$, we say $\mathbf{z}$ is weak-majorized from above *by $\mathbf{z}'$, and denote this as $\mathbf{z} \prec^w \mathbf{z}'$.*

The dominance and majorization have an associated stochastic version, defined below.

Definition 4. *Consider random vectors $\mathbf{Z}$ and $\mathbf{Z}'$. If there exist random vectors $\tilde{\mathbf{Z}}$ and $\tilde{\mathbf{Z}}'$ such that $\mathbf{Z}$ and $\tilde{\mathbf{Z}}$ are identically distributed, $\mathbf{Z}'$ and $\tilde{\mathbf{Z}}'$ are identically distributed, and $\tilde{\mathbf{Z}}' \leq \tilde{\mathbf{Z}}'$ almost surely, then we say that $\mathbf{Z}$ is* stochastically dominated *by $\mathbf{Z}'$, and denote this as $\tilde{\mathbf{Z}} \leq^{st} \tilde{\mathbf{Z}}'$.*

Instead, if $\tilde{\mathbf{Z}}' \prec_w \tilde{\mathbf{Z}}'$, then we say that $\mathbf{Z}$ stochastically weak-majorized from below *by $\mathbf{Z}'$, and denote this as $\tilde{\mathbf{Z}} \prec_w^{st} \tilde{\mathbf{Z}}'$.*

In the sequel, it will be useful to introduce following notation. Recall, $\mathbf{r}(\mathbf{x}) = (r_i(\mathbf{x}) : i \in F)$ is the vector of rates allocated to various classes. We define $r_{(k)}(.)$ for each $k \in \{1, \ldots, n\}$ as follows: For a given state $\mathbf{x}$, let i_k be the class corresponding to $x_{[k]}$. Then, $r_{(k)}(\mathbf{x}) = r_{i_k}(\mathbf{x})$. In words, $r_{(k)}(\mathbf{x})$ is the rate allocated to the class with the kth largest number of ongoing jobs.

Notation for scaling: Consider sequences of numbers $(f_n : n \in \mathbb{N})$ and $(g_n : n \in \mathbb{N})$. We say that $f_n = O(g_n)$ if there exists a constant $k > 0$ and an integer n_0 such that for each $n \geq n_0$, we have $f_n \leq k g_n$. We say that $f_n = \Omega(g_n)$ if there exists a constant $k > 0$ and an integer n_0 such that for each $n \geq n_0$, we have $f_n \geq k g_n$.

We say that $f_n = o(g_n)$ if $\lim_{n\to\infty} \frac{f_n}{g_n} = 0$. Similarly, we say that $f_n = \omega(g_n)$ if $\lim_{n\to\infty} \frac{g_n}{f_n} = 0$.

Several notations above are borrowed from [16], [24] and [22].

3. RATE ALLOCATION POLICIES: A BACKGROUND

There are several possible rate allocation policies, each resulting in potentially different user-perceived delays. Below, we introduce three different policies studied in literature, each with its own merits.

1) Greedy rate allocation: Roughly, the Greedy rate allocation policy on a polymatroid capacity region $\mathcal{C}$ assigns the maximum possible rate to the largest queues subject to the capacity constraints. We denote the Greedy rate allocation by $\mathbf{r}^G(.)$ and define it as follows: for each state $\mathbf{x}$, we let

$$r^G_{(k)}(\mathbf{x}) = \mu(\{[1],[2],\ldots,[k]\}) - \mu(\{[1],[2],\ldots,[k-1]\}) \quad \text{if } k \in \{1,2,\ldots,|A_{\mathbf{x}}|\},$$
$$= 0 \text{ otherwise.}$$

Equivalently, the sum rate assigned to the k largest queues, namely $\sum_{l=1}^{k} r^G_{(l)}(\mathbf{x})$, is equal to $\mu(\{[1],[2],\ldots,[k]\})$. Using a quadratic Lyapunov function, one can show that Greedy rate allocation results in a stationary state process if $\boldsymbol{\rho} \in \hat{\mathcal{C}}$, where $\hat{\mathcal{C}}$ is defined in (1). The Greedy rate allocation for symmetric polymatroid capacity regions was first studied in [24] where the following result was shown.

PROPOSITION 1. ([24]) *Suppose the capacity region $\mathcal{C}$ is a symmetric polymatroid and the load $\boldsymbol{\rho} \in \hat{\mathcal{C}}$ is homogeneous, i.e., $\rho_i = \rho$ for each $i \in F$. Then the following statements hold:*

1. *Let $(\mathbf{X}^G(t) : t \geq 0)$ and $(\tilde{\mathbf{X}}(t) : t \geq 0)$ be state processes under Greedy and an arbitrary feasible rate allocation, respectively. If $\mathbf{X}^G(0) \prec^{st}_{w} \tilde{\mathbf{X}}(0)$ then $\mathbf{X}^G(t) \prec^{st}_{w} \tilde{\mathbf{X}}(t)$ for each $t \geq 0$.*
2. *The mean job delay under Greedy rate allocation is less than or equal to that under any feasible rate allocation.*

Unfortunately, this optimality result for symmetric systems does not provide any explicit performance characterization or bound. Further, the result is brittle to heterogeneity in load or capacity.

2) α-fair rate allocation: As introduced in [19], this policy allocates rates based on maximizing a concave sum utility function subject to the system's capacity region. Formally, for a given $\alpha > 0$, the α-fair (αF) rate allocation $\mathbf{r}^\alpha(.)$, can be defined as follows: for each state $\mathbf{x}$, let

$$\mathbf{r}^\alpha(\mathbf{x}) = \begin{cases} \arg\max_{\hat{\mathbf{r}} \in \mathcal{C}} \sum_{i\in F} \frac{x_i^\alpha \, \hat{r}_i^{1-\alpha}}{1-\alpha} & \text{for } \alpha \in (0,\infty)\backslash\{1\}, \\ \arg\max_{\hat{\mathbf{r}} \in \mathcal{C}} \sum_{i\in F} x_i \log(\hat{r}_i) & \text{for } \alpha = 1. \end{cases} \tag{2}$$

This generalizes various notions of fairness across jobs, e.g., proportional fair and max-min fair allocations are equivalent to the α-fair policy for $\alpha = 1$ and $\alpha \to \infty$, respectively [19]. However, for polymatroid capacity regions the following result has been established.

PROPOSITION 2. ([22]) *All α-fair rate allocations are equivalent for polymatroid capacity regions.*

Further, the stability result in [7] implies that the αF rate allocation results in a stationary state process when $\boldsymbol{\rho} \in \hat{\mathcal{C}}$. The α-fair rate allocation is attractive in that it it is amenable to distributed implementation [12, 15] and satisfies natural axioms for fairness [13]. Unfortunately, little is known regarding their performance under stochastic loads. What has been shown is that for α-fair allocations, the performance is *sensitive* to the distribution of service requirements [3]. Thus, it will be hard to make general claims. This leads us to the Balanced fair rate allocation below.

3) Balanced fair rate allocation: As introduced in [3], the Balanced fair (BF) rate allocation is 'insensitive', i.e., performance depends on the job service distribution only through its mean. Further, as we will see, it is more amenable to performance analysis under stochastic loads. Formally, Balanced fair rate allocation $\mathbf{r}^B(.)$ for a polymatroid capacity region $\mathcal{C}$ can be defined as follows, see [3]: for each state $\mathbf{x}$, we have

$$r_i^B(\mathbf{x}) = \frac{\Phi(\mathbf{x} - \mathbf{e}_i)}{\Phi(\mathbf{x})}, \ \forall i \in F \tag{3}$$

where the function Φ is called a balance function and is defined recursively as follows: $\Phi(\mathbf{0}) = 1$, and $\Phi(\mathbf{x}) = 0$ $\forall \mathbf{x}$ s.t. $x_i < 0$ for some i, otherwise,

$$\Phi(\mathbf{x}) = \max_{A \subset F} \left\{ \frac{\sum_{i\in A} \Phi(\mathbf{x} - \mathbf{e}_i)}{\mu(A)} \right\}. \tag{4}$$

As shown in [3], (3) ensures the property of insensitivity, while (4) ensures that $\mathbf{r}(\mathbf{x})$ for each $\mathbf{x}$ lies in the capacity region, i.e., the constraints $\sum_{i\in A} r_i(\mathbf{x}) \leq \mu(A)$ are satisfied for each A. It also ensures that there exists a set $B \subset A_{\mathbf{x}}$ for which $\sum_{i\in B} r_i(\mathbf{x}) = \mu(B)$. In fact the BF allocation is the unique policy satisfying the above properties.

It was shown in [2, 3] that if $\boldsymbol{\rho} \in \hat{\mathcal{C}}$, the state process $(\mathbf{X}^B(t) : t \geq 0)$ is asymptotically stationary. Further, under this condition, its stationary distribution is given by

$$\pi(\mathbf{x}) = \frac{\Phi(\mathbf{x})}{G(\boldsymbol{\rho})} \prod_{i \in A_{\mathbf{x}}} \rho_i^{x_i} \quad \text{where} \quad G(\boldsymbol{\rho}) = \sum_{\mathbf{x}'} \Phi(\mathbf{x}') \prod_{i \in A_{x'}} \rho_i^{x'_i}.$$

The existence of such an expression for stationary distribution makes balanced fairness amenable for time-averaged performance analysis, a property we will use extensively in the sequel. While, in general, BF may result in wasteful resource allocation, e.g., BF is not Pareto efficient for certain triangle networks studied in [3], for polymatroid capacity regions BF has been shown to be Pareto efficient which leads us to following two results.

PROPOSITION 3. ([22]) *For polymatroid capacity regions $\mathcal{C}$, BF rate allocation is Pareto efficient, i.e., $\sum_{i\in A_{\mathbf{x}}} r_i^B(\mathbf{x}) = \mu(A_{\mathbf{x}})$ for each $\mathbf{x}$.*

In [22], the following easily computable *exact* expression for mean delay was provided for homogeneous loads.

PROPOSITION 4. ([22]) *Consider a system with symmetric polymatroid capacity region $\mathcal{C}$ and with homogenous load $\boldsymbol{\rho} \in \hat{\mathcal{C}}$, i.e., for all $j \in F$ we have $\rho_j = \rho$. Then, the mean delay under balanced fair resource allocation to serve the jobs is given by,*

$$E[D^B_{\boldsymbol{\rho}}] = \frac{\nu \hat{F}(\rho)}{F(\rho)}, \tag{5}$$

where, $F(\rho)$ and $\hat{F}(\rho)$ can be recursively obtained as follows:

$$F(\rho) = \sum_{k=0}^{n} F_k(\rho), \tag{6}$$

where, $F_0(\rho) = 1$, and for $k \geq 1$,

$$F_k(\rho) = \frac{(n-k+1)\rho F_{k-1}(\rho)}{h(k) - k\rho}. \tag{7}$$

Also,

$$\hat{F}(\rho) = \sum_{k=0}^{n} \frac{k}{n} \hat{F}_k(\rho), \tag{8}$$

where, $\hat{F}_0(\rho) = 0$, and for $k \geq 1$,

$$\hat{F}_k(\rho) = \frac{F_k(\rho) + \frac{n-k+1}{k} F_{k-1}(\rho) + \frac{(n-k+1)(k-1)}{k} \rho \hat{F}_{k-1}(\rho)}{h(k) - k\rho}. \tag{9}$$

An expression for mean delay for a system with an arbitrary polymatroid capacity region and arbitrary load is also provided in [22], but has exponential computation complexity.

4. PERFORMANCE BOUNDS

Recall that for each rate allocation policy considered in Section 3, namely Greedy, αF, and BF, the underlying state process is asymptotically stationary if the load $\boldsymbol{\rho} \in \hat{\mathcal{C}}$. Thus the corresponding mean delays of the system's jobs are finite. In this section, we assume that the **capacity region $\mathcal{C}$ is symmetric**, and develop explicit and easily computable bounds on the mean delay of jobs in systems with Greedy or αF rate allocation under potentially heterogeneous load $\boldsymbol{\rho}$ within a subset of the stability region $\hat{\mathcal{C}}$.

Our goal here is to enable performance analysis for a general enough class of systems so as to allow us to develop quantitative and qualitative insights for large-scale systems prevalent today. For example, the bounds developed below will enable us to later characterize user-performance in downloading files from heterogeneous (in loads and service capacities) large-scale content delivery systems supporting parallel servicing of downloads.

Below we develop performance bounds for the following three cases:

(i) Homogeneous loads: We provide an upper bound for mean delay for loads $\boldsymbol{\rho} \in \hat{\mathcal{C}}$ which are *homogeneous across classes with non-zero entries*, i.e., if A is the set of classes such that $\rho_i > 0$ for each $i \in A$, then $\rho_i = \rho_j$ for each $i, j \in A$.

(ii) Dominance bound: For loads $\boldsymbol{\rho}, \boldsymbol{\rho}' \in \hat{\mathcal{C}}$ such that $\boldsymbol{\rho} \leq \boldsymbol{\rho}'$ we show that the system with load $\boldsymbol{\rho}$ has lower mean delay than that with load $\boldsymbol{\rho}'$. Thus, if $\boldsymbol{\rho}'$ is homogeneous across non-zero entries as described above then we have an upper bound for mean delay for $\boldsymbol{\rho}$ as well, even if $\boldsymbol{\rho}$ is heterogeneous.

(iii) Majorization bound: We consider loads $\boldsymbol{\rho}, \boldsymbol{\rho}' \in \hat{\mathcal{C}}$ such that $\boldsymbol{\rho} \prec \boldsymbol{\rho}'$. Further, suppose that $\boldsymbol{\rho}'$ is homogeneous across non-zero entries as described above. Then, we show that the system with load $\boldsymbol{\rho}$ has lower mean delay than that with load $\boldsymbol{\rho}'$.

Using the above majorization bound, we can bound mean delay for a larger subset of heterogeneous loads as compared to the dominance bound. For example, consider $\boldsymbol{\rho} = (\rho, \frac{1}{2}\rho, \frac{1}{2}\rho)$. Recall, for symmetric rank functions we have $\mu(A) = h(|A|)$ for each $A \subset F$, where $h(.)$ is concave. Now, if $\frac{1}{3}h(3) < \rho < \frac{1}{2}h(2)$, then $\boldsymbol{\rho}' = (\rho, \rho, 0)$ is in $\hat{\mathcal{C}}$ but $\boldsymbol{\rho}'' = (\rho, \rho, \rho)$ is not. Then the majorization bound holds for $\boldsymbol{\rho}$ but the dominance bound does not. Further, even if $\boldsymbol{\rho}''$ is in $\hat{\mathcal{C}}$, the bound obtained through $\boldsymbol{\rho}'$ may be tighter.

The bounds for each case will be obtained through coupling arguments on the corresponding state processes, followed by an application of Little's law.

4.1 Homogeneous Loads

Consider the following set of loads:

$$\mathcal{B}_H \triangleq \{\boldsymbol{\rho} \in \hat{\mathcal{C}} : \exists A \subset F \text{ s.t. } \rho_i = \rho_j \ \forall i, j \in A \text{ and } \rho_i = 0 \ \forall i \in F \backslash A\}.$$

Since by Proposition 1 the Greedy rate allocation is delay optimal for homogeneous loads, for each $\boldsymbol{\rho} \in \mathcal{B}_H$ one can immediately conclude that the performance of BF as obtained in Proposition 4 is an upper bound for Greedy. Below we show that this performance upper bound via BF also holds for αF rate allocation.

To that end we show a coupling result for systems under αF and BF rate allocations. In the process, we prove and use the property that αF is more greedy than BF in the following sense: if the state process corresponding to αF is the same as or more balanced than that of BF, then αF assigns larger rate to bigger queues than BF. This in turn keeps the state process for αF more balanced in the future. For a proof of the theorem below see the Appendix.

Theorem 1. *Consider a system with symmetric polymatroid capacity region and load $\boldsymbol{\rho} \in \mathcal{B}_H$, i.e., $\boldsymbol{\rho}$ is homogeneous across classes with non-zero entries. Then the following statements hold:*

1. *Let $(\mathbf{X}^\alpha(t) : t \geq 0)$ and $(\mathbf{X}^B(t) : t \geq 0)$ be state processes under αF and BF rate allocation. If $\mathbf{X}^\alpha(0) \prec_w \mathbf{X}^B(0)$ then we have $\mathbf{X}^\alpha(t) \prec_w^{st} \mathbf{X}^B(t)$ for each $t \geq 0$.*

2. *The mean delays for systems with αF and BF rate allocation for load $\boldsymbol{\rho} \in \mathcal{B}_H$ satisfy the following:*

$$E[D^\alpha_{\boldsymbol{\rho}}] \leq E[D^B_{\boldsymbol{\rho}}].$$

4.2 Dominance Bounds

The result below maintains that for αF and Greedy rate allocations, if $\boldsymbol{\rho} \leq \boldsymbol{\rho}'$ then the state process of a system under load $\boldsymbol{\rho}$ is stochastically dominated by that under $\boldsymbol{\rho}'$. The result can be shown using a per class coupling argument, along with the following per-class rate monotonicity which is satisfied by both αF and Greedy: for each $i \neq j$ we have $r_i(\mathbf{x}) \geq r_i(\mathbf{x} + \mathbf{e}_j)$. We omit the proof for brevity.

Theorem 2. *Consider a system with symmetric polymatroid capacity region $\mathcal{C}$. The rate allocation $\mathbf{r}(.)$ is either αF or Greedy. Let $\boldsymbol{\rho} \leq \boldsymbol{\rho}'$. Then the following statements hold:*

1. *Let $(\mathbf{X}(t) : t \geq 0)$ and $(\mathbf{X}'(t) : t \geq 0)$ be state processes under loads $\boldsymbol{\rho}$ and $\boldsymbol{\rho}'$. If $\mathbf{X}(0) \leq \mathbf{X}'(0)$, then we have $\mathbf{X}(t) \leq^{st} \mathbf{X}'(t)$ for each $t \geq 0$.*

2. *The mean delays for systems with loads $\boldsymbol{\rho}$ and $\boldsymbol{\rho}'$ satisfy the following:*

$$E[D_{\boldsymbol{\rho}}] \leq E[D_{\boldsymbol{\rho}'}]$$

Theorem 2 along with Theorem 1 allows us to bound the mean delay for any load in the following region:

$$\mathcal{B}_D \triangleq \{\boldsymbol{\rho} \in \hat{\mathcal{C}} : \exists \boldsymbol{\rho}' \in \mathcal{B}_H \text{ s.t. } \boldsymbol{\rho} \leq \boldsymbol{\rho}'\},$$

or equivalently,

$$\mathcal{B}_D \triangleq \left\{\boldsymbol{\rho} \in \hat{\mathcal{C}} : \max_i \rho_i < \frac{h(k)}{k} \text{ where } k = |\{i : \rho_i > 0\}|\right\}.$$

Theorem 2 implies that for αF and Greedy rate allocations, the mean delay for each load $\boldsymbol{\rho} \in \mathcal{B}_D$ can be bounded by that for a corresponding load $\boldsymbol{\rho}' \in \mathcal{B}_H$, which in turn has an easily computable bound through Theorem 1. Thus, we get the following corollary.

Corollary 1. *Consider a system with symmetric polymatroid capacity region and load $\boldsymbol{\rho} \in \mathcal{B}_D$. Let $\rho' = \max_i \rho_i$. Let $\boldsymbol{\rho}'$ be such that for each $i \in F$ we have $\rho'_i = \rho'$ if $\rho_i > 0$ and $\rho'_i = 0$ if $\rho_i = 0$. Then, mean delays for systems with Greedy and αF rate allocations for load $\boldsymbol{\rho}$ satisfy the following:*

$$E[D^G_{\boldsymbol{\rho}}] \leq E[D^B_{\boldsymbol{\rho}'}], \text{ and } E[D^\alpha_{\boldsymbol{\rho}}] \leq E[D^B_{\boldsymbol{\rho}'}].$$

4.3 Majorization Bounds

The theorem below generalizes the Dominance bound to provide a mean delay bound for a system with load $\boldsymbol{\rho}$ such that there exists $\boldsymbol{\rho}' \in \mathcal{B}_H$ which satisfies $\boldsymbol{\rho} \prec \boldsymbol{\rho}'$.

Its proof is similar to that of Theorem 1, where instead of relative greediness between rate allocations, we use the following balancing property satisfied by both αF and Greedy: if state $\mathbf{x}$ is more balanced than state $\mathbf{x}'$, than the rate allocation $\mathbf{r}(.)$ would provide larger rates to longer queues in state $\mathbf{x}$ as compared to $\mathbf{x}'$, and thus balancing it even further. For a brief discussion of this property, see the Appendix. We omit the proof for brevity.

Theorem 3. *Consider a system with symmetric polymatroid capacity region $\mathcal{C}$. The rate allocation $\mathbf{r}(.)$ is either αF or Greedy. Let $\boldsymbol{\rho}, \boldsymbol{\rho}' \in \hat{\mathcal{C}}$ be such that $\boldsymbol{\rho} \prec \boldsymbol{\rho}'$ and $\boldsymbol{\rho}' \in \mathcal{B}_H$, i.e., $\boldsymbol{\rho}'$ is homogeneous across classes with non-zero entries. Then the following statements hold:*

1. *Let $(\mathbf{X}(t) : t \geq 0)$ and $(\mathbf{X}'(t) : t \geq 0)$ be state processes under loads $\boldsymbol{\rho}$ and $\boldsymbol{\rho}'$. If $\mathbf{X}(0) \prec_w \mathbf{X}'(0)$, then we have $\mathbf{X}(t) \prec^{st}_w \mathbf{X}'(t)$ for each $t \geq 0$.*

2. *The mean delays for systems with loads $\boldsymbol{\rho}$ and $\boldsymbol{\rho}'$ satisfy the following:*

$$E[D_{\boldsymbol{\rho}}] \leq E[D_{\boldsymbol{\rho}'}]$$

Theorem 3 above is stronger than Theorem 2 in the sense that it only requires the condition $\boldsymbol{\rho} \prec_w \boldsymbol{\rho}'$ instead of $\boldsymbol{\rho} \leq \boldsymbol{\rho}'$. However, it is weaker in the sense that it requires $\boldsymbol{\rho}'$ to be in $\mathcal{B}_H$ and that it gives stochastic weak-majorization of the corresponding state processes instead of stochastic dominance.

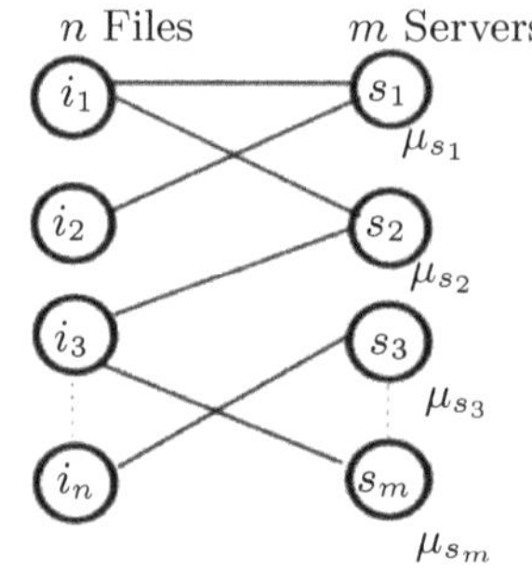

Figure 1: Graph $G^{(n)} = (F^{(n)} \cup S^{(n)}; E^{(n)})$ modeling the placement of copies of n files across $m = \lceil bn \rceil$ servers with finite service capacities in a CDN-like infrastructure.

For both $\mathbf{r}^G(.)$ and $\mathbf{r}^\alpha(.)$, Theorem 3, along with Theorem 1 and Proposition 1, allows us to bound the mean delay for any load in the following region:

$$\mathcal{B}_M \triangleq \{\boldsymbol{\rho} \in \hat{\mathcal{C}} : \exists \boldsymbol{\rho}' \in \mathcal{B}_H \text{ s.t. } \boldsymbol{\rho} \prec \boldsymbol{\rho}'\},$$

or equivalently,

$$\mathcal{B}_M \triangleq \left\{\boldsymbol{\rho} \in \hat{\mathcal{C}} : \exists k \leq n \text{ s.t. } \max_i \rho_i < \frac{h(k)}{k} \text{ and } |\boldsymbol{\rho}| < h(k)\right\}.$$

Theorem 3 implies that for αF and Greedy rate allocation, the mean delay for each load $\boldsymbol{\rho} \in \mathcal{B}_M$ can be bounded by that for a corresponding load $\boldsymbol{\rho}' \in \mathcal{B}_H$, which in turn has an easily computable bound through Theorem 1. Thus, we get the following corollary.

Corollary 2. *Consider a system with symmetric polymatroid capacity region and load $\boldsymbol{\rho} \in \mathcal{B}_M$. Let $\rho' = \max_{i \in F} \rho_i$. Let $k = \min\{l : \rho' \leq \frac{h(l)}{l}$ and $|\boldsymbol{\rho}| \leq h(l)\}$. Let A be an arbitrary subset of F of size k and $\boldsymbol{\rho}'$ be such that $\rho'_i = \rho'$ $\forall i \in A$ and $\rho'_i = 0$ otherwise. Then, the mean delays for systems with Greedy and αF rate allocations for load $\boldsymbol{\rho}$ satisfy the following:*

$$E[D^G_{\boldsymbol{\rho}}] \leq E[D^B_{\boldsymbol{\rho}'}], \text{ and } E[D^\alpha_{\boldsymbol{\rho}}] \leq E[D^B_{\boldsymbol{\rho}'}].$$

It is easy to check that for each $\boldsymbol{\rho} \in \mathcal{B}_M$ the computation of the mean delay upper bound as given by Corollary 2 has complexity $O(n)$ when computed using Proposition 4.

5. UNIFORM SYMMETRY IN LARGE SYSTEMS

Large content delivery infrastructure, where servers can jointly serve file-download requests, not only have polymatroid capacity but under appropriate assumptions become approximately symmetric.

Consider a sequence of bipartite graphs $G^{(n)} = (F^{(n)} \cup S^{(n)}; E^{(n)})$ where $F^{(n)}$ is a set of n files, $S^{(n)}$ is a set of $m = \lceil bn \rceil$ servers for some constant b, and each edge $e \in E^{(n)}$ connecting a file $i \in F^{(n)}$ and server $s \in S^{(n)}$ implies that a copy of file i is available at server s. For each node $s \in S^{(n)}$, let $N_s^{(n)}$ denote the set of neighbors of server s, i.e., the set of files it stores and can serve. Henceforth, wherever possible, we will avoid the use of ceil and floor notations to avoid clutter.

We associate each file in $F^{(n)}$ with a class of job arrivals each corresponding to a file download request. The arrival processes and service requirements are as described in Section 2, with $\boldsymbol{\lambda}^{(n)}$ and $\boldsymbol{\rho}^{(n)}$ representing the corresponding arrival rates and loads. Further, we let the service capacity of each server $s \in S^{(n)}$ be μ_s bits per second.

We allow each server $s \in S^{(n)}$ to concurrently serve the jobs with classes $N_s^{(n)}$ as long as the total service rate does not exceed μ_s. The service rate for each job is the sum of the rates it receives from different servers. For any $A \subset F^{(n)}$, let $\mu^{(n)}(A)$ be the maximum sum rate at which jobs with file-class in A could be served, i.e.,

$$\mu^{(n)}(A) \triangleq \sum_{s \in S^{(n)}} \mathbf{1}_{\{A \cap N_s^{(n)} \neq \emptyset\}} \mu_s.$$

Clearly any rate allocation $\mathbf{r}(.)$ for such a system must satisfy the following constraints for each state $\mathbf{x}$: $\forall A \subset F^{(n)}$,

$$\sum_{i \in A} r_i(\mathbf{x}) \leq \mu^{(n)}(A).$$

It was shown in [22] that $\mu^{(n)}(.)$ is submodular and that the corresponding polymatroid

$$\mathcal{C}^{(n)} \triangleq \left\{ \mathbf{r} \geq \mathbf{0} : \sum_{i \in A} r_i \leq \mu^{(n)}(A),\ \forall A \subset F^{(n)} \right\}$$

is indeed the capacity region for such a system, i.e., each $\mathbf{r} \in \mathcal{C}^{(n)}$ is achievable.

Note that $\mathcal{C}^{(n)}$ will in general be an asymmetric polymatroid depending upon edges $E^{(n)}$ and service capacities μ_s for each $s \in S^{(n)}$. However, we show below that if copies of files are stored across servers at random and scaled appropriately with n then, as n increases, $\mathcal{C}^{(n)}$ gets uniformly close to a symmetric polymatroid, subject to the following assumptions:

Assumption 1 (Heterogeneous server capacities). *$S^{(n)}$ is partitioned into a finite number of groups where each group has $\Omega(n)$ number of servers. Within each group, the server capacities are homogeneous. The server capacities across groups may be heterogeneous such that average of service capacity across servers*

$$\xi \triangleq \frac{1}{m} \sum_{s \in S^{(n)}} \mu_s$$

is independent of n.

Assumption 2 (Randomized file placement). *Let $(c_n : n \in \mathbb{N})$ be a sequence such that*

$$c_n = \omega(\log n).$$

For each file $i \in F^{(n)}$, store a copy in c_n different servers chosen uniformly and independently at random.

A randomized placement of file copies implies a random system configuration, i.e., a random graph. Let $\mathcal{E}^{(n)}$ denote the random set of edges resulting Assumption 2. Similarly, for each $s \in S^{(n)}$, let $\mathcal{N}_s^{(n)}$ denote the random set of neighbors of s, i.e., the random set of files stored in server s. Let $M^{(n)}(.)$ denote the corresponding random rank function, and $\mu^{(n)}(.)$ a possible realization. Then, for each $A \subset F^{(n)}$, we have

$$M^{(n)}(A) = \sum_{s \in S^{(n)}} \mathbf{1}_{\{A \cap \mathcal{N}_s^{(n)} \neq \emptyset\}} \mu_s,$$

where $\mathbf{1}_{\{A \cap \mathcal{N}_s^{(n)} \neq \emptyset\}}$ is now a Bernoulli random variable indicating if a copy of at least one of the files in A is placed in s. In fact, for each $A \subset F^{(n)}$ such that $|A| = k$, the set $\left\{ \mathbf{1}_{\{A \cap \mathcal{N}_s^{(n)} \neq \emptyset\}} : s \in S^{(n)} \right\}$ is a set of m negatively associated Bernoulli$(p_k^{(n)})$ random variables [8] where $p_k^{(n)}$ is the probability that a given server is assigned at least one of the kc_n copies of files in A and is given by

$$p_k^{(n)} \triangleq 1 - \left(1 - \frac{1}{m}\right)^{kc_n} \quad \forall k = 0, 1, \ldots, n.$$

By linearity of expectation, for each $A \subset F^{(n)}$, we have

$$\bar{\mu}^{(n)}(A) \triangleq E[M^{(n)}(A)] = \xi m p_{|A|}^{(n)}.$$

Note, $\bar{\mu}^{(n)}(A)$ depends on A only through $|A|$ and is thus symmetric. The theorem below shows that with high probability we can bound the random rank function $M^{(n)}(.)$ uniformly over all $A \subset F^{(n)}$, from above as well as from below, with a symmetric rank function which is close to $\bar{\mu}^{(n)}(A)$. See Section 5.1 for a proof.

Theorem 4. *Fix ϵ independent of n such that $0 < \epsilon < 1$. Consider a sequence of systems with n files and $m = \lceil bn \rceil$ servers, where $b > 0$ is a constant. Under Assumptions 1 and 2, let $M^{(n)}(.)$ be the corresponding random rank function. Then, there exists a sequence $(g_n : n \in \mathbb{N})$ such that $g_n = \omega(\log n)$, and*

$$P\left(\exists A \subset F^{(n)} \text{ s.t. } M^{(n)}(A) \leq (1-\epsilon)\bar{\mu}^{(n)}(A) \right) \leq e^{-g_n},$$

and

$$P\left(\exists A \subset F^{(n)} \text{ s.t. } M^{(n)}(A) \geq (1+\epsilon)\bar{\mu}^{(n)}(A) \right) \leq e^{-g_n}.$$

This result gives us following corollary on the random capacity region associated with $M^{(n)}(.)$ generated by random file placement. Recall, $\bar{\mu}^{(n)}(A) = E[M^{(n)}(A)]$ for all $A \subset F^{(n)}$, and let

$$\bar{\mathcal{C}}^{(n)} \triangleq \left\{ \mathbf{r} \geq \mathbf{0} : \sum_{i \in A} r_i \leq \bar{\mu}^{(n)}(A),\ \forall A \subset F^{(n)} \right\}.$$

Thus $\bar{\mathcal{C}}^{(n)}$ is the (symmetric) capacity region associated with the average rank function $\bar{\mu}(.)$. Then, the following holds:

Corollary 3. *Fix ϵ independent of n such that $0 < \epsilon < 1$. Under Assumptions 1 and 2, the random capacity region associated with randomized file placement is a subset of $(1+\epsilon)\bar{\mathcal{C}}^{(n)}$ and a superset of $(1-\epsilon)\bar{\mathcal{C}}^{(n)}$ with high probability.*

Further, under Assumption 1, there exists a deterministic file placement where $c_n = \omega(\log n)$ copies of each file are stored across servers such that the corresponding capacity region $\mathcal{C}^{(n)}$ is a subset of $(1+\epsilon)\bar{\mathcal{C}}^{(n)}$ and a superset of $(1-\epsilon)\bar{\mathcal{C}}^{(n)}$.

5.1 Proof of Theorem 4

Here, we will only show

$$P\left(\exists A \subset F^{(n)} \text{ s.t. } M^{(n)}(A) \leq (1-\epsilon)\bar{\mu}^{(n)}(A) \right) \leq e^{-g_n},$$

The other bound follows in similar fashion.

For now, suppose $\mu_s = \xi$ for each $s \in S^{(n)}$. We relax this assumption later.

We first provide a bound for $P\left(M^{(n)}(A) \leq (1-\epsilon)\bar{\mu}^{(n)}(A)\right)$ for each $A \subset F^{(n)}$. Then, for each $k = 1, 2, \ldots, n$, we use the union bound to obtain a uniform bound over all sets $A \subset F^{(n)}$ such that $|A| = k$. The bound we provide for $P\left(M^{(n)}(A) \leq (1-\epsilon)\bar{\mu}^{(n)}(A)\right)$ is small enough so that the above union bound is small too. Then, yet another use of the union bound would give us the uniform result over all sets $A \subset F^{(n)}$.

Now, if the random variables $\left\{\mathbf{1}_{\{A\cap\mathcal{N}_s^{(n)}\neq\emptyset\}} : s \in S^{(n)}\right\}$ were independent Bernoulli($p_k^{(n)}$), then the following two concentration results would hold [18]: Fix $k \in \{1, \ldots, n\}$. For each set $A \subset F^{(n)}$ such that $|A| = k$, we have

$$P\left(M^{(n)}(A) \leq (1-\epsilon)\bar{\mu}^{(n)}(A)\right) \leq e^{-\frac{\epsilon^2}{2}mp_k^{(n)}}, \quad (10)$$

and,

$$P\left(M^{(n)}(A) \leq (1-\epsilon)\bar{\mu}^{(n)}(A)\right) \leq e^{-mH\left(p_k^{(n)}(1-\epsilon)||p_k^{(n)}\right)}, \quad (11)$$

where $H(p||q)$ is the KL divergence between Bernoulli(p) and Bernoulli(q) random variables, given by

$$H(p||q) = p\log\left(\frac{p}{q}\right) + (1-p)\log\left(\frac{1-p}{1-q}\right).$$

However, in reality, since $\left\{\mathbf{1}_{\{A\cap\mathcal{N}_s^{(n)}\neq\emptyset\}} : s \in S^{(n)}\right\}$ are negatively associated Bernoulli($p_k^{(n)}$) random variables, the above Chernoff bounds still apply [8].

In the sequel, we will use the following two technical lemmas. Their proofs are provided in the Appendix A.3.

Lemma 1. *Let a sequence $(g_n : n \in \mathbb{N})$ be such that $g_n = o(c_n)$. Let δ_1 be a positive constant independent of n such that $\delta_1 < 1$. Then, for large enough n, we have*

$$p_k^{(n)} \geq \frac{\delta_1 g_n}{n}k \quad \forall k \in \left\{0, 1, \ldots, \left\lfloor\frac{n}{g_n}\right\rfloor\right\}.$$

Lemma 2. *There exists a positive constant δ such that $H\left(p_k^{(n)}(1-\epsilon)||p_k^{(n)}\right) \geq -\delta + \epsilon\frac{kc_n}{m}$.*

Now, let $(g_n : n \in \mathbb{N})$ be a sequence such that $g_n \triangleq (c_n \log n)^{1/2}$ for each n. The following properties of g_n can be easily checked:

$$g_n = \omega(\log n) \text{ and } g_n = o(c_n). \quad (12)$$

We now provide a uniform bound over all sets $A \subset F^{(n)}$ such that $|A| = k$ for each $k \in \{1, \ldots, n\}$, under following two cases.

<u>**Case 1**</u> $0 \leq k \leq \frac{n}{g_n}$: From Lemma 1, for each k we have

$$p_k^{(n)} \geq \delta_1\frac{kg_n}{n},$$

for a suitably chosen positive constant δ_1 independent of n. In the sequel, δ_i for any $i \geq 1$ will be a suitably chosen positive constant independent of n.

Using the concentration result (10), for $|A| = k$ we get

$$P\left(M^{(n)}(A) \leq (1-\epsilon)\bar{\mu}^{(n)}(A)\right) \leq e^{-\frac{\epsilon^2}{2}\delta_1 bkg_n},$$

and using the union bound, we get

$$P\left(\exists A \subset F^{(n)} \text{ s.t. } |A| = k \text{ and } M^{(n)}(A) \leq (1-\epsilon)\bar{\mu}^{(n)}(A)\right)$$
$$\leq e^{-\frac{\epsilon^2}{2}\delta_1 bkg_n}\binom{n}{k} \leq e^{-\frac{\epsilon^2}{2}\delta_1 bkg_n + k\log n} \leq e^{-\delta_2 kg_n}.$$

<u>**Case 2**</u> $\frac{n}{g_n} < k \leq n$: In this case, we use the concentration result (11). From Lemma 2, we get

$$P\left(M^{(n)}(A) \leq (1-\epsilon)\bar{\mu}^{(n)}(A)\right) \leq e^{(\delta_6 m - \epsilon kc_n)}.$$

Since $g_n = o(c_n)$, for n large enough we get $\delta_6 m \leq (\epsilon/2)\frac{nc_n}{g_n}$. Also, for each $k > \frac{n}{g_n}$, we have $(\epsilon/2)\frac{nc_n}{g_n} \leq (\epsilon/2)kc_n$. Thus, for large enough n, $\delta_6 m - \epsilon kc_n \leq -(\epsilon/2)kc_n$ for each k such that $\frac{n}{g_n} < k \leq n$, and consequently,

$$P\left(M^{(n)}(A) \leq (1-\epsilon)\bar{\mu}^{(n)}(A)\right) \leq e^{-\delta_7 kc_n}$$

By using the union bound, for large enough n, we get

$$P\left(\exists A \subset F^{(n)} \text{ s.t. } |A| = k \text{ and } M^{(n)}(A) \leq (1-\epsilon)\bar{\mu}^{(n)}(A)\right)$$
$$\leq e^{-\delta_7 kc_n}\binom{n}{k} \leq e^{-\delta_7 kc_n + k\log n} \leq e^{-\delta_8 kc_n}.$$

Combining the above two cases, we can show that for large enough n there exists a positive constant δ_9 such that for each $k \in \{1, \ldots, n\}$ we have

$$P\left(\exists A \subset F^{(n)} \text{ s.t. } |A| = k \text{ and } M^{(n)}(A) \leq (1-\epsilon)\bar{\mu}^{(n)}(A)\right)$$
$$\leq e^{-\delta_9 g_n}.$$

Using the union bound again, we get

$$P\left(\exists A \subset F^{(n)} \text{ s.t. } M^{(n)}(A) \leq (1-\epsilon)\bar{\mu}^{(n)}(A)\right)$$
$$\leq ne^{-\delta_9 g_n} \leq e^{-\delta_9 g_n + \log n} \leq e^{-\delta_{10} g_n}.$$

Now, we relax the assumption $\mu_s = \xi$ for each $s \in S^{(n)}$ with Assumption 1. The above proof can then be used to show a similar concentration result for individual groups. The overall result follows by linearity of expectation and yet another use of the union bound. □

6. PERFORMANCE ROBUSTNESS

We now combine results from Section 4 and Section 5 to exhibit performance robustness in large systems. In Section 5, we showed that large systems support symmetric polymatroid capacity regions. This allows us to apply the performance bounds developed in Section 4 for symmetric polymatroid capacity regions.

However, there is one more hurdle to overcome before we can apply our bounds from Section 4. Recall, from Corollary 3, under Assumptions 1 and 2 the random capacity region *contains* and is *contained by* symmetric polymatroids with high probability. The realizations of the random capacity region, themselves, may still not be symmetric. We thus need to show that if the capacity region is bigger then the corresponding mean delay is smaller when subject to the same load.

Intuitively, larger capacity regions may imply larger service rates for each class, and may thus provide better performance. Although intuitively obvious, such results are not always straightforward. We show below that such a comparison result indeed holds under the following monotonicity conditions for rate allocations.

Definition 5 (Monotonicity w.r.t. capacity region). *We say that a rate allocation satisfies monotonicity w.r.t. capacity region if for any state* $\mathbf{x}$*, the rate allocation per class for a system with a larger capacity region dominates that with a smaller one.*

Recall, $\frac{r_i(\mathbf{x})}{x_i}$ is the rate allocated to each job in class i when the system is in state $\mathbf{x}$.

Definition 6 (Per-job rate monotonicity). *We say that a rate allocation* $\mathbf{r}(.)$ *satisfies per-job rate monotonicity if the following holds for all states* $\mathbf{x}$ *and* $\mathbf{x}'$ *such that* $\mathbf{x} \geq \mathbf{x}'$*: for each class* i*, we have* $\frac{r_i(\mathbf{x})}{x_i} \leq \frac{r_i(\mathbf{x}')}{x'_i}$*. In words, adding jobs into the system only decreases the rate allocated to each job.*

Note that the condition of per-job rate monotonicity is stronger than that of per-class rate monotonicity used in Section 4.2. Per-job rate monotonicity was first used in [4] to provide a comparison result similar to the lemma below. The following lemma can be shown to hold through a simple coupling argument across jobs for arbitrary polymatroid capacity regions.

Lemma 3. *Consider systems with arbitrary polymatroid capacity regions* $\mathcal{C}$ *and* $\tilde{\mathcal{C}}$ *such that* $\mathcal{C} \subset \tilde{\mathcal{C}}$*. Consider a rate allocation which satisfies monotonicity w.r.t. capacity region as well as per-job rate monotonicity. Then, the mean delay for capacity region* $\mathcal{C}$ *under arbitrary load* $\boldsymbol{\rho}$ *upper bounds that for capacity region* $\tilde{\mathcal{C}}$ *under the same load.*

It is easy to check that α-fair rate allocation satisfies per-job rate monotonicity as well as monotonicity w.r.t. capacity region. Thus, Lemma 3 holds for α-fair rate allocation. However, one can show that Greedy rate allocation may not satisfy either property for arbitrary polymatroid capacity regions. This further highlights the brittleness of Greedy rate allocation to asymmetries. Even for Balanced fair rate allocation it is not directly clear if the lemma holds. Thus, henceforth we will only consider α-fair rate allocation.

Now we are indeed ready with all the tools required to exhibit robustness in large scale systems.

Assumption 3 (Load Heterogeneity). *We consider a sequence of systems where load* $\boldsymbol{\rho}^{(n)}$ *for each* n *is allowed to be within a set* $\mathcal{B}^{(n)}$ *defined as follows: Consider a sequence* $(\theta_n : n \in \mathbb{N})$ *such that* $\theta_n = \omega(1)$*,* $\theta_n = o(\frac{n}{\log n})$*, and* $\theta_n = o(c_n)$*. Also, fix a constant* $\gamma < 1$ *independent of* n*. For each* n*:*

$$\mathcal{B}^{(n)} \triangleq \left\{ \boldsymbol{\rho} : \max_{i \in F^{(n)}} \rho_i \leq \theta_n \text{ and } |\boldsymbol{\rho}| \leq \gamma \xi m \right\}.$$

The condition $|\boldsymbol{\rho}| \leq \gamma\xi m$ implies that we allow load to increase linearly with system size. Also, since $\theta_n = \omega(1)$, the condition $\max_i \rho_i \leq \theta_n$ implies that we allow load across servers to be increasingly heterogeneous. The condition $\theta_n = o(\frac{n}{\log n})$ limits the heterogeneity allowed in the system. Further, the condition $\theta_n = o(c_n)$ would allow us to claim stability, and to show that the mean delay of the system tends to 0 as n increases.

The following is the main result of this section.

Theorem 5. *Consider a sequence of systems with* n *files* $F^{(n)}$ *and* $m = \lceil bn \rceil$ *servers* $S^{(n)}$*, where* b *is a constant. For each* n*, let the total service capacity of servers be* ξm*, where* ξ *is independent of* n*.* $S^{(n)}$ *is partitioned into a finite number of heterogeneous groups, each with* $\Omega(n)$ *servers and equal per-server capacity. Let* $(c_n : n \in \mathbb{N})$ *be a sequence such that* $c_n = \omega(\log n)$*. We allow* c_n *copies of each file to be placed across the servers.*

Let the mean service requirement of file-download jobs be ν*, where* ν *is independent of* n*. Let* $(\theta_n : n \in \mathbb{N})$ *be such that* $\theta_n = \omega(1)$*, but* $o\left(\min(\frac{n}{\log n}, c_n)\right)$*. Fix a constant* $\gamma < 1$*. Let* $\mathcal{B}^{(n)} = \{\boldsymbol{\rho} : \max_i \rho_i \leq \theta_n \text{ and } |\boldsymbol{\rho}| \leq \gamma\xi m\}$*. For each* n*, let load across file classes be* $\boldsymbol{\rho}^{(n)} \in \mathcal{B}^{(n)}$*.*

Fix a constant $\delta > 1$*. Then, there exists an integer* n_δ *such that for each* $n \geq n_\delta$ *the following holds: there exists at least one file placement policy such that the mean delay for file-download jobs with* α*-fair rate allocation satisfies the following bound:*

$$E[D^{(n)}] \leq \delta \frac{\nu \theta_n}{\xi c_n} \frac{1}{\gamma} \log\left(\frac{1}{1-\gamma}\right).$$

Further, for each $n \geq n_\delta$*, if the* c_n *copies of each file are stored uniformly at random across servers, then the above bound holds with high probability.*

6.1 Proof of Theorem 5

We first show the existence of a file placement policy such that the mean delay bound is satisfied. Without loss of generality, assume $\delta < \frac{1}{\gamma}$.

From Corollary 3, and definitions of $\bar{\mathcal{C}}^{(n)}$ and $\bar{\mu}^{(n)}(.)$, for large enough n there exists a file placement such that the corresponding capacity region contains the following symmetric polymatroid:

$$\tilde{\mathcal{C}}^{(n)} \triangleq \left\{ \mathbf{r} \geq \mathbf{0} : \sum_{i \in A} r_i \leq h^{(n)}(|A|),\ \forall A \subset F^{(n)} \right\},$$

where

$$h^{(n)}(k) \triangleq (1/\delta)\xi m \left(1 - e^{-\frac{kc_n}{m}}\right) \quad \forall k = 0, 1, \ldots, n.$$

Thus, from Lemma 3, for α-fair rate allocations it is sufficient to consider $\tilde{\mathcal{C}}^{(n)}$. Further, since $\tilde{\mathcal{C}}^{(n)}$ is monotonic in c_n, it is sufficient to assume that $c_n = o(\frac{n}{\log n})$ since, if it is not, we can set c_n to be equal to $\sqrt{\frac{n}{\log n}\theta_n}$ and all the assumptions still hold. Thus, henceforth we assume that

$$c_n = o(\frac{n}{\log n}).$$

Let $\xi' \triangleq \xi/\delta$. Thus, we get

$$h^{(n)}(k) = \xi' m \left(1 - e^{-\frac{kc_n}{m}}\right) \quad \forall k = 0, 1, \ldots, n.$$

Since $\gamma\xi m < \xi' m$ and $\theta_n = o(c_n)$, one can check that $B^{(n)}$ is a subset of $\tilde{\mathcal{C}}^{(n)}$ for large enough n, and we get stability.

Let $t_n \triangleq \left\lceil \frac{\gamma\xi' m}{\theta_n} \right\rceil$. Let $A^{(n)}$ be an arbitrary subset of $F^{(n)}$ such that $|A^{(n)}| = t_n$. Let $\hat{\boldsymbol{\rho}}^{(n)} = (\hat{\rho}_i^{(n)} : i \in F^{(n)})$ where

$\hat{\rho}_i^{(n)} = \theta_n$ if $i \in A^{(n)}$ and 0 otherwise. Then, it is easy to show that for each n, we have

$$B^{(n)} \subset \left\{\boldsymbol{\rho} : \boldsymbol{\rho} \prec_w \hat{\boldsymbol{\rho}}^{(n)}\right\}.$$

Thus, from Theorem 3, it is sufficient to show that the bound on mean delay holds for balanced fair rate allocation under load $\boldsymbol{\rho}^{(n)} = \hat{\boldsymbol{\rho}}^{(n)}$.

Henceforth, we assume BF rate allocation and let load $\boldsymbol{\rho}^{(n)} = \hat{\boldsymbol{\rho}}^{(n)}$. For each n, we invoke Proposition 4 with ρ replaced by θ_n and n replaced by t_n, where for each $k = 0, 1, \ldots, t_n$ we let[1]

$$\pi_k^{(n)} \triangleq \frac{F_k(\theta_n)}{F(\theta_n)}, \text{ and } \tau_k^{(n)} \triangleq \frac{\hat{F}_k(\theta_n)}{F(\theta_n)}.$$

Then, we have

$$E[D^{(n)}] = \nu \sum_{k=1}^{t_n} \frac{k}{t_n} \tau_k^{(n)}. \tag{13}$$

Also, we have $\tau_0^{(n)} = 0$, $\pi_0^{(n)} = 1/F(\theta_n)$, and for each $k = 1, \ldots, t_n$ we have

$$\pi_k^{(n)} = \frac{(t_n - k + 1)\theta_n}{h^{(n)}(k) - k\theta_n} \pi_{k-1}^{(n)}, \tag{14}$$

and

$$\tau_k^{(n)} = \frac{\pi_k^{(n)} + \frac{t_n - k + 1}{k}\pi_{k-1}^{(n)} + \frac{(t_n - k + 1)(k-1)}{k}\theta_n \tau_{k-1}^{(n)}}{h^{(n)}(k) - k\theta_n}. \tag{15}$$

First, we show the following result.

Theorem 6. *For any positive constants $\epsilon > 1$ and $\epsilon' < 1$ independent of n, there exists a constant $\delta' < 1$ such that for large enough n we have*

$$\sum_{k=\epsilon' b \log(\frac{1}{1-\gamma})\frac{n}{c_n}}^{\epsilon b \log(\frac{1}{1-\gamma})\frac{n}{c_n}} \pi_k^{(n)} \geq 1 - \delta'^{\frac{m}{c_n}}. \tag{16}$$

PROOF. Fix a constant $0 < \delta_{11} < 1$. Let

$$k_\downarrow^{(n)} = \frac{m}{c_n} \log\left(\frac{1}{1 - \gamma\delta_{11}}\right).$$

Then, we have $h^{(n)}(k_\downarrow) = \gamma\delta_{11}\xi' m$. In fact, we have $h^{(n)}(k) \leq \gamma\delta_{11}\xi' m, \ \forall k \leq k_\downarrow^{(n)}$. Using (14), for each $k \leq k_\downarrow^{(n)}$, we have

$$\begin{aligned}\pi_k^{(n)} \geq \frac{(t_n - k + 1)\theta_n}{\gamma\delta_{11}\xi' m - k\theta_n}\pi_{k-1}^{(n)} &\geq \frac{t_n\theta_n - (k_\downarrow^{(n)} - 1)\theta_n}{\gamma\delta_{11}\xi' m}\pi_{k-1}^{(n)} \\ &= \frac{\gamma\xi' m - o(n)}{\gamma\delta_{11}\xi' m}\pi_{k-1}^{(n)} \geq \frac{1}{\delta_{12}}\pi_{k-1}^{(n)},\end{aligned}$$

for a positive constant δ_{12} such that $\delta_{11} < \delta_{12} < 1$, and large enough n. Equivalently, $\pi_k^{(n)} \leq \delta_{12}\pi_{k+1}^{(n)} \ \ \forall k < k_\downarrow^{(n)}$. Fix a positive constant $\epsilon_1 < 1$. Then, for all $k < \epsilon_1 k_\downarrow^{(n)}$, we have

$$\pi_k^{(n)} \leq \delta_{12}^{(1-\epsilon_1)k_\downarrow^{(n)}} \pi_{k_\downarrow^{(n)}}^{(n)}$$

Similarly, for a constant δ_{13} such that $\gamma < \delta_{13} < 1$, a constant $\epsilon_2 > 1$, and $k_\uparrow^{(n)} = \frac{m}{c_n}\log\left(\frac{1}{1-\gamma/\delta_{13}}\right)$ one can show that there exists a constant $\delta_{14} < 1$ such that

$$\pi_k^{(n)} \leq \delta_{14}^{(\epsilon_2 - 1)k_\uparrow^{(n)}} \pi_{k_\uparrow^{(n)}}^{(n)} \ \ \forall k > \epsilon_2 k_\uparrow^{(n)}$$

Thus, we get

$$\begin{aligned}1 = \sum_{k=0}^{t_n}\pi_k^{(n)} &= \sum_{k=0}^{\epsilon_1 k_\downarrow^{(n)} - 1}\pi_k + \sum_{k=\epsilon_1 k_\downarrow^{(n)}}^{\epsilon_2 k_\uparrow^{(n)}}\pi_k^{(n)} + \sum_{\epsilon_2 k_\uparrow^{(n)}+1}^{t_n}\pi_k^{(n)} \\ &\leq (\epsilon_1 k_\downarrow^{(n)})\delta_{12}^{(1-\epsilon_1)k_\downarrow^{(n)}} + \sum_{k=\epsilon_1 k_\downarrow^{(n)}}^{\epsilon_2 k_\uparrow^{(n)}}\pi_k^{(n)} + \left(t_n - \epsilon_2 k_\uparrow^{(n)}\right)\delta_{14}^{(\epsilon_2 - 1)k_\uparrow^{(n)}} \\ &\leq n\delta_{12}^{(1-\epsilon_1)k_\downarrow^{(n)}} + n\delta_{14}^{(\epsilon_2-1)k_\uparrow^{(n)}} + \sum_{k=\epsilon_1 k_\downarrow^{(n)}}^{\epsilon_2 k_\uparrow^{(n)}}\pi_k^{(n)} \\ &= \delta_{12}^{\delta_{15}\frac{m}{c_n} - \log_{\delta_{12}} n} + \delta_{14}^{\delta_{17}\frac{m}{c_n} - \log_{\delta_{14}} n} + \sum_{k=\epsilon_1 k_\downarrow^{(n)}}^{\epsilon_2 k_\uparrow^{(n)}}\pi_k^{(n)},\end{aligned}$$

for suitably chosen positive constants δ_{15}, and δ_{17}. Thus, the theorem follows by noting that $\epsilon_1, \epsilon_2, \delta_{11}$, and δ_{13} can be chosen arbitrarily close to 1. □

We now use (15) to provide a slightly simpler bound on $\tau_k^{(n)}$.

Lemma 4. *For large enough n, we get,*

$$\tau_k^{(n)} \leq \frac{(t_n - k + 1)\theta_n}{h^{(n)}(k) - k\theta_n}\left(\frac{1}{k}\pi_{k-1}^{(n)} + \frac{k-1}{k}\tau_{k-1}^{(n)}\right),$$

for each $k = 1, \ldots, t_n$.

PROOF. Using (14) in (15), we get

$$\begin{aligned}\tau_k^{(n)} &= \frac{\left(\begin{aligned}&\frac{(t_n - k + 1)\theta_n}{h^{(n)}(k) - k\theta_n}\pi_{k-1}^{(n)} + \frac{t_n - k + 1}{k}\pi_{k-1}^{(n)} \\ &\qquad + \frac{(t_n - k + 1)(k-1)}{k}\theta_n\tau_{k-1}^{(n)}\end{aligned}\right)}{h^{(n)}(k) - k\theta_n} \\ &= \frac{(t_n - k + 1)\theta_n}{h^{(n)}(k) - k\theta_n}\left(\left(\frac{1}{h^{(n)}(k) - k\theta_n} + \frac{1}{k\theta_n}\right)\pi_{k-1}^{(n)} \right. \\ &\qquad \left. + \frac{k-1}{k}\tau_{k-1}^{(n)}\right).\end{aligned}$$

Now, we have the lemma if we show that for large enough n, we have $\left(\frac{1}{h^{(n)}(k) - k\theta_n} + \frac{1}{k\theta_n}\right) \leq \frac{1}{k}$ for each $k = 1, \ldots, t_n$. This can be shown as follows.

One can show that Lemma 1 holds even when $p_k^{(n)} = 1 - e^{-\frac{kc_n}{m}}$. Using $g_n = \frac{\theta_n}{\gamma\xi' b}$, we get $h^{(n)}(k) = \xi' bnp_k^{(n)} \geq \frac{\delta_{20}}{\gamma}k\theta_n$ for large enough n and some constant δ_{20} such that $\gamma < \delta_{20} < 1$. Thus, $(h^{(n)}(k) - k\theta_n) \geq (\frac{\delta_{20}}{\gamma} - 1)k\theta_n$. For large enough n, $(\frac{\delta_{20}}{\gamma} - 1)\theta_n \geq 2$, and thus, $(h^{(n)}(k) - k\theta_n) \geq 2k$. Similarly, for large enough n, $k\theta_n \geq 2k$. Hence the lemma. □

---

[1] If $\pi^{(n)}(\mathbf{x})$ stationary distribution of the queue length process for the nth system, then $\pi_k^{(n)}$ has the following interpretation: $\pi_k^{(n)} = \sum_{\mathbf{x}:|A_\mathbf{x}|=k}\pi^{(n)}(\mathbf{x})$ for $k = 1, \ldots, t_n$.

Following lemma provides an even simpler bound on $\tau_k^{(n)}$.

Lemma 5. *For large enough n, we get,*

$$\tau_k^{(n)} \leq \pi_k^{(n)}$$

for each $k \in \{1, \ldots, t_n\}$.

PROOF. Fix n large enough such that the bound in Lemma 4 holds. We prove the result using induction on k. Consider the base case of $k = 1$. From Lemma 4 and (14) we have

$$\tau_1^{(n)} \leq \frac{(t_n - 1 + 1)\theta_n}{h^{(n)}(1) - \theta_n} \pi_0^{(n)} = \pi_1^{(n)}.$$

Now, let us assume that the lemma holds for $k = k' - 1$, i.e., $\tau_{k'-1}^{(n)} \leq \pi_{k'-1}^{(n)}$. Using this, we show below that the lemma holds for $k = k'$ as well.

From Lemma 4 and induction hypothesis we have

$$\tau_{k'}^{(n)} \leq \frac{(t_n - k' + 1)\theta_n}{h^{(n)}(k') - k'\theta_n} \left(\frac{1}{k'} \pi_{k'-1}^{(n)} + \frac{k'-1}{k'} \pi_{k'-1}^{(n)} \right) = \pi_{k'}^{(n)},$$

where the last equality follows from (14). Hence, the lemma. □

Using above lemma and (13), we get

$$E[D^{(n)}] \leq \nu \sum_{k=1}^{t_n} \frac{k}{t_n} \pi_k^{(n)}.$$

Or equivalently,

$$\frac{1}{\nu} E[D^{(n)}] = \sum_{k=1}^{\epsilon b \log(\frac{1}{1-\gamma})\frac{n}{c_n}} \frac{k}{t_n} \pi_k^{(n)} + \sum_{k=\epsilon' b \log(\frac{1}{1-\gamma})\frac{n}{c_n}+1}^{t_n} \frac{k}{t_n} \pi_k^{(n)}.$$

We now use Theorem 6 to prove the main result. From Theorem 6, we have

$$\begin{aligned}
\frac{1}{\nu} E[D^{(n)}] &\leq \sum_{k=1}^{\epsilon b \log(\frac{1}{1-\gamma})\frac{n}{c_n}} \frac{k}{t_n} \pi_k^{(n)} + \delta'^{\frac{m}{c_n}} \\
&\leq \epsilon b \log\left(\frac{1}{1-\gamma}\right) \frac{n}{c_n t_n} \sum_{k=1}^{\epsilon b \log(\frac{1}{1-\gamma})\frac{n}{c_n}} \pi_k^{(n)} + \delta'^{\frac{m}{c_n}} \\
&\leq \epsilon \log\left(\frac{1}{1-\gamma}\right) \frac{\theta_n}{\gamma \xi' c_n} + \delta'^{\frac{m}{c_n}},
\end{aligned}$$

where in last inequality we used definition of t_n. The first part of the theorem thus follows from definition of ξ', and the fact that ϵ and δ' where chosen arbitrarily.

Further, from Corollary 3, upon randomly placing c_n copies of each file, the associated random capacity region contains $\tilde{\mathcal{C}}^{(n)}$ with high probability. Hence, the second part follows as well. □

7. CONCLUSIONS

Our main conclusions address both practical and theoretical aspects associated with such systems. CDN systems address potential high demands by maintaining multiple copies of content – server diversity. At the same time there has been increasing interest in adopting multipath transport protocols to improve reliability and throughput. Our results show that infrastructure combining multipath transport with server diversity scales well even when subject to substantial variations in per file demands. Specifically, if CDN capacity (servers) scale with total load, and memory per server is proportional to worst case per file demand variability then average download delays will scale, i.e., are asymptotically negligible. This suggests a scalable approach towards addressing the delivery of popular content without requiring complex caching strategies.

On the theoretical side we have established: (1) basic new results linking fairness in resource allocation to delays and (2) the asymptotic symmetry of randomly configured large-scale systems with heterogenous components. Together these results suggest large systems might eventually be robust to heterogeneity and fairness criterion.

8. REFERENCES

[1] T. Bonald. Throughput performance in networks with linear capacity contraints. In *Proceedings of CISS*, pages 644–649, 2006.

[2] T. Bonald, L. Massoulié, A. Proutière, and J. Virtamo. A queueing analysis of max-min fairness, proportional fairness and balanced fairness. *Queueing Systems*, 53:65–84, 2006.

[3] T. Bonald and A. Proutière. Insensitive bandwidth sharing in data networks. *Queueing Systems*, 44:69–100, 2003.

[4] T. Bonald and A. Proutière. On stochastic bounds for monotonic processor sharing networks. *Queueing Systems*, 47:81–106, 2004.

[5] T. Bonald, A. Proutière, J. Roberts, and J. Virtamo. Computational aspects of balanced fairness. In *Proceedings of ITC*, 2003.

[6] T. Bonald and J. Virtamo. Calculating the flow level performance of balanced fairness in tree networks. *Perform. Eval.*, 58(1):1–14, Oct. 2004.

[7] G. de Veciana, T.-J. Lee, and T. Konstantopoulos. Stability and performance analysis of networks supporting elastic services. *IEEE/ACM Transactions on Networking*, 9(1):2–14, Feb. 2001.

[8] D. Dubhashi and D. Ranjan. Balls and bins: A study in negative dependence. *Random Structures & Algorithms*, 13(2):99–124, 1998.

[9] J. Edmonds. Submodular functions, matroids, and certain polyhedra. In *Proceedings of Calgary International Conference on Combinatorial Structures and Applications*, pages 69–87, 1969.

[10] B. Frank, I. Poese, G. Smaragdakis, A. Feldmann, B. M. Maggs, S. Uhlig, V. Aggarwal, and F. Schneider. Collaboration opportunities for content delivery and network infrastructures. In H. Haddadi and O. Bonaventure, editors, *Recent Advances in Networking*, pages 305–377. ACM SIGCOMM ebook, 2013.

[11] V. Joseph and G. de Veciana. Stochastic networks with multipath flow control: Impact of resource pools on flow-level performance and network congestion. In *Proceedings of the ACM Sigmetrics*, pages 61–72, 2011.

[12] F. P. Kelly, A. K. Maulloo, and D. K. H. Tan. Rate control for communication networks: Shadow prices, proportional fairness and stability. *The Journal of the Operational Research Society*, 49(3):237–252, 1998.

[13] T. Lan, D. Kao, M. Chiang, and A. Sabharwal. An axiomatic theory of fairness in network resource

allocation. In *Proceedings of IEEE Infocom*, pages 1–9, March 2010.

[14] M. Leconte, M. Lelarge, and L. Massoulié. Adaptive replication in distributed content delivery networks. *arXiv preprint arXiv:1401.1770*, 2014.

[15] X. Lin and N. Shroff. Utility maximization for communication networks with multipath routing. *IEEE Transactions on Automatic Control*, 51(5):766 – 781, May 2006.

[16] A. W. Marshall, I. Olkin, and B. C. Arnold. *Inequalities: Theory of Majorization and Its Applications*. Springer, 2nd edition, 2011.

[17] L. Massoulié and J. Roberts. Bandwidth sharing and admission control for elastic traffic. *Telecommunication Systems*, 15(1-2):185–201, 2000.

[18] M. Mitzenmacher and E. Upfal. *Probability and Computing: Randomized Algorithms and Probabilistic Analysis*. Cambridge University Press, 2005.

[19] J. Mo and J. Walrand. Fair end-to-end window-based congestion control. *IEEE/ACM Transactions on Networking*, 8(5):556 –567, Oct. 2000.

[20] S. Moharir, J. Ghaderi, S. Sanghavi, and S. Shakkottai. Serving content with unknown demand: The high-dimensional regime. In *Proceedings of ACM Sigmetrics*, pages 435–447, 2014.

[21] G. L. Nemhauser and L. A. Wolsey. *Integer and combinatorial optimization*, volume 18. Wiley, 1988.

[22] V. Shah and G. de Veciana. Performance evaluation and asymptotics for content delivery networks. In *IEEE Infocom*, pages 2607–2615, 2014.

[23] J. N. Tsitsiklis and K. Xu. Queueing system topologies with limited flexibility. In *Proceedings of ACM Sigmetrics*, pages 167–178, 2013.

[24] E. Yeh. *Multiaccess and fading in communication networks*. PhD thesis, Massachusetts Institute of Technology, 2001.

APPENDIX

A.1 Proof of Theorem 1

Consider the following lemma regarding relative greediness of αF and BF.

Lemma 6. *Consider states* $\mathbf{x}$ *and* $\mathbf{y}$ *such that* $\mathbf{x} \prec_w \mathbf{y}$. *For each* k *such that* $\sum_{l=1}^{k} x_{[l]} = \sum_{l=1}^{k} y_{[l]}$, *we have* $\sum_{l=1}^{k} r_{(l)}^{\alpha}(\mathbf{x}) \geq \sum_{l=1}^{k} r_{(l)}^{B}(\mathbf{y})$.

Roughly, it asserts that if state $\mathbf{x}$ is same or more balanced than state $\mathbf{y}$, then the sum rate assigned to larger queues by αF to state $\mathbf{x}$ is greater than that by BF to state $\mathbf{y}$. Proof of this lemma is summarized in A.2. Below, we provide a detailed coupling argument showing stochastic weak-majorization using this lemma.

Coupling Argument: Without loss of generality, assume $\nu = 1$. Suppose $\mathbf{X}^{\alpha}(0) \prec_w \mathbf{X}^{B}(0)$. Below, we couple the arrivals and departures of processes $(\mathbf{X}^{\alpha}(t) : t \geq 0)$ and $(\mathbf{X}^{B}(t) : t \geq 0)$ such that their marginal distributions remain intact and $\mathbf{X}^{\alpha}(t) \prec_w \mathbf{X}^{B}(t)$ almost surely for each $t \geq 0$.

LetΠ_a be a Poisson point process with rate $\sum_{i \in F} \lambda_i$, and letΠ_d be Poisson point process with rate $\mu(F)$. The points in these processes are the times of 'potential events' in $(\mathbf{X}^{B}(t) : t \geq 0)$ and $(\mathbf{X}^{\alpha}(t) : t \geq 0)$. We use$\Pi_a$ to couple arrivals andΠ_d to couple departures. For each time t' when a potential event occurs, let $\epsilon_{t'}$ be a small enough number such that no potential event occurred in the time interval of $[t' - \epsilon_{t'}, t')$.

Coupling of arrivals: For each point t' inΠ_a, do the following: Choose a random variable $Z_{t'}$ independently and uniformly from $\{1, \ldots, n\}$. Let an arrival occur in $(\mathbf{X}^{\alpha}(t) : t \geq 0)$ at time t' in the $Z_{t'}^{\text{th}}$ largest queue of $\mathbf{X}^{\alpha}(t' - \epsilon_{t'})$. Ties are broken uniformly at random. Similarly, let an arrival occur in $(\mathbf{X}^{\alpha}(t) : t \geq 0)$ at time t' in the $Z_{t'}^{\text{th}}$ largest queue of $\mathbf{X}^{\alpha}(t' - \epsilon_{t'})$. Again, ties are broken uniformly at random.

Coupling of departures: For each point t' of increment inΠ_d, do the following: Choose a random variable $Z_{t'}$ independently and uniformly from interval $(0, \mu(F)]$. For k such that

$$Z_{t'} \in \left(\sum_{l=1}^{k-1} r_{(l)}^{\alpha}(X^{\alpha}(t' - \epsilon_{t'})), \sum_{l=1}^{k} r_{(l)}^{\alpha}(X^{\alpha}(t' - \epsilon_{t'})) \right],$$

let a departure occur in $(\mathbf{X}^{\alpha}(t) : t \geq 0)$ at time t' in the kth largest queue of $\mathbf{X}^{\alpha}(t' - \epsilon_{t'})$, with ties broken uniformly and independently at random.

Similarly, for k such that

$$Z_{t'} \in \left(\sum_{l=1}^{k-1} r_{(l)}^{B}(\mathbf{X}^{B}(t' - \epsilon_{t'})), \sum_{l=1}^{k} r_{(l)}^{B}(\mathbf{X}^{B}(t' - \epsilon_{t'})) \right],$$

let a departure occur in $(\mathbf{X}^{B}(t) : t \geq 0)$ at time t' in the kth largest queue of $\mathbf{X}^{B}(t' - \epsilon_{t'})$, with ties broken uniformly and independently at random. Note that in both cases it is possible that no such k exists since some classes may not be active and the total service rate may be less than $\mu(F)$. In that case, no departure occurs.

It can be checked that the marginal distributions of $(\mathbf{X}^{\alpha}(t) : t \geq 0)$ and $(\mathbf{X}^{B}(t) : t \geq 0)$ remain intact. We now show that $\mathbf{X}^{\alpha}(t) \prec_w \mathbf{X}^{B}(t)$ almost surely for each t.

It is easy to check that if an arrival occurred at time t' and if $\mathbf{X}^{\alpha}(t) \prec_w \mathbf{X}^{B}(t)$ for each $t < t'$, then $\mathbf{X}^{\alpha}(t') \prec_w \mathbf{X}^{B}(t')$ as well. We now show that the same holds for points ofΠ_d as well.

Suppose a potential departure occurred at t', and $\mathbf{X}^{\alpha}(t) \prec_w \mathbf{X}^{B}(t)$ for each $t < t'$. We show below that $\sum_{l=1}^{k} X_{[l]}^{\alpha}(t') \leq \sum_{l=1}^{k} X_{[l]}^{B}(t')$ for each k. Here, we use Lemma 6. Following two cases arise.

Case 1: $\sum_{l=1}^{k} X_{[l]}^{\alpha}(t' - \epsilon_{t'}) < \sum_{l=1}^{k} X_{[l]}^{B}(t' - \epsilon_{t'})$. A maximum of one departure occurs at time t' in either processes. Thus we have $\sum_{l=1}^{k} X_{[l]}^{\alpha}(t') \leq \sum_{l=1}^{k} X_{[l]}^{B}(t')$.

Case 2: $\sum_{l=1}^{k} X_{[l]}^{\alpha}(t' - \epsilon_{t'}) = \sum_{l=1}^{k} X_{[l]}^{B}(t' - \epsilon_{t'})$. By using $\mathbf{X}^{\alpha}(t - \epsilon_{t'}) \prec_w \mathbf{X}^{B}(t - \epsilon_{t'})$ in Lemma 6 and from the definition of the coupling at time t', it can be shown that if a departure occurs from any of the k largest queues in $\mathbf{X}^{B}(t' - \epsilon_{t'})$, then it also occurs in one of the k largest queues in $\mathbf{X}^{\alpha}(t' - \epsilon_{t'})$. Thus, $\sum_{l=1}^{k} X_{[l]}^{\alpha}(t') \leq \sum_{l=1}^{k} X_{[l]}^{B}(t')$.

Hence the result. □

A.2 Relative greediness and other rate allocation properties

Below, we outline a proof of Lemma 6 which asserts that αF is more greedy than BF. Along the way, we develop several other properties of the rate allocation policies.

Proof of Lemma 6 stems on the following two fundamental properties of per-job rate assignment for αF and BF.

1.) *αF gives the most balanced per-job rate allocation:* The property follows from the fact that αF is equivalent to max-min fair rate allocation, see Proposition 2. Formally, this property implies the following:

Lemma 7. *Let $\mathbf{b}^\alpha$ represent a vector of rates assigned to a set of flows under αF rate allocation. Let $\tilde{\mathbf{b}}$ be the rates assigned to the same set of flows under any other feasible rate allocation. Then, $\mathbf{b}^\alpha \prec^w \tilde{\mathbf{b}}$, i.e., weak majorized from above.*

2.) *In αF and BF, the longest queues have smaller per-job rates:* For αF, this property again follows from the fact that it is equivalent to max-min fair, and that the capacity region is convex and symmetric. For BF, the proof for this property is technical and we omit its discussion here for brevity. Formally, this property implies the following:

Lemma 8. *αF and BF rate allocations satisfy the following property for any state $\mathbf{x}$: if $x_i > x_j$ then $\frac{r_i(\mathbf{x})}{x_i} \leq \frac{r_j(\mathbf{x})}{x_j}$.*

Now, let us study what the above properties imply for per-class rate allocation. Consider a state $\mathbf{x}$. Lemma 8 above implies that the most disadvantaged jobs are the ones which belong to longest queues for both, BF and αF. This, along with Lemma 8, implies that αF provides larger rate to longest queues. Thus we get the following property.

3.) *αF gives larger rate to the longest queues as compared to BF:* Formally, this property implies the following:

Lemma 9. *For any state $\mathbf{x}$, $\sum_{l=1}^k r^\alpha_{(l)}(\mathbf{x}) \geq \sum_{l=1}^k r^B_{(l)}(\mathbf{x})$ for each $k \in \{1, 2, \ldots, n\}$.*

Now, we focus on αF and study how it allocates rates across classes for states $\mathbf{x}$ and $\mathbf{y}$ such that $\mathbf{x} \prec \mathbf{y}$. Intuitively, jobs in longer queues in state $\mathbf{y}$ are more constrained than those in $\mathbf{x}$. Again using the fact that αF is equivalent to max-min fair, the most constrained jobs in state $\mathbf{y}$ have smaller rate than those in state $\mathbf{x}$. By monotonicity of αF, this holds even when $\mathbf{x} \prec_w \mathbf{y}$. When translated to per-class rate allocation in states $\mathbf{x}$ and $\mathbf{y}$, this argument leads us to the following property:

4.) *αF gives larger rate to longer queues in more balanced states:* Formally, this property implies the following:[2]

Lemma 10. *Consider states $\mathbf{x}$ and $\mathbf{y}$ such that $\mathbf{x} \prec_w \mathbf{y}$. For each k such that $\sum_{l=1}^k x_{[l]} = \sum_{l=1}^k y_{[l]}$, we have $\sum_{l=1}^k r^\alpha_{(l)}(\mathbf{x}) \geq \sum_{l=1}^k r^\alpha_{(l)}(\mathbf{y})$.*

Finally, we are ready to study relative greediness of αF and BF.

5.) *αF is more greedy than BF:* We now prove Lemma 6. Consider states $\mathbf{x}$ and $\mathbf{y}$ such that $\mathbf{x} \prec_w \mathbf{y}$. From Lemma 10 we have $\sum_{l=1}^k r^\alpha_{(l)}(\mathbf{x}) \geq \sum_{l=1}^k r^\alpha_{(l)}(\mathbf{y})$, and from Lemma 9 we have $\sum_{l=1}^k r^\alpha_{(l)}(\mathbf{y}) \geq \sum_{l=1}^k r^B_{(l)}(\mathbf{y})$. Hence, Lemma 6 holds.

A.3 Technical Lemmas for proof of Theorem 4

Lemma 1. Let a sequence $(g_n : n \in \mathbb{N})$ be such that $g_n = o(c_n)$. Let δ_1 be a positive constant independent of n such that $\delta_1 < 1$. Then, for large enough n, we have

$$p_k^{(n)} \geq \frac{\delta_1 g_n}{n} k \quad \forall k \in \left\{0, 1, \ldots, \left\lfloor \frac{n}{g_n} \right\rfloor \right\}.$$

PROOF. Consider a sequence of functions $\left(f^{(n)}(.)\right)_{n\geq 1}$ where for each n, $f^{(n)}(t) = 1 - (1 - 1/(bn))^{tc_n}$ for each $t \in \mathbb{R}_+$. Then,

$$f^{(n)}(n/g_n) = 1 - (1 - 1/(bn))^{\frac{nc_n}{g_n}} \stackrel{n\to\infty}{\longrightarrow} 1.$$

Thus, there exists an integer n' such that $f^{(n)}(n/g_n) \geq \delta_1$ for all $n \geq n'$. Also, $f^{(n)}(0) = 0$ for each n. Using concavity of $f^{(n)}(.)$, for each $n \geq n'$ we have

$$f^{(n)}(t) \geq \frac{f^{(n)}(n/g_n)}{(n/g_n)} t, \quad \forall t \text{ s.t. } 0 \leq t \leq n/g_n.$$

Hence, the lemma. □

Lemma 2. There exists a positive constant δ such that $H\left(p_k^{(n)}(1-\epsilon)||p_k^{(n)}\right) \geq -\delta + \epsilon\frac{kc_n}{m}$.

PROOF. From definition,

$$H\left(p_k^{(n)}(1-\epsilon)||p_k^{(n)}\right) = p_k^{(n)}(1-\epsilon)\log(1-\epsilon) + (1 - p_k^{(n)}(1-\epsilon))\log\left(\frac{1-p_k^{(n)}(1-\epsilon)}{1-p_k^{(n)}}\right)$$

Here, the term $p_k^{(n)}(1-\epsilon)\log(1-\epsilon)$, while negative, is greater than $(1-\epsilon)\log(1-\epsilon)$, a constant. Similarly, the term $(1-p_k^{(n)}(1-\epsilon))\log\left(1-p_k^{(n)}(1-\epsilon)\right)$ is negative, but can be upper-bounded by a constant as follows:

$$\begin{aligned}(1-p_k^{(n)}(1-\epsilon))\log\left(1-p_k^{(n)}(1-\epsilon)\right) &\geq \log\left(1-p_k^{(n)}(1-\epsilon)\right)\\ &\geq \log(1-(1-\epsilon)) = \log\epsilon\end{aligned}$$

Thus, we have

$$\begin{aligned}H\left(p_k^{(n)}(1-\epsilon)||p_k^{(n)}\right) &\geq -\delta + (1-p_k^{(n)}(1-\epsilon))\log\left(\frac{1}{1-p_k^{(n)}}\right)\\ &\geq -\delta + (1-(1-\epsilon))\log\left(\frac{1}{1-p_k^{(n)}}\right)\\ &= -\delta + \epsilon\log\left(\frac{1}{1-p_k^{(n)}}\right)\\ &\geq -\delta + \epsilon\frac{kc_n}{m},\end{aligned}$$

where in the last inequality we used the fact that $1 - p_k^{(n)} \leq e^{-\frac{kc_n}{m}}$. □

[2]This property is also used to prove Majorization bound described in Section 4.3. Also, one can check that this property is satisfied by Greedy rate allocation as well.

Fisher Information-based Experiment Design for Network Tomography *

Ting He‡, Chang Liu†, Ananthram Swami§, Don Towsley†,
Theodoros Salonidis‡, Andrei Iu. Bejan*, and Paul Yu§
‡IBM T. J. Watson Research Center, Yorktown Heights, NY, USA. {the, tsaloni}@us.ibm.com
†University of Massachusetts, Amherst, MA, USA. {cliu, towsley}@cs.umass.edu
§Army Research Laboratory, Adelphi, MD, USA. {ananthram.swami, paul.l.yu}.civ@mail.mil
*University of Cambridge, Cambridge, UK. aib29@cam.ac.uk

ABSTRACT

Network tomography aims to infer the individual performance of networked elements (e.g., links) using aggregate measurements on end-to-end paths. Previous work on network tomography focuses primarily on developing estimators using the given measurements, while the design of measurements is often neglected. We fill this gap by proposing a framework to design probing experiments with focus on probe allocation, and applying it to two concrete problems: packet loss tomography and packet delay variation (PDV) tomography. Based on the Fisher Information Matrix (FIM), we design the distribution of probes across paths to maximize the best accuracy of unbiased estimators, asymptotically achievable by the maximum likelihood estimator. We consider two widely-adopted objective functions: determinant of the inverse FIM (D-optimality) and trace of the inverse FIM (A-optimality). We also extend the A-optimal criterion to incorporate heterogeneity in link weights. Under certain conditions on the FIM, satisfied by both loss and PDV tomography, we derive explicit expressions for both objective functions. When the number of probing paths equals the number of links, these lead to closed-form solutions for the optimal design; when there are more paths, we develop a heuristic to select a subset of paths and optimally allocate probes within the subset. Observing the dependency of the optimal design on unknown parameters, we further propose an algorithm that iteratively updates the design based on parameter estimates, which converges to the design based on true parameters as the number of probes increases. Using packet-level simulations on real datasets, we verify that the proposed design effectively reduces estimation error compared with the common approach of uniformly distributing probes.

*Research was sponsored by the U.S. Army Research Laboratory and the U.K. Ministry of Defence and was accomplished under Agreement Number W911NF-06-3-0001. The views and conclusions contained in this document are those of the authors and should not be interpreted as representing the official policies, either expressed or implied, of the U.S. Army Research Laboratory, the U.S. Government, the U.K. Ministry of Defence or the U.K. Government. The U.S. and U.K. Governments are authorized to reproduce and distribute reprints for Government purposes notwithstanding any copyright notation hereon.

SIGMETRICS'15, June 15–19, 2015, Portland, OR, USA.

http://dx.doi.org/10.1145/2745844.2745862.

Categories and Subject Descriptors

C.2.3 [**Computer-communication Networks**]: Network Operations—*Network Monitoring*; G.3 [**Probability and Statistics**]: Experimental Design

General Terms

Theory, Algorithms

Keywords

Network Tomography; Experiment Design; Fisher Information Matrix

1. INTRODUCTION

Network management in complex networks (e.g., MANET-cellular hybrid networks, coalition networks) often suffers from inefficiencies imposed by protocol/policy barriers between different administration domains, where one notable example is the lack of common monitoring services that provide global state of all the networked components (e.g., links). This limitation motivates the need for external approaches that allow one domain to infer the *internal* state (e.g., link loss rates) of another domain by measuring its *external* performance (e.g., end-to-end losses between a set of vantage points). The methodology of such inference is called *network tomography* [5].

Network tomography has been an active research area in the recent past. Compared with the approach of directly measuring the performance at individual network components, it provides an alternative approach that does not require privileged access to the components. The challenge is that since the measurements are generally functions of the states of multiple components, one has to "invert" these functions. Moreover, the states of interest are usually persistent performance indicators such as mean delays and packet loss rates, while the measurements are functions of the delay/loss instances, and thus the "inversion" has to be robust against randomness in the measurements.

By modeling the performance of each link as a random variable with a (partially) unknown probability distribution, one can apply statistical techniques to estimate the parameter of this distribution from path measurements [4, 7, 10].

While most existing work focuses on designing estimators, the accuracy of estimation is fundamentally bounded by the amount of "information" contained in measurements. It is crucial that the probing experiments generate measurements that are most informative for estimating link parameters.

It is not straightforward to quantify the information in measurements. On the one hand, measurements from different paths provide different amounts of information as they traverse different sets of links, each exhibiting a different level of uncertainty; on the other hand, measurements from a single (multi-hop) path alone do not provide sufficient information for uniquely determining link performances. To address this issue, we apply a notion from estimation theory called the *Fisher Information Matrix (FIM)* [13]. The FIM combines knowledge of paths and link parameters into a single measure of how much "information" a measurement provides for the parameter of interest. By the *Cramér-Rao bound (CRB)* [13], the inverse of the FIM establishes a lower bound on the error covariance matrix of any unbiased estimator.

Based on the FIM, an intuitive formulation of experiment design is to allocate probes on paths to maximize the total information. Turning this intuition into a precise formulation requires an objective function that maps a matrix (FIM) to a scalar that can be uniquely optimized. The theory of optimal experiment design [2] has established a set of such objective functions. In particular, maximizing the determinant of FIM (aka *D-optimality*) leads to a design that minimizes (a bound on) the volume of the error ellipsoid, and minimizing the trace of the inverse FIM (aka *A-optimality*) leads to a design that minimizes (a bound on) the average *mean squared error (MSE)*. Both objective functions lead to convex optimization problems that can, in theory, be solved to obtain the optimal experiment design [3]. Solving these optimizations for practical networks, however, is highly nontrivial, as its solution space (i.e., all possible probe allocations) has a dimension that is at least the size of the network. In this work, we develop efficient solutions for tomographic experiment design using the above objective functions, and apply our results to two concrete tomography problems with multiplicative/additive link metrics.

1.1 Related Work

Based on the model of link metrics, existing work can be classified into algebraic tomography and statistical tomography. Algebraic tomography models each link metric as an unknown constant (e.g., fixed link delay) and each path measurement as a deterministic function of link metrics (e.g., fixed path delay). The goal of experiment design for algebraic tomography is to construct paths whose measurements can uniquely determine link metrics, e.g., n linearly independent paths for an n-link network [12].

Statistical tomography models each link metric as a random variable with a (partially) unknown probability distribution, and applies various estimation techniques to infer the distribution from path measurements. When multicast is supported, techniques have been proposed to estimate link loss rates and delays from multicast losses and delays [4, 7, 10]. Similar results have been obtained for multi-source measurements [9]. Variants based on subtree, unicast, and striped unicast have also been developed to improve the flexibility of probing [15, 6].

Most existing work in statistical tomography has focused on developing estimators, while the problem of experiment design is often ignored. Unlike algebraic tomography where it suffices to find paths that result in a unique solution of link metrics, statistical tomography also needs to deal with randomness in link metrics and possibly measurement noise. There has been a rich theory of experiment design for general statistical inference, which casts the problem as an optimization of a set of design objectives that capture various aspects of estimation accuracy [2]. The approach has recently been applied to design experiments for network monitoring, e.g., to design link sampling rates for flow size estimation [16], or design probing experiments for estimating link delays/loss rates from delays/losses of multicast or correlated unicast probes [8, 18]. In particular, [8, 18] measure the quality of an experiment design by the FIM and try to design probing experiments such that certain optimality criteria based on the FIM can be optimized (A-optimality in [8], D-optimality in [18]). Their solutions, however, either rely on numerical solvers [18] or a coarse approximation that ignores off-diagonal elements of the FIM [8]. We have a similar goal of designing the optimal allocation of probes based on certain functions of the FIM that capture the overall estimation accuracy, but we identify special structures of the objective functions that allow for exact, closed-form solutions.

1.2 Summary of Contributions

Given a fixed number of probes and a set of measurement paths, we want to allocate the probes to the paths so that the measurements can provide the most accurate estimate of the link parameters of interest. Our contributions are:

1. We propose a general experiment design framework for network tomography, where we use the FIM to allocate probes across paths for inferring link parameters using path measurements, with illustrative applications to loss and packet delay variation (PDV) tomography.

2. We derive closed-form estimators for loss and PDV tomography, which, in conjunction with the optimal experiment design, provide asymptotically optimal estimates of the link parameters of interest.

3. For two well-adopted design criteria, *D-optimality* and *A-optimality*, we derive explicit formulas for the design objectives as functions of probe allocation. We also propose a novel criterion, *weighted A-optimality*, that extends A-optimality to incorporate heterogeneity in importance of links. We show how to evaluate these formulas in closed form for loss and PDV tomography.

4. Based on the derived formulas, we develop closed-form solutions for optimal probe allocation when measurement paths form a basis of the vector space of all links. In particular, our solutions show that the D-optimal design leads to a uniform allocation of probes, while the A-optimal design is generally non-uniform. When extra paths are available, we propose a two-step heuristic that first selects a proper basis and then optimizes probe allocation over the basis. Compared with numerical optimization, the proposed solutions significantly improve scalability wrt the number of paths.

5. Observing the dependency of the optimal design on the unknown link parameters, we propose an iterative

algorithm that periodically updates the design using refined estimates of the parameters. We show that the result converges to a design based on the true parameters with high probability.

6. We evaluate the proposed designs on real network datasets for both loss and PDV tomography. Our results show that the proposed design based on the A-optimal criterion can effectively reduce the MSE compared with uniform probing, even when the CRB is loose.

The rest of the paper is organized as follows. Section 2 formulates the problem of experiment design for network tomography. Section 3 introduces the FIM and its basic properties. Section 4 presents estimators of link parameters. Section 5 defines objectives of experiment design, and Section 6 presents algorithms to optimize the objectives. Section 7 evaluates the proposed design algorithms via simulations based on real data. Then Section 8 concludes the paper. All proofs are deferred to the appendix.

2. PROBLEM FORMULATION

2.1 Network Model

Let $\mathcal{G} = (V, L)$ denote a network with nodes V and links L. Each link $l \in L$ is associated with a performance metric (e.g., delay, loss) that varies stochastically according to a distribution with unknown parameter θ_l. Let P be a given set of candidate probing paths in $\mathcal{G}$. Each path $p_y \in P$ consists of one or more pairwise adjacent links in[1] $\mathcal{G}$. We assume that the monitoring system can inject probes on all paths in P and observe their end-to-end performance. We also introduce a $|P| \times |L|$ matrix $A := [A_{y,l}]$ defined by P, called the *measurement matrix*, where $A_{y,l} = 1$ if link l is on path p_y and $A_{y,l} = 0$ otherwise. Without loss of generality, we assume that each link is on at least one path in P. Additional assumptions on A (and hence P) will be introduced later as needed. At run time, probes are injected on paths selected according to our experiment design. We consider a probabilistic design model, where each probe is sent over a path randomly selected from P, with probability ϕ_y of selecting path p_y. Here $\boldsymbol{\phi} := (\phi_y)_{y=1}^{|P|}$, satisfying $\phi_y \geq 0$ and $\sum_{y=1}^{|P|} \phi_y = 1$, is a design parameter.

2.2 Stochastic Link Metric Tomography

Given a family of link metric distributions with unknown parameters $\boldsymbol{\theta} := (\theta_l)_{l \in L}$, the goal of (parametric) stochastic link metric tomography is to infer $\boldsymbol{\theta}$ from observations of the corresponding performance metrics over probed paths. Let $f_y(x; \boldsymbol{\theta})$ denote the conditional probability of observing path metric x, given that the probe is sent on path p_y and the link parameters are $\boldsymbol{\theta}$. Then the problem of stochastic link metric tomography is to infer the parameter $\boldsymbol{\theta}$ from the observations $(\mathbf{x}, \mathbf{y}) := (x_t, y_t)_{t=1}^{N}$, where x_t is the outcome of the t-th probe and y_t the corresponding path index. Under the assumption that the performance experienced by probes is independent both across probes and across links, the observations are i.i.d., each with the following distribution:

$$f(x, y; \boldsymbol{\theta}, \boldsymbol{\phi}) = \phi_y f_y(x; \boldsymbol{\theta}). \tag{1}$$

[1]We do not impose constraints on paths except that a path traverses each link at most once.

As concrete examples, we will address in detail two representative performance metrics as follows.

2.2.1 Packet Loss Tomography

Packet loss is a typical performance metric that is multiplicative over links on a path. Packet loss tomography aims to infer loss rates on individual links by observing end-to-end packet losses on probed paths. Let the parameter of interest $\boldsymbol{\theta}$ be the vector of link success rates (i.e., complements of loss rates), and each probe outcome x be an indicator that the probe successfully reaches its destination. Assume that losses of the same probe on different links and of different probes on the same link are both independent. Then the observation model becomes:

$$f(x, y; \boldsymbol{\theta}, \boldsymbol{\phi}) = \phi_y(\prod_{l \in p_y} \theta_l)^x (1 - \prod_{l \in p_y} \theta_l)^{1-x}. \tag{2}$$

2.2.2 Packet Delay Variation Tomography

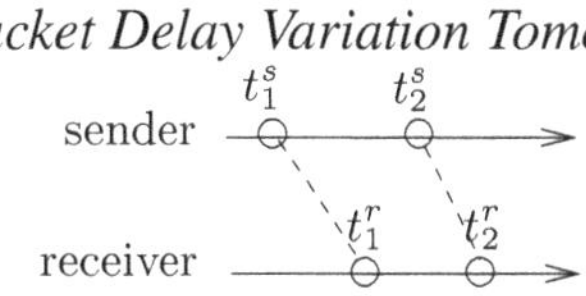

Figure 1: Illustration of PDV: t_i^s (t_i^r) is the timestamp of the i-th packet at the sender (receiver).

Packet delay variation (PDV), aka *delay jitter*, is a typical performance metric that is additive over links on a path[2]. PDV between a sender and receiver pair is defined as the difference in sender-to-receiver delays between different packets, i.e., as illustrated in Fig. 1, PDV $= (t_2^r - t_2^s) - (t_1^r - t_1^s)$; equivalently, it is the difference between the inter-packet delays at the sender and the receiver, i.e., PDV $= (t_2^r - t_1^r) - (t_2^s - t_1^s)$. The latter definition has the advantage that its evaluation does not require clock synchronization across nodes (assuming the difference in clock speeds is negligible). One can verify that the end-to-end PDV on a path equals the sum of the PDVs at each link. Suppose that PDVs on individual links follow the normal distribution $\mathcal{N}(0, \theta_l)$ with zero mean and *unknown* variance θ_l ($l \in L$), and that PDVs experienced by the same probe on different links and by different probes on the same link are both independent. PDV tomography aims to infer $\boldsymbol{\theta}$ from the observed end-to-end PDV x based on the following observation model:

$$f(x, y; \boldsymbol{\theta}, \boldsymbol{\phi}) = \phi_y \frac{1}{\sqrt{2\pi \sum_{l \in p_y} \theta_l}} \exp\left(-\frac{x^2}{2\sum_{l \in p_y} \theta_l}\right). \tag{3}$$

2.3 Main Problem: Experiment Design

Our goal is to develop a systematic framework to optimally allocate probes over measurement paths such that the overall error in estimating $\boldsymbol{\theta}$ is minimized. Specifically, given an error measure $C(\hat{\boldsymbol{\theta}}, \boldsymbol{\theta})$ (e.g., L_2-norm) and a total number of probes N, we want to design the probe distribution $\boldsymbol{\phi}$, such that in conjunction with an appropriate estimator $\hat{\boldsymbol{\theta}}$, the expected error $\mathbb{E}[C(\hat{\boldsymbol{\theta}}, \boldsymbol{\theta})]$ after making N probes is minimized. The specific form of $C(\hat{\boldsymbol{\theta}}, \boldsymbol{\theta})$ will determine the design criterion, and will be specified later (Section 5).

[2]Delay is also a typical additive performance metric, where the parameter of interest is usually the mean link delay. We study PDV instead because it has a greater impact on streaming applications.

3. PRELIMINARIES

In preparation for FIM-based experiment design, we first review FIM and its important properties.

3.1 FIM and CRB

Given the observation model (1), the (per-measurement) FIM wrt $\boldsymbol{\theta}$ is an $|L| \times |L|$ matrix, whose (i, j)-th entry is defined by

$$\mathbb{E}\left[\left(\frac{\partial}{\partial\theta_i}\log f(x, y; \boldsymbol{\theta}, \boldsymbol{\phi})\right)\left(\frac{\partial}{\partial\theta_j}\log f(x, y; \boldsymbol{\theta}, \boldsymbol{\phi})\right)\Big|\boldsymbol{\theta}, \boldsymbol{\phi}\right]. \quad (4)$$

We denote this matrix by $I(\boldsymbol{\theta}; \boldsymbol{\phi})$ to highlight its dependence on both the (unknown) parameter $\boldsymbol{\theta}$ and the design parameter $\boldsymbol{\phi}$. All subsequent references to "FIM" mean this per-measurement FIM.

The significance of the FIM is that it provides a fundamental bound on the error of unbiased estimators. Specifically, if $\hat{\boldsymbol{\theta}}$ is an unbiased estimator of $\boldsymbol{\theta}$ using N i.i.d. measurements, then the covariance matrix of $\hat{\boldsymbol{\theta}}$ satisfies[3] $\text{cov}(\hat{\boldsymbol{\theta}}) \succeq \frac{1}{N}I^{-1}(\boldsymbol{\theta}; \boldsymbol{\phi})$, known as the *Cramér-Rao bound (CRB)* [13]. In particular, the MSE in estimating θ_l, given by $\text{cov}(\hat{\boldsymbol{\theta}})_{l,l}$, is lower bounded by $I^{-1}_{l,l}(\boldsymbol{\theta}; \boldsymbol{\phi})/N$.

3.2 Identifiability and Invertibility of FIM

The CRB has an implicit assumption that the FIM is invertible. In our problem, we will show that this assumption follows from the identifiability of link parameters. We say that an unknown parameter $\boldsymbol{\theta}$ is *identifiable* from observations $\mathbf{x}$ if and only if the observation model satisfies that $f(\mathbf{x}; \boldsymbol{\theta}) \neq f(\mathbf{x}; \boldsymbol{\theta}')$ at some $\mathbf{x}$ for any $\boldsymbol{\theta} \neq \boldsymbol{\theta}'$. In network tomography, the identifiability of link parameters $\boldsymbol{\theta}$ has direct implication on the measurement matrix and the FIM.

Specifically, suppose that a stochastic link metric tomography problem can be cast as a linear system $A\mathbf{z}(\boldsymbol{\theta}) = \mathbf{w}$, where A is the measurement matrix, $\mathbf{z}(\boldsymbol{\theta})$ is a bijection of $\boldsymbol{\theta}$, and $\mathbf{w}$ is a vector of path performance parameters such that the probe outcomes depend on $\boldsymbol{\theta}$ only through $\mathbf{w}$. Suppose that $\mathbf{w}$ can be estimated consistently from probes[4]. Then the following statements hold:

- $\boldsymbol{\theta}$ is identifiable if and only if A has full column rank;
- if $\boldsymbol{\theta}$ is identifiable, then $I(\boldsymbol{\theta}; \boldsymbol{\phi})$ is invertible.

The first statement can be easily proved by an argument of contradiction, and the second statement is a direct implication of the equivalence between the invertibility of the FIM and the *local identifiability*[5] of $\boldsymbol{\theta}$ [14].

Both loss tomography and PDV tomography admit a linear system model $A\mathbf{z} = \mathbf{w}$, where $z_l = \log\theta_l$, $w_y = \log\left(\prod_{l\in p_y}\theta_l\right)$ for loss tomography according to (2), and $z_l = \theta_l$, $w_y = \sum_{l\in p_y}\theta_l$ for PDV tomography according to (3) (the same applies to delay).

Discussion: The aspect of experiment design focusing on path construction has been extensively studied in the literature. If the routing of probes is controllable (subject to cycle-free constraint), then identifiability can be guaranteed by constructing paths using the *Spanning Tree-based Path Construction (STPC)* algorithm in [12]; if the routing is uncontrollable and the default routes between monitors cannot identify all link parameters, then we can transform the topology into a logical topology as in [19], whose links represent the *Minimal Identifiable Link Sequences (MILS)*, such that parameters of the logical links are identifiable.

In this work, we focus on a different aspect of designing probe allocation. Intuitively, identifiability is a basic requirement for the inference problem to be solvable with infinite measurements, and probe allocation maximizes the inference accuracy with finite measurements. Therefore, we will assume in the sequel that *the link parameters of interest are identifiable* using the given paths. By the above statements, this implies that the measurement matrix A has full column rank and the FIM $I(\boldsymbol{\theta}; \boldsymbol{\phi})$ is invertible. Conceptually, probe allocation among all possible paths generalizes path construction because it specifies not only which paths are used for probing but also how often each path is probed.

3.3 Example

We illustrate FIM-based experiment design by a simple example in Fig. 2, where we want to use end-to-end losses on paths p_1, p_2, and p_3 to infer loss rates of links l_1 and l_2. Consider three candidate designs $\boldsymbol{\phi}_1 = (\frac{1}{3}, \frac{1}{3}, \frac{1}{3})$, $\boldsymbol{\phi}_2 = (0.5, 0.5, 0)$, and $\boldsymbol{\phi}_3 = (0.15, 0.85, 0)$. The average CRB for loss rate estimation, given by the average of diagonal elements of the inverse FIM, equals 0.6, 0.5, and 0.98 respectively for the three designs, if the actual link loss rates are (0.5, 0.5); however, if the link loss rates are (0.99, 0.5), the CRB becomes 0.21, 0.26, and 0.18 respectively (see (16) in Section 5.4.1 for computation of the FIM and hence the CRB). The example demonstrates that: (i) the usual approach of uniformly allocating probes (i.e., $\boldsymbol{\phi}_1$) is generally suboptimal, and (ii) the optimal allocation depends not only on the paths but also on the link parameters. Moreover, although the preferred design ($\boldsymbol{\phi}_2$ or $\boldsymbol{\phi}_3$) in the above cases does not use p_3, it is not clear whether this is always true, as a measurement on p_3 provides information about both links.

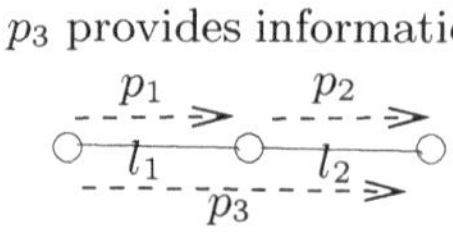

Figure 2: Example: loss tomography using three paths.

4. LINK PARAMETER ESTIMATION

Fundamental to experiment design is how the collected measurements will be used to estimate the parameters of interest. To this end, we review a well-known estimator and its special relationship with FIM-based experiment design.

4.1 Maximum Likelihood Estimator (MLE)

Given observations, the MLE solves for the parameter value that maximizes the likelihood of these observations and uses this value as an estimate of the parameter. The MLE plays a significant role in FIM-based experiment design. Using the FIM in experiment design implies an implicit assumption that the adopted estimator is *efficient* (i.e., unbiased and achieves the CRB), and thus the CRB characterizes estimation error. In this regard, the MLE has a superior property that it is the only candidate for efficient estimator, i.e., if an efficient estimator exists, it must be the MLE [17].

[3]For matrices A and B, $A \succeq B$ means that $A - B$ is positive semi-definite.

[4]That is, there exists an estimator $\hat{\mathbf{w}}$ that converges to $\mathbf{w}$ in probability as the number of probes goes to infinity.

[5]That is, there exists an open neighborhood of $\boldsymbol{\theta}$ such that no $\boldsymbol{\theta}'$ ($\boldsymbol{\theta}' \neq \boldsymbol{\theta}$) in this neighborhood leads to the same observation model.

Moreover, although efficient estimators may not exist for finite sample sizes, the MLE is asymptotically efficient under regularity conditions, i.e., its expectation converges to the true parameter at a rate approximating the CRB. Therefore, using the MLE to estimate link parameters guarantees that our FIM-based experiment design will optimize the error decay rate as the number of probes becomes large.

4.2 MLE for Packet Loss Tomography

The MLE has a unique property that it is *invariant under one-to-one parameter transformations*. That is, if $\hat{\theta}$ is an MLE of θ and $\eta = g(\theta)$ is a one-to-one transformation, then $\hat{\eta} = g(\hat{\theta})$ is an MLE of η. For tomography problems, this property can be leveraged to greatly simplify the derivation of the MLE. Specifically, let $\alpha_y(\boldsymbol{\theta}) := \prod_{l \in p_y} \theta_l$ denote the success probability of path p_y, $n_{1,y}$ the number of successfully received probes, and $n_{0,y}$ the number of lost probes. It is known that the MLE of $\alpha_y(\boldsymbol{\theta})$ is simply the empirical path success probability $\hat{\alpha}_y := n_{1,y}/(n_{1,y}+n_{0,y})$, as $n_{1,y}$ can be viewed as a sum of $n_{0,y} + n_{1,y}$ i.i.d. Bernoulli random variables with success probability $\alpha_y(\boldsymbol{\theta})$. Moreover, when A has full column rank, the link success rates $\boldsymbol{\theta}$ and the path success rates $\boldsymbol{\alpha} := (\alpha_y(\boldsymbol{\theta}))_{y=1}^{|P|}$ form a one-to-one mapping $\log \boldsymbol{\theta} = (A^T A)^{-1} A^T \log \boldsymbol{\alpha}$ (assume $\boldsymbol{\alpha} > 0$). Using the invariance property of MLE, we can obtain the MLE of $\boldsymbol{\theta}$ from the MLE of $\boldsymbol{\alpha}$ as follows. Without loss of generality, we assume that $n_{1,y} + n_{0,y} > 0$ for $y = 1, \ldots, |P|$.

Proposition 1. *If the measurement matrix A has full column rank and there is at least one successful probe per path (i.e., $n_{1,y} > 0$ for $y = 1, \ldots, |P|$), then the MLE for loss tomography equals*[6]*:*

$$\hat{\boldsymbol{\theta}} = \exp\left((A^T A)^{-1} A^T \log \hat{\boldsymbol{\alpha}}\right), \tag{5}$$

where $\hat{\boldsymbol{\alpha}}$ is the vector of empirical path success rates.

Remark: The MLE for loss tomography is only asymptotically unbiased (verified in Section 7.2) because of the non-linear operators (log, exp).

4.3 MLE for PDV Tomography

We follow a similar approach to derive the MLE for PDV tomography. Specifically, let $\sigma_y(\boldsymbol{\theta}) := \sum_{l \in p_y} \theta_l$ denote the PDV variance on path p_y. Under the zero-mean assumption, it is known that the MLE of $\sigma_y(\boldsymbol{\theta})$ is the empirical path variance $\hat{\sigma}_y := \frac{1}{n_y} \sum_{k=1}^{n_y} x_{y,k}^2$, where n_y is the number of probes sent on path p_y and $x_{y,k}$ the end-to-end PDV for the k-th probe on p_y; this MLE is unbiased. When A has full column rank, the link PDV variances $\boldsymbol{\theta}$ and the path PDV variances $\boldsymbol{\sigma} := (\sigma_y(\boldsymbol{\theta}))_{y=1}^{|P|}$ form a one-to-one transformation $\boldsymbol{\theta} = (A^T A)^{-1} A^T \boldsymbol{\sigma}$. We can then obtain the MLE of $\boldsymbol{\theta}$ as follows (assuming $n_y > 0$ for $y = 1, \ldots, |P|$).

Proposition 2. *If the measurement matrix A has full column rank, then the MLE for PDV tomography equals:*

$$\hat{\boldsymbol{\theta}} = (A^T A)^{-1} A^T \hat{\boldsymbol{\sigma}}, \tag{6}$$

where $\hat{\boldsymbol{\sigma}}$ is the vector of empirical path PDV variances.

[6]For ease of presentation, we use $g(\mathbf{z})$ to denote the vector obtained by applying a scalar function $g(\cdot)$ to each element of a vector $\mathbf{z}$.

Remark: The MLE for PDV tomography is unbiased (verified in Section 7.3).

Requirements on probing experiment: Applying the MLE formulas in Propositions 1 and 2 imposes certain requirements on the probing experiment: the set of paths for which there is at least one successful probe per path should form a full-column-rank measurement matrix (note that each probe for PDV measurement contains at least two packets). One way to satisfy this requirement is to employ an *initialization phase*, where we send one probe per path (recall that the entire path set P is assumed to give a full-column-rank measurement matrix). In the case of loss tomography, we also need to ensure non-zero empirical path success rates; we find a modified estimate $\tilde{\alpha}_y = 1/(1 + n_{0,y})$ for paths without a successful probe performs well[7] (note that the error caused by this modification diminishes as the number of probes increases).

5. OBJECTIVE OF EXPERIMENT DESIGN

The essence of FIM-based experiment design is to treat the CRB as an approximation of the estimation error matrix and select the design parameter $\boldsymbol{\phi}$ to optimize a given objective function based on the CRB. Given an estimate of $\boldsymbol{\theta}$, the FIM (and hence the CRB) only depends on $\boldsymbol{\phi}$, which in theory allows us to optimize $\boldsymbol{\phi}$. Solving this optimization, however, is highly nontrivial as it is an optimization of a $|P|$-dimensional vector, making numerical solutions infeasible for larger $|P|$ (i.e., larger networks). In this section, we will show that under certain conditions, satisfied by both loss and PDV tomography, the objective function has a special structure that allows for closed-form solutions.

5.1 D-Optimal Design

In D-optimal experiment design, we seek to minimize the determinant of the inverse FIM, $\det(I^{-1}(\boldsymbol{\theta}; \boldsymbol{\phi}))$, or equivalently maximize $\det(I(\boldsymbol{\theta}; \boldsymbol{\phi}))$. The CRB implies that this design minimizes the volume of the error ellipsoid.

We begin by establishing a special structure of $\det(I(\boldsymbol{\theta}; \boldsymbol{\phi}))$ that holds for any network topology and any set of probing paths, under certain conditions on the observation model. We first show a general property of the FIM as follows.

Lemma 3. *The FIM for the observation model (1) is a convex combination of per-path FIMs:*

$$I(\boldsymbol{\theta}; \boldsymbol{\phi}) = \sum_{y=1}^{|P|} \phi_y I^{(y)}(\boldsymbol{\theta}), \tag{7}$$

where $I^{(y)}(\boldsymbol{\theta})$ is the FIM for path p_y based on the observation model $f_y(x; \boldsymbol{\theta})$. Note that $I^{(y)}(\boldsymbol{\theta})$ is independent of $\boldsymbol{\phi}$ and is only a function of $\boldsymbol{\theta}$.

Based on this decomposition, we can show that the determinant of the FIM has a particular structure as follows.

Theorem 4. *Let $\mathcal{S}_n$ be the collection of all size-n subsets of $\{1, \ldots, |P|\}$. If the per-path FIM satisfies*

$$I_{i,k}^{(y)}(\boldsymbol{\theta}) I_{j,l}^{(y)}(\boldsymbol{\theta}) = I_{i,l}^{(y)}(\boldsymbol{\theta}) I_{j,k}^{(y)}(\boldsymbol{\theta}) \tag{8}$$

[7]Alternatively, one may keep probing each path until obtaining a success; this procedure is however not robust for paths with low success rates.

for any $y \in \{1, \ldots, |P|\}$ and any $i, j, k, l \in \{1, \ldots, |L|\}$, then there exist functions $B_C(\boldsymbol{\theta})$ ($C \in \mathcal{S}_{|L|}$) such that

$$\det(I(\boldsymbol{\theta};\boldsymbol{\phi})) = \sum_{C \in \mathcal{S}_{|L|}} B_C(\boldsymbol{\theta}) \prod_{i \in C} \phi_i. \tag{9}$$

Functions $B_C(\boldsymbol{\theta})$ ($C \in \mathcal{S}_{|L|}$) do not depend on $\boldsymbol{\phi}$.

Remark: This theorem describes a generic structure of $\det(I(\boldsymbol{\theta};\boldsymbol{\phi}))$ that applies to any tomography problem where condition (8) holds. In words, condition (8) states that any 2×2 submatrix of the per-path FIM formed by removing $|L|-2$ rows and $|L|-2$ columns has a determinant of zero, i.e., *any 2×2 minor of the per-path FIM (and the overall FIM) is zero*[8] (note that the condition holds trivially if $i = j$ or $k = l$). We will see in Section 5.4 that this condition holds for both loss and PDV tomography.

The essence of this theorem is that under condition (8), the determinant of the FIM, when viewed as a function of $\boldsymbol{\phi}$, can be written as a weighted sum of order-$|L|$ terms, where each term is a product of $|L|$ (out of $|P|$) *distinct* ϕ_i's. We will show later that this property helps to simplify our FIM-based experiment design. Theorem 4 implies, in particular, that when $|P| = |L|$, the determinant of the FIM equals:

$$\det(I(\boldsymbol{\theta};\boldsymbol{\phi})) = B(\boldsymbol{\theta}) \prod_{k=1}^{|L|} \phi_k. \tag{10}$$

Analogous arguments can be used to show a formula for any minor of the FIM as follows.

Corollary 5. *Let M be an n-dimensional submatrix of $I(\boldsymbol{\theta};\boldsymbol{\phi})$ after removing $|L|-n$ rows and columns, and $\mathcal{S}_n$ be defined as in Theorem 4. Then under condition (8), there exist functions $B_C(\boldsymbol{\theta})$ ($C \in \mathcal{S}_n$) such that the determinant of M (i.e., a* minor *of $I(\boldsymbol{\theta};\boldsymbol{\phi})$) equals:*

$$\det(M(\boldsymbol{\theta};\boldsymbol{\phi})) = \sum_{C \in \mathcal{S}_n} B_C(\boldsymbol{\theta}) \prod_{i \in C} \phi_i. \tag{11}$$

Functions $B_C(\boldsymbol{\theta})$ ($C \in \mathcal{S}_n$) do not depend on $\boldsymbol{\phi}$.

5.2 A-Optimal Design

In A-optimal experiment design, we seek to minimize the trace of the inverse FIM, $\mathrm{Tr}(I^{-1}(\boldsymbol{\theta};\boldsymbol{\phi}))$. The CRB states that this design minimizes the average mean squared error (MSE) for estimating $\boldsymbol{\theta}$.

We observe a special structure of $\mathrm{Tr}(I^{-1}(\boldsymbol{\theta};\boldsymbol{\phi}))$ as follows. When $|P| = |L|$, the result in (10) together with Corollary 5 can be used to prove the following structure of $\mathrm{Tr}(I^{-1}(\boldsymbol{\theta};\boldsymbol{\phi}))$.

Theorem 6. *Suppose $|P| = |L|$ and the FIM is invertible. If condition (8) holds, then the trace of the inverse FIM $\mathrm{Tr}(I^{-1}(\boldsymbol{\theta};\boldsymbol{\phi}))$ admits the following representation:*

$$\mathrm{Tr}(I^{-1}(\boldsymbol{\theta};\boldsymbol{\phi})) = \sum_{i=1}^{|L|} \frac{1}{\phi_i} \mathcal{A}_i(\boldsymbol{\theta}), \tag{12}$$

where $\mathcal{A}_1(\boldsymbol{\theta}), \ldots, \mathcal{A}_{|L|}(\boldsymbol{\theta})$ are only functions of $\boldsymbol{\theta}$.

[8]The $k \times k$ minor of an $m \times n$ matrix is the determinant of a submatrix obtained by removing $m-k$ rows and $n-k$ columns.

Remark: The proof actually gives a more general structure of $\mathrm{Tr}(I^{-1}(\boldsymbol{\theta};\boldsymbol{\phi}))$ for any $|P| \geq |L|$:

$$\mathrm{Tr}(I^{-1}(\boldsymbol{\theta};\boldsymbol{\phi})) = \frac{\sum_{C' \in \mathcal{S}_{|L|-1}} \prod_{i \in C'} \phi_i \left[\sum_{k=1}^{|L|} B_{C',k}(\boldsymbol{\theta})\right]}{\sum_{C \in \mathcal{S}_{|L|}} B_C(\boldsymbol{\theta}) \prod_{i \in C} \phi_i}, \tag{13}$$

where $B_{C',k}(\boldsymbol{\theta})$ and $B_C(\boldsymbol{\theta})$ are only functions of $\boldsymbol{\theta}$. We only highlight the special case of $|P| = |L|$ because it allows for efficient optimization of $\boldsymbol{\phi}$; see Section 6.1.

5.3 Weighted A-Optimal Design

In practice, applications may place different weights on the links. We extend the A-optimal design to account for this by introducing a *weight vector* $\boldsymbol{\omega} := (\omega_k)_{k=1}^{|L|}$, where ω_k denotes the importance of link l_k. Introducing weights changes the objective from minimizing $\mathrm{Tr}(I^{-1}(\boldsymbol{\theta};\boldsymbol{\phi}))$ to minimizing a *weighted trace* of $I^{-1}(\boldsymbol{\theta};\boldsymbol{\phi})$, i.e., the weighted sum of the diagonal elements of $I^{-1}(\boldsymbol{\theta};\boldsymbol{\phi})$: $\sum_{k=1}^{|L|} \omega_k I^{-1}_{k,k}(\boldsymbol{\theta};\boldsymbol{\phi})$. By the CRB, this design minimizes the weighted average MSE for estimating $\{\theta_l\}_{l \in L}$. We refer to this design as the *weighted A-optimal design.*

Using analogous arguments, we can easily extend Theorem 6 to the following result.

Corollary 7. *Under the conditions in Theorem 6, the weighted trace of the inverse FIM admits the following representation:*

$$\sum_{k=1}^{|L|} \omega_k I^{-1}_{k,k}(\boldsymbol{\theta};\boldsymbol{\phi}) = \sum_{i=1}^{|L|} \frac{1}{\phi_i} \widetilde{\mathcal{A}}_i(\boldsymbol{\theta}), \tag{14}$$

where $\widetilde{\mathcal{A}}_1(\boldsymbol{\theta}), \ldots, \widetilde{\mathcal{A}}_{|L|}(\boldsymbol{\theta})$ are only functions of $\boldsymbol{\theta}$.

Remark: Since the weighted A-optimal design contains the A-optimal design as a special case, we only consider the weighted A-optimal design in the sequel, simply referred to as "A-optimal".

5.4 Application to Loss/PDV Tomography

We now apply our generic results to concrete tomography problems. To apply these results, we need to answer two questions: (i) Does condition (8) hold for the problem at hand? (ii) Can we evaluate the coefficient functions in the derived formulas (i.e., $B_C(\boldsymbol{\theta})$, $\mathcal{A}_i(\boldsymbol{\theta})$, and $\widetilde{\mathcal{A}}_i(\boldsymbol{\theta})$) for a given value of $\boldsymbol{\theta}$? In this subsection, we give positive answers to both questions for loss tomography and PDV tomography.

5.4.1 Application to Packet Loss Tomography

Based on the observation model (2), we can obtain the per-path FIM $I^{(y)}(\boldsymbol{\theta})$ for loss tomography, whose (i, j)-th entry equals

$$I^{(y)}_{i,j}(\boldsymbol{\theta}) = \frac{\alpha_y(\boldsymbol{\theta})}{\theta_i \theta_j (1-\alpha_y(\boldsymbol{\theta}))} \{i, j \in p_y\}, \tag{15}$$

where $\{\cdot\}$ is the indicator function. It is easy to verify that this FIM satisfies condition (8), and thus the formulas in Theorem 4, Theorem 6, and Corollary 7 apply.

To derive explicit expressions for their coefficients, we take a detailed look at the FIM, which leads to a decomposition into a product of matrices with special structures. Substituting (15) into (7) gives the (i,j)-th entry of the FIM:

$$I_{i,j}(\boldsymbol{\theta};\boldsymbol{\phi}) = \sum_{y=1}^{|P|} \phi_y \frac{\alpha_y(\boldsymbol{\theta})}{\theta_i \theta_j (1-\alpha_y(\boldsymbol{\theta}))} \{i, j \in p_y\}. \tag{16}$$

We introduce two auxiliary matrics[9]: $D = \text{diag}\left((d_y)_{y=1}^{|P|}\right)$ for $d_y := \phi_y \alpha_y(\boldsymbol{\theta})/(1-\alpha_y(\boldsymbol{\theta}))$, and $\Theta = \text{diag}(\boldsymbol{\theta})$. Then the above FIM can be written in matrix form as

$$I(\boldsymbol{\theta};\boldsymbol{\phi}) = \Theta^{-1}A^T D A \Theta^{-1}, \tag{17}$$

where A is the measurement matrix.

Based on this decomposition, we can evaluate its determinant and trace of the inverse as functions of Θ, A, and D, leading to the following results.

Lemma 8. *Let A_C denote a $|L| \times |L|$ submatrix of the measurement matrix A formed by rows with indices in C ($C \in \mathcal{S}_{|L|}$). Then $\det(I(\boldsymbol{\theta};\boldsymbol{\phi}))$ for loss tomography can be expressed as (9) with coefficients*

$$B_C(\boldsymbol{\theta}) = \frac{\det(A_C)^2}{\prod_{l\in L}\theta_l^2}\prod_{i\in C}\frac{\alpha_i(\boldsymbol{\theta})}{1-\alpha_i(\boldsymbol{\theta})} \tag{18}$$

for each $C \in \mathcal{S}_{|L|}$.

Moreover, if $|P| = |L|$ and $I(\boldsymbol{\theta};\boldsymbol{\phi})$ is invertible, then $\text{Tr}(I^{-1}(\boldsymbol{\theta};\boldsymbol{\phi}))$ *can be expressed as (12) with coefficients*

$$\mathcal{A}_i(\boldsymbol{\theta}) = \frac{1-\alpha_i(\boldsymbol{\theta})}{\alpha_i(\boldsymbol{\theta})}\sum_{k=1}^{|L|}\theta_k^2 b_{k,i}^2 \tag{19}$$

for $i = 1,\dots,|L|$, where $b_{k,i}$ is the (k,i)-th entry of[10] *A^{-1}. Similarly, the weighted sum of the diagonal elements of $I^{-1}(\boldsymbol{\theta};\boldsymbol{\phi})$ can be expressed as (14) with coefficients*

$$\widetilde{\mathcal{A}}_i(\boldsymbol{\theta}) = \frac{1-\alpha_i(\boldsymbol{\theta})}{\alpha_i(\boldsymbol{\theta})}\sum_{k=1}^{|L|}\omega_k\theta_k^2 b_{k,i}^2, \tag{20}$$

where ω_k is the weight of link l_k.

5.4.2 Application to PDV Tomography

Similarly, from the observation model (3), we can derive the per-path FIM for PDV tomography as

$$I_{i,j}^{(y)}(\boldsymbol{\theta}) = \frac{1}{2\left(\sum_{l\in p_y}\theta_l\right)^2} \quad \{i,j \in p_y\}, \tag{21}$$

which also satisfies condition (8).

Applying (21) to (7) gives an expression for individual entries of the FIM for PDV tomography. Observing its similarity to the FIM for loss tomography, we again write it in matrix form by introducing another auxiliary matrix $E = \text{diag}\left((e_y)_{y=1}^{|P|}\right)$ for $e_y := \phi_y/[2(\sum_{l\in p_y}\theta_l)^2]$. It can be verified that the FIM for PDV tomography satisfies $I(\boldsymbol{\theta};\boldsymbol{\phi}) = A^T E A$. This decomposition leads to the following results.

Lemma 9. *For PDV tomography, $\det(I(\boldsymbol{\theta};\boldsymbol{\phi}))$ can be expressed as (9) with coefficients*

$$B_C(\boldsymbol{\theta}) = \frac{\det(A_C)^2}{2^{|L|}\prod_{i\in C}\left(\sum_{l\in p_i}\theta_l\right)^2} \tag{22}$$

for each $C \in \mathcal{S}_{|L|}$ (A_C defined as in Lemma 8).

Moreover, if $|P| = |L|$ and $I(\boldsymbol{\theta};\boldsymbol{\phi})$ is invertible, then $\text{Tr}(I^{-1}(\boldsymbol{\theta};\boldsymbol{\phi}))$ *can be expressed as (12) with coefficients*

$$\mathcal{A}_i(\boldsymbol{\theta}) = 2\left(\sum_{l\in p_i}\theta_l\right)^2\sum_{k=1}^{|L|}b_{k,i}^2 \tag{23}$$

for $i = 1,\dots,|L|$ ($b_{k,i}$ is the (k,i)-th entry of A^{-1}). Similarly, the weighted sum of the diagonal elements of $I^{-1}(\boldsymbol{\theta};\boldsymbol{\phi})$ can be expressed as (14) with coefficients

$$\widetilde{\mathcal{A}}_i(\boldsymbol{\theta}) = 2\left(\sum_{l\in p_i}\theta_l\right)^2\sum_{k=1}^{|L|}\omega_k b_{k,i}^2. \tag{24}$$

6. EXPERIMENT DESIGN ALGORITHMS

The special structures of the design objectives established in Section 5 enable us to compute the design parameter $\boldsymbol{\phi}$ efficiently. In the sequel, we will first derive closed-form solutions for the case of $|P| = |L|$, i.e., all probing paths are linearly independent, and then address the case of $|P| > |L|$.

6.1 Closed-form Solution for $|P| = |L|$

For the D-optimal design, Theorem 4 implies that when $|P| = |L|$, the determinant of the FIM is proportional to the product of ϕ_i's as shown in (10). Since $\sum_{i=1}^{|L|}\phi_i = 1$, by the inequality of arithmetic and geometric means, we see that (10) is maximized by setting $\phi_i = 1/|L|$ for all $i = 1,\dots,|L|$.

Claim 10. *Uniform probing (i.e., $\phi_i = 1/|P|$) is D-optimal when $|P| = |L|$.*

For the A-optimal design, it is easy to show, using the Lagrange Multiplier method, that a closed-form solution for minimizing (12) wrt $\boldsymbol{\phi}$ is the following:

$$\phi_i = \frac{\sqrt{\mathcal{A}_i(\boldsymbol{\theta})}}{\sum_{j=1}^{|L|}\sqrt{\mathcal{A}_j(\boldsymbol{\theta})}}, \tag{25}$$

for $i = 1,2,\dots,|L|$. The solution for the weighted A-optimal design is analogous, except that $\mathcal{A}_i(\boldsymbol{\theta})$ is replaced by $\widetilde{\mathcal{A}}_i(\boldsymbol{\theta})$.

6.2 Heuristic Solution for $|P| > |L|$

When $|P| > |L|$, the computation of the optimal design becomes more complicated. From the example in Fig. 2, we see that uniform probing is no longer D-optimal. Computing the exact D/A-optimal design involves optimizing a $|P|$-variable function (9) or (13), which can only be solved numerically for very small networks. To develop a scalable solution, we leverage the closed-form solution in the case of $|P| = |L|$. We illustrate our idea by a small example in Fig. 3. Suppose links l_1, l_2, and l_3 have success rates 0.2, 0.1, and 0.3, respectively. Numerical calculation gives the A-optimal design for inferring these link success rates in the last row of the table. Alternatively, we can select a basis of paths[11] and use the solution in (25) to compute the optimal design when only probing paths in the basis; see the first four rows of the table. We see that although the optimal design may use all paths, a design that only optimizes $\boldsymbol{\phi}$ for a properly selected basis can achieve near-optimal performance (see Figs. 9 and 12 for more comprehensive evaluations).

[9]Here diag $(\mathbf{d})$ denotes a diagonal matrix with the main diagonal $\mathbf{d}$.

[10]Given identifiability of $\boldsymbol{\theta}$, A must be invertible in this case; see Section 3.2.

[11]Here, 'basis' means a subset of $|L|$ paths that provide an invertible measurement matrix.

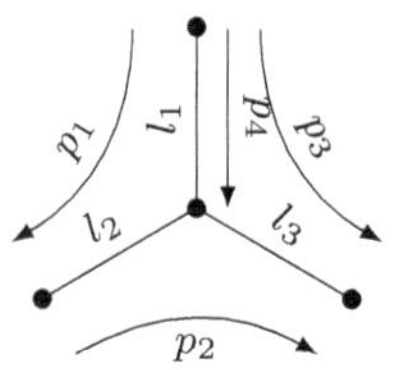

ϕ_1	ϕ_2	ϕ_3	ϕ_4	$\mathrm{Tr}(I^{-1})$
0.42	0.34	0.24	0	9.70
0.47	0.37	0	0.16	21.79
0.27	0	0.45	0.28	6.95
0	0.22	0.49	0.29	6.60†
0.17	0.15	0.44	0.24	5.94*

Figure 3: Example for heuristic solution. *: A-optimal; †: A-optimal on the best basis.

Algorithm 1 Two-step Experiment Design for Given $\boldsymbol{\theta}$

```
1: P_B ← P
2: for iteration i = 1, ..., |P| − |L| do
3:     for path p ∈ P_B do
4:         if P_B \ p has rank |L| then
5:             evaluate design objective when only using paths
               in P_B \ p
6:             record path p* that yields the optimal objective
7:     P_B ← P_B \ p*
8: compute optimal φ_y for p_y ∈ P_B; set φ_y to 0 for p_y ∉ P_B
```

Algorithm 2 Iterative Experiment Design

```
1: φ_y ← 1/|P| for y = 1, ..., |P|
2: for iteration i = 1, ..., N/k do
3:     send k probes according to φ
4:     update θ̂ based on probing results
5:     compute a new design parameter φ̂ by Algorithm 1
       using the updated θ̂
6:     update design parameter φ ← (1 − ik/N)φ + (ik/N)φ̂
```

This observation motivates a two-step heuristic solution, where we first pick a basis of paths that gives the optimal objective value among all bases, and then optimize $\boldsymbol{\phi}$ using solutions in Section 6.1 for paths in the basis, while setting $\phi_y = 0$ for paths not in the basis. However, optimizing the basis is itself a combinatorial optimization that is hard to solve exactly. To select a basis, we propose a backward greedy algorithm, given in Algorithm 1. Starting with all $|P|$ paths, it iteratively deselects one path at a time to optimize the design objective (determinant, trace, or weighted trace of $I^{-1}(\boldsymbol{\theta};\boldsymbol{\phi})$), and the iteration continues until the remaining paths form a basis (lines 2–7). To evaluate the design objective (line 5) before calculating $\boldsymbol{\phi}$, we assume uniform $\boldsymbol{\phi}$ for the selected paths.

6.3 Iterative Design Algorithm

In general, the optimal design depends on the unknown parameter $\boldsymbol{\theta}$, which can only be estimated after collecting some measurements. This motivates an iterative design algorithm, presented in Algorithm 2. Specifically, we conduct probing in N/k iterations of k probes each. In each iteration, we send k probes on paths selected according to the current $\boldsymbol{\phi}$ (line 3), update the estimate $\hat{\boldsymbol{\theta}}$ based on the probing results (line 4), and then compute a new design parameter $\hat{\boldsymbol{\phi}}$ using the updated estimate (line 5). During first few iterations, we may not have sufficient measurements to accurately estimate $\boldsymbol{\theta}$, which can mislead our design. To improve robustness against estimation error, we use a combination of the current $\boldsymbol{\phi}$ (obtained from the previous iteration) and the new $\hat{\boldsymbol{\phi}}$ (computed by line 5), and give increasing weight to $\hat{\boldsymbol{\phi}}$ as we obtain more measurements (line 6).

How does the iteratively designed $\hat{\boldsymbol{\phi}}$ converge to the $\boldsymbol{\phi}$ designed based on the true value of $\boldsymbol{\theta}$? Intuitively, as we obtain more measurements, the estimated $\hat{\boldsymbol{\theta}}$ will converge to $\boldsymbol{\theta}$, and thus the iteratively designed $\hat{\boldsymbol{\phi}}$ will converge to the $\boldsymbol{\phi}$ optimized for $\boldsymbol{\theta}$. Formalizing this intuition requires two steps: first, we need to show that the design objectives (e.g., trace of the inverse FIM) computed from $\hat{\boldsymbol{\theta}}$ and $\boldsymbol{\theta}$ will converge so that we will select the correct basis P_B; moreover, we need to show that for a fixed P_B, the optimal ϕ_y ($p_y \in P_B$) based on $\hat{\boldsymbol{\theta}}$ and $\boldsymbol{\theta}$ will converge. We now provide concrete analysis for loss and PDV tomography. We only consider the A-optimal design due to space limitation, as results are analogous for the other design objectives.

Theorem 11. *For both loss and PDV tomography, as the number of probes per path increases, the estimated objective of the A-optimal design (i.e., trace of the inverse FIM based on $\hat{\boldsymbol{\theta}}$) converges to the true objective with high probability. Moreover, for a fixed basis P_B, the A-optimal design on P_B based on $\hat{\boldsymbol{\theta}}$ converges to the true A-optimal design on P_B based on $\boldsymbol{\theta}$ with high probability.*

7. PERFORMANCE EVALUATION

We evaluate different experiment designs by packet-level simulations on real network topologies and link parameters. Our goal in the evaluation is two-fold: (i) evaluating the performance of (iterative) A-optimal design compared with uniformly allocating probes (*uniform probing*), and (ii) evaluating the impact of system parameters such as link weights, number of monitors, and number of paths.

To guarantee identifiability of all the link parameters, we first place a minimum set of monitors by the *Minimum Monitor Placement (MMP)* algorithm in [11] and then place the remaining monitors, if any, randomly. Given the monitors, we first construct $|L|$ linearly independent paths by the *Spanning Tree-based Path Construction (STPC)* algorithm in [12] and then construct additional paths if needed by a random walk[12]. We consider two types of link weights: *homogeneous* link weights, where all links have unit weight, and *heterogeneous* link weights, where a randomly selected subset of K links have a larger weight Ω ($\Omega > 1$), and the rest of the links have unit weight. In the case of heterogeneous link weights, we set $K = 1$ and $\Omega = 500$.

We measure the performance of an experiment design by the (weighted) average MSE and bias over all estimated link parameters when applying the MLE (Section 4) to measurements collected using this design. Furthermore, we evaluate the CRB and the design parameter $\boldsymbol{\phi}$ to gain insights on the internal behaviors of various designs. All results are averaged over 5 instances of monitor locations, measurement paths, and link weights, and 100 Monte Carlo runs of probing simulations per instance. In each Monte Carlo run, we simulate 10^5 probes, which is divided into 100 iterations of 1000 probes each for the iterative design.

7.1 Dataset for Evaluation

To evaluate our experiment design in a realistic scenario, we use the Roofnet dataset [1], which contains topologies and link measurements from a 38-node wireless mesh network. The dataset contains four subsets of data, correspond-

[12]We remove cycles from the random-walk paths so that all paths are cycle-free, although this is not required for the design of probe allocation.

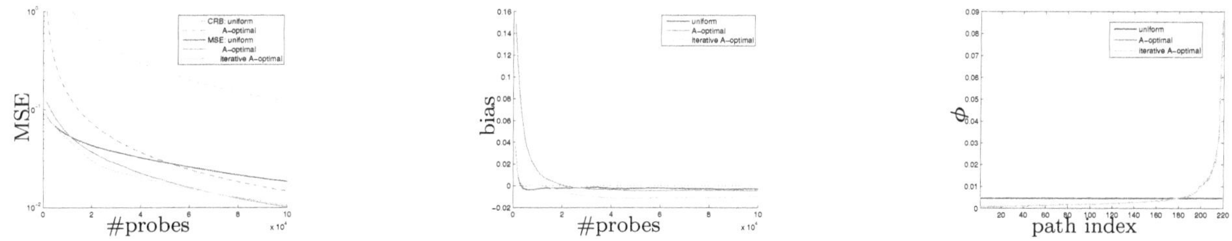

(a) MSE and CRB (b) Bias (c) ϕ

Figure 6: Loss tomography, homogeneous link weights (20 monitors, 219 paths)

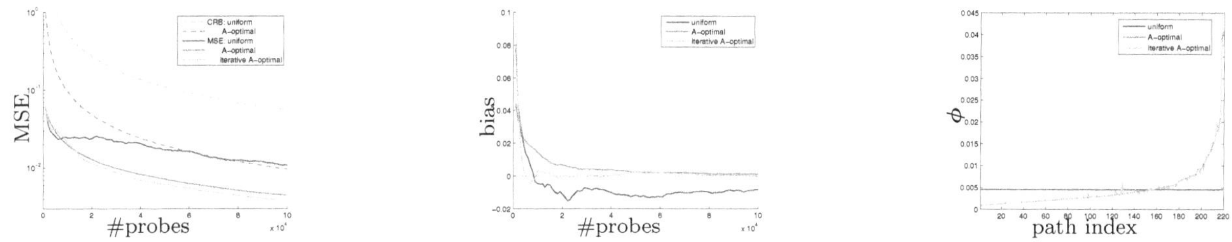

(a) MSE and CRB (b) Bias (c) ϕ

Figure 7: Loss tomography, heterogeneous link weights (20 monitors, 219 paths)

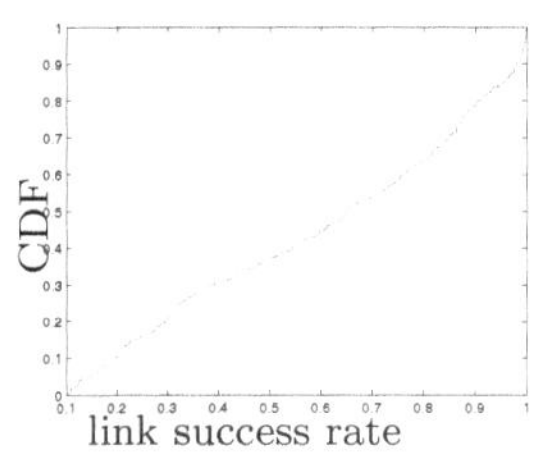

Figure 4: Distribution of Roofnet link success rates.

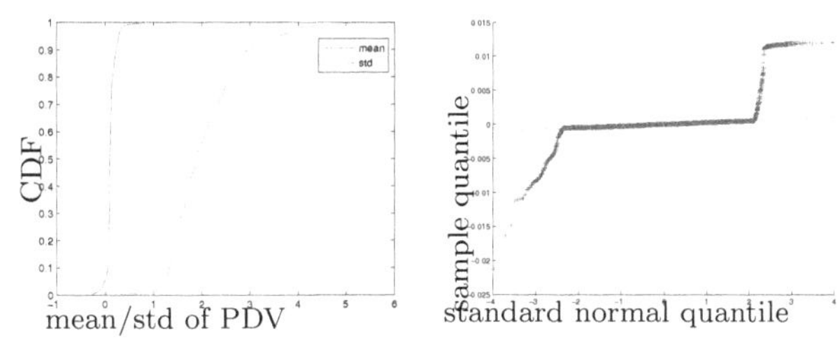

(a) mean/std of link PDV (ms) (b) Q-Q plot

Figure 5: Distribution of Roofnet link PDVs.

Table 1: Relative Performance for Loss Tomography (20 monitors, 10^5 probes)

Link weights	$\frac{CRB^A}{CRB^U}$	$\frac{MSE^A}{MSE^U}$	$\frac{MSE^I}{MSE^U}$
homogeneous	0.12	0.55	0.58
heterogeneous	0.18	0.41	0.35

ing to data rates 1, 2, 5.5, and 11 Mbps. We only present results based on the 1-Mbps data, as the results are similar to those for the other data rates. The raw dataset contains sent/received packet sequence numbers and timestamps between all pairs of nodes within communication range.

This dataset is suitable for evaluating both loss tomography and PDV tomography. For loss tomography, we extract link success rates by computing the fraction of packets sent by a first node that are received by a second node. For PDV tomography, we extract link PDVs by computing the difference between inter-packet delays at a sender and a receiver (ignoring lost packets). We then take the average of both directions of transmission as the parameter of a link[13]. We also filter out links with success rates below 0.1 to only focus on useful links. After filtering, we obtain a topology with 38 nodes and 219 (undirected) links; see Fig. 4 and 5 (a) for distributions of the link parameters. We also compare the empirical PDV distribution per link with the normal distribution; see Fig. 5 (b) for the Quantile-Quantile (Q-Q) plot for a sample link (dashed line corresponds to a true normal distribution). We see that the mean PDVs are much smaller than the standard deviations (std's), and that the majority (90%+) of the PDV values fit a normal distribution (similar results are observed for other links), both confirming our zero-mean normal assumption in Section 2.2.2.

7.2 Evaluation of Loss Tomography

We first evaluate the performance of different designs as the number of probes increases; see Fig. 6 for results under homogeneous link weights, and Fig. 7 for results under heterogeneous link weights. From Fig. 6 (a) and 7 (a), we see that the A-optimal design and its iterative version achieve lower MSE than uniform probing, and the improvement is greater under heterogeneous link weights. Examining the design parameter ϕ under each design (Fig. 6 (c) and 7 (c)) verifies that this improvement is achieved through nonuniformly allocating probes to better measure the paths that provide more information for estimating link success rates (paths are sorted in the order of increasing probing probabilities under the A-optimal design). The same figure also verifies that the iterative design is able to converge to the true A-optimal design (their curves essentially overlap); we will evaluate the rate of convergence later. Interestingly, for loss tomography, the MLE (Eq. (5)) is biased at finite sample sizes as shown in Fig. 6 (b) and 7 (b), and thus the CRB does not provide a true lower bound on the MSE as shown in

[13]Note that the realizations of link losses/PDVs for each probe are generated according to our model, using parameters extracted from the dataset.

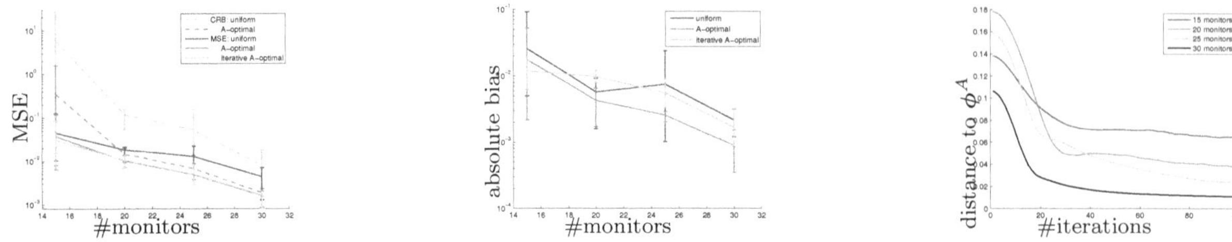

(a) MSE and CRB (b) Absolute bias (c) Convergence of ϕ^I

Figure 8: Loss tomography, varying number of monitors (219 paths, 10^5 probes, homogeneous link weights)

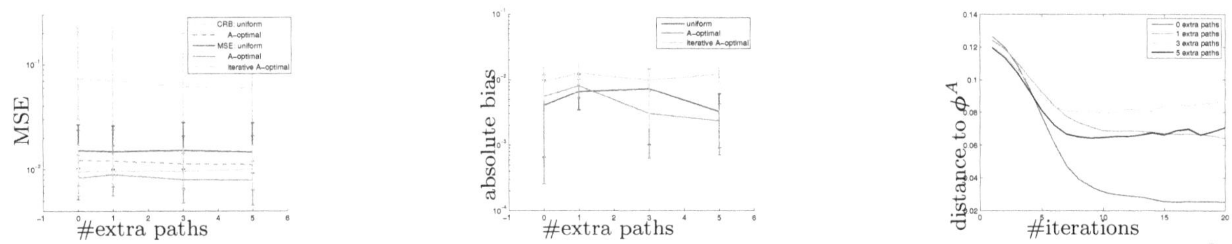

(a) MSE and CRB (b) Absolute bias (c) Convergence of ϕ^I

Figure 9: Loss tomography, varying number of paths (20 monitors, 10^5 probes, homogeneous link weights)

Table 2: Relative Performance for PDV Tomography (20 monitors, 10^5 probes)

Link weights	$\frac{CRB^A}{CRB^U}$	$\frac{MSE^A}{MSE^U}$	$\frac{MSE^I}{MSE^U}$
homogeneous	0.47	0.47	0.48
heterogeneous	0.38	0.39	0.39

Fig. 6 (a) and 7 (a). Nevertheless, the CRB captures trends of the MSE so that minimizing the CRB provides a design (i.e., A-optimal design) with low MSE.

To better appreciate the advantage of A-optimal design, we summarize the relative performance of the A-optimal and the iterative A-optimal designs compared with uniform probing, measured by ratios of their CRB and MSE (the lower, the better); see Table 1, where $\{\cdot\}^A$ stands for A-optimal, $\{\cdot\}^U$ for uniform, and $\{\cdot\}^I$ for iterative A-optimal. We see that although the CRB overestimates performance improvement, our iterative design algorithm used in conjunction with the A-optimal criterion indeed achieves a much lower MSE than uniform probing (40–65% lower). Since our design takes into account different link weights, it achieves greater improvement in the case of heterogeneous link weights.

Next, we study the impact of system parameters on estimation performance. We first vary the number of monitors and repeat the probing simulation under each instance of monitor placement. Figs. 8 (a)–(b) show the error bar plots of MSE/CRB and absolute bias computed over different instances of monitor placement and path construction. The result shows that all probing methods benefit as we place more monitors. Intuitively, this is because with more monitors, paths become shorter, making the measurements less aggregated and more informative for inferring parameters of individual links. We also evaluate the impact on convergence rate of the iterative design by measuring the L_2-distance of the iterative design (ϕ^I) to the A-optimal design (ϕ^A) across iterations; see Fig. 8 (c). The result verifies that the iterative design algorithm is able to quickly converge to the true A-optimal design. Moreover, the convergence becomes faster as the number of monitors increases, because a larger number of monitors allows more accurate estimation of the link parameters and thus closer approximation of the true A-optimal design. We only show the results under homogeneous link weights, as the observations are analogous under heterogeneous link weights.

So far we have limited probing to a basis of paths. To evaluate the impact of probing extra paths, we add paths constructed by a random walk (#extra paths $= |P| - |L|$) and repeat the simulations; see Fig. 9. Since when $|P| > |L|$, the A-optimal design can no longer be computed in closed form, we only compute a constrained A-optimal design on a basis selected by Algorithm 1 (based on the true value of $\boldsymbol{\theta}$), simply referred to as 'A-optimal'. Due to the higher complexity of Algorithm 1 in this case, we reduce the number of iterations to 20, each with 5000 probes. We see that although the constrained A-optimal design given by Algorithm 1 only probes a subset of paths (i.e., a basis), it still performs notably better than uniform probing which probes all the paths by strategically allocating probes (Fig. 9 (a)–(b)). In contrast to adding monitors, adding paths does not significantly impact the MSE; we do not observe a clear trend in bias. Meanwhile, we see from Fig. 9 (c) that having extra paths significantly slows down convergence of the iterative design. Detailed examination shows that this is due to near-tie between some bases in terms of the objective value (trace of the inverse FIM). Nevertheless, Fig. 9 (a) shows that the iterative design outperforms uniform probing in terms of MSE. We have obtained similar results under heterogeneous link weights (omitted due to space limitation).

7.3 Evaluation of PDV Tomography

We have evaluated PDV tomography in a similar manner. Specifically, Fig. 10 shows the performance wrt number of probes in a basic setting with homogeneous link weights, Fig. 11 shows the impact of placing more monitors, and Fig. 12 shows the impact of probing more paths. We have obtained similar results under heterogeneous link weights (omitted). Overall, the relative performances of different

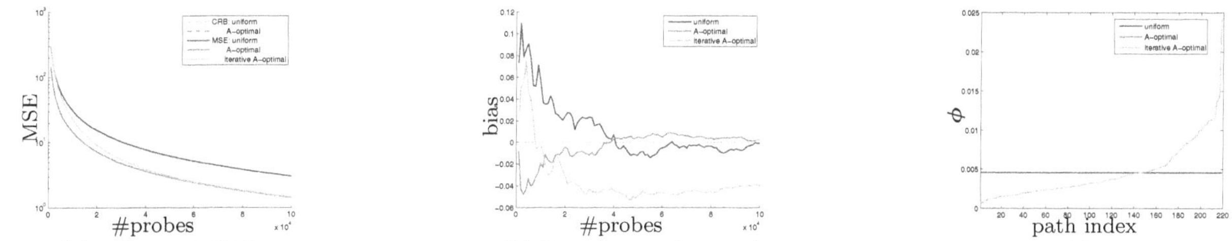

(a) MSE and CRB (b) Bias (mean $\theta_l = 4.8$) (c) ϕ

Figure 10: PDV tomography, varying number of probes (20 monitors, 219 paths, homogeneous link weights)

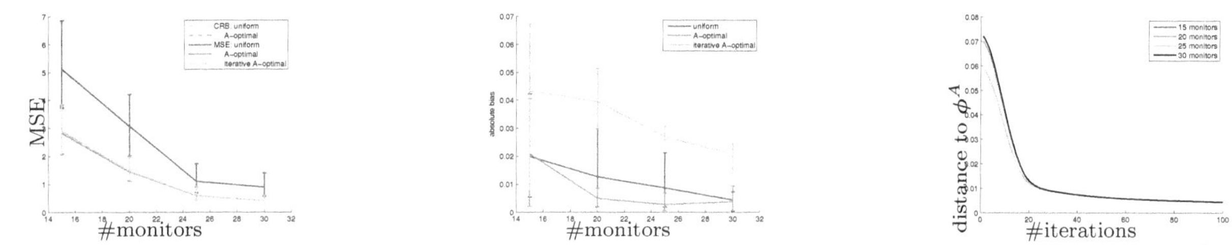

(a) MSE and CRB (b) Absolute bias (c) Convergence of ϕ^I

Figure 11: PDV tomography, varying number of monitors (219 paths, 10^5 probes, homogeneous link weights)

designs are similar to those for loss tomography, but the absolute performances differ.

Specifically, the estimation error for PDV tomography decays faster than that for loss tomography as the number of probes increases, as each measurement (path PDV) contains more fine-grained information about the links. As a consequence, the MSE values in Fig. 10 (a) are much smaller than those in Fig. 6 (a) for the same number of probes. A more striking difference between the two plots is that instead of being a loose approximation of MSE as in loss tomography, the CRB accurately predicts the MSE in PDV tomography (the curves overlap). This is because the estimator for PDV tomography (Eq. (6)) is unbiased, as verified by Fig. 10 (b); note that the empirical bias is negligible compared to the parameters of interest (link PDV variances). As in loss tomography, the A-optimal design for PDV tomography leads to a highly skewed distribution of probes across paths, as shown in Fig. 10 (c). Similar to Table 1 for loss tomography, we summarize the relative performance for PDV tomography in Table 2, which shows that the iterative design achieves a similar improvement of 50–60% for PDV tomography, but the performance predicted by the CRB is much more accurate.

As we vary the number of monitors, we again see a clear trend of decreasing CRB/MSE in Fig. 11 (a). A key difference from the results for loss tomography (Fig. 8 (a)) is that the CRB accurately predicts the value of the MSE. A more subtle difference is that as we increase the number of monitors, the gap between (iterative) A-optimal and uniform probing becomes narrower, instead of becoming wider as in loss tomography. We also see a trend of slightly decreasing absolute bias, and that the iterative design incurs a slightly larger bias; see Fig. 11 (b). Note, however, that the difference in bias is insignificant as the estimator is statistically unbiased. Another difference from loss tomography is that the convergence rate of iterative design for PDV tomography is largely independent of the number of monitors, as shown in Fig. 11 (c).

As we vary the number of paths, we see from Fig. 12 (a) that the MSE of uniform and A-optimal probing (on a basis selected by Algorithm 1) remains largely the same, so does their CRB. We notice a mild but notable increase in the MSE of the iterative A-optimal design, because having extra paths slows down the convergence of the design parameter, as shown in Fig. 12 (c). Note that the convergence is much faster than that in loss tomography (Fig. 9 (c)), because the parameters of interest (link PDV variances) can be estimated more accurately using the same number of probes (see Fig. 10 (a) and 6 (a)). As in loss tomography, increasing the number of paths does not have monotone impact on the bias as shown in Fig. 12 (b).

8. CONCLUSION

We propose a general framework of optimal experiment design for inferring parameters of stochastic link metrics using path measurements, with two concrete case studies on loss tomography and PDV tomography. Using the FIM to measure the amount of information contained in each measurement, we formulate the problem as an optimization of probe distribution across paths, with two widely-adopted objectives known as D-optimality and A-optimality. We are particularly interested in A-optimal design since it is directly linked to MSE and can be easily extended to incorporate different link weights. Under certain conditions on the FIM, satisfied for both loss and PDV tomography, we derive explicit expressions for both objectives as functions of the design parameter, which enable closed-form solution of the optimal design when the probing paths are linearly independent. Using this solution as a building block, we develop a two-step heuristic and an iterative algorithm to address the issues of linearly dependent paths and dependency on unknown parameters. Our evaluations on real datasets verify the effectiveness of the proposed solution in reducing MSE, even if the FIM-based bound can be loose.

Discussion: While our design is based on probabilistic allocation of probes, our solution can be easily modified for deterministic probe allocation. Specifically, our formulas for the design objectives derived in Section 5 remain valid when replacing the probing probability ϕ_y by the allocated num-

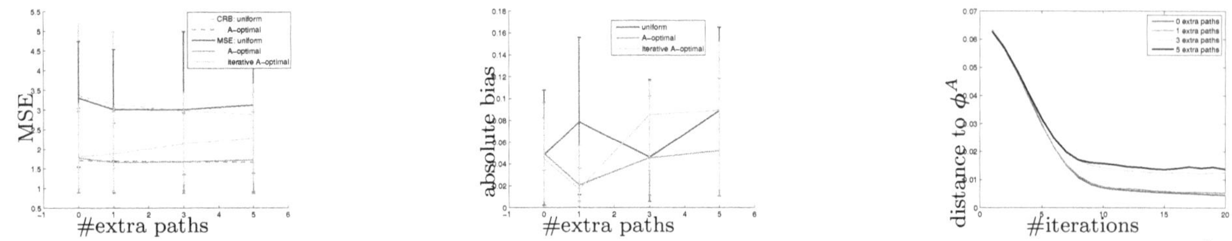

(a) MSE and CRB (b) Absolute bias (c) Convergence of ϕ^I

Figure 12: PDV tomography, varying number of paths (20 monitors, 10^5 probes, homogeneous link weights)

ber of probes N_y for each path p_y. Based on these formulas, one can derive analogous solutions to $(N_y)_{y=1}^{|P|}$, under the new constraints that $\sum_{y=1}^{|P|} N_y = N$ (N: total number of probes) and N_y's are integers. Relaxing the integer constraint yields $N_y = \phi_y N$, where ϕ_y is the design parameter computed by our current solution, the rounding of which leads to a deterministic probe allocation. However, deterministic probe allocation faces an additional challenge in iterative design, where the *order* of probing also needs to be optimized to obtain useful estimates as early as possible. In this regard, the probabilistic design framework simplifies the design process.

9. REFERENCES

[1] D. Aguayo, J. Bicket, S. Biswas, G. Judd, and R. Morris. Link-level measurements from an 802.11b mesh network. In *SIGCOMM*, 2004.

[2] A.C. Atkinson and A.N. Donev. *Optimum Experimental Designs*. Clarendon Press, 1992.

[3] S. Boyd and L. Vandenberghe. *Convex Optimization*. Cambridge University Press, 2004.

[4] R. Caceres, N.G. Duffield, J. Horowitz, D. Towsley, and T. Bu. Multicast-based inference of network-internal characteristics: Accuracy of packet loss estimation. *IEEE Trans. Info. Thy*, 45:2462–2480, 1998.

[5] M. Coates, A. O. Hero, R. Nowak, and B. Yu. Internet tomography. *IEEE Signal Processing Magzine*, 19:47–65, 2002.

[6] N. Duffield, F. Lo Presti, V. Paxson, and D. Towsley. Network loss tomography using striped unicast probes. *IEEE/ACM Trans. Networking*, 14(4):697–710, Aug 2006.

[7] N.G. Duffield and F. Lo Presti. Multicast inference of packet delay variance at interior network links. In *IEEE INFOCOM*, 2000.

[8] T. Gu, G. Jiang, V. Singh, and Y. Zhang. Optimal probing for unicast network delay tomography. In *IEEE INFOCOM*, 2010.

[9] A. Krishnamurthy and A. Singh. Robust multi-source network tomography using selective probes. In *IEEE INFOCOM*, 2012.

[10] F. Lo Presti, N.G. Duffield, J. Horowitz, and D. Towsley. Multicast-based inference of network-internal delay distributions. *IEEE/ACM Trans. Networking*, 10(6):761–775, Dec. 2002.

[11] L. Ma, T. He, K.K. Leung, A. Swami, and D. Towsley. Identifiability of link metrics based on end-to-end path measurements. In *ACM IMC*, 2013.

[12] L. Ma, T. He, K.K. Leung, D. Towsley, and A. Swami. Efficient identification of additive link metrics via network tomography. In *ICDCS*, 2013.

[13] H.V. Poor. *An Introduction to Signal Detection and Estimation*. Springer, 1994.

[14] T. J. Rothenberg. Identification in parametric models. *Econometrica*, 39:577–591, May 1971.

[15] M. Shih and A. Hero. Unicast inference of network link delay distributions from edge measurements. In *IEEE ICASSP*, 2001.

[16] H. Singhal and G. Michailidis. Optimal sampling in state space models with applications to network monitoring. In *ACM SIGMETRICS*, 2008.

[17] H. L. Van Trees. *Detection, estimation, and modulation theory*. John Wiley&Sons, 2004.

[18] B. Xi, G. Michailidis, and V. N. Nair. Estimating network loss rates using active tomography. *Journal of the American Statistical Association*, 101:1430–1448, December 2006.

[19] Y. Zhao, Y. Chen, and D. Bindel. Towards unbiased end-to-end network diagnosis. In *SIGCOMM*, 2006.

Appendix

Proof of Lemma 3. Let $\mathcal{L}(\boldsymbol{\theta})$ and $\mathcal{L}_y(\boldsymbol{\theta})$ be the log-likelihood functions for the overall experiment and path p_y, respectively (both are implicitly functions of x and $\boldsymbol{\phi}$). Since $\mathcal{L}(\boldsymbol{\theta}) = \log \phi_y + \mathcal{L}_y(\boldsymbol{\theta})$, applying the definition of FIM in (4) yields:

$$I_{i,j}(\boldsymbol{\theta};\boldsymbol{\phi}) = \sum_{y=1}^{|P|} \phi_y \mathbb{E}\left[\left(\frac{\partial}{\partial\theta_i}\mathcal{L}_y(\boldsymbol{\theta})\right)\left(\frac{\partial}{\partial\theta_j}\mathcal{L}_y(\boldsymbol{\theta})\right)\middle|\boldsymbol{\theta},\boldsymbol{\phi},y\right],$$

and $\mathbb{E}\left[(\frac{\partial\mathcal{L}_y(\boldsymbol{\theta})}{\partial\theta_i})(\frac{\partial\mathcal{L}_y(\boldsymbol{\theta})}{\partial\theta_j})\middle|\boldsymbol{\theta},\boldsymbol{\phi},y\right]$ equals $I_{i,j}^{(y)}(\boldsymbol{\theta})$ by definition. □

Proof of Theorem 4. Applying the Leibniz formula for determinant to the decomposed FIM in (7) shows that

$$\begin{aligned}\det(I(\boldsymbol{\theta};\boldsymbol{\phi})) &= \sum_{\boldsymbol{\pi}\in\Pi_{|L|}} \operatorname{sgn}(\boldsymbol{\pi}) \prod_{i=1}^{|L|} I_{i,\pi_i}(\boldsymbol{\theta};\boldsymbol{\phi}) \\ &= \sum_{\boldsymbol{\pi}\in\Pi_{|L|}} \operatorname{sgn}(\boldsymbol{\pi}) \left(\sum_{y_1=1}^{|P|}\cdots\sum_{y_{|L|}=1}^{|P|}\prod_{i=1}^{|L|}\phi_{y_i} I_{i,\pi_i}^{(y_i)}(\boldsymbol{\theta})\right),\end{aligned} \tag{26}$$

where $\boldsymbol{\pi}$ is a permutation of $\{1,\ldots,|L|\}$ ($\Pi_{|L|}$ is the set of all permutations), and $\operatorname{sgn}(\boldsymbol{\pi})$ is a sign function that equals 1 if $\boldsymbol{\pi}$ is achievable by an even number of pairwise swaps, and -1 if it is achievable by an odd number of swaps. Equation (26) shows that the determinant of the FIM can be written as a sum of order-$|L|$ terms of $\boldsymbol{\phi}$ (i.e., $\prod_{i=1}^{|L|}\phi_{y_i}$), weighted by functions of $\boldsymbol{\theta}$. Each term in the summation is uniquely determined by $\boldsymbol{\pi}$ and $\mathbf{y}$.

The key to the proof is to show that after combining these order-$|L|$ terms, the remaining terms only contain product of $|L|$ *distinct* ϕ_y's, i.e., terms containing duplicate variables ($y_i = y_j$ for $i \neq j$) all disappear. We prove this by showing that terms with duplicate variables will combine to zero.

For each term with at least one duplicate variable, i.e., the corresponding $\boldsymbol{\pi}$ and $\mathbf{y}$ satisfy: $\exists i,j \in \{1,\ldots,|L|\}$ ($i \neq j$) such that $y_i = y_j = y_0$ for some $y_0 \in \{1,\ldots,|P|\}$, there must exist a corresponding term, referred to as the *opposite term*, for the same $\mathbf{y}$ and a slightly different permutation $\boldsymbol{\pi}'$ that is identical to $\boldsymbol{\pi}$ except that $\pi'_i = \pi_j$ and $\pi'_j = \pi_i$. The absolute value of this opposite term equals

$$\left(\prod_{k\neq i,j}\phi_{y_k} I_{k,\pi'_k}^{(y_k)}(\boldsymbol{\theta})\right)\phi_{y_0}^2 I_{i,\pi'_i}^{(y_0)}(\boldsymbol{\theta}) I_{j,\pi'_j}^{(y_0)}(\boldsymbol{\theta}),$$

which equals the absolute value of the first term

$$\left(\prod_{k\neq i,j}\phi_{y_k} I_{k,\pi_k}^{(y_k)}(\boldsymbol{\theta})\right)\phi_{y_0}^2 I_{i,\pi_i}^{(y_0)}(\boldsymbol{\theta}) I_{j,\pi_j}^{(y_0)}(\boldsymbol{\theta})$$

because $I_{i,\pi'_i}^{(y_0)}(\boldsymbol{\theta}) I_{j,\pi'_j}^{(y_0)}(\boldsymbol{\theta}) = I_{i,\pi_i}^{(y_0)}(\boldsymbol{\theta}) I_{j,\pi_j}^{(y_0)}(\boldsymbol{\theta})$. Meanwhile, $\operatorname{sgn}(\boldsymbol{\pi})$ and $\operatorname{sgn}(\boldsymbol{\pi}')$ must differ as the permutations differ by one pairwise swap. Therefore, the two terms sum up to zero.

Moreover, if we define the *opposite term* of a term containing duplicate variables as the term obtained by swapping π_i and π_j for the first two duplicate variables (i.e., for the smallest i,j with $y_i = y_j$), then it is easy to see that the opposite term of the opposite term is the original term, and thus no two different terms can have the same opposite term. Therefore, after combining terms, only terms consisting of a product of $|L|$ distinct ϕ_y's remain, implying formula (9). □

Proof of Theorem 6. Let us denote the (i,j)-element of $I^{-1}(\boldsymbol{\theta};\boldsymbol{\phi})$ by $I_{i,j}^{-1}(\boldsymbol{\theta};\boldsymbol{\phi})$. Applying Cramer's rule of calculating the inverse of a matrix, we can write

$$I_{i,j}^{-1}(\boldsymbol{\theta};\boldsymbol{\phi}) = (-1)^{i+j}\frac{\det(M_{ji}(\boldsymbol{\theta};\boldsymbol{\phi}))}{\det(I(\boldsymbol{\theta};\boldsymbol{\phi}))},$$

where $\det(M_{ji}(\boldsymbol{\theta};\boldsymbol{\phi}))$ is the minor of element (j,i) of $I(\boldsymbol{\theta};\boldsymbol{\phi})$ (i.e., the determinant of the submatrix after removing row j and column i). In particular, the diagonal elements of $I^{-1}(\boldsymbol{\theta};\boldsymbol{\phi})$ have the following form:

$$I_{k,k}^{-1}(\boldsymbol{\theta};\boldsymbol{\phi}) = \frac{\det(M_{kk}(\boldsymbol{\theta};\boldsymbol{\phi}))}{\det(I(\boldsymbol{\theta};\boldsymbol{\phi}))},\ k = 1,\ldots,|L|.$$

By Corollary 5, the numerator can be written as:

$$\det(M_{kk}(\boldsymbol{\theta};\boldsymbol{\phi})) = \sum_{C\in\mathcal{S}_{|L|-1}} B_{C,k}(\boldsymbol{\theta})\prod_{i\in C}\phi_i.$$

The trace of $I^{-1}(\boldsymbol{\theta};\boldsymbol{\phi})$ is thus equal to

$$\begin{aligned}\operatorname{Tr}(I^{-1}(\boldsymbol{\theta};\boldsymbol{\phi})) &= \sum_{k=1}^{|L|} I_{k,k}^{-1}(\boldsymbol{\theta};\boldsymbol{\phi}) \\ &= \sum_{C\in\mathcal{S}_{|L|-1}} \frac{\prod_{i\in C}\phi_i}{\prod_{s=1}^{|L|}\phi_s}\left(\sum_{k=1}^{|L|}\frac{B_{C,k}(\boldsymbol{\theta})}{B(\boldsymbol{\theta})}\right),\end{aligned}$$

where we have used the representation (10) for $\det(I(\boldsymbol{\theta};\boldsymbol{\phi}))$. Next, we observe that $\mathcal{S}_{|L|-1}$ has exactly $|L|$ members $C_1,\ldots,C_{|L|}$, where each C_i is the subset of $\{1,\ldots,|L|\}$ that excludes i. Thus,

$$\operatorname{Tr}(I^{-1}(\boldsymbol{\theta};\boldsymbol{\phi})) = \sum_{i=1}^{|L|}\frac{1}{\phi_i}\left(\sum_{k=1}^{|L|}\frac{B_{C_i,k}(\boldsymbol{\theta})}{B(\boldsymbol{\theta})}\right) = \sum_{i=1}^{|L|}\frac{1}{\phi_i}A_i(\boldsymbol{\theta}),$$

where $A_i(\boldsymbol{\theta}) := \sum_{k=1}^{|L|}\frac{B_{C_i,k}(\boldsymbol{\theta})}{B(\boldsymbol{\theta})}$. □

Proof of Lemma 8. To derive $B_C(\boldsymbol{\theta})$, we evaluate the determinant of the FIM by $\det(\Theta^{-1})^2\det(A^TDA)$. Applying the Cauchy-Binet formula to $\det(A^T(DA))$ gives

$$\det(I(\boldsymbol{\theta};\boldsymbol{\phi})) = \frac{1}{\prod_{l\in L}\theta_l^2}\sum_{C\in\mathcal{S}_{|L|}}\det(A_C)\det((DA)_C), \tag{27}$$

where similar to A_C, $(DA)_C$ is a $|L|\times|L|$ submatrix of DA formed by rows with indices in C. Since D is diagonal, we can further decompose $\det((DA)_C)$ into $\det(D_C)\det(A_C)$, where $D_C = \operatorname{diag}((d_y)_{y\in C})$. Since the only term depending on $\boldsymbol{\phi}$ is $\det(D_C)$, we can rewrite (27) as a function of $\boldsymbol{\phi}$ as

$$\det(I(\boldsymbol{\theta};\boldsymbol{\phi})) = \sum_{C\in\mathcal{S}_{|L|}}\left[\frac{\det(A_C)^2}{\prod_{l\in L}\theta_l^2}\prod_{i\in C}\frac{\alpha_i(\boldsymbol{\theta})}{1-\alpha_i(\boldsymbol{\theta})}\right]\prod_{i\in C}\phi_i,$$

which matches formula (9) with $B_C(\boldsymbol{\theta})$ defined as in (18).

To derive $A_i(\boldsymbol{\theta})$, we evaluate the inverse of the FIM by $\Theta A^{-1}D^{-1}A^{-T}\Theta$. Denoting A^{-1} as $(b_{i,j})_{i,j=1}^{|L|}$, we can evaluate the k-th diagonal entry as $I_{k,k}^{-1}(\boldsymbol{\theta};\boldsymbol{\phi}) = \theta_k^2\sum_{i=1}^{|L|}b_{k,i}^2 d_i^{-1}$

since Θ and D^{-1} are diagonal. Plugging in the definition of d_i^{-1} yields

$$\begin{aligned}\mathrm{Tr}(I^{-1}(\boldsymbol{\theta};\boldsymbol{\phi})) &= \sum_{k=1}^{|L|}\theta_k^2\sum_{i=1}^{|L|}\frac{b_{k,i}^2(1-\alpha_i(\boldsymbol{\theta}))}{\alpha_i(\boldsymbol{\theta})}\cdot\frac{1}{\phi_i}\\ &= \sum_{i=1}^{|L|}\frac{1}{\phi_i}\left[\frac{1-\alpha_i(\boldsymbol{\theta})}{\alpha_i(\boldsymbol{\theta})}\sum_{k=1}^{|L|}\theta_k^2 b_{k,i}^2\right],\end{aligned}$$

which matches formula (12) with $A_i(\boldsymbol{\theta})$ defined as in (19). The same derivation will give the expression for $\widetilde{A}_i(\boldsymbol{\theta})$. □

Proof of Lemma 9. The proof is analogous to that of Lemma 8 by evaluating $\det(A^TEA)$ and $A^{-1}E^{-1}A^{-T}$. □

Proof of Theorem 11 . Fundamental to our proof is the convergence of empirical path parameters to the true parameters. For loss tomography, these are path success rates, denoted by $\boldsymbol{\alpha}$; for PDV tomography, these are path PDV variances, denoted by $\boldsymbol{\sigma}$. Based on the *Chernoff-Hoeffding bound*, the empirical parameters converge exponentially fast as the number of probes n_i for each path p_i $(i = 1,\ldots,|P|)$ increases, i.e., both $\Pr\{|\hat{\alpha}_i - \alpha_i| \le \delta\}$ and $\Pr\{|\hat{\sigma}_i - \sigma_i| \le \delta\}$ are lower bounded by $1 - 2e^{-2\delta^2 n_i}$ $(i = 1,\ldots,|P|)$. What remains is to bound the error in the design objective and $\boldsymbol{\phi}$, given δ-error in estimating α_i and σ_i. Due to space limitation, we only detail the analysis for loss tomography, as the analysis for PDV tomography is analogous but simpler.

Let $T(\boldsymbol{\theta})$ denote the trace of inverse FIM based on uniform $\boldsymbol{\phi}$ (as assumed in line 5 of Algorithm 1). For a function $x(\boldsymbol{\theta})$, we use $\hat{x}$ to denote $x(\hat{\boldsymbol{\theta}})$. We will show that for any sufficiently small $\delta > 0$, $\exists\epsilon_1(\delta)$, $\epsilon_2(\delta)$ that go to 0 as $\delta \to 0$ such that $|\hat{\alpha}_i - \alpha_i| \le \delta$ $(i = 1,\ldots,|P|)$ implies $|\hat{T} - T| \le \epsilon_1(\delta)$, and $|\hat{\phi}_i - \phi_i| \le \epsilon_2(\delta)$ for all $p_i \in P_B$.

For loss tomography, a derivation similar to Lemma 8 shows that

$$T = \frac{|P|\sum_{C'\in\mathcal{S}_{|L|-1}}\left[\sum_{k=1}^{|L|}\theta_k^2\det(A_{C'}^{(k)})^2\right]\prod_{i\in C'}\frac{\alpha_i}{1-\alpha_i}}{\sum_{C\in\mathcal{S}_{|L|}}\det(A_C)^2\prod_{i\in C}\frac{\alpha_i}{1-\alpha_i}}, \tag{28}$$

where $A^{(k)}$ denotes the submatrix of A by removing the k-th column and $A_C^{(k)}$ the submatrix of $A^{(k)}$ formed by rows with indices in C. Denoting the numerator of (28) by f_1 and the denominator by f_2 (both functions of $\boldsymbol{\theta}$). It can be shown that δ-error in α_i implies $|\hat{\theta}_k - \theta_k| \le e^{\delta'} - 1 := c_0(\delta)$ $(k = 1,\ldots,|L|)$, where δ' is the largest absolute value for entries of $(A^TA)^{-1}A^T\frac{\delta}{\boldsymbol{\alpha}-\delta}$ ($\frac{\delta}{\boldsymbol{\alpha}-\delta}$ is a column vector defined as $(\frac{\delta}{\alpha_i-\delta})_{i=1}^{|P|}$). Moreover, $|\prod_{i\in C}\frac{\hat{\alpha}_i}{1-\hat{\alpha}_i} - \prod_{i\in C}\frac{\alpha_i}{1-\alpha_i}| \le \max(\prod_i\alpha_i - \prod_i(\alpha_i-\delta), \prod_i(\alpha_i+\delta) - \prod_i\alpha_i)/\prod_i(1-\alpha_i-\delta)(1-\alpha_i) := c_1(\delta;C)$. Based on these results, we have

$$\begin{aligned}|f_1 - \hat{f}_1| \le &|P|\sum_{C'\in\mathcal{S}_{|L|-1}}\left[\sum_{k=1}^{|L|}\theta_k^2\det(A_{C'}^{(k)})^2 c_1(\delta;C')\right.\\ &\left.+ 2c_0(\delta)(\prod_{i\in C'}\frac{\alpha_i}{1-\alpha_i} + c_1(\delta;C'))\sum_{k=1}^{|L|}\det(A_{C'}^{(k)})^2\right] := c_2(\delta),\end{aligned}$$

and $|f_2 - \hat{f}_2| \le \sum_{C\in\mathcal{S}_{|L|}}\det(A_C)^2 c_1(\delta;C) := c_3(\delta)$. Together, these bounds yield

$$|T - \hat{T}| \le \frac{f_1c_3(\delta) + f_2c_2(\delta)}{f_2(f_2 - c_3(\delta))} := \epsilon_1(\delta),$$

which goes to 0 as $\delta \to 0$ since $c_i(\delta) \to 0$ $(i = 0,\ldots,3)$.

Given a basis P_B, the A-optimal designs on P_B, calculated by (25), based on $\hat{\boldsymbol{\theta}}$ and $\boldsymbol{\theta}$ satisfy

$$|\phi_i - \hat{\phi}_i| \le \frac{\epsilon\left(|L|\sqrt{A_i(\boldsymbol{\theta})} + \sum_{j=1}^{|L|}\sqrt{A_j(\boldsymbol{\theta})}\right)}{\left(\sum_{j=1}^{|L|}\sqrt{A_j(\boldsymbol{\theta})}\right)\left(\sum_{j=1}^{|L|}\sqrt{A_j(\boldsymbol{\theta})} - \epsilon|L|\right)} \tag{29}$$

if $|\sqrt{A_i(\boldsymbol{\theta})} - \sqrt{A_i(\hat{\boldsymbol{\theta}})}| \le \epsilon$ for all $p_i \in P_B$ for a sufficiently small $\epsilon > 0$. Based on the expression of $A_i(\boldsymbol{\theta})$ in Lemma 8, we can show that $|\hat{\alpha}_i - \alpha_i| \le \delta$ implies

$$|A_i(\boldsymbol{\theta}) - A_i(\hat{\boldsymbol{\theta}})| \le \frac{2(1-\alpha_i)\beta_i c_0(\delta)}{\alpha_i} + \frac{\beta_i\delta}{\alpha_i(\alpha_i - \delta)},$$

where $\beta_i := \sum_k b_{k,i}^2$. Hence, $|\sqrt{A_i(\boldsymbol{\theta})} - \sqrt{A_i(\hat{\boldsymbol{\theta}})}| \le \epsilon(\delta)$ for $\epsilon(\delta) := \max_i \frac{2(1-\alpha_i)\beta_i c_0(\delta)}{\alpha_i\sqrt{A_i(\boldsymbol{\theta})}} + \frac{\beta_i\delta}{\alpha_i(\alpha_i-\delta)\sqrt{A_i(\boldsymbol{\theta})}}$. Plugging $\epsilon(\delta)$ into (29) gives a bound on $|\phi_i - \hat{\phi}_i|$, denoted by $\epsilon_2(\delta)$, that goes to 0 as $\delta \to 0$. □

When Virtual Meets Physical at the Edge: A Field Study on Datacenters' Virtual Traffic

Robert Birke
IBM Research Zurich Lab
Saümerstrasse 4
Rüschlikon, Switzerland
bir@zurich.ibm.com

Mathias Björkqvist
IBM Research Zurich Lab
Saümerstrasse 4
Rüschlikon, Switzerland
mbj@zurich.ibm.com

Cyriel Minkenberg
IBM Research Zurich Lab
Saümerstrasse 4
Rüschlikon, Switzerland
sil@zurich.ibm.com

Martin Schmatz
IBM Research Zurich Lab
Saümerstrasse 4
Rüschlikon, Switzerland
mrt@zurich.ibm.com

Lydia Y. Chen
IBM Research Zurich Lab
Saümerstrasse 4
Rüschlikon, Switzerland
yic@zurich.ibm.com

ABSTRACT

The wide deployment of virtualization in datacenters catalyzes the emergence of virtual traffic that delivers the network demands between the physical network and the virtual machines hosting clients' services. Virtual traffic presents new opportunities for reducing physical network demands, as well as challenges of increasing management complexity. Given the plethora of prior art on virtualization technologies in datacenters, surprisingly little is still known about such virtual traffic, and its dependence on the physical network and virtual machines. This paper provides a multi-faceted analysis of the patterns and impacts of multiplexing the virtual traffic onto the physical network, particularly from the perspective of the network edge. We use a large collection of field data from production datacenters hosting a large number of diversified services from multiple enterprise tenants. Our first focus is on uncovering the temporal and spatial characteristics of the virtual and physical traffic, i.e., network demand growth and communication patterns, with special attention paid to the traffic of migrating virtual machines. The second focus is on characterizing the effect of network multiplexing in terms of communication locality, traffic load heterogeneity, and the dependency on CPU processing power at the edges of the network. Last but not least, we conduct a mirroring analysis on service QoS, defined by the service unavailability induced by network related issues, e.g., loads. We qualitatively and quantitatively discuss the implications and opportunities that virtual traffic presents for network capacity planning of virtualized networks and datacenters.

Categories and Subject Descriptors

C.4 [**Performance of Systems**]: Performance attributes; Reliability, availability, and serviceability; C.2.3 [**Computer-Communication Networks**]: Network Operations; Network monitoring

SIGMETRICS'15, June 15–19, 2015, Portland, OR, USA.

ACM 978-1-4503-3486-0/15/06 ...$15.00.
DOI: http://dx.doi.org/10.1145/2745844.2745865.

Keywords

Bandwidth demand; Virtual traffic; Migration; Growth; Datacenter

1. INTRODUCTION

The advancement and wide adoption of virtualization technologies has heavily influenced the recent development of network design and management. This is especially true for datacenters, where physical resources are typically multiplexed in the form of virtual machines (VMs) running on physical servers (termed *boxes*) to cater a large number of services. The virtual traffic that transports network demand generated from VMs to the physical network is central to determine the quality of services [34] hosted in cloud datacenters.

To cater to datacenter traffic with a compounded annual growth rate of 25% [13], innovation continues especially in the areas of network virtualization [3, 19, 21, 42], e.g., software defined networks, and traffic aware resource management [22,26,27]. The former centers on network architecture and traffic engineering, which aim at increasing the efficiency of physical networks and ease the management complexity coming from a plethora of additional network devices, e.g., virtual switches. The latter tries to minimize the network latency by exploring VM network demands and communication patterns, such as migrating VMs across boxes. The interdependency among virtual traffic, the physical network, and virtual machines is the fundamental knowledge required to achieve both objectives [4].

In highly virtualized datacenters, the performance of the network depends on the volume of virtual as well as physical traffic. On the one hand, the physical traffic can be reduced by leveraging communication patterns among VMs [27], such as intra-box communication, and the traffic burstiness can be mitigated by statistical aggregation, i.e., by (mis)matching the peaks and dips of VMs' demands [14]. On the other hand, managing and routing virtual traffic requires extensive CPU resources, leading to the recent trend of offloading functionality related to the data plane [30] to hardware. Moreover, the quality of service (QoS), e.g., the duration of service unavailability, can be highly affected by the network performance [34]. Overall, the advantages of virtual traffic comes at the cost of higher management complexity and the dependency on physical shared resources.

While there exists a large body of prior art centering on optimizing the management of datacenter virtual traffic [2,4], few present a characterization of bandwidth demands in production datacenters, which can provide crucial understanding of workloads and operation practices. Most of them focus on the flows of physical traffic [5,6], or of virtual traffic only [10,26]. Little is known of the dependency of virtual traffic on physical traffic and CPU, in terms of volume and communication patterns – the key aspect of network design and management at virtualized datacenters.

The aim of this paper is to provide a multi-faceted study analyzing the patterns and impact of virtual traffic, with special attention paid to its interdependency on the physical network and virtual machines. Our analysis is based on a large number of network edges, i.e., virtual machines and boxes hosted in production datacenters, catering to several tens of thousands of services and covering a wide range of enterprise tenants, over a time span of one year. Our study presents a broad overview of how bandwidth demands at production systems are driven by virtualization, including multiplex level and VM migration. Limited by a shortage of information regarding the network topology, this study derives an approximation of communication patterns driven by data from the network edges, and VM migrations — the key enabling technology in cloud computing.

This study consists of four main parts: (1) the spatial characteristics of resources and demand growth; (2) the communication analysis driven by migrations of virtual machines, including radius and overhead; (3) the impact of traffic multiplexing on communication locality, load heterogeneity, traffic burstiness, and CPU loads from the perspective of physical edges; (4) the impact of network issues on the service unavailability. The communication radius is defined by boxes and geographic zones, a combination of country and time zone. The traffic locality is defined as the percentage of virtual traffic mapped to physical traffic, and the heterogeneity as the relationship between average and maximum bandwidth demands of co-located VMs across time. The burstiness looks at how consolidation levels affect the peaks in the network traffic, and we also investigate how CPU utilization may depend on the virtual traffic. For the QoS analysis, we leverage service performance tickets and compare network- and non-network-induced service unavailability, at the level of the datacenter and single service VMs.

In addition to providing critical network traffic statistics, our analysis also shows many useful findings. First of all, VM migration has a dominant effect on traffic volume and requires a communication radius of up to 26 boxes and 9 geographic zones. In terms of network overhead, VM migration results in a traffic volume of approximately twice the size of the active VM memory. The benefit of intra-box communication is not fully harvested, and services with very different bandwidth demands are co-located, resulting in the average max-mean ratio being 6. Correlating CPU loads and traffic, we derive that the cost of processing a single packet is roughly 0.26 Mcycles/packet, or 98.7 μs on a 2.6 GHz CPU. Moreover, the occurrences of service unavailability caused by network issues is 2.5 to 10 times lower than non-network related issues at the datacenter level. The impact the network load has on network-induced service unavailability is positive with loads measured in kilopackets per second, but neutral in terms of megabits per second.

In terms of contribution, we provide a first-of-a-kind virtual traffic analysis, uncovering its dependence on the physical network and virtual machines. In contrast to existing flow-based traffic analysis, our analysis takes the unique perspective of network edges, containing rich information on how virtual meets physical resources. Our migration analysis shows the communication patterns and overhead required in production systems, providing key parameterizations for migration driven network design. We also show the impact of network-related issues on service unavailability, using performance tickets.

The outline of this work is as follows. In Section 2, we provide an overview of the presented dataset. The temporal analysis of virtual traffic, and the spatial analysis of migration traffic, are introduced in Section 3 and Section 4, respectively. The impact of network multiplexing on traffic locality, heterogeneity, and CPU dependency is detailed in Section 5. The influence of network related issues on service unavailability is discussed in Section 6. Section 7 presents related work. A summary of our findings in Section 8 concludes this paper.

2. STATISTICS COLLECTION

We use a large collection of field data from ninety thousands VMs, hosted on eight thousand physical servers in different production datacenters located around the globe, serving more than 300 corporate clients, over intermittent observation periods between April 2013 and April 2014. The VMs, belonging to clients from different industries, are used to host different kinds of service components, and run various operating systems. In the rest of this paper we interchangeably use VMs and services. The boxes in this study are well equipped with virtualization technologies from major vendors, such as VMware and IBM, and employ various service management policies for, e.g., VM consolidation, turning VMs on/off, and VM migration. Our statistics are divided into two categories: network-related and service VM-related. In terms of presentation, we focus on presenting the entire distributions, the means, and some particular percentiles, e.g., the 25th, 50th and 75th percentiles, due the nature of long tails in our statistics of interests.

2.1 Network Statistics

The statistics collection is performed using standard utilities such as `netstat` and `vmstat` for network demands and CPU usage, respectively, depending on the operating system and hypervisor. In particular, we extract information about the number of network interface cards (NICs), the inbound/outbound rates in megabits per second (Mbps) per NIC, kilopackets per second (Kpps) per NIC, and the number of VMs per box. We define the *virtual traffic* as the bandwidth associated with VMs, and the *physical traffic* as the traffic of the boxes. To obtain the amount of virtual (physical) traffic for a VM (box), we aggregate over all its NICs. Our base data is an hourly average between April 2013 and April 2014. To simplify the presentation, most statistics presented here are from first week of April, and from a single day, April 17, 2013, except when computing the growth rates, which require monthly averages over the entire one year period. To study the dependency of virtual and physical traffic on VM consolidation, we focus on comparing the virtual traffic generated from VMs co-located on the same box, to the physical traffic of the underlying box.

Geographic Zones: For each box, we have information about which country it is located in, as well as its Coordinated Universal Time zone. Using this pair of information, we give geographic identifiers to VMs and boxes. An example information can be a VM providing mail service for a financial enterprise hosted on a box located in (USA, Pacific time). Both the VM and the box are given the identifier (USA, Pacific time). Due to business confidentiality, we do not have access to the exact location of VMs and boxes - instead, we resort to the above mentioned geographic identifiers to derive the dispersion of network edges per enterprise, and the communication patterns of migrating traffic.

Table 1: Statistics of VM consolidation levels.

Percentiles	25th	50th	75th	90th	99th
VMs per box [#]	4	8	16	35	60

2.2 VM Statistics

Generally, VMs considered by this study host a wide range of services, such as application servers, web servers, mail servers, backup servers, and database servers. We also consider the following attributes related to the VMs, in terms of their management and QoS:

VM Consolidation: As the degree of virtualization of boxes is fairly dynamic, the data processing complexity is non-negligible. For each box, we associate the consolidation level of the box to its weekly average, computed from the first week of April, 2013. The distribution of the consolidation level per box can be found in Table 1. One can also see the consolidation traffic as the multiplexing level of network traffic, i.e., at which degree the network of the box is shared by the traffic of VMs hosted on the box. On average, 11 VMs, each configured with 2 CPUs and 4.8 GB memory, are consolidated on a single physical box with 15 CPUs and 60 GB of memory. We refer interested readers to [8] for the detailed statistics.

VM Migration: Using finer-grained data of VM resource usage, collected at 15-minute intervals, we are able to track how frequently VMs are migrated in a one month observation period (April 2013). A VM migration is defined by the change of the hosting box. The percentage of boxes and VM experiencing at least one occurrence of migration is 56.3% and 30.8%, respectively. The percentage of boxes is roughly double that of VMs, as we consider both directions of migration for boxes, i.e., VMs migrated in and out. Due to the granularity of the data available to us, we consider migrations whose processes completed within 15 minutes as on-line migrations, and the rest as off-line migrations, where VM is first turned off or suspended and then turned on on the other machine.

Quality of Services: The service QoS is defined by the fraction of time a service running on a VM is interrupted and becomes unavailable, the so-called service unavailability (SU). To derive the statistics of interest, we leverage the performance tickets, [11], collected both directly from users and via automatic ticketing systems. Here, we focus on a subset of five specific enterprises, accounting for roughly 3000 boxes and 4000 VMs. The tickets also provide a coarse grained root cause analysis, including both network and non-network related ones, such as software, disk, and OS. Thus, we consider network-induced SU and non-network induced SU, as measurements of service QoS.

Limitation: Due to the nature of the data available to us, our study has some limitations. Because of the aggregation of data into time averages, we inevitably lose information on fine-grained resolution, in particular the traffic peaks. For example, the maximum Mbps identified in this study is based on a one hour window, and is much lower than the instantaneous maximum Mbps. Moreover, we have limited information on the communication affinity of each VM, and therefore we only provide approximate communication analysis, from the perspective of a network edge, and service migration. However, the coarseness of the information gathered is contrasted by the huge dataset the study is based on: 8000 boxes and 90000 VMs over an extended observation period.

3. TEMPORAL ANALYSIS

In this section, we present a bird's-eye view on virtual and physical traffic, generated from VMs and boxes, respectively, and highlight their differences. In particular, we focus on the provisioning of network resources, i.e., network interface cards (NICs), and bandwidth demands, including short-term and long-term views. Note that NICs here are the network interfaces as seen by the operating system of VMs or boxes. As the resource provisioning and bandwidth dynamically change over time, we use the averages computed over a week as the base statistics.

Table 2: Network resource and traffic of boxes and VMs: no. of NICs, no. of inactive NICs, and daily traffic volume [GB].

	Boxes			VMs		
	Mean	50th	99th	Mean	50th	99th
NICs [#]	8.5	7	22	2.3	1	19
Inact. NICs [#]	4.2	4	16	1.0	0	14
Volume [GB]	259	70	2700	18	2	305

3.1 Virtual Traffic Demands

We first present a short term overview collected from the first week of April 2013. Table 2 summarizes the snapshot results: number of NICs, number of inactive NICs, and daily bandwidth demand in GB. We split the NICs by their transmitted packets over a day, using different threshold values, η. We consider a NIC inactive if its transmission never exceeded the threshold value over the entire day. We do not consider received packets since the NIC could still receive broadcast packets from the network. We avoid $\eta = 0$ pps as being too conservative since it does not allow for any spurious packet transmission. Using $\eta \in 5, 10, 25$ pps only slightly varies the statistics, i.e., variations in the mean within 10%. Hence, hereon we present the results with $\eta = 10$ pps.

Due to the long tail of the distribution, we present the mean, the 50th, and the 99th percentiles. Not surprisingly, boxes not only have a higher number of NICs, but also a slightly higher redundancy in NICs, i.e., less than 10% of boxes have all their NICs active, especially when looking at the 50th percentile.

The mean virtual traffic of both inbound and outbound sums up to 18 GB, whereas boxes have a mean daily traffic volume of 259 GB. The bandwidth demands of VMs are lower than that of boxes, roughly by a factor of 14.3, which is slightly higher than the mean number of 11 VMs per box. However, one has to take into account that the box traffic includes also management traffic, such as VM migration traffic, which does not contribute to the virtual traffic.

3.2 Growth Analysis

To compute the long term growth, we compute the differences between the first weeks of April 2013 and April 2014.

3.2.1 Growth of NICs

In this study, we use NICs as channels for statistics collection, but also study the availability of NICs at VMs and boxes as resource provisioning vehicles. We are thus interested in seeing how the provisioning of NICs changes over the year, and the multiplexing level of the NICs, i.e., how many NICs associated with co-located VMs share the NICs associated with the hosting box.

Figure 1 (a) depicts the CDF/PDF of changes in number of NICs between April 2013 and 2014. Roughly 90% (80%) of boxes (VMs) do not change their number of NICs, and the majority of the remaining boxes and VMs increase their number of NICs. The increasing trend can be observed on a slightly higher number of VMs, due to the ease of VM re-configuration. A possible explanation of constant NIC provisioning is that the redundancy of NICs, i.e.,

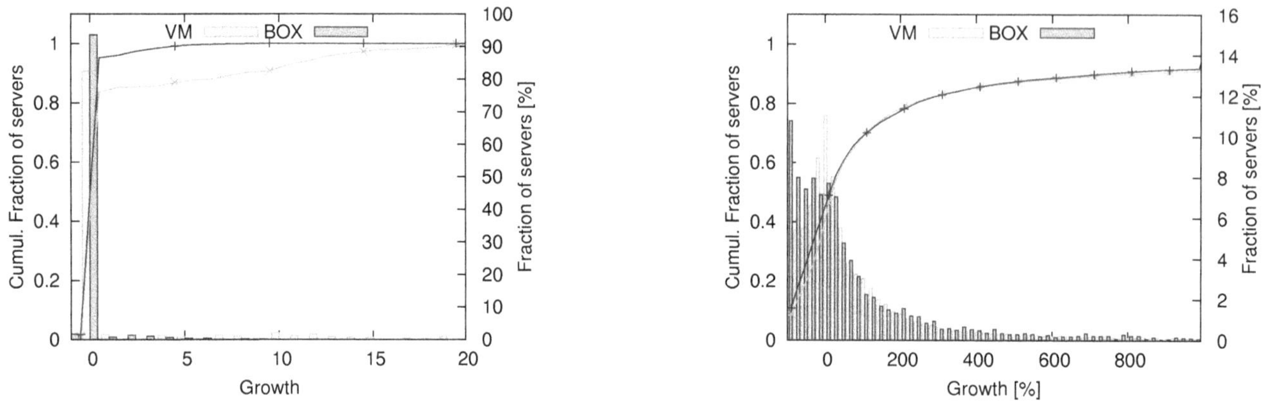

(a) Growth of NICs [#]

(b) Growth of volume [%]

Figure 1: Yearly growth of network resources and traffic: cumulative density function (CDF) and probability density function (PDF).

Table 3: Yearly traffic volume growth [%].

Boxes			VMs		
Mean	Median	99th	Mean	Median	99th
7674	22	20081	24425	27	76174

number of inactive NICs, is very high in today's boxes and VMs. Extra NICs are used to increase the reliability (hot standby), and as a management interface to connect external devices, such as a laptop to do extraordinary maintenance on the server. Moreover, additional NICs can easily be aggregated into faster logical links for smaller link capacity upgrades, instead of going to the next generation of network technology. As a result, there are sufficient numbers of NICs to cater the traffic growth discussed in the following section.

Another criterion for evaluating the provisioning of NICs is the multiplexing level of NICs, defined as the total number of virtual NICs of co-located VMs, divided by the number of physical NICs of the underlying box. This ratio tells us how many virtual NICs on VMs are supported by a physical NIC on a box. An intuitive guess might be that such a ratio is greater than one for most of boxes – indeed, the average value of such a ratio computed from our dataset is roughly 3. In comparison, our previous work [8] shows that the average multiplex levels for CPU and memory are 1.56 and 0.96. However only 60% of boxes have the ratio greater than one, meaning there are more virtual NICs than physical ones. Surprisingly, the remaining 40% of boxes have more NICs associated with the box than for the VMs hosted on it. This can be explained by the fact that some boxes host only a very low number of VMs, while having high provisioning of NICs at the box level.

3.2.2 *Growth of Traffic Volume*

Taking advantage of the vast amount of data in our study, we verify the common belief that datacenter network demands have roughly 25% compounded annual growth rate every year [13], from the perspective of individual VMs and boxes. We compute the yearly growth of daily average traffic volume in GB between April 2013 and April 2014.

We summarize the distribution of the 1-year growth for individual VMs and boxes in Figure 1 (b) and the statistics in Table 3. A significant fraction of VMs and boxes, i.e., roughly 50%, have their growth rate lower than zero, indicating that their network demand decreased, e.g., due to business reasons. The remaining half of the VMs and boxes have positive and strong network demand growth rates – the 50th percentile of growth rates for VMs is 27%. As for boxes, the 50th percentile of growth rates is 22%.This implicitly hints at an improvement of communication locality in datacenters.

Our findings show that the median growth rates every year for VMs and boxes traffic are 22% and 27%, respectively. While contradicting older beliefs, these growth rates are in line with revised growth estimate. The growth rate information provided here is critical for dimensioning network resources, such as the deployment of routers and links, which are very difficult to upgrade in datacenters, compared to CPU and memory.

4. MIGRATION TRAFFIC

Migrating VMs is one of key features of enabling elastic service computing, and the network is the main vehicle for achieving the migration of VMs within and across datacenters. A large number of studies [26,27] try to optimize the network topology and routing algorithms such that the network overhead of migration is minimized. From our data, we see that migrations are not frequent, but also not negligible, i.e., roughly 30% and 45% of VMs and boxes, respectively, experienced at least one migration during our observation period. In this section, using the information about geographic zones covered by tenants' VMs, we for the first time uncover migration practices in the real world, in terms of traffic volume, communication matrix, and overhead. We first give an overview of the migration traffic and investigate the relationship between the number of migrations and the average network volume of VMs, using simple statistics and visual inspection. We then present the migration communication matrix based on the migration patterns, and derive their characteristics. By zooming in on a subset of servers experiencing frequent migrations, we estimate the network overhead per migrating volume, in terms of active VM memory size. Last but not least, we discover how migration can drive the network traffic in reality.

4.1 Tenant's Edge Network Radius

Prior to presenting a detailed migration analysis, we show the geographical dispersion of tenants' virtual machines, as an approximation of the upper bound of the communication radius. We note that due to business confidentiality, we are only able to provide anonymous information on datacenter physical locations. Using the definition of geographical zones defined in Section 2, we sum-

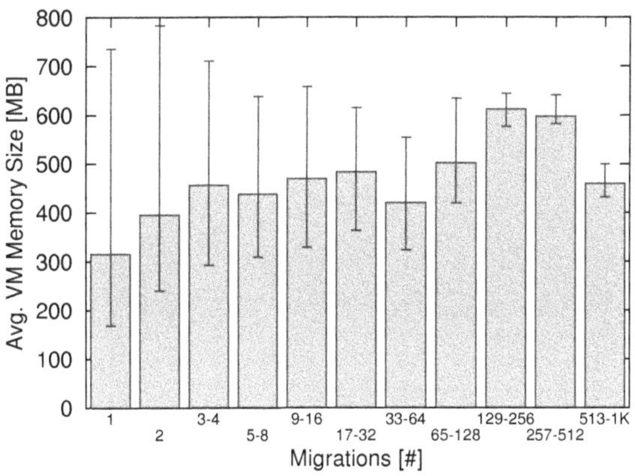

(a) Boxes' migration

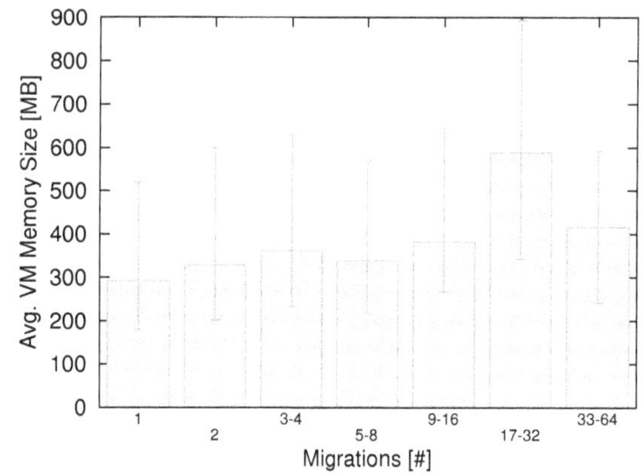

(b) VMs' migration

Figure 2: Migration volume vs. migration frequencies.

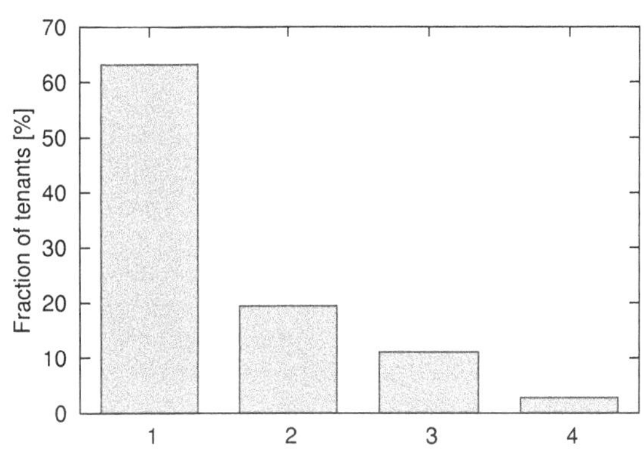

Figure 3: Geographic zones of tenant's edge network.

marize the distribution of number of zones covered by a tenant's edge network in Figure 3. Note that a geographic zone, as defined in this study, can contain multiple physical datacenters. A significant number of clients' networks, i.e., 62%, are within one geographic zone, and the rest of clients' networks span 2 to 4 zones, representing non-negligible communication distances. Dispersion over multiple geographical zones has multiple benefits, especially for increased service availability and reliability in the case of catastrophic events. Moreover, the probability of being closer to users is higher, and thus there is greater potential for reducing the end-to-end latency. However, maintaining a tenant edge network in a single physical location, such as a datacenter and cluster, is already shown challenging [4], and having the network expand to multiple geographic zones manifold increases the management complexity with the additional physical and virtual network layers.

4.2 Classification of Migration: Timings, Distance and Volume

Here, we first classify migration by the their timings and geographic distances. In terms of timing, each migration takes place *off-line* or *on-line*, depending on the fact if VMs are first turned off or suspended before migration or not. By the geographic distances, we also consider *near* and *far* migrations, for which happen within the same geographic zone or across zones, respectively. Essentially, migrations can be divided into four classes, as shown in Table 4. First of all, one can see that migration is almost evenly divided between on-line and off-line migration. Unsurprisingly, only a small percentage of migration happens across multiple zones, i.e., roughly 4.54%. The on-line and far migrations, accounting for 2.82%, pose a difficult challenge for network operation.

Table 4: Distribution and migration volume of four classes of migration: combinations of {far, near} $\times$ {on-line, off-line}.

	On-line		Off-line	
	Near	Far	Near	Far
Distribution [%]	50.75	2.83	44.71	1.72
Migration volume [MB]	724	454	575	458

Furthermore, we compute the average migration volumes, approximated by VMs' active memories, and summarize them in Table 4. On the one hand, the volume for far migration is visibly lower than the near migration, so as to avoid occurrences of high migration latency. On the other hand, the volume that needs to be transmitted via on-line migration is surprisingly higher than off-line, roughly by 26%. This implies that on-line migration happens on relatively larger VMs, instead of smaller ones. Moreover, due to different memory migration policies, such as retransmission of dirty memory pages, the actual migration traffic caused by on-line migration can be higher than the size of active memory, potentially resulting in higher migration traffic. In the subsequent subsections, we present an estimate on the traffic overhead, given the VM memory sizes. In summary, roughly 50% of migration is on-line and aims to transmit 724 MB, whereas the other 50% of migration is off-line to transmit 575 MB of active memory size.

4.2.1 *Migration Volume vs. Frequency*

To better understand the bandwidth demands of migration in terms of spatial distribution, we report the average volume per migration relative to different migration frequencies during the observation period of April 2013. We consider the perspective of VMs as well as boxes. When calculating the total number of migrations at boxes, we include migrations in both directions, i.e., in- and out-migrating. We first group VMs/boxes by their migration frequencies and then obtain the 25th, 50th, and 75th percentiles of average migration volume in each frequency group. We summarize the results in box plots for boxes and VMs in Figure 2 (a) and (b), respectively. The bar presents the 50th percentile and two whiskers the 25th and 75th percentiles. For both boxes and VMs, one can observe a clear increasing trend of average migration vol-

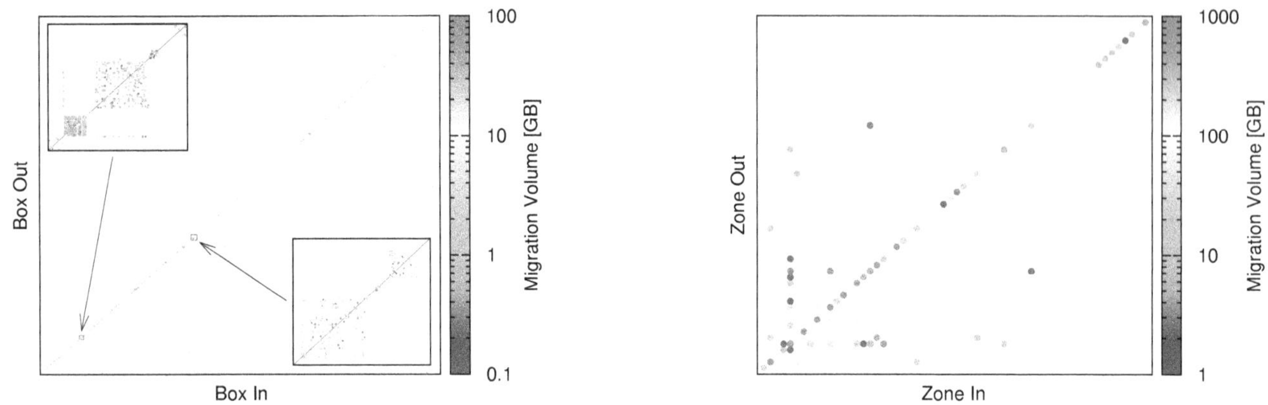

(a) By boxes (b) By zones

Figure 4: Migration communication matrix: the color shows the migration volume between source (x-axes) and destination (y-axes).

Table 5: Migration radius in terms of boxes/zones and migration volumes across boxes/zones.

	Boxes				Zones			
	Mean	Median	p99	Max	Mean	Median	p99	Max
Communicating boxes/zones [#]	3.57	3	15	26	1.94	1	9	9
Migration volume [GB]	11.85	3.48	100.38	605.52	820.60	107.64	5128.97	7353.37

ume with respect to increasing migration frequencies, especially for the first few categories of frequencies. This observation implies that VMs/boxes which migrate higher volumes of memory also migrate more frequently. Combining the results in Table 4, we conclude that frequently migrated VMs have higher migration volume and often require on-line migration.

4.3 Migration Communication Matrix

We construct the migration communication matrix which is defined by the migrated volume of active memory between different boxes and zones. We first present the heatmap of the migration matrix, where each point represents the aggregated migrated memory volume between different boxes/zones, during a one month observation window in April 2013. Here, we only consider out-migrating traffic from the source to the destination. Boxes/zones are sorted by their unique IDs, and servers belonging to the same tenant tend to have adjacent IDs. We present the result for boxes in Figure 4 (a), where the x-axes (y-axes) represent the source (destination) box, and provide two inset figures to highlight two of the largest communication clusters, and make the following key observations: First of all, shown by the dominance of diagonal elements in Figure 4 (a), VMs tend to migrate among adjacent boxes. Secondly, the communication matrix is quite symmetric, in terms of patterns and intensities, implying that a similar amount of VM memory tend to migrate back and forth among a certain set of boxes. Note that there is no point on the diagonal line, but adjacent to it. Figure 4 (b) shows the migration communication matrix for geographic zones. The diagonal line represents migration happening within the zone. The observations for boxes also hold true for zones: migrations tend to happen between adjacent zones and the symmetry in the communication matrix indicates groups of zones exchanging similar amounts of VM memories. Another observation worth noting is that there are clusters of dots, grouped in horizontal and vertical lines, meaning that certain boxes (zones) are very hot in terms of migration radius and migration volume.

Motivated by the observation that some boxes are especially hot, we zoom into boxes/zones that experience at least one migration and summarize their statistics, i.e., the number of boxes/zones and the migrated memory volume across boxes/zones, in Table 5. For each such a box/zone, we compute the number of boxes to which it migrates VMs and the aggregated active memory volume of the migrated VMs. Note that one can see that Table 5 presents the numerical values for hot boxes/zones, shown in Figure 4. Through presenting the average, mean, 99th percentile, and maximum value, we focus on discussing the tail values for boxes/zones. We further stress that the migrated volume presented here is a kind of lower bound, as different memory migration policies may require retransmission of dirty memory pages. One can see that a hot box/zone can chat with up to 26/9 boxes/zones and the migration volume from those hot boxes/zones can be as high as 605/7353 GB. Such values are critical to estimate the network performance, such as the network transfer time required, which might translate into non-negligible delays at the service level under a given network technology and/or network topology. For example, migrating 0.5 GB of active memory over a 10 Gbps Ethernet link will take at least 0.4 seconds, assuming no extra network load/overhead. Overall, our statistics presented above provide simple but crucial design parameters for the network, such that migration-driven communication needs of hot boxes/zones can be well addressed by realistic workloads.

4.4 Migration Overhead

To further quantitatively measure the migration overhead per migration volume, we focus on the set of boxes that experience migrations. More precisely, for the boxes of interest, we collect the active memory sizes associated with migrated-out VMs, and the network bandwidths of the box during that hourly time interval. As the original data is widely spread, we aggregate boxes having a similar level of migration and apply fitting on this aggregate set, where each point represents network bandwidth and migration frequency of aggregated boxes. Figure 5 depicts such a filtered dataset and the fitting results. We apply multiple parametric models, i.e., linear, higher order polynomial, and exponential, and based on the

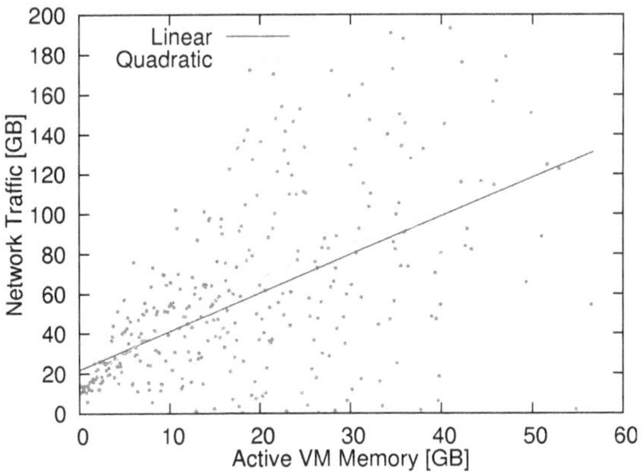

Figure 5: Estimating network overhead per migrating volume for boxes: network traffic vs. active memory sizes.

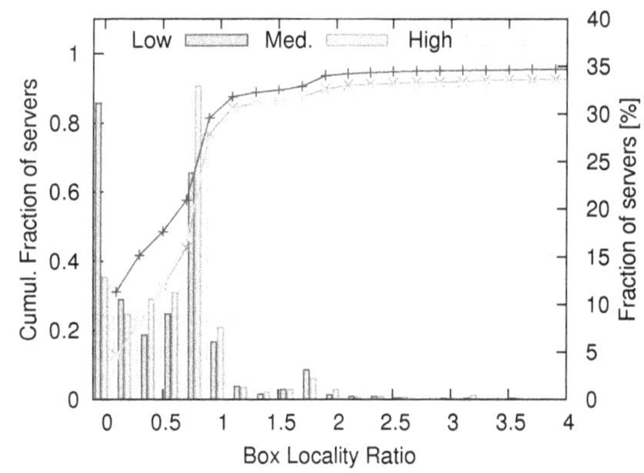

Figure 6: Distribution of boxes' locality ratios by low, medium and high consolidation levels.

sum of square errors and P-values, the linear model

$$Traffic = 21.79 + 1.93 \cdot M_{migrated}$$

where $M_{migrated}$ denotes active memory, returns the best fit. The convex second order model is the second best. As the information on the underlying VM memory migration strategies, i.e., pre-copy v.s. post-copy, are not available to us, we provide in the following a discussion on both models, though the linear model has a lower mean square error.

The linear model shows a gradient value of 1.93, which implies that migrating 1 GB of memory incurs 1.93 GB of box traffic volume. Essentially, network migration overhead roughly accounts for $0.93x$ of the migrated data, on top of the minimum migrated memory volume, i.e., the VM's active memory set. Such an overhead can be explained by the memory migration strategies, in particular, pre-copy memory migration, which tends to stress network resources to keep the memory most up-to-date. As for the quadratic model, it shows an increasing trend of network traffic up to a memory size of 40 GB, and then flattens out. A possible explanation is that a different mix of memory migration strategies is adopted at boxes, depending on the migration requirement. Actually, the gradient of the increasing part is roughly 2, taken from the point of a memory size of 25 GB, which is very close to the case of the linear model. Thus, we conclude that the upper bound of migrating one unit of VM memory can induce roughly $2x$ unit of traffic volume. Combing the observation in Section 4.2, a VM migration needs to transmit roughly 724 MB memory, resulting into 1448 MB of traffic.

5. VIRTUAL TRAFFIC MULTIPLEX

In today's datacenters, the network bandwidth demands of virtual and physical traffic are highly affected by the level of multiplexing, i.e., the level of VM consolidation at boxes. We are interested in answering the following questions through the state-of-the-practice at today's datacenters, especially from the perspective of network edges: (1) What is the degree of intra-box vs. inter-box communication when co-locating VMs with frequent bilateral communication on a box where the hypervisor can either manifest or reduce the bandwidth of virtual and physical traffic? (2) How do the bandwidth demands of co-located VMs differ from each other over time, and how do the total virtual and physical traffic volumes on a box vary with respect to different degrees of virtualization levels? (3) How can the aggregation of virtual traffic impact the burstiness of the network traffic, and what are the implications from a network resource provisioning point of view? (4) What is the CPU overhead when forwarding/receiving network packets and their dependency on virtualized datacenters?

To such an end, we use the bandwidth demands of consolidated VMs and boxes and derive the statistics of interest. To study the efficacy of intra-box communication of consolidated VMs, we propose communication locality ratios for each box. Using the max-mean ratio, we study the heterogeneity of virtual traffic generated from co-located VMs. To get an understanding of how the burstiness behaves, we combine the two aforementioned results, and for the CPU and network dependency, we look at the correlation between CPU usage and total virtual traffic for a box.

5.1 Communication Locality: Intra- vs. Inter-box Traffic

Local intra-box VM traffic is cheaper to forward than inter-box traffic, because it does not involve any physical network resource. This is even more so under recent communication layers which aim at a zero-copy or near zero-copy operation [36]. To find out the traffic locality, we use the ratio between the volume of total virtual traffic from co-located VMs to the physical traffic of the underlying box. We term such a value the box *locality ratio*, and use it to explain the relationship between inter- and intra-box traffic.

The rational behind is the following. From the communication layer viewpoint, the VMs, the hypervisor and the external world are all seen as edge nodes of a box-internal virtual network. Assuming that such a layer is lossless, its input and output traffic must be balanced. This assumption is reasonable since in normal conditions there is no reason to drop packets and degrade network performance. Unfortunately, we lack one component of the balancing equation, which is the hypervisor traffic. To infer the locality from the proposed statistics, we assume that the aforementioned hypervisor traffic is negligible.

Under the assumption of negligible hypervisor traffic and no packet losses, we consider three distinct cases for the locality ratio: (1) the locality ratio is equal to 1, meaning that VMs co-located on the same box do not communicate with other local VMs. (2) the locality ratio is between 0 and 1, implying that VMs generate very little traffic in comparison to the underlying physical traffic. In other words, the box has more inter-box than intra-box communication. This can be explained by significant traffic being generated by the hypervisor, e.g., during a migration. (3) The locality ratio is greater than 1, indicating that a box has a good mix of inter- and intra-box communication. As an extreme case, where the locality ratio is

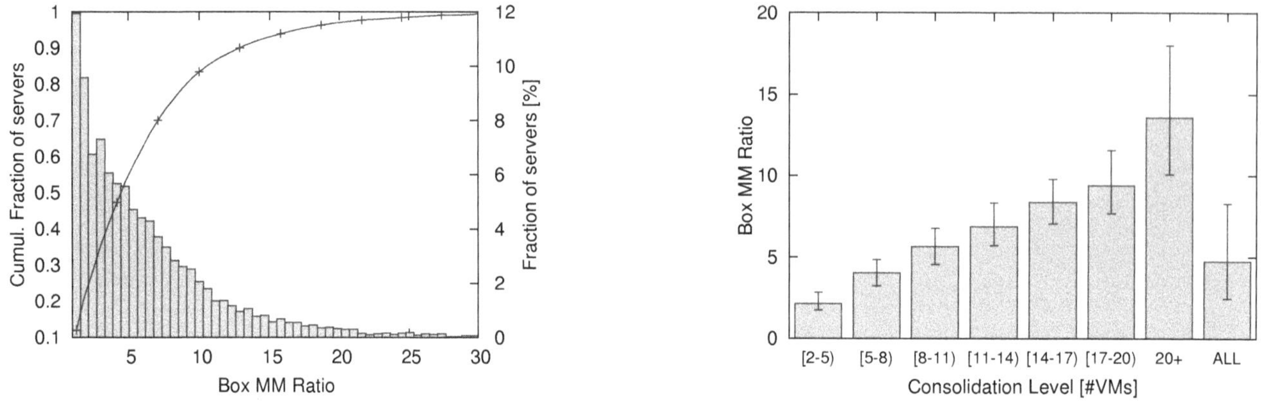

(a) Distribution of MM ratio

(b) Dependency on the consolidation level

Figure 7: Heterogeneity by average Max-Min ratios, MM_i.

close to infinity, only intra-box traffic exists, meaning that the box does not communicate with the outside world. The locality ratio defined here acts as a lower bound, as we assume hypervisor traffic is negligible. In the case the hypervisor traffic is indeed significant, our proposed locality ratio then underestimates the intra-box traffic. Overall, we consider higher locality ratio values to imply a communication advantage for the current VM placement.

In the following, we show the distribution of the locality ratios of boxes, and its relationship with the consolidation level. We present three distribution lines of locality ratios in Figure 6. The three groups are low, medium and high consolidation levels, which correspond to boxes hosting $1-5$, $6-15$ and >15 VMs, respectively. For all three groups, one can observe that there are two masses around 0 and 0.8, accounting for roughly 80% of boxes. Indeed, the median value of the locality ratios is roughly 0.88, meaning that the bandwidth demands of aggregated virtual traffic is only 88% of its underlying physical traffic. The remaining 12% of the bandwidth demands of boxes is attributed to network management and control traffic. This further implies that only roughly 15% of boxes have aggregated virtual traffic demands higher than their aggregated physical traffic demand, which is the most desirable condition from the viewpoint of taking advantage of stronger intra-box communication. Even so, the locality ratios of those boxes have long tails, which drive up the average value. We note that the presence of boxes with very low locality ratios indicate that our coarse assumption on the supervisor traffic being negligible does not hold well. Therefore, boxes with a locality ratio close to zero means that the inter-box traffic observed at boxes is mainly consumed and generated by the hypervisor, and thus the hypervisor traffic is non-negligible.

Though the percentage of high locality ratios, i.e., greater than one, is roughly the same across the three consolidation levels, boxes with low consolidation have a distinct distribution of locality ratio from boxes with medium and high consolidation levels. This can be observed from the fractions of boxes with ratios of 0 and 0.8 among these three groups. The statistics presented here lead to one key observation: the consolidation level indeed affects the communication locality. However, boxes with high consolidation levels may not necessarily guarantee that the volume of intra-box traffic is higher than inter-box traffic, i.e., that the locality ratio is greater than one. Our observation leads us to conclude that there are still plenty of opportunities for traffic-aware VM placement to enhance the communication locality and take advantage of the cheaper traffic forwarding.

5.2 Heterogeneity by Max-Mean Ratio

The previous subsection illustrates the difference between the total bandwidth of aggregate virtual and physical traffic at edges. This subsection highlights how bandwidth demands of co-located VMs differ from each other over time. The objective here is to quantify the heterogeneity of co-located virtual traffic. The interest is in light of the fact that high levels of heterogeneity may lead to fairness and/or isolation issues for the network resources.

We compute a max-mean ratio for each box i at each time window t, denoted as MM_i^t, using their bandwidth demand of all co-located VM j, denoted as B_j^t MM_i. More precisely,

$$MM_i^t = \frac{\max_{j \in \Omega_i} B_j^t}{\frac{1}{|\Omega_i^t|} \sum_{j \in \Omega_i^t} B_j^t}$$

where Ω_i^t is the set of co-located VMs on box i at time t. Furthermore, we compute the time average of MM_i^t across observation periods, i.e., the 24 hours of a day. Note that we only use information of virtual traffic to study the heterogeneity by MM ratios. As the MM_i ratio is the average across time, it reveals the bandwidth heterogeneity over time as well as across VMs. When co-located VMs have similar demands, the MM ratio is close to one, whereas the further away from one the ratio is, the higher the heterogeneity, implying uneven network demands.

We depict the PDF/CDF of the average MM ratios for all boxes in Figure 7 (a). One can see that 12% of boxes have an MM ratio close to one. After that, the fraction of boxes decreases with the MM ratios, as indicated by the monotonically decreasing PDF. However, the distribution has a long tail, with a 99th percentile of 27.5, increasing the mean to 6.3. Indeed, there is a non-negligible fraction of boxes where a VM with high traffic demand shares the network resource with a number of VMs with low traffic demands.

Intuitively, the MM ratio depends on the consolidation level, i.e., when there are more VMs consolidated on a box, the probability of finding VMs with different network demands is higher. To quantitatively show this dependency, we plot a box plot of the median, 25th and 75th percentiles of MM ratios computed at different groups of consolidation levels in Figure 7 (b). One can clearly see that boxes with low consolidation levels show a lower degree of heterogeneity, i.e., lower MM ratio values, while the MM ratios grow almost linearly with the consolidation level. The observation of high heterogeneity further stresses the challenge of managing virtual traffic in highly consolidated datacenters.

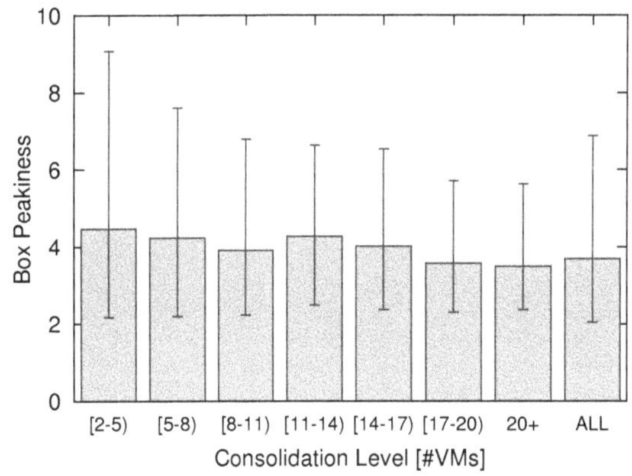

Figure 8: Network burstiness by average peakiness across different consolidation levels.

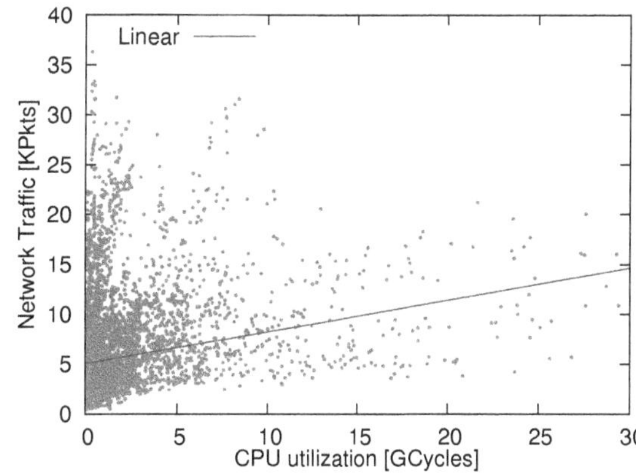

Figure 9: Estimating CPU overhead per network traffic for boxes consolidating eight VMs.

Furthermore, we also look at the standard deviation of MM ratios across time. The values are rather low, and get even lower with increasing consolidation levels. The conclusion here is that the MM ratio for each box is rather stable over the time, when looking at hourly bandwidth demands.

Overall, the MM ratio is not low, i.e., the mean across boxes is roughly 6.3, indicating that the "elephant" VM can generate many times more network demands than the average VMs. Overall, VMs with very different bandwidth demands compete for the underlying network resources. The statistics provided here not only support the studies [21,33] addressing fairness and performance of isolation in network sharing, but also provide key parameters for their proposed solutions.

5.3 Network Burstiness

Here we analyze the effects of statistical traffic aggregation to counter network demand burstiness at the physical network level. Bursty workloads have been found to dramatically degrade performance, and much work has been done to mitigate it [25,38]. However, since peaks of individual services are typically uncorrelated, the aggregate peak network load grows much more slowly than the sum of the individual peak loads. Therefore, provisioning costs can be lowered by aggregating the traffic of a larger number of services [14].

Virtual traffic provides opportunities to mitigate workload burstiness, due to consolidation. To quantify such an effect, we again resort to a max-mean statistic, looking from the perspective of physical traffic. This statistic is termed *peakiness*, P, to avoid confusion with MM ratios in the previous subsection. More in detail, given the physical box network demand N_i^t in Mbps of box i at time t, the box peakiness P_i observed during the observation period, T, is:

$$P_i^t = \frac{\max_{t \in T} N_i^t}{\frac{1}{|T|} \sum_{t \in T} N_i^t}$$

where T are the observation periods, i.e., the 24 hours of a day. Using such values, we try to see traffic smoothing effect measured during a day.

Figure 8 depicts the box plot of the peakiness P, categorized into different groups of consolidation levels. One can see that there is a minor decreasing trend in peakiness with increasing consolidation levels, particularly the 50th percentile decreases from 4.4 to 3.5. This implies that the peak load of a day is 4.4 times the average load, and then drops to 3.5 times when the consolidation level increases, showing an improvement of 33%. Moreover, the standard deviation also decreases, as can be inferred from the reduced span between the whiskers representing the 25th and 75th percentiles. This indicates that co-locating multiple VMs on the same box effectively smoothens the burstiness of the box. Our data shows that increasing the multiplex level of virtual traffic indeed smoothens the physical traffic, with a reduction of roughly 30% on the peak loads. Hence, while our observation on heterogeneity emphasizes the management complexity of consolidation levels, the burstiness of physical traffic can effectively be smoothed by aggregating the traffic of a large number of virtual machines.

5.4 Dependency on CPU Usage

There has been a long debate over which resource is the bottleneck at datacenters, particularly between CPU and network. Considering the virtual traffic in today's virtualized datacenters, these two resources are no longer decoupled. In fact, the virtual switch, which acts as an access layer providing inter- and intra-VM connectivity, is most of the time implemented in software [28,31,39]. Hence, network and CPU are directly intertwined. To provide a more complete view, we try to quantify this dependency.

More precisely, we collect the hourly averages of the box CPU utilization, and compare them to the total virtual traffic exchanged by the VMs within the hour. Since the CPU is also directly related to the computation activity of the VMs, we create separate datasets aggregating boxes with similar VM consolidation levels. Each point in the sub-datasets represents the virtual network demand versus the box CPU utilization. Since the packet forwarding operation in software is mainly dominated by a per-packet rather then per-byte cost [7], we measure the exchanged traffic in packets, while the CPU utilization is in cycles used. We apply fitting on each of these sub-datasets using multiple parametric models, i.e., linear, higher order polynomial, and exponential. Based on the sum of square errors and P-values, the linear model $U = aT + b$ returns the best fit, where U denotes used CPU cycles and T represents the traffic in packets. The slope a models the dependency between box CPU utilization and virtual traffic, while b gathers any other CPU activity performed by the hypervisor and VMs. Figure 9 shows the dataset (U,T) pairs and the resulting linear model fit for boxes consolidating exactly eight VMs. We report the model parameters a and b for all other levels of consolidation in Table 6. We observe that a shows a constant trend fluctuating around a mean value of 0.26 Mcycles/packet, while b increases with consolidation levels. As expected, the more VMs, the higher the constant aggregate CPU activity.

Table 6: Linear Model Parameters: a in [Pkts/MCycles] and b in [MCycles] under different consolidation levels, n.

n	1	2	3	4	5	6	7	8	9	10	11	12	13	14	15	16	17	18	Mean
a	0.40	0.21	0.31	0.31	0.37	0.22	0.37	0.32	0.25	0.25	0.23	0.01	0.21	0.22	0.05	0.27	0.43	0.36	0.26
b	497	936	1868	2320	3087	3452	3371	5046	5967	6050	6610	7279	7693	8408	8396	8923	8428	9082	

Table 7: Service unavailability (SU) due to network and non-network issues.

	Mean	Median	99th
	Network		
Time between SU [d]	27.54	19.58	140.90
Down Times [h]	28.79	5.75	567.48
No. of Servers [#]	1.44	1.00	4.00
	Non-network		
Time between SU [d]	12.06	1.97	128.03
Down Times [h]	18.67	3.23	291.52
No. of Servers [#]	1.19	1.00	5.00

To give a more concrete idea of the dependency, an estimated cost of 0.26 Mcycles/packet translates into a packet processing time of 98.7 μs, assuming a 2.6 GHz CPU and no parallelism. Moreover, with an additional assumption on 1500 byte MTU Ethernet frames, one can further translate it into an estimated maximum bandwidth of 121 Mbps. Hence if the VMs perform very network-intensive workloads, the host might spend non-negligible resources in forwarding the virtual traffic. One has to consider, however, that the cost estimated by a is not solely the forwarding cost incurred by the hypervisor, but also accounts for any CPU load triggered by the packet inside the VMs. Nevertheless, this hints to the fact that when consolidating VMs, their network demand must be taken into account to insure that no performance penalties are incurred. Moreover, depending on CPU performance isolation and provisioning, very chatty VMs might affect the performance of other VMs, even of those not directly having high network demands, by simply reducing the available CPU capacity of the host.

6. SERVICE QOS

In this section, we provide an analysis on how network traffic affects the quality of service, which is defined by the probabilities and percentages of service unavailability. To such an end, we leverage the service tickets used in [11]. Service tickets record how services hosted on physical and virtual machines fail and recover. Root causes considered are network, hardware, software, power, reboot, and the rest. In particular, network-induced service unavailability (SU) is related to network issues compromising the reachability of a server. To study the impact of network on service QoS, we here categorize service unavailability into network-induced and non-network induced, the latter encompassing all other root causes. We start out our analysis by providing overview statistics related to both types from the datacenter provider's perspective, and further highlight the significance of network issues on service unavailability of a single VM. Finally, we investigate if network loads affect the network-induced service unavailability, and contrast our findings with previous studies on network failures [34,37].

6.1 Datacenter Level

Here, we focus on how network and non-network induced service unavailability takes place at the datacenter level. We consider all the service tickets collected, and compute the time between consecutive SUs at the same datacenter, the service down times, and the number of servers involved. The service down time includes both the waiting time in the queue and the repair time. We present the mean, median and 99th percentile of the network-induced and non-network induced SUs statistics in Table 7. We note that as we consider multiple specific causes in the non-network induced SU, we only compute the time between SUs having the same root cause for fair comparison.

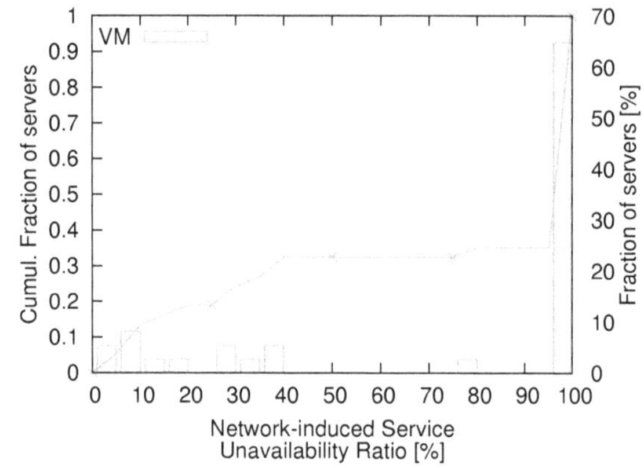

Figure 10: The relative impact of network on service unavailability: the CDF of network-induced SU ratio per VM.

From Table 7, we see that a datacenter in our study experiences service unavailability due to network issues every 27.5 days on average, with almost 1.2 days of service down time, affecting 1.44 servers. Non-network induced SUs happen on average a bit more than twice as frequently, i.e., every 12 days, with a lower service down time (18.7 hours), and affecting a slightly lower number of servers (1.19). Similar differences between non-network- and network-induced SUs can also be observed from the median and 99th percentile values. We would like to point out that the mean values of service down times and times between non-network SUs are much higher than the medians (roughly by a factor of 10) due to the heavy tails of the data. Moreover, the difference between the two types of SUs are much more dominant when using the median values. For example, the time between a network-induced SU is higher than a none-network one by 2.3x and 9.8x when evaluating by mean and median values, respectively. In the following, to avoid being biased by the heavy tail, we derive most of our key findings from the median values. Overall, large datacenters experience network-induced service unavailabilities with a much lower frequency, i.e., in the factor of one tenth, but a visibly higher service down time, i.e., 1.8x, compared to non-network induced ones.

6.2 Single Service Level

In this subsection, we zoom in to individual servers that have experienced at least one occurrence of network-induced SU. Our aim here is to quantify the significance of network-induced SUs, compared to the overall duration of SUs. For each server, we define a network-induced SU ratio, computed as the network-induced service down time percentage with respect to the total service down time. Such a ratio illustrates the relative impact of network related issues on individual server QoS. As only very few boxes were af-

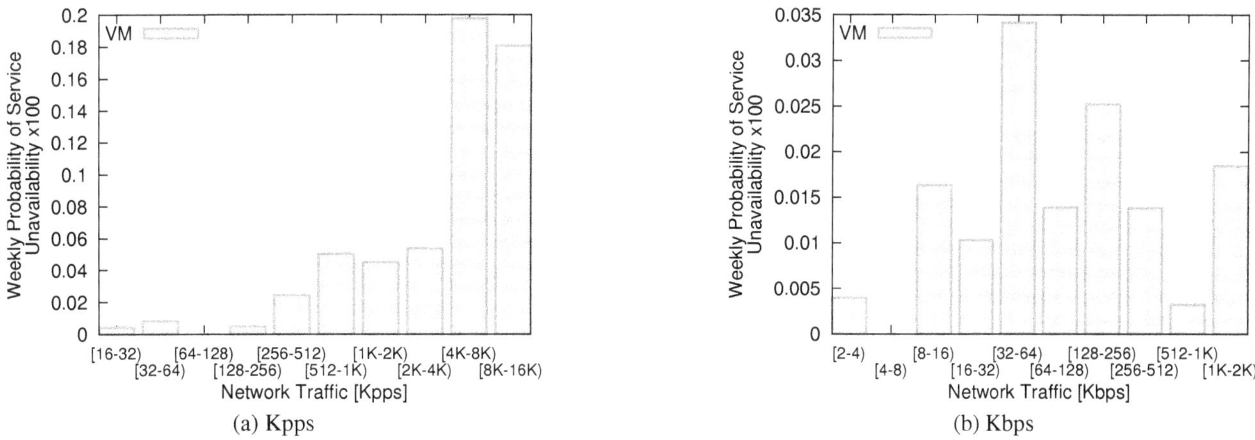

Figure 11: The impact of network loads on the probability of service unavailability: by two types of load measurement.

fected by network outages, we consider only VMs and present the CDF of their network-induced SU ratios in Figure 10.

The network-induced SU ratios cluster around three masses. The first and most prominent one, accounting for 65% of all VMs, locates at 100%. Hence 65% of VMs were affected only by network induced SUs. The other two masses are around low network-induced SU ratio values, i.e., the second peak centers at around 10% and the third at around 35%. Moreover they account for 20% and 15% of VMs, respectively.

Our results lead us to conclude that for the majority of VMs with network-related issues, the network is the sole cause of issues, while only 35% of VMs suffer from more diverse SUs such as software or unexpected reboot issues.

6.3 Virtual Network Loads Make (in)Differences

Finally, we revisit a debate on network loads causing network-induced service unavailability. One study claims the positive correlation [37] using experimental data, where another study argues otherwise [34], citing field data. We compute the probability of service unavailability relative to VMs with different ranges of virtual traffic. The probability of network-induced service unavailability is the occurrences of such SU divided by the number of VMs that have a particular range of virtual traffic loads. We particularly present the weekly probability which is the average over multiple weeks in the observation period. In Figure 11 (a) and (b) we show two results of virtual traffic loads measured in Kpps and Mbps, respectively.

One can see that the probability of network-induced SU grows with the Kpps, whereas there is no visible trend with respect to Mbps. On the one hand, the load in Kpps is more prominent for virtual systems since forwarding operations within the hypervisor typically have a per packet cost and are often independent on the actual packet size, hence the dependency seen in Figure 11 (a). On the other hand, packet payloads are typically either very small for acknowledgements like the one used by TCP, or fully sized to reduce the packet header overhead. Here the mix of small and big packets defines the Mbps load, hence there is less direct correlation between network-induced SUs and the Mbps load as seen in Figure 11 (b). Essentially, our data supports both arguments in the related work, depending on the network traffic metrics considered.

7. RELATED WORK

In the past years, there have been tremendous research efforts focused on improving datacenter networking from the perspective of physical and virtual traffic, leveraging information about bandwidth demands and communication patterns, using simulation or small-scale testbeds. Bandwidth allocation reservation via various virtual network abstraction techniques [2,42] and deployment frameworks [6] have been proposed to increase the utilization of the entire datacenter network, and lower the cost for tenants, especially in the context of cloud computing, to extract workloads exhibiting complimentary time variability [42] and desired sets of properties [32]. Novel datacenter network architectures and management techniques have been designed for various communication patterns, such as multi-layer fat tree [1] for heterogeneous traffic, LV2 [17] for uniform traffic, and [41] for one to many traffic.

Additionally, there is another host of studies trying to address performance of services by adopting network-aware VM management. A purely network centric approach places VMs with strong communication needs on adjacent boxes, such that the network demands on the physical network [26] and the routing overhead [22] are minimized as far as possible. VM placement and migration decisions that take multi-resource and bandwidth demands into thorough consideration [15, 27, 40] are shown to result in significant efficiency gains not only for the network, but also for the entire datacenter. Li et al. [24] benchmark and compare the computing and storage services performance across different public cloud providers. The aforementioned work is typically evaluated using synthetic benchmarks, and therefore lacks the overview of a broader spectrum of real-life service demands.

Large scale characterizations of datacenter networks aim to fill the gap by providing diversified workload statistics on production systems. Most of the related work focuses on the "flow" of physical traffic and collects statistics at the network aggregation points, e.g., switches and routers, from enterprise [18,29] and cloud-like datacenters [5,12,23]. Motivated by the wide adoption of virtualization and cloud computing, a few studies characterize virtual traffic at public cloud datacenters, e.g., Amazon EC2 [16], as well as enterprise datacenters [9, 10, 26], capturing the network demands from the perspectives of both virtual and physical traffic. Recently, a few network studies [20,34,35] have been conducted from the perspective of services. However, none of the aforementioned studies correlate the virtual traffic with physical traffic, resource management of virtual machines, and CPU requirements in virtualized datacenters.

Our study provides a characterization of virtual traffic from the perspective of network edges, where virtual meets physical resources. We derive a special kind of communication matrix and network overhead – migrating VMs. Focusing on VMs co-located on a single physical host, we address the pattern of network demands due to network multiplex and their CPU demands. We quantitatively evaluate the impact the network has on service unavailability.

8. SUMMARY AND CONCLUSION

Using a large collection of field data and correlating VM management, service QoS, and bandwidth demands of co-located VMs and the hosting box, our analysis develops a sound understanding on the patterns, dependencies, and impact of virtual traffic from the perspective of datacenters network edges. In particular, we highlight the differences between virtual and physical traffic, communication patterns of migration, the communication locality and heterogeneity of co-located services, CPU overhead per packet forwarding, and the impact of network-induced service unavailability at the datacenter and service level.

- VMs show a higher average annual increase in bandwidth than boxes, i.e., 27% vs. 22%. The number of NICs remains constant for the majority of boxes and VMs, but has a higher tendency to increase for VMs.

- Roughly 3% of migrations are live and across multiple geographic zones. Frequently migrated VMs tend to have higher migration volume of memory. The ratio between migration traffic and migrated volume in terms of active memory is roughly two-to-one. The migration-driven communication radius can be up to 26 boxes or 9 zones.

- Roughly 15% of boxes show strong intra-box communication, indicated by a locality ratio greater than one. There is still plenty of opportunities for communication-aware VM management.

- Daily bandwidth demands of co-located VMs are very different, showing that elephant VMs can generate roughly 6 times more network demands than the average VMs. The hourly peak load of box network demands can be reduced by up to 30% when increasing the consolidation level of virtual traffic.

- The processing cost to forward one packet of virtual traffic is approximately 0.26 Mcycles/packet, or 98.7 μs on a 2.6 GHz CPU.

- At the datacenter level, network-induced service unavailability occurs at much lower frequency, but causes slightly higher down time durations, than non-network induced ones. The impact of network issues is low for VMs suffering from diversified service unavailabilities. Traffic loads measured in Kpps (Mbps) have a positive (no) impact on network-induced service unavailability.

Overall, our study provides a multi-faceted analysis of virtual traffic, demystifying the ways virtual traffic meets and interacts with physical resources. Our findings are crucial for developing service-aware network design and traffic-aware resource management.

9. ACKNOWLEDGMENTS

This work has been supported by the Swiss National Science Foundation (project 200021 141002) and partly funded by the EU commission under the FP7 GENiC project (Grant Agreement No 608826).

10. REFERENCES

[1] M. Al-Fares, A. Loukissas, and A. Vahdat. A scalable, commodity data center network architecture. In *ACM SIGCOMM*, pages 63–74, 2008.

[2] H. Ballani, P. Costa, T. Karagiannis, and A. I. T. Rowstron. Towards predictable datacenter networks. In *ACM SIGCOMM*, pages 242–253, 2011.

[3] H. Ballani, K. Jang, T. Karagiannis, D. Gunawardena, C. Kim, and G. O'Shea. Chatty tenants and the cloud network sharing problem. In *NSDI*, pages 171–184, 2013.

[4] M. F. Bari, R. Boutaba, R. P. Esteves, L. Z. Granville, M. Podlesny, M. G. Rabbani, Q. Zhang, and M. F. Zhani. Data center network virtualization: A survey. *IEEE Commun. Surveys Tuts*, 15(2):909–928, 2013.

[5] T. Benson, A. Akella, and D. A. Maltz. Network traffic characteristics of data centers in the wild. In *ACM IMC*, pages 267–280, 2010.

[6] T. Benson, A. Akella, A. Shaikh, and S. Sahu. CloudNaaS: a cloud networking platform for enterprise applications. In *ACM SoCC*, pages 8:1–8:13, 2011.

[7] A. Bianco, R. Birke, L. Giraudo, and M. Palacin. Openflow switching: Data plane performance. In *IEEE ICC*, pages 1–5, 2010.

[8] R. Birke, , A. Podzimek, L. Y. Chen, and E. Smirni. State-of-the-practice in data center virtualization: Toward a better understanding of vm usage. In *IEEE/IFIP DSN*, 2013.

[9] R. Birke, M. Bjoerkqvist, L. Y. Chen, E. Smirni, and T. Engbersen. (big)data in a virtualized world: Volume, velocity, and variety in cloud datacenters. In *USENIX FAST*, pages 177–189, 2014.

[10] R. Birke, L. Y. Chen, and C. Minkenberg. A datacenter network tale from a server's perspective. In *IEEE IWQoS*, 2013.

[11] R. Birke, I. Giurgiu, L. Y. Chen, D. Wiessmann, and T. Engbersen. Failures analysis of virtual and physical machines: Patterns, causes and characteristics: Toward a better understanding of vm usage. In *IEEE/IFIP DSN*, 2014.

[12] Y. Chen, S. Jain, V. K. Adhikari, Z.-L. Zhang, and K. Xu. A first look at inter-data center traffic characteristics via yahoo! datasets. In *IEEE INFOCOM*, pages 1620–1628, 2011.

[13] Cisco. Cisco Global Cloud Index, 2014. [Online].

[14] D. Clark, W. Lehr, and I. Liu. Provisioning for bursty internet traffic: Implications for industry and internet structure. In *Proc. MIT ITC Workshop on Internet QoS*, 1999.

[15] Y. Feng, B. Li, and B. Li. Bargaining towards maximized resource utilization in video streaming datacenters. In *IEEE INFOCOM*, pages 1134–1142, 2012.

[16] G. G. Wang and E. Ng. The impact of virtualization on network performance of Amazon EC2 data center. In *IEEE INFOCOM*, pages 1163–1171, 2010.

[17] A. Greenberg, J. Hamilton, N. Jain, S. Kandula, C. Kim, P. Lahiri, D. Maltz, P. Patel, and S. Sengupta. VL2: a scalable and flexible data center network. In *ACM SIGCOMM*, pages 51–62, 2009.

[18] S. Guha, J. Chandrashekar, N. Taft, and K. Papagiannaki. How healthy are today's enterprise networks? In *ACM IMC*, pages 145–150, 2008.

[19] C. Guo, G. Lu, H. J. Wang, S. Yang, C. Kong, P. Sun, W. Wu, and Y. Zhang. SecondNet: a data center network virtualization architecture with bandwidth guarantees. In *ACM CoNEXT*, page 15, 2010.

[20] K. He, A. Fisher, L. Wang, A. Gember, A. Akella, and T. Ristenpart. Next stop, the cloud: understanding modern web service deployment in EC2 and Azure. In *ACM IMC*, pages 177–190, 2013.

[21] V. Jeyakumar, M. Alizadeh, D. Mazières, B. Prabhakar, A. G. Greenberg, and C. Kim. EyeQ: Practical network performance isolation at the edge. In *USENIX NSDI*, pages 297–311, 2013.

[22] J. W. Jiang, T. Lan, S. Ha, M. Chen, and M. Chiang. Joint VM placement and routing for data center traffic engineering. In *IEEE INFOCOM*, pages 2876–2880, 2012.

[23] S. Kandula, S. Sengupta, A. G. Greenberg, P. Patel, and R. Chaiken. The nature of data center traffic: Measurements & analysis. In *ACM IMC*, pages 202–208, 2009.

[24] A. Li, X. Yang, S. Kandula, and M. Zhang. Cloudcmp: comparing public cloud providers. In *ACM IMC*, pages 1–14, 2010.

[25] C. Maltzahn, K. J. Richardson, D. Grunwald, and J. H. Martin. On bandwidth smoothing. In *IWCW*. Citeseer, 1999.

[26] X. Meng and V. P. L. Zhang. Improving the scalability of data center networks with traffic-aware virtual machine placement. In *IEEE INFOCOM*, pages 1154–1162, 2010.

[27] M. Moshref, M. Yu, A. Sharma, and R. Govindan. Scalable rule management for data centers. In *NSDI*, 2013.

[28] F. Ning, C. Weng, and Y. Luo. Virtualization i/o optimization based on shared memory. In *IEEE Big Data*, pages 70–77, 2013.

[29] R. Pang, M. Allman, M. Bennett, J. Lee, V. Paxson, and B. Tierney. A first look at modern enterprise traffic. In *ACM IMC*, pages 2–2, 2005.

[30] S. Peter, J. Li, I. Zhang, D. R. K. Ports, D. Woos, A. Krishnamurthy, T. Anderson, and T. Roscoe. Arrakis: The operating system is the control plane. In *USENIX OSDI*, pages 1–16, 2014.

[31] B. Pfaff, J. Pettit, K. Amidon, M. Casado, T. Koponen, and S. Shenker. Extending networking into the virtualization layer. In *ACM HotNets*, 2009.

[32] L. Popa, A. Krishnamurthy, S. Ratnasamy, and I. Stoica. FairCloud: sharing the network in cloud computing. In *ACM HotNets*, page 22, 2011.

[33] L. Popa, G. Kumar, M. Chowdhury, A. Krishnamurthy, S. Ratnasamy, and I. Stoica. Faircloud: sharing the network in cloud computing. In *ACM SIGCOMM*, pages 187–198. ACM, 2012.

[34] R. Potharaju and N. Jain. Demystifying the dark side of the middle: A field study of middlebox failures in datacenters. In *ACM IMC*, pages 9–22, 2013.

[35] R. Potharaju and N. Jain. When the network crumbles: an empirical study of cloud network failures and their impact on services. In *ACM SoCC*, page 15, 2013.

[36] L. Rizzo and G. Lettieri. Vale, a switched ethernet for virtual machines. In *ACM CoNEXT*, pages 61–72. ACM, 2012.

[37] J. Sherry, S. Hasan, C. Scott, A. Krishnamurthy, S. Ratnasamy, and V. Sekar. Making middleboxes someone else's problem: network processing as a cloud service. In *ACM SIGCOMM*, pages 13–24, 2012.

[38] J. Tai, J. Zhang, J. Li, W. Meleis, and N. Mi. Ara: Adaptive resource allocation for cloud computing environments under bursty workloads. In *IEEE IPCCC*, pages 1–8, 2011.

[39] J. Wang, K.-L. Wright, and K. Gopalan. Xenloop: a transparent high performance inter-vm network loopback. In *ACM HPDC*, pages 109–118, 2008.

[40] T. Wood, K. Ramakrishnan, P. Shenoy, and J. Van der Merwe. CloudNet: dynamic pooling of cloud resources by live WAN migration of virtual machines. In *ACM SIGPLAN Notices*, volume 46, pages 121–132, 2011.

[41] H. Wu, Z. Feng, C. Guo, and Y. Zhang. ICTCP: Incast congestion control for TCP in data-center networks. *IEEE/ACM Trans. Netw.*, 21(2):345–358, 2013.

[42] D. Xie, N. Ding, Y. C. Hu, and R. R. Kompella. The only constant is change: incorporating time-varying network reservations in data centers. In *ACM SIGCOMM*, pages 199–210, 2012.

Hyper-Compact Virtual Estimators for Big Network Data Based on Register Sharing

Qingjun Xiao[†‡] Shigang Chen[†] Min Chen[†] Yibei Ling[§]
[†]Department of Computer & Information Science & Engineering, University of Florida, Gainesville, FL, USA
[‡]Key Lab of Computer Network and Information Integration (Southeast University), Ministry of Education, China
[§]Telcordia Technologies & Applied Research, Ericsson, USA
Email: csqjxiao@seu.edu.cn {sgchen, min}@cise.ufl.edu yibei.ling@gmail.com

ABSTRACT

Cardinality estimation over big network data consisting of numerous flows is a fundamental problem with many practical applications. Traditionally the research on this problem focused on using a small amount of memory to estimate each flow's cardinality from a large range (up to 10^9). However, although the memory needed for each flow has been greatly compressed, when there is an extremely large number of flows, the overall memory demand can still be very high, exceeding the availability under some important scenarios, such as implementing online measurement modules in network processors using only on-chip cache memory. In this paper, instead of allocating a separated data structure (called *estimator*) for each flow, we take a different path by viewing all the flows together as a whole: Each flow is allocated with a virtual estimator, and these virtual estimators share a common memory space. We discover that sharing at the register (multi-bit) level is superior than sharing at the bit level. We propose a framework of virtual estimators that allows us to apply the idea of sharing to an array of cardinality estimation solutions, achieving far better memory efficiency than the best existing work. Our experiment shows that the new solution can work in a tight memory space of less than 1 bit per flow or even one tenth of a bit per flow — a quest that has never been realized before.

Categories and Subject Descriptors

C.4 [**Performance of Systems**]: [Measurement Techniques]; C.2.3 [**Computer Communication Networks**]: Network Operations – Network Management

Keywords

Big Network Data, Flow Monitoring, Cardinality Estimation

1. INTRODUCTION

Cardinality estimation is one of the fundamental problems in network traffic measurement [9,10,14,17,25,26]. In a general definition, it is to estimate the number of *distinct* elements in each flow during a measurement period. The *flows* under measurement may be per-source flows, per-destination flows, per-source/destination flows, TCP flows, WWW flows, P2P flows, or abstract flows. The *elements* may be destination addresses, source addresses, ports, values in other header fields, or even keywords that appear in the payload of packets in the flow.

SIGMETRICS'15, June 15–19, 2015, Portland, OR, USA.

http://dx.doi.org/10.1145/2745844.2745870 .

Practical Importance: The cardinality problem has many practical applications. For example, if we treat all packets sent from the same *source address* as a flow (per-source flow), we may use a cardinality estimation module at a gateway or firewall to detect scanners by measuring the number of *distinct destination addresses* in each flow. In this case, packets belonging to a flow are identified by their common source address (also called *flow label*). The elements under measurement are the destination addresses in the headers of the packets. In the opposite example, we may treat all packets to a common destination as a flow and count the number of distinct source addresses in each flow. When we observe the cardinality of a certain flow suddenly surges, it may signal a DDoS attack against the destination address of the flow. For other applications, a large server farm may learn the popularity of its content by tracking the number of distinct users that access each file, where all accesses to a file form an (abstract) flow; an institutional gateway may determine the popularity of external web content for caching priority by tracking the number of outbound web requests for each web content, where all requests from different users to a common URL form a flow.

In yet another example, if Google treats all client IPs that query a keyword as a flow, the cardinality of the flow suggests the popularity of the keyword being searched. In this case, the flow label is the keyword under query. The estimator that works on per-keyword flows may be implemented as a function module at the web server. According to a recent paper [14], various data analysis systems at Google, such as Sawzall, Dremel and PowerDrill, estimate the cardinalities of very large data sets on a daily basis. As pointed out in [14], cardinality estimation over large data sets presents a challenge in terms of computational resources, and memory in particular; for the PowerDrill system, a non-negligible fraction of queries historically could not be computed because they exceeded the available memory.

State of the Art: To deal with big data consisting of a very large number of flows, we must conserve memory space when designing a cardinality estimation module. For this purpose, a series of solutions were developed in the past, including PCSA [12], MultiresolutionBitmap [10] (which is a generalization of LinearCounting [22]), MinCount [3], LogLog [8], and HyperLogLog [11]. They all allocate a separate data structure, called *estimator*, for every flow. Each estimator contains a certain number of registers, bitmaps or other elementary data structures. The most compact estimator in [11] requires hundreds of bytes to ensure a large estimation range and a good estimation accuracy.

Challenges: However, as the Internet moves into the era of big network data, hundreds of bytes per flow can be too much in some important scenarios — Modern high-speed routers forward packets at the speed of hundreds of Gigabits or even hundreds of Terabits per second [13]. The number of data flows that traverse a core router can be in tens of millions. Simultaneous tracking of such a large number of flows (each of which needs hundreds of bytes) brings a great challenge. The reason is that, in order to sustain high throughput, routers forward packets from incoming ports to outgoing ports via switching fabric, bypassing main memory and CPU. If one wants to apply cardinality estimation as an online module to process packets in real time, one way is to implement it on network processors at the incoming/outgoing ports and use on-chip cache memory. However, the commonly-used cache on processor chips is SRAM, typically a few megabytes, which may have to be shared among multiple functions for routing, performance, measurement, and/or security purposes. In such a context, the memory that can be allocated for the function of cardinality estimation may be even less than 1 bit per flow.

In another scenario, suppose a major web search company wants to know how many different users have searched the same phrase (question or sentence) each day, which provides information on phrase popularity, useful in optimizing search performance or studying social trends on the Internet [2]. This is a cardinality estimation problem, where all search records for a given phrase form a flow. The number of flows (phrases, questions, sentences) can be in billions. Of course, we can resort to a data center for such big data, but it will certainly be welcome if one can find a novel solution that deals with an extremely large number of flows in the memory of a cheap commodity computer.

Our Contribution: After decades of development [3, 8, 10–12, 22], it appears to be very difficult to further compress the size of an individual estimator much below hundreds of bits, without sacrificing estimation range or accuracy. Recently, an interesting idea was proposed to let different estimators (each for one flow) share bits [16, 17, 25], so that bits unused by one can be picked up by another. Along this line, we make three new contributions: First, we discover that sharing bits is actually inefficient because of too much noise introduced between estimators. Sharing space is good, but it should be done differently at the register level, not at the bit level, where a register is a multi-bit data structure that will be introduced later. Second, sharing has only been applied to bitmap and PCSA [12], an early work dated back to 1985. We develop a framework of virtual estimators which enables memory sharing for the recent cardinality estimation solutions, including LogLog [8] and HyperLogLog [11], with the latter being the best existing work. Third, we fully develop the virtual HyperLogLog solution, with a new procedure for recording per-flow information in the shared space, a set of formulas for estimating per-flow cardinality with noise removal, and the analytical results for estimation error under register sharing. We show that the new solution can work in a tight memory space of less than 1 bit per flow or even one tenth of a bit per flow — a quest that has never been realized before.

The rest of the paper is organized as follows: Section 2 discusses the related work. Section 3 introduces our new design of register sharing. Section 4 proposes a framework for constructing virtual estimators based on register sharing. Section 5 presents the detailed design of a memory-efficient cardinality estimation solution under the framework, and Section 6 analyzes the new solution's mean and variance. Section 7 evaluates the performance of the proposed estimation solution through experiments based on real traffic traces. Section 8 draws the conclusion.

2. RELATED WORK

Cardinality estimation is different from the related problem of *flow-size estimation* [15], which measures the number of elements (e.g., packets or bytes) in each flow through CountMin Sketches (a generalized tool for estimating the frequency of each element in a multiset) [5], Counter Braids [18, 19], Probabilistic Lossy Counting [7], Randomized Counter Sharing [15], etc., with the goal of learning flow distribution or identifying heavy hitters. Consider all packets from a source address as a flow. Suppose the source sends 10,000 packets to a single destination address. The flow size is 10,000 when we measure the number of packets, but the flow cardinality is just one if we measure the *distinct* number of destination addresses in this flow. In short, cardinality estimation needs to remove duplicates, which makes it a more difficult problem because it has to somehow "remember" the observed elements for duplicate removal, while measuring a flow size only needs a counter.

Hash table and Bitmap: It is too costly to design an estimator based on a hash table that stores all elements to remove duplicates. Instead, we may use a bitmap [22]: Initially all bits are zeros. Each arrival element is hashed to a bit which is then set to one. Duplicates are automatically filtered out since they are mapped to the same bit. At the end of a measurement period, the cardinality estimation is $\hat{n} = -b \ln V$ [22], where b is the number of bits used, V is the fraction of bits whose values remain zeros, and $\hat{n}$ is the estimated flow cardinality.

The problem of bitmap is that the estimation range is bounded by $b \ln b$. Hence, the bitmap has to be huge to handle a very large flow. Fig. 1 shows the simulation results, where the bitmap size is 1280 bits per flow in the leftmost plot, 96 bits per flow in the second plot, and 32 bits per flow in the third, respectively. Each flow is represented by a point, whose x-coordinate is the true cardinality and y-coordinate is the estimated cardinality. The equality line is also shown. The closer a point is to the line, the more accurate the estimation is. The leftmost plot clearly shows a limited estimation range. As the bitmap size shrinks, the range shrinks quickly, as shown by plots (b)-(d). Note that "less than 1 bit" per flow will not work for the bitmap approach. Variants of the bitmap approach also have the problem of limited estimation range [23–26].

MultiResolutionBitmap and PCSA: Sampling is one of the main methods in the literature for dealing with the estimation range problem. MultiResolutionBitmap [10] is essentially the concatenation of multiple bitmaps, each having a different sampling probability. If we let the sampling probabilities be $\frac{1}{2}$, $(\frac{1}{2})^2$, ..., $(\frac{1}{2})^w$ and set each bitmap to its minimum size (a single bit), then we have the smallest MultiResolutionBitmap, equivalent to an FM sketch of the earlier PCSA [12]. An FM sketch, also referred to as a *register* in the literature, can give an estimation up to 2^w, where w is the number of bits in the register. For example, $w = 32$ for an estimation range up to 2^{32}.

However, the estimation result from a single register is very inaccurate. To improve accuracy, FM uses multiple registers and returns the average of their estimations. Fig. 2 presents the simulation results of FM. It clearly has a larger estimation range, but its estimation accuracy is low even when there are 40 registers in the first plot. The estimation results are discrete when there are just a few registers in the second and third plots.

LogLog and HyperLogLog: LogLog [8] and HyperLogLog [11] were proposed to compress the size of each register from 32 bits to

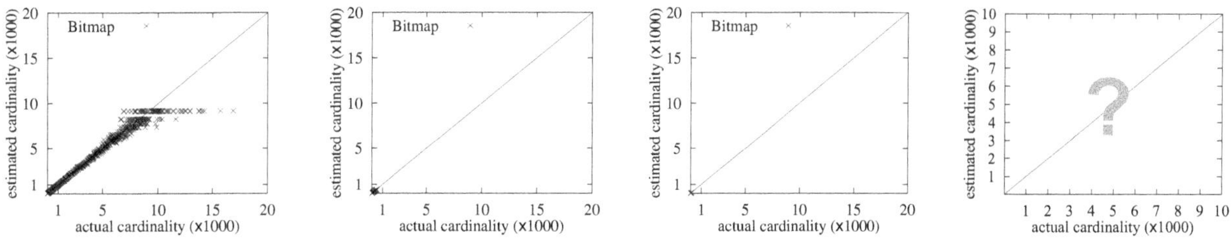

(a) 1280 bits per flow (b) 96 bits per flow (c) 32 bits per flow (d) less than 1 bit per flow

Figure 1: Measurement results of the bitmap approach, whose estimation range is limited. Each flow is represented by one point. The x-coordinate is the true cardinality, and the y-coordinate is the estimated cardinality. The closer a point is to the equality line, the more accurate the estimation is.

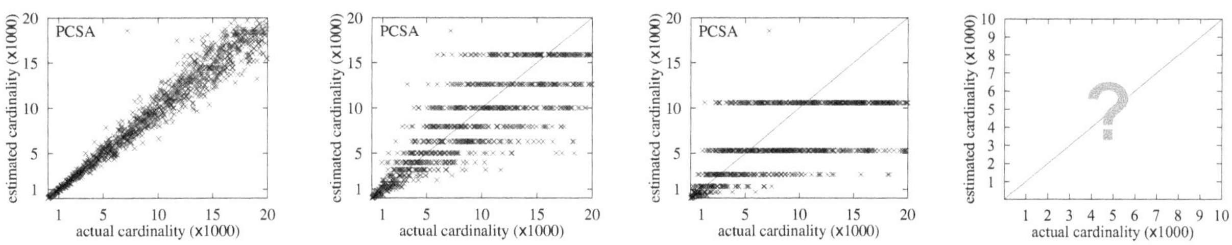

(a) 1280 bits per flow, 40 registers of 32 bits each, 13% error (b) 96 bits per flow, 3 registers of 32 bits each (c) 32 bits per flow, 1 register of 32 bits (d) less than 1 bit per flow

Figure 2: Measurement results of FM or PCSA.

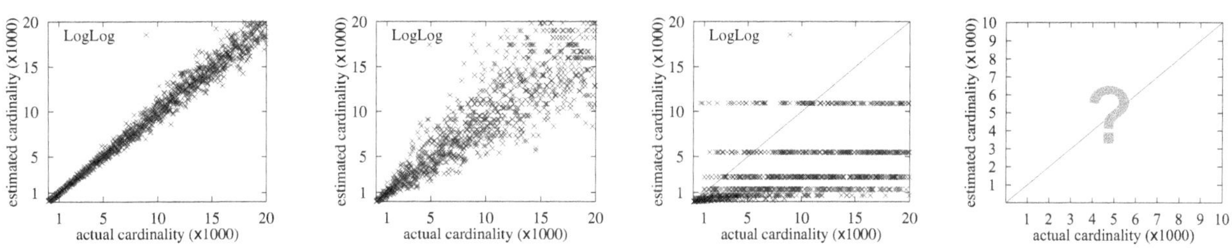

(a) 1280 bits per flow, 256 registers of 5 bits each, 8.1% error. (b) 80 bits per flow, 16 registers of 5 bits each, 33% error. (c) 5 bits per flow, 1 register of 5 bits (d) less than 1 bit per flow

Figure 3: Measurement results of LogLog.

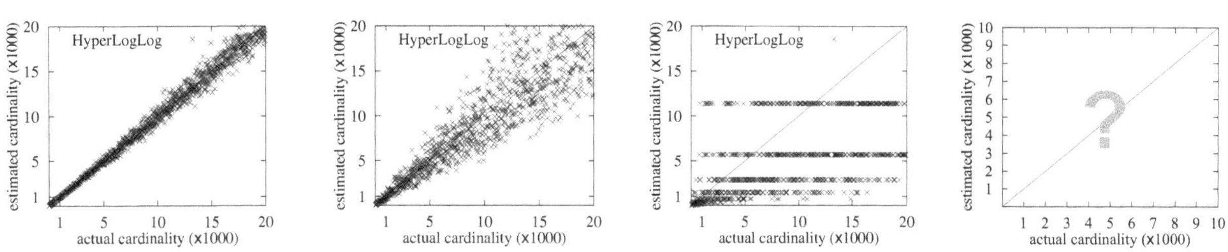

(a) 1280 bits per flow, 256 registers of 5 bits each, 6.5% error (b) 80 bits per flow, 16 registers of 5 bits each, 26% error (c) 5 bits per flow, 1 register of 5 bits (d) less than 1 bit per flow

Figure 4: Measurement results of HyperLogLog.

5 bits for the same estimation range of 2^{32}. Their performance is presented in Fig. 3 and Fig. 4. The estimation accuracy of LogLog and HyperLogLog (HLL) is much improved as compared with PCSA, because smaller registers mean there are more of them under the same memory constraint, which drives the estimation variance down. However, they do not work well for 80 bits in the second plot of Fig. 3 and Fig. 4 (with the relative standard error being 33% for LogLog and 26% for HLL), let alone less than one bit per flow. The accuracy of HLL is a little better than that of LogLog.

Performance Summary: The performance of the traditional cardinality estimators is summarized in Table 1, where MinCount [3, 4] takes a different approach by hashing each arrival element and keeping a number of smallest hash values, from which the estimation is made (using the range of the smallest hash values). In the second column, m is the number of smallest hash values kept by MinCount for each flow, the number of bits used by MultiResolutionBitmap, or the number of registers used by other approaches. The total memory cost is m multiplied by the size of each memory unit (hash value, bit or register).

Table 1: Comparison of the prior art.

Solution	Std. Err. (σ)	Mem Units	Mem (σ=5%)
MinCount	$1.00/\sqrt{m}$	≤32 bits	1600 bytes †
MultiResBitmap	$\approx 4.4/\sqrt{m}$	1 bit	968 bytes
PCSA	$0.78/\sqrt{m}$	32-bit registers	974 bytes
LogLog	$1.30/\sqrt{m}$	5-bit registers	423 bytes
HyperLogLog	$1.04/\sqrt{m}$	5-bit registers	271 bytes

† For MinCount, we assume the size of its memory units is 32 bits, and each unit stores the 32-bit hash value of a stream element.

For a single flow, the memory needed to control the standard error within 5% of the actual cardinality is given in the last column, which shows the progress in memory saving over the past decades: If we use PCSA as the initial benchmark, the seminal work of LogLog cuts the memory requirement by more than half. The followup HyperLogLog cuts the memory further by more than 30%. HyperLogLog has made great impact on IT industry and was adopted by Google [14], PostgreSQL, file-sharing P2P systems [21], and DDoS attack detection systems [11].

3. OUR NEW APPROACH OF REGISTER SHARING AND VIRTUAL ESTIMATORS

3.1 Motivation: Waste of Space

The traditional solutions allocate one estimator for each flow, which is however a serious waste of space. As an example, we download traffic traces from CAIDA (Cooperative Association for Internet Data Analysis) [1]. Consider per-source flows. The cardinality of each flow is the number of distinct destination addresses contacted by a source. We illustrate the distribution of the flow cardinalities in Fig. 5, where the measurement period is 10 minutes and each point shows the number (y-coordinate) of flows that have a certain cardinality (x-coordinate). A roughly straight line on a log-log plot is often considered as the signature of a power law distribution. In this figure, the line is roughly $y = 3 \cdot 10^4 \cdot x^{-1.7}$. This log-scale figure demonstrates that the vast majority of flows have small cardinalities, while a small number of flows have large cardinalities.

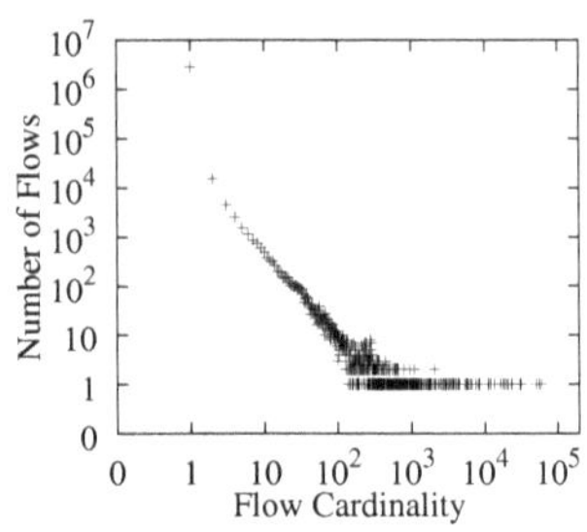

Figure 5: Flow distribution: each point shows the number (y-coordinate) of flows having a certain cardinality (x-coordinate). The average cardinality of all flows is about two.

Without knowing the flows' cardinalities beforehand (which are in fact what we want to figure out), the estimators of all flows are set according to the maximum range of cardinality, requiring hundreds of bits even for the best estimator. However, if a flow turns out to be small, e.g., with a cardinality of 1, most of the bits will be wasted.

3.2 Sharing at bit level?

One way to make use of unused bits is to share bits among the estimators. Two solutions were proposed for sharing among

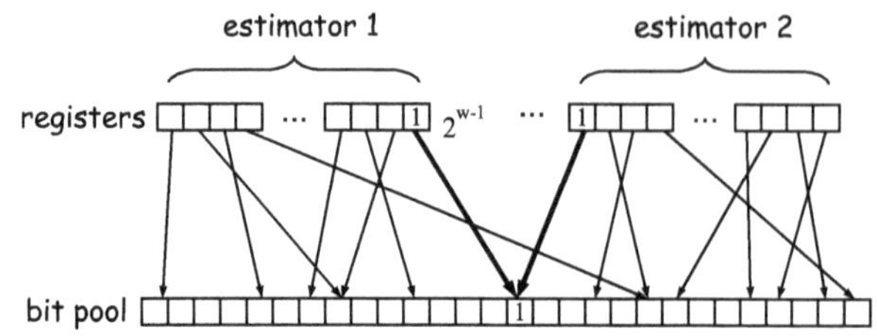

Figure 6: Bit sharing in [17], where the FM sketches (registers) share their individual bits from a common bit pool.

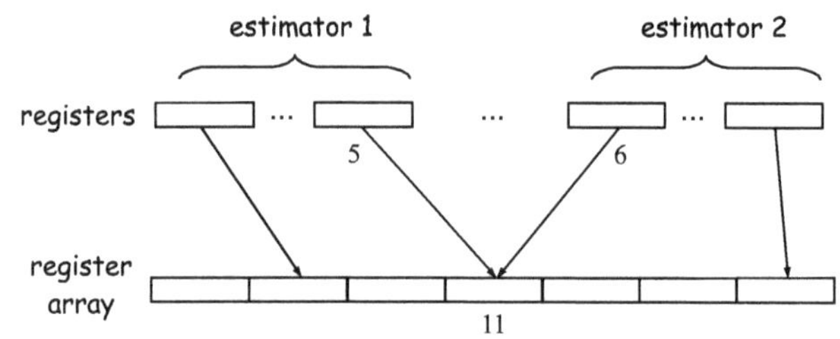

Figure 7: Register sharing, where the estimators share their registers from a common register pool.

bitmaps [25] and FM sketches [17]. In the compact spread estimator (CSE) [25], a bitmap is allocated for each flow, but all bitmaps share their bits from a common bit pool. The problem is that it is difficult to extend the estimation range of bitmaps without incurring large overhead or causing estimation inaccuracy.

In the probabilistic multiplicity counting solution (PMC) [17], an estimator with multiple FM sketches is allocated to each flow. In fact, PMC was originally designed for estimating the flow size (i.e., the number of packets in each flow), but it can be easily modified for estimating the flow cardinality, which is not commonly true for other flow-size estimators. As illustrated in Figure 6, the FM sketches (called registers) of all estimators share their *bits* from a common bit pool uniformly at random, so that mostly unused higher-order bits in the registers can be utilized. However, sharing introduces noise across estimators, which we explain through an example: Without going into too much technical details which can be found in the original paper [17], roughly speaking, when the ith bit in a register (FM sketch) is set to one, it means 2^i packets are recorded by the register on average, where $0 \leq i < w$ and w is the number of bits in each register. In the Figure 6, suppose estimator 1 is for a small flow. So the high-order bits in its sketches should be zeros. If a high-order bit in estimator 1 happens to share the same bit in the common pool with a low-order bit in estimator 2, when the low-order bit is set to one by estimator 2, the high-order bit in estimator 1 will also become one. The low-order bit in estimator 2 only represents one element, but the noise it induces represents 2^{w-1} elements for estimator 1. Although novel statistical methods can be used to remove noise, the noise of bit-level sharing is too high to take the full potential of the sharing idea, which we will demonstrate through experiments. Sharing high-order bits only with high-order bits will not work well either because the underutilized high-order bits will remain underutilized.

3.3 Register Sharing and Virtual Estimators

Our idea is to share at the register level, as illustrated in Figure 7. The estimators of different flows share their registers from a common register array M. Given a fixed register array, we dynamically create an estimator for a new flow by randomly drawing a number of registers from the array. In a sense, the array of registers are physical, but the estimators are logical because they are created on the fly without additional memory allocation. Hence, they are called *virtual estimators*.

Suppose a system allocates a certain amount of physical memory to the function of cardinality estimation. The number of bits available may be smaller than the number of flows. If this is the case, the number of registers in M will certainly be even smaller. Each register is thus shared by many virtual estimators, ensuring that the register is fully utilized.

Consider the virtual estimator of an arbitrary flow. What it estimates is actually the cardinality of the flow plus the noise introduced by other flows that share its registers. Refer to Figure 7 where estimator 1 and estimator 2 share a common register. If the register records 5 elements from the flow of estimator 1 and 6 elements from the flow of estimator 2, the final result will be 11 elements recorded. From the viewpoint of estimator 1, the register carries its flow's information as well as noise from other flows. The same is true from the viewpoint of estimator 2.

Because the registers in all virtual estimators are randomly picked, there is an equal opportunity for any two registers from different estimators to be mapped to the same physical register in M. Hence, as one virtual estimator records an element of its flow into one of its registers, the probability for this operation to cause noise to any other virtual estimator is the same. When there are a large number of virtual estimators and each of them randomly chooses a large number of registers, the noise that they cause to each other will be roughly uniform. Such uniform noise can be measured and removed.

One may argue that similar noise also exists for register-level sharing. An estimator of a small flow may share a register with an estimator of a large flow. First, the elements of the large flow will be spread among its hundreds of registers. Each register carries much smaller noise than a single bit in PMC can do. Second, the number of large flows is often exponentially fewer than the number of small flows; see Fig. 5 for example. That means the number of registers that carry large noise account for a small fraction of all registers in M. If the estimator of a small flow contains one or a few registers of large noise, the technique of harmonic averaging can be used to remove the effect of such outliers (which is already done by [8, 11]). On the contrary, for PMC, all bits that are set to ones in V can cause large noise.

3.4 Counter Sharing for Flow Size — A Different Problem

We have explained in the previous section that flow-size estimation is a different problem than cardinality estimation. Sharing counters has been applied to reduce memory overhead for estimating the sizes of a large number of flows [5, 15, 18]. Take CountMin [5] as example, which resembles a segmented counting Bloom filter (organized in a two-dimensional matrix), where the arrival of each packet of a flow causes the k counters of the flow to increase by one. The minimal value of the k counters is used as an estimation of the flow size. This approach cannot solve the problem of cardinality estimation because the counter does not "remember" the elements that it has seen for duplicate removal. As a minor note, although the minimal value of the k counters has the least noise, it does have noise, which can be significant when the number of bits is smaller than the number of flows — Because each counter has multiple bits, the number of counters will be far smaller than the number of flows. Therefore it is highly probable that most counters are shared by multiple flows, and thus even the minimal value of the k counters carries the combined size of multiple flows.

4. A FRAMEWORK FOR VIRTUAL-ESTIMATOR SOLUTIONS

We propose a unified framework for developing virtual-estimator solutions that enable register-level sharing for mainstream sketches such as PCSA [12], LogLog [8], and HyperLogLog [11]. In the next section, we will show as an example how to apply the framework to HLL for a virtual-estimator solution denoted as vHLL. The notations used are summarized in Table 2 for quick reference.

Table 2: Notations

M	a physical array of registers
m	number of registers in M
M_f	a subset of registers from M used by the virtual estimator of flow f
s	number of registers used by a virtual estimator
$H_i(f)$	a hash function that maps the ith register of M_f to a physical register in M
n_f	true cardinality of flow f
$\hat{n_f}$	estimated cardinality of flow f
$\hat{n_s}$	an estimation made based on M_f, which record both elements of flow f and elements from other flows as noise
n	true combined cardinality of all flows
$\hat{n}$	an estimated value of n

In the framework, we use a single array M of m registers to store the cardinality information of all flows. The ith register in the array is denoted by $M[i]$, $0 \le i < m$. The size of the registers is set based on the type of estimators used [8, 11, 12] and the maximum range of cardinality to be estimated. For example, in the vHLL solution, the size of registers is five bits, in order to measure big cardinalities up to 4×10^9. Each flow has s virtual registers that are randomly selected from M through hash functions. These registers logically form a virtual estimator, denoted as M_f, where f is the label of the flow. The ith register of the virtual estimator, denoted as $M_f[i]$, $0 \le i < s$, is selected from M as follows:

$$M_f[i] = M[H_i(f)], \tag{1}$$

where $H_i(...)$ is a hash function whose range is $[0, m)$. We want to stress that M_f is not a separate data structure. It is merely a logical construction based on registers selected from M, and it is not explicitly constructed during online operation. In all our later formulas, one should treat the notation $M_f[i]$ simply as $M[H_i(f)]$, referring to a register in M.

The hash function H_i, $0 \le i < s$, can be implemented from a master function $H(...)$ as follows:

$$\begin{aligned} H_i(f) &= H(f \oplus R[i]) \quad \text{or} \\ H_i(f) &= H(f \,|\, i), \end{aligned} \tag{2}$$

where '|' is the concatenation operator, '⊕' is the XOR operator, and $R[i]$ is a constant whose bits differ randomly for different indexes i. The master hash function H we have adopted in our experiments is 64-bit MURMUR3 hash. According to an online technical document, MURMUR3 performs better than many other hash functions, including JENKINS' LOOKUP3, CITY, and SPOOKY [20].

At the beginning of each measurement period, all registers are reset to zeros. The arrival stream of elements is abstracted as a sequence of $\langle f, e\rangle$ pairs, where f is a flow label and e is an element of the flow. For example, if a router measures per-source flows for their numbers of distinct destination addresses, it extracts the source address of each arrival packet as the flow label and the destination address from the IP header as the element to be recorded. For each pair $\langle f, e \rangle$, we record e in one of the registers of M_f based on the methods in [12], [8] or [11], depending on which one is used.

At the end of a measurement period, the register array M is offloaded by a server for long-term storage. Given a flow label f in offline query, we reconstruct its virtual estimator M_f by copying s registers from M at indices $H_i(f), 0 \le i < s$. Let n_s be the number of distinct elements recorded by M_f, which is the flow's cardinality plus the noise introduced by other flows due to register sharing. Let n_f be the actual cardinality of flow f. The noise term is $n_s - n_f$. We use the estimation formula from [12], [8] or [11] (depending on which one is used) to give an estimation $\hat{n_s}$ of n_s. Below we focus on noise estimation.

Let n be the sum of all flows' cardinalities. From the flow f's point of view, the elements of all other flows, $(n - n_f)$ of them, are noise. Let Y be a random variable for the number of noise elements recorded by an arbitrary register in M. When the number of flows and the number of registers per estimator are both sufficiently large and the cardinality of any flow is negligibly small when comparing with n, Y approximately follows the binomial distribution $Bino(n - n_f, \frac{1}{m})$, because each noise element has approximately an equal chance to be recorded by any register due to the random selection of registers by virtual estimators. Hence,

$$E(Y) = \frac{n - n_f}{m}.$$

The total noise, $n_s - n_f$, is the sum of individual noises in the s registers of M_f. Hence, $n_s - n_f$ can be considered as the sum of s independent random variables of $Bino(n - n_f, \frac{1}{m})$.

$$E(n_s - n_f) = s\,E(Y) = s\frac{n - n_f}{m} \tag{3}$$

By the law of large numbers in the probability theory, the relative variance $Var(\frac{n_s - n_f}{E(n_s - n_f)})$ approaches to zero when s is large. In this case, $E(n_s - n_f)$ can be approximated by an instance value, $n_s - n_f$. We have

$$\begin{aligned} n_s - n_f &\approx \frac{n - n_f}{m} s \\ n_f &\approx \frac{ms}{m - s}\left(\frac{n_s}{s} - \frac{n}{m}\right). \end{aligned} \tag{4}$$

We define a *grand flow* as the combination of all flows. With a few hundreds of extra bytes and applying the HyperLogLog, we can obtain an accurate estimation $\hat{n}$ for n (see Table 1), while the additional memory overhead is negligible when comparing with the memory space M. Alternatively, since the elements of the grand flow distribute approximately in uniform over M, we can use the entire register array M as an estimator to give an estimation for n (using HyperLogLog, for example).

Let $\hat{n_f}$ be our estimation of n_f. We have the following estimation formula from (4).

$$\hat{n_f} = \frac{ms}{m - s} \cdot \left(\frac{\hat{n_s}}{s} - \frac{\hat{n}}{m}\right) \tag{5}$$

In the next section, we will select vHLL, i.e., virtual HyperLogLog, to discuss its operations and performance in details.

5. VIRTUAL HYPERLOGLOG ESTIMATOR

In this section, as an example, we apply the framework of virtual estimators on HyperLogLog for a new solution, vHLL, based on register-level sharing. This solution consists of two components: one for recording the stream of packets in the virtual HyperLogLog estimators, and the other for estimating the cardinality of an arbitrary flow f.

5.1 Record Flow Elements in Virtual Estimator

Consider a flow f. When a measurement period begins, all registers in its virtual estimator M_f are reset to zeros. For each arrival element e of flow f, we perform the hashing below:

$$\begin{aligned} H(e) &= \langle x_1 x_2 ... \rangle \\ p &= \langle x_1 x_2 \ldots x_b \rangle \\ q &= \langle x_{b+1} x_{b+2}, \ldots \rangle, \end{aligned} \tag{6}$$

where $\langle x_1 x_2 ... \rangle$ is binary format of the hash output $H(e)$, p denotes the leading b bits with b equal to $\log_2 s$, and q represents the remaining bits. Using the value of p, we can map e pseudo-randomly to a register $M_f[p \bmod s]$. For clarity, we will breviate $M_f[p \bmod s]$ simply as $M_f[p]$ afterwards.

The operation of recording e is simple: Let $\rho(q)$ be the number of leading zeros in q plus one; for example, if $q = 001...$, then $\rho(q) = 3$. Clearly, the probability of $\rho(q) = i$ is $(\frac{1}{2})^i$, for $\forall i > 0$. We update $M_f[p]$ if its current value is smaller than $\rho(q)$. Namely,

$$M_f[p] := \max\big(M_f[p],\, \rho(q)\big), \tag{7}$$

where $:=$ is assignment operator. Hence, $M_f[p]$ has recorded (one plus) the longest run of leading zeros from any element mapped to the register. Suppose $M_f[p] = M[H_p(f)]$ as in (1), and $H_p(f) = H(f \mid p)$ as in (2). Combining (7), (1) and (2), we have

$$M[H(f \mid p)] := \max\big(M[H(f \mid p)],\, \rho(q)\big). \tag{8}$$

This assignment requires two hash operations: $H(e)$ for p and q in (6), and $H(f \mid p)$. It also requires at most two memory accesses, reading $M[H(f \mid p)]$ and writing $M[H(f \mid p)]$ back if its value changes. Note that the writing operation happens rarely since the likelihood for $\rho(q) > M[H(f \mid p)]$ to happen will decrease exponentially as the register's value increases.

Eq. (8) shows that the operations are actually performed on the physical register array M, and the virtual estimator is logical in the online recording phase.

5.2 Flow Cardinality Estimation

Given a flow label f for offline query, we construct M_f from the stored M. Consider an arbitrary register $M_f[i]$, $0 \le i < s$. Any element mapped to this register had a probability of $\frac{1}{2^{M_f[i]}}$ to set the register to its current value. Hence, the estimation for the number of elements mapped to this register is $2^{M_f[i]}$ [11].

Recall that n_s is the total number of distinct elements that have been recorded by the estimator M_f, including both elements in flow f and those in other flows that share registers in M_f. In order to estimate n_s, the normalized harmonic mean is applied to aggregate the estimations from all registers in M_f:

$$\hat{n_s} = \alpha_s \cdot s^2 \cdot \Big(\sum_{j=0}^{s-1} 2^{-M_f[j]}\Big)^{-1}, \tag{9}$$

where α_s is a bias correction constant that equals

$$\alpha_s = \Big(s \int_0^\infty \Big(\log_2\Big(\frac{2+u}{1+u}\Big)\Big)^m du\Big)^{-1}. \tag{10}$$

The above equation for constant α_s is complicated. Numerical values are often used in practice: $\alpha_{16} = 0.673$, $\alpha_{32} = 0.697$, $\alpha_{64} = 0.709$, and $\alpha_s = 0.7213/(1 + 1.079/s)$ for $s \ge 128$.

The estimator in (9) is good for large cardinalities, but it is severely biased when dealing with small cardinalities [11]. For a small cardinality, we treat M_f as a bitmap of s bits, with each register $M_f[i]$ converted to one bit, whose value is 1 when $M_f[i] > 0$ or zero otherwise. The estimation formula is $\hat{n_s} = -s \log_2 V$, where V is the fraction of bits in the bitmap that are zeros [22]. This formula is used when the cardinality estimation by (9) is smaller than $2.5s$.

Recall that we can estimate the sum $\hat{n}$ of all flow cardinalities based on a separate estimator or simply from the whole array M using (10) where $\hat{n_s}$ is replaced with $\hat{n}$, s is replaced with m, and M_f is replaced with M. After computing both $\hat{n_s}$ and $\hat{n}$, we use (5) to compute the estimated flow cardinality $\hat{n_f}$.

6. ESTIMATION BIAS AND VARIANCE

This section analyzes the bias and standard error of our vHLL estimator. From [11], we have the following theorem.

THEOREM 1. *Let n_s be the number of distinct elements that are mapped to a HyperLogLog estimator M_f. Suppose the number s of registers in M_f is more than 16.*

- *If n_s is sufficiently large, the estimate $\hat{n_s}$ by (9) is asymptotically almost unbiased in the sense that*

$$\frac{1}{n_s}E(\hat{n_s}) = 1 + \delta_1(n_s) + o(1),$$

  where $|\delta_1(n_s)| < 5 \times 10^{-5}$ as soon as $s \geq 16$.

- *The standard error defined as $\frac{1}{n_s}\sqrt{Var(\hat{n_s})}$ satisfies*

$$\frac{1}{n_s}\sqrt{Var(\hat{n_s})} = \frac{\beta_s}{\sqrt{s}} + \delta_2(n_s) + o(1),$$

  where $|\delta_2(n_s)| < 5 \times 10^{-4}$ as soon as $s \geq 16$. The constants β_s being bounded, with $\beta_{16} = 1.106$, $\beta_{32} = 1.070$, $\beta_{64} = 1.054$, $\beta_{128} = 1.046$, and $\beta_\infty = 1.039$.

As stated in the HyperLogLog paper [11], the functions δ_1 and δ_2 represent oscillating functions of a tiny amplitude, and they can be safely neglected for all practical purposes.

6.1 Estimation Bias

Given an arbitrary flow f, we know from Section 4 that n_s is the sum of the flow cardinality n_f and a noise random variable $n_s - n_f$ with a binomial distribution of $Bino(n - n_f, \frac{s}{m})$. For $\forall i \in [0, n - n_f]$, we have

$$Prob\{n_s - n_f = i\} = \binom{n - n_f}{i}(\frac{s}{m})^i(1 - \frac{s}{m})^{n-n_f-i}. \quad (11)$$

Under the condition of $n_s - n_f = i$, by Theorem 1, we have

$$\begin{aligned} E(\hat{n_s} \mid n_s - n_f = i) &= (n_f + i)(1 + \delta_1(n_f + i) + o(1)) \\ &\approx n_f + i, \end{aligned} \quad (12)$$

with a small error bounded by a ratio of 5×10^{-5}. Hence,

$$\begin{aligned} E(\hat{n_s}) &= \sum_{i=0}^{n-n_f} E(\hat{n_s} \mid n_s - n_f = i) \times Prob\{n_s - n_f = i\} \\ &\approx \sum_{i=0}^{n-n_f} (n_f + i) \times \binom{n - n_f}{i}(\frac{s}{m})^i(1 - \frac{s}{m})^{n-n_f-i} \\ &= n_f + (n - n_f)\frac{s}{m}. \end{aligned} \quad (13)$$

The value of $\hat{n}$ is estimated based on the entire array M or through a separate estimator with hundreds of bytes (i.e., much more than 16 registers). From Theorem 1, we have $E(\hat{n}) = n(1 + \delta_1(n) + o(1)) \approx n$, with a very small error bounded by a ratio of 5×10^{-5}. From the estimation formula (5), we have

$$\begin{aligned} E(\hat{n_f}) &= \frac{ms}{m - s}\Big(\frac{E(\hat{n_s})}{s} - \frac{E(\hat{n})}{m}\Big) \\ &\approx \frac{ms}{m - s}\Big(\frac{n_f + (n - n_f)\frac{s}{m}}{s} - \frac{n}{m}\Big) = n_f. \end{aligned} \quad (14)$$

Therefore, the vHLL estimator is approximately unbiased.

6.2 Estimation Variance

Next we derive the variance of $\hat{n_f}$.

$$\begin{aligned} Var(\hat{n_f}) &= (\frac{ms}{m - s})^2\Big(\frac{Var(\hat{n_s})}{s^2} + \frac{Var(\hat{n})}{m^2}\Big) \quad (15) \\ &= (\frac{ms}{m - s})^2\Big(\frac{E(\hat{n_s}^2) - \big(E(\hat{n_s})\big)^2}{s^2} + \frac{Var(\hat{n})}{m^2}\Big) \\ &= (\frac{m}{m - s})^2\Big(E(\hat{n_s}^2) - \big(E(\hat{n_s})\big)^2 + (\frac{s}{m})^2 Var(\hat{n})\Big) \end{aligned}$$

With $\forall i \in [0, n - n_f)$, under the condition of $n_s - n_f = i$, by Theorem 1, we have

$$\begin{aligned} \tfrac{1}{n_f+i}\sqrt{Var(\hat{n_s} \mid n_s - n_f = i)} &= \tfrac{\beta_s}{\sqrt{s}} + \delta_2(n_f + i) + o(1) \\ &= \frac{\beta_s}{\sqrt{s}} \approx \frac{1.04}{\sqrt{s}}, \end{aligned} \quad (16)$$

where we use 1.04 to approximate β_s, assuming $s \geq 128$, which is always the case in our experiments later. Hence,

$$Var(\hat{n_s} \mid n_s - n_f = i) \approx \frac{1.04^2}{s}(n_f + i)^2. \quad (17)$$

Similarly, we have

$$Var(\hat{n}) \approx \frac{1.04^2}{m}n^2, \quad (18)$$

where m is the number of registers in the physical estimator for n, and we let $m \geq 128$. Because $E(\hat{n_s}^2 \mid n_s = n_f + i) = Var(\hat{n_s} \mid n_s - n_f = i) + \big(E(\hat{n_s} \mid n_s - n_f = i)\big)^2$, from (12) and (17), when s is sufficiently large, we have

$$\begin{aligned} E(\hat{n_s}^2 \mid n_s = n_f + i) &\approx \frac{1.04^2(n_f + i)^2}{s} + (n_f + i)^2 \\ &= (\frac{1.04^2}{s} + 1)(n_f + i)^2. \end{aligned}$$

Combining (11) with the above equation, we have

$$\begin{aligned} E(\hat{n_s}^2) &= \sum_{i=0}^{n-n_f} E(\hat{n_s}^2 \mid n_s - n_f = i)Prob\{n_s - n_f = i\} \quad (19) \\ &\approx \sum_{i=0}^{n-n_f} (\frac{1.04^2}{s} + 1)(n_f + i)^2\binom{n - n_f}{i}(\frac{s}{m})^i(1 - \frac{s}{m})^{n-n_f-i} \\ &= (\frac{1.04^2}{s} + 1)\big(n_f^2 + 2n_f E(n_s - n_f) + E((n_s - n_f)^2)\big) \\ &= (\frac{1.04^2}{s} + 1)\Big(n_f^2 + 2n_f(n - n_f)\frac{s}{m} \\ &\qquad + (n - n_f)\frac{s}{m}(1 - \frac{s}{m}) + (n - n_f)^2(\frac{s}{m})^2\Big) \\ &= (\frac{1.04^2}{s} + 1)\Big((n_f + (n - n_f)\frac{s}{m})^2 + (n - n_f)\frac{s}{m}(1 - \frac{s}{m})\Big). \end{aligned}$$

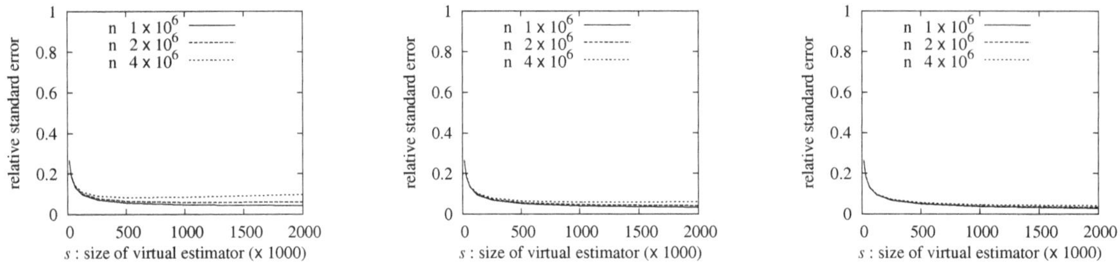

(a) Flow cardinality n_f=1 × 10^4 (b) Flow cardinality n_f=2 × 10^4 (c) Flow cardinality n_f=4 × 10^4

Figure 8: Relative standard error with respect to s, n, and n_f

Applying (13), (18) and (19) to (15), we have

$$Var(\hat{n_f}) \approx \Big(\frac{m}{m-s}\Big)^2\Big(\frac{1.04^2}{s}\big(n_f + (n-n_f)\frac{s}{m}\big)^2 + (n-n_f)\frac{s}{m}(1-\frac{s}{m}) + (\frac{s}{m})^2\frac{1.04^2}{m}n^2\Big). \quad (20)$$

Consider the three terms between the parentheses after $\big(\frac{m}{m-s}\big)^2$. We know that the noise $n_s - n_f$ follows a binomial distribution $Bino(n-n_f, \frac{s}{m})$, whose mean is given by (3) as $(n-n_f)\frac{s}{m}$. Hence, the first term is the estimation variance for the flow cardinality plus the mean noise. The noise variance is $(n-n_f)\frac{s}{m}(1-\frac{s}{m})$, which is captured by the second term. The third term $(\frac{s}{m})^2\frac{1.04^2}{m}n^2$ is caused by the estimation $\hat{n}$ for the grand flow.

6.3 Relative Standard Error

We define the relative standard error as

$$StdErr\Big(\frac{\hat{n_f}}{n_f}\Big) = \frac{\sqrt{Var(\hat{n_f})}}{n_f}. \quad (21)$$

From (20) and (21), we also observe that the relative standard error (or error in short) increases as the cardinality of grand flow n increases, and it decreases as the cardinality of target flow n_f grows.

Below we use some numerical examples to illustrate the above observations and the interplay between different sources of estimation error. Suppose the allocated memory is $m = 256K$. Consider a target flow cardinality of $n_f = 10^4$. Figure 8(a) shows the numerically computed estimation error by (21) with respect to s (the number of registers per virtual estimator) along the horizontal axis and n (the combined cardinality of all flows) for different curves. Starting from 16, as s increases, the error drops quickly, thanks to improved estimation accuracy from the virtual estimator M_f as predicted by Theorem 1. However, when s becomes further larger (more than 256 in the figure), the rate of improvement drops significantly, which can also be predicted by Theorem 1 with its factor of improvement being $\frac{1}{\sqrt{s}}$. Moreover, as s increases, the error caused by noise increases. Combining these two factors, we observe that when s is relatively large (for a wide range from 500 to 2000 in the figure), its impact on the error becomes more or less stabilized.

From Figure 8(a) to Figure 8(c), we increase n_f and observe that the error decreases, which means that the *relative* standard error is smaller for flows of larger cardinalities (although their *absolute* errors can still be larger). When n increases, the error increases, as predicted.

7. EXPERIMENTAL EVALUATION

We have implemented the vHLL solution and the most related work PMC [17]. vHLL is based on register-sharing, while PMC is based on bit-level sharing. We compare their performance through experiments using real network traces downloaded from CAIDA [1]. The traces are captured by a high-speed monitor named equinix-sanjose (located in San Jose, CA, US), which is connected to a 10-Gbit/s Ethernet backbone link. Each trace file captures the packets in 1 minute. In order to create larger traces for our experiments, we download 60 traces and combine them into 6 larger ones, each for 10 consecutive minutes. The statistics of the large traces can be found in Table 3.

Table 3: Trace Statistics

time(min)	num of flows	total cardinality	mean flow cardinality
1-10	1473306	2675506	1.8
11-20	1013517	1856676	1.8
21-30	1648779	3005649	1.8
31-40	1562288	2881330	1.8
41-50	1612709	3280242	2.0
51-60	1612605	3280138	2.0

We consider per-source flows and measure the number of distinct destinations that each source sends packets to. The distribution of the flows with respect to the cardinality has been shown previously in Figure 5. We stress that the purpose of our experiments is primarily technical — evaluating how accurate our vHLL is on cardinality estimation, while the case study of measuring per-source flows may find use in profiling scanners, identifying popular hosts on the Internet (server sources send data to a large number of clients), and detecting anomaly based on measurement over consecutive periods, such as the detection of a worm-infected host by observing that it suddenly deviates from normal behavior by probing a large number of different destination addresses [6,27].

7.1 Estimation Accuracy in Tight Memory

We evaluate the impact of memory space on the accuracy of cardinality estimation for vHLL and PMC. To make a fair comparison between the two, they are allocated with the same memory to process the CAIDA traces. For the proposed vHLL, we configure the value of s to 512 by default, but will vary its value in later experiments. Recall that m is the total number of registers in the common pool. Its value depends on the overall available memory. The average number of flows in all six traces is about 1.5 millions. We vary the available memory space from 1.5 Mb to 0.75 Mb to 0.375 Mb to 0.15 Mb, such that the average memory per flow is about 1 bit, 0.5 bit, 0.25 bit, and 0.1 bit, respectively. The corresponding experimental results are presented in Figures 9, 10, 11, and 12, respectively. Again, each flow is represented by a point, whose x-coordinate is the true cardinality and y-coordinate is the estimated cardinality. The equality line is also shown. The closer a point is to the line, the more accurate the estimation is.

In Figure 9, plot (a) shows the performance of vHLL with average memory of 1 bit per flow. The points are clustered around the equality line ($y = x$), indicating good accuracy. Plot (b) shows the performance of PMC with the points scattering away from the equality line. Plot (c) compares the two solutions in terms of estimation bias. The vertical axis is the relative bias defined as $E(\frac{n_f - \hat{n_f}}{n_f})$. Since there are too few flows for some cardinalities (especially the large ones) in our Internet trace, we divide the horizontal axis into measurement bins of width from 5000 on the high end in the plots to 1000 in the low end to ensure that each bin has a sufficient number of flows 25, and measure the bias and standard deviation in each bin. In general, PMC has larger bias than vHLL. Plot (d) compares the two solutions in terms of accuracy. The vertical axis is the relative standard error of the estimation results, which is defined as $\frac{\sqrt{Var(\hat{n_f})}}{n_f}$. The measurement also uses the bin method as previously explained. vHLL has much smaller error than PMC. This result is expected because according to [17], the performance of PMC is related to the so-called fill rate, i.e., the fraction of bits that are set to ones in the common bit pool. The intended fill rate for PMC to perform well is in the range of $(0, 0.5)$. When the memory is 0.5 bit per flow, the fill rate is about 0.76 in our experiment, which explains why PMC performs relatively poor. Specifically, when the actual cardinality is 10000, 20000 and 30000, the measured errors by PMC are 0.22, 0.28 and 0.23, respectively, while those by vHLL are 0.055, 0.043 and 0.044, respectively.

Figure 10 makes the same set of comparison with 0.5 bit per flow. The performance of vHLL remains good, whereas PMC no longer works as its fill rate becomes 0.9. For example, when the actual cardinality is 10000, 20000 and 30000, the measured errors by PMC are 0.74, 0.67 and 0.87, respectively, while those by vHLL are 0.073, 0.065 and 0.049, respectively.

As the average memory per flow decreases to 0.25 bit and further to 0.1 bit, Figures 11-12 show that vHLL still works with gradually deteriorating accuracy. For 0.25 bit per flow, when the actual cardinality is 10000, 20000 and 30000, the measured errors by vHLL are 0.10, 0.095 and 0.096, respectively. For 0.25 bit per flow, when the actual cardinality is 10000, 20000 and 30000, the measured errors by vHLL are 0.15, 0.13 and 0.10, respectively. We also point out that although the relative standard errors for small flows are higher, it does not entirely diminish the usefulness of these estimations because the absolute errors for small flows are in fact much smaller than those of large ones. For example, by examining the first plot of each figure, one will not mistaken a small flow for a large one due to the modest absolute error.

7.2 Impact of Value s on vHLL

Our second set of experiments evaluate the impact of s (number of registers per virtual estimator) on estimation accuracy. We repeat the experiment in Figure 10(a) with average memory of 0.5 bit per flow, but change s from 512 to values: 128, 256 and 1024. The results are shown in Fig. 13(a)-(c), respectively. Corresponding relative standard errors are shown in Figure 14(a)-(c), respectively.

We observe that when s is relatively small at 128, the estimation accuracy in Figure 13(a) is noticeably worse than that in Figure 10(a), which is evident from the fact that the points of the former surround the equality line less tightly. Quantitatively, the errors in Figure 14(a) with $s = 128$ are larger than those in Figure 14(d) for vHLL with the default $s = 512$. For example, when the actual cardinality is 20000, the relative standard error under $s = 128$ is 10.9%, while that under $s = 512$ is 6.5%.

However, when s becomes large enough (more than 256), for a wide range of values, the impact of s on the estimation accuracy stabilizes, which is evident when comparing Figure 13(b), Figure 13(c), and Figure 10(a), whose s values are 256, 512 and 1024, respectively. For example, when the actual cardinality is 20000, their errors are 8.1%, 6.5% and 5.2%, based on from Figure 14(b), Figure 14(c) and Figure 10(d), respectively.

The above observations are consistent with our analysis in Section 6 and the numerical results in Figure 8 (which has different parameters though). The reasons for these observations have been explained in Section 6.3 and will not be repeated here.

7.3 Impact of Overall Traffic

Our third set of experiments investigate how the overall traffic volume affects estimation accuracy. The overall traffic volume is characterized by n, the sum of all flows' cardinalities, because duplicates in the traffic must be removed in our context. The greater the value of n is, the larger the average noise level on each register will be, which will in turn negatively affect the estimation accuracy of a virtual estimator consisting of s registers.

We artificially increase the cardinality of each flow by a factor randomly chosen from the range of $[1, 3]$, which doubles the cardinality on average. The value of n is thus expected to be doubled. We then repeat the experiment in Figure 10(a) with average memory of 0.5 bit per flow. The results are presented in Figure 15, where plot (a) shows raw estimated cardinalities, plot (b) shows the estimation bias, and plot (c) shows the relative standard error. The bias remains close to zero, particularly for large flows. The error is modest, but larger than that in Figure 10(d) where the value of n is half, which confirms our prediction above.

We further enlarge n by increasing the cardinality of each flow with a factor randomly chosen from the range of $[1, 7]$. The value of n is expected to be increased by four folds. The results are presented in Figure 16. Again the bias is close to one, but the error increases.

7.4 A Case Study: Detect Super Destinations

Our last set of experiments compare vHLL and PMC based on a hypothetical application for detecting so-called super destinations. In this case study, we consider per-destination flows and measure the number of distinct sources that access a destination address in each measurement period, using the same Internet traces. Suppose the policy is to report all the destinations that have been accessed by 5,000 or more sources within a measurement period. These *super destinations* may be used for profiling the popular servers (or services) in the network or triggering anomaly warnings (such as potential DDoS attacks) if they were never reported as super destinations before.

If a destination with a cardinality less than 5,000 is reported, it is called a *false positive*. If a destination with a cardinality 5,000 or above is not reported, it is called a *false negative*. We define the false positive ratio (FPR) as the number of false positives divided by the total number of destinations reported. Based on this definition, if FRP is 0.1, it means 10% of the reported destinations should not have been reported. We define the false negative ratio (FNR) as the number of false negatives divided by the number of destinations whose cardinalities are 5,000 or more.

The experimental results are shown in Table 4. Clearly, vHLL outperforms PMC by a wide margin when we take both FPR and FNR into consideration. The FNR is close to zero for PMC when the memory is 0.5 bit per flow or less. That is because PMC becomes a positively biased estimator in such a small memory as depicted in Fig. 10(b). Its FPR is 73.7% for 0.5 bit per flow and 99.2% for 0.25 bit per flow.

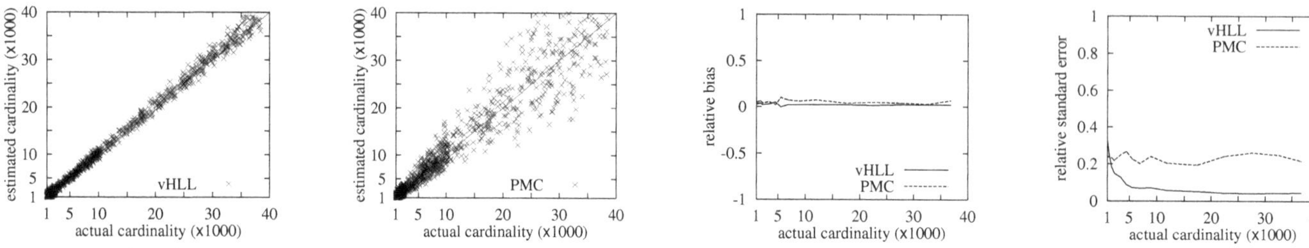

(a) vHLL with 1 bit per flow (b) PMC with 1 bit per flow (c) Estimation bias (d) Estimation accuracy

Figure 9: Compare vHLL and PMC with 1 bit per flow.

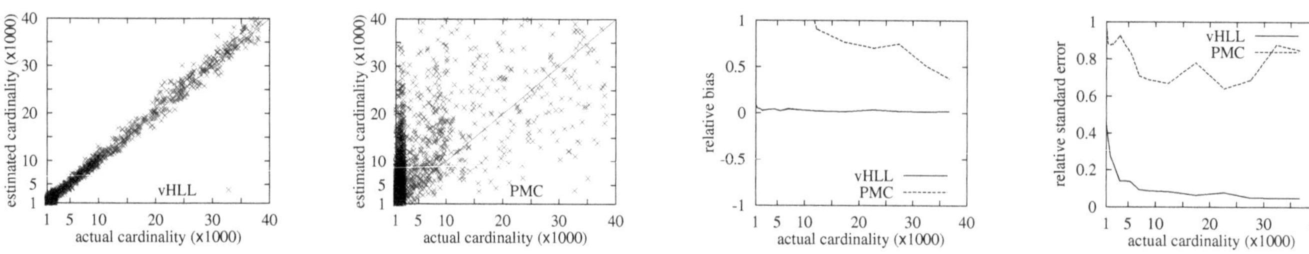

(a) vHLL with 0.5 bit per flow (b) PMC with 0.5 bit per flow (c) Estimation bias (d) Estimation accuracy

Figure 10: Compare vHLL and PMC with 0.5 bit per flow.

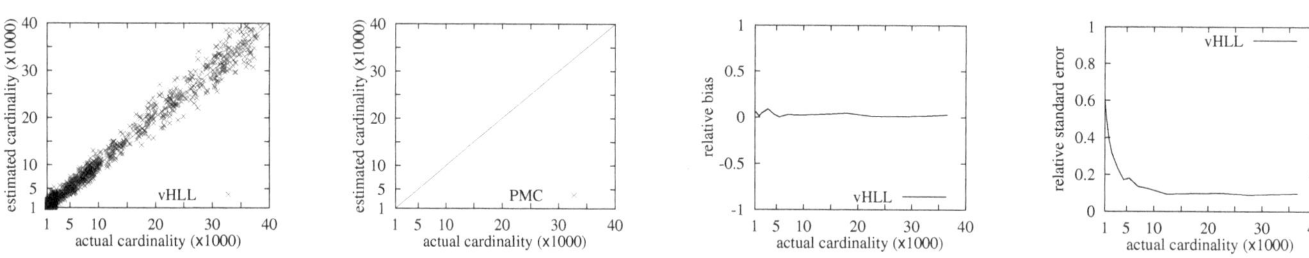

(a) vHLL with 0.25 bit per flow (b) PMC with 0.25 bit per flow (c) Estimation bias (d) Estimation accuracy

Figure 11: Compare vHLL and PMC with 0.25 bit per flow

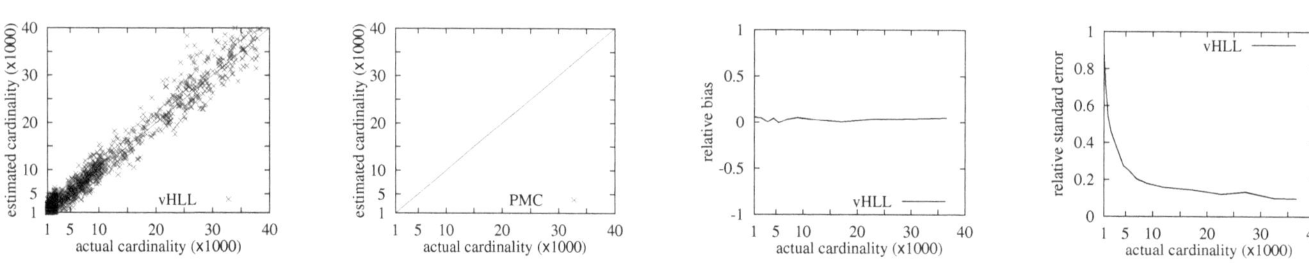

(a) vHLL with 0.1 bit per flow (b) PMC with 0.1 bit per flow (c) Estimation bias (d) Estimation accuracy

Figure 12: Compare vHLL and PMC with 0.1 bit per flow.

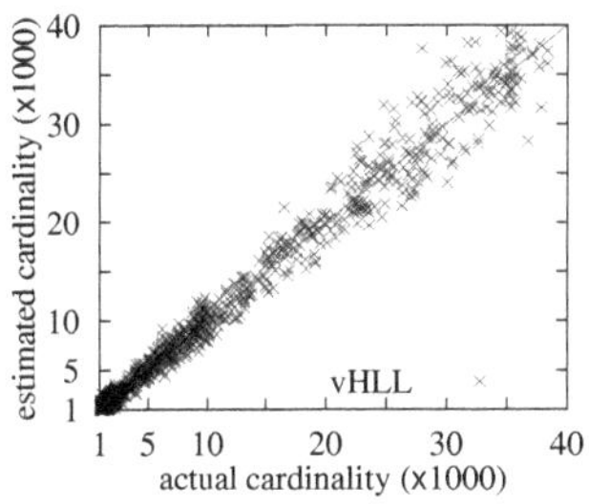

(a) $s = 128$.

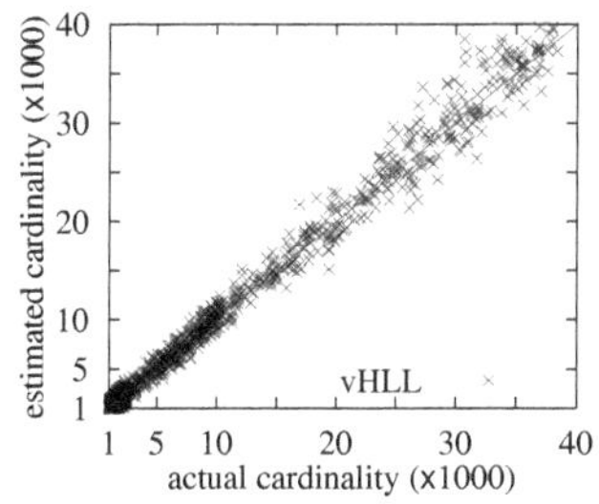

(b) $s = 256$

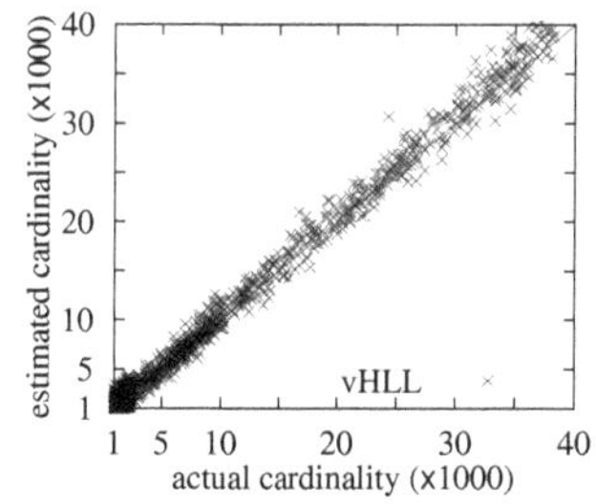

(c) $s = 1024$

Figure 13: Cardinality estimation with different values of s under average memory of 0.5 bit per flow

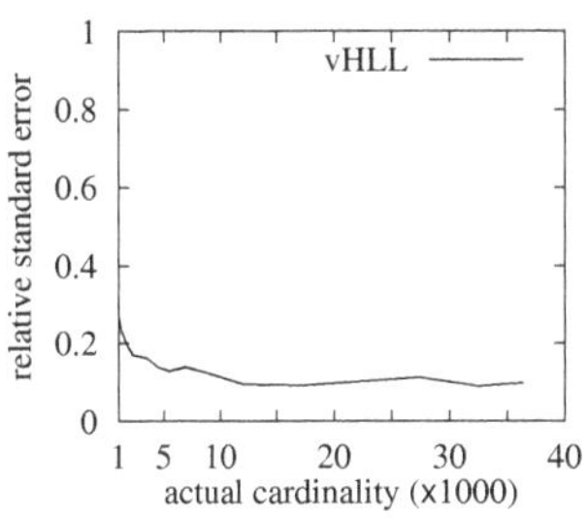

(a) $s = 128$

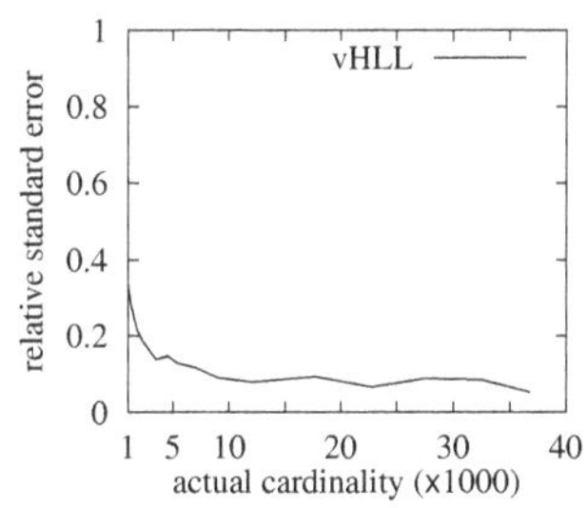

(b) $s = 256$

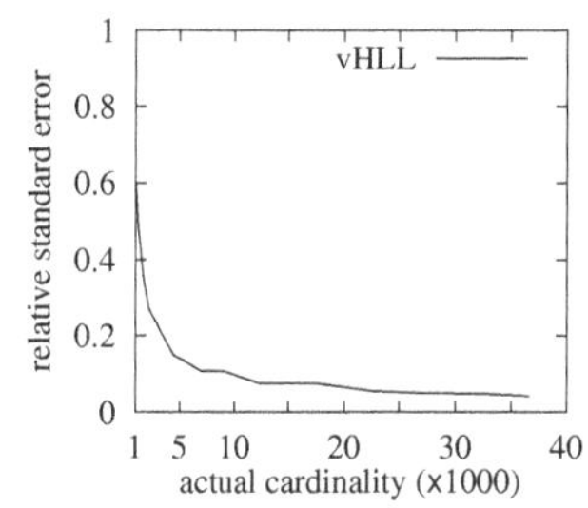

(c) $s = 1024$

Figure 14: Relative standard errors of cardinality estimation with different values of s under average memory of 0.5 bit per flow

Table 4: False positive ratio and false negative ratio with respect to memory cost

Memory (bit per flow)	PMC		vHLL	
	FPR	FNR	FPR	FNR
0.25	0.992	0.048	0.039	0.026
0.5	0.737	0.045	0.034	0.013
1	0.039	0.044	0.012	0.014

vHLL also has non-negligible FPR and FNR since its estimated cardinality is not exactly the true cardinality. To confine impreciseness to a certain degree, the policy may be relaxed to report all destinations whose estimated cardinalities are $5000 \times (1 - \epsilon)$ or above, where $0 \leq \epsilon < 1$. If a destination less than $5000 \times (1 - 2\epsilon)$ gets reported, it is called an *ϵ-false positive*. If a destination with a true cardinality 5,000 or more is not reported, it is called an *ϵ-false negative*. The FPR and FNR are defined the same as before. The experimental results for $\epsilon = 10\%$ are shown in Table 5, and those for $\epsilon = 20\%$ are shown in Table 6, where the FPR and FNR for vHLL are merely 0.7% and 0.6%, respectively, when the memory is 0.25 bit per flow. In Table 6, when the memory grows to at least 0.5 bit per flow, FPR and FNR for vHLL become zeros.

Table 5: $\epsilon = 10\%$, False positive ratio and false negative ratio with respect to memory cost

Memory (bit per flow)	PMC		vHLL	
	FPR	FNR	FPR	FNR
0.25	0.992	0.010	0.014	0.010
0.5	0.846	0.029	0.003	0.003
1	0.013	0.017	0.003	0.002

Table 6: $\epsilon = 20\%$, False positive ratio and false negative ratio with respect to memory cost

Memory (bit per flow)	PMC		vHLL	
	FPR	FNR	FPR	FNR
0.25	0.991	0.003	0.007	0.006
0.5	0.953	0.021	0.0	0.0
1	0.010	0.002	0.0	0.0

8. CONCLUSION

In this paper, we have proposed a unified framework for developing efficient solutions to the problem of estimating cardinalities for a very large number of streaming flows. From this framework, we examine a particularly powerful solution called virtual HyperLogLog (vHLL) in details. Through analysis and experimental evaluation, we show that vHLL can use a compact memory space (down to 0.1 bit per flow on average) to estimate the cardinalities of flows with wide range and reasonable accuracy. This new capability enables on-chip implementation of cardinality estimation needed for online applications that can keep up with the line speed of modern routers, or allow efficient processing of big data by using low-cost commodity computers instead of expensive high-performance computing systems.

9. ACKNOWLEDGMENTS

This work is supported in part by National Science Foundation of United States under grants CNS-1115548 and CNS-1409797. The authors also would like to thank the Key Laboratory of Computer Network and Information Integration (Southeast University), Education Ministry of China, for financial support.

10. REFERENCES

[1] CAIDA UCSD anonymized 2013 internet traces on Jan. 17. http://www.caida.org/data/passive/passive_2013_dataset.xml.

[2] Google trends. *http://www.google.com/trends/*.

[3] Z. Bar-yossef, T. S. Jayram, R. Kumar, D. Sivakumar, L. Trevisan, and Luca. Counting distinct elements in a data stream. *Proc. of RANDOM: Workshop on Randomization and Approximation*, 2002.

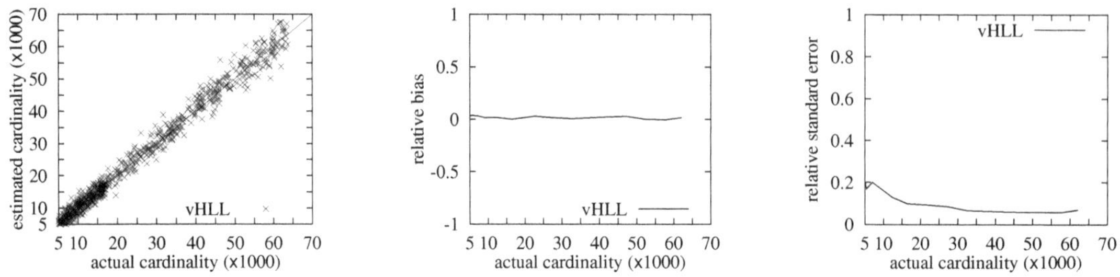

(a) n is doubled (b) Estimation bias (c) Estimation accuracy

Figure 15: Cardinality estimation with n doubled under average memory of 0.5 bits per flow

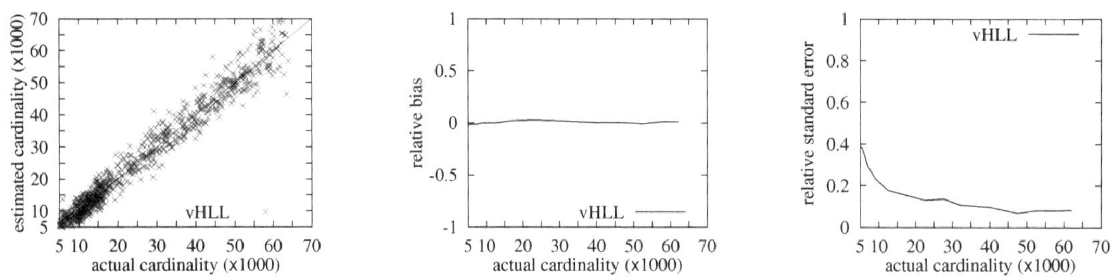

(a) n is increased by four folds (b) Estimation bias (c) Estimation accuracy

Figure 16: Cardinality estimation with n increased four folds under average memory of 0.5 bits per flow

[4] K. Beyer, P. J. Haas, B. Reinwald, Y. Sismanis, and R. Gemulla. On synopses for distinct-value estimation under multiset operations. *Proc. of ACM SIGMOD*, 2007.

[5] G. Cormode and S. Muthukrishnan. An improved data stream summary: the Count-Min sketch and its applications. *Proc. of LATIN*, 2004.

[6] M. Costa, J. Crowcroft, M. Castro, A. Rowstron, L. Zhou, L. Zhang, and P. Barham. Vigilante: End-to-end containment of internet worms. *SIGOPS Operating Systems Review*, 39(5), October 2005.

[7] X. Dimitropoulos, P. Hurley, and A. Kind. Probabilistic lossy counting: An efficient algorithm for finding heavy hitters. *ACM SIGCOMM Computer Communication Review*, 38(1), 2008.

[8] M. Durand and P. Flajolet. Loglog counting of large cardinalities. *ESA: European Symposia on Algorithms*, pages 605–617, 2003.

[9] C. Estan and G. Varghese. New directions in traffic measurement and accounting. *Proc. of ACM SIGCOMM*, August 2002.

[10] C. Estan, G. Varghese, and M. Fish. Bitmap algorithms for counting active flows on high-speed links. *IEEE/ACM Transactions on Networking (TON)*, 14(5):925–937, 2006.

[11] P. Flajolet, E. Fusy, O. Gandouet, and F. Meunier. HyperLogLog: The analysis of a near-optimal cardinality estimation algorithm. *Proc. of AOFA: International Conference on Analysis Of Algorithms*, 2007.

[12] P. Flajolet and G. N. Martin. Probabilistic counting algorithms for database applications. *J. Comput. Syst. Sci.*, 31(2), 1985.

[13] W. D. Gardner. Researchers transmit optical data at 16.4 Tbps. *InformationWeek*, February 2008.

[14] S. Heule, M. Nunkesser, and A. Hall. HyperLogLog in practice: Algorithmic engineering of a state-of-the-art cardinality estimation algorithm. *Proc. of EDBT*, 2013.

[15] T. Li, S. Chen, and Y. Ling. Fast and compact per-flow traffic measurement through randomized counter sharing. *in Proc. of IEEE INFOCOM*, 2011.

[16] T. Li, S. Chen, W. Luo, M. Zhang, and Y. Qiao. Spreader classification based on optimal dynamic bit sharing. *IEEE/ACM Transactions on Networking*, 21(3):817–830, 2013.

[17] P. Lieven and B. Scheuermann. High-speed per-flow traffic measurement with probabilistic multiplicity counting. *Proc. of IEEE INFOCOM*, pages 1–9, 2010.

[18] Y. Lu, A. Montanari, B. Prabhakar, S. Dharmapurikar, and A. Kabbani. Counter braids: A novel counter architecture for per-flow measurement. *Proc. of ACM SIGMETRICS*, June 2008.

[19] Y. Lu and B. Prabhakar. Robust counting via counter braids: An error-resilient network measurement architecture. *Proc. of IEEE INFOCOM*, April 2009.

[20] Neustar.biz. How to choose a good hash function: Part 3. http://research.neustar.biz/2012/02/02/choosing-a-good-hash-function-part-3.

[21] N. Ntarmos, P. Triantafillou, and G. Weikum. Counting at large: Efficient cardinality estimation in internet-scale data networks. *Proc. of ICDE*, pages 40–40, 2006.

[22] K.-Y. Whang, B. T. Vander-Zanden, and H. M. Taylor. A linear-time probabilistic counting algorithm for database applications. *ACM Transactions on Database Systems*, 15(2):208–229, 1990.

[23] Q. Xiao, Y. Qiao, M. Zhen, and S. Chen. Estimating the persistent spreads in high-speed networks. *Proc. of IEEE ICNP*, pages 131–142, 2014.

[24] Q. Xiao, B. Xiao, and S. Chen. Differential estimation in dynamic RFID systems. In *Proc. of INFOCOM (mini-conference)*, pages 295–299, 2013.

[25] M. Yoon, T. Li, S. Chen, and J.-K. Peir. Fit a spread estimator in small memory. *Proc. of IEEE INFOCOM*, 2009.

[26] Q. Zhao, J. Xu, and A. Kumar. Detection of super sources and destinations in high-speed networks: Algorithms, analysis and evaluation. *IEEE JASC*, 24(10):1840–1852, 2006.

[27] C. C. Zou, L. Gao, W. Gong, and D. Towsley. Monitoring and early warning for internet worms. *Proc. of the 10th ACM Conference on Computer and Communications Security*, 2003.

Investigating the Potential of the Inter-IXP Multigraph for the Provisioning of Guaranteed End-to-End Services

Vasileios Kotronis, Rowan Klöti, Panagiotis Georgopoulos, Bernhard Ager
ETH Zurich, Switzerland

Matthias Rost, Stefan Schmid
TU Berlin, Germany

Xenofontas Dimitropoulos
FORTH, Greece
ETH Zurich, Switzerland

ABSTRACT

In this work, we propose utilizing the rich connectivity between IXPs and ISPs for inter-domain path stitching, supervised by centralized QoS brokers. In this context, we highlight a novel abstraction of the Internet topology, i.e., the inter-IXP multigraph composed of IXPs and paths crossing the domains of their shared member ISPs. This can potentially serve as a dense Internet-wide substrate for provisioning guaranteed end-to-end (e2e) services with high path diversity and global IPv4 address space reach. We thus map the IXP multigraph, evaluate its potential, and introduce a rich algorithmic framework for path stitching on such graph structures.

Categories and Subject Descriptors

C.2.2 [**Network Protocols**]: Routing Protocols

Keywords

Internet Exchange Point; QoS; Embedding; EuroIX

1. INTRODUCTION

Modern Internet applications, from HD video-conferencing to telesurgery and remote control of power-plants, pose increasing demands on network latency, bandwidth and availability. Presently, ISPs are able to provide certain QoS guarantees only in intra-domain settings based on technologies such as leased circuits and VPN tunnels, e.g., over MPLS. Such services provide an important revenue stream for ISPs. However, despite several research and standardization efforts, providing QoS guarantees at the inter-domain level has seen very limited success so far.

Centralized inter-domain path brokers have been explored in the literature [8, 11, 12] and the industry [1], as an approach to support the requirements of demanding applications across domains. In these setups, ISPs provide QoS-enabled pathlets [6], which are stitched together by an inter-domain routing mediator, e.g., a bandwidth broker mediating the exchange of transit bandwidth between ISPs [12]. This work explores logically centralized inter-domain QoS routing mediators for the provisioning of inter-domain path guarantees in light of ongoing changes in the Internet ecosystem. In particular, *(i)* the Internet is becoming denser and more flat [3] due to richer interconnectivity at Internet eXchange Points (IXPs) [4], and *(ii)* there is a gradual paradigm shift towards network virtualization and Software Defined Networking (SDN), also in the context of IXPs [7]. Our main proposal is that a rich inter-IXP overlay fabric opens interesting traffic engineering flexibilities which can be exploited, e.g., for inter-domain QoS.

SIGMETRICS'15, June 15-19, 2015, Portland, OR, USA.
ACM 978-1-4503-3486-0/15/06.
http://dx.doi.org/10.1145/2745844.2745877.

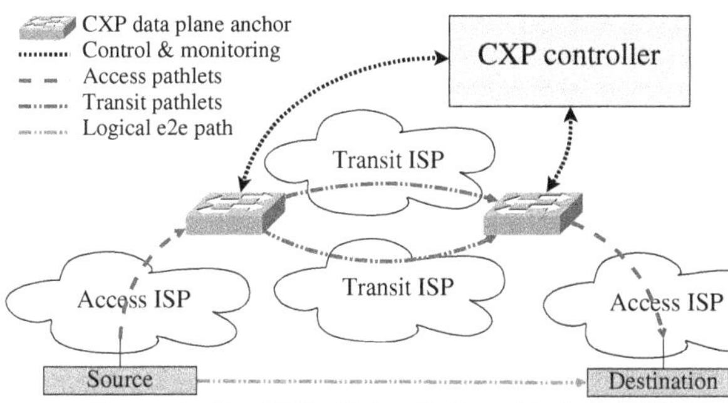

Figure 1: The CXP stitches QoS-enabled e2e paths.

2. CXPS: PATH BROKERS OVER IXPS

We propose performing inter-domain QoS routing over a novel abstraction of the Internet topology, in which vertices are IXPs and edges are virtual links connecting two IXPs over an ISP. We call this abstraction the *IXP multigraph* because two IXPs can be connected with multiple edges over different ISPs. The choice of IXPs as switching points exploits their rich connectivity to geo-diverse ISPs, enabling high path diversity and global client reach with a deployment of only of a few well-placed switching points as we show in Section 3. We call the routing brokers and controllers that are deployed over IXP multigraphs *Control eXchange Points (CXPs)*. CXPs stitch pathlets [6] across multiple administrative domains to construct global paths. The pathlets are provided by ISPs and are annotated with specific properties, such as bandwidth and latency guarantees. The incentive for ISPs to provide pathlets is the revenue generated by their use for e2e services. As shown in Fig. 1, the ISPs of the source and the destination offer access pathlets to connect to ISP-adjacent data plane anchors, i.e., programmable CXP switching points, while the intermediary ISPs offer transit pathlets between those points.

A CXP performs the following tasks: it *(i)* handles new requests for QoS-enabled paths (admission control), *(ii)* computes and sets up suitable paths (embeddings), *(iii)* monitors pathlet availability and compliance with QoS guarantees, and *(iv)* performs re-embedding, if required. A client negotiates her request directly with her access ISP, which selects a suitable CXP for establishing the inter-domain route

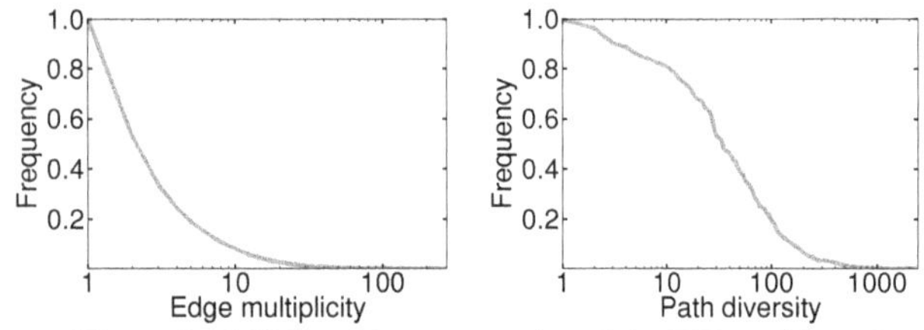

Figure 2: CCDFs of key properties of the IXP multigraph

out of a set of available CXPs. The ISP forwards the client's request to the chosen CXP, which in turn computes a suitable e2e path. The CXP reserves capacity on the selected pathlets and then configures the respective data plane anchors. Accordingly, the client's ISP has to configure its network such that the quality sensitive traffic is sent via a pathlet to the correct data plane anchor. A CXP monitors the bandwidth, latency and availability of a path for the duration of the client's reservation. If the client's requirements are violated or a pathlet becomes unavailable, the CXP chooses and configures an alternate path for the affected part(s) of the traffic; this can even be a "hot-standby" backup path carrying traffic duplicates. Besides, the CXP may choose to better utilize the available pathlets by re-embedding paths and defragmenting the substrate resources. CXPs and ISPs may use MPLS, SDN or PCE mechanisms for the execution of their associated tasks, such as Traffic Engineering (TE).

3. POTENTIAL OF IXP MULTIGRAPHS

Motivated by the CXP concept, we analyze the properties of the resulting IXP multigraph by extracting ISP membership data for 229 IXPs from the EuroIX dataset [4]. We find *49k* inter-connections of type: IXP_A, ISP_X, IXP_B. These form a dense multigraph, where a few pairs of IXPs are interconnected by hundreds of distinct ASes, each of which is in a position to offer one or multiple pathlets between each pair. In Fig. 2, we observe that the resulting pathlet-wise path diversity is one order of magnitude larger than the direct IXP connectivity, assuming that all the member ASes provide one pathlet each per IXP pair. In terms of AS-level path diversity, in our accompanying technical report [9] we show that the application of generalized inter-domain routing policies can lead to an increase of up to *29* times, as compared to classic valley-free practices [5]. More disjoint paths indicate potentially higher availability for demanding applications. In contrast, classic BGP-based routing is known to use a limited number of suboptimal inter-domain paths [10], as they normally cross up to one peering link in an IXP. Furthermore, in terms of IP address coverage, we discovered that even a small deployment ($\sim$5 IXP anchors) could directly cover a high fraction ($\sim$40%) of the Internet IPv4 address space. This increases to $\sim$91% of announced addresses if we also consider the 1-hop customer cone of the IXP members, assuming access pathlets over the member ISPs. This allows an initial deployment of just a few IXPs to serve large sets of IPv4 addresses and enables incremental adoption. Further use of private peering points might selectively extend the graph and augment coverage, where required.

4. PATH STITCHING ALGORITHMS

Given the interesting properties of the IXP-based multigraph, we devised algorithms which leverage its flexibility in the context of CXP-like QoS mediators. The problem is essentially a path embedding problem: CXPs embed e2e paths on dense inter-IXP multigraphs, subject to bandwidth and latency constraints. The objective is to exploit the rich path diversity in order to maximize the number of concurrently embeddable routes. These routes are requested by the client IPv4 endpoints that connect to the multigraph via their access ISPs. In our accompanying technical report [9], we formally introduce the e2e routing problem considered in this work as the QoS Multigraph Routing Problem (QMRP), together with an optimal offline formulation. This problem is complex for several reasons. *(i)* Requests from the large client base dynamically arrive over time in a non-predictable manner, necessitating the use of online algorithms. *(ii)* While a single suitable e2e path can be found in polynomial time, the IXP-based graph offers many choices and requires to carefully select which of the edges between two IXPs is used. In fact, in such multigraphs the number of available edges can be 3 orders of magnitude larger than the number of nodes (IXPs) [9]. *(iii)* The online selection of e2e paths should reflect multiple conflicting high-level objectives, namely accepting as many requests as possible, avoiding the usage of scarce low-latency, high-bandwidth links, and preventing resource fragmentation.

We thus propose a *sample-select* approach to heuristically tackle the QMRP in an online manner. In particular, given the NP-hardness of the *optimal path* calculations, we employ a sample-select process, where in the first stage, a set of *feasible* paths is sampled (i.e., generated) in polynomial time, and subsequently one of them is selected for the actual embedding. The techniques for the sampling process may range from modified Dijkstra-based approaches to random walks. Moreover, we propose a hybrid online-offline algorithm to support reconfigurations of pre-generated embeddings in order to accommodate further online requests. Using simulations based on the mapped IXP multigraph, we show that our algorithms scale to the sizes of the measured graphs and can serve diverse path request mixes. The full set of online, offline and hybrid algorithmic variants, together with the results and insights stemming from their application on the EuroIX-based multigraph, can be found in our technical report [9]. The software that we used is publicly available [2].

Acknowledgments. This work was partly funded by European Research Council Grant Agreement no. 338402.

5. REFERENCES

[1] GEANT Bandwidth-on-Demand Provisioning Tool. http://geant3.archive.geant.net/service/autobahn/about_autoBAHN/Pages/About_autoBAHN.aspx.
[2] Software for CXP-based Experimentation. https://bitbucket.org/vkotronis/cxp_experimentation.
[3] DHAMDHERE, A., AND DOVROLIS, C. The Internet is Flat: Modeling the Transition from a Transit Hierarchy to a Peering Mesh. In *ACM CONEXT* (2010).
[4] EUROIX. European Internet Exchange Association. https://www.euro-ix.net/. Dataset acquired on 2014-04-09.
[5] GAO, L., AND REXFORD, J. Stable Internet Routing Without Global Coordination. In *ACM SIGMETRICS* (2000).
[6] GODFREY, P. B., GANICHEV, I., SHENKER, S., AND STOICA, I. Pathlet Routing. In *ACM SIGCOMM* (2009).
[7] GUPTA, A., VANBEVER, L., SHAHBAZ, M., DONOVAN, S. P., SCHLINKER, B., FEAMSTER, N., REXFORD, J., SHENKER, S., CLARK, R., AND KATZ-BASSETT, E. SDX: A Software Defined Internet Exchange. In *ACM SIGCOMM* (2014).
[8] KOTRONIS, V., DIMITROPOULOS, X., AND AGER, B. Outsourcing the Routing Control Logic: Better Internet Routing Based on SDN Principles. In *ACM HotNets* (2012).
[9] KOTRONIS, V. ET AL. Investigating the Potential of the Inter-IXP Multigraph for the Provisioning of Guaranteed End-to-End Services. Tech. Rep. 360, ETH Zurich, Laboratory TIK, Feb 2015. ftp://ftp.tik.ee.ethz.ch/pub/publications/TIK-Report-360.pdf.
[10] LUMEZANU, C., BADEN, R., SPRING, N., AND BHATTACHARJEE, B. Triangle Inequality and Routing Policy Violations in the Internet. In *PAM* (2009).
[11] SPRINTSON, A., YANNUZZI, M., ORDA, A., AND MASIP-BRUIN, X. Reliable Routing with QoS Guarantees for Multi-Domain IP/MPLS Networks. In *IEEE INFOCOM* (2007).
[12] VALANCIUS, V., FEAMSTER, N., JOHARI, R., AND VAZIRANI, V. MINT: A Market for INternet Transit. In *ACM CONEXT* (2008).

MaxWeight Scheduling: Asymptotic Behavior of Unscaled Queue-Differentials in Heavy Traffic

Rahul Singh
ECE Department
Texas A&M University
College Station, TX 77843
rsingh1@tamu.edu

Alexander Stolyar
ISE Department
Lehigh University
Bethlehem, PA 18015
stolyar@lehigh.edu

ABSTRACT

The model is a "generalized switch", serving multiple traffic flows in discrete time. The switch uses MaxWeight algorithm to make a service decision (scheduling choice) at each time step, which determines the probability distribution of the amount of service that will be provided. We are primarily motivated by the following question: in the heavy traffic regime, when the switch load approaches critical level, will the service processes provided to each flow remain "smooth" (i.e., without large gaps in service)? Addressing this question reduces to the analysis of the asymptotic behavior of the unscaled queue-differential process in heavy traffic. We prove that the stationary regime of this process converges to that of a positive recurrent Markov chain, whose structure we explicitly describe. This in turn implies asymptotic "smoothness" of the service processes.

Categories and Subject Descriptors

C.2.1 [**Network Architecture and Design**]: Centralized networks; G.3 [**Probability and Statistics**]: Markov processes, Queueing theory, Stochastic processes

General Terms

Algorithms, Performance, Theory

Keywords

Dynamic scheduling; MaxWeight algorithm; Heavy traffic asymptotic regime; Markov chain; Queue length differentials; Smooth service process

1. INTRODUCTION

Suppose we have a system in which several data traffic flows share a common transmission medium (or channel). Sharing means that in each time slot a scheduler chooses a transmission mode – the subset the flows to serve and corresponding transmission rates; the outcome of each transmission is random. Scheduler has two key objectives: (a) the time-average (successful) transmission rate of each flow i has to be at least some $\lambda_i > 0$; (b) the successful transmissions for each flow need to be spread out "smoothly" in time – without large time-gaps between successful transmissions. Such models arise, for example, when the goal is *timely delivery* of information over a shared wireless channel [5].

A very natural way to approach this problem is to treat the model as a queueing system, where services (transmissions) are controlled by a so called MaxWeight scheduler (see [3, 9, 10]), which serves a set of *virtual queues* (one for each traffic flow), each receiving new work at the rate λ_i. (See e.g. [1].) This automatically achieves objective (a), if this is feasible at all; MaxWeight is known to be *throughput optimal* – stabilize the queues if this is feasible at all. The MaxWeight stability results, however, do not tell whether or not the objective (b) is achieved. Specifically, when the system is heavily loaded, i.e. the vector $\boldsymbol{\lambda} = (\lambda_i)$ is within the system *rate region* $\boldsymbol{V}$, but close to its boundary, the steady-state queue lengths under MaxWeight are necessarily large, and it is conceivable that this may result in large time-gaps in service for individual flows. (Note that, if (a) and (b) are the objectives and the queues are virtual, the large queue lengths in themselves are not an issue. As long as (a) and (b) are achieved, minimizing the queue lengths is not important.) Our main results show that this is *not* the case. Namely, in the heavy traffic regime, when $\boldsymbol{\lambda} \to \boldsymbol{\lambda}^\star$, where $\boldsymbol{\lambda}^\star$ is a point on the outer boundary of rate region $\boldsymbol{V}$, the service process remains "smooth", in the sense that its stationary regime converges to that of a positive recurrent Markov chain, whose structure is given explicitly.

We emphasize two features of our model. First, our heavy traffic results do *not* require the *complete resource pooling* (cf. [3, 9]), namely the condition that there is a unique outer normal vector to region $\boldsymbol{V}$ at point $\boldsymbol{\lambda}^\star$. Second, we assume that the (random) amounts of new work arriving into the queues have *absolutely continuous* distribution; this assumption is non-restrictive if we create virtual queues, artificially, for the purpose of applying MaxWeight algorithm – in this case the structure of the virtual arrival process is within our control.

The details of our results and proofs are in [11].

2. MODEL

We consider a system of N flows served by a "switch", which evolves in discrete time $t = 0, 1, \ldots$. At the beginning of each time-slot, the scheduler has to choose from a finite number K of "service-decisions". If the service decision k is chosen, then independently of the past history the flows get an amount of

SIGMETRICS'15, June 15-19, 2015, Portland, OR, USA.
ACM 978-1-4503-3486-0/15/06.
http://dx.doi.org/10.1145/2745844.2745878.

service, given by a random non-negative vector. Furthermore, we assume that (if decision k is chosen), there is a finite number $\mathcal{O}_k$ of possible service-vector outcomes, i.e. with probability $p^{k,j}$, it is given by a non-negative vector $\boldsymbol{v}^{k,j}$. The expected service vector for decision k is denoted $\boldsymbol{\mu}^k$. We assume that vectors $\boldsymbol{\mu}^k$ are non-zero and different from each other; and that for each i there exists k such that $\mu_i^k > 0$.

We denote by $\boldsymbol{S}(t) = (S_1(t), \ldots, S_N(t))$ the (random) service vector at time t, and call $\boldsymbol{S}(\cdot)$ the service process.

After the service at time t is completed, a random amount of work arrives into the queues, and it is given by a non-negative vector $\boldsymbol{A}(t)$. The values of $\boldsymbol{A}(t)$ are i.i.d. across times t, and $\boldsymbol{A}(\cdot)$ is called the arrival process. The mean arrival rates of this process are given by vector $\boldsymbol{\lambda}$.

If $\boldsymbol{Q}(t)$ is the vector of queue lengths at time t, then for each i, $Q_i(t+1) = \max\{Q_i(t) - S_i(t),\ 0\} + A_i(t)$.

Let parameters $\gamma_i > 0$ be fixed for all i. MaxWeight scheduling algorithm chooses, at each time t, a service decision

$$k \in \arg\max_l \sum_i \gamma_i Q_i(t) \mu_i^l,$$

with ties broken according to any well defined rule.

We will consider a sequence of systems, indexed by $n \to \infty$, operating under MaxWeight scheduling. (Variables pertaining to n-th system will be supplied superscript (n).) The switch parameters will remain unchanged, but the distribution of $\boldsymbol{A}^{(n)}(t)$ changes with n, for each n it has density $f^{(n)}$, and $f^{(n)}$ uniformly converges to some density $f^\star$. The arrival process $\boldsymbol{A}^\star(\cdot)$, such that the distribution of $\boldsymbol{A}^\star(t)$ has density $f^\star$, has the arrival rate vector $\boldsymbol{\lambda}^\star$. Correspondingly, $\boldsymbol{\lambda}^{(n)} \to \boldsymbol{\lambda}^\star$.

We assume that $\boldsymbol{\lambda}^\star$ has positive components and is a maximal element of rate region $\boldsymbol{V}$. We further assume that for each n, $\boldsymbol{\lambda}^{(n)}$ lies in the *interior* of $\boldsymbol{V}$; therefore, the system is stable for each n (under the MaxWeight algorithm).

3. MAIN RESULTS

We define the notion of *asymptotic smoothness* of the steady-state service process. Informally, it means the property that as the system load approaches critical, the steady state service processes are such that for each flow the probability of a T-long gap (without any service at all) uniformly vanishes, as $T \to \infty$.

For each n, consider the cumulative service process $\boldsymbol{G}^{(n)}(\cdot)$ in steady state. Namely,

$$\boldsymbol{G}^{(n)}(t) \triangleq \sum_{\tau=1}^{t} \boldsymbol{S}^{(n)}(\tau), \quad t = 1, 2, \ldots$$

DEFINITION 1. *We call the service process asymptotically smooth, if*

$$\max_i \lim_{T\to\infty} \left(\limsup_{n\to\infty} P\left(G_i^{(n)}(T) = 0 \right) \right) = 0.$$

Our key result, Theorem 21 in [11], is concerned with the following "queue-differential" process $\boldsymbol{Y}^{(n)}(t)$, which is the orthogonal projection of Markov process $(\gamma_1 Q_1^{(n)}(t), \ldots, \gamma_N Q_N^{(n)}(t))$ on the subspace orthogonal to the outer normal cone to $\boldsymbol{V}$ at point $\boldsymbol{\lambda}^\star$. We prove that the stationary version of the *non-Markov* process $\boldsymbol{Y}^{(n)}(\cdot)$ converges to that of the positive Harris recurrent *Markov* process $\boldsymbol{Y}^\star(\cdot)$, which, informally speaking, can be thought of as the queue-differential process of the critically loaded system (with mean arrival rates given by $\boldsymbol{\lambda}^\star$). The structure of the process $\boldsymbol{Y}^\star(\cdot)$ is defined explicitly. Moreover, as $n \to \infty$, the steady-state probability that the choice of a scheduling decision is uniquely determined by the current queue-differential $\boldsymbol{Y}^{(n)}(t)$ converges to 1. These results, in particular, imply the following

THEOREM 2. *Consider the sequence of systems described in Section 2, in the heavy traffic regime. Under MaxWeight scheduling, the service process is asymptotically smooth.*

4. REFERENCES

[1] M. Andrews, K. Kumaran, K. Ramanan, A. L. Stolyar, R. Vijayakumar, P. Whiting. Providing Quality of Service over a Shared Wireless Link. *IEEE Communications Magazine*, 2001, Vol.39, No.2, pp.150-154.

[2] M. Andrews, K. Jung, A. L. Stolyar. Stability of the Max-Weight Routing and Scheduling Protocol in Dynamic Networks and at Critical Loads. STOC'07, San Diego, CA, June 11-13, 2007.

[3] A. Eryilmaz and R. Srikant. Asymptotically Tight Steady-State Queue Length Bounds Implied by Drift Conditions. *Queueing Systems*, 2012, Vol.72, No.3-4, pp.311-359.

[4] B. Hajek. Hitting-Time and Occupation-Time Bounds Implied by Drift Analysis with Applications. *Advances in Applied Probability*, 1982, Vol.14, No.3, pp. 502-525.

[5] I-H. Hou, V. Borkar and P.R. Kumar. A Theory of QoS for Wireless. *INFOCOM 2009*.

[6] R. Li, A. Eryilmaz, B. Li. Throughput-Optimal Wireless Scheduling with Regulated Inter-Service Times. *INFOCOM 2013*.

[7] B. Li, R. Li, A. Eryilmaz. Heavy-Traffic-Optimal Scheduling with Regular Service Guarantees in Wireless Networks. *MobiHoc 2013*.

[8] S. P. Meyn and R.L. Tweedie. Stability of Markovian Processes I: Criteria for Discrete-Time chains. *Advances in Applied Probability*, 1992, Vol.24, No. 3, pp. 542-574.

[9] A.L. Stolyar. Max Weight Scheduling in a Generalized Switch: State Space Collapse and Workload Minimization in Heavy Traffic. *Annals of Applied Probability*, 2004, Vol.14, No. 1, pp. 1-53.

[10] L. Tassiulas, E. Ephremides. Stability properties of constrained queueing systems and scheduling policies for maximum throughput in multihop radio networks. *IEEE Trans. Automat. Control*, 1992, Vol. 37, No. 1, pp. 1936 - 1948.

[11] R. Singh and A. Stolyar. MaxWeight Scheduling: Asymptotic Behavior of Unscaled Queue-Differentials in Heavy Traffic. `http://arxiv.org/abs/1502.03793`

Kraken: Towards Elastic Performance Guarantees in Multi-tenant Data Centers

Carlo Fuerst⋆, Stefan Schmid⋆†, Lalith Suresh⋆, and Paolo Costa‡
⋆ TU Berlin, Germany † Telekom Innovation Laboratories, Germany
‡ Microsoft Research, United Kindom
{carlo,stefan,lalith}@inet.tu-berlin.de, paolo.costa@microsoft.com

ABSTRACT

It is well-known that without strict network bandwidth guarantees, application performance in multi-tenant cloud environments is unpredictable. While recently proposed systems support explicit bandwidth reservation mechanisms, they require the resource schedules to be announced *ahead of time*. We argue that this is not practical in today's cloud environments, where application demands are inherently unpredictable, e.g., due to stragglers. We in this paper present KRAKEN, a system that allows tenants to dynamically request and *update* minimum resource guarantees for both network bandwidth and compute resources *at runtime*. Unlike previous work, Kraken does not require prior knowledge about the resource needs of the tenants' applications but allows tenants to modify their reservation at runtime. Kraken achieves this through an *online resource reservation scheme*, and by optimally embedding and reconfiguring virtual networks.

1. INTRODUCTION

Cloud-based applications, including MapReduce and scale-out databases, generate significant amount of network traffic and a considerable fraction of their runtime is due to network activity. Unfortunately, as reported in previous studies [1], in existing cloud infrastructures, the bandwidth available to the tenants varies significantly over time, even within the same day. Given the time spent in network activity by these applications, this variability has a non-negligible impact on the application performance, which makes it impossible for tenants to accurately estimate the execution time in advance [3].

Several systems have been proposed which leverage admission control and support explicit bandwidth reservations to overcome this problem. [1, 4] Many of these systems offer *virtual cluster* abstractions, which provides the tenants with the illusion of having their own dedicated network: A virtual cluster offers the tenant the illusion for all her *Compute Units (CUs)* to be attached to a single non-oversubscribed switch with a minimum bandwidth b guaranteed. A virtual cluster VC(n, b) has two parameters: n, the number of (identical) CUs in the cluster, and b, the bandwidth reservation from each CU to the virtual switch.

SIGMETRICS'15, June 15-19, 2015, Portland, OR, USA.
ACM 978-1-4503-3486-0/15/06.
http://dx.doi.org/10.1145/2745844.2745879 .

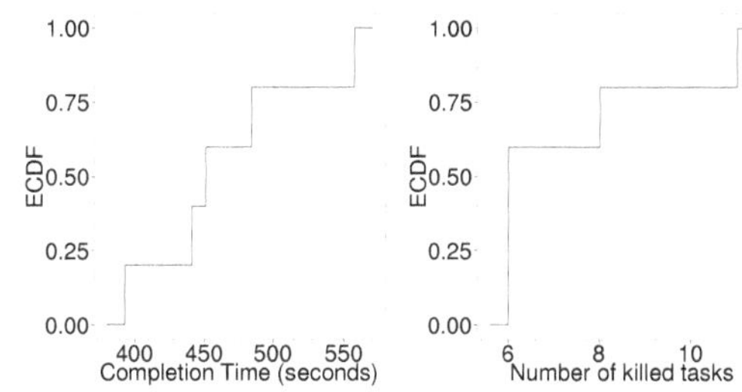

Figure 1: Execution unpredictability—Completion times of jobs in the presence of speculative execution (*left*) and the number of speculated tasks (*right*).

However, *all* existing solutions providing absolute bandwidth guarantees are based on *offline reservations schemes* [1, 2, 4]: they require that tenants announce the entire resource reservation schedule *ahead of time*, i.e., at job submission time.

We argue that in most cases it is very hard to accurately estimate application resource needs ahead of time, rendering offline reservation schemes inadequate. To highlight this point, we demonstrate that even with the same workload and a dataset of the same size being re-executed, it is difficult to predict how a job progresses over time. Concretely, we conduct an "idealized" experiment wherein we run a Hadoop cluster in our OpenStack-based testbed; environments such as Amazon EC2 are far more noisy. We use five physical servers (8 CPU cores) with one virtual machine each. Each virtual machine is allocated 4 virtual cores. Each node of the Hadoop cluster is mapped to a virtual machine each (one master, four slaves). The Hadoop workload consists of a TeraSort job. We repeat the experiment five times with speculative execution enabled. Figure 1 (*left*) indicates the variance in job completion times across the runs: a range of 150 seconds. This observation is also supported by Figure 1 (*right*) which shows the variable number of straggling tasks speculatively re-executed by the Hadoop cluster.

2. KRAKEN

Kraken introduces virtual clusters whose resource guarantees can be adjusted over time, in an online fashion. Since the objectives of the execution (e.g., deadlines) depend on the context and the need of the tenant, we argue that the tenant itself should be responsible for the specific scheduling strategy, and Kraken simply exposes an interface which allows to (1) upgrade a virtual cluster VC(n,b) consisting of n CUs and with a bandwidth guarantee b, both in *size* (i.e., number of CUs) as well as in the minimum *bandwidth*, that is, to a virtual cluster with $x \geq 0$ more nodes and a factor $\delta \geq 1$ more bandwidth, i.e., to VC$(n + x, b \cdot \delta)$; (2) downgrade a virtual cluster in both size and bandwidth; (3) or a combination of both (e.g., upgrade size and downgrade bandwidth).

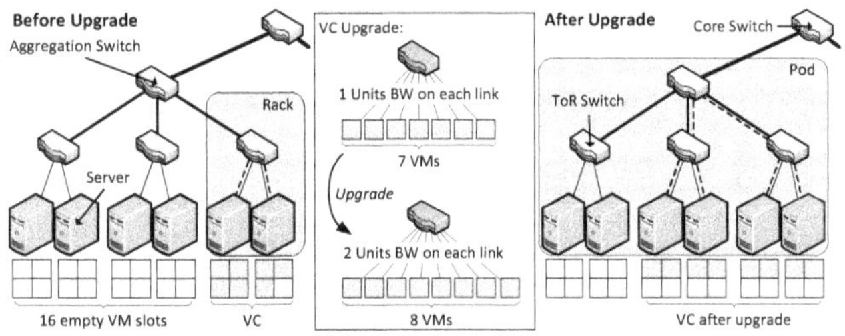

Figure 2: Example: upgrade of virtual cluster requiring migration.

How to support such reconfigurations is also an algorithmic problem. We would like to avoid or at least minimize migrations in order to satisfy a reconfiguration request; moreover, the resulting embeddings should have small network *footprints*, in the sense that CUs are embedded close to each other and unnecessary bandwidth reservations (on substrate links) are avoided.

Example. To illustrate both the model and the challenge, let us consider an example. Figure 2 (*left*) shows a part of a fat-tree data center topology, i.e., a single pod consisting of three racks with two servers each; each server has 4 CU slots. We assume that the uplinks of the servers have a capacity of 4 units and the fat-tree provides full bisection bandwidth, resulting in a capacity of 8 units on the ToR switches' uplinks and a capacity of 24 units on the links between the aggregation switches and the core switch. On the right most rack, currently a virtual cluster VC is embedded; the dashed line indicates the path along with bandwidth is reserved to connect the CUs. At some point, VC is upgraded, from VC(7,1) to VC(8,2), see Figure 2 (*middle*).

How can this request be implemented? Theoretically, the right server in the rack still has a free CU slot which could be used to accommodate the additional CU; however, doubling the bandwidth reservations for each of the CUs will violate the bandwidth capacities on the uplinks of the servers. Hence it becomes necessary to distribute the CUs in the substrate, in order to reduce the bandwidth utilization of the uplinks of the two servers. Thus, in this scenario, some CUs need to be migrated to satisfy the request. Figure 2 (*right*) shows a solution: the resulting embedding is valid.

Theoretical Contribution. Kraken is based on the observation that by first fixing the logical switch of the virtual cluster, optimal tradeoffs between small footprints and reconfiguration costs can be computed efficiently, using dynamic programming (namely bottom-up, from the substrate-tree leaves to the core switch). Since also the number of possible logical switch locations is small (linear in the substrate size), Kraken is fast.

THEOREM 2.1. *Kraken efficiently computes provably optimal virtual cluster embeddings and minimizes reconfiguration costs.*

Previous Work: Static Embeddings only and Suboptimal Footprints. Previous systems such as Oktopus [1] and Proteus [4] do not support online reconfigurations and migrations. Moreover, the static embeddings computed by these systems can be suboptimal (large footprints): In the case of Oktopus, a small virtual cluster which could be hosted by a single server (Kraken footprint: 0) may be embedded across multiple servers (footprint > 1). In the case of Proteus, the ratio of the optimal footprint computed by Kraken and the footprint by Proteus can be as high as $n/3$: such an example can be constructed by exploiting the fact that Proteus will only consider cross-pod embeddings if a request cannot be fit in a single pod. Thus, in case $n-1$ slots are available on a single server in one pod and n times one slot is available on servers in another pod, the Proteus footprint is $2n$ while the footprint of Kraken is 6.

Preliminary Evaluation. Hadoop-YARN is an interesting application for Kraken, as the MapReduce tasks inform the Application Master about the progress of a task periodically. This information is used, for instance, to speculate tasks that are straggling. To demonstrate a basic version of Kraken (without support for elastic computations or migrations), we implemented a simple controller that runs inside a virtual machine and uses the Linux `tc` utility in order to make bandwidth reservations. We then instrumented the Hadoop source code such that tasks inform the controller prior to executing a shuffle. If there is spare bandwidth to be allocated, the controller increases the corresponding endpoint's bandwidth reservation. Once the shuffle is completed, the Hadoop framework informs the controller of the same in order to release its reservations. (Migrations are not supported yet.)

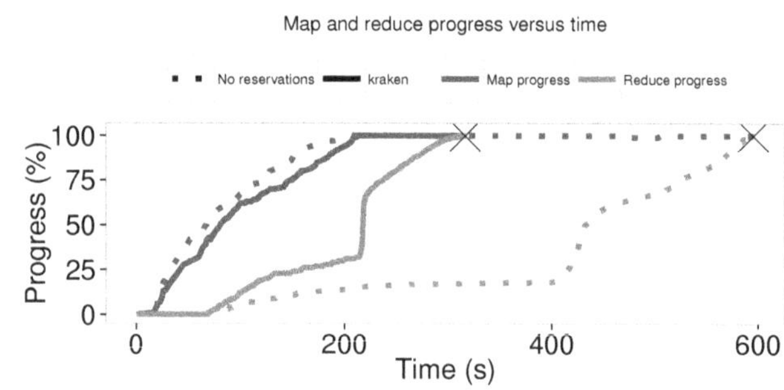

Figure 3: Map and reduce progress of a TeraSort job in best effort conditions (*dotted*) and when using Kraken (*solid lines*). The X marks indicate the point of job completion.

Using this framework, we executed the TeraSort benchmark against a dataset size of 100 million 100 byte records (a total of ~10 GB of data). We co-locate the Hadoop datanodes against a set of VMs that generate UDP flows on the network using `iperf`. The UDP flows are set to last 400 seconds at a throughput of 600 Mbps and thus significantly stresses the underlying 1 Gbps network. Hadoop is initially allocated only 100 Mbps of bandwidth, but requests additional bandwidth when shuffles are to be executed (with the UDP tenant given best-effort service, and left to consume the remaining bandwidth throughout). Figure 3 indicates the map and reduce progress with and without Kraken's online reservations. Without online reservations, the UDP tenant interferes heavily with Hadoop's network usage, thus prolonging the TeraSort job until the UDP flows terminate. With online reservations however, Hadoop requests bandwidth when it needs it, leading to just under 300 seconds of improvement in job completion time.

Research Funding. BMBF Software Campus grant 01IS12056, Bigfoot FP7-ICT-317858, G.I.F. No I-1245-407.6/2014.

3. REFERENCES

[1] H. Ballani, P. Costa, T. Karagiannis, and A. Rowstron. Towards predictable datacenter networks. In *Proc. ACM SIGCOMM*, 2011.

[2] C. Guo, G. Lu, H. J. Wang, S. Yang, C. Kong, P. Sun, W. Wu, and Y. Zhang. SecondNet: A data center network virtualization architecture with bandwidth guarantees. In *Proc. ACM CoNEXT*, 2010.

[3] J. C. Mogul and L. Popa. What we talk about when we talk about cloud network performance. *SIGCOMM CCR*, 42(5):44–48, 2012.

[4] D. Xie, N. Ding, Y. C. Hu, and R. Kompella. The only constant is change: incorporating time-varying network reservations in data centers. In *Proc. ACM SIGCOMM*, 2012.

Latency in Software Defined Networks: Measurements and Mitigation Techniques

Keqiang He†, Junaid Khalid†, Sourav Das†, Aaron Gember-Jacobson†, Chaithan Prakash†, Aditya Akella†, Li Erran Li*, Marina Thottan*
†University of Wisconsin-Madison, *Bell Labs

ABSTRACT

We conduct a comprehensive measurement study of switch control plane latencies using four types of production SDN switches. Our measurements show that control actions, such as rule installation, have surprisingly high latency, due to both software implementation inefficiencies and fundamental traits of switch hardware. We also propose three measurement-driven latency mitigation techniques—optimizing route selection, spreading rules across switches, and reordering rule installations—to effectively tame the flow setup latencies in SDN.

Categories and Subject Descriptors

C.2.0 [**Computer-Communication Network**]: General

Keywords

Software-defined Networks; Latency; Measurement; Mitigation

1. INTRODUCTION

Software defined networking (SDN) advocates for the separation of control and data planes in network devices, and provides a logically centralized platform to program data plane state [5]. This has opened the door to rich network control applications that can adapt to changes in network topology or traffic patterns more flexibly and more quickly than legacy control planes [1, 2]. For such applications, timely interaction between the logically central SDN control plane and network switches is crucial. However, it is unknown whether SDN can provide sufficiently responsive control to support the aforementioned applications.

To this end, we present a thorough systematic exploration of latencies in four types of production SDN switches from three different vendors—Broadcom, Intel, and IBM—using a variety of workloads. Key highlights from our measurements are as follows: (1) We find that *inbound latency*, i.e., the latency involved in the switch generating packet events to the controller can be high (8 ms per packet on average on Intel). We find the delay is particularly high whenever the switch is simultaneously processing forwarding rules received from the controller. (2) We find that *outbound latency*, i.e.,

SIGMETRICS'15, June 15–19, 2015, Portland, OR, USA.
ACM 978-1-4503-3486-0/15/06.
http://dx.doi.org/10.1145/2745844.2745880.

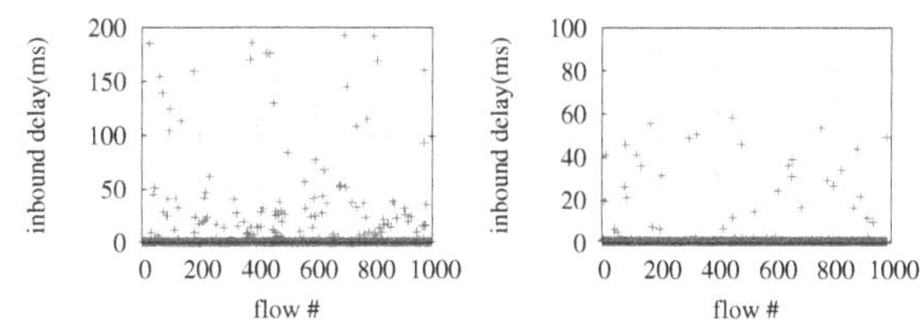

(a) with flow_mod/pkt_out (b) w/o flow_mod/pkt_out
Figure 1: Inbound delay on Intel switch, flow arrival rate = 200/s

the latency involved in the switch installing/modifying/deleting forwarding rules, is high as well (3ms and 30ms per rule for insertion and modification, respectively, in Broadcom).

Some of our findings show that poor switch software design contributes significantly to observed latencies (affirming [4, 6]). We believe that near term work will address these issues; our measurements with an early release of Broadcom's OpenFlow 1.3 software exemplify this. More crucially, our measurements also reveal latencies that appear to be fundamentally rooted in hardware design: e.g., rules must be organized in switch hardware tables in priority order, and simultaneous switch control actions must contend for limited bus bandwidth between a switch's CPU and ASIC. Unless the hardware significantly changes—and our first-of-a-kind in-depth measurement study may engender such changes—we believe these latencies will manifest even in next generation switches.

To mitigate the impact of outbound latency, and support the needs of SDN apps, we propose three immediately deployable techniques: flow engineering (FE), rule offload (RO), and rule reordering (RR). Simulation for fast fail-over and responsive traffic engineering applications shows our techniques can improve the time taken to update network state in these scenarios by factors of 1.6-5X. Detailed results can be found in [3].

2. LATENCY MEASUREMENTS

We conduct measurements on four types of switches from three vendors—Broadcom 956846K with OpenFlow 1.0 firmware (BCM-1.0) and OpenFlow 1.3 firmware (BCM-1.3), Intel FM6000 (Intel) and IBM G8264 (IBM). We craft our experiments to ensure the latency impact of various factors can be measured directly from the data plane with the exception of packet_in generation latency.

2.1 Inbound Latency

Representative results for inbound latency are shown in Figure 1a and 1b, respectively, for the Intel FM6000 switch. For the first experiment, we see that the inbound latency is quite variable with a mean of 8.33ms, a median of 0.73ms, and a standard deviation of

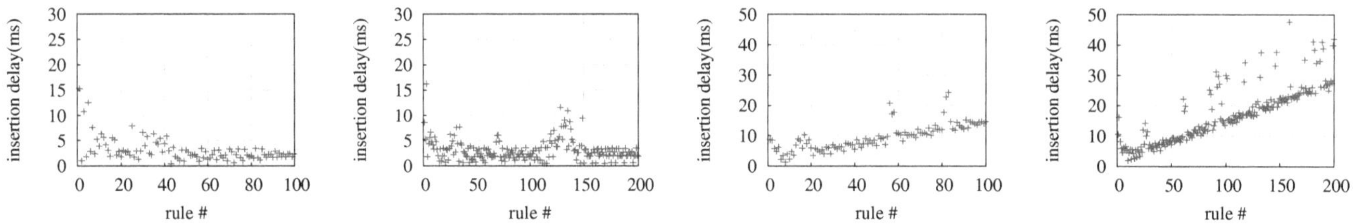

(a) burst size 100, same priority (b) burst size 200, same priority (c) burst size 100, incr. priority (d) burst size 200, incr. priority

Figure 2: BCM-1.0 per-rule insertion latency

31.34ms. For the second experiment, the inbound delay is lower (mean of 1.72ms, median of 0.67ms) and less variable (standard deviation of 6.09ms). We also observe that inbound latency depends on the *packet_in* rate: e.g., in first experiment the mean is 3.32 ms for 100 flows/s (not shown) vs. 8.33ms for 200 flows/s (Figure 1a). Our conversations with the switch vendor suggest that the limited bus bandwidth between the ASIC and switch CPU is the primary factor contributing to inbound latency.

2.2 Outbound Latency

We study the outbound latencies for three different *flow_mod* operations: insertion, modification, and deletion. For each operation, we examine the latency impact of key factors, including flow table occupancy and rule priority.

2.2.1 *Insertion Latency*

Figure 2 shows representative results on BCM-1.0 switch. We observe that: (1) rule complexity does not affect insertion delay; (2) same priority insertions in BCM-1.0, BCM-1.3, Intel and IBM are fast and not affected by flow table occupancy; and (3) priority insertion patterns can affect insertion delay very differently. For Intel, increasing priority insertion is similar to same priority insertion, but decreasing priority incurs much higher delay. For BCM-1.3 and IBM the behavior is inverted: decreasing priority insertion is similar to same priority insertion and increasing priority insertion incurs higher delay. For BCM-1.0, insertions with different priority patterns are all much higher than insertions with same priority. Key root causes for observed latencies are: (1) how rules are organized in the TCAM, and (2) the number of TCAM slices. *Both of these are intrinsically tied to switch hardware.* Even in the best case (Intel), per-rule insertion latency of 1ms is higher than what native TCAM hardware can support. Thus, in addition to the above two causes, there appears to be an *intrinsic switch software overhead* contributing to all latencies.

2.2.2 *Modification Latency*

We observe that the per-rule modification latency on BCM-1.0 and IBM is impacted purely by table occupancy, not by rule priority structure. Conversations with Broadcom indicated that TCAM modification should ideally be fast and independent of table size, so the underlying cause appears to be less optimized switch software in BCM-1.0. For BCM-1.3 and Intel, the per-rule modification delay is independent of rule priority, table occupancy, and burst size; BCM-1.3's per-rule modification delay is 2X higher than insertion.

2.2.3 *Deletion Latency*

For BCM-1.0, BCM-1.3, Intel and IBM, deletion latency is not affected by the priorities of rules in the table or the order of deletion. However, deletion delay is affected by table occupancy—it decreases with rule number in all the switches we measured. Thus we infer that deletion is incurring TCAM reordering.

3. MITIGATION TECHNIQUES

We propose three techniques to mitigate the outbound latencies imposed by current switches: *Flow engineering* (FE) leverages our empirical latency models to compute paths such that the latency of installing forwarding state at any switch is minimized. *Rule offloading* (RO) computes strategies for opportunistically offloading installation of some forwarding state to downstream switches. Finally, *rule reordering* (RR) sends rule installation requests in an order that is optimal for the switch in question. By reducing installation latency per switch (FE + RR) and enabling network-wide parallel updates (RO), rule updates can finish much faster. We evaluated our mitigation techniques for three applications: failover in a tunneled WAN, two-level responsive traffic engineering, and MicroTE [2]. Our simulations show we can improve the time taken to update network state in these scenarios by factors of 1.6-5X.

4. CONCLUSION

Our measurements across four OpenFlow-based switches show that the latencies underlying the generation of control messages (pkt_in's) and execution of control operations (flow_mod's) can be quite high, and variable. We find that the underlying causes are linked both to software inefficiencies, as well as pathological interactions between switch hardware properties (shared resources and how forwarding rules are organized) and the control operation workload (the order of operations issues, and concurrent switch activities). Finally, to mitigate the challenges these latencies create for SDN in supporting critical management applications, we present three measurement-driven techniques. Our evaluation shows that these mechanisms can tame flow setup latencies effectively.

Acknowledgement

This work is supported in part by NSF grants CNS-1302041, CNS-1314363 and CNS-1040757.

5. REFERENCES

[1] M. Al-Fares, S. Radhakrishnan, B. Raghavan, N. Huang, and A. Vahdat. Hedera: Dynamic flow scheduling for data center networks. In *NSDI*, 2010.

[2] T. Benson, A. Anand, A. Akella, and M. Zhang. Microte: Fine grained traffic engineering for data centers. In *CoNEXT*, 2011.

[3] K. He, J. Khalid, S. Das, A. Akella, E. L. Li, and M. Thottan. Mazu: Taming latency in software defined networks. *University of Wisconsin-Madison Technical Report*, 2014.

[4] D. Y. Huang, K. Yocum, and A. C. Snoeren. High-fidelity switch models for software-defined network emulation. In *HotSDN*, 2013.

[5] N. McKeown, T. Anderson, H. Balakrishnan, G. Parulkar, L. Peterson, J. Rexford, S. Shenker, and J. Turner. Openflow: enabling innovation in campus networks. *SIGCOMM CCR*, 2008.

[6] C. Rotsos, N. Sarrar, S. Uhlig, R. Sherwood, and A. W. Moore. Oflops: An open framework for openflow switch evaluation. In *PAM*, 2012.

Tree-structured Bloom Filters for Joint Optimization of False Positive Probability and Transmission Bandwidth

Yongquan Fu
Science and Technology Laboratory of Parallel and Distributed Processing
School of Computer
National Univ. of Defense Technology
yongquanf@nudt.edu.cn

Ernst Biersack
www.e-biersack.eu
erbi@e-biersack.eu

ABSTRACT

Bloom filters are frequently used to perform set queries that test the existence of some items. However, Bloom filters face a dilemma: the transmission bandwidth and the accuracy cannot be optimized simultaneously. This dilemma is particularly severe for transmitting Bloom filters to remote nodes when the network bandwidth is limited. We propose a novel Bloom filter **BloomTree** that consists of a tree-structured organization of smaller Bloom filters, each one using a set of independent hash functions. BloomTree spreads items across levels that are compressed to reduce the transmission bandwidth need. We investigate in detail under which conditions BloomTree performs better than the compressed Bloom filter and the standard Bloom filter.

Categories and Subject Descriptors

C.2.0 [**Computer Systems Organization**]: Data communications

Keywords

Bloom filter; tree

1. INTRODUCTION

A Bloom filter (BF) [1] is a space-efficient compact data structure answering the approximate set queries [2, 3]. The Standard Bloom Filter (denoted as **SBF**) represents the set by randomly hashing each item into k bit locations into a bit array, where k denotes the number of hash functions. The Bloom filter incurs a certain false positive (FP) probability, since the hash locations may be already be set to ones by different items. However, a Bloom filter never has false negatives, i.e. an item is hashed to the bit array, but the query fails to report the existence of this item. To control the false positive probability, the size of the Bloom filter must grow linearly with the number of items in the set. Further, when Bloom filters must be exchanged among remote nodes, the transmission bandwidth is an important performance metric. In this case, using a Compressed Bloom Filter (denoted as **CBF**) may decrease the transmission cost [4]. However, CBF usually has two hash functions, which significantly degrades the accuracy compared to the Bloom filters with the optimal hash functions. As a result, there is still a gap between the space efficiency and the accuracy.

SIGMETRICS'15, June 15-19, 2015, Portland, OR, USA.
ACM 978-1-4503-3486-0/15/06.
http://dx.doi.org/10.1145/2745844.2745881.

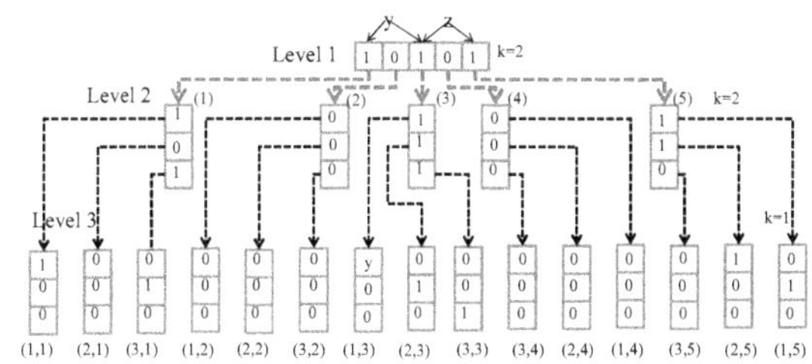

Figure 1: A three-level BloomTree instance. We represent a BloomTree with a tuple: $\{n_{\max}, d, \rho_1, k_1, m_{i,i>1}, k_{i,i>1}\}$, where $n_{\max}$ denotes the maximal number of items to be inserted, d represents the depth of the BloomTree, ρ_1 denotes the ratio between the number of bits and the number of items in the first-level filter, k_1 is the number of hash functions of the filter in the first level, $m_{i,i>1}$ is the size of the filter in the second and higher levels, and $k_{i,i>1}$ denotes the number of hash functions of the filter in the second and higher levels.

There exists a performance dilemma for BF based approximate set queries: *Given a fixed-size bit array, selecting the optimal number of hash functions that minimizes the FP probability will make compression ineffective, while selecting fewer hash functions will increase the compression efficiency but degrade the FP probability*. By how much a Bloom filter can be compressed depends on the probability $p \in [0, 1]$ that a bit in the array is zero [4]. For $p = 0.5$ the entropy of the bit array is at its maximum and no compression is possible: This is the case for the SBF when it uses the optimal number of hash functions. The closer p gets to either one or to zero, the higher the potential for compression.

We designed and implemented a novel Bloom filter called BloomTree (BT for short) that simultaneously decreases the average FP probability and optimizes the transmission cost. A BloomTree is a hierarchical organization of Bloom filters, as shown in Figure 1. Each vertex is a small-size filter. For each bit in the filter, this vertex has one separate descendent filter in the next level. BloomTree determines whether an item is hashed into it via independent tests. The number of such tests increases exponentially increasing with the number of levels in the tree, resulting in an exponentially decreasing FP probabilities as the tree grows in hight.

The tree structure provides novel opportunities for optimizing the FP probabilities, by improving the locality of the hash locations

Table 1: Some optimal configurations for BloomTree. The size n of the item set is set to $n_{\max} = 10^8$. Let W_{BT} denote the transmission size of a BloomTree instance. Let W_{CBF} and W_{SBF} be the transmission sizes of the CBF and SBF instances with the same geometric-mean FP probability with the BloomTree instance.

d	ρ_1	m_2	m_3	m_4	k_1	k_2	k_3	k_4	Posterior FP	$\frac{W_{BT}}{W_{CBF}}$	$\frac{W_{BT}}{W_{SBF}}$
2	0.5	3	–	–	6	1	–	–	0.84	0.33	0.39
3	0.5	4	3	–	5	3	2	–	0.21	0.43	0.55
4	0.5	5	3	3	6	3	2	2	1.02×10^{-5}	0.67	0.71

of data items, which in turn reduces the false positive probabilities of querying the items.

2. DESIGN

The BloomTree optimizes the false positives and decreases the transmission size through a novel tree-structured Bloom filter. As shown in Figure 1, a logical structure of the BloomTree has d levels of Bloom filters that are organized as a **tree**. The root of the tree is a SBF in the first level. For each bit in a SBF at level i, a **descendent** Bloom filter is appended at level $(i+1)$, $i < d$. The i-th level is also called the **ancestor level** for the $(i+1)$-th level. The level d is called the **leaf level**.

To insert an item, we first insert the item in the first-level Bloom filter like the SBF. We also record the hash positions of the item. We next insert the item into each descendent Bloom filter at these hash positions. The inserting process is recursively run until we complete the insertion on the bottom level. The query process is also a recursive process, where an item is said to be in the set *iff* all visited Bloom filters report that the item is in the set. Accordingly, a FP event occurs for a membership query *iff the visited Bloom filters all report that the item is in the set*.

Time Complexity: To ensure constant time complexity, the physical storage of the BloomTree is stored into a one-dimensional bit array. In the bit array, the ancestor-descendent links are computed on-th-fly with low time complexity. As a result, the storage structure of BloomTree is identical to that of the SBF. Thanks to the doubling hash method, we only use two hash functions to generate the hash values for all filters in the tree, as a result, we keep the hashing time of the overall query time on the BloomTree to be constant.

Accuracy: To control the number of bits that are set to ones, we recursively map each item to a small number of descendent filters layer by layer. As a result, some of the bits set for a given item have common prefixes through the tree, so those bits tend to be more clustered than for a traditional flat Bloom Filter.

The FP probability for an incoming item is a random variable, since the computed hash locations of each filter may lead to different branches in the hierarchical structure, as shown in Figure 1. As a result, optimizing the FP probability of the BloomTree is a stochastic-programming problem. We present a light-weight parameter tuning method with the sample average approximation method that minimizes the transmission size while limiting the FP probability to be under a fixed threshold with 95% confidence. As a result, we guarantee the FP probability for each incoming query "on average".

Space Efficiency: Observing that the bits that are set to ones are biased towards a subset of all possible bits to be set, the bit array can be efficiently compressed. For example, from Figure 1, we see that in the second and third level, many filters have all-0 bits or all-1 bits. As a result, the whole level can be efficiently compressed.

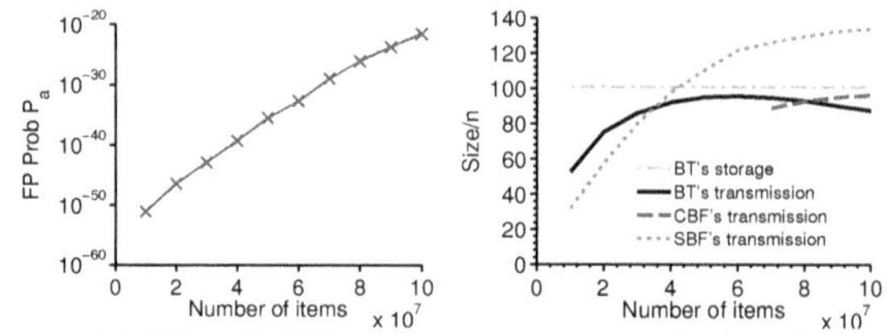

(a) FP probability (b) Transmission size

Figure 2: The FP probabilities and the transmission sizes as functions of the numbers of set items. The upper bound $n_{\max}$ of the set size is set to 10^8. We set d =4, ρ_1 = 1, m_2 = 4, m_3 = 4, m_4 = 5, k_1 = 6, k_2 = 3, k_3 = 3, k_4 = 2.

Results: We compare BloomTree with the standard Bloom filter and the Compressed Bloom filter. For a fair comparison, we create CBF and SBF instances whose geometric-mean posterior FP probabilities amount to those of the BloomTree instances. BloomTree's accuracy is determined by Bloom filters that are close to the leaves. The filters in the middle levels of the BloomTree serve as selectors for the SBFs close to the leaves. Increasing the number d of levels means that an exponential number of close-to-leaves Bloom filters are added. Therefore, BloomTree has exponentially decreasing FP probabilities as the depth d increases. From Table 1 we see that the BloomTree improves the space efficiency by 30-40% compared to the Compressed Bloom filter.

From Figure 2, we see that BloomTree's FP probability increases as we keep adding new items, since the percent of bits set to one at each level monotonically increases due to the constant storage of the BloomTree. We see that BloomTree requires the smallest transmission size compared to the CBF and the SBF as we continue to add more items. Moreover, the Compressed Bloom filters do not have a feasible parameter region for a wide range of experiments, since its transmission size becomes infinite due to too few hash functions.

Acknowledgments: This work was supported by the National Natural Science Foundation of China (Grant No. 61402509 and 61379052), the National High Technology Research and Development 863 Program of China (Grant No.2013AA01A213), the Natural Science Foundation for Distinguished Young Scholars of Hunan Province (Grant No.14JJ1026), Specialized Research Fund for the Doctoral Program of Higher Education (Grant No.20124307110015).

3. REFERENCES

[1] A. Z. Broder and M. Mitzenmacher. Network Applications of Bloom Filters: A Survey. *Internet Mathematics*, 1(4), 2003.

[2] Y. Fu and Y. Wang. BCE: A Privacy-preserving Common-friend Estimation Method for Distributed Online Social Networks without Cryptography. In *Proc. of CHINACOM*, pages 212–217, 2012.

[3] Y. Fu, Y. Wang, and W. Peng. CommonFinder: A Decentralized and Privacy-preserving Common-friend Measurement Method for the Distributed Online Social Networks. *Computer Networks*, 64:369–389, 2014.

[4] M. Mitzenmacher. Compressed Bloom Filters. *IEEE/ACM Trans. Netw.*, 10:604–612, 2002.

Scheduling Storms and Streams in the Cloud

Javad Ghaderi
Columbia University
New York, NY
jghaderi@columbia.edu

Sanjay Shakkottai
University of Texas
Austin, TX
shakkott@austin.utexas.edu

Rayadurgam Srikant
University of Illinois
Urbana, IL
rsrikant@illinois.edu

ABSTRACT

Motivated by emerging big *streaming* data processing paradigms (e.g., Twitter Storm, Streaming MapReduce), we investigate the problem of scheduling graphs over a large cluster of servers. Each graph is a job, where nodes represent compute tasks and edges indicate data-flows between these compute tasks. Jobs (graphs) arrive randomly over time, and upon completion, leave the system. When a job arrives, the scheduler needs to partition the graph and distribute it over the servers to satisfy load balancing and cost considerations. Specifically, neighboring compute tasks in the graph that are mapped to different servers incur load on the network; thus a mapping of the jobs among the servers incurs a cost that is proportional to the number of "broken edges". We propose a low complexity randomized scheduling algorithm that, without service preemptions, stabilizes the system with graph arrivals/departures; more importantly, it allows a smooth trade-off between minimizing average partitioning cost and average queue lengths. Interestingly, to avoid service preemptions, our approach does not rely on a Gibbs sampler; instead, we show that the corresponding limiting invariant measure has an interpretation stemming from a loss system.

Categories and Subject Descriptors

G.3 [**Probability and Statistics**]: Queuing theory, Markov processes, Probabilistic algorithms

General Terms

Theory, Performance

Keywords

Graph Partitioning, Dynamic Resource Allocation

1. PROBLEM SETUP

Consider a collection of machines $\mathcal{L}$. Each machine $\ell \in \mathcal{L}$ has a set of slots m_ℓ which it can use to run at most $|m_\ell|$ processes in parallel. These machines are inter-connected by a communication network. Let $M = \sum_\ell |m_\ell|$ be the total number of slots in the cluster. There is a collection of *jobs types* $\mathcal{J}$, where each job type $j \in \mathcal{J}$ is described by a *graph* $\mathcal{G}_j(V_j, E_j)$ consisting of a set of nodes V_j and a set of edges E_j. Each graph $\mathcal{G}_j$ represents how the computation is split among the set of nodes V_j. Nodes correspond to computation with each node requiring a slot on some machine; edges represent data flows between these computations (nodes). We assume graphs of type j arrive according to a Poisson process with rate λ_j, and will remain in the system for an exponentially distributed amount of time with mean $1/\mu_j$. Node of the graph must be assigned to an empty slot on one of the machines. Thus a graph of type $\mathcal{G}_j$ requires a total number of $|V_j|$ free slots ($|V_j| < M$). For each graph, data center needs to decide how to partition the graph and distribute it over the machines. When jobs arrive, they can either be immediately served, or queued and served at a later time. Thus, there is a set of queues $\mathbf{Q}(t) = (Q^{(j)}(t) : j \in \mathcal{J})$ representing existing jobs in the system either waiting for service or receiving service. For any job, we assume that the cost of data exchange between two nodes that are inside the same machine is zero, and the cost of data exchange between two nodes of a graph on different machines is one. This models the cost incurred by the data center due to the total traffic exchange among different machines.

An important construct in this paper is the concept of template. Observe that for any graph $\mathcal{G}_j$, there are several ways (exponentially large number) in which it can be *partitioned* and *distributed* over the machines. A *template* corresponds to one possible way in which a graph $\mathcal{G}_j$ can *partitioned* and *distributed* over the machines. Rigorously, a template A for graph $\mathcal{G}_j$ is an injective function $A : V_j \to \bigcup_{\ell \in \mathcal{L}} m_\ell$ which maps each node of $\mathcal{G}_j$ to a unique slot in one of the machines. We use $\mathcal{A}^{(j)}$ to denote the set of all possible templates for graph $\mathcal{G}_j$. Tying back to the cost model, for $A \in \mathcal{A}^{(j)}$, let $b_A^{(j)}$ be the cost of partitioning $\mathcal{G}_j$ according to template A. There is a template in the system corresponding to each job that is being served on a set of machines. Further, when a new job arrives or departs, the system can (potentially) create a new template that is a pattern of *empty slots* across machines that can be "filled" with a specific job type (i.e., one particular graph topology). We call the former as *actual templates*, and the latter as *virtual templates*. Further, when a job departs, the system can potentially destroy the associated template.

Given any stationary (and Markov) algorithm for scheduling arriving graphs, the system state evolves as an irre-

This work is partially supported by the Simons Foundation Chair at UT Austin and NSF Grant ECCS-1202065.

SIGMETRICS'15, June 15-19, 2015, Portland, OR, USA.
ACM 978-1-4503-3486-0/15/06.
http://dx.doi.org/10.1145/2745844.2745882

ducible and aperiodic Markov chain. Our goal is to minimize the average partitioning cost, i.e.,

$$\begin{aligned} \text{minimize} \quad & \mathbb{E}\Big[\sum_{j\in\mathcal{J}} \sum_{A\in\mathcal{A}^{(j)}} x_A b_A^{(j)}\Big] \qquad (1) \\ \text{subject to} \quad & \text{system stability} \end{aligned}$$

where x_A is a random variable denoting the fraction of time that a template A is used in steady state. The system stability in (1) means that the average delay (or average queue size) remains bounded. There is an inherent tradeoff between the average delay and the average partitioning cost. For more lenient delay constraints, the algorithm can defer the scheduling of jobs further until a feasible template with low partitioning cost becomes available.

2. ALGORITHM

Our low complexity algorithm can be used to solve (1) without interrupting/migrating the ongoing services. Given the vector of queue sizes $\mathbf{Q}(t)$, and a function $f(x) = \log^{1-b}(x)$, $b \in (0,1)$, the weight of template $A \in \mathcal{A}^{(j)}$, $j \in \mathcal{J}$, is defined as

$$\tilde{w}_A^{(j)}(t) = \alpha f^{(j)}\Big(\mathbf{h} + \mathbf{Q}(t)\Big) - b_A^{(j)}, \qquad (2)$$

where $f^{(j)} : \mathbb{R}_+{}^{|\mathcal{J}|} \to \mathbb{R}_+$ is

$$f^{(j)}(x) = \max\Big\{f(x_j), \frac{\epsilon}{8M} f(x_{\max})\Big\};\ x_{\max} = \max_{j\in\mathcal{J}} x_j, \qquad (3)$$

where $\mathbf{h} = h\mathbb{1}_{|\mathcal{J}|}$, and $\alpha, h \in \mathbb{R}_+$, and $\epsilon \in (0,1)$ are the parameters of the algorithm.

At the instances of job arrivals and departures, the algorithm makes decisions on the templates that are added to/removed from the system configuration. It is important that the addition/removal of templates by the algorithm *does not* disrupt the ongoing service of existing jobs in the configuration.

The low complexity algorithm is a randomized algorithm in which the candidate template to be added to the configuration is chosen randomly among the set of feasible templates. In particular, the following *Random Partition Procedure* is used as a subroutine in our low complexity algorithm.

Algorithm 1 Random Partition Procedure

Input: current configuration C, and a graph $\mathcal{G}(V,E)$, $V = \{v_1, \cdots, v_{|V|}\}$
Output: a virtual template A for distributing $\mathcal{G}$ over the machines.

$k \leftarrow 1$
slot-available $\leftarrow 1$
while $k \le |V|$ and slot-available **do**
  if there are no free slots available on any of the machines **then**
    slot-available $\leftarrow 0$; $A \leftarrow \varnothing$
  else
    place v_k uniformly at random in one of the free slots
    $A(v_k)$ = index of the slot containing v_k
    $k \leftarrow k+1$
  end if
end while

When a random template is generated according to Random Partition Procedure, the decision to keep or remove the template is made probabilistically based on the weight of the template. The description of the low complexity algorithm (called *Dynamic Graph Partitioning (DGP) algorithm*) is as follows. In the the description, $\beta > 0$ is a fixed parameter.

Algorithm 2 Dynamic Graph Partitioning (DGP)

Arrival instances. Suppose a graph (job) $\mathcal{G}_j$ arrives at time t, then:

1: This job is added to queue $Q^{(j)}$.
2: A virtual graph $\mathcal{G}_j$ is randomly distributed over the machines, if possible, using *Random Partition Procedure*, which creates a virtual template $A^{(j)}$ for distributing a graph $\mathcal{G}_j$ over the machines with some partitioning cost $b_A^{(j)}$. Then, this virtual template is added to the current configuration with probability $\frac{\exp(\frac{1}{\beta}\tilde{w}_A^{(j)}(t^+))}{1+\exp(\frac{1}{\beta}\tilde{w}_A^{(j)}(t^+))}$, otherwise, it is discarded and the configuration does not change. The virtual templates of type j leave the system after an exponentially distributed time duration with mean $1/\mu_j$.
3: If there is one or more virtual templates available for accommodating graphs of type $\mathcal{G}_j$, a job from $Q^{(j)}$ (e.g., the head-of-the-line job) is placed in one of the virtual templates chosen arbitrarily at random. This converts the virtual template to an actual template.

Departure instances. Suppose a departure of a (virtual or actual) template $A^{(j)}$ occurs at time t, then:

1: If this an actual template, the job departs and queue $Q^{(j)}(t^+)$ is updated.
2: A virtual template of the same type $A^{(j)}$ is added back to the configuration with probability $\frac{\exp(\frac{1}{\beta}\tilde{w}_A^{(j)}(t^+))}{1+\exp(\frac{1}{\beta}\tilde{w}_A^{(j)}(t^+))}$.
3: If a virtual template for accommodating a graph $\mathcal{G}_j$ is available in the system, and there are jobs in $Q^{(j)}(t^+)$ waiting to get service, a job from $Q^{(j)}$ (e.g. the head-of-the line job) is placed in one of the virtual templates chosen arbitrarily at random. This converts the virtual template to an actual template.

The main result regarding the performance of our algorithm for any choices of $\alpha, \beta, \epsilon, h$ can be found in our full paper [1]. Here, we only mention a corollary to give an interpretation of the main result for a particular choice of the parameters.

COROLLARY 1. *Choose* $\alpha = \beta^2$, $h = \exp\Big((\frac{1}{\beta})^{1/(1-b)}\Big)$, $\epsilon = \beta^{b^2/4}$, *then as* $\beta \to 0$,

$$\sum_{j\in\mathcal{J}} \mathbb{E}\Big[f(Q_j(\infty))\Big] \le \Theta((\frac{1}{\beta})^2),$$

$$\mathbb{E}\Big[\sum_{j\in\mathcal{J}} \sum_{A\in\mathcal{A}^{(j)}} x_A(\infty) b_A^{(j)}\Big] \le G(x^\star) + \Theta(\beta^{b^2/4}),$$

where $x^\star$ *is the optimal solution to (1)*

3. REFERENCES

[1] J. Ghaderi, S. Shakkottai, and R. Srikant. Scheduling Storms and Streams in the Cloud. *ArXiv 1502.05968*, Feb. 2015.

Localized Epidemic Detection in Networks with Overwhelming Noise

Eli A. Meirom†, Chris Milling♯, Constantine Caramanis♯, Shie Mannor†,
Sanjay Shakkottai♯, Ariel Orda†
† Dept. Of Electrical Engineering, Technion - Israel Institute of Technology, Haifa, Israel
♯ Dept. Of Electrical and Computer Engineering, University of Texas, Austin, Texas, USA

ABSTRACT

We consider the problem of detecting an epidemic in a population where individual diagnoses are extremely noisy. We show that exculsively local, approximate knowledge of the contact network suffices to accurately detect the epidemic. The motivation for this problem is the plethora of examples (influenza strains in humans, or computer viruses in smartphones, etc.) where reliable diagnoses are scarce, but noisy data plentiful. In flu or phone-viruses, exceedingly few infected people/phones are professionally diagnosed (only a small fraction go to a doctor) but less reliable *secondary signatures* (e.g., people staying home, or greater-than-typical upload activity) are more readily available.

Our algorithm requires only local-neighbor knowledge of this graph, and in a broad array of settings that we describe, succeeds even when false negatives and false positives make up an overwhelming majority of the data available. Our results show it succeeds in the presence of partial information about the contact network, and also when are many (hundreds, in our examples) of initial patients-zero.

1. INTRODUCTION

Any study, analysis or curbing of an epidemic begins with the fundamental question: is the phenomenon that we experience indeed an epidemic? The identification of such processes, be they malicious malware spreading on computer networks, memes on social networks, or trends in public opinion, is of major interest across several disciplines.

A common characteristic is a stark absence of reliable information: patients with flu-like symptoms rarely visit a medical professional. More typical, however, is the availability of significant amounts of information indicating a secondary signature of the outbreak: flu patients may stay home from work, infected computers may exhibit somewhat encumbered performance, adopters of a new technological trend (e.g., smart-watch) may show new usage patterns, or may simply "self-report." While more plentiful, such data may be riddled with false positives and negatives. Further complicating the problem is the fact that the underlying network is rarely fully known and in practice it may be possible to recover only a local subgraph near any infected node. In an epidemic setting, there may be multiple epidemic sources rather than a single "patient zero."

How can we obtain accurate *population-diagnoses* from unreliable single-node information, and only local (and possibly approximate) knowledge of the contact network? We consider the basic problem in the most dire setting: at some instant in time we are informed that a given subset of nodes exhibiting unusual behavior (in the computer setting) or are sick. Exact reporting times are inaccessible. Moreover, we assume we are unable to observe the time evolution of the sickness reporting process. Even if there is an epidemic, we may have a large (possibly an overwhelming) fraction of false positives and false negatives among the reporting subset and its complement, respectively. Given this single (and very noisy) snapshot in time, the statistical inference problem is to determine if there is an epidemic which propagates through the network from one or possibly many initial nodes, or rather nodes have become infected via an independent, external mechanism.

We do not wish to require each node to know more than its local neighborhood (and in fact, our simulations show that this too need only be approximate). We provide the only algorithm, to the best of our knowledge, that has these key properties. Our theoretical results show that our algorithm succeeds in successfully solving the hypothesis testing problem even when the fractions of false negatives and positives go to 1. Our simulation results corroborate this finding.

2. PROBLEM DEFINITION

Consider a graph $G = (V, E)$, where the number of nodes is $N = |V|$. The decision making task is distinguishing between the two following alternative scenarios.

An epidemic: At time $t = 0$, an arbitrary subset of nodes is infected. Infected nodes infect their neighbors according to an exponential clock set on each edge. At this time, each infected node *reports it is infected* with probability $q(N)$. The number of reporting nodes is $|S_r|$. The non-reporting nodes are *false negatives*. In addition, there are $f(N)|S_r|$ nodes, picked uniformly over the network, that also report infected. Each node that is not infected yet reports infection constitutes a *false positive*.

Uniform reporting: Each node, independently of all others, reports an infection with some probability. The problem is most challenging when the expected numbers of reporting

SIGMETRICS'15, June 15?19, 2015, Portland, OR, USA.
ACM 978-1-4503-3486-0/15/06.
http://dx.doi.org/10.1145/2745844.2745883.

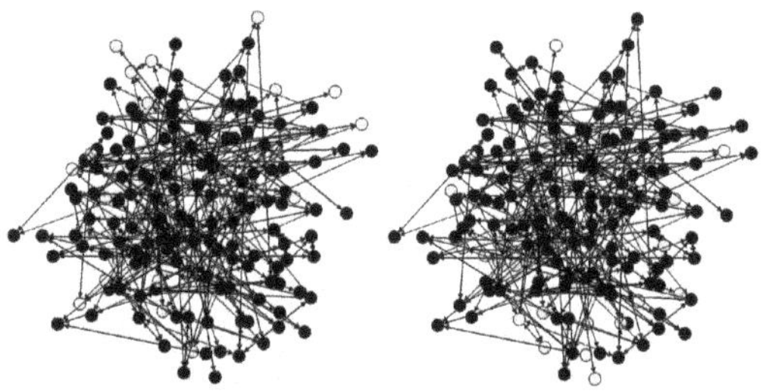

Figure 1: Reporting map samples. Reporting nodes are in yellow. (left) A reporting sample in a uniform reporting setting. (right) An epidemic reporting scenario map. It is virtually impossible to distinguish between the two hypotheses visually.

nodes in each scenario match, as otherwise simple counting would solve the problem.

When the reporting probability increases there exists a large connected component with a ball-like shape about the set of "patient-zero"s, the initial sources of the epidemic, and the problem is easier. Likewise, the problem is more difficult when the ratio of the number of falsely reporting to the number of truly reporting nodes, $f(N)$, tends to infinity, as the truly reporting nodes are washed out by the sea of falsely reporting nodes. We describe an algorithm that is shown to converge correctly even in settings where the reporting probability tends to zero and $f(N) \to \infty$.

While we present the epidemic dynamics using the concrete example of an SI (susceptible-infected) model, our algorithm may be applied to other infection models as well. Indeed, the algorithm and proofs are diffusion-model-agnostic – they assume no knowledge of the diffusion mechanics.

The problem we consider here was first introduced in [1]. However, the algorithm and analysis used in this paper is fundamentally different. In [1], the authors rely on tools from first passage percolation, which in some settings (for some graph topologies, for initial infection conditions) may be fragile. For example, it is not clear if the algorithms given there are able to handle large numbers of initial seeds. Additionally, our algorithm is inherently local and easily parallelizable. Most significantly, our algorithm requires only local knowledge of the graph: each infected node is required to know only information about its local neighborhood.

3. ALGORITHM: HOTSPOT AGGREGATOR

The intuition is simple: neighbors of infected nodes are more likely to be infected in an epidemic, when compared to the baseline of random illness. Let $H_i^{NN}(K, s)$ be an indicator equal to one if there are more than s reporting nodes within the the K nearest neighbors of node i.

If the indicator evaluates to 1, we call node i a *hotspot*, and the sum of these indicators gives the number of hotspots. Note that the evaluation of these, and hence the counting of hotspots, can be done in a distributed fashion, with each reporting infected node requiring only local network information. Our Hotspot Aggregator Algorithm counts the number of hotspots, and then performs a threshold test: if there are more than T hotspots, it declares an epidemic.

The algorithm depends on the local neighborhood size K, and the threshold T. The theorems that make up our main results [2], demand a choice for K and T that requires only approximate knowledge of the false positive rate and the graph topology. Computing the correct values for K and T is straightforward for essentially all topologies, and in fact, for some topologies the values for K and T can be computed analytically [2]. Our experimental results suggest that the algorithm's performance is quite stable. For instance, choosing K corresponding to the r-hop neighborhood, for $r = 2, 3$ yields uniformly good computational results.

Algorithm Information and Complexity. The complete graph information (its global structure) requires $O(N^2)$ to encode. In contrast, our algorithm requires only the number of reporting nodes within each local environment. For many cases of interest, $N_{\text{reporting}}$ can be as small as $O(\log(N))$ or even lower. The algorithm's complexity is $O(N_{\text{reporting}})$ and it scales with the number of reporting nodes (which, again, is typically vanishingly small compared to the number of nodes in the network).

Algorithm Performance. The conditions on the size of the local neighborhoods our algorithm must consider depend on level of noise. We show that our algorithm succeeds even in the extreme setting where the number of falsely reporting nodes is $\Theta(N)$ and the number of truly reporting nodes is $\omega(1)$. In this case, we require $\Theta(\log N)$-size local neighborhoods in order to guarantee convergence. If there are only $o(N)$ falsely reporting nodes, we show we can do much better:, a local environment containing only a constant number of nodes is sufficient.

Statistical Performance: We provide sufficient conditions w.r.t. the topology, the number of infected nodes, and the number of false negatives and positives, for our algorithm to correctly identify the infection cause (epidemic or random). Among our results, we show that our algorithm succeeds even when the number of infected nodes is $O(N)$, i.e., a constant fraction of all the nodes, and also in the setting where the false positives grossly outnumber the true positives. We also consider the small-infection regime. We show here that our algorithm succeeds *even if each node only knows the graph up to its 1-hop neighbors.*

Experiments: we provide experiments on random graphs, as well as real-world graphs. We show that our algorithm's performance is at least as good as the theory predicts. Moreover, its efficiency allows it to scale easily to very large networks. We compare to state-of-the-art and demonstrate that our algorithm is both faster and more accurate.

Acknowledgments

This research was supported in part by the European Union through the CONGAS project in the 7th Framework Programme, NSF Grants CNS-1017525, CNS-1320175, EECS-1056028, DTRA grant HDTRA 1-08-0029, ARO Grants W911NF-11-1-0265 and W911NF-14-1-0387, and the US DOT supported D-STOP Tier 1 UTC.

4. REFERENCES

[1] C. Milling, C. Caramanis, S. Mannor, and S. Shakkottai, "Network forensics," in *SIGMETRICS '12*, vol. 40, no. 1, Jun. 2012, p. 223.

[2] E. A. Meirom, C. Milling, C. Caramanis, S. Mannor, A. Orda, and S. Shakkottai, "Localized epidemic detection in networks with overwhelming noise." [Online]. Available: http://arxiv.org/abs/1402.1263

Pricing Bilateral Electricity Trade between Smart Grids and Hybrid Green Datacenters

Zhi Zhou, Fangming Liu*
Services Computing Technology & System Lab
School of Computer Science and Technology
Huazhong University of Science and Technology
{zhiz, fmliu}@hust.edu.cn

Zongpeng Li
Department of Computer Science
University of Calgary
zongpeng@ucalgary.ca

ABSTRACT

Datacenter demand response is envisioned as a promising approach for mitigating operational instability faced by smart grids. It enables significant potentials in peak load shedding and facilitates the incorporation of distributed generation and intermittent energy sources. This work considers two key aspects towards realtime electricity pricing for eliciting demand response: (i) Two-way electricity flow between smart grids and large datacenters with hybrid green generation capabilities. (ii) The geo-distributed nature of large cloud systems, and hence the potential competition among smart grids that serve different datacenters of the cloud. We propose a pricing scheme tailored for geo-distributed green datacenters, from a multi-leader single-follower game point of view. At the cloud side, in quest for performance, scalability and robustness, the energy cost is minimized in a distributed manner, based on the technique of alternating direction of multipliers (ADMM). At the smart grid side, a practical equilibrium of the pricing game is desired. To this end, we employ mathematical programming with equilibrium constraints (MPEC), equilibrium problem with equilibrium constraints (EPEC) and exact linearization, to transform the multi-leader single-follower pricing game into a mixed integer linear program (MILP) that can be readily solved. The effectiveness of the proposed solutions is evaluated based on trace-driven simulations.

Categories and Subject Descriptors

C.4 [**Performance of Systems**]: Design studies; Modeling techniques; C.2.4 [**Computer-Communication Networks**]: Distributed Systems

Keywords

Geo-distributed Cloud; Hybrid Green Datacenters; Smart Grid; Demand Response; Multi-leader Single-follower Game

*Corresponding Author

SIGMETRICS'15, June 15-19, 2015, Portland, OR, USA.
ACM 978-1-4503-3486-0/15/06.
http://dx.doi.org/10.1145/2745844.2745884.

1. INTRODUCTION

The recent years have witnessed new technology advances in the ICT sector, two of which are of practical significance and of particular interest to this work. The first is the Internet-scale cloud services deployed over geographically distributed datacenters, serving enterprises and end users, indispensable for a wide variety of applications. The second is the evolution of the traditional power grids to smart grids, enabling sustainable, cost-effective, and environmental-friendly electric power generation and consumption.

Further developments of both cloud computing and smart grids are facing their respective challenges. In smart grids, the integration of a large number of generation units (*e.g.*, wind turbines and solar arrays) incurs operation stability concerns and hence economic issues, due to the intermittent nature of such distributed generation. For example, the enormous wind generation in Germany in May 2014 resulted in continuous negative electricity prices for five hours [5]. Furthermore, the soaring of peak demand exacerbates the vulnerability and price fluctuation of a power grid. These operational issues can be addressed by demand response from large loads, among whom datacenters are natural candidates. For a datacenter, the power drawn from the smart grid is often of very large volumes yet exhibiting an elastic nature. An individual datacenter can make up 50% of the load of a distribution grid nowadays [3] (*e.g.*, Facebook's datacenter in Crook County, Oregon). Despite its sheer volume, datacenter power consumption is a natural target in demand response since it is driven by user requests that can be split to geo-distributed datacenters, and be served by multiple energy sources. Thus, the power drawn by a datacenter from the smart grid can be flexibly adjusted by changing the workload routed to the former, or modulating the output of on-site generation.

Table 1: Renewable Generation at Large Datacenters.

Company	Location	Type	Capacity
Microsoft	Chicago, IL	Wind	175MW
Facebook	Altoona, IA	Wind	138MW
Google	Mayes, OK	Wind	48MW
Apple	Maiden, NC	Solar	40MW
Google	Council Bluffs, IA	Wind	114MW
Microsoft	San Antonio, TX	Wind	110MW

In response to escalating pressure from economic and environmental concerns, large-scale cloud providers such as Google and Microsoft start to install hybrid renewable energy systems that include off-site wind, solar farms and onsite fuel cell generators [4]. For economies of scale, the installed capacity of wind and solar generation is often very large, as illustrated in Table 1. The farms are constructed mostly at locations with desirable climate. However, storing the excess wind or solar power in energy storage device (ESD) is still technically challenging, and large capacity lead-acid ESD is not environment friendly. Fortunately, by participating in the existing *net metering* [2] program, the excess renewable power can be sold back to the smart grid, eliminating the need of expensive large capacity ESDs. Such an option is already adopted in reality, including the cloud providers in Table 1. Such backward flow of renewable energy is particularly desirable as a response to energy deficit within the smart grid, easing the latter's burden at peak-hour. Furthermore, thanks to rapid developments in fuel cell technology in the recent past, fuel cell generation is emerging as a reliable complement to intermittent renewable energy such as wind or solar, with predictable and controllable output levels. Compared to traditional onsite stand-by generation (*e.g.*, diesel generators), fuel cell generation running on direct biogas is carbon neutral, and hence much more environment-friendly [4].

A hybrid datacenter not only draws energy from the smart grid, but also sells excess renewable energy back to the latter. A datacenter can provide great potential to demand response, by setting the appropriate amount of energy drawn from or sold back to the smart grid. Unfortunately, despite the fact that datacenter demand response can be obtained by adjusting the electricity and/or net metering price in a real-time manner, eliciting a desired amount of demand response from the hybrid green datacenter is of great challenge to a smart grid. In particular, when a cloud runs on top of geo-distributed datacenters and couples multiple smart grids, a smart grid needs not only to anticipate the corresponding cloud's response to the price decisions, but also to consider the impact of other smart grids' price decisions on the cloud's response. In such competition scenarios, an efficient pricing strategy is needed by each smart grid to optimize its objective.

We study the pricing of the bilateral electricity trade between a cloud that runs on geo-distributed hybrid green datacenters and the smart grids that serve it, aiming to determine the electricity and net metering prices for each datacenter. In such price computation, each smart grid needs to anticipate how the cloud would response to a given price, by minimizing the latter's energy cost via *geographically load balancing*, *i.e.*, at each front-end server, determining the amount of workload distributed to each datacenter, and *green capacity planning*, *i.e.*, determining the amount of fuel cell generation, net metering and power drawn from the corresponding smart grid. Note that the price strategy of one smart grid can influence the demand response at another smart grid. Consequently, the pricing process becomes a non-cooperative game. If we further consider the cloud's response to the prices, the entire process can then be captured by a two-stage *multi-leader single-follower game* [1], in which each smart grid acts as a leader and sets the prices, while the cloud acts as the follower and responses to the prices by minimizing its cost.

2. CONTRIBUTIONS

At the cloud side, in quest for performance, scalability and robustness, the energy cost of the cloud is expected to be minimized in a distributed manner. We show that the green capacity planning subproblems at each datacenter can be decoupled from the master geographical load balancing problem. We first solve the green capacity planning subproblems at each datacenter analytically, and obtain the master geographical load balancing problem explicitly. Then, such global master problem is solved in a fully distributed manner, based on the technique of alternating direction method of multipliers (ADMM) [5]. ADMM is a simple yet powerful tool for large-scale convex optimization that has enjoyed successful applications in image processing, machine learning and applied statistics. The proposed distributed geographical load balancing algorithm follows a decomposition-coordination approach. Each facility (front-end servers and datacenters) first solves a small-scale subproblem, and then these local solutions are coordinated to find the global optimum of the energy cost minimization problem.

At the smart grid side, it is desirable to discover and analyze a practical equilibrium of the multi-leader single-follower game, at which point no player can improve his/her objective by changing his/her strategy unilaterally. However, detecting an equilibrium of a multi-leader single-follower game is particularly challenging, since each leader's strategy space is non-convex, ruling out direct applications of results on classic Nash games [1]. To address this challenge, we first replace the lower-level energy cost minimization for the cloud with its first-order optimality conditions that are represented as a primal-dual formulation. The resulting problem for each smart grid is a mathematical program with equilibrium constraints (MPEC) [1]. The joint consideration of all MPECs, one per smart grid, constitutes an equilibrium problem with equilibrium constraint (EPEC) [1]. The equilibrium associated with the EPEC is analyzed by solving the Karush-Kuhn-Tucker conditions of all MPECs, which can be linearized without approximation loss by mixed-integer linear programming (MILP) techniques. The resulting mixed-integer linear system allows determining a meaningful equilibrium that meets certain pre-established criteria through an auxiliary MILP problem.

3. ACKNOWLEDGMENTS

The Corresponding Author is Fangming Liu. The research was supported in part by a grant from The National Natural Science Foundation of China (NSFC) under grant No.61370232, by a grant from National Basic Research Program (973 program) under grant No.2014CB347800. Zongpeng Li's work was supported by Wedge Networks Inc.

4. REFERENCES

[1] S. A. Gabriel, A. J. Conejo, J. D. Fuller, B. F. Hobbs, and C. Ruiz. Complementarity modeling in energy markets. *International Series in Operations Research and Management Science*, 180:1–629, 2012.

[2] F. Kong, X. Liu, and L. Rao. GreenPlanning: Optimal Energy Source Selection and Capacity Planning for Green Datacenters. In *Proc. of ACM SIGMETRICS*, 2014.

[3] Z. Liu, I. Liu, S. Low, and A. Wierman. Pricing Data Center Demand Response. In *Proc. of ACM SIGMETRICS*, 2014.

[4] Z. Zhou, F. Liu, B. Li, B. Li, H. Jin, R. Zou, and Z. Liu. Fuel Cell Generation in Geo-Distributed Cloud Services: A Quantitative Study. In *Proc. of IEEE ICDCS*, 2014.

[5] Z. Zhou, F. Liu, Z. Li, and H. Jin. When Smart Grid Meets Geo-distributed Cloud: An Auction Approach to Datacenter Demand Response. In *Proc. of IEEE INFOCOM*, 2015.

Detecting Sponsored Recommendations

Subhashini Krishnasamy, Rajat Sen and Sanjay Shakkottai
Dept. of Electrical and Computer Engineering, UT Austin

Sewoong Oh
Dept. of Industrial and Enterprise Systems Engineering, UIUC

ABSTRACT

Personalized recommender systems provide great opportunities for targeted advertisements, by displaying ads alongside genuine recommendations. We consider a *biased* recommendation system where such ads are displayed without any tags (disguised as genuine recommendations), rendering them indistinguishable to users. We consider the problem of detecting such a bias and propose an algorithm that uses statistical analysis based on binary feedback data from a subset of users. We prove that the proposed algorithm detects bias with high probability for a broad class of recommendation systems with sufficient number of feedback samples.

General Terms

Recommender systems, anomaly detection, bias detection

1. INTRODUCTION

The growth of online services has provided a vast variety of choices to users. This choice exists today in multiple domains including retail market, search engines, social networking websites, online news portals etc. With users having to choose from an overwhelming set of items, personalized recommender systems have become indispensable in easing the information overload and search complexity. Such recommender systems serve as an attractive platform for advertisers to reach their targeted consumers. It is now customary to see ads alongside other genuine recommendations in many of the websites that provide recommendation services. One can distinguish these ads from genuine recommendations, for example, by the location of their placement or by their special tags.

But recommendation engines are not legally obliged to facilitate such distinction and could possibly serve these ads mixed with genuine recommendations in a manner that renders them indistinguishable to users. Such a *biased recommender system* can have far reaching consequences, including user dissatisfaction with the recommendations [1]. Social and political consequences of bias in the context of media and online content have also been studied [2]. A basic question of interest to the users of such systems is whether or not such a biased recommender system can be detected.

We say a recommendation engine is *biased*, if it systematically favors a small set of items over other items in the database irrespective of users' preferences. On the other hand, we say that a recommendation engine is *objective*, if it satisfies a simple monotonic property in its recommendations to users – better suited items are given higher priority (in a statistical sense). The primary goal of this paper is then to develop algorithms to answer the following question: *Can a meaningful distinction be drawn between objective and biased recommendation engines?*

2. SYSTEM MODEL

The recommendation engine recommends products to users from a large database of m items indexed from 1 to m. A user's opinion about an item is represented by a numerical value that we call the user's *rating* of that item. We denote the user-item rating matrix for the entire database by $\mathbf{R}$, where rows indicate users and columns indicate items. We introduce a parameter called the *efficacy threshold*, denoted by η which is used to represent opinions on a binary scale. We assume that a user is satisfied with a recommendation if the rating of the recommended item is greater than or equal to η. We refer to such a recommendation and item as being *effective* for that user.

DEFINITION 1 (EFFECTIVE & INEFFECTIVE). *An item i is effective for a user u if the rating of that item by the user, R_{ui} is at least η. Similarly, a recommendation is said to be effective for a user if the recommended item is effective. An item or recommendation that is not effective is said to be ineffective.*

We next describe the behavior of a recommendation engine using a probabilistic model. Let $\mathbb{1}_{ui}(t)$ indicate whether item i has been recommended to user u at time t, i.e.,

$$\mathbb{1}_{ui}(t) := \begin{cases} 1 & \text{if item } i \text{ is recommended to user } u \text{ at time } t, \\ 0 & \text{otherwise.} \end{cases}$$

We make the following assumption about any recommender system: An item that has been recommended to a user once is not recommended to the same user again, i.e., for any user, u and item, i, $\sum_{t=1}^{\infty} \mathbb{1}_{ui}(t) \leq 1$.

Objective Recommendation Engine An *objective* recommendation engine is considered to consist of two components - one is the *learning* strategy which estimates the

SIGMETRICS'15, June 15 –19, 2015, Portland, OR, USA.
ACM 978-1-4503-3486-0/15/06.
http://dx.doi.org/10.1145/2745844.2745885.

user-item rating matrix by the means of available feedback from users, and another is the *recommendation* strategy which generates recommendations based on the estimated user preferences. Our model does not specify the details of the learning strategy except requiring that the output of the strategy, that is the estimate of the user-item matrix, be close to the original rating matrix, $\mathbf{R}$. Therefore, this model could be applied to a wide class of recommendation engines which estimate users' preferences fairly well. Let the estimate of the rating matrix at time t be denoted by $\hat{\mathbf{R}}(t) = \left[\hat{R}_{ui}(t)\right]$.

The recommendation strategy uses the estimated user-item rating matrix $\hat{\mathbf{R}}(t)$ to make recommendations at time t. The following model characterizes the behavior of an *objective* recommendation strategy:

1. Recommendations are made based on a user-item weight matrix, denoted by $\mathbf{W}(t) = [W_{ui}(t)]$. This is a stochastic matrix (rows sum to one), which is updated based on the current estimate of the rating matrix, $\hat{\mathbf{R}}(t)$.
2. Given the weight matrix, a user is given a recommendation by choosing an item randomly, independent of everything else, with weights given by the row corresponding to the user in the user-item weight matrix.
3. At any time t, the weight matrix $\mathbf{W}(t)$ satisfies the following *monotonic* property: if i and j are two items that have not been shown to user u and the ratings are such that $\hat{R}_{ui}(t) \geq \hat{R}_{uj}(t)$, then the weights satisfy $W_{ui}(t) \geq W_{uj}(t)$.

Biased Recommendation Engine A *biased* recommendation engine marks a small set of items, $\mathcal{A}$ ($\subseteq [m]$) from the item database as *ads*. To make a recommendation to a user, with probability γ, independent of everything else, it chooses an item that has not been shown from the ad-pool, $\mathcal{A}$. And with probability $1-\gamma$, it can follow any recommendation algorithm (for example, an *objective* recommendation algorithm). We refer to γ as the *bias probability*. Note that the strategy for showing ad items is unspecified except that no item is shown to a user twice. In particular, the engine may even customize its ad recommendations according to users' tastes.

3. ALGORITHM: BiAD

The problem is to design a test to detect if a recommendation engine is *biased*. In other words, the test has to decide between the following two hypotheses:

- H_1 : "The recommendation engine is *biased*," and
- H_0 : "The recommendation engine is not *biased*."

We now describe an algorithm called *Bi*nary feedback *A*nomaly *D*etector (*BiAD*), that uses the recommendations made to the players and their feedback to decide between one of the two hypotheses. In every *round* of recommendation, each player is recommended an item by the recommendation engine. In round t, the algorithm uses the feedback from the players and computes for each item, the total number of players until that round who have been recommended that item and found the item ineffective. This number is denoted

Algorithm 1 *Bi*nary feedback *A*nomaly *D*etector (*BiAD*)

```
Initialize t = 1 (round 1).
while t ≤ Q(m) do
   Compute B_i(t) = number of players who have rated
item i ineffective upto round t for all i ∈ [m].
   Compute S(t) = sum of the largest Â(t) among
{B_i(t)}_{i=1}^m.
   if S(t) ≥ T(t) then
      Stop and accept H_1.
   else
      t ← t + 1.
   end if
end while
Stop and reject H_1.
```

by $B_i(t)$ for item i. If the sum of the largest $\hat{A}(t)$ of these numbers among all the items is greater than or equal to a threshold $T(t)$, the recommendation engine is declared to be *biased*. Otherwise, the same procedure is repeated in the next round. If the algorithm does not declare the engine to be *biased* in $Q(m)$ rounds, then the hypothesis that the engine is *biased* is rejected. Here, $\hat{A}(t)$, $T(t)$ and $Q(m)$ in the algorithm are appropriately designed parameters. The pseudocode for this algorithm is shown in Algorithm 1.

The principal idea underlying this algorithm is that it searches for concentration of large number of ineffective items in a small set. Since the number of potential ads is unknown, the algorithm makes decisions in real-time as it gets feedback from the players. Larger the size of the ad-pool, larger is the number of feedback samples required to detect a *biased* engine. Thus, the algorithm increases the size of the search set with progressing rounds of recommendation. Also, note that it requires only binary feedback from the players.

Details on how to choose the algorithm parameters $\hat{A}(t)$, $T(t)$, $Q(m)$ and related performance can be found in [3]. We show, in [3], that appropriate choice of these parameters results in error probability that tends to zero with increasing size of the database and the number of feedback samples. We provide extensive simulation results with real data sets and practical recommendation algorithms, which confirm the trade offs deduced from theoretical analysis. In addition, we describe how such an anomaly detector can be applied to real world issues such as identification of search engine bias and pharmaceutical lobbying.

Acknowledgements

This work was supported by the NSF grant CNS-1320175 and the ARO grant W911NF-14-1-0387.

4. REFERENCES

[1] J. Beel, S. Langer, and M. Genzmehr, "Sponsored vs. organic (research paper) recommendations and the impact of labeling," in *Research and Advanced Technology for Digital Libraries*. Springer, 2013, pp. 391–395.

[2] L. D. Introna and H. Nissenbaum, "Shaping the web: Why the politics of search engines matters," *The information society*, vol. 16, no. 3, pp. 169–185, 2000.

[3] S. Krishnasamy, R. Sen, S. Oh, and S. Shakkottai, "Detecting sponsored recommendations," *arXiv preprint arXiv:1504.03713*, 2015.

Understanding Parallel Performance under Interferences in Multi-tenant Clouds

Yong Zhao, Jia Rao, Xiaobo Zhou, Qing Yi
Dept. of Computer Science
University of Colorado, Colorado Springs
{yzhao, jrao, xzhou, qyi}@uccs.edu

ABSTRACT

The performance of parallel programs is notoriously difficult to reason in virtualized environments. Although performance degradations caused by virtualization and interferences have been well studied, there is little understanding why different parallel programs have unpredictable slowdowns. We find that unpredictable performance is the result of complex interplays between the design of the program, the memory hierarchy of the hosting system, and the CPU scheduling in the hypervisor. We develop a profiling tool, `vProfile`, to decompose parallel runtime into three parts: compute, steal and synchronization. With the help of time breakdown, we devise two optimizations at the hypervisor to reduce slowdowns.

Categories and Subject Descriptors

D.4.8 [**Performance**]: Measurements, Modeling and prediction

General Terms

Management, Measurement, Performance

Keywords

Cloud computing, Scheduling, Parallel computing

1. INTRODUCTION

While the cloud is believed to be an ideal platform for hosting parallel applications, its nature of multi-user sharing and resource over-commitment makes parallel performance often quite disappointing and unpredictable. Although many studies [1, 2, 4] have identified the excessive synchronization delays due to multi-tenant interferences as the culprit, there lacks a full understanding of the quantitative relationship between changes in synchronization and the overall performance loss. As performance modeling plays a fundamental role in designing traditional parallel systems, a systematic and quantitative study of parallel performance under cloud interferences would help improve the resource and power management in datacenters.

SIGMETRICS'15, June 15-19, 2015, Portland, OR, USA.
ACM 978-1-4503-3486-0/15/06.
http://dx.doi.org/10.1145/2745844.2745886 .

In this paper, we find that the contention on CPU time at synchronizing threads is the primary cause of performance unpredictability. It leads to out-of-sync execution and changes in the original program behavior. Program profiling with synthetic workloads reveals that (1) programs have varying resilience to interference depending on the granularity of synchronization and user-level work balancing. Some programs are immune to further slowdowns if the level of interference increases, making good candidates for overcommitment; (2) preemptions between co-running parallel applications are especially detrimental to performance; (3) interference can surprisingly accelerate parallel execution due to the alleviation of intra-program contentions in memory-intensive parallel applications. Our findings identify opportunities for performance optimization and resource management guidelines for datacenter administrators.

2. PROFILING PARALLEL PROGRAMS

In a virtualized environment, program execution can stall waiting for virtual CPUs (vCPUs) to be scheduled by the hypervisor. Steal time is the time a vCPU waits to run on a physical CPU (pCPU) while the hypervisor is servicing another vCPU. Therefore, we decompose parallel runtime into *compute*, *synchronization* and *steal* time. We design `vProfile` to report the breakdown of parallel runtime and record important scheduling statistics in the hypervisor. vProfile tracks per-vCPU runtime state changes, i.e., `running`, `runnable`, `blocked`, and `offline`, in the hypervisor to decompose parallel runtime. For workloads using blocking primitives, such as `pthread_barrier_wait` and `pthread_mutex_lock`, synchronization time is simply the time a vCPU stays in the blocked state. For spinning synchronization, we used a lightweight spin detection in our previous work [3] to separate compute and spinning.

Event	Description
YIELD	Voluntary yield to other vCPUs due to idling
PREEMPT	Involuntary preemption by the scheduler
IDLE	The time the pCPU in the idle state
MPKI	Last-level cache misses per thousand instruction
OFFCORE_STALL	Stalls due to data accesses that miss the L2 Cache

Table 1: vProfile performance events.

The breakdown of execution time alone is not sufficient to identify the causes of slowdown. Detailed execution statistics can help find the root cause and develop approaches to mitigate slowdowns. vProfile reports per-vCPU statistics of the scheduling and hardware performance events listed in Table 1 at the end of a profiling period. Events `YIELD` and `PREEMPT` shed light on the contentions between co-located

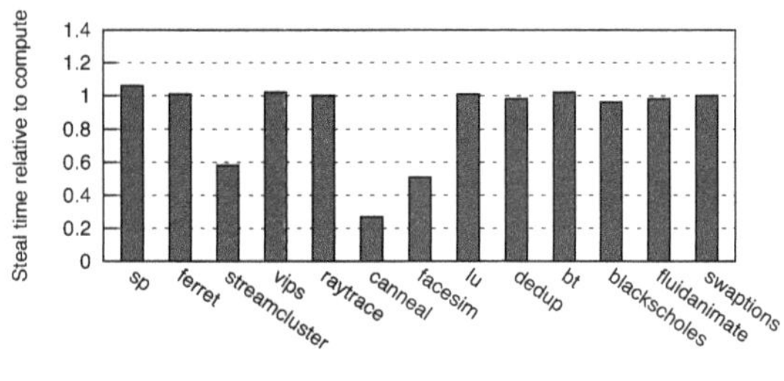

Figure 1: Varying resilience to interference.

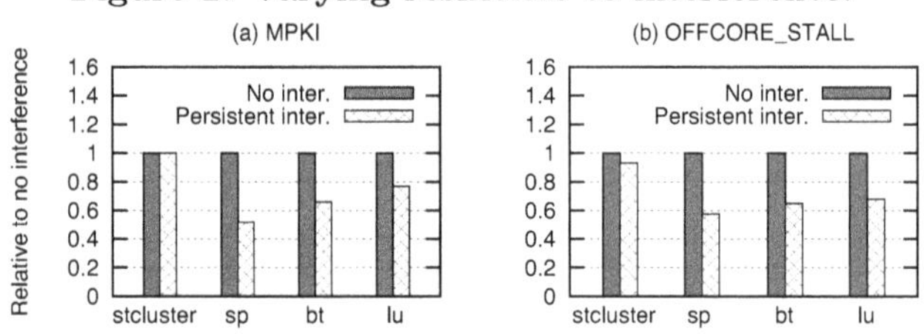

Figure 2: Interference mitigates intra-program contentions.

VMs while `IDLE` reflects the overall utilization of the pCPU as well as the efficiency of the scheduler. Hardware events `MPKI` and `OFFCORE_STALL` track changes in program behaviors due to interference. Changes of `MPKI` indicate that interference affects intra or inter-thread data re-use; `OFFCORE_STALL` measures the overall cost of data access.

We design **synthetic** workloads to emulate interferences and study slowdowns under different scenarios. *Persistent* interference comprises of simple `while(1)` loops demanding 100% of CPU time. *Periodic* interference demands CPU at regular intervals and otherwise stays idle. *Intermittent* interference demands CPU at irregular intervals.

3. IMPORTANT FINDINGS

We ran representative shared-memory multiprocessor programs from the PARSEC and NPB benchmarks in a Xen environment with three types of interference. We configured the VM running parallel programs with 4GB memory and 4 vCPUs, each pinned to a separate core in a quad-core Intel Xeon E5620 processor. We make the following important observations:

Varying resilience to interference. Figure 1 shows the steal time of individual benchmarks reported by vProfile when co-ran with one persistent loop. Surprisingly, programs with fine-grained blocking synchronization suffer less steal time and thereby are more resilient to interference. Xen prioritizes vCPUs waking up from sleep and assigns them high priorities (i.e., the *boost* priority). vCPUs performing frequent blocking synchronization tend to block more frequently and thus are prioritized over the persistent interference loop. The **implication** for datacenter management is that programs with fine-grained synchronization would suffer additional slowdowns as interference ramps up because they are no longer frequently blocked thus do not gain advantages over interference.

Changes in execution behavior. Some programs show little or no slowdown under interference. The contention on one or more vCPUs can also be absorbed by other sibling vCPUs if a parallel program (e.g., *raytrace*) dynamically re-balances work among threads at runtime. Even more surprising is that some programs, especially memory-bound ones, have inherent changes in execution under interference.

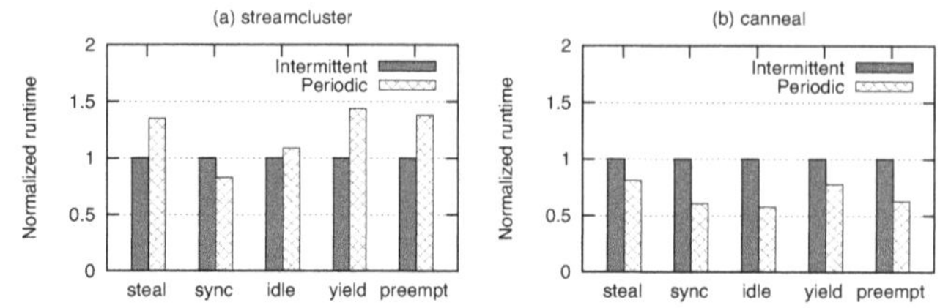

Figure 3: Low-level metrics under interference.

For example, although benchmarks *sp*, *lu*, and *bt* suffer steal time and long synchronization under interference, the compute time needed to complete the job decreases significantly, leading to little overall slowdown. Figure 2 shows that both the number of last-level cache (LLC) misses (i.e., `MPKI`) and the cost to access uncore memory (i.e., `OFFCORE_STALL`) drop under interference. The explanation is that the out-of-sync execution caused by interference alleviates the pressure sibling threads put on the memory hierarchy, resulting in less capacity misses at LLC and less coherence misses at the L2 cache. This observation **suggests** a new group of symbiotic datacenter workloads, in which seemly destructive competitions help constructively mitigate intra-program contentions on shared resources.

Complex interactions with the scheduler. Performance is even harder to characterize if all threads of the parallel program are affected by interference and the interference demands CPU time in different ways. The difficulty lies in the complex interactions among the parallel program, the interference, and the scheduler. Figure 3 shows the low-level metrics under different types of interference. We found a strong correlation between high-level performance and the low-level metrics: `IDLE` and `PREEMPT`. When the Xen scheduler performs less involuntary preemptions and there is less idling on pCPUs, the performance is higher. One **implication** from the observations is that reducing the number of preemptions would help improve performance under interference.

4. OPTIMIZATIONS

Our analysis found that involuntary preemptions are especially detrimental to performance and randomness in CPU scheduling help mitigate intra-program contentions on shared resources. Inspired by these findings, we envision two simple optimizations, *delayed preemption* and *differential scheduling*, at the hypervisor to improve parallel performance under interference. Our preliminary results show that the two optimizations derived from our analysis with the synthetic workloads are effective in reducing performance slowdowns when real parallel applications are co-located.

Acknowledgement This work was supported in part by U.S. NSF grants CNS-1320122 and CNS-1422119.

5. REFERENCES

[1] X. Ding, P. B. Gibbons, M. A. Kozuch, and J. Shan. Gleaner: Mitigating the blocked-waiter wakeup problem for virtualized multicore applications. In *Proc. of USENIX ATC*, 2014.

[2] H. Kim, S. Kim, J. Jeong, J. Lee, and S. Maeng. Demand-based coordinated scheduling for smp vms. In *Proc. of ASPLOS*, 2013.

[3] J. Rao and X. Zhou. Towards fair and efficient smp virtual machine scheduling. In *Proc. of PPoPP*, 2014.

[4] O. Sukwong and H. S. Kim. Is co-scheduling too expensive for smp vms? In *Proc. of EuroSys*, 2011.

Clustering and Inference from Pairwise Comparisons

Rui Wu
University of Illinois at Urbana-Champaign
ruiwu1@illinois.edu

Jiaming Xu
University of Illinois at Urbana-Champaign
jxu18@illinois.edu

Rayadurgam Srikant
University of Illinois at Urbana-Champaign
rsrikant@illinois.edu

Laurent Massoulié
INRIA
laurent.massoulie@inria.fr

Marc Lelarge
INRIA
marc.lelarge@ens.fr

Bruce Hajek
University of Illinois at Urbana-Champaign
b-hajek@illinois.edu

ABSTRACT

Given a set of pairwise comparisons, the classical ranking problem computes a single ranking that best represents the preferences of all users. In this paper, we study the problem of inferring individual preferences, arising in the context of making personalized recommendations. In particular, we assume users form clusters; users of the same cluster provide similar pairwise comparisons for the items according to the Bradley-Terry model. We propose an efficient algorithm to estimate the preference for each user: first, compute the *net-win* vector for each user using the comparisons; second, cluster the users based on the net-win vectors; third, estimate a single preference for each cluster separately. We show that the net-win vectors are much less noisy than the high dimensional vectors of pairwise comparisons, therefore our algorithm can cluster the users reliably. Moreover, we show that, when a cluster is only approximately correct, the maximum likelihood estimation for the Bradley-Terry model is still close to the true preference.

Categories and Subject Descriptors

G.3 [**Probability and Statistics**]: Multivariate statistics

Keywords

ranking; clustering; inference; Bradley-Terry model

1. INTRODUCTION

The question of ranking items using pairwise comparisons is of interest in many applications, and is usually studied using the Bradley-Terry model [1] where each item i is associated with a score θ_i measuring its competitiveness and

$$\mathbb{P}\left[\text{item } i \text{ is preferred over item } j\right] = \frac{e^{\theta_i}}{e^{\theta_i} + e^{\theta_j}},$$

and the goal is to rank the items from pairwise comparisons.

SIGMETRICS'15, June 15-19, 2015, Portland, OR, USA.
ACM 978-1-4503-3486-0/15/06.
http://dx.doi.org/10.1145/2745844.2745887.

However, in many applications, it is more appropriate to assume individuals can have different preferences over the same set of items. For example, when typing in the same keywords on a search engine, users tend to click the returned results differently. Similarly, customers shopping at the online retailer end up buying different products. Therefore, a single global ranking of the items does not help much in understanding an individual's preference.

In this work, we assume user preferences come from the more general mixture Bradley-Terry model, and would like to infer each user's preference from the pairwise comparisons the users provide. More specifically, consider a system with r user clusters of sizes K and m items. Each user u has a score vector for the items $\theta_u = (\theta_{u,1}, \ldots, \theta_{u,m})$, and he/she compares items according to the Bradley-Terry model. Assume users in cluster k have the same score vector θ_k. Let $n = rK$ be the total number of users. The overall comparison result is represented by an $n \times \binom{m}{2}$ sample comparison matrix R. The u-th row R_u is the comparison vector of user u. The columns are indexed by two numbers $i, j = 1, \ldots, m$ with $i < j$, and the ij-th column corresponds to the comparisons for item i and j. For each user u, and items i and j with $i < j$, user u's comparison result of item i and j is sampled with probability $1 - \epsilon$ independently, where ϵ is the erasure probability. Let $R_{u,ij} = 1$ if u prefers i over j, $R_{u,ij} = -1$ if u prefers j over i, and $R_{u,ij} = 0$ if u's comparison is not sampled. Then

$$R_{u,ij} = \begin{cases} 1 & \text{w.p. } (1-\epsilon)\frac{e^{\theta_{u,i}}}{e^{\theta_{u,i}} + e^{\theta_{u,j}}} \\ 0 & \text{w.p. } \epsilon \\ -1 & \text{w.p. } (1-\epsilon)\frac{e^{\theta_{u,j}}}{e^{\theta_{u,i}} + e^{\theta_{u,j}}} \end{cases}$$

To simplify the analysis, we will assume θ_k's are generated independently as follows: for each k and i, generate $\theta^0_{k,i}$ i.i.d. uniformly in $[0, b]$, and then define

$$\theta_{k,i} = \theta^0_{k,i} - \frac{1}{m}\sum_{i=1}^{m} \theta_{k,i}.$$

Our goal is to estimate the score vectors θ_u from R.

The algorithm we propose first clusters the users using the comparison vectors R_u's, and then estimate a score vector for each cluster. There are two challenges. First, for each user u, the comparison vector R_u lies in a high dimensional space , but only a small number of entries are observed. If one directly clusters the vectors R_u, the resulted clusters will be very noisy, which is demonstrated in our numerical experiment [5]. Second, existing algorithms for estimating the score vector [3,4] assume the users to have the same preference, and it is unclear how to estimate the score vectors when the clusters are only approximately recovered.

Our first contribution is to propose and show the effectiveness of clustering users according to their *net-win* vectors. For user u, the net-win of item i is defined as

$$S_{u,i} = \frac{1}{\sqrt{m}} \sum_{j \neq i} \left[\mathbb{I}_{\{u \text{ prefers } i \text{ over } j\}}(R) - \mathbb{I}_{\{u \text{ prefers } j \text{ over } i\}}(R) \right],$$

where $\mathbb{I}_{\{\cdot\}}(R)$ is the indicator function given R. We call the vector S_u the net-win vector of user u. The key observation is that, even though the comparison vectors R_u are of dimension $\binom{m}{2}$, the expectations $\mathbb{E}[R_u]$ are close to some $(m-1)$-dimensional linear subspace, and the net-win vectors S_u are essentially the projection of R_u onto this low-dimensional linear subspace. In particular, we show that S_u preserve the distance among R_u but are much less noisy. Therefore, we can further show that a standard spectral clustering algorithm approximately recovers the user clusters.

Our second contribution is to show that, when a cluster only has small fraction of erroneously assigned users, if we pretend the users are from the same cluster and apply the maximum likelihood estimation for the Bradley-Terry model, the resulted score vector is close to the true score vector for this cluster. As we only expect to approximately recover the user clusters, this robustness result ensures that we can still approximately recover the score vectors for most users.

In the next section, we present a sketch of our algorithm and the main results. For more details, see [5].

2. ALGORITHM AND MAIN RESULTS

A sketch of our algorithm for clustering users and inferring their preferences is presented as Algorithm 1. For the complete algorithm, see [5]. The basic idea is to estimate θ in two steps: cluster the users and then estimate a score vector for each cluster separately.

The difficulty lies in the clustering step. Recall that, each user provides a comparison vector R_u of length $\binom{m}{2}$, but only roughly $(1-\epsilon)\binom{m}{2}$ of its entries are observed. When the erasure probability $\epsilon \to 1$, R_u is a very noisy observation of the underlying score vector θ_u. We overcome this difficulty by representing each user u by its net-win vector S_u, defined in the previous section, instead. The effectiveness of S_u lies in the nontrivial fact that $\mathbb{E}[R_u]$ are close to an $(m-1)$-dimensional linear subspace [5], therefore one can reduce the noise of R_u by projecting it onto this linear subspace.

We show in [5] that, for any two users v and w in two different clusters, $||\mathbb{E}[S_v] - \mathbb{E}[S_w]||_2 \approx ||\mathbb{E}[R_v] - \mathbb{E}[R_w]||_2$ and for $u = v$ or w, $||S_u - \mathbb{E}[S_u]||_2 \approx \frac{1}{\sqrt{m}}||R_u - \mathbb{E}[R_u]||_2$, which implies that the net-win vectors S_u are much less noisy thus easier to separate than the comparison vectors R_u. The overall performance of Algorithm 1 is characterized by the following theorem.

Algorithm 1 Multi-Cluster Projected Ranking

Step 0: Sampling splitting. Split the observed comparisons in R randomly into two sets and get two comparison matrices $R^{(1)}$ and $R^{(2)}$.

Step 1: Denoising. Let S be the net-win matrix, where the u-th row of S is the net-win vector of user u based on $R^{(1)}$.

Step 2: User clustering. Let $\widetilde{S}$ be the rank r approximation of S. Construct the clusters $\widehat{C}_1, \ldots, \widehat{C}_r$ sequentially. For $1 \le k \le r$, after $\widehat{C}_1, \ldots, \widehat{C}_{k-1}$ have been selected, choose an initial user u not in the first $k-1$ clusters uniformly at random, and let $\widehat{C}_k = \{u' : ||\widetilde{S}_u - \widetilde{S}_{u'}||_2 \le \tau\}$ where the threshold τ is specified later. Assign each remaining unclustered user to a cluster arbitrarily.

Step 3: Score vector estimation. Let $D_{u,ij} = \mathbb{I}_{\{R^{(2)}_{u,ij}=1\}}$ and $D_{u,ji} = \mathbb{I}_{\{R^{(2)}_{u,ij}=-1\}}$ for any u and $i < j$. For users in cluster $\widehat{C}_k$, the estimated score vector is given by $\widehat{\theta}_k = \arg\max_\gamma L_k(\gamma)$, where

$$L_k(\gamma) = \sum_{u \in \widehat{C}_k, i, j} D_{u,ij} \log \frac{e^{\gamma_i}}{e^{\gamma_i} + e^{\gamma_j}}$$

THEOREM 1. *Define*

$$\eta_1 = \frac{r \max\{m,n\} \log m \log n}{(1-\epsilon)Km^2}, \quad \eta_2 = \sqrt{\frac{\log m}{(1-\epsilon)Km}}.$$

Assume $b \in [b_0, 5]$ for any arbitrarily small constant $b_0 > 0$. Then there exists a constant $C > 0$ such that

$$\frac{||\widehat{\theta}_u - \theta_u||_2}{||\theta_u||_2} \le \frac{C(e^b+1)^2}{be^b} \max\{\eta_1, \eta_2\}$$

except for $512K\eta_1$ users with high probability. In particular, if $Km^2(1-\epsilon) > r\max\{m,n\}\log m \log^2 n$, then $\frac{||\widehat{\theta}_u - \theta_u||_2}{||\theta_u||_2} = O(\frac{1}{\log n})$ except for $O\left(\frac{K}{\log n}\right)$ users.

REMARK 1. *The lower bounds in [4] and [2] show that at least $\Omega(m)$ pairwise comparisons per type are needed to ensure $\frac{||\widehat{\theta}_u - \theta_u||_2}{||\theta_u||_2} = o(1)$ even when clusters are known. Also, a user needs to provide at least one pairwise comparison for us to infer his/her preference, which means that at least $\Omega(n)$ pairwise comparisons in total are required to infer the preferences for most users. Theorem 1 shows that Algorithm 1 needs roughly $(1-\epsilon)K\binom{m}{2} = O(r\max\{m,n\}\log m \log^2 n)$ comparisons per cluster, which matches the lower bounds up to logarithmic factors if r is poly-logarithmic in n or m.*

3. REFERENCES

[1] R. A. Bradley and M. E. Terry. Rank Analysis of Incomplete Block Designs: I. The Method of Paired Comparisons. *Biometrika*, 39(3/4), 1952.

[2] B. Hajek, S. Oh, and J. Xu. Minimax-optimal inference from partial rankings. *Advances in Neural Information Processing Systems*, 2014.

[3] D. R. Hunter. MM algorithms for generalized Bradley-Terry models. *The Annals of Statistics*, 32:384–406, 2004.

[4] S. Negahban, S. Oh, and D. Shah. Rank centrality: Ranking from pair-wise comparisons. 2014.

[5] R. Wu, J. Xu, R. Srikant, L. Massoulié, M. Lelarge, and B. Hajek. Clustering and inference from pairwise comparisons. 2015. http://arxiv.org/abs/1502.04631.

Deterministic Near-Optimal P2P Streaming

Shaileshh Bojja Venkatakrishnan
Department of Electrical and Computer Engineering
University of Illinois Urbana-Champaign
bjjvnkt2@illinois.edu

Pramod Viswanath
Department of Electrical and Computer Engineering
University of Illinois Urbana-Champaign
pramodv@illinois.edu

ABSTRACT

We consider live-streaming over a peer-to-peer network in which peers are allowed to enter or leave the system adversarially and arbitrarily. Previous approaches for streaming have either used randomized distribution graphs or structured trees with randomized maintenance algorithms. Randomized graphs handle peer churn well but have only probabilistic connectivity guarantees, while structured trees have good connectivity but have proven hard to maintain under peer churn. We improve upon both approaches by presenting a novel distribution structure with a *deterministic* and distributed algorithm for maintenance under peer churn. The algorithm has a constant repair time for connectivity, and near optimal delay. As opposed to order results, the guarantees provided by our algorithm are exact and hold for any network size.

Categories and Subject Descriptors

C.2.1 [**Computer-Communication networks**]: Network Architecture and Design—*Distributed networks, Network topology*; C.2.4 [**Distributed Systems**]: Distributed Applications

Keywords

Peer-to-peer, Streaming, Deterministic, One-to-many content distribution

1. INTRODUCTION

In peer-to-peer (P2P) live-streaming, a low-capacity server uploads live-content to a small number of clients which, together with the other clients (a total of n peers), then exchange the content among themselves. Peers are often limited in their resources such as bandwidth, number of connections they can make to other peers, and available memory. Further, they are not guaranteed to stay in the system and can arrive or depart from the system at any time (also called *peer churn*). With these constraints, the problem now is how to construct, maintain and schedule the P2P network in order to effectively utilize the available upload capacity for a high *rate* and to ensure playback with a small *delay*.

Several approaches have been presented towards the management of P2P networks in the above setting, such as using a centralized controller [2], distributed lookup protocols [3] or random sampling [1]. Our main result is the design of a distribution structure and algorithm that is (i) distributed, (ii) deterministic and (iii) has constant repair time to ensure connectivity under peer arrival and departure. As far as the authors are aware, no other algorithm in the literature has all of the above properties. The tradeoff is that the algorithm has a sub-optimal rate and delay, however we show that the losses incurred are only small. Let us now present the system model.

SIGMETRICS'15, June 15-19, 2015, Portland, OR, USA.
ACM 978-1-4503-3486-0/15/06.
http://dx.doi.org/10.1145/2745844.2745888.

2. SYSTEM MODEL

We model the P2P overlay network as a directed node capacitated graph G. Each peer has an upload capacity of C, a constant degree bound of Δ and a total memory of M. We incorporate peer churn by allowing peers to arrive or depart from the system *arbitrarily*. In particular, we do not require the peers to announce their arrival or departure apriori. Whenever a peer departs, the node and all edges connected to it are lost immediately; only the neighbors of the departing peer are aware of this event. We also assume communication happens as a flow. In addition to the upload capability, we let the nodes be able to communicate control messages through the edges. The terms peer, node and client have been used interchangeably.

3. ALGORITHM AND PERFORMANCE

In the following we let $C = 1$ and consider streaming at a rate of $R \leq 1$. To do this we divide the stream, and distribute it over $m = \lceil R/(1-R) \rceil$ distribution graphs. Let $G_1, G_2, \ldots, G_m$ denote the m distribution graphs with each distribution graph carrying a rate of R/m. Figure 1 shows the steady-state distribution graphs G_1, G_2 and G_3 for a network with 11 users, $R = 3/4$ and $m = 3$.

Steady-state Topology: The structure of the distribution graphs in the steady-state can be described as follows. Each of the G_i comprises of a tree T_i (rooted at the server and spanning all the nodes) and additional edges U_i that connect the leaves of the tree to its interior nodes. For example, the distribution graph G_1 shown in Figure 1 can be decomposed into a tree and redundant edges as shown in Figure 2(a) and 2(b) respectively. The latter edges are *redundant* because they carry streaming packets that have been

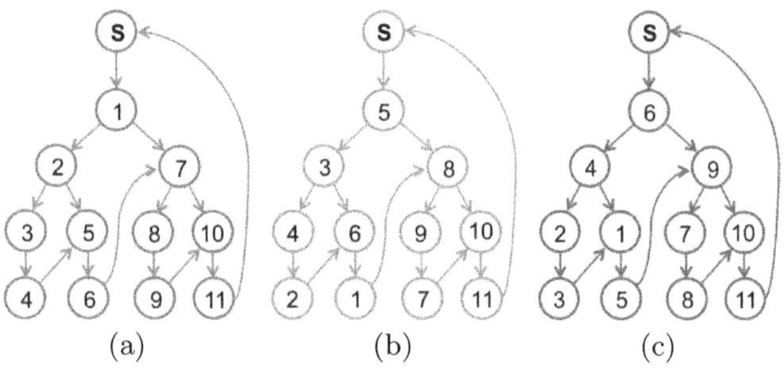

Figure 1: An example showing a steady state topology of G_1, G_2 and G_3 for $n = 11$ and $R = 3/4$ ($m = 3$). S is the server, and the users are numbered 1 to 11.

potentially already received at the other end. Structurally the tree T_i consists of a balanced binary tree of roughly n/m nodes, plus additional nodes forming chains (i.e. line graphs) of length roughly $m-1$ that hang from the leaves of the binary tree. This has also been illustrated in Figure 2(a), where the nodes hanging from the leaves of the binary tree are of depth 2 ($= m - 1$ for $m = 3$). Now, for any degree two node let the left (resp. right) edge and child be called the *primary* (resp. *secondary*) edge and child respectively of that node. Then, the redundant edges U_i consist of edges that go from the left to the right sub-tree of each degree 2 node – the rightmost leaf of the left sub-tree is connected to the secondary child of the degree 2 node. For the G_1 of Figure 1(a) this has been illustrated in Figure 2(b).

Now, given a distribution graph with the above structure (say G_1), the other $m-1$ distribution graphs $G_2, \ldots, G_m$ can be deterministically constructed from G_1 as follows. Consider any degree 2 node in the binary tree portion of T_1. The secondary child of that degree 2 node receives a redundant edge from a leaf node of T_1. Now consider the chain of degree 1 nodes (in T_1) to which that leaf belongs. We associate the degree 2 node to that chain of degree 1 nodes. Now, to construct the other substream graphs $G_2, \ldots, G_m$, we simply swap a member in the degree 1 chain of T_1 with it's associated degree two node. For example, in Figure 1(a) nodes 3,4 are associated with 2, nodes 5,6 with 1 and nodes 8,9 with 7. As such, in G_2 we have node 3 taking the position of node 2, while node 2 becomes part of the degree 1 chain. Similarly, node 5 takes the place of node 1, while node 1 becomes part of the corresponding degree 1 chain.

Thus, our P2P overlay (i) has redundancy and (ii) is symmetric – features that facilitate very fast and robust maintenance of the network under churn. Whenever a peer departs, the child of this peer in any G_i can connect to his parent in that G_i. If the departing peer has a degree 2 in any G_i, then the primary child of the peer can connect to his parent, while the secondary child continues to receive the stream via the redundant edge. Similarly, whenever a peer enters the system, it can simple break a single edge to insert itself between two nodes in each of the G_i. Thus connectivity is maintained at all times. With this guarantee, balancing of the G_i's to ensure small delay can now be performed via the use of node labels. The delay provided by our algorithm is given by the following.

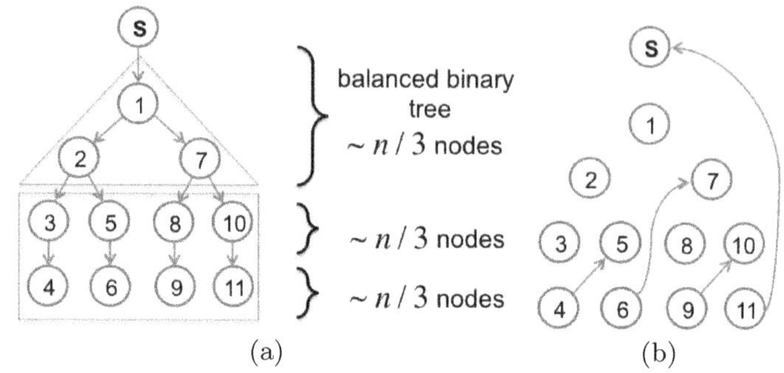

Figure 2: Decomposition of G_1 in Figure 1(a) showing (a) tree T_1 and (b) redundant edges U_1. The structure of T_1 with a binary tree on the top, and a chain of $m-1$ nodes from each leaf of the binary tree has also been illustrated in (a).

THEOREM 1. *In the steady state with n peers in the system, the streaming delay is bounded by* $\log_2(n+1) + \frac{2R}{C-R} + \log_2(1 - \frac{R}{C}) - 2$ *for a rate* $R \in (0, C)$.

Hence, by using a slightly sub-optimal rate we are able to greatly improve the churn handling capability while incurring only a small penalty on the delay (here each edge is assumed to contribute 1 unit of delay). In our second result, we show that for the amount of redundancy used, the delay guarantee of the algorithm is order optimal.

THEOREM 2. *For structed streaming in which multiple spanning graphs each carry partial flows, the maximum delay across the substream graphs is at least* $\log_\Delta(n) + \frac{R}{2(C-R)} + \log_\Delta\left(\frac{2(C-R)}{R}\right) - c'$, *where* $c' = (\Delta - 2)\log_\Delta\left(\frac{\Delta!}{2}\right) + \log_e(\Delta - 1) + 2$, *for a rate R, degree bound* Δ *and* $n \geq \frac{3R}{C-R}$, *if the partial flow graphs have enough capacity redundancy to handle arbitrary node departures.*

Thus, we claim that the $R/(C-R)$ term in the delay is fundamental for all algorithms guaranteeing continuity of playback.

4. ACKNOWLEDGMENTS

This work was supported by Army grant W911NF-14-1-0220 and NSF grant CCF-1409106.

5. REFERENCES

[1] J. Kim and R. Srikant. Real-time peer-to-peer streaming over multiple random hamiltonian cycles. *Information Theory, IEEE Transactions on*, 59(9):5763–5778, 2013.

[2] V. N. Padmanabhan, H. J. Wang, and P. A. Chou. Resilient peer-to-peer streaming. In *Network Protocols, 2003. Proceedings. 11th IEEE International Conference on*, pages 16–27. IEEE, 2003.

[3] I. Stoica, R. Morris, D. Karger, M. F. Kaashoek, and H. Balakrishnan. Chord: A scalable peer-to-peer lookup service for internet applications. In *Proceedings of the 2001 Conference on Applications, Technologies, Architectures, and Protocols for Computer Communications*, SIGCOMM '01, pages 149–160, New York, NY, USA, 2001. ACM.

Flexible Transformations for Learning Big Data

Azalia Mirhoseini Ebrahim M. Songhori Bita Darvish Rouhani
Farinaz Koushanfar

azalia, ebrahim, bita, farinaz@rice.edu

Electrical and Computer Engineering, Rice University, Houston TX 77005, USA

ABSTRACT

This paper proposes a domain-specific solution for iterative learning of big and *dense (non-sparse)* datasets. A large host of learning algorithms, including linear and regularized regression techniques, rely on iterative updates on the data connectivity matrix in order to converge to a solution. The performance of such algorithms often severely degrade when it comes to large and dense data. Massive dense datasets not only induce obligatory large number of arithmetics, but they also incur unwanted message passing cost across the processing nodes. Our key observation is that despite the seemingly dense structures, in many applications, data can be transformed into a new space where sparse structures become revealed. We propose a scalable data transformation scheme that enables creating versatile sparse representations of the data. The transformation can be tuned to benefit the underlying platform's cost and constraints. Our evaluations demonstrate significant improvement in energy usage, runtime, and memory footprint, within guaranteed user-defined error bounds.

Categories and Subject Descriptors

I.1.2 [**Computing Methodologies**]: Symbolic and algebraic manipulation—*Algorithms*

Keywords

Big and dense data, Sparse factorization, Subspace sampling, Performance optimization

1. INTRODUCTION

Since finding a direct solution to a matrix-based analysis problem requires the (unscalable) matrix inversion, most contemporary data analysis methods use iterative computing to converge to a solution [3]. The major bottleneck of iterative algorithms is the costly operations on the correlation matrix. Let us denote the *data matrix* by $\mathbf{A} \in \mathcal{R}^{m\times n}$, where n is the total number of samples and m is the number of features per sample. We denote the *correlation matrix* by $\mathbf{G} \in \mathcal{R}^{n\times n}$, where $\mathbf{G} = \mathbf{A}^T\mathbf{A}$. At each iteration t, the following process is applied to update a *solution vector*, $\mathbf{x}$: $\mathbf{x}^{t+1} = \Phi(\mathbf{G}\mathbf{x}^t, \mathbf{x}^t)$, where Φ is a lightweight operator determined by the algorithm. The update is applied iteratively until convergence is achieved.

The complexity of the update arises from computing the matrix-vector product $\mathbf{G}\mathbf{x}^t$ at each step. Computing and storing $\mathbf{G}$ for massive datasets with dense correlations become infeasible as it requires $\mathcal{O}(n^3)$ arithmetic operations and $\mathcal{O}(n^2)$ storage. To circumvent this, only $\mathbf{A}$ is stored. Thus, the $\mathbf{G}\mathbf{x}^t$ computation is instead done using $\mathbf{A}^T\mathbf{A}\mathbf{x}^t$. In settings where $\mathbf{A}$ has to be partitioned across distributed processing nodes, computing the correlations between data samples that reside on different nodes incur communication overhead.

Several classes of fast-growing data, including the image and video content, contain dense (non-sparse) dependencies, i.e., a large number of non-zeros in the data correlation matrix. While available approaches such as [5] rely sparsity of the data connectivity matrix for efficient partitioning, when data exhibits dense dependencies, it is inherently impossible to find efficient cuts.

This work aims to address the challenges that arise due to the large number of arithmetic and message passing operations required for executing iterative algorithms on massive and densely correlated data. We propose a tunable data transformation scheme that enables producing versatile sparse representations of the same dataset, within a user-defined approximation error. The degree of freedom in transformation can be leveraged to optimize the performance cost of iterative updates in terms of energy usage, runtime, and memory on the pertinent platform.

2. A FLEXIBLE AND SPARSIFYING DATA TRANSFORMATION

Here we present our parametric data transformation methodology. Our objective is to find an approximate solution to the following NP hard problem:

$$\min_{L,\mathbf{B}_{m\times L},\mathbf{C}_{L\times n}} \|\mathbf{c}\|_0 \ \text{ s.t. } \ \|\mathbf{a_i} - \mathbf{B}\mathbf{c_i}\|_F \leq \delta, \ \textbf{for } \mathbf{1 \leq i \leq n}. \quad (1)$$

where $\mathbf{a}_i$'s and $\mathbf{c}_i$'s are columns of $\mathbf{A}$ and $\mathbf{C}$, $\|\cdot\|_0$ measures the total number of non-zeros, $\|\cdot\|_F$ measures the Frobenius norm, and δ is an approximation error. Equation 1 naturally expresses our goal to find sparse transformations of the dense data.

SIGMETRICS'15, June 15-19, 2015, Portland, OR, USA.
ACM 978-1-4503-3486-0/15/06.
http://dx.doi.org/10.1145/2745844.2745889.

Algorithm 1 : Parametric sparsifying data transformation

Input: Matrix $\mathbf{A} \in \mathbb{R}^{m \times n}$, error tolerance δ, and the maximum number of columns to select L.

Output: A sparse matrix $\mathbf{C} \in \mathbb{R}^{L \times n}$ and a dense matrix $\mathbf{B} \in \mathbb{R}^{m \times L}$ such that $\|\mathbf{a}_i - \mathbf{B}\mathbf{c}_i\|_\mathbf{F} \leq \delta$ for each $1 \leq i \leq n$.

1. Update $\mathbf{B}$ by selecting L columns uniformly at random from $\mathbf{A}$
2. Normalize columns of $\mathbf{B}$: $\|b_i\|_2 = 1$.
3. For each $1 \leq i \leq n$, compute $\mathbf{c}_i$ by applying OMP to solve Equation 1 within error bound δ: $\mathbf{a}_i - B\mathbf{c}_i \leq \delta$.

Our approach to solve Equation 1 consists of 2 steps. First matrix $\mathbf{B}$ is created by using a random Column-Subset-Selection (CSS) approach; a set of L columns of $\mathbf{A}$ are selected at random to create $\mathbf{B}$. L should be large-enough such that the error criteria is met. We refer to the general results on random CSS, provided in [4], for bounds on L for a given error. Oncer $\mathbf{B}$ is formed, Equation 1 becomes equivalent to a sparse approximation problem. Each column $\mathbf{c}_i$ is a sparse approximation of the corresponding column $\mathbf{a}_i$, with respect to $\mathbf{B}$ and the user-specified approximation error δ. We solve this problem using an efficient greedy routine called *Orthogonal Matching Pursuit* (OMP) [2].

Sparsity guarantees for C. When a dataset lives in a union of lower dimensional subspaces, as it is the case in many large-scale scenarios, each data point corresponds to a superposition of a few points from its own subspace [6]. More precisely, let us assume that $\mathbf{A}$ lives in a union of s subspaces of $\mathbb{R}^n$, where each subspace is k_i-dimensional $(1 \leq i \leq s)$. Then the columns of $\mathbf{A}$ that belong to each subspace i will be represented by at most k_i non-zeros in $\mathbf{c}$. Note that the low-rank model is an instance of the union-of-subspace model where $s = 1$. In Algorithm 1, matrix $\mathbf{B}$ is the collection of all subspaces that $\mathbf{A}$ lives in. The OMP routine greedily approximates each $\mathbf{a}_i$, as a superposition of few columns of $\mathbf{B}$ that best represent $\mathbf{a}_i$.

Platform-aware tuning of transformation . Once the transformation is completed, subsequent iterative analysis on $\mathbf{A}^T\mathbf{A}$ are replaced by $(\mathbf{BC})^T\mathbf{BC}$. The sparsity of $\mathbf{C}$ enables efficient partitioning and computation. One can exploit the existing work in the field of high performance computing to optimally distribute and apply the updates on matrices $\mathbf{B}$ and $\mathbf{C}$. In particular, if n is much larger than both m and the number of columns in $\mathbf{x}$, as it is the case in many large-scale learning problems, the number of communicated words increases linearly with L [1].

On the other hand, increasing parameter L results in sparser transformations. The larger sparsity is achieved due to the higher redundancy in $\mathbf{B}$. Thus, there is a trade-off between the number of non-zeros (or the cost of computation and the memory footprint) of the transformed data and the communication overhead. We can leverage this property to adaptively tune the transformation for the target platform.

3. EVALUATIONS

We performed our evaluations on IBM iDataplex computer cluster. Our test datasets include a database of video frames (size 1764×100000) and a database of light-field image patches (size 18496×100000).

Table 1: Performance improvement in terms of number of floating point operations per iteration and memory usage.

Method	Video	Light field
Ours (GFLOP-per-iteration)	0.061	0.068
Baseline (GFLOP-per-iteration)	0.227	3.69
Ours (Memory MB)	244.64	275.71
Baseline (Memory MB)	1280.00	14797.96

Tunable sparse representations. We tested Algorithm 1 on light field data by setting $\delta = 0.1$. Figure 1 shows the average number of non-zeros per column of C as L increases. At first the number of non-zeros increases with L until the transformation error criteria is met. Afterwards, increasing L further sparsifies $\mathbf{C}$. Since L governs the communication cost, depending on the relative cost of arithmetics and communication on a platform, optimal L can be chosen.

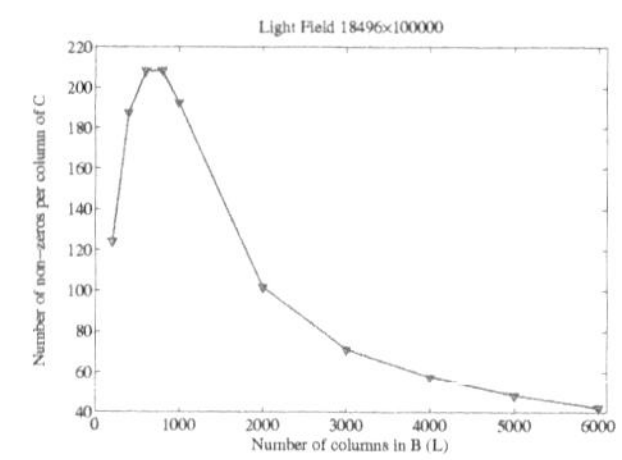

Figure 1: By varying the number of columns in $\mathbf{B}$ in our transformation, various sparsity levels in coefficient matrix $\mathbf{C}$ can be achieved. This property can be used to tune data representation w.r.t costs of the pertinent platform.

Energy and memory efficiency. Table 1 provides the cost in terms of number of floating point operations (FLOPs) per iteration using our approach i.e., $(\mathbf{BC})^T\mathbf{BCx}$ vs. the baseline, i.e., $\mathbf{A}^T\mathbf{Ax}$. It also provides the cost in terms of memory usage using our approach (memory for storing $\mathbf{B}$ and $\mathbf{C}$) vs. the baseline (memory for storing $\mathbf{A}$). The error is set to $\delta = 0.1$. Since energy usage is highly dependent on the number of FLOPs, drastic reductions in the number of FLOPs (e.g., more than 54 times for Light Field data) is an indication of significant energy performance improvement.

4. REFERENCES

[1] G. Ballard, A. Buluc, J. Demmel, L. Grigori, B. Lipshitz, O. Schwartz, and S. Toledo. Communication optimal parallel multiplication of sparse random matrices. SPAA '13, pages 222–231.

[2] G. Davis, S. Mallat, and Z. Zhang. Adaptive time-frequency decompositions. *Opt. Engin SPIE*, pages 2183–2191, 1994.

[3] C. Fowlkes et al. Spectral grouping using the nystrom method. *TPAMI*, pages 214–225, 2004.

[4] Alex Gittens and Michael Mahoney. Revisiting the nystrom method for improved large-scale machine learning. *JMLR.*, 28(3):567–575, 2013.

[5] Y. Low et al. GraphLab: A new parallel framework for machine learning. *UAI*, pages 340–349, 2010.

[6] A. Mirhoseini, E. Dyer, E. Songhori, E. Baraniuk, and F. Koushanfar. Rankmap: A platform-aware framework for distributed learning from dense datasets. In *arXiv:1503.08169*, 2015.

Energy Coupon: A Mean Field Game Perspective on Demand Response in Smart Grids

Jian Li‡, Bainan Xia‡, Xinbo Geng*, Hao Ming‡,
Srinivas Shakkottai‡, Vijay Subramanian†, and Le Xie*
‡*Dept. of ECE, Texas A&M University, †Dept. of EECS, University of Michigan
Email: ‡{lj0818, xiabainan, mingming511, sshakkot}@tamu.edu,
*{gengxbtamu, lxie}@ece.tamu.edu, †vgsubram@umich.edu

1. INTRODUCTION

There has recently been much interest in understanding *societal networks,* consisting of interconnected communication, transportation, energy and other networks that are important to the functioning of society. Research into these networks often takes the form of behavioral studies on decision making by the participants, and whether it is possible to provide incentives to modify their resource usage pattern in such a way that the society as a whole benefits [5].

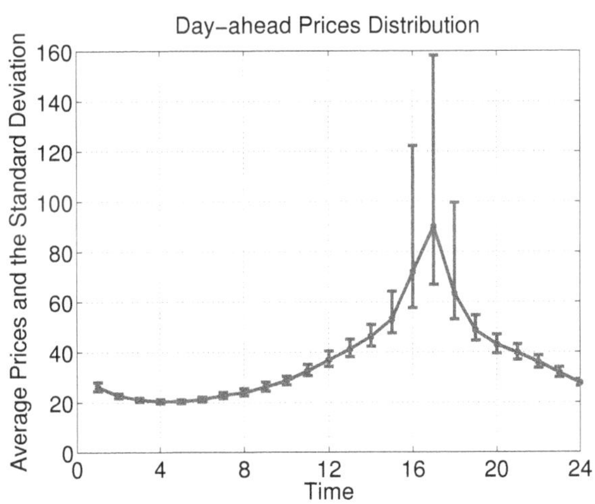

Figure 1: Day-ahead electricity market prices in dollars per MWh on an hourly basis between 12 AM to 12 PM, measured between June–August, 2013 in Austin, TX. Standard deviations above and below the mean are indicated separately.

Our candidate application in this paper is that of a Load Aggregator (LA) (*e.g.,* a utility company) trying to reduce its exposure to daily electricity market volatility by incentivizing demand response in a Smart Grid setting. For instance, consider Figure 1, which shows the (wholesale) price of electricity at different hours of day during the summer months in Texas. The data was obtained from the Electric Reliability Council of Texas (ERCOT) [1], an organization that manages the deregulated wholesale energy market in the state. The price shows considerable variation during the day, and peaks at about 5 PM, which is the time at which maximum demand occurs. A major source of this demand in Texas is air conditioning, which in each home is of the order of 30 kWh per day [2]. Incentivizing customers to move a few kWh of peak-time usage to the sides of the peak each day could lead to much reduced risks of peak price borne by the LA. Such demand shaping could also have a positive effect on environmental impact of power plant emissions.

Changing the energy usage pattern could potentially cause a small increase in the mean and deviation of the internal home temperature, which is a discomfort cost borne by the customer. In our system, the LA awards a number of "Energy Coupons" to the customer in proportion to his usage at the non-peak times, and these coupons are used as tickets at a lottery conducted by the LA. A higher number of coupons would be obtained by choosing an option that potentially entails more discomfort, and would also imply a higher probability of winning at the lottery.

2. ANALYTICAL MODEL

In our analytical model, each agent has a set of actions that it can take in each play of a repeated game, with each action having a corresponding cost. Higher cost actions yield a higher number of coupons. At the end of each play, the agents participate in a lottery in which they are randomly permuted into groups, and one or more prizes are given in each group. The state of each agent is measured using his surplus, which captures the history of plays experienced by the agent, and is a proxy to capture his interest in participating in the incentive system. Each win at the lottery increases the surplus, and each loss decreases it. Furthermore, we assume that the agent is risk neutral and the surplus is translated to value/utility using a concave and increasing function. This captures the idea that each successive win yields a reduced marginal happiness to the agent. Any agent could depart from the system with a fixed probability, and a departing agent is replaced by a new entrant with a randomly drawn surplus. In this setting, we would like to understand how agents would decide on their actions.

Our model is well suited to large scale systems in which any given subset of agents interact only rarely. This is the setting of a Mean Field Game (MFG) [3], which we will use as a framework to study equilibria in societal networks.

SIGMETRICS'15, June 15-19, 2015, Portland, OR, USA.
ACM 978-1-4503-3486-0/15/06.
http://dx.doi.org/10.1145/2745844.2745890 .

Here, the system is viewed from the perspective of a single agent, who assumes that each opponent's action would be drawn independently from an assumed distribution, and plays a best response action. We say that the system is at a Mean Field Equilibrium (MFE) if this best response action turns out to be a sample drawn from the assumed distribution.

Our first result is to characterize the best response policy of the mean field agent, using a dynamic programming formulation. We find that under our assumptions the value function of certain state of surplus is increasing, continuous and submodular. Further, we show using this result that given our ordering in which higher cost actions result in a higher probability of winning the lottery (due to more coupons being given), the choice of one action versus another depends on threshold values the surplus.

The probability of winning the lottery defines the transition kernel (along with the regeneration distribution) of the Markov process of the surplus, and hence maps an assumed distribution across competitors states to a resultant stationary distribution. We show the existence of a fixed point of this kernel, which is the MFE. Since we have a discrete action and state space, showing a fixed point in the space of stationary distributions is quite intricate, which follows Nash's original argument for the existence of mixed equilibria. The proofs of main results are available in [4].

3. NUMERICAL MODEL

We conduct a data-based simulation in the context of electricity usage for home air conditioning to illustrate the performance our system.

Home model: We model the usage of electricity for air conditioning by an average home in Texas over the course of a day. Given the ambinent temperature, from [2] we calculate the ON-OFF pattern of our typical air conditioner.

Actions: We pick a reasonable discrete subset of the action space for our study. We assume that the actions available to the customer involve transfering energy from maximum price period 3 ($5-6$ PM) to the cheaper periods indexed by $1, 2, 4$, and 5. Transferring energy is equivalent to increasing/decreasing the ON time of the AC. We choose a transfer unit of 5 minutes, and candidate actions are shown in Table 2.

Costs: We measure the state of the home under action a by the tuple consisting of the mean tempurature and the standard deviation, denoted by $[\bar{\tau}_a, \sigma_a]$. The baseline state is under action 0, denoted by $[\bar{\tau}_0, \sigma_0]$. The cost of taking action a is $\theta_a = |\bar{\tau}_0 - \bar{\tau}_a| + \lambda|\sigma_0 - \sigma_a|$, where we choose $\lambda = 10$ to make the numerical values of the mean and standard deviation comparable to each other.

Hazard: We measure the hazard experienced by the LA per unit load as the weighted sum of the mean and standard deviation of the day-ahead price of electricity. Denoting the mean price at time period j by π_j and the standard deviation by ϕ_j, we define the *hazard* of peroid j measured in dollars/MWh as $h_j(\pi_j, \phi_j) = \pi_j + \alpha\phi_j$, where α models the risk that the LA perceives. The hazard values for each period are shown in Table 1.

Coupons: Coupons are assigned heuristically to promote consumption in off-peak time. We identified 6 actions that appeared to have the most promise of being used, and these are shown in Table 2 with their attendant costs and number of coupons received.

Table 1: Hazards

Index	Period	Hazard/MWh
1	$3-4$ PM	\$61.2
2	$4-5$ PM	\$120.2
3	$5-6$ PM	\$154.2
4	$6-7$ PM	\$101.3
5	$7-8$ PM	\$54.05

The LA conducts an auction each week across clusters of M homes (we take $M = 50$ in our study) in each auction. For each cluster, there are K prizes (we take $K = 1$ here) for winning the lottery with a value of \$40 (we will see below that this choice is viable). We assume that customers are likely to remain in the system for an average of 50 lotteries.

Table 2: Actions, Costs and Energy Coupons

Index	Action Vector	Cost	Coupons
0	$(0, 0, 6, 0, 0)$	0	13.92
1	$(1, 0, 0, 0, 5)$	2.495	243.92
2	$(2, 0, 0, 0, 4)$	2.328	233.92
3	$(3, 0, 0, 1, 2)$	1.950	187.92
4	$(4, 0, 0, 1, 1)$	1.829	177.92
5	$(3, 0, 0, 2, 1)$	1.747	151.92

MFE: Given the above parameters, we numerically determine the properties of the MFE generated by our system. The mean field distribution of surplus indicates that customers win at a lottery between 1 and 2 times over an average lifetime of 50 time intervals, as is to be expected with a cluster size of 50 customers at each lottery. From the mean field action distribution, we find that the best action from the LA's perspective is action 1, which is chosen with probability 0.6. We use the mean field action distribution to find that the net reduction in hazard over 50 homes is \$82 per week. Thus, incentivizing customers by offering a prize of \$40 each week is certainly feasible. The MFE illustrates that even as small a shift as 30 minutes of AC usage each day over several homes can yield significant benefits.

4. ACKNOWLEDGEMENTS

This work was funded in part by NSF grants CNS-1149458, EFRI-1440969, AST-1443891, III-1219071, AST-1443972, AST-1343381, ECCS-1150944 and CCF-1331863.

5. REFERENCES

[1] Electric Reliability Council of Texas (ERCOT). Data set available at `http://www.ercot.com/`.

[2] Pecan Street. Data set available at `https://dataport.pecanstreet.org/`.

[3] J. M. Lasry and P. Lions. Mean field games. *Japanese Journal of Mathematics*, 2(1):229–260, 2007.

[4] J. Li, B. Xia, X. Geng, H. Ming, S. Shakkottai, V. Subramanian, and L. Xie. Energy coupon: A mean field game perspective on demand response in smart grids. *Arxiv preprint arXiv:1503.02951*, 2015.

[5] B. Prabhakar. Designing large-scale nudge engines. In *Proceedings of the ACM SIGMETRICS*, 2013.

DeltaTree: A Locality-aware Concurrent Search Tree

Ibrahim Umar
Department of Computer Science
University of Tromsø, Norway
ibrahim.umar@uit.no

Otto J. Anshus
Department of Computer Science
University of Tromsø, Norway
otto@cs.uit.no

Phuong Hoai Ha
Department of Computer Science
University of Tromsø, Norway
phuong@cs.uit.no

ABSTRACT

Like other fundamental abstractions for high-performance computing, search trees need to support both high concurrency and data locality. However, existing locality-aware search trees based on the van Emde Boas layout (vEB-based trees), poorly support *concurrent* (update) operations.

We present DeltaTree, a practical locality-aware concurrent search tree that integrates both locality-optimization techniques from vEB-based trees, and concurrency-optimization techniques from highly-concurrent search trees. As a result, DeltaTree minimizes data transfer from memory to CPU and supports high concurrency. Our experimental evaluation shows that DeltaTree is up to 50% faster than highly concurrent B-trees on a commodity Intel high performance computing (HPC) platform and up to 65% faster on a commodity ARM embedded platform.

Categories and Subject Descriptors

D.1.3 [**Concurrent programming**]: Parallel programming; D.4.8 [**Performance**]: Measurements—*performance evaluation, concurrent performance*; G.1.0 [**General**]: Parallel algorithms—*complexity measures, performance measures*

Keywords

Performance evaluation; concurrent algorithms; data locality; multi-core processors; memory systems

1. INTRODUCTION

The conventional van Emde Boas (vEB) layout based trees are examples of locality-aware search trees found in several research on cache-oblivious (CO) data structure [1, 2, 3, 4, 5].

The main feature of the vEB layout is that the cost of any search is $O(\log_B N)$ memory transfers, where N is the tree size and B is the *unknown* memory block size in the CO model [5]. As such, its search is cache-oblivious. The search cost is optimal and matches that of B-trees. However, B-trees requires the memory block size B to be *known in advance*. To accomplish optimal search cost, at any level of detail each subtree in the vEB layout is stored in a contiguous block of memory.

Although the conventional vEB layout benefits from data locality, it poorly supports *concurrent* update operations. Inserting (or deleting) a node at position i in the contiguous block of memory storing the tree may trigger a restructure of a large part of the tree. Even worse, we will need to allocate a new contiguous block of memory for the whole tree if the previously allocated block of memory for the tree runs out of space [4]. Note that we cannot use dynamic node allocation via pointers since at *any* level of detail, each subtree in the vEB layout must be stored in a *contiguous* block of memory.

SIGMETRICS'15, June 15–19, 2015, Portland, OR, USA.
ACM 978-1-4503-3486-0/15/06.
http://dx.doi.org/10.1145/2745844.2745891.

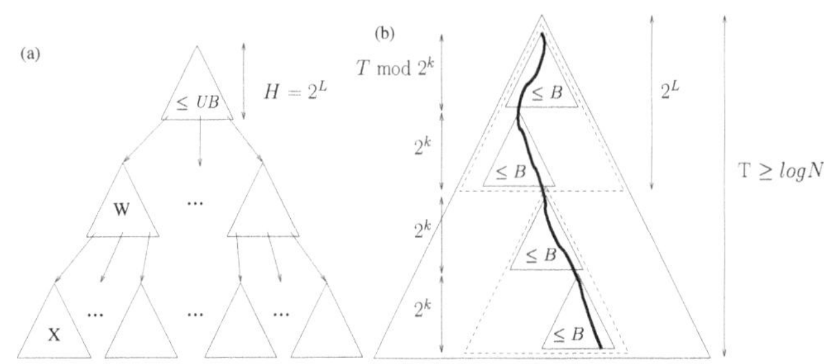

Figure 1: ***(a)*** **New concurrency-aware vEB layout.** ***(b)*** **Search using concurrency-aware vEB layout.**

2. RELAXED CO MODEL AND CONCURRENCY-AWARE VEB LAYOUT

In order to make the vEB layout suitable for highly concurrent data structures with concurrent update operations, we introduce a novel *concurrency-aware* dynamic vEB layout. Our key idea is that if we know an *upper bound UB* on the unknown memory block size B, we can support dynamic node allocation via pointers while maintaining the optimal search cost of $O(\log_B N)$ memory transfers without knowing B (cf. Lemma 2.1). This idea is based on that in practice it is not feasible to keep the vEB layout in a contiguous block of physical memory greater than some upper bound set by the underlying system physical page size (frame size) and cache-line size.

Figure 1a illustrates the new concurrency-aware vEB layout based on the relaxed CO model. The memory transfer cost for search operations in the new concurrency-aware vEB

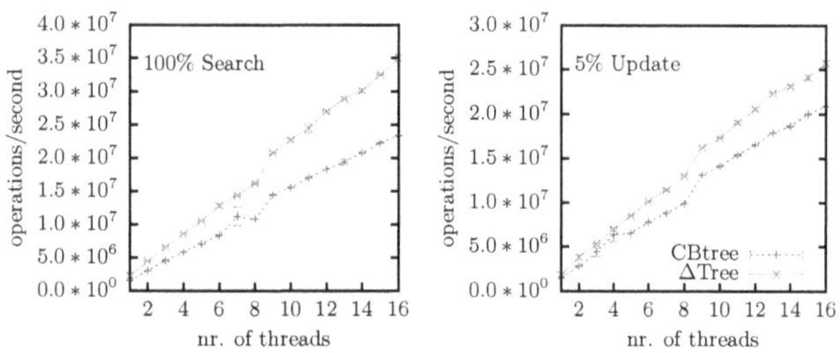

Figure 2: Performance comparison using 2^{22} initial values on an Intel HPC platform with dual Intel Xeon E5-2670 CPUs.

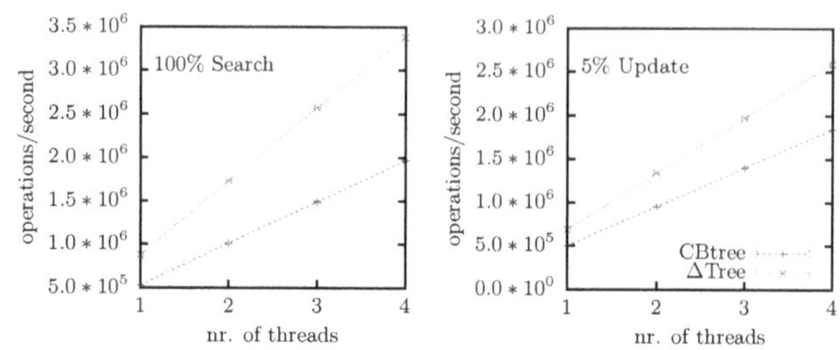

Figure 3: Performance comparison using 2^{21} initial values on an ARM platform with a Samsung Exynos 5410 octa-core ARM CPU.

layout is the same as that of the conventional vEB layout (cf. Lemma 2.1). However, the concurrency-aware vEB supports high concurrency for update operations.

We define *relaxed cache-oblivious* algorithms as cache-oblivious (CO) algorithms with the restriction that an upper bound UB on the unknown memory block size B is known in advance. As long as an upper bound on all the block sizes of multilevel memory is known, the new relaxed CO model maintains the key features of the original CO model [5]. This enables algorithm designs that can utilize fine-grained data locality in the multilevel memory hierarchy of modern architectures.

LEMMA 2.1. *For any upper bound UB on the* unknown *memory block size B, a search in a complete binary tree with the concurrency-aware vEB layout achieves the optimal memory transfer $O(\log_B N)$, where N and B are the tree size and the* unknown *memory block size in the CO model, respectively.*

PROOF. (Sketch) Figure 1b illustrates the proof. Let k be the coarsest level of detail such that every recursive subtree contains at most B nodes. Since $B \leq UB$, $k \leq L$, where L is the coarsest level of detail at which every recursive subtree (ΔNodes) contains at most UB nodes. Consequently, there are at most 2^{L-k} subtrees along the search path in a ΔNode and no subtree of depth 2^k is split due to the boundary of ΔNodes. Namely, triangles of height 2^k fit within a dashed triangle of height 2^L in Figure 1b.

Because at any level of detail $i \leq L$ in the concurrency-aware vEB layout, a recursive subtree of depth 2^i is stored in a contiguous block of memory, each subtree of depth 2^k *within* a ΔNode is stored in at most two memory blocks of size B (depending on the starting location of the subtree in memory). Since every subtree of depth 2^k fits in a ΔNode (i.e., no subtree is stored across two ΔNodes), every subtree of depth 2^k is stored in at most two memory blocks of size B.

Since the tree has height T, $\lceil T/2^k \rceil$ subtrees of depth 2^k are traversed in a search and thereby at most $2\lceil T/2^k \rceil$ memory blocks are transferred.

Since a subtree of height 2^{k+1} contains more than B nodes, $2^{k+1} \geq \log_2(B+1)$, or $2^k \geq \frac{1}{2}\log_2(B+1)$.

We have $2^{T-1} \leq N \leq 2^T$ since the tree is a *complete* binary tree. This implies $\log_2 N \leq T \leq \log_2 N + 1$.

Therefore, the number of memory blocks transferred in a search is $2\lceil T/2^k \rceil \leq 4\lceil \frac{\log_2 N+1}{\log_2(B+1)} \rceil = 4\lceil \log_{B+1} N + \log_{B+1} 2 \rceil$ $= O(\log_B N)$, where $N \geq 2$. □

3. CONTRIBUTIONS

We devised a new *relaxed* cache-oblivious model and a novel *concurrency-aware* vEB layout that makes the vEB layout suitable for highly-concurrent data structures even with update operations (cf. Figure 1). The concurrency-aware vEB layout supports dynamic node allocation via pointers while maintaining the optimal search cost of $O(\log_B N)$ memory transfers without knowing the exact value of block size B (cf. Lemma 2.1).

Based on the new concurrency-aware vEB layout, we developed a new locality-aware concurrent search tree called DeltaTree (ΔTree).

We experimentally evaluated[1] ΔTree on a commodity Intel HPC platform (cf. Figure 2) and an ARM embedded platform (cf. Figure 3). ΔTree is up to 50% and 65% faster than CBtree [6], a highly-concurrent B-tree, on Intel HPC and ARM platforms, respectively.

4. ACKNOWLEDGMENTS

This research work has received funding from the European Union Seventh Framework Programme (grant n°611183) and from the Research Council of Norway (grant n°231746/F20). The authors would like to thank the Norwegian Metacenter for Computational Science for giving us access to HPC clusters.

5. REFERENCES

[1] M. Bender, E. D. Demaine, and M. Farach-Colton. Cache-oblivious b-trees. *SIAM Journal on Computing*, 35:341, 2005.

[2] M. A. Bender, M. Farach-Colton, J. T. Fineman, Y. R. Fogel, B. C. Kuszmaul, and J. Nelson. Cache-oblivious streaming b-trees. In *Proc. 19th annual ACM Symp. Parallel algorithms and architectures*, SPAA '07, pages 81–92, 2007.

[3] M. A. Bender, J. T. Fineman, S. Gilbert, and B. C. Kuszmaul. Concurrent cache-oblivious b-trees. In *Proc. 17th annual ACM Symp. Parallelism in algorithms and architectures*, SPAA '05, pages 228–237, 2005.

[4] G. S. Brodal, R. Fagerberg, and R. Jacob. Cache oblivious search trees via binary trees of small height. In *Proc. 13th annual ACM-SIAM Symp. Discrete algorithms*, SODA '02, pages 39–48, 2002.

[5] M. Frigo, C. E. Leiserson, H. Prokop, and S. Ramachandran. Cache-oblivious algorithms. In *Proc. 40th Annual Symp. Foundations of Computer Science*, FOCS '99, page 285, 1999.

[6] P. L. Lehman and s. B. Yao. Efficient locking for concurrent operations on b-trees. *ACM Trans. Database Syst.*, 6(4):650–670, Dec. 1981.

[1]Using 5 million operations in two micro-benchmarks: 100% search and 5% update (95% search) using random numbers.

Detecting and Localizing End-to-End Performance Degradation for Cellular Data Services

Faraz Ahmed[†], Jeffrey Erman[‡], Zihui Ge[‡], Alex X. Liu[†], Jia Wang[‡], He Yan[‡],
[†]Department of Computer Science and Engineering, Michigan State University, East Lansing, MI, USA
[‡]AT&T Labs - Research, Bedminster, NJ, USA
{farazah,alexliu}@cse.msu.edu, {erman,gezihui,jiawang,yanhe}@research.att.com

ABSTRACT

Nowadays mobile device (e.g., smartphone) users not only have a high expectation on the availability of the cellular data service, but also increasingly depend on the high end-to-end (E2E) performance of their applications. Since the E2E performance of individual application sessions may vary greatly, depending on factors such as the cellular network condition, the content provider, the type/model of the mobile devices, and the application software, detecting and localizing service performance degradations in a timely manner at large scale is of great value to cellular service providers. In this paper, we build a holistic measurement system that tracks session-level E2E performance metrics along with the service attributes for these factors. Using data collected from a major cellular service provider, we first model the expected E2E service performance with a regression based approach, detect performance degradation conditions based on the time series of fine-grained measurement data, and finally localize the service degradation using association-rule-mining techniques. Our deployment experience reveals that in 80% of the detected problem instances, performance degradation can be attributed to non-network-location specific factors, such as a common content provider, or a set of applications running on certain models of devices.

Categories and Subject Descriptors

C.2.3 [**Computer Communication Networks**]: Network Operations—*Network monitoring*

Keywords

Cellular Network, End-to-end, Performance

1. INTRODUCTION

Cellular data services are increasingly being used from smartphones to tablets in every aspect of everyday life such as emailing, web browsing, video streaming, and online shopping. Nowadays mobile users using smartphones and cellular data services have a high expectation not only on the service availability but also on their application performance, i.e., the end-to-end (E2E) service performance. The E2E performance may vary significantly depending on application, content provider, device type, geographic location, time of day and day of week [1–3]. Providing high E2E performance is critical for cellular service providers to best serve their customers and maintain their competitive edge. In this context, E2E performance means the performance that users experience for a specific user location, content provider, device type, and application type.

In this work, we study the detection and localization of E2E performance degradation (such as slow webpage loading and unsmooth video playback) at cellular service providers across four different administrative domains: cellular service providers, content providers, device manufacturers, and application developers. For detection, we want to proactively detect E2E performance degradations before users call the customer service of cellular service providers to complain. For localization, we want to find the causes (user location, content provider, device type, and/or application type) of the E2E performance degradation. Detecting and localizing E2E performance degradation is crucial for cellular service providers, content providers, device manufactures, and application developers to jointly troubleshoot root causes. When users experience E2E performance degradation, they have no clue who is responsible. For example, when a user at New York experiences performance degradation for email application A provided by a content provider C on his device D, he does not know whether it is the cellular provider, the content provider, the device, or his email client app, that is causing the problem. Often when such E2E performance degradation arises, users blankly ascribe all the faults to their cellular service providers and may call customer service centers to complain, which may cause both reputation damage and financial losses for the providers. Furthermore, when cellular service providers receive such calls, it is a lengthy, manual, labor intensive process for them to locate where the issue is, and the actual issue may not be the cellular service provider's problem. The localization findings allow cellular service providers to quickly mitigate service issues, effectively communicate with customers complaining about service problems, and engage content providers, device manufactures, or application developers and operators to jointly troubleshoot for root causes.

2. PROPOSED APPROACH

In this paper, we propose a holistic approach to detecting and localizing E2E performance degradation at cellular service providers across the four dimensions of user locations, content providers, device types, and application types. We

SIGMETRICS'15, June 15-19, 2015, Portland, OR, USA.
ACM 978-1-4503-3486-0/15/06.
http://dx.doi.org/10.1145/2745844.2745892.

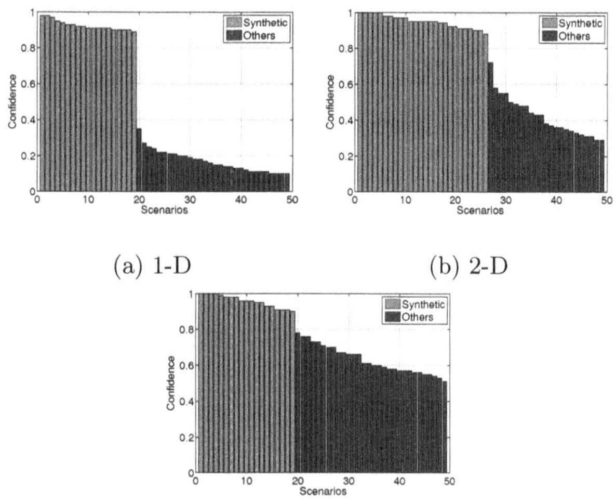

(a) 1-D (b) 2-D

(c) 3-D

Figure 1: Synthetic anomaly detection

utilize anonymized flow level data collected from the core network of a major cellular service provider in the United States to compute TCP loss ratio and Round Trip Time (RTT) as E2E performance metrics. For each TCP flow, we capture information such as standard coordinated universal time (UTC), the serving RNC that describes the user access point (L), the handheld device type (D), the application type (A), and the content provider being accessed (P). First, we use training data to build regression based models that capture the normal performance of every *E2E instance*, which means the flows corresponding to a user location, content provider, device type, and application type. We use robust regression for this baseline modeling because it can minimize the impact of extreme outlier data points on the produced model. Specifically, we represent E2E performance in a four dimensional matrix that is called *E2E matrix* and is denoted $E_I = [1..L, 1..P, 1..D, 1..A]$. We build a baseline model for all E2E instances, identify the E2E instance groups that have significantly different performance, and then model these groups separately, leaving the rest of E2E instances still being modeled by the baseline model. Second, we use our models to detect performance degradation for each E2E instance on an hourly basis. For each E2E instance, if the real performance in the testing phase is significantly much worse than the expected performance based on our models, we label it as degrading. Third, after each E2E instance has been labeled as non-degrading or degrading, we use association rule mining to localize the source of performance degradation. For example, rule `Device - D, Email` $\rightarrow$ `degrading` shows that for a particular hour, for all locations and content providers, the cellular users of Device-D are experiencing significantly degraded performance for their email application.

3. EVALUATION

For evaluation purposes, we created three different synthetic sets of scenarios. The first set consists of 19 scenarios involving only one of the four dimensions, the second set involves 26 scenarios with two dimensions and the third set involves 19 scenarios with three dimensions. Each scenario corresponds to a one-hour anomaly associated with a group of instances in the E2E performance matrix. Figure 1 shows that all 64 synthetic anomaly scenarios that we injected into the collected operational data are successfully detected and localized. For one dimensional scenarios, we obtain all scenarios as association rules with more than 90% confidence. For two dimensional scenarios we achieved 0 false positives for a minimum confidence threshold of 70% and for three dimensional scenarios we got 0 false positives for a minimum confidence threshold of 80%.

We implemented and deployed our detection and localization tool on an operational network and separately examined performance anomalies for packet loss ratio and RTT. We monitored 78 different user locations, 51 device types, 13 application types and 36 content providers for a period of two weeks. We did not observe performance anomalies in the user location dimension, which means that a single user location cannot be blamed for the anomalies occurring during the one week time period. We observe 16 and 27 one dimensional anomalous events for content providers and device types respectively, which is small when compared to anomalous events in the application domain. It is highly unlikely that the performance of a content provider will degrade across all user locations. This is because content providers utilize content distribution networks for serving content at different user locations. Therefore, a problematic content server can only affect the performance of a subset of user locations. For applications, we observe 180 single dimension anomalies. This could be attributed to application patches and bug fixes that are released periodically and frequently. Software bugs in these updates can cause performance issues across all user locations, device types and content providers.

For multi-dimensional cases, we detected a total of 8415 E2E instances as anomalous. In 83% of these instances, a content provider was involved, 86% involved device types, and 86% involved application types. Overall, 80% of these instances do not have location as one of the dimensions. In other words, 80% of the time the anomalies are not due to issues in the cellular network. This composition indicates that most of the time content providers, device types and applications are involved in the performance degradations. These results are extremely useful for network operators as they point network operators to the problematic dimensions and reduce the search space of root causes.

4. REFERENCES

[1] J. Huang, F. Qian, A. Gerber, Z. M. Mao, S. Sen, and O. Spatscheck. A close examination of performance and power characteristics of 4g lte networks. In *Proceedings of the 10th International Conference on MobiSys*, pages 225–238, 2012.

[2] J. Huang, F. Qian, Y. Guo, Y. Zhou, Q. Xu, Z. M. Mao, S. Sen, and O. Spatscheck. An in-depth study of lte: Effect of network protocol and application behavior on performance. In *Proceedings of the ACM SIGCOMM*, pages 363–374, 2013.

[3] M. Z. Shafiq, L. Ji, A. X. Liu, and J. Wang. Characterizing and modeling internet traffic dynamics of cellular devices. In *Proceedings of the ACM SIGMETRICS*, pages 305–316, San Jose, California, June 2011.

Speeding up Glauber Dynamics for Random Generation of Independent Sets

Rémi Varloot
Inria - Microsoft Research
France

Ana Bušić
Inria Paris-Rocquencourt
France

Anne Bouillard
École Normale Supérieure
Paris, France

ABSTRACT

The maximum independent set (MIS) problem is a well-studied combinatorial optimization problem that naturally arises in many applications, such as wireless communication, information theory and statistical mechanics.

MIS problem is NP-hard, thus many results in the literature focus on fast generation of maximal independent sets of high cardinality. One possibility is to combine Gibbs sampling with coupling from the past arguments to detect convergence to the stationary regime. This results in a sampling procedure with time complexity that depends on the mixing time of the Glauber dynamics Markov chain.

We propose an adaptive method for random event generation in the Glauber dynamics that considers only the events that are effective in the coupling from the past scheme, accelerating the convergence time of the Gibbs sampling algorithm.

The full paper is available on arXiv.

Categories and Subject Descriptors

G.2.2 [**Discrete Mathematics**]: Graph theory—*graph algorithms*; G.3 [**Probability and Statistics**]: Markov processes, Probabilistic algorithms (including Monte Carlo)

Keywords

Glauber dynamics; exact sampling; independent sets

1. COUPLING FROM THE PAST

Propp and Wilson [4] introduced in 1996 the coupling from the past (CFTP) algorithm, a perfect sampling technique for the stationary distribution of an ergodic finite state space Markov chain. CFTP generates an unbiased sample from the stationary distribution in finite expected time.

Formally, given a finite state space $\mathcal{S}$ of cardinality n and a $n \times n$ transition matrix M, a Markov chain over $\mathcal{S}$ with transition matrix M can be represented as

$$X_t = X_0 \cdot u_1 \cdot \ldots \cdot u_t,$$

SIGMETRICS'15, June 15–19, 2015, Portland, OR, USA
ACM 978-1-4503-3486-0/15/06.
http://dx.doi.org/10.1145/2745844.2745893.

where the u_i are i.i.d. letters from a finite alphabet A, drawn according to a distribution D defined such that the operator $\cdot : \mathcal{S} \times A \to \mathcal{S}$ satisfies

$$\forall x, y \in \mathcal{S}, \quad \mathbf{P}_{u \sim D}(x \cdot u = y) = M_{xy}.$$

Consider an i.i.d. sequence of letters $(u_{-t})_{t \in \mathbb{N}}$ drawn according to D, and define the chains $(B_{-i}^{-t})_{i \in \mathbb{N}}$ by

$$B_{-i}^{-t} = \{x \cdot u_{-t} \cdot \ldots \cdot u_{-i-1} : x \in \mathcal{S}\}.$$

THEOREM 1 (PROPP AND WILSON [4]). *If there exists a $T \in \mathbb{N}$ such that B_0^{-T} is a singleton, then:*

1. *For all $-t \leq -T$, $B_0^{-t} = B_0^{-T}$;*
2. *The unique element of B_0^{-T} is distributed according to the stationary distribution of M.*

A key element in their proof is that

$$\forall t, \forall i, \quad B_{-i}^{-t-1} \subseteq B_{-i}^{-t} \tag{1}$$

CFTP algorithm consists in drawing the letters u_{-i} one by one until B_0^{-t} is a singleton, then returning the unique element of B_0^{-t}. The main drawback is that at each time step $-i$, the algorithm computes $x \cdot u_{-i}$ for all $x \in B_{-i}^{-t}$, which is often prohibitive due to the cardinality of $\mathcal{S}$. The complexity of this one step transition can be improved through the use of bounding chains and we assume here the approach in [2].

2. EXPANDING AND CONTRACTING

The complexity of the CFTP algorithm is closely linked to the rate at which the Markov chain changes state: for a given set of states B, call a letter u passive if $B = \{x \cdot u : x \in B\}$. The main contribution of this paper is to propose a variant of the algorithm that avoids considering the passive letters, while still producing an unbiased sample from the stationary distribution.

Whereas such a modification is easily achievable in a simple Markov chain Monte Carlo dynamic, it is not immediate to adapt it to the CFTP approach. The main reason is that letters passive for B_{-i}^{-t} are not necessarily passive for B_{-i}^{-t-s}. This is illustrated in Figure 1.

The proposed method removes passive letters as it proceeds, while reinserting active letters where they may have been removed due to being passive at some earlier stage of the algorithm. The insertion is done in a randomized manner that preserves the distribution of the output of the algorithm.

We define two operations, contraction and expansion, that remove and add passive letters in a given word. These are illustrated in Figure 2.

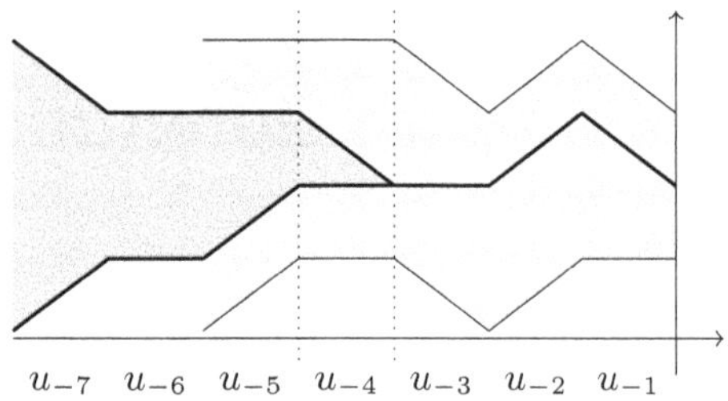

Two bounding chains starting at times −5 and −7.
u_{-4} is passive for the former but becomes active for the later.

Figure 1: Passive events become active

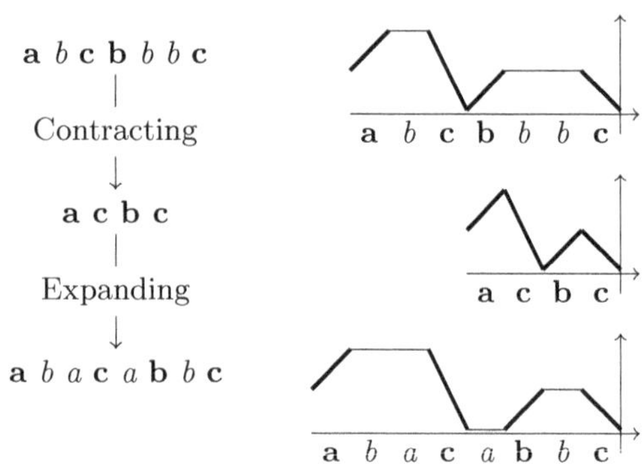

Active letters are shown in bold font.

Figure 2: Contracting and Expanding

Contraction is straightforward. Expansion, on the other hand, is more complex as it should not introduce a bias in the distribution of the output. The key element here is to make sure that the inclusion (1) is still valid despite new letters being introduced. Also, when starting a new chain from further back in time, the number of new letters must be geometrically distributed. Due to space constraints, we do not give all the details of this procedure here.

The proposed algorithm, called CFTP with oracle skipping (OS-CFTP), is obtained by adapting the CFTP algorithm so as to expand the current word before going back in time, adding letters, then contracting the result. A reduction in complexity is obtained by merging the expansion and contraction phases so as never to work with a fully expanded word. The gain depends greatly on the proportion of passive letters.

THEOREM 2. *OS-CFTP returns a state that is distributed according to the stationary distribution* π.

For details concerning the algorithm, its complexity, and a proof of Theorem 2, see the full paper.

One of the main assumptions here is that it is always possible to draw letters conditioned to being active for a given set of states. Identifying passive letters is in general not straightforward. In the case of local dynamics on graphs, such as the independent set example from Section 3, this can be done efficiently under some reasonable assumptions. Note that we can also remove only a subset of passive eventsa tradeoff between the complexity of finding passive events and the gain obtained by eliminating them.

An iterative approach to find passive events was considered in [3].

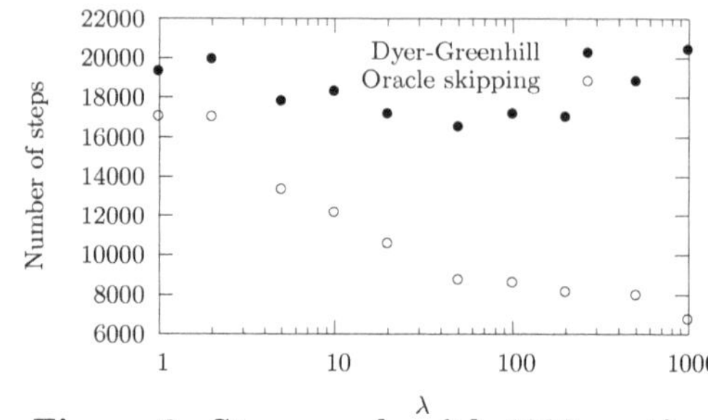

Figure 3: Star graph with 1000 vertices

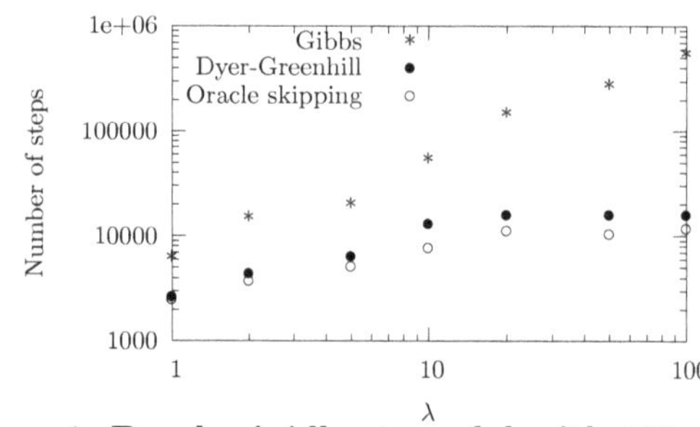

Figure 4: Barabasi-Albert model with 100 vertices

3. GENERATING INDEPENDENT SETS

We illustrate the efficiency of the OS-CFTP algorithm for independent sets. An independent set in a graph is a subset I of the vertices of that graph, no two of which are linked by an edge. The target distribution is given by

$$\pi(I) = \frac{\lambda^{\mathrm{card}(I)}}{Z_\lambda},$$

where λ is a parameter, called the fugacity, and Z_λ is a normalization constant. It is possible to express π as the stationary distribution of a Markov chain by using a Gibbs sampler. This method was furthermore refined by Dyer and Greenhill [1, 2].

Simulation results for different graph models are given in Figures 3 and 4. Theoretical bounds for the star topology are given in the full paper. Overall, oracle skipping does better than previous methods, though the gain is strongly linked to the model studied.

4. ACKNOWLEDGMENTS

The work presented in this paper has been carried out at LINCS (www.lincs.fr) and is supported by the French National Research Agency grant ANR-12-MONU-0019.

5. REFERENCES

[1] M. Dyer and C. Greenhill. On Markov chains for independent sets. *J. Algorithms*, 35(1):17–49, 2000.

[2] M. Huber. Perfect sampling using bounding chains. *Ann. Appl. Probab.*, 14(2):734–753, 2004.

[3] F. Pin, A. Bušić, and B. Gaujal. Acceleration of perfect sampling by skipping events. In *Proceedings of the 5th International Conference on Performance Evaluation Methodologies and Tools (Valuetools)*, 2011.

[4] J. G. Propp and D. B. Wilson. Exact sampling with coupled Markov chains and applications to statistical mechanics. *Random Structures & Algorithms*, 9(1-2):223–252, 1996.

Online Electricity Cost Saving Algorithms for Co-Location Data Centers

Linquan Zhang†, Zongpeng Li†, Chuan Wu‡, Shaolei Ren*
†Department of Computer Science, University of Calgary
‡Department of Computer Science, The University of Hong Kong
*School of Computing and Information Sciences, Florida International University
{linqzhan,zongpeng}@ucalgary.ca, cwu@cs.hku.hk, sren@fiu.edu

ABSTRACT

This work studies the online electricity cost minimization problem at a co-location data center. A co-location data center serves multiple tenants who rent the physical infrastructure within the data center to run their respective cloud computing services. Consequently, the co-location operator has no direct control over power consumption of its tenants, and an efficient mechanism is desired for eliciting desirable consumption patterns from the co-location tenants. Electricity billing faced by a data center is nowadays based on both the total volume consumed and the peak consumption rate. This leads to an interesting new combinatorial optimization structure on the electricity cost optimization problem, which also exhibits an online nature due to the definition of peak consumption. We model and solve the problem through two approaches: the *pricing* approach and the *auction* approach. For the former, we design an offline 2-approximation algorithm as well as an online algorithm with a small competitive ratio in most practical settings. For the latter, we design an efficient $(2+c)-$competitive online algorithm, where c is a system dependent parameter close to 1.49, and then convert it into an efficient mechanism that executes in an online fashion, runs in polynomial time, and guarantees truthful bidding and $(2+2c)-$competitive in social cost.

Categories and Subject Descriptors

C.4 [**Performance of Systems**]: Design studies; Modeling techniques; I.1.2 [**Algorithms**]: Analysis of algorithms

Keywords

Co-Location Data Center; Mechanism Design; Approximation Algorithms; Online Algorithms

1. INTRODUCTION

Co-location data centers (or *co-locations*) rent physical space and infrastructure support, *e.g.*, reliable power supply and cooling service, to multiple tenants for hosting their servers at a common site. Co-locations have become an indispensable part for today's cloud computing industry, offering a flexible data center solution to small and medium users who wish to run their own 'cloud' but are otherwise deterred by the daunting cost of constructing and maintaining their own data center. Even large users, as exemplified by Google and Akamai, rely on co-locations as a cost-effective complement to their own data centers for achieving a global presence, particularly in regions of relatively low demand that do not justify a dedicated data center.

Electricity charges paid by a co-location is computed by an interesting formula that includes two components: i) the *peak charge*, which is determined by the peak demand within a billing cycle, *e.g.*, the maximum average power consumption measured over each 15-minute interval; ii) the *volume charge*, which is based on total energy consumption in the billing cycle [1, 3]. The volume charge is relatively intuitive. The rationale behind the peak charge is that peak consumption shedding is critical to a power grid; even a small reduction in peak demand can provide significant cost savings, reduce greenhouse gas emission, and help balance grid-wide demand and supply. In practice, the peak charge component is seen to account for over 30% of the total electricity bill [3]. For example, consider a co-location data center located in British Columbia, Canada, powered by BC Hydro [1] with 24 MW peak demand and 15 MW average demand. The monthly peak charge is \$238,800, while the volume charge is \$524,880. In this case, the peak charge is 31% of the total monthly payment. This suggests that *a well designed algorithm for shaping the power consumption profile and controlling the peak demand has a great potential in helping cut electricity cost at a co-location.*

However, different from the case of private data centers, the co-location operator has no direct control on which machines are on/off, since its role is to offer basic services such as stable power supply and cooling. The individual tenants at a co-location manage their own servers and control the corresponding power consumption. While the co-location has a strong incentive to cut peak consumption and therefore save cost, its tenants may or may not share that same interest, depending on the contract between the two sides.

Typical electricity pricing today between a co-location and its tenants is flat-rate based, and does not depend on the real consumption volume or pattern [2, 4]. The tenants have little incentive to reduce their electricity usage by shutting down under-utilized servers, or by modulating their consumption pattern via shifting computing jobs in the temporal domain to reduce peak consumption rate. Such actions desired by the co-location will not automatically happen without appropriate incentives. Co-locations are sometimes so desperate to cut peak consumption that they start their own stand-by generators to cover part of the demand from its tenants [3]. Such quick-start stand-by generation (*e.g.*, using diesel generators) is often not economical, nor is it environment friendly. Auction based demand response mechanisms are natural approaches that have the

SIGMETRICS'15, June 15-19, 2015, Portland, OR, USA.
ACM 978-1-4503-3486-0/15/06.
http://dx.doi.org/10.1145/2745844.2745894.

potential of efficiently providing incentive for tenants to cooperate, eliciting desired electricity consumption patterns with remuneration paid in return. A well designed auction may represent a win-win solution for both the co-location operator and its tenants, such that both enjoy a higher utility.

The maximum power demand is dependent on the power consumption in all time intervals during a billing cycle. Decisions in different time slots are therefore coupled, leading to an inherent online nature of the problem of demand shaping. Appropriate control of the peak demand helps reduce electricity cost while inappropriate control might incur a high cost. For a quick illustration, assume the energy demand pattern is $(D, D/2, D/2, D/2)$, possible savings by tenants are $(D/2, 0, 0, 0)$, the price for energy reduction is $f/2$, peak and volume charges are f and $f/4$, respectively. The optimal algorithm reduces the peak demand to $D/2$ at the beginning by using energy reduction from tenants, so that the total cost is $5Df/4$; while an online algorithm without future information might anticipate high demand in the future and refuse to use energy reduction from tenants, which makes the total cost $13Df/8$, 30% higher than the optimum. Even for the offline version of the problem (future prices and demands are perfectly known), computing the optimal solution efficiently is still highly non-trivial, since its underlying optimization problem is an integer program, which is NP-hard in general. The challenge escalates when one seeks to design an *online solution* for practical application, as knowledge on the demands, unit power prices as well as tenants' bids in the future are completely unknown.

2. RESULTS OVERVIEW

In this work, we model and solve the electricity cost saving problem in a co-location data center through two approaches: the *pricing* approach and the *auction* approach. In the pricing approach, the co-location data center offers a price it is willing to pay for unit energy reduction by tenants, and the tenants decide and submit how much energy they are willing to save at that price. Finally the co-location data center determines which tenants' energy reductions are accepted. In the auction approach, the co-location data center invites the tenants to submit energy reduction bids including the amount of energy consumption to shed and the amount of remuneration asked. The co-location then conducts a reverse auction to determine winning bids along with their corresponding payments. The pricing approach is relatively simple and has been applied in real world demand response solutions, implemented in electric appliances on the market. It is simple but requires the co-location to first come up with a good estimate on a unit reduction offer. The auction approach eliminates the need of such ad hoc guesses and resorts to the power of the market instead for automatic fair price revelation based on demand and supply. However, the auction design is considerably more complex than the algorithm design in the pricing approach, and our solution to the former borrows techniques from the latter.

Pricing Approach. We first study the offline cost minimization problem, find a piecewise linear function between the peak demand and the total electricity cost, and then propose a 2-approximation algorithm with future information assumed. By applying the approximation algorithm on the information currently available to decide the amount of energy obtained from the grid, and the primal-dual framework on the remaining linear integer program, we then proceed to design an online algorithm, which strives to increase the peak demand gracefully as requests and bids arrive. The online algorithm achieves a competitive ratio of $(1 + 2(\kappa + 1)/\rho + 2)$, where κ and ρ are system dependent parameters. The ratio is 6.2 when $\kappa = 3$ and $\rho \approx 2.5$ in our empirical studies. The ratio has two parts: the term 2 results from addressing the computational complexity in the integer programming nature of the problem, while the term $1 + 2(\kappa + 1)/\rho$ results from addressing the challenge of the online nature of peak demand control.

Auction Approach. A reverse auction is conducted by the co-location data center. We model social cost minimization using a natural mixed integer program. We first analyze the social cost minimization problem by deriving the dual of its linear program relaxation. We design a $(2+\xi/(1-\frac{1}{\rho}))$-competitive online algorithm, by applying the primal-dual framework to iteratively compute primal and dual solutions that are feasible to the primal and dual problems, respectively. The dual solution acts as a lower bound of the primal optimum, which helps analyze the competitive ratio. In empirical studies, we find $\xi \approx 1.2$ and $\rho \approx 2.5$, resulting in a competitive ratio of 4. Similar to the pricing approach, 2 comes from addressing challenges in computational complexity while $\xi/(1-\frac{1}{\rho})$ comes from coping with lack of future information.

We study improvements to reduce the competitive ratio of the online algorithm, by keeping track of the maximum demand that has happened so far, and carefully exploiting that extra piece of information in decision making. That reduces the competitive ratio to $(2 + c)$, where c is a system dependent parameter. We find $c \approx 1.49$ in our empirical studies, and therefore the competitive ratio is 3.49, which is improved from 4. The new online algorithm solves two sub-problems: i) deciding the energy drawn from the grid based on historic information as well as current demand; ii) using the bids from tenants to fill the gap between current demand and the energy drawn from the grid. The second sub-problem is a general version of the integer program in the pricing approach, and a similar approximation algorithm is applied.

Since the tenants decide their bidding prices, a strategic tenant may submit a falsified price in the hope of a higher payment from the co-location. A *truthful* auction is desired, in which it is a dominant strategy for each tenant to bid its true cost. The celebrated Vickrey-Clarke-Groves (VCG) auction guarantees both truthfulness and social cost minimization. Unfortunately, a VCG auction requires solving the underlying optimization problem, which is NP-hard in our work, for multiple times, making it impractical. We resort to a randomized auction design framework, which decomposes a fractional optimal solution to the second sub-problem into a convex combination of feasible integer solutions. The framework runs in polynomial time, ensures the winning probability of a bid is monotonically non-increasing in its bidding price, and therefore is truthful in expectation. Combining the randomized auction framework with the online algorithm, we obtain an online auction with a competitive ratio of $(2 + 2c)$, which has only a small loss over that of the online algorithm.

Acknowledgments. This work has been supported by Wedge Networks, NSERC, AITF, HK RGC (HKU 718513), and NSF (CNS-1423137 and CNS-1453491).

3. REFERENCES

[1] BC Hydro. https://www.bchydro.com/.

[2] Enaxis Consulting. Pricing Data Center Co-location Services, 2009, http://enaxisconsulting.com.

[3] Z. Liu, A. Wierman, Y. Chen, B. Razon, and N. Chen. Data Center Demand Response: Avoiding the Coincident Peak via Workload Shifting and Local Generation. In *Proc. of ACM SIGMETRICS*, 2013.

[4] A. Qureshi, R. Weber, H. Balakrishnan, J. Guttag, and B. Maggs. Cutting the Electric Bill for Internet-scale Systems. In *Proc. of ACM SIGCOMM*, 2009.

Web Transparency for Complex Targeting: Algorithms, Limits, and Tradeoffs

Guillaume Ducoffe, Mathias Lécuyer, Augustin Chaintreau, Roxana Geambasu
Inria & U. Nice Sophia Antipolis, Columbia U.
guillaume.ducoffe@inria.fr, {mathias,augustin,roxana}@cs.columbia.edu

Big Data promises important societal progress but exacerbates the need for due process and accountability. Companies and institutions can now discriminate between users at an individual level using collected data or past behavior. Worse, today they can do so in near perfect opacity. The nascent field of *web transparency* aims to develop the tools and methods necessary to reveal how information is used, however today it lacks robust tools that let users and investigators identify targeting using multiple inputs.

Here, we formalize for the first time the problem of detecting and identifying targeting on *combinations of inputs* and provide the first algorithm that is asymptotically exact. This algorithm is designed to serve as a theoretical foundational block to build future scalable and robust web transparency tools. It offers three key properties. First, our algorithm is *service agnostic* and applies to a variety of settings under a broad set of assumptions. Second, our algorithm's analysis delineates a *theoretical detection limit* that characterizes which forms of targeting can be distinguished from noise and which cannot. Third, our algorithm establishes *fundamental tradeoffs* that lead the way to new metrics for the science of web transparency. Understanding the tradeoff between effective targeting and targeting concealment lets us determine under which conditions predatory targeting can be made unprofitable by transparency tools.

1. QUICK OVERVIEW

A primer on web transparency tools.

To address the big-data web's untenable opacity, a new set of transparency tools have been proposed recently [7, 4, 5, 6, 3, 9]. Generally speaking, they assume no insider information about how the data-driven web service operates and instead rely on a specific form of *black box testing* [2] to detect data use. Briefly, a transparency tool works as follows. First, it collects the results of a series of tests in which *inputs* vary, *e.g.*, browsing history [7], search history [4], emails [6], locations [9], or explicit profile information [3]. Second, by examining the observed *outputs* – *e.g.*, search results [4, 9], ads seen [3, 6], recommendations [6, 5], or prices [7, 5] – the tool deduces how the system personalizes its behavior based on this input. Finally, the tool's deductions are used as *hypotheses* that are further analyzed for implications by the tool's users, such as end users, journalists, privacy watchdogs, or federal investigators.

To be valuable to their users, transparency tools strive to meet three requirements:

1. **Scalability:** Each test may involve multiple preliminary steps to open a new web account and populating its inputs. These steps cannot always be automated and may be expensive (e.g., creating a Google account requires buying a new phone number). It is also important to keep resources to a minimum as the size of outputs/inputs grows.
2. **Accuracy:** The deduction that the tool provides should be *sound*, which means that it can be trusted not to originate from noise or other limitations of the experiments. The tool should also be *complete* which specifies that it rarely misses an important deduction.
3. **Broad Applicability:** Ideally, the same tool should apply not only to many different services but also various forms of data usage within those services, with only minor and intellectually simple changes.

Perhaps unsurprisingly, the first two requirements are often in conflict. The third makes the problem extremely challenging, and has barely been considered to date. With few exceptions [6, 3], previous transparency tools were designed for a specific service or usage in order to detect a particularly sensitive topic: price discrimination [7], search results personalization [4], censorship [9]. Only recently has development of widely-applicable, generic tools begun to be considered to allow generic data collections [5] and service-agnostic detection methods [6, 3]. Despite appearences, however, we find that even the latest transparency tools are limited in the kind of data uses they can support accurately and scalably. We believe that the biggest roadblock is the lack of support for detecting complex, multi-input targeting, which we find mandatory for building scalable, accurate, and broadly applicable tools.

Our new findings.

We prove that targeting that uses one or several combinations of N inputs can be detected and identified with asymptotically perfect accuracy, and that this only requires

SIGMETRICS'15, June 15–19, 2015, Portland, OR, USA.
ACM 978-1-4503-3486-0/15/06.
http://dx.doi.org/10.1145/2745844.2745896.

a logarithmic order $O(\ln(N))$ of experimental observations. To place our contribution in respect to prior work, this shows that a web transparency tool can remain scalable and accurate, without being strictly restricted to single input targeting. However, and this is where our contribution contrasts the most with previous results, it comes at a cost: the intensity of targeting (defined below) needs to be sufficiently large. In other words, web transparency need not always be blind to combined targeting, however as the inherent complexity of targeting increases, targeting becomes easier to conceal. Our results open a new chapter in the understanding of Big Data: to determine sufficient and necessary conditions under which one can prevent its opacity.

2. PROBLEM FORMULATION & RESULTS

We formalize the following intuitive problem: given a set of N inputs representing possible information items present in a user's account (such as emails or searches), we wish to determine how they affect occurence of one particular output of interest (such as an ad or a recommendation).

Our main assumption is that the output is affected through an unknown targeting function f of the inputs, to be determined. The function f is defined separately for each output. The targeting function f is a mapping from the set of all combinations to $\{0; 1\}$. By convention, $f(\mathcal{C}) = 1$ indicates that an account containing $\mathcal{C}$ is targeted, and we denote $f(.) = 0$ if the ad is untargeted.

Experiments and outcome properties.

Because in practice we have no access to the targeting function, we rely on experiments to observe its reaction to various inputs. Intuitively, these experiments collect outputs from a set of accounts that contain subsets of the inputs and produce a set of observations of f. For example, experiments could collect ads for accounts with different subsets of emails. More formally, the experimental infrastructure we assume is similar to an *oracle* from function learning theory [8, 1]. We assume that our experimental oracle satisfies the following axiom. There exist two probabilities p_{in}, p_{out} such that:

$$\mathbb{P}\left[\mathcal{O}(\mathcal{C}_i)=1|f(\mathcal{C}_i)=1\right] \geq p_{\text{in}} > p_{\text{out}} \geq \mathbb{P}\left[\mathcal{O}(\mathcal{C}_j)=1|f(\mathcal{C}_j)=0\right].$$

where p_{in} is a minimal bound on the probability that an account receives an output that is relevant for it and p_{out} is a maximal bound on the probability that an account receives an output that is not relevant for it. This axiom properly states that f is related to the outcome we study. It allows the variables to also depend on other factors: hidden inputs that are not in the set of N we study, external sources of randomness such as availability of ad-slot, competition. One experimental design used in practice [6, 3] and that fits this axiom is to populate each account randomly so that an input independently appears with probability α.

Under the assumptions above, we say that an algorithm using m observations solves the targeting detection problem if it can correctly decide whether $f(.) \neq 0$ and hence that the output is targeted using at most m queries to $\mathcal{O}$. Going further, an algorithm solves the targeting identification problem if it correctly returns the function f. Naturally, both problems rely on random observations and hence our goal is to design algorithms whose detection/identification error is arbitrarily small for large N.

Since one should distinguish (at least) between N inputs, it seems that a minimum of $\Omega(\ln(N))$ binary observations are absolutely necessary at least for the identification. This is hence what we assume and we aim at keeping it at this absolute minimum.

THEOREM 1. *Assuming that f is a monotone DNF with size at most s and width at most w, and that ratio p_{out}/p_{in} is below a predetermined bound, we provide a targeting detection algorithm that for any $\varepsilon > 0$ requires $O(\ln(N/\varepsilon))$ observations, $O(N^s \ln(N/\varepsilon))$ operations and is correct with probability $(1 - \varepsilon/N)$.*

THEOREM 2. *Under the same assumption, we provide a targeting identification algorithm that for any $\varepsilon > 0$ requires $O(\ln(N/\varepsilon))$ observations, $O(N^{s+w} \ln(N/\varepsilon))$ operations and is correct with probability $(1 - \varepsilon/N)$.*

3. ACKNOWLEDGEMENTS

This work was supported by DARPA Contract FA8650-11-C-7190, NSF CNS-1351089 and CNS-1254035, Google, and Microsoft.

4. REFERENCES

[1] D. Angluin. Queries and concept learning. *Machine Learning*, 2(4):319–342, Apr. 1988.

[2] B. Beizer. *Black-Box Testing.* Techniques for Functional Testing of Software and Systems. John Wiley & Sons, May 1995.

[3] A. Datta, M. C. Tschantz, and A. Datta. Automated Experiments on Ad Privacy Settings: A Tale of Opacity, Choice, and Discrimination. *arXiv.org*, Aug. 2014.

[4] A. Hannak, P. Sapiezynski, A. M. Kakhki, B. Krishnamurthy, D. Lazer, A. Mislove, and C. Wilson. Measuring personalization of web search. In *WWW '13: Proceedings of the 22nd international conference on World Wide Web.* International World Wide Web Conferences Steering Committee, May 2013.

[5] A. Hannak, G. Soeller, D. Lazer, A. Mislove, and C. Wilson. Measuring Price Discrimination and Steering on E-commerce Web Sites. In *IMC '14: Proceedings of the 2014 Conference on Internet Measurement Conference.* ACM Request Permissions, Nov. 2014.

[6] M. Lecuyer, G. Ducoffe, F. Lan, A. Papancea, T. Petsios, R. Spahn, A. Chaintreau, and R. Geambasu. XRay: Enhancing the Web's Transparency with Differential Correlation . In *23rd USENIX Security Symposium (USENIX Security 14)*, San Diego, CA, 2014. USENIX Association.

[7] J. Mikians, L. Gyarmati, V. Erramilli, and N. Laoutaris. Detecting price and search discrimination on the internet. In *HotNets-XI: Proceedings of the 11th ACM Workshop on Hot Topics in Networks.* ACM Request Permissions, Oct. 2012.

[8] R. A. Servedio. On learning monotone DNF under product distributions. *Information and Computation*, 193(1):57–74, Aug. 2004.

[9] X. Xing, W. Meng, D. Doozan, N. Feamster, W. Lee, and A. C. Snoeren. Exposing Inconsistent Web Search Results with Bobble. *Passive and Active Measurements Conference*, 2014.

Lagrangian-based Online Stochastic Bin Packing

Varun Gupta
University of Chicago
varun.gupta@chicagobooth.edu

Ana Radovanovic
Google
anaradovanovic@google.com

ABSTRACT

Motivated by the problem of packing Virtual Machines on physical servers in the cloud, we study the problem of online stochastic bin packing under two settings – packing with permanent items, and packing under item departures.

In the setting with permanent items, we present the first truly distribution-oblivious bin packing heuristic that achieves $O(\sqrt{n})$ regret compared to OPT for all distributions. Our algorithm is essentially gradient descent on suitably defined Lagrangian relaxation of the bin packing Linear Program. We also prove guarantees of our heuristic against non *i.i.d.* input using a randomly delayed Lyapunov function to smoothen the input.

For the setting where items eventually depart, we are interested in minimizing the steady-state number of bins. Our algorithm extends as is to the case of item departures. Further, leveraging the Lagrangian approach, we generalize our algorithm to a setting where the processing time of an item is inflated by a certain known factor depending on the configuration it is packed in.

Categories and Subject Descriptors

F.2.2 [**Nonnumerical Algorithms and Problems**]: Sequencing and Scheduling; G.3 [**Probability and Statistics**]: Stochastic Processes

Keywords

Stochastic bin packing; Primal-Dual algorithm; Best Fit

1. MODEL NOTATION AND DEFINITIONS

There is a sequence of items that are packed online using algorithm A. Items can be of different types $j \in [J] = \{1, \ldots, J\}$. Each arrival is of type j i.i.d. with probability p_j. We abbreviate this distribution by F. The set $\mathcal{C}$ denotes the feasible set of configurations for the bins, where each $c \in \mathcal{C}$ is a multiset of items with x_{cj} representing the number of type j items in configuration c. Denote the empty configuration by $\emptyset$, a configuration with a single type j item by e_j, and $c \cup j$ and $c \backslash j$ denotes configurations with one more and one less item j respective (assuming they are in $\mathcal{C}$). We assume that we have an infinite number of bins available, and we use $N_c^A(n)$ to denote the number of bins in configuration c after nth item has been packed.

The performance metric that we want to minimize is the number of bins opened by a packing algorithm on distribution F, i.e.,

$$N_F^A(n) \triangleq \sum_{c \in \mathcal{C} \backslash \emptyset} N_c^A(n)$$

Departure Model: In Section 2.2 we extend our model to the case where items depart after spending some random time in the system. We assume that items arrive according to a Poisson process in time with rate $0 < \lambda < \infty$ and leave after some random time with finite mean $1/\mu_j$ and $M \triangleq \{1/\mu_1, \ldots, 1/\mu_J\}$, and finite higher moments.Additionally, an item packed in configuration c experiences a slowdown, so that the departure rate of a type j item which is currently in configuration c becomes $\mu_j s_{cj}$. We are interested in both the steady-state behavior (the number of bins used is parameterized by λ in this case), as well as the transient behavior (convergence rate to steady-state).

1.1 Review of Bin Packing Literature

Online bin packing with infinite collection of bins and permanent items: The Sum of Squares (SS) rule [2, 1] is the current state-of-the-art bin packing policy when item sizes and bin size B are integral. However, for certain class of distributions ("linear waste") SS achieves a constant factor more waste than OPT, and in [1] the authors fix this problem by essentially learning some information about the distribution. Our proposed policy achieves $O(\sqrt{n})$ regret for all distributions and is truly distribution-oblivious.

Bin packing with infinitely many bins and item departures: Stolyar [5] proposes a greedy packing heuristic that achieves $OPT \times (1+\epsilon)$ number of bins in steady state for arbitrarily small $\epsilon > 0$, which was improved to $OPT + o(\lambda)$ by Stolyar and Zhong [6]. Ghaderi et al. [3] propose a randomized Best Fit heuristic which also achieves $OPT \times (1+\epsilon)$ number of bin for arbitrary $\epsilon > 0$. However, due to specialized nature of the proposed algorithms, none of the above extend to the case of congestion-dependent slowdown.

2. ALGORITHMS

2.1 Bin Packing with Permanent Items

Given the item size distribution F, the optimal *bin rate* for

SIGMETRICS'15, June 15-19, 2015, Portland, OR, USA

http://dx.doi.org/10.1145/2745844.2745897.

F (that is, the average number of bins used per item) can be computed by solving the following Linear Program (called the configuration LP):

$$b(F) = \min_{n_c} \sum_{c \in \mathcal{C}} n_c \qquad (\mathbf{P_{nodep}})$$

subject to

$$\forall c \in \mathcal{C} : n_c \geq 0$$

$$\forall j \in [J] : \sum_c n_c x_{cj} = P_j$$

The variable n_c denote the expected number of configuration c bins opened per item from F. (In a prior unpublished technical report [4], we had looked at the 1-d level packing problem via *flow LP* which is a more compact representation of the configuration LP in that setting, and gives slightly better constants in suboptimality gap).

The algorithm PD-exp is a straightforward Lagrangian minimization of P_{nodep} with exponential penalty function:

Algorithm PD-exp : At time t

- Define configuration potentials:

$$V_c(t) = 1 - \kappa e^{-\epsilon(t) N_c(t)}$$

with $V_\emptyset \doteq 0$.

- Place arriving item, say of type j, in configuration c^* to create $c^* \cup j$, where:

$$c^* = \arg\min_c V_{c \cup j}(t) - V_c(t)$$

THEOREM 1. *For the PD-exp algorithm with* $\epsilon(t) = \sqrt{\frac{|\mathcal{C}|}{2(|\mathcal{C}|+t)}}$,

$$\mathbf{E}\left[N_F^{PD}(n)\right] \leq \mathbf{E}\left[N_F^{OPT}(n)\right] + \sqrt{8|\mathcal{C}|(n+|\mathcal{C}|)}$$

2.1.1 *Guarantees against non-i.i.d. input*

Adversarial Model: At time t, the adversary samples an item size S_t from distribution F_t that is a function of the history of samples generated by him. That is:

$$F_t = f_t(S_1, \ldots, S_{t-1}) \qquad (1)$$

Let $\{\mathcal{F}_t\}$ denote the filtration generated by $\{S_1, \ldots, S_t\}$ where as is usual $\mathcal{F}_0 = \{\emptyset, \Omega\}$.

THEOREM 2. *For a given window size* L, *define the* smoothed arrival distribution *at time* k *conditioned on* $\mathcal{F}_t$ *as:*

$$\hat{F}_{k|t} \doteq \mathbf{E}\left[\frac{1}{L+1} \sum_{m=k}^{k+L} F_m \,\middle|\, \mathcal{F}_t\right]$$

Denote the optimal bin-rate of the bin packing LP for $\hat{F}_k$ *by* $\hat{b}_{k|t}$. *For succinctness,* $\hat{b}_k \doteq \hat{b}_{k|0}$.
If $L, \epsilon, \kappa, |\mathcal{C}|$ *satisfy (i)* $\epsilon L < 1$ *and (ii)* $L \leq \frac{1}{\epsilon} \log \frac{\kappa|\mathcal{C}|}{|\mathcal{C}|-1}$ *then*

$$\mathbf{E}\left[N^{PD}(n)|\mathcal{F}_t\right] \leq \sum_{k=1}^{n} \hat{b}_{k|t} + n\kappa\epsilon\left(\frac{2L+3}{4}\right) + \frac{|\mathcal{C}|\kappa}{\epsilon} + L.$$

COROLLARY 1. *If* $L = \Theta(n^c)$ *for arbitrary* $0 \leq c < 1$, *choosing* $\epsilon = \Theta(n^{\frac{1+c}{2}})$*:*

$$\mathbf{E}\left[N^{PD}(n)\right] \leq \sum_{k=1}^{n} \hat{b}_k + O(n^{\frac{1+c}{2}}).$$

2.2 Bin Packing with item departures

Our proposed heuristics extend almost as-is to the case of item departures. As before we define configuration potentials as:

$$V_c(t) = 1 - \frac{1}{\epsilon(t)} e^{-\epsilon(t) N_c(t)}$$

where we set $\epsilon(t) = \sqrt{\frac{|\mathcal{C}|}{2(|\mathcal{C}|+n(t))}}$, $n(t)$ denoting the total number of items in the system.

2.2.1 *Packing with Heterogeneous slowdowns: The Proxy Dual method*

In this section we consider the more general problem of heterogeneous slowdowns: the departure rate of a type j item in configuration c is given by $\mu_j s_{cj}$. Our convention will be $s_{e_j,j} = 1$, that is the slowdown of an item type when it is the only item in a bin is the benchmark of slowdown.

Algorithm PD$_{\mathbf{het}}$:

- Define configuration duals:

$$\alpha_c(t) = 1 - \kappa e^{-\epsilon(t) N_c(t)}$$

where $\kappa \geq m \times \max_{c, j \in c} \frac{1}{s_{cj}}$ (m denotes the maximum number of items in any configuration).

- Define configuration potentials:

$$V_c(t) = (1 - \alpha_c(t)) - \sum_j x_{cj} s_{cj} (1 - \alpha_{e_j})$$

with $V_\emptyset \doteq 0$.

- Place arriving item, say of type j, in configuration c^* to create $c^* \cup j$, where:

$$c^* = \arg\min_c V_{c \cup j}(t) - V_c(t)$$

Figure 1: Primal-Dual algorithm for heterogeneous slowdowns

3. REFERENCES

[1] János Csirik, David S. Johnson, Claire Kenyon, James B. Orlin, Peter W. Shor, and Richard R. Weber. On the sum-of-squares algorithm for bin packing. *J. ACM*, 53(1):1–65, 2006.

[2] János Csirik, David S. Johnson, Claire Kenyon, Peter W. Shor, and Richard R. Weber. A self organizing bin packing heuristic. In *ALENEX*, pages 246–265, London, UK, 1999. Springer-Verlag.

[3] Javad Ghaderi, Yuan Zhong, and R. Srikant. Asymptotic optimality of bestfit for stochastic bin packing. *SIGMETRICS Perform. Eval. Rev.*, 42(2):64–66, September 2014.

[4] Varun Gupta and Ana Radovanovic. Online stochastic bin packing. *CoRR*, abs/1211.2687, 2012.

[5] Alexander L. Stolyar. An infinite server system with general packing constraints. *Operations Research*, 61(5):1200–1217, 2013.

[6] Alexander L. Stolyar and Yuan Zhong. A large-scale service system with packing constraints: Minimizing the number of occupied servers. In *ACM SIGMETRICS*, pages 41–52, New York, NY, USA, 2013. ACM.

Towards Cooling Internet-Scale Distributed Networks on the Cheap

Vani Gupta†, Stephen Lee†, Prashant Shenoy†, Ramesh K. Sitaraman†‡, Rahul Urgaonkar¶
†University of Massachusetts, Amherst ‡Akamai Technologies ¶IBM Research
{vani,stephenlee,shenoy,ramesh}@cs.umass.edu rurgaon@us.ibm.com

ABSTRACT

Internet-scale Distributed Networks (IDNs) are large distributed systems that comprise hundreds of thousands of servers located around the world. IDNs consume significant amounts of energy to power their deployed server infrastructure, and nearly as much energy to cool that infrastructure. We study the potential benefits of using renewable open air cooling (OAC) in an IDN. Our results show that by using OAC, a global IDN can extract 51% cooling energy reducing during summers and a 92% reduction in the winter.

Categories and Subject Descriptors

C.2.4 [**Computer-Communication Networks**]: Distributed Systems

Keywords

Internet-Scale Distributed Systems, Load Balancing, Energy

1. INTRODUCTION

Internet-scale distributed Networks (IDNs) deliver web content, streaming media to clients via thousands of servers located in data centers throughout the world. These data centers consume significant amount of energy to power their servers and cool them. While the energy bills incurred in these data centers may run into millions of dollars per month, the environmental impact of IDNs is also substantial. With carbon emissions from data centers growing by 15% every year, it is imperative to re-design IDNs with energy as a key design consideration in order to ensure the sustainable growth of these networks. Since the energy bill spent in cooling an IDN is nearly as large as the portion used to power its servers, we focus explicitly on the problem of reduction in cooling energy usage using *open air cooling* (OAC) to reduce costs.

To our knowledge, OAC has not been studied in an IDN context and is distinctive for the following reasons. IDNs such as CDNs have two defining characteristics: (i) *global deployment* of servers in multiple data centers around the world, and (ii) *replication* of services across these data centers. The global deployment is often driven by the need for an IDN to have servers "proximal" to the end-users. Hence, it is not possible for IDNs to deploy data centers *only* in places where weather is cold most of the year, or where electricity is cheap. However, IDNs often replicate their services across their data centers, so that the workload of serving users can be easily shifted from one data center to another, albeit with a potential for performance degradation. A combination of these two characteristics provide an IDN the flexibility to move its workload across data centers to exploit climatic variations to optimize the use of OAC, a flexibility that services employing a single or a few data centers do not possess. Our algorithms orchestrate both the movement of load (i.e, load balancing) as well as energy drawn from the grid (i.e., power management) to decrease an IDN's cooling costs.

SIGMETRICS'15, June 15 -19, 2015, Portland, OR, USA.
ACM 978-1-4503-3486-0/15/06.
http://dx.doi.org/10.1145/2745844.2745898.

2. BACKGROUND

Internet-scale Distributed Networks: A recent study of data center energy consumption showed that servers and cooling consumed 56% and 30% of the total energy respectively. Since cooling energy is a significant portion of the total energy consumption, we examine the potential for employing OAC to reduce the energy usage in an IDN. We assume that an IDN (or, its proxy) has the ability to deploy or exploit advanced cooling technologies in all of its data centers locations. With increasing trend towards modular self-contained containers, it is reasonable to assume that IDNs will have greater control over how a data center is built and cooled.

Renewable Cooling using Open Air: A promising approach to reduce the cooling energy of a data center is to use the outside air, instead of chillers, to cool servers within the data center. However, OAC is feasible only when the air is "cold and dry enough". As a result, OAC may not be possible everywhere and may not be possible during all times of the day. In our work, we use (i) the instantaneous weather outside each of the IDN's data center locations, and (ii) the recommendations in Table 1 from the American Society of Heating, Refrigeration, and Air-conditioning Engineers (ASHRAE) to determine whether the outside air can be used to cool the data center at any point in time. To determine whether a data center can employ OAC at any point in time, we follow the methodology presented in the GreenGrid consortium whitepaper[3].

Data center Class	Dry-Bulb Temp (° C)	Humidity Range	Max Dew Point (° C)
A1	15 to 32	20% to 80%	17
A2	10 to 35	20% to 80%	21
A3	5 to 40	8% to 85%	24
A4	5 to 45	8% to 90%	24

Table 1: ASHRAE's allowable ranges suitable for cooling [3].

Energy Consumption Model: We use the standard linear model of server power consumption where the power (in Watts) consumed by a server serving load λ equals $P_{idle} + (P_{peak} - P_{idle})\lambda$, where

P_{idle} is the power consumed by an idle server, P_{peak} is the power consumed by the server under peak load, and λ is the load served by the server as a fraction of its capacity. Clearly, cooling energy is roughly proportional to the amount of heat dissipated in the data center, which in turn is governed largely by server energy. The proportionality factor is a measure of the effectiveness of the cooling system deployed at the data center and is captured by its power usage effectiveness (PUE) that is ratio of the total energy consumed by the facility to the energy consumed by the servers and other IT equipment. In our evaluation, we assume the average PUE is 1.80

3. EVALUATION

To evaluate the benefit of OAC, we used extensive load data from across Akamai's CDN for the period of one month, and global weather traces provided by the National Oceanic and Atmospheric Administration (NOAA) for the year 2012. We use a simple greedy algorithm that modifies the load assignments made by the (non-weather-aware) load balancer as reflected in our Akamai load traces by moving user load from data centers that have no OAC to nearby data centers that do, subject to performance constraints. Specifically, our greedy algorithm does the following for each of the IDN's data centers at each time step: if the weather conditions at a data center location permits OAC, then user load mapped to that location is unchanged; however, if the weather conditions at a data center location do not permit OAC to be employed, the load balancer attempts to greedily re-assign the load destined for that location to other nearby data centers (in increasing order of distance) with spare server capacity where OAC may be available. After our algorithm moves as much of the load as it can to open-air coolable data centers, the residual load must be cooled using chillers. Each unit of load that is cooled using OAC is a direct reduction in energy usage for the IDN, since chillers are not used. The energy savings can be computed by comparing the energy used with OAC to the energy used to cool the original load *entirely* with chillers.

3.1 Empirical Results

We evaluate the potential for OAC using our greedy algorithm outlined above on our IDN load and weather traces for a full year.

Reduction in global energy usage: Figure 1 depicts the average energy savings obtained across the entire CDN for different months of the year and for different values of distance r. The savings from OAC is higher during the cooler winter, with lower savings during the warmer summer months (May to September). Note that our analysis includes savings from data centers in both the hemispheres. However, Internet traffic from northern hemisphere dominate the global Internet traffic, hence the seasonal benefits from the northern hemisphere dominate the global trends. Overall, our result shows that even during summer, a global IDN can extract significant cooling energy reduction of more than 51% *with no performance impact* ($r = 0$) and the savings due to OAC increase to over 92% during winter months; when $r =$ 1000km, an additional 13% savings during the warmest month of July. For $r =$ 5000km, (allows trans-continental load redirection), the savings increase to nearly 100% throughout the year. We observed that the savings in USA broadly follow the global trends, indicating that USA not only contributes a significant portion of the global traffic, but also has its seasons aligned with the dominant northern hemisphere.

Regional and Seasonal Variations in Savings: Our results show significant regional and seasonal differences in the savings obtained from OAC. Japan (Figure 2(a)) has the most significant seasonal variations in OAC benefits—with nearly 100% energy savings from employing OAC during the winter months to a zero savings in the summer month of August for the no load redirection scenario of $r = 0$. The savings do not increase significantly even when load can be redirected to other data centers with a radius of $r =$ 1000km. While Japan exhibits the extreme seasonal variations in OAC benefits, Singapore (Figure 2(b)) sees the worst year-round benefits. While Singapore is itself a small country, it is a key regional "hub" with significant traffic. Since Singapore is located near the equator, it has warm and humid weather throughout the year with nearly no seasons. Consequently OAC is not possible in Singapore during any month of the year, yielding zero savings. Even allowing Singapore traffic to be sent to data centers within a 1000km radius yields no benefits.

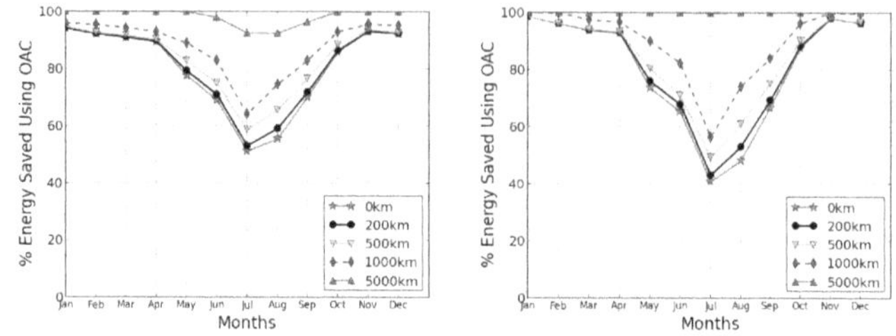

(a) Global (b) USA

Figure 1: Energy savings for the entire global IDN

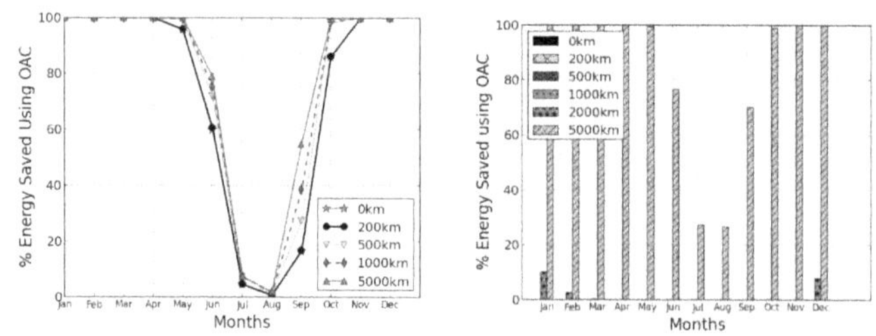

(a) Japan (b) Singapore

Figure 2: Regional and seasonal variations in OAC savings

4. CONCLUSIONS

In this poster we presented the potential benefits of using open air cooling to reduce the energy usage incurred by an IDN. We empirically evaluated the efficacy of OAC using extensive traces from Akamai's global CDN and global weather data from NOAA. Our results showed that, by using free OAC, a global IDN can extract 51% cooling energy reducing during summers and a 92% reduction in the winter.

5. ACKNOWLEDGEMENTS

This research is supported in part by National Science Foundation grants 1422245, 1229059 and 1413998.

6. REFERENCES

[1] Z. Liu, M. Lin, A. Wierman, S. Low, and L. Andrew. Greening geographical load balancing. In *Proc of ACM Sigmetrics*, 2011.

[2] Asfandyar Qureshi, Rick Weber, Hari Balakrishnan, John Guttag, and Bruce Maggs. Cutting the Electric Bill for Internet-Scale Systems. In *Proceedings of SIGCOMM, 2009.*

[3] Michael Patterson Tom Harvey and John Bean. Updated air-side free cooling maps: The impact of ASHRAE 2011 allowable ranges. *The Green Grid*, 2012.

A Simple Model to Quantify the Impact of Memory Latency and Bandwidth on Performance

Russell Clapp, Intel Corporation, Hillsboro, Oregon
Martin Dimitrov, Intel Corporation, Chandler, Arizona
Karthik Kumar, Intel Corporation, Chandler, Arizona
Vish Viswanathan, Intel Corporation, Hillsboro, Oregon
Thomas Willhalm, Intel Gmbh, Walldorf, Germany
{Russell.M.Clapp, Martin.P.Dimitrov, Karthik.Kumar, Vish.Viswanathan, Thomas.Willhalm}@intel.com

ABSTRACT

In recent years, DRAM technology improvements have scaled at a much slower pace than processors. While server processor core counts grow from 33% to 50% on a yearly cadence, DDR4 memory channel bandwidth has grown at a slower rate, and memory latency has remained relatively flat for some time. Meanwhile, new computing paradigms have emerged, which involve analyzing massive volumes of data in real time and place pressure on the memory subsystem. The combination of these trends makes it important for computer architects to understand the sensitivity of the workload performance to memory bandwidth and latency. In this paper, we outline and validate a methodology for quick and quantitative performance estimation using a real-world workload.

Categories and Subject Descriptors

C.4 [**Performance of Systems**]: Modeling techniques, Design studies; D.4.8 [**Performance**]: Measurements

Keywords

Performance Modeling, Workload Characterization

1. INTRODUCTION

As data volumes grow and as compute capabilities continue to increase with Moore's Law, memory (DRAM) density scaling has begun to lag far behind. Emerging memory technologies [1] may address the capacity issue but have different latency and bandwidth characteristics from conventional DRAM. The implication is clear: as computer architects look toward alternative memory technologies that provide more capacity at the expense of latency and bandwidth, it is paramount that performance models exist to quantify those tradeoffs. Higher-level quick-turn estimation models that enable faster evaluation of architectural alternatives are required to set direction before developing new, more detailed simulation models of new technologies. Further, as the adoption of these new technologies increases, it is natural that there will be hybrid memory systems – that contain more than one type of memory technology – in tiered or non-tiered configurations. The key factor in determining how an application may use or benefit from such systems is performance. This paper demonstrates how we can vary the latency and bandwidth characteristics of the memory subsystem and determine the impact of that subsystem on performance. To do so, we outline and validate a methodology that uses classic analytic equations for quick, quantitative performance estimation.

SIGMETRICS'15, June 15–19, 2015, Portland, OR, USA.
ACM 978-1-4503-3486-0/15/06.
http://dx.doi.org/10.1145/2745844.2745900

2. RELATED WORK

Previous researchers have also extensively addressed performance modeling [2-6]. Sorin et al. [2] present an analytical model for evaluating various types of architectural alternatives for shared-memory systems, exploiting instruction level parallelism. Emma [4] provides an analytical framework for estimating performance using CPI, breaking it down into both infinite cache and memory subsystem effects, which is consistent with our model. In particular, [5,6] describe the impact of *memory-level parallelism* (MLP) in modeling. Our paper builds on these approaches with equations that provide quick and quantitative analytical performance estimation. We demonstrate and validate the modeling methodology using a real-world workload.

3. METHODOLOGY

We use the number of clock *cycles per instruction* (CPI) as the measure of processor performance, as recommended in [4]. CPI is the inverse of instruction throughput, and a lower value of CPI indicates better performance. We define the *pathlength* of a workload as the required number of instructions to complete a unit of work. Thus the pathlength depends on the software code path that is executed in order to complete such a unit of work. The combination of pathlength and CPI then determines the performance of the workload, whether it is quantified as run time or throughput. Thus, if the pathlength is fixed, the CPI per processor and the number of processors can directly be converted into a workload measure of throughput. To simplify our analysis, we will consider the case of a fixed pathlength below.

Let's assume we have a processor with a two-level memory hierarchy; one level of cache followed by main memory. $\boldsymbol{CPI_{eff}}$ stands for Effective Cycles per Instruction and denotes the inverse of the effective rate of instruction execution. Thus for a single-thread of execution in its simplest form:

$$CPI_{eff} = CPI_{cache} + MPI * MP * BF \quad [1]$$

Here $\boldsymbol{CPI_{cache}}$ is the CPI if all memory references were satisfied by the processor cache, $\boldsymbol{MPI}$ are the misses per instruction at the processor cache (either demand or prefetch), $\boldsymbol{MP}$ is the cache miss penalty, and $\boldsymbol{BF}$ is the "blocking factor", or percentage of the miss penalty that contributes to $\boldsymbol{CPI_{eff}}$. Thus, the equation takes as input the effective CPI with an infinite cache, and adds incremental CPI based on the number of cache misses, the latency to satisfy those misses, and a factor that reflects the impact of that latency. If an application is truly *core bound*, it will have no sensitivity to memory latency, and the *blocking factor* in our equation will be zero. This is possible if prefetching ensures that data is readily available in the processor cache once the core requires it. On the other hand, if the workload is *bandwidth bound*, the equation should still hold, as queuing theory informs us that latency increases dramatically as available bandwidth becomes saturated.

Table 1: Computed versus measured CPI for In-memory Analytics.

Core Speed (GHz)	2.1	2.1	2.4	2.4	2.7	2.7	3.1	3.1
MPI	0.0056	0.0056	0.0056	0.0056	0.0059	0.0055	0.0057	0.0055
MP **(core cycles)**	402	383	462	448	543	502	631	598
CPI_{eff} **(computed)**	1.33	1.31	1.39	1.38	1.52	1.43	1.60	1.53
CPI_{eff} **(measured)**	1.32	1.32	1.38	1.39	1.47	1.44	1.60	1.57
Error	1.0%	-1.1%	0.9%	-0.6%	3.0%	-0.6%	-0.1%	-2.5%

Our Eq. 1 is consistent with the observations made in [5,6], which states that the core stall time resulting from multiple simultaneous outstanding long latency cache misses, call this value ***MLP***, is derived from the miss penalty ***MP*** divided by the ***MLP***. Eq. 2 is taken from [5] and shows this explicitly:

$$CPI_{eff} = CPI_{cache} * (1 - Overlap_{CM}) + \frac{MPI * MP}{MLP} \quad [2]$$

Our ***BF*** then, is proportional to ***1/MLP***, but offset by $Overlap_{CM}$, which represents the overlap of core execution with cache misses. We choose to use Eq. 1, since $Overlap_{CM}$ and ***MLP*** are not directly measureable from hardware performance counters.

Once we have computed the effective CPI for a given program phase using Eq. 1, we can use Eq. 3 to compute the bandwidth demand in bytes per cycle on the memory subsystem. In Eq. 3, ***WBR*** is the percentage of cache misses that require writeback of a dirty victim, ***LS*** is the line size in bytes, and ***CPS*** is the core speed in cycles per second.

$$BW = \frac{(MPI * (1 + WBR) * LS) * CPS}{CPI_{eff}} \quad [3]$$

This equation can be easily extended to account for IO events that also consume memory bandwidth. By scaling Eq. 3 with total core count, we can compute the total system-wide bandwidth required. Using this value, we can estimate the average ***MP*** using queuing theory or characterization data that provides a relationship between queuing delay and bandwidth utilization. Further, by changing the denominator in Eq. 3 to the available memory bandwidth, we can compute a *bandwidth-limited* CPI.

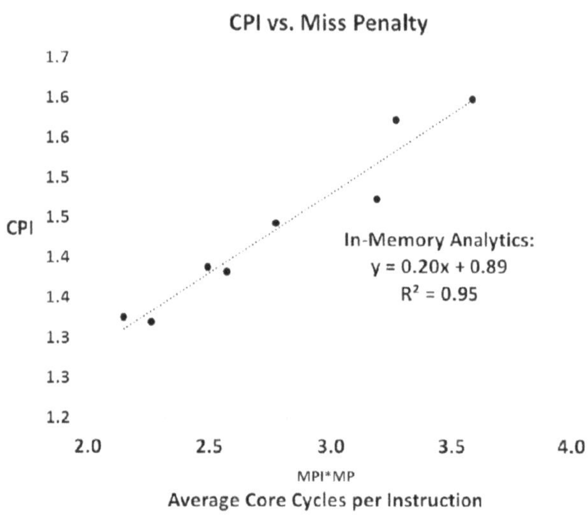

Figure 1: Example fit for CPI_{cache} and *BF*.

4. VALIDATING THE MODEL

To demonstrate and validate the model, we need to determine CPI_{cache} and ***BF*** in Eq. 1 for workloads of interest. We can estimate these parameters by measuring a workload's CPI_{eff} at different miss penalties, which are achieved by varying the core speed and memory speed of the system under test. Thus we get data points with different $(MPI * MP)$, and we measure CPI_{eff} for each of these datapoints using hardware performance counters. We estimate CPI_{cache} and ***BF*** in Eq. 1 by obtaining a fit for these data points – as shown in Fig. 1 for an in-memory analytics workload. Table 1 shows the detailed measurements we made to construct Fig. 1, taking multiple measurements at each core speed to account for any run-to-run variation. Using the values for CPI_{cache} and ***BF*** determined in Fig. 1, we compute the CPI_{eff} and compare it to the measured value. The error is shown in last row of the table, and is less than 3%. We have found similar error rates across many workloads that we have measured.

5. OBSERVATIONS

We have applied this methodology to establish CPI_{cache} and ***BF*** for several Big Data workloads, and compare them to well-known HPC and Enterprise workloads. We see that there is a similarity within each workload class between the values for ***BF*** and $(MPI*(1+WBR))/CPI_{cache}$, the second term representing the injection rate of memory requests coming from the processor. Based on this observation, we created synthetic parameter sets for each workload class, and computed CPI sensitivity to changes in memory latency and bandwidth. We have observed that, while the HPC workloads we selected are more sensitive to changes in memory bandwidth, and Enterprise class workloads are more sensitive to changes in memory latency, and Big Data workloads fall in between, with sensitivity to latency only in configurations where sufficient bandwidth is provided. We plan to publish these results in the near future. The ability to derive these model parameters from measured data and apply them to hypothetical systems is exactly what is required to evaluate the insertion of new memory technologies into system designs.

6. REFERENCES

[1] A. Makarov et al. "Emerging memory technologies: Trends, challenges, and modeling methods," *Microelectronics Reliability*, vol. 52, no. 4, pp. 628--634, 2012.

[2] D. Sorin et al. "Analytic evaluation of shared-memory systems with ilp processors", *25th ISCA*, pp. 380-391, 1998.

[3] B. Fields et al. "Using interaction costs for microarchitectural bottleneck analysis," *36th MICRO*, pp. 228-239, 2003.

[4] P. Emma. "Understanding some simple processor-performance limits," *IBM J. Res. Dev.* 41: 3, 215-232, 1997.

[5] Y. Chou et al, "Microarchitecture optimizations for exploiting memory-level parallelism," *31st ISCA*, pp. 76-87, 2004.

[6] T. Karkhanis et al. "A first-order superscalar processor model," *31st ISCA*, pp. 338—349, 2004.

Performance Characterization of Hyperscale Applications on NVMe SSDs

Qiumin Xu*, Huzefa Siyamwala‡, Mrinmoy Ghosh†, Manu Awasthi†,
Tameesh Suri†, Zvika Guz†, Anahita Shayesteh†, Vijay Balakrishnan†
*Univeristy of Southern California, ‡ San Jose State University, †Samsung Semiconductor Inc., Milpitas, CA
qiumin@usc.edu, mrinmoy.g@ssi.samsung.com

ABSTRACT

The storage subsystem has undergone tremendous innovation in order to keep up with the ever-increasing demand for throughput. NVMe based SSDs are the latest development in this domain, delivering unprecedented performance in terms of both latency and peak bandwidth. Given their superior performance, NVMe drives are expected to be particularly beneficial for I/O intensive applications in datacenter installations. In this paper we identify and analyze the different factors leading to the better performance of NVMe SSDs. Then, using databases as the prominent use-case, we show how these would translate into real-world benefits. We evaluate both a relational database (MySQL) and a NoSQL database (Cassandra) and demonstrate significant performance gains over best-in-class enterprise SATA SSDs: from 3.5× for TPC-C and up to 8.5× for Cassandra.

Categories and Subject Descriptors

C.4 [**Computer Systems Organization**]: [Performance Of Systems][Measurement Techniques]

Keywords

SSD, NVMe, Hyperscale Applications, NoSQL Databases, Performance Characterization

1. INTRODUCTION

The vast majority of today's web-based services require a datacenter installation in the background. There has been an explosion of the amount of data being stored, and an increasing demand for processing this volumes of data faster. To meet the ever-increasing performance demands, storage subsystems and data-storage devices have been evolving. Solid State Drives (SSDs) were the first technology leap: using traditional interfaces like Serial-ATA (SATA) and SAS, they provide significantly better performance than hard disk drives (HDDs). In the next technology leap, SSDs were connected to the host via PCIe interconnect to provide a higher bandwidth and lower latency interface. PCIe-based solutions provided higher performance, but their adoption was hindered by the lack of standardization and inter-vendor compatibility [3].

SIGMETRICS'15, June 15-19, 2015, Portland, OR, USA.
ACM 978-1-4503-3486-0/15/06.
http://dx.doi.org/10.1145/2745844.2745901.

The NVMe standard was designed to enable fast and widespread adoption of PCIe SSDs. NVMe was architected from the ground up for non-volatile memory devices over PCIe, focusing on latency, performance, and request parallelism. Being a widely used standard which driver authors conform to, NVMe has contributed towards eliminating dependencies on a single vendor, allowing standard drivers to be written across different vendors, and increasing interoperability between cross-vendor PCIe based SSD storage solutions. The next section provides an overview of the benefits of the NVMe standard.

2. BENEFITS OF NVME

NVMe devices are able to leverage scalable bandwidth advantages of the fast PCIe interconnect, while being able to build additional features like multipath IO and shared namespaces. The performance benefit of NVMe stems from three main factors:

Interface capabilities: PCIe supports much higher throughput compared to SATA: while SATA supports up to 600 MB/s, a single PCIe 3.0 lane allows transfers of up to 1GB/s. Typical PCIe based SSDs are ×4 PCIe generation 3 devices and support up to 4 GB/s.

Hardware data path: SATA drives connect to the system through the host bus: the data path traverses the AHCI driver, the host bus, and an AHCI host bus adapter (HBA). NVMe SSDs, on the other hand, connect directly through the PCIe root complex port. Therefore, an NVMe I/O access has a much shorter data path, resulting in a reduced overall access latency.

Simplified Software stack: In the conventional SATA I/O path, an I/O request arriving at the block layer is first inserted into a queue where requests are merged and reordered. Since, from a performance standpoint, reordering only benefits HDDs, for most modern SSDs, the block layer applies the *noop* scheduler to the request queue. By bypassing the block layer, NVMe SSDs eliminates this queue which is a single point of contention and significantly improves the overall access latency.

The NVMe standard introduced many changes to the I/O software stack. Figure 1 provides a high level representation of the differences between the I/O stacks of SATA and NVMe. An NVMe based request bypasses the conventional block layer request queue and instead implements a paired *Submission* and *Completion* queue mechanism [1]. The standard supports up to 64K I/O queues and up to 64K commands per queue. These queues are saved in host memory and are managed by the NVMe driver and the NVMe controller cooperatively: new commands are placed by the host software into the submission queue (SQ) and completions are placed by the NVMe controller into an associated completion queue (CQ).

[1]The 3.17 linux kernel has a re-architected block layer for NVMe drives. NVMe accesses no longer bypass the kernel. The results shown in this paper are for the 3.14 kernel.

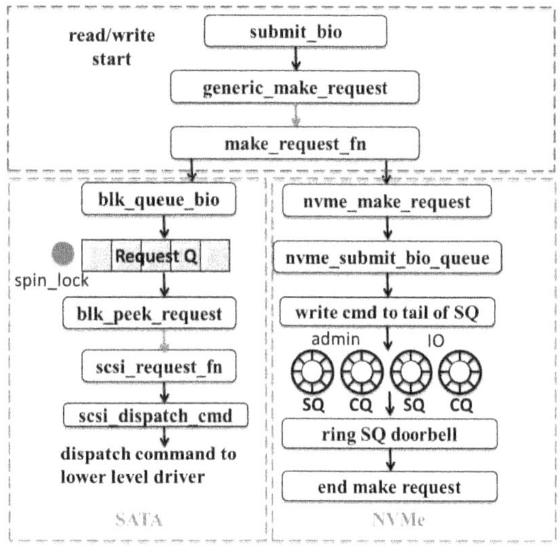

Figure 1: An illustration of the I/O software stacks of SATA SSD and NVMe SSD.

The controller fetches commands from the front of the queue, processes the commands, and rings the completion queue doorbell to notify the host. This asynchronous handshake reduces CPU time spent going through many different kernel modules and prevents resource sharing with other block devices.

3. NVME DRIVES CHARACTERIZATION

To analyze the performance of NVMe drives as compared to SATA SSDs, we first perform a detailed latency characterization of the raw devices. We then demonstrate the benefits of the raw performance for different database applications. The `blktrace` tool is adequate for doing this analysis for SATA devices. In order to extract a detailed latency analysis for NVMe SSDs, we instrument the NVMe driver to add tracing events, and use the `blktrace` tool to capture timestamps of events during an NVMe I/O access. Using this tool in conjunction with `fio` for generating requests, we are able to estimate the time spent at different layers of the software stack during an I/O access.

The measured random read latency for the SATA SSD (Samsung 843T) we tested at low loads is 500μs. We found that system software accounts for a whopping 28% of the overall access latency, and that the block layer alone accounts for 5% of the total latency. In contrast, the measured latency for the tested NVMe SSD (Samsung XS1715) is only 110μs, and the total system software overhead in NVMe drives is significantly reduced to only 7.3%. Considering absolute latencies, our analysis indicates that NVMe SSD consumes 4.5$\times$ less time for random reads compared to the SATA SSD. By reducing system software inefficiencies, breaking interface bottlenecks, innovation in FTL design, and better NAND device characteristics, NVMe devices under test were able to sustain a maximum throughput of 750 K IOPS of 4 KB random read accesses , compared to 100K IOPS for SATA SSDs.

Next, we show how real world applications can benefit from the improved raw performance of NVMe SSDs. We use two example database workloads: (i) TPC-C [1] with MySQL, and (ii) YCSB with Cassandra [6]. TPC-C is an extensively used online transaction processing (OLTP) workload, composed of several operations that best represent a complex web based application environment. Cassandra is an open-source, production quality NoSQL data store. Cassandra provides a number of features similar to Google's BigTable [4] and is used in a number of production datacenters [2].

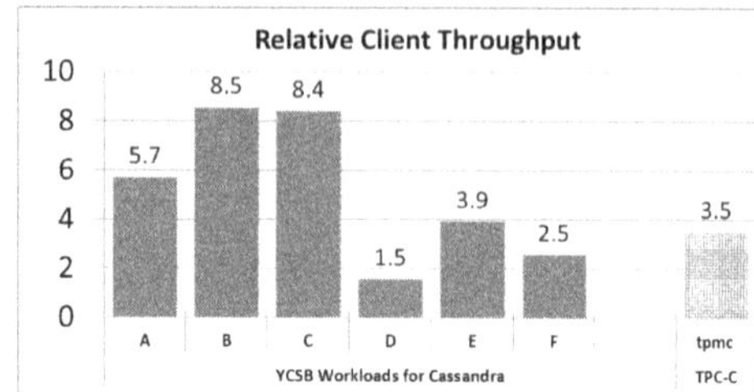

Figure 2: Relative performance improvement for different databases when using one NVMe compared to one SATA SSD.

Figure 2 shows the relative client-side throughput gains when using Samsung XS1715 NVMe drives compared to a system that uses enterprise class Samsung 843T SATA SSDs. The metric of interest in case of databases is client side performance, measured in transactions per second. We show that NVMe delivers speedup of 3.5$\times$ for TPC-C (tpmC) using MySQL, and up to 8.5$\times$ for YCSB [5] using the Cassandra database.

In summary, the reduction of access latency, the asynchronism between request and completion queues, and the high bandwidth of the PCIe interface, all result in tremendous performance gains for real-world applications, especially for disk bound database applications.

4. CONCLUSIONS

Scale-out systems are driving the need for high performance storage solutions with high available bandwidth and low access latencies. To address this need, newer standards are being developed exclusively for non-volatile storage devices like SSDs. In this paper, we present a characterization of SSDs based on the NVMe standard for storage subsystems, and make a number of important contributions.

Firstly, we instrument the Linux NVMe driver and the popular `blktrace` tool and quantify the benefits of a leaner I/O stack. Secondly, using this instrumentation tool, we show that the NVMe access stack allows the I/O requests to bypass most of the legacy I/O layers, resulting in a 4.5$\times$ decrease in access latencies. Lastly, using databases as an example class of applications, we show that NVMe's hardware and software redesign of the storage subsystem translates into *real world* benefit for relational and scale-out database applications. In particular, we show that, as compared to a single SATA SSD, NVMe based SSDs can provide performance benefits of up to 8.5$\times$.

5. REFERENCES

[1] "TPC-C Benchmark Standard Specification, Revision 5.11," http://www.tpc.org/tpcc/spec/tpcc_current.pdf, 2010.

[2] "Benchmarking Cassandra Scalability on AWS - Over a million writes per second," http://techblog.netflix.com/2011/11/benchmarking-cassandra-scalability-on.html, 2011.

[3] "NVM Express Explained," http://nvmexpress.org/wp-content/uploads/2013/04/NVMe_whitepaper.pdf, 2013.

[4] F. Chang, J. Dean, S. Ghemawat, W. C. Hsieh, D. A. Wallach, M. Burrows, T. Chandra, A. Fikes, and R. E. Gruber, "Bigtable: A Distributed Storage System for Structured Data," in *Proceedings of OSDI*, 2006.

[5] B. F. Cooper, A. Silberstein, E. Tam, R. Ramakrishnan, and R. Sears, "Benchmarking Cloud Serving Systems with YCSB," in *SoCC*, 2010.

[6] A. Lakshman and P. Malik, "Cassandra: A Decentralized Structured Storage System," *SIGOPS Oper. Syst. Rev.*, vol. 44, no. 2, Apr. 2010.

Author Index

www.ingramcontent.com/pod-product-compliance
Ingram Content Group UK Ltd.
Pitfield, Milton Keynes, MK11 3LW, UK
UKHW051414290926
15471UKWH00009B/1595

9 781450 338738